lonely planet

KT-512-960

Australia

Hugh Finlay
Lindsay Brown
Andrew Humphreys
Jon Murray
Denis O'Byrne
Tom Smallman
Dani Valent
Jeff Williams
Steve Womersley

Australia

9th edition

Published by
    Lonely Planet Publications
    Head Office: PO Box 617, Hawthorn, Vic 3122, Australia
    Branches: 150 Linden Street, Oakland, CA 94607, USA
                  10a Spring Place, London NW5 3BH, UK
                  71 bis rue du Cardinal Lemoine, 75005 Paris, France

Printed by
    The Bookmaker Pty Ltd
    Printed in China

Photographs
    Many of the images in this guide are available for licensing from Lonely Planet Images.
    email: lpi@lonelyplanet.com.au

    All DESART slides in the Aboriginal Art section by Barry Skipsey

    Front cover: Kata Tjuta (The Olgas), Northern Territory (Pete Turner, The Image Bank)

First Published
    February 1977

This Edition
    September 1998

**Although the authors and publisher have tried to make the information as
accurate as possible, they accept no responsibility for any loss, injury or
inconvenience sustained by any person using this book.**

National Library of Australia Cataloguing in Publication Data

    Australia

    9th edition
    Includes index.
    ISBN 0 86442 546 5.

    1. Australia - Guidebooks.
    2. Australia - Description and travel - 1976-1990.
    I. Finlay, Hugh.

919.40465

Hugh Finlay

Deciding there must be more to life than civil engineering, Hugh took off around Australia in the mid-70s, working at everything from spray painting to diamond prospecting before hitting the overland trail. He joined Lonely Planet in 1985 and has written *Jordan & Syria* and *Northern Territory*, co-authored *Morocco, Algeria & Tunisia* and *Kenya* and updated *Nepal*. Hugh coordinated this edition of *Australia*, wrote the Aboriginal Art and Fauna & Flora sections, and updated the introductory and Northern Territory chapters and the northern Queensland section. Hugh lives in central Victoria with partner, Linda, and daughters Ella and Vera.

Lindsay Brown

Lindsay grew up on NSW's south coast and in sunny Melbourne. A promising career in fisheries conservation biology remained just that, and after a brief stint in science publishing he landed a job with Lonely Planet as an editor and resident flora & fauna expert. Lindsay updated the Tasmania chapter of this book and has written the Kerala chapter for Lonely Planet's *South India* guide.

Andrew Humphreys

Andrew is a big fan of rugby league, cold Castlemaine XXXX and a hot sun. He's far too widely travelled to even think about listing the countries here and he's worked in journalism since 1991. He has authored, co-authored and updated some 10 titles for Lonely Planet, although under pressure he'll give way and admit that none of it would have been possible without the assistance of his wife Gadi. She also sat next to him in a lot of buses and cars while he updated southern Queensland for this edition of *Australia*.

Jon Murray

Jon spent time alternating between travelling and working with various publishing companies in Melbourne, Australia, before joining Lonely Planet as an editor and then author. He co-authored LP's *South Africa, Lesotho & Swaziland* and has written and updated books to destinations including West Africa, Papua New Guinea and Bangladesh. He lives near Daylesford, Victoria, on a bush block he shares with quite a few marsupials and a diminishing number of rabbits. Jon updated the Victoria chapter for this book.

Denis O'Byrne

Denis was born in the Adelaide Hills, South Australia, and raised at Robe in the state's south-east. He left SA when he was 17 but returns home often to visit family in Adelaide or to go fishing on the Eyre Peninsula. He describes his career as a zigzag path leading nowhere, having worked as a surveyor, plant operator, national park ranger, builder's labourer, building consultant and freelance writer among other things. Denis has worked on Lonely Planet's *Outback Australia* and *Vanuatu* guides. He updated the South Australia chapter for this book.

Tom Smallman

Tom was born and raised in the UK and now lives in Melbourne, Australia. He had a number of jobs before joining Lonely Planet as an editor and now works full time researching guidebooks. He has worked on *Canada*, *Ireland*, *Dublin*, *New York*, *New Jersey & Pennsylvania*, *New South Wales*, *Sydney* and *Britain*. For this edition of *Australia*, Tom updated southern NSW.

Dani Valent

Working for Lonely Planet has prevented Dani from sailing across the Atlantic on a dog trampoline, mapping the human genome, and hosting her own cooking show (Oh Naughty Wok). Other than that, she doesn't reckon it's too bad. Dani supports native title for Australia's aborigines and the Carlton Football Club. For this edition, she updated Sydney and the Blue Mountains.

Jeff Williams

Jeff is from Greymouth on New Zealand's wild west coast. He thinks he has now found a use for his university degrees by working as a Lonely Planet author. When not enthusing over 'that bird', 'this mountain' or 'a great place to stay', he hikes, skis and climbs over whichever country will have him. He is author, co-author or contributor to Lonely Planet's *New Zealand*, *Tramping in New Zealand*, *Outback Australia*, *South Africa*, *Lesotho & Swaziland*, *Washington DC & the Capital Region*, *Africa* and *West Africa*. His dream is to write a guide to the South Pacific, accompanied by his wife Alison and son Callum. Jeff updated the Western Australia chapter for this edition.

Steve Womersley

Steve updated the northern NSW section of this book, covering ground he first discovered as a child on summer holidays. He lives in St Kilda, Melbourne, and is a publications worker with the Tenants Union of Victoria.

From the Authors

Hugh Finlay In addition to the many people who helped generally, thanks to Yidumduma Bill Harney, Philippa Davidson, Alan Withers and Brits:Australia for all their hospitality and assistance while I was on the road.

Lindsay Brown Thanks to the staff at Tasmania's Travel Centre in Melbourne and the Travel & Information Centres in Tasmania. Thanks also to the many helpful National Parks rangers and to the numerous people involved in tourism and hospitality in Tasmania who make travelling there so special. A special thanks to Jenny, Patrick and Sinead.

Andrew Humphries Many people gave up their time to help me in my research without any money ever changing hands – some of them even bought *me* drinks. Some of those who must be singled out for thanks and praise include Nick Earls (buy his books, they'll make you laugh); David Gibson, Brisbane historian and the best man to ride a City Cat with; Mark the singing ranger of Fraser Island; Dominque White of the QTTC; Casey O'Hare of Brisbane Tourism; Denis J Casey of Queensland Rail; Gerard Ross of the Queensland Writers' Association; and Brett Murray of IndyCar Australia. Extra special thanks go to Jeff, Alison and Callum for their reckless loan of a house, car and computer. The BBQs and Westcoasters were much appreciated, too.

Denis O'Byrne Thanks to Phil Brennan and Jan Matthew.

Jon Murray Thanks to Naomi, Rose and Vivienne Richards, and Margaret, Maggie, Saffron and Yolande Finch.

Tom Smallman My thanks to Narelle Graefe and Lindy Spindler for their hospitality in Canberra, to Steve Womersley, to the Denson family, to all those people in the travel industry who patiently answered my questions and to Sue Graefe for her patience and support.

Dani Valent Thanks to Kath Kenny, Hazel and Cass for Australia St turret hospitality; Leon, Joy and Michael; Justin 'Mr Mint' Cvitan; Karen, Ben and Ingrid from Sydney Visitors Centre; Barbara Brisenden from Darling Harbour Visitor Centre; Jo Bremner; Julie, Paul, Ariel and Amy Valent; Emma Black; my bicycle; and Stephen Kernahan for ten inspirational years.

Jeff Williams To my mate Russell Wilson for looking after Callum when I was trying to work; Alison in Melbourne; and to my four-year-old son Callum for his company and surprise statements – a very special thanks. Thanks also to Pete Flavelle from Perth; Thomas from Switzerland; Janet from California; Sharon from England; Rowan for his advice on Fremantle; Mal Toole of Exmouth Dive; Helen the Bushtucker Lady in Margaret River (Callum still loves you); Cervantes Pinnacles Adventure Tours for the 4WD thrill; the folk at the Wander Inn in Bunbury; the friendly folk (but not the mosquitoes) at Eco Beach, Cape Villaret; Rory at his backpackers' in Northbridge; the staff of the Broome, Kununurra, Exmouth, Denham, Denmark, Port Hedland, Karratha, Kalbarri, Northam, York, Margaret River, Albany, Kalgoorlie-Boulder, Geraldton, Newman, Carnarvon, Esperance, Norseman, Dunsborough and Busselton tourist bureaus and offices and the WATC Perth for the wildflower photos. And last but certainly not least – to the LP staff in Melbourne.

Steve Womersley Thanks to Sera Jane and my mum for the reassuring phone calls whilst I nursed a swollen gum in the Dubbo RSL bridal suite; Jain, Snake and Saddlebags for protecting me from Sydney axe murderers; and the stranger in Wilcannia with an eye for dodgy tyres.

This Book

Australia was first written by Tony Wheeler in 1977 and has been through successive transformations. Among the major contributors to past editions were Susan Forsyth, John Noble, Hugh Finlay, Richard Nebesky and Peter Turner (5th edition), Alan Tiller, Hugh Finlay and Charlotte Hindle (6th edition), Hugh Finlay, Mark Armstrong, Michelle Coxall, Jon Murray and Jeff Williams (7th edition), and Hugh, Mark, Jeff, David Willett, Denis O'Byrne, David Collins, Dani Valent and John & Monica Chapman (8th edition).

From the Publisher

This edition was edited at Lonely Planet in Melbourne by Bethune Carmichael, Rebecca Turner, Paul Harding, Anne Mulvaney, Sarah Mathers and Lou Callan. Mapping and design were coordinated by Matt King with the assistance of Mark Griffiths, Jenny Jones, Tony Fankhauser and Jacqui Schiff. Matt King compiled the material for the Aboriginal Arts section, the Australian Ecosystems section was written by Lindsay Brown and the cover was designed by Simon Bracken. Thanks to Mary Neighbour, Jane Hart and Rob van Driesum. Thanks also to the readers whose letters helped with this update. Their names are listed at back of the book.

Warning & Request

Things change – prices go up, schedules change, good places go bad and bad places go bankrupt – nothing stays the same. So, if you find things better or worse, recently opened or long since closed, please tell us

and help make the next edition even more accurate and useful.

We value all of the feedback we receive from travellers. Julie Young coordinates a small team who read and acknowledge every letter, postcard and email, and ensure that every morsel of information finds its way to the appropriate authors, editors and publishers.

Everyone who writes to us will find their name in the next edition of the appropriate guide and will also receive a free subscription to our quarterly newsletter, *Planet Talk*. The very best contributions will be rewarded with a free Lonely Planet guide.

Excerpts from your correspondence may appear in new editions of this guide; in our newsletter, *Planet Talk*; or in updates on our Web site – so please let us know if you don't want your letter published or your name acknowledged.

Contents

NORTHERN TERRITORY 347

QUEENSLAND 434

TASMANIA...688

VICTORIA 767

Boxed Asides

Map Index

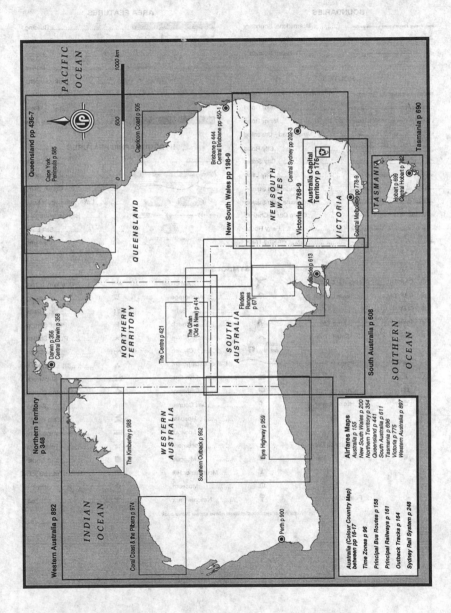

Map Legend

PACIFIC OCEAN

1000 km

500

0

Cape York Peninsula p 585

Queensland pp 436-7

Capricorn Coast p 505

Brisbane p 444
Central Brisbane pp 450-1

New South Wales pp 198-9

Central Sydney pp 202-3

QUEENSLAND

NEW SOUTH WALES

Australia Capital Territory p 176

Victoria pp 768-9

VICTORIA

Central Melbourne pp 778-9

Tasmania p 690

TASMANIA

Hobart p 699
Central Hobart p 702

Northern Territory p 348

Darwin p 356
Central Darwin p 358

NORTHERN TERRITORY

The Centre p 421

The Ghan (Old & New) p 414

SOUTH AUSTRALIA

Flinders Ranges p 671

Adelaide p 613

South Australia p 608

SOUTHERN OCEAN

Western Australia p 892

The Kimberley p 988

WESTERN AUSTRALIA

Southern Outback p 952

Eyre Highway p 959

Coral Coast & the Pilbara p 974

Perth p 900

INDIAN OCEAN

Australia (Colour Country Map) between pp 16-17
Time Zones p 96
Principal Bus Routes p 158
Principal Railways p 161
Outback Tracks p 164
Sydney Rail System p 248

Airfares Maps
Australia p 155
New South Wales p 200
Northern Territory p 354
Queensland p 441
South Australia p 611
Tasmania p 696
Victoria p 775
Western Australia p 897

Map Legend

BOUNDARIES

▬▪▬▪▬▪▬▪▬	International Boundary
▬ ▬ ▬ ▬ ▬	State Boundary
▬ ▬ ▬ ▬	Disputed Boundary

ROUTES

A25	Freeway, with Route Number
	Major Road
	Minor Road
==========	Minor Road - Unsealed
	City Road
	City Street
	City Lane
▬▬◉▬▬	Train Route, with Station
▬▬Ⓜ▬▬	Metro Route, with Station
▬▪▬▪▬▪	Cable Car or Chairlift
▬ ▬ ▬ ▬	Ferry Route
	Walking Track

AREA FEATURES

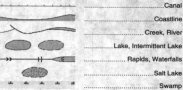

	Building
+ + + +	Cemetery
	Beach
	Market
✿	Park, Gardens
	Pedestrian Mall
	Reef
	Urban Area

HYDROGRAPHIC FEATURES

	Canal
	Coastline
	Creek, River
	Lake, Intermittent Lake
»»»⊢⊣	Rapids, Waterfalls
	Salt Lake
⊥ ⊥ ⊥ ⊥	Swamp

SYMBOLS

Symbol	Name	Symbol	Name	Symbol	Name
✪ CAPITAL	National Capital	✈	Airport	←	One Way Street
◉ CAPITAL	State Capital	⊕	Anchorage	P	Parking
● CITY	City	$	Bank	)(	Pass
● Town	Large Town	⚲	Beach		Petrol Station
● Town	Small Town	∩	Cave	★	Police Station
		✝	Church	✉	Post Office
■	Place to Stay	∿	Cliff or Escarpment	⁘	Ruins
▲	Camping Ground	▧	Dive Site	⚓	Shipwreck
⌂	Caravan Park	◎	Embassy	❖	Shopping Centre
⌂	Hut or Chalet	⚑	Golf Course	⊚	Spring
		⊕	Hospital	⚐	Surf Beach
		✳	Lookout	⊞	Swimming Pool
▼	Place to Eat	⚑	Monument	☎	Telephone
☗	Pub or Bar	☪	Mosque	⊟	Temple
		▲	Mountain or Hill	ⓘ	Tourist Information
		⛪	Museum	⊖	Transport
○	Point of Interest	⚘	National Park	⚲	Zoo

Note: not all symbols displayed above appear in this book

Introduction

Most people harbour a particular image of Australia, such as the Sydney Opera House or Ayers Rock, yet these famous icons do scant justice to the richness of Australia's natural treasures and its cultural diversity. Australia offers a wealth of travel experiences, from the drama of the outback and the spectacle of the Great Barrier Reef to cosmopolitan Sydney and arguably the best beaches in the world.

To really get to grips with the country, you must get away from the cities. Australian society may be largely urban but, myth or not, it's in the outback, in 'the bush', where you really find Australia – endless skies and red dirt, and laconic Aussie characters. For those adventurous and independent travel-

lers who really want to experience travel off the beaten track, Australia has plenty to offer, from World Heritage listed rainforests to desert national parks.

However, Australia can also be far from the rough and ready country its image might indicate. In the big cities you'll find some of the prettiest Victorian architecture anywhere; Australian restaurants serve an astounding variety of cuisines with the freshest ingredients you could ask for (it's all grown here) and it's no problem at all to fall in love with Australian wines.

Australia is exciting and invigorating, and it's hard to think of another country that offers such variety and opportunity for the short or long-term visitor.

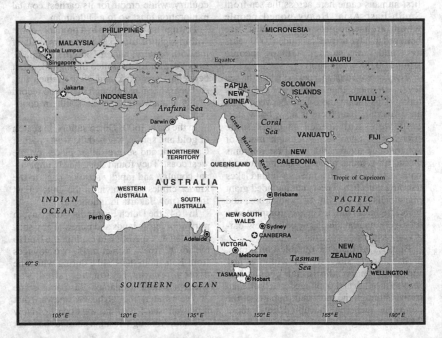

15

Facts about the Country

HISTORY

Australia was the last great landmass to be discovered by the Europeans. Long before the British claimed it as their own, European explorers and traders had been dreaming of the riches to be found in the unknown – some said mythical – southern land (terra australis) that was supposed to form a counterbalance to the landmass north of the equator. The continent they eventually found had already been inhabited for tens of thousands of years.

Aboriginal Settlement

Australian Aboriginal (which literally means 'indigenous') society has the longest continuous cultural history in the world, with origins dating to the last Ice age. Although mystery shrouds many aspects of Australian prehistory, it seems almost certain that the first humans came here across the sea from South-East Asia. Heavy-boned people whom archaeologists call 'Robust' are believed to have arrived around 70,000 years ago, and more slender 'Gracile' people around 50,000 years ago.

They arrived during a period when the sea level was more than 50m lower than it is today. This meant more land between Asia and Australia than there is now, but watercraft were still needed to cross some stretches of open sea. Although much of Australia is today arid, the first migrants would have found a much wetter continent, with large forests and numerous inland lakes teeming with fish. The fauna included giant marsupials such as 3m-tall kangaroos, and huge, flightless birds. The environment was relatively nonthreatening – only a few carnivorous predators existed.

Because of these favourable conditions, archaeologists suggest that within a few thousand years Aboriginal people had moved through and populated much of Australia, although the most central parts of the continent were not occupied until about 24,000 years ago.

The last Ice age came to an end 15,000 to 10,000 years ago. The sea level rose dramatically with the rise in temperature, and an area of Greater Australia the size of Western Australia was flooded during a process that would have seen strips of land 100km wide inundated in just a few decades. Many of the inland lakes dried up, and vast deserts formed. Thus, although the Aboriginal population was spread fairly evenly throughout the continent 20,000 years ago, the coastal areas became more densely occupied after the end of the last Ice age and the stabilisation of the sea level 5000 years ago.

European 'Discovery' & Exploration

Captain James Cook is popularly credited with Australia's discovery, but a Portuguese was probably the first European to sight the country, while credit for its earliest coastal exploration must go to a Dutchman.

Portuguese navigators had probably come within sight of the coast in the first half of the 16th century; and in 1606 the Spaniard, Luis Vaez de Torres, sailed through the strait between Cape York and New Guinea that still bears his name, though there's no record of his actually sighting the southern continent.

In the early 1600s Dutch sailors, in search of gold and spices, reached the west coast of Cape York and several other places on the west coast. They found a dry, harsh, unpleasant country, and rapidly scuttled back to the kinder climes of Batavia in the Dutch East Indies (now Jakarta in Indonesia).

In 1642 the Dutch East India Company, in pursuit of fertile lands and riches of any sort, mounted an expedition to explore the land to the south. Abel Tasman made two voyages from Batavia in the 1640s, during which he discovered the region he called Van Diemen's Land (renamed Tasmania some 200 years later), though he was unaware that it was an island, and the west coast of New Zealand. Although Tasman charted the coast

RICHARD I'ANSON

RICHARD I'ANSON

From the snowcapped peaks of Mt Feathertop in the Victorian Alps to the red rock domes of Kata Tjuta in the heart of the desert, Australia offers a breathtaking variety of landscapes.

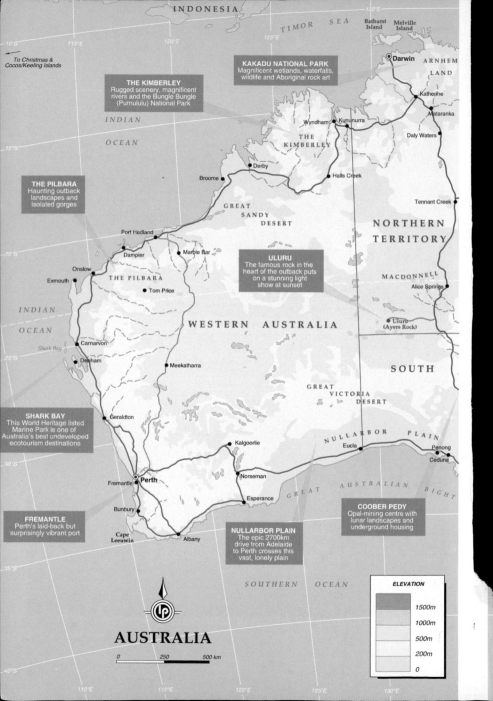

INDONESIA

TIMOR SEA

Bathurst Island
Melville Island

To Christmas & Cocos/Keeling Islands

KAKADU NATIONAL PARK
Magnificent wetlands, waterfalls, wildlife and Aboriginal rock art

Darwin

ARNHEM LAND

THE KIMBERLEY
Rugged scenery, magnificent rivers and the Bungle Bungle (Purnululu) National Park

Katherine

Mataranka

INDIAN

OCEAN

Wyndham Kununurra

Daly Waters

THE KIMBERLEY

Derby

Halls Creek

THE PILBARA
Haunting outback landscapes and isolated gorges

Broome

GREAT SANDY DESERT

Tennant Creek

NORTHERN

TERRITORY

Port Hedland

Dampier Marble Bar

ULURU
The famous rock in the heart of the outback puts on a stunning light show at sunset

MACDONNELL

Onslow

THE PILBARA

Tom Price

Alice Springs

Exmouth

INDIAN

OCEAN

WESTERN AUSTRALIA

Uluru
(Ayers Rock)

Shark Bay

Carnarvon

SOUTH

Denham

Meekatharra

GREAT VICTORIA DESERT

SHARK BAY
This World Heritage listed Marine Park is one of Australia's best undeveloped ecotourism destinations

Geraldton

NULLARBOR PLAIN

Kalgoorlie

Eucla

Penong

Ceduna

Fremantle Perth

Norseman

GREAT AUSTRALIAN BIGHT

Bunbury

Esperance

FREMANTLE
Perth's laid-back but surprisingly vibrant port

COOBER PEDY
Opal-mining centre with lunar landscapes and underground housing

Cape Leeuwin

Albany

NULLARBOR PLAIN
The epic 2700km drive from Adelaide to Perth crosses this vast, lonely plain

SOUTHERN OCEAN

ELEVATION	
	1500m
	1000m
	500m
	200m
	0

AUSTRALIA

0   250   500 km

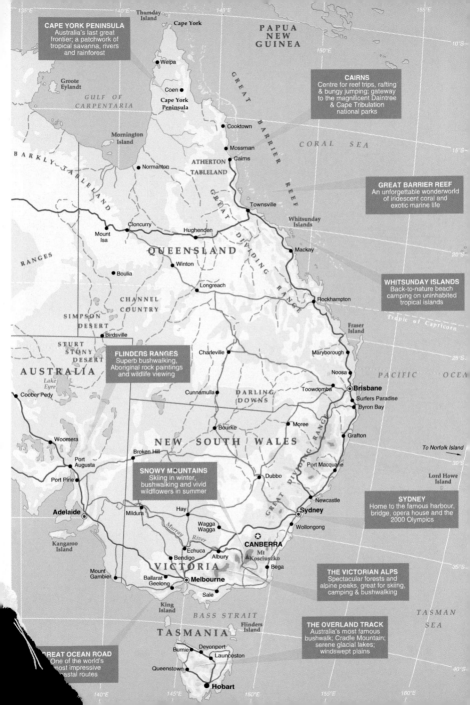

CAPE YORK PENINSULA
Australia's last great frontier; a patchwork of tropical savanna, rivers and rainforest

CAIRNS
Centre for reef trips, rafting & bungy jumping; gateway to the magnificent Daintree & Cape Tribulation national parks

GREAT BARRIER REEF
An unforgettable wonderworld of iridescent coral and exotic marine life

WHITSUNDAY ISLANDS
Back-to-nature beach camping on uninhabited tropical islands

FLINDERS RANGES
Superb bushwalking, Aboriginal rock paintings and wildlife viewing

SNOWY MOUNTAINS
Skiing in winter, bushwalking and vivid wildflowers in summer

SYDNEY
Home to the famous harbour, bridge, opera house and the 2000 Olympics

THE VICTORIAN ALPS
Spectacular forests and alpine peaks, great for skiing, camping & bushwalking

THE OVERLAND TRACK
Australia's most famous bushwalk; Cradle Mountain; serene glacial lakes; windswept plains

GREAT OCEAN ROAD
One of the world's most impressive coastal routes

PAPUA NEW GUINEA

Thursday Island
Cape York
Weipa
Coen
Cape York Peninsula
Groote Eylandt
GULF OF CARPENTARIA
Mornington Island
Cooktown
Mossman
Cairns
ATHERTON TABLELAND
CORAL SEA
BARKLY TABLELAND
Normanton
Townsville
Whitsunday Islands
GREAT DIVIDING RANGE
Cloncurry
Hughenden
Mackay
Mount Isa
QUEENSLAND
RANGES
Winton
Boulia
Longreach
Rockhampton
SIMPSON DESERT
CHANNEL COUNTRY
Fraser Island
Tropic of Capricorn
Birdsville
STURT STONY DESERT
Charleville
Maryborough
AUSTRALIA
Lake Eyre
DARLING DOWNS
Noosa
PACIFIC OCEA
Coober Pedy
Cunnamulla
Toowoomba
Brisbane
Surfers Paradise
Byron Bay
Woomera
Bourke
Moree
Grafton
Port Augusta
Broken Hill
NEW SOUTH WALES
To Norfolk Island
Lord Howe Island
Port Pirie
Dubbo
Port Macquarie
Mildura
Hay
Wagga Wagga
Newcastle
Sydney
Adelaide
Murray River
Wollongong
Kangaroo Island
Echuca
Albury
CANBERRA
Bendigo
Mt Kosciuszko
Bega
Mount Gambier
Ballarat
Geelong
VICTORIA
Melbourne
Sale
King Island
BASS STRAIT
TASMAN SEA
Flinders Island
Burnie
Devonport
Launceston
TASMANIA
Queenstown
Hobart

TONY WHEELER

JAMES LYON

RICHARD I'ANSON

Australian Capital Territory
Left: National Gallery of Australia, Canberra
Right: Waterfall near Canberra
Bottom: Parliament House, Canberra

Archaeological Treasures

The early Aboriginal people left no stone buildings or statues to tickle our fancy, but archaeologists have unearthed many other treasures. The best known site by far is **Lake Mungo**, in the dry Willandra Lakes system in the south-west of New South Wales.

Mungo (the name is Scottish) is a living, evolving excavation. The true archaeologists here are time and weather. This area was once a vast system of inland lakes, dry now for some 20,000 years. The embankment of sand and mud on the eastern fringe of the ancient lake system, named the 'Walls of China' by homesick Chinese workers, has been eroded by wind in recent years, revealing human and animal skeletal remains, ancient campfires and evidence of intertribal trading.

The remains prove that ritual burial was practised here 15,000 years before the construction of the Egyptian pyramids. The fireplaces reveal that sophisticated, tertiary-chipped stone implements were fashioned by the dwellers at the edge of this now dry lake. The food they ate can be discovered in the fireplaces, and the long-extinct animals they preyed on are found in skeletal form on the dunes. This area is so important that the Willandra Lakes are now a UN World Heritage area.

Another fascinating area of study has been **Kow Swamp** in northern Victoria. This site has a rich collection of human remains that date from the late Pleistocene epoch. One body, buried 12,000 years ago, had a headband of kangaroo incisor teeth. In the lunette of **Lake Nitchie**, in western New South Wales, a man was buried 7000 to 6500 years ago with a necklace of 178 pierced Tasmanian-devil teeth.

The west and north of Australia have many significant sites. Groove-edged axes dating back 23,000 years have been found in the **Malangangerr** rock-shelter in Arnhem Land. Other rich sources of artefacts are the **Miriwun** rock-shelter on the Ord River in the Kimberley; the **Mt Newman** rock-shelter in the Pilbara; and the **Devil's Lair** near Cape Leeuwin in the far south-west of the continent. Fragments and stone tools dating back 38,000 years were found in the nearby **Swan Valley**.

Ice-age rock engravings (petroglyphs) have been found throughout the continent. Those in **Koonalda Cave**, on the Nullarbor in South Australia, are perhaps the oldest. Flint miners often visited the cave 24,000 to 14,000 years ago, and unexplained patterns were left on the wall – perhaps it's art, perhaps not. Other places where petroglyphs are easily seen are on the **Burrup Peninsula** near Dampier, Western Australia; **Mootwingee National Park**, between Tibooburra and Broken Hill in far western New South Wales; the **Lightning Brothers** site, Flora River, Northern Territory; and at the **Early Man shelter** near Laura in Queensland.

Josephine Flood's *Archaeology of the Dreamtime* (Collins, Sydney, 1983) provides a fascinating account of archaeological research into Australia's first inhabitants.

Warning: In Australia it is illegal to remove archaeological objects or to disturb human remains. Look but don't touch. ∎

of New Holland from Cape York to the Great Australian Bight, as well as the southern reaches of Van Diemen's Land, he did not sight the continent's east coast.

The prize for being Australia's original Pom goes to the enterprising pirate William Dampier, who made the first investigations ashore, about 40 years after Tasman and nearly 100 years before Cook.

Dampier's records of New Holland, from visits made to Shark Bay on the west coast in 1688 and 1698, influenced the European idea of a primitive and godless land, and that perspective remained unchanged until Cook's more informed and better documented voyages spawned romantic and exotic notions of the South Seas and the idealised view of the 'noble savage'.

The dismal continent was forgotten until 1768, when the British Admiralty instructed Captain James Cook to lead a scientific expedition to Tahiti, to observe the transit of the planet Venus, and then begin a search for the Great South Land. On board his ship *Endeavour* were also several scientists, including an astronomer and a group of naturalists and artists led by Joseph Banks.

After circumnavigating both islands of New Zealand, Cook set sail in search of the Great South Land, planning to head west until he found the unexplored east coast of New Holland.

On 19 April 1770 the extreme south-eastern tip of the continent was sighted and named Point Hicks, and when the *Endeavour* was a navigable distance from shore Cook turned north to follow the coast and search for a suitable landfall. It was nine days before an opening in the cliffs was sighted and the ship and crew found sheltered anchorage in a harbour they named Botany Bay.

During their forays ashore the scientists recorded descriptions of plants, animals and birds, the likes of which they had never seen, and attempted to communicate with the few native inhabitants, who all but ignored the first white people to set foot on the east coast. Cook wrote of the blacks: 'All they seemed to want was for us to be gone'.

After leaving Botany Bay, Cook continued north, charting the coastline and noting that the fertile east coast was a different story from the inhospitable land earlier explorers had seen to the south and west. When the *Endeavour* was badly damaged on a reef off north Queensland, Cook was forced to make a temporary settlement. It took six weeks to repair the ship, during which time Cook and the scientists investigated their surroundings further, this time making contact with the local Aboriginal people.

After repairing the *Endeavour*, navigating the Great Barrier Reef and rounding Cape York, Cook again put ashore to raise the Union Jack, rename the continent New South Wales and claim it for the British in the name of King George III.

James Cook was resourceful, intelligent, and popularly regarded as one of the greatest and most humane explorers of all time. His incisive reports of his voyages make fascinating reading even today. By the time he was killed, in the Sandwich Islands (now Hawaii) in 1779, he had led two further expeditions to the South Pacific.

Convicts & Settlement

Following the American Revolution, Britain was no longer able to transport convicts to North America. With jails and prison hulks already overcrowded, it was essential that an alternative be found quickly. In 1779 Joseph

The British colonisation of Australia was based on the brutal exploitation of convict labour.

Banks suggested New South Wales as a fine site for a colony of thieves and in 1786 Lord Sydney announced that the king had decided upon Botany Bay as a place for convicts under sentence of transportation. That the continent was already inhabited was not considered significant.

Less than two years later, in January 1788, the First Fleet sailed into Botany Bay under the command of Captain Arthur Phillip, who was to be the colony's first governor. Phillip was immediately disappointed with the landscape and sent a small boat north to find a more suitable landfall. The crew soon returned with the news that in Port Jackson they had found the finest harbour in the world and a good sheltered cove.

The fleet comprised 11 ships carrying about 750 male and female convicts, 400 sailors, four companies of marines and enough livestock and supplies for two years. It weighed anchor again and headed for Sydney Cove to begin settlement.

For the new arrivals, New South Wales was a harsh and horrible place. The crimes punished by transportation were often minor and the sentences, of no less than seven years with hard labour, were tantamount to life sentences as there was little hope of returning home.

Although the colony of soldiers, sailors, pickpockets, prostitutes, sheep stealers and petty thieves managed to survive the first difficult years, the cruel power of the military guards made the settlement a prison hell.

At first, until farming could be developed, the settlers were dependent upon supplies from Europe and a late or, even worse, a wrecked supply ship would have been disastrous. The threat of starvation hung over the colony for at least 16 years.

The Second Fleet arrived in 1790 with more convicts and some supplies, and a year later, following the landing of the Third Fleet, the population increased to around 4000.

As crops began to yield, New South Wales became less dependent on Britain for food. There were still, however, huge social gulfs in the fledgling colony: officers and their families were in control and clinging desperately to a modicum of civilised British living; soldiers, free settlers and even emancipated convicts were beginning to eke out a living; yet the majority of the population was still in chains, regarded as the dregs of humanity and living in squalid conditions.

Little of the country was explored during those first years; few people ventured farther than Sydney Cove, and though Governor Phillip had instructed that every attempt should be made to befriend the blacks, this was not to be.

Phillip believed New South Wales would not progress if the colony continued to rely solely on the labour of convicts, who were already busy constructing government roads and buildings. He believed prosperity depended on attracting free settlers, to whom convicts could be assigned as labourers, and in the granting of land to officers, soldiers and worthy emancipists (convicts who had served their time).

This had begun by the time Phillip returned to England and his second in command, Grose, took over. In a classic case of 'jobs for the boys', Grose tipped the balance of power further in favour of the military by granting land to officers of the New South Wales Corps.

With money, land and cheap labour suddenly at their disposal the officers became exploitative, making huge profits at the expense of the small farmers. To encourage convicts to work, the officers paid them in rum. The officers quickly prospered and were soon able to buy whole shiploads of goods and resell them for many times their original value. New South Wales was becoming an important port on trade routes, and whaling and sealing were increasing.

Meeting little resistance, the officers did virtually as they pleased. In particular, one John Macarthur managed to upset, defy, outmanoeuvre and outlast three governors, including William Bligh of the *Bounty* mutiny fame.

As governor, Bligh actually faced a second mutiny in 1808 when the officers rebelled and ordered his arrest. The Rum Rebellion, as it became known, was the final straw for the British government, which dispatched Lieutenant-Colonel Lachlan Macquarie with his own regiment and orders for the return to London of the New South Wales Corps.

John Macarthur, incidentally, was to have far-reaching effects on the colony's first staple industry, wool. His understanding of the country's grazing potential fostered his own profitable sheep-breeding concerns and prompted his introduction of the merino, in the belief that careful breeding could produce wool of exceptional quality. Though it was his vision, his wife, Elizabeth, did most of the work – Macarthur remained in England for nearly a decade for his part in the Rum Rebellion.

Governor Macquarie, having broken the stranglehold of the Corps, set about laying the groundwork for significant social reforms. He felt that the convicts who had served their time should be allowed rights as citizens, and began appointing emancipists to public positions.

While this meant the long-term future for convicts didn't appear quite so grim, by the end of Macquarie's term in 1821 New South Wales was still basically a convict society and there were often clashes between those who had never been imprisoned and those who had been freed.

During the 1830s and 1840s the number

of free settlers to the colonies of New South Wales, Western Australia, Van Diemen's Land (present-day Tasmania) and Port Phillip (Victoria) was increasing, although it was the discovery of gold in the 1850s that was truly to change the face of the young country.

By the time transportation was abolished (1852 in the eastern colonies and 1868 in the west) more than 168,000 convicts had been shipped to Australia.

Colonial Exploration & Expansion

Australia never experienced the systematic push westward that characterised the European settlement of America. Exploration and expansion basically took place for one of three reasons: to find suitable places of secondary punishment, like the barbaric penal settlement at Port Arthur in Van Diemen's Land; to occupy land before anyone else arrived; or in later years because of the quest for gold.

By 1800 there were only two small settlements in Australia – at Sydney Cove and Norfolk Island. While unknown areas on world maps were becoming few and far between, most of Australia was still one big blank. It was even suspected that it might be two large, separate islands and it was hoped there might be a vast sea in the centre.

The ensuing 40 years was a great period of discovery, as the vast inland was explored and settlements were established at Hobart, Brisbane, Perth, Adelaide and Melbourne. Some of the early explorers, particularly those who braved the hostile centre, suffered great hardship.

George Bass had charted the coast south of Sydney almost down to the present location of Melbourne during 1797 and 1798. Also in 1798, he sailed around Van Diemen's Land with Matthew Flinders, establishing that it was an island. Flinders went on in 1802 to sail right round Australia.

The first settlement in Van Diemen's Land, in 1803, was close to the present site of Hobart; by the 1820s Hobart Town rivalled Sydney in importance. The island was not named Tasmania, after its original

European discoverer, until 1856 when, after the end of transportation, the inhabitants requested the name be changed to remove the stigma of what had been a vicious penal colony.

On the mainland, the Blue Mountains at first proved an impenetrable barrier, fencing in Sydney to the sea, but in 1813 a track was finally forced through and the western plains were reached by the explorers Blaxland, Wentworth and Lawson.

Port Phillip Bay in Victoria was originally considered as the site for a second settlement in Australia but was rejected in favour of Hobart, so it was not looked at again until 1835 when settlers from Tasmania, in search of more land, selected the present site of Melbourne. Perth was first settled in 1829, but as it was isolated from the rest of the country, growth there was very slow.

The first settlement in the Brisbane area was made by a party of convicts sent north from Sydney because the (by then) good citizens of that fair city were getting fed up with having all those crims about the place. By the time the Brisbane penal colony was abandoned in 1839, free settlers had arrived in force.

Adelaide, established in 1837, was initially an experiment in free-enterprise colonisation. It failed due to bad management and the British government had to take over from the bankrupt organisers and bail the settlement out of trouble.

In 1824 the explorers Hume and Hovell, starting from near present-day Canberra, made the first overland journey southwards, reaching the western shores of Port Phillip Bay. On the way they discovered a large river and named it after Hume, although it was later renamed the Murray by another great explorer, Charles Sturt. In 1829, Sturt established how the Murrumbidgee and Darling river systems tied in with the Murray, and where the Murray met the sea. Until that time there had been much speculation that many of the inland rivers might in fact drain the anticipated inland sea.

Twelve years later the colony's surveyor-general, Major Mitchell, wrote glowing reports of the beautiful and fertile country he had crossed in his expedition across the Murray River and as far south as Portland Bay. He dubbed the region (now Victoria) Australia Felix, or 'Australia Fair'.

In 1840 Edward Eyre left Adelaide to try to reach the centre of Australia. He gave up at Mt Hopeless and then attempted a crossing to Albany in Western Australia. This formidable task nearly proved too much as both food and water were virtually unobtainable and Eyre's companion, Baxter, was killed by two Aboriginal guides. Eyre struggled on, encountering a French whaling ship in Rossiter Bay; reprovisioned, he managed to reach Albany. The road across the Nullarbor Plain from South Australia to Western Australia is named the Eyre Highway.

From 1844 to 1845 a German scientist by the name of Ludwig Leichhardt travelled through northern Queensland, skirting the Gulf of Carpentaria, to Port Essington, near modern-day Darwin. He failed in 1846 and 1847 to cross Australia from east to west, and disappeared on his second attempt; he was never seen again.

In 1848 Edmund Kennedy set out to travel by land up Cape York Peninsula while a ship, HMS *Rattlesnake*, explored the coast and islands. Starting from Rockingham Bay, south of Cairns, the expedition almost immediately struck trouble when its heavy supply carts could not be dragged through the swampy ground around Tully. The rugged land, harsh climate, lack of supplies, hostile Aboriginal people and missed supply drops, all took their toll and nine of the party of 13 died. Kennedy himself was speared to death by Aboriginal people when he was only 30km from the end of the fearsome trek. His Aboriginal servant, Jacky Jacky, was the only expedition member to finally reach the supply ship.

Beginning in Melbourne in 1860, the legendary attempt by Robert Burke and William Wills to cross the continent from south to north was destined to be one of the most tragic. Unlike earlier explorers, they tried to manage without Aboriginal guides. After reaching a depot at Cooper Creek in Queens-land they intended to make a dash north to the Gulf of Carpentaria with a party of four. Their camels proved far slower than anticipated in the swampy land close to the gulf and on their way back one of the party died of exhaustion.

Burke, Wills and the third member, John King, eventually struggled back to Cooper Creek, at the end of their strength and nearly two months behind schedule, only to find the depot group had given up hope and left for Melbourne just hours earlier. They remained at Cooper Creek, but missed a returning search party and never found the supplies that had been left for them. Burke and Wills finally starved to death, literally in the midst of plenty; King was able to survive on food provided by local Aboriginal people until a rescue party arrived.

Departing from Adelaide in 1860, and chasing a £2000 reward for the first south-north crossing, John McDouall Stuart reached the geographical centre of Australia, Central Mt Stuart, but shortly after was forced to turn back. In 1861 he got much closer to the Top End before he again had to return. Finally in 1862 Stuart reached the north coast near Darwin. The overland telegraph line, completed in 1872, and the modern Stuart Highway follow a similar route.

Devastation of the Aborigines

When Sydney Cove was first settled by the British, it is believed there were about 300,000 Aboriginal people in Australia and around 250 different languages, many as distinct from each other as English is from Chinese. Tasmania alone had eight languages, and tribes living on opposite sides of present-day Sydney Harbour spoke mutually unintelligible languages.

In such a society, based on family groups with an egalitarian political structure, a coordinated response to the European colonisers was not possible. Despite the presence of the Aboriginal people, the newly arrived Europeans considered the new continent to *terra nullius* – a land belonging to no Conveniently, they saw no recogn system of government, no commerce or permanent settlements and no evidence of landownership. (Had there been such systems, and if the Aboriginal people had offered coordinated resistance, the British might have been forced to legitimise their colonisation by entering into a treaty with the Aboriginal landowners, as happened in New Zealand with the Treaty of Waitangi.)

Many Aboriginal people were driven from their land by force, and many more succumbed to exotic diseases such as smallpox, measles, venereal disease, influenza, whooping cough, pneumonia and tuberculosis. Others voluntarily left their lands to travel to the fringes of settled areas to obtain new commodities such as steel and cloth, and experience hitherto unknown drugs such as tea, tobacco and alcohol.

The delicate balance between Aboriginal people and nature was broken, as the European invaders cut down the forests and introduced numerous feral and domestic animals – by 1860 there were 20 million sheep in Australia. Sheep and cattle destroyed water holes and ruined the habitats which had for tens of thousands of years sustained mammals, reptiles and vegetable foods. Many species of plants and animals disappeared altogether.

There was still considerable conflict between Aboriginal people and white settlers. Starving Aboriginal people speared sheep and cattle and then suffered fierce reprisal raids which often left many dead. For the first 100 years of 'settlement' very few Europeans were prosecuted for killing Aboriginal people, although the practice was widespread.

In many parts of Australia, Aboriginal people could only defend their lands with desperate guerrilla tactics. Warriors including Pemulwy, Yagan, Dundalli, Jandamarra (known to the whites as 'Pigeon') and

courtesy of the National Library of Australia

control of Aboriginal land necessitated the systematic slaughter and repression of its traditional Aboriginal people suffered inhuman treatment with dignity, and often fought back.

Nemarluk were feared by the colonists for a time, and some settlements had to be abandoned. Until the 1850s, when Europeans had to rely on inaccurate and unreliable flintlock rifles, Aboriginal people sometimes had the benefit of superior numbers, weapons and tactics. However, with the introduction of breach-loading repeater rifles in the 1870s, armed resistance was quickly crushed (although on isolated occasions into the 1920s, whites were still speared in central and northern Australia). Full-blood Aboriginal people in Tasmania were wiped out almost to the last individual, and Aboriginal society in southern Australia suffered terribly. Within 100 years of European settlement all that was left of traditional Aboriginal society consisted of relatively small groups in central and northern Australia.

Gold, Stability & Growth

The discovery of gold in the 1850s brought about the most significant changes in the social and economic structure of Australia, particularly in Victoria, where most of the gold was found.

Earlier gold discoveries had been all but ignored, partly because they were only small finds and mining skills were still undeveloped, but mostly because the law stated that all gold discovered belonged to the government.

The discovery of large quantities near Bathurst in 1851, however, caused a rush of hopeful miners from Sydney and forced the government to abandon the law of ownership. Instead, it introduced a compulsory diggers' licence fee of 30 shillings a month, whether the miners found gold or not, to ensure the country earned some revenue from the incredible wealth that was being unearthed. Victorian businesspeople at the time, fearing their towns would soon be devoid of able-bodied men, offered a reward for the discovery of gold in their colony.

In 1851 one of the largest gold discoveries in history was made at Ballarat, followed by others at Bendigo and Mt Alexander (near Castlemaine), starting a rush of unprecedented magnitude.

While the first diggers at the goldfields that soon sprang up all over Victoria came from the other Australian colonies, it wasn't long before they were joined by thousands of migrants. The Irish, Scots and English, as well as other Europeans and Americans, began arriving in droves, and within 12 months there were about 1800 hopeful diggers disembarking at Melbourne every week.

Similar discoveries in other colonies, particularly in Western Australia in the 1890s, further boosted populations and levels of economic activity.

The gold rushes also brought floods of diligent Chinese miners and market gardeners onto the Australian diggings, where violent white opposition led to race riots and a morbid fear of Asian immigration which persists, to some extent, to this day. Although few people actually made their fortunes on the goldfields, many stayed to settle, as farmers, workers and shopkeepers. At the same time the Industrial Revolution in England started to produce a strong demand for raw materials. With its vast agricultural and mineral resources, Australia's economic base became secure.

Besides the population and economic growth that followed the discovery of gold, the rush contributed greatly to the development of a distinctive Australian folklore. The music brought by the Scots, English and Irish, for instance, was tuned to life on the diggings, while poets, singers and writers told stories of the people, the roaring gold towns and the boisterous hotels, the squatters and their sheep and cattle stations, the swagmen, and the derring-do of the notorious bushrangers, many of whom became folk heroes.

Federation & WWI

During the 1890s calls for the separate colonies to federate became increasingly strident. Supporters argued that it would improve the economy and the position of workers by enabling the abolition of intercolonial tariffs and protection against competition from foreign labour.

Each colony was determined, however, that its interests should not be overshadowed by those of the other colonies. For this reason, the constitution that was finally adopted gave only very specific powers to the Commonwealth, leaving all residual powers with the states. It also gave each state equal representation in the upper house of parliament (the Senate) regardless of size or population. Today Tasmania, with a population of less than half a million, has as many senators in Federal parliament as New South Wales, with a population of around six million. As the Senate is able to reject legislation passed by the lower house, this legacy of Australia's colonial past has had a profound effect on its politics, entrenching state divisions and ensuring that the smaller states have remained powerful forces in the government of the nation.

With federation, which came on 1 January 1901, Australia became a nation, but its loyalty and many of its legal and cultural ties to Britain remained. The mother country still expected military support from its Commonwealth allies in any conflict, and Australia fought beside Britain in battles as far from Australia's shores as the Boer War in South Africa. This willingness to follow western powers to war would be demonstrated time and again during the 20th century. Seemingly unquestioning loyalty to Britain and later the USA was only part of the reason. Xenophobia – born of isolation, an Asian location and a vulnerable economy – was also to blame.

The extent to which Australia regarded itself as a European outpost became evident with the passage of the Immigration Restriction Bill of 1901. The bill, known as the White Australia policy, was designed to prevent the immigration of Asians and Pacific Islanders. Prospective immigrants were required to pass a dictation test in a European language. This language could be as obscure a tongue as the authorities wished. The dictation test was not abolished until 1958.

The desire to protect the jobs and conditions of white Australian workers that had helped bring about the White Australia policy did, however, have some positive results. The labour movement had been a strong political force for many years, and by 1908 the principle of a basic wage sufficient to enable a male worker to support himself, a wife and three children had been established. By that time also, old age and invalid pensions were being paid.

When war broke out in Europe in 1914, Australian troops were again sent to fight thousands of kilometres from home. From Australia's perspective, the most infamous of the WWI battles in which Diggers took part was that intended to force a passage through the Dardanelles to Constantinople. Australian and New Zealand troops landed at Gallipoli only to be slaughtered by well-equipped and strategically positioned Turkish soldiers. The sacrifices made by Australian soldiers are commemorated annually on Anzac Day, 25 April, the anniversary of the Gallipoli landing.

Interestingly, while Australians rallied to the aid of Britain during WWI, the majority of voters were prepared to support voluntary military service only. Efforts to introduce conscription during the war led to bitter debate, both in parliament and in the streets, and in referenda compulsory national service was rejected by a small margin.

Australia was hard hit by the Depression; prices for wool and wheat – two mainstays of the economy – plunged. In 1931 almost a third of breadwinners were unemployed and poverty was widespread. Swagmen became a familiar sight, as they had been in the 1890s depression, as thousands of men took to the 'wallaby track' in search of work in the countryside. By 1933, however, Australia's economy was starting to recover, a result of rises in wool prices and a rapid revival of manufacturing.

Also on the rise was the career of Joseph Lyons, who had become prime minister after defeating the Labor government, headed by James Scullin, at elections in 1932. Lyons, a former Labor minister, had defected and formed the conservative United Australia Party, which stayed in power through the

The Flying Doctor

Before the late 1920s the outback's far-flung residents had little or no access to medical facilities. The nearest doctor was often weeks away over rough tracks, so if you fell seriously ill or met with a bad accident, your chances of recovery were slim. Difficult pregnancies and illnesses such as rheumatic fever and acute appendicitis were almost a death sentence. If you were lucky, you fell ill near a telegraph line, where your mates could treat you – or even operate – under instructions received in Morse code.

In 1912 the Reverend John Flynn of the Presbyterian Church helped establish the outback's first hospital at Oodnadatta. Flynn was appalled by the tragedies resulting from the lack of medical facilities and was quick to realise the answer lay in radios and aircraft. However, these technologies – particularly radio – were still very much in their infancy.

Flynn knew nothing of either radios or aviation but his sense of mission inspired others who did, such as radio engineer Alfred Traeger. In 1928, after years of trial and error, Traeger developed a small, pedal-powered radio transceiver that was simple to use, inexpensive and could send and receive messages over 500km. The outback's great silence was broken at last.

Aircraft suitable for medical evacuations had become available in 1920 but it was the lack of a radio communication network that delayed their general use for this purpose. Traeger's invention was the key to the establishment of Australia's first Flying Doctor base in Cloncurry, Queensland, in 1928. Cloncurry was then the base for the Queensland & Northern Territory Aerial Services (Qantas), which provided the pilot and an aircraft under lease.

The new service proved an outstanding success and areas beyond the reach of Cloncurry soon began to clamour for their own Flying Doctor. However, the Presbyterian Church had insufficient resources to allow a rapid expansion. In 1933 it handed the aerial medical service over to 'an organisation of national character' and so the Royal Flying Doctor Service (RFDS) was born. Flynn's vision of a 'mantle of safety' over the outback had become a reality.

Today, 12 RFDS base stations provide a sophisticated network of radio communications and medical services to an area as large as Western Europe and about two-thirds the size of the USA. Emergency evacuations of sick or injured people are still an important function, but these days the RFDS provides a comprehensive range of medical services, including routine clinics at communities that are unable to attract full-time medical staff. It also supervises numerous small hospitals that normally operate without a doctor; such hospitals are staffed by registered nurses who communicate by telephone or radio with their RFDS doctor.

The administration of RFDS bases is divided between seven nonprofit organisations funded by government grants and private donations. ■

1930s. The death of Lyons in 1939 saw the emergence of a figure who was set to dominate the Australian political scene for the next 25 years – Robert Gordon Menzies. He was prime minister from 1939 until forced by his own party to resign in 1941, after which time he formed a new conservative party, the Liberal Party, before regaining office in 1949, a post which he held for a record 16 years.

'Protection' of Aboriginal People

By the early 1900s, legislation designed to segregate and 'protect' Aboriginal people was passed in all states. The legislation imposed restrictions on the Aboriginal people's rights to own property and seek employment, and the Aboriginals Ordinance of 1918 even allowed the state to remove children from Aboriginal mothers if it was suspected that the father was not an Aboriginal. In these cases the parents were considered to have no rights over the children, who were placed in foster homes or childcare institutions.

Many Aboriginal people are still bitter about having been separated from their families and forced to grow up apart from their people – they have come to be known as the 'Stolen Generation'. An upside of the ordinance was that it gave a degree of protection for 'full-blood' Aboriginal people who were living on reserves, as non-Aboriginal people could enter only with a permit, and mineral exploration was forbidden.

WWII & Postwar Australia

In the years before WWII Australia became increasingly fearful of Japan. When war did break out, Australian troops fought alongside the British in Europe but after the Japanese bombed Pearl Harbor, Australia's own national security finally began to take priority.

Singapore fell, the northern Australian towns of Darwin and Broome and the New Guinean town of Port Moresby were all bombed, the Japanese advanced southward, and still Britain called for more Australian troops. This time the Australian prime minister, John Curtin, refused. Australian soldiers were needed to fight the Japanese advancing over the mountainous Kokoda Trail towards Port Moresby. In appalling conditions Australian soldiers confronted and defeated the Japanese at Milne Bay, east of Port Moresby, and began the long struggle to push them from the Pacific.

Ultimately it was the USA, not Britain, that helped protect Australia from the Japanese, defeating them in the Battle of the Coral Sea. This event was to mark the beginning of a profound shift in Australia's allegiance away from Britain and towards the USA. Although Australia continued to support Britain in the war in Europe, its appreciation of its own vulnerability had been sharpened immeasurably by the Japanese advance.

One result of this was the postwar immigration program, which offered assisted passage not only to the British but also to refugees from eastern Europe in the hope that the increase in population would strengthen Australia's economy and its ability to defend itself. 'Populate or Perish' became the catch phrase. Between 1947 and 1968 more than 800,000 non-British European migrants came to live in Australia. They have since made an enormous contribution to the country, enlivening its culture and broadening its vision.

The standard of living improved rapidly after the war (due largely to rapid increase in the demand for Australian raw materials), and the Labor government of Ben Chifley put in place a reconstruction program, which saw, among other things, the establishment of the massive Snowy Mountains Hydroelectric Scheme.

Postwar Australia came to accept the American view that it was not so much Asia but *communism* in Asia that threatened the increasingly Americanised Australian way of life. Accordingly Australia, again under Menzies by this stage, followed the USA into the Korean War and joined it as a signatory to the treaties of ANZUS and the anti-

20th-Century Exploration

Around the turn of the century, Baldwin Spencer, a biologist, and Francis Gillen, an anthropologist, teamed up to study the Aboriginal people of central Australia and Arnhem Land. Other expeditions to northern Australia and Arnhem Land were led by the British polar explorer GH Wilkins (in 1923) and Donald Mackay (in 1928). Donald Thomson led his first expedition to Arnhem Land in 1935 and his work in northern Australia still receives accolades from anthropologists and naturalists.

In the 1930s, aerial mapping of the Centre began in earnest, financed by Mackay. Surveys were carried out over the Simpson Desert, the only large stretch of the country still to be explored on foot. In 1939, CT Madigan led an expedition that crossed this forbidding landscape from Old Andado to Birdsville.

In 1948 the largest scientific expedition ever undertaken in Australia was led by Charles Mountford into Arnhem Land. Financed by the National Geographic Society and the Australian government, it collected over 13,000 fish, 13,500 plant specimens, 850 birds and over 450 animal skins, along with thousands of Aboriginal implements and weapons.

During the 1950s the Woomera Rocket Range and the atomic-bomb test sites of Emu Junction and Maralinga were set up. This vast region was opened up by the surveyor Len Beadell, who is widely regarded as the last Australian explorer. ∎

communist Southeast Asia Treaty Organization (SEATO). During the 1950s Australia also provided aid to South-East Asian nations under the Colombo Plan of 1950, a scheme initiated by Australia but subscribed to by many other countries (including the USA, Britain, Canada and Japan) as a means to prevent the spread of communism throughout the region.

In the light of Australia's willingness to join SEATO, it is not surprising that the Menzies government applauded the USA's entry into the Vietnam War and, in 1965, committed troops to the struggle. Support for involvement was far from absolute, however. Arthur Calwell, the leader of the Australian Labor Party, for example, believed the Vietnam conflict to be a civil war in which Australia had no part. Still more troubling for many young Australian men was the fact that conscription had been introduced in 1964 and those undertaking national service could now be sent overseas. By 1967 as many as 40% of Australians serving in Vietnam were conscripts.

'Assimilation' of Aboriginal People

The process of social change for Aboriginal people was accelerated by WWII. After the war 'assimilation' of Aboriginal people became the stated aim of the government. To this end, the rights of Aboriginal people were subjugated even further – the government had control over everything, from where they could live to whom they could marry. Many people were forcibly moved from their homes to townships, the idea being that they would adapt to European culture, which would in turn aid their economic development. This policy was a dismal failure.

In the 1960s the assimilation policy came under a great deal of scrutiny, and white Australians became increasingly aware of the inequity of their treatment of Aboriginal people. In 1967 non-Aboriginal Australians voted to give Aboriginal people and Torres Strait Islanders the status of citizens, and gave the Federal government power to legislate for them in all states. The states had to provide them with the same services as were available to other citizens, and the Federal government set up the Department of Aboriginal Affairs to identify and legislate for the special needs of Aboriginal people.

The assimilation policy was finally dumped in 1972, to be replaced by the government's policy of self-determination, which for the first time enabled Aboriginal people to participate in decision-making processes by granting them rights to their land. (See the Government & Politics section later in this chapter for more on Aboriginal land rights.)

Although the outcome of the Mabo case (see Aboriginal Land Rights under Government & Politics later in this chapter) gives rise to cautious optimism, many Aboriginal people still live in appalling conditions, and alcohol and drug abuse remain widespread problems, particularly among young and middle-aged men. Aboriginal communities have taken up the challenge to try and eradicate these problems – many communities are now 'dry', and there are a number of rehabilitation programs for alcoholics, petrol-sniffers and others with drug problems. Thanks for much of this work goes to Aboriginal women, many of whom have found themselves on the receiving end of domestic violence.

The 1970s & Beyond

The civil unrest aroused by conscription was one factor that contributed to the rise to power, in 1972, of the Australian Labor Party, under the leadership of Gough Whitlam, for the first time in more than 25 years. The Whitlam government withdrew Australian troops from Vietnam, abolished national service and higher-education fees, instituted a system of free and universally available health care, and supported land rights for Aboriginal people.

The government, however, was hampered by both a hostile Senate and much talk of mismanagement. On 11 November 1975, the governor-general (the British monarch's representative in Australia) dismissed the parliament and installed a caretaker government led by the leader of the opposition

Liberal Party, Malcolm Fraser. Labor supporters were appalled. Such action was unprecedented in the history of the Commonwealth of Australia and the powers that the governor-general had been able to invoke had long been regarded by many as an anachronistic vestige of Australia's now remote British past.

Nevertheless, it was a conservative coalition of the Liberal and National Country parties that won the ensuing election. A Labor government was not returned until 1983, when a former trade union leader, Bob Hawke, led the party to victory. In 1990 Hawke won a third consecutive term in office (a record for a Labor prime minister), thanks in no small part to the lack of better alternatives offered by the Liberals. He was replaced as prime minister by Paul Keating, his long-time treasurer, in late 1991.

By 1991 Australia was in recession, mainly as a result of domestic economic policy but also because Australia is particularly hard hit when demand (and prices) for primary produce and minerals falls on world markets. Unemployment was the highest it had been since the early 1930s, hundreds of farmers were forced off the land because they couldn't keep afloat financially, there was a four-million-bale wool stockpile that no-one seemed to know how to shift, and the building and manufacturing industries faced a huge slump amid a general air of doom and gloom. The Federal election in 1993 was won by Paul Keating, against all expectations. The economy took a slight turn for the better, but not enough for the electorate to maintain its faith in the Labor government. With unemployment remaining high at around 9%, in early 1996 Keating was defeated in a landslide victory to the Coalition, led by John Howard.

Despite the economic problems, however, most non-Aboriginal Australians have a

Cutting Ties With Britain

With the turn of the millennium looming, and with it the 2000 olympic games in Sydney followed closely by the centenary anniversary of Australian federation, the debate about Australia's national identity has become one of the major issues of the day. At the core of the debate is the current constitution which sees Britain's Queen Elizabeth as the Australian head of state. On one side are the republicans, who want an Australian as head of state, on the other side the monarchists, who favour the status quo.

In a nutshell, the republican argument is that Australia over the past 40 years has become a multicultural society, with immigrants from at least 100 countries, a far cry form the Anglo-Celtic-dominated population of a century ago. Therefore, the current constitutional set up is an anachronism. The monarchists believe that the system has served Australia well, and if it ain't broke why fix it?

The republic issue has been simmering since the mid-90s when it became a hobby horse of the prime minister at the time, Paul Keating. It seemed back then that a republic was a sure bet, and that it was just a matter of time, and probably sooner rather than later. However, with the victory of John Howard, an avowed monarchist, in the 1996 elections, the process slowed.

In 1997, Howard grudgingly set up a constitutional convention slated for early 1998, but put the onus on the 152 delegates at the convention to come up with a 'workable' republic model. If they were able to do this, and the model was passed by a referendum to be held in 1999, Australia would become a republic on 1 January 2001, exactly 100 years after the current constitution, which saw the federation of the six colonies, came into being.

The constitutional convention saw a frenzy of activity which did eventually lead to the adoption of a republic model. This model allowed for an Australian president chosen by the prime minister from a list prepared by a 15-member committee from public nominations, and the choice agreed to by the Opposition leader and a two-thirds majority of parliament.

While this model is not the one favoured by the majority of the roughly 60% of Australians who want a republic (they would prefer to see a president directly elected by popular vote), it is the one that will be put to the referendum vote in 1999. Changes to the constitution don't come easily, and it remains to be seen whether Australians are willing to accept the compromise model, cut the ties with Britain and move into the next century as a republic. ■

standard of living which is extremely high; it's a disgrace that the same can't be said for most of their Aboriginal counterparts. Many Aboriginal people still live in deplorable conditions, with outbreaks of preventable diseases and infant mortality running at a rate higher even than in many Third World countries. While definite progress has been made with the Federal government's Native Title legislation (see the Government & Politics section in this chapter for details), there's still a long way to go before Aboriginal people can enjoy an improved standard of living.

Socially and economically, Australia is still coming to terms with its strategic location in Asia. While it has accepted large numbers of Vietnamese and other Asian immigrants during the past two decades, it has never really considered itself a part of Asia, nor has it exploited the area's economic potential. One of the key aims of the former Labor government was to make Australia a more important player in the Asia-Pacific arena, shifting the focus away from traditional ties with Britain, the USA and Europe. John Howard's government places far less importance on this, and few would dispute the fact that Australia's image in Asia has recently taken a severe battering following the highly publicised, racist sentiments of the independent parliamentarian, Ms Pauline Hanson.

Another issue dominating Australian thinking in the late 1990s is that of republicanism, as increasing numbers of people feel that constitutional ties to Britain are no longer relevant. This is especially true with Sydney having been awarded the Olympic Games in the year 2000. Many feel it would be fitting that the games be opened by the constitutional head of a new Republic of Australia. But the election in 1996 of a conservative prime minister with apparently strong traditional ties to the monarchy means it may be a long time yet before the governor-general is done away with.

GEOGRAPHY

Australia is an island continent whose landscape – much of it uncompromisingly bleak and inhospitable – is the result of gradual changes wrought over millions of years. Although there is still seismic activity in the eastern and western highland areas, Australia is one of the most stable land masses, and for about 100 million years has been free of the forces that have given rise to huge mountain ranges elsewhere.

From the east coast a narrow, fertile strip merges into the greatly eroded Great Dividing Range, that is almost continent-long. The mountains are mere reminders of the mighty range that once stood here. Only in the section straddling the New South Wales border with Victoria, and in Tasmania, are they high enough to have winter snow.

West of the range the country becomes increasingly flat and dry. The endless flatness is broken only by salt lakes, occasional mysterious protuberances like Uluru (Ayers Rock) and Kata Tjuta (the Olgas), and some starkly beautiful mountains like the Mac-Donnell Ranges near Alice Springs. In places, the scant vegetation is sufficient to allow some grazing. However, much of the Australian outback is a barren land of harsh, stone deserts and dry lakes with evocative names like Lake Disappointment.

The extreme north of Australia, the Top End, is a tropical area within the monsoon belt. Although its annual rainfall looks adequate on paper, it comes in more or less one short, sharp burst. This has prevented the Top End from becoming seriously productive agriculturally.

The west of Australia consists mainly of a broad plateau. In the far west a mountain range and fertile coastal strip heralds the Indian Ocean, but this is only to the south. In the north-central part of Western Australia, the dry country runs right to the sea. The rugged Kimberley region in the state's far north is spectacular.

Australia is the world's sixth largest country. Its area is 7,682,300 sq km, about the same size as the 48 mainland states of the USA and half as large again as Europe, excluding the former USSR. It constitutes approximately 5% of the world's land surface. Lying between the Indian and Pacific oceans, Australia is about 4000km from east to west and 3200km from north to south, with a coastline 36,735km long.

GEOLOGY

Along with Africa, South America, Antarctica and India, Australia once formed part of the supercontinent Gondwana, which was formed about 600 million years ago when its various components bumped into each other and bonded together. Australia only became a continent in its own right about 100 million years ago when it broke away from Antarctica. Since then it has been drifting north – its current rate of drift is about 55mm per year.

Australia can be divided into two broad geological zones: the Tasman Fold Belt and the Australian Craton. These are situated east and west, respectively, of a line drawn roughly between Kangaroo Island in South Australia and Princess Charlotte Bay, near Cooktown in far north Queensland.

The Australian Craton is geologically ancient, its basement metamorphic and igneous rocks ranging in age from 570 million to 3.7 billion years. Its oldest rock formations – in Western Australia's Pilbara region – contain crystals that formed 4.3 billion years ago, making them part of the earth's original crust. At North Pole, also in the Pilbara, are the fossil remains of stromatolites that lived 3.5 billion years ago.

The Australian Craton is actually made up of several small crustal blocks of igneous material such as granite that became welded together about a billion years ago. Today these blocks are mostly buried by sedimentary material, although they emerge at places like Mt Isa, Broken Hill and in the Tanami Desert. All these areas contain rich mineral deposits that today sustain major mining developments. The eroded remnants of the original sandstone blanket form the rugged landscapes we now admire in the north-west Kimberley region and Kakadu, in the Top End.

About 500 million years ago, the first of a series of mountain-building episodes threw up an Andes-like mountain range along the Australian Craton's eastern side. Over a period of 110 million years these events gradually pushed the coastline 1000km eastwards.

Most of the Australian Craton was dry land between 250 and 140 million years ago, after which a major rise in sea level created an inland sea covering a third of the continent. Marine siltstones from this period contain precious opal, now mined at a number of places including Coober Pedy in South Australia and White Cliffs in New South Wales. Another inundation occurred 10 to 15 million years ago, creating the limestone deposits that today make up the Nullarbor Plain.

The Great Artesian Basin, one of the world's largest groundwater resources, underlies about 20% of the continent, and much of eastern inland Australia is almost totally reliant on it for its water needs.

CLIMATE

Australian seasons are the antithesis of those in Europe and North America. It's hot in December and many Australians spend Christmas at the beach, while in July and August it's midwinter. Summer starts in December, autumn in March, winter in June and spring in September.

The climatic extremes aren't too severe in most parts of Australia. Even in Melbourne, the southernmost capital city on the mainland, it's a rare occasion when the mercury hits freezing point, although it's a different story in Canberra, the national capital. Tasmanians, farther to the south, have a good idea of what cold is.

As you head north the seasonal variations become fewer until, in the far north around Darwin, you are in the monsoon belt where there are just two seasons – hot and wet, and hot and dry. In the Snowy Mountains of southern New South Wales and the high country of north-east Victoria there's a snow season with good skiing. The centre of the continent is arid – hot and dry during the day, but often bitterly cold at night.

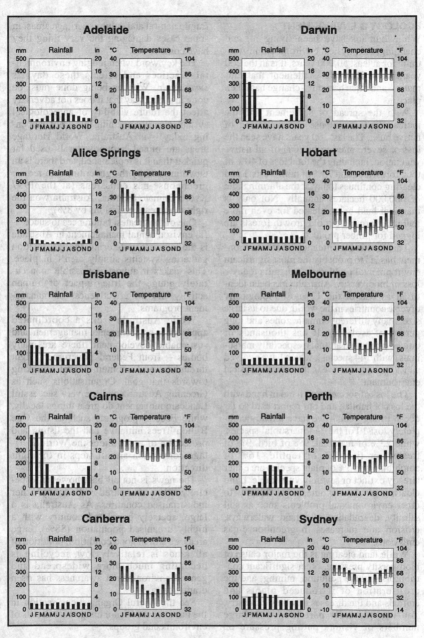

ECOLOGY & ENVIRONMENT

While humans have been living in, and changing, the physical environment in Australia for at least 50,000 years, it is in the 200 years since European settlement that dramatic – and often harmful – change has taken place.

With the spread of settlement and the increase in pastoral use came clearing of native bush. The last 200 years have seen the loss or severe altering of 70% of all native vegetation, including the total loss of 40% of total forest area and 75% of rainforests. Land clearing continues today at the alarming rate of 600,000 hectares annually. Not only is marginal land being cleared for even more marginal farming but old growth forests are logged for timber products.

This drastic modification of the environment has led to probably the most significant environmental problem in Australia today – loss of biodiversity. Australia has been identified as one of the 12 most biologically diverse countries in the world, due to its large size, many different climatic zones and long period of isolation. It has thousands of unique plants and animals, especially marsupials (with 144 species), which have evolved and adapted to survive in the unique physical environment.

The loss of species goes hand in hand with the loss of habitat, and our report card so far doesn't look good – we have already completely lost 10 of the 144 marsupial species, while 23% of mammal, 9% of bird, 9% of freshwater fish, 7% of reptile, 16% of amphibian and 5% of plant species are either already extinct or severely vulnerable. Land clearing also contributes significantly to other environmental problems such as soil salinity, degradation of inland waterways, erosion and increases in greenhouse-gas emissions.

While land clearing is the major cause of biodiversity pressure, other significant contributors include pollution, mining, and the proliferation of introduced plants and animals and the diseases that they can carry. Tourism plays its part too, with large numbers of visitors putting pressure on fragile natural and cultural heritage areas, in some cases damaging the very thing they have come to see.

The key word when judging environmental practices and effects these days is *sustainable*. What is being done must be done in such a way that it does not adversely affect the future viability of an ecological system, clearly something that is not happening today – in Australia, World Heritage areas are mined, groundwater is used far quicker than it is replenished, and there is an unwillingness by the government to reduce greenhouse-gas emissions (at the 1997 Kyoto Climate Summit, Australia won the right to increase emissions by 8%).

One of the greatest hindrances to successful environmental management in Australia is the fact that monitoring and information gathering systems simply aren't in place. This makes it almost impossible to accurately gauge the true impact of human activity and the effectiveness of management programs.

While Australia lacks a coordinated approach to environmental management and sustainable development, there are many bodies – from Federal government right through to local community level – working towards that goal. Organisations such as Greening Australia and the very successful Landcare movement do great things locally, while Federal programs such as the One Billion Trees initiative and the listing and protection of areas under the World Heritage convention are all steps in the right direction.

The news is not all bad, however, especially when compared with many other industrialised countries. As Australia is a large, sparsely populated country with a highly urbanised population (88%), large areas are still in good condition, pollution of all kinds is relatively low, recycling is becoming much more widespread and general environmental awareness has risen dramatically.

See the Useful Organisations section in the Facts for the Visitor chapter for details of environmental groups.

Australian Ecosystems

The expanse of the island continent embraces a variety of ecosystems: dynamic interactions of the physical environment and living organisms. The following representations are composed 'snapshots'. Tropical rainforests and wetlands are found in the north of Australia, as are offshore coral reefs; eucalypt forests dominate in the south-east and south-west; and deserts and arid lands feature in the vast centre.

The typical image of Australia, of a mostly dry and harsh landscape, is largely true; but it wasn't always this way. The familiar arid-land flora and fauna had rainforest-dwelling ancestors – their fossil remains are imprinted in the rocks of the outback. Living and recognisable descendants of this wetter past flourish in the wet tropics of the north and the temperate rainforests of the south-east; a few reside in the deep gorges of central Australia. Contemporary ecosystems reflect this Gondwanan ancestry, the effects of continental drift and a gradually drying climate, the influence of Ice-age events, and, more recently, migrations of other animals (including humans) and plants from the Eurasian continent.

Nourlangie Rock and Anbangbang Billabong,
Kakadu National Park

Tropical Wetland

The tropical wetlands of northern Australia witness remarkable seasonal change. Growing, flowering, feeding and breeding are all governed by the annual cycle of Wet and Dry. Towards the end of the Dry, the receding swamps and lagoons attract thousands of water birds; noisy flocks of whistling ducks and magpie geese are joined by fish-hunting jabiru and pied herons. A series of spectacular storms precedes the Wet. By the end of December heavy rains have arrived, signalling the estuarine crocodiles to nest and forcing the antilopine wallaroos to higher ground. In the warm, wet environment, plant growth is rapid. Many water birds now nest among the rushes and wild rice. Further storms flatten the tall grasses, and by about May, the Wet is over. As the land dries, natural fires and Aboriginal hunting fires continue to shape this environment.

DAVID CURL

DAVID CURL

Left: Brolgas and magpie geese
Right: Darter drying its wings in the sunshine

DAVID CURL

DAVID CURL

Left: Red lily
Right: Magpie geese and egrets gather on the edge of a drying floodplain

DAVID CURL

DAVID CURL

Left: Estuarine crocodile eating a file snake
Right: Kakadu's floodplains during the Wet

A diverse rainforest understorey of palms, ferns and
saplings at Cape Tribulation National Park

Tropical Rainforest

There is scarcely a niche in the warm, damp environment that is not occupied by lush, green
vegetation. The tree canopy filters sunlight and resounds to the calls of birds and fruit bats.
The trunks of trees support lichens, ferns and orchids, and the understorey and forest floor
are a profusion of palms, more ferns and the essential fungi and micro-organisms that
decompose the rich forest litter. Pythons, bandicoots, cassowaries and native mice are the
largest inhabitants of the forest floor, while among the tree branches clamber possums,
clumsy tree kangaroos and monkey-like cuscuses. Interrupting the almost uniform green
are brightly coloured birds and butterflies, often seen near water or displaying themselves
in patches of sunlight.

Most of Australia's tropical rainforest is restricted to a few mountain ranges and along
river courses on the north-east coast. The wet tropic region supports many endemic species
of plants and animals, some of which closely resemble the inhabitants of the cool rainforest
that once covered much of Australia.

DAVID SHERMAN

QUEENSLAND TOURIST & TRAVEL CORPORATION

Left: King parrot
Right: The brightly coloured cassowary

TONY WHEELER

RICHARD I'ANSON

Left: Bracket fungi
Right: Epiphytic ferns and vines in the rainforest midstorey

DAVID CURL

QUEENSLAND TOURIST & TRAVEL CORPORATION

Left: Green tree frog
Right: Ulysses butterfly

The coral environment offers a dazzling array of colours

Coral Reef

Unlike other ecosystems of great diversity, coral reefs do not have a conspicuous flora. There are, however, symbiotic algae living within coral, encrusting coralline algae which help to hold the reefs together, and a thin algal turf covering most of the reef. Close to the mainland, in shallows protected from ocean swells by the reef, are seagrass meadows, home to dugongs and a nursery for many fish. Six of the world's seven species of sea turtle feed and breed in these waters. Swimming and crawling among the coral are many unrecorded varieties of fish, crustaceans, echinoderms and molluscs. Above and along the reef edge prowl barracuda, sharks and sailfish. Overhead, gannets, terns, shearwaters, gulls and frigatebirds search for a feed of fish; the isolated coral cays provide a relatively safe nesting ground for thousands of seabirds.

MARK NORMAN

GBRMPA

Left: Gorgonian coral
Right: False clown anemonefish

MARK NORMAN

GREAT BARRIER REEF MARINE PARK AUTHORITY

Left: Regal angelfish
Right: Dugong and calf

ROGER FENWICK

TONY WHEELER

Left: Green turtle
Right: Black noddy

Mountain ash with a fern understorey

Eucalypt Forest

The eucalypt tree is typically Australian but there is no typical eucalypt forest. Depending on climate and soil, you may find mountain ash (the world's tallest flowering plant), stunted alpine gum, hardy arid land ironbark or desert gum. Understorey ranges from moist ferns to dry acacias, sedges and grasses. Eucalypt-associated faunas reveal similar variety. Although there are over 600 species of eucalypt, only a handful of species in the south-east of the continent are eaten by the koala. Less particular are the common possums, the brushtail and the ringtail, who both supplement their diets of eucalypt leaves with fruits and insects. Announcing its presence with a familiar laugh, the kookaburra is a daytime hunter of lizards, snakes, frogs and small mammals. Grey kangaroos and wallabies may be seen moving into open forest in the evenings to browse shrubs and graze native grasses. Also out for a nightly forage, the common wombat, a relative of the koala, grazes its home range before returning to one of its large and conspicuous burrows.

RICHARD I'ANSON

Alpine gums are hardy enough to survive the climatic extremes
of Australia's alpine regions

RICHARD TIMBURY

Eucalypt forest covers vast expanses of Australia's landscape.
There are over 600 varieties of eucalypt, or gum tree.

Right: Despite there
being hundreds of
species of eucalypt in
Australia, the koala
only eats the leaves of
a select few

Far Right: Eucalypt in
flower

RICHARD I'ANSON

RICHARD I'ANSON

Typical flora of the Red Centre: mulga, spinifex and desert oaks

Central Desert

In the arid centre of Australia life is most conspicuous in shaded gorges and along dry river courses where river red gums, home to colourful and noisy parrots, are able to tap deep reserves of water. On this ancient, eroded landscape, sparse vegetation and red sandy soils are infrequently and temporarily transformed by rain into a carpet of wildflowers. Tell-tale tracks in the sand lead to clumps of spinifex grass and burrows. Small marsupials and mice are mostly nocturnal; the rare and endangered bilby was once common to much of Australia but is now only found in the deserts of central Australia. A few of the lizards, such as the thorny devil, will venture out into the heat of the day for a feed of ants. Among the scattered mulga and desert oak, mobs of kangaroos, the males brick-red and over two metres tall, seek shelter from the sun; but seemingly impervious to the heat, emus, with an insulating double layer of feathers, continue the search for seeds and fruit. In the evenings rock-wallabies emerge from rocky outcrops to browse on nearby vegetation. Most animals breed in the cooler winter – their eggs and young attracting the attention of dingoes, eagles and perenties.

BERNARD NAPTHINE

RICHARD I'ANSON

RON & VIV MOON

Flora and fauna of the central deserts – emus, Sturt's desert pea
and kangaroos

DENIS O'BYRNE

RICHARD I'ANSON

Left: River red gums line a dry creek bed
Right: Major Mitchell cockatoos

BERNARD NAPTHINE

DAVID CURL

BERNARD NAPTHINE

Thousands of years ago, as the climate changed and lakes dried up,
animals like the thorny devil adapted to life in the arid desert

NATIONAL PARKS & RESERVES

Australia has more than 500 national parks – non-urban protected wilderness areas of environmental or natural importance. Each state defines and runs its own national parks, but the principle is the same throughout Australia. National parks include rainforests, vast tracts of empty outback, strips of coastal dune land and long, rugged mountain ranges.

Public access is encouraged if safety and conservation regulations are observed. In all parks you're asked to do nothing to damage or alter the natural environment. Approach roads, camping grounds (often with toilets and showers), walking tracks and information centres are often provided for visitors. In most national parks there are restrictions on bringing in pets.

Some national parks are so isolated, rugged or uninviting that you wouldn't want to go there unless you were an experienced, well-prepared bushwalker or climber. Other parks, however, are among Australia's major attractions and some of the most beautiful have been included on the World Heritage List (a United Nations list of natural or cultural places of world significance that would be an irreplaceable loss to the planet if they were altered).

Internationally, the World Heritage List includes more than 400 sites such as the Taj Mahal and the Grand Canyon, and 13 Australian areas: the Great Barrier Reef; Kakadu and Uluru-Kata Tjuta national parks in the Northern Territory; the Willandra Lakes region of far western New South Wales; the Lord Howe Island group off New South Wales; the Tasmanian Wilderness (the Franklin-Gordon Wild Rivers and Cradle Mountain-Lake St Clair national parks); the Central Eastern Rainforest Reserves (15 national parks and reserves, covering 1000 sq km in the eastern highlands of New South Wales); the Wet Tropics of far north Queensland, in the Daintree-Cape Tribulation area; Shark Bay on the Western Australian coast; Fraser Island off the Queensland coast; the fossil-mammal sites of Riversleigh (north-western Queensland) and Naracoorte (coastal South Australia); Macquarie Island (Australian external territory near Antarctica); and Heard Island and the McDonald Islands group (also external territories off Antarctica).

The Great Barrier Reef, the Tasmanian Wilderness, the Wet Tropics of Queensland and Shark Bay meet all four World Heritage criteria for natural heritage, with Kakadu National Park, Uluru-Kata Tjuta National Park, Willandra Lakes and the Tasmanian Wilderness being listed for both natural and cultural criteria. These sites are among the

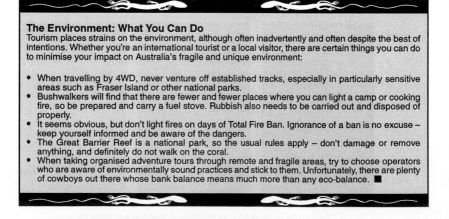

The Environment: What You Can Do

Tourism places strains on the environment, although often inadvertently and often despite the best of intentions. Whether you're an international tourist or a local visitor, there are certain things you can do to minimise your impact on Australia's fragile and unique environment:

- When travelling by 4WD, never venture off established tracks, especially in particularly sensitive areas such as Fraser Island or other national parks.
- Bushwalkers will find that there are fewer and fewer places where you can light a camp or cooking fire, so be prepared and carry a fuel stove. Rubbish also needs to be carried out and disposed of properly.
- It seems obvious, but don't light fires on days of Total Fire Ban. Ignorance of a ban is no excuse – keep yourself informed and be aware of the dangers.
- The Great Barrier Reef is a national park, so the usual rules apply – don't damage or remove anything, and definitely do not walk on the coral.
- When taking organised adventure tours through remote and fragile areas, try to choose operators who are aware of environmentally sound practices and stick to them. Unfortunately, there are plenty of cowboys out there whose bank balance means much more than any eco-balance. ■

very few on the World Heritage List selected for both natural and cultural heritage reasons, or because they meet all four natural criteria.

Before a site or area is accepted for the World Heritage List it has first to be proposed by its country and then must pass a series of tests at the UN, culminating, if it is successful, in acceptance by the UN World Heritage Committee, which meets at the end of each year. Any country proposing one of its sites or areas for the list must agree to protect the selected area, keeping it for the enjoyment of future generations even if to do so requires help from other countries.

While state governments have authority over their own national parks, the Federal government is responsible for ensuring that Australia meets its international treaty obligations, and in any dispute arising from a related conflict between a state and the Federal government, the latter can override the former.

In this way the Federal government can force a state to protect an area with World Heritage listing, as it did in the early 1980s when the Tasmanian government wanted to dam the Gordon River in the south-west of the state and thereby flood much of the wild Franklin River.

For national park authority addresses see Useful Organisations in the Facts for the Visitor chapter.

State Forests

Another form of nature reserve is the state forest. These are owned by state governments and have fewer regulations than national parks. In theory, state forests can be logged, but often they are primarily recreational areas with camping grounds, walking trails and signposted forest drives. Some permit horses and dogs.

The logging of state forests for woodchips has long been a contentious issue in Australia, and in recent times has once again come to the fore. The Federal government issues the woodchip licences and decides which forests will go and which will stay. Its current policy sets aside a number of areas

for woodchipping, while protecting others. The loggers say more should be logged, the conservationists naturally enough say it should be less, and the confrontation often gets quite ugly. One of the more high-profile campaigns by the pro-logging lobby in recent years saw hundreds of logging trucks descend on Canberra, blockading Parliament House and forcing the politicians to walk the last bit to work.

GOVERNMENT & POLITICS

Australia is a federation of six states and two territories. Under the written Constitution, which came into force on 1 January 1901 when the colonies joined to form the Commonwealth of Australia, the Federal government is mainly responsible for the national economy and Reserve Bank, customs and excise, immigration, defence, foreign policy and the postal system. The state governments are chiefly responsible for health, education, housing, transport and justice. There are both Federal and State police forces.

Australia has a parliamentary system of government based on that of the UK, and the state and Federal structures are broadly similar. In Federal parliament, the lower house is the House of Representatives, the upper house the Senate. The House of Representatives has 148 members, divided among the states on a population basis (NSW 50, Victoria 37, Queensland 27, South Australia 12, Western Australia 14, Tasmania five, ACT two and Northern Territory one). Elections for the House of Representatives are held at least every three years. The Senate has 12 senators from each state, and two each from the ACT and the Northern Territory. State senators serve six-year terms, with elections for half of them every three years; territory senators serve only three years, their terms coinciding with elections for the House of Representatives. Queensland's upper house was abolished in 1922. The Federal government is run by a prime minister, while the state governments are led by a premier and the Northern Territory by a chief minister. The party holding the greatest number of lower-house seats forms the government.

Australia is a monarchy, but although Britain's king or queen is also Australia's, Australia is fully autonomous. The British sovereign is represented by the governor-general as well as state governors, whose nominations for their posts by the respective governments are ratified by the monarch of the day.

Federal parliament is based in Canberra, the capital of the nation. Like Washington DC in the USA, Canberra is in its own separate area of land, the Australian Capital Territory (ACT), and is not under the rule of one of the states. Geographically, however, the ACT is completely surrounded by New South Wales. The state parliaments are in each state capital.

The Federal government is elected for a maximum of three years but elections can be (and often are) called earlier. Voting is by secret ballot and is compulsory for persons 18 years of age and over. Voting can be somewhat complicated as a preferential system is used whereby each candidate has to be listed in order of preference. This can result, for example, in Senate elections with 50 or more candidates to be ranked.

The Constitution can only be changed by referendum, and only if a majority of voters in at least four states favour it. Since federation in 1901, of the 42 proposals that have been put to referendum, only eight have been approved.

In Federal parliament, the two main political groups are the Australian Labor Party (ALP) and the coalition between the Liberal Party and the National Party. These parties also dominate state politics but sometimes the Liberal and National parties are not in coalition. The latter was once known as the National Country Party since it mainly represents country seats.

The only other political party of any real substance is the Australian Democrats, which has largely carried the flag for the ever-growing 'green' movement. The Democrats have been successful in recent times. Although the 1996 election gave a massive majority to the Coalition in the House of Representatives, the balance of power is held in the Senate by the Democrats and four independent Senators.

The Cabinet, presided over by the prime minister, is the government's major policy-making body, and it comprises about half of the full ministry. It's a somewhat secretive body which meets in private (usually in Canberra) and its decisions are ratified by the Executive Council, a formal body presided over by the governor-general.

Aboriginal Land Rights

Britain founded the colony of New South Wales on the legal principle of *terra nullius*, a land belonging to no-one, which meant that Australia was legally unoccupied. The settlers could take land from Aboriginal people without signing treaties or providing compensation. The European concept of land ownership was completely foreign to Aboriginal people and their view of the world in which land did not belong to individuals: people belonged to the land, were formed by it and were a part of it like everything else.

After WWII, Australian Aboriginal people became more organised and better educated, and a political movement for land rights developed. In 1962 a bark petition was presented to the Federal government by the Yolngu people of Yirrkala, in north-east Arnhem Land, demanding that the government recognise Aboriginal peoples' occupation and ownership of Australia since time immemorial. The petition was ignored, and the Yolngu people took the matter to court – and lost. In the famous Yirrkala Land Case 1971, Australian courts accepted the government's claim that Aboriginal people had no meaningful economic, legal or political relationship to land. The case upheld the principle of *terra nullius*, and the common-law position that Australia was unoccupied in 1788.

Because the Yirrkala Land Case was based on an inaccurate (if not outright racist) assessment of Aboriginal society, the Federal government came under increasing pressure to legislate for Aboriginal land rights. In 1976 it eventually passed the Aboriginal Land Rights (Northern Territory) Act – often referred to as the Land Rights Act.

Land Rights Acts The Aboriginal Land Rights (NT) Act of 1976, which operates in the Northern Territory, remains Australia's most powerful and comprehensive land rights legislation. Promises were made to legislate for national land rights, but these were abandoned after opposition from mining companies and state governments. The act established three Aboriginal Land Councils, which are empowered to claim land on behalf of traditional Aboriginal owners.

However, under the act the only land claimable is unalienated Northern Territory land outside town boundaries – land that no-one else owns or leases, usually semi-desert or desert. Thus, when the traditional Anangu owners of Uluru (Ayers Rock) claimed traditional ownership of Uluru and Kata Tjuta (the Olgas), their claim was disallowed because the land was within a national park and thus alienated. It was only by amending two acts of parliament that Uluru-Kata Tjuta National Park was handed back to traditional Anangu owners on the condition that it be immediately leased back to the then Australian Nature Conservation Agency (formerly the Australian National Parks & Wildlife Service, now Parks Australia North). At present, almost half of the Northern Territory has either been claimed, or is being claimed, by its traditional Aboriginal owners. The claim process is extremely tedious and can take many years to complete, largely because almost all claims have been opposed by the NT government. A great many elderly claimants die before the matter is resolved. Claimants must prove that under Aboriginal law they are responsible for the sacred sites on the land being claimed.

Once a claim is successful, Aboriginal people have the right to negotiate with mining companies and ultimately to accept or reject exploration and mining proposals. This right is strongly opposed by the mining lobby, despite the fact that traditional Aboriginal owners in the Northern Territory only reject about a third of these proposals outright.

The Pitjantjatjara Land Rights Act 1981 (South Australia) is Australia's second-most powerful and comprehensive land rights law. This gives Anangu Pitjantjatjara and Yankunytjatjara people freehold title to 10% of South Australia. The land, known as the Anangu Pitjantjatjara Lands, is in the far north of the state.

Just south of the Anangu Pitjantjatjara Lands lie the Maralinga Lands, which comprise 8% of South Australia. The area, largely contaminated by British nuclear tests in the 1950s, was returned to its Anangu traditional owners by virtue of the Maralinga Tjarutja Land Rights Act 1984 (South Australia).

Under these two South Australian acts, Anangu can control access to land and liquor consumption. However, if Anangu traditional owners cannot reach agreement with mining companies seeking to explore or mine on their land, they cannot veto mining activity; an arbitrator decides if mining will go ahead. If mining is given the green light, the arbitrator will bind the mining company with terms and conditions and ensure that reasonable monetary payments are made to Anangu.

In South Australia, other Aboriginal reserves exist by virtue of the Aboriginal Land Trust Act 1966 (South Australia). However, this act gives Aboriginal people little control over their land.

Outside the Northern Territory and South Australia, Aboriginal land rights are extremely limited. In Queensland, less than 2% of the state is Aboriginal land and, what's more, the only land that can be claimed under the Aboriginal Land Act 1991 (Queensland) is land which has been gazetted by the government as land available for claim. Under existing Queensland legislation, 95% of the state's Aboriginal people can't claim their traditional country.

Since the passing of the Nature Conservation Act 1992 (Queensland), Aboriginal people in the state also have very limited claim to national parks. If Aboriginal people successfully claim a Queensland park, they must permanently lease it back to the government without a guarantee of a review of the lease arrangement or a majority on the board of management. This is quite different to the arrangements at Uluru-Kata Tjuta National Park, where the traditional owners have a majority on the board, with a 99-year lease-back that is renegotiated every five years.

In Western Australia, Aboriginal reserves comprise about 13% of the state. Of this land about one-third is granted to Aboriginal people under 99-year leases; the other two-thirds is controlled by the government's Aboriginal Affairs Planning Authority. Control of mining and payments to communities are a matter of ministerial discretion.

In New South Wales, the Aboriginal Land Rights Act 1983 (New South Wales) transferred freehold title of existing Aboriginal reserves to Aboriginal people and gave them the right to claim a minuscule amount of other land. Aboriginal people also have limited rights to the state's national parks, but these rights fall short of genuine control and don't permit Aboriginal people to live inside parks. In Victoria and Tasmania, land rights are extremely limited.

Mabo & the Native Title Act It was only very recently that the non-Aboriginal community, including the Federal government, came to grips with the fact that a meaningful reconciliation between white Australia and its indigenous population was vital to the psychological well-being of all Australians.

In May 1982, five Torres Strait Islanders led by Eddie Mabo began an action for a declaration of native title over the Queensland Murray Islands. They argued that the legal principle of *terra nullius* had wrongfully usurped their title to land, as for thousands of years Murray Islanders had enjoyed a relationship with the land that included a notion of ownership. In June 1992 the High Court of Australia rejected *terra nullius* and the myth that Australia had been

unoccupied. In doing this, it recognised that a principle of native title existed before the arrival of the British.

The High Court's judgment became known as the Mabo decision, one of the most controversial decisions ever handed down by an Australian court. It was ambiguous, as it didn't outline the extent to which native title existed in mainland Australia. It received a hostile reaction from mining and other industry groups, but was hailed by Aboriginal people and the prime minister of the time, Paul Keating, as an opportunity to create a basis of reconciliation between Aboriginal and non-Aboriginal Australians.

To define the principle of native title, the Federal parliament passed the Native Title Act in December 1993. Despite protest from the mining industry, the act gives Australian Aboriginal people very few new rights. It limits the application of native title to land which no-one else owns or leases, and also to land with which Aboriginal people have continued to have a physical association. The act states that existing ownership or leases extinguish native title, although native title may be revived after mining leases have expired. If land is successfully claimed by Aboriginal people under the act, they will have no veto over developments, including mining.

The Wik Decision Several months prior to the Native Title Act becoming law, the Wik and Thayorre peoples had made a claim for native title in the Federal Court to land on Cape York Peninsula. The area claimed included two pastoral leases. Neither had ever been permanently occupied for that purpose, but the Wik and Thayorre peoples had been in continuous occupation of them. They argued that native title coexisted with the pastoral leases.

In January 1996 the Federal Court decided that the claim could not succeed as the granting of pastoral leases under Queensland law extinguished any native title rights. The Wik people appealed that decision in the High Court, which subsequently overturned it.

The High Court determined that, under the

law that created pastoral leases in Queensland, native title to the leases in question had not been extinguished. Further, it said that native title rights could continue at the same time that land was under lease, and that pastoralists did not have exclusive right of possession to their leases. Importantly, it also ruled that where the two were in conflict, the rights of the pastoralists would prevail.

Despite the fact that lease tenure was not threatened, the Wik decision brought a hue and cry from pastoral lessees across Australia, who demanded that the Federal government step in to protect them by legislating to limit native title rights, as was intended in the original act. Aboriginal leaders were equally adamant that native title must be preserved.

In late 1997 the government responded with its so-called 10 Point Plan, a raft of proposed legislative amendments to the Native Title Act which only further entrenches the pastoralists' position and effectively extinguishes native title, something the Wik judgement does not do. Whatever the outcome of the Federal government's response to Wik, it's obvious that failure to resolve the native title issue will put new and extravagant meaning into the phrase 'lawyers' picnic', and will make reconciliation less rather than more likely.

ECONOMY

Australia is a relatively affluent and industrialised nation but much of its wealth still comes from agriculture and mining. It has a small domestic market and its manufacturing sector is comparatively weak. Nevertheless, a substantial proportion of the population is employed in manufacturing, and for much of Australia's history it has been argued that these industries need tariff protection from imports to ensure their survival.

Today, however, tariff protection is on the way out and efforts are being made to increase Australia's international competitiveness. This has become more important as prices of traditional primary exports have become more volatile. During the 1980s and early 90s, Labor sought to restrain the growth of real wages with the assistance of the Australian Council of Trade Unions (ACTU), to make Australian products more competitive overseas, but this Accord, as it was known, ended with the 1996 election of the conservative Howard government.

An increasingly important source of income is the tourism industry, with the numbers of visitors rising each year and projections for even greater numbers in the future. That vision has been dampened somewhat by the downturn that hit the once booming economies of South-East Asia in late 1997, however Australia remains well positioned to enter these markets – more than half of Australia's exports go to the Asian region.

Agriculture, formerly the cornerstone of the Australian economy, today accounts for about 4% of production, while mining contributes about 8% and manufacturing about 16%. Major commodity exports include wool (Australia is the world's largest supplier), wheat, barley, sugar, coal and iron ore.

Japan is Australia's biggest trading partner, but the economies of China, Korea and Vietnam are becoming increasingly important. Regionally, Australia recently initiated the establishment of the Asia-Pacific Economic Cooperation (APEC) group, a body aimed at furthering the economic interests of the Pacific nations.

The Australian economy is growing at the rate of around 3% per year and inflation is low, at around 1%.

POPULATION & PEOPLE

Australia's population is about 18.3 million. The most populous states are New South Wales (6.2 million) and Victoria (4.6 million), which also have the two largest cities respectively – Sydney (3.28 million) and Melbourne (2.87 million). The population is concentrated along the east coast from Adelaide to Cairns and in a similar, but much smaller, coastal region in the south-western corner of Western Australia. The centre of the country is very sparsely populated.

Until WWII Australians were mostly of

British and Irish descent but that has changed dramatically. Since the war, heavy migration from Europe has created major Greek and Italian populations, also adding Germans, Dutch, Maltese, Yugoslavs, Lebanese, Turks and other groups.

More recently Australia has had large influxes of Asians, particularly Vietnamese after the Vietnam War. In comparison to its population, Australia probably has taken more Vietnamese refugees than any other western nation. On the whole these 'new Australians' have been remarkably well accepted and 'multiculturalism' is a popular concept in Australia.

According to the 1996 census there are around 350,000 people who identified themselves as Aboriginal or being of indigenous origin. This is a large increase on previous census figures, a reflection of the fact that these days people are far more willing to declare their indigenous origins. They are concentrated in northern and central Australia. Most of the 28,000 Torres Strait Islanders, primarily a Melanesian people, live in north Queensland and on the islands of Torres Strait between Cape York and Papua New Guinea.

If you come to Australia in search of a real Australian you will find one quite easily. He or she may be a Lebanese cafe owner, an English used-car salesperson, an Aboriginal artist, a Malaysian architect or a Greek greengrocer. And you will find them in pubs, on beaches, at barbecues, in mustering yards and at art galleries. And yes, you may meet a Mick (Crocodile) Dundee or two telling the same tall stories – a popular activity in outback pubs.

ARTS
Music
Popular Music Australia's participation in the flurry of popular music since the 1950s has been a frustrating mix of good, indifferent, lousy, parochial and excellent. In the early days the local industry suffered from severe cultural cringe, the highest praise being that it was 'good enough to have come from the UK/USA'. Fortunately that has all

changed. The 1970s saw music with a distinctly Australian flavour start to emerge, and bands such as Skyhooks lead the way. The music has since evolved to the stage where the local scene is flooded with great talent playing Australian rock. Popular bands and performers to look out for include: Midnight Oil, Cruel Sea, You Am I, The Black Sorrows, Spider Bait, Silverchair, Magic Dirt, Custard, Regurgitator, Stephen Cummings, Hunters & Collectors, Mark Seymour, Deborah Conway, Screamfeeder, Paul Kelly, The Earthmen, Deadstar, Dave Graney and Nick Cave.

The last decade or so has also seen huge success for Aboriginal music and performers. The most obvious name that springs to mind is Yothu Yindi. Their song about the dishonoured white-man's agreement, *Treaty*, perhaps did more than anything else to popularise Aboriginal land-rights claims. The band's lead singer, Mandawuy Yunupingu, was named Australian of the Year in 1993.

Other Aboriginal names include Nokturnl, Blekbala Mujik, Coloured Stone, Kev Carmody, Archie Roach, Ruby Hunter, Blackstorm, Bart Willoughby, Scrap Metal, the Sunrise Band, Christine Anu (from the Torres Strait Islands), and the bands that started it all but no longer exist, No Fixed Address and Warumpi Band.

White country music owes much to Irish heritage and American country influences, often with a liberal sprinkling of dry outback humour. Names to watch out for include Slim Dusty, Ted Egan, John Williamson, Chad Morgan, Lee Kernaghan, Neil Murray, Dirty Hanks, Trailblazers, Gondwanaland and Smokey Dawson.

Folk Music Australian folk music is derived from English, Irish and Scottish roots. Bush bands, playing fast-paced and high-spirited folk music for dancing, can be anything from performers trotting out standards such as *Click Go the Shears* to serious musicians who happen to like a rollicking time.

Fiddles, banjos and tin whistles feature prominently, plus there's the indigenous 'lagerphone', a percussion instrument made from a great many beer bottle caps nailed to a stick, which is then shaken or banged on the ground. If you have a chance to go to a bush dance or folk festival, don't pass it up.

Literature
Bush Ballads & Yarns The 'bush' was a great source of inspiration for many popular ballads and stories. These were particularly in vogue at the turn of the century but they have an enduring quality.

Adam Lindsay Gordon was the forerunner of this type of literature, having published *Bush Ballads and Galloping Rhymes* in 1870. This collection includes his popular *The Sick Stockrider*.

The two most famous exponents of the ballad style were AB 'Banjo' Paterson and Henry Lawson. Paterson grew up in the bush in the second half of the 19th century and became one of Australia's most important bush poets. His pseudonym 'The Banjo' was the name of a horse on his family's station. His horse ballads were regarded as some of his best, but he was familiar with all aspects of station life and wrote with great optimism. *Clancy of the Overflow* and *The Man From Snowy River* are both well known, but The Banjo is probably best remembered as the author of Australia's alternative national

anthem, *Waltzing Matilda*, in which he celebrates an unnamed swagman, one of the anonymous wanderers of the bush.

Henry Lawson was a contemporary of Paterson, but was much more of a social commentator and political thinker and less of a humorist. Although he wrote a good many poems about the bush – pieces such as *Andy's Gone with Cattle* and *The Roaring Days* are among his best – his greatest legacy is his short stories of life in the bush, which seem remarkably simple yet manage to capture the atmosphere perfectly. Good examples are *A Day on a Selection* (a selection was a tract of crown land for which annual fees were paid) and *The Drover's Wife;* the latter epitomises one of Lawson's 'battlers' who dreams of much better things as an escape from the ennui of her isolated circumstances.

There were many other balladeers. George Essex Evans is the author of a tribute to Queensland's women pioneers, *The Women of the West*; Will Ogilvie wrote of the great cattle drives; and Barcroft Boake's *Where the Dead Men Lie* celebrates the people who opened up never-never country where 'heat-waves dance forever'.

Standing apart from the romanticism of these writers is Barbara Baynton. She is

Waltzing Matilda
Written in 1895 by the 'bard of the bush', Banjo Paterson, *Waltzing Matilda* is Australia's unofficial national anthem. Most people know it as a catchy but meaningless ditty about a jolly swagman who stole a jumbuck (a sheep) and later drowned himself in a billabong rather than be arrested, but historians have suggested that Paterson actually wrote the tune as a political anthem. The Waltzing Matilda Centenary Festival, held in Winton in 1995, fuelled the controversy over the origins of the song.

The 1890s was a period of social and political upheaval in Queensland. Along with nationalistic calls for the states to amalgamate and form a federation, the decade was dominated by an economic crisis, mass unemployment and a series of shearers' strikes in outback Queensland which led to the formation of the Australian Labor Party to represent workers' interests.

Patterson visited Winton in 1895, and during a picnic beside the Combo Waterhole he heard stories about the violent 1894 shearers' strike on Dagworth Station. During the strike, rebel shearers had burned down seven woolsheds, leading the police to declare martial law and place a reward of £1000 on the head of their leader, Samuel Hofmeister. Rather than face arrest, Hofmeister drowned himself in a billabong.

While there is no direct proof that Paterson was writing allegorically about the strikes, the song's undeniable anti-authoritarianism and the fact that it was adopted as an anthem by the rebel shearers weigh heavily in support of the theory. ■

uncompromising in her depiction of the outback as a cruel, brutal environment, and the romantic imagery of the bush is absent in the ferocious depiction of the lot of *Squeaker's Mate* in *Bush Studies* (1902).

Outback Novelists The author's name if not the content would have encouraged many overseas visitors to read DH Lawrence's *Kangaroo* (1923), which, in places, presents his frightened images of the bush. Later, Nevil Shute's *A Town Like Alice* (1950) would have been the first outback-based novel that many people read. Other Shute titles with outback themes are *In the Wet* (1953) and *Beyond the Black Stump* (1956).

Perhaps the best local depicter of the outback was Katharine Susannah Prichard. She produced a string of novels with outback themes into which she wove her political thoughts. *Black Opal* (1921) was the study of the fictional opal mining community of Fallen Star Ridge; *Working Bullocks* (1926) examined the political nature of work in the karri forests of Western Australia; and *Moon of Desire* (1941) follows its characters in search of a fabulous pearl from Broome to Singapore. Her trilogy of the Western Australian goldfields was published separately as *The Roaring Nineties* (1946), *Golden Miles* (1948) and *Winged Seeds* (1950).

Xavier Herbert's *Capricornia* (1938) stands as one of the great epics of outback Australia, with its sweeping descriptions of the northern country. His second epic, *Poor Fellow My Country* (1975), is a documentary of the fortunes of a northern station owner. Through the characters, Herbert voices his bitter regret at the failure of reconciliation between the white despoilers of the land and its indigenous people.

One of the great nonfiction pieces is Mary Durack's family chronicle, *Kings in Grass Castles* (1959), which relates the white settlement of the Kimberley ranges. Her sequel was *Sons in the Saddle* (1983).

Australia's Nobel prize-winner, Patrick White, used the outback as the backdrop for a number of his monumental works. The most prominent character in *Voss* (1957) is an explorer, perhaps loosely based on Ludwig Leichhardt; *The Tree of Man* (1955) has all the outback happenings of flood, fire and drought; and the journey of *The Aunt's*

Australia's Literary Hoaxes

Australia has a rich tradition of literary hoaxes; a tradition that began in the 1940s with the Ern Malley Hoax. An edition of the literary magazine, *Angry Penguins*, edited by Adelaide poet Max Harris, featured 16 poems grouped under the title *The Darkening Ecliptic* – the entire works of the newly discovered (but supposedly deceased) Australian poet, Ern Malley. It was soon revealed that Malley was a hoax, created by two young poets James McAuley and Harold Stewart, who had concocted the poems in a single afternoon. It seems their aim was to expose Harris and others like him who McAuley and Stewart felt were responsible for 'the gradual decay of meaning and craftsmanship in poetry'.

In 1995 the winner of the prestigious Miles Franklin Award was the author Helen Demidenko. Her winning work, *The Hand that Signed the Paper*, supposedly related events experienced by her allegedly Ukrainian family during famine in the Ukraine in the 1930s. Initially the quality of the work was the subject of debate, but this became a furore when it was later discovered that Demidenko was in fact the very un-Ukrainian Helen Darville, who not only had no experience of the subject matter but also plagiarised much of her material from a wide variety of sources. Amazingly, the judges stood by their decision and the award stood; the book was initially withdrawn, then republished with the author's correct name.

More recently the Wanda Koolmatrie deception has been the one to capture the spotlight. Wanda Koolmatrie was supposedly a Kimberley Aboriginal woman and author of the book *In My Own Sweet Time*. The book had won an award for the best first publication by a female writer and was set to become part of the NSW secondary school syllabus. It was only when the book's publisher insisted on actually meeting the author that 'she' confessed to being Leon Carmen, a non-Aboriginal man from Sydney! ∎

Story (1948) begins on an Australian sheep station.

Kenneth Cook's nightmarish novel set in outback New South Wales, *Wake in Fright* (1961), has been made into a film.

20th-Century Writers Miles Franklin was one of Australia's early feminists and decided early in life to become a writer rather than the traditional wife and mother. Her best-known book, *My Brilliant Career*, was also her first. It was written at the turn of the century when the author was only 20, and brought her both widespread fame and criticism. On her death she endowed an annual award for an Australian novel; today the Miles Franklin Award is the most prestigious in the country.

Peter Carey is one of Australia's most successful contemporary writers and all his books are worth looking for. His rambling novel *Illywhacker* (1985) is set mostly in Melbourne, while *The Tax Inspector* (1991) is set in an outer suburb of Sydney. His most recent offering is *Jack Maggs* (1997).

Other writers with a strong sense of place include Helen Garner *(Monkey Grip*, 1987 – Melbourne), Peter Corris (the Cliff Hardy stories, including *Matrimonial Causes*, 1994, *Beware of the Dog*, 1992, and *Wet Graves*, 1990 – Sydney) and David Ireland *(The Glass Canoe*, 1993 – Sydney).

Thomas Keneally is well-known for his novels which deal with the suffering of oppressed peoples, for example *The Chant of Jimmy Blacksmith* (1972) and the Booker Prize-winning *Schindler's Ark* (1982), upon which the Spielberg film *Schindler's List* was based.

Thea Astley is far from a household name, yet she is one of the finest writers in the country. Her books include *Vanishing Points* (1992), *The Slow Natives* (1965), *An Item from the Late News* (1982) and *It's Raining in Mango* (1987), the last of which is probably her finest work and expresses her outrage at the treatment of Aboriginal people.

Elizabeth Jolley is well known as a short-story writer and novelist with a keen eye for the eccentric. Her works include *Mr Scobie's Riddle* (1983), *My Father's Moon* (1989), *Cabin Fever* (1990) and *The Georges' Wife* (1993).

David Malouf has won just about every award there is to be won in Australian literature, including the NSW Premier's Literary Award for *An Imaginary Life* (1978) in 1979, the *Age* Book of the Year Award in 1982 for *Fly Away Peter* (1981), the Miles Franklin Award in 1991 and the 1991 Commonwealth Prize for fiction for *The Great World* (1991).

David Foster, until recently a largely overlooked writer, won the 1997 Miles Franklin Award for his impenetrable, rambling and complex novel *The Glade Within the Grove* (1996), his ninth book. Other works by him include *Dog Rock* (1989) and *The Pale Blue Crochet Coathanger Cover* (1998).

Christopher Koch is a writer who has for many years been exploring Australia's relationship with Asia. Although *The Year of Living Dangerously* (1978) is probably his best known work, *The Doubleman* (1985) won him the Miles Franklin Award in 1985, and *Highways to a War* (1996), which looks at Australia's role in Vietnam, was the 1996 winner.

Tim Winton is widely regarded as one of the best writers in Australia today. Winton's evocation of coastal WA is superb, particularly in works such as *Cloudtsreet* (1991), *The Riders* (1994), *Shallows* (1982) and *An Open Swimmer* (1984).

Australia also has some great poets, including Dorothy Porter and Les Murray.

Architecture

Australia's first European settlers arrived in the country with memories of Georgian grandeur, but the lack of materials and tools meant that most of the early houses were almost caricatures of the real thing. One of the first concessions to the climate, and one which was to become a feature of Australian houses, was the addition of a wide verandah which kept the inner rooms of the house dark and cool.

The prosperity of the gold rush era in the second half of the last century saw a spate of grand buildings in the Victorian style in most major towns. Many of these buildings survive, and are a fine reminder of a period of great wealth, confidence and progress. The houses of the time became much more elaborate, with ornamentation of all sorts gracing the facades.

Increasing population in the major towns saw the rise of the terrace house, simple single and later double-storey houses which, although cramped at the time, today provide comfortable dwellings for thousands of inner-city residents.

By the turn of the century, at a time when the separate colonies were now combining to form a new nation, a simpler, more 'Australian' architectural style evolved, and this came to be known as Federation style. Built between about 1890 and 1920, Federation houses typically feature red-brick walls, and an orange-tiled roof decorated with terracotta ridging and chimney pots. Another feature was the rising-sun motif on the gable ends, symbolic of the dawn of a new age for Australia.

The Californian bungalow, a solid house style which developed in colonial British India, became the rage in the 1920s and 30s, and its simple and honest style fitted well with the emerging Australian tendency towards a casual lifestyle.

Differing climates led to some interesting regional variations. In the tropical north the style known as the Queenslander evolved – elevated houses with plenty of ventilation to make the most of cooling breezes. In the 1930s the first buildings in Darwin appeared with the same features, and have developed into the modern 'Troppo' (tropical) style of architecture.

The immigration boom which followed WWII led to urban sprawl – cities and towns expanded rapidly, and the 'brick veneer' became the dominant housing medium, and remains so today. On the fringe of any Australian city you'll find acres of new, low-cost, brick-veneer suburbs – as far as the eye can see it's a bleak expanse of terracotta roofs and bricks in various shades.

Modern Australian architecture struggles to maintain a distinctive style, with overseas trends dominating large projects. Often the most interesting 'modern' buildings are in fact recycled Victorian or other era buildings. There are some exceptions, notable ones being the Convention Centre at Sydney's Darling Harbour, which was designed by Phillip Cox, and the Cultural Centre at Uluru-Kata Tjuta National Park in central Australia, which was designed in consultation with the traditional owners of the national park.

Film

The Australian film industry began as early as 1896, a year after the Lumiere brothers opened the world's first cinema in Paris. Maurice Sestier, one of the Lumieres' photographers, came to Australia and made the first films in the streets of Sydney and at Flemington Racecourse during the Melbourne Cup.

Cinema historians regard an Australian film, *Soldiers of the Cross*, as the world's first 'real' movie. It was originally screened at the Melbourne Town Hall in 1901, cost £600 to make and was shown throughout the USA in 1902.

The next significant Australian film, *The Story of the Kelly Gang*, was screened in 1907, and by 1911 the industry was flourishing. Low-budget films were being made in such quantities that they could be hired out or sold cheaply. Over 250 silent feature films were made before the 1930s when the talkies and Hollywood took over.

In the 1930s, film companies like Cinesound sprang up. Cinesound made 17 feature films between 1931 and 1940, many based on Australian history or literature. *Forty Thousand Horsemen*, directed by Cinesound's great film maker Charles Chauvel, was a highlight of this era of locally made and financed films which ended in 1959, the year of Chauvel's death. Early Australian actors who became famous both at home and overseas include Errol Flynn and Chips Rafferty (born John Goffage).

Before the introduction of government subsidies during 1969 and 1970, the Australian film industry found it difficult to compete with US and British interests. The New Wave era of the 1970s, a renaissance of Australian cinema, produced films like *Picnic at Hanging Rock*, *Sunday Too Far Away*, *Caddie* and *The Devil's Playground*, which appealed to large local and international audiences.

Since the 70s, Australian actors and directors such as Mel Gibson, Nicole Kidman, Judy Davis, Greta Scacchi, Paul Hogan, Geoffrey Rush, Bruce Beresford, Peter Weir, Gillian Armstrong and Fred Schepisi have gained international recognition. Films like *Gallipoli*, *The Year of Living Dangerously*, *Mad Max*, *Malcolm*, *Crocodile Dundee*, *Proof*, *Holidays on the River Yarra*, *The Year My Voice Broke*, *Strictly Ballroom*, *Priscilla – Queen of the Desert*, *Muriel's Wedding*, *Babe* and most recently *Shine* have entertained and impressed audiences worldwide.

Painting

In the 1880s a group of young artists developed the first distinctively Australian style of watercolour painting. Working from a permanent bush camp in Melbourne's (then) outer suburb of Box Hill, the painters captured the unique qualities of Australian life and the bush. The work of this group is generally referred to as the Heidelberg School, although the majority of the work was done at Box Hill. In Sydney a contemporary movement worked at Sirius Cove on Sydney Harbour. Both groups were influenced by the French plein-air painters, whose practice of working outdoors to capture the effects of natural light led directly to Impressionism. The main artists were Tom Roberts, Arthur Streeton, Frederick McCubbin, Louis Abrahams, Charles Conder, Julian Ashton and, later, Walter Withers. Their works can be found in most of the major galleries and are well worth seeking out.

In the 1940s, under the patronage of John and Sunday Reed at their home in suburban Melbourne, a new generation of artists redefined the direction of Australian art. This group included some of Australia's most famous contemporary artists, such as Sir Sidney Nolan and Arthur Boyd.

More recently the work of painters such as Fred Williams, John Olsen and Brett Whiteley has made an impression on the international art world. Whiteley, probably Australia's most well-known modern artist, died in 1992.

RELIGION

A shrinking majority of people in Australia (around 58%) are at least nominally Christian. Most Protestant churches have merged to become the Uniting Church, although the Church of England has remained separate. The Catholic Church is popular (almost half of Australia's Christians are Catholics), with the original Irish adherents now joined by large numbers of Mediterranean immigrants.

Non-Christian minorities abound, the main ones being Buddhists (1.13% of the total population), Jews (0.45%) and Muslims (1.13%). Almost 20% of the population describe themselves as having no religion.

LANGUAGE

While English is the main language of Australia, as you'd expect in a country with such a diverse ethnic mix, languages other than English are in common use. The 1996 census found that 240 languages other than English were being spoken at home, and almost 50 of these were indigenous languages. This amounts to a language other than English being used in 15% of Australian households.

The most commonly used non-English languages are, in order, Italian, Greek, Cantonese, Arabic and Vietnamese. Languages rapidly growing in use are Mandarin, Vietnamese and Cantonese, while those most in decline include Dutch, German, Italian and Greek.

Australian English

Any visitor from abroad who thinks Australian (that's 'Strine') is simply a weird variant of English/American will soon have a few surprises. For a start many Australians don't even speak Australian – they speak Italian, Lebanese, Vietnamese, Turkish or Greek.

Those who do speak the native tongue are liable to lose you in a strange collection of Australian words. Some have completely different meanings in Australia than they have in English-speaking countries north of the equator; some commonly used words have been shortened almost beyond recognition. Others are derived from Aboriginal languages, or from the slang used by early convict settlers.

There is a slight regional variation in the Australian accent, while the difference between city and country speech is mainly a matter of speed. Some of the most famed Aussie words are hardly heard at all – 'mates' are more common than 'cobbers'. If you want to pass for a native try speaking slightly nasally, shortening any word of more than two syllables and then adding a vowel to the end of it, making anything you can into a diminutive (even the Hell's Angels can become mere 'bikies') and peppering your speech with as many expletives as possible. Lonely Planet publishes an *Australian phrasebook*, which is an introduction to both Australian English and Aboriginal languages, and the list that follows may also help:

arvo – afternoon
avagoyermug – traditional rallying call, especially at cricket matches
award wage – minimum pay rate

back o' Bourke – back of beyond, middle of nowhere
bail out – leave
bail up – hold up, rob, earbash
banana bender – resident of Queensland
barbie – barbecue (BBQ)
barrack – cheer on team at sporting event, support (ie 'who do you barrack for?')
bastard – general form of address which can mean many things, from high praise or respect ('He's the bravest bastard I know') to dire insult ('You rotten bastard!'). Only use on males, and avoid if unsure!
bathers – swimming costume (Victoria)

battler – hard trier, struggler
beaut, beauty, bewdie – great, fantastic
big mobs – a large amount, heaps
bikies – motorcyclists
billabong – water hole in dried up riverbed, more correctly an ox-bow bend cut off in the dry season by receding waters
billy – tin container used to boil tea in the bush
bitumen – surfaced road
black stump – where the '*back o' Bourke*' begins
block, do your – lose your temper
bloke – man
blow-in – stranger
blowies, blow flies – large flies
bludger – lazy person, one who refuses to work
blue – to have an argument or fight (ie 'have a blue')
bluey – *swag*, or nickname for a red-haired person; a jacket, common to the building trade
bonzer – great, *ripper*
boogie board – half-sized surf board
boomer – very big; a particularly large male kangaroo
boomerang – a curved flat wooden instrument used by Aboriginal people for hunting
booze bus – police van used for random breath testing for alcohol
bot – to scrounge or obtain by begging or borrowing
bottle shop – liquor shop
Buckley's – no chance at all
bug (Moreton Bay bug) – a small, edible crustacean
bull dust – fine and sometimes deep dust on outback roads, also bullshit
bunyip – mythical bush spirit
burl – have a try (ie 'give it a burl')
bush, the – country, anywhere away from the city
bushbash – to force your way through pathless bush
bushranger – Australia's equivalent of the outlaws of the American wild west (some goodies, some baddies)

bush tucker – native foods, found in the *outback*

BYO restaurant – one that allows you to 'bring your own' alcohol

camp oven – large, cast-iron pot with lid, used for cooking on an open fire

cark it – to die

cask – wine box (a great Australian invention)

Chiko roll – vile Australian junk food

chocka – completely full, from 'chock-a-block'

chook – chicken

chuck a U-ey – do a U-turn, turn a car around within a road

clobber – to hit, also clothes

clout – to hit

cobber – friend, *mate* (archaic)

cocky – small-scale farmer

come good – turn out all right

compo – compensation such as workers' compensation

counter meal, countery – pub meal

cow cocky – small-scale cattle farmer

cozzie – swimming costume (New South Wales)

crack the shits – lose your temper, also 'crack a mental'

crook – ill, badly made, substandard

crow eater – resident of South Australia

cut lunch – sandwiches

dag, daggy – dirty lump of wool at back end of a sheep; also an affectionate or mildly abusive term for a socially inept person

daks – trousers

damper – bush loaf made from flour and water and cooked in a camp oven

dead horse – tomato sauce

dead set – true, *dinkum*

deli – milk bar in South Australia & Western Australia, but a delicatessen elsewhere.

didjeridu – cylindrical wooden musical instrument traditionally played by Aboriginal men

dill – idiot

dinkum, fair dinkum – honest, genuine

dinky-di – the real thing

dip out – to miss out or fail

divvy van – police divisional van

dob in – to tell on someone

down south – the rest of Australia, according to anyone north of Brisbane

drongo – worthless or stupid person

Dry, the – dry season in northern Australia (April to October)

duco – car paint

dunny – outdoor lavatory

dunny budgies – large flies, *blowies*

earbash – talk nonstop

eastern states – the rest of Australia viewed from Western Australia

esky – large insulated box for keeping beer etc cold

fair crack of the whip! – give us a break

fair dinkum – see *dinkum*

fair go! – give us a break

flake – shark meat, used in fish & chips

flat out – very busy or fast

floater – meat pie floating in pea soup – yuk

flog – sell, steal

fossick – hunt for gems or semiprecious stones

freshie – freshwater crocodile (the harmless, unless provoked, one); new *tinny*

from arsehole to breakfast – all over the place

furphy – a rumour or false story

galah – noisy parrot, thus noisy idiot

game – brave (ie 'game as Ned Kelly')

gander – look (ie 'have a gander')

garbo – person who collects your garbage

g'day – good day, traditional Australian greeting

gibber – Aboriginal word for a stone or rock, hence gibber plain or desert

give it away – give up

good on ya – well done

grazier – large-scale sheep or cattle farmer

grog – general term for alcoholic drinks

grouse – very good

homestead – residence of a station owner or manager

hoon – idiot, hooligan, yahoo

how are ya? – standard greeting (expected answer: 'good, thanks, how are *you*?')

icy-pole – frozen lollipop, ice lolly

iffy – dodgy, questionable

jackaroo – young male trainee on a station (farm)

jillaroo – young female trainee on an outback station

jiffy – a very short time

jocks – men's underpants

journo – journalist

jumped-up – full of self-importance, arrogant

jumper – sweater

kick the bucket – to die

kiwi – New Zealander

knacker – testicle

knackered – broken; tired

knock – criticise, deride

knocker – one who knocks; woman's breast

Koori – Aboriginal person (mostly south of the Murray River)

lair – layabout, ruffian

lairising – acting like a *lair*

lamington – square of sponge cake covered in chocolate icing and coconut

larrikin – hooligan, mischievous youth

lay-by – put a deposit on an article so the shop will hold it for you

lemon – faulty product, a dud

lob in – drop in (to see someone)

lollies – sweets, candy

lurk – a scheme

mate – general term of familiarity, whether you know the person or not

milk bar – general store

milko – milkman

mozzies – mosquitoes

never-never – remote country in the outback

no hoper – hopeless case

no worries – no problems; that's OK

north island – mainland Australia, viewed from Tasmania

northern summer – summer in the northern hemisphere

ocker – an uncultivated or boorish Australian; a *knocker* or derider

off-sider – assistant or partner

OS – overseas (ie 'he's gone OS')

outback – remote part of the bush, *back o' Bourke*

paddock – a fenced area of land, usually intended for livestock

pastoralist – large-scale grazier

pavlova – traditional Australian meringue and cream dessert, named after the Russian ballerina Anna Pavlova

perve – to gaze with lust

piker – someone who doesn't pull their weight or chickens out

pinch – steal

piss – beer

piss turn – boozy party, also piss up

pissed – drunk

pissed off – annoyed

piss weak – no good, gutless

plonk – cheap wine

pokies – poker machines

Pom – English person

postie – mailman

pot – large beer glass (Victoria); beer gut; to sink a billiard ball

ratbag – friendly term of abuse

ratshit, (RS) – lousy

rapt – delighted, enraptured

reckon! – you bet!, absolutely!

rego – car registration (ie 'car rego')

rellie – family relative

ridgy-didge – original, genuine

ring-in – a substitute or outsider

ripper – good (also 'little ripper')

road train – a large truck, a semitrailer towing several trailers

root – have sexual intercourse

rooted – tired, broken

ropable – very bad-tempered or angry

rubbish – deride, tease (ie 'to rubbish')

saltie – saltwater crocodile (the dangerous one)

Salvo – member of the Salvation Army

sandgroper – resident of Western Australia

scallops – fried potato cakes (Queensland, New South Wales), shellfish (elsewhere)

schooner – large beer glass (New South Wales, South Australia)

scrub – bush

sea wasp – deadly box jellyfish

sealed road – bitumen road

session – lengthy period of heavy alcohol drinking

Shanks's pony – to travel on foot

shark biscuit – an inexperienced surfer

sheila – woman

shellacking – comprehensive defeat

she'll be right – no problems, *no worries*

shonky – unreliable

shoot through – leave in a hurry

shout – buy a round of drinks (ie 'it's your shout')

sickie – day off work ill (or malingering)

slab – carton of beer bottles or cans

smoko – tea break

snag – sausage

sparrow's fart – dawn

squatter – pioneer farmer who occupied land as a tenant of the government

station – large farm

sticky beak – nosy person

stinger – (deadly) box jellyfish

strides – trousers, *daks*

stroppy – bad tempered

stubby – 375ml bottle of beer

Stubbies – popular brand of mens' work shorts

sunbake – sunbathe (well, the sun's hot in Australia)

swag – canvas-covered bed roll used in the *outback*; also a large amount

tall poppies – achievers (*knockers* like to cut them down)

tea – evening meal

thingo – thing, whatchamacallit, doovelacki, thingamajig

thongs – flip-flops, an *ocker*'s idea of formal footwear

tinny – 375ml can of beer; also a small, aluminium fishing dinghy (Northern Territory)

togs – swimming costume (Queensland, Victoria)

too right! – absolutely!

Top End – northern part of the Northern Territory

trucky – truck driver

true blue – *dinkum*

tucker – food

two-pot screamer – person unable to hold their drink

two-up – traditional heads/tails gambling game

uni – university

up north – New South Wales and Queensland when viewed from Victoria

ute – utility, pick-up truck

wag – to skip school or work (ie to wag)

wagon – station wagon, estate car

walkabout – lengthy walk away from it all

wallaby track, on the – to wander from place to place seeking work (archaic)

weatherboard – wooden house

Wet, the – the rainy season in the north

wharfie – dockworker

whinge – complain, moan

wobbly – disturbing, unpredictable behaviour (ie 'throw a wobbly')

woomera – stick used by Aboriginal people for throwing spears

woop-woop – *outback*, miles from anywhere

yabbie – small freshwater crayfish

yahoo – noisy and unruly person

yakka – work (from an Aboriginal language)

yobbo – uncouth, aggressive person

yonks – ages, a long time

youse – plural of you, pronounced 'yooze', only used by the grammatically challenged

Aboriginal Culture

TRADITIONAL SOCIETY

Australia's Aboriginal people were tribal, living in extended family groups or clans, with clan members descending from a common ancestral being. Tradition, rituals and laws linked the people of each clan to the land they occupied and each clan had various sites of spiritual significance, places to which their spirits would return when they died. Clan members came together to perform rituals to honour their ancestral spirits and the creators of the Dreaming. These beliefs were the basis of the Aboriginal peoples' ties to the land they lived on.

It is the responsibility of the clan, or particular members of it, to correctly maintain and protect the sites so that the ancestral beings are not offended and continue to protect the clan. Traditional punishments for those who neglect these responsibilities can still be severe, as their actions can easily affect the well-being of the whole clan – food and water shortages, natural disasters or mysterious illnesses can all be attributed to disgruntled or offended ancestral beings.

Many Aboriginal communities were semi-nomadic, others sedentary, one of the deciding factors being the availability of food. Where food and water were readily available, the people tended to remain in a limited area. When they did wander, however, it was to visit sacred places to carry out rituals, or to take advantage of seasonal foods available elsewhere. They did not, as is still often believed, roam aimlessly and desperately in the search for food and water.

The traditional role of the men was that of hunter, tool-maker and custodian of male law; the women reared the children, and gathered and prepared food. There was also female law and ritual for which the women were responsible. Ultimately, the shared efforts of men and women ensured the continuation of their social system.

Wisdom and skills obtained over millennia enabled Aboriginal people to use their environment to the maximum. An intimate knowledge of the behaviour of animals and the correct time to harvest the many plants they utilised ensured that food shortages were rare. As is the case with other hunter-gatherer peoples, Aboriginal people were true ecologists.

Although Aboriginal people in northern Australia had been in regular contact with the fishing and farming peoples of Indonesia for at least 1000 years, the cultivation of crops and the domestication of livestock held no appeal. The only major modification of the landscape practised by Aboriginal people was the selective burning of undergrowth in forests and dead grass on the plains. This encouraged new growth, which in turn attracted game animals to the area. It also prevented the build-up of combustible material in the forests, making hunting easier and reducing the possibility of major bushfires. Dingoes were domesticated to assist in the hunt and to guard the camp from intruders.

Similar technology – for example the boomerang and spear – was used throughout the continent, but techniques were also adapted to the environment and the species being hunted. In the wetlands of northern Australia, fish traps hundreds of metres long made of bamboo and cord were built to catch fish at the end of the wet season. In the area now known as Victoria, permanent stone weirs many kilometres long were used to trap migrating eels, while in the tablelands of Queensland finely woven nets were used to snare herds of wallabies and kangaroos.

Contrary to the common image, some tribes did build permanent dwellings, varying widely depending on climate, the materials available and likely length of use. In western Victoria the local Aboriginal people built permanent stone dwellings; in the deserts semicircular shelters were made with arched branches covered with native grasses or leaves; and in Tasmania large conical thatch shelters which could house up to 30 people were constructed. Such dwellings were used mainly for sleeping.

The early Australian Aboriginal people were also traders. Trade routes crisscrossed the country, dispersing goods and a variety of produced items. Many items traded, such as certain types of stone or shell, were rare and had great ritual significance. Boomerangs and ochre were other important items. Along the networks which developed, large numbers of people would meet for 'exchange ceremonies', where not only goods but also songs and dances were passed on.

BELIEFS & CEREMONIES

Early European settlers and explorers usually dismissed the entire Aboriginal population as 'savages' and 'barbarians', and it was some time before the Aboriginal peoples' deep, spiritual bond with the land, and their relationship to it, was understood by white Australians.

The perceived simplicity of the Aboriginal peoples' technology contrasts with the sophistication of their cultural life. Religion, history, law and art are integrated in complex ceremonies which depict the activities of their ancestral beings, and also prescribe codes of behaviour and responsibilities for looking after the land and all living things. The link between the people and the ancestral beings are totems, each person having their own totem, or Dreaming. These totems take many forms, such as caterpillars, snakes, fish and magpies. Songs explain how the landscape contains these powerful creator ancestors, who can exert either a benign or a malevolent influence. They tell of the best places and the best times to hunt, and where to find water in drought years. They can also specify kinship relations and identify correct marriage partners.

Ceremonies are still performed in many parts of Australia; many of the sacred sites are believed to be dangerous and entry is prohibited under traditional Aboriginal law. These restrictions may seem merely the result of superstition, but in many cases they have a pragmatic origin. One site in northern Australia was believed to cause sores to break out all over the body of anyone visiting the area. Subsequently, the area was found to have a dangerously high level of radiation from naturally occurring radon gas. In another instance, fishing from a certain reef was traditionally prohibited. This restriction was scoffed at by local Europeans until it was discovered that fish from this area had a high incidence of ciguatera, which renders fish poisonous if eaten by humans.

While many Aboriginal people still live in rural areas, those living an urban life remain distinctively Aboriginal – they still speak their indigenous language (or a creolised mix) on a daily basis, and mix largely with other Aboriginal people. Much of their knowledge of the environment, bush medicine and food ('bush tucker') has been retained, and many traditional rites and ceremonies are being revived.

See the Religion section later in this chapter for more on Aboriginal beliefs, ceremonies and sacred sites. See also the Aboriginal Art section starting on page 129.

SONG & NARRATIVE

Aboriginal oral traditions are loosely and misleadingly described as 'myths and legends'. Their single uniting factor is the Dreamtime, when the totemic ancestors formed the landscape, fashioned the laws and created the people who would inherit the land. Translated and printed in English, these renderings of the Dreamtime often lose much of their intended impact. Gone are the sounds of sticks, dijeridu and the rhythm of dance that accompany each poetic line; alone, the words fail to fuse past and present, and the spirits and forces to which the lines refer lose much of their animation.

At the turn of the century, Catherine Langloh Parker was collecting Aboriginal legends and using her outback experience to interpret them sincerely but synthetically. She compiled *Australian Legendary Tales: Folklore of the Noongah-burrahs* (1902).

Professor Ted Strehlow was one of the first methodical translators, and his *Aranda Traditions* (1947) and *Songs of Central Australia* (1971) are important works. Equally important is the combined effort of Catherine & Ronald Berndt. There are 188 songs in the Berndt collection *Djanggawul* (1952), and 129 sacred and 47 secular songs in the collection *Kunapipi* (1951). *The Land of the Rainbow Snake* (1979) focuses on children's stories from western Arnhem Land.

More recently, many Dreamtime stories have appeared in translation, illustrated and published by Aboriginal artists. Some representative collections are *Joe Nangan's Dreaming: Aboriginal Legends of the North-West* (Joe Nangan & Hugh Edwards, 1976); *Milbi: Aboriginal Tales from Queensland's Endeavour River* (Tulo Gordon & J B Haviland, 1980); *Visions of Mowanjum: Aboriginal Writings from the Kimberley* (Kormilda Community College, Darwin, 1980); and *Gularabulu* (Paddy Roe & Stephen Muecke, 1983).

Modern Aboriginal Literature

Modern Aboriginal writers have fused the English language with aspects of their traditional culture. The result is often carefully fashioned to expose the injustices they have been subjected to, especially as urban dwellers. The first Aboriginal writer to be published was David Unaipon in 1929 *(Native Legends)*.

Aboriginal literature now includes drama, fiction and poetry. The poet Oodgeroo Noonuccal (Kath Walker), one of the most well-known of modern Aboriginal writers, was the first Aboriginal woman to have work published *(We Are Going*, 1964). *Paperbark: A collection of Black Australian writings* (1990) presents a great cross-section of modern Aboriginal writers, including dramatist Jack Davis and novelist Mudrooroo Narogin (Colin Johnson). The book has an excellent bibliography of black Australian writing.

There are a number of modern accounts of Aboriginal life in remote parts of Australia. *Raparapa Kularr Martuwarra: Stories from the Fitzroy River Drovers* (1988) is a Magabala Books production. This company, based in Broome, energetically promotes Aboriginal literature.

Autobiography and biography have become an important branch of Aboriginal literature – look for *Moon and Rainbow* (Dick Roughsey, 1971) and *My Country of*

the Pelican Dreaming (Grant Ngabidj, 1981).

The Aboriginal in White Literature

Aboriginal people have often been used as characters in white outback literature. Usually the treatment was patronising and somewhat short-sighted. There were exceptions, especially in the subject of interracial sexuality between white men and Aboriginal women.

Rosa Praed, in her short piece *My Australian Girlhood* (1902), drew heavily on her outback experience and her affectionate childhood relationship with Aboriginal people. Jeannie Gunn's *Little Black Princess* was published in 1904, but it was *We of the Never Never* (1908) which brought her renown. Her story of the life and trials on Elsey Station includes an unflattering, patronising depiction of the Aboriginal people on and around the station.

Catherine Martin, in 1923, wrote *The Incredible Journey*. It follows the trail of two black women, Iliapo and Polde, in search of a little boy who had been kidnapped by a white man. The book describes in careful detail the harsh desert environment they traverse.

Katharine Susannah Prichard contributed a great deal to outback literature in the 1920s. A journey to Turee station in the cattle country of the Ashburton and Fortescue rivers, in 1926, inspired her lyric tribute to the Aborigine, *Coonardoo* (1929), which delved into the then almost taboo love between an Aboriginal woman and a white station boss. Later, Mary Durack's *Keep Him My Country* (1955) explored the theme of a white station manager's love for an Aboriginal girl, Dalgerie.

More recent works incorporating Aboriginal themes include Rodney Hall's *The Second Bridegroom* (1991), Thomas Keneally's *Flying Hero Class* (1991) and David Malouf's *Remembering Babylon* (1993).

RELIGION

Traditional Aboriginal cultures either have

very little religious component or are nothing but religion, depending on how you look at it. Is a belief system which views every event, no matter how trifling, in a non-material context a religion? The early Christian missionaries certainly didn't think so. For them a belief in a deity was an essential part of a religion, and anything else was mere superstition.

Sacred Sites

Aboriginal sacred sites are a perennial topic of discussion. Their presence can lead to headline-grabbing controversy when they stand in the way of developments such as roads, mines and dams. This is because most other Australians still have great difficulty understanding the Aboriginal peoples' deep spiritual bond with the land.

Aboriginal religious beliefs centre on the continuing existence of spirit beings that lived on Earth during the Dreamtime, which occurred before the arrival of humans. These beings created all the features of the natural world and were the ancestors of all living things. They took different forms but behaved as people do, and as they travelled about they left signs to show where they had passed.

Despite being supernatural, the ancestors were subject to ageing and eventually they returned to the sleep from which they'd awoken at the dawn of time. Here their spirits remain as eternal forces that breathe life into the newborn and influence natural events. Each ancestor's spiritual energy flows along the path it travelled during the Dreamtime and is strongest at the points where it left physical evidence of its activities, such as a tree, hill or claypan. These features are sacred sites.

Every person, animal and plant is believed to have two souls – one mortal and one immortal. The latter is part of a particular ancestral spirit and returns to the sacred sites of that ancestor after death, while the mortal soul simply fades into oblivion. Each person is spiritually bound to the sacred sites that mark the land associated with his or her ancestor. It is the individual's obligation to help care for these sites by performing the necessary rituals and singing the songs that tell of the ancestor's deeds. By doing this, the order created by that ancestor is maintained.

Unfortunately, Aboriginal sacred sites are not like Christian churches, which can be desanctified before the bulldozers move in. Neither can they be bought, sold or transferred. Other Australians find this difficult to accept because they regard land as belonging to the individual, whereas in Aboriginal society land is regarded as belonging to the community. In a nutshell, Aboriginal people believe that to destroy or damage a sacred site threatens not only the living but also the spirit inhabitants of the land. It is a distressing and dangerous act, and one that no responsible person would condone. See Aboriginal Beliefs & Ceremonies earlier in this section for more on sacred sites.

Throughout much of Australia, when pastoralists were breaking the Aboriginal peoples' subsistence link to the land, and sometimes shooting them, many Aboriginal people sought refuge on missions and became Christian. However, becoming Christian has not, for most Aboriginal people, meant renouncing their traditional religion. Many senior Aboriginal law men are also devout Christians, and in many cases ministers.

LANGUAGE

At the time of European contact there were around 250 separate Australian languages, comprising about 700 dialects. Often three or four adjacent tribes would speak what amounted to dialects of the same language, but another adjacent tribe might speak a completely different language.

It is believed that all the languages evolved from a single language family as the Aboriginal people gradually moved out over the entire continent and split into new groups. There are a number of words that occur right across the continent, such as *jina* (foot) and *mala* (hand), and similarities also exist in the often complex grammatical structures.

Following European contact the number

of Aboriginal languages was drastically reduced. At least eight separate languages were spoken in Tasmania alone, but none of these was recorded before the native speakers either died or were killed. Of the original 250 or so languages, only around 30 are now regularly spoken and taught to children.

Aboriginal Kriol is a new language which has developed since European arrival in Australia. It is spoken across northern Australia and has become the 'native' language of many young Aboriginal people. It contains many English words, but the pronunciation and grammatical usage are along Aboriginal lines, the meaning is often different, and the spelling is phonetic. For example, the English sentence 'He was amazed' becomes 'I bin luk kwesjinmak' in Kriol.

There are a number of generic terms which Aboriginal people use to describe themselves, and these vary according to the region. The most common of these is Koori, used for the people of south-east Australia. Nunga is used to refer to the people of coastal South Australia, Murri for those from the north-east, and Nyoongah is used in the country's south-west.

Lonely Planet's excellent *Australian phrasebook* gives a detailed account of Aboriginal languages.

Fauna & Flora

The Australian landmass is one of the most ancient on earth. The sea has kept it cut off from other continents for more than 50 million years, and its various indigenous plants and animals have experienced an unusually long, uninterrupted period of evolution in isolation.

Australia's characteristic vegetation began to take shape about 55 million years ago when Australia broke from the supercontinent of Gondwanaland. At this time, Australia was completely covered by cool-climate rainforest, but as the continent drifted towards warmer climes, it gradually dried out, the rainforests retreated, plants like eucalypts and wattles (acacias) took over and grasslands expanded, resulting in the distinctive habitats found today.

FAUNA

Australia is blessed with a fascinating mix of native fauna, which ranges from the primitive to the highly evolved – some creatures are unique survivors from a previous age, while others have adapted so acutely to the natural environment that they can survive in areas which other animals would find uninhabitable.

Since the European colonisation of Australia, 17 species of mammal have become extinct and at least 30 more are endangered. Many introduced non-native animals have been allowed to run wild, causing a great deal of damage to native species and to Australian vegetation. Introduced animals include the fox, cat, pig, goat, camel, donkey, water buffalo, horse, starling, blackbird, cane toad and the notorious rabbit. Foxes and cats kill small native mammals and birds, rabbits denude vast areas of land, pigs carry disease and introduced birds take over the habitat of the local species.

MONOTREMES

The monotremes are often regarded as living fossils, and although they display some intriguing features from their reptile ancestors, such as laying eggs, they are now recognised as a distinct mammalian lineage rather than a primitive stage in mammalian evolution. It's an exclusive little club with just two members – the platypus, found solely in Australia, and the echidna, which is also found in the highlands of Papua New Guinea. The newly hatched young are suckled on milk. They are both superbly adapted and consequently fairly common within their distributions.

Platypus

The platypus *(Ornithorhynchus anatinus)* is certainly well equipped for its semi-aquatic lifestyle. It has a duck-like bill, which is actually quite soft, short legs, webbed feet and a short but thick, beaver-like tail. Adult males are about 50 cm long, not including the 10 to 13-cm tail, and weigh around two kg; the females are slightly smaller.

A platypus spends most of its time in the extensive burrows which it digs along the river banks; it spends the rest of its time in the water foraging for food with its electrosensitive bill or sunning itself in the open. Its diet is mainly small crustaceans, worms and tadpoles.

The platypus is confined to eastern, mainland Australia and Tasmania.

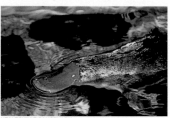

HEALESVILLE SANCTUARY

Platypus, as seen at Healesville Sanctuary's 'Sidney Myer World of the Platypus' exhibit

Echidna

The short-beaked echidna (or spiny anteater; *Tachyglossus aculeatus*) is a small monotreme which is covered on the back with long, sharp spines and on the underside with fur. When fully grown it weighs around 4.5 kg and measures around 45 cm long. The elongated, beak-like snout is around 7.5 cm long and it has a long, sticky tongue which it can whip out some 15 cm beyond the snout – perfect for catching ants and termites, which comprise the major portion of its diet. At the first sign of danger, the echidna rapidly buries its body in the dirt, leaving only its formidable spines exposed.

Short-beaked echidnas are found in a great range of habitats, from hot, dry deserts to altitudes of 1800 metres in the Alps.

CHRIS KLEP

Echidna

MARSUPIALS

Marsupials are mammals which raise their young inside a pouch, or *marsupium*. Marsupials are largely confined to Australia, and included in this group of around 120 species are some of the country's most distinctive and well-known animals – kangaroos, wallabies, koalas, wombats and possums – as well as others less well-known, such as the numerous bandicoots, the predatory quoll and the now-extinct thylacine (or Tasmanian tiger).

Marsupial young are usually very tiny at birth and need to spend a good deal of time in the pouch before being sufficiently developed to live independently of their mothers.

Kangaroos & Wallabies

Kangaroos are probably the most instantly recognisable Australian mammal and hardly need a description, although the name is applied to dozens of species.

There are now greater numbers of kangaroos in Australia than there were when Europeans arrived, a result of the better availability of water and the creation of grasslands for sheep and cattle. Certain species, however, are threatened with extinction through habitat destruction and predation from feral cats and foxes. About three million kangaroos are culled legally each year but many more are killed for sport or by those farmers who believe the cull is insufficient to protect their paddocks from overgrazing by the animals. Kangaroo meat has been exported for some time but it is only in recent years that it has started to appear on Australian menus.

Red kangaroo

DENIS O'BYRNE

Red Kangaroo The distinctive red kangaroo *(Macropus rufus)* is the largest and most widespread of the kangaroos. A fully grown male can be 2.4 metres long and up to two metres high. It's usually only the males that are brick-red; females are often a blue-grey colour. They range over most of arid Australia.

Grey Kangaroo The eastern grey kangaroo *(M. giganteus)* is about the same size as the red, and is found throughout the dry sclerophyll forests of south-eastern Australia, from Queensland to Tasmania. The western grey *(M. fuliginosus)* is very similar, although slightly darker in colour, and is common in the southern regions of Western Australia and South Australia, central and western New South Wales and western Victoria. Mixed populations of eastern and western greys occur in Victoria and New South Wales but there have been no recordings of natural hybrids.

Eastern grey kangaroo

TONY WHEELER

Wallaby Wallabies come in a variety of shapes and sizes. The most commonly seen are the red-necked *(M. rufogriseus)*, agile *(M. agilis)* and the swamp wallaby *(Wallabia bicolor)*, all of which are about 1.7 metres long when fully grown.

Agile wallaby

DAVID CURL

DAVID CURL

Bilby

JOHN TURBILL

Common brushtail possum

DAVID CURL

Sugar glider

The various rock-wallabies are small (around one metre long) and are confined to cliffs and rocky habitats around the country. One of the most widespread is the brush-tailed rock-wallaby *(Petrogale penicillata)*, which is found along the Great Dividing Range in eastern Australia.

Quokka The quokka *(Setonix brachyurus)* is a small, nocturnal mammal found only in the south-western corner of Western Australia, including Rottnest Island, where it is found in large numbers. They are gregarious creatures and move in groups which can number more than 100.

Tree Kangaroo The two Australian species of tree kangaroo, Bennett's *(Dendrolagus bennettianus)* and Lumholtz's *(D. lumholtzi)*, are about the size of a cat and, as the name suggests, have given up life on the ground for life in the trees. Unlike other kangaroos they have strong forelimbs, but are rather ungainly climbers.

Both species are restricted to the north Queensland rainforest, and their habitat has come under extreme pressure from logging activities.

Bandicoots & Bilbies

The small, rat-like bandicoots and bilbies have been among the principal victims of domestic and feral cats.

Bandicoots are largely nocturnal, but can occasionally be seen scampering through the bush. They are mainly insect eaters but also eat some plant material.

One of the most common varieties is the southern brown bandicoot *(Isoodon obesulus)*, which is found in eastern and western Australia. Others, such as the eastern barred bandicoot *(Perameles gunnii)*, are these days found in very limited areas. The rare bilby *(Macrotis lagotis)* is found mainly in the Northern Territory and major efforts have been made to ensure its survival. Its rabbit-like ears have recently caused it to be promoted as Australia's own Easter animal: the Easter bilby versus the Easter bunny!

Possums

There is an enormous range of possums (or phalangers) in Australia – they have adapted to all sorts of habitats, including that of the city, where you'll often find them in parks. Some large species are found living in suburban roofs and will eat garden plants and food scraps. Possums are also common visitors at camp sites in heavily treed country, and will often help themselves to any food left out.

Probably the most familiar of all possums is the common brushtail (or grey) possum *(Trichosurus vulpecula)*, which occurs widely throughout the mainland and Tasmania.

The sugar glider *(Petaurus breviceps)* has membranes between its front and rear legs, which when spread out are used for gliding from the tip of one tree to the base of the next, covering up to 100 metres in one swoop – quite a remarkable sight.

Koala

Australia's other instantly recognisable mammal is the much-loved koala *(Phascolarctos cinereus)*. The name is an Aboriginal word meaning 'no water', which refers to the koala's alleged ability to meet all its moisture requirements from gum leaves, although it does drink water from pools.

Although they are protected today and their survival assured, large numbers of females are infertile due to chlamydia, a sexually transmitted disease. Their cuddly appearance also belies an irritable nature, and they will scratch and bite if sufficiently provoked.

When fully grown a koala measures about 70 cm and weighs around 10 kg. Their most distinctive features are their tufted ears and hard, black nose.

Koalas feed only on the leaves of certain types of eucalypt and are particularly sensitive to changes to their habitat. They are found along the east coast from around Townsville down to Melbourne, and have been reintroduced in South Australia, where they had previously been driven to extinction.

Wombats

Wombats are slow, solid, powerfully built marsupials with broad heads and short, stumpy legs. These fairly placid and easily tamed creatures are legally killed by farmers, who object to the damage done by wombats digging large burrows and tunnelling under fences.

Adult wombats are about one metre long and weigh up to 35 kg. Their strong front legs are excellent burrowing tools, and the rear legs are used for pushing the earth away. Their diet consists of grasses, roots and tree barks.

There are three species of wombat, the most prevalent being the common wombat *(Vombatus ursinus)*, which is distributed throughout the forested areas of south-eastern Australia. The other species are the rare and endangered northern hairy-nosed wombat *(Lasiorhinus krefftii)*, and the southern hairy-nosed wombat *(Lasiorhinus latifrons)*, which is also vulnerable and lives inland of the Great Australian Bight.

Koala   CHRIS KLEP

DAVID CURL

Common wombat

DAVID CURL

Northern quoll

DAVID CURL

Tasmanian devil

Dasyuroids

Members of the Dasyuroidea are predatory marsupials, such as quolls, numbats and the Tasmanian devil. The main distinguishing feature of Dasyuroids is a pointy, elongated snout.

Quoll Australia's spotted quolls, or native cats, are about the size of domestic cats and are probably even more efficient killers. Being nocturnal creatures which spend most of their time in trees, they are not often seen.

The native cats include the eastern quoll *(Dasyurus viverrinus)*, western quoll *(D. geoffroii)* and the northern quoll *(D. hallucatus)*. The eastern is now largely extinct on the mainland but is still found in numbers in Tasmania. The spotted-tailed quoll *(D. maculatus)*, also known as the tiger cat, is one of the most ferocious hunters in the Australian bush.

Tasmanian Devil The carnivorous Tasmanian devil *(Sarcophilus harrisii)* is the largest of the dasyuroids, and is as fierce as it looks. It's solitary and nocturnal and has a fierce whining growl. The body is black with a white stripe across the chest, and measures around 60 cm long, while the tail is around 25 cm long. Its diet consists of small birds and mammals, insects and carrion.

Numbat The attractive numbat *(Myrmecobius fasciatus)*, is a pouchless marsupial and is unusual in that it is most active during the day rather than at night. It has striking rust-red fur with six or seven white stripes across the rump. Adult numbats are about the size of a rat and weigh around half a kg.

Numbats live in hollow, fallen wandoo trees *(Eucalyptus redunca)* found in the forests of south-western Australia; their numbers are dwindling.

DAVID CURL

Numbat

EUTHERIANS

The largest mammalian group on earth is the placental mammals or eutherians. Australia's native eutherians include the marine mammals and the 'recent' invaders, having arrived no more than 15 million years ago, which include numerous species of bats, rodents and the native dog or dingo.

Dingo

The dingo *(Canis familiaris dingo)*, is Australia's native dog. It's thought to have arrived in Australia around 6000 years ago, and was domesticated by Aboriginal people. It differs from the domestic dog in that it howls rather than barks and breeds only once a year (rather than twice), although the two can interbreed.

Dingoes prey on rabbits, rats and mice, although when other food is scarce they sometimes attack livestock (usually unattended sheep or calves), and for this reason are considered vermin by many farmers. Efforts to control dingo numbers have been largely unsuccessful.

JOHN TURBILL
Grey headed flying fox

Marine Mammals

Humpback Whale Now a regular visitor to the east and west coasts of Australia, this massive marine mammal *(Megaptera novaeangliae)* is a joy to behold. It migrates northwards from feeding grounds in the polar seas to breed in subtropical waters in winter. Adult humpbacks range from 14 to 19 metres in length and can live for over 30 years.

Southern Right Whale The southern right whale *(Eubalaena australis)*, so-called because it was the 'right' whale to kill, was hunted almost to the point of

JOHN CHAPMAN
Dingo

WESTERN AUSTRALIAN TOURISM COMMISSION
Humpback whale

RICHARD I'ANSON

Emu

DAVID CURL

Laughing kookaburra

DAVID CURL

Blue-winged kookaburra

extinction but, since the cessation of whaling, has started to return to Australian waters. It can be seen in the Great Australian Bight, and is easily recognised by its strongly down-turned mouth with long baleen plates (these filter water for planktonic krill).

Dugong This is a herbivorous aquatic mammal *(Dugong dugon)*, often known as the 'sea cow', found along the northern Australian coast, from Shark Bay in Western Australia to the Great Barrier Reef in Queensland. The Shark Bay population is estimated to be over 10,000, about 10% of the world's dugong population. The dugong is found in shallow tropical waters where it feeds on seagrasses, supplemented by algae.

BIRDS

Australia's birdlife is as beautiful as it is varied, with over 750 recorded species, many of them endemic.

The Royal Australasian Ornithologists Union runs bird observatories in New South Wales, Victoria and Western Australia, which provide accommodation and guides. Contact the RAOU (☎ (03) 9882 2622) at 415 Riversdale Rd, Hawthorn East, Victoria 3123.

Emu

The emu *(Dromaius novaehollandiae)* is a shaggy feathered bird that stands two metres high. The only bird larger than the emu is the African ostrich, also flightless. Emus are found across the country, but only in areas away from human habitation. After the female lays her six to 12 large, dark green eggs the male hatches them and raises the young.

Kookaburra

The laughing kookaburra *(Dacelo novaeguinae)* is common throughout coastal Australia, but particularly in the east and south-west of the country. The blue-winged kookaburra *(D. leachii)* is found in northern coastal woodlands. Kookaburras are the largest members of the kingfisher family. The kookaburra is heard as much as it is seen – you can't miss its loud, cackling laugh. Kookaburras can become quite tame and pay regular visits to friendly households, but only if the food is excellent.

Bowerbird

The stocky, stout-billed bowerbird, of which there are at least half a dozen species, is best known for its unique mating practice. The brightly coloured male builds a bower which he decorates with various coloured objects to attract the less showy female. The female is impressed by the male's neatly built bower and attractively displayed treasures, but once they've mated all the hard work is left to her.

The three most common species are the great *(Chlamydera nuchalis)*, the spotted *(C. maculata)* and the satin *(Ptilonorhynchus violaceus)*.

Magpie

The black and white magpie (*Gymnorhina* spp) is one of the most widespread birds in Australia, being found virtually throughout the country. One of the most distinctive sounds of the Australian bush is the melodious song of the magpie, which is heard at any time of day, but especially at dawn. One of the magpie's less endearing traits is the way it swoops at people who approach its nest too closely in spring. The several geographic species of magpie all look much alike to the untrained eye but differ in the arrangement of their black and white markings.

Wedge-Tailed Eagle

The wedge-tailed eagle *(Aquila audax)* is Australia's largest bird of prey. It has a wing span of up to two metres, and is easily identified in flight by its distinctive wedge-shaped tail. 'Wedgies' are often seen in outback Australia, either soaring to great heights, or feeding on road-kill carcasses.

Parrots, Rosellas, Lorikeets & Cockatoos

There is an amazing variety of these birds throughout Australia. Some, such as the galah, are fairly plain, while others have vivid colouring.

Rosella There are a number of species of rosella (*Platycercus* spp), most of them brilliantly coloured and not at all backward about taking a free feed from humans. The mainly red, yellow and blue eastern rosella *(P. eximius)* is the most widespread and is found throughout rural south-eastern Australia.

Galah The pink and grey galah *(Cacatua roseicapilla)* is amongst the most common, and is often sighted scratching for seeds on the roadside.

Rainbow Lorikeet The rainbow lorikeet *(Trichoglossus haematodus)* is so extravagantly colourful that it is hard to imagine until you've seen one, with its blue head, orange breast and green body. Lorikeets have a brush-like tongue for extracting nectar from flowers.

CHRIS KLEP

Wedge-tailed eagle

JOHN TURBILL

Galah at nest hollow

DAVID CURL

Rainbow lorikeets

Jabiru

Magpie goose

Brolga

Black swan

Budgerigar Budgies *(Melopsittacus undulatus)* are widespread over inland Australia where they can be seen in flocks of thousands flying in tight formation. Budgies are probably the most widely kept cage bird in the world.

Black Cockatoo There are six species of black cockatoo, the most widespread being the large red-tailed black cockatoo *(Calyptorhynchus magnificus)* and the yellow-tailed black cockatoo *(C. funereus)*.

Sulphur-Crested Cockatoo This noisy cocky *(Cacatua galerita)*, often seen in loud, raucous flocks, is found throughout eastern and northern Australia. When the flock is feeding on the ground, several individuals will fly to a high vantage point to watch over the flock and signal if there is any danger.

Lyrebird

The shy superb lyrebird *(Menura novaehollandiae)* is a ground-dwelling rainforest bird found in south-eastern Australia. The male has tail feathers which form a lyre shape when displayed to attract a mate. The similar Albert lyrebird *(M. alberti)* is found in the rainforests of southern Queensland and northern New South Wales. Lyrebirds have a beautiful song and are also clever mimics.

Jabiru

The jabiru (or black-necked stork, *Xenorhynchus asiaticus*) is found throughout northern and eastern Australia, although it is not often seen. It stands over one metre high, and has an almost iridescent green-black neck, black and white body, and orange legs.

Magpie Goose

The magpie (or pied) goose *(Anseranas semipalmata)* is commonly seen in the tropical wetlands of northern Australia – indeed when water becomes scarce towards the end of the dry season (October) they often gather in huge numbers on the retreating wetlands.

Brolga

Another bird commonly seen in wetland areas of northern and, to a lesser extent, eastern Australia, is the tall crane known as the brolga *(Grus rubicundus)*. They stand over one metre high, are grey in colour and have a distinctive red head colouring.

Black Swan

Commonly seen on stretches of water from the Top End to Tasmania are black swans *(Cygnus atratus)*. They are usually seen in large flocks near fresh or brackish water. Black swans nest among reeds or on islands in lakes and both parents take on nesting duties.

REPTILES

Snakes

Australian snakes are generally shy and avoid confrontations with humans. A few, however, are deadly. The most dangerous are the taipan and tiger snake, although death adders, copperheads, brown snakes and red-bellied black snakes should also be avoided. Tiger snakes will actually attack.

Crocodiles

There are two types of crocodile in Australia: the extremely dangerous saltwater crocodile *(Crocodylus porosus)*, or 'saltie' as it's known, and the less aggressive freshwater crocodile *(C. johnstoni)*, or 'freshie'. It is important to be able to tell the difference between them, as both are prolific in northern Australia.

Saltwater Crocodile Salties are not confined to salt water. They inhabit estuaries, and following floods may be found many km from the coast. They may even be found in permanent fresh water more than 100 km inland. Salties, which can grow to seven metres, will attack and kill humans.

Freshwater Crocodile Freshies are smaller than salties – anything over four metres should be regarded as a saltie. Freshies are also more finely constructed and have much narrower snouts and smaller teeth. Freshies, though unlikely to seek human prey, have been known to bite, and children in particular should be kept away from them.

Lizards

Goanna Goannas are large and sometimes aggressive lizards, up to two metres long. With their forked tongues and loud hiss they can be quite formidable, and are best left undisturbed as they will stand their ground. The largest goanna is the carnivorous perentie *(Varanus giganteus)*, found in central Australia.

Frilled Lizard The frilled lizard *(Chlamydosaurus kingii)* is Australia's most famous lizard, and is commonly seen in bushland in eastern and northern Australia. The frill is a loose flap of skin which normally hangs flat around the neck. When alarmed or threatened, the lizard raises its frill and opens its mouth to give a more ferocious appearance.

SPIDERS

The redback *(Latrodectus hasselti)* is Australia's most notorious spider. It is generally glossy black with a red streak down its back. Woodheaps and garden sheds are favourite hang-outs, and its bite can be lethal. The funnel-web (Dipluridae family) is a large, aggressive ground-dwelling spider found mainly in New South Wales. Funnel-webs from around Sydney are particularly venomous; their bite can be fatal.

DAVID CURL

Saltwater crocodile

WESTERN AUSTRALIAN TOURISM COMMISSION

Freshwater crocodile

DAVID CURL

Perentie

DAVID CURL

Frilled lizard

FLORA

Despite vast tracts of dry and barren land, much of Australia is well vegetated. Forests cover 5%. or 410,000 sq km. Plants can be found even in the arid centre, though many of them grow and flower erratically.

The arrival of Europeans 200 years ago saw the introduction of new flora, fauna and tools. Rainforests were logged, new crops and pasture grasses spread, hoofed animals such as cows, sheep and goats damaged the soil, and watercourses were altered. Irrigation, combined with excessive tree clearing, gradually resulted in salination of the soil. Human activities seriously threaten Australian flora but to date most species have survived.

JEFF WILLIAMS
Spinifex country, the Kimberley, WA

DAVID CURL
Spear grass *(Sorghum intrans)*, Kakadu NP, NT

NATIVE GRASSES

There are more than 700 native Australian grasses found in a variety of habitats across the country.

Spinifex

The hardiest and most common desert plants belong to the group of desert grasses called spinifex. They are a dense, dome-shaped mass of long, needle-like leaves found on sandy soils and rocky areas. Spinifex grasslands are very difficult to walk through – the explorer Ernest Giles called the prickly spinifex 'that abominable vegetable production'. They cover vast areas of central Australia and support large populations of reptiles.

The resin from spinifex was used by Aboriginal people to fasten spear heads and as a general adhesive.

Mitchell Grass

Mitchell grass covers huge areas of arid land in northern Australia, and is the saviour of the cattle industry in the Top End. It has a well-developed root system and is therefore very drought resistant. The grass usually grows in tussocks on clay soils which develop huge cracks when dry and become quagmires when wet.

SHRUBS & FLOWERS

Callistemons

Callistemons, or bottlebrushes (after the brush-like flowers), are found across the country, but especially in New South Wales. They are attractive, hardy and draw many native birds. There are about 25 different species, which grow from one to 10 metres high. Some of the most common are the crimson bottlebrush *(C. citrinus)*, the weeping bottlebrush *(C. viminalis)* and the prickly bottlebrush *(C. brachycandrus)*.

Grevilleas

Grevilleas are another major family of shrubs. Of the 250 or so varieties, all but 20 are native to Australia. Like bottlebrushes, they come in a variety of sizes and flower colours. Most grevilleas are small to medium shrubs, such as Banks grevillea *(G. banksii)*, which has beautiful red flower spikes. When in flower, the silky oak *(G. robusta)*, which can grow to a height of 30 metres, is one of Australia's most spectacular trees.

Kangaroo Paw

Kangaroo paw (*Anigozanthos* spp) grows wild only in the south-western corner of Western Australia; Mangle's kangaroo paw *(A. manglesii)* is that state's floral emblem. Because they are unusual and attractive they are commonly seen in gardens in the eastern states. The plant takes its name from the distinctive, tubular flowers which are covered in velvet-like hair and come in a variety of colours – from black through to red, green and yellow. The plants were used for medicinal purposes by Aboriginal people.

Sturt's Desert Pea

Sturt's desert pea *(Clianthus formosus)* is a small, annual flower which flourishes in the drier areas of inland Australia, particularly after heavy rain soaks the ground. The plant is the floral emblem of South Australia, and has distinctive red flowers with black centres.

Saltbush

Millions of sheep and cattle living in the arid zone owe their survival to dry shrubby plants called saltbush, named for their tolerance to saline conditions. Saltbush is extremely widespread and can be dominant over vast areas. There are 30 different species.

CYCADS & FERNS

MacDonnell Ranges Cycad

The MacDonnell Ranges cycad *(Macrozamia macdonnelli)* is one of 18 species in Australia belonging to the ancient cycad family. It is a very slow-growing plant, often seen high up on rocky hillsides and gorges. Seed cones grow at the tip of the short trunk on female plants, while male cones carry the pollen. The seeds are poisonous but were eaten by Aboriginal people after the toxins had been leached out.

WESTERN AUSTRALIAN TOURISM COMMISSION

Mangle's kangaroo paw

WESTERN AUSTRALIAN TOURISM COMMISSION

Sturt's desert pea

JOHN TURBILL

MacDonnell Ranges cycad

DENIS O'BYRNE
Cabbage palms

Tree Ferns

The beautifully ornate rough tree fern (*Cyathea* spp) and the soft tree fern *(Dicksonia antarctica)* are found in the temperate rainforests of eastern Australia. Some varieties can be as much as 20 metres high, and all are topped by a crown of green fronds.

TREES
Cabbage Palms

The most well-known of Australia's 40 palm species is the cabbage palm *(Livistona mariae)* of Palm Valley in the Finke Gorge National Park near Alice Springs. The tree grows up to 30 metres high, and is unique to this area. The growing tip of the tree consists of tender green leaves, and these were a source of bush tucker to Aboriginal people. The mature leaves were also woven into hats by early European inhabitants of the Centre.

Acacias

The Australian species of the genus *Acacia* are commonly known as wattle – and they are common indeed, with over 660 species known to exist in Australia. They vary from small shrubs to towering blackwoods.

Most species flower during late winter and spring. At this time the countryside is often ablaze with yellow flowers, and it's easy to see why a wattle is Australia's floral emblem.

WESTERN AUSTRALIAN TOURISM COMMISSION
Cootamundra wattle

Blackwood The largest of the acacias, the blackwood *(A. melanoxylon)* can grow up to 30 or more metres high in good soil and is generally found on the ranges of eastern and southern Australia.

Mulga The mulga *(A. aneura)* is the dominant species in huge areas of inland Australia. It is very drought tolerant, and the hard wood was preferred by Aboriginal people for making spears and other implements.

Golden Wattle The golden wattle *(A. pycnantha)* is Australia's floral emblem, and is one of the most widespread acacias. It grows best in hot and arid areas, but is common throughout south-eastern Australia.

Banksias

Banksias (*Banksia* spp) take their name from Sir Joseph Banks, the botanist who accompanied Captain James Cook on his exploratory voyage of eastern Australia. There are about 60 species in Australia, and they are often found in poor soils unsuitable for most other plants. Most of them sport upright flower spikes covered with brilliant orange, red or yellow flowers, one of the most spectacular being the scarlet banksia *(B. coccinea)*. These flowers were a favourite source of nectar for Aboriginal people, who would dip the spikes in water to make a sweet drink.

WESTERN AUSTRALIAN TOURISM COMMISSION
Scarlet banksia

Casuarinas

Also known as sheoaks, these hardy trees are almost as much a part of the Australian landscape as eucalypts. They grow in a variety of habitats, and are characterised by feather-like 'leaves', which are actually branchlets; the true leaves are small scales at the joints of the branchlets.

Desert Oak Its height, broad shady crown, dark weeping foliage and the sighing music of the wind in its leaves make the desert oak *(Allocasuarina decaisneana)* an inspiring feature of its sand-plain habitat. These magnificent trees are confined to the western arid zone of central Australia and are common around Uluru and Kings Canyon, near Alice Springs. Young desert oaks resemble tall hairy broomsticks; they don't look anything like the adult trees and many people think that they're a different species altogether.

Desert oak   DAVID CURL

River Sheoak The river sheoak *(Casuarina cunninghamania)* is a tall tree, highly valued for its ability to bind river banks, which greatly reduces erosion.

Eucalypts

The eucalypt *(Eucalyptus* spp), or gum tree, is ubiquitous in Australia except in the deepest rainforests and the most arid regions. Of the 700 species of the genus eucalyptus, 95% occur naturally in Australia, the rest in New Guinea, the Philippines and Indonesia.

Gum trees vary in form and height from the tall, straight hardwoods such as jarrah, karri and mountain ash to the stunted, twisted, shrub-like Mallee gum.

LINDSAY BROWN
Snow gum *(Eucalyptus pauciflora)*

River Red Gum River red gums *(E. camaldulensis)* are generally confined to watercourses where their roots have access to a reliable water source. They are massive trees which can grow up to 40 metres high and can live for up to 1000 years.

Coolabah Coolabah trees *(E. Microtheca)* are widespread throughout inland and northern Australia. They grow to about 20 metres high, and are not the prettiest tree around, usually having an uneven, spreading form and a twisted trunk. The coolabah was immortalised in Banjo Paterson's poem, *Waltzing Matilda.*

Ghost Gum The ghost gum *(E. papuana)* is one of the most attractive eucalypts and is found throughout central and northern Australia. Its bright green leaves and smooth white bark contrast with the red rocks and soil of the Centre; and, not surprisingly, it is a common subject for artists.

Melaleucas

The paperbarks, or *Melaleucas*, are generally easily recognised by the loose, papery bark which hangs in thin sheets around the trunk. This is actually dead bark which stays on the tree, insulating the trunk from extreme temperature and moisture loss. The trees

JOHN TURBILL
Ghost gum

TOURISM NEW SOUTH WALES

Waratah

DENIS O'BYRNE

Boab

LINDSAY BROWN

Pencil pine

have for centuries been put to many uses by Aboriginal people – drinkable water is obtainable from the trunk, and the bark has been used for water carriers, rafts, shelters and food coverings.

Some of the most common varieties are the swamp paperbark *(M. ericifolia)*, the bracelet honey-myrtle *(M. armillaris)* and the long-leaved paperbark *(M. leucadendron)*.

Waratah

The waratah *(Telopea Speciosissima)* has a spectacular red flower. The scientific name, *Telopea*, means 'seen from afar', which gives some idea of the impact it makes in the bush. The small tree is limited to New South Wales and Victoria and is the floral emblem of NSW. Genera other than *Telopea* are also given the name waratah, such as the waratah tree *(Oreocallis pinnata)* of Queensland and NSW.

Boab

The boab *(Adansonia gregorii)* is Australia's most grotesque tree and is found only from the south-western Kimberley to the Northern Territory's Victoria River, where it grows on flood plains and rocky areas. Its huge, grey, swollen trunk topped by a mass of contorted branches makes it a fascinating sight, particularly during the dry season when it loses its leaves and becomes 'the tree that God planted upside-down'. Although boabs rarely grow higher than 20 metres, their moisture-storing trunks can be over 25 metres in girth.

Conifers

There are several families of native Australian conifers; however, conifers rarely dominate the vegetation in the way some pines and spruces do in parts of the northern hemisphere.

Bunya Pine One of the most unusual pines is the bunya pine *(Araucaria bidwillii)*, which is often found in older botanic gardens. The huge cones can weigh up to seven kg, so take care before taking a rest under one! The seeds found inside these cones were a favourite food of Aboriginal people.

Norfolk Island Pine The Norfolk Island pine *(A. heterophylla)* is native to Norfolk Island, an external territory of Australia about 1600 km north-east of Sydney. These tall, straight trees were first noted by Captain Cook in 1774, and he suggested they would make excellent masts. Their very symmetrical form has made them a popular tree for streets and parks, particularly close to the seashore.

Pencil Pine Endemic to Tasmania, the pencil pine *(Athrotaxis cupressoides)* is found in high-altitude rainforests. Native pines are vulnerable to fire and stands of dead pencil pines are unfortunately a common site.

Facts for the Visitor

PLANNING
When To Go

Any time is a good time to be in Australia, but as you'd expect in a country this large, different parts are at their best at different times.

The southern states are most popular during summer (December through February), as it's warm enough for swimming and it's great to be outdoors. In the centre of the country it's just too damn hot to do anything much, while in the far north the summer is the Wet season and, even though it is usually not as hot as down south, the heat and humidity can make life pretty uncomfortable. To make matters worse, swimming in the sea in the north is not possible due to the 'stingers' (box jellyfish) which frequent the waters at this time. On the other hand, if you want to see the Top End green and free of dust, be treated to some spectacular electrical storms and have the best of the barramundi fishing while all the other tourists are down south, this is the time to do it.

In winter (June through August) the focus swings to the north, when the humidity has faded and the temperature is perfect. This is the time for visits to far north Queensland and the Top End. Central and outback Australia are also popular at this time, as the extreme heat of summer has been replaced by warm sunny days and surprisingly cool – even cold – nights. The cooler weather also deters the bush flies, which in the warmer months can be an absolute nightmare. The southern states, however, are not without their own attractions in winter. Snow skiers can head for the Victorian Alps or the Snowy Mountains in New South Wales for good cross-country or downhill skiing – although snow cover ranges from excellent one year to virtually nonexistent the next.

Spring and autumn give the greatest flexibility for a short visit as you can combine highlights of the whole country while avoiding the extremes of the weather. Spring is the time for wildflowers in the outback (particularly central and Western Australia) and these can be absolutely stunning after rains and are worth going a long way to see.

The other major consideration when travelling in Australia is school holidays. Australian families take to the road (and air) en masse at these times and many places are booked out, prices rise and things generally get a bit crazy. (See the Holidays section for details.)

Maps

There's no shortage of maps available, although many of them are of pretty average quality. For road maps the best are probably those published by the various oil companies – Shell, BP, Mobil etc, and these are available from service stations. The various state motoring organisations are another good source of maps, and theirs are often a lot cheaper than the oil company maps (see Useful Organisations later in this chapter for addresses). Commercially available city street guides, such as those produced by Melways, Gregorys and UBD are also useful.

For bushwalking, ski-touring and other activities that require large-scale maps, the topographic sheets put out by the Australian Surveying & Land Information Group (AUSLIG) are the ones to get. Many of the more popular sheets are usually available over the counter at shops that sell specialist bushwalking gear and outdoor equipment. AUSLIG also has special-interest maps showing various types of land use, population densities or Aboriginal land. For more information, or a catalogue, you can contact AUSLIG, the Department of Administrative Services, Scrivener Bldg, Fern Hill Park, Bruce, ACT 2617 (☎ (02) 6201 4201).

SUGGESTED ITINERARIES

The toughest part about visiting Australia is deciding what to see now and what to leave for next time. The biggest influence on any decisions you make will be whether you are travelling by land or air. In a country where it takes a week or more to drive from coast to coast, clearly a driving or coach holiday of a couple of weeks is going to limit you to a relatively small area (Tasmania, for instance), whereas by air you could hop between a number of widely spaced points.

The main thing to bear in mind when trying to plan ahead is that Australia is *big* – that line on the map between two cities may look like an easy day's drive, but it may be 1000km or more! A leisurely trip through a small area is going to be much more enjoyable (and safer) than a mad, 500km-a-day dash around the place. In the outback and in sparsely populated country areas, 500km is not an unrealistic day's driving if you don't plan to stop much along the way; on the east coast you can halve that.

While everybody travels at a different pace, the following suggestions assume that you want to see things along the way, don't want to spend 12 hours a day behind the wheel and would like to finish your trip feeling more relaxed than when you started.

One Month
One of the most popular routes is the run up (or down) the east coast between Sydney and Cairns. To drive (or bus) this comfortably would take about a month, although you could easily spend three months doing it. Another four-week drive could be from Cairns across Queensland to Darwin and Kakadu, and even down to the centre to Alice Springs, with a side trip to Uluru. You could also attack the centre from the other direction, starting in Sydney or Melbourne and heading north via Adelaide and the Flinders Ranges. You could also do the trek between Perth and the east coast in a comfortable four weeks, but that wouldn't allow for much time at either end.

Three Months
With three months at your disposal you can start getting serious: Sydney to Cairns via the centre and Darwin; Sydney to Adelaide via Cairns, Darwin and the centre; Perth to Cairns via the Kimberley and Darwin; or Melbourne to Cairns via the coast.

Six Months
Six months gives you enough time to do the big loop which takes in the east coast, Darwin,

central Australia, Adelaide and Melbourne, with perhaps a stop for a month to work or hang out somewhere along the way. Cairns to Perth via the eastern and southern coasts would also be a viable proposition.

HIGHLIGHTS
In a country as broad and geographically diverse as Australia the list of highlights is virtually endless, although one person's highlight can easily be another's disappointment. However, a number of features in each state shouldn't be missed:

ACT
The national capital is a picturesque, planned city, the focal point being Lake Burley Griffin and impressive, modern buildings such as Parliament House and the High Court. The fine National Gallery should not be missed.

New South Wales
Sydney, the capital and host for the year 2000 Olympic Games, has simply one of the most stunning locations you're likely to come across, as well as the beautiful Blue Mountains nearby. The coastal beaches, northern rainforests, Snowy Mountains National Park and the wide expanse of the interior also have plenty to offer.

Northern Territory
The obvious attraction is Uluru (Ayers Rock), probably Australia's most readily identifiable symbol after the Sydney Opera House. There's also the World Heritage-listed Kakadu National Park with its abundant flora and fauna and superb wetlands. The Territory is also where Australia's Aboriginal cultural heritage is at its most accessible – the rock-art sites of Kakadu, and a number of Aboriginal-owned and run tours of Arnhem Land, Manyallaluk (near Katherine) and Uluru are just a few of the possibilities.

Queensland
The Great Barrier Reef, and its many water-based activities, is outstanding. The state's varied terrain offers visitors secluded beach and island resorts, the rainforested Daintree, inland deserts and 'one-horse towns', cattle country and the remote Cape York Peninsula.

South Australia
The big drawcards here are the Barossa Valley, with its excellent wineries, and the Flinders Ranges, which offer superb bushwalking and stunning scenery. In the northern areas of South Australia you can get a real taste of the outback along famous tracks such as the Strzelecki, Oodnadatta and Birdsville, while the opal-mining town of Coober Pedy, where many people not only work underground but also live in subterranean houses, is totally unique.

Tasmania
There's the rich heritage of the convict era at places such as Port Arthur, as well as some of the most beautiful wilderness areas in the country. The Cradle Mountain-Lake St Clair World Heritage area is popular with bushwalkers, as is the rugged south-west corner of the state.

Victoria
No visit to Victoria would be complete without an exploration of the enchanting Grampians mountain range, famous for its natural beauty and great bushwalks. Other highlights include the fairy penguins at Phillip Island, the re-created gold-mining township of Sovereign Hill at Ballarat, the snowfields and forests of the Victorian Alps and the Great Ocean Road, one of the world's most spectacular coastal routes. Melbourne, too, is often overlooked, yet it has a charm not found in other Australian cities.

Western Australia
Vast distances and wide open spaces are the big attractions here. In the south of the state is Fremantle, an eclectic little port city not far from the state capital, Perth. The eucalypt forests of the south coast are spectacular, while the Kimberley region in the far north is ruggedly picturesque – the Bungle Bungle (Purnululu) National Park here is unforgettable.

TOURIST OFFICES

There are a number of information sources for visitors to Australia and, like many other tourist-conscious western countries, you can easily drown yourself in brochures and booklets, maps and leaflets.

Local Tourist Offices

Within Australia, tourist information is handled by various state and local offices. Each state and the ACT and Northern Territory has a tourist office of some kind and you will find information about these centres in the state chapters. Apart from a main office in the capital cities, they often have regional offices in main tourist centres and also in other states. Tourist information in Victoria is handled by the Royal Automobile Club of Victoria (RACV) in Melbourne.

As well as supplying brochures, price lists, maps and other information, the state offices will often book transport, tours and accommodation for you. Unfortunately, very few of the state tourist offices maintain information desks at the airports and, furthermore,

the opening hours of the city offices are too often the 9-to-5-weekdays and Saturday-morning-only variety. Addresses of the main state tourist offices and government tourist bodies are:

Australian Capital Territory
Canberra Tourist Bureau, Jolimont Centre, Northbourne Ave, Canberra City, ACT 2601 (☎ 1800 026 166)
Canberra Tourism, Canberra Visitors' Centre, Northbourne Ave, Dickson, ACT (☎ (02) 6205 0666, 1800 026 166; www.canberratourism.com.au/welcome.html)

New South Wales
NSW Government Travel Centre, 19 Castlereagh St, Sydney, NSW 2000 (☎ 13 2077; www.tourism.nsw.gov.au)

Northern Territory
Darwin Region Tourism Association, Cnr Mitchell and Knuckey Sts, Darwin, NT 0800 (☎ (08) 8981 4300)
Northern Territory Tourism Commission, Tourism House, GPO Box 1155, Darwin, 0801 (☎ 1800 621 336; www.world.net/Travel/Australia/NTinfo/NTTC)

Queensland
Queensland Government Travel Centre, Cnr Adelaide and Brisbane Sts, Brisbane, Qld 4000 (☎ 13 1801; www.qttc.com.au)

South Australia
South Australian Travel Centre, 1 King William St, Adelaide, SA 5000 (☎ 1300 366 770)
South Australian Tourism Commission, PO Box 1972, Adelaide 5001, South Australia (☎ (08) 8303 2033; sthaustour@tourism.sa.gov.au; www.tourism.sa.gov.au)

Tasmania
Tasmanian Travel & Information Centre, Cnr Davey and Elizabeth Sts, Hobart, Tas 7000 (☎ (03) 6230 8233)
Tourism Tasmania, GPO Box 399, Hobart, Tasmania (☎ (03) 6230 8227; fax 6230 8307; www.tourism.tas.gov.au)

Victoria
RACV Travel Centre, 230 Collins St, Melbourne, Vic 3000 (☎ 1800 337 743)
Victorian Tourism Information Service, Melbourne Town Hall, Cnr Little Collins & Swanston Sts, Melbourne, Vic (☎ (03) 13 2842; fax 9790 2955; www.tourism.vic.gov.au)

Western Australia
Western Australian Tourist Centre, Forrest Place, Perth, WA 6000 (☎ (1800 812 818)
Western Australian Tourism Commission, 16 St Georges Tce, Perth, WA (☎ (08) 9220 1700; fax 9220 1702; www.wa.gov.au/gov/watc)

A step down from the state tourist offices are the local or regional offices. Almost every major town in Australia seems to maintain a tourist office or centre of some type or other and in many cases these are really excellent, with much local information not readily available from the state offices. This particularly applies where there is a strong local tourist trade.

Tourist Offices Abroad
The Australian Tourist Commission (ATC) is the government body intended to inform potential visitors about the country. There's a very definite split between promotion outside and inside Australia. The ATC is strictly an external operator; it does minimal promotion within the country and has little contact with visitors to Australia. Within the country, tourist promotion is handled by state or local tourist offices.

ATC offices overseas have a useful free magazine-style periodical booklet called *Australia Travellers Guide* which has some handy info for potential visitors. The ATC also publishes *Australia Unplugged*, a good introduction to Australia for young people, giving some information about the country in general and snapshots of major cities.

As well, it publishes a number of Fact Sheets on various topics, such as camping, fishing, skiing, disabled travel and national parks – and these can be a useful introduction to the subject. They have a handy map of the country, which is available for a small fee. This literature is intended for distribution overseas only; if you want copies, get them before you come to Australia, or find them on the Web at www.aussie.net.au/pl/atc:1.

The ATC maintains a number of Helplines (often toll-free), which independent travellers can ring or fax to get specific information about Australia. All requests for information should be directed through these numbers:

France
   ☎ toll-free 0591 5626
Germany
   ☎ toll-free 0130 825 182

Hong Kong
   ☎ 2802 7817; fax 2802 8211
Japan
   ☎ /fax (03) 5229 0021
New Zealand
   ☎ toll-free 0800 650 303
Singapore
   ☎ 250 6277; fax 253 8431
UK
   ☎ 0990 022 000
USA
   ☎ (847) 296 4900; fax 635 3718

VISAS & DOCUMENTS
Visas
All visitors to Australia need a visa. Only New Zealand nationals are exempt, and even they receive a 'special category' visa on arrival.

Visa application forms are available from either Australian diplomatic missions overseas or travel agents, and you can apply by mail or in person. There are several different types of visas, depending on the reason for your visit.

Tourist Visas Tourist visas are issued by Australian consular offices abroad; they are the most common visa and are generally valid for a stay of either three or six months. Three-month visas are free; for six-month visas there is a $35 fee.

The visa is valid for use within 12 months of the date of issue and can be used to enter and leave Australia several times within that 12 months.

When you apply for a visa, you need to present your passport and a passport photo, as well as sign an undertaking that you have an onward or return ticket and 'sufficient funds' – the latter is obviously open to interpretation.

You can also apply for a long-stay visa, which is a multiple-entry, four-year visa allowing stays of up to six months on each visit. These also cost $35.

Electronic Travel Authority (ETA) Visitors who require a tourist visa of three months or less can make the application through an IATA-registered travel agent (no form required), who can then make the application direct and issue the traveller with an ETA, which replaces the usual visa stamped in your passport. This system was only introduced in late 1997, and the nationalities it is available to are so far limited to passport holders of the UK, the USA, most European and Scandinavian countries, Malaysia and Singapore. The list is likely to grow rapidly.

Working Holiday Visas Young, single visitors from the UK, Canada, Korea, Holland and Japan may be eligible for a 'working holiday' visa. 'Young' is fairly loosely interpreted as around 18 to 25, although people up to 30 and young married couples without children may sometimes be given a working holiday visa.

A working holiday visa allows for a stay of up to 12 months, but the emphasis is supposed to be on casual employment rather than a full-time job. For this reason you are only supposed to work for one employer for three months, but there's nothing to stop you from working for more than one employer in the 12 months. This visa can only be applied for from outside Australia (preferably but not necessarily in your country of citizenship), and you can't change from a visitor visa to a working holiday visa.

You can apply for a working holiday visa up to 12 months in advance, and it's a good idea to do it as early as possible as there is a limit on the number issued each year. Conditions attached to a working holiday visa include having sufficient funds for a ticket out, and taking out private medical insurance; a fee of $145 is charged when you apply for the visa.

See the section on Work later in this chapter for details of what sort of work is available and where.

Visa Extensions The maximum stay allowed to visitors is one year, including extensions.

Visa extensions are made through Department of Immigration & Ethnic Affairs offices in Australia and, as the process takes some time, it's best to apply about a month

---

Travel Insurance

A travel insurance policy to cover theft, loss and medical problems is a good idea. The policies handled by STA Travel and other student travel organisations are usually good value. Some policies offer lower and higher medical-expense options; the higher ones are chiefly for countries that have extremely high medical costs, such as the USA. There is a wide variety of policies available: compare the small print.

Some policies specifically exclude 'dangerous activities' such as scuba diving, motorcycling and even trekking. A locally acquired motorcycle licence is not valid under some policies.

You may prefer a policy which pays doctors or hospitals direct rather than you having to pay on the spot and claim later. If you have to claim later make sure you keep all documentation. Some policies ask you to call back (reverse charges) to a centre in your home country where an immediate assessment of your problem is made.

Check that the policy covers ambulances or an emergency flight home. ■

---

before your visa expires. There is an application fee of $145 – and even if they turn down your application they can still keep your money. To qualify for an extension you are required to take out private medical insurance to cover the period of the extension, and have a ticket out of the country.

If you're trying to stay for longer in Australia the books *Temporary to Permanent Resident in Australia* and *Practical Guide to Obtaining Permanent Residence in Australia*, both of which are published by Longman Cheshire, might be useful.

Medicare Card

Under reciprocal arrangements, residents of the UK, New Zealand, the Netherlands, Finland, Malta and Italy are entitled to free or subsidised medical treatment under Medicare, Australia's compulsory national health insurance scheme. To enrol you need to show your passport and health-care card or certificate from your own country, and you are then given a Medicare card.

Once you have a card you can get free

necessary public-hospital treatment, and visits to a private doctor's practice are also claimable under Medicare, although depending on the claim method used by the doctor you may have to pay the bill first and then make a claim yourself from Medicare. You also need to find out how much the doctor's consultation fee is, as Medicare only covers you for a certain amount and you will need to pay the balance. Clinics which advertise 'bulk billing' are the easiest to use as they charge Medicare direct.

For more information phone Medicare on ☎ 13 2011.

Driving Licence

You can use your own foreign driving licence in Australia, as long as it is in English (if it's not, a translation must be carried). As an International Licence cannot be used alone and must be supported by your home licence, there seems little point in getting one.

EMBASSIES
Australian Embassies Abroad

Australian consular offices overseas include:

Canada
Suite 710, 50 O'Connor St, Ottawa, Ontario K1P 6L2 (☎ (613) 236 0841; fax 236 4376)
Also in Vancouver
France
4 Rue Jean Rey, 75015 Cedex 15, Paris (☎ (01) 4059 3300; fax 4059 3310)
Germany
Godesberger Allee 105-7, Bonn 53175 (☎ (0228) 81 030; fax 373 145)
Indonesia
Jalan HR Rasuna Said Kav C15-16, Kuningan, Jakarta Selatan 12940 (☎ (021) 522 7111; fax 522 7101)
Jalan Prof Moh Yamin 4, Renon, Denpasar, Bali (☎ (0361) 23 5092; fax 23 1990)
Ireland
6 Fitzwilton House, Wilton Terrace, Dublin 2 (☎ (01) 676 1517; fax 661 3576)
Malaysia
6 Jalan Yap Kwan Seng, Kuala Lumpur 50450 (☎ (03) 2423 122; fax 2414 495)
Netherlands
Carnegielaan 4, The Hague 2517 KH (☎ (070) 310 8200; fax 364 3807)

New Zealand
72-78 Hobson St, Thorndon, Wellington (☎ (04) 473 6411; fax 498 7103)
Union House, 132-38 Quay St, Auckland (☎ (09) 303 2429; fax 303 2431)
Papua New Guinea
Godwit St, Waigani, Port Moresby (☎ 325 9183; fax 325 3528)
Philippines
Dona Salustiana Ty Tower, 104 Paseo de Roxas Ave, Makati, Metro Manila (☎ (02) 750 2850; fax 287 2029)
Singapore
25 Napier Rd, Singapore 258507 (☎ 737 9311; fax 735 1242)
Thailand
37 South Sathorn Rd, Bangkok 10120 (☎ (02) 287 2680; fax 213 1177)
UK
Australia House, The Strand, London WC2B 4LA (☎ (0171) 379 4334; fax 465 8218)
Also in Manchester
USA
1601 Massachusetts Ave NW, Washington DC 20036-2273 (☎ (202) 797 3000; fax 797 3100)
Also in Los Angeles and New York
Vietnam
Van Thuc Compound, Ba Dinh District, Hanoi (☎ (04) 831 7755; fax 831 7711)
Also in Ho Chi Minh City

Foreign Embassies in Australia

The principal diplomatic representations to Australia are in Canberra. There are also representatives in various other major cities, particularly from countries with major connections with Australia like the USA, UK or New Zealand; or in cities with important connections, like Darwin which has an Indonesian consulate.

Big cities like Sydney and Melbourne have nearly as many consular offices as Canberra, although visa applications are generally handled in Canberra. Addresses of important offices follow (look under Consulates & Legations in the *Yellow Pages* telephone book for more):

Canada
Commonwealth Ave, Yarralumla, ACT 2600 (☎ (02) 6273 3844)
Level 5/111 Harrington St, Sydney 2000 (☎ (02) 9364 3050)

France
> 6 Perth Ave, Yarralumla, ACT 2600 (☎ (02) 6216 0100)
>
> 31 Market St, Sydney 2000 (☎ (02) 9261 5779)
>
> 492 St Kilda Rd, Melbourne 3004 (☎ (03) 9820 0921)

Germany
> 119 Empire Circuit, Yarralumla, ACT 2600 (☎ (02) 6270 1911)
>
> 13 Trelawney St, Woollahra, NSW 2025 (☎ (02) 9327 9624)
>
> 280 Punt Rd, South Yarra, Vic 3141 (☎ (03) 9828 6888)

Indonesia
> 8 Darwin Ave, Yarralumla, ACT 2600 (☎ (02) 6250 8600)
>
> 236 Maroubra Rd, Maroubra, NSW 2035 (☎ (02) 9344 9933)
>
> 20 Harry Chan Ave (PO Box 1953), Darwin, NT 0801 (☎ (08) 8941 0048)
>
> 22 Queens Rd, Melbourne 3004 (☎ (03) 9525 2755)

Ireland
> 20 Arkana St, Yarralumla, ACT 2600 (☎ (02) 6273 3022)

Malaysia
> 7 Perth Ave, Yarralumla, ACT 2600 (☎ (02) 6273 1543)
>
> 67 Victoria Rd, Bellevue Hill, NSW 2023 (☎ (02) 9327 7565)
>
> 492 St Kilda Rd, Melbourne 3004 (☎ (02) 9867 5339)

Netherlands
> 120 Empire Circuit, Yarralumla, ACT 2600 (☎ (02) 6273 3111)
>
> 500 Oxford St, Bondi Junction, Sydney 2022 (☎ (02) 9387 6644)
>
> 9499 St Kilda Rd, Melbourne 3004 (☎ (03) 9867 7933)

New Zealand
> Level 14/1 Alfred St, Circular Quay, Sydney 2000 (☎ (02) 9247 1511)

Papua New Guinea
> 39-41 Forster Crescent, Yarralumla, ACT 2600 (☎ (02) 6273 3322)
>
> 100 Clarence St, Sydney 2000 (☎ (02) 9299 5151)
>
> Level 15/15 Lake St, Cairns, Qld 4870 (☎ (070) 521 033)

Singapore
> 17 Forster Crescent, Yarralumla, ACT 2600 (☎ (02) 6273 3944)

Thailand
> 111 Empire Circuit, Yarralumla, ACT 2600 (☎ (02) 6273 1149)
>
> 131 Macquarie St, Sydney 2000 (☎ (02) 9241 2542)
>
> 101 Wickham Tce, Brisbane 4000 (☎ (07) 3832 1999)

> 277 Flinders Ln, Melbourne 3000 (☎ (03) 9650 1714)

UK
> Commonwealth Ave, Yarralumla, ACT 2600 (☎ (02) 6270 6666)
>
> 17/90 Collins St, Melbourne 3000 (☎ (03) 9650 3699)
>
> 16/1 Macquarie Pl, Sydney Cove, Sydney 2000 (☎ (02) 9247 7521)

USA
> 21 Moonah Place, Yarralumla, ACT 2600 (☎ (02) 6270 5000)
>
> 19 Martin Place, Sydney 2000 (☎ (02) 9373 9200)
>
> 553 St Kilda Rd, Melbourne 3004 (☎ (03) 9526 5900)

CUSTOMS

When entering Australia you can bring most articles in free of duty provided that Customs is satisfied they are for personal use and that you'll be taking them with you when you leave. There's also a duty-free, per-person quota of 1125ml of alcohol, 250 cigarettes and dutiable goods up to the value of A\$400.

With regard to prohibited goods, there are two areas that need particular attention. Number one is, of course, drugs – Australian Customs can be extremely efficient when it comes to finding them. Unless you want to make first-hand investigations of conditions in Australian jails, don't bring illegal drugs with you, particularly if you are arriving from South-East Asia or India.

Problem two is animal and plant quarantine. You will be asked to declare all goods of animal or vegetable origin – wooden spoons, straw hats, the lot – and show them to an official. The authorities are naturally keen to prevent weeds, pests or diseases getting into the country – Australia has so far managed to escape many of the agricultural pests and diseases prevalent in other parts of the world. Fresh food is also unpopular, particularly meat, fruit, vegetables and flowers, and there are restrictions on taking fruit and vegetables between states (see the aside on Interstate Quarantine in the Getting Around chapter).

Weapons and firearms are either prohibited or require a permit and safety testing. Other restricted goods include products made from protected wildlife species (such as ivory), unapproved telecommunications devices and live animals.

There are duty-free stores at the international airports and their associated cities. Treat them with healthy suspicion: 'duty-free' is one of the world's most overworked catch phrases, and it is often just an excuse to sell things at prices you can easily beat by a little shopping around.

MONEY
Currency

Australia's currency is the Australian dollar, which comprises 100 cents. There are 5c, 10c, 20c, 50c, $1 and $2 coins, and $5, $10, $20, $50 and $100 notes.

Although the smallest coin in circulation is 5c, prices are still marked in single cents, and then rounded to the nearest 5c when you come to pay.

There are no notable restrictions on importing or exporting travellers cheques. Cash amounts in excess of the equivalent of A$5000 (any currency) must be declared on arrival or departure.

In this book, unless otherwise stated, all prices given in dollars refer to Australian dollars.

Exchange Rates

The Australian dollar fluctuates quite markedly against the US dollar, but it seems to stay pretty much in the 65c to 80c range.

Canada	C$1	=	$1.05
France	FF10	=	$2.44
Germany	DM1	=	$0.82
Hong Kong	HK$10	=	$1.92
Ireland	IR£1	=	$2.05
Japan	¥100	=	$1.16
New Zealand	NZ$1	=	$0.87
UK	UK£1	=	$2.47
USA	US$1	=	$1.49

Changing Money

Changing foreign currency or travellers cheques is no problem at almost any bank or at licensed moneychangers such as Thomas Cook or American Express.

Travellers Cheques

There is a variety of ways to carry your money. If your stay is limited, then travellers cheques are the most straightforward and generally enjoy a better exchange rate than foreign cash in Australia.

American Express, Thomas Cook and other well-known international brands of travellers cheques are all widely used. A passport will usually be adequate for identification; it would be sensible to carry a driver's licence, credit cards or other form of identification in case of problems.

Fees for changing foreign currency travellers cheques seem to vary from bank to bank and from year to year. Currently, of the 'big four' (ANZ, Commonwealth, National and Westpac), ANZ charges $6.50 for up to the equivalent of A$3000 (free when it's above that amount or if they are Visa travellers cheques), Westpac charges $7 up to A$500 (free above that amount), while at the National and the Commonwealth it's $5, regardless of amount or number of cheques.

Buying Australian dollar travellers cheques is an option worth looking at. These can be exchanged immediately with the bank teller without being converted from a foreign currency and incurring commissions, fees and exchange rate fluctuations.

Credit Cards

Credit cards are widely accepted in Australia and are an alternative to carrying large numbers of travellers cheques. Visa, MasterCard, Diners Club and American Express are all widely accepted.

Cash advances from credit cards are available over the counter and from many automatic teller machines (ATMs), depending on the card.

If you're planning to rent cars, a credit card makes life much simpler; they're looked upon with much greater favour by rent-a-car agencies than nasty old cash, and many agencies simply won't rent you a vehicle if you don't have a card.

Bank Accounts & ATMs

If you're planning to stay longer than just a

month or so, it's worth considering other ways of handling money that give you more flexibility and are more economical.

Most travellers these days opt for an account that includes a cash card, which you can use to access your cash from ATMs all over Australia. Westpac, ANZ, National and Commonwealth bank branches are found nationwide, and in all but the most remote town there'll be at least one place where you can withdraw money from a hole in the wall.

ATMs can be used day or night, and it is possible to use the machines of some other banks: Westpac ATMs accept Commonwealth Bank cards and vice versa; National Bank ATMs accept ANZ cards and vice versa. There is a limit on how much you can withdraw (usually around $1000 per day).

Many businesses, such as service stations, supermarkets and convenience stores, are linked into the EFTPOS system (Electronic Funds Transfer at Point Of Sale), and here you can use your bank cash card to pay for services or purchases direct, and often withdraw cash as well. Credit cards can also be used to make local, STD and international phone calls in special public telephones, found in most towns throughout the country.

Opening an account at an Australian bank is easy for overseas visitors if they do it within the first six weeks of arrival. You simply present your passport and away you go. After six weeks (and for Australian citizens) it's much more complicated. A points system operates and you need to score a minimum of 100 points before you can have the privilege of letting the bank take your money. Passports, driver's licences, birth certificates and other 'major' IDs earn you 40 points; minor ones such as credit cards get you 20 points. Just like a game show really!

If you don't have an Australian Tax File Number (see Work later in this chapter), interest earned from your funds will be taxed at the rate of 47%.

Costs

Compared to the USA, Canada and European countries, Australia is cheaper in some ways and more expensive in others. Manu-factured goods tend to be more expensive: if they are imported they have the additional costs of transport and duties, and if they're locally manufactured they suffer from the extra costs entailed in making things in com-paratively small quantities. Thus you pay more for clothes, cars and other manufac-tured items. On the other hand, food is both high in quality and low in cost.

Accommodation is also very reasonably priced. In virtually every town where back-packers are likely to stay there'll be a backpackers' hostel with dorm beds from $10 to $15, or a caravan park with on-site vans from around $30 for two people.

The biggest cost in any trip to Australia will be transport, simply because it's such a vast country. If there's a group of you, buying a second-hand car is probably the most economical way to go.

On average you can expect to spend about $30 per day if you budget fiercely and *always* take the cheapest option; $50 gives you much greater flexibility. Obviously if you stay for longer periods in each place and can take advantage of discounts given on long-term accommodation – or even move into a share-house with other people – this helps keep your costs to a minimum.

Tipping

In Australia tipping isn't entrenched. It's only customary to tip in more expensive restaurants and only then if you feel it's necessary. If the service has been especially good and you decide to leave a tip, 10% of the bill is the usual amount. Taxi drivers don't expect tips (of course, they don't hurl it back at you if you decide to leave the change).

POST & COMMUNICATIONS
Postal Rates

Letters Australia's postal services are rela-tively efficient and reasonably cheap. It costs 45c to send a standard letter or postcard within Australia.

Internationally, aerograms cost 70c to any country, air-mail letters/postcards cost 75/70c to New Zealand, 85/80c to Singapore and Malaysia, 95/90c to Hong Kong and India, $1.05/95c to the USA and Canada, and $1.20/1 to Europe and the UK.

Parcels The rates for parcels are not too extortionate. By sea mail a 1/2/5kg parcel costs $11/21/33 to India, and $13/25/43 to the USA, Europe or the UK. Each kg over 5kg costs $4 for India, and $6 for the USA, Europe or the UK, with a maximum of 20kg for all destinations. Air-mail rates are considerably more expensive.

To New Zealand, air mail is the only option. A 1/2/5kg parcel sent by 'economy air' costs $11/21/33, with a maximum of 20kg.

Sending Mail

Post offices are open from 9 am to 5 pm Monday to Friday, but you can often get stamps from local post offices operated from newsagencies or from Australia Post shops, found in large cities, on Saturday mornings as well.

Receiving Mail

All post offices will hold mail for visitors, and some city GPOs (main post offices) have very busy poste-restante sections. You can also have mail sent to you at American Express offices in big cities if you have an Amex card or carry Amex travellers cheques.

There are also a number of companies that, for a fee, will hold and forward mail to you.

Telephone

The Australian telecommunications industry is deregulated and there are a number of providers offering various services. Private phones are serviced by the two main players, Telstra and Optus, but it's in the mobile phone and payphone markets that other companies such as Vodafone, One.Tel, Unidial, Global One and AAPT are also operating, and it's where you'll find the most competition.

Payphones & Phonecards There are a number of different cards issued by the

various telecommunications companies, and these can be used in any Telstra public phone that accepts cards (virtually all do these days), or from a private phone by dialling a toll-free access number.

Long-distance calls made from payphones are generally considerably more expensive than calls made from private phones. If you will be using payphones to make a large number of calls it pays to look into the various cards available from providers other than Telstra.

The important thing is to know exactly how your calls are being charged, as the charges for calls vary from company to company. An explanatory booklet should be available from the card outlet – usually a newsagent or other shop.

Some public phones are set up to take only credit cards, and these too are convenient, although you need to keep an eye on how much the call is costing as it can quickly mount up. The minimum charge for a call on one of these phones is $1.20.

Local Calls Local calls from public phones cost 40c for an unlimited amount of time. Local calls from private phones cost 30c. Calls to mobile phones attract higher rates.

Long-Distance Calls & Area Codes It's also possible to make long-distance (sometimes known as STD – Subscriber Trunk Dialling) calls from virtually any public phone. Long-distance calls are cheaper in off-peak hours (basically outside normal business hours), and different service providers have different charges.

For the purpose of area (or STD) codes, Australia is divided into just four areas. All regular numbers (ie numbers other than mobiles or information services) have one of four area codes followed by an eight digit number. Long-distance calls (ie more than about 50km) within these areas are charged at long-distance rates, even though they have the same area code. The 02 code covers NSW, 03 is for Victoria and Tasmania, 07 covers Queensland and 08 is for South Australia, Western Australia and the Northern Territory.

Confusingly, when making calls within one area-code area, you still have to dial the area code for that area if the call is a long-distance one. However, as of March 1999 all calls within one STD area (ie origin and destination in the same STD area) can be dialled without using the area code.

International Calls From most payphones you can also make ISD (International Subscriber Dialling) calls, although calls are generally cheaper if using a provider other than Telstra.

When making overseas calls, the international dialling code varies depending on which provider you are using – 0011, 0012.

International calls from Australia are among the cheapest you'll find anywhere, and there are often specials which bring the rates down even further. Off-peak times, if available, vary depending on the destination – see the back of any *White Pages* telephone book, or call ☎ 0102 for more details. Sunday is often the cheapest day to ring.

Country Direct is a service that gives callers in Australia direct access to operators in nearly 60 countries, to make collect or credit-card calls. For a full list of the countries hooked into this system, check any local White Pages telephone book.

Toll-Free Calls Many businesses and some government departments operate a toll-free service, so no matter where you are ringing from around the country, it's a free call. These numbers have the prefix 1800 and we've listed them wherever possible throughout this book.

Many companies, such as the airlines, have numbers beginning with 13 or 1300, and these are charged at the rate of a local call. Often these numbers are Australia-wide, or may be applicable to a specific state or STD district only. Unfortunately, there's no way of telling without actually ringing the number.

Calls to these services still attract charges if you are calling from a mobile phone.

Mobile Phones As the costs come down, mobile phones have become an increasingly popular option for travellers on all budgets. They are an excellent way to keep in touch, and the costs are reasonable if you are careful about when you call and for how long. The digital mobile network covers more than 90% of the population, but this still leaves vast tracts of the country not covered, so be sure to check that the company you choose gives adequate coverage for the areas in which you want to use the phone. Basically the whole of the east coast is covered; it's when you start moving inland that it thins out. The older analogue network is less extensive and is to be wound up at the end of 1999.

Phone numbers with the prefixes 014, 015, 018, 019 or 041 are mobile phones. The three main mobile operators are the (mostly) government-owned Telstra, and the two private companies Optus and Vodafone.

Information Calls Other odd numbers you may come across are those starting with 190x. These numbers, usually recorded information services and the like, are provided by private companies, and your call is charged at anything from 35c to $5 or more per minute (more from mobile and payphones).

Email & Internet Access
If you want to surf the Net, even if it's only to access your email, there are service providers in all the capital cities, and in many regional areas too. Online costs vary, but a typical price structure is a $20 registration fee (which may include a few hours of online time), plus $20 per month for 10 hours online time. A few of the current major players include:

Australia On Line
    ☎ toll-free 1800 621 258; www.ozonline.com.au
Microsoft Network
    ☎ (02) 9870 2100; www.au.msn.com
Oz Email
    ☎ 1800 805 874; www.ozemail.com.au
Telstra Big Pond
    ☎ 1800 804 282; www.onaustralia.com.au

CompuServe users who want to access the service locally should phone CompuServe (☎ 1300 307 072) to get the local log-in numbers.

BOOKS

In almost any bookshop in the country you'll find a section devoted to Australiana with books on every Australian subject you care to mention. Australia has a lot of bookshops and some of the better-known ones are mentioned in the various city sections.

At the Wilderness Society shops in each capital city and the Government Printing offices in Sydney and Melbourne you'll find a good range of wildlife posters, calendars and books.

Lonely Planet

For more detail than is provided in this guide, Lonely Planet also has *Victoria*, *Western Australia*, *New South Wales*, *Queensland*, *Northern Territory*, *South Australia* and *Tasmania* state guides, *Melbourne* and *Sydney* city guides and the *Great Barrier Reef* guide.

Lonely Planet's *Bushwalking in Australia* describes 35 walks of different lengths and difficulty in various parts of the country.

Sean & David's Long Drive, a hilarious, offbeat road book by young Australian author Sean Condon, is one of the titles in Lonely Planet's 'Journeys' travel literature series.

For trips into the outback in your own vehicle Lonely Planet's *Outback Australia* is the book to get.

Also part of the Lonely Planet stable are the Pisces diving guides. The Australian titles are *Coral Sea & Great Barrier Reef* and *Southeast Coast & Tasmania*.

Other Guidebooks

Burnum Burnum's Aboriginal Australia is subtitled 'a traveller's guide'. If you want to explore Australia from the Aboriginal point of view, this large and lavish hardback is the book for you.

Brian Sheedy's *Outback on a Budget* includes lots of practical advice. There are a number of other books about vehicle prepa-

ration and driving in the outback, including *Explore Australia by Four-Wheel Drive* by Peter & Kim Wherrett.

Surfing Australia's East Coast by Aussie surf star Nat Young is a slim, cheap, comprehensive guide to the best breaks from Victoria to Fraser Island. He's also written the *Surfing & Sailboard Guide to Australia*, which covers the whole country. Surfing enthusiasts can also look for the expensive coffee-table book *Atlas of Australian Surfing*, by Mark Warren.

For the complete story on the Great Barrier Reef the *Reader's Digest Book of the Great Barrier Reef* is the one to go for. It's a hefty but comprehensive volume. There's also a cheaper abbreviated paperback version. *Australia's Wonderful Wildlife* is the shoestringer's equivalent of a coffee-table book – a cheap paperback published by the Womens Weekly with lots of great photos of the animals you didn't see, or those that didn't stay still when you pointed your camera at them.

There are state-by-state Reader's Digest guides to coasts and national parks, such as the *Coast of New South Wales*, and Gregory's guides to national parks, such as *National Parks of New South Wales* (a handy reference listing access, facilities, activities and so on for all parks).

Travel

Other accounts of travels in Australia include the marvellous *Tracks*, by Robyn Davidson. It's the amazing story of a young woman who set out alone to walk from Alice Springs to the Western Australia coast with her camels – proof that you can do anything if you try hard enough. It almost single handedly inspired the current Australian interest in camel safaris!

Quite another sort of travel is Tony Horwitz's *One for the Road*, an entertaining account of a high-speed hitchhiking trip around Australia (Oz through a windscreen). In contrast, *The Ribbon and the Ragged Square*, by Linda Christmas, is an intelligent, sober account of a nine-month investigatory trip round Oz by a *Guardian* journalist from

England. There's lots of background, history, first-hand reporting and interviews.

Howard Jacobson's *In the Land of Oz* recounts his circuit of the country. It's amusing at times, but through most of the book you're left wondering when the long-suffering Ros is finally going to thump the twerp!

The late Bruce Chatwin's *The Songlines* tells of his experiences among central Australian Aboriginal people. It probably reveals more about the author than Aboriginal people, its best feature probably being some excellent pithy anecdotes about modern Australia.

The journals of the early European explorers can be fairly hard going but make fascinating reading. The hardships that many of these men (and they were virtually all men) endured is nothing short of amazing. These accounts are usually available in main city libraries. Men such as Sturt, Eyre, Leichhardt, Davidson, King (on the Burke and Wills expedition), Stuart and many others all kept detailed journals.

History & Politics
For a good introduction to Australian history, read *A Short History of Australia*, a most accessible and informative general history by the late Manning Clark, the respected Aussie historian, or *The Fatal Shore*, Robert Hughes' bestselling account of the convict era.

Geoffrey Blainey's *The Tyranny of Distance* is an engrossing study of the problems of transport in this harsh continent and how they shaped the pattern of White settlement: transporting produce 100 miles by bullock cart from an inland farm to a port, cost more than shipping it from there around the globe to Europe – a handicap only wool, and later gold, was profitable enough to overcome.

Finding Australia, by Russel Ward, traces the period from the first Aboriginal arrivals up to 1821. It's strong on Aborigines, women and the full story of foreign exploration, not just Cook's role. There's lots of fascinating detail, including information about the

appalling crooks who ran the early colony, and it's intended to be the first of a series.

The Exploration of Australia, by Michael Cannon, is a coffee-table book in size, presentation and price, but it's a fascinating reference book about the gradual European uncovering of the continent.

The Fatal Impact, by Alan Moorehead, begins with the voyages of Cook, regarded as one of the greatest and most humane explorers, and tells the tragic story of the European impact on Australia, Tahiti and Antarctica in the years that followed. It details how good intentions and the economic imperatives of the time led to disaster, corruption and annihilation. *Cooper's Creek*, also by Moorehead, is a classic account of the ill-fated Burke and Wills expedition; it dramatises the horrors and hardships faced by the early explorers.

John Pilger's *A Secret Country* is a vividly written book which deals with Australia's historical roots, its shabby treatment of Aboriginal people and the current political complexion. It also posits an interesting theory on the dismissal of the Whitlam government in 1975.

To get an idea of life on a Kimberley cattle station last century, *Kings in Grass Castles* and *Sons in the Saddle*, both by Dame Mary Durack, are well worth getting hold of. Other books giving an insight into the pioneering days in the outback include *Packhorse & Waterhole* by Gordon Buchanan, son of legendary drover Nat Buchanan who opened up large areas of the Northern Territory; *The Big Run*, by Jock Makin, a history of the Victoria River Downs cattle station in the Northern Territory; and *The Cattle King* by Ion Idriess, which details the life of the remarkable Sir Sidney Kidman, who set up a chain of stations in the outback early this century.

Aboriginal People
The Australian Aborigines by Kenneth Maddock is a good cultural summary. The award-winning *Triumph of the Nomads*, by Geoffrey Blainey, chronicles the life of Australia's original inhabitants, and it convincingly demolishes the myth that

Aboriginal people were 'primitive' people trapped on a hostile continent. They were in fact extremely successful in adapting to and overcoming the difficulties presented by the climate and seeming lack of resources – it's an excellent read.

For a sympathetic historical account of what's happened to the original Australians since Europeans arrived read *Aboriginal Australians* by Richard Broome. *A Change of Ownership*, by Mildred Kirk, covers similar ground to Broome's book, but does so more concisely, focusing on the land rights movement and its historical background.

The Other Side of the Frontier, by Henry Reynolds, uses historical records to give a vivid account of an Aboriginal view of the arrival and takeover of Australia by Europeans. His *With the White People* identifies the essential Aboriginal contributions to the survival of the early white settlers. *My Place*, Sally Morgan's prize-winning autobiography, traces her discovery of her Aboriginal heritage. *The Fringe Dwellers*, by Nene Gare, describes just what it's like to be an Aborigine growing up in a white-dominated society.

Don't Take Your Love to Town by Ruby Langford and *My People* by Oodgeroo Noonuccal (Kath Walker) are also recommended reading for people interested in the experiences of Aboriginal people.

Songman, by Allan Baillie, is a fictional account of the life of an adolescent Aboriginal boy growing up in Arnhem Land in the days before white settlement.

General

If you want a souvenir of Australia, such as a photographic record, try one of the numerous coffee-table books like *A Day in the Life of Australia*. *Local Color – Travels in the Other Australia* by Bill Bachman is a photographic essay which includes fine prose by Tim Winton.

There are many other Australian books which make good gifts: books for children, with very Australian illustrations, like Julie Vivar and Mem Fox's *Possum Magic*,

Norman Lindsay's *The Magic Pudding*, Dorothy Wall's *Blinky Bill*, and *Snugglepot & Cuddlepie* by May Gibbs (one of the first bestselling Australian children's books), or cartoon books by excellent Australian cartoonists such as Michael Leunig and Kaz Cooke.

INTERNET RESOURCES

As you would expect, the World Wide Web is full of interesting (and not so interesting) sites relevant to Australia. The following is a selection:

Australian Tourist Commission (www.aussie.net.au)
    The Australian Tourist Commission's comprehensive site has plenty of information and some good links.
Guide to Australia (www.csu.edu.au/education/australia.html)
    This site, maintained by the Charles Sturt University in NSW, is a mine of information, with links to Australian government departments, weather information, books, maps etc.
The Aussie Index (www.aussie.com.au/aussie.htm)
    A fairly comprehensive list of Australian companies, educational institutions and government departments that maintain Web sites.
Australian Government (www.gov.info.au)
    The Federal government has a site, which is predicably unexciting, but it is wide-ranging and a good source for things like visa information.
Lonely Planet (www.lonelyplanet.com.au)
    Our own site is not specific to Australia but is still definitely worth a look. Well, we would say that, wouldn't we?

NEWSPAPERS & MAGAZINES

Australia's print media is dominated by a few big companies (Rupert Murdoch's News Corporation and Kerry Packer's Publishing & Broadcasting Limited being the best-known).

Each major city tends to have at least one important daily, often backed up by a tabloid and also by evening papers. The Fairfax group's *Sydney Morning Herald* and Melbourne *Age* are two of the most important dailies. There's also the *Australian*, a Murdoch-owned paper and the country's only national daily. The *Australian Financial Review* is the country's business daily.

Weekly newspapers and magazines

include an Australian edition of *Time* and a combined edition of the Australian news magazine the *Bulletin* and *Newsweek*. The *Guardian Weekly* is widely available and good for international news, while the *Business Review Weekly* explores business matters in depth on a weekly basis.

Good outdoor and adventure magazines include *Wild* and *Outdoor Australia*, published quarterly, and *Rock*, published monthly.

Magazines from the UK and USA are also available, but usually with a delay of a month or so.

RADIO & TV

The national advertising-free TV and radio network is the Australian Broadcasting Corporation (ABC). In most places there are a couple of ABC radio stations and a host of commercial stations, both AM and FM, featuring the whole gamut of radio possibilities. Triple J is the ABC's youth FM radio station; it broadcasts nationally and is an excellent place to hear music (Australian and overseas) that's outside the pop mainstream, and plug in to Australia's youth culture.

In Sydney and Melbourne there are the ABC, three commercial TV stations (Nine, Ten and Seven networks) and SBS, a government-sponsored multicultural TV station beamed to the capital cities and main regional centres. Around the country the number of TV stations varies from place to place; there are regional TV stations but in some remote areas the ABC may be all you can receive.

Imparja is an Aboriginal-owned and run commercial TV station which operates out of Alice Springs and has a 'footprint' which covers one-third of the country (mainly the Northern Territory, South Australia and western NSW). It broadcasts a variety of programs, ranging from soaps to pieces made by and for Aboriginal people.

Pay TV is still in its infancy in Australia, with the major players (Murdoch's Foxtel and Optus Vision) still jockeying for position and market share. Austar is the only provider outside the metropolitan areas.

VIDEO SYSTEMS

Australia uses the PAL system, and so pre-recorded videos purchased in Australia may be incompatible with overseas systems. Check this before you buy.

PHOTOGRAPHY & VIDEO
Film & Equipment

Australian film prices are not too far out of line with those of the rest of the western world. Including developing, 36-exposure Kodachrome 64 or Fujichrome 100 slide film costs around $25, but with a little shopping around you can find it for around $20 – even less if you buy it in quantity.

There are plenty of camera shops in all the big cities and standards of camera service are high. Processing standards are also high, with many places offering one-hour developing of print film. Sydney is the main centre for developing Kodachrome slide film in the South-East Asian region.

Photography

In the outback you have to allow for the exceptional intensity of the light. Best results are obtained early in the morning and late in the afternoon. As the sun gets higher, colours appear washed out. You must also allow for the intensity of reflected light when taking shots on the Barrier Reef or at other coastal locations. Especially in the summer, allow for temperature extremes and do your best to keep film as cool as possible, particularly after exposure. Other film and camera hazards are dust in the outback and humidity in the far north tropical regions.

Photographing People

As in any country, politeness goes a long way when taking photographs; ask before taking pictures of people. Note that many Aboriginal people don't like having their photo taken, even from a distance.

TIME

Australia is divided into three time zones: Western Standard Time is GMT/UTC plus eight hours (Western Australia), Central Standard Time is plus 9½ hours (Northern

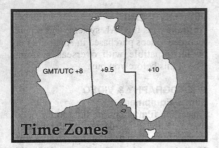

Time Zones

Territory, South Australia) and Eastern Standard Time is plus 10 (Tasmania, Victoria, New South Wales, Queensland). When it's noon in Western Australia it's 1.30 pm in the Northern Territory and South Australia and 2 pm in the rest of the country.

During the summer things get slightly screwed up as daylight saving time (when clocks are put forward an hour) does not operate in Western Australia, the Northern Territory or Queensland, and in Tasmania it starts a month earlier and finishes up to a month later than in the other states.

ELECTRICITY
Voltage is 220-240V and the plugs are three-pin, but not the same as British three-pin plugs. Users of electric shavers or hairdriers should note that, apart from in fancy hotels, it's difficult to find converters to take either US flat two-pin plugs or the European round two-pin plugs. Adaptors for British plugs can be found in good hardware shops, chemists and travel agents. You can easily bend the US plugs to a slight angle to make them fit.

WEIGHTS & MEASURES
Australia uses the metric system. Petrol and milk are sold by the litre, apples and potatoes by the kg, distance is measured by the metre or km, and speed limits are in kilometres per hour (km/h). Colloquially, distance is often measured in the time it takes to get there, rather than in km, eg Geelong is two hours drive away.

For those who need help with metric there's a conversion table at the back of this book.

HEALTH
Australia is a remarkably healthy country in which to travel, considering that such a large portion of it lies in the tropics. Tropical diseases such as malaria and yellow fever are unknown, diseases of insanitation such as cholera and typhoid are unheard of, and even some animal diseases such as rabies and foot-and-mouth disease have yet to be recorded.

Travel health depends on your predeparture preparations, your daily health care while travelling and how you handle any medical problem that does develop. Few travellers experience anything more than upset stomachs.

Health Insurance
Make sure that you have adequate health insurance. See the boxed text Travel Insurance earlier in this chapter for details.

Environmental Hazards
Fungal Infections Fungal infections occur more commonly in hot weather and are usually found on the scalp, between the toes or fingers, in the groin and on the body (ringworm). You get ringworm (which is a fungal infection, not a worm) from infected animals or other people. Moisture encourages these infections.

To prevent fungal infections wear loose, comfortable clothes, avoid artificial fibres, wash frequently and dry carefully. If you do get an infection, wash the infected area at least daily with a disinfectant or medicated soap and water, and rinse and dry well. Apply an antifungal cream or powder like tolnaflate (Tinaderm). Try to expose the infected area to air or sunlight as much as possible and wash all towels and underwear in hot water, change them often and let them dry in the sun.

Heat Exhaustion Dehydration and salt deficiency can cause heat exhaustion. Take time to acclimatise to high temperatures, drink sufficient liquids and do not do anything too physically demanding.

Salt deficiency is characterised by fatigue, lethargy, headaches, giddiness and muscle cramps; salt tablets may help, but adding extra salt to your food is better.

Anhydrotic heat exhaustion, caused by an inability to sweat, is quite rare. It is likely to strike people who have been in a hot climate for some time, rather than newcomers.

Heat Stroke This serious, occasionally fatal, condition can occur if the body's heat-regulating mechanism breaks down and the body temperature rises to dangerous levels. Long, continuous periods of exposure to high temperatures and insufficient fluids can leave you vulnerable to heat stroke.

The symptoms are feeling unwell, not sweating very much (or at all) and a high body temperature (39°C to 41°C or 102°F to 106°F). Where sweating has ceased the skin becomes flushed and red. Severe, throbbing headaches and lack of coordination will also occur, and the sufferer may be confused or aggressive. Eventually the victim will become delirious or convulse. Hospitalisation is essential, but in the interim get victims out of the sun, remove their clothing, cover them with a wet sheet or towel and then fan continually. Give fluids if they are conscious.

Hypothermia Too much cold can be just as dangerous as too much heat. If you are trekking in cold areas, such as the alpine areas of NSW, Victoria and Tasmania, you should always be prepared.

Hypothermia occurs when the body loses heat faster than it can produce it and the core temperature of the body falls. It is surprisingly easy to progress from very cold to dangerously cold due to a combination of wind, wet clothing, fatigue and hunger, even if the air temperature is above freezing. It is best to dress in layers; silk, wool and some of the new artificial fibres are all good insulating materials. A hat is important, as a lot of heat is lost through the head. A strong, waterproof outer layer (and a 'space' blanket

Everyday Health
Normal body temperature is up to 37°C or 98.6°F; more than 2°C (4°F) higher indicates a high fever. The normal adult pulse rate is 60 to 100 per minute (children 80 to 100, babies 100 to 140). As a general rule the pulse increases about 20 beats per minute for each °C (2°F) rise in fever.

Respiration (breathing) rate is also an indicator of illness. Count the number of breaths per minute: between 12 and 20 is normal for adults and older children (up to 30 for younger children, 40 for babies). People with a high fever or serious respiratory illness breathe more quickly than normal. More than 40 shallow breaths a minute may indicate pneumonia. ■

for emergencies) are essential. Carry basic supplies, including food containing simple sugars to generate heat quickly and fluid to drink.

Symptoms of hypothermia are exhaustion, numb skin (particularly toes and fingers), shivering, slurred speech, irrational or violent behaviour, lethargy, stumbling, dizzy spells, muscle cramps and violent bursts of energy. Irrationality may take the form of sufferers claiming they are warm and trying to take off their clothes.

To treat mild hypothermia, first get the person out of the wind and/or rain, remove their clothing if it's wet and replace it with dry, warm clothing. Give them hot liquids – not alcohol – and some high-kilojoule, easily digestible food. Do not rub victims, instead allow them to slowly warm themselves. This should be enough to treat the early stages of hypothermia. The early recognition and treatment of mild hypothermia is the only way to prevent severe hypothermia, which is a critical condition.

Motion Sickness Eating lightly before and during a trip will reduce the chances of motion sickness. If you are prone to motion sickness try to find a place that minimises movement – near the wing on aircraft, close to midships on boats, near the centre on buses. Fresh air usually helps; reading and cigarette smoke don't. Commercial motion-sickness preparations, which can cause drowsiness, have to be taken before the trip commences. Ginger (available in capsule form) and peppermint (including mint-flavoured sweets) are natural preventatives.

Prickly Heat Prickly heat is an itchy rash caused by excessive perspiration trapped under the skin. It usually strikes people who have just arrived in a hot climate. Keeping cool, bathing often, drying the skin and using a mild talcum or prickly heat powder or resorting to air-conditioning may help.

Sunburn In the tropics, the desert or at high altitude you can get sunburnt surprisingly quickly, even through cloud. Use a sunscreen, hat, and barrier cream for your nose and lips. Calamine lotion or Stingose are good for mild sunburn. Protect your eyes with good quality sunglasses, particularly if you will be near water, sand or snow.

Diseases of Insanitation

Diarrhoea Poor food hygiene or simply a change of water, food or climate can all cause a mild bout of diarrhoea, but a few rushed toilet trips with no other symptoms is not indicative of a major problem.

Dehydration is the main danger with any diarrhoea, particularly in children or the elderly as dehydration can occur quite quickly. Under all circumstances *fluid replacement* is the most important thing to remember. Weak black tea with a little sugar, soda water, or soft drinks allowed to go flat and diluted 50% with clean water are all good. With severe diarrhoea a rehydrating solution is preferable to replace minerals and salts lost. Commercially available oral rehydration salts (ORS) are very useful; add them to boiled or bottled water. In an emergency you can make up a solution of six teaspoons of sugar and a half teaspoon of salt to a litre of boiled or bottled water. You need to drink at least the same volume of fluid that you are losing in bowel movements and vomiting. Urine is the best guide to the adequacy of

replacement – if you have small amounts of concentrated urine, you need to drink more. Keep drinking small amounts often. Stick to a bland diet as you recover.

Lomotil or Imodium can be used to bring relief from the symptoms, although they do not actually cure the problem. Only use these drugs if you do not have access to toilets, eg if you *must* travel. For children under 12 years Lomotil and Imodium are not recommended. Do not use these drugs if the person has a high fever or is severely dehydrated.

Intestinal Worms These parasites are most common in rural, tropical areas. The different worms have different ways of infecting people. Some may be ingested on food including undercooked meat and some enter through your skin. Infestations may not show up for some time, and although they are generally not serious, if left untreated some can cause severe health problems later. Consider having a stool test when you return home to check for these and determine the appropriate treatment.

Tetanus Tetanus occurs when a wound becomes infected by a germ which lives in soil and in the faeces of horses and other animals. It enters the body via breaks in the skin. All wounds should be cleaned promptly and adequately and an antiseptic cream or solution applied. Use antibiotics if the wound becomes hot, throbs or pus is seen. The first symptom may be discomfort in swallowing, or stiffening of the jaw and neck; this is followed by painful convulsions of the jaw and whole body. The disease can be fatal.

Sexually Transmitted Diseases

HIV & AIDS The Human Immunodeficiency Virus (HIV) can develop into Acquired Immune Deficiency Syndrome (AIDS), which is a fatal disease. HIV is a major problem in many countries. Any exposure to blood, blood products or body fluids may put the individual at risk. The disease is often transmitted through sexual contact or dirty needles – vaccinations, acupuncture, tattooing and body piercing can be potentially as dangerous as intravenous drug use. HIV/AIDS can also be spread through infected blood transfusions, although blood is thoroughly screened in Australia.

Fear of HIV infection should never preclude treatment for serious medical conditions.

Gonorrhoea, Herpes and Syphilis Sores, blisters or rashes around the genitals, discharges or pain when urinating are common symptoms of these diseases. In some STDs, such as wart virus or chlamydia, symptoms may be less marked or not observed at all, especially in women. Syphilis symptoms eventually disappear completely but the disease continues and can cause severe problems in later years. While abstinence from sexual contact is the only 100% effective prevention, using condoms is also effective. The treatment of gonorrhoea and syphilis is with antibiotics. The different sexually transmitted diseases each require specific antibiotics. There is no cure for herpes or AIDS.

Bites & Stings
Many spiders and snakes, the box jellyfish, blue-ringed octopus and Barrier Reef cone shell can sting dangerously or even fatally: for information on first-aid treatment for such bites see Dangers & Annoyances later in this chapter.

Bee and wasp stings are usually painful rather than dangerous. However, in people who are allergic to them severe breathing difficulties may occur and require urgent medical care. Calamine lotion or Stingose spray will give relief and ice packs will reduce the pain and swelling. Scorpion stings are notoriously painful. Scorpions often shelter in shoes or clothing. There are various fish and other sea creatures which can be dangerous to eat; seek local advice.

Ross River Fever This viral disease, properly known as epidemic polyarthritis, is transmitted by some species of mosquitoes. The disease is mostly found in eastern Aus-

tralia and outbreaks are most likely to occur in January and February, but risk of infection is very low. Flu-like symptoms (muscle and joint pain, rashes, fever, headache, tiredness) are possible indicators, but blood tests are necessary for positive detection. Unfortunately there is no treatment for Ross River Fever, although relief of symptoms can be achieved. Conventional wisdom has it that the symptoms do not last more than a few months, although there are now serious doubts about this, with some people still feeling the effects (mainly chronic fatigue) some years after contracting the disease. Avoid mozzie bites is the best advice.

Cuts & Scratches
Wash well and treat any cut with an antiseptic. Where possible avoid bandages and Band-aids, which can keep wounds wet. Coral cuts are notoriously slow to heal and if they are not adequately cleaned small pieces of coral can become embedded in the wound. Avoid coral cuts by not walking on reefs – barefoot or with shoes as it damages the coral. If you do sustain a cut, clean it thoroughly with an antiseptic. Coral cuts may result in serious infections: severe pain, throbbing, redness, fever or generally feeling unwell suggest infection and the need for antibiotics promptly.

Women's Health
Antibiotic use, synthetic underwear, sweating and contraceptive pills can lead to fungal vaginal infections when travelling in hot climates. Maintaining good personal hygiene, and loose-fitting clothes and cotton underwear will help to prevent these infections.

Fungal infections, characterised by a rash, itch and discharge, can be treated with a vinegar or lemon-juice douche, or with yoghurt. Nystatin, miconazole or clotrimazole pessaries or vaginal cream are the usual treatment.

Sexually transmitted diseases are a major cause of vaginal problems. Symptoms include a smelly discharge, painful intercourse and sometimes a burning sensation when urinating.

WOMEN TRAVELLERS

Australia is generally a safe place for women travellers, although it's probably best to avoid walking alone late at night in any of the major cities. Sexual harassment is unfortunately still second nature to some Aussie males and it's hard to say when you might be confronted by these individuals. It's generally true to say that the farther you get from 'civilisation' (ie the big cities), the less enlightened your average Aussie male is going to be about women's issues; you're far more likely to meet an 'ocker' than a snag (sensitive new-age guy)!

Female hitchers should exercise care at all times (see the section on hitching in the Getting Around chapter).

GAY & LESBIAN TRAVELLERS

Australia is a popular destination for gay and lesbian travellers. Certainly the profile of gay and lesbian travel has risen significantly in the last few years, partly as a result of the publicity surrounding the Gay & Lesbian Mardi Gras in Sydney. Throughout the country, but especially on the east coast, there is a number of tour operators, travel agents, airlines, resorts and accommodation places that are exclusively gay and lesbian, or gay friendly.

Certain areas are the focus of the gay and lesbian communities: Cairns and Noosa in Queensland, the Blue Mountains and the south coast in New South Wales, and Melbourne, Daylesford and Hepburn Springs in Victoria, are all popular areas.

As is the case with the attitude to women, the farther into the country you get, the more likely you are to run into fairly rampant homophobia. Homosexual acts are legal in all states, but only Tasmania and Western Australia have legislation prohibiting discrimination on the basis of sexual preference.

Publications

There's a wide range of publications produced by the gay community. All major cities have free gay newspapers, available through subscription, from major gay and lesbian

venues and some newsagents in gay and lesbian residential areas.

The *G'day Guide* gives state by state listings of a whole range of items which may be of interest to the gay traveller, such as transport, bars, pubs, entertainment and tours. The *G'day Accommodation Guide* lists gay-friendly accommodation across the country. Both can be purchased from newsagencies in Australia and New Zealand and gay book shops in Europe and the USA.

National gay lifestyle magazines include *OutRage*, *Campaign*, *Lesbians on the Loose* and the art magazine, *Blue*.

Tour Operators

A number of tour operators cater exclusively or partly for gay and lesbian travellers. They include:

BreakOut Travel & Tours
    10 Roseby St, Marrickville, Sydney, NSW 22041
    (☎ (02) 9558 8229; fax 9558 7140; break-out.com.au)
Destination DownUnder
    40 Miller Street, (PO Box 429) North Sydney,
    NSW 2060 (☎ (02) 9957 3811)
    Also has offices in Europe, the UK and the USA
Beyond the Blue
    Suite 205, 275 Alfred St, North Sydney, NSW
    2060 (☎ (02) 9955 6755; fax 9922 6036)

Organisations

The Australian Gay & Lesbian Tourism Association (☎ (02) 9955 6755; fax 9922 6036; aglta.asn.au/index.htm), PO Box 208, Darlinghurst, NSW 2010, promotes gay and lesbian travel within Australia and is well worth contacting.

USEFUL ORGANISATIONS
National Parks Organisations

The Biodiversity Group of Environment Australia (EABG), formerly the Australian Nature Conservation Agency, is a commonwealth body responsible for Kakadu and Uluru national parks in the Northern Territory, national parks in the ACT, some offshore areas such as the Cocos (Keeling) Islands and Norfolk Island, and also international conservation issues such as whaling and migratory bird conventions. It's based at 153 Emu Bank, Belconnen, ACT 2617; GPO Box 636, Canberra 2601; (☎ (02) 6250 0200; www.biodiversity.environment.gov. au).

The individual national park organisations in each state are state-operated, not nationally run. They can be hidden away in their capital-city locations, but if you search them out they have excellent literature and maps on the parks. In the bush, national park offices are much more up-front – they are usually the best places for local information. The state offices for outback parks are:

New South Wales
National Parks & Wildlife Service, 41 Bridge St, Hurstville, NSW 2220 (☎ (02) 9585 6333)

Northern Territory
Parks & Wildlife Commission of the Northern Territory, Gaymark Building, Mansfield Lane, Palmerston, NT 0830 (PO Box 496, Palmerston 0831; ☎ (08) 8999 4401)
Parks Australia North (an arm of Environment Australia), 81 Smith St, Darwin, NT 0800 (GPO Box 1260, Darwin 0801; ☎ (08) 8946 4300)

Queensland
Department of Environment & Heritage, 160 Ann St, Brisbane, Qld 4000 (PO Box 155, Brisbane Albert St 4002; ☎ (07) 3227 8186)

South Australia
Department of Environment & Natural Resources, 77 Grenfell St, Adelaide, SA 5000 (GPO Box 1047, Adelaide 5001; ☎ (08) 8204 1910)

Tasmania
Department of Parks, Wildlife & Heritage, 134 Macquarie St, Hobart, Tas 7000 (PO Box 44A, Hobart, Tas 7001 (☎ (03) 6233 6191)

Victoria
Department of Conservation & Natural Resources, 240 Victoria Parade, East Melbourne, Vic 3002 (PO Box 41, East Melbourne, Vic 3002 (☎ (03) 9412 4011)

Western Australia
Department of Conservation & Land Management, 50 Hayman Rd, Como, Perth, WA 6152 (Locked Bag 104, Bentley DC, WA 6983; ☎ (08) 9334 0333)

Australian Conservation Foundation

The Australian Conservation Foundation (ACF) is the largest nongovernment organisation involved in conservation. Only 9% to 10% of its income is from government; the rest comes from memberships, subscriptions and from donations, which come mainly from individuals.

The ACF covers a wide range of issues, including the greenhouse effect and depletion of the ozone layer, the negative effects of logging, the preservation of rainforests, the problems of land degradation, and the protection of the Antarctic. It frequently works in conjunction with the Wilderness Society and other conservation groups.

With the growing focus on conservation issues and the increasing concern of the Australian public in regard to their environment, the conservation vote is increasingly important to all political parties.

The contact address is ACF (☎ (03) 9416 1166; fax 9416 0767; www.peg.apc.org/-acfenv), 340 Gore St, Fitzroy, Vic 3065.

Wilderness Society

The Tasmanian Wilderness Society was formed by conservationists who had been unsuccessful in preventing the damming of Lake Pedder in south-west Tasmania but who were determined to prevent the destruction of the Franklin River. The Franklin River campaign was one of Australia's first major conservation confrontations and it caught the attention of the international media. In 1983, after the Australian High Court ruled against damming the Franklin, the group changed its name to the Wilderness Society because of its Australia-wide focus.

The Wilderness Society is involved in issues such as forest management and logging. Like the ACF, government funding is only a small percentage of its income, the rest coming from memberships, donations and merchandising. There are Wilderness Society shops in all states (not in the Northern Territory) where you can buy books, T-shirts, posters, badges etc.

The Wilderness Society is at 130 Davey St, Hobart, Tas 7000 (☎ (03) 6234 9799; fax 6224 1497; www.peg.apc.org/twsnat).

Australian Trust for Conservation Volunteers

This nonpolitical, nonprofit group organises practical conservation projects (such as tree

Australia for the Traveller with a Disability

Disability awareness in Australia is high, especially in the lead-up to the 2000 Paralympics in New South Wales. Information about accessible tourist attractions and accommodation is becoming more available, while legislation requires that new accommodation must meet accessibility standards and tourist operators must not discriminate.

Information Reliable information is the key ingredient for travellers with a disability, and the best source is the ACT-based National Information Communication and Recreation Network or NICAN (☎/TTY toll-free (02) 6285 3713; TTY 1800 806 769; fax (02) 6285 3714; nican@spirit.com.au), PO Box 407, Curtin, ACT. It's an Australia-wide directory providing information on access issues, accessible accommodation, sporting and recreational activities, transport and specialist tour operators.The Australian Tourist Commission (see the Tourist Offices section earlier in this chapter for contact details) publishes an information fact sheet *Travel in Australia for People with Disabilities* containing travel tips, transport and contact addresses of organisations on a state-by-state basis. The Australian Council for the Rehabilitation of Disabled, ACROD (☎(02) 6282 4333; fax 6281 3488), PO Box 60, Curtin, ACT 2605, can provide information on ACROD state offices, state-based help organisations, care, and has some accommodation information.

Other sources of quality information are the Disability Information Resource Centre (DIRC) in SA (☎(08) 8223 7522; dirc@dircsa.org.au), and the Independent Living Centre in WA (☎(08) 9382 2011; ilcwa@iinet.com.au). Tourism Tasmania (☎(03) 6230 8301; aleitch@tourism.tas.gov.au), has created *Tasmania – Tourist Information for People with Disabilities*, and the Queensland Travel & Tourism Corp (☎(07) 3406 5455; millerg@qttc.com.au) is undertaking a similar project. AbleTours (☎(08) 9295 4665; abletours@worldview.com.au) runs adventures from Perth in an accessible 4WD.

Publications to look for include:

Access in Brisbane and *Darwin Without Steps*, both available from local councils in those cities
Accessing Sydney, available from ACROD NSW
Accessing Melbourne, available from RACV outlets and the Melbourne Information Centre
Easy Access Australia – A Travel Guide to Australia
($24.85), a book researched and written by wheelchair users (order from PO Box 218, Kew, Victoria 3101)
A Wheelie's Handbook of Australia, another book written by a wheelchair user (order from Colin James, 3 Furner Ave, Bell Park Vic., 3215).

Places to Stay Accommodation in Australia is generally good and the best sources of information are NICAN and the state-based disability organisations. It's worth asking at information centres for lists of accessible accommodation and tourist attractions (but beware that the information may not have been independently assessed). Capital cities are well serviced by international hotel chains such as Hyatt, Hilton, Sheraton etc, which provide accessible rooms. More affordable are the Novotel and Ibis Hotels, while motel chains such as Flag and Best Western have many properties, and many with accessible rooms (but of varying quality – check first).

Some other accommodation providers have accessible rooms and most proprietors will do what they can to assist you. Accommodation guides published by the state motoring organisations are very comprehensive and give wheelchair-access information. However, it is best to confirm that the facilities suit your needs.

A few YHA youth hostels have accessible accommodation. Contact YHA Travel Membership (☎(02) 9261 1111), 422 Kent St, Sydney, NSW 2001. YHA Central in Sydney (☎(02) 9281 9111), opposite Central Station, opened in 1997 with seven excellent accessible rooms.

Two wheelchair-accessible resorts are *Clark Bay Farm* (☎(02) 4476 1640) at Narooma, Southern NSW, where you can go whale-watching, fish the ocean or the Wagonga Inlet and visit the local

planting, track construction and flora and fauna surveys) for volunteers. Travellers are welcome and it's an excellent way to get involved with the conservation movement

and, visit some of the more interesting areas of the country. Past volunteers have found themselves working in places such as Tasmania, Kakadu and Fraser Island.

Umburra Aboriginal Community. The other is *The Wheel Resort* (☎(02) 6685 6139; fax 6685 8754), at 39-51 Broken Head Rd, Byron Bay in NSW, designed by wheelchair users for travellers with a disability.

Getting Around Bus travel is not an option for wheelchair users. However, there are good facilities on other forms of transport

Air The Carers Concession Card was developed by NICAN and Qantas but is also accepted by Ansett. It entitles a carer to travel for a 50% discount; call NICAN for eligibility and an application form. Ansett also has its ANSACARE system of recording your details and needs – once only, eliminating repetition. Both Qantas (13 13 13; TTY 1800 652 660) and Ansett (13 13 10; TTY 1800 623 195) welcome passengers with a disability and some of their aircraft have a larger 'accessible' toilet. All of Australia's major airports have dedicated parking spaces, wheelchair access to terminals, accessible toilets and skychairs to convey passengers onto planes via airbridges. At some regional airports a forklift arrangement is used to lift wheelchair passengers to the plane.

Train NSW Countrylink (☎(02) 9379 4850; reservations 13 23 32) operates the XPT from Sydney to Melbourne, Brisbane (via Murwillumbah), Coffs Harbour, Dubbo and Wagga Wagga, while the Xplorer travels to Tamworth and Canberra. Each train has at least one carriage with a seat removed for a wheelchair and an accessible toilet. Countrylink's *Guide for People with Special Requirements* details this and other services.

The Indian Pacific (national reservations 13 22 32) runs twice-weekly between Sydney, Adelaide and Perth; a journey of 65 hours (including three nights). One 'cabin' in each carriage provides wheelchair access but will not suit everyone. Train doorways are narrow so a skychair-type chair is used for boarding; an en-suite bathroom has grab rails.

In Victoria *Public Transport Disability Services* is available from Disability Services (☎(03) 9610 5535) at Flinders St train station. Melbourne's suburban rail network is accessible and V/Line's country trains and stations are equipped with ramps while some rural services employ hoist-equipped accessible coaches. Twenty-four hours advance booking is required; V/Line Reservations & Enquiries (☎13 22 32; ask for wheelchair reservations) are at Spencer St station. The Travellers Aid Society (☎(03) 9670 2873) at Spencer St Station provides a meet-and-greet service (arrange in advance), and there is a cafe (☎(03) 9654 2600) with assistance and accessible toilets at Level 2, 169 Swanston Walk.

Accessible public transport in Sydney is limited but the monorail from Darling Harbour and Sydney light rail from Central Station cover parts of the city.

Car Rental Avis (1800 225 533) and Hertz (13 30 39) offer hire cars with hand controls at no extra charge for pick-up at capital cities and the major airports, but advance notice is required.

Parking The International Wheelchair Symbol (blue on a white background) for parking in allocated bays is recognised. Mobility maps of central business districts showing accessible routes, toilets etc are available from major city councils, some regional areas and at information centres.

Taxi Most taxi companies in the major cities and towns have modified vehicles that take wheelchairs. In Melbourne, Norden Transport Equipment (☎(03) 9793 1066) has a self-drive van equipped with a lift and lock-down attachments for up to three wheelchairs; this is available for long or short-term rentals. TL Engineering (☎(08) 9279 5466) in Perth has a rental van for two wheelchairs.

Ferry TT Line's *Spirit of Tasmania* (reservations 13 20 10) operates between Melbourne and Devonport in Tasmania. It has four accessible cabins and wheelchair access to the public areas on the ship.

Bruce Cameron

Most projects are either for a weekend or a week and all food, transport and accommodation is supplied in return for a small contribution to help cover costs. Most travellers who take part in ATCV join a Banksia Package, which lasts six weeks and includes six different projects. The cost is $650, and further weeks can be added for $105.

Contact the head office (☎ (03) 5333 1483; users.netconnect.com.au/atcv) at PO Box 423, Ballarat, Vic 3350, or the state offices listed below:

New South Wales
2 Holt St, Stanmore, Sydney, NSW 2048 (☎ (02) 9564 1244)
Northern Territory
Box 2358, Darwin, NT 0801 (☎ (08) 8981 3206)
Queensland
Old Government House, QUT Grounds, George St, Brisbane, Qld 4000 (☎ (07) 3210 0330)
South Australia
PO Box 419, Campbelltown, Adelaide, SA 5074 (☎ (08) 8207 8747)
Tasmania
Box 940, Hobart, Tas 7001 (☎ (03) 6224 4911)
Victoria
534 City Rd, South Melbourne, Vic 3205 (☎ (03) 9686 5554)
Western Australia
39 Canning Hwy, East Fremantle, WA 6158 (☎ (08) 9339 3902)

National Trust

The National Trust is dedicated to preserving historic buildings in all parts of Australia. It owns and manages a number of buildings throughout the country, which are open to the public. Many other buildings are 'classified' by the National Trust to ensure their preservation.

The National Trust produces some excellent literature, including a fine series of walking-tour guides to many cities, large and small. These guides are often available from local tourist offices or from National Trust offices and are usually free whether you're a member of the National Trust or not. Membership is well worth considering, however, because it entitles you to free entry to any National Trust property for your year of membership.

If you're a dedicated visitor of old buildings this could soon pay for itself. Annual membership costs $49 for individuals ($35 concession) and $68 for families ($49 concession), and includes the monthly or quarterly magazine put out by the state organisation that you join. Addresses of the National Trust state offices are:

Australian Capital Territory
2 Light St, Griffith, ACT 2603 (☎ (02) 6239 5222)
New South Wales
Observatory Hill, Sydney, NSW 2000 (☎ (02) 9258 0123)
Northern Territory
4 Burnett Place, Myilly Point, Darwin, NT 0800 (☎ (08) 8981 2848)
Queensland
Old Government House, QUT Grounds, George St, Brisbane, Qld 4000 (☎ (07) 3229 1788)
South Australia
452 Pulteney St, Adelaide, SA 5000 (☎ (08) 8223 1655)
Tasmania
Brisbane St, Hobart 7000 (☎ (03) 6223 5200)
Victoria
Tasma Terrace, 4 Parliament Place, Melbourne, Vic 3002 (☎ (03) 9654 4711)
Western Australia
Old Observatory, 4 Havelock St, West Perth, WA 6005 (☎ (08) 9321 6088)

WWOOF

WWOOF (Willing Workers on Organic Farms) is a relatively new organisation in Australia, although it is well established in other countries. The idea is that you do a few hours work each day on a farm in return for bed and board. Some places have a minimum stay of a couple of days but many will take you for just a night. Some will let you stay for months if they like the look of you, and you can get involved in some interesting large-scale projects.

Becoming a WWOOFer is a great way to meet people and to travel cheaply. There are about 200 WWOOF associates in Australia, mostly in Victoria, New South Wales and Queensland.

As the name says, the farms are supposed to be organic but that isn't always so. Some places aren't even farms – you might help out at a pottery or do the books at a seed wholesaler. There are even a few commercial farms that exploit WWOOFers as cheap harvest labour, although these are rare. Whether they have a farm or just a vegie patch, most participants in the scheme are concerned to some extent with alternative lifestyles.

To join WWOOF send $20 to WWOOF,

Mt Murrindal Coop, Buchan, Vic 3885 (☎ (03) 5155 0218; www.earthink.com.au/wwoof), and they'll send you a membership number and a booklet that lists WWOOF places all over Australia.

DANGERS & ANNOYANCES
Animal Hazards
There are a few unique and sometimes dangerous creatures, although it's unlikely that you'll come across any of them, particularly if you stick to the cities. Here's a rundown just in case.

Snakes The best-known danger in the Australian outback, and the one that captures the imagination of visitors, is snakes. Although there are many venomous snakes there are few that are aggressive, and unless you have the bad fortune to stand on one it's unlikely that you'll be bitten. Taipans and tiger snakes, however, will attack if alarmed. Sea snakes can also be dangerous.

To minimise your chances of being bitten always wear boots, socks and long trousers when walking through undergrowth where snakes may be present. Don't put your hands into holes and crevices, and be careful when collecting firewood.

Snake bites do not cause instantaneous death and antivenenes are usually available. Keep the victim calm and still, wrap the bitten limb tightly, as you would for a sprained ankle, and then attach a splint to immobilise it. Then seek medical help, if possible with the dead snake for identification. Don't attempt to catch the snake if there is even a remote possibility of being bitten again. Tourniquets and sucking out the poison are now comprehensively discredited.

Spiders There are a couple of nasty spiders too, including the funnel-web, the redback and the white-tail, so it's best not to play with any spider. The funnel-web spider is found in New South Wales and its bite is treated in the same way as snake bite. For redback bites, apply ice and seek medical attention.

Insects Among a splendid variety of biting insects the mosquito and march fly are the most common. The common bush tick (found in the forest and scrub country along the east coast of Australia) can be dangerous if left lodged in the skin, as the toxin the tick excretes can cause paralysis and sometimes death – check your body for lumps every night if you're walking in tick-infested areas. The tick should be removed by dousing it with methylated spirits or kerosene and levering it out intact.

Leeches are common, and while they will suck your blood they are not dangerous and are easily removed by the application of salt or heat.

Crocodiles Up north, saltwater crocodiles ('salties') can be a real danger and each year kill a number of people. They are found in river estuaries and large rivers, sometimes a long way inland, so before diving into that inviting, cool water find out from the locals whether it's croc-free.

Box Jellyfish In the sea, the box jellyfish, also known as the sea wasp or 'stinger' can be fatal. It appears during summer north of Great Keppel Island (see the Queensland chapter). The stinging tentacles spread several metres away from the sea wasp's body; by the time you see it you're likely to have been stung. If someone is stung, they are likely to run out of the sea screaming and collapse on the beach, with weals on their body as though they've been whipped. They may stop breathing. Douse the stings with vinegar (available on many beaches or try a nearby house), do not try to remove the tentacles from the skin, and treat as for snake bite (see the Snakes entry earlier in this section). If there's a first-aider present, they may have to apply artificial respiration until the ambulance gets there. Above all, stay out of the sea when the sea wasps are around – the locals are ignoring that lovely water for an excellent reason.

Stings from most other jellyfish are simply rather painful and dousing in vinegar will deactivate any stingers that have not 'fired'. Calamine lotion, antihistamines and analgesics may reduce the reaction and relieve the pain.

Other Sea Creatures The blue-ringed octopus and Barrier Reef cone shells can also be fatal so don't pick them up. If someone is stung, apply a pressure bandage, monitor breathing carefully and conduct mouth-to-mouth resuscitation if breathing stops.

When reef walking you must always wear shoes to protect your feet against coral. In tropical waters there are stonefish – venomous fish that look like a flat piece of rock on the sea bed. Also watch out for the scorpion fish, which has venomous spines.

Flies & Mosquitoes For four to six months of the year you'll have to cope with those two banes of the Australian outdoors – the fly and the mosquito ('mozzie').

In the cities the flies are not too bad; it's in the country that it starts getting out of hand, and the further 'out' you get the worse the flies seem to be. In central Australia the flies start to come out with the warmer spring weather (late August), particularly if there has been any amount of spring rain, and last until winter. They are such a nuisance that virtually every shop sells the Genuine Aussie Fly Net (made in Korea), which fits on a hat and is rather like a string onion bag but is very effective. It's either that or the 'great Australian wave' to keep them away. Repellents such as Aerogard and Rid go some way to deterring the little bastards.

Mozzies, too, can be a problem, especially in warmer tropical areas. Fortunately none of them are malaria carriers, although some are carriers of Ross River Fever (see the Health section earlier in this chapter).

On the Road
Kangaroos and wandering stock can be a real hazard to the driver. A collision with one will badly damage your car and probably kill the animal. Unfortunately, other drivers are even more dangerous, particularly those who drink. Australia has its share of fatal road accidents, particularly in the countryside, so don't drink and drive. The dangers posed by stray animals and drunks are particularly enhanced at night, so it's best to avoid travelling after dark. See the Getting Around chapter for more on driving hazards.

Bushfires & Blizzards
Bushfires happen every year in Australia. Don't be the mug who starts one. In hot, dry, windy weather, be extremely careful with any naked flame – cigarette butts thrown out of car windows have started many a fire. On a Total Fire Ban Day (listen to the radio or watch the billboards on country roads), it is forbidden even to use a camping stove in the open. The locals will not be amused if they catch you breaking this particular law; they'll happily dob you in, and the penalties are severe.

If you're unfortunate enough to find yourself driving through a bushfire, stay inside your car and try to park off the road in an open space, away from trees, until the danger has passed. Lie on the floor under the dashboard and cover up with a wool blanket or protective clothing – heat radiation is the big killer in bushfire situations. The front of the fire should pass quickly, and you will be much safer than if you were out in the open.

Bushwalkers should take local advice before setting out. On a day of total fire ban, don't go – delay your trip until the weather has changed. Chances are that it will be so unpleasantly hot and windy, you'll be better off anyway in an air-conditioned pub sipping a cool beer.

If you're out in the bush and you see smoke, even at a great distance, you should take it seriously. Go to the nearest open space, downhill if possible. A forested ridge is the most dangerous place to be. Bushfires move very quickly and change direction with the wind.

Having said all that, more bushwalkers die of cold than in bushfires! Even in summer, temperatures can drop below freezing at night in the mountains (see the Health section earlier in this chapter). Blizzards in Tasmanian, Victorian and NSW mountains can occur at almost any time of the year, even January!

Swimming

Ocean Beaches Be aware that many surf beaches can be dangerous places to swim if you are not used to the conditions. Undertows (or 'rips') are the main problem, but a number of people are paralysed each year by diving into waves in shallow water and hitting a sand bar – check first.

Many popular beaches are patrolled by surf lifesavers, and patrolled areas are marked off by flags. If you swim between the flags help should arrive quickly if you get into trouble; raise your arm if you need help. Outside the flags and on unpatrolled beaches you are on your own.

If you find yourself being carried out by a rip, the main thing to do is just keep afloat; don't panic or try to swim against the rip. In most cases the current stops within a couple of hundred metres of the shore, and you can then swim parallel to the shore for a short way to get out of the rip and then make your way back to the shore.

BUSINESS HOURS

Most shops close at 5 or 5.30 pm weekdays, and either noon or 5 pm on Saturday. Sunday trading is becoming increasingly common, but it's currently limited to the major cities and, to a lesser extent, regional Victoria. In most towns there are usually one or two late shopping nights each week, when the doors stay open until 9 or 9.30 pm. Usually it's Thursday and/or Friday night.

Banks are open from 9.30 am to 4 pm Monday to Thursday, and until 5 pm on Friday. Some large city branches are open 8 am to 6 pm Monday to Friday. Some are also open to 9 pm on Friday. Of course there are some exceptions to Australia's unremarkable opening hours and all sorts of places stay open late and all weekend – particularly milk bars, convenience stores, supermarkets, delis and city bookshops. The big chain supermarkets in large city shopping centres are also often open 24 hours.

PUBLIC HOLIDAYS & SPECIAL EVENTS

School Holidays

The Christmas holiday season, from mid-December to late January, is part of the long, summer, school vacation and the time you are most likely to find accommodation booked out and long queues. There are three other shorter school holiday periods during the year but they vary by a week or two from state to state, falling from early to mid-April, late June to mid-July, and late September to early October.

Public Holidays

Public holidays also vary quite a bit from state to state. The following is a list of the main national and state public holidays; for precise dates (which vary from year to year), check locally (* indicates holidays are only observed locally):

National

New Year's Day
 1 January
Australia Day
 26 January
Easter
 (Good Friday and Easter Saturday, Sunday and Monday) March/April
Anzac Day
 25 April
Queen's Birthday(except WA)
 2nd Monday in June
Queen's Birthday (WA)
 Last Monday in September
Christmas Day
 25 December
Boxing Day
 26 December

ACT

Canberra Day
 March
Bank Holiday
 1st Monday in August
Labour Day
 1st Monday in October

New South Wales

Bank Holiday
 1st Monday in August
Labour Day
 1st Monday in October

Northern Territory

May Day
    1st Monday in May
Alice Springs Show Day
    1st Friday in July *
Tennant Creek Show Day
    2nd Friday in July *
Katherine Show Day
    3rd Friday in July *
Darwin Show Day
    4th Friday in July *
Picnic Day
    1st Monday in August

Queensland

Labour Day
    1st Monday in May
RNA Show Day (Brisbane)
    August *

South Australia

Adelaide Cup Day
    May *
Labour Day
    1st Monday in October
Proclamation Day
    Last Tuesday in December

Tasmania

Regatta Day
    14 February
Launceston Cup Day
    February *
Eight Hours Day
    1st Monday in March
Bank Holiday
    Tuesday following Easter Monday
Launceston Show Day
    October *
Hobart Show Day
    October *
Recreation Day(northern Tasmania only)
    1st Monday in November *

Victoria

Labour Day
    2nd Monday in March
Melbourne Cup Day
    1st Tuesday in November *

Western Australia

Labour Day
    1st Monday in March
Foundation Day
    1st Monday in June

Special Events

Some of the most enjoyable Australian festivals are, naturally, the most typically Australian ones – like the surf-lifesaving competitions on beaches all around the country during summer; or the outback race meetings, which draw together isolated townsfolk, tiny communities from the huge stations and more than a few eccentric bush characters.

There are happenings and holidays in Australia year-round – the following is just a brief overview (enquire at relevant state tourist authorities for precise dates and more details):

January

Sydney to Hobart Yacht Race – Tas
    The arrival (29 December to 2 January) in Hobart of the yachts competing in this annual New Year race is celebrated with a mardi gras. The competitors in the *Melbourne to Hobart Yacht Race* arrive soon after.
Huon Folk & Music Festival – Tas
    Popular music festival with a great setting at Port Cygnet by the Huon River.
Sardine Festival – WA
    Great music festival held at historic Fremantle, south of Perth, also features distinctively Australian food and street theatre.
Sydney Fringe Festival – NSW
    Multi-arts festival based around the pavilion at Bondi Beach.
Tunarama Festival – SA
    Held at Port Lincoln, this festival features, among other things, a tuna tossing competition.
Australia Day
    This national holiday, commemorating the arrival of the First Fleet, in 1788, is observed on 26 January.
Sydney Festival & Carnivale – NSW
    A three-week arts, music, food and dance festival.
Australasian Country Music Festival – NSW
    Tamworth *is* country music in Australia, and this festival held on the Australia Day long weekend is the showcase for the country's top C & W artists.
International Jazz Festival – Vic
    Australia's biggest jazz festival is held in Melbourne.
Alpine Wildflower Festival – NSW
    Held at the skiing village of Thredbo, this festival focuses on arts and the environment.

Midsumma Festival – Vic

Melbourne's gay festival runs through January and February, starts with a street party in Brunswick St, includes the famous Red Raw dance party and ends with Midsumma Carnival in early February.

February

Royal Hobart Regatta – Tas

This is the largest aquatic carnival in the southern hemisphere, with boat races and other activities.

Sydney Gay & Lesbian Mardi Gras – NSW

It's fun – there's a huge procession, with extravagant costumes, and an incredible party along Oxford St.

Festival of Perth – WA

This huge cultural festival features three weeks of performances by local and international artists.

Melbourne Music Festival – Vic

The main contemporary music festival in the country.

Hunter Vintage Festival – NSW

Wine enthusiasts flock to the Hunter Valley (north of Sydney) for wine tasting, and grape-picking and treading contests. Runs throughout February and March.

Antipodes International Festival – Vic

Melbourne's Greek community celebrates its culture and achievements.

March

Adelaide Festival – SA

Held on even-dated years, this is three weeks of music, theatre, opera, ballet, art exhibitions, light relief and plenty of parties. The *Adelaide Fringe Festival* accompanies the main festival.

Moomba – Vic

This week-long festival in Melbourne features cultural and sporting events and culminates in a huge evening street procession.

Port Fairy Folk Festival – Vic

Every Labour Day weekend the small coastal town of Port Fairy comes to life with music, dancing, workshops, storytelling, spontaneous entertainment and stalls. Australia's biggest folk music festival attracts all sorts of people and for three days the population swells from 2500 to over 10,000.

Australian Formula One Grand Prix – Vic

This premier motor race takes place on a circuit around Albert Park Lake in inner suburban Melbourne.

Canberra Festival – ACT

Ten-day festival to mark the founding of Canberra.

March to April

Melbourne International Comedy Festival – Vic

No joke, one of the largest comedy festivals in the world.

Royal Easter Show – NSW

Livestock contests and exhibits, ring events, sideshows and rodeos are features of the Sydney show, which is held at Easter.

Bell's Beach Surf Classic – Vic

The longest-running professional surfing event in the world is held over the Easter weekend at Bell's Beach, south-west of Melbourne.

National Folk Festival – ACT

Large music festival held at Easter in Canberra.

Port Fairy Folk Festival – Vic

Another major folk festival.

Queer Film & Video Festival – Vic

Showcase festival for film and video work by gay artists.

April

Anzac Day – This national public holiday on 25 April commemorates the landing of Anzac troops at Gallipoli in 1915. Memorial marches by the returned soldiers of both world wars and the veterans of Korea and Vietnam are held all over the country.

Great Goat Race – NSW

Annual wild goat race through the main street of Lightning Ridge in outback NSW!

Bright Autumn Festival – Vic

Two-week festival in country Victoria, main feature being a prestigious art exhibition.

May

Outback Muster – Qld

Held at the famed Stockman's Hall of Fame in Longreach, this unusual three-day festival features a variety of events related to droving.

June

Barunga Wugularr Sports & Cultural Festival – NT

For the four days over the Queen's Birthday long weekend in June, Barunga, 80km south-east of Katherine, becomes a gathering place for Aboriginal people from all over the Territory. There's traditional arts and crafts, as well as dancing and athletics competitions.

Merrepen Arts Festival – NT

In June or July, Nauiyu Nambiyu on the banks of the Daly River is the venue for this festival where several Aboriginal communities from around the district, such as Wadeye, Nauiyu and Peppimenarti, display their arts and crafts.

Blackrock Stakes – WA
Held in the iron-ore mining region of the Pilbara, the Blackrock Stakes is a 122km race where contestants (teams or solo) push a wheelbarrow weighted down with a large chunk of iron ore.

July

Melbourne International Film Festival – Vic
This is Australia's longest-running international film event, presenting the best in contemporary world cinema.
Alice Springs Camel Cup – NT
Camel races and charity fundraising day.
NT Royal Shows – Agricultural shows in Darwin, Katherine, Tennant Creek and Alice Springs.

August

Darwin Rodeo – NT
This includes international team events between Australia, the USA, Canada and New Zealand.
Darwin Beer Can Regatta – NT
Races for boats constructed entirely out of beer cans, of which there are plenty in this heavy drinking city.
Yuendumu Festival – NT
Aboriginal people from the central and western desert region meet in Yuendumu, north-west of Alice Springs, over a long weekend in early August. There's a mix of traditional and modern sporting and cultural events.
Sydney City to Surf – NSW
Australia's biggest foot race takes place with up to 25,000 competitors running the 14km from Hyde Park to Bondi Beach.
Oenpelli Open Day – NT
Oenpelli is in Arnhem Land, not far from Jabiru in Kakadu National Park. On the first Saturday in August an open day is held where there's a chance to purchase local artefacts and watch the sports and dancing events.

August to September

Shinju Matsuri (Festival of the Pearl) – WA
Held in the old pearling port of Broome during the week of the full moon, this week-long festival is a great event and highlights the town's Asian cultural heritage.

September

AFL Grand Final – Vic
Sporting attention turns to Melbourne with the Grand Final of Aussie rules football, when a crowd close to 100,000 assembles at the MCG. It's the biggest sporting event in Australia.
Royal Melbourne Show – Vic
This attracts agricultural folk for the judging of livestock and produce, and lots of families for the sideshows and showbags.

Royal Perth Show – WA
Has agricultural displays and demonstrations, with sideshows, novelty rides etc.
Royal Adelaide Show – SA
One of the oldest royal shows in the country, with major agricultural and horticultural exhibits and entertainment.
Birdsville Races – Qld
Famous outback race meeting where visitors flock in from around the country for a weekend of horse races and heavy drinking. Proceeds go to the Royal Flying Doctor Service.
Floriade – ACT
Month-long spring festival in Canberra with thousands of bulbs and annuals in bloom, and activities.

October

Land of the Beardies Festival – NSW
Country festival with performances by Aboriginal and non-Aboriginal singers, dancers and musicians at Glen Innes; long beard competition.
Melbourne Writers Festival – Vic
Readings and discussions of works by Australian and international authors.
Melbourne Festival – Vic
An annual festival offering some of the best of opera, theatre, dance and the visual arts from around Australia and the world.
Melbourne Fringe Festival – Vic
Three weeks of theatre, dance, comedy, cabaret, readings, exhibitions and other events help Melbourne celebrate the 'alternative' arts.
Henley-on-Todd Regatta – NT
A series of races for leg-powered bottomless boats on the (usually) dry Todd River.
Bathurst 1000 Touring Car Race – NSW
Motor racing enthusiasts flock to Bathurst for the annual 1000km, touring car race on the superb Mt Panorama circuit.
Royal Shows – Tas
The royal agricultural and horticultural shows of Hobart and Launceston are held this month.
Australian Motorcycle Grand Prix – Vic
The last round of the 500cc world championships is held at the Phillip Island circuit.

November

Melbourne Cup – Vic
On the first Tuesday in November Australia's premier horse race is run at Flemington Racecourse. It's a public holiday in Melbourne but the whole country comes to a virtual standstill for the three minutes or so when the race is on.
Festival of the Bogong Moth – NSW
Held at Albury Wodonga on the Murray River, this three-day Aboriginal festival features the art,

music, dance and language of seven regional Aboriginal groups.

December to January
These are the busiest summer months with Christmas, school holidays and lots of beach activities, rock and jazz festivals, international sporting events, including tennis and cricket, a whole host of outdoor activities and lots of parties.

Sydney to Hobart Yacht Race – NSW
Sydney Harbour is a sight to behold on Boxing Day (26 December) when boats of all shapes and sizes crowd its waters to farewell the yachts competing in this gruelling race. It's a fantastic sight as the yachts stream out of the harbour and head south. In Hobart there's a mardi gras to celebrate the finish of the race.

Woodford Folk Festival – Qld
Held between Christmas and New Year, this five-day festival is the largest folk festival in the country, attracting up to 70,000 people.

ACTIVITIES
There are plenty of activities that you can take part in while travelling round the country. Here we've just given an idea of what's available; for specifics, check the Activities section at the start of each chapter.

Skiing
Australia has a flourishing ski industry – a fact that takes a number of travellers by surprise – with snowfields straddling the New South Wales-Victoria border. There's ski information in the Victorian Alps section of the Victoria chapter, and in the Snowy Mountains section of the New South Wales chapter. Tasmania's snowfields aren't as developed as those of Victoria and New South Wales, but if you do want to ski while in Tassie you can read all about it in the Activities section of the Tasmania chapter.

Bushwalking
One of the best ways of really getting away from it all in Australia is to go bushwalking. There are many fantastic walks in the various national parks around the country and information on how to get there is in Lonely Planet's *Bushwalking in Australia*.

Some walks include the Overland and South-West Tracks in Tasmania; the Bogong High Plains Circuit in Victoria's High Country; Fraser Island and Bellenden Ker in Queensland; the Flinders Ranges in South Australia; and the Larapinta Trail west of Alice Springs in the Centre.

Surfing
If you're interested in surfing you'll find great beaches and surf in various states (see the accompanying boxed text on surfing in Australia).

Scuba Diving
There's great scuba diving at a number of places around the coast but particularly along the Great Barrier Reef where there are also many dive schools. Airlie Beach and Cairns both have a handful of dive schools, but there are at least a dozen other places along the coast where you can learn to dive while on the reef. Open-water PADI courses typically cost $250 to $400, depending on how much time you actually spend on the reef.

Diving courses are available in all other states as well, but you don't have the major attraction of the Barrier Reef to go with it.

Horse Riding
Horseback is a great way to get out into the bush and experience the silence and space in a way not possible by vehicle. You can find horses to hire at any number of places around the country, and you can opt for anything from a half-hour stroll to extended trail rides.

In Victoria you can go horse riding in the High Country and follow the spectacular routes of the Snowy Mountains cattle people, whose lives were the subject of the film *The Man from Snowy River*, which in turn was based on the poem by Banjo Paterson. Rides in the Alps in NSW are also popular.

In northern Queensland you can ride horses through rainforests and along sand dunes and swim with them in the sea.

The Northern Territory has a dedicated riding station (Bonrook) near Katherine as well as operators in central Australia (Ooraminna Bush Camp and Ossie's Trail Rides) offering extended trail rides.

In Western Australia, Kimberley Pursuits has riding tours lasting from two to 11 days and exploring remote country with 4WD back-up. The South West Timber Trekking Company does similar things in the south-west corner of the state.

Cycling

You can cycle all around Australia; for the athletic there are long, challenging routes and for the not so masochistic there are plenty of great day trips. In most states there are excellent roads and helpful bicycle societies, which have lots of maps and useful tips and advice. Around the country there are a number of specialist bicycle tour companies. One of the most ambitious is Remote Outback Cycle, a company offering trips through some superb areas of outback Australia, with 4WD back-up. Other companies include: Out the Back Mountain Adventures (Cooma, NSW); Boomerang Bicycle Tours (Sydney, NSW); The Adventure Company (Cairns, Qld); Freewheelin Cycle Tours

---

Considerations for Responsible Bushwalking

The popularity of bushwalking is placing great pressure on wilderness areas. Please consider the following tips when trekking and help preserve the ecology and beauty of the Australian bush.

Rubbish

- Carry out all your rubbish. If you've carried it in you can carry it out. Don't overlook those easily forgotten items, such as silver paper, orange peel, cigarette butts and plastic wrappers. Empty packaging weighs very little anyway and should be stored in a dedicated rubbish bag. Make an effort to carry out rubbish left by others.
- Never bury your rubbish: digging disturbs soil and ground-cover and encourages erosion. Buried rubbish will more than likely be dug up by animals such as dingoes, which may be injured or poisoned by it. On the other hand, it may take years to decompose.
- Minimise the waste you must carry out by taking minimal packaging and taking no more than you will need. If you can't buy in bulk, unpack small-portion packages and combine their contents in one container before your trek. Take re-useable containers or stuff sacks.
- Sanitary napkins, tampons and condoms should also be carried out despite the inconvenience. They burn and decompose poorly.

Human Waste Disposal

- Contamination of water sources by human faeces can lead to the transmission of hepatitis, typhoid and intestinal parasites, such as giardiasis, amoebas and round worms. It can cause severe health risks not only to members of your party, but also to local residents and wildlife.
- Where there is a toilet, please use it.
- Where there is none, bury your waste. Dig a small hole 15cm deep and at least 100m from any watercourse. Consider carrying a lightweight trowel for this purpose. Cover the waste with soil and a rock. Use toilet paper sparingly and bury it with the waste. In snow, dig down to the soil otherwise your waste will be exposed when the snow melts. If the area is inhabited, ask local people if they have any concerns about your chosen toilet site.
- Ensure that these guidelines are applied to a portable toilet tent if one is being used by a large trekking party. Encourage all party members to use the site.

Washing

- Don't use detergents or toothpaste in or near watercourses, even if they are biodegradable. For personal washing, use biodegradable soap and a water container (or even a lightweight, portable basin) at least 50m away from the watercourse. Widely disperse the waste water to allow the soil to filter it fully before it finally makes it back to the watercourse.
- Wash cooking utensils 50m from watercourses using a scourer, sand or snow instead of detergent.

Erosion

- Hillsides and mountain slopes are prone to erosion. It is important to stick to existing tracks and

(Adelaide, SA); Tasmanian Expeditions (Launceston, Tas); and Bogong Jack Adventures (SA).

See the Getting Around and individual state chapters for more details.

Camel-Riding
Camel-riding has taken off around the country but especially in and around Alice Springs in the Northern Territory. If you've done it in India or Egypt or you just fancy yourself as the explorer/outdoors type, then here's your chance. You can take anything from a five-minute stroll to a 14-day expedition.

Bird-Watching
The Royal Australasian Ornithologists Union (☎ (03) 9882 2622) runs bird observatories in New South Wales, Victoria and Western Australia. Its headquarters are at 415 Riversdale Rd, Hawthorn East, Victoria.

---

avoid short cuts that bypass a switchback. If you blaze a new trail straight down a slope it will turn into a watercourse with the next heavy rainfall and eventually cause soil loss and deep scarring.
- If a well-used track passes through a mud patch, walk through the mud: walking around the edge will increase the size of the patch.
- Avoid removing the plant life that keeps topsoils in place.

Fires & Low Impact Cooking
- Don't depend on open fires for cooking. The cutting of wood for fires in popular trekking areas can cause rapid deforestation. Cook on a light-weight kerosene, alcohol or Shellite (white gas) stove and avoid those powered by disposable butane gas canisters. Fires are banned in many Australian national parks.
- Fires may be acceptable in areas that get very few visitors. If you light a fire, use an existing fireplace rather than create a new one. Don't surround fires with rocks as this creates a visual scar. Use only dead, fallen wood. Remember the adage 'the bigger the fool, the bigger the fire'. Use minimal wood, just what you need for cooking. In huts leave wood for the next person.
- Ensure that you fully extinguish a fire after use. Spread the embers and douse them with water. A fire is only truly safe to leave when you can comfortably place your hand in it.

Wildlife Conservation
- Do not engage in or encourage hunting. It's illegal in all parks and reserves.
- Don't buy items made from endangered species.
- Don't assume animals in huts to be nonindigenous vermin and attempt to exterminate them. In wild places they are likely to be protected native animals.
- Discourage the presence of wildlife by not leaving food scraps behind you. Place gear out of reach and tie packs to rafters or trees.
- Do not feed the wildlife as this can lead to animals becoming dependent on trekker hand-outs, to unbalanced populations and to diseases such as 'lumpy jaw'.

Camping & Walking on Private Property
- Seek permission to camp from landowners.
- Public access to private property without permission is acceptable where public land is otherwise inaccessible, so long as safety and conservation regulations are observed.

Park Regulations
- Take note of and observe any rules and regulations particular to the national or state reserve that you are visiting.

Environmental Organisations
- See Useful Organisations later in this chapter for the contact addresses of active environmental groups in Australia. ■

Where to Surf in Australia

In the summer of 1915, Hawaiian surfer Duke Kahanamoku came to Australia and introduced the art of surfboard riding. He fashioned a board from local timbers and gave a demonstration at Freshwater, on Sydney's north shore. From that point on the sport grew steadily and today Australia boasts several world champions and many world class breaks.

Queensland Surfers Paradise, located south of Brisbane, is not what the name suggests. The Gold Coast, however, is generally a good place to surf – Burleigh Heads and Kirra are the more well known breaks with good rights on a solid ground swell. Also check Coolangatta's Greenmount Point and Duranbah on the other side of the Point Danger headland.

Just north of Surfers Paradise, check out South Stradbroke Island for some big and powerful beach breaks.

North of Brisbane is the Sunshine Coast, which has a variety of breaks at Caloundra and Maroochydore.

When it works, Noosa Heads National Park has a good right but does draw large crowds. Double Island Point, north of Noosa, is worth checking but you'll need a 4WD.

New South Wales Name practically any coastal town in New South Wales and there will be good surf nearby.

Sydney's northern beaches are well known for their good surf, with Manly, Dee Why, Narrabeen and Avalon the more popular. To the east of Sydney check out the areas around Bondi; to the south of Sydney there's good surf around Cronulla.

On the far north coast check out Byron Bay, Lennox Head and Angourie, Coffs Harbour and Nambucca Heads on the mid-north coast and the beaches off Newcastle on the lower north coast. Down on the south coast check out the beaches off Wollongong, Jervis Bay, Ulladulla, Merimbula and Pambula.

Victoria Bells Beach has become synonymous with surfing in Australia and does have a classic right-hander if the swell is up. There are many other excellent breaks throughout the state.

Phillip Island, the Mornington Peninsula and the West Coast are all within a two-hour drive from Melbourne. On Phillip Island check Woolamai, Surfies Point, Smiths Beach and Cat Bay. The Mornington Peninsula's best spots are Point Leo, Flinders, Gunamatta, Rye and Portsea. While on the West Coast you can try Barwon Heads, Torquay, Bells Beach and the Great Ocean Road.

In Gippsland try Lakes Entrance and Wilsons Promontory.

There is also the big and powerful shipwreck coast near Port Campbell, which only experienced surfers should attempt.

Tasmania Despite the cold water, Tasmania has some fine surfing. The best spots to check on the exposed west coast are around Marrawah. There are many quality spots along the east coast. Check north and south of St Helens, around Eaglehawk Neck on the Tasman Peninsula and Shelly Beach near Orford. Bruny Island also has some surfable waves and closer to Hobart try Cremorne Point and Clifton Beach.

South Australia Cactus Beach, west of Ceduna on remote Point Sinclair, is South Australia's best known surf spot, and is also renowned worldwide as one of Australia's best remote waves. Other places to check are the Eyre and York peninsulas, while closer to Adelaide and near Victor Harbour there are good waves on the east and west side of the Fleurieu Peninsula.

Western Australia Western Australia's best known surfing spot is probably Margaret River and the surf here can get huge. The beaches and points north and south of Margaret River also offer some excellent surf.

Trig and Scarborough beaches north of Perth have beginners surf and Rottnest Island has some good waves, too.

Further North, Geraldton, Kalbarri and Carnarvon are also well worth checking out. However, you may need a 4WD on the coast road north of Carnarvon, and only experienced surfers should attempt these waves.

Andrew Tudor

Considerations for Responsible Diving

The popularity of diving is placing immense pressure on many sites on the Great Barrier Reef. Please consider the following tips when diving and help preserve the ecology and beauty of the reef:

- Do not use anchors on the reef, and take care not to ground boats on coral. Encourage dive operators and regulatory bodies to establish permanent moorings at popular dive sites.
- Avoid touching living marine organisms with your body or dragging gauges across the reef. Polyps can be damaged by even the gentlest contact. Never stand on corals, even if they look solid and robust. If you must secure yourself to the reef, only hold fast to exposed rock or dead coral.
- Be conscious of your fins. Even without contact the surge from heavy fin strokes near the reef can damage delicate organisms. When treading water in shallow reef areas, take care not to kick up clouds of sand. Settling sand can easily smother delicate organisms.
- Practise and maintain proper buoyancy control. Major damage can be done by divers descending too fast and colliding with the reef. Make sure you are correctly weighted and that your weight belt is positioned so that you stay horizontal. If you have not dived for a while, have a practice dive in a pool before taking to the reef. Be aware that buoyancy can change over the period of an extended trip: initially you may breathe harder and need more weighting; a few days later you may breathe more easily and need less weight.
- Take great care in underwater caves. Spend as little time within them as possible as your air bubbles may be caught within the roof and thereby leave previously submerged organisms high and dry. Taking turns to inspect the interior of a small cave will lessen the chances of damaging contact.
- Resist the temptation to collect or buy corals or shells. Aside from the ecological damage, taking home marine souvenirs depletes the beauty of a site and spoils the enjoyment of others.
- The same goes for marine archaeological sites (mainly shipwrecks). Respect their integrity; they may even be protected from looting by law.
- Ensure that you take home all your rubbish, and any litter you may find as well. Plastics in particular are a serious threat to marine life. Turtles will mistake plastic for jellyfish and eat it.
- Resist the temptation to feed fish. You may disturb their normal eating habits, encourage aggressive behaviour or feed them food that is detrimental to their health.
- Minimise your disturbance of marine animals. In particular, do not ride on the backs of turtles as this causes them great anxiety. ■

Other Activities

Windsurfing, paragliding, rafting, hot-air ballooning, bungee-jumping and hang-gliding are among the many other outdoor activities enjoyed by Australians and available to travellers. The places with the most activities available are usually also those with the most backpackers, so places like Airlie Beach and Cairns in Queensland have a huge range.

WORK

If you come to Australia on a tourist visa then strictly you shouldn't work. Many travellers on tourist visas do in fact find casual work, usually in the tourism industry. The work is not well paid and as you are not working legally you are open to being exploited.

With a working holiday visa (see the Visa section earlier in this chapter), the possibilities are many. With the current boom in tourism, work is often easy to find in the peak season at the major tourist centres. Places like Alice Springs, Cairns and various other places along the Queensland coast, and the ski fields of Victoria and NSW, are all good prospects, but opportunities are usually limited to the peak holiday seasons.

Other good prospects for casual work include factory work, bar work, waiting on tables, washing dishes (kitchenhand), other domestic chores at outback roadhouses, nanny work, fruit picking, station hands (jackaroo/jillaroo) and collecting for charities. People with computing or secretarial skills should have little difficulty finding work in the major cities, and for qualified nurses agency work is often available. We even got one letter from a traveller who was employed as an ostrich babysitter!

The various backpacker magazines, newspapers and hostels are good information sources – some local employers even advertise on their notice boards. Try the classified section of the daily papers under Situations Vacant, especially on Saturday and Wednesday. The government Centrelink offices are of virtually no help.

Workabout Australia, by Barry Drebner, gives a comprehensive state by state breakdown of the seasonal work opportunities.

Tax File Number

If you have a working holiday visa, it's important to apply for a Tax File Number (TFN), not because it's a condition of employment, but because without a TFN tax will be deducted from any wages you receive at the maximum rate, which is currently set at 47%! To get a TFN, contact the local branch of the Australian Taxation Office (☎ 13 2861) for a form. It's a straightforward procedure, and you will have to supply adequate identification, such as a passport, and show that you have a work visa. The issuing of a TFN takes about four weeks.

Paying Tax

Yes, it's one of the certainties in life! If you have supplied your employer with a Tax File Number, tax will be deducted from your wages at the rate of 29% if your weekly income is below $397. As your income increases, so does the tax rate, with the maximum being 47% for weekly incomes over $961. For nonresident visitors, tax is payable from the first dollar you earn, unlike residents who have something like a $6000 tax-free threshold. For this reason, if you have had tax deducted at the correct rate as you earn, it is unlikely you'll be entitled to a tax refund when you leave.

If you have had tax deducted at 47% because you have not submitted a Tax File Number, chances are you will be entitled to a partial refund if your income was less than $50,000. Once you lodge a tax return (which must include a copy of the Group Certificate all employers issue to salaried workers at the end of the financial year or within seven days

of leaving a job), you will be refunded the extra tax you have paid. Before you can lodge a tax return, however, you must have a Tax File Number.

Superannuation

As part of the government's compulsory superannuation scheme, employers must make contributions to a superannuation fund on your behalf. These contributions are made at the rate of 7% of your wage, and the money must remain in the fund until you reach 'preservation age' (sounds nasty!), which is currently 55.

The only escape from this is if you earn less than $900 per month, in which case you can decide to opt-out of superannuation and instead receive the 7% payment as part of your regular salary or wages.

Casual Employment Seasons

The table below lists the main times and regions where casual employment, mainly fruit-picking, is a possibility:

New South Wales

Job	Time	Region/s
Apples	Feb-Apr	Orange
	Dec-Jan	Forbes
Bananas	Nov-Jan	North Coast
Cherries	Nov-Jan	Orange
Citrus	Dec-Mar	Griffith
Grapes	Feb-Mar	Griffith,
		Hunter Valley
Tomatoes	Jan-Mar	Forbes

Northern Territory

Job	Time	Region/s
Mangoes	Oct-Nov	Darwin
Tourism	May-Sep	Darwin,
		Alice Springs,
		Katherine

Queensland

Job	Time	Region/s
Apples	Feb-Mar	Warwick
Asparagus	Aug-Dec	Warwick
Bananas	year-round	Tully
Fishing trawlers	May-Aug	Cairns
Grapes	Jan-Apr	Stanthorpe
Mangoes	Dec-Jan	Atherton
Tomatoes	Oct-Dec	Bundaberg
Tourism	Apr-Oct	Cairns
Various veg	May-Nov	Bowen

South Australia

Job	Time	Region/s
Apples/pears	Feb-July	Adelaide Hills
Apricots	Dec	Riverland
Grapes	Feb-Apr	Riverland, Barossa, Clare
Peaches	Feb-June	Riverland
Pruning	Aug-Dec	Adelaide Hills
Tomatoes	Jan-Feb	Riverland

Tasmania

Job	Time	Region/s
Apples/pears	Mar-Apr	Huon Valley, Tamar Valley
Cherries	Dec-Jan	Huonsville
Grapes	Mar-Apr	Tamar Valley
Strawberries/ raspberries	Jan-Apr	Huonville

Victoria

Job	Time	Region/s
Apples	Mar-May	Bendigo
Cherries	Nov-Dec	Dandenongs
Grapes	Feb-Mar	Mildura
Peaches/pears	Feb-Mar	Shepparton
Strawberries	Oct-Dec	Echuca, Dandenongs
Tomatoes	Jan-Mar	Shepparton, Echuca
Ski fields work	June-Oct	Wangaratta/Alps

Western Australia

Job	Time	Region/s
Apples/pears	Feb-Apr	Manjimup
Bananas	Apr-Dec	Kununurra
	Year round	Carnarvon
Flowers	Sep-Nov	Midlands
Grapes	Feb-Mar	Albany, Mt Barker, Manjimup
Lobsters	Nov-May	Esperance
Prawn trawlers	Mar-June	Carnarvon
Tourism	May-Dec	Kununurra
Vegies	May-Nov	Kununurra, Carnarvon

ACCOMMODATION

Australia is very well equipped with youth hostels, backpacker hostels and caravan parks with camp sites – the cheapest shelter you can find. Furthermore, there are plenty of motels around the country, and in holiday regions like the Queensland coast intense competition tends to keep the prices down.

A typical town of a few thousand people will have a basic motel at around $50 for a double, an old town centre pub with rooms (shared bathrooms) at say $30, and a caravan park – probably with camp sites for around $10 and on-site vans or cabins for $35 for two. If the town is on anything like a main road or is bigger, it will probably have several of each. You'll rarely have much trouble finding *somewhere* to lay your head in Oz, even when there are no hostels, although some surprisingly small and seemingly insignificant towns have backpacker hostels. If there's a group of you, the rates for three or four people in a room are always worth checking. Often there are larger 'family' rooms or units with two bedrooms.

There are a couple of free backpacker newspapers and booklets available at hostels around the country, and these have fairly up-to-date listings of hostels, although they give neither prices nor details of each hostel.

For more comprehensive accommodation listings, the state automobile clubs produce directories listing caravan parks, hotels, motels, holiday flats and a number of backpacker hostels in almost every city and town in the country. They're updated every year so the prices are generally fairly current. They're available from the clubs for a nominal charge if you're a member, or if you're a member of an affiliated club enjoying reciprocal rights. Alternatively, some state tourist offices (notably Tasmania and Western Australia) also put out frequently updated guides to local accommodation.

There's a wide variation in seasonal prices for accommodation. At peak times – school holiday in particular – prices are at their peak, whereas at other times useful discounts can be found. This particularly applies to the Top End, where the Wet season (summer) is the low season and prices can drop by as much as 30%. In this book high-season prices are used unless indicated otherwise, and all prices are quoted in Australian dollars.

Camping & Caravanning

The camping story in Australia is partly excellent and partly rather annoying! The excellent side is that there is a great number of caravan parks and you'll almost always find space available. If you want to get around Australia on the cheap then camping is the cheapest way of all, with nightly costs for two of around $10 to $15, slightly more if you want power.

On the downside, camp sites are often intended more for caravanners (house trailers for any North Americans out there) than for campers. The fact that most of the sites are called 'caravan parks' indicates who gets most attention. In many Australian caravan parks gravel is laid down to make the ground more suitable for cars and caravans, so pitching a tent becomes very hard work.

Equally bad is that in most big cities sites are well away from the centre. This is not inconvenient in small towns, but in general if you're planning to camp around Australia you really need your own transport. Brisbane is the worst city in Australia in this respect because council regulations actually forbid tents within a 22-km radius of the centre. Although there are some sites in Brisbane within that radius, they're strictly for caravans – no campers allowed.

Still, it's not all gloom; most Australian caravan parks are well kept, conveniently located and excellent value. Many caravan parks also have on-site vans which you can rent for the night. These give you the comfort of a caravan without the inconvenience of actually towing one of the damned things. On-site cabins are also widely available, and these are more like a small self-contained unit. They usually have one bedroom, or at least an area which can be screened off from the rest of the unit – just the thing if you have small kids. Cabins also have their own bathroom and toilet, although this is sometimes an optional extra. They are also much less cramped than a caravan, and the price difference is not always that great – say $25 to $30 for an on-site van, $40 to $50 for a cabin. In winter, if you're going to be using this sort of accommodation on a regular basis, it's worth investing in a small heater of some sort as many vans and cabins are unheated.

Camping in the bush, either in national parks and reserves or in the open, is for many

people one of the highlights of a visit to Oz. In the outback you won't even need a tent – swags are the way to go, and nights spent around a campfire under the stars are unforgettable.

Youth Hostels

Australia has a very active Youth Hostel Association (YHA) and you'll find hostels all over the country, with more official hostels and backpacker hostels popping up all the time.

YHA hostels provide basic accommodation, usually in small dormitories or bunk rooms although more and more are providing twin rooms for couples. The nightly charges are very reasonable – usually between $14 and $18 a night.

Very few YHA hostels still have the old fetishes for curfews and doing chores, but many retain segregated dorms. Most also take non-YHA members, although their price is typically a couple of dollars more. To become a full YHA member in Australia costs $27 a year (there's also a $17 joining fee, although if you're an overseas resident joining in Australia you don't have to pay this). You can join at a state office or at any youth hostel.

There's also the introductory membership, where you pay no initial membership, but instead pay an additional $3 at any hostel. Once you have stayed for nine nights, you get a full membership.

The YHA also has Accommodation Packs, whereby you can prepay accommodation and get healthy discounts. The '20 for $250' and '10 for $130' give you 20 and 10 nights respectively at any Australian YHA hostel.

Youth hostels are part of an international organisation, the International Youth Hostel Federation (IYHF, also known as HI, Hostelling International), so if you're already a member of the YHA in your own country, your membership entitles you to use Australian hostels. Hostels are great places for meeting people and great travellers' centres. In many busier hostels the foreign visitors will outnumber the Australians. The annual *YHA Accommodation & Discounts*

Guide booklet, which is available from any YHA office in Australia and from some YHA offices overseas, lists all YHA hostels in Australia, with useful maps showing how to find them. It also lists the handy discounts on things such as car hire, activities, accommodation etc which members are entitles to.

You must have a regulation sheet ,sleeping bag or bed linen – for hygiene reasons a regular sleeping bag will not do. If you haven't got sheets they can be rented at many hostels (usually for $3), but it's cheaper, after a few nights stay, to have your own. YHA offices and some larger hostels sell the official YHA sheet bag.

All hostels have cooking facilities and 24-hour access, and there's usually some communal area where you can sit and talk. There are usually laundry facilities and often excellent notice boards. Many hostels have a maximum-stay period (usually five to seven days).

The YHA classes its main hostels as simple, standard or superior, and rural hostels also get a gum-leaf rating, from one to three gum leaves depending on how much of a wilderness experience the visitor can expect.

Hostels range from tiny places to big modern buildings, from historic convict buildings to a converted railway station. Most hostels have a manager who checks you in when you arrive and keeps the peace. Because you have so much more contact with a hostel manager than the person in charge of other styles of accommodation they can really make or break the place. Good managers are often great characters and well worth getting to know.

Accommodation can usually be booked directly with the manager or through a Membership & Travel Centre – see the YHA handbook for details.

The Australian head office is in Sydney, at the Australian Youth Hostels Association, 10 Mallett St, Camperdown, NSW 2050 (☎ (02) 9565 1699). If you can't get a YHA hostel booklet in your own country write to them but otherwise deal with the Membership & Travel centres:

New South Wales
    422 Kent St, Sydney, NSW 2001 (☎ (02) 9261 1111; fax 9261 1969)
Northern Territory
    Darwin City Hostel, 69A Mitchell St, Darwin, NT 0800 (☎ (08) 8981 6344; fax 8981 6674)
Queensland
    154 Roma St, Brisbane, Qld 4000 (☎ (07) 3236 1680; fax 3236 1702)
South Australia
    38 Sturt St, Adelaide, SA 5000 (☎ (08) 8231 5583; 8231 4219; yhasa@ozemail.com.au)
Tasmania
    1st floor, 28 Criterion St, Hobart, Tas 7000 (☎ (03) 6234 9617; fax 6234 7422)
Victoria
    205 King St, Melbourne, Vic 3000 (☎ (03) 9670 7991; fax 9670 9840)
Western Australia
    236 William St, Northbridge, Perth, WA 6003 (☎ (08) 9227 5122; fax 9227 5123)

Not all of the 130-plus hostels listed in the handbook are actually owned by the YHA. Some are 'associate hostels' which generally abide by hostel regulations but are owned by other organisations or individuals. You don't need to be a YHA member to stay at an associated hostel. Others are 'alternative accommodation' and do not totally fit the hostel blueprint. They might be motels which keep some hostel-style accommodation available for YHA members, caravan parks with an on-site van or two kept aside, or even places just like hostels but where the operators don't want to abide by all the hostel regulations.

Backpacker Hostels
Australia has a large number of backpacker hostels, and the standard of these hostels varies enormously. Some are run-down, inner-city hotels where the owners have tried to fill empty rooms; unless renovations have been done, these places are generally pretty gloomy and depressing. Others are former motels, so each unit, typically with four to six beds, will have fridge, TV and bathroom. When the climate allows, there's usually a pool too, and they're often air-conditioned, at least at night. The drawback with these places is that the communal areas and cooking facilities are often lacking, as motels

were never originally designed for communal use. You may also find yourself sharing a room with someone who wants to watch TV all night – it happens a lot!

Still other hostels are purpose-built as backpacker hostels; these are usually the best places in terms of facilities, although sometimes they are simply too big and therefore lack any personalised service. As often as not the owners have backpackers running the places, and usually it's not too long before standards start to slip. Some of these places, particularly along the Queensland coast, actively promote themselves as 'party' hostels, so if you want a quiet time, they're not the place to be. The best places are often the smaller, more intimate hostels where the owner is also the manager. These are usually the older hostels which were around long before the 'backpacker boom'.

With the proliferation of hostels has also come intense competition. Hop off a bus in any town on the Queensland coast and chances are there'll be at least three or four touts from the various hostels, all trying to lure you in. To this end many have introduced inducements, such as the first night free, and virtually all have courtesy buses. Even the YHA hostels have had to resort to this to stay in the race in some places.

Prices at backpacker hostels are generally in line with YHA hostels – typically $12 to $18, although discounts can reduce this.

There's at least one organisation (VIP) which you can join where, for a modest fee (typically $15), you'll receive a discount card (valid for 12 months) and a list of participating hostels. This is hardly a great inducement to join but you do also receive useful discounts on other services, such as bus passes, so they may be worth considering.

Nomads Backpackers (☎ (08) 8224 0919; fax 8232 2911) is another organisation which runs a number of revamped pubs and hostels around the country.

As with YHA hostels, the success of a hostel largely depends on the friendliness and willingness of the managers. Some places will only admit overseas backpackers.

This happens mostly in cities and when it does it's because the hostel in question has had problems with locals treating the place more as a dosshouse – drinking too much, making too much noise, getting into fights and the like. Hostels which discourage or ban Aussies say it's only a rowdy minority that makes trouble, but they can't take the risk. If you're an Aussie and encounter this kind of reception, the best you can do is persuade the desk people that you're genuinely travelling the country, and aren't just looking for a cheap place to crash for a while.

Guesthouses & B&Bs

This is the fastest growing segment of the accommodation market. New places are opening all the time, and the network of alternatives throughout the country includes everything from restored miners' cottages, converted barns and stables, renovated and rambling old guesthouses, upmarket country homes and romantic escapes to a simple bedroom in a family home. Many of these places are listed throughout the book. Tariffs cover a wide range, but are typically in the $40 to $100 (per double) bracket.

Hotels & Pubs

For the budget traveller, hotels in Australia are generally older places – new accommodation is usually motels. Every place called a hotel does not necessarily have rooms to rent, although many in the country still do. A 'private hotel', as opposed to a 'licensed hotel', really is a hotel and does not serve alcohol. A 'guesthouse' is much the same as a 'private hotel'.

New hotels being built today are mainly of the Hilton variety; smaller establishments will usually be motels. So, if you're staying in a hotel, it will normally mean an older place, usually in a country town, and often with rooms without private facilities. You'll find hotels all around the town centres in smaller towns, while in larger towns the hotels that offer accommodation are often to be found close to the railway stations. In some older towns, or in historic centres like the gold-mining towns, the old hotels can be really magnificent. The rooms themselves may be pretty old-fashioned and unexciting, but the hotel facade and entrance area will often be quite extravagant. The plus side of staying in country hotels is that these places are often the social focus of a town (especially in smaller towns) and so staying in the local pub is the best way to find out what makes the town tick. Generally, hotels will have twin rooms for around $25 to $35.

In airports and bus and railway stations, there are often information boards with direct-dial phones to book accommodation. These are generally for the more expensive hotels, but these will sometimes offer discounts if you use the direct phone to book. The staff at bus stations are helpful when it comes to finding cheap and convenient places to stay.

Motels, Serviced Apartments & Holiday Flats

If you've got transport and want a more modern place with your own bathroom and other facilities, then you're moving into the motel bracket. Motels cover the earth in Australia, just like in the USA, but they're usually located away from the city centres. Prices vary and with the motels, unlike hotels, singles are often not much cheaper than doubles. The reason is quite simple – in the old hotels many of the rooms really are singles, relics of the days when single men travelled the country looking for work. In motels, the rooms are almost always doubles. You'll sometimes find motel rooms for less than $40, but in most places they'll be at least $50.

Holiday flats are found in holiday areas, and serviced apartments in cities. A holiday flat is much like a motel room but usually has a kitchen or cooking facilities. Usually holiday flats are not serviced like motels – you don't get your bed made up every morning and the cups washed out. In some holiday flats you actually have to provide your own sheets and bedding but others are operated just like motel rooms with a kitchen. Most motels in Australia provide at least tea and coffee-making facilities and a small fridge.

Holiday flats are often rented on a weekly basis but even in these cases it's worth asking if daily rates are available. Paying for a week, even if you stay only for a few days, can still be cheaper than having those days at a higher daily rate. If there are more than just two of you, another advantage of holiday flats is that you can often find them with two or more bedrooms. A two-bedroom holiday flat is typically priced at about $1\frac{1}{2}$ times the cost of a comparable single-bedroom flat.

In holiday areas like the Queensland coast, motels and holiday flats will often be virtually interchangeable terms – there's nothing really to distinguish one from the other. In big cities, on the other hand, the serviced apartments are often a little more obscure, although they may be advertised in the daily newspaper's classified ads.

Other Possibilities

There are lots of less conventional accommodation possibilities. You don't have to camp in caravan parks, for example. There are plenty of parks where you can camp for free, or (in Queensland at least) roadside rest areas where short-term camping is permitted. Australia has lots of bush where nobody is going to complain about you sleeping in the back of your car or rolling out a swag for a night – or even notice you.

Australia is a land of farms (known as 'stations' in the outback) and one of the best ways to come to grips with Australian life is to spend a few days on one. Many farms offer accommodation where you can just sit back and watch how it's done, while others like to get you more actively involved in day-to-day activities. With commodity prices falling daily, mountainous wool stockpiles and a general rural crisis, tourism offers the hope of at least some income for farmers, at a time when many are being forced off the land. The state tourist offices can advise you on what's available; prices are pretty reasonable.

Finally, how about life on a houseboat? See the Murray River sections in the Victoria and South Australia chapters.

Long-Term Accommodation

In the cities, if you want to stay longer, the first place to look for a shared flat or a room is the classified ad section of the daily newspaper. Wednesday and Saturday are the best days for these ads. Notice boards in universities, hostels, certain popular bookshops and cafes, and other contact centres are good places to look for flats/houses to share or rooms to rent.

FOOD

The culinary delights can be one of the real highlights of Australia. There was a time – like 25 years ago – when Australia's food (mighty steaks apart) had a reputation for being like England's, only worse. But mira-cles happen and Australia's miracle was immigration. The Greeks, Yugoslavs, Italians, Lebanese and many others who flooded into Australia in the 50s and 60s brought their food with them. More recent arrivals include the Vietnamese, whose communities are thriving in several cities.

In Australia today you can have excellent Greek moussaka (and a bottle of retsina to wash it down), delicious Italian saltimbocca and pasta, or good, heavy German dumplings; you can perfume the air with garlic after stumbling out of a French bistro, or try all sorts of Middle Eastern treats. The Chinese have been sweet & souring since the gold-rush days, while more recently Indian, Thai and Malaysian restaurants have been all

The Kangaroo-Meat Debate

Kangaroos – should we eat them? On one hand, the animal rights lobby claims that killing kangaroos is cruel and that the meat itself may not be disease-free. Yet farmers, ecologists, meat industry representatives and others say the legitimate culling of kangaroos is a humane way to bring population numbers down to levels the environment can tolerate, and that the meat harvested this way is properly inspected, safe and indeed a healthy low-cholesterol alternative to, say, cow or sheep meat.

A lot is at stake. The kangaroo meat and hide industry employs about 4000 people in Australia and generates more than A\$200 million a year. In Britain kangaroo meat sales have been booming, helped along by fears of mad-cow disease which have put people off beef. However, in September 1997 giant British supermarket chain Tesco banned kangaroo meat from 350 stores after a Sunday newspaper ran a disturbing feature, with pictures, on a kangaroo hunt in the Australian outback. The farmer involved was not a licensed hunter and was not working in the meat industry. Nevertheless, kangaroo meat was taken off the shelves, leaving Australian meat-industry representatives fuming, as the meat sold in supermarkets and restaurants comes from licensed hunters governed by a code of practice, and is subject to strict hygiene standards.

Kangaroos are indigenous to Australia but are not endangered. Government estimates put the total population at between 15 million and 25 million (depending on the availability of food and water from one season to another). Each year the government earmarks a certain number (about 10% to 15% of the total) for harvesting. State and territory governments issue permits to shooters who may then, with landholders' consent, hunt on private property (national parks and reserves are off-limits).

While emus and crocodiles are farmed for their meat, the kangaroo is shot in the field at night, using spotlights, four-wheel drives, high calibre rifles and telescopic sights. Hunters and wildlife authorities claim that a bullet shot straight into the head is quick and humane; certainly better than steel traps or poison. However, animal rights advocates claim otherwise. They say the hunt itself (with its lights and noise), let alone the killing, is highly stressful.

Unfortunately, a fair amount of killing goes on by unlicensed hunters who aren't working for the meat industry, and distressing tales of cruelty surface from time to time. The RSPCA and conservation agencies prosecute occasionally, but it's difficult to positively identify the perpetrators.

Formerly seen as a pest, the kangaroo is now increasingly viewed as a resource to be managed along with other variables to ensure the land remains fertile and productive. For the kangaroo this could mean more room to roam, as graziers are encouraged to take cloven-hoofed animals off marginal land that should never have been conventionally farmed anyway. The payoff for farmers would be money earned from harvesting kangaroos when they become too numerous and destructive, and for the environment, a chance to regenerate.

Christine Niven

the rage. And for cheap eats, you can't beat some of the Vietnamese places.

In this book, all food prices are quoted in Australian dollars.

Australian

Although there is no real Australian cuisine there is certainly some excellent Australian food to try. In recent years there's been a great rise in popularity of exotic local and 'bush' foods, and for the adventurous these dishes offer something completely different. So in a swish Melbourne restaurant or Sydney bistro you might find braised kangaroo tail samosas, emu pâté, gum-leaf smoked venison, salt-bush lamb, native aniseed frittata, Warrigal-greens salad or wattle-seed ice cream.

All major cities also have a selection of cafes and restaurants serving food which can be termed 'modern Australian'. These are dishes which borrow heavily from a wide range of foreign cuisines, but have a definite local flavour. At these places seemingly anything goes, so you might find Asian-inspired curry-type dishes sharing a menu with European or Mediterranean-inspired dishes. It all adds up to exciting dining.

Australia also has a superb range of seafood: fish like John Dory and the esteemed barramundi, or superb lobsters and other crustaceans like the engagingly named Moreton Bay bugs! Yabbies are freshwater crayfish and very good.

Another positive aspect of Australian food is the fine ingredients. Nearly everything is grown locally so you're not eating food that has been shipped halfway around the world.

At the bottom end of the food scale is the meat pie – an awful concoction of anonymous meat and dark gravy in a soggy pastry case. You'll have to try one though; the number consumed in Australia each year is phenomenal, and they're a real part of Australian culture. A pie 'n sauce at the 'footy' on a Saturday afternoon in winter is something plenty of Aussies can relate to.

Even more a part of Australian food culture is Vegemite. This strange, dark yeast extract looks and spreads like thick tar and smells like, well, Vegemite. Australians spread Vegemite on bread and become positively addicted to the stuff.

Vegetarian

Vegetarians are generally well catered for in most areas. While there are few dedicated vegetarian restaurants, most modern cafes and restaurants have a few vegetarian dishes on the menu.

Where to Eat

Takeaway Food Around the country you'll find all the well-known international fast-food chains – *McDonald's, KFC, Pizza Hut* etc – typically conspicuous.

On a more local level, you'll find a milk bar on (almost) every corner, and most of them sell pies, pasties, sandwiches and milkshakes. There are speciality sandwich bars, delicatessens and health-food shops worth seeking out if you want something a little more exotic than a pie.

Most shopping centres have a fish & chip shop and a pizza joint, and most of the latter seem to do home deliveries.

Absolute rock-bottom is the kept-luke-warm-for-hours food found at roadside cafes and roadhouses across the country. Give it a miss unless you have absolutely no choice.

Restaurants & Cafes The best Australian eateries serve food as exciting and as innovative as any you'll find anywhere, and it doesn't need to cost a fortune. Best value are the modern and casual cafes, where for less than $20 you can get an excellent feed.

Restaurants – and there's no shortage of them – range from the ordinary to the utterly extraordinary, and it's just a matter of finding one which suits your tastes and budget.

While eating out is a pleasure in the big cities, in many smaller country towns it can be something of an ordeal. The food will be predictable and unexciting, and is usually of the 'meat and three veg' variety.

All over Australia, but particularly in Melbourne, you'll find restaurants advertising that they're BYO. This stands for 'Bring Your Own' and means they're not licensed to serve alcohol but you are permitted to bring your own. This is a real boon to wine-loving but budget-minded travellers because you can buy a bottle from the local bottle shop or from that winery you visited last week and not pay any mark-up. Most restaurants have only a small 'corkage' charge (typically $1 to $1.50 per person) if you bring your own.

Pubs Most pubs serve two types of meals: bistro meals, which are usually in the $10 to $15 range and are served in the dining room or lounge bar, where there's usually a self-serve salad bar; and bar (or counter) meals which are filling, simple, no-frills afairs eaten in the public bar; these usually cost less than $10, and sometimes as little as $4.

The quality of pub food varies enormously, and while it's usually fairly basic and unimaginative, it's generally pretty good value. The usual meal times are from noon to 2 pm and 6 to 8 pm.

Markets Where the climate allows there are often outdoor food stalls and markets, and these can be an excellent place to sample a variety of cuisines, with Asian being the most popular. Darwin's Thursday evening Mindil Beach market is probably the largest of its type in the country, and the range of cuisines is very impressive.

DRINKS
Beer
Australian beer will be fairly familiar to North Americans; it's also similar to what's known as lager in the UK. It may taste like lemonade to the European real-ale addict, but it packs quite a punch. It is invariably chilled before drinking.

Fosters is the best-known international brand with a worldwide reputation, but there's a bewildering array of Australian beers. Among the most well-known are XXXX (pronounced 'four-ex'), Tooheys Red, Fosters, Carlton Draught and VB (Victoria Bitter). Recent additions to the stable of old favourites include lower alcohol beers such as Fosters Light Ice, and styles other

than your average Aussie lager, such as Blue Bock and Old Black Ale, both made by Tooheys.

The smaller breweries generally seem to produce better beer – Cascade (Tasmania) and Coopers (South Australia) being two examples. Coopers also produces a stout, popular among connoisseurs, and their Black Crow is a delicious malty, dark beer.

Small 'boutique' beers have become very popular so you'll find one-off brands scattered around the country. Beers such as Redback, Dogbolter and Eumundi, while being more expensive than the big commercial brands, are definitely worth a try. For the homesick European, there are a few pubs in the major cities that brew their own bitter. Guinness is occasionally found on draught.

Standard beer generally contains around 4.9% alcohol, although the trend in recent years has been towards low-alcohol beers, with an alcohol content of between 2% and 3.5%. Tooheys Blue is a particularly popular light beer. And a warning: people who drive under the influence of alcohol and get caught lose their licences (unfortunately, drink-driving is a real problem in Australia). The maximum permissible blood-alcohol concentration level for drivers in most parts of Australia is 0.05%.

While Australians are generally considered to be heavy beer drinkers, per capita beer consumption has fallen quite considerably in recent years. In the past decade per capita consumption has decreased by 20%.

Wine
If you don't fancy Australian beer, then turn to wines. Australia has a great climate for wine producing and Australian wine is rapidly gaining international recognition – it's also one of our fastest-growing exports.

The best-known wine-growing regions are the Hunter Valley of New South Wales and the Barossa Valley of South Australia, but there are plenty of other areas too. In Victoria the main region is the Rutherglen/Milawa area of the north-east, but there's also the Yarra Valley (where the French company, Moët et Chandon, makes top-quality

A Beer, By Any Other Name ...

All around Australia, beer, the containers it comes in, and the receptacles you drink it from are called by different names. The standard bottle is 750ml, and costs around $2. Cans (or tinnies) hold 375ml and come in cartons of 24, known as a slab, and these cost around $20, although you can of course buy them singly.

Half-size bottles with twist-top caps are known as stubbies (echoes in South Australia), except in the Northern Territory where a stubby is also a 1.25 litre bottle, although these are not in everyday use and are really only a novelty souvenir. Low-alcohol beer is marginally cheaper than full-strength beer. Boutique beers generally only come in stubbies, and are significantly more expensive than your average common or garden variety.

Ordering at the bar can be an intimidating business for the uninitiated. Beer by the glass basically comes in three sizes – 200, 285 and 425ml – but knowing what to ask for when the barman/maid queries you with an eloquent 'Yeah, mate?' is not quite so simple. A 200ml (seven oz) beer is a 'glass' (Vic and Qld), a 'butcher' (SA) or a 'beer' (WA or NSW). Tasmanians like to be different, and so there they have a six oz glass. A 285ml (10 oz) beer is a 'pot' (Vic and Qld), a 'schooner' (SA), a 'handle' (NT), a 'middie' (NSW and WA) or a '10 ounce' (Tasmania – they're very original down there!). Lastly, there's the 425ml (15 oz) glass, which is a 'schooner' (NSW and NT) or a 'pint' (SA). ∎

sparkling wines), the Mornington Peninsula and the Geelong area, all within easy reach of Melbourne. South Australia also has the beautifully picturesque Clare Valley, and the Coonawarra area south of Adelaide. In Western Australia increasingly sophisticated wines are being produced in the Margaret River area, and there's even a winery in Alice Springs in the Northern Territory.

Australia's wines are cheap and readily available. For $10 you can get a perfectly acceptable bottle of wine which you could happily take to someone's place without having to hide the label; $20 gets you something very good indeed.

It takes a little while to become familiar with Australian wineries and their styles but it's an effort worth making. The best – and most enjoyable – way to do this is to get out to the wineries and sample the wine at the cellar door. Most wineries have tastings: you just zip straight in and say what you'd like to try. However, free wine tastings do not mean open slather drinking – the glasses are generally thimble-sized and it's expected that you will buy something if, for example, you taste every Chardonnay that vineyard has ever produced. Many wineries, particularly in the main areas, have decided that enough is enough and now have a small 'tasting fee' of a couple of dollars, refundable if you buy.

Each wine-growing area is generally renowned for a particular style of wine, although there's much more experimentation and blending of grapes these days. The Hunter Valley is famous for its whites, especially Chardonnay, the Clare Valley and Coonawarra regions produces excellent reds and fortified wines, and the Rutherglen region of Victoria is great for port and Muscat.

Other Alcoholic Drinks

So-called 'designer drinks' (or 'alcopops') are all the rage in the hip cafes and bars. Two Dogs Lemonade, an alcoholic lemonade, was the first on the scene in what was thought to be a novelty part of the market. This was followed by the phenomenally popular Sub Zero, a basically tasteless alcoholic soda which, when mixed with the obligatory dash of raspberry cordial, is *de rigueur*.

Other alcoholic oddities include Strongbow White, a cider with a real kick; Stolichnaya Lemon Ruski (vodka and lemon soda); a shandy (half beer, half lemonade) called Razorback Draught; XLR8, an alcoholic cola; Finlandia Vodka Pulp, Cactus, and Rhubarb Rhubarb.

Nonalcoholic Drinks

Australians knock back Coke and flavoured

milk like there's no tomorrow and also have some excellent mineral water brands. Coffee enthusiasts will be relieved to find good Italian cafes serving cappuccino, caffe latte and other coffees, often into the wee small hours and beyond.

ENTERTAINMENT
Cinema
In main cities there are commercial cinema chains, such as Village, Hoyts and Greater Union, usually in two to 10-screen complexes. Smaller towns have just the one cinema, and many of these are almost museum pieces in themselves. Seeing a new-release mainstream film costs around $14 ($8 for children under 15) in the big cities, less in country areas and less on certain nights at the bigger cinema chains.

Also in the cities you'll find art-house and independent cinemas, and these places generally screen either films that aren't made for mass consumption or specialise purely in re-runs of classics and cult movies. Cinemas such as the Kino and Astor in Melbourne, the Valhalla and Paddington Academy Twin in Sydney, the Chelsea in Adelaide and the Astor in Perth all fall into this category.

Discos & Nightclubs
Yep, no shortage of these either, but they are confined to the larger cities and towns. Clubs range from the exclusive 'members only' variety to barn-sized discos where anyone who wants to spend the money is welcomed with open arms. Admission charges range from around $6 to $12.

Some places have certain dress standards, but it is generally left to the discretion of the people at the door – if they don't like the look of you, bad luck. The more 'upmarket' nightclubs attract an older, more sophisticated and affluent crowd, and generally have stricter dress codes, smarter décor – and higher prices.

Live Music
Many suburban pubs have live music, and these are often great places for catching bands, either nationally well-known names

or up-and-coming performers trying to make a name for themselves – most of Australia's popular bands started out on the pub circuit.

The best way to find out about the local scene is to get to know some locals, or travellers who have spent some time in the place. Otherwise, there are often comprehensive listings in newspapers, particularly on Friday. Free street papers are also good places to look – check out *Drum Media*, *Beat* and *3D World* in Sydney; *Son of Barfly* in Cairns; *Beat* and *Inpress* in Melbourne; *Xpress* in Perth; *Time Off*, *Rave* and *The Scene* in Brisbane and *Pulse* in Darwin.

SPECTATOR SPORTS
If you're an armchair – or wooden bench – sports fan, Australia has plenty to offer. Australians play at least four types of football, each type being called 'football' by its aficionados. The seasons run from about March to September.

Aussie Rules (Footy)
Aussie Rules is unique – only Gaelic football is anything like it. It's played by teams of 18 on an oval field with an oval ball that can be kicked, caught, hit with the hand or carried and bounced. You get six points for kicking the ball between two central posts (a goal) and one point for kicking it through side posts (a behind). A game lasts for four quarters of 25 minutes each. To take a 'mark' players must catch a ball on the volley from a kick – in which case they then receive a free kick. A typical final score for one team is between 70 and 110.

Players cannot be sent off in the course of a game; disciplinary tribunals are usually held the following week. Consequently there can be spectacular brawls on field – while the crowds, in contrast, are noisy but remarkably peaceful (a pleasant surprise for visiting soccer fans).

Melbourne is the national (and world) centre for Australian Rules, and the Australian Football League (AFL) is the national competition. Nine of its 16 teams are from Melbourne; the others are from Geelong, Perth, Fremantle, Sydney, Brisbane, and

Adelaide (two teams), which is also a stronghold of Aussie Rules. But it's nowhere near as big-time there as it is in Melbourne, where crowds regularly exceed 30,000 at top regular games and 80,000 at finals.

The top eight sides compete in the finals in September, and the season culminates with the AFL Grand Final on the last Saturday in September.

Australian Rules is a great game to get to know. Fast, tactical, skilful, rough and athletic, it can produce gripping finishes when even after 80 minutes of play the outcome hangs on the very last kick. It also inspires fierce spectator loyalties and has made otherwise obscure Melbourne suburbs (such as Hawthorn, Essendon, Collingwood, St Kilda etc) national names.

Soccer

Soccer is a bit of a poor cousin: it's widely played on an amateur basis but the national league is only semiprofessional and attracts a pathetically small following. It's slowly gaining popularity thanks in part to the success of the national team. At the local level, there are ethnically based teams representing a wide range of origins.

Rugby

Rugby is the main game in New South Wales and Queensland, and it's rugby league, the 13-a-side version, that attracts the crowds. The Australian Rugby League (ARL) was the original competition, but recently Rupert Murdoch has split the game with the introduction of his Super League competition, luring away many ARL players with lucrative contracts. Many fans were so disgusted they have simply given up following the game.

The ARL (which has financial backing from Australia's other major media player, Kerry Packer), has six Sydney teams, two from elsewhere in NSW and two from Queensland. In the Super League competition there are three Sydney teams, two from Queensland and one each from country NSW, the ACT, South Australia, Victoria and New Zealand.

A rapprochement between the two sides (ARL and Super League) was announced in late 1997, which proposed a combined 20-team league in 1998, dropping to 14 teams by 2000.

Rugby union, the 15-a-side game originally for amateurs but now professional, also has a growing following.

Cricket

During the other (nonfootball) half of the year there's cricket. The Melbourne Cricket Ground (MCG) is the world's biggest, and international Test and one-day matches are played every summer there and in Sydney, Adelaide, Perth, Brisbane and Hobart. There is also an interstate competition (the poorly attended Sheffield Shield) and state-wide district cricket.

Basketball & Hockey

Basketball too is growing in popularity and there is a national league, the NBL. Australia's women's netball team won the world cup in 1995, and Australia also has world-class hockey teams (both men and women).

Horse Racing

Australians love a gamble, and hardly any town of even minor import is without a horse-racing track or a Totalisator Agency Board (TAB) betting office or pub. Melbourne and Adelaide must be amongst the only cities in the world to give a public holiday for horse races. The prestigious Melbourne Cup is held on the first Tuesday in November.

Motor Sports

The Australian Formula One Grand Prix is held in Melbourne each March, and the Australian round of the World 500cc Motorcycle Grand Prix is held at Phillip Island in Victoria annually in October.

Other major events are the Bathurst 1000 held at the Mt Panorama circuit in NSW every October, the Targa Tasmania race in April, and the Finke Desert Race in central Australia (June).

Other Sports

The grand slam tennis event, the Australian Open, is played in Melbourne in January.

Surfing competitions, such as that held each year at Bell's Beach, Victoria, are world-class.

Booking & Tickets

Tickets for most major events in each state, including concerts, are handled by one or two central booking agencies in that state.

ACT Ticketek	☎ (02) 6248 7666
NSW Ticketek	☎ (02) 9266 4848
First Call (NSW)	☎ (02) 9320 9000
Qld Ticketek	☎ (07) 3223 0444
Bass Adelaide	☎ (08) 8400 2205
Tas Centretainment	☎ (03) 6231 0303
VicTicketmaster Bass	☎ 1800 338 998
Ticketek (Vic)	☎ 1800 062 849
WA BOCS Ticketing	☎ 1800 193 300
Red Ticket (WA)	☎ 1800 199 991

THINGS TO BUY

There are lots of things definitely not to buy – like plastic boomerangs, fake Aboriginal ashtrays and T-shirts, and all the other terrible souvenirs which fill the tacky souvenir shops in the big cities. Most of them come from Taiwan or Korea anyway. Before buying an Australian souvenir, turn it over to check that it was actually made here.

Australiana

The term 'Australiana' is a euphemism for all those things you buy as gifts for all the friends, aunts and uncles, nieces and nephews, and other sundry bods back home. They are supposedly representative of Australia and its culture, although many are extremely dubious as such.

The seeds of many native plants are on sale all over the place. Try growing kangaroo paws back home (if your own country will allow them in).

For those last-minute gifts, drop into a deli. Australian wines are well known overseas, but why not try honey (leatherwood honey is one of a number of powerful local varieties), macadamia nuts (native to Queensland) or Bundaberg rum with its unusual sweet flavour.

Also gaining popularity are 'bush tucker' items such as tinned witchetty grubs, or honey ants.

Opals

The opal is Australia's national gemstone, and opals and jewellery made with it are popular souvenirs. It's a beautiful stone, but buy wisely and shop around – quality and prices can vary widely from place to place.

Aboriginal Art

Aboriginal art has been 'discovered' by the international community, and prices are correspondingly high.

For most people the only thing remotely affordable are small carvings and some very beautiful screen-printed T-shirts produced by Aboriginal craft cooperatives. Didjeridus and boomerangs are also popular purchases, but just be aware that unless you pay top dollar, what you are getting is something made purely for the tourist trade – these are certainly not the real thing.

See the following Aboriginal Art section for more information on buying Aboriginal art and artefacts.

Aboriginal Art

Art has always been an integral part of Aboriginal life, a connection between past and present, between the supernatural and the earthly, between people and the land. The initial forms of artistic expression were rock carvings, body painting and ground designs, and the earliest engraved designs known to exist date back at least 30,000 years.

Aboriginal art has undergone a major revival in the last decade or so, with artists throughout the country finding a means to express and preserve ancient Dreaming values, and a way to share this rich cultural heritage with the wider community.

While the so-called dot paintings of the central deserts are among the more readily identifiable and probably most popular form of contemporary Aboriginal art, there's a huge range of material being produced – bark paintings from Arnhem Land, wood carving and silk-screen printing from the Tiwi Islands north of Darwin, batik printing and wood carving from central Australia, dijeridus and more.

*Title Page: **Devil Devil Man** by Djambu Barra Barra; acrylic on canvas; 1997; Ngukurr, NT; represented by Alcaston House Gallery, Melbourne*

Below: Ewaniga rock engravings, south of Alice Springs; courtesy of the NT Tourist Commission

Art & the Dreaming

All early Aboriginal art was based on the various peoples' ancestral Dreaming – the 'Creation', when the earth's physical features were formed by the struggles between powerful supernatural ancestors such as the Rainbow Serpent, the Lightning Men and the Wandjina. Codes of behaviour were also laid down in the Dreaming, and although these laws have been diluted and adapted in the last 200 years, they still provide the basis for today's Aborigines. Ceremonies, rituals and sacred paintings are all based on the Dreaming.

A Dreaming can relate to a person, an animal or a physical feature, while others are more general, relating to a region, a group of people, or natural forces such as floods and wind. Australia is covered by a vast network of Dreamings, and any one person may have connections to several. ■

Rock Art

Arnhem Land

Arnhem Land, in Australia's tropical Top End, is possibly the area with the richest artistic heritage. Recent finds suggest that rock paintings were being made as early as 60,000 years ago, and some of the rock art galleries in the huge sandstone Arnhem Land plateau are at least 18,000 years old.

The art of Arnhem Land is vastly different from that of the central deserts. Here, Dreaming stories are depicted far more literally, with easily recognisable (though often stylised) images of ancestors, animals, and even Macassans – early Indonesian mariners who regularly visited the north coast long before Europeans arrived.

The paintings contained in the Arnhem Land rock art sites range from hand prints to paintings of animals, people, mythological beings and European ships, constituting one of the world's most important and fascinating rock art collections. They provide a record of changing environments and lifestyles over the millennia.

In some places they are concentrated in large galleries, with paintings from more recent eras sometimes superimposed over older paintings. Some sites are kept secret – not only to protect them from damage, but also because they are private or sacred to the Aboriginal owners. Some

Hollow-Log Coffins

Hollowed-out logs were often used for reburial ceremonies in Arnhem Land, and were also a major form of artistic expression. They were highly decorated, often with many of the Dreaming themes, and were known as *dupun* in eastern Arnhem Land and *lorrkon* in western Arnhem Land.

In 1988 a group of Arnhem Land artists made a memorial as their contribution to the movement highlighting injustices against Aborigines – this was, of course, the year when non-Aboriginal Australians were celebrating 200 years of European settlement. The artists painted 200 log coffins – one for each year of settlement – with traditional clan and Dreaming designs, and these now form a permanent display in the National Gallery in Canberra.

are believed to be inhabited by dangerous beings, who must not be approached by the ignorant. However, two of the finest sites have been opened up to visitors, with access roads, walkways and explanatory signs. These are Ubirr and Nourlangie in Kakadu National Park.

The rock paintings show how the main styles succeeded each other over time. The earliest hand or grass prints were followed by a 'naturalistic' style, with large outlines of people or animals filled in with colour. Some of the animals depicted, such as the thylacine (Tasmanian tiger), have long been extinct on mainland Australia.

After the naturalistic style came the 'dynamic', in which motion was often cleverly depicted (a dotted line, for example, to show a spear's path through the air). In this era the first mythological beings appeared, with human bodies and animal heads.

The next style mainly showed simple human silhouettes, and was followed by the curious 'yam figures', in which people and animals were drawn in the shape of yams (or yams in the shape of people and animals!). Many fish were depicted in the art of this period, and the so-called 'x-ray' style, which showed the creatures' bones and internal organs, made its appearance.

Below: Rock paintings, Nourlangie Rock, Kakadu National Park; courtesy of the NT Tourist Commission

By about 1000 years ago many of the salt marshes had turned into freshwater swamps and billabongs. The birds and plants which provided new food sources in this landscape appeared in the art of this time.

From around 400 years ago, Aboriginal artists also depicted the human newcomers to the region – Macassan fisherpeople and, more recently, the Europeans – and the things they brought, or their modes of transport such as ships or horses.

The Kimberley

The art of the Kimberley is most famous for its images of the Wandjina, a group of ancestor beings who came from the sky and sea and were associated with fertility. They controlled the elements and were responsible for the formation of the country's natural features.

Wandjina images are found painted on rock as well as on more recent portable art media, with some of the rock images being more than 6m long. They generally appear in human form, with large black eyes, a nose but no mouth, a halo around the head (representative of both hair and clouds), and a black oval shape on the chest.

North Queensland

In North Queensland rock art again predominates. The superb Quinkan galleries at Laura on the Cape York Peninsula, north-west of Cairns, are among the best known in the country. Among the many creatures depicted on the walls, the main ones are the Quinkan spirits, which are shown in two forms – the long and stick-like Timara, and the crocodile-like Imjim with their knobbed, club-like tails.

Local Aboriginal people run tours of the Quinkan rock art sites; for further information call ☎ 1800 633933.

Quinkan rock art, Laura, far north Queensland; photograph reproduced with the permission of the Aboriginal community of the Quinkan district, Cape York Peninsula

Painting

Western Desert Painting

The current renaissance in Aboriginal painting began in the early 1970s at Papunya ('honey ant place'), at the time a small, depressed community 240km north-west of Alice Springs, which had grown out of the government's 'assimilation' policy. Here the local children were given the task of painting a traditional-style mural on the school wall. The elders took interest in the project, and although the public display of traditional images gave rise to much debate among the elders, they eventually participated and in fact completed the *Honey Ant Dreaming* mural. This was the first time that images which were originally confined to rock and body art came to be reproduced in a different medium.

Other murals followed this first one, and the desire to paint spread through the community. In the early stages paintings were produced on small boards on the ground or balanced on the artist's knee, but this soon gave way to painted canvasses and acrylic paints. Canvas was an ideal medium as it could be easily rolled and transported, yet large paintings were possible. With the growing importance of art, both as an economic and a cultural activity, an association was formed to help the artists sell their work. The Papunya Tula company in Alice Springs is still one of the relatively few galleries in central Australia to be owned and run by Aboriginal people.

Painting in central Australia has flourished to such a degree that it is now an important educational activity for children, through which they can learn different aspects of religious and ceremonial knowledge. This

Possum Dreaming by Eunice Woods; acrylic on canvas; 100cm x 102cm; 1997; Kaltjiti Crafts, Fregon; courtesy of DESART

Possum, Snake, Potato Dreaming by Paddy Japaljarri Sims and Bessie Nakamarra Sims; acrylic on linen; 91 x 153cm; 1992; Warlukurlangu Artists Association, Yuendumu, NT; courtesy of DESART

is especially true now that women are so much a part of the painting movement.

Dot-painting partly evolved from 'ground paintings', which formed the centrepiece of dances and songs. These were made from pulped plant material, and the designs were made on the ground using dots of this mush. Dots were also used to outline objects in rock paintings, and to highlight geographical features or vegetation.

While dot paintings may look random and abstract, they usually depict a Dreaming journey, and so can be seen almost as aerial landscape maps. Many paintings feature the tracks of birds, animals and humans, often identifying the ancestor. Subjects are often depicted by the imprint they leave in the sand – a simple arc depicts a person (as that is the print left by someone sitting), a *coolamon* (wooden carrying dish) is shown by an oval shape, a digging stick by a single line, a camp fire by a circle. Males or females are identified by the objects associated with them – digging sticks and coolamons for women, spears and boomerangs for

Kadaitja Man by Ronnie Tjampitjinpa; acrylic on linen; 122 x 61cm; 1993; Papunya Tula Artists Pty Ltd, Alice Springs, NT; courtesy of DESART

Albert Namatjira

Australia's most well-known Aboriginal artist was probably Albert Namatjira (1902-59). He lived at the Hermannsburg Lutheran Mission, about 130km west of Alice Springs, and was introduced to European-style watercolour painting by a non-Aboriginal artist, Rex Batterbee, in the 1930s.

Namatjira successfully captured the essence of the Centre using a heavily European-influenced style. At the time his paintings were seen purely as picturesque landscapes. These days, however, it is thought he chose his subjects carefully, as they were Dreaming landscapes to which he had a great bond.

Namatjira supported many of his people on the income from his work, as was his obligation under tribal law. Because of his fame he was allowed to buy alcohol at a time when this was otherwise illegal for Aborigines. In 1957 he was the first Aborigine to be granted Australian citizenship, but in 1958 he was jailed for six months for supplying alcohol to Aborigines. He died the following year aged only 57.

Although Namatjira died very disenchanted with white society, he did much to change the extremely negative views of Aborigines which prevailed at the time. At the same time he paved the way for the Papunya painting movement which emerged just over a decade after his death.

men. Concentric circles usually depict Dreaming sites, or places where ancestors paused in their journeys.

While these symbols are widely used, their meaning within each individual painting is known only by the artist and the people closely associated with him or her – either by group or by the Dreaming – and different groups apply different interpretations to each painting. So sacred stories can be publicly portrayed, as the deeper meaning is not evident to most viewers.

The colours used in dot paintings from central Australia include reds, blues and purples which may seem overly vivid but which can be seen in the outback landscape.

Bark Paintings

While bark painting is a more recent art form, it is still an important part of the cultural heritage of Arnhem Land Aboriginal people. It's difficult to establish when bark was first used, partly because it is perishable and old pieces simply don't exist. European visitors in the early 19th century noted the practice of painting the inside walls of bark shelters.

The bark used is from the stringybark tree (*Eucalyptus tetradonta*), and it is taken off the tree in the wet season when it is moist and supple. The rough outer layers are removed and the bark is dried by placing it over a fire and then under weights on the ground to keep it flat. In a couple of weeks the bark is dry and ready for use. A typical bark painting made today has sticks across the top and bottom of the sheet to keep it flat.

The pigments used in bark paintings are mainly red and yellow (ochres), white (kaolin) and black (charcoal). The colours were gathered from special sites by the traditional owners, and they were then traded. Even today these natural pigments are used, giving the paintings their superb soft and earthy finish. Binding agents such as birds' egg yolks, wax and plant resins were added to the pigments. Recently these have been replaced by synthetic agents such as wood glue. Similarly, the brushes used in the past were obtained from the bush materials at hand – twigs, leaf fibres, feathers, human hair and the like – but these too have largely been replaced by modern brushes.

One of the main features of Arnhem Land bark paintings is the use of

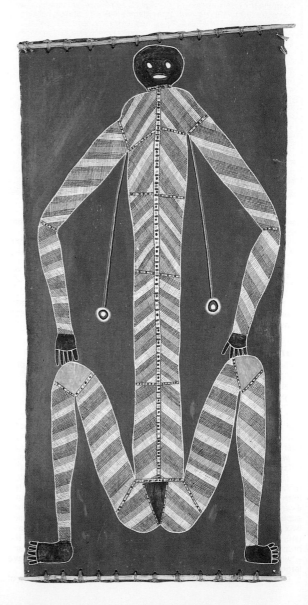

Namarrkon, Lightning Spirit by Curly Bardagubu, c. 1931-87, Born clan; Kunwinjku language, Namokardabu, western Arnhem Land; earth pigments on bark; 156 x 75cm; 1987; purchased through the Art Foundation of Victoria with assistance from Alcoa of Australia Limited, Governor 1990; National Gallery of Victoria

Kumoken (Freshwater Crocodile) with Mimi Spirits by Djawida, b.c. 1935, Yulkman clan; Kunwinjku language, Kurrudjmuh, western Arnhem Land; earth pigments on bark; 151 x 71cm; 1990; purchased 1990; National Gallery of Victoria

Tiwi Island Art

Due to their isolation, the Aborigines of the Tiwi Islands (Bathurst and Melville islands, off the coast of Darwin) have developed art forms – mainly sculpture – not found anywhere else, although there are some similarities with the art of Arnhem Land.

The *pukumani* burial rites are one of the main rituals of Tiwi religious life, and it is for these ceremonies that many of the art works are created – *yimwalini* (bark baskets), spears and *tutini* (burial poles). These carved and painted ironwood poles, up to 2.5m long, are placed around the grave, and represent features of the deceased person's life.

In the last 50 or so years the Tiwi islanders have been producing sculptured animals and birds, many of these being Creation ancestors (the Darwin Museum of Arts & Sciences has an excellent display). More recently, bark painting and silk-screen printing have become popular, and there are workshops on both islands where these items are produced. ■

cross-hatching designs. These designs identify the particular clans, and are based on body paintings of the past. The paintings can also be broadly categorised by their regional styles. In the west the tendency is towards naturalistic images and plain backgrounds, while to the east the use of geometric designs is more common.

The art reflects Dreaming themes that vary by region. In eastern Arnhem Land the prominent ancestor beings are the Djangkawu, who travelled the land with elaborate *dilly* bags (carry bags) and digging sticks (for making waterholes), and the Wagilag Sisters, who are associated with snakes and waterholes. In western Arnhem Land the Rainbow Serpent, Yingarna, is the significant being (according to some clans), but one of her offspring, Ngalyod, and Nawura are also important. The *mimi* spirits are another feature of western Arnhem Land art, both on bark and rock. These mischievous spirits are attributed with having taught the Aborigines of the region many things, including hunting, food gathering and painting skills.

Contemporary Painting

Ngukurr Since the late 1980s the artists of Ngukurr ('nook-or'), near Roper Bar in south-eastern Arnhem Land, have been producing works using acrylic paints on canvas. Although ancestral beings still feature prominently, the works are generally much more modern, with free-flowing forms and often little in common with traditional formal structure.

The Kimberley Contemporary art in the eastern Kimberley also features elements of the works of the desert peoples of central Australia, a legacy of the forced relocation of people during the 1970s. The community of Warmun at Turkey Creek on the Great Northern Highway has been particularly active in ensuring that Aboriginal culture through painting and dance remains strong.

Facing page: Pukamani funerary poles and bark baskets installation; Milikapiti, Melville Island, NT; represented by Alcaston House Gallery, Melbourne

Urban Art While traditional works by rural artists have a higher profile, city-based Aboriginal people also produce some important work. Much of this work has strong European influences and it was once regarded as an inauthentic form of Aboriginal art, but this view has changed.

A major impetus in the development of urban art was the Aboriginal land rights movement, which started to gain momentum in the 1970s. Images depicting the dispossession of the Aborigines and the racist

treatment they had received became powerful symbols in their struggle for equality.

Although much of the work being produced still carries strong political and social comment, these days the range has become broader.

Artefacts & Crafts

Objects traditionally made for practical or ceremonial uses, such as weapons and musical instruments, often featured intricate and symbolic decoration. In recent years many communities have also developed non-traditional craft forms that have created employment and income, and the growing tourist trade has seen demand and production increase steadily.

Dijeridus

*Top: **Pelican Story** by Amy Jirwulurr Johnson; acrylic on canvas; 185 x 175cm; 1994; Ngukurr, NT; represented by Alcaston House Gallery, Melbourne*

Above & right: Dijeridu by Djambu Barra Barra; private collection; Ngukurr, NT; represented by Alcaston House Gallery, Melbourne

The most widespread craft items seen for sale these days are dijeridus. There has been a phenomenal boom in popularity and they can be found in shops around the country.

Originally they were used as ceremonial musical instruments by Aboriginal people in Arnhem Land (where they are known as *yidaki*). The traditional instrument was made from particular eucalypt branches which had been hollowed out by termites. The tubes were often fitted with a wax mouthpiece made from sugarbag (native honey bee wax) and decorated with traditional designs.

Although they may look pretty, most dijeridus made these days bear little relation to traditional ones: they may be made from the wrong or inferior wood, have been hollowed out using mechanical or other means, have poor sound quality, and most have never had an Aboriginal person anywhere near them! (See Buying Aboriginal Art & Artefacts, below.)

Boomerangs

Boomerangs are curved wooden throwing sticks used for hunting and also as ceremonial clapping sticks. Contrary to popular belief, not all boomerangs are designed to return when thrown – the idea is to hit the animal being hunted! Returning boomerangs were mostly used in south-eastern and western Australia. Although they all follow the same fundamental design, boomerangs come in a huge range of shapes, sizes and decorative styles, and are made from a number of different wood types.

Wooden Sculptures

Traditionally most wooden sculptures were made to be used for particular ceremonies and then discarded. Arnhem Land artists still produce soft-wood carvings of birds, fish, animals and ancestral beings, which were originally used for ceremonial purposes. The lightweight figures are engraved and painted with intricate symbolic designs.

Early in this century, missionaries encouraged some communities and groups to produce wooden sculptures for sale.

Scorched Carvings

Also very popular are the wooden carvings which have designs scorched into them with hot fencing wire. These range from small figures, such as possums, up to quite large snakes and lizards, although none of them have any Dreaming significance. In central Australia one of the main outlets for these is the Maruku Arts & Crafts centre at the Uluru-Kata Tjuta National Park Cultural Centre, where it's possible to see the crafts

Below: Decorative central Australian scorched carvings made from river red gum root; Maraku Arts & Crafts; Uluru (Ayers Rock), NT; courtesy of DESART

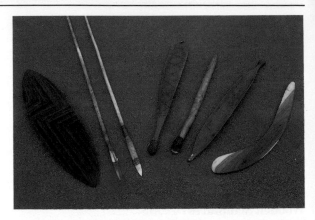

being made. Although much of the artwork is usually done by women, men are also involved at the Maruku centre. The Mt Ebenezer Roadhouse, on the Lasseter Highway (the main route to Uluru), is another Aboriginal-owned enterprise and one of the cheapest places for buying sculpted figures.

Ceremonial Shields

Around the country many types of weapons were traditionally produced, including spears, spear-throwers (*woomeras*), clubs (*nulla nullas*) and shields. The shields were made from timber or bark in different shapes and sizes, and were often richly decorated with carved and painted surfaces showing the owner's ancestry or Dreaming. They were mainly used for ceremonial purposes, but they were also put to practical use when fighting between clans occurred.

Fibre Craft

Articles made from fibres are a major art form among women. String or twine was traditionally made from bark, grass, leaves, roots and other materials, hand-spun and dyed with natural pigments, then woven to make dilly bags, baskets, garments, fishing nets and other items. Strands or fibres from the leaves of the pandanus palm (and other palms or grasses) were also woven to make dilly bags and mats. While all these objects have utilitarian purposes, many also have ritual uses.

Textiles

The women of Utopia, 260km north-east of Alice Springs, have become known in recent years for their production of batik material. In the mid-1970s the Anmatyerre and Alyawarre people started to reoccupy their traditional lands around Utopia cattle station, and this was given a formal basis in 1979 when they were granted title to the station. A number of scattered outstations, rather than a central settlement, were set up, and around this time the women were introduced to batik as part of a self-help program. The art form flourished and Utopia Women's Batik Group was formed in 1978 (the group was later incorporated and is now called Utopia Awely Batik Utopia Women's Centre Aboriginal Corporation, trading as Utopia Silks). The brightly coloured silk batiks were based on traditional women's body-painting designs called *awely*, and on images of flora and fauna.

In the late 1980s techniques using acrylic paints on canvas were introduced at Utopia, and Utopian art is now receiving international acclaim.

Other Crafts

The Ernabella Presbyterian Mission in northern South Australia was another place where craftwork was encouraged. A 1950 mission report stated that: 'A mission station must have an industry to provide work for and help finance the cost of caring for the natives'. As the mission had been founded on a sheep station, **wool craft** techniques of spinning, dyeing and weaving were introduced. The Pitjantjatjara ('pigeon-jara') women made woollen articles such as rugs, belts, traditional dilly bags and scarves, using designs incorporating aspects of women's law (*yawilyu*). With the introduction of batik fabric dyeing in the 1970s, weaving at Ernabella virtually ceased.

The Arrernte people from Hermannsburg have recently begun to work with **pottery**, a craft which is not traditionally Aboriginal. They have incorporated moulded figures and surface treatments adapted from Dreaming stories.

Bush Tucker and Flowers, silk scarf by Rosemary Petyarre; courtesy of Utopia Cultural Centre and , Utopia Awely Batik Aboriginal Corporation, NT

Another art form from the western Kimberley is the engraved **pearl-shell pendants** which come from the Broome area. It is believed that the Aboriginal people of the area were using pearl shell for decoration before the arrival of Europeans, but with the establishment of the pearling industry in Broome late last century the use of pearl shell increased markedly. The highly prized shells were engraved and used for ceremonial purposes, as well as for personal decoration and trade – examples of this art have been found as far away as Queensland and South Australia.

The designs engraved into the shells were usually fairly simple geometric patterns which had little symbolic importance. The practice of pearl-shell engraving has largely died out, although the decorated shells are still highly valued.

Buying Aboriginal Art & Artefacts

One of the best and most evocative reminders of your trip is an Aboriginal work of art or artefact. By buying *authentic* items you are supporting Aboriginal culture and helping to ensure that traditional skills and designs endure. Unfortunately much of the so-called Aboriginal art sold as souvenirs is either ripped off from Aboriginal people or is just plain fake. Admittedly it is often difficult to tell whether an item is genuine, or whether a design is being used legitimately, but it is worth trying to find out.

The best place to buy artefacts is either directly from the communities which have craft outlets or from galleries and shops which are owned and operated by Aboriginal communities (see the list below for some suggestions). This way you can be sure that the items are genuine and that the money you spend goes to the right people. There are many Aboriginal artists who get paid very small sums for their work, only to find it being sold for thousands in big city galleries.

Below: Detail of hand-painted silk fabric, Kathleen Wallace; 1997; Keringke Arts; Santa Teresa, NT; courtesy of DESART

Dijeridus are the hot item these days, and you need to decide whether you want a decorative piece or an authentic and functional musical instrument. Many of the dijeridus sold are not made by Aboriginal people, and there are even stories of backpackers in Darwin earning good money by making or decorating dijeridus. From a community outlet such as Injalak or Manyallaluk in the Northern Territory you could expect to pay $100 to $200 for a functional dijeridu which has been painted with ochre paints, and you may even get to meet the maker. On the other hand, from a souvenir shop in Darwin or

Cairns you could pay anything from $200 to $400 or more for something which looks pretty but is really little more than a painted bit of wood.

Dot paintings are also very popular, although they tend to be expensive. As with any art, works by lesser known artists are cheaper than big-name works. A dot painting measuring 1 sq m could be as little as $200, but you can be sure it's no masterpiece. Bargains are hard to find and basically it comes down to whether you think you are getting value for money.

Above: A collection of handpainted gumnut necklaces; 1993; Keringke Arts; Santa Teresa, NT; courtesy of DESART

*Left: **My Country** by Elaine Namatjira; terracotta with underglazes; Hermannsburg, NT; represented by Alcaston House Gallery, Melbourne*

Major Aboriginal Craft Outlets

The following are some Aboriginal owned and operated places where you can buy artefacts and crafts:

Alice Springs

Aboriginal Art & Culture Centre

86 Todd St (☎ (08) 8952 3408, email: aborart@ozemail.com.au) – gallery and craft outlet with a good variety of dot paintings and other desert crafts

Papunya Tula Artists

78 Todd St (☎ (08) 8952 4731; fax 8953 2509) – specialising in western desert dot paintings; high prices but good quality

DESART

Suite 1, Heenan Building, Gregory Tce (☎ (08) 8953 4736) – a resource and advocacy organisation representing 22 owner-operated Aboriginal art centres in central Australia

Cairns

Tjapukai Aboriginal Cultural Park

Kamerunga Rd, Smithfield (☎ (07) 4042 9999; fax 4042 9900) – located at the Skyrail terminus in Cairns with a good range of art, craft and fabrics from a variety of sources

Darwin

Raintree Aboriginal Art Gallery

18 Knuckey St (☎ (08) 8981 2732; fax 8981 8333) – one of the major commercial outlets in Darwin, with medium to high prices but top quality paintings and artefacts

Kakadu National Park

Injalak Arts & Crafts

Oenpelli (☎ (08) 8979 0190; fax 8979 0119) – just over the East Alligator River from Ubirr in Kakadu National Park, Injalak has probably the best selection of Top End arts and crafts anywhere; prices are very reasonable and the staff can pack and ship orders (permits required to visit, but easily available on the spot)

Warradjan Aboriginal Cultural Centre

Kakadu National Park (☎ (08) 8979 0051) – high exposure and consequently high prices, but good fabrics, T-shirts and dijeridus

Katherine Region

Manyallaluk Community

PMB 134, Katherine (☎ (08) 8975 4727; fax 8975 4724) – this small community of Top End Aboriginal people, 100km from Katherine, has a small but impressive array of artefacts including dijeridus and bark paintings, and some of the best prices you'll come across anywhere

Uluru National Park

Maruku Arts & Crafts

Uluru-Kata Tjuta Cultural Centre (☎ (08) 8956 2153; fax 8956 2410) – good for artefacts, especially scorched wood carvings, and craftspeople usually work on the site.

Getting There & Away

AIR

Getting to Australia basically means flying and Australia is a long way from anywhere. Coming from Asia, Europe or North America there are lots of competing airlines and a wide variety of air fares, but there's no way you can avoid those great distances. Australia's current international popularity adds another problem – flights are often heavily booked. If you want to fly to Australia at a particularly popular time of year (the middle of summer, ie Christmas time, is notoriously difficult) or on a particularly popular route (like Hong Kong or Singapore to Sydney or Melbourne) then you need to plan well ahead.

Australia has a large number of international gateways. Sydney and Melbourne are the two busiest. Perth also gets many flights from Asia and Europe and has direct flights to New Zealand and Africa. Other international airports include Hobart in Tasmania (New Zealand only), Adelaide, Port Hedland (Bali only), Darwin, Cairns and Brisbane. One place you can't arrive at directly from overseas is Canberra, the national capital.

Although Sydney is the busiest gateway it makes a lot of sense to avoid arriving or departing there. Sydney's airport is stretched way beyond its capacity and flights are frequently delayed on arrival and departure. Even if you can organise your flights to avoid Sydney, unfortunately many intercity flights (Melbourne in particular) still go via Sydney. If you're planning to explore Australia seriously then starting at a quieter entry port like Cairns, in far north Queensland, or Darwin, in the Northern Territory, is worth considering.

Tickets

Discount Tickets Buying airline tickets these days is like shopping for a car, a stereo or a camera – five different travel agents will quote you five different prices. Rule number one if you're looking for a cheap ticket is to go to an agent, not directly to the airline. The airline can usually only quote you the absolutely by-the-rule-book regular fare. An agent, on the other hand, can offer all sorts of special deals, particularly on competitive routes.

Ideally, an airline would like to fly all its flights with every seat in use and every passenger paying the highest fare possible. Fortunately, life usually isn't like that and airlines would rather have a half-price passenger than an empty seat. When faced with the problem of too many seats, they will either let agents sell them at cut prices, or occasionally make one-off special offers on particular routes – watch the travel ads in the press.

Of course what's available and what it costs depends on what time of year it is, what route you're flying and who you're flying with. If you're flying on a popular route (like Hong Kong) or one where the choice of flights is very limited (like South America or, to a lesser extent, Africa) then the fare is likely to be higher or there may be nothing available but the official fare.

Similarly, the dirt-cheap fares are likely to be less conveniently scheduled, go by a less convenient route or be with a less popular airline. Flying London-Sydney, for example, is most convenient with airlines like Qantas, British Airways, Thai International or Singapore Airlines. They have flights every day, they operate the same flight straight through to Australia and they're good, reliable, comfortable, safe airlines. At the other extreme you could fly from London to an Eastern European or Middle Eastern city on one flight, switch to another flight to Asia, and change to another airline from there to Australia. It takes longer, there are delays and changes of aircraft along the way, the airlines may not be so good and furthermore the connection only works once a week and that means leaving London at 1.30 on a Wednesday morning. The flip side is it's cheaper.

Round-the-World Tickets Round-the-World (RTW) tickets are very popular and many of these will take you through Australia. The airline RTW tickets are often real bargains and since Australia is pretty much at the other side of the world from Europe or North America it can work out no more expensive, or even cheaper, to keep going in the same direction right round the world rather than U-turn to return.

The official airline RTW tickets are usually put together by a combination of two

---

Air Travel Glossary

Apex Tickets Apex stands for Advance Purchase Excursion fare. These tickets are usually 30% to 40% cheaper than the full economy fare, but there are restrictions. You must purchase the ticket at least 21 days in advance and must be away for a minimum period (normally 14 days) and return within a maximum period (90 or 180 days). Stopovers are not allowed, and if you have to change your destination or dates of travel there will be extra charges. As well, if you have to cancel your trip, the refund is often considerably less than what you paid for the ticket. Take out travel insurance to cover yourself in case you have to cancel your trip unexpectedly.

Baggage Allowance This will be written on your ticket; you are usually allowed one 20kg item to go in the hold, plus one item of hand luggage. Some airlines which fly trans-Pacific and trans-Atlantic routes allow for two pieces of luggage (there are limits on dimension and weight).

Bucket Shops At certain times of the year and/or on certain routes, many airlines fly with empty seats. As it's more cost-effective for them to fly full, even if that means having to sell a certain number of drastically discounted tickets, the airlines off-load tickets onto bucket shops (UK) or consolidators (USA), travel agents who specialise in discounted fares. The agents, in turn, sell the tickets at reduced prices. These tickets are often the cheapest you'll find, but you can't purchase them directly from the airlines. Availability varies widely, so you'll have to be flexible in your travel plans.

Bucket shop agents advertise in newspapers and magazines and there's a lot of competition – especially in places like Amsterdam and London – so it's a good idea to telephone first to ascertain availability before rushing from shop to shop. You have to be quick off the mark, as by the time you get there the tickets may be sold out.

Bumped Just because you have a confirmed seat doesn't mean you're going to get on the plane – see Overbooking.

Cancellation Penalties If you have to cancel or change an Apex or other discount ticket, there may be heavy penalties. However, insurance can sometimes be taken out against these penalties. Be aware that some airlines impose penalties on regular tickets as well, particularly against 'no show' passengers.

Check In Airlines ask you to check in a certain time before the flight departure (usually two hours on international flights). If you fail to check in on time and the flight is overbooked, the airline can cancel your booking and give your seat to somebody else.

Confirmation Having a ticket written out with the flight and date on it doesn't mean you have a seat until the agent has confirmed with the airline that your status is 'OK'. Prior to this confirmation, your status is 'on request'.

Courier Fares Businesses often need to send urgent documents or freight securely and quickly. They do this through courier companies which hire people to accompany the package through customs and, in return, offer a discount ticket – sometimes a phenomenal bargain. In effect, what the companies do is ship their freight as your luggage on a regular commercial flight. This is perfectly legal, but there are two shortcomings: the short turnaround time of the ticket is usually not longer than a month; and you may be required to surrender all your baggage allowance for the use of the courier company, and be only allowed to take carry-on luggage.

Discounted Tickets There are two types of discounted fares – officially discounted (such as Apex; see Promotional Fares) and unofficially discounted (see Bucket Shops). The latter can save you more than money – you may be able to pay Apex prices without the associated Apex advance booking and other requirements. The lowest prices often impose drawbacks, such as flying with unpopular airlines, inconvenient schedules, or unpleasant routes and connections.

Economy-Class Tickets These tickets are usually not the cheapest way to go, though they do give you maximum flexibility and are valid for 12 months. Most unused tickets are fully refundable, as are unused sectors of a multiple ticket.

Lost Tickets If you lose your ticket, an airline will usually treat it like a travellers' cheque and, after

airlines, and permit you to take a flight anywhere you want on their route systems so long as you do not backtrack. Other restrictions are that you (usually) must book the first sector in advance and cancellation penalties then apply. There may be restrictions on how many stops you are permitted and usually the tickets are valid from 90 days up to a year. A typical price for a South Pacific RTW ticket is around US$2000.

An alternative type of RTW ticket is one put together by a travel agent using a combi-

enquiries, issue a replacement. Legally, however, an airline is entitled to treat it like cash, so if you lose a ticket, it could be forever. Take good care of your tickets.

MCO An MCO (Miscellaneous Charges Order) is a voucher for a value of a given amount, which resembles an airline ticket and can be used to pay for a specific flight with any IATA (International Air Transport Association) airline. MCOs, which are more flexible than a regular ticket, may satisfy the onward ticket requirement, but some countries are now reluctant to accept them. MCOs are fully refundable if unused.

No Shows No shows are passengers who fail to show up for their flight for whatever reason. Full-fare no shows are sometimes entitled to travel on a later flight. The rest of us are penalised (see Cancellation Penalties).

Open Jaw Tickets These are return tickets which allow you to fly to one place but return from another, and travel between the two 'jaws' by any means of transport at your own expense. If available, this can save you backtracking to your arrival point.

Overbooking Airlines hate to fly with empty seats, and since every flight has some passengers who fail to show up (see No Shows), they often book more passengers than they have seats available. Usually the excess passengers balance those who fail to show up, but occasionally somebody gets bumped. If this happens, guess who it is most likely to be? The passengers who check in late.

Reconfirmation You must contact the airline at least 72 hours before departure to 'reconfirm' that you intend to be on the flight. If you don't do this, the airline can delete your name from the passenger list and you could lose your seat.

Restrictions Discounted tickets often have various restrictions on them, such as necessity of advance purchase, limitations on the minimum and maximum period you must be away, restrictions on breaking the journey or changing the booking or route etc.

Round-the-World Tickets These tickets have become very popular in the last few years; basically, there are two types – airline tickets and agent tickets. An airline RTW ticket is issued by two or more airlines that have joined together to market a ticket which takes you around the world on their combined routes. It permits you to fly pretty well anywhere you choose using their combined routes as long as you don't backtrack, ie you must keep moving in approximately the same direction east or west. Other restrictions are that you (usually) must book the first sector in advance and cancellation penalties then apply. There may be restrictions on how many stopovers you are permitted. The RTW tickets are usually valid for 90 days to up to a year.

The agent ticket is a combination of cheap fares strung together by a travel agent. These may be cheaper than airline RTW tickets, but the choice of routes will be limited.

Standby This is a discounted ticket where you only fly if there is a seat free at the last moment. Stand-by fares are usually only available directly at the airport, but sometimes may also be handled by an airline's city office. To give yourself the best possible chance of getting on the flight you want, get there early and have your name placed on the waiting list. It's first come, first served.

Student Discounts Some airlines offer student-card holders 15% to 25% discounts on their tickets. The same often applies to anyone under the age of 26. These discounts are generally only available on ordinary economy-class fares. You wouldn't get one, for instance, on an Apex or an RTW ticket, as these are already discounted.

Transferred Tickets Airline tickets cannot be transferred from one person to another. Travellers sometimes try to sell the return half of their ticket, but officials can ask you to prove that you are the person named on the ticket. This may not be checked on domestic flights, but on international flights, tickets are usually compared with passports.

Travel Periods Some officially discounted fares, Apex fares in particular, vary with the time of year. There is often a low (off-peak) season and a high (peak) season. Sometimes there's an intermediate or shoulder season as well. At peak times both officially and unofficially discounted fares will be higher, or there may simply be no discounted tickets available. Usually the fare depends on your outward flight – if you depart in the high season and return in the low season, you pay the high-season fare. ■

nation of discounted tickets from a number of airlines. A UK agent like Trailfinders can put together interesting London-to-London RTW combinations including Australia for between £799 and £1099.

The UK

The cheapest tickets in London are from the numerous 'bucket shops' (discount ticket agencies) which advertise in magazines and papers such as *Time Out*, *TNT* and *Southern Cross*. Pick up one or two of these publications and ring a few bucket shops to find the best deal. The magazine *Business Traveller* also has good advice on air-fare bargains. Most bucket shops are trustworthy and reliable but the occasional sharp operator appears – *Time Out* and *Business Traveller* give useful advice on precautions to take.

Trailfinders (☎ (0171) 938 3366) at 194 Kensington High St, London W8 7RC, and STA Travel (☎ (0171) 581 4132) at 86 Old Brompton Rd, London SW7 3LQ, and 117 Euston Rd, London NW1 2SX (☎ (0171) 465 0484), are good, reliable agents for cheap tickets.

The cheapest flights from London to Sydney, Melbourne or Adelaide are Britannia Airways charter flights which operate from November through March for an amazing £399 return.

The cheapest bucket-shop (not direct) tickets to both Melbourne and Sydney are about £339/550 one way/return. Cheap fares to Perth are around £309/549 one way/return. Such prices are usually only available if you leave London in the low season (March to June). In September and mid-December fares go up by about 30%, while the rest of the year they're somewhere in between. Average direct high-season fares to Sydney and Melbourne are £554/700 one way/return and for Perth £459/699 one way/return.

From Australia you can expect to pay around A$895/1075 one way/return to London and other European capitals (with stops in Asia on the way) in the low season and A$1399/1870 in the high season.

North America

There is a variety of connections across the Pacific from Los Angeles, San Francisco and Vancouver to Australia, including direct flights, flights via New Zealand, island-hopping routes and more circuitous Pacific rim routes via nations in Asia. Qantas, Air New Zealand and United fly USA-Australia; Qantas, Air New Zealand and Canadian Airlines International fly Canada-Australia. An interesting option from the east coast is Northwest's flight via Japan.

To find good fares to Australia check the travel ads in the Sunday travel sections of papers like the *Los Angeles Times*, *San Francisco Chronicle-Examiner*, *New York Times* or Toronto *Globe & Mail*. You can typically get a one-way/return ticket from the west coast for US$998/1498 in the low season, US$1058/1558 in the high season (Australian summer/Christmas period) or from the east coast for US$1179/1378 one way/return in the low season and US$1609/1878 in the high season. In the USA good agents for discounted tickets are the two student travel operators, Council Travel and STA Travel, both with lots of offices around the country. Canadian west-coast fares out of Vancouver will be similar to those from the US west coast. From Toronto fares go from around C$1790/2200 one way/return during the low season and C$2055/2550 in the high season; from Vancouver they cost C$1370/1610 during low season and C$1790/2110 during high season.

If Pacific island-hopping is your aim, check out the airlines of Pacific island nations, some of which have good deals on indirect routings. Qantas can give you Fiji or Tahiti along the way, while Air New Zealand can offer both and the Cook Islands as well.

One-way/return fares available from Australia include: San Francisco A$1030/1530 low season, A$1030/1830 high season, New York A$1200/1780 low season, A$1200/2080 high season, and Vancouver A$1030/1530 low season A$1030/1830 high season.

New Zealand

Air New Zealand and Qantas operate a

network of trans-Tasman flights linking Auckland, Wellington and Christchurch in New Zealand with most major Australian gateway cities. You can fly directly between a lot of places in New Zealand and a lot of places in Australia.

Fares vary depending on which cities you fly between and when you do it but from New Zealand to Sydney you're looking at around NZ$345/459 one way/return in high season, NZ$425/650 high season, and to Melbourne NZ$470/529 low season, NZ$495/730 high season. There is a lot of competition on this route, with United, British Airways, Qantas and Air New Zealand all flying it, so there is bound to be some good discounting going on.

Cheap fares to New Zealand from Europe will usually be for flights via the USA. A straightforward London-Auckland return bucket-shop ticket costs around £599 in the low season, £800 high season. Coming via Australia you can continue right around on a RTW ticket which will cost from around £895 for a ticket with a comprehensive choice of stopovers.

Asia

Ticket discounting is widespread in Asia, particularly in Singapore, Hong Kong, Bangkok and Penang. There are a lot of fly-by-nights in the Asian ticketing scene so a little care is required. Also, the Asian routes have been particularly caught up in the capacity shortages on flights to Australia. Flights between Hong Kong and Australia are notoriously heavily booked while flights to or from Bangkok and Singapore are often part of the longer Europe-Australia route so they are also sometimes full. Plan ahead. For more information on South-East Asian travel, and travel on to Australia, see Lonely Planet's *South-East Asia on a shoestring*.

Typical one-way fares to Australia from Singapore are S$638 to Darwin or Perth, S$895 to Sydney or Melbourne.

From east-coast Australia return fares to Singapore, Kuala Lumpur and Bangkok range from A$700 to A$1200, and to Hong Kong from A$1065.

The cheapest way out of Australia is to take one of the flights operating between Darwin and Kupang (Timor, Indonesia). Current one-way/return fares are $244/396. See the Darwin Getting There & Away section for full details.

Africa

There are a number of possibilities between Africa and Australia with direct flights each week, but only between Perth and Harare or Johannesburg (both routes cost around A$1060/1590 one way/return low season, A$1200/1890 high season). Fares from Harare to Perth cost around US$910/1000 low season, US$910/1310 high season, and from Johannesburg to Perth they go for around US$870/1220 low season and US$990/1400 high season. Qantas, South African Airways and Air Zimbabwe all fly these routes.

Other airlines which connect southern Africa and Australia include Malaysia Airlines (via Kuala Lumpur), Singapore Airlines (via Singapore) and Air Mauritius (via Mauritius).

From East Africa the options are to fly via Mauritius or Zimbabwe, or via the Indian subcontinent and on to South-East Asia, then connect from there to Australia.

South America

Two routes operate between South America and Australia. The Chile connection involves Lan Chile's Santiago-Easter Island-Tahiti twice-weekly flight, from where you fly Qantas or another airline to Australia. This costs around US$1830 to Sydney, US$1920 to Melbourne and Brisbane. Alternatively there is the route which skirts the Antarctic circle, flying from Buenos Aires to Auckland and Sydney, operated twice-weekly by Aerolineas Argentinas.

SEA

It *is* quite possible to make your way to other countries like New Zealand, Papua New Guinea or Indonesia by hitching rides or crewing on yachts. Ask around at harbours, marinas, yacht or sailing clubs. Good places on the east coast include Coffs Harbour, Great Keppel Island, Airlie Beach/Whitsundays, Cairns – anywhere where boats call. Usually you have to chip something in for food. A lot of boats move north to escape the winter, so April is a good time to look for a berth in the Sydney area.

DEPARTURE TAXES
There is a $27 departure tax when leaving Australia, but this is incorporated into the price of your air ticket so is not paid separately.

WARNING
The information in this chapter is particularly vulnerable to change – prices for international travel are volatile, routes are

introduced and cancelled, schedules change, rules are amended, special deals come and go. Airlines and governments seem to take a perverse pleasure in making price structures and regulations as complicated as possible: you should check directly with the airline or travel agent to make sure you understand how a fare (and any ticket you may buy) works. In addition, the travel industry is highly competitive and there are many lurks and perks.

The upshot of this is that you should get quotes and advice from as many airlines and travel agents as possible before you part with your hard-earned cash. The details given in this chapter should be regarded only as pointers and cannot be any substitute for your own careful, up-to-date research.

Getting Around

Schedules for land and sea transport services throughout Australia appear in the *Travel Times*, which is published twice yearly and available from newsagents ($7.95).

AIR

Australia is so vast (and at times so empty) that unless your time is unlimited you will probably have to take to the air at some stage.

There are only two main domestic carriers within Australia – Qantas and Ansett – despite the fact that the airline industry is deregulated. A third airline, Aussie Airlines, is set to start flights in direct competition with the two biggies. Note that all domestic flights in Australia are nonsmoking. Because Qantas flies both international and domestic routes, flights leave from both the international and domestic terminals at Australian airports. Flights with flight numbers from QF001 to QF399 operate from international terminals; flight numbers QF400 and above operate from domestic terminals.

Cheap Fares

Random Discounting A major feature of the deregulated air-travel industry is random discounting. As the airlines try harder to fill planes, they often offer substantial discounts on selected routes. Although this seems to apply mainly to the heavy-volume routes, that's not always the case.

To make the most of the discounted fares, you need to keep in touch with what's on offer, mainly because there are usually conditions attached to cheap fares – such as booking 14 or so days in advance, or only flying on weekends or between certain dates and so on. Also the number of seats available is usually fairly limited. The further ahead you can plan the better.

The places to which this sort of discounting generally applies are the main centres – Melbourne, Sydney, Brisbane, Cairns, Adelaide and Perth – but deals come and go all the time.

It is fair to say that on virtually any route in the country covered by Qantas or Ansett the full economy fare will not be the cheapest way to go. Because the situation is so fluid, the special fares will more than likely have changed by the time you read this. For that reason we list full one-way economy fares throughout the book, although you can safely assume that there will be a cheaper fare available.

Discounts are generally greater for return rather than one-way travel.

Some Possibilities If you're planning a return trip and you have 21 days up your sleeve then you can save around 55% by travelling Apex. You have to book and pay for your tickets 21 days in advance and you must stay away at least one Saturday night. Flight details can be changed at any time (with 21 days notice), but the tickets are nonrefundable. If you book 14 days in advance the saving is 50% off the full fare. With five days advance notice you can save 10% off the full one way or return fares.

University or other higher education students under the age of 26 can get a 25% discount off the regular economy fare. An airline tertiary concession card (available from the airlines) is required for Australian students. Overseas students can use their International Student Identity Card.

All nonresident international travellers can get up to a 30% discount on internal Qantas flights and 25% on Ansett flights simply by presenting their international ticket when booking. It seems there is no limit to the number of domestic flights you are allowed to take, it doesn't matter which airline you fly into Australia with, and it doesn't have to be on a return ticket. Note that the discount applies only to the full economy fare, and so in many cases it will be cheaper to take advantage of other discounts offered. The best advice is to ring around and explore the options before you buy.

Air Passes

With discounting being the norm these days, air passes do not represent the value they did in pre-deregulation days. However, there are a few worth checking out.

Qantas Qantas offers two passes. The Boomerang Pass can only be purchased overseas and involves purchasing coupons for either short-haul flights (eg Hobart to Melbourne)

at $200 one way, or for long-haul sectors (eg from just about anywhere to Uluru) for $250. You must purchase a minimum of four coupons before you arrive in Australia from the USA, two if you're coming from the UK or Europe, and once here you can buy up to four more.

There is also the Qantas Backpackers Pass, which can only be bought in Australia with proof of membership of the YHA, VIP Backpackers, Independent Backpackers, Nomads Australia, or with a Greyhound Pioneer Aussie or Kilometre Pass. You must purchase a minimum of three sectors and

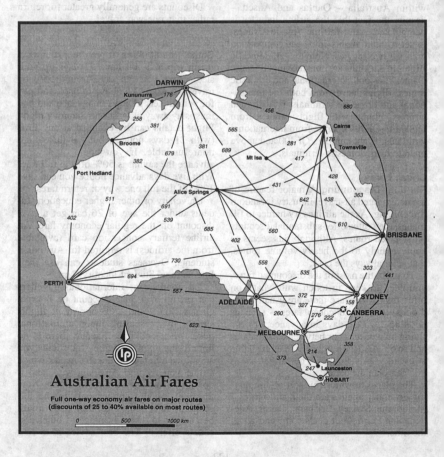

Australian Air Fares

Full one-way economy air fares on major routes
(discounts of 25 to 40% available on most routes)

stay a minimum of two nights at each stop. The discount is quite substantial; a sample fare using this pass is Sydney to Uluru for $292 one way, as against the full economy fare of $542.

Ansett Ansett has its Kangaroo Airpass, which gives you two options – 6000km with two or three stopovers for $949 ($729 for children) and 10,000km with three to seven stopovers for $1499 ($1149 for children). A number of restrictions apply to these tickets, although they can be a good deal if you want to see a lot of the country in a short period of time. You do not need to start and finish at the same place; you could start in Sydney and end in Darwin, for example, and you can upgrade from 6000 to 10,000 at any time on payment of the difference.

Restrictions include a minimum travel time (10 nights) and a maximum (45 nights). One of the stops must be at a non-capital-city destination and be for at least four nights, and you can only stay overnight at each destination once. All sectors must be booked when you purchase the ticket, although these can be changed without penalty unless the ticket needs rewriting, in which case there's a $50 charge. Refunds are available in full before travel commences but not at all once you start using the ticket.

On a 6000km air pass you could, for example, fly Sydney-Alice Springs-Cairns-Brisbane-Sydney. That gives you three stops and two of them are in non-capital cities. The regular fare for that circuit would be $1708, but with current discounts (five day advance purchase) it's $1538, so you save $589. A one-way route might be Adelaide-Melbourne-Sydney-Alice Springs-Perth. There are three stops, of which one is a non-capital city. The regular cost for that route would be $1635, but with discounts it's $1472, so the saving is $523.

Other Airline Options

There are a number of secondary airlines. In Western Australia there's Ansett WA with an extensive network of flights to the mining towns of the north-west and to Darwin in the

---

Interstate Quarantine

When travelling throughout Australia, whether by land or air, you may well come across signs (mainly in airports, interstate railway stations and at state borders) warning of the possible dangers of carrying fruit, plants and vegetables (which may be infected with a disease or pest) from one area to another. Certain pests and diseases – such as fruit fly, cucurbit thrips, grape phylloxera and potato cyst nematodes, to name a few – are prevalent in some areas but not in others, and so for obvious reasons authorities would like to limit their spread.

For the traveller this presents few problems; while there are quarantine inspection posts on some state borders and occasionally elsewhere, most quarantine control relies on honesty and the posts are not actually staffed. However, there are a few places where you may be inspected, and at these places the officers are entitled to search your car for undeclared items. ■

Northern Territory. Kendell Airlines services country areas of Victoria, South Australia and Tasmania, as well as Broken Hill (NSW) and Uluru (NT).

There are numerous other smaller operators. Sunstate operates services in Queensland including some to a number of islands. They also have a couple of routes in the south to Mildura and Broken Hill. Skywest has a number of services to remote parts of Western Australia.

Eastern Australia Airlines operates up and down the New South Wales coast and also inland from Sydney as far as Bourke and Cobar. Airnorth connects Darwin and Alice Springs with many small towns in the Northern Territory.

These smaller airlines are usually affiliated with either Qantas or Ansett, and their flights can be booked through that affiliate.

Airport Transport

There are private or public bus services between every major town and its airport, and they are economical and convenient. Quite often, a taxi shared between three or more people can be cheaper than the bus. In one or two places you may have to depend on taxis.

BUS

Bus travel is generally the cheapest way from A to B, other than hitching of course, but the main problem is to find the best deal.

There is only one truly *national* bus network – Greyhound Pioneer Australia (☎ 13 2030). McCafferty's (☎ 13 1499), operating out of Brisbane, is certainly the next biggest, with services in all mainland states except Western Australia.

There are also many smaller bus compa-nies operating locally or specialising in one or two main intercity routes. These often offer the best deals – Firefly costs $45 for Sydney to Melbourne, for example. In South Australia, Stateliner operates around the state including services to the Flinders Ranges. Westrail in Western Australia and V/Line in Victoria operate bus services to places trains no longer go.

A great many travellers see Australia by bus because it's one of the best ways to come to grips with the country's size and variety of terrain, and because the bus companies have such comprehensive route networks –

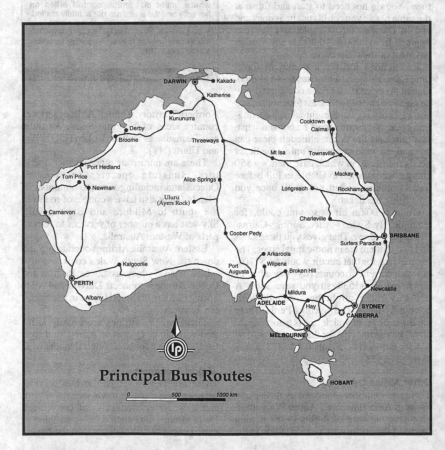

Principal Bus Routes

0   500   1000 km

far more comprehensive than the railway system. The buses all look pretty similar and are equipped with air-con, toilets and videos.

In most places there is just one bus terminal. Big city terminals are usually well equipped with toilets, showers and other facilities.

Greyhound Pioneer and McCafferty's have a variety of passes available, so it's a matter of deciding which suits your needs. One possible problem with the longer passes is that you are locked into one mode of travel, and this may not be convenient if there are more interesting alternatives (eg see Other Bus Options later in this section) to straight A to B travel.

Greyhound Pioneer Passes

Aussie Kilometre Pass This gives you a specified amount of travel to be completed within 12 months, the shortest being 2000km ($176), going up in increments of 1000km to a maximum of 20,000km ($1344), with a 10% discount for YHA and VIP members. The advantage of these passes is that they allow you to travel one route as many times as you like. The disadvantage is that you may feel obliged to travel farther than you might otherwise like to, simply because you have the kilometres free to do so. As an indication, 2000km will get you from Cairns to Brisbane, 4000km ($311) from Cairns to Melbourne, and 12,000km ($832) will get you a loop from Sydney to Melbourne, Adelaide, central Australia, Darwin, Cairns and back to Sydney.

Aussie Day Passes These are like the Kilometre passes, except that you are limited by days of travel rather than by km. Passes for seven ($499), 10 ($640) and 15 ($745) days of travel are valid for 30 days; 21 day passes ($982) are valid for two months.

Aussie Explorer Passes These set-route passes are more popular, giving you three, six or 12 months to cover a set route. You haven't got the go-anywhere flexibility of the Kilometre Pass but if you can find a set route which suits you – and there are 25 to

choose from – it generally works out cheaper than the Kilometre Pass. When a pass follows a circular route, you can start anywhere along the loop, and finish at the same spot.

The main limitation is that you can't backtrack, except on 'dead-end' short sectors such as Darwin to Kakadu, Townsville to Cairns or the Stuart Highway to Uluru.

The Aussie Highlights pass allows you to loop around the eastern half of Australia from Sydney taking in Melbourne, Adelaide, Coober Pedy, Uluru, Alice Springs, Darwin (and Kakadu), Cairns, Townsville, the Whitsundays, Brisbane and Surfers Paradise for $882, including tours of Uluru-Kata Tjuta and Kakadu national parks. Or there are one-way passes, such as the Reef & Rock, which goes from Sydney to Alice Springs (and Uluru) via Cairns and Darwin (and Kakadu) for $683; or Top End Explorer which takes in the Cairns to Darwin (and Kakadu) section only, for $279; or Country Road which takes you from Cairns to Sydney via Alice Springs, Adelaide and Melbourne, for $415. There's even an All Australia Pass which takes you right around the country, including up or down through the Centre, for $1491.

McCafferty's Passes

McCafferty's has eight set-route passes to choose from, including one in Tasmania.

The Best of the East & Centre is the equivalent of Greyhound Pioneer's Aussie Highlights, and costs $795 ($890 including Uluru and Kakadu tours). The Outback Wanderer goes from Cairns to Sydney via the centre for $440 ($480 including tours), or there's the Sun & Centre, from Sydney to Alice Springs via Cairns and Darwin, for $585 ($695 including tours).

Other Bus Options

There are other companies which offer transport options in various parts of the country. While most of these are really organised tours, they do also get you from A to B, and are a good alternative to the big bus companies. Their trips are generally aimed at budget travellers and so are good fun. The buses are generally smaller and not necessarily as comfortable as those of the big companies, but it's a much more interesting way to travel. The following is a selection:

The Wayward Bus (☎ 1800 882 823)

This award-winning company (they won a 1997 Australian Tourism Award) has an excellent reputation and offers a number of trips. Face the Outback is an eight day run from Adelaide to Alice Springs via the Oodnadatta Track, Coober Pedy and Uluru for $640. The return trip (Mad Cow) is a simple two-day dash down the Stuart Highway for $75, which is a good deal if you are in a hurry. The Classic Coast is a three-day trip along the spectacular Great Ocean Road between Adelaide and Melbourne, running twice a week in each direction ($160). During summer they also have a six-day trip which does a loop up into the Grampians in Victoria. These trips include sight-seeing, meals and accommodation (camping). Their third route is the Snowball Express, a twice weekly three-day run between Melbourne and Sydney via the Alpine Way and the Snowy Mountains ($140 including lunches).

Oz Experience (☎ 1300 300 028)

Basically a cross between a bus line and an organised group tour, Oz Experience offers frequent service along the east coast and up the centre to Darwin, with off-the-beaten-track detours to cattle stations and national parks. You buy one of their 22 passes, which range from $165 to $930 depending on the distance, and are valid for six to 12 months. Their buses travel set routes, but your pass entitles you to unlimited stops, which means you can get on and off whenever and wherever you like. The drivers act as guides, providing commentary and advice, and they can also prebook your hostels, stop at supermarkets so you can do your shopping, and arrange discounts on most tours and activities along the way.

Nullarbor Traveller (☎ 1800 816 858)

This is a small company running 10-day trips across the Nullarbor and around the south-west coast between Adelaide and Perth. The trips operate roughly once a month in each direction, and cost $750, which includes all meals, accommodation (camping and hostels) and entry fees.

Heading Bush Adventures (☎ 1800 639 933)

This company also does the route from Adelaide to Alice Springs, taking 10 days and going via the western edge of the Simpson Desert. The small group size (10 maximum) makes this a good personal tour, and the cost is $695.

TRAIN

Rail travel in Australia today is basically something you do because you really want to – not because it's cheaper, and certainly not because it's fast. It's generally the slowest way to get around. On the other hand the trains are comfortable and you certainly see Australia at ground level in a way no other means of travel permits.

Rail services within each state are run by that state's rail body, either government or private. The three major interstate services in Australia (the Ghan between Adelaide and Alice Springs, the Indian Pacific from Sydney to Perth and the Overland between Melbourne and Adelaide) are run by Great Southern Railways, a private consortium which took over the passenger services of the federal rail body, Australian National, when it was privatised in late 1997.

Australia is also one of the few places in the world where new lines are still being laid or are under consideration; the task of finally completing the north-south, transcontinental rail link between Alice Springs and Darwin is still being considered.

Rail Passes

There are a number of passes that allow unlimited rail travel either across the country or just in one state. With the Austrail Pass you can travel in economy class anywhere on the rail network during a set period. The cost is $485 for a 14-day pass, $625 for 21 days and $755 for 30 days. A seven-day extension to any of these passes costs $250.

The Austrail Flexipass allows a set number of economy-class travelling days within a six-month period. The cost is $400 for eight days of travel, $575 for 15 days, $810 for 22 days and $1045 for 29 days. The eight-day pass cannot be used for travel between Adelaide and Perth or between Adelaide and Alice Springs.

These two national passes are only available to holders of non-Australian passports and must be purchased prior to arrival in Australia. For travel within a limited area, passes which just cover travel in one state may be more suitable. These are available for

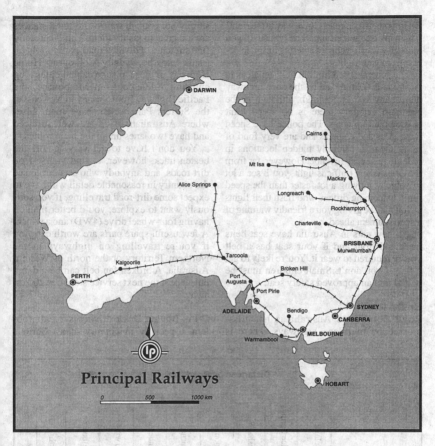

Principal Railways

0   500   1000 km

Victoria, Queensland, NSW and Western Australia (see the Getting Around sections in chapters covering those states for details).

As the railway booking system is computerised, any station (other than those on metropolitan lines) can make a booking for any journey throughout the country. For reservations telephone ☎ 13 2232 during office hours; this will connect you to the nearest mainline station.

CAR

Australia is a big, sprawling country with large cities where public transport is not always very comprehensive or convenient – the car is the accepted means of getting from A to B. More and more travellers are also finding it the best way to see the country; with three or four of you the costs are reasonable and the benefits many, provided of course you don't have a major mechanical problem.

Road Rules

Driving in Australia holds few real surprises. Australians drive on the left-hand side of the road just like in the UK, Japan and most countries in South-East Asia and the Pacific.

An important road rule is 'give way to the right' – if an intersection is unmarked (unusual), you must give way to vehicles entering the intersection from your right.

The general speed limit in built-up areas in Australia is 60km/h and on the open highway it's usually 100 or 110km/h, although in the Northern Territory there is no speed limit outside built-up areas. The police have speed radar guns and cameras and are very fond of using them in carefully hidden locations in order to raise easy revenue. However, far from the cities where traffic is light, you'll see a lot of vehicles moving a lot faster than the speed limit. Oncoming drivers who flash their lights at you may be giving you a friendly warning of a speed camera ahead.

All new cars in Australia have seat belts back and front and if your seat has a belt you're required to wear it. You're lkely to get a fine if you don't. Small children must be belted into an approved safety seat.

On the Road

Road Conditions Australia is not criss-crossed by multilane highways. There is simply not enough traffic and the distances are too great to justify them. You'll certainly find stretches of divided road, particularly on roads like the Sydney-Melbourne Hume Highway or close to state capital cities – eg entering Adelaide from Melbourne, the Pacific Highway from Sydney to Newcastle, the Surfers Paradise-Brisbane road. Elsewhere Australian roads are well-surfaced and have two lanes on all the main routes.

You don't have to get very far off the beaten track, however, to find yourself on dirt roads, and anybody who sets out to see the country in reasonable detail will have to expect some dirt-road travelling. If you seriously want to explore, you'd better plan on having four-wheel drive (4WD) and a winch. A few useful spare parts are worth carrying if you're travelling on highways in the Northern Territory or the north of Western Australia. A broken fan belt can be a damn nuisance if the next service station is 200km away.

Drink-Driving Drink-driving is a real problem, especially in country areas. Serious

Distances by Road (km)								
	Adelaide	Alice Springs	Brisbane	Broome	Cairns	Canberra	Darwin	Melbourne	Perth
Alice Springs	1690								
Brisbane	2130	3060							
Broome	4035	2770	4320						
Cairns	2865	2418	1840	4126					
Canberra	1210	2755	1295	5100	3140				
Darwin	3215	1525	3495	1965	2795	4230			
Melbourne	755	2435	1735	4780	3235	655	3960		
Perth	2750	3770	4390	2415	6015	3815	4345	3495	
Sydney	1430	2930	1030	4885	2870	305	4060	895	3990

These are the shortest distances by road; other routes may be considerably longer. For distances by coach, check the companies' leaflets.

attempts have been made in recent years to reduce the resulting road toll – random breath tests are not uncommon in built-up areas. If you're caught with a blood-alcohol level of more than 0.05 then be prepared for a hefty fine and the loss of your licence.

Fuel Fuel (super, diesel and unleaded) is available from stations sporting the well-known international brand names. Prices vary from place to place and from price war to price war but generally they're in the range of 65c to 80c. Once away from the major cities, however, prices soar to between 80c and $1 a litre. Some outback service stations are not above exploiting their monopoly position. Distances between fill-ups can be long in the outback.

Hazards Cows and kangaroos are two common hazards on country roads, and a collision is likely to kill the animal and seriously damage your vehicle. Kangaroos are most active around dawn and dusk, and they often travel in groups. If you see one hopping across the road in front of you, slow right down – its friends may be just behind it. Many Australians try to avoid travelling altogether after dark because of the hazards posed by animals. Finally, if one hops out right in front of you, hit the brakes and only swerve to avoid the animal if it is safe to do so. The number of people who have been killed in accidents caused by swerving to miss an animal is high – better to damage your car and probably kill the animal than kill yourself and your passengers.

Outback Travel
You can drive all the way round Australia on Highway 1 or through the centre from Adelaide to Darwin without ever leaving sealed road. However, if you really want to see outback Australia, there are lots of roads where the official recommendation is that you report to the police before you leave one end, and again when you arrive at the other, so if you fail to turn up they can send out search parties.

Nevertheless many of these tracks are

fairly well maintained and you don't need 4WD or fancy expedition equipment to tackle them. You do need to be carefully prepared and to carry important spare parts. Backtracking a couple of hundred kilometres to pick up some minor component or, much worse, to arrange a tow, is unlikely to be easy or cheap.

When travelling to the really remote areas it is advisable to travel with a high-frequency outpost radio transmitter equipped to pick up the Royal Flying Doctor Service bases in the area, or a satellite phone. A GPS position finder is also handy.

You will of course need to carry a fair amount of water in case of disaster – around 20 litres a person is sensible – stored in more than one container. Food is less important – if space is tight it might be better allocated to an extra spare tyre.

The state automobile associations can advise on preparation, and supply maps and track notes. Most tracks have an ideal time of year – in the centre it's not wise to attempt the tough tracks during the heat of summer (November-March) when the dust can be severe, chances of mechanical trouble are much greater and water will be scarce and hence a breakdown more dangerous. Similarly, travel during the wet season in the north may be hindered by flooding and muddy roads.

If you do run into trouble in the back of beyond, stay with your car. It's easier to spot a car than a human being from the air, and you wouldn't be able to carry your 20 litres of water very far anyway. For the full story on safe outback travel, get hold of Lonely Planet's *Outback Australia*.

Some of the favourite outback tracks are:

Birdsville Track
> Running 499km from Marree in South Australia to Birdsville just across the border in Queensland, this is one of the best-known routes in Australia and these days is quite feasible in any well-prepared, conventional vehicle.

Strzelecki Track
> This track covers much the same territory, starting south of Marree at Lyndhurst and going to Innamincka, 473km north-east and close to the

Queensland border. From there you can loop down to Tibooburra in New South Wales. The route has been much improved due to work on the Moomba gas fields. It was at Innamincka that the hapless early explorers Burke and Wills died.

Oodnadatta Track

Parallel to the old Ghan railway line to Alice Springs, this track is comprehensively bypassed by the sealed Stuart Highway to the west and south. It's 465km from Marree to Oodnadatta then another 202km from there to the Stuart Highway at Marla. Any well-prepared vehicle should be able to manage this route.

Simpson Desert

Crossing the Simpson Desert from Birdsville to the Stuart Highway is becoming increasingly popular but this route is still a real test. Four-wheel drive is definitely required and you should be in a party of at least three or four vehicles equipped with long-range two-way radios.

Warburton Road/Gunbarrel Highway

This route runs west from Uluru by the Aboriginal settlements of Docker River and Warburton to Laverton in Western Australia. From there you can drive down to Kalgoorlie and on to Perth. The route passes through Aboriginal reserves and permission to enter them must be obtained in advance if you want to leave the road. A well-prepared conventional vehicle can complete this route although ground clearance can be a problem, and it is very remote. From the Yulara resort at Uluru to Warburton is 567km, and it's

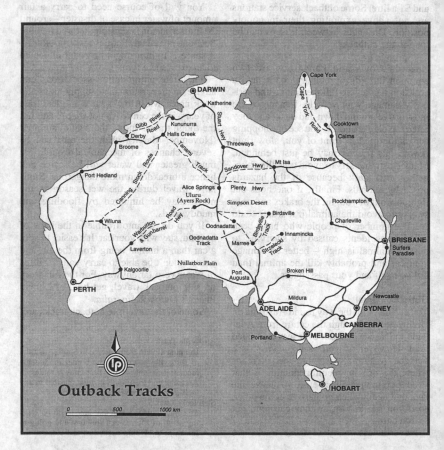

Outback Tracks

another 568km from there to Laverton. It's then 361km on a sealed road to Kalgoorlie. For 300km near the Giles Meteorological Station the Warburton Road and the Gunbarrel Highway run on the same route. Taking the old Gunbarrel (to the north of the Warburton) all the way to Wiluna in Western Australia is a much rougher trip requiring 4WD. The Warburton Road is now commonly referred to as the Gunbarrel – just to make life simple.

Tanami Track

Turning off the Stuart Highway just north of Alice Springs this track goes north-west across the Tanami Desert to Halls Creek in Western Australia. It's a popular short-cut for people travelling between the centre and the Kimberley. The road has been extensively improved in recent years and conventional vehicles are quite OK, although there are occasional sandy stretches on the WA section. Be warned that the Rabbit Flat roadhouse in the middle of the desert is only open from Friday to Monday.

Canning Stock Route

This old stock trail runs south-west from Halls Creek to Wiluna in Western Australia. It crosses the Great Sandy and Gibson Desert, and since the track has not been maintained for over 30 years it's a route to be taken seriously. Like the Simpson Desert crossing, you should only travel in a well-equipped party and careful navigation is required.

Plenty & Sandover Highways

These two routes run east from the Stuart Highway, to the north of Alice Springs, to Mt Isa in Queensland. They're suitable for conventional vehicles.

Cape York

The Peninsula Developmental Road (Cape York Road) up to the top of Cape York, the most northerly point in Australia, is a popular route with a number of rivers to cross. It can only be attempted in the dry season when water levels are lower. The original Cape York Road along the old telegraph line definitely requires 4WD. Conventional vehicles can take the new 'Heathlands' road to the east beyond the Wenlock River, bypassing the difficult sections, but the Wenlock River itself can be a formidable obstacle.

Gibb River Road

This is the 'short cut' between Derby and Kununurra, and runs through the heart of the spectacular Kimberley in northern Western Australia. Although fairly badly corrugated in places, it can be easily negotiated by conventional vehicles in the dry season and is 720km, compared with about 920km via the bitumen Northern Highway.

Rental

If you've got the cash there are plenty of car rental companies ready and willing to put you behind the wheel. Competition is pretty fierce so rates tend to be variable and lots of special deals pop up and disappear again. Whatever your mode of travel on the long stretches, it can be very useful to have a car for some local travel. Between a group it can even be reasonably economical. There are some places – like around Alice Springs – where if you haven't got your own transport you really have to choose between a tour and a rented vehicle since there is no public transport and the distances are too great for walking or even bicycles.

The three major companies are Budget, Hertz and Avis, with offices in almost every town that has more than one pub and a general store. A second-string company which is also represented almost everywhere in the country is Thrifty. Then there are a vast number of local firms, or firms with outlets in a limited number of locations. The big operators will generally have higher rates than the local firms but it ain't necessarily so, so don't jump to conclusions.

The big firms have a number of big advantages, however. First of all Avis, Budget, Hertz and, quite often, Thrifty, are represented at most airports. If you want to pick up a car or leave a car at the airport then they're the best ones to deal with. In some, but not all, airports other companies will also arrange to pick up or leave a car there for you. It tends to depend on how convenient the airport is.

The second advantage is if you want to do a one-way rental – pick up a car in Adelaide and leave it in Sydney, for example. There are, however, a variety of restrictions on this. Usually it's a minimum-hire period rather than repositioning charges. Only certain cars may be eligible for one-way trips. Check the small print on one-way charges before deciding on one company rather than another. One-way rentals are generally not available into or out of the Northern Territory or Western Australia.

The major companies offer a choice of

Sydney to Melbourne via the Princes Highway

(Total distance 1041 km)

★ *93* ★ Distances between locations in km
(diagram not to scale)

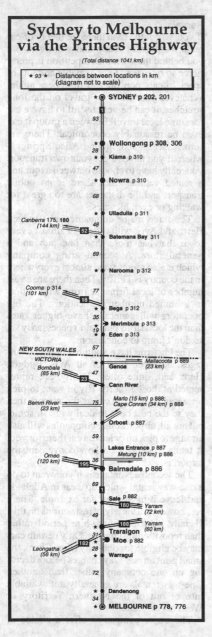

★ ◉ **SYDNEY p 202, 201**

93

★ ● **Wollongong p 308, 306**

28

★ ● **Kiama** p 310

47

★ ● **Nowra** p 310

68

★ ● **Ulladulla** p 311

Canberra 175, 180
(144 km) — **52** — 48

★ ● **Batemans Bay** 311

69

★ ● **Narooma** p 312

Cooma p 314
(101 km) — **18** — 77

★ ● **Bega** p 312

35

★ ● **Merimbula** p 313
19
★ ● **Eden** p 313

NEW SOUTH WALES 57
VICTORIA

Bombala ● *Genoa*   *Mallacoota* p 889
(85 km) — **23** — 47   *(23 km)*

★ ● **Cann River**

Bemm River — 75   *Marlo (15 km) p 888;*
(23 km)   *Cape Conran (34 km)* p 888

★ ● **Orbost** p 887

59

★ ● **Lakes Entrance** p 887
Omeo ● *Metung (10 km)* p 886
(120 km) — **195** — 36

★ ● **Bairnsdale** p 886

69

★ ● **Sale** p 882

180 — *Yarram*
49   *(72 km)*

188 — *Yarram*
★ ● **Traralgon**   *(60 km)*
31
Leongatha — **182** — ★ ● **Moe** p 882
(56 km)   28

★ ● **Warragul**

72

● **Dandenong**

34

★ ◉ **MELBOURNE p 778, 776**

deals, either unlimited kilometres or a flat charge plus so many cents per km. On straightforward off-the-card city rentals they're all pretty much the same price. It's on special deals, odd rentals or longer periods that you find the differences. Weekend specials – usually three days for the price of two – are usually good value. If you just need a car for three days to drive around Sydney try to make it the weekend rather than midweek. Budget offers 'stand-by' rates and you may see other special deals available.

Daily rates are typically about $50 a day for a small car (Holden Barina, Ford Festiva, Daihatsu Charade, Suzuki Swift), about $75 a day for a medium car (Mitsubishi Magna, Toyota Camry, Nissan Pulsar) or about $100 a day for a big car (Holden Commodore, Ford Falcon), all including insurance. You must be at least 21 years old to hire from most firms.

There is a whole collection of other factors to bear in mind about this rent-a-car business. For a start, if you're going to want it for a week, a month or longer then they all have significantly lower rates. If you're in Tasmania there are often lower rates, especially in the low season.

OK, that's the big hire companies, what about all the rest of them? Well, some of them are still pretty big in terms of numbers of shiny new cars. In Tasmania, for example, the car-hire business is huge since many people don't bring their cars with them. There's a plethora of hire companies and lots of competition. In many cases local companies are markedly cheaper than the big boys, but in others what looks like a cheaper rate can end up quite the opposite if you're not careful. In the Northern Territory, Territory Rent-a-Car is at least as big as the others, and its rates are very competitive.

And don't forget the 'rent-a-wreck' companies. They specialise in renting older cars and have a variety of rates, typically around $35 a day. If you just want to travel around the city, or not too far out, they can be worth considering.

Be aware when renting a car in Australia

that if you are travelling on dirt roads you are generally not covered by insurance. So if you have an accident, you'll be liable for all the costs involved. This applies to all companies, although they don't always point this out. This does not apply to 4WDs.

4WD Rental Having 4WD enables you to get right off the beaten track and out to some of the Australian natural wonders that most travellers miss.

Renting a 4WD is within a reasonable budget range if a few people get together. Something small like a Suzuki, or similar, costs around $100 per day; for a Toyota Landcruiser you're looking at around $150, which should include insurance and some free kilometres (typically 100km per day). Check the insurance conditions, especially the excess, as they can be onerous – in the Northern Territory $4000 is typical, although this can often be reduced to around $1000 on payment of an additional daily charge (around $20). Even for a 4WD the insurance of most companies does not cover damage caused when travelling 'off-road', which basically means anything that is not a maintained bitumen or dirt road.

Hertz and Avis have 4WD rentals, with one-way rentals possible between the eastern states and the Northern Territory. Budget also rents 4WDs from Darwin and Alice Springs. Brits:Australia (☎ 1800 331 454) is a company which hires fully equipped 4WDs fitted out as campervans. These have proved extremely popular in recent years, and cost around $130 per day for unlimited km, plus insurance ($20 per day, or $40 to cover everything, including windscreen and tyres). Brits:Australia has offices in all the mainland capitals, as well as in Cairns and Alice Springs, so one-way rentals are also possible.

Renting Other Vehicles There are lots of vehicles you can rent apart from cars and motorcycles. In many places you can rent campervans – they're particularly popular in Tasmania. Motorscooters are also available in a number of locations – they are popular on Magnetic Island and in Cairns for

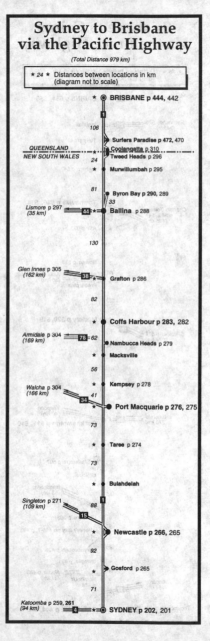

Sydney to Brisbane via the Pacific Highway

(Total Distance 979 km)

★ *24* ★ Distances between locations in km (diagram not to scale)

★ ● BRISBANE p 444, 442

106

➤ Surfers Paradise p 472, 470
Coolangatta p 310
QUEENSLAND
NEW SOUTH WALES
24 ➤ Tweed Heads p 296

★ ➤ Murwillumbah p 295

81
➤ Byron Bay p 290, 289
33
Lismore p 297 (35 km) — 44 ★ Ballina p 288

130

Glen Innes p 305 (162 km) — 38 ★ Grafton p 286

82

★ Coffs Harbour p 283, 282

Armidale p 304 (169 km) — 78 ➤ 62 Nambucca Heads p 279

★ Macksville

56

Walcha p 304 (166 km) — 41 ★ Kempsey p 278
— 34 ★ Port Macquarie p 276, 275

73

★ Taree p 274

73

★ Bulahdelah

Singleton p 271 (109 km) — 88 ■
— 15

★ ● Newcastle p 266, 265

92

★ ➤ Gosford p 265

71

Katoomba p 259, 261 (94 km) — 4 ★ ● SYDNEY p 202, 201

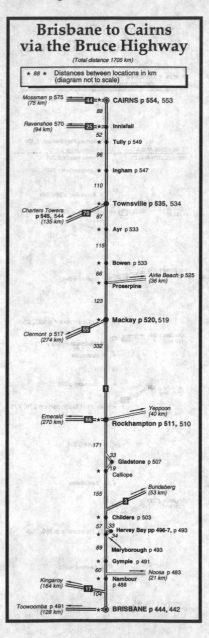

Brisbane to Cairns
via the Bruce Highway

(Total distance 1705 km)

★ *88* ★ Distances between locations in km
(diagram not to scale)

Mossman p 575
(75 km) ━━━━ 44 ★● **CAIRNS p 554,** 553

88

Ravenshoe 570
(94 km) ━━━━ 25 ● **Innisfail**

52

★ **Tully** p 549

96

★ **Ingham** p 547

110

Charters Towers ━━ 78 ★● **Townsville p 535,** 534
p 545, 544
(135 km) 87

★ **Ayr** p 533

115

● **Bowen** p 533

66

Airlie Beach p 525
★ **Proserpine** *(36 km)*

123

Clermont p 517 ━ 55 ★● **Mackay p 520,** 519
(274 km)

332

🅱

Emerald ━━ 66 ★● *Yeppoon
(270 km)* *(40 km)*
Rockhampton p 511, 510

171

33
● **Gladstone** p 507
/19
★ Calliope

Bundaberg
155 *(53 km)*
3

★ **Childers** p 503

57 *33*
● **Hervey Bay pp 496-7,** p 493
★ *34*

89 **Maryborough** p 493

★ **Gympie** p 491

60 *Noosa* p 483
Kingaroy ● **Nambour** *(21 km)*
(164 km) p 488
17
104

Toowoomba p 491 ━━━ ★● **BRISBANE p 444,** 442
(128 km)

example – and you only need a car licence to ride one. Best of all, in many places you can rent bicycles.

Purchase

New Australian cars are not cheap – a result of the small population. Locally manufactured cars are made in small, uneconomic numbers and imported cars are heavily taxed so they won't undercut the local products. If you're buying a second-hand vehicle reliability is all important. Mechanical breakdowns way out in the outback can be very inconvenient (not to mention dangerous) – the nearest mechanic can be a hell of a long way down the road.

Secondhand cars in Australia are relatively cheap. It's possible to pick up a 1982 to 1984 XE Falcon station wagon (a very popular model with backpackers) in good condition for around A$2500 to A$3000. An XD Falcon (1979 to 1982) costs around $2000. Although there are plenty for sale, anything older than that and you're getting into the seriously used category. Japanese cars of a similar age are considerably more expensive.

Shopping around for a used car involves much the same rules as anywhere in the Western world but with a few local variations. First of all, used-car dealers in Australia are just like used-car dealers from Los Angeles to London – they'd sell their mother into slavery if it turned a dollar. You'll probably get any car cheaper by buying privately through newspaper small ads rather than through a car dealer. Buying through a dealer does have the advantage of some sort of guarantee, but a guarantee is not much use if you're buying a car in Sydney and intend setting off for Perth next week. Used-car guarantee requirements vary from state to state – check with the local automobile organisation.

There's a great deal of discussion among travellers about where the best place is to buy used cars. It's quite possible that prices do vary but don't count on turning it to your advantage. See the section on buying cars in

Sydney for the situation at that popular starting/finishing point.

What is rather more certain is that the further you get from civilisation, the better it is to be in a Holden or a Ford. New cars can be a whole different ball game of course, but if you're in an older vehicle that's likely to have the odd hiccup from time to time, life is much simpler if it's a car for which you can get spare parts anywhere from Bourke to Bulamakanka.

In Australia third-party personal injury insurance is always included in the vehicle registration cost. This ensures that every vehicle (as long as it's currently registered) carries at least minimum insurance. You'd be wise to extend that minimum to at least third-party property insurance as well – minor collisions with other cars can be amazingly expensive.

When you come to buy or sell a car there are usually some local regulations. In Victoria, for example, a car has to have a compulsory safety check (Road Worthy Certificate – RWC) before it can be registered in the new owner's name – usually the seller will indicate if the car already has a RWC. In New South Wales and the Northern Territory, on the other hand, safety checks are compulsory every year when you come to renew the registration. Stamp duty has to be paid when you buy a car and, as this is based on the purchase price, it's not unknown for buyer and seller to agree privately to understate the price. It's much easier to sell a car in the same state that it's registered in, otherwise you (or the buyer) must re-register it in the new state, and that's a hassle. Vehicles with interstate plates are particularly hard to get rid of in WA.

One way of getting around the hassles of buying and selling a vehicle privately is to enter into a buy-back arrangement with a car or motorcycle dealer. However, dealers will often find ways of knocking down the price when you return the vehicle, even if it was agreed to in writing – often by pointing out expensive repairs that allegedly will be required to gain the dreaded RWC needed to transfer the registration. The cars on offer have often been driven around Australia a number of times, often with haphazard or minimal servicing, and are generally pretty tired. The main advantage of these schemes is that you don't have to worry about being able to sell the vehicle quickly at the end of your trip, and can usually arrange insurance, which short-term visitors may find hard to get. See the Sydney Getting There & Away section in the New South Wales chapter for more details.

A company that specialises in buy-back arrangements on cars and motorcycles, with fixed rates and no hidden extras, is Car Connection Australia (☎ (03) 5473 4469; fax (03) 5473 4520). Here a second-hand Ford Falcon or Holden Kingswood station wagon or Yamaha XT600 trail bike will set you back a fixed sum of $1950 for any period up to six months; a Toyota Landcruiser Troopcarrier, suitable for serious outback exploration, is $3500 ($4500 for an air-con station wagon), also for up to six months. Information and bookings are handled by its European agent: Travel Action GmbH (☎ (0276) 47824; fax 7938), Einsiedeleiweg 16, 57399 Kirchhundem, Germany.

Finally, make use of automobile associations. They can advise you on local regulations you should be aware of, give general guidelines about buying a car and, most importantly, for a fee (around $70) will check over a used car and report on its condition before you agree to purchase it. They also offer car insurance to their members.

Automobile Associations

The national Australian Automobile Association is an umbrella organisation for the various state associations and maintains links with similar bodies throughout the world. Day-to-day operations are handled by the state organisations, which provide an emergency breakdown service, literature, excellent maps and detailed guides to accommodation and camp sites.

The state organisations have reciprocal arrangements with other states in Australia and with similar organisations overseas. So, if you're a member of the National Roads &

Motorists Association in New South Wales, you can use the Royal Automobile Club of Victoria's facilities in Victoria. Similarly, if you're a member of the AAA in the USA, or the RAC or AA in the UK, you can use any of the state organisations' facilities. Bring proof of membership with you.

Some of the material these organisations publish is of a very high standard. In particular there is a good set of regional maps to Queensland produced by the Royal Automobile Club of Queensland. The most useful state offices are:

New South Wales
National Roads & Motorists Association (NRMA), 151 Clarence St, Sydney, NSW 2000 (☎ 13 2132; fax 15 3132)
Northern Territory
Automobile Association of the Northern Territory (AANT), 79-81 Smith St, Darwin, NT 0800 (☎ (08) 8981 3837; fax 8941 2965)
Queensland
Royal Automobile Club of Queensland (RACQ), 300 St Pauls Terrace, Fortitude Valley, Qld 4006 (☎ (07) 3361 2444; fax 3849 0610)
South Australia
Royal Automobile Association of South Australia (RAA), 41 Hindmarsh Square, Adelaide, SA 5000 (☎ (08) 8202 4600; fax 8202 4521)
Tasmania
Royal Automobile Club of Tasmania (RACT), Cnr Patrick and Murray Sts, Hobart, Tas 7000 (☎ (03) 6232 6300; fax 6234 8784)
Victoria
Royal Automobile Club of Victoria (RACV), 360 Bourke St, Melbourne, Vic 3000 (☎ 13 1955; fax (03) 9790 2844)
Western Australia
Royal Automobile Club of Western Australia (RAC), 228 Adelaide Terrace, Perth, WA 6000 (☎ (08) 9421 4444; fax 9221 2708)

MOTORCYCLE

Motorcycles are a very popular way of getting around. The climate is just about ideal for bikes for much of the year, and the many small trails from the road into the bush often lead to perfect spots to spend the night.

The long, open roads are really made for large-capacity machines above 750cc, which Australians prefer once they outgrow their 250cc learner restrictions. But that doesn't stop enterprising individuals from tackling

the length and breadth of the continent on 250cc trail bikes. Doing it on a small bike is not impossible, just tedious at times.

If you want to bring your own motorcycle into Australia you'll need a *carnet de passages*, and when you try to sell it you'll get less than the market price because of restrictive registration requirements. Shipping from just about anywhere is expensive.

However, with a little bit of time up your sleeve, getting mobile on two wheels in Australia is quite feasible, thanks largely to the chronically depressed motorcycle market. The beginning of the southern winter is a good time to strike out. Australian newspapers and the lively local bike press have extensive classified advertisement sections where $2500 gets you something that will easily take you around the country if you know a bit about bikes. The main drawback is that you'll have to try and sell it again afterwards.

An easier option is a buy-back arrangement from a large motorcycle dealer in a major city (Elizabeth St in Melbourne is a good hunting ground). They're keen to do business, and basic negotiating skills allied with a wad of cash (say, $4000) should secure an excellent second-hand bike with a written guarantee that they'll buy it back in good condition minus $1500 or $2000 after your four-month, round-Australia trip. Popular brands are BMWs, large-capacity, shaft-driven Japanese bikes and possibly Harley-Davidsons (very popular in Australia). The percentage drop on a trail bike will be much greater (though the actual amount you lose should be similar), but very few dealers are interested in buy-back schemes on trail bikes.

You'll need a rider's licence and a helmet. A fuel range of 350km will cover fuel stops up the centre and on Highway 1 around the continent. Beware of dehydration in the dry, hot air – force yourself to drink plenty of water, even if you don't feel thirsty. If riding in Tasmania (a top cycling and motorcycling destination) you should be prepared for rotten weather in winter, and rain any time of year.

The 'roo bars' (outsize bumpers) seen on

interstate trucks and many outback cars tell you one thing: never ride on the open road from early evening until after dawn. Marsupials are nocturnal, sleeping in the shade during the day and feeding at night, and road ditches often provide lush grass. Cows and sheep also stray onto the roads at night.

It's worth carrying some spares and tools even if you don't know how to use them, because someone else often does. If you do know, you'll probably have a fair idea of what to take. The basics include: a spare tyre tube (front wheel size, which will also fit on the rear but a rear tube usually won't fit the front); puncture repair kit with levers and a pump (or tubeless tyre repair kit with at least three carbon dioxide cartridges), a spare tyre valve, and a valve cap with which you can unscrew the valve; the bike's standard tool kit for what it's worth (nonstandard tools will be of a better quality); spare throttle, clutch and brake cables; tie wire, cloth tape ('gaffer' tape) and nylon 'zip-ties'; a handful of bolts and nuts in the usual emergency sizes (M6 and M8), along with a few self-tapping screws; one or two fuses in your bike's ratings; a bar of soap for fixing tank leaks (knead to a putty with water and squeeze into the leak); and, most important of all, a workshop manual for your bike (even if you can't make sense of it, the local motorcycle mechanic can). You'll never have enough elastic (octopus) straps to tie down your gear.

Make sure you carry water – at least two litres on major roads in central Australia, more off the beaten track. And finally, if something does go hopelessly wrong in the back of beyond, park your bike where it's clearly visible and observe the cardinal rule: *don't leave your vehicle.*

BICYCLE

Whether you're hiring a bike to ride around a city or wearing out your Bio-Ace chainwheels on a Melbourne-Darwin marathon, you'll find that Australia is a great place for cycling. There are bike tracks in most cities, and in the country you'll find thousands of kilometres of good roads which carry so little traffic that the biggest hassle is waving back

to the drivers. Especially appealing is that in many areas you'll ride a very long way without encountering a hill.

Bicycle helmets are compulsory in all states and territories.

It's possible to plan rides of any duration and through almost any terrain. A day or two cycling around South Australia's wineries is popular, or you could meander along beside the Murrumbidgee River for weeks. Tasmania is very popular for touring, and mountain bikers love Australia's deserts – and its mountains, for that matter.

Cycling has always been popular here, and not only as a sport: some shearers would ride for huge distances between jobs, rather than use less reliable horses. It's rare to find a good sized town that doesn't have a shop stocking at least basic bike parts.

If you're coming specifically to cycle, it makes sense to bring your own bike. Check your airline for costs and the degree of dismantling/packing required. Within Australia you can load your bike onto a bus or train to skip the boring bits. Note that bus companies require you to dismantle your bike, and some don't guarantee that it will travel on the same

Cycling is a cheap and healthy way to get off the beaten track and discover the real Australia

bus as you. Trains are easier, but supervise the loading and if possible tie your bike upright, otherwise you may find that the guard has stacked crates of Holden spares on your fragile alloy wheels.

You can buy a good steel-framed touring bike in Australia for about $400 (plus panniers). It may be possible to rent touring bikes and equipment from a few of the commercial touring organisations.

Much of eastern Australia seems to have been settled on the principle of not having more than a day's horse ride between pubs, so it's possible to plan even ultra-long routes and still get a shower at the end of each day. Most people do carry camping equipment, but, on the east coast at least, it's feasible to travel from town to town staying in hostels, hotels or on-site vans.

You can get by with standard road maps, but as you'll probably want to avoid both the highways and the low-grade unsealed roads, the Government series is best. The 1:250,000 scale is the most suitable but you'll need a lot of maps if you're covering much territory. The next scale up, 1:1,000,000, is adequate. They are available in capital cities and elsewhere.

Until you get fit you should be careful to eat enough to keep you going – remember that exercise is an appetite suppressant. It's surprisingly easy to be so depleted of energy that you end up camping under a gum tree just 10km short of a shower and a steak.

No matter how fit you are, water is vital. Dehydration is no joke and can be life threatening. One Lonely Planet author rode his first 200km day on a bowl of cornflakes and a round of sandwiches, but the Queensland sun forced him to drink nearly five litres. Having been involved in a drinking contest with stockmen the night before may have had something to do with it, though.

It can get very hot in summer, and you should take things slowly until you're used to the heat. Cycling in 35°C-plus temperatures isn't too bad if you wear a hat and plenty of sunscreen, and drink *lots* of water. In the eastern states, be aware of the blistering hot 'northerlies', the prevailing winds

that make a north-bound cyclist's life uncomfortable in summer. In April, when the south-east's clear autumn weather begins, the southerly trade winds prevail, and you can have (theoretically at least) tailwinds all the way to Darwin.

Of course, you don't have to follow the larger roads and visit towns. It's possible to fill your mountain bike's panniers with muesli, head out into the mulga, and not see anyone for weeks. Or ever again – outback travel is very risky if not properly planned. Water is the main problem in the 'dead heart', and you can't rely on it where there aren't settlements. That tank marked on your map may be dry or the water from it unfit for humans, and those station buildings probably blew away years ago. That little creek marked with a dotted blue line? Forget it – the only time it has water is when the country's flooded for hundreds of km.

Check with locals if you're heading into remote areas, and notify the police if you're about to do something particularly adventurous. That said, don't rely too much on local knowledge of road conditions – most people have no idea of what a heavily loaded touring bike needs. What they think of as a great road may be pedal-deep in sand or bull dust, and cyclists have happily ridden along roads that were officially flooded out.

Useful Organisations
In each state there are touring organisations which can help with information and put you in touch with touring clubs:

Australian Capital Territory
    Pedal Power ACT, PO Box 581, Canberra, ACT 2601 (☎ (02) 6248 7995; www.sunsite.anu.edu.au/community/pedalpower)
New South Wales
    Bicycle Institute of New South Wales, 209 Castlereagh St, Sydney, NSW 2000 (☎ (02) 9283 5200; www.ozemail.com.au/bikensw)
Queensland
    Bicycle Institute of Queensland, PO Box 8321, Woolloongabba, Brisbane, Qld 4102 (☎ (07) 3844 1144; www.modeling.ctpm.uq.edu.au/biq)
South Australia
    Bicycle Institute of South Australia, GPO Box

792, Adelaide 5000 (☎ (08) 8346 7534; www. dove.net.au/rday/bisa/welcome.htm)

Tasmania

Bicycle Tasmania, c/o Environment Centre, 102 Bathurst St, Hobart, Tas 7000 (☎ (03) 6233 6619; www.netspace.net.au/spoke/biketas.html)

Victoria

Bicycle Victoria, 19 O'Connell St, North Melbourne, Vic 3051 (☎ (03) 9328 3000; www. sofcom.com.au/BicycleVic/index.html)

Western Australia

Bicycle Transportation Alliance, PO Box 8295 PBC, Perth, WA 6849 (☎ (08) 9470 4007; www.sunsite.anu.edu.au/wa/bta)

Organised Bicycle Tours

There are many organised tours available of varying lengths, and if you get bored talking to sheep as you ride along, it might be a good idea to include one or more tours in your itinerary. Most provide a support vehicle and take care of accommodation and cooking, so they can be a nice break from solo chores.

Remote Outback Cycle Tours (☎ (08) 9244 4614; fax 9244 4615; www.omen.com. au/roc) based in Perth has tours through some really remote country, such as the Great Victoria Desert and the Kimberley, and when you're not riding the mountain bikes (supplied) they are carried on the 4WD support vehicle. The cost works out at about $100 per day all inclusive.

HITCHING

Hitching is never entirely safe in any country in the world. It is in fact illegal in most states of Australia (which doesn't stop people doing it) and we don't recommend it. Travellers who decide to hitch should understand that they are taking a small but potentially serious risk. Australia is not exempt from danger (Queensland in particular is notorious for attacks on women travellers), and even people hitching in pairs are not entirely safe. Before deciding to hitch, talk to local people about the dangers, and it is a good idea to let someone know where you are planning to hitch to before you set off. If you do choose to hitch, the advice that follows should help to make your journey as fast and safe as possible.

Factor one, for safety and speed, is num-

bers. More than two people hitching together will make things very difficult, and solo hitching is unwise for men as well as women. Two women hitching together may be vulnerable, and two men hitching together can expect long waits. The best option is for a woman and a man to hitch together.

Factor two is position – look for a place where vehicles will be going slowly and where they can stop easily. A junction or freeway slip road is a good place if there is stopping room. Position goes beyond just where you stand. The ideal location is on the outskirts of a town – hitching from way out in the country is as hopeless as from the centre of a city. Take a bus out to the edge of town.

Factor three is appearance. The ideal appearance for hitching is a sort of genteel poverty – threadbare but clean. Don't carry too much gear – if it looks like it's going to take half an hour to pack your bags aboard you'll be left on the roadside.

Factor four is knowing when to say no. Saying no to a car-load of drunks is pretty obvious, but you should also be prepared to abandon a ride if you begin to feel uneasy for any reason. Don't sit there hoping for the best; make an excuse and get out at the first opportunity.

It can be time-saving to say no to a short ride that might take you from a good hitching point to a lousy one. Wait for the right, long ride to come along. On a long haul, it's pointless to start walking as it's not likely to increase the likelihood of your getting a lift and it's often an awfully long way to the next town.

Trucks are often the best lifts but they will only stop if they are going slowly and can get started easily again. Thus, the ideal place is at the top of a hill where they have a downhill run. Truckies often say they are going to the next town and if they don't like you, will drop you anywhere. As they often pick up hitchers for company, the quickest way to create a bad impression is to jump in and fall asleep. It's also worth remembering that while you're in someone else's vehicle, you are their guest and should act accordingly –

many drivers no longer pick up people because they have suffered from thoughtless hitchers in the past. It's the hitcher's duty to provide entertainment!

Of course people do get stuck in outlandish places but that is the name of the game. If you're visiting from abroad a nice prominent flag on your pack will help, and a sign announcing your destination can also be useful. Uni and hostel notice boards are good places to look for hitching partners. The main law against hitching is 'thou shalt not stand in the road' – so when you see the law coming, step back.

Just as hitchers should be wary when accepting lifts, drivers who pick up fellow travellers to share the costs should also be aware of the risks involved.

BOAT

Not really. Once upon a time there was quite a busy coastal shipping service but now it only applies to freight, and apart from specialised bulk carriers, even that is declining rapidly. The only regular shipping service is between Victoria and Tasmania and unless you are taking a vehicle with you the very cheapest ticket on that often choppy route is not all that much cheaper than the air fare.

ORGANISED TOURS

There are all sorts of tours around Australia including some interesting camping tours. Adventure tours include 4WD safaris in the Northern Territory and up into far north Queensland. Some of these go to places you simply couldn't get to on your own without large amounts of expensive equipment. You can also walk, ski, boat, raft, canoe, ride a horse or camel or even fly.

YHA tours are good value – find out about them at YHA Travel offices in capital cities (see Accommodation in the Facts for the Visitor chapter for addresses). In major centres like Sydney, Darwin and Cairns there

are many tours aimed at backpackers – good prices, good destinations, good fun.

There are several good operators offering organised motorcycling tours in Australia. One of these is Bike Tours Australia, which also operates under the name Car Connection Australia (see Car earlier in this chapter for contact details). Another company that offers tours is Motorcycle Safaris Australia (☎ (02) 9552 6910; teammc@marcut.com.au).

STUDENT TRAVEL

STA Travel is the main agent for student travellers in Australia. They have a network of travel offices around the country and apart from selling normal tickets also have special student discounts and tours. STA Travel doesn't only cater to students, they also act as normal travel agents to the public in general. The STA Travel head office is in Melbourne, but there are a number of other offices around the various cities and at the universities. The national telephone sales number is ☎ 1300 360 960, and the main offices are:

Australian Capital Territory
    13-15 Garema Place, Canberra, ACT 2601
    (☎ (02) 6247 8633)
New South Wales
    1st floor, 730 Harris St, Ultimo, Sydney 2077
    (☎ (02) 9281 5259)
Northern Territory
    Shop T17, Smith St Mall, Darwin 0800 (☎ (08) 8941 2955)
Queensland
    Shop 25-26, Brisbane Arcade, 111 Adelaide St, Brisbane 4000 (☎ (07) 3221 9388)
South Australia
    235 Rundle St, Adelaide 5000 (☎ (08) 8223 2426)
Victoria
    222 Faraday St, Carlton, Melbourne 3053 (☎ (03) 9349 2411)
Western Australia
    100 James St, Northbridge, Perth 6003 (☎ (08) 9227 7569)

Australian Capital Territory

When the separate colonies of Australia were federated in 1901 and became States, a decision to build a national capital was included in the constitution. The site was selected in 1908, diplomatically situated between arch rivals Sydney and Melbourne, and American architect Walter Burley Griffin won an international competition to design the city. In 1911 the Commonwealth government bought land for the Australian Capital Territory (ACT) and in 1913 decided to call the capital Canberra, believed to be an Aboriginal term for 'meeting place'.

Development of the site was slow and until 1927, when parliament was first convened here, Melbourne was the seat of the national government. The Depression virtually halted development and things really only got under way after WWII. In 1960 the ACT's population topped 50,000, reaching 100,000 by 1967. Today it has around 308,000 people.

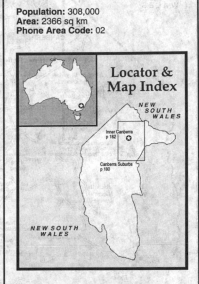

Population: 308,000
Area: 2366 sq km
Phone Area Code: 02

Locator &
Map Index

NEW SOUTH WALES

Inner Canberra
p 182

Canberra Suburbs
p 180

NEW SOUTH WALES

Highlights

- Taking a tour of the architecturally fascinating, grass-topped Parliament House
- Following the Aboriginal plant trail through the Australian National Botanic Gardens
- The Australian art collection at the National Gallery of Australia
- The display of Canberra's spring flowers at the Floriade Festival in October and November
- Cycling around Lake Burley Griffin
- Bushwalking in Tidbinbilla Nature Reserve or the dense forest of Namadgi National Park

Canberra

- *Pop 299,000*

Canberra is well worth visiting. The first things you'll notice about it are the space and how green it is. Some of the best modern architecture and exhibitions in Australia are here, and the city is fascinating because, unlike so much of Australia, it is totally planned and orderly. Canberra is a place of government with few local industries so it has a unique atmosphere only found in dedicated national capitals. It also has a beautiful setting, surrounded by hills, and is close to good bushwalking and skiing country.

Canberra has all the furnishings of a national centre – the exciting National Gallery of Australia, the splendid Parliament House and the excellent Australian National Botanic Gardens. What's more, Canberra has quite a young population, including a lot

of students, and its entertainment scene is livelier than we're usually led to believe. Finally, this is the only city in Australia where it really is possible to bump into kangaroos – they've been spotted swimming

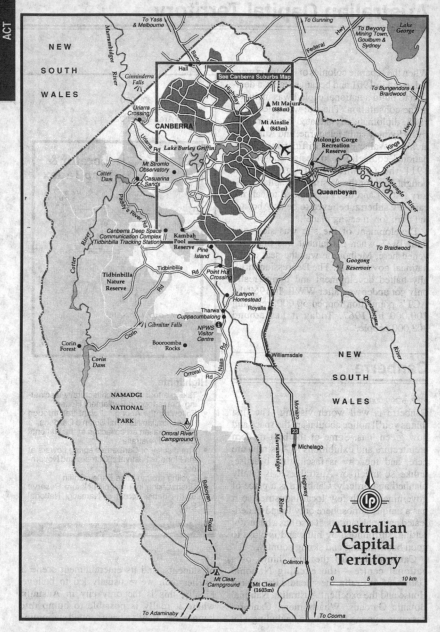

Australian
Capital
Territory

0   5   10 km

across Lake Burley Griffin and grazing in the grounds of Parliament House.

Orientation

The city is arranged around the natural-looking (but artificial) Lake Burley Griffin. On the north side is Canberra's city centre known as Civic, the heart of which is Vernon Circle, with the post office, banks and bus terminals nearby. The pedestrian malls east of the circle are Canberra's main shopping areas. The mirror-image Sydney and Melbourne buildings flank the beginning of Northbourne Ave, the main artery north of the lake.

South of Vernon Circle, Northbourne Ave becomes Commonwealth Ave and runs over Lake Burley Griffin to Capital Circle. This circular road surrounds the new Parliament House on Capital Hill and is the apex of Burley Griffin's parliamentary triangle, formed by Commonwealth Ave, Kings Ave (crossing the lake on the north-north-eastern side) and Constitution Ave. Within the parliamentary fringe, the so-called national triangle encompasses a number of important buildings such as the National Library of Australia, the High Court, the National Gallery of Australia and the old Parliament House.

South-east of Capital Hill is Manuka Circle, a pleasant shopping and dining district.

As well as the city centre and its surrounding neighbourhoods, Canberra includes the 'towns' of Belconnen, Woden and Tuggeranong.

Maps The NRMA (☎ 13 2132), 92 Northbourne Ave, has an excellent map of Canberra; the Visitor Information Centre (see the following Information entry) has a B&W version as well as topographic maps of the ACT. The ACT Government City Shop on the corner of Mort and Bunda Sts, near the Civic bus interchange and the Travellers Maps & Guides (☎ 6249 6006) shop in the Jolimont Centre also have a wide range of maps.

Information

Tourist Offices The Visitor Information Centre (☎ 6205 0044, 1800 026 166), on Northbourne Ave near the corner of Morphett St, Dickson, about 2km north of Vernon Circle, is open daily from 9 am to 6 pm. The friendly Travellers Maps & Guides (☎ 6249 6006) in the Jolimont Centre on Northbourne Ave is an excellent source of information on Canberra. Tune to 98.9FM for tourist information.

There's a Women's Information & Referral Centre (☎ 6205 1075) on the ground floor of the North Building on London Circuit.

Post & Communications Have mail addressed to poste restante at Canberra City Post Office, 53-73 Alinga St, Civic, ACT 2601. It's open Monday to Friday from 8.30 am to 5.30 pm. There are payphones and credit-card phones outside the post office and in the nearby Jolimont Centre (and elsewhere).

Bookshops Canberra has many good bookshops. Dalton's Bookshop, 54 Marcus Clarke St, Civic, specialises in computer, business and limited-edition titles. The Commonwealth Government Bookshop, 10 Mort St, has useful publications plus some glossy ones that make good souvenirs. Smith's Bookshop, 76 Alinga St, is a good alternative bookshop, while Paperchain Bookstore on Furneaux St in Manuka is more general.

Electric Shadows on City Walk, near the cinema of the same name, has books on theatre, films and the arts. It's open daily.

Book Lore, 94 Wattle St near Tilley Devine's bar in the Lyneham shopping centre, is an excellent second-hand bookshop.

Cultural Centres Canberra is well stocked with overseas information centres and clubs including Alliance Francaise (☎ 6247 5027) on McCaughey St, Turner; the British Council (☎ 9326 2365) at the British High Commission (see the earlier Foreign Embassies section); the Goethe Institute (☎ 6247 4472) in NatWest House, 40 Allara St; and

ACT

the Spanish-Australia Club (☎ 6295 6506) on Jerrabomberra Ave, Narrabundah.

Medical Services The Travellers' Medical & Vaccination Centre (☎ 6257 7154), upstairs in the City Walk Arcade near the Civic bus interchange, is open on weekdays from 9 am to 5 pm. Treatment is by appointment only. Several other clinics are nearby.

Emergency Emergency phone numbers are ☎ 000 for ambulance, fire and police; ☎ 13 1114 for Lifeline (emergency counselling); and ☎ 1800 424 017 for the Rape Crisis Centre.

Lookouts
There are fine views of Canberra from the surrounding hills. West of Civic, **Black Mountain** rises to 812m and is topped by the 195m **Telstra Tower**, complete with revolving restaurant. There's also a display on telecommunications history. The tower is open daily from 9 am to 10 pm ($3, children

$1). There are also splendid vistas from the approach road. Bus No 904 runs to the tower or you can walk up a 2km trail through bush, starting on Frith Rd. Other bushwalks, accessible from Belconnen Way and Caswell Drive, wander to the north-west round the back of the mountain. The information centre in town has a brochure with a map.

Other lookouts, all with road access, are **Mt Ainslie** (843m), **Red Hill** (720m) and **Mt Pleasant** (663m). Mt Ainslie is close to and north-east of the city and has particularly fine views, day or night. There are foot trails up Mt Ainslie from behind the Australian War Memorial, and out behind (north-west) Mt Ainslie to **Mt Majura** (888m) 4km away. You may see kangaroos on the hike up.

Lake Burley Griffin
The lake was named after Canberra's designer but wasn't created until the Molonglo River was dammed in 1963. Swimming in the lake is not recommended,

---

Canberra Walking Tour
Canberra is widely spread out, but many of the major attractions are near or around Lake Burley Griffin, within the 'parliamentary triangle' bounded by the lake, Commonwealth Ave and Kings Ave. You'll need to allow three to four hours for the following walk.

The focus of the triangle is **Parliament House** on Capital Hill. Starting from there, if you head north toward the lake along Commonwealth Ave you'll pass the Canadian, New Zealand and British **high commissions** on your left. Turning right (east) at Coronation Drive brings you to King George Terrace and **Old Parliament House**, which also houses the **National Portrait Gallery**, and the **Aboriginal Tent Embassy** on the lawns in front of Old Parliament House.

Crossing diagonally (north-westward) across the lawn in front of Old Parliament House to King Edward Terrace you arrive at the **National Library of Australia** near the lake. Beside the library is the **National Science & Technology Centre** (aka Questacon), the city's interesting interactive science museum. Along King Edward Terrace towards Kings Ave is the grand **High Court** with its ornamental watercourse burbling alongside the path leading up to the entrance. Next door across Parkes Place is the wonderful **National Gallery of Australia**.

From there follow King Edward Terrace onto Kings Ave, turn left (north-east) and follow the avenue over the lake to the other side. As you cross over you'll see on your left-hand side the **Carillon** on Aspen Island. The avenue ends at the **Australian-American Memorial**, but before you reach it, turn left (north-west) at the roundabout onto Parkes Way, which follows the northern side of the lake. After about a kilometre and off Parkes Way to the left (south) you'll come across the modest **Blundell's Farmhouse**.

Continuing along Parkes Way you'll come to another roundabout. **Anzac Parade** travels north-east from there and has a number of memorials, ending with the largest of them all, the **Australian War Memorial**. Back on Parkes Way, follow it to Commonwealth Ave. Turn left (south) and after about 500m, turn left (east) again onto Albert St and follow the path to the **National Capital Exhibition** at Regatta Point. From there you can see the **Captain Cook Memorial Water Jet** out on the lake.

If you continue south on Commonwealth Ave you will eventually come back to Parliament House.

but you can go boating on it (beware of sudden strong winds) or cycle around it. You can hire boats, bikes and in-line skates at the Acton Park ferry terminal, on the northern side of the lake.

There are many places of interest around the lake's 35km shore. The most visible is the **Captain Cook Memorial Water Jet** which flings a six-tonne column of water 147m into the air and gives you a free shower if the wind is blowing from the right direction (despite an automatic switch-off if wind speeds get too high). The jet, built in 1970 to commemorate the bicentenary of Captain Cook's visit to Australia, operates daily from 10 am to noon and 2 to 4 pm (plus 7 to 9 pm during daylight-saving time). At **Regatta Point**, nearby on the north shore, is a skeleton globe with Cook's three great voyages traced onto it.

The **National Capital Exhibition**, also at Regatta Point, is open daily from 9 am to 6 pm and has displays on the growth of the capital (admission is free). It's interesting. Further around the lake, to the east, is **Blundell's Farmhouse** (c1860). This simple stone-and-slab cottage, a reminder of the area's early farming history, is open from Tuesday to Sunday from 10 am to 4 pm ($2).

A little further around the lake, at the far end of Commonwealth Park which stretches east from the Commonwealth Ave Bridge, is the **Carillon** on Aspen Island. The 53-bell tower was a gift from Britain in 1963 for Canberra's 50th anniversary. The bells weigh from 7kg to six tonnes. There are recitals on Wednesday from 12.45 to 1.30 pm and on weekends and public holidays from 2.45 to 3.30 pm.

The southern shore of the lake, along which are the impressive National Gallery of Australia and High Court, forms the base of the national triangle.

Parliament House

South of the lake, the four-legged flag mast on top of Capital Hill marks Parliament House, at the end of Commonwealth Ave. This, the most recent aspect of Burley Griffin's vision to become a reality, sits at the apex of the parliamentary triangle. Opened in 1988, it cost $1.1 billion, took eight years to build and replaced the 'temporary' parliament house down the hill on King George Terrace, which served for 11 years longer than its intended 50-year life. The new parliament was designed by the US-based Italian Romaldo Giurgola, who won a competition entered by more than 300 architects.

It's built into the top of the hill and the roof has been grassed over to preserve the shape of the original hill top. The interior design and decoration is splendid. A different combination of Australian timbers is used in each of the main sections. Seventy Australian art and craftworks were commissioned and a further 3000 were bought for the building.

Its main axis runs from north-east to south-west and in a direct line from the old parliament, the Australian War Memorial across the lake and Mt Ainslie. On either side of this axis, two high, granite-faced walls curve out from the centre to the corners of the site. The House of Representatives is to the east of these walls, the Senate to the west. They're linked to the centre by covered walkways.

Extensive areas of Parliament House are open daily to the public from 9 am to 5 pm. You enter through the white-marble **Great Verandah** at the north-eastern end of the main axis, where Michael Tjakamarra Nelson's *Meeting Place* mosaic, within the pool, represents a gathering of Aboriginal tribes.

Inside, the grey-green marble columns of the foyer symbolise a forest, while marquetry panels on the walls depict Australian flora. From the 1st floor you look down on the **Great Hall**, with its 20m-long Arthur Boyd tapestry. A public gallery above the Great Hall has a 16m-long embroidery work, created by over 500 people.

Beyond the Great Hall you reach the gallery above the Members' Hall, the central 'crossroads' of the building, with the flag mast above it and passages to the debating chambers on each side. One of only four known originals of the **Magna Carta** is on display here. Committee rooms and

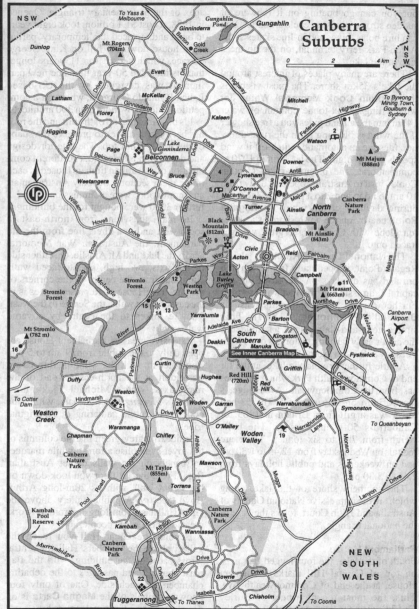

Canberra Suburbs

ministers' offices are south of the Members' Hall. The public can view the committee rooms and attend some of the proceedings. You can also wander over the grassy top of the building. If you want to ensure a place in the **House of Representatives** gallery, book by phone (☎ 6277 4890) or write to the principal attendant, House of Representatives, Parliament House, Canberra. Some seats are left unbooked, but on sitting days you have to queue early to get one. Seats in the **Senate** gallery are usually available.

On nonsitting days there are free **guided tours** every half-hour; on sitting days there's a talk on the building in the Great Hall gallery every half-hour.

Bus Nos 231, 234, 235 and 901 run from the city centre to Parliament House.

Old Parliament House

On King George Terrace, halfway between the new Parliament House and the lake, this building was the seat of government from 1927 to 1988. Its parliamentary days ended in style: as the corridors of power echoed to the defence minister's favourite Rolling Stones records, the prime minister and leader of the opposition sang together arm in arm, and bodies were seen dragging themselves away well after dawn the next morning – and that's just what got into print!

There are tours of the building and regular exhibitions from the collections of the National Museum and the Australian Archives. The building is also home to the **National Portrait Gallery** (☎ 6273 4723).

Old Parliament House is open daily from 9 am to 4 pm ($2, children $1).

On the lawn in front of Old Parliament House is the **Aboriginal Tent Embassy**. Established in 1972 to persuade the federal government to recognise the legitimacy of Australian and Torres Strait Islander land claims, its now recognised by the Australian Heritage Commission as a site of special cultural significance. It was here that the Aboriginal flag first gained prominence.

National Gallery of Australia

This excellent art gallery (☎ 6240 6411/ 6502) is on Parkes Place beside the High Court and the south bank of Lake Burley Griffin. The Australian collection ranges from traditional Aboriginal art to 20th-century works by Arthur Boyd, Sidney Nolan and Albert Tucker. Aboriginal works include bark paintings from Arnhem Land, *pukumani* burial poles from the Tiwi people of Melville and Bathurst islands off Darwin, printed fabrics by the women of Utopia and Ernabella in central Australia, and paintings from Yuendumu, also in central Australia. There are often temporary exhibitions from the Kimberley and other areas where Aboriginal art is flourishing.

In addition to works from the early decades of European settlement and the 19th-century romantics, there are examples of the early nationalistic statements of Charles Conder, Arthur Streeton and Tom Roberts. The collection is not confined to paintings: sculptures, prints, drawings, photographs, furniture, ceramics, fashion, textiles and silverware are all on display. The

ACT

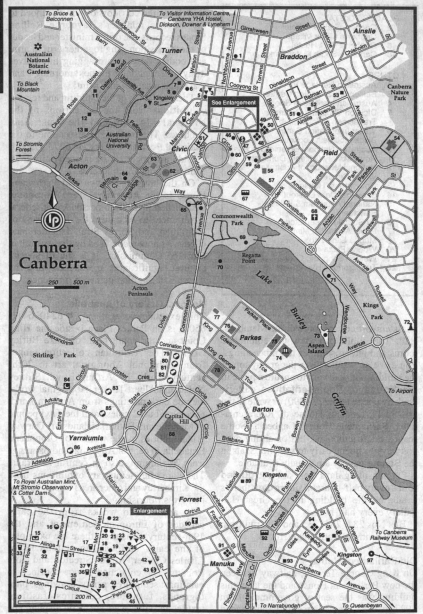

To Bruce &
Belconnen

To Visitor Information Centre,
Canberra YHA Hostel,
Dickson, Downer & Lyneham

Australian
National Botanic
Gardens

To Black
Mountain

To Stromlo
Forest

Turner

Ainslie

Braddon

Canberra
Nature
Park

Civic

Australian
National University

Acton

See Enlargement

Reid

**Inner
Canberra**

0   250   500 m

Acton
Peninsula

Commonwealth
Park

Regatta
Point

Lake

Burley

Kings
Park

Alexandrina

Stirling   Park

Parkes

Aspen
Island

Coronation Dve

Barton

To Airport

Griffin

Arkana

Capital
Hill

Yarralumia

Kingston

To Royal Australian Mint,
Mt Stromlo Observatory
& Cotter Dam

Forrest

To Canberra
Railway Museum

Manuka

Kingston

Enlargement

To Narrabundah

To Queanbeyan

0   200 m

Sculpture Garden (always open) has a variety of striking sculptures. The garden is a great place to listen to carillon recitals.

The gallery is open daily from 10 am to 5 pm ($3, admission is free for children and full-time students). There are free tours at 11 am and 2 pm; every Thursday and Sunday at 11 am a free tour focuses on Aboriginal art.

PLACES TO STAY
2 Downtown Spero's Motel
7 Toad Hall
10 Bruce Hall
11 Burton & Garran Hall
12 Ursula College
13 Burgmann College
18 City Walk Hotel
52 Acacia Motor Lodge
53 Olim's Canberra Hotel
89 Macquarie Private Hotel
93 Kingston Hotel
95 Motel Monaro
96 Victor Lodge

PLACES TO EAT
3 Psychedeli
4 Fringe Benefits
9 University Union
23 Mama's Cafe & Bar
24 Sammy's Kitchen; Gus's Cafe
25 Ali Baba; Heaven Nite Club
27 Noshes Cafe
34 Lemon Grass
37 Thai Lotus; Canberra Vietnamese
39 Bailey's Corner; Tosolini's
40 Antigo Cafe
42 Red Sea Restaurant & Club Asmara; Tutu Tango
49 Sizzle City
59 Anarkali Pakistani Restaurant

OTHER
1 NRMA
5 Dalton's Bookshop
6 Environment Centre
8 Drill Hall Gallery
14 Canberra Workers' Club
15 Main Post Office
16 Jolimont Centre (Countrylink, Airlines, Bus Station, Travellers Maps & Guides)
17 Pandora's

19 Travellers' Medical & Vaccination Centre
20 Civic Cinemas 3
21 Center Cinema
22 ACT Government City Shop
26 Wilderness Society Shop
28 ACT Government City Shopfront
29 Police Kiosk
30 Civic Bus Interchange
31 Private Bin
32 Smith's Bookshop
33 Wig & Pen
35 Moosehead's Pub
36 Asylum & Phoenix
38 Commonwealth Government Bookshop
41 ANZ Bank
43 Commonwealth Bank
44 Merry-go-round
45 Westpac Bank
46 Women's Information & Referral Centre
47 National Australia Bank
48 Canberra Centre
50 City Market
51 Gorman House Community Arts Centre & Cafe Luna
54 Australian War Memorial
55 Canberra Blade Centre
56 Casino Canberra
57 National Convention Centre
58 Electric Shadows Cinema & Bookshop
60 Canberra Theatre Centre
61 Canberra City Police Station
62 Australian Academy of Science
63 National Film & Sound Archive

64 University House
65 Acton Park Ferry Terminal & Boat Hire
66 Mr Spokes Bike Hire
67 Olympic Swimming Pool
68 Church of St John the Baptist; St John's Schoolhouse Museum
69 National Capital Exhibition
70 Captain Cook Memorial Water Jet
71 Blundell's Farmhouse
72 Australian-American Memorial
73 Carillon
74 National Gallery of Australia
75 High Court
76 National Science & Technology Centre
77 National Library of Australia
78 Old Parliament House
79 UK High Commission
80 NZ High Commission
81 Canadian High Commission
82 PNG High Commission
83 Indonesian Embassy
84 Canberra Mosque
85 US Embassy
86 Thai Embassy
87 The Lodge
88 Parliament House
90 Serbian Orthodox Church
91 Manuka Shopping Centre
92 Manuka Swimming Pool
94 Kingston Shopping Centre
97 Train Station

ACT

The gallery often provides free lectures relating to its exhibitions and presents films on Friday at 12.45 pm. Phone the gallery for details or check Saturday's *Canberra Times*.

Foreign Consulates There are about 60 embassies and high commissions in Canberra. A few are worth looking at, although many operate from nondescript suburban houses. Most are in Yarralumla, west and north of Parliament House. Some have an open day when the public can visit; ask the Visitor Information Centre staff if any are scheduled.

The US Embassy is a facsimile of a southern mansion, in the style of those in Williamsburg, Virginia. Opposite is the Mughal-inspired Indian High Commission. The Thai Embassy, with its pointed, orange-tile roof, is in a style similar to that of Bangkok temples. Beside the dull Indonesian Embassy building is a small display centre exhibiting the country's colourful culture. It's open on weekdays from 9.30 am to 12.30 pm and 2 to 4 pm. Papua New Guinea's high commission looks like a 'haus tambaran' (spirit house) from the Sepik region. A display room containing colour photographs and artefacts is open on weekdays from 10 am to 12.30 pm and 2 to 4.30 pm.

See the Embassies section in the Facts for the Visitor chapter for the addresses of embassies and high commissions.

High Court
The High Court building (☎ 6270 6811) on King Edward Terrace by the lake and next to the National Gallery of Australia is open daily from 9.45 am to 4.30 pm (admission is free). Opened in 1980, its grandiose magnificence caused it to be dubbed 'Gar's Mahal', a reference to Sir Garfield Barwick, Chief Justice during the building's construction. High Court sittings are open to the public (call for times) and, because of the good acoustics, music is often played in the foyer on weekends.

National Science & Technology Centre (Questacon)
This is a 'hands-on' science museum in the snappy white building between the High Court and the National Library of Australia. There are 200 'devices' in the centre's five galleries and outdoor areas where you can use 'props' to get a feeling for a scientific concept and then see it applied to an everyday situation. It might be educational but it's also great fun.

It's open daily from 10 am to 5 pm ($8, children $4, concessions $5).

National Library of Australia
Also on Parkes Place beside the lake is the National Library of Australia (☎ 6262 1111), one of the most elegant buildings in Canberra. The visitor information desk is staffed on weekdays from 9 am to 5 pm.

The library has more than five million books and among its displays are rare books, paintings, early manuscripts and maps, Captain Cook's *Endeavour* journal, a fine model of the ship itself and special exhibitions. There are guided tours at 2 pm from Tuesday to Thursday and free films on Thursday at 7 pm. You can access the Internet at a terminal in the foyer and in the Brindabella Bistro on the 4th floor.

The library is open from Monday to Thursday from 9 am to 9 pm, on Friday and Saturday from 9 am to 5 pm and on Sunday from 1.30 to 5 pm.

Royal Australian Mint
The mint (☎ 6202 6999), south of the lake on Denison St, Deakin, produces Australia's coins. Through plate-glass windows (to keep you at arm's length) you can see the process from raw materials to finished coins. There's a collection of rare coins in the foyer. The mint is open on weekdays from 9 am to 4 pm and on weekends from 10 am to 3 pm (admission is free). Bus Nos 230, 231 and 267 run past.

Australian War Memorial
The massive war memorial, north of the lake and at the foot of Mt Ainslie, looks along

Anzac Parade to old Parliament House across the lake. It was conceived in 1925 and finally opened in 1941. It houses an amazing collection of pictures, dioramas, relics and exhibitions. For the less military-minded, the memorial has an excellent **art collection**. The **Hall of Memory** is the focus of the memorial. Entombed here is the Unknown Australian Soldier, whose remains were returned from a WWI battlefield in 1993.

The memorial is open daily from 10 am to 5 pm (when the *Last Post* is played) and admission is free. Several free tours are held each day, some focusing on the artworks. Phone ☎ 6243 4268 for times. Bus Nos 233, 302, 303, 362, 363, 436 and 901 stop nearby.

There are memorials along Anzac Parade to several conflicts and campaigns.

Australian National University (ANU)
The ANU's attractive grounds take up most of the area between Civic and Black Mountain and are pleasant to wander through. University House (☎ 6249 2229) on Balmain Crescent is open on weekdays. The University Union on University Ave offers a variety of cheap eats and entertainment. On Kingsley St near the junction with Hutton St is the **Drill Hall Gallery** (☎ 6249 5832), an offshoot of the National Gallery of Australia with changing exhibitions of contemporary art. It's open from Wednesday to Sunday from noon to 5 pm (admission is free).

National Film & Sound Archive
The archive (☎ 6209 3111) is in an Art Deco building on McCoy Circuit at the southeastern edge of the university area. There are interesting exhibitions (some interactive) from the archive's collections. It is open daily from 9 am to 5 pm (admission is free).

Over the road is the **Australian Academy of Science** (not open to the public), known locally as the Martian Embassy – it looks like a misplaced flying saucer.

Australian National Botanic Gardens
On the lower slopes of Black Mountain, behind the ANU, the beautiful 50-hectare botanic gardens are devoted to Australian

flora. There are educational walks, including one among plants used by Aborigines. A highlight is the **rainforest area**, achieved in this dry climate by a 'misting' system, while the **eucalypt lawn** has 600 species of this ubiquitous Australian tree.

There are **guided walks** from Monday to Friday at 11 am and on weekends at 11 am and 2 pm. The information centre (☎ 6250 9540; open daily from 9.30 am to 4.30 pm) has an introductory video about the gardens. Near where the walks start and finish is the *Kookaburra Cafe* with a pleasant outdoor section.

The gardens are open daily from 9 am to 5 pm and are reached from Clunies Ross St (take bus No 904).

Australian Institute of Sport (AIS)
The AIS (☎ 6252 1111) is on Leverrier Crescent in the northern suburb of Bruce. It provides training facilities for the country's top athletes, who lead hour-long tours of the institute daily at 11 am and 2 pm ($7, children $3). The tennis courts and swimming pools are open to the public; phone ☎ 6252 1281 for times. Bus No 431 runs to the AIS from the city centre.

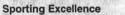

Sporting Excellence
Although Australians had done well at international sporting events during the 1950s and 60s, their success had declined considerably by the 1970s. Out of this slump the Australian Institute of Sport (AIS) was born in 1981.

Supplied with the country's top coaches and some of the best facilities in the world, the AIS's aim was achieving sporting excellence in areas such as athletics, swimming and tennis. It later expanded its range of sports and also helped to develop sports institutes at a state level. Its methods proved successful: in the 1990s Australian sportspeople have performed well at major sporting occasions like the Commonwealth and Olympic games. This success has drawn international attention and the AIS's main focus is now on the 2000 Sydney Olympics. ■

ACT

National Aquarium & Wildlife Sanctuary

The impressive aquarium is about 6km south-west of the city centre on Lady Denman Drive near Scrivener Dam, at the western end of Lake Burley Griffin. It also has a sanctuary for native fauna. It's open daily from 9 am to 5.30 pm ($10, children $6). Take bus No 904 from the Civic bus interchange.

National Museum of Australia

A site for this long-awaited museum might have finally been found on Acton Peninsula, west of the Commonwealth Ave Bridge. Meanwhile, the visitor centre on Lady Denman Drive north of Yarralumla displays items from the museum's collection; it's open on weekdays from 10 am to 4 pm and on weekends from 1 to 4 pm.

Other Attractions

You can do no more than drive by and peek through the gates of the prime minister's official Canberra residence, The Lodge, on Adelaide Ave, Deakin. The same is true of Government House, the residence of the Governor-General, which is on the south-western corner of Lake Burley Griffin, but there's a lookout beside Scrivener Dam at the end of the lake, giving a good view of the building. The Governor-General is the representative of the Australian monarch – who lives in London and also happens to be the British monarch.

The Australian-American Memorial at the eastern end of Kings Ave is a 79m-high pillar topped by an eagle. It recognises US support for Australia during WWII.

The Church of St John the Baptist in Reid, just east of Civic, was built between 1841 and 1845. The stained-glass windows were donated by pioneering families of the region. The adjoining St John's Schoolhouse Museum has some early relics and is open on Wednesday from 10 am to noon and on weekends from 2 to 4 pm ($1.50).

The Royal Military College, Duntroon, was once a homestead, with sections dating from the 1830s. Between April and October, free guided tours start at the sign in Starkey Park on Jubilee Ave on Tuesday and Thursday (except public holidays) at 2.30 pm. Bookings (☎ 6275 9408) are advised.

The enterprising Tradesmen's Union Club, 2 Badham St off Antill St, Dickson, has a large collection of 'old and unusual bicycles'. The club also runs the Downer Club nearby on Hawdon St, home to 'the world's largest beer collection', although it has been put in storage indefinitely. There's also an Antarctic igloo on display. Not interested? Well, what about an observatory with an astronomer on duty nightly from 7 pm? A new planetarium is being built. Admission to all this is free.

Bushwalking

Tidbinbilla Nature Reserve, south-west of the city centre, has marked trails; see the Around Canberra section later in the chapter for details of this and other bushwalking places. Contact the Canberra Bushwalking Club through the Environment Centre (☎ 6247 3064) on Kingsley St on the ANU campus. Here you can buy *Above the Cotter*, which details walks and drives in the area. Graeme Barrow's *Exploring Namadgi National Park and Tidbinbilla Nature Reserve* is useful for planning day walks. (There are also some good rock climbing areas in Namadgi National Park.)

Bushwalking information is also available from the ACT Government City Shop on the corner of Mort and Bunda Sts.

Water Sports

Dobel Boat Hire (☎ 6249 6861) at the Acton Park ferry terminal on the northern shore of Lake Burley Griffin rents out canoes at $12 an hour and catamarans at $35 an hour, as well as paddle-boats, sailboards and surf skis. Canoeing on the Murrumbidgee River, about 20km west of Canberra at its closest point, is also popular.

Swimming pools around the city include the Olympic Swimming Pool on Allara St, Civic, and the pool in Manuka. Swimming in Lake Burley Griffin is not recommended.

River Runners (☎ 6288 5610) offers a 5½-hour white-water rafting trip on the

Shoalhaven River, 1½ hours drive east of Canberra, for $115 – or less if you can meet them there.

Cycling
Canberra has a great series of bicycle tracks – probably the best in Australia. See the Getting Around section later in the chapter for more information.

In-Line Skating
Several places hire out skates. Mr Spokes Bike Hire (☎ 6257 1188) near the Acton Park ferry terminal charges $15 for the first hour and $5 for subsequent hours. Canberra Blade Centre (☎ 6257 7233), 38 Akuna St, Civic, charges $15 for the first two hours and $5 for subsequent hours. Fees at both include all safety wear.

Organised Tours
The Visitor Information Centre (☎ 6205 0044, 1800 026 166) has details of the many tours of the city and ACT. Half-day city tours start at around $30. Canberra Cruises (☎ 6295 3544) has 1½-hour cruises on Lake Burley Griffin for $12 (children $6). Umbrella Tours (☎ 6285 2605), 1 Bailey Place, Yarralumla, offers 1½-hour walking tours ($9) and three-hour cycling tours ($45) of the city.

Taking a flight is a good way of seeing the grand scale of the city's plan and several outfits offer aeroplane flights. The Canberra Flight Training Centre (☎ 6248 6766) based at the airport has 40-minute scenic flights for $80 (minimum of two people).

Special Events
The Canberra Festival takes place over 10 days in March and celebrates the city's birthday with fun events, many of which are held in Commonwealth Park. In September and October the Floriade Festival concentrates on Canberra's spectacular spring flowers but has many other events, including music, dance and circus-type entertainment.

Places to Stay
Camping *Canberra Motor Village* (☎ 6247

5466), 6km north-west of the city centre on Kunzea St, O'Connor, has a bush setting and charges $17 for sites and $62 a double for on-site vans and cabins. There's a restaurant, kitchen, tennis court and swimming pool.

Canberra South Motor Park (☎ 6280 6176) is 8km south-east of the city in Fyshwick, on Canberra Ave, the main road to Queanbeyan. A tent site costs $12 or $16 with power; cabins are from $35 to $75 a double.

Hostels In the centre of Canberra, the *City Walk Hotel* (☎ 6257 0124), 2 Mort St on the corner of City Walk, has dorm beds for $16 and singles/doubles for $37/42. Most rooms share bathrooms but this place is a reasonable option, with a spacious TV lounge and kitchen facilities.

The *Canberra YHA Hostel* (☎ 6248 9155), 191 Dryandra St, O'Connor, about 6km north-west of Civic, has been named the second most popular YHA hostel worldwide. It's purpose built, and well designed and equipped. There is a travel desk which handles domestic and international travel and you can hire bicycles. Dorm beds cost $16, twin rooms $21/23 per person with shared/private bathroom. (Add $3 if you aren't a YHA member.) The office is open from 7 am to 10.30 pm but you can check in up until midnight if you give advance warning. Bus No 304 runs regularly from the Civic bus interchange to the Scrivener St stop on Miller St, O'Connor. From there, follow the signs. From the Jolimont Centre, take bus No 307 or 308 to the corner of Scrivener and Brigalow Sts, head north-east up Scrivener St to Dryandra St and turn right.

The *Kingston Hotel* (☎ 6295 0123) is a large, popular pub on the corner of Canberra Ave and Giles St in Manuka, about 2km south-east of Parliament House. It offers shared accommodation for $12 with optional linen hire ($4). There are cooking facilities, although counter meals are available. Bus No 238 from the city runs past.

Colleges The Australian National University (ANU) in Acton, just west of Civic, is a pleasant place to stay. A selection of residential colleges rents out rooms during university holidays in Easter (one week), June/July and September (two weeks), and late-November to late-February.

Toad Hall (☎ 6267 4999) on Kingsley St near the corner of Barry Drive is the closest to the city centre and has basic rooms for $16.50/98 a day/week.

Most other colleges are along Daley Rd at the western end of the campus near Clunies Ross St. At *Burgmann College* (☎ 6267 5222) rates for students/nonstudents are $30/40 with breakfast or $38/48 for full board. *Bruce Hall* (☎ 6267 4050) and *Burton & Garran Hall* (☎ 6267 4333) have rooms for $30 a night for the first two nights (it costs less per night if you stay longer). *Fenner Hall* (☎ 6279 9000) has basic rooms for $25/110 a day/week. *Ursula College* (☎ 6279 43 00) has rooms at a similar price.

Guesthouses & Private Hotels *Victor Lodge* (☎ 6295 7777) is a clean and friendly place at 29 Dawes St, Kingston, about 500m from the train station and 2km south-east of Parliament House. Rooms with shared bathrooms are $35/44 a single/double or you can share a four-bunk room for $16, including a light breakfast. It has a barbecue and offers bike rental. Several travellers have reported enjoying their stay here. From the city take bus No 352 to the nearby Kingston shops, or phone to see if lodge staff can pick you up.

Also south of the lake, the modern *Macquarie Private Hotel* (☎ 6273 2325), 18 National Circuit on the corner of Bourke St, has over 500 rooms, all with shared bathrooms. Singles cost $39 to $50, while doubles are $60. Breakfast deals are available but aren't great value. Bus No 310 from the city stops at the front door.

Entering Canberra from the north, there's a cluster of guesthouses on the east side of Northbourne Ave in Downer, south of where the Barton Highway from Yass and the Federal Highway from Goulburn meet. All are clean, straightforward and comfortable. It's 4km or so into town, but buses run past and Dickson shopping centre isn't far away.

At No 524 *Blue & White Lodge* (☎ 6248 0498), which also runs the similarly priced *Blue Sky* at No 528, has singles/doubles for from $46/60 to $60/75. Prices include a cooked breakfast, and rooms have TV and a fridge, but most bathrooms are shared. Its staff can probably pick you up from the bus station. *Chelsea Lodge* (☎ 6248 0655) at No 526 also does pick-ups and charges $60/75 with private bathroom; rates include cooked breakfast. *Northbourne Lodge* (☎ 6257 2599) at No 522 is a pleasant place with rooms, including breakfast, for $55/68 or $65/80 with bathroom.

Motels Most motels are expensive and few resemble those seen elsewhere in Australia; many are ex-government guesthouses. You might do better than the prices listed here if you book at the visitor information centre which often has special rates.

The *Acacia Motor Lodge* (☎ 6249 6955), 65 Ainslie Ave, Braddon, is near the centre but the rooms are small. It charges from $69/75 for a single/double including a light breakfast. South of the centre next to Victor Lodge is *Motel Monaro* (☎ 6295 2111), 27 Dawes St, Kingston, which has rooms for $76/79.

Other places are scattered throughout the suburbs, with a cluster of mid-range motels about 8km south-east of the city in Narrabundah, most on Jerrabomberra Ave.

More-expensive places include the old but pleasant *Olim's Canberra Hotel* (☎ 6248 5511) on the corner of Ainslie and Limestone Aves, Braddon. Rooms cost from $95 a single or double.

Places to Eat

Canberra has a fine eating scene. Most places are around Civic, with an upmarket selection in Manuka, an Asian strip in Dickson and other possibilities scattered around the suburbs. Smoking isn't allowed in Canberra's eateries.

City Centre There's a food hall in the lower section of the *Canberra Centre* on City Walk where you can fill up on burgers, pasta, croissants and more for $4 to $7. There's a smaller food hall in *City Market* on Bunda St, where the excellent *Sizzle City* has cheap Japanese lunch packs.

Upstairs in the Sydney building at 27 East Row, *Thai Lotus* is one of the best places to eat. It's open nightly for dinner and lunch from Tuesday to Friday. The food is excellent and prices reasonable; most meat mains cost $12.50, while vegetable dishes are $9.50. Nearby at No 21, the *Canberra Vietnamese Restaurant* has main courses for less than $10.

Bailey's Corner, on the corner of East Row and London Circuit, has a couple of places with outdoor tables. *Tosolini's* is an Italian-based bistro, good for a drink or a meal, including breakfast. Lunch-time specials start at $10 and in the evening pasta dishes are $9 and mains $14. The cakes here are to die for. Around the corner in Petrie Plaza, the *Antigo Cafe* is a cafe and bar open daily until late. The diverse menu includes a seafood barbecue for $15.90 and pasta for $12.90.

On the southern end of the Melbourne building, *Lemon Grass* is a Thai restaurant with seafood mains for $14 and a good selection of vegetarian dishes for $11. Behind the Westpac Bank on the corner of London Circuit and Akuna St, the cosy *Anarkali Pakistani Restaurant* has lunch specials for $15 and dinner specials for $19.

Garema Place, just north-east of London Circuit, is full of restaurants and cafes. Popular with students, *Noshes Cafe* has breakfast all day for $4, decent coffee and cheap pasta. *Happy's* is a popular, reasonably priced Chinese restaurant with noodle dishes for $7.50 to $9.50. Nearby, *Mama's Cafe & Bar* serves home-made pasta for $9 and other meals for around $12 in a good atmosphere.

Around the corner on Bunda St, *Gus's Cafe* has outdoor tables and serves unpretentious food (no sun-dried tomato has ever darkened this door). Soup is $6 and pasta is $8.50. Gus's is open until midnight during the week and later on weekends. Not far away, the Chinese/Malaysian *Sammy's Kitchen* has a good reputation and many dishes between $7 and $11. *Ali Baba*, on the corner of Bunda St and Garema Place's southern arm, does Lebanese takeaways, including shawarma and felafel for around $4 and meals for $9 to $10.50.

The *Red Sea Restaurant* at Club Asmara, 121 Bunda St, has interesting decor and main courses, some African, for from $13 to $15. It's closed on Sunday. *Tutu Tango* at No 124 is a cafe and bar with a varied menu: pizzas are $12 and vegetarian tostados are $15.50.

There are a couple of good eating options on Marcus Clarke St, north-west of Civic. The excellent *Fringe Benefits*, 54 Marcus Clarke St, is a brasserie which has regularly won national wine and food awards, and has main courses for around $20. Nearby at No 60, *Psychedeli* has good coffee, foccacia and pizza.

Manuka South of the lake, not far from Capital Hill, is the Manuka shopping centre, which services the diplomatic corps and well-heeled bureaucrats from surrounding neighbourhoods. There are plenty of cafes and restaurants on Franklin, Fourneaux and Bougainville Sts and on Flinders Way.

Several bars-cum-cafes stay open late. *On Fourneaux*, 2 Furneaux St on the corner of Franklin St, has pizzas for $12.90 and burgers for $13.90; it also serves good gelati. The stylish *La Grange* bar and brasserie further south on Franklin St has main courses for around $16 and live music on weekends.

Across Franklin St is *My Cafe*, with bagels and foccacia for $4.50 and main courses for between $8.50 and $10.50. Upstairs in the nearby Style Arcade, *Alanya* is a good Turkish restaurant with starters for $8 to $10 and mains (including vegetarian) for between $10 and $15. Also here is *Chez Daniel*, one of Canberra's better restaurants, serving French and Moroccan food. Its creative main courses usually cost around $20, but it has a lunch-time three-course special for $27.90.

Timmy's Kitchen on Furneaux St is a popular Malaysian/Chinese place with main courses for $7.50 to $12.70; it has a good vegetarian selection.

Dickson The Dickson shopping area, a few kilometres north of Civic, is a thriving restaurant district sometimes called Little China because of its many Asian restaurants.

Dickson Asian Noodle House, 19 Woolley St, is a popular Lao and Thai cafe with dishes for around $9. The Japanese *Sakura* at No 51, opposite the BP service station, has lunch specials for under $10. The Malaysian *Rasa Sayang* at No 43 charges reasonable prices, with noodles for $8.80 and a good vegetarian selection. *Pho Phu Quoc*, 4-6 Cape St, is a good Vietnamese restaurant with wonton soup for $2.50 and beef and rice noodles for $6.

La Lupa is a popular cafe with outside tables and jazz on Sunday mornings.

Elsewhere There's cheap food at the student union *Refectory* on University Ave at the ANU.

In Lyneham, *Tilley Devine's*, 96 Wattle St on the corner of Brigelow St, is a well-known cafe and bar. The food is healthy (if you don't count the great cakes), the clientele is diverse and there is often entertainment. Burgers are $6.90 and salads are $9.80.

Entertainment

Canberra is more lively than its reputation suggests. Liberal licensing laws allow hotels unlimited opening hours and there are some 24-hour bars. Underage drinking is strictly policed; if you don't have ID proving you're over 18, forget it. The 'Good Times' section in the Thursday *Canberra Times* has entertainment listings and the free monthly *BMA* magazine lists bands and other events.

If you're tired of Australian leagues clubs and workers' clubs, phone one of the clubs catering to Australians of foreign descent to find out if visitors are welcome – see the *Yellow Pages* under the heading 'Clubs, Social & General'. Also check with the foreign cultural organisations (see under the Cultural Centres heading in the earlier Information section) to find out what's on.

Cinemas There are several cinemas in the Civic Square and London Circuit area. *Electric Shadows* is an art-house cinema on City Walk near Akuna St; entry is $12.

The *National Library of Australia* shows free films on Thursday night at 7 pm. The *National Gallery of Australia* has screenings on art-related topics on Friday at 12.45 pm.

Performing Arts The *Canberra Theatre Centre* (☎ 6257 1077) on Civic Square has several theatres with a varied range of events. *Gorman House Community Arts Centre* (☎ 6249 7377), Ainslie Ave, Braddon, is home to several theatre and dance companies which put on occasional performances and exhibitions.

Pubs, Bars & Nightclubs Friday night is the big drinking night in Canberra when everyone winds down after a hard week.

There's live music two or three nights a week during term at the *ANU union bar*, which is a good place for a drink even when there's no entertainment. Big touring acts often play at the *Refectory* here.

In Civic, the Sydney building has a number of venues including the popular *Moosehead's Pub* on the south side at 105 London Circuit. Around the corner, *Private Bin*, 50 Northbourne Ave, is a big bar and nightclub that's popular with younger dancers. The *Phoenix*, 21 East Row, has poetry and quiz nights. *Asylum*, upstairs at No 23, has live music most nights; entry costs $4 to $8, depending on who's playing. Not far away, *Pandora's* on the corner of Alinga and Mort Sts has a bar downstairs and a dance club upstairs.

Heaven Nite Club on Garema Place is popular with gays. *Club Asmara*, 121 Bunda St near Garema Place, is home to the Red Sea Restaurant. The musical emphasis is on African, Latin and reggae rhythms. After about 9 pm you can listen to music, sometimes live, without ordering a meal; on Friday and Saturday, however, there's a $5 cover charge. The *Wig & Pen* on the corner of West Row and Alinga St is a British-style pub serving real ale.

Olim's Canberra Hotel, on the corner of Limestone and Ainslie Aves, Braddon, has a piano bar (free jazz performances on Thursday night) and a popular beer garden.

In Kingston in the Green Square shopping area, *Filthy McFadden's*, 62 Jardine St, is an Irish pub with music most nights. Nearby, the *Durham Castle Arms* occasionally has live bands performing jazz and blues.

In Lyneham, *Tilley Devine's*, 96 Wattle St on the corner of Brigelow St, has live music, usually a cut above pub bands, on weekend nights. It also has poetry nights and talks by guest writers.

The *Canberra Southern Cross Club*, on the corner of Corinna St and Hindmarsh Drive in Phillip, south-west of the city, has local bands on Friday night and sometimes good jazz.

Other places that occasionally have bands include the *Canberra Workers' Club* on Childers St in Civic and the *Tradesmen's Union Club*, 2 Badham St, in Dickson.

Casino The *Casino Canberra*, 21 Binara St near the National Convention Centre, is open daily from noon to 6 am. It's a fairly casual place: before 7 pm T-shirts, jeans and sports shoes are OK, but after 7 pm men have to wear a shirt with a collar and shoes other than runners.

Things to Buy
Artwares Gift Gallery at Gorman House Community Arts Centre on Ainslie Ave sells craftwork by local and international artisans. There's also an interesting craft market at the centre on Sunday.

The Old Bus Depot Market on Wentworth Ave in Kingston is held every Sunday, with stalls selling art and craft with a New Age slant, as well as food from around the world.

The Wilderness Society Shop on Garema Place and the Bogong Environment Shop in the Environment Centre on Kingsley St sell books, gifts and other products with an ecological theme.

Getting There & Away
Air Canberra doesn't have an international airport. Sydney is about half an hour away and a standard one-way fare with the two

major airlines is $158; Melbourne is about an hour's flight ($222) away, while direct flights to Adelaide and Brisbane cost $327 and $329 respectively. These prices drop dramatically when you book in advance, and other special deals are often available. Ansett Express (☎ 13 1300) offers a night flight to Sydney for $178 return.

Qantas Airways (☎ 13 1313) and Ansett Australia (☎ 13 1300) are both in the Jolimont Centre.

Although fares with Eastern Australia Airlines (☎ 13 1313) and Ansett Express are the same as regular Qantas and Ansett flights, services are more frequent. Other smaller airlines fly to NSW country destinations. Air Facilities (☎ 6041 1210) flies daily to Albury.

Bus Several bus lines have booking offices and their main stop is at the Jolimont Centre. Greyhound Pioneer Australia (☎ 13 2030) has the most frequent Sydney service ($32), which takes four to five hours. It also runs to Adelaide ($99) and Melbourne ($50). Services to Cooma ($16) and to Thredbo in the New South Wales snowfields ($38, including park entry fees) are frequent in winter, less so at other times.

Murrays (☎ 6295 3611) also has daily express buses to Sydney (under four hours) for $28 and to the NSW coast at Batemans Bay ($22) and connects with buses running up to Nowra ($39). Capital Coachlines (☎ 6292 9412) runs to Bathurst ($36); book through the Countrylink Travel Centre (see under the later Bus & Train heading).

McCafferty's (☎ 13 1499) has buses to Sydney ($28), Melbourne ($45) and Adelaide ($96); you can book through the Travellers Maps & Guides shop in the Jolimont Centre.

Transborder Express (☎ 6226 1378) runs to Yass for $10 one way; a same-day return is $12. Sid Fogg's (☎ 4928 1088) runs between Newcastle and Canberra on Monday, Wednesday and Friday for $45 one way.

Bus & Train The train station (☎ 6239 7039)

is south of Lake Burley Griffin on Wentworth Ave in Kingston. You can make bookings for trains and connecting buses at the Countrylink Travel Centre (☎ 6257 1576) in the Jolimont Centre. There are two trains making the four-hour trip to Sydney ($40 one way) daily.

There's no direct train to Melbourne. The daily V/Line Canberra Link service involves a train between Melbourne and Wodonga and a connecting bus to Canberra ($44, about nine hours). A longer, more interesting bus/train service to Melbourne is the V/Line Capital Link which runs via Cooma and the forests of Victoria's East Gippsland, then down the Princes Highway to Sale, where you catch a train. This trip takes over 11 hours and costs $47.

Car & Motorcycle The Hume Highway, connecting Sydney and Melbourne, passes about 50km north of Canberra. The Federal Highway runs north to the Hume near Goulburn, while the Barton Highway meets the Hume near Yass. To the south, the Monaro Highway connects Canberra with Cooma.

Major car-rental companies with offices in the city, as well as desks at the airport, are:

Avis
   (☎ 6249 6088) 17 Lonsdale St, Braddon
Budget
   (☎ 6257 1305) On the corner of Mort and Girrahween Sts, Braddon
Hertz
   (☎ 6257 4877) 32 Mort St, Braddon
Thrifty
   (☎ 6247 7422) 29 Lonsdale St, Braddon

Cheaper outfits include Rumbles (☎ 6280 7444), 157 Gladstone St in Fyshwick, and Rent a Dent (☎ 6257 5947), 8 Ijong St in Braddon, whose staff will pick you up from the Jolimont Centre. Expect to pay from $35 or $40 a day with the first 200km free of charge on longer rentals.

Getting Around
To/From the Airport The airport is 7km south-east of the city centre. Note all the

government cars lined up outside waiting to pick up 'pollies' and public servants. The only airport bus service is ACT Minibuses (☎ 6291 4592), which charges $8 and picks up from the Jolimont Centre, various hotels and the YHA; you have to book. The taxi fare from the airport to Civic is around $10.

Bus Buses operated by the Australian Capital Territory Internal Omnibus Network (ACTION; ☎ 6207 7611) run fairly frequently.

The main interchange is along Alinga St between Northbourne Ave and East Row/Mort St in Civic, not far from the Jolimont Centre. The information kiosk on the corner of Alinga St and East Row is open daily until about 11.30 pm, though it only sells tickets until about 5.30 pm. If you'll be using buses a lot it's worth buying the *ACTION Bus Book* ($2) here.

The flat 'one route' fare is $2 and you need the correct change. Fares on the commuter express buses – the No 700 series – are $4. You can save money with pre-purchase tickets, available from newsagents and elsewhere but not on buses. A book of 10 FareGo tickets costs $14; a weekly ticket is $24. Daily Tickets are great value as they offer unlimited travel for $6.

Special Services The free Downtowner service is a bus disguised as a tram, which runs around the Civic shopping centre, stopping at specially designated stops.

Sightseeing Bus No 901 runs to the Australian War Memorial, Regatta Point, Questacon, the National Gallery of Australia, Parliament House and several embassies in Yarralumla; bus No 904 goes to the Australian National Botanic Gardens, National Museum, National Aquarium and Telstra Tower. Both services depart hourly from the Civic interchange: bus No 901 operates between 9.35 am and 4.05 pm and bus No 904 between 10.20 am and 3.20 pm. You'll need a day ticket ($6) to ride these services.

Murray's Canberra Explorer (☎ 13 2251) runs a 25km route around 19 points of interest; you can get on and off wherever you like. This daily service departs hourly from the Jolimont Centre between 10.15 am and 4.15 pm, and tickets ($18, children $8) are sold on the bus. If you want to make one circuit without getting off – a good way to orient yourself – buy a one-hour tour ticket ($7, children $5).

Car & Motorcycle Canberra's wide and relatively uncluttered main roads make driving a joy, although once you enter the maze of curving roads in the residential areas things become more difficult. Take a map, but expect to get lost in Canberra's roundabout system.

Taxi Call Aerial Taxi Cabs (☎ 6285 9222).

Bicycle Canberra is a cyclist's paradise, with bike paths making it possible to ride around the city hardly touching a road. One popular track circles the lake; there are also peaceful stretches of bushland along some suburban routes. Get a copy of the *Canberra Cycleways* map ($6.40) from bookshops or the Visitor Information Centre.

Mr Spokes Bike Hire (☎ 6257 1188), near the Acton Park ferry terminal, charges $8 an hour and $7 for subsequent hours. Another company is Dial a Bicycle (☎ 6286 5463) which delivers and picks up your bike. It hires out 10-speed mountain bikes including helmet and lock for $25 for a day, $40 for two days and $80 for a week.

Around Canberra

The ACT is about 88km long from north to south and about 30km wide. There's plenty of unspoiled bush just outside the urban area and a network of roads into it. The NRMA's *Canberra & District* map and the Visitor Information Centre's *Canberra Sightseeing Guide with Tourist Drives* are helpful.

The plains and isolated hills around Canberra rise to rugged ranges in the south and west of the ACT. The Murrumbidgee River flows across the ACT from south-east to north-west. Namadgi National Park in the south covers 40% of the ACT and adjoins Kosciuszko National Park. The information centre has leaflets on walking trails, swimming spots and camp sites.

Picnic, Swimming & Walking Areas
Picnic and barbecue spots, many with gas facilities, are scattered throughout and around Canberra. There's no public transport to most of them. **Black Mountain**, west of the city, is convenient for picnics and there are swimming spots along the Murrumbidgee and Cotter rivers. Other riverside areas include **Uriarra Crossing**, 24km north-west of the city, on the Murrumbidgee near its meeting with the Molonglo River; **Casuarina Sands**, 19km west of the city at the meeting of the Cotter and Murrumbidgee rivers; **Kambah Pool Reserve** about 14km farther upstream (south) on the Murrumbidgee; the **Cotter Dam**, 23km west of the city on the Cotter River, which also has a camping area ($10); **Pine Island** and **Point Hut Crossing** on the Murrumbidgee upstream of Kambah Pool Reserve; and **Gibraltar Falls**, roughly 45km south-west of the city, which also has a camping area.

There are good walking tracks along the Murrumbidgee from Kambah Pool Reserve to Pine Island (7km) or Casuarina Sands (about 14km).

The spectacular **Ginninderra Falls** (☎ 6257 6633) at Parkwood, north-west of Canberra and across the NSW border is open daily ($5, concession $2); there are gorges and a nature trail, and you can canoe and camp here.

Tidbinbilla Nature Reserve, 45km south-west of the city in the hills beyond Canberra Deep Space Communication Complex (see the Observatories & Tracking Stations section later in the chapter), has bushwalking tracks, some leading to interesting rock formations. The reserve is open from 9 am to 6 pm (later during daylight-saving time); the visitor centre is open on weekdays from 11 am to 3 pm and on weekends from 9 am to 6 pm. Round About Tours

ACT

(☎ 6258 9354) has day ($38) and night ($14) bushwalking tours of the reserve and provides food and a pick-up/drop-off service.

South-west of the reserve in **Corin Forest**, there's a 1km-long metal 'bobsled' run open on weekends and during school holidays; you can get three rides for $15. There's also a flying fox.

Other good walking areas include **Mt Ainslie** to the north-east of the city and **Mt Majura** behind it (the combined area forms part of Canberra Nature Park), and **Molonglo Gorge** near Queanbeyan.

Namadgi National Park, occupying the south-west of the ACT and partly bordering NSW's mountainous Kosciuszko National Park, has seven peaks higher than 1600m and offers challenging bushwalking. Two kilometres south of **Tharwa** is the NPWS visitor centre (☎ 6237 5222) on Naas Rd. Wild Thing Tours (☎ 6254 6303) has half-day bushwalking tours ($25) of Namadgi where you get to see lots of animals in the wild.

Round About Tours (☎ 6258 9354) also has tours of the park. There are picnic and camping facilities at the Orroral River crossing and Mt Clear. To the south, Naas Rd becomes the partly surfaced Boboyan Rd which leads to **Adaminaby** on the eastern edge of the Snowy Mountains in NSW.

Observatories & Tracking Stations
The ANU's **Mt Stromlo Observatory**, 16km south-west of Canberra, has a 188cm telescope plus a visitors' annexe open daily from 9.30 am to 4 pm. A joint US-Australian deep-space tracking station, the **Canberra Deep Space Communication Complex**, also called the Tidbinbilla Tracking Station, is 40km south-west of Canberra. The visitor centre has displays of spacecraft and tracking technology. It's open daily from 9 am to 5 pm (to 8 pm during daylight-saving time; admission is free). The area is popular for bushwalks and barbecues.

Gold Creek
Near the Barton Highway and about 11km

north-west of the city, Gold Creek has a number of attractions. Hard to resist is the **National Dinosaur Museum**. This is a private collection with replica skeletons of 10 dinosaurs and many other bones and fossils. It's open daily from 10 am to 5 pm (from 9 am during school holidays); admission is $8 (children $5).

Ginninderra Village is a collection of craft workshops and galleries open daily from 10 am to 5 pm (admission is free). Next door, **Cockington Green** is a miniature replica of an English village and is open daily from 9.30 am to 4 pm ($8, children $4).

Other Attractions
Bywong Mining Town, about 30km north-east of Canberra on Millyn Rd off the Federal Highway in NSW, is a re-creation of a mining settlement. It's open daily from 10 am to 4 pm with tours at 10.30 am and 12.30 and 2 pm ($7, children $4.50).

The beautifully restored **Lanyon Homestead**, on Tharwa Drive off the Monaro Highway beside the Murrumbidgee River, is about 30km south of Canberra. The early stone cottage on the site was built by convicts and the grand homestead was completed in 1859.

A major attraction at this National Trust homestead, which documents the life of the region before Canberra existed, is the **Nolan Gallery** which contains a collection of Sidney Nolan's paintings. The homestead and gallery are open from Tuesday to Sunday from 10 am to 4 pm (combined admission is $6; concession $3).

Cuppacumbalong, on Naas Rd near Tharwa, is another old homestead, but now a craft studio and gallery, and is open from Wednesday to Sunday from 11 am to 5 pm.

Day Trips
A popular drive is the journey on the Kings Highway east into NSW through **Bungendore**, which has craft galleries and some old buildings, to pretty **Braidwood** (an hour or so from Canberra) with its many antique shops, craft stores and restaurants.

Another good route takes in **Tharwa** in hilly grazing lands.

QUEANBEYAN (pop 27,000)

Across the NSW border about 12km southeast of Canberra is Queanbeyan, now virtually a suburb of the capital it predates. It was known as 'Queen Bean' until 1838, when it was proclaimed a township. The Queanbeyan Information & Tourist Centre (☎ 1800 026 192) is at 1 Farrer Place.

There's a **museum** with displays on the town's history and good lookouts on **Jerrabomberra Hill** (5km west) and **Bungendore Hill** (4km east). Motel accommodation here is slightly cheaper than in Canberra.

New South Wales

Population: 6.2 million
Area: 802,000 sq km
Phone Area Code: 02

Highlights

- Cruising on Sydney Harbour, the best way to view the harbour city
- Bushwalking in the Blue Mountains
- Skiing in the Snowy Mountains beneath Mt Kosciuszko, Australia's highest mainland peak
- Catching a wave at Byron Bay, Australia's surfing mecca
- Touring the wineries of the Hunter Valley region
- Visiting the extraordinary archaeological record of Lake Mungo
- Heading into the remote outback, 'back of Bourke'

New South Wales is the site of Captain Cook's original landing in Australia, and the place where the first permanent European settlement was established. Today it's

Australia's most populous state and it has the country's largest city, Sydney. Those expecting NSW to be little more than Sydney's hinterland are in for a real surprise. The state is rich in history, some of it tainted with the brutality of the early penal settlement, but much of it bound up with the gold rush and expansion westward. The state has fabulous coastal and mountain scenery and dry western plains stretching all the way to the 'back of Bourke'.

The state capital, with its opera house, harbour and bridge, is a good place to start your exploration of NSW. It was at Sydney Cove, where the ferries run from Circular Quay today, that the first European settlement was established in 1788, so it's not surprising that Sydney has an air of history which is missing from many Australian cities. That doesn't stop the city being far brasher and more lively than many of its younger Australian counterparts though.

The Pacific Highway runs north from Sydney and is the gateway to the great beaches, surf and scenery of NSW's northern coastal strip. The Princes Highway heads south from the capital along the state's less-developed southern coast.

GEOGRAPHY & CLIMATE

The state divides neatly into four regions. The narrow coastal strip runs between Queensland and Victoria and has many beaches, national parks, inlets and coastal lakes. The Great Dividing Range also runs the length of the state, about 100km inland from the coast, and includes the New England tablelands north of Sydney, the spectacular Blue Mountains west of Sydney, and, in the south of the state, the Snowy Mountains, which offer excellent winter skiing and summer bushwalking.

West of the Great Dividing Range is the farming country of the western slopes and the dry western plains, which cover two-thirds of the state. The plains fade into the outback in the far west.

The major rivers are the Murray and the Darling, which meander westward across the plains. As a general rule of thumb, it gets hotter the further north you go and drier the further west. In winter, the Snowy Mountains are, not surprisingly, covered with snow.

INFORMATION

NSW travel information is distributed to travel agents nationally or you can telephone ☎ 13 2077 for recorded information. There's also a major information centre at Albury, on the Victorian border, and a smaller one at Tweed Heads, on the Queensland border. Most towns have tourist information centres.

NATIONAL PARKS

The state's 70-odd national parks include stretches of coast, vast forested inland tracts, the peaks and valleys of the Great Dividing Range, and some epic stretches of outback. Most parks can be reached by conventional vehicles in reasonable weather. With the exception of those surrounding Sydney, public transport into most parks is scarce.

Entry to most national parks is $7.50 per car – less for motorcycles and pedestrians. However, entry to more remote national parks is often free. The $60 annual pass, which gives unlimited entry to the state's parks, is worth considering, especially if you plan to visit Mt Kosciuzko National Park, where the daily fee is $12.50. Many parks have camp sites with facilities, costing between $5 and $15 a night for two people. Camp sites at popular parks are often booked out during school holidays. Bush camping is allowed in some parks; call the nearest NSW National Parks & Wildlife Service (NPWS) office for regulations.

The NPWS information line is ☎ 9585 6533. The NPWS has a shop and information centre at 43 Bridge St, Hurstville. Cadman's Cottage (☎ 9247 5033), 110 George St, The Rocks, Sydney has information on Sydney Harbour National Parks. Also handy is Gregory's *National Parks NSW* ($18.95).

The state forests – owned by the NSW government and used for logging – have drives, camp sites, picnic areas and walking tracks. The State Forests of NSW head office (☎ 9980 4296) is at Building 2, 423 Pennant Hills Rd, Pennant Hills, Sydney.

ACTIVITIES
Bushwalking

Close to Sydney, there are dramatic cliff-top walks in the Royal National Park, bushwalks around the inlets of Broken Bay in Ku-ring-gai Chase National Park, and all the sandstone bluffs, eucalyptus forests and fresh air you could wish for in the Blue Mountains. Further south, Kosciuszko National Park, in the Snowy Mountains, has excellent alpine walks in summer.

The NSW Confederation of Bushwalking Clubs (☎ 9548 1228), GPO Box 2090, Sydney 1043, and the NPWS have information on bushwalking. The Department of Land & Water Conservation (DLWC; ☎ 9228 6111), 23-33 Bridge St, Sydney, has free brochures and discovery kits ($10) on the 250km Great North Walk, linking Sydney with the Hunter Valley, and the Hume & Hovell Track running through High Country between Yass and Albury.

Lonely Planet's *Bushwalking in Australia* details some walks in NSW. Other useful books are *100 Walks in New South Wales* by Tyrone Thomas and *Sydney and Beyond* by Andrew Mevissen.

Water Sports

Swimming & Surfing The state's 1900km coastline is liberally sprinkled with beaches offering excellent swimming (see the Sydney section for surf beaches within the metropolitan area). North of Sydney, surfing spots include Newcastle, Port Macquarie, Seal Rocks, Crescent Head, Nambucca Heads, Coffs Harbour, Angourie, Lennox Head and Byron Bay. South of Sydney, you could try Wollongong, Jervis Bay, Ulladulla, Merimbula or Eden. Contact the NSW Surfriders Association (☎ 9518 9410), PO Box 330, Manly, NSW 2095, for detailed information.

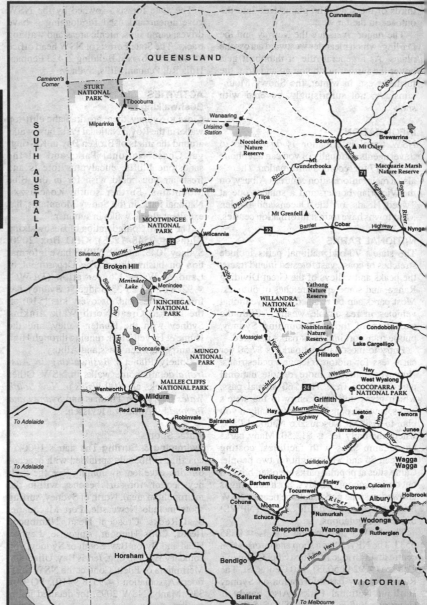

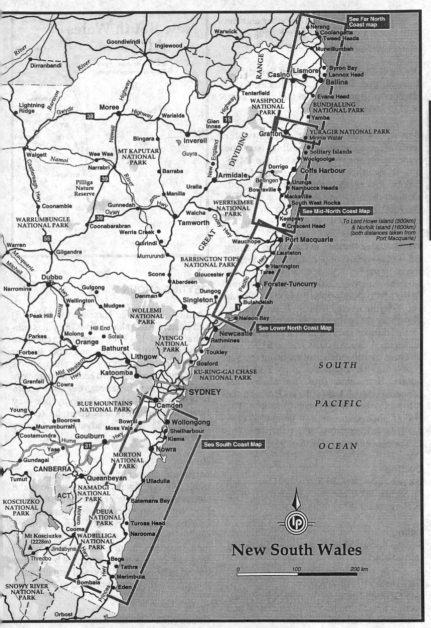

Surf carnivals start in December and run until April. Contact Surf Life Saving NSW (☎ 9597 5588) for dates and venues.

Diving & Snorkelling North of Sydney, try Terrigal, Port Stephens, Seal Rocks, Coffs Harbour or Byron Bay. On the south coast, head to Jervis Bay, Merimbula or Eden.

Sailing Sydney Harbour and Pittwater both offer exceptional sailing (see the Sydney section for details). Lake Macquarie, south of Newcastle, and Myall Lakes, just to the north, are also good. Contact the Yachting Association of NSW (☎ 9660 1266) for information on sailing clubs and courses.

White-Water Rafting & Canoeing Rafting takes place on the upper Murray and Snowy rivers in the Snowy Mountains, and on the Shoalhaven River, 220km south of Sydney. In the north, there's rafting on the Nymboida and Gwydir rivers. Albury, Jindabyne and Nowra are the centres for the southern rivers; Coffs Harbour and Nambucca Heads for the northern. A day trip costs around $100.

There's an abundance of canoeing spots in NSW, but you might like to try Port Macquarie, Barrington Tops (for white-water canoeing), Myall Lakes, Jervis Bay, and the Murrumbidgee River near Canberra. The NSW Canoe Association (☎ 9660 4597) can provide information, and publishes *The Canoeing Guide to NSW* ($24.95).

Cycling
Bicycle NSW (☎ 9283 5200), 209 Castlereagh St, Sydney 2000, can provide information on cycling routes throughout the state.

Skiing
See the Snowy Mountains section for skiing information.

GETTING THERE & AWAY
See Getting There & Away in the Sydney section for information on international and interstate air, rail and bus links.

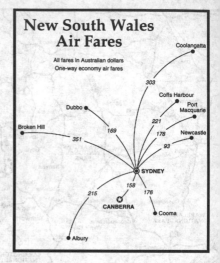

New South Wales Air Fares

All fares in Australian dollars
One-way economy air fares

Coolangatta
303
Coffs Harbour
Dubbo
Port Macquarie
Broken Hill
221
351
169
178 Newcastle
93
SYDNEY
158
215   176
CANBERRA
Cooma
Albury

GETTING AROUND
Air
Smaller airlines like Hazelton (☎ 13 1713) and Eastern Australia Airlines (a Qantas subsidiary, ☎ 13 1313) operate comprehensive networks within the state, and other airlines serve particular regions. The chart shows some routes and standard economy one-way fares. In many instances, discount return tickets are as cheap as economy one-way fares. Discounted tickets generally require purchase 21 days in advance and carry restrictions.

Bus
Buses are often quicker and cheaper than trains, but not always. If you want to make stops on the way to your ultimate destination, look for cheap stopover deals rather than buying separate tickets. Once you've reached your destination, there are usually local bus lines, though services may not be frequent. In remote areas, school buses may be the only option. They will usually pick you up, but they aren't obliged to do so.

Train
Countrylink has the most comprehensive

state rail service in Australia and will, in conjunction with connecting buses, take you quite quickly to most sizeable towns in NSW. All Countrylink services have to be booked in advance (☎ 13 2242 daily between 7 am and 9 pm). You can do this in person at Central Station or the Countrylink Travel Centre, corner York and Margaret Sts (both in Sydney). Passage for bicycles ($20) and surfboards ($10) must also be reserved in advance.

The frequency of services and their value for money is variable so compare options with private bus services. Countrylink offers first and economy-class tickets and a quota of discount tickets; return fares are double the single fare. Australian students travel for half the economy fare.

Intrastate services and one-way economy fares from Sydney include Albury, 643km, $73; Armidale, 569km, $67; Bathurst, 223km, $31; Bourke, 835km, $82; Broken Hill, 1125km, $92; Byron Bay, 883km, $82; Canberra, 326km, $41; Coffs Harbour, 608km, $67; Cooma, 441km, $55; Dubbo, 462km, $55; Port Macquarie, 474km, $61; and Tamworth, 455km, $60.

Frequent commuter-type trains run between Sydney and Wollongong ($6.80), Katoomba ($9.40), Lithgow ($14.20), Newcastle ($14.20) and, less frequently, Goulburn ($22).

A one-month NSW Discovery Pass offers economy-class travel and unlimited stopovers on the state network for $249 (YHA members pay $199).

Sydney

• *Pop 3,276,200*

Australia's oldest and largest settlement is a vibrant city built around one of the most spectacular harbours in the world. Instantly recognisable thanks to its opera house, harbour and bridge, Sydney also boasts lesser-known attractions like the historic Rocks, Victorian-era Paddington, excellent beaches such as Bondi and Manly, and two superb coastal national parks on the city fringe.

The city is built on land once occupied by the Iora tribe, whose presence lingers in the place names of many suburbs and whose artistic legacy can be seen at many Aboriginal engraving sites around the city. After its brutal beginnings, and a long period when it seemed content to be a second-rate facsimile of a British city, Sydney has finally come of age. Selected to host the 2000 Olympic Games, it is undergoing a period of rejuvenation as it strives to put its cityscape on a level with its natural charms.

An array of ethnic groups contribute to the city's social life – the dynamism of the Chinese community in particular has played an important role in altering the city's Anglo-Mediterranean fabric, and preparing it to become a key player in Asia.

Orientation

The harbour divides Sydney into northern and southern halves, with the Sydney Harbour Bridge and the Harbour Tunnel joining the two shores. The city centre and most places of interest are south of the harbour. The central area is long and narrow, stretching from the Rocks and Circular Quay in the north to Central Station in the south. It is bounded by Darling Harbour to the west and a string of pleasant parks to the east.

East of the city centre are the innercity suburbs of Darlinghurst, Kings Cross and Paddington. Further east again are exclusive suburbs such as Double Bay and Vaucluse. To the south-east of these are the ocean-beach suburbs of Bondi and Coogee. Sydney's Kingsford-Smith airport is in Mascot, 10km south of the city centre, jutting into Botany Bay.

West of the centre is the radically changing suburb of Pyrmont, and the peninsula suburbs of Glebe and Balmain. The inner west includes Newtown and Leichhardt.

Suburbs stretch a good 20km north and south of the centre, their extent limited by national parks. The suburbs north of the bridge are known collectively as the North

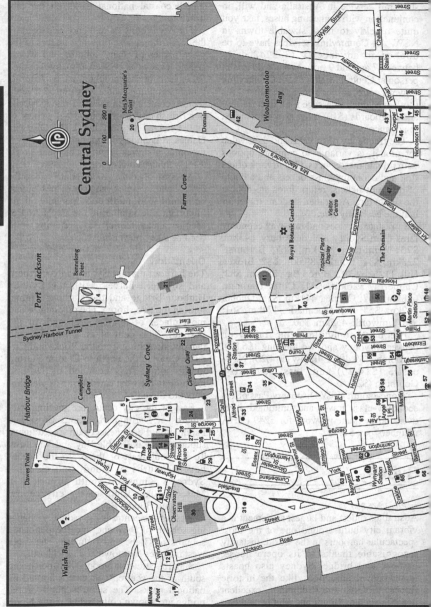

Central Sydney

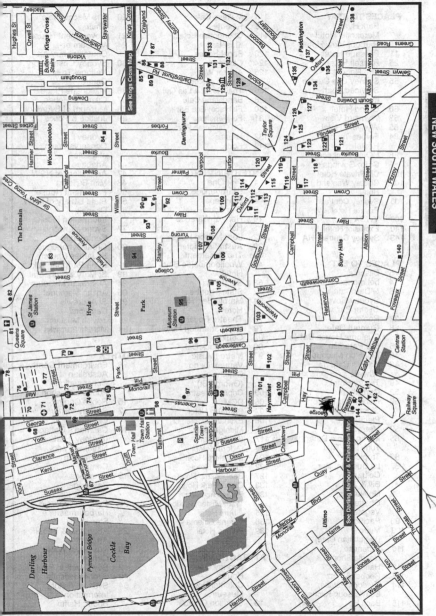

NEW SOUTH WALES

PLACES TO STAY
3 Park Hyatt
7 Mercantile Hotel
8 Harbour View Hotel
11 Palisade Hotel
25 Russell Hotel
32 The Regent
55 Sydney City Centre
    Serviced Apart-
    ments
60 Grand Hotel
63 Wynyard Vista
65 Wynyard Hotel
84 Forbes Terrace
    Hostel
88 L'Otel; Backdoor
    Cafe; Govinda's
101 CB Private Hotel
102 Citistay Westend
    Hotel
103 Sydney Central
    Private Hotel
105 YWCA
140 Excelsior Hotel
143 Sydney Central YHA

PLACES TO EAT
5 Bilson's
14 bel mondo & anti bar
16 G'Day Cafe
22 Sydney Cove
    Oyster Bar
27 Rockpool
28 Gumnut Cafe;
    Customs House Bar
35 Bar Paradiso
40 Kiosk on Macquarie
43 Harry's Cafe de
    Wheels
45 Tilbury Hotel
52 Carruthers
56 Dendy Bar Bistro;
    Cinema (Martin
    Place)
59 Metro Bar
85 Indian Home Diner;
    Tum Tum Thai
86 Tropicana
87 La Bussola; Bar
    Coluzzi
91 Bill & Toni's
92 No Names;
    Chatters
    Vegetaran
93 Pacifico
109 Metro
    (Vegetarian Cafe)
110 Japanese
    Noodle Shop
112 Hanover's
113 Roobar & Fatz
114 Tandoori Palace;
    Betty's Soup Kitchen
115 Bach Hy

116 Maltese Cafe
118 Riberries
119 Courthouse Hotel;
    Kinselas
123 Bagel House
124 Cafe 191
125 Angkor Wat;
    Balkan seafood
126 Thai-Nesia & Lan Qui
128 Bandstand Cafe
130 Fishface; Eca Bar
131 Fu-Manchu;
    Oh Calcutta!; Fez
132 Lauries
142 Bodhi

ENTERTAINMENT
1 Pier One
    (Harbourside
    Brasserie)
2 Pier Four
10 Hero of Waterloo
    Hotel
12 Lord Nelson Hotel
29 Australian Hotel
34 The Basement
46 Woolloomooloo Bay
    Hotel
68 Soup Plus
72 State Theatre
74 Marble Bar; Hilton
    Hotel
78 Theatre Royal
79 Riva; Sheraton Hotel
89 Cauldron
90 Hard Rock Caf
97 Metro (Music
    Venue); Dendy
    Cinema
    (George St)
100 Capitol Theatre
106 DCM
107 Burdekin Hotel
108 Exchange Hotel; Q
111 Midnight Shift
117 Bentley Bar
120 Oxford Hotel
121 Beresford Hotel
122 Flinders Hotel
127 Beauchamp Hotel
133 Green Park Hotel
134 Palace Academy
    Twin; Mister Goodbar
135 Albury Hotel
136 Verona Cinema
139 Palace Hotel

ATTRACTIONS
4 Sydney Opera
    House
9 Colonial House
    Museum
13 Garrison Church

20 Mrs Macquarie's
    Chair
21 Government House
24 Museum of
    Contemporary Art
30 Sydney Observatory
31 National Trust
    Centre
36 Macquarie Place
37 Customs House
38 Museum of Sydney
39 Justice & Police
    Museum
41 Sydney
    Conservatorium
    of Music
44 Artspace
47 Art Gallery of NSW
48 Mint Building
50 Parliament House
51 State Library of NSW
53 Olympic
    Information Kiosk
77 Sydney Tower &
    Centrepoint
80 Great Synagogue
81 St James Church
82 Hyde Park Barracks
83 St Mary's Cathedral
94 Australian Museum
95 Anzac Memorial
98 St Andrew's
    Cathedral
129 Jewish Museum
138 Victoria Barracks

OTHER
6 Environment Centre;
    Australian
    Conservation
    Foundation shop
15 Rocks Centre
17 Sydney Visitors
    Centre
18 Cadman's Cottage
    (Sydney Harbour
    National Parks
    Information
    Centre)
19 Overseas
    Passenger
    Terminal
23 Commissioners &
    Harbourmaster's
    Steps
26 Aboriginal & Tribal
    Art Centre
33 Australian Wine
    Centre
42 Boy Charlton Pool
49 Sydney Hospital
54 Sydney Visitors
    Information
    Booth; Halftix

NEW SOUTH WALES

NEW SOUTH WALES

Shore and are somewhat loosely considered the territory of Sydney's middle classes. The western suburbs sprawl 50km to reach the foothills of the Blue Mountains, encompassing the once separate settlements of Parramatta and Penrith.

Maps Just about every brochure you pick up includes a map of the city centre, but the *UBD Sydney Tourist* map ($4.50) has good coverage of the city centre and inner suburbs. If you're intending to drive around the city, the *Sydney UBD* street directory ($32) is invaluable. For topographic maps, go to the DLWC (☎ 9228 6111), 23-33 Bridge St.

Information
Tourist Offices The Sydney Visitors Information Booth (☎ 9235 2424) is in Martin Place (sharing a booth with Halftix) and is open 9 am to 5 pm weekdays (closed weekends). Tourism NSW (☎ 13 2077) is at 11 York St.

The Travellers Information Service in the international terminal at the airport (☎ 9669 5111) is open daily from 6 am to 10.30 pm. It can book hotel rooms and will help arrange hostel accommodation.

There's another helpful Travellers Information Service (☎ 9281 9366) in the Sydney coach terminal, outside Central Station. It's open daily from 6 am until 10.30 pm and makes bus and accommodation bookings.

The Sydney Visitors Centre (☎ 9255 1788), 106 George St, the Rocks, has heaps of information about Sydney in general, as well as the Rocks.

Some areas, like Kings Cross and Manly, have their own tourist offices (see those sections for details).

Kings Cross hostel notice boards offer everything from flat-shares and job opportunities to cars and unused air tickets.

Foreign Consulates Sydney has nearly as many consular offices as Canberra. See Foreign Embassies in Australia in the Facts for the Visitor chapter for details.

Money There are six Thomas Cook bureaux in the airport's international terminal, which are open daily from around 5.15 am until after the last flight. There's an American Express branch at 92 Pitt St and Thomas Cook branches at 175 Pitt St, in the lower level of the Queen Victoria Building on York St, and in the Kingsgate shopping centre in Kings Cross, but they are all closed Saturday afternoon and Sunday.

Seven-day change bureaux include the one in the coach terminal at Central Station (8 am to 8 pm), another opposite Wharf 6 at Circular Quay (8 am to 9 pm) and one at the pedestrian juncture of Springfield Ave and Darlinghurst Rd, Kings Cross (8 am to 11 pm and till 1 am Saturday).

Post The GPO (counter service) is at 130 Pitt St. Poste restante is at 310 George St, on the 3rd floor of the Hunter Connection shopping centre. Poste restante is open weekdays and there are computer terminals that indicate if mail is being held for you. You can have your mail redirected to any suburban post office for $5 a month.

There are several travel agencies, offering mail-holding and forwarding services, including Travellers Contact Point (☎ 9221 8744), 7th floor, 428 George St and Backpackers World (☎ 9380 2700), 212 Victoria St, Kings Cross.

Telephone & Fax The Telstra Payphone Centre at 130 Pitt St has phones and faxes. You can make discounted calls and send faxes from Backpackers World.

Internet A lot of hostels have coin-operated Internet machines. You can check email and use the computers at Travellers Contact Point, 7th floor, 428 George St and at Backpackers World, 212 Victoria St, Kings Cross. There's a net cafe (closed Sunday) upstairs at the Hotel Sweeney, 236 Clarence St. Kinko's, 175 Liverpool St opposite Hyde Park, is a copy shop with Internet access open 24 hours daily. The Idle Tank at 84 Campbell St, Bondi Beach is a cruisy book and CD shop with an Internet-connected computer. Well Connected, 35 Glebe Point Rd, Glebe, is a surf-and-snack cafe.

Travel Agencies The YHA Membership & Travel Centre (☎ 9261 1111), 422 Kent St, between Market and Druitt Sts, offers normal travel agency services and enables travellers to make national and international hostel bookings. There's another travel centre in the Sydney Central YHA (☎ 9281 9444) on the corner of Pitt St and Rawson Place.

Left-Luggage There are cloakrooms at Central and Town Hall train stations, costing $1.50 per item per day for the first day and $4.50 per day for subsequent days. Luggage lockers at the Sydney coach terminal, on the corner of Pitt St and Eddy Ave, cost $4 a day. Lockers at the airport's international terminal cost from $4 to $8 per day depending on

how big your swag is. Travellers Contact Point (☎ 9221 8744), 7th floor, 428 George St, will store luggage for $10 per piece per month.

Bookshops The Travel Bookshop, 175 Liverpool St, has the most comprehensive range of guidebooks and travel literature in Sydney. Dymocks Booksellers, 424-426 George St, claims to be the largest bookshop in the southern hemisphere. Other good bookshops are Gleebooks, 49 Glebe Point Rd, Glebe, and Ariel, 42 Oxford St, Paddington. Gould's, 33 King St, Newtown, is an amazing muddle of second-hand tomes; it's open daily till midnight.

Laundry Most hostels have laundry facilities and all hotels provide a laundry service.

Publications *TNT* is a free monthly magazine aimed at backpackers. It's full of stuff to know, budget accommodation and activities and is available from hostels and tourist offices. *OVG* ('overseas visitors guide') is a free monthly that combines maps, stories and places of interest with what's-on listings. *This Month in Sydney* is similar, if a bit twee.

The *Metro* lift-out in Friday's *Sydney Morning Herald* provides a comprehensive listing of what's on in the city over the coming week. The free music and entertainment newspapers delivered to pubs, cafes and record shops have listings for those clubs that open and close so fast that you never actually find out where they are. They include *Drum Media, Beat, 3D World* (rave and dance), and *Capital Q Weekly* (gay). *Sydney City Hub* is full of culturally savvy listings for the innercity groover.

There are plenty of guidebooks to Sydney. Lonely Planet's *Sydney city guide* and *New South Wales & the ACT* are general guides. *Untourist Sydney* by Jacqueline Huié is a difficult to navigate 'insider's guide' to the city.

A great piece of travel literature to read while visiting the city is *Sydney* by Jan Morris. For a literary journey through the mean streets of Sydney, try one of Peter Corris' Cliff Hardy thrillers.

Medical Services The Travellers Medical & Vaccination Centre (☎ 9221 7133), Level 7, 428 George St, and the Kings Cross Travellers' Clinic (☎ 9358 3066), Suite 1, 13 Springfield Ave, Kings Cross, are both open weekdays and Saturday mornings. It's best to book. If you break a leg in central Sydney, hobble up to Sydney Hospital (☎ 9382 7111) on Macquary St.

Other Services The National Roads & Motorists Association (NRMA) head office is at 151 Clarence St (☎ 9260 9222).

If your backpack needs repairing, try Custom Luggage, 317 Sussex St. Cameras can be repaired at Whilton Camera Service, 251 Elizabeth St, opposite Hyde Park.

If you just need a damn good wash, get a shower at Travellers Aid in Central Station for $3 on weekdays between 7 am and 4.30 pm.

Emergency The Wayside Chapel (☎ 9358 6577), 29 Hughes St, Kings Cross, is a crisis centre which can handle personal problems.

Other emergency support services include Lifeline (☎ 13 1114) and the Rape Crisis Centre (☎ 9819 6565).

Dangers & Annoyances Sydney isn't an especially dangerous city but you should remain alert. The usual big-city rules apply: never leave luggage unattended, never flaunt money and never get drunk in the company of strangers. Harassment of gays, lesbians and non-Anglo-Saxons is not rife but it does happen. Use extra caution in Kings Cross, which attracts shady characters.

Sydney Harbour

The harbour has melded and shaped the Sydney psyche since the first days of settlement, and today it's both a major port and the city's playground. Its waters, beaches, islands and waterside parks offer all the swimming, sailing, picnicking and walking you could wish for.

Officially called **Port Jackson**, the harbour stretches some 20km inland to join the mouth of the Parramatta River. The headlands at the entrance are known as North Head and South Head. The city centre is about 8km inland and the most scenic part of the harbour is between the Heads and the Harbour Bridge. **Middle Harbour** is a large

---

The 2000 Olympics

Sydney will take its place on the world stage when it hosts the Olympic Games in September 2000 and the Paralympic Games in October 2000. There's a tangible sense of expectation as energies are harnessed, key areas are given face-lifts, and politicians cat-fight over budget blowouts. There's also a smudge of Sydney fatalism in the air, which reasons that no matter what happens, it will all be worth it in the end because the major star of the games will, of course, be the city itself.

Facilities are being constructed at Olympic Park on Homebush Bay, where existing sport, aquatic and athletic centres will be supplemented by an 80,000-seat Olympic Stadium and an Olympic Village. New show grounds, also at Homebush, will first be used for the 1998 Royal Easter Show.

Homebush Bay is 12km west of the Harbour Bridge on the Parramatta River. The Homebush Bay Corporation operates daily guided 35-minute bus tours of the Olympic site. Tours depart from Strathfield railway station at 9.30 and 10.30 am and 12.30 pm on Bus No 401 and cost $5 ($2.50 concession). CTA Cycle Tours (☎ 1800 353 004) operates a cycle tour of Olympic Park.

There is a rail link through the Homebush Bay site and the Parramatta RiverCat ferry has been stopping at Homebush Bay since mid-1998.

For more information contact the Sydney Organising Committee for the Olympic Games (SOCOG) (☎ 9297 2000), 207 Kent St or check the web at www.sydney.olympic.org. The Olympic Information Kiosk in the NSW Government Information Service, on the corner of Elizabeth and Hunter Sts, has touch-screen info about Olympic events, PR publications and not particularly well-briefed staff. ∎

inlet which heads north-west a couple of kilometres inside the Heads.

The best way to view the harbour is to persuade someone to take you sailing, to take a boat cruise or to catch one of the numerous ferries that ply its waters. The Manly ferry offers vistas of the harbour east of the bridge, while the Parramatta RiverCats cover the west.

Sydney's **harbour beaches** are generally sheltered, calm coves with little of the frenetic activity of the ocean beaches. On the south shore, they include Lady Bay (nude), Camp Cove and Nielsen Park; all accessible by bus No 325 from Watsons Bay.

On the North Shore, there are harbour beaches at Manly Cove, Reef Beach (nude but not very secluded), Clontarf, Chinaman's Beach and Balmoral. The Manly ferry docks at Manly Cove, and Reef Beach is a couple of kilometres walk along the Manly Scenic Walkway.

All the other beaches are accessible, with a bit of walking, by catching bus Nos 169, 175, 185 and 248, which depart from Wynyard Park, travel along Military Rd and cross Spit Bridge.

Sydney Harbour National Park This park protects the scattered pockets of bushland around the harbour and includes several small islands. It offers some great walking tracks, scenic lookouts, Aboriginal carvings and a handful of historic sites. On the south shore, it incorporates South Head and Nielsen Park; on the North Shore, it includes North Head, Dobroyd Head, Middle Head and Ashton Park. Fort Denison, Goat, Clark, Rodd and Shark islands are also part of the park. Pick up information at Cadman's Cottage (☎ 9247 5033) in the Rocks.

Previously known as Pinchgut, **Fort Denison** is a small fortified island off Mrs Macquarie's Point, originally used to isolate troublesome convicts. The fort was built during the Crimea War amid fears of a Russian invasion.

Tours leave from Cadman's Cottage at noon and 2 pm, and also at 10 am on weekends. A one to two-hour tour costs $9 ($6.50 concession). There are also tours of **Goat Island**, just west of the Harbour Bridge, which has been a shipyard, quarantine station, gunpowder depot and, more recently, part of the set for the popular Water Rats television show. Depending on your obsessions, you can take a Water Rats tour ($13 to $16), a heritage tour ($11) or a Ghastly Tales supper tour ($16). Ask at Cadman's Cottage for details.

Clark Island, off Darling Point, and **Shark Island**, off Rose Bay, are great picnic spots, but you should book your getaway in advance (☎ 9247 5033).

Harbour Walks

The 10km **Manly Scenic Walkway** from Manly Cove to Spit Bridge is one of the best ways for landlubbers to experience the harbour. It passes through native bushland at Dobroyd Head, runs close to several hideaway beaches, passes Aboriginal engravings and a charming lighthouse at Grotto Point, and has panoramic views of Sydney Harbour and Middle Harbour. It can be a complicated walk to follow, so pick up a leaflet at Cadman's Cottage in the Rocks or at the Manly Visitors Information Bureau on South Steyne, Manly. Bus Nos 169, 175, 185 and 248 run from Spit Bridge back to the city centre. The best way to get to Manly Cove is by ferry from Circular Quay.

There's a 4km walking track in **Ashton Park**, south of Taronga Zoo, which passes Bradleys Head and Taylor Bay. Bradleys Head has military fortifications and memorabilia. Take the Taronga Zoo ferry from Circular Quay to get to Ashton Park.

The walking track along the **Hermitage Foreshore** in Nielsen Park has spectacular views back to the city, and you can cool off at netted Shark Beach (known locally by the less scary name of Nielsen Park Beach). Bus No 325 from the city passes Nielsen Park via Kings Cross and terminates at Watsons Bay. **South Head**, near Watsons Bay, is a good spot for a cliff-top stroll. ■

The Rocks

Sydney's first white settlement was on the rocky spur of land on the western side of Sydney Cove, from which the Harbour Bridge now crosses to North Shore. It was a squalid, raucous place of convicts, whalers, prostitutes and street gangs, though in the 1820s the nouveaux riches inexplicably built three-storey houses on the ridges overlooking the slums.

It later became an area of warehouses and maritime commerce and then fell into decline as modern shipping and storage facilities moved away from Circular Quay. An outbreak of bubonic plague at the turn of this century led to whole streets being razed and the construction of the Harbour Bridge resulted in further demolition.

Since the 1970s, redevelopment has turned the Rocks into a sanitised, historical tourist precinct, full of narrow cobbled streets, fine colonial buildings, converted warehouses, tea rooms and stuffed koalas. If you ignore the kitsch, it's a delightful place to stroll around, especially in the backstreets and in the less developed, tight-knit, contiguous community of Millers Point.

Pick up a self-guided tour map ($1) of the area from the Sydney Visitors Centre (☎ 9255 1788) in the old Sailors Home at 106 George St. The best guided tour of the Rocks is Master Christopher's atmospheric night tour (phone ☎ 9555 2700 or ask at the Visitors Centre). Tours run at 5 and 7 pm and cost $13 ($10 concession). If you'd rather soak it up at your own pace, hire a Rocks Walking Adventure cassette for $8 (☎ 018 111 011).

Next door to the Heritage Centre, at 110 George St, is **Cadman's Cottage** (1816), the oldest house in Sydney. It once housed longboats and was home to the last Government Coxswain, John Cadman, but it's now home to the Sydney Harbour National Parks Information Centre (☎ 9247 5033).

Despite all the helpful tourist infrastructure, the beauty of the Rocks is that it's as much fun to wander aimlessly around as it is to see particular attractions. Soak up the atmosphere, sample the frequent entertainment in The Rocks Square on Playfair St, browse around the vibrant **Rocks Centre** for that Aussie present you must go home with, dine at an outdoor cafe, admire the views of Circular Quay and **Campbell Cove**, and join the melee at the weekend **Rocks Market**.

A short walk west along Argyle Street, through the convict-excavated **Argyle Cut**, takes you to the other side of the peninsula and **Millers Point**, a delightful district of early colonial homes with a quintessential English village green. Close at hand are the **Garrison Church** and the more secular delights of the Lord Nelson Hotel and the Hero of Waterloo Hotel, which vie for the title of Sydney's oldest pub. The **Colonial House Museum** on Lower Fort St is crammed with period bric-a-brac, reminiscent of a rampant Great Aunt's attic. It's open daily from 10 am to 5 pm ($1).

Sydney Observatory (☎ 9217 0485) has a commanding position atop Observatory Hill overlooking Millers Point and the harbour. The observatory is open from 10 am to 5 pm ($5, $2 concession). Night visits ($8, $3 concession) must be booked in advance.

In the old military hospital building close by, the **National Trust Centre** houses an art gallery, bookshop and cafe. It's open Tuesday to Friday from 11 am to 5 pm, and weekends from 12 to 5 pm. Admission charges apply for the gallery.

At Dawes Point on Walsh Bay, just west of the Harbour Bridge, are several renovated wharves. **Pier One** is an under-used shopping and leisure complex: **Pier Four** is beautifully utilised as the home of the prestigious Sydney Theatre and Sydney Dance companies.

Sydney Harbour Bridge

The much-loved, imposing 'old coat hanger' crosses the harbour at one of its narrowest points, linking the southern and northern shores and joining central Sydney with the satellite business district in North Sydney. The bridge was completed in 1932 at a cost of $20 million and has always been a favourite icon, partly because of its sheer size, partly because of its function in uniting the city and partly because it kept a lot of people in work during the Depression.

You can climb inside the south-eastern stone pylon, which houses the Harbour Bridge Museum (see the earlier City Views aside).

Cars, trains, cyclists, joggers and pedestrians use the bridge. The cycleway is on the western side and the pedestrian walkway on the eastern; stair access is from Cumberland St in the Rocks and near Milsons Point Station on the North Shore.

The best way to experience the bridge is undoubtedly on foot; don't expect much of a view crossing by car or train. Driving south (only) there's a $2 toll.

The **Harbour Tunnel** now shoulders some of the bridge's workload. It begins about half a kilometre south of the opera house, crosses under the harbour just to the east of the bridge, and rejoins the highway on the northern side. There's a southbound (only) toll of $2. If you're heading from the North Shore to the eastern suburbs, it's much easier to use the tunnel.

Sydney Opera House

The Sydney Opera House is dramatically situated on the eastern headland of Circular Quay. Its soaring sail-like, shell-like roofs were actually inspired by palm fronds, but may remind you of turtles engaging in sexual congress. It's a memorable experience to see a performance here, and just as fulfilling to sit at one of the outdoor cafes and watch harbour life go by.

The opera house has four auditoriums and hosts classical music, ballet, theatre and film, as well as opera. On Sunday, there is free music on the building's 'prow' and a bustling craft market in the forecourt.

Popular operas sell out quickly (despite the three-figure sums for the best seats) but there are often 'restricted view' tickets available for $35 for those with a long neck or a good imagination. Decent seats to see a play or hear the Sydney Symphony Orchestra are more affordable at around $40. The box office (☎ 9250 7777) is open Monday to Saturday between 9 am and 8.30 pm and 2½ hours prior to a Sunday performance.

Worthwhile one-hour tours of the building run daily between 9 am and 4 pm (☎ 9250 7250). They depart from the concourse and cost $9 ($6 students). Not all tours can visit all theatres because of rehearsals, but you're more likely to see everything if you take an early tour. There are irregular backstage tours on Sunday.

Circular Quay

Circular Quay, built around Sydney Cove, is one of the city's major focal points. The first European settlement grew around the Tank Stream, which now runs underground into the harbour here near Wharf 6. For many years this was the shipping centre of Sydney, but it's now both a commuting hub and a recreational space, combining ferry quays, a

---

The Soap Opera House

The hullabaloo surrounding construction of the Sydney Opera House was an operatic blend of personal vision, long delays, bitter feuding, cost blowouts and narrow-minded politicking. Construction began in 1959 after Danish architect Joørn Utzon won an international design competition with his plans for a $7 million building. After political interference, Utzon quit in disgust in 1966, leaving a consortium of Australian architects to design a compromised interior. The parsimonious state government financed the eventual $102 million bill through a series of lotteries. The building was finally completed in 1973, but it was lumbered with an internal design impractical (too small, for one thing) for staging operas.

After all the brawling, the first public performance at the Opera House was, appropriately, Prokofiev's *War & Peace*. The preparations were reported to be a debacle and a possum appeared on stage during one of the dress rehearsals. An opera, *The Eighth Wonder*, has even been written about the building of the Opera House – it was performed here by the Australian Opera in 1995. ■

train station and the Overseas Passenger Terminal with harbour walkways, restaurants, buskers, fisherfolk and parks.

The **Museum of Contemporary Art** (MCA) is in the stately Art Deco building dominating Circular Quay West. It shows eclectic modern art and is open daily from 10 am to 6 pm; entry is $9 ($6 concession). The grand **Customs House** fronting Circular Quay is awaiting redevelopment, possibly as a cultural centre.

Macquarie Place & Surrounds

Narrow lanes lead south from Circular Quay towards the centre of the city. At the corner of Loftus and Bridge Sts, under the shady Moreton Bay figs in Macquarie Place, are a cannon and anchor from the First Fleet flagship, HMS *Sirius*. There is also an **obelisk**, erected in 1818, indicating road distances to various points in the nascent colony. The square has a couple of pleasant outdoor cafes and is overlooked by the rear facade of the imposing 19th-century **Lands Department building** on Bridge St.

The excellent **Museum of Sydney** is east of here, on the corner of Bridge and Phillip Sts, on the site of the first and infamously fetid Government House built in 1788. Sydney's early history comes to life here in whisper, argument, gossip and artefacts. It's open daily ($6, $4 concession).

The **Justice & Police Museum** is in the old Water Police Station on the corner of Phillip and Albert Sts. It's set up as a turn-of-the-century police station, and is open Sunday from 10 am to 5 pm ($5, $3 concession).

City Centre

Central Sydney stretches from Circular Quay in the north to Central Station in the south. The business hub is towards the northern end, but most redevelopment is occurring at the southern end and this is gradually shifting the focus of the city.

Sydney lacks a true civic centre, but **Martin Place** lays claim to the honour, if only by default. This grand pedestrian mall extends from Macquarie St to George St and is impressively lined by the monumental buildings of financial institutions and the

---

A Sydney Walking Tour

Setting out on foot is a good way to explore Australia's largest city. This walk covers about 7km and takes about ½ to three hours.

Start in **Hyde Park** at Museum Station's Liverpool St exit. Walk north-east through the park past the **Anzac Memorial**. On the right, on College St, is the **Australian Museum**. From here William St (the eastward extension of Park St) heads east to **Kings Cross**. Across Park St, at the end of the avenue of trees is the wonderful **Archibald Fountain**. To the east on College St is the impressive **St Mary's Cathedral**.

Keep going north to reach **Macquarie St** with its collection of early colonial buildings and, after a few blocks, **Circular Quay** and the **Sydney Opera House**. On the west side of Circular Quay, behind the **Museum of Contemporary Art**, George St runs through **the Rocks**.

Walk north on George St, which curves around under the **Harbour Bridge** into Lower Fort St. Turn right (north) for the waterfront or left to climb **Observatory Hill**. From here Argyle St heads east, through the **Argyle Cut** and back to the Rocks.

Nearby on Cumberland St you can climb stairs to the Harbour Bridge and walk across to **Milsons Point** on the North Shore, from where you can take a train back to the city.

It's also worth walking along Oxford St from Hyde Park's south-eastern corner to **Paddington**. You can catch a bus back to the city from Paddington, or, if you keep going to **Bondi Junction**, catch a train.

West of Hyde Park you can walk along Market St, which leads to Pyrmont Bridge (for pedestrians and the monorail only) and **Darling Harbour**. Pyrmont Bridge Rd crosses Darling Harbour and leads to **Glebe Island Bridge**, the **Pyrmont Fish Markets** and eventually to **Glebe** itself.

See The Rocks and Organised Tours later in this chapter for guided walks. ∎

colonnaded Victorian post office (undergoing renovation). The street has a couple of fountains, plenty of public seating, a Cenotaph commemorating Australia's war dead and an amphitheatre which is a popular lunchtime entertainment spot.

The **Town Hall**, a few blocks south of here, on the corner of George and Druitt Sts, was built in 1874. Its outrageously ornate exterior is matched by the elaborate chamber room and concert hall inside. The Anglican **St Andrew's Cathedral** was built around the same time and is the oldest cathedral in Australia. Free organ recitals are held on Thursday lunchtimes.

The city's most sumptuous shopping complex, the Byzantine **Queen Victoria Building** (QVB), is next to the Town Hall and takes up an entire city block bordered by George, Druitt, York and Market Sts. Other interesting shopping centres include the lovingly restored Strand Arcade and the modern Skygarden arcade nearby.

Opposite the QVB, underneath the Royal Arcade linking George and Pitt Sts, is a bar and extravagant piece of Victoriana called the **Marble Bar**. The **State Theatre**, just to the north at 49 Market St, is just as ostentatious; it's worth going to see a concert or musical here just to loiter in the lobby and marvel at the pomp-and-ceremony decor.

To the south-west are **Spanish Town** and **Chinatown**, two lively areas in a part of the city that includes a number of unsightly holes in the ground where development projects in the 1980s fell foul of economic downturn. Chinatown is booming though, fuelled by an influx of money from Hong Kong, and this dynamic part of the city is spreading to breathe life into the city's dead south-eastern zone, where Central Station lies isolated on the southern periphery.

Darling Harbour

This huge, purpose-built waterfront leisure park on the western edge of the city centre was once a thriving dockland area (see the Darling Harbour & Chinatown map). Having declined to being an urban eyesore, it was reinvented in the 1980s by a combina-

tion of vision, politicking, forbearance and huge amounts of cash. The emphasis is on casual fun of the kind appreciated by families and coach tourists. The supposed centrepiece is the **Harbourside Festival Marketplace** – a graceful structure crammed with shops and tacky food outlets – but the real attractions are the stunning aquarium, excellent museums, the Chinese Garden and nifty water sculptures.

The **monorail** and **light rail** link Darling Harbour to the city centre.

Ferries leave from Circular Quay and stop at Darling Harbour's Aquarium Wharf every 30 minutes ($3). The Rocket Express ferry departs every 20 minutes from the Harbourmaster's Steps at Circular Quay West ($3.15). The Sydney Explorer bus (see the Sydney Getting Around section) stops at four points around Darling Harbour every 20 minutes. A dinky People Mover snakes around Darling Harbour's attractions – a ride costs $2.50.

The main pedestrian approaches are across footbridges from Market and Liverpool Sts. The one from Market St leads to **Pyrmont Bridge**, now a pedestrian-and-monorail-only route, but once famous as the world's first electrically operated swingspan bridge.

The Darling Harbour Visitors Centre (☎ 9286 0111) is under the highway, and is open daily.

Sydney Aquarium This aquarium, displaying the richness of Australian marine life, should not be missed. Three 'oceanariums' are moored in the harbour with sharks, rays and big fish in one, and Sydney Harbour marine life and seals in the others. There are also informative and well-presented exhibits of freshwater fish and coral gardens. The transparent underwater tunnels are spectacular.

The aquarium is near the eastern end of Pyrmont Bridge and is open daily from 9.30 am to 10 pm ($15.90, students $10).

Australian National Maritime Museum
This thematic museum tells the story of

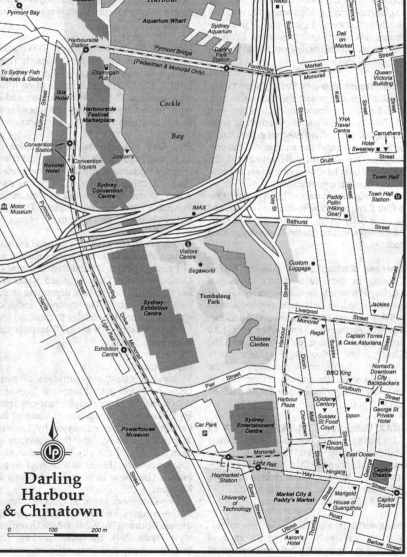

NEW SOUTH WALES

Darling Harbour & Chinatown

0   100   200 m

Australia's relationship with the sea, from Aboriginal canoes and the First Fleet to surf culture and the America's Cup. A naval destroyer, a racing yacht and a Vietnamese refugee boat are moored outside awaiting exploration. Free guided tours take place on the hour between 11 am and 2 pm. The museum is near the western end of Pyrmont Bridge and is open daily from 10 am to 5 pm ($7, $4.50 concession).

Powerhouse Museum Sydney's most spectacular museum covers the decorative arts, social history, science and technology with exhibits covering just about anything from costume jewellery and Australian rock music to locomotives and space capsules. The collections are superbly displayed and the emphasis is on hands-on interaction and education through enjoyment.

The museum is behind the Sydney Exhibition Centre, at 500 Harris St, Ultimo, and is open daily from 10 am to 5 pm ($8, $3 concession, free on the first Saturday of each month).

Chinese Garden The exquisite Chinese Garden in the south-eastern corner of Darling Harbour is an oasis of tranquillity. It was designed by landscape architects from NSW's Chinese sister province, Guangdong, and it's worth every cent of the $3 ($1.50 concession) entrance fee. Enter through the Courtyard of Welcoming Fragrance, circle the Lake of Brightness and round off the experience with tea and cake in the Chinese teahouse. The garden is open daily from 9.30 am to 5 pm.

IMAX Panasonic's IMAX Theatre (☎ 13 3462) is the world's biggest movie screen. If you're into being wowed by massive images, some in 3D, then the IMAX gets a big tick – it's a blast. Movies shown tend to be either thrill-fests or nature docos; tickets are $13.95 ($10.95 concession).

Segaworld If you like your fun otherworldly, or likely to bring on an acid flashback, Sega's indoor entertainment complex is the place to come. Rides (cool) and cinema-style entertainment are included in a day pass ($20 weekdays, $25 weekends) or you can buy your fun for $5 a pop on top of the $5 admission charge. Segaworld is open weekdays from 11 am; weekends from 10 am.

Motor Museum There are over 100 vehicles on display at the Motor Museum, from vintage beauties to Morris Minors. It's at level 1, 320 Harris St, Ultimo, a fume-filled walk from the Powerhouse Museum, and is open Wednesday to Sunday and school holidays from 10 am to 5 pm ($8, $4 concession).

Star City This massive new complex of wavy buildings, cones and cages has taken shape in Pyrmont on the north-eastern headland of Darling Harbour. Star City includes a **casino** and two **theatres** as well as the inevitable hotel and retail outlets. The light rail conveniently runs right to the casino.

Sydney Fish Markets Fish auctions are held on weekdays at these markets, on the corner of Pyrmont Bridge Rd and Bank St, west of Darling Harbour. They begin at 5.30 am and last from three to six hours, depending on the size of the catch. The complex includes eateries (dinner Wednesday to Sunday) and fabulous all-day fish shops. The light rail stops here.

Macquarie St

Sydney's greatest concentration of early public buildings grace Macquarie St, which runs along the eastern edge of the city from Hyde Park to the opera house. Many of the buildings were commissioned by Lachlan Macquarie, who was the first governor to have a vision of the city beyond that of a convict colony. He enlisted convict forger Francis Greenway as an architect to realise his plans.

Two Greenway gems on Queens Square, at the northern end of Hyde Park, are **St James Church** (1819-24) and the Georgian-style **Hyde Park Barracks** (1819). The barracks were built originally as convict quarters, then became an immigration depot, and later a court. They now house a museum which concentrates on the history of the building and provides an interesting perspective on Sydney's social history. The museum (☎ 9223 8922) is open daily from 10 am to 5 pm ($5, $3 concession).

Next to the barracks is the lovely **Mint Building** (1814), which was originally the southern wing of the infamous Rum Hospital built by two Sydney merchants in return for a monopoly on the rum trade. It became a branch of the Royal Mint in 1854.

The Mint's twin is **Parliament House**, which was originally the northern wing of the Rum Hospital. This simple, proud building is now home to the Parliament of NSW. It's open to the public on weekdays between 9.30 am and 4 pm (admission is free). There are free tours of the chambers at 10 and 11 am and 2 pm on nonsitting days. The public gallery is open on sitting days.

Next to Parliament House is the **State Library of NSW**, which is more of a cultural centre than a traditional library. It houses the Australian Research Collections, which document early life in Australia, and hosts innovative temporary exhibitions in its galleries. The library is open daily, except the Australian Research Collection, which is closed on Sunday. There are free guided tours at 11 am and 2 pm (2 pm only on weekends).

The **Sydney Conservatorium of Music** was built by Greenway as the stables and servants' quarters of Macquarie's planned new government house. Macquarie was replaced as governor before the house could be finished, partly because of the extravagance of this project. The conservatorium is now a centre of musical studies and hosts performances, including free lunchtime concerts – phone ☎ 9230 1263 to see what's cooking.

Art Gallery of NSW

This gallery (☎ 9225 1744) has an excellent permanent display of Australian, Aboriginal, European and Asian art, and some inspired temporary exhibits. It's in the Domain, east of Macquarie St, and is open daily from 10 am to 5 pm. Admission is free but fees may apply to special exhibitions. There are free guided tours at noon, 1 and 2 pm most days.

Australian Museum

This natural history museum has an excellent Australian wildlife collection and a gallery tracing Aboriginal history from the Dreamtime to the present. It's on the eastern flank of Hyde Park, on the corner of College and William Sts. It's open daily from 9.30 am to 5 pm ($5, $3 concession). There are free tours on the hour between 10 am and 3 pm.

Parks

The city's favourite picnic spot, jogging route and place to stroll is the enchanting **Royal Botanic Gardens**, which border Farm Cove, east of the opera house. The gardens were established in 1816 and feature plant life from the South Pacific. They include the site of the colony's first paltry vegetable patch, which has been preserved as the First Farm exhibit.

The tropical plant display in the Arc and Pyramid glasshouses is worth seeing ($5). The visitor centre (☎ 9231 8125) is open daily from 9.30 am to 4.30 pm. Free guided walks begin at the centre daily at 10.30 am.

Government House dominates the western headland of Farm Cove. Until early 1996 this was the home of the Governor of NSW, but in the new spirit of republicanism the NSW government has made the governor's post a part-time, live-at-home position. The grounds are open to the public from 10 am to 4 pm daily. The house is open from 10 am to 3 pm Friday to Sunday – there's a gallery on the 1st floor (admission is free).

The **Domain** is a grassy area east of Macquarie St which was set aside by Governor Phillip for public recreation. Today it's used by city workers for lunchtime sports and as a place to escape the hubbub. On Sunday afternoons it's the gathering place for soapbox speakers who do their best to entertain or enrage their listeners.

On the eastern edge of the city centre is the formal **Hyde Park**, which was originally the colony's first racetrack and cricket pitch. It has a grand avenue of trees, delightful fountains, and a giant public chess board. It contains the dignified **Anzac Memorial**, which has a free exhibition on the ground floor covering the nine overseas conflicts Australians have fought in. **St Mary's Cathedral** overlooks the park from the east and the **Great Synagogue** from the west. There are free tours of the synagogue on Tuesday and Thursday at noon (enter from 166 Castlereagh St).

Sydney's biggest park is **Centennial Park**, which has running, cycling, skating and horse tracks, duck ponds, barbecue sites and sports pitches. It's 5km from the centre, just east of Paddington. You can hire bikes from several places on Clovelly Rd near the south-eastern edge of the park (see Getting Around), inline skates (see Activities), or horses ($30) from Superior Horse Hire (☎ 0417 250 025) on Lang Rd, just west of Centennial Park.

Moore Park abuts the eastern flank of Centennial Park and contains sports pitches, a golf course, an equestrian centre, the Sydney Football Stadium (SFS) and the Sydney Cricket Ground (SCG). Sportspace (☎ 9380 0383) offers behind-the-scenes guided tours (1¾ hours) of the SCG and SFS. Tours are held at 10 am and 1 and 3 pm Monday to Saturday (unless they conflict with a sporting event) and cost $18 ($12 concession). A Fox film studio and entertainment complex is due to open on the old Show Ground site in 1999.

Pyrmont Point Park is a bit sterile, but it's not a bad place to fish (there are fish-gutting benches), picnic and contemplate the changing face of Sydney. Take the light rail to John St Square and walk downhill along Harris St towards the water.

On the North Shore, **Davidson Park** is an 8km corridor of bushland stretching north-west from Middle Harbour to Ku-ring-gai Chase National Park.

The **Lane Cove National Park** runs between the suburbs of Ryde and Chatswood, and has extensive walking tracks along the picturesque but polluted Lane Cove River. Entry to the park costs $7.50 per car.

See the Sydney Harbour section for information on the parks and bushland areas which comprise the Sydney Harbour National Park.

City Views

Sydney is an ostentatious city that offers visitors a dramatic spectacle. You can see the complete panorama by whooshing to the top of **Sydney Tower**, a needle-like column that has an observation deck and a revolving restaurant set 305m above the ground. The view, extending as far as the Blue Mountains to the west, gives you an idea of the city's geography. The tower is on top of the Centrepoint complex on Market St, between Pitt and Castlereagh Sts. It's open daily from 9.30 am to 9.30 pm (11.30 pm on Saturday); entry costs $10 ($8 concession).

The Harbour Bridge is another obvious vantage point, but even many locals have never visited the small **Harbour Bridge Museum** and climbed the 200 stairs inside the south-eastern pylon to enjoy the dazzling view. The pylon and museum are open daily between 10 am and 5 pm; admission is $2. Enter from the bridge's pedestrian walkway, accessible from Cumberland St in the Rocks, or from near Milsons Point station on the North Shore. There are impressive ground-level views of the city and harbour from **Mrs Macquarie's Point**, and from **Observatory Hill** in Millers Point. **Blues Point Reserve** and **Bradleys Head** are the best vantage points on the North Shore.

The most enjoyable and atmospheric way to view Sydney is by boat. If you can't persuade someone to take you sailing, jump aboard a ferry at Circular Quay. The Manly ferry offers an unforgettable cruise down the length of the harbour east of the bridge for a mere $4. If you really want to have your breath taken away, Heli-Scenic (☎ 9317 3402) offers 25-minute helicopter flights over the harbour daily for a cool $140. ■

Kings Cross

The Cross is a cocktail of strip joints, prostitution, crime and drugs, shaken and stirred with a handful of classy restaurants, designer cafes, international hotels and backpacker hostels. It attracts an odd mix of low-life, sailors, travellers, Japanese tourists, inner-city trendies and suburbanites looking for a big night out.

The Cross has always been a bit raffish, from its early days as a centre of bohemianism to the Vietnam War era, when it became the vice centre of Australia. While the vice is real and nasty enough, Sydneysiders are quite fond of the Cross. It appeals to the larrikin spirit, which always enjoys a bit of devil-may-care and 24-hour drinking. Many travellers begin and end their Australian adventures in the Cross, and it's a good place to swap information, meet up with friends, pick up work, browse the hostel notice boards and buy or sell a car.

Darlinghurst Rd is the trashy main drag. This doglegs into Macleay St which continues into the more upmarket suburb of Potts Point. Most of the hostels are on Victoria St, which diverges from Darlinghurst Rd just north of William St, near the iconic Coca-Cola sign. The thistle-like **El Alamein Fountain** in Fitzroy Gardens is the psychological centre of the area, and there's a market here every Sunday.

The helpful Kings Cross Tourist Information Service (☎ 9368 0479) operates from the new Rex Hotel on the edge of the Fitzroy Gardens. You can book tours and bus tickets here and the staff know the area well and will recommend places to stay.

In the dip between the Cross and the city is **Woolloomooloo**, one of Sydney's oldest areas. Sensitive urban restoration has made it a lovely place to stroll around. Its huge disused wharf is awaiting redevelopment. Harry's Cafe de Wheels is next to the wharf and must be one of the few pie carts in the world to be a tourist attraction. It opened in 1945, stays open 18 hours a day and is *the* place to go for a late-night chicken and mushroom fill-up. The innovative Artspace gallery is opposite.

The easiest way to get to the Cross from the city is by train ($1.80 one way). It's the first stop outside the city loop on the line to Bondi Junction. Bus Nos 324, 325 and 327 from Circular Quay pass through the Cross. You can walk from Hyde Park along William St in 15 minutes. A prettier, longer route involves crossing the Domain, descending the hill behind the Art Gallery of NSW, walking past Woolloomooloo's wharf and climbing McElhone Stairs to the northern end of Victoria St.

Inner East

The lifeblood of Darlinghurst, Surry Hills and Paddington, **Oxford St** is one of the more exciting places for late-night action. It's a strip of shops, cafes, bars and nightclubs whose flamboyance and spirit can be largely attributed to the vibrant and vocal gay community. The route of the Sydney Gay & Lesbian Mardi Gras parade passes this way.

The main drag of Oxford St runs from the south-eastern corner of Hyde Park to the north-western corner of Centennial Park, though it continues in name up to Bondi Junction. Taylor Square is the hub of social life in the area. Oxford St street numbers restart west of the junction with South Dowling and Victoria Sts, on the Darlinghurst-Paddington border. Bus Nos 380 and 382 from Circular Quay, and No 378 from Railway Square, run the length of the street.

The innercity Mecca for bright young things wanting to be close to the action and live on nothing but cafe lattes is **Darlinghurst**. It's a vital area of urban cool that's fast developing a cafe monoculture, and there's no better way to soak up its studied ambience than to loiter in a few sidewalk cafes and do as the others do. Darlinghurst encompasses the vibrant 'Little Italy' of Stanley St in East Sydney, and is wedged between Oxford and William Sts. Sydney's **Jewish Museum**, on the corner of Darlinghurst Rd and Burton St, has evocative exhibits on Australian Jewish history and the Holocaust. It's open daily except

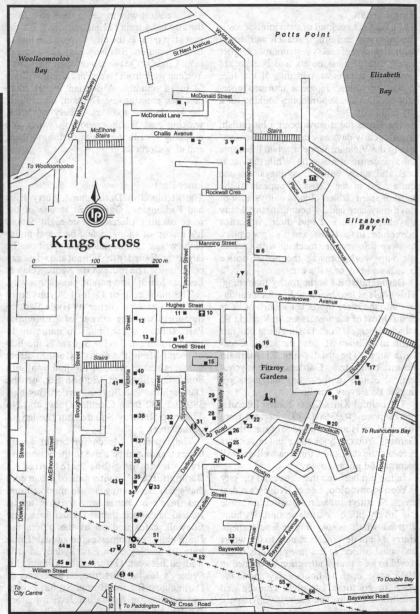

NEW SOUTH WALES

Woolloomooloo
Bay

Potts Point

St Neot Avenue

Wylde Street

Elizabeth
Bay

Cooper Wharf Roadway

McElhone
Stairs

To Woolloomooloo

McDonald Street
McDonald Lane
1

Challis Avenue
2   3
4

Stairs

Madeay Street

Onslow
Place
5

Kings Cross

0   100   200 m

Rockwall Cres

Manning Street

6

Elizabeth
Bay

Tusculum Street

7

8   9
Greenknowe   Avenue

Hughes Street
11   10

12

13   14

Orwell Street

15   16

Fitzroy
Gardens

Earl Street

Stairs

40
39
41

38   32

37   31
30

42

36

43   35
34   33

49

Springfield Ave

Llankelly Place

29
28

Darlinghurst Road

27

26
25
24

22
23

21

17
18

19

20
Barncleuth Square

To Rushcutters Bay

Roslyn

Kellett Street

Roslyn Street

Gardens

Ward Avenue

Barncleuth Avenue

To Double Bay

Brougham Street

McElhone Street

Dowling Street

Victoria Street

51

50

47

44

45   46

William Street

To
City Centre

53
Bayswater

54

Bayswater Avenue

52

48

Victoria St

To Paddington

Kings Cross Road

55

56

Bayswater Road

Saturday and closes at 2 pm on Friday ($6, $4 concession).

South of Darlinghurst is **Surry Hills**, home to a mishmash of innercity residents and a swag of good pubs. Once the undisputed centre of Sydney's rag trade and print media, many warehouses have been converted or razed to make way for expensive yuppie dogboxes. The Surry Hills Market is held on the first Saturday of the month in Shannon Reserve on the corner of Crown and Foveaux Sts. The Brett Whiteley Studio, 2 Raper St, is in the artist's old home and studio, and is open on weekends between 10 am and 4 pm ($6, $4 concession). Surry Hills is a short walk east of Central Station or south from Oxford St. Catch bus No 301, 302 or 303 from Circular Quay.

Next door to Surry Hills is **Paddington**, an attractive residential area of leafy streets and tightly packed Victorian terrace houses. It was built for aspiring artisans, but during the lemming-like rush to the outer suburbs after WWII the area became a slum. A renewed interest in Victorian architecture and the pleasures of innercity life led to its restoration during the 1960s and today these modest terraces swap hands for a decent portion of a million dollars.

Most facilities, shops, cafes and bars are on Oxford St but the suburb doesn't really have a geographic centre. Most of its streets cascade down the hill north of here towards Edgecliff and Double Bay. It's a lovely place to wander around at any time, but the best time to visit is Saturday when the **Paddington Village Bazaar** is in full swing on the corner of Newcombe and Oxford Sts.

There are over 20 art galleries in Paddington; pick up a copy of *Paddington Galleries & Environs* at the first one you stumble upon. Free tours of the stately **Victoria Barracks** on Oxford St are held on Thursday at 10 am, including a performance by the military band on the first and third Thursdays of each month. The Army Museum is open on Sunday between 10 am and 3 pm (admission is free).

NEW SOUTH WALES

Eastern Suburbs

A short walk north-east of the Cross is the harbour-front suburb of **Elizabeth Bay**. Elizabeth Bay House, 7 Onslow Ave, is one of Sydney's finest colonial homes. It's open daily except Monday from 10 am to 4.30 pm ($5, $3 concession).

Beautiful **Rushcutters Bay** is the next bay east. Its handsome harbourside park is just a five-minute walk from the Cross and is the closest place for cooped-up backpackers to stretch their legs. The tennis courts (☎ 9357 1675) on Waratah St can be hired for $16 an hour. This is the yachting centre of Sydney and is one of the best places to learn to sail (see the Sailing & Boating section).

Further east is the manicured suburb of **Double Bay**, which is over-endowed with smart cafes and designer stores. The views from the harbour-hugging New South Head Rd as it leaves Double Bay, passes **Rose Bay** and climbs east towards wealthy **Vaucluse**, are up there with the best. Vaucluse House, in Vaucluse Park, is an attractive colonial villa open daily except Monday from 10 am to 4.30 pm ($5).

At the entrance to the harbour is **Watsons Bay**, a snug community composed of harbourside restaurants, a palm-lined park and a couple of nautical churches. It makes a great day trip if you want to forget you're in the middle of a large city. Nearby **Camp Cove** is one of Sydney's best harbour beaches, and there's a nude beach near South Head at **Lady Bay**. South Head has great views across the harbour entrance to North Head and Middle Head. **The Gap** is a dramatic cliff-top lookout on the ocean side (it's also Sydney's favourite suicide spot).

Bus Nos 324 and 325 from Circular Quay service the eastern suburbs via Kings Cross. Sit on the left side heading east to make the most of the views.

Southern Beaches

The grande dame of Sydney's beaches is **Bondi**, which has a majesty all its own. The focus is on the sand 'n' surf, but the suburb has a unique flavour blended from the mix of old Jewish and Italian communities, dyed-in-the-wool Aussies, New Zealand and UK expats, working travellers and surf rats who live here bonded by their love for the beach. They'll be playing volleyball for gold here in the 2000 Olympics.

In recent years Bondi has shed much of its tired facade and a new lick of paint, some landscaping and a rash of new cafes has been enough for it to be suddenly 'rediscovered' by innercity trendies.

The ocean road is Campbell Parade, where most of the shops, cafes and hotels are. The Bondi Beach Market is held every Sunday at the Bondi Beach Public School, at the northern end of Campbell Parade. There are Aboriginal rock engravings on the golf course in North Bondi.

Catch bus Nos 380 or 382 from the city to get to the beach or, if you're in a hurry, catch a train to Bondi Junction and pick up one of these buses as they pass through the Bondi Junction bus station.

Just south of Bondi is **Tamarama**, a lovely cove with strong surf. Get off the bus as it kinks off Bondi Rd onto Fletcher St, just before it reaches Bondi Beach. Tamarama is a five-minute walk down the hill.

There's a superb beach hemmed in by a bowl-shaped park and sandstone headlands at **Bronte**, south of Tamarama. Cafes with outdoor tables on the edge of the park make it the perfect place for a day of rest and relaxation. Catch bus No 378 from the city or catch a train to Bondi Junction and pick the bus up there; sit on the left side heading to the beach and wait for the breathtaking view as the bus descends Macpherson St. You can walk here along the wonderful cliff-top footpath from Bondi Beach or from Coogee via Gordon's Bay, Clovelly and the sun-bleached Waverley Cemetery.

Clovelly Bay is the narrow scooped-out beach to the south. As well as the saltwater baths here, there's a wheelchair-access boardwalk to make it easier for the chairbound to have a sea dip. A submersible fibreglass wheelchair is available from the council (☎ 9399 0999) if you don't fancy wetting your own wheels.

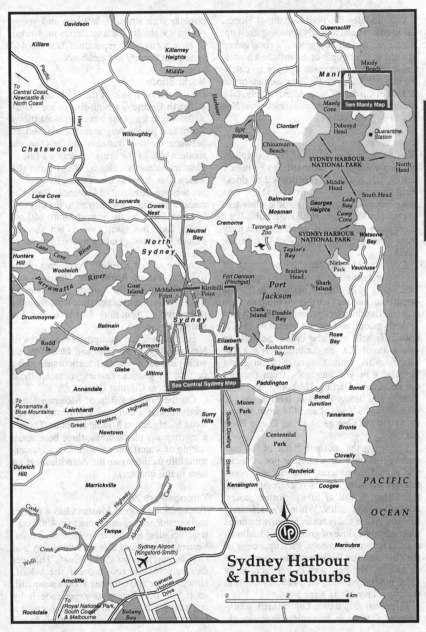

Sydney Harbour
& Inner Suburbs

Traditionally the poor cousin of Bondi, **Coogee** has been recently sprucing itself up. It has a relaxed air, few graces, a good sweep of sand and a couple of established hostels and hotels. You can reach Coogee by catching bus No 372 from Railway Square or No 373 from Circular Quay. Alternatively, take a train to Bondi Junction and pick up bus Nos 314 or 315 from there.

Inner West

West of the centre is the higgledy-piggledy peninsula suburb of **Balmain**. It was once a notoriously rough neighbourhood of dockyard workers but gentrification has transformed it into an arty, middle-class area of restored Victoriana flush with pubs. It's a great place for a casual stroll. Catch a ferry from Circular Quay or bus No 442 from the QVB.

Cosy, bohemian **Glebe** is south-west of the centre, bordering the northern edge of the University of Sydney. It has a large student population, a cruisy cafe-lined main street, a tranquil Buddhist temple, aroma therapy and crystals galore, and several decent hostels. A market is held at Glebe Public School, on Glebe Point Rd, on Saturday. It's a 10-minute walk from Central Station along Broadway or you can walk from the city centre across Darling Harbour's Pyrmont Bridge and along Pyrmont Bridge Rd (20 minutes). Bus Nos 431 and 434 from Millers Point run via George St along Glebe Point Rd.

Bordering the southern flank of the university is **Newtown**, a melting pot of social and sexual subcultures, students and home renovators. King St, its relentlessly urban main drag, is full of funky clothes stores, bookshops and cafes. While it's definitely moving up the social scale, Newtown comes with a healthy dose of grunge, and harbours several live-music venues. Pick up a copy of the *Newtown Art Walk* pamphlet from a cafe or gallery. The best way to get there is by train, but bus No 422, 423, 426 or 428 from the city all run along King St.

Predominantly Italian **Leichhardt**, southwest of Glebe, is becoming increasingly popular with students, lesbians and young professionals. Its Italian eateries on Norton St have a city-wide reputation. Bus No 440 runs from the city to Leichhardt.

North Shore

On the northern side of the Harbour Bridge is **North Sydney**, a high-rise office centre with little to tempt the traveller. **McMahons Point** is a lovely, forgotten suburb wedged between the two business districts, on the western side of the bridge. There's a line of pleasant sidewalk cafes on Blues Point Rd, which runs down to Blues Point Reserve on the western headland of Lavender Bay. The reserve has fine views across to the city.

Luna Park, on the eastern shore of Lavender Bay, has been closed, but the big mouth still grins, pending redevelopment of the site.

At the end of Kirribilli Point, east of the bridge, stand **Admiralty House** and **Kirribilli House**, the Sydney residences of the governor-general and the prime minister respectively (Admiralty House is the one nearer the bridge).

East of here are the upmarket suburbs of **Neutral Bay**, **Cremorne** and **Mosman**, all with pleasant coves and harbourside parks perfect for picnics. Ferries go to all these suburbs from Circular Quay.

On the northern side of Mosman is the pretty beach suburb of **Balmoral**, which faces Manly across Middle Harbour. There's a promenade, picnic areas, three beaches, a couple of waterfront restaurants and watersport hire facilities (see the Activities section later in this chapter).

Taronga Park Zoo

Taronga Park Zoo in Mosman has a superb harbourside setting and more than 4000 critters, including lots of native Australian ones. Ferries leave Wharf 2 at Circular Quay and stop at the Taronga Park Wharf. The rear entrance to the zoo is near the wharf. However, the zoo complex is on a steep hill, so if you don't want to experience it by constantly walking uphill, you can catch a bus to the main entrance at the top of the hill and walk down. An alternative is catch the cable car from the rear (bottom) entrance to the main (top) one. The cable car costs $2.50 one way.

The zoo (☎ 9969 2777) is open daily from 9 am to 5 pm ($15); night visits are scheduled seasonally. A Zoo Pass, sold at the ferry ticket counters at Circular Quay, costs $21 and includes a return ferry ride, zoo admission and either the bus or the cable car to the top entrance.

Manly

The jewel of the North Shore, Manly is on a narrow peninsula which ends at the dramatic cliffs of North Head. It boasts harbour and ocean beaches, a ferry wharf, all the trappings of a full-scale holiday resort and a great sense of community identity. It's a sun-soaked place not afraid to show a bit of tack and brashness to attract visitors, and makes a refreshing change from the prim upper-middle-class harbour enclaves nearby.

The Manly Visitors Information Bureau (☎ 9977 1088) on the promenade at South Steyne is open daily from 10 am to 4 pm. It has useful, free pamphlets on the 10km Manly Scenic Walkway and sells Manly Heritage Walk booklets for $3.50. There's a bus information booth at the entrance to the wharf. Both ferries and JetCat catamarans ply between Circular Quay and Manly. The JetCats seem to traverse the harbour before you get a chance to blink, so jump on one of the stately Manly ferries. These navigate the length of the harbour in a cool 30 minutes and offer fantastic views of the city.

The ferry wharf is on Manly's harbour shore. A short walk along Manly's pedestrian mall, the Corso, brings you to the ocean beach lined by towering Norfolk Pines. North and South Steyne are the roads running along the foreshore. A footpath follows the shoreline from South Steyne around the small headland to Fairy Bower

NEW SOUTH WALES

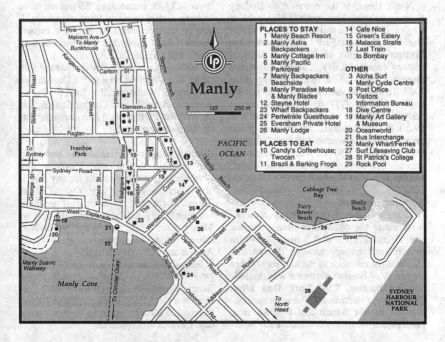

Manly

0   125   250 m

PACIFIC OCEAN

PLACES TO STAY
1 Manly Beach Resort
2 Manly Astra Backpackers
5 Manly Cottage Inn
6 Manly Pacific Parkroyal
7 Manly Backpackers Beachside
8 Manly Paradise Motel & Manly Blades
12 Steyne Hotel
23 Wharf Backpackers
24 Periwinkle Guesthouse
25 Eversham Private Hotel
26 Manly Lodge

PLACES TO EAT
10 Candy's Coffeehouse; Twocan
11 Brazil & Barking Frogs

14 Cafe Nice
15 Green's Eatery
16 Malacca Straits
17 Last Train to Bombay

OTHER
3 Aloha Surf
4 Manly Cycle Centre
9 Post Office
13 Visitors Information Bureau
18 Dive Centre
19 Manly Art Gallery & Museum
20 Oceanworld
21 Bus Interchange
22 Manly Wharf/Ferries
27 Surf Lifesaving Club
28 St Patrick's College
29 Rock Pool

Cabbage Tree Bay

Fairy Bower Beach

Shelly Beach

Manly Scenic Walkway

Manly Cove

To Circular Quay

To North Head

SYDNEY HARBOUR NATIONAL PARK

Beach and the picturesque cove of **Shelly Beach**.

The **Manly Art Gallery & Museum** focuses on the suburb's special relationship with the beach. The museum is on West Esplanade, on the Manly Cove foreshore, and is open Tuesday to Sunday from 10 am to 5 pm; entry is $2.

The excellent **Oceanworld** is next door. The big drawcards are the sharks and stingrays, and the best time to visit is 11.15 am and 2 pm (plus 4 pm on weekends) when divers enter the tanks to feed the bigger fish. An underwater perspex tunnel offers dramatic (but dry) close encounters with the fish. If that's still not close enough for your thrill levels, certified Scuba divers can dive with the sharks in the evenings for $65. Oceanworld is open daily from 10 am to 5.30 pm. Entry is $13.50 ($10 concession). Behind Oceanworld is the wonderful 10km-long Manly Scenic Walkway (see the Harbour Walks aside).

North Head, at the entrance to Sydney Harbour, is about 3km south of Manly. Most of the dramatic headland is in Sydney Harbour National Park. The **Quarantine Station** represents an interesting slice of Sydney's social history; it housed suspected disease carriers from 1832 right up until 1984. To visit the station you have to book a guided tour (☎ 9977 6522). These depart daily at 1.10 pm, take 1½ hours and cost $9.50 ($7 concession). Night-time 'ghost tours' take place Wednesday and Friday to Sunday at about 7.30 pm. A three hour spook session costs $17 and includes supper. Catch bus No 135 from Manly Wharf.

Northern Beaches

A string of ocean-front suburbs stretches north along the coast from Manly, ending after 30km on at beautiful, well-heeled **Palm Beach** and the spectacular Barrenjoey Heads at the entrance to Broken Bay. There are plenty of beaches along the way, including **Freshwater, Curl Curl, Dee Why, Collaroy** and **Narrabeen**. The most spectacular are **Whale Beach** and **Bilgola**, near Palm Beach; both have dramatic, steep head-

lands. Several of the northernmost beach suburbs also back onto **Pittwater,** a lovely inlet off Broken Bay and a favoured sailing spot.

Bus Nos 136 and 139 run from Manly to Freshwater and Curl Curl. Bus No 190 from Wynyard in the city runs to Newport and north to Palm Beach. The thrice daily Palm Beach Ferry Service (☎ 9918 2747) runs between Palm Beach and Patonga on the Central Coast ($6 one way).

Activities

Swimming Sydney's harbour beaches offer sheltered water conducive to swimming. But if you just want to frolic, nothing beats being knocked around in the waves that pound the ocean beaches, where swimming is safe if you follow instructions and swim within the 'flagged' areas patrolled by lifeguards. There are some notorious but clearly signposted rips even at Sydney's most popular beaches, so don't underestimate the surf just because it doesn't look threatening. Efforts are made to keep surfers separate from swimmers. If you're worried about sharks, just remind yourself that Sydney has only had one fatal shark attack since 1937.

Outdoor pools in the city include the salt-water Boy Charlton pool in the Domain, on the edge of Woolloomooloo Bay; the Prince Alfred Park pool, near Central Station; and the Victoria Park pool on Broadway, next to the University of Sydney.

Surfing South of the Heads, the best spots are Bondi, Tamarama, Coogee and Maroubra. Cronulla, south of Botany Bay, is also a serious surfing spot. On the North Shore, there are a dozen surf beaches between Manly and Palm Beach; the best are Manly, Curl Curl, Dee Why, North Narrabeen, Mona Vale, Newport Reef, North Avalon and Palm Beach itself.

Shops such as the Bondi Surf Company (☎ 9365 0870), 72 Campbell Parade, Bondi Beach, and Aloha Surf (☎ 9977 3777), 44 Pittwater Rd, Manly, hire equipment. Expect to pay $25 for a board and a wetsuit for the day. Lessons are available.

RICHARD I'ANSON

New South Wales
Top: Sydney and the Harbour Bridge, seen from Milson's Point
Bottom: Sydney's skyline and harbourside, from Novotel, Darling Harbour

RICHARD NEBESKY

RICHARD I'ANSON

JON MURRAY

New South Wales
Left: An Aborigine busking, Circular Quay, Sydney
Right: Ferries & Opera House, Circular Quay, Sydney
Bottom: The magnificent Blue Mountains

Sailing & Boating There are plenty of sailing schools in Sydney and even if you're not serious about learning the ropes, an introductory lesson can be a fun way of getting out on the harbour. Hiring a motorboat is even easier.

Sydney By Sail (☎ 9371 6228) offers a 90-minute introductory sail for $39 departing daily from the National Maritime Museum in Darling Harbour.

The Elizabeth Bay Marina (☎ 9358 2057), close to Kings Cross, hires easy-to-operate five-metre boats with outboards for $65 for a half-day. They supply a map, instructions and can even whip up a picnic.

The sociable East Sail Sailing School (☎ 9327 1166) at d'Albora Marina, New Beach Rd, Rushcutters Bay, runs a huge range of courses from introductory to racing level.

Northside Sailing School (☎ 9969 3972), at the southern end of the Spit Bridge in Mosman, also offers courses and rents sailboards and dinghies.

Rose Bay Aquatic Centre (☎ 9371 7036) and Balmoral Marine (☎ 9969 6006) offer tuition and rent sailboards ($15), catamarans ($25) and motor boats ($20) by the hour.

Pittwater and Broken Bay offer excellent sailing. Scotland Island Schooners (☎ 9999 3954) at Church Point runs intensive two-day yachting courses ($220) and offers generous discounts to travellers and YHA members.

Diving The best shore dives in Sydney are the Gordons Bay Underwater Nature Trail, north of Coogee; Shark Point, Clovelly; and Ship Rock, Cronulla. Popular boat dive sites are Wedding Cake Island, off Coogee; around the Sydney Heads; and off the Royal National Park.

Plenty of outfits will take you diving and many run dive courses, including Pro Dive (☎ 9264 6177) at 428 George St in the city and 27 Alfreda St, Coogee (☎ 9665 6333), and Dive Centre Manly (☎ 9977 4355) at 10 Belgrave St, Manly. Days out start at $65. Qualified divers can also dive with the sharks at Manly's Oceanworld (see the Manly section).

Canoeing & Kayaking The NSW Canoe Association (☎ 9660 4597) provides information on canoe courses, hire and tours. Canoe Specialists (☎ 9969 4590) at the southern end of Spit Bridge in Mosman rents sea kayaks for $10 for the first hour and $5 for each subsequent hour. Natural Wanders (☎ 9555 9788) has kayak tours of the harbour which go under the bridge and stop in secluded bays. A five-hour tour costs $75 including lunch; no experience is necessary.

Inline Skating The beach promenades at Bondi, Manly and Centennial Park are the most favoured spots for skating. Manly Blades (☎ 9976 3833), 49 North Steyne, hires skates for $10 for the first hour and $5 for each subsequent hour, or $25 per day; Bondi Boards & Blades (☎ 9365 6555), 148 Curlewis St, Bondi Beach, has the same hourly rate and charges $28 a day. Protective gear is free and there's a free lesson every Tuesday afternoon. Total Skate (☎ 9380 6356), 36 Oxford St, Paddington, near Centennial Park, is slightly cheaper.

Organised Tours

Conventional city and country tour operators include Australian Pacific (☎ 13 1304), Clipper Gray Line (☎ 9252 4499) and Murrays (☎ 13 2251). A half-day city tour costs around $35, and a one-day tour costs around $70. Tours of the Blue Mountains cost around $80, the Hunter Valley $90 and Canberra $75.

Maureen Fry (☎ 9660 7157) offers a variety of guided walking tours of Sydney for around $12. CTA Cycle Tours (☎ 1800 353 004) runs cycling day tours of Sydney on weekends for $45, including cycle and helmet hire and ferry transport. Sydney Bike Tours (☎ 9241 5990) offers trips from one hour ($15) to all day ($75).

Sydney Aboriginal Discoveries (☎ 9566 4816) run bus tours, walks and cruises, but they cater mostly to groups.

See the Olympics boxed aside for tours of Homebush Bay.

Cruises There's a wide range of relatively inexpensive cruises on the harbour, from ferry boats and cruisers to paddle-wheelers and sailing ships. You can book most at the Quayside Booking Centre (☎ 9555 2700) opposite Wharf 6, Circular Quay. Captain Cook Cruises (☎ 9206 1111) has its own booking office at Wharf 6.

STA ferries offer some good-value cruises, such as the 2½-hour Ferry Cruise, which departs Circular Quay at 1 pm on weekdays and 1.30 pm on weekends and visits Middle Harbour. Tickets cost $17.50 and can be purchased from the ticket office opposite Circular Quay's Wharf 4.

The Sydney Harbour Explorer is a hop-on/hop-off service which stops at Circular Quay, the opera house, Watsons Bay, Taronga Zoo and Darling Harbour. Boats run two-hourly from 9.30 am until 3.30 pm and the fare is $20 ($15 concession).

For about $40 you can take a two-hour weekday lunch cruise on the *Bounty* (☎ 9247 1789), a replica of the ship lost by Captain Bligh, which departs Campbell Cove in the Rocks at 12.30 pm.

Special Events
Call the City Events Infoline (☎ 9265 9007) for info on current events.

The massive **Sydney Festival** floods the city with art in January, including free outdoor concerts in the Domain. **Chinese New Year** is celebrated in Chinatown with fireworks in January or February. Surf lifesaving carnivals are held at Sydney's ocean beaches from mid-November to May.

The highlight of the month-long **Gay & Lesbian Mardi Gras** is the outrageous parade along Oxford St which ends in a bacchanalian party at the Hordern Pavilion in Moore Park in early March.

The 12-day **Royal Easter Show** is an agricultural show and funfair held at Homebush Bay.

The 14-day **Sydney Film Festival** is held in June at the State Theatre and other cinemas. The **Biennale of Sydney** is an international art festival held between July and September in even-numbered years at the Art Gallery of NSW, the Powerhouse Museum and other venues.

The 14km **City to Surf Run** takes place on the second Sunday in August and attracts a mighty 40,000 entrants who run from Hyde Park to Bondi Beach.

Carnivale is an ethnic arts festival held in early spring. The **Manly Jazz Festival** is held over the Labour Day long weekend in early October and the **Kings Cross Carnival** takes place in late October or early November.

Thousands of backpackers descend on **Bondi Beach** for a booze fest on Christmas Day, much to the consternation of the powers-that-be and the overworked lifesavers. Sydney Harbour is a fantastic sight on Boxing Day as boats of all shapes and sizes farewell the competitors in the gruelling Sydney to Hobart Yacht Race. The Rocks, Kings Cross and Bondi Beach are all traditional gathering places for alcohol-sodden celebrations on **New Year's Eve** although alcohol-free zones and a massive police presence aims to discourage the rowdier elements.

Various **Olympics Arts Festivals** are scheduled in the lead up to the Olympics. 'A Sea Change' is the theme for the June to October 1998 festival; 'Reaching the World' will take place from November 1998 to January 2000 and 'Harbour of Life' will run concurrent with the Olympics in August 2000.

Places to Stay
Sydney has a huge variety of accommodation, including a large selection of travellers' hostels. Prices listed below are winter rates. In summer, prices rise and special deals vanish. At these times, expect hostel rates to increase by just the odd dollar; hotel rooms at beachside suburbs can increase by as much as 50%. A 'bed tax' of up to 10% applies to hotel and guesthouse (not hostel) beds in the city centre to raise funds for the Olympics.

Bed & Breakfast Sydneyside (☎ 9449 4430), PO Box 555, Turramurra, 2074, arranges accommodation in private homes for $45 to $70 a night a single, or $65 to $100 a double.

If you want to find long-stay accommodation, peruse the 'flats to let' and 'share accommodation' ads in the *Sydney Morning Herald* on Wednesday and Saturday. Hostel notice boards are also good sources of information.

Camping Sydney's caravan parks are a long way out of town, but those listed below are within 25km of the city centre:

East's Lane Cove River Van Village (☎ 9805 0500), Plassey Rd, North Ryde, has sites/vans/cabins from $18/47/52 a double.

Sheralee Tourist Caravan Park (☎ 9567 7161), 88 Bryant St, Rockdale, offers sites/vans from $12/35 a double.

Lakeside Caravan Park (☎ 9913 7845), Lake Park Rd, North Narrabeen, has sites/cabins from $16/67 a double.

Grand Pines Caravan Park (☎ 9529 7329), 289 Grand Parade, San Souci, rents vans and cabins from $45 a double.

Hostels The largest concentration of hostels is in Kings Cross, but there are clusters in Glebe, Manly and Coogee. The average price for a dorm bed is $16, but in the peak summer period they can rise to $20. Facilities vary from dorms with en-suite, TV, fridge and cooking facilities to just a plain room with a couple of bunks. Some hostels have set hours for checking in and out, although all have 24-hour access once you've paid.

Things to think about when you're shopping around include whether a key deposit is required; whether alcohol is permitted; phone, Internet and satellite TV access; whether free pick-up is available, if visitors are allowed, and the standard of security on the premises.

City Centre *Sydney Central YHA* (☎ 9281 9111) is on the corner of Pitt St and Rawson Place opposite Central Station. It's a big whizz-bang place with excellent facilities (pool, sauna, cafe) in a heritage building. Dorms start at $18; twins with en-suite are a bargain $31 per person. Wheelchair-access rooms are available.

Nomad's Downtown City Backpackers (☎ 9211 8801), on the corner of Goulburn and George Sts (see the Darling Harbour & Chinatown map), is a happening hostel with lots of activities. Dorm beds start at $17; twin rooms are $25 per person.

The *YWCA* hostel (☎ 9264 2451) on Wentworth Ave allows both men and women to stay. A dorm bed costs $24 a night. Rooms go for $60/80 for singles/twins; $90/110 with bathroom.

Kings Cross Area There are heaps of hostels in the Cross and little to distinguish between many of them. Eva's has the best reputation, followed by Backpackers Headquarters. The Pink House is for those who like their hostels a little more lived-in and cosy. The Jolly Swagman hostels have the best organised social life.

Heading north along Victoria St from Kings Cross Station, the first hostel you come to is *Plane Tree Lodge* (☎ 9356 4551) at No 172. This is an average Kings Cross hostel, with a variety of rooms. Rates start at $15 ($95 weekly) in a six-bed dorm with TV and fridge, $16 ($100 weekly) in a four-bed with own bathroom. Singles/twins/doubles with en-suite cost $25/35/40. Next down the street at No 166 is *Highfield House* (☎ 9326 9539), another average place with three-bed dorms for $15 ($95 weekly) and singles/doubles for $30/45 ($180/250 weekly).

The *Original Backpackers* (☎ 9356 3232) in the lovely Victorian building at No 162 *is* the original hostel in this part of the world. It's a reasonably clean, lived-in place with a courtyard and a pleasant kitchen-dining area. The dorms are large and cost $16 ($94 weekly); twins/doubles are $38 ($230 weekly).

Travellers Rest (☎ 9358 4606) at No 156 has clean dorms with fridge and TV for $17, twins/doubles for $36/38, singles for $30 ($135 weekly) and twins/doubles that include en-suite for $40 ($230 weekly). Shared facilities are spic and span and the owner/operators are friendly and helpful.

Potts Point House (☎ 9368 0733) at No 154 is a cut above average. Bedding down in a sleek dorm is $18 ($110 weekly); doubles start at $40 ($260 weekly).

One of the three busy *Jolly Swagman* (☎ 9357 4733) hostels is at No 144. The others are at 16 Orwell St (☎ 9358 6600) and 27 Orwell St (☎ 9358 6400). They all charge $17 ($99 weekly) for bright dorms with kitchenettes and fridge, and $40 ($240 weekly) for doubles. Organised entertainment includes barbecues, tennis matches and trips. Across the road at No 141 is the basic *Kanga House* (☎ 9357 7897), which charges $14 ($75 weekly) for dorms and $16/36 ($90/200 weekly) for singles/doubles.

Eva's Backpackers (☎ 9358 2185) at 6-8 Orwell St is a clean, friendly, well-run place. Dorms cost $18 and doubles $42. It's so popular that it's often full, even in winter. The secure, squeaky-clean *Backpackers Headquarters* (☎ 9331 6180) at 79 Bayswater Rd has dorms from $15 (10 beds) or $16 (six beds) and is also often full.

One of the most popular hostels in the Cross is the mellow, homely *Pink House* (☎ 9358 1689), which has a lovely patio, a rear courtyard and a social atmosphere. It's east of Darlinghurst Rd at 6 Barncleuth Square. Dorm beds cost $15 ($90 weekly) and twins are $19 per person ($110 weekly).

Funk House (☎ 9358 6455), 23 Darlinghurst Rd (enter from Llankelly Place), is a relative newcomer but rates high on the fun scale. It's a colourful, busy place with dorm beds at $16 ($96 weekly), and doubles $19 ($114 weekly). If you'd rather things a bit quieter, *Backpackers Connection* (☎ 9358 4844), 2 Roslyn St, is an impressive hostel with $17 dorm beds and doubles for $24. Every room has its own bathroom and TV.

Rucksack Rest (☎ 9358 2348), 9 McDonald St, Potts Point, is a quiet hostel. Dorm beds cost $16 ($96 weekly) and singles/doubles $25/35. *Forbes Terrace* (☎ 9358 4327), 153 Forbes St, Woolloomooloo, four streets east of Victoria St is a clean, quiet

hostel with a courtyard area. Dorms cost from $16 ($84 weekly), singles/twins go for $45/50.

South of the Centre *Kangaroo Bakpak* (☎ 9319 5915) at 665 South Dowling St, Surry Hills, has dorm beds for $15 ($90 weekly). Bus Nos 372, 393 and 395 run along Cleveland St from Central Station; bus Nos 301, 302 and 303 run along Bourke St from Circular Quay. *Nomad's Backpackers* (☎ 9331 6487) in the renovated Captain Cook Hotel, 162 Flinders St, Surry Hills, has dorms for $16. It's only a few minutes walk from Taylor Square.

The *Excelsior Hotel* (☎ 9211 4945), 64 Foveaux St, Surry Hills, is a small pub only a few blocks from Central Station with dorms for $15 ($90 weekly) and singles for $35 ($190 weekly).

The *Alfred Park Private Hotel* (☎ 9319 4031), 207 Cleveland St, is just a short stroll from Central Station. It has a pleasant courtyard and kitchen, and dorms with en-suite, TV and fridge for $16 ($98 weekly). Singles/doubles cost $40/50 and doubles with en-suite $65.

Billabong Gardens (☎ 9550 3236), 5 Egan St, Newtown, is a quiet hostel with a pool, spa and happy-looking guests. Dorms with en-suite cost $16 ($100 weekly) and doubles from $40. Take a train to Newtown Station, turn right into King St and Egan St is about four blocks along on the left.

Glebe *Glebe Point YHA Hostel* (☎ 9692 8418) at 262 Glebe Point Rd is large and squeaky clean. Five-bed dorms cost $21, four-bed $23 and twin rooms $54. The staff here have lots of ideas about what to check out in Sydney, and they store luggage.

The friendly *Glebe Village Backpackers* (☎ 9660 8133), 256 Glebe Point Rd, is a ramshackle hostel in two big houses. Facilities range from scruffy to sparkling and the vibe is cruisy. Dorms cost from $17 and doubles $48.

Delightful *Wattle House* (☎ 9552 4997), 44 Hereford St, has dorm beds for $19 ($115 weekly) and twin or double rooms from $44.

The *Alishan International Guesthouse* (☎ 9566 4048) at 100 Glebe Point Rd is a lovely, civilised guesthouse with a few dorm beds for $20 ($126 weekly).

Nomad's Forest Lodge (☎ 9660 1872), 117 Arundel St, is near the university above a small pub. The kitchen facilities are lacking but there are good $5 pasta dinners available. Beds start at $15.

Bondi Bondi has a range of hostel accommodation, not all of it particularly appealing, but with the consolation of the beach on your doorstep you're unlikely to spend much time staring at the paint peeling in your room. This is a popular base for long-term working travellers so there are plenty of cheap flats available if you plan on sticking around for a while.

Indy's (☎ 9365 4900), 35a Hall St, is a social backpackers with funky murals you might not want to look at when drunk. Dorm beds are $16 ($100 weekly), the kitchen is big and clean and the staff have good work connections. Ask here about Indy's couples-only love shack further up the beach.

Bondi Lodge (☎ 9365 2088), 63 Fletcher St, is a short, sharp walk up the hill from the southern end of the beach, but it's well placed to get to neighbouring Tamarama Beach. Dinner B&B costs $30 in a dorm ($140 weekly) and from $50/80 in singles/doubles.

The *Bondi Beach Guest House* (☎ 9389 8309), 11 Consett Ave, is two blocks from the beach, and has unpromising dorms for $15.

Coogee It's worth ringing before setting off to Coogee because some hostels have limited office hours. *Surfside Backpackers Coogee* (☎ 9315 7888), on the corner of Arden and Alfreda Sts, is conveniently just across the road from the beach and the main bus stop. Dorms cost $17 ($95 per week).

The popular *Coogee Beach Backpackers* (☎ 9315 8000), 94 Beach St, is a short but stiff walk up the hill at the northern end of the beach. The hostel sprawls over three buildings. It's clean, and has good common

areas and a deck with great views of the ocean. Spacious dorms cost $17. These people also run two smaller hostels: *Sydney Beachside* (☎ 9315 8511) at 178 Coogee Bay Rd and *Wizard of Oz Backpackers* (☎ 9315 7876) at 172 Coogee Bay Rd. Beds, once again, are $17 ($95 weekly).

Coogee Bunkhouse (☎ 9665 9254; fax 9338 2553), 15 Waltham St, is an atmospheric house, nicely spruced up. Beds are $16 or $100 weekly. Turn right off Arden St up the hill at the southern end of the beach. *Indy's* (☎ 9315 7644) is further up the hill at 302 Arden St. Four-bed dorms cost from $14 ($95 weekly) which includes breakfast. There are free bikes and surfboards available.

In nearby Clovelly is *Nomad's Clovelly Beach Backpackers* (☎ 9665 1214) at 381 Clovelly Rd. Dorms are $15, doubles from $24 per person and each room has its own bathroom. *Packers at Clovelly* (☎ 9665 3333), 272 Clovelly Rd, is a secure hostel with four-bed dorms, each with its own bathroom, TV and phone. A bed goes for $18 ($105 weekly); twins/doubles are $45 ($270 weekly).

Manly This is the best place to stay if you want to be free of city hassles, experience Sydney's beach culture and still be within commuting distance of the city.

Manly Backpackers Beachside (☎ 9977 3411), 28 Raglan St, has modern dorms costing from $15. Doubles cost $42 ($48 with en-suite). The older *Manly Astra Backpackers* (☎ 9977 2092) is nearby at 68-70 Pittwater Rd. Dorms cost $15 ($78 weekly) and doubles/twins $34 ($190 weekly). *Manly Cottage Inn* (☎ 9976 0297) is a small-ish hostel with average facilities at 25 Pittwater St. Dorms cost $15 ($85 weekly).

The *Wharf Backpackers*, (☎ 9977 2800), 48 East Esplanade, is a spacious alcohol-free hostel opposite the ferry terminal. Dorms start at $15 ($100 weekly); twins are $40 ($280 weekly).

The *Manly Bunkhouse* (☎ 9976 0472; fax 9938 2553), 46 Malvern Ave, offers apartment-style accommodation. Each room has a small kitchen and bathroom but communal areas are lacking. Dorm beds are $16 ($100 weekly).

The huge *Steyne Hotel* (9977 4977) on the Corso has squashy four-bed dorms for $25, which includes 'a big hearty Australian breakfast'.

North Shore *Kirribilli Court Private Hotel* (☎ 9955 4344), 45 Carabella St, Kirribilli, has dorm beds for $15 ($80 weekly) and singles/doubles with shared bathroom and kitchen for $25/40.

The *Harbourside Hotel* (☎ 9953 7977), 41 Cremorne Rd, Cremorne Point, is a large hostel that looks like a NSW north coast commune. Dorms cost $14 ($97 weekly). It's close to Cremorne Wharf, but a long hike from facilities on Military Rd.

For a break from innercity life, try the relaxed, northern beachside suburb of Avalon, where the *Avalon Beach Hostel* (☎ 9918 9709), 59 Avalon Parade, offers the nicest hostel accommodation in Sydney. It has an open-plan common area, couches around a fire, a big balcony, and the atmosphere of a beachside rainforest lodge. There are surfboards and bikes for hire. Dorms cost from $18 a night ($110 weekly) and doubles are $44. Take bus No L90 from Wynyard Park, York St, and ask for Avalon Beach (1¼ hours, $4). Make sure you phone in advance because it's often full.

Hotels & Guesthouses – bottom end
Sydney has some fine budget hotels and guesthouses, which work out only fractionally more expensive than hostels if you're travelling with friends. A refundable key deposit of around $10 is often required.

City Centre & the Rocks The *George St Private Hotel* (☎ 9211 1800), 700a George St (see the Darling Harbour & Chinatown map), is the best of the budget innercity hotels. It's clean, equipped with cooking and laundry facilities, and doesn't have the slightest whiff of seediness. Spartan singles/doubles with shared bathroom cost $34/52 ($204/312 weekly), doubles with en-suite and TV cost $75.

The nearby *CB Private Hotel* (☎ 9211 5115), 417 Pitt St, opened in 1908 and was once the largest hotel in the country. It's fairly well maintained, but gets a lot of wear. Singles/doubles with shared bathroom are $32/52 (cheaper by the week).

The *Sydney Central Private Hotel* (☎ 9212 1005), 75 Wentworth Ave, is a basic hotel with cooking and laundry facilities, just a short walk from Central Station and Oxford St. Singles/doubles cost $30/50 with shared bathroom, or $65 with en-suite.

The small *Harbour View Hotel* (☎ 9252 3769) on the corner of Lower Fort and Cumberland Sts is a community pub on the fringes of the Rocks. There's some noise from trains on the bridge, but with clean singles/doubles with views for $45/55, it's great value and a great location. The *Mercantile Hotel* (☎ 9247 3570), 25 George St, has good pub rooms from $65/95 a single/double including breakfast.

The *Palisade Hotel* (☎ 9247 2272) stands like a sentinel at 35 Bettington St, Millers Point. It has bright pub rooms with shared bathroom, and views of the city, bridge, harbour and dockyard, for $80 a double or triple.

Kings Cross Area One of the accommodation bargains near the Cross is *Challis Lodge* (☎ 9358 5422), 21-23 Challis Ave, which occupies a pair of cavernous terraces in Potts Point. It's a low-key, well-run establishment offering singles/doubles with fridge and TV for $30/36 ($150/180 weekly) or $42/49 ($210/245 weekly) with en-suite. Rooms on the upper floors are quieter and get better light. Nearby *Macleay Lodge* (☎ 9368 0660), 71 Macleay St, Potts Point, has good-value, bright singles/doubles with TV, fridge and shared bathroom from $35/40. En-suite rooms start at $55.

Springfield Lodge (☎ 9358 3222), 9 Springfield Ave, has similar rooms but they're a tad depressing. Singles/doubles with shared bathroom start at $32/40

($160/200 weekly) and with en-suite cost $45/55 ($225/275 weekly).

Nearby, the recommended *Bernly Private Hotel* (☎ 9358 3122), 15 Springfield Ave, has light, modern singles/doubles with TV and shared bathroom for $40/50. Rooms with en-suite and phone are $70/80.

The *Cross Court Tourist Motel* (☎ 9368 1822) is a terrace house at 201-3 Brougham St, which offers smart, tasteful singles/doubles with shared bathroom from $40/58. Beds in a four-share dorm are $18 ($110 weekly). En-suite rooms start at $75.

The *Gala Hotel* (☎ 9357 1199), 23 Hughes St, is a welcoming guesthouse with a TV lounge and communal kitchen. Singles/doubles with fridge and shared bathroom cost $40/50, doubles with en-suite $60.

Newtown The clean, pleasant *Australian Sunrise Lodge* (☎ 9550 4999), 485 King St, has motel-style singles/doubles with TV and fridge from $45/55, or $65 with en-suite.

Watsons Bay If you want to enjoy the harbour in a quiet locale and still be within a short ferry ride of the city, try the harbourside *Watsons Bay Hotel* (☎ 9337 4299), 1 Military Rd, Watsons Bay, which has singles/doubles for $50/80, which includes breakfast.

Bondi Bondi's hotels are prone to summer price rises like most other beachside suburbs. Rates below are for the low season.

The *Biltmore Private Hotel* (☎ 9130 4660), 110 Campbell Parade, is a big rooming house with a hotch-potch of rooms – some with sea views, some poky and smelly, so check a few rooms out before you commit. Dorms are $15 ($90 weekly). Singles/doubles are $30/35/50 ($170/190 weekly). The *Hotel Bondi* (☎ 9130 3271) is the peach-coloured layer-cake at 178 Campbell Parade. It has OK single rooms for $45 with shared facilities (men only), and doubles for $75 with en-suite or $85 with en-suite and an ocean view.

The *Thellelen Lodge* (☎ 9130 1521), 11a Consett Ave, is a modest operation in a ren-ovated suburban house two blocks back from the beach. It's clean, has a good communal kitchen and a friendly feel. Single/double rooms cost from $35/39.

Coogee The *Grand Pacific Private Hotel* (☎ 9665 6301), Carr St, overlooks the southern end of the beach. Scungy old-style singles/doubles with TV and fridge are $35/45 ($25/35 a night for stays of three nights or more). Some rooms have views.

Manly The *Eversham Private Hotel* (☎ 9977 2423), 27-29 Victoria Parade, is a huge, somewhat depressing place more reminiscent of an Edwardian boarding school than accommodation at a beach resort. Scruffy singles/doubles cost $28/46 ($123/150 weekly) and triples $69 ($225 weekly).

North Shore *St Leonards Mansions* (☎ 94 39 6999), 7 Park Rd, St Leonards, has singles/doubles with TV, cooking facilities and telephone for $45/65 with shared bathroom or $55/75 with en-suite, including breakfast. From St Leonards station, turn left (west) along the Pacific Highway and Park Rd is the second street on the left.

Kirribilli Court Private Hotel (☎ 9955 4344), 45 Carabella St, has dorm beds for $12 ($70 weekly) and singles/doubles with shared bathroom and kitchen for $25/30.

Tremayne Private Hotel (☎ 9955 4155), 89 Carabella St, Kirribilli, is a guesthouse with singles/doubles with shared bathroom for $150/220 weekly (no daily rates).

The *Neutral Bay Motor Lodge* (☎ 9953 4199), on the corner of Kurraba Rd and Hayes St in Neutral Bay, has motel-style singles/doubles for $55/65.

Hotels, Motels, Guesthouses & Serviced Apartments – middle Some mid-range hotels and guesthouses offer top-value facilities at little more than budget prices.

City Centre & The Rocks The *Sydney City Centre Serviced Apartments* (☎ 9233 6677), 7 Elizabeth St, offers the best-value accommodation in the city. It's in the heart of the

NEW SOUTH WALES

financial district, between Martin Place and Hunter St. The apartments are fully equipped with kitchenette, TV, phone, en-suite, washing machine and drier, and cost $60 a double.

The *Wynyard Hotel* (☎ 9299 1330), on the corner of Clarence and Erskine Sts, is a pub with singles/doubles with shared bathroom for $50/60. Another city pub, the *Grand Hotel* (☎ 9232 3755), 30 Hunter St, has singles/doubles with TV and fridge for $60/80. In the south of the city, *Citistay Westend Hotel* (☎ 9211 4822), 412 Pitt St, offers doubles for $95.

Aarons Hotel (☎ 9281 5555), 37 Ultimo Rd, Haymarket, is close to Chinatown and Darling Harbour (see the Darling Harbour & Chinatown map). Renovated doubles start at about $90. There's a great rooftop courtyard.

The *Lord Nelson Hotel* (☎ 9251 4044), on the corner of Kent and Argyle Sts, Millers Point, is a boutique pub on the edge of the Rocks. It has three doubles with shared bathroom for between $60 and $100.

Kings Cross *O'Malley's Hotel* (☎ 9357 2211) is a friendly Irish pub at 228 William St, downhill from the Coca-Cola sign. It has excellent singles/doubles with fridge, TV and en-suite from $70/75 including breakfast.

The *Barclay Hotel* (☎ 9358 6133), 17 Bayswater Rd, has a wide range of air-con singles/doubles from $70/80. At 40 Bayswater Rd there's a *Metro Motor Inn* (☎ 9356 3511) charging $95 a double.

The *Kingsview Motel* (☎ 9358 5599), 30 Darlinghurst Rd, has air-con rooms for $75 on weekends and $95 during the week.

In Potts Point, the *De Vere Hotel* (☎ 9358 1211), 46 Macleay St, has air-con rooms from $105. The lovely Art-Deco *Manhattan Hotel* (☎ 9358 1288), 8 Greenknowe Ave, has doubles from $145. The comfortable, quiet *Victoria Court Hotel* (☎ 9357 3200), 122 Victoria St, has doubles from $99, including breakfast.

The very hip *L'Otel* (☎ 9360 6868), 114 Darlinghurst Rd, is on the Darlinghurst side of the huge William St-Victoria St-

Darlinghurst Rd junction (see the Central Sydney map). It's a stylish, small hotel charging from $90 a double.

The *Lodge* (☎ 9327 8511), 38-44 New South Head Rd, Rushcutters Bay, has studio apartments with TV, kitchenette and en-suite for $75 a double. Check-in is at the Bayside Motel diagonally opposite.

Glebe The *Alishan International Guest-house* (☎ 9566 4048), 100 Glebe Point Rd, is a guesthouse and upmarket hostel, with good common areas and a small garden. Singles/doubles with en-suite cost $75/85.

The *Rooftop Motel* (☎ 9660 7777), 146 Glebe Point Rd, is a pleasant motel charging $85 for air-con rooms with TV, fridge, telephone and en-suite.

The *Haven Inn* (☎ 9660 6655), 196 Glebe Point Rd, has excellent rooms with en-suite from $110. There's a heated swimming pool, spa and secure parking.

Trickett's Bed & Breakfast (☎ 9552 1141), 270 Glebe Point Rd, is exceptionally pleasant. Homely double rooms (all en-suite) cost $140 including breakfast.

Bondi The *Bondi Beachside Inn* (☎ 9130 5311), 152 Campbell Parade, is the kind of architectural monstrosity that gave Bondi a bad name, but inside it's a delightful place with apartment-style rooms which have TV, phone, kitchen, en-suite and balcony. Standard doubles cost $72, or $78 with an ocean view (worth paying for). Renovated rooms are $78, or $91 with a view. There's plenty of room for three people to stay in the room ($10 extra).

Plage Bondi (☎ 9387 1122), 212 Bondi Rd, is a 15-minute lungburster from the beach. The front rooms have amazing views. Single or double-occupancy apartments with more than adequate facilities cost $95, dropping to $70 by the week and $50 for a month-long stay.

Ravesi's (☎ 9365 4422), on the corner of Campbell Parade and Hall St, is a classy boutique hotel indicative of the emerging smarter Bondi. Rooms start at $95 and climb to $155 depending on your angle to the ocean.

Coogee The *Coogee Bay Hotel* (☎ 9665 0000), on the corner of Arden St and Coogee Bay Rd, has air-con singles/doubles with fridge, TV, telephone and en-suite for $80/85, and doubles with ocean view from $120.

Manly Like all beach suburbs, Manly is susceptible to price rises in summer and on weekends. The prices below are for midweek rates in winter.

Manly Lodge (☎ 9977 8655), 22 Victoria Parade, offers B&B in good rooms with TV, fridge and en-suite for $69/89 for singles/doubles or $110 for a family room which sleeps four. The *Steyne Hotel* (☎ 9977 4977) on the Corso has OK singles from $49, and twins/doubles from $84, including breakfast. En-suite rooms are also available.

Reasonable motel rooms at *Manly Beach Resort* (☎ 9977 4188), 6 Carlton St, cost $90/95 for a single/double, including breakfast.

Periwinkle Guesthouse (☎ 9977 4668), 18-19 East Esplanade, is an elegant guesthouse on Manly Cove with singles/doubles/triples from $75/95/95, most with en-suite. Rooms with harbour view cost an extra $5.

The *Manly Paradise Motel* (☎ 9977 5799), 54 North Steyne, is on the beachfront. It has a rooftop pool and air-con motel double rooms for $85, or $115 with an oblique view of the ocean.

Hotels & Serviced Apartments – top end
There are lots of hotels and serviced apartments charging between $100 and $200 a double but many cater to business people so their rates might be lower on weekends. Serviced apartments sometimes sleep more than two people and with lower weekly rates they can be inexpensive if shared by a group.

The boutique *Russell Hotel* (☎ 9241 3543), 143 George St, the Rocks, has singles/doubles with shared bathroom from $95/105 and with en-suite from $155/165.

In the city centre, the *Wynyard Vista* (☎ 9290 1840), 7 York St, has rooms from $155. In the Cross, the *Sebel Town House* (☎ 9358 3244), Elizabeth Bay Rd, charges from $189.

Beachside hotels include the *Swiss Grand Hotel* (☎ 9365 5666), Cnr Campbell Pde and Beach Rd, Bondi Beach (from $210); the *Holiday Inn* (☎ 9315 7600), 242 Arden St, Coogee (from $160); and the *Manly Pacific Parkroyal* (☎ 9977 7666), 55 North Steyne, Manly (from $150).

The international heavyweights include the *Regent* (☎ 9238 0000), 199 George St; the *Park Hyatt* (☎ 9241 1234), 7 Hickson Rd, the Rocks; and the plush *Ritz-Carlton* (☎ 9362 4455), 33 Cross St, Double Bay.

Colleges Many colleges at the University of Sydney (☎ 9351 2222) and the University of NSW (☎ 9385 1000) are eager for casual guests during vacations. Most places quote B&B or full-board rates but it's often possible to negotiate a lower bed-only rate.

University of Sydney This is south-west of the city centre, close to Glebe and Newtown. A sample of colleges offering accommodation includes:

International House (☎ 9950 9800); full board in singles for $40 ($240 weekly); twins for $30 ($185 weekly)
St Johns College (☎ 9394 5200); B&B singles for $65, doubles/twins for $90, mostly en-suite
Women's College (☎ 9516 1642); B&B singles/twins for $42/62
Sancta Sophia College (☎ 9577 2100); B&B singles for $45 ($50 en-suite)

University of NSW This is further from the centre but not far from Oxford St and the southern ocean beaches.

International House (☎ 9663 0418); full-board singles for $40
New College (☎ 9662 6066); singles from $40, or $35 for students

Places to Eat
With great local produce, innovative chefs, inexpensive prices and BYO licensing laws,

it's no surprise that eating out is one of the great delights of a visit to Sydney.

If you're going to explore Sydney's food options, *Cheap Eats in Sydney* ($7.95) lists affordable places. An excellent, critical book is the Sydney Morning Herald's *Good Food Guide* ($17.95).

City Centre There's no shortage of places for a snack or meal in the city, especially on weekdays. They are clustered around train stations, in shopping arcades and tucked away in the food courts to be found in just about every office building higher than 20 storeys.

Bodhi is a vegan cafe in the coach terminal at Central Station – perfect for a pre-bus-odyssey light meal.

Bar Paradiso has outdoor tables in the historic precinct of Macquarie Place. Breakfasts start at $2.50, bagels around $5. The *Customs House Bar* nearby is more ragey. Gourmet pies and hearty roasts are $8.

Deli on Market, a large cafe on the corner of Clarence and Market Sts, serves a range of breakfasts from $2.50 and wholesome lunches from $5.

The *Metro Bar* at 123 Pitt St has standard cafe fare from as cheap as $2.50. *Angel Espresso Bar* nearby at 125 Pitt St has tasty snacks and modish meals for between $10.50 and $15.50.

The *Dendy Bar & Bistro* is a vibey space in the MLC Centre, Martin Place. The uncomplicated menu includes pastas, burgers and steaks for between $10.50 and $15. There are pool tables here and free music on Thursday nights – the bar is open till 1 am. *Carruthers* on Macquarie St has cheap vegetarian fare, salads and juices. There's a second Carruthers at 68 Druitt St.

Kiosk on Macquarie at the Macquarie St entrance to the Royal Botanic Gardens is a nice spot for lunch on a sunny day. Cafe fare at the outdoor tables costs between $5 and $10.

Spanish Town consists of a cluster of seven or eight Spanish restaurants and bars on Liverpool St between George and Sussex Sts. *Casa Asturiana*, 77 Liverpool St, is

reputed to have the best tapas in the city (from $5.50). *Captain Torres*, at No 73, has good seafood and a great bar. *Jackies* is the only non-Spanish place in the strip. It's a groovy espresso bar at No 86 serving honest cafe fare until midnight.

Planet Hollywood, 600 George St opposite the cinemas, is overpriced and overcrowded.

Chinatown Chinatown has expanded well beyond the confines of the officially designated pedestrian mall on Dixon St (see the Darling Harbour & Chinatown map). You can spend a small fortune at some outstanding Chinese restaurants or eat well for next to nothing in a food hall.

The best place to start is the *Sussex St Food Court*, which has counters of Chinese, Malay, Vietnamese, Thai and Japanese food. It's the most hectic, bubbly food court in the city at lunchtime when it's one of the best and most atmospheric places to eat. A full meal costs between $4 and $7. There are also food courts in *Dixon House*, on the corner of Dixon and Little Hay Sts, and the *Harbour Plaza*, on the corner of Dixon and Goulburn Sts.

Hingara, 82 Dixon St, is a classic low-budget Chinese eatery. *BBQ King*, 18 Goulburn St, is a sociable, high-turnover joint open into the early hours of the morning; expect to pay between $9 and $12 for a main. *House of Guangzhou*, on the corner of Thomas St and Ultimo Rd, is a popular, established restaurant with mains around $12.

If you're looking for quality, expect to pay a little more or choose from the cheaper dishes on the menu. *Marigold*, 4th & 5th floors, 683 George St, and *East Ocean*, 421 Sussex St, have great yum-cha. The *Regal*, on the corner of Liverpool and Sussex Sts, is a huge dim place with a lovely seasonal menu. The *Golden Century* (☎ 9212 3901), 393 Sussex St, is the king of Sydney's Cantonese restaurants. Seafood mains cost from $20.

Ippon, 404 Sussex St, is a fun Japanese sushi bar where you choose your dishes as they pass by on a conveyor belt. Pieces start at $1.

Darling Harbour Eating at Darling Harbour is mostly a food-court affair. The *Ettamogah Pub* in the Harbourside Shopping Centre does meals of the burger ($8.50) and steak ($10) variety. Of the restaurants with outdoor tables and water views, *Jordon's* is well-known for its seafood (mains are around $25).

Wockpool in the IMAX building is wonderful, expensive and *the* place to be seen wielding chopsticks.

The Rocks & Circular Quay Restaurants and cafes in the Rocks are overtly aimed at tourists, but there are still some good deals available, especially in the pubs where most bar meals are still under $10.

The friendly *G'Day Cafe* at 83 George St, just north of Argyle St, has good-value cooked breakfasts from $4, and focaccia from $2. The *Gumnut Cafe* has a rear courtyard and serves breakfast for around $5, lunches from $6.50 and Devonshire Tea on weekends. It's on Harrington St, near the junction with Argyle St.

The la-de-dahling *MCA Cafe*, in the foyer of the Museum of Contemporary Art on Circular Quay West, has a terrace overlooking the ferry wharves and the Sydney Opera House.

There are several average cafes and kiosks amid the ferry wharves notable mainly for being open 24 hours. The *Sydney Cove Oyster Bar* on Circular Quay East has one of the best views in the city. Mains are a tad expensive, but half-a-dozen oysters will set you back only $11.50, so crack open a bottle of wine and toast the spectacular vista.

If you're looking for excellence, the Sydney Opera House's *Bennelong* is a culinary institution. *Rockpool* (☎ 9252 1888), at 107 George St, and *Bilson's* (☎ 9251 5600), perched above the Overseas Passenger Terminal at Circular Quay West, have formidable reputations and require a formidable amount of cash. *Bel mondo* (☎ 9241 3700), in the Argyle Department Store, is

similarly cash-splashy, but you can eat for under $15 in the attached *anti bar*.

Darlinghurst & East Sydney Victoria St is the main cafe and restaurant strip in Darlinghurst (see the Central Sydney map). If you're just looking for a caffeine hit, *Bar Coluzzi* at No 322 is a Sydney institution, and *Tropicana*, over the road, is not far behind.

If you can't subsist on caffeine alone, the nearby *Backdoor Cafe* has fat toast and thin people. *La Bussola* at No 324 dishes up great pizzas from $10.50.

Fu-Manchu at No 249 Victoria St is a gregarious noodle bar with famed soups for around $10. Next door is *Oh Calcutta!*, a quality Indian restaurant with mains from $10 and a balcony for balmy nights. Also here is *Fez* where you can mix and match mezze from $3.50.

Lauries, on the corner of Victoria and Burton Sts, has simple vegetarian lunches for about $7 and evening mains for around $12. There's more vegetarian food at *Govinda's*, the Hare Krishna restaurant at 112 Darlinghurst Rd, just south of William St and Kings Cross. A $13.90 all-you-can-eat smorgasbord also gives you free admission to the cinema upstairs.

In Green Park, the *Bandstand Cafe's* menu is kind of dull but the setting is lovely.

Tum Tum Thai at No 199 Darlinghurst Rd is an eat-in or takeaway place which has curries and stir-fries from $6 and queues out the door. The *Indian Home Diner* on the corner of William St has goodish curry combos from $4.50 and they stay open late. *Fishface* at No 132 is an unlikely place for the best affordable seafood in the city, but it has all manner of marine life all seared with a hiss for around $14. *Eca Bar* next door is a cheaper-than-it-looks trendoid cafe.

There's a second cluster of restaurants in Stanley St, East Sydney, just south of William St, between Crown and Riley Sts. This strip used to be an Italian monoculture but it's increasingly multicultural. The classic Italian cheapies are *Bill & Toni's* at No 74 and *No Names* above the Arch Coffee Lounge at No 81. *Chatters Vegetarian* is cheapish but less than adventurous. *Pacifico* is a Mexican cantina just around the corner in a 1st-floor warehouse at No 95 Riley St.

Oxford St The mish-mash of restaurants on Oxford St, east of Taylor Square, moves from Asia to southern Europe and from gold coin to gold card territory. The popular *Thai-Nesia* at No 243 and *Lan Qui* at No 233 are $10 cheapies. The Cambodian *Angkor Wat* at No 227 and *Balkan Seafood* at No 215 are more expensive.

The *Bagel House*, 7 Flinders St, just off Taylor Square, is a friendly cafe above a bakery. A filled bagel is around $7. The *Courthouse Hotel*, which dominates Taylor Square, has hearty pub fare in the upstairs bar for between $9 and $15. *Cafe 191*, which also fronts Taylor Square, is a prime people-watching spot.

The city end of Oxford St has a rash of nondescript cafes and fast-food Asian eateries, some relying on desperate clubbers and night owls, others on passing trade, so choose selectively. *Bach Hy* at No 139 is a good place to slurp a soup before or after glamming it up. *Hanover's* at No 103 is a faux-European coffee house with pastas around $10. The *Tandoori Palace* at No 86 is a fine budget Indian restaurant with mains for about $10. The country-style *Betty's Soup Kitchen* at No 84 has goulash or soup and damper for $5.50. The cheap and chatty *Japanese Noodle Shop* is at No 80. At No 26 Burton St, just to the north, the landmark *Metro* has innovative vegetarian mains for $6, but it's only open Wednesday to Friday and Sunday evenings.

There's a concentration of budget restaurants just to the south on Crown St. They include the cosy retro *Roobar* at No 253, which does great brekkies all day. *Fatz* next door manages to do new things with pasta. The modest *Maltese Cafe* at No 310 has pastas under $5 and pastizzi snacks for 30c.

If you want to eat Australian flora and fauna, try *Riberries*, 411 Bourke St, near Taylor Square, where Australian produce meets French cuisine. Although a couple of courses will set you back around $35, it's cheaper than a trip to the outback to see the real thing.

Kings Cross The Cross has a mixture of fast-food joints serving edible fare designed mainly to soak up beer, tiny cafes servicing locals and travellers, and some swanky eateries among the city's best.

On William St, near the Coca-Cola sign, *William's on William* has eggs, bacon, chips and toast for $3.90 and pasta lunches for $5. *Mamma Maria*, just down the hill, offers similar cheap fare. Other bargain eateries include the teeny *Peninsula Cafe* in Highfield House hostel on Victoria St, where an-all-you-can-stomach Asian combo costs $4.50; *Hwang So* a cheap Korean BBQ place at 142 Victoria St; and *Pad Thai* on Llankelly Place, where noodles and rice dishes cost between $5 and $8. *Tokyo Roll* in the thick of it on Darlinghurst Rd, has nori rolls for $1.50 – they kept this author going!

Lovely little *Cleo's Cafe* at 7 Roslyn St serves brekkies and lunches from $4 and has a $3.50 afternoon special for coffee and cake. *Roys Famous* on Victoria St, open breakfast through to supper, is a good place to grab a booth and fill up on Mediterranean-style mains for around $12. Next door, *Out of India* has $10 thalis if you're out by 7 pm – not bad value unless you've come straight from Delhi.

The two most prominent eateries in the Cross are the *Fountain Cafe*, a plate-of-meat kind of place, and the nearby *Bourbon & Beefsteak*, which is just for the tourists unless it's 4 am and you develop the munchies.

The *Japanese Noodles Shop* on Macleay St has a small selection of noodles and soups for between $6 and $9. *India Down Under*, 46 Macleay St, is a mid-priced restaurant with a good reputation. *Deliciosa*, over the Fitzroy Gardens at 27 Elizabeth Bay Rd, is a sit-down deli as yummy as its name.

Mere Catherine, 146 Victoria St, is an unpretentious French restaurant, so intimate that you have to knock on the door to gain admittance. Main courses are around $15. The fabulous *Wockpool Noodle Bar*, 155 Victoria St, has phó for a flat $10.

Hard Coffee, under the Metro Motor Inn on Bayswater Rd, is a popular spot for breakfast all day. Meals are about $7. The *Hotel 59 Cafe* at (don't tell me) 59 Bayswater Rd has $5 meals of the chilli con carne and jacket-potato variety. The *Waterlily Cafe* nearby has a pleasing New Age ambience; you can eat well here for under $10.

If you want to try some of Sydney's best restaurants, and can afford main courses nudging $25, the *Bayswater Brasserie* on Bayswater Rd is a welcoming institution with great food and impeccable service. *Darley Street Thai*, next door, has excellent Thai food (there's a cheaper takeaway outlet here, too). *Cicada*, 29 Challis Ave, has kept Sydney's foodies entranced for a couple of years now.

Surry Hills Crown St is the main thoroughfare through Surry Hills but it's a long street and the restaurants occur in fits and starts. It's worth a wander, though, with interesting shops and eateries always springing up.

Prasits at No 395, near the corner with Foveaux St, is a nifty box-like Thai place where you can get great curries and stir-fries from $10. *Nile 2* at No 553 is a north African place where it's easy to eat for under $10. *Alt* is an espresso bar with damn fine coffee and arty happenings.

A second smattering of eateries on Devonshire St includes the much-loved *Passion du Fruit*, which is on the corner of Devonshire and Bourke Sts. On the corner of Devonshire and Crown Sts is the *Rustic Cafe*, a hearty Mediterranean eatery that you need sunglasses to look at; mains are around $15. The elegant *Elephant's Foot* hotel is opposite. It serves unchallenging but pleasant Italian fare for around $15. *Mohr Fish* at No 202 is a designer fish & chip shop; seafood mains are around $15.

There are half-a-dozen nondescript Lebanese eateries around the corner of Cleveland and Elizabeth Sts, at the southern end of Surry Hills, where dishes are between $4 and $6. The best of them is *Gazal's* at No 286.

Indian and Turkish places spice up Cleveland St between Crown and Bourke Sts.

Dhaba at No 466 has good north Indian fare; *Maya* is a lovely Indian sweet shop almost next door. Just on the Redfern side of Crown St at 650 Bourke St, *Casa Pueblo* does highly-praised South American food in an intimate atmosphere. There's a good vegetarian selection and nothing is over $14.

Paddington *Anastasia's Japanese Cosmopolitan*, 288 Oxford St, does mid-price Japanese and pasta dishes and you can contemplate global cuisine in the pleasant rear garden. *Sloane Ranger* at No 312 is an intimate cafe offering light meals for $8 and Mediterranean mains for $12.

Caffe Centaur at No 19 is a whisper-quiet coffee and dessert spot upstairs in the wonderful Berkelouw bookshop.

La Mensa Cafeteria at No 257 is a bright 'n' breezy cafe and deli doing beautiful dishes for beautiful people. The *Beehive Deli-Cafe* at No 212 comes back down to earth with a modern and classic pasta, focaccia and risotto menu, with nothing over $12.

The *Paddington Inn* at No 338 has a reputable bistro with mains for around $15 and bar meals under $10. At No 388, the *Golden Dog* has Italian sandwiches for $7.50 and pizza for $12. The very lovely *Hot Gossip* deli and cafe at No 438 is one of the nicest hangouts in Paddington.

The *Ritz Hotel* on the corner of Oxford and Jersey Sts is a stylish pub with wood-fired pizzas from $8. The *Centennial Park Cafe*, a five-minute walk inside the park from the Centennial Square entrance off Oxford St, serves expensive food in glorious surroundings.

Glebe Glebe Point Rd was Sydney's original 'eat street' but it's managed to retain a laid-back, unfaddish atmosphere, good-value food and warm conversation.

IKU Wholefoods at No 25 serves inexpensive macrobiotic dishes and snacks. *Lolita's* at No 29 is a student hangout, which has open philosophy meets on Sunday afternoons. *Badde Manors* at No 37, on the corner of Francis St, is the mellow neighbourhood favourite. Cafe fare and vegetarian meals are under $10. *Cafe Otto* at No 79 has a lovely front courtyard garden but meals can get up around $15. Nearby, *Dakhni* is a traditional Indian place. Main dishes are either side of $10.

Juba Cafe, at No 197, has an African slant. You can eat your $6 cous cous on a cushion in the front window.

AD 163, at No 92 is a quirky gallery cafe with meals around $8.

The *Pudding Shop*, near the corner of Glebe Point and Bridge Rds, is a budget haven with delicious pies and quiches for under $3. *Craven*, at No 166, next to the Valhalla cinema, is an inexpensive joint with that oh-so Glebe, jumble-sale aura. It's a popular spot for a relaxing coffee, snack or meal.

Lien at No 331 has good value Thai, Vietnamese and Malaysian mains for around $7, and *Lilac* at No 333 has Chinese, Malaysian, Indonesian and vegetarian fare mostly under $9. *That's It Thai* at No 381 is another of those popular eat-in/takeaway, closet-sized Thai places. Budget vegetarian and meat dishes are only $7.

The secret gem of Glebe is the *Blackwattle Canteen* in the Blackwattle Studios, a converted wharf at the end of Glebe Point Rd, overlooking Rozelle Bay. It's among the studios of artists, sculptors and picture framers and has mega breakfasts and comfort food under $10.

Newtown A swag of funky cafes and restaurants (which include an excess of virtually indistinguishable Thai eateries and Indian diners) lining Newtown's King St offer an interesting introduction to the suburb's community life. The *Green Iguana Cafe* at No 6 is a down-home vegetarian place with a rear courtyard offering cheap cafe fare.

Cafe Solea at No 182 serves basic but tasty pastas, salads and frittatas for under $10 and sometimes has free acoustic music (there's a moneybox on your table). Serious coffeeheads make for *Has Beans* at No 153a, a coffee shop and pasta place. *Peasants Feast* at No 121a does hearty old faves with a new

twist. Entrees are $8, mains $13 and there's a good vegetarian selection. *Old Saigon* is kookily decorated but the Vietnamese food is spot on.

Le Kilamanjaro at No 280 is a bustling, high-turnover African eatery with mains around $7.50. *Sumalee Thai* is in the (heated) beer garden of the Bank Hotel. It's not cheap but the servings are massive and the food delicious.

The *Old Fish Shop* at No 239 is a wonderful spot for lunch (no shortage of rocket). *Cafe 381* at No 381 is a loungeroomy, feral hangout. *Camo's* at No 397 has $8.50 dinner deals. *70 Please In My Kitchen* (you ask!), 275 Australia St, just off King St, is a teeny cafe serving kiddy food.

Saray is a low-key Turkish restaurant at 18 Enmore Rd. The Turkish pizza ($7) is excellent.

Leichhardt You can still get a cheap spag bol in Norton St, but the classic bistros are now rubbing shoulders with the classy, plus Greek, Chinese and Thai interlopers.

Bar Italia at No 169 Norton St is everyone's old favourite. Almost everything is under $10 and the gelati is renowned. *L'Epoca Cafe* at No 167 and *Elio* at No 159 are more expensive with more varied menus. *Portofino* at No 166 has pizzas and pastas around $12. *Bar Galante* at No 138 is full of bright young things proving that black is the new black. *Mezzapica* at No 128 is popular with local families.

Closer to Parramatta Rd, *La Cremeria* at No 110 scoops amazing gelati made on the premises.

Bondi The grill joints and takeaway greasebuckets are being squeezed away from the foreshore of Bondi by cafes, bistros and a slew of serious foodie joints. You can still eat well in Bondi for under $10 but you might have to go without a sea view. Of course, you can always do as the locals do and take a steaming paper package down to the beach: the best fish & chips are at *Bondi Surf Seafood*, 128 Campbell Pde.

The lovely *Gusto* delicatessen, a block

back from the beach at 16 Hall St, is a great spot to perch for a laid-back breakfast (try the OJ-soaked muesli for a $5 gunshot start to the day). *Le Paris-Go Cafe* on the corner of Hall St and Consett Ave is a chatty baguette hangout. The *Earth Food Store*, 81 Gould St (off Hall St), sells organic fruit 'n' vegies and does sustaining takeaways. *Thai Terrific* at 147 Curlewis St has cheap, tasty curries.

Closer to the surf, *Toriyoshi* at 224 Campbell Pde is a cheap Japanese eatery with yakitori sticks from $1.50. *Liberty Lunch* at No 106 is a breezy licensed cafe with mains from $15. *Hugo's* at No 70 has serious food for the white tablecloth brigade.

There's a strip of trendy cafe-bars on Campbell Parade at the southern end of the beach. The groovy *Sports Bar(d)* at No 32 and *Urchin* next door are happening drinking and shouting spots. *Bondi Tratt* at No 34 is a popular place with outdoor seating, ocean views and Mediterranean-influenced bistro fare around the $12 mark. *GPK* at No 80 is a new wave pizza joint where the combos include kangaroo, tiger prawns and as much marinated this 'n' that as a crust can bear.

The beautiful people have colonised the northern end of the beach, too. *Jackie's* is a classy cafe on the corner of Warners and Wairoa Aves. Brekkies (weekends only) go for around $8 but main dishes sneak up to $15. *Raw*, opposite, serves bistro-style Japanese. Further north, *Diggers Cafe*, 232 Campbell Parade, is cheaper, serving breakfasts from 7 am and soups ($6) and salads ($7) until dark. The restaurant in the *Digger's Club* upstairs has $3 roast lunches.

There are a stack of restaurants up Bondi Rd away from the beach. *Quaint* at No 195 has croissants and salads for around $7. *Lauries Vegetarian* at No 286 is tucked in amidst Thai, Indian and Italian cheapies. Curries, pastas and stir fries start at $3.

Coogee There are a number of takeaways on Coogee Bay Rd offering cheap eats, but you're better off hitting the cafes, which have healthier food, sunnier demeanours and outdoor tables. The exuberant *Congo Cafe*

faces the beach at 208 Arden St. Pizzas, focaccias, bagels, melts and salads all cost $7. *La Casa*, a few doors along, has $7 pasta and focaccias for under $5. On a fine day, the buzzy *Sun of a Beach Bar* on Beach Plaza is as close as you can eat to the ocean without getting sand in your food.

There are several bright, pleasant places on Coogee Bay Rd serving standard cafe fare costing between $5 and $10. They include the nautical *Coogee Cafe* at No 221, the more interesting *Globe* at No 203 and *Cafe Blah Blah* at No 198, which has a small but thoughtful menu of light, modern fare. If you want something more substantial, the *Coogee Bay Hotel* has a better-than-average pub brasserie with mains around $13.

Bronte For beachside body-filler, mix it with the locals at *Sejuiced*, 472 Bronte Rd. One of a string of goodish cafes in this strip by the park, Sejuiced is a great place for sipping on those liquid vitamins, munching on a focaccia and drying off. If you can't get a table, try flicking your fringe at *Cafe Q* or the *Bogey Hole*.

Manly The ocean end of the Corso is jam-packed with takeaways and outside tables. Manly Wharf and South Steyne have plenty of eateries, but you're often paying more for the view than the food.

If you want good value and don't need to see the ocean while you eat, head to Belgrave St where *Candy's Coffeehouse* serves inexpensive food in a cosy, book-lined cafe more reminiscent of Glebe than a beachside suburb. *Twocan*, 27 Belgrave St, serves sparky Mod Oz – dinners are up around $18 but lunch can be had for well under $10. *Last Train to Bombay*, 11 Belgrave St, serves carefully prepared Indian food, mostly under $10.

Green's Eatery in the mall section of Sydney Rd adjoining the Corso has a sunny atmosphere and serves light meals for around $5. For more spicy food, try *Malacca Straits* on the corner of Sydney Rd and Whistler St, where Malay and Thai dishes cost $9 to $12. If you're in the mood for cheap 'n' cheerful pub food, try the *Steyne Hotel* on the Corso.

Brazil, 46 North Steyne, and *Barking Frogs* next door vie for the waterfront's trendiest food. It's all corn-fed-this and goat-cheese-that, but you can still eat for under $15. The South Steyne cafes and restaurants are overpriced, but if you're feeling groovy, *Cafe Nice* serves good coffee in steel cups.

North Sydney The *North Sydney Noodle Market* is a praiseworthy attempt to capture the flavour of Asian street-food markets. It's held on Sunday lunchtimes during autumn and winter, and on Friday nights during spring and summer, in the park on Miller St, between McClaren and Ridge Sts, North Sydney.

Entertainment
The *Sydney Morning Herald* lift-out *Metro* is published on Friday and lists events in town for the coming week. Free newspapers, such as *Drum Media* and *Beat*, are available from shops, bars and record stores and also have useful listings.

Halftix sells half-price seats to shows from its booth on Martin Place near Elizabeth St. Tickets are only available for shows that night and they can't tell you where you'll be sitting. The booth is also a Ticketek agency (☎ 9266 4800), so if you miss out on cheap

seats you can always buy full-price ones. Halftix is open weekdays from noon to 5.30 pm and Saturday from 10.30 am to 5 pm. The Ticketek side of the business is open weekdays from 9 am to 5 pm and Saturday from 10.30 am to 5 pm. City Stubs sells half-price tickets to major exhibitions and performances every Saturday at Paddington Market.

Pubs There are plenty of good pubs in Sydney's inner suburbs.

The Rocks Two interesting pubs in this district are the *Lord Nelson*, on the corner of Argyle Place and Kent St, which brews its own ale, and the friendly *Hero of Waterloo*, on the corner of Lower Fort and Windmill Sts.

Molly Bloom's Bar at the *Mercantile Hotel*, 25 George St, is a nice place to sink a Guinness. The *Australian Hotel*, on the corner of Gloucester and Cumberland Sts, has renowned local brews on tap.

Darling Harbour The *Ettamogah Bar*, Harbourside Shopping Centre, lays on the ocker to pull in the crowds. Tuesday is backpacker night.

Kings Cross The Cross has plenty of hotels, though many are in less than salubrious sur-

---

The Best Things in Life are Free
There's plenty of free entertainment in Sydney for those who want fun without having to splash their hard-earned cash around. The Art Gallery of NSW has no admission charge for its permanent exhibitions. The Powerhouse Museum has no admission charge on the first Saturday of the month.

Lunchtime offers a feast of free music, from bands who play regularly in the Martin Place amphitheatre to classical music at the Conservatorium of Music (Wednesday and Friday during term). There are plenty of buskers and free weekend performances at Circular Quay, Playfair St in the Rocks and in Darling Harbour's Tumbalong Park. There's also free music on the 'prow' of the Opera House on Sunday afternoon.

The Paddington Village Bazaar is a spectacle in itself, and there are often performers strutting their stuff in Oxford St. 'Speakers Corner' in the Domain attracts the mad, the dangerous and the erudite on Sunday afternoons.

Don't forget the simple pleasures. It costs nothing to stroll across the Harbour Bridge, walk around the Royal Botanic Gardens, lie on the beach or frolic in the surf.

Saturday's *Sydney Morning Herald* lists freebies for the week ahead. ■

roundings. The 24-hour *Kings Cross Hotel*, at the junction of William and Victoria Sts, is a backpacker favourite. It's the spooky-looking building in the shadow of the Coca-Cola sign.

O'Malley's, on the corner of William and Brougham Sts, is a convivial Irish pub which has live music seven nights (free entry). The *Soho Bar*, 171 Victoria St, is a discreet, neighbourhood watering hole.

The *Bourbon & Beefsteak*, on the dogleg of Darlinghurst Rd, is a 24-hour institution still suffering a hangover from the Vietnam War. *Barons* is a snug, late-night alternative tucked above a Thai restaurant at 5 Roslyn St. There's also a strip of late-night hybrid bar-restaurant-clubs on Kellett St.

A five-minute walk from the Cross is the huge *Woolloomooloo Bay Hotel*, 2 Bourke St, Woolloomooloo. It has free-for-alls Wednesday to Sunday with crowd-pleasing live music.

Darlinghurst The *Green Park Hotel*, on the corner of Liverpool and Victoria St, is the haunt of dark-clothed, pool-playing, inner-city groovers. The *Hard Rock Cafe*, 121 Crown St, is for those who feel the need to add to their T-shirt collection.

On Oxford St, the cavernous shell of the *Burdekin Hotel* at No 2 attracts a lively, mixed crowd, especially on Friday and Saturday night. The *Lizard Lounge*, upstairs in the Exchange Hotel at No 34, is a hip melting pot of straights, gays and lesbians. *Q* is a hard-to-find pool hall cum bar at No 46, above Central Station Records.

The *Bentley Bar*, on the corner of Crown and Campbell Sts, has DJs six nights and Sunday recovery from 10 am. See the Out & About in Gay Sydney aside for gay pubs and clubs near Oxford St.

Surry Hills There's a batch of decent pubs here, including the *Palace Hotel*, 122 Flinders St; the *Cricketers Arms*, 106 Fitzroy St; the *Hopetoun Hotel* on the corner of Fitzroy and Bourke Sts; and the *Forresters Hotel* on the corner of Foveaux and Riley Sts.

Paddington The *Paddington Inn*, 338 Oxford St, is a sociable local. The *Lord Dudley*, 236 Jersey St, Woollahra, is as close as Sydney gets to English pub atmosphere.

Glebe The *Friend in Hand* at 58 Cowper St has crab racing (Wednesday), live music (Thursday and Sunday) and pool comps. The legendary *Harold Park Hotel*, 115 Wigram Rd, should win an award for its packed entertainment program, which includes theatre, comedy, bands, poetry readings and chess competitions. The *Excelsior Hotel*, 101 Bridge St, has music seven nights.

Bondi The *Icebergs Club* is an excellent place for a cheap beer and million-dollar ocean views. It's above the southern end of the beach down Nott Ave; cover bands play on weekends.

Clubs Sydney's club scene is thriving, eclectic and tribal. Some of the more established venues are:

Cauldron, 207 Darlinghurst Rd, Darlinghurst; flashy funk-house club-restaurant
DCM, 33 Oxford St, Darlinghurst; nominally gay, muscular and sweaty
Mister Goodbar, 11 Oxford St, Paddington; cool basement club with super-strict door
Kinselas, 383 Bourke St, Taylor Square, Darlinghurst; hip, triple-decked funk mecca
Riva, Sheraton on the Park, Castlereagh St, Sydney; glitzy city crowd
EP1, 1 Earl Place, Kings Cross; writhing bodies, flashing lights

Live Music Sydney doesn't have a dynamic pub music scene, but there are still places where you can count on something most nights of the week. For detailed listings of venues and acts, see the listings in the papers mentioned in the Entertainment introduction.

Rock There's sometimes no charge for young local bands, a charge of between $5 and $10 for more well-known local acts, around $20 for top Australian bands, and up

Out & About in Gay Sydney

Sydney has vibrant, vocal and well-organised gay and lesbian communities, which throw some spectacular parties and provide a range of social-support services. There are large gay and lesbian populations in Darlinghurst, Paddington and Surry Hills and growing communities in Newtown, Leichhardt and Alexandria. Light tans and, for men, heavy pecs are the rage, so hit the beach and the gym a few weeks before arriving.

Gay social life is predominantly focussed on Oxford St, where many cafes, restaurants and businesses are gay-owned and operated. Major entertainment venues include:

Albury Hotel, 6 Oxford St, Paddington (drag show heaven)

DCM, 33 Oxford St, Darlinghurst (mixed, real muscles, fake tatts)

Exchange Hotel, 34 Oxford St, Darlinghurst (glam, mixed, basement disco)

Midnight Shift, 85 Oxford St, Darlinghurst (1st-floor disco with trippy light show)

Oxford Hotel, 134 Oxford St, Darlinghurst (boozy bar, blokey basement & 1st-floor cocktail lounge)

Other gay and lesbian haunts include the *Beauchamp Hotel*, 267 Oxford St, Darlinghurst (mainly men); the *Beresford Hotel*, 354 Bourke St, Surry Hills; and the *Flinders Hotel*, 63 Flinders St, Surry Hills (mainly men). In Newtown, try the *Bank Hotel*, 342 King St (mainly women), or the *Newtown Hotel*, 174 King St. There's a strong lesbian scene in Leichhardt – the *Leichhardt Hotel*, 126 Balmain Rd, is a starting point. Gay beach life is focussed on Lady Bay (nude) and Tamarama (also known as Glamarama).

The major social events of the year are the month-long Sydney Gay & Lesbian Mardi Gras, which culminates in an outrageous parade and party in March, and the Sleaze Ball, which takes place in early October. The parties for both events are held in Moore Park. Tickets are restricted to Mardi Gras members. Gay and lesbian international visitors wishing to attend the parties should contact the Mardi Gras office well in advance (☎ 9557 4332).

The free gay press includes the *Sydney Star Observer* and *Capital Q*, which can be found in shops and cafes in the inner east and west. Both papers have excellent listings of gay and lesbian organisations, services and events.The Australian Gay & Lesbian Tourism Association publishes a Tourism Services Directory listing all Australian members, including tour operators and accommodation. It's available by writing to PO Box 208, Darlinghurst, NSW 2010. Break Out Tours (☎ 9558 8229) is a gay-operated tour company offering trips to the Blue Mountains, the Hunter Valley vineyards and Jervis Bay ($115). ∎

to $50 for international performers. Venues worth considering are:

Annandale Hotel, corner of Nelson and Parramatta Rds, Annandale (☎ 9550 1078); indie institution

Enmore Theatre, 130 Enmore Rd, Newtown (☎ 9550 3666); major Australian and overseas acts

Excelsior Hotel, 64 Foveaux St, Surry Hills (9211 4945); neighbourhood pub with young bands

The *Globe*, 379 King St, Newtown (☎ 9519 0220); indie pop and DJs till late

Hopetoun Hotel, corner of Fitzroy and Bourke Sts, Surry Hills (☎ 9361 5257); comfy local with original music Thursday to Sunday

Hordern Pavilion, Moore Park (☎ 9331 9263); major Australian and overseas acts

Metro, 624 George St, Sydney (☎ 9264 1581); major local and international acts

Phoenician Club, 173 Broadway, Ultimo (☎ 9212 5955); young bands and occasional touring gems

Rose, Shamrock & Thistle Hotel (aka 'the three weeds'), 139 Evans St, Rozelle (☎ 9810 2244); folk, blues and light rock

Sandringham Hotel, 387 King St, Newtown (☎ 9557 1254); breeding ground of Aussie pub rock

Selinas (in the Coogee Bay Hotel), Coogee Bay Rd, Coogee Bay; touring Aussie and international bands

Sydney Entertainment Centre, Darling Harbour (☎ 1900 957 333); for the Elton Johns and Billy Joels of this world

Jazz Sydney has a healthy and innovative jazz circuit. Venues worth a swing include:

anti bar, Argyle Department Store, The Rocks; Friday evening nibble and wiggle

The *Basement*, 29 Reiby Place, Circular Quay (☎ 9251 2797); good venue with a mix of local and international acts

Bondi Surf Lifesavers Club, Bondi Beach; Monday night fun, especially in summer

Harbourside Brasserie, Pier One, Walsh Bay (☎ 9252 3000); established local acts and international bands

Kinselas, 383 Bourke St, Taylor Square, Darlinghurst (☎ 9331 3299); groove, funk and acid jazz – the hip end of the spectrum

Round Midnight, 2 Roslyn St, Kings Cross (☎ 9356 4045); cocktail jazz venue with stiff drink prices

Soup Plus, 383 George St, Sydney (☎ 9299 7728); live jazz every lunch and dinner, cheap food, casual atmosphere

Strawberry Hills Hotel, corner of Devonshire and Elizabeth Sts, Surry Hills (☎ 9698 2997); piano bar or jazzy duos nightly

Tilbury Hotel, corner of Forbes Esplanade and Nicholson St, Woolloomooloo (☎ 9368 1955); Sunday afternoon jazz and funk

Classical The best classical music venues are the *Concert Hall* in the Sydney Opera House (☎ 9250 7777), the *Sydney Town Hall* (☎ 9265 9555), the *Sydney Conservatorium of Music* (☎ 9230 1263) and the ABC's *Eugene Goosens Hall* (☎ 9333 1500), 700 Harris St, Ultimo.

Musica Viva Australia (☎ 9698 1711) presents an ambitious program of Australian and international chamber music at various city venues.

Theatre The top theatre company is the *Sydney Theatre Company* (☎ 9250 1777), which has its own theatre at Pier Four, Hickson Rd, Walsh Bay. The similarly prestigious *Sydney Dance Company* is also here.

The *Drama Theatre* in the Sydney Opera House (☎ 9250 7777) stages innovative plays.

Mainstream theatres specialising in blockbusters and musicals include the *Capitol Theatre* (☎ 9320 9122) on the corner of George and Campbell Sts; the *Theatre Royal* (☎ 9320 9111) in the MLC Centre, King St; the *State Theatre* (☎ 9373 6655), 49 Market St, and the *Lyric Theatre* in Star City, Darling Harbour. If you like your musicals with a little less sugar, see what's happening at the *Footbridge Theatre* (☎ 9692 9955), Parramatta Rd, Sydney University.

There are invariably interesting productions at the *Belvoir Theatre* (☎ 9699 3444), 25 Belvoir St, Surry Hills; the *Seymour Centre* (☎ 9364 9400) on the corner of Cleveland St and City Rd, Chippendale; and the *Performance Space* (☎ 9319 5091), 199 Cleveland St, Redfern.

Comedy & Cabaret The heart and home of Sydney comedy is the *Comedy Store* (☎ 9564 3900) on the corner of Parramatta Rd and Crystal St, Petersham. It's open Tuesday to Sunday and has a different show each night.

Best supporting role goes to the *Harold Park Hotel*, 115 Wigram Rd, Glebe, which hosts 'Comics in the Park' on Monday and various stand-up gigs throughout the week.

Cinemas Commercial cinemas line George St between Liverpool and Bathurst Sts. The average ticket price is $11 (students $9).

For art-house and commercial films, try independent cinemas such as the *Dendy* at 624 George St, in the MLC Centre in Martin Place, and 261 King St, Newtown; the *Palace Academy Twin* at 3 Oxford St, Paddington; the nearby *Verona* at 17 Oxford St, Paddington; and the *Chauvel Cinema* in the Paddington Town Hall, on the corner of Oxford St and Oatley Rd. On the North Shore, try the Art-Deco *Cremorne Hayden*, 180 Military Rd; and the *Manly Twin* opposite Manly Wharf.

Places to catch independent films or cult reruns include the *Valhalla Cinema*, 166 Glebe Point Rd, Glebe; and the *Movie Room* above Govinda's at 112 Darlinghurst Rd.

The *State Movie Theatre* on Market St between Pitt and George Sts hosts the Sydney Film Festival in June.

Spectator Sports

Sydney is one of rugby league's world capitals. Games are played from April to September; finals are played at the Sydney Football Stadium in Moore Park in September.

The Sydney Cricket Ground in Moore Park is the venue for sparsely attended Sheffield Shield matches, well-attended five-day Test matches and sell-out one-day World

Series cricket matches. It's also the home ground of the high-flying Sydney Swans, NSW's only contribution to the Australian Football League. Aussie rules matches are played between March and September.

A spectator boat leaves the Sydney Flying Squadron at McDougall St, Milsons Point, on Saturday at 1.30 pm to follow the spectacular, honed-down 18-foot skiffs that race on the harbour between late September and April ($10).

The sporting year ends with the start of the Sydney to Hobart Yacht Race on Boxing Day. A huge fleet of spectator boats follow the racing yachts to the Heads as they set sail for the three to five-day voyage to Tasmania.

Things to Buy

Shopping complexes in the city include the Queen Victoria Building, Piccadilly, Centrepoint, Skygarden, the Strand Arcade and Market City in Haymarket. David Jones and Grace Brothers are the biggest department stores. The hub of shopping is the Pitt St mall. For outdoor gear, head to the corner of Kent & Bathurst Sts, where Paddy Pallin is one of several outdoor suppliers in the area. Late-night shopping is on Thursday night, when most stores stay open until 9 pm.

Aboriginal Art The Aboriginal & Tribal Art Centre (☎ 9247 9625) at Level One, 117 George St, the Rocks, has paintings and crafts. Prices range from $5 to $5000.

The Boomali Aboriginal Artists Cooperative (☎ 9698 2047) at 27 Abercrombie St, Chippendale is an interesting Aboriginal-run gallery, showroom and resource centre.

Australiana There are plenty of shops selling Australian arts, crafts and souvenirs in the Rocks and in Darling Harbour's Harbourside Festival Marketplace, but you're more likely to pick up bargains at the city's markets (see the next entry).

The Rocks Centre on Playfair St in the Rocks has one of the best selections of goods aimed at tourists. The Environment Centre, 39 George St, and the Australian Conservation Foundation shop, 33 George St, cater for

those shopping beyond cliches, and your bucks go to good causes. For bush gear, try RM Williams, 389 George St, or Thomas Cook, 790 George St.

Street-smart goods can be found on the upper floors of the Strand Arcade, where several leading Australian designers have shops.

The Australian Wine Centre in Goldfields House, 1 Alfred St, stocks wine from every Australian wine-growing region and can send wine overseas.

Markets Sydney has lots of weekend 'flea' markets. The most interesting is the trendy Paddington Village Bazaar, held in the grounds of the church on the corner of Oxford and Newcombe Sts on Saturday.

The weekend Rocks Market in George St in the Rocks is more tourist oriented but it's still a colourful affair. The arty-farty Sunday Tarpeian Market is at a fantastic site, on the concourse of the Sydney Opera House.

There are bric-a-brac markets in Glebe (Saturday; Glebe Public School, Glebe Point Rd); Balmain (Saturday; St Andrews Church, Darling St); Kings Cross (Sunday; Fitzroy Gardens); and Bondi Beach (Saturday; Bondi Public School, Campbell Parade).

The biggest innercity market is Paddy's Market (Friday to Sunday), in Market City. It's a smorgasbord of tack in a gloomy dungeon, but it can be an interesting place to stroll around if you're not allergic to fake Calvin Klein T-shirts and fluffy slippers.

Getting There & Away

Air Sydney's Kingsford-Smith airport is Australia's busiest and the most inadequate for handling demand, so expect delays. It's only 10km south of the city centre making access easy, but this also means that flights cease between 11 pm and 5 am due to noise regulations.

You can fly into Sydney from all the usual international points and from all over Australia. Both Qantas (☎ 13 1313) and Ansett (☎ 13 1300) have frequent flights to other capital cities and major airports. Smaller airlines, linked to the major ones, fly within NSW.

Cheap international flights are advertised in the Saturday *Sydney Morning Herald*.

Bus The private bus operators are competitive and service is efficient. Make sure you shop around for discounts – backpackers get 30% concession on Pioneer Motor Service (☎ 9281 2233) services to Brisbane, for example. Always compare private operator prices to the government's Countrylink network of trains and buses (☎ 13 2242), which has discounts of up to 40% on economy fares.

The Sydney coach terminal (☎ 9281 9366) deals with all companies and can advise you on the best prices. It's on the corner of Pitt St and Eddy Ave, outside Central Station. Coach operators have offices either in the terminal or nearby. Most buses stop in the suburbs on the way in and out of cities.

To Brisbane It generally takes about 16 hours to reach Brisbane either along the coastal Pacific Highway or inland via the New England Highway. The standard fare is around $67. It's best to book in advance. Companies running the Pacific Highway route include Greyhound Pioneer (☎ 13 2030) and McCafferty's (☎ 13 1499).

Some typical fares from Sydney to towns along the way are Port Macquarie $42 (seven hours), Coffs Harbour $46 (nine hours), Byron Bay $66 (12 hours) and Surfers Paradise $67 (15 hours). Not all buses stop in all main towns en route.

The backpacker-friendly Oz Experience (☎ 9368 1766) offers hop-on/hop-off four-day trips between Sydney and Brisbane for $165. The Pioneering Spirit (☎ 1800 672 422) runs from Sydney to Brisbane ($215) via Byron Bay ($175), taking a leisurely four days. Dinner, breakfast and accommodation are included.

Ando's Outback Adventure (☎ 9559 2901) travels between Sydney and Byron Bay via a week-long outback detour for

$395. Ando is quite a character and his tour gets good reports.

To Canberra Murrays (☎ 13 2251) has three daily express buses to Canberra taking under four hours for $28, or around $22 if you pay in advance. Greyhound Pioneer (☎ 13 2030) runs almost hourly to Canberra and costs $32 one way or $58 return.

To Melbourne It's a 12 to 13-hour journey to Melbourne if you travel via the Hume Highway. Firefly Express (☎ 9211 1644) charges $45, while most other companies charge around $50. Greyhound Pioneer (☎ 13 2030) runs along the Hume and the prettier, but much longer (up to 18 hours), coastal Princes Highway for $64.

If that all sounds too rushed, the Wayward Bus (☎ 1800 882 823) offers flexible backroads packages and string a trip to Melbourne over three days ($140).

To Adelaide The cheapest way to get to Adelaide is with Firefly's $85 bus running Sydney-Melbourne-Adelaide, and you can break your journey in Melbourne (☎ 9211 1644). Countrylink's daily Speedlink service is the fastest option (☎ 13 2242). It takes just under 20 hours and involves catching a train to Albury, then a connecting bus to Adelaide. The fare is $103.

Elsewhere To the Snowy Mountains, Greyhound Pioneer (☎ 13 2030) runs to Cooma ($45) and Jindabyne ($58). The 53-hour trip to Perth costs $313. To Alice Springs it's $247 and takes 42 hours – check if you're up for a wait in Adelaide.

Train The government's Countrylink rail network is complemented by coaches. All interstate and principal regional train and bus services operate to and from Central Station. Tickets must be booked in advance. Call the Central Reservation Centre (☎ 13 2242).

Discounts of up to 40% are possible, subject to availability, making prices comparable to the private bus lines; Australian students get a 50% discount on economy

NEW SOUTH WALES

fares. Discount tickets are operated on a first-come/first-served quota basis. As long as it's not a public or school holiday, you stand a pretty good chance of getting one, even if you purchase your ticket on the day of departure; book in advance to be sure.

Interstate trains can be faster than buses, and on interstate journeys you can arrange free stopovers on economy and student tickets, but not on discounted tickets.

Three trains run daily to Canberra taking about four hours and costing $41/56 in economy/1st class.

Two trains run between Sydney and Melbourne, one leaving in the morning and travelling throughout the day, and the other departing in the evening and travelling overnight. The trip takes 10½ hours and the economy/1st-class fare is $93/130; a 1st-class sleeper is $225. Discounted tickets can bring the economy fare down to $56.

The nightly train to Brisbane takes about 13½ hours. Economy/1st class costs $93/130; a sleeper costs $225. There's also a daily morning train to Murwillumbah in northern NSW with connecting buses to either the Gold Coast or Brisbane (16 hours).

A daily Speedlink train/bus service between Sydney and Adelaide via Albury costs $103 economy and takes 20 hours. You can also travel on the twice-weekly Indian Pacific via Broken Hill, but this takes 25 hours. The economy fare is $148, an economy sleeper is $271 and a 1st-class sleeper $414.

See the Perth section in the Western Australia chapter for details of the three-day train-trip between Sydney and Perth on the Indian Pacific.

There's an extensive rail network within the state – see the NSW introductory Getting Around section for details.

Car Rental There are Avis, Budget, Delta, Hertz and Thrifty branches, and a number of local operators, on William St. The larger companies' daily metropolitan rates are typically about $60 a day for a small car (Holden Barina), about $85 for a medium car (Toyota Corolla), or about $95 for a big car (Holden Commodore), all including insurance and unlimited kilometres. Some places require you to be over 23 years old.

There's no shortage of outfits renting older cars, which offer reasonable transport as long as your expectations are modest. Check for things like bald tyres and bad brakes before you sign, and check the fine print regarding insurance excess. Cut Price Rent-a-Car (☎ 9380 5122), 85 William St, is reputable and has adequate cars. A mid-80s sedan costs only $180 per week, if you're prepared to risk a $1000 excess.

Buying/Selling a Car or Motorcycle

Sydney is a good place for this; Parramatta Rd is lined with used car lots. There's a daily car market (☎ 9358 5000) at the Kings Cross Car Park on the corner of Ward Ave and Elizabeth Bay Rd, which charges sellers $35 a week (if the car has a roadworthy certificate known as a pink slip). This place can help with paperwork and arrange third-party property insurance. Although it's a dismal spot, it's becoming something of a travellers' rendezvous. The Flemington Car Market (☎ 0055 21122) near Flemington station operates on Sunday and charges sellers $60.

Several dealers will sell you a car with an undertaking to buy it back at an agreed price, but make sure you read the small print and don't accept any verbal guarantees – get it in writing. Better Bikes (☎ 9718 6668), 605 Canterbury Rd, Belmore, sometimes has buy-back deals on motorcycles and can help arrange insurance.

Before you buy a vehicle, it's worth having it checked by a mechanic. The NRMA (☎ 13 2132) does this for members for $105; nonmembers $125. Some service stations conduct inspections for less.

Getting Around

Securing the Olympics has prompted Sydney to undertake much-needed transport improvements such as new roads and expanded rail and ferry lines. For information on buses, ferries and trains, phone ☎ 13 1500 between 6 am and 10 pm daily.

To/From the Airport Sydney airport is 10km south of the city centre. The international and domestic terminals are a 4km bus trip apart on either side of the runway.

The Airport Express is a special STA service operating every 10 minutes from Central Station, with bus No 300 going to the airport via Circular Quay and No 350 going via Kings Cross. Airport Express buses have their own stops, extra-large luggage racks, and are painted green and yellow. The one-way fare is $5 and a return ticket, valid for two months, is $9. It's about 15 minutes from the airport to Central Station; add another 15 minutes to reach Circular Quay or Kings Cross.

Kingsford Smith Transport (KST) (☎ 9667 0663) runs a door-to-door service between the airport and places to stay (including hostels) in the city, Kings Cross, Darling Harbour and Glebe. The fare is $6. When heading to the airport, book at least three hours before you want to be collected. The Sydney Airporter (☎ 9667 3800) runs a similar service.

There are car rental agencies in the terminals. A taxi from the airport to Circular Quay should cost between $20 and $25.

A rail link between the city and the airport is scheduled to open in 2000.

Bus Sydney's bus network extends to most suburbs. Fares depend upon the number of 'sections' you pass through, so consult the driver. As a rough guide, short jaunts cost $1.20, and most other fares in the inner suburbs are $2.50. Regular buses run between 5 am and midnight when Nightrider buses take over.

The major starting points for bus routes are Circular Quay, Argyle St in Millers Point, Wynyard Park and the Queen Victoria Building on York St, and Railway Square. Most buses head out of the city on George or Castlereagh Sts, and take George or Elizabeth Sts coming in. Pay the driver as you enter, or dunk your prepaid ticket in the ticket machines by the door.

The bus information kiosk on the corner of Alfred and Loftus Sts at Circular Quay is open daily. There are other information offices on Carrington St and in the Queen Victoria Building on York St.

Special Bus Services The Sydney Explorer, a red STA tourist bus, navigates the innercity on a route designed to pass most central attractions. A bus departs from Circular Quay every 20 minutes between 8.40 am and 5.25 pm daily, but you can board at any of the 22 clearly marked, red bus stops on the route. Tickets are sold on board the bus and at STA offices, and entitle you to get on and off the bus as often as you like. They cost $20, so the service is really only worthwhile if you don't want the hassle of catching ordinary buses.

The Bondi & Bay Explorer operates along similar lines, running a much larger circuit from Circular Quay to Kings Cross, Double Bay, Rose Bay, Vaucluse, Watsons Bay, the Gap, Bondi Beach and Coogee, returning to the city along Oxford St. Just riding around the circuit takes two hours, so if you want to get off at many of the 18 places of interest along the way you'll need to start early. The buses depart half-hourly from Circular Quay daily between 9.15 am and 4.20 pm; tickets cost $20.

Nightrider buses provide an hourly service after regular buses and trains stop running. They operate from Town Hall station and service suburban train stations. Most trips cost $2.70.

Train Sydney has a vast suburban rail network and frequent services, making trains much quicker than buses. The underground City Circle comprises seven city-centre stations. Lines radiate from the City Circle, but the rail network does not extend to the northern and southern beaches, Balmain or Glebe. All suburban trains stop at Central Station, and usually one or more of the other City Circle stations as well (a ticket to the City will take you to any station on the City Circle). Trains run from around 5 am to midnight.

After 9 am on weekdays and at any time on weekends, you can buy an off-peak return ticket for not much more than a standard

NEW SOUTH WALES

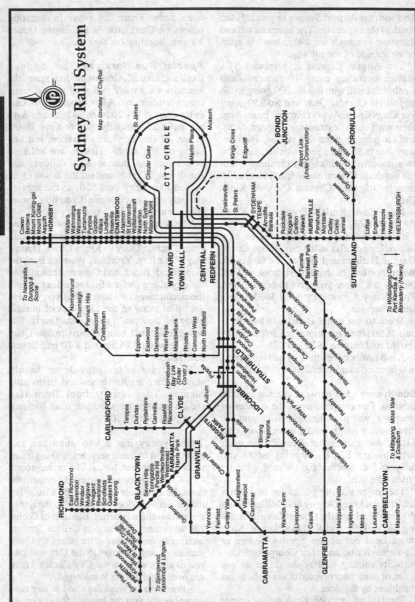

Sydney Rail System

Map courtesy of CityRail

one-way fare. A trip anywhere on the City Circle or to a nearby suburb such as Kings Cross is $1.80 single, $2 off-peak return and $3.20 day return. A City Hopper costs $5.40 and gives you a day of unlimited rides in the central area after 9 am on weekdays and at any time on weekends. You can go as far north as North Sydney, as far south as Central and as far east as Kings Cross on this ticket.

Staffed ticket booths are supplemented by automatic ticket machines at busy stations. If you have to change trains, it's cheaper to buy a ticket to your ultimate destination; however, don't leave an intermediary station en route to your destination or your ticket will be invalid.

For rail information, ask at any station or drop by the rail information booth near the ferry ticket office at Circular Quay.

Ferry Sydney's ferries are one of the most enjoyable and sensible ways of getting around. Many people use ferries to commute so there are frequently connecting bus services. Some ferries operate between 6 am and midnight, although ferries servicing tourist attractions operate much shorter hours. Popular places accessible by ferry include Darling Harbour, Balmain, Hunters Hill and Parramatta to the west; McMahons Point, Kirribilli, Neutral Bay, Cremorne, Mosman, Taronga Zoo and Manly on the North Shore; and Double Bay, Rose Bay and Watsons Bay in the eastern suburbs.

There are four types of ferry: the regular STA ferries; fast, modern JetCats which go to Manly ($5.20); RiverCats which traverse the Parramatta River to Parramatta ($4.80); and small private operators. All ferries depart from Circular Quay. There's a ferry information office next to the ticket booths on the concourse behind Wharf 4 (☎ 9207 3166). Most regular harbour ferries cost $3, although the longer trip to Manly costs $4.

Privately operated ferries include the Rocket Express (☎ 9264 7377), which shuttles from Harbourmaster's Steps at Circular Quay West to the Casino and Darling Harbour every 20 minutes for $3.15;

Hegarty's Ferries (☎ 9206 1167), which run during the day from Wharf 6 at Circular Quay to wharves directly across the harbour at Milson's Point, Lavender Bay, McMahons Point, and Kirribilli ($2.40); and Doyles Ferries (☎ 9337 2007), which run to Watsons Bay from Commissioners Steps between 11.30 am and 3 pm weekdays for $5.

Monorail The monorail circles Darling Harbour and the south-western quarter of the city centre, travelling at 1st-floor level. It operates between 7 am (8 am Sunday) and 9 pm (midnight Thursday to Saturday). The entire loop takes just over 10 minutes, with a train roughly every three or four minutes. A single loop or a portion of a loop costs $3; a day pass costs $7. Unless you're heading for Darling Harbour, consider it a novelty rather than a mode of transport.

Light Rail Sydney's snazzy new light rail glides from Central Station, through Haymarket, behind Darling Harbour, under the Casino and past the fish markets to Wentworth Park. It's strictly for the tourists at the moment, although proposed extensions through to Glebe and the inner west, and a loop through the city to Circular Quay, should make it more useful. A single ride costs $2.80; a day pass is $6.

Fare Deals The Sydney Pass offers three, five or seven-day unlimited travel over a seven-day period on all STA buses and ferries, and the red Travel Pass zone (inner suburbs) of the rail network. The passes cover the Airport Express, the Explorers, the JetCats, RiverCats and three STA-operated harbour cruises. They cost $66 (three days); $88 (five days) and $99 (seven days), which is good value compared to buying the components separately. Passes are available in many places including STA offices, train stations, and from Airport Express and Explorer bus drivers.

Travel Passes are designed for commuters and offer cheap weekly travel. There are various colour-coded grades offering combinations of distance and service. The Green

Travel Pass is valid for extensive train and bus travel and all ferries, except the Manly JetCat during the day. It's a bargain at $28 for a week. Travel Passes are sold at train stations, STA offices and major newsagents.

If you're just catching buses, get a Travel Ten ticket which gives a sizeable discount on 10 bus trips. There are various colour codes for distances so check which is the most appropriate for your travel patterns. A red Metro Ten costs $17.20 and can be used to reach most places mentioned in this section. Metro Tens are available from larger newsagents and STA offices. Insert the ticket in the ticket machine as you board the bus.

Ferry Ten tickets are similar and cost $17 for 10 innerharbour (ie short) ferry trips, or $28 including the Manly ferry. They can be purchased at the Circular Quay ferry ticket office.

Several transport-plus-entry tickets are available, which work out cheaper than catching a ferry and paying entry separately. They include the Zoo Pass, Aquarium Pass and Ocean Pass (to Manly's Oceanworld aquarium).

Taxi There are heaps of taxis in Sydney. The four big taxi companies offer a reliable telephone service: Legion (☎ 13 1451), Premier Cabs (☎ 13 1017), RSL Taxis (☎ 13 1581) and Taxis Combined (☎ 9332 8888).

Water taxis are pricey but fun ways of getting around the harbour. Companies include Taxis Afloat (☎ 9955 3222) and Harbour Taxi Boats (☎ 9555 1155). The Beachhopper (☎ 9326 9546) will drop you at any harbour beach from Elizabeth Bay, Double Bay or Circular Quay for $10 per person one way.

Bicycle Bicycle NSW (☎ 9283 5200), 209 Castlereagh St, Sydney 2000, publishes a handy book *Cycling Around Sydney* ($10), which details routes and cycle paths.

Bicycle Hire Most cycle hire shops require a hefty deposit (up to $500) or a credit card.

Inner City Cycles (☎ 9660 6605), 31 Glebe Point Rd, Glebe, rents quality moun-

tain bikes for $30 a day, $50 a weekend (Friday afternoon to Monday morning) and $120 a week. The Australian Cycle Company (☎ 9399 3475), 28 Clovelly Rd, Randwick, is handy for Centennial Park and rents bikes for $8 an hour, $12 for two hours and $25 a day. Manly Cycle Centre (☎ 9977 1189), 36 Pittwater Rd, Manly, charges $10 for two hours ($5 for each subsequent hour), $25 a day or $60 a week.

Around Sydney

There are superb national parks to the north and south of Sydney and historic small towns to the west, which were established in the early days of European settlement but survive today as pockets engulfed by urban sprawl.

BOTANY BAY

It's a common misconception that Sydney is built around Botany Bay. But Sydney Harbour is actually Port Jackson and Botany Bay is 10 to 15km south on the fringe of the city. This area is a major industrial centre so don't expect too many unspoilt vistas. Despite this, the bay has pretty stretches and holds a special place in Australian history. This was Captain Cook's first landing point in Australia, and it was named by Joseph Banks, the expedition's naturalist, for the many botanical specimens he found here.

The **Botany Bay National Park** encompasses both headlands of the bay. At Kurnell, on the southern headland, Cook's landing place is marked by monuments. The 436-hectare park has bushland and coastal walking tracks, picnic areas and an 8km cycle track. The Discovery Centre (☎ 9668 9923) in the park describes the impact of European arrival, and has information on the surrounding wetlands. It's open from 11 am to 3 pm daily. The park is open from 7 am to 7.30 pm. Entry costs $7.50 per car but pedestrians are not charged so you may as well park outside – the centre, monuments and most walking tracks are close to the entrance.

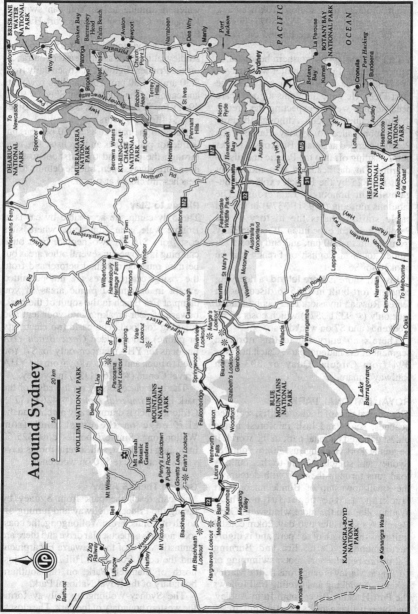

Around Sydney

0   10   20 km

To Bathurst

To Newcastle

PACIFIC OCEAN

BRISBANE WATER NATIONAL PARK

DHARUG NATIONAL PARK

MURRAMARRA NATIONAL PARK

KU-RING-GAI CHASE NATIONAL PARK

WOLLEMI NATIONAL PARK

BLUE MOUNTAINS NATIONAL PARK

KANANGRA-BOYD NATIONAL PARK

ROYAL NATIONAL PARK

HEATHCOTE NATIONAL PARK

BOTANY BAY NATIONAL PARK

Sydney

Gosford
Woy Woy
Spencer
Broken Bay
Barrenjoey Head
Palm Beach
Avalon
Newport
Narrabeen
Dee Why
Manly
Port Jackson
Pittwater
Brooklyn
West Head
Patonga
Church Point
Terrey Hills
St Ives
North Ryde
Bobbin Head
Berowra Waters
Mt Colah
Hornsby
Pennant Hills
Parramatta
Homebush Bay
Auburn
Liverpool
La Perouse
Botany Bay
Kurnell
Port Hacking
Cronulla
Bundeena
Audley
Loftus

Wisemans Ferry
Hawkesbury River
Putty Rd
Pitt Town
Wilberforce
Hawkesbury Heritage Farm
Windsor
Richmond
Castlereagh
Kurrajong
Bells Line of Rd
Mt Tomah Botanic Gardens
Mt Wilson
Bell
Mt Victoria
Blackheath
Hargreaves Lookout
Mt Blackheath Lookout
Medlow Bath
Katoomba
Leura
Wentworth Falls
Megalong Valley
Woodford
Lawson
Faulconbridge
Springwood
Glenbrook
Blaxland
Elizabeth's Lookout
Riverview Lookout
Marge's Lookout
Penrith
Nepean River
St Mary's
Western Motorway
Riverstone
Featherdale Wildlife Park
Australia's Wonderland
Leppington
Campbelltown
Narellan
Camden
The Oaks
Warragamba
Wallacia
Lake Burragorang
Jenolan Caves
Kanangra Walls

Zig Zag Railway
Lithgow
Hartley
Great Western Hwy
Perry's Lookdown
Pulpit Rock
Govetts Leap
Evan's Lookout

Vale Lookout
Panorama Point Lookout

Pacific Hwy
Old Northern Rd

To Melbourne Via Coast

Princes Hwy

Hume Hwy

South Western Fwy (Hume)

Northern Road

M7
M5
M2
M4
32
31
1

40

From Cronulla train station (10km away), catch Kurnell Bus Co (☎ 9524 8977) bus No 987 ($2.80). Services are limited on weekends.

La Perouse, on the northern headland, is named after the French explorer who arrived in 1788, just six days after the arrival of the First Fleet. He gave the Poms a good scare because they weren't expecting the French to turn up quite so soon. Although the First Fleet soon sailed to Sydney Harbour, La Perouse camped at Botany Bay for six weeks before sailing off into the Pacific and disappearing. On the headland is a monument built in 1825 by the French explorer Bougainville in honour of La Perouse. The fabulous museum (☎ 9311 3379) in the old cable station charts the history of La Perouse's fateful expedition. It's open daily from 10 am to 4.30 pm, and entry costs $2; guided tours in English or French can be booked for $6.

Just off shore is **Bare Island**, a decaying concrete fort built in 1885 to discourage a feared Russian invasion. Entry is by guided tour only (☎ 9331 3379) which costs $5 on weekends and $7 on weekdays.

There's no entry fee to this northern segment of the national park. Catch bus Nos 394 from Circular Quay or 393 from Railway Square.

ROYAL NATIONAL PARK

This coastal park of dramatic cliffs, secluded beaches, scrub and lush rainforest is the oldest gazetted national park in the world. It begins at Port Hacking just 30km south of Sydney and stretches 20km to the south. A road runs through the park with detours to the small township of Bundeena on Port Hacking, to the beautiful beach at Wattamolla, and the more windswept Garie Beach. A spectacular two-day, 26km coastal trail runs the length of the park and is highly recommended. Garie, Era and Burning Palms are popular surf spots; swimming or surfing at Marley is dangerous (Little Marley is safe). A walking and cycling trail follows the Port Hacking River south from Audley, and other walking tracks pass tranquil, fresh-water swimming holes. You can swim in Kangaroo Creek but not the Port Hacking River.

There is a visitor centre (☎ 9542 0648) at Audley, at the park's north-eastern entrance, off the Princes Highway. It's open daily from 8.30 am to 4.30 pm. You can hire rowboats and canoes at the Audley Boat Shed (☎ 9545 4967) for $12 an hour or $24 a day. Bikes cost $14 for two hours.

Entry to the park costs $7.50 per car, but is free for pedestrians and cyclists. The road through the park and the offshoot to Bundeena are always open, but the detours to the beaches are closed at sunset.

Places to Stay

The only camp site accessible by car is at Bonnie Vale, near Bundeena, where sites cost from $10 for two people. Free bush camping is allowed in several other areas but permits must be obtained beforehand from the visitor centre. Fires are not permitted except in designated picnic areas. If you camp at Era Beach in the south of the park, beware of deer breaking into your tent and foraging for food. The basic (no electricity or phone) and secluded *Garie Beach YHA* has beds for YHA members only for $7. You need to book and collect a key from the YHA Travel Centre (☎ 9261 1111) in Sydney.

The best place to stay on the edge of the park is the *Imperial Hotel* (☎ 4267 1177), Clifton, which is dramatically perched on the cliff edge on the coast road from Wollongong. Singles/doubles cost $25/60 including breakfast, and several rooms have views. Doubles are $70 on weekends.

Getting There & Away

You can reach the park from Sydney by taking the Princes Highway and turning off south of Loftus. From Wollongong, the coast road north is a spectacular drive and there are fantastic views of the Illawarra Escarpment and the coast from Bald Hill Lookout, just north of Stanwell Park, on the southern boundary of the Royal National Park.

The Sydney-Wollongong railway forms the western boundary of the park. The closest station is at Loftus, 4km from the park entrance and another 2km from the visitor centre. Bringing a bike on the train is a good idea. Engadine, Heathcote, Waterfall and Otford are on the park boundary and have walking trails leading into the park.

A scenic way to reach the park is to take a train from Sydney to the southern beach suburb of Cronulla ($3.80) then a Cronulla National Park Ferries (☎ 9523 2990) boat to **Bundeena** in the north-eastern corner of the park. Bundeena is the starting-point of the 26km long coastal walk. Ferries depart from the Cronulla wharf, just below the train station, hourly on the half-hour (except 12.30 pm) and return from Bundeena hourly on the hour (except 1 pm); the fare is $2.40 one way.

HEATHCOTE NATIONAL PARK

This forgotten 2000-hectare heath land national park adjoins the western boundary of the Royal National Park and is administered from the Audley visitor centre. It has rugged scenery, great bushwalking and plenty of pools suitable for swimming. Bush camping permits are available from the Audley visitor centre. Walking trails enter the park from Heathcote and Waterfall, both on the Princes Highway and the Sydney-Wollongong railway line.

PARRAMATTA

Parramatta, 24km west of Sydney, was the second European settlement in Australia and contains a number of historic buildings dating from the early days of the colony. When Sydney proved to be a very poor area for farming, Parramatta was selected in 1788 for the first farm settlement. Despite its rural beginnings, the settlement has been consumed by Sydney's westward sprawl and is now a thriving but undistinguished commercial centre.

The Parramatta visitor centre (☎ 9630 3703) is on the corner of Church and Market Sts. It's open weekdays from 10 am to 4 pm, Saturday from 9 am to 1 pm, and Sunday from 10.30 am to 3.30 pm.

On the western edge of the city, **Parramatta Park** was the site of the area's first farm and contains a number of relics. The elegant **Old Government House** sits atop a rise overlooking the Parramatta River. It was built from 1799 as a country retreat for the early governors of NSW, and is the oldest remaining public building in Australia. It now houses a museum and is open Tuesday to Thursday from 10 am to 4 pm and weekends from 11 am to 4 pm ($5). The park has several other relics from the early days of settlement and is the starting point for a 15km cycle track that runs east to Putney along the foreshore of the Parramatta River.

St John's Cathedral and the **Town Hall** form a pleasant civic centre near the junction of Church and Macquarie Sts. St John's Cemetery, on O'Connell St between the cathedral and the park, contains the graves of many of the first settlers.

There are more historic buildings east of the city centre. **Elizabeth Farm**, 70 Alice St, is the oldest surviving home in the country. It was built in 1793 by the founders of Australia's wool industry, John and Elizabeth Macarthur, and its deep verandah and simple lines became the prototype for early Australian homesteads. The house is open daily from 10 am to 4.30 pm; entry is $5 ($3 concession).

Experiment Farm Cottage, 9 Ruse St, is an exquisite colonial bungalow built on the site of the first land grant issued in Australia. The cottage is open Tuesday to Thursday from 10 am to 4 pm, and on Sunday from 11 am to 4 pm ($5, $3 concession).

Getting There & Away

The best way to reach Parramatta is by RiverCat from Circular Quay ($4.80), otherwise catch a train from Central Station ($3). By car, exit the city via Parramatta Rd and detour onto the Western Motorway tollway ($1.50) at Strathfield.

AROUND PARRAMATTA

There are two mainstream tourist attractions halfway between Parramatta and Penrith, further west. The **Featherdale Wildlife Park**, 217 Kildare Rd, Doonside, has plenty of native fauna. Featherdale is open daily from 9 am to 5 pm and costs $9.50. Take a train to Blacktown and bus No 725 from there. **Australia's Wonderland**, Wallgrove Rd, Eastern Creek, is a large amusement park complex with a wildlife park. It's open daily ($31.95, admission to the wildlife park only is $9.95). Shuttle buses meet trains at Rooty Hill on weekends.

PENRITH

Penrith, on the serene Nepean River, is at the base of the forested foothills of the Blue Mountains. Despite being 50km west of the city centre, it's virtually an outer suburb of Sydney. The Penrith Tourist Office (☎ 4732 7671) is in the car park of the huge Panthers World of Entertainment complex on Mulgoa Rd. It's open daily from 9 am to 4.30 pm.

Cables Waterski Park (☎ 4732 1044), next to Panthers, offers cable-towed skiing ($22 for two hours), waterslides and pools. If you like water, but not necessarily dipping, you can take a cruise through the **Nepean Gorge** on the *Nepean Belle* paddle-wheeler (☎ 4733 1274). There are day cruises ($12) on Sunday and Wednesday and dinner cruises ($44) on Friday and Saturday. There are fine views of the Nepean Gorge from the **Rock Lookout**, 5km west of the town of Mulgoa. Mulgoa is 10km south of Penrith on Mulgoa Rd. There's limited public access to the new regatta centre north of Penrith, purpose built for Olympic rowing, canoeing and rafting.

You can reach Penrith by train from Central Station ($5) or by driving west along Parramatta Rd and taking the Western Motorway tollway at Strathfield ($1.50).

CAMDEN AREA

Camden is promoted as the 'birthplace of the nation's wealth' because it was here that John and Elizabeth Macarthur conducted the sheep-breeding experiments which laid the foundation for Australia's wool industry. Camden is on the urban fringe, 50km south-west of the city centre via the Hume Highway. The Camden visitor centre (☎ 4658 1370), Camden Valley Way, has free walking-tour leaflets.

The surrounding countryside has attractions aimed primarily at families and coach tourists, including the **Gledswood** historic homestead at nearby Narellan and the **Australiana Park** tourist complex next door.

The 400-hectare **Mount Annan Botanic Garden** is the native plant garden of Sydney's Royal Botanic Gardens and is midway between Camden and Campbelltown, to the east. It's open daily ($5 per car, $2 for pedestrians). Take a train to Campbelltown station ($4.60) and a Busways bus No 894/5/6 from there.

South of Camden is the small town of **Picton**. The 1839 *George IV Inn* (☎ 4677 1415) here is one of the nicest places to stay around Sydney if you need to recharge your batteries. Basic singles/doubles built around a courtyard cost $25/38. In nearby Thirlmere, the **Rail Transport Museum** has a huge collection of steam trains. It's open daily ($8).

KU-RING-GAI CHASE NATIONAL PARK

This 15,000-hectare national park, 24km north of the city centre, borders the southern edge of Broken Bay and the western shore of Pittwater. It has that classic Sydney mixture of sandstone, bushland and water vistas, plus walking tracks, horse-riding trails, picnic areas, Aboriginal rock engravings and spectacular views of Broken Bay, particularly from West Head at the park's north-eastern tip. There are several roads through the park and four entrances. Entry is $7.50 per car.

The Kalkari visitor centre (☎ 9457 9853) is on Ku-ring-gai Chase Rd, about 4km into the park from the Mt Colah entrance. It's open daily from 9 am to 4.30 pm. The road descends from the visitor centre to the picnic area at Bobbin Head on Cowan Creek. Halvorsen (☎ 9457 9011) rents rowboats for $10 for the first hour and $4 for subsequent hours; motor boats that seat eight cost $30 for the first hour and $6 for subsequent hours. There are also boats for hire at the Akuna Bay marina on Coal & Candle Creek.

Recommended walks include the America Bay Trail and the Gibberagong and Sphinx tracks. The best places to see Aboriginal engravings are on the Basin Trail and the Garigal Aboriginal Heritage Walk at West Head. There's a mangrove boardwalk at Bobbin Head. It's unwise to swim in Broken Bay because of sharks, but there are safe, netted swimming areas at Illawong Bay and the Basin.

Places to Stay

Camping is allowed only at the Basin (☎ 9457 9853), on the western side of Pittwater. It's a 2.5km walk from the West Head road or a ferry ride from Palm Beach. It costs $10 for two people; book in advance and pay at the site. There is safe swimming in the lagoon at the Basin, and basic supplies are brought over by ferry from Palm Beach.

The *Pittwater YHA* (☎ 9999 2196) is on the shore of Pittwater, a couple of kilometres south of the Basin. It's noted for its idyllic setting and friendly wildlife. Dorms cost $16, and twins $20 per person. Nonmembers pay $3 more. Canoes and sailboats are available. Book in advance and bring food.

Getting There & Away

There are four road entrances to the park: Mt Colah, on the Pacific Highway; Turramurra, in the south-west; and Terrey Hills and Church Point, in the south-east. Shoreline Buses' (☎ 9457 8888) bus No 577 runs every 30 minutes from Turramurra station to the nearby park entrance ($2.10) on weekdays; one bus enters the park as far as Bobbin Head. The schedule changes on weekends with less frequent buses to the entrance but more to Bobbin Head.

The Palm Beach Ferry Service (☎ 9918 2747) runs to the Basin hourly (except 1 pm) from 9 am to 5 pm for $7 one way. It also departs Palm Beach daily at 11 am for Bobbin Head via Patonga, returning at 3.30 pm. The one-way fare is $25.

To reach the Pittwater YHA, take a ferry from Church Point to Halls Wharf ($6 return). The hostel is a short walk from here. Bus No 156 runs from Manly to Church Point. From the city centre, Bus No E86 is a direct service, or catch Bus No L88, L90 or

190 from Wynyard Park as far as Warringah Mall and transfer to No 156 from there.

HAWKESBURY RIVER

The mighty Hawkesbury River enters the sea 30km north of Sydney at Broken Bay. It's dotted with coves, beaches and picnic spots, making it one of Australia's most attractive rivers. Before entering the ocean, the river expands into bays and inlets like Berowra Creek, Cowan Creek and Pittwater on the southern side, and Brisbane Water on the northern. The river flows between a succession of national parks – Murramarra and Ku-ring-gai Chase to the south; and Dharug, Brisbane Water and Bouddi to the north. Windsor (see below) is about 120km upstream.

An excellent way to get a feel for the river is to catch the *Riverboat Postman* (☎ 9985 7566) mail boat, which does a 40km round trip every weekday, running upstream as far as Marlow, near Spencer. It departs from Brooklyn at 9.30 am and returns at 1.15 pm. A shorter afternoon run on Wednesday and Friday departs at 1.30 pm and returns at 4 pm. It costs $25 ($20 concession). The 8.16 am train from Sydney's Central Station ($4.60) will get you to Brooklyn's Hawkesbury River Station in time to join the morning boat.

You can hire houseboats in Brooklyn, Berowra Waters and Bobbin Head. These aren't cheap but renting midweek during low season is affordable for a group. Halvorsen (☎ 9457 9011) at Bobbin Head has four berths for $230 for three days during this period. No experience is necessary.

The settlements along the river have their own distinct character. Life in **Brooklyn** revolves totally around boats and the river. The town is on the Sydney-Newcastle railway line, just east of the Pacific Highway. **Berowra Waters** is a quaint community further upstream, clustered around a free 24-hour winch ferry which crosses Berowra Creek. There are a couple of cafes overlooking the water and a marina, which hires outboards for $50 for a half-day. Berowra Waters is 5km west of the Pacific Highway;

there's a train station at Berowra, but it's a 6km hike down to the ferry.

Wisemans Ferry is a tranquil settlement overlooking the Hawkesbury River roughly halfway between Windsor and the mouth of the river. A free 24-hour winch ferry is the only means of crossing the river here. The historic *Wisemans Ferry Inn* (☎ 4566 4301) has rooms from $55 a double. The *Rosevale Farm Resort* (☎ 4566 4207) has tent sites for $7 per person and on-site vans from $27. It's a couple of kilometres north of the town, on the opposite bank of the river.

The **Yengo National Park**, a rugged sandstone area covering the foothills of the Blue Mountains, stretches from Wisemans Ferry to the Hunter Valley. It's a wilderness area with no facilities and limited road access. A scenic road leads east from Wisemans Ferry to the Central Coast, following the course of the river before veering north through bushland and orange groves. An early convict-built road leads north from Wisemans Ferry to **St Albans**. The friendly *Settlers Arms Inn* (☎ 4568 2111) here dates from 1836 and has pleasant rooms from $100 a double. There's a basic camp site opposite the hotel.

Note that it may be unwise to swim in the Hawkesbury River between Windsor and Wisemans Ferry during the summer due to blue-green algae. Call the EPA Pollution Line (☎ 9325 5555) for information.

WINDSOR

Windsor, Richmond, Wilberforce, Castlereagh and Pitt Town are the five 'Macquarie Towns' established on rich agricultural land on the upper Hawkesbury River in the early 19th century by Governor Lachlan Macquarie. You can see them on the way to or from the Blue Mountains if you cross the range on the Bells Line of Road – an interesting alternative to the Great Western Highway.

The Hawkesbury visitor centre (☎ 4588 5895) is on Richmond Rd, between Richmond and Windsor, and is open daily. Windsor has its own tourist information

centre (☎ 4577 2310) in the 1843 Daniel O'Connell Inn on Thompson Square.

Windsor has some fine old buildings, notably those around the picturesque Thompson Square on the banks of the Hawkesbury River. The Daniel O'Connell Inn houses the **Hawkesbury Museum of Local History**, which is open daily from 10 am to 4 pm ($2.50, $1.50 concession). The **Macquarie Arms Hotel** (1815) has a nice terrace fronting the square and is reckoned to be the oldest pub in Australia, but there are a few 'oldest pubs' around. Other old buildings include the convict-built **St Matthew's Church of England**, completed in 1822 and designed, like the **courthouse**, by the convict architect Francis Greenway. Windsor River Cruises (☎ 9831 6630) offers cruises on the Hawkesbury on Sunday and Wednesday from $15.

If you want to stay overnight in Windsor, the historic *Clifton Cottage* (☎ 4587 7135), 22 Richmond Rd, is the best value at $30/55 for a single/double with shared facilities midweek, and $35/58 on weekends.

You can reach Windsor by train from Sydney's Central Station ($4.60) but public transport to the other Macquarie Towns (apart from Richmond) is scarce. By car, exit the city on Parramatta Rd and head northwest on the Windsor Rd from Parramatta.

AROUND WINDSOR

The next largest of the Macquarie Towns is **Richmond**, which has its share of colonial buildings and a pleasant village-green-like park. It's 6km west of Windsor, at the end of the metropolitan railway line and at the start of the Bells Line of Road across the Blue Mountains. There's a NPWS office (☎ 4588 5247) open on weekdays at 370 Windsor Rd.

The **Hawkesbury Heritage Farm** is a theme park which contains Rose Cottage (1811), probably the oldest surviving timber building in the country. It's in Wilberforce, 6km north of Windsor, and is open daily ($10). The pretty **Ebenezer Church** (1809), 5km north of Wilberforce, is the oldest church in Australia still used as a place of worship.

DAVID COLLINS

JON MURRAY

JON MURRAY   JON MURRAY

JON MURRAY

New South Wales
A: Megalong Valley, Blue Mountains
B: Sunset, Darling River
C: Protesters' Falls, near Nimbin

D: Border Ranges National Park
E: Abandoned farmhouse, Cooma

JON MURRAY

RICHARD I'ANSON

New South Wales
Top: Ghost town in the Riverina
Bottom: Late afternoon at Mungo National Park

Wilberforce is the starting point for the Putty Rd, a 160km isolated back road that runs north to Singleton in the Hunter Valley. The **Colo River**, 15km north along this road, is a picturesque spot popular for swimming, canoeing and picnicking. There's a caravan park (☎ 4575 5253) on the river bank where tent sites cost $7 per person, and on-site vans are $28 a double. Canoes can be hired for $12 an hour.

Blue Mountains

The Blue Mountains, part of the Great Dividing Range, were an impenetrable barrier to White expansion from Sydney. Despite many attempts to find a route through – and a bizarre belief among many convicts that China, and freedom, was just on the other side – it took 25 years before a successful crossing was made by Europeans. A road was built soon afterwards which opened the western plains to settlement.

The first whites into the mountains found evidence of Aboriginal occupation but few Aboriginal people. It seems likely that European diseases had travelled from Sydney long before the explorers and wiped out most of the indigenous people.

The Blue Mountains National Park has some truly fantastic scenery, excellent bushwalks and all the gorges, gum trees and cliffs you could ask for. The foothills begin 65km inland from Sydney and rise as high as 1100m. The blue haze which gave the mountains their name is a result of the fine mist of oil given off by eucalyptus trees.

For the past century, the area has been a popular getaway for Sydneysiders seeking to escape the summer heat. Despite the intensive tourist development, much of the area is so precipitous that it's still only open to bushwalkers.

Be prepared for the climatic difference between the Blue Mountains and the coast – you can swelter in Sydney but shiver in Katoomba. It usually snows sometime between June and August and the region has

a Yuletide Festival during this period, complete with Christmas decorations and dinners.

Bushfires in 1994 burned large areas of the Grose Valley but the Blue Gum Forest escaped almost intact. The YHA hostel at North Springwood was destroyed in the fires but there are plans to rebuild it. Contact the YHA Travel Centre (☎ 9261 1111) in Sydney for further information.

Orientation

The Great Western Highway from Sydney follows a ridge running on an east-west axis through the Blue Mountains. Along this less-than-beautiful road, the Blue Mountains towns merge into each other – Glenbrook, Springwood, Woodford, Lawson, Wentworth Falls, Leura, Katoomba (the main accommodation centre), Medlow Bath, Blackheath, Mt Victoria and Hartley. On the western fringe of the mountains is Lithgow – see the Central West section later in this chapter.

To the south and north of the highway's ridge, the country drops away into precipitous valleys, including the Grose Valley to the north, and the Jamison Valley south of Katoomba.

The Bells Line of Road is a much more scenic and less congested alternative to the Great Western Highway. It's the more northerly of the two crossings, beginning in Richmond (see the Around Windsor section) and running north of the Grose Valley to emerge in Lithgow, although you can cut across from Bell to join the Great Western Highway at Mt Victoria.

Information

There are Blue Mountains information centres open daily on the highway at Glenbrook and at Echo Point in Katoomba (☎ 4739 6266). The Blue Mountains Heritage Centre (☎ 4787 8877) is a NPWS visitor centre on Govetts Leap Rd, Blackheath, about 3km off the Great Western Highway.

There are plenty of books on the Blue Mountains. For a general introduction, try the *Blue Mountains of Australia*. Lonely

Planet's *Bushwalking in Australia* by John & Monica Chapman includes Blue Mountains treks. Cyclists can check out Robert Sloss's *Bushwalking-Hiking-Cycling in the Blue Mountains*. Books and maps and individual walking-track guides are sold at visitor centres.

You can hire any camping gear you may need from Mountain Designs (☎ 4782 5999), 190 Katoomba St, Katoomba.

National Parks

The **Blue Mountains National Park** protects large areas to the north and south of the Great Western Highway. It's the most popular and accessible of the three national parks in the area, and offers great bushwalking, scenic lookouts, breathtaking waterfalls and Aboriginal stencils. **Wollemi National Park**, north of the Bells Line of Road, is the state's largest forested wilderness area and stretches all the way to Denman in the Hunter Valley. It has limited access and the park's centre is so isolated that a new species of tree, named the Wollemi pine, was discovered as recently as 1994.

Kanangra-Boyd National Park is southwest of the southern section of the Blue Mountains National Park. It has bushwalking opportunities, limestone caves and grand scenery, and includes the spectacular Kanangra Walls Plateau, which is surrounded by sheer cliffs and can be reached by unsealed road from Oberon or Jenolan Caves.

Entry to these national parks is free unless you enter the Blue Mountains National Park at Bruce Rd, Glenbrook, where it costs $7.50 per car; walkers are not charged.

Bushwalking

The roads across the mountains offer tantalising glimpses of the majesty of the area, but the only way to really experience the Blue Mountains is to start walking. There are walks lasting from a few minutes to several days. The two most popular areas are Jamison Valley, south of Katoomba, and Grose Valley, north-east of Katoomba and west of Blackheath. The area south of Glenbrook is another good place.

Visit an NPWS visitor centre for information or, for shorter walks, ask at one of the tourist information centres. It's very rugged country and walkers sometimes get lost, so it's highly advisable to get reliable information, to not go alone, and to tell someone where you're going. Most Blue Mountains watercourses are polluted, so you have to sterilise water or take your own. Be prepared for rapid weather changes.

Adventure Activities

The cliffs and gorges of the Blue Mountains offer excellent abseiling, climbing and canyoning. Mountain-bike touring is also popular. See the Katoomba Activities section for details.

Organised Tours

Wonderbus (☎ 9247 5151) runs backpacker-friendly day tours to the Blue Mountains for $48. It's possible to arrange a one-night stopover in Katoomba and catch the tour back to Sydney the next day, depending on seating availability. Wildframe (☎ 9314 0658) runs reportedly good tours with an ecological slant ($55). Book at the YHA Travel Centre (☎ 9261 1111) in Sydney.

Places to Stay

Accommodation ranges from camp sites and hostels to guesthouses and luxury hotels. Katoomba is the main centre. Prices are fairly stable throughout the year, but most places charge more on weekends. Prices listed below are winter rates. If you intend to camp in the national parks, check with the NPWS first.

Getting There & Away

Katoomba is 109km from Sydney's city centre, but it's still almost a satellite suburb. Trains run approximately hourly from Central Station. The trip takes two hours ($9.20 single), and there are stops at plenty of Blue Mountains townships on the way.

By car, exit the city via Parramatta Rd and detour onto the Western Motorway tollway

($1.50) at Strathfield. The motorway becomes the Great Western Highway west of Penrith. To reach the Bells Line of Rd, exit the city on Parramatta Rd and from Parramatta head north-west on the Windsor Rd to Windsor. The Richmond Rd from Windsor becomes the Bells Line of Rd west of Richmond.

Getting Around

Mountainlink (☎ 4782 3333) runs between Katoomba, Medlow Bath, Blackheath and (infrequently) Mt Victoria, with some services running down Hat Hill Rd and Govetts Leap Rd, which lead respectively to Perrys Lookdown and Govetts Leap. The buses take you to within about 1km of Govetts Leap but for Perrys Lookdown you have to walk about 6km from the last stop. Services are sparse on Saturday and don't run on Sunday. In Katoomba, the bus leaves from the top of Katoomba St, opposite the Carrington Hotel.

The Blue Mountains Bus Company (☎ 4782 4213) runs between Katoomba, Leura, Wentworth Falls, and east as far as Woodford. There's roughly one service an hour from Katoomba train station.

There are train stations in most Blue Mountains towns along the Great Western Highway. Trains run roughly hourly between stations east of Katoomba and roughly two-hourly between stations to the west.

Thrifty (☎ 4784 2888), 80 Megalong St, Leura, rents cars from about $60 a day.

GLENBROOK TO KATOOMBA

From Marge's and Elizabeth's lookouts, just north of Glenbrook, there are good views east to Sydney. The section of the Blue Mountains National Park south of Glenbrook contains **Red Hand Cave**, an old Aboriginal shelter with hand stencils on the walls. It's an easy 7km return walk, south-west of the NPWS visitor centre.

The artist and author Norman Lindsay lived in **Springwood** from 1912 until he died in 1969. His home at 14 Norman Lindsay Crescent is now a gallery and museum, with exhibits of his paintings, cartoons, illustrations and sculptures. It's open daily except Tuesday from 10 am to 4 pm ($5, $2.50 concession).

Just south of the town of **Wentworth Falls**, there are great views of the Jamison Valley. You can see the spectacular 300m Wentworth Falls from Falls Reserve, which is the starting point for a network of walking tracks.

Leura is a quaint tree-lined centre full of country stores and cafes. Leuralla is an Art-Deco mansion which houses a toy and model railway museum ($6). Sublime Point, south of Leura, is a great cliff-top lookout. Nearby, Gordon Falls Reserve is a popular picnic spot, and from here you can take the cliff-top path or Cliff Drive 4km west past Leura Cascades to Katoomba's Echo Point.

Places to Stay & Eat

There are NPWS camp sites accessible by car at Euroka Clearing near Glenbrook, Murphys Glen near Woodford, and Ingar near Wentworth Falls. You need a permit to camp at Euroka Clearing from the NPWS office in Richmond (☎ 4588 5247 Monday to Friday). The tracks to Ingar and Murphys Glen may be closed after heavy rain.

Leura Village Caravan Park (☎ 4784 1552), on the corner of the Great Western Highway and Leura Mall, has tent sites (from $18), on-site vans (from $37) and cabins (from $47). There are plenty of guesthouses and expensive hotel accommodation; expect to pay from around $50 per person for guest-house B&B.

Country-style cafes lining Leura Mall serve light meals for around $8. Try *Gracie's on the Mall* at No 174. *Baker's Cafe* at No 179 has sweet and savoury pastries to die for. If you want something special, *Le Gobelet* at the top of the mall has beluga caviar for a mere $98.50.

KATOOMBA (pop 17,700)

Katoomba and the adjacent centres of Wentworth Falls and Leura form the tourist centre of the Blue Mountains. Katoomba is where the Sydney 'plains-dwellers' escape the summer heat, and has long catered to visitors. Despite the number of tourists and its proximity to Sydney, Katoomba has an uncanny, otherworldy ambience, an atmosphere accentuated by its Art Deco and Art Nouveau guesthouses and cafes, its thick mists and occasional snowfalls. An alternative new-agey scene has also embraced Katoomba: there are lots of yoga classes, meditation centres and incense. On a quiet day you can almost hear the chakras realigning.

Steep Katoomba St is the main drag. The major tourist attraction is at **Echo Point**, near the southern end of Katoomba St, about a kilometre from the shopping centre. Here you'll find some of the best views of the Jamison Valley and the magnificent **Three Sisters** rock formation.

To the west of Echo Point, at the junction of Cliff Drive and Violet St, are the **Scenic Railway** and **Scenic Skyway** (☎ 4782 2699). The railway runs to the bottom of the Jamison Valley (one way $3, return $4.50), where the popular six-hour walk to the **Ruined Castle** rock formation begins. The railway was built in the 1880s to transport coal-miners and its 45° incline is one of the steepest in the world. The Scenic Skyway is a cable car, which travels some 200m above the valley floor traversing Katoomba Falls gorge ($4.50 return).

If you want to experience the thrills of the Blue Mountains without leaving the comfort of a cushioned seat, The Edge-Blue Mountains Maxvision Cinema (☎ 4782 8928), 235 Great Western Highway, is a giant-screen cinema which shows a stunning 38-minute Blue Mountains documentary as well as feature films. Sessions cost $12 ($10 concession).

Activities
There are several companies offering rock climbing, abseiling, canyoning and caving adventure activities. The Australian School of Mountaineering (☎ 4782 2014), 166b Katoomba St, offers introductory rock climbing ($95), abseiling ($69), and canyoning (from $95). High 'n Wild (☎ 4782 6224),

opposite the train station, on the corner of Main and Katoomba Sts, offer the highest introductory abseil. Half-day abseiling or rock climbing excursions start at $49. The Blue Mountains Adventure Company (☎ 4782 1271), 84a Main St, offers similar activities. Break Away Bikes (☎ 4787 6630), in Mountain Designs, 190 Katoomba St, has full and half-day mountain-bike tours from $48.

Places to Stay
Camping *Katoomba Falls Caravan Park* (☎ 4782 1835) on Katoomba Falls Rd has tent sites for $7 per person and on-site vans from $31 for two people.

Hostels The *Katoomba YHA* (☎ 4782 1416) is in a pleasant old guesthouse on the corner of Lurline and Waratah Sts. Many rooms have attached bathrooms and there are good communal areas. Dorms cost from $12 and doubles are $25; nonmembers pay $3 more.

Nearby, *Katoomba Mountain Lodge* (☎ 4782 3933), 31 Lurline St, is a cosy hostel and guesthouse charging from $11 for dorm beds and $28/42 for singles/doubles with shared bathrooms.

Blue Mountains Backpackers (☎ 4782 4226), 190 Bathurst Rd, is a short walk from the train station. It's a friendly hostel reminiscent of a large student house. Dorms cost $15, and twins/doubles $40. *Nomads Gearin's Hotel* and the *Katoomba Hotel* also have backpacker rooms (see below).

Hotels & Motels The *Katoomba Hotel* (☎ 4782 1106), on the corner of Parke and Main Sts, is a smoky Aussie local with uninspiring singles/doubles for $20/45 midweek and $25/50 on weekends. A night in a dorm costs $12.

The *Clarendon Guesthouse* (☎ 4782 1322), on the corner of Lurline and Waratah Sts, has excellent budget singles/doubles with TV from $38/48 midweek and $68/88 on weekends. There's a great old-time atmosphere here, helped along by log fire, games room, cocktail bar and cabaret-style entertainment.

NEW SOUTH WALES

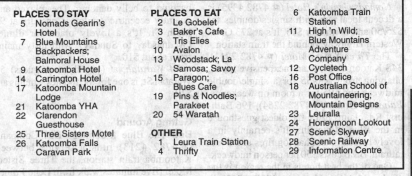

PLACES TO STAY
5 Nomads Gearin's Hotel
7 Blue Mountains Backpackers; Balmoral House
9 Katoomba Hotel
14 Carrington Hotel
17 Katoomba Mountain Lodge
21 Katoomba YHA
22 Clarendon Guesthouse
25 Three Sisters Motel
26 Katoomba Falls Caravan Park

PLACES TO EAT
2 Le Gobelet
3 Baker's Cafe
8 Tris Elies
10 Avalon
13 Woodstack; La Samosa; Savoy
15 Paragon; Blues Cafe
19 Pins & Noodles; Parakeet
20 54 Waratah

OTHER
1 Leura Train Station
4 Thrifty

6 Katoomba Train Station
11 High 'n Wild; Blue Mountains Adventure Company
12 Cycletech
16 Post Office
18 Australian School of Mountaineering; Mountain Designs
23 Leuralla
24 Honeymoon Lookout
27 Scenic Skyway
28 Scenic Railway
29 Information Centre

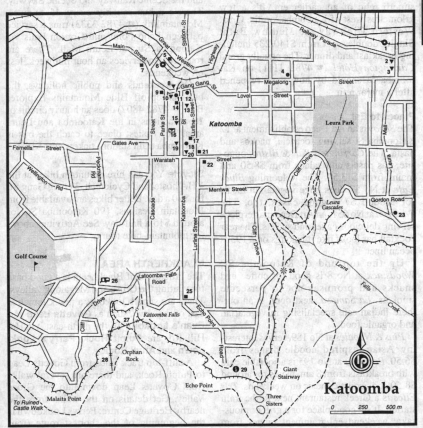

Katoomba

Nomads Gearin's Hotel (☎ 4782 4395) is a decent local pub with singles/doubles for $25/50 and dorms for $15. It's at 273 Great Western Highway, behind the train station.

The *Three Sisters Motel* (☎ 4782 2911), 348 Katoomba St, is an inexpensive motel, charging from $50/55 for a single/double midweek and $95 for a room on weekends. *Balmoral House* (☎ 4782 2264), 196 Bathurst Rd, claims to be the oldest guesthouse in the Blue Mountains. It's certainly in a lovely building, and has log fires and a restaurant. B&B costs $50 per person midweek.

One of the best hotels in the region is the *Hydro Majestic Hotel* (☎ 4788 1002), a superb relic of an earlier era. It's a few kilometres west of Katoomba, on the Great Western Highway, at Medlow Bath. Singles/doubles cost from $140/235 including breakfast and dinner. The equally grand *Carrington Hotel* (☎ 4782 1111) on Katoomba St should by now have reopened after a major refit.

Places to Eat

The *Savoy* is an Art Deco establishment at 12 Katoomba St serving focaccia, nachos and pasta. The *Carrington Bar & Bistro*, opposite, has pastas and salads from $8.50 and mains from $13.50. The welcoming *Blues Cafe* at No 57 does huge vegetarian meals for around $7 – good cakes, too. The *Paragon* at No 65 is an Art Deco masterpiece serving delicious cakes and sweets. The rear cocktail bar looks like it belongs on a 1930s ocean liner.

Up the top end of Katoomba St, *Woodstack* at No 8 is good for coffee and snacks and promises not to persecute smokers. *La Samosa*, next door, is an out-there Indian cafe specialising in vegetarian and organic food.

Pins & Noodles at No 189, serves interesting Asian-inspired noodle dishes from $6.50. *Parakeet* at No 195 is a sociable cafe with breakfasts from 8 am, meals for around $8.50 and acoustic music on weekends. *Tris Elies* is a Greek restaurant next to the train station. It's a good place for a grill or moussaka; weekend entertainment ranges from

bazouki to belly dancing. The relaxed and quaintly eccentric *Avalon* is upstairs at 98 Main St. It's a lovely place for dinner (Wednesday to Sunday), with tasty mains from about $10.

54 Waratah, at (you'll never guess) 54 Waratah St, is one for the foodies – mains are $19.

Getting Around

Bus The Blue Mountains Bus Company (☎ 4782 4213) runs a service between Katoomba train station, the Three Sisters Motel (five minutes walk from Echo Point), and the Scenic Railway and Scenic Skyway. There's a bus roughly every 45 minutes. Mountainlink (☎ 4782 3333) runs a service between Echo Point and Gordon Falls via Katoomba St and Leura Mall. There are roughly two services an hour midweek, less on weekends.

On weekends and public holidays, the hop-on/hop-off Blue Mountains Explorer Bus (☎ 4782 4807) does an hourly circuit of 18 attractions in the Katoomba and Leura area. The easiest place to catch the bus is Katoomba train station; tickets cost $16.

Bicycle You can hire mountain bikes at the YHA hostel and Cycletech, 3 Gang Gang St, for $20 a day. Better bikes are available from Mountain Designs, 190 Katoomba St, for around $15 a half-day. See Activities above for mountain-bike tours.

BLACKHEATH AREA

The little town of Blackheath is a good base for visiting the Grose and Megalong valleys. There are superb lookouts a few kilometres east of the town, such as **Govetts Leap** and **Evan's Lookout**. To the north-east, via Hat Hill Rd, are **Pulpit Rock**, **Perry's Lookdown** and **Anvil Rock**.

A cliff-top track leads from Govetts Leap to Pulpit Rock, and there are several walks from Govetts Leap down into the Grose Valley. Get details on the walks from the nearby Heritage Centre. Perrys Lookdown is the beginning of the shortest route (four hours return) to the beautiful **Blue Gum Forest** in the valley bottom.

The **Megalong Valley**, south of Blackheath, is largely cleared farmland but it's still a beautiful place with fabulous sandstone escarpments. The road down from Blackheath passes through pockets of rainforest and you can get a taste of the beauty of the Blue Mountains by following the 600m Coachwood Glen Nature Trail, which is a couple of kilometres before the small valley settlement of Werribee. There are several horse-riding outfits in the valley, such as Werriberri Trail Rides (☎ 4787 9171), on Megalong Rd. Two-hour rides cost $35.

Blackheath is on the railway line from Sydney, two stops past Katoomba, or a short drive along the Great Western Highway. From Blackheath, it's a 15-minute winding drive into the Megalong Valley via Shipley and Megalong Rds.

Places to Stay & Eat

The nearest NPWS camp site is Acacia Flat, in the Grose Valley near the Blue Gum Forest. It's a steep walk down from Govetts Leap or Perrys Lookdown. You can also camp at Perrys Lookdown, which has a car park and is a convenient base for walks into the Grose Valley.

The *Blackheath Caravan Park* (☎ 4787 8101) has tent sites from $7 and vans from $31. It's on Prince Edward St, off Govetts Leap Rd, about 500m from the Great Western Highway.

The cosy *Gardners Inn* (☎ 4787 8347), on the Great Western Highway in Blackheath, is the oldest hotel in the Blue Mountains (1831). It charges $20 per person midweek and $25 on weekends. There are cheap bar meals here (try roast on a roll for $3), a bistro, and a more upmarket steakhouse.

The *Lakeview Holiday Park* (☎ 4787 8534), 63 Prince Edward St, has cabins with en-suite for $45 a double midweek and $50 on weekends.

The *Wattle Cafe*, on the corner of the Great Western Highway and Govetts Leap Rd, has meals for $7 and a wood-heater to warm yourself by. The *Piedmont Inn*, on the highway near Gardners Inn, has pizzas and fettucine for under $9.

MT VICTORIA & HARTLEY

A few kilometres west of Blackheath is the pretty National Trust classified town of Mt Victoria. The museum at the train station is open on weekends and school holidays between 2 and 5 pm. Interesting buildings include the Victoria & Albert guesthouse, the 1849 tollkeeper's cottage and the 1870s church.

The *Mt Vic Flicks* (☎ 4787 1577) is a lovely little cinema on Harley Ave, near the Victoria & Albert guesthouse. Movies ($7) are shown from Thursday to Sunday and there are various meal and movie tickets in conjunction with restaurants in the area for around $20.

Off the highway at **Mt York** is a memorial to the explorers who first crossed the Blue Mountains. A short stretch of the original road crosses the mountains here.

About 11km past Mt Victoria, on the western slopes of the range, is the tiny, sandstone ghost town of **Hartley**, which flourished from the 1830s but declined when it was bypassed by the railway in 1887. There are several buildings of historic interest, including the 1837 courthouse and a quaint church and presbytery. There's a NPWS information centre (☎ 6355 2117) in the Farmers Inn in the centre of town. It's open daily between 10 am and 4.30 pm (closed between 1 and 2 pm) and tours of the town and courthouse run from here.

Places to Stay

The *Imperial Hotel* (☎ 4787 1233) on the Great Western Highway in Mt Victoria is a Blue Mountains institution. It's a fine old hotel, with expensive dorm beds for $27 and singles/doubles from $49/78 midweek all including breakfast. It has a coffee shop with snacks and light meals, and a bistro.

Nearby, the *Victoria & Albert* (☎ 4787 1241), 19 Station St, is a lovely guesthouse that could be straight out of an Agatha Christie mystery. It offers B&B from $45 per person midweek. The stately *Manor House*

(☎ 4787 1369) on Montgomery St also has B&B from $49 per person midweek.

JENOLAN CAVES
South-west of Katoomba, on the north-western fringe of the Kanangra-Boyd National Park, are the Jenolan Caves (☎ 6359 3311), the best-known limestone caves in Australia. One cave has been open to the public since 1867, although parts of the system are still unexplored. Three 'arches' are open for independent viewing, but you can visit the caves by guided tour only. Tours run from about 9.30 am to 5 pm plus there's a ghost tour on Saturday at 8 pm. Tours last between one and two hours, and prices vary from $12 to $20.

Places to Stay
You can camp near Jenolan Caves House for $10 per site. There's decent dorm accommodation at the *Gatehouse* (☎ 6359 3042) for $15 ($20 on weekends). Ask in Trails Cafe. *Binda Bush Cabins* (☎ 6359 3311) is on the road from Hartley, about 8km north of the caves, and accommodates six people in bunks for $75 per night midweek and $90 on weekends and school holidays. *Jenolan Caves House* (☎ 6359 3322) has dinner, B&B packages from $195 a double midweek.

Getting There & Away
The caves are on plenty of tour itineraries from Sydney and Katoomba. By car, turn off the Great Western Highway at Hartley and they're a 45-minute drive along Jenolan Caves Rd. Parking costs $2. The Six Foot Track from Katoomba to Jenolan Caves is a fairly easy three-day walk, but make sure you get information from an NPWS visitor centre.

BELLS LINE OF ROAD
This back road between Richmond and Lithgow is the most scenic route across the Blue Mountains. It's highly recommended if you have your own transport. There are fine views towards the coast from Kurrajong Heights on the eastern slopes of the range,

orchards around Bilpin, and sandstone cliff and bush scenery all the way to Lithgow.

There are grass skiing and karting at **Kurrajong Heights Grass Ski Park** on weekends for $15 for two hours. Roughly midway between Richmond and Lithgow is the exquisite **Mt Tomah Botanic Gardens**, the cool-climate annexe of Sydney's Royal Botanic Gardens. It's open daily ($5 per car, $2 for pedestrians); late October and late April are the most spectacular times to visit.

North of the Bells Line of Road is the quaint town of **Mt Wilson**, which has formal gardens and a nearby remnant of rainforest known as the **Cathedral of Ferns**. The **Zig Zag Railway** is at Clarence, 10km east of Lithgow. It was built in 1869 and was quite an engineering wonder in its day. Trains used to descend from the Blue Mountains by this route until 1910, when a series of tunnels made the line redundant. A section has been restored and several steam trains run daily. The fare is $12. Call ☎ 6351 4826 for time-table information.

North Coast

The popular NSW north coast has excellent beaches, and several national parks offering wildlife, superb scenery and challenging bushwalks, including the 14-day Great North Walk, which runs from Newcastle to Sydney: contact tourist offices and the Department of Land & Water Conservation (☎ 9228 6315; fax 9221 5980) for details.

The Pacific Highway runs north along the narrow coastal strip into Queensland, passing a string of resorts, including Byron Bay – a surfing mecca and an established travellers' haunt. Scenic roads lead inland into the Great Dividing Range and onto the New England tableland.

SYDNEY TO NEWCASTLE
The area between Broken Bay and Newcastle is known as the Central Coast. It's a densely populated area of rampant suburban

housing, superb beaches, inland waterways and national parks.

The largest town in the area is **Gosford**, an undistinguished settlement on the shores of Brisbane Water, some 85km north of Sydney. It's easily accessible by train from Sydney and Newcastle. A visitor information centre (☎ 4325 2835) is open daily at 200 Mann St, near the train station. Gosford makes a sensible base from which to explore the region if you don't have transport because bus services radiate from here. The *Gosford Hotel* (☎ 4324 1634) on the corner of Mann and Erina Sts has singles/doubles from $30/40.

Brisbane Water National Park (☎ 4324 4911), a few kilometres south-east of Gosford, includes the northern inlets of the Hawkesbury River. It has good bushwalking, Aboriginal engravings, and is renowned for its spring wildflowers. The **Bouddi National Park** extends north along the coast from the mouth of Brisbane Water and offers excellent coastal bushwalking.

There are several beach and river-side towns worth exploring. One of the best is the National Trust classified township of **Pearl Beach**, south of Gosford on the eastern edge of the Brisbane Water National Park. It's a heavenly enclave with a lovely beach and spectacular views. The most attractive of the Central Coast beach resorts is **Terrigal**, 12km east of Gosford. The *Terrigal Beach Backpackers Lodge* (☎ 4385 3330), 10 Campbell Crescent, is one block from the beach and has a five-backpack rating. Dorms cost $17, singles $35 and doubles $42. The small township of **Brooklyn**, on the banks of the Hawkesbury, is a calm backwater offering fishing, boating, kayaking tours and bushwalking. The helpful visitors centre on Bridge St (at the rear of the cafe) has a wealth of information on accommodation and activities in the area.

Further north is a series of large saltwater lakes, including **Tuggerah Lake**, which offer fine boating and fishing opportunities. Further north again, and just south of Newcastle, is **Lake Macquarie**, Australia's biggest saltwater lake. It's a popular centre for sailing, water-skiing and fishing. The Lake Macquarie visitor centre (☎ 4972 1172) is on the Pacific Highway just north of Swansea.

The Sydney to Newcastle freeway is the major road link between the two cities, but it skirts the Central Coast. If you want to explore this area, it's best to take the Pacific Highway between Gosford and Newcastle. You can reach the southern part of the Central Coast from Sydney's Palm Beach by catching the thrice-daily ferry to Patonga. There are two buses from Patonga to Gosford on weekdays run by Busways (☎ 4368 2277); it costs $3.

NEWCASTLE (pop 270,300)

Newcastle, 167km north of Sydney at the mouth of the Hunter River, is the state's second-largest city and one of Australia's largest ports. It's a major industrial and commercial centre, the export port for the Hunter Valley coalfields and for grain from the north-west.

For many, Newcastle conjures up images of belching smokestacks. It's an image that locals resent, and quite rightly. Newcastle is a relaxed and friendly place. The city centre has wide, leafy streets and some fine early colonial buildings. There are clean surf beaches only a few hundred metres away.

Originally named Coal River, the city was founded in 1804 as a place for the most intractable of Sydney's convicts and was known as the 'hell of New South Wales'. The breakwater out to Nobbys Head, with its lighthouse, was built by convicts. The Bogey Hole, a swimming pool cut into the rock on the ocean's edge below the pleasant King Edward Park, was built for Major Morriset, a strict disciplinarian. It was Australia's first ocean baths and it's still a great place for a dip.

In late 1989, Newcastle suffered Australia's most destructive recorded earthquake, with 12 people killed and severe property damage. The props and scaffolding are disappearing, but in mid-1997 Newcastle was struck another blow when BHP announced it was to cease steel-making, with

NEW SOUTH WALES

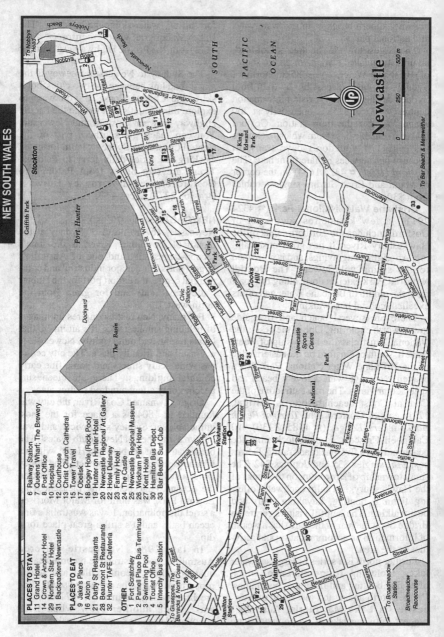

Newcastle

PLACES TO STAY
11 Grand Hotel
14 Crown & Anchor Hotel
29 Northern Star Hotel
31 Backpackers Newcastle

PLACES TO EAT
9 Jake's Place
16 Alcron
21 Darby St Restaurants
28 Beaumont St Restaurants
32 Hunter TAFE Cafeteria

OTHER
1 Fort Scratchley
2 Parnell Place Bus Terminus
3 Swimming Pool
4 Tourist Office
5 Intercity Bus Station

6 Railway Station
7 Queens Wharf; The Brewery
8 Post Office
10 Hospital
12 Courthouse
13 Christ Church Cathedral
15 Tower Travel
17 Obelisk
18 Bogey Hole (Rock Pool)
19 Hunter on Hunter Hotel
20 Newcastle Regional Art Gallery
22 Hotel Delaney
23 Family Hotel
24 The Castle
25 Newcastle Regional Museum
26 Wickham Park Hotel
27 Kent Hotel
30 Hamilton Bus Depot
33 Bar Beach Surf Club

the loss of more than 2500 jobs. Still, spirits lifted when the Newcastle Knights won the 1997 NSW rugby-league premiership.

Orientation

The city centre is a peninsula bordered by the ocean on one side and the Hunter River on the other. It tapers down to the long sandspit leading to Nobbys Head. Hunter St is the 3km-long main street, forming a pedestrian mall between Newcomen and Perkins Sts.

The train station, the long-distance bus stop, the post office, banks and some fine old buildings are at the north-eastern end of the city centre. Cooks Hill rises steeply behind the centre and offers good views. Apart from checking out the sights, there's not a lot to do in the city centre. Most travellers head for the lively inner western suburb of Hamilton, centred on Beaumont St.

There are good views over Newcastle's industrial landscape from Queens Wharf Tower and 360° views from the obelisk above King Edward Park.

Just across the river from the city centre is Stockton, a modest suburb with beaches and good views back to Newcastle city. It's minutes from the city by ferry but by road you have to wind through the docks and some dramatic industrial landscapes, a trip of about 20km.

Information

The tourist office (☎ 4929 9299) occupies the Old Stationmaster's Cottage (built 1858) at 92 Scott St, just beyond the station. It's open weekdays from 9 am to 5 pm and weekends from 10 am to 3.30 pm. It sells excellent heritage-walk maps.

Pepperina bookshop in Bolton St, 50m north of the Grand Hotel, is open daily. There's a left-luggage office at the train station, near the Watt St entrance ($1.50 per item). There is a laundrette (open daily) in Cleary St, just off Beaumont St near the Kent Hotel.

Things to See & Do

The **Newcastle Regional Museum** at 787 Hunter St, Newcastle West, is open Tuesday

to Sunday 10 am to 5 pm and daily in school holidays (admission is free). It includes the Supernova hands-on science display and hosts temporary exhibitions. The **Fort Scratchley Military & Maritime Museum** is open Tuesday to Sunday from noon to 4 pm (admission is free). The tunnels under the fort are said to run all the way to King Edward Park.

The **Newcastle Regional Art Gallery** is on Laman St next to Civic Park. The collection isn't extensive, but there are some decent pieces by Brett Whiteley and some excellent drawings and paintings by Lloyd Rees and Grace Cossington Smith. Entry is by donation and it's open Tuesday to Sunday, 10 am to 5 pm.

Blackbutt Reserve (☎ 4952 1449) is a 182-hectare bushland reserve at New Lambton Heights, approximately 10km south-west of the centre. It has bushwalks and aviaries, wildlife enclosures and fern houses. It also has a koala enclosure. It's open daily from 10 am to 5 pm (admission is free). Bus Nos 232 and 363 run past the upper entrance, Nos 216 and 217 past the lower. To allow yourself plenty of time, it may be worth getting an all-day pass ($6).

About 10km west of the centre near Sandgate train station, the **Shortlands Wetlands Centre** (☎ 4951 6466) on the edge of Hexham Swamp has lots of birdlife as well as walks and canoe trails. It's open daily from 9 am to 5 pm (admission is by a $2 donation).

Surf Beaches Newcastle's favourite surfing son is former world champ Mark Richards, and many come to seek out the breaks where Richards cut his teeth. The main beach, **Newcastle Beach**, is just a couple of minutes walk from the city centre. It has an ocean pool and good surf. Just north of here is **Nobbys Beach**, more sheltered from the southerlies and often open when other beaches are closed. At the northern end of Nobbys is a fast left-hander known as The Wedge. The most popular surfing break is about 5km south at **Bar Beach**, and it's floodlit at night in summer. Nearby,

Merewether Beach has two huge pools. Bus 207 from the Parnell St terminus in the city runs to Merewether Beach every half-hour via Bar Beach.

Organised Tours
The *William the Fourth*, a replica of an old steamship, leaves Merewether St Wharf at 11 am and 2 pm on the third Sunday of the month ($20/10/5 families/adults/children) for cruises on the harbour. Newcastle's Famous Tram departs from the Newcastle train station on the hour from 10 am till 3pm daily. The 45-minute tour of Newcastle's historic sites with commentary costs $10/5 for adults/children.

Special Events
Beaumont St hosts a Jazz & Arts Fair in March, and August sees the Newcastle Jazz Festival and the Newcastle Fringe Festival.

Places to Stay
Camping *Stockton Beach Caravan Park* (☎ 4928 1393) is on the beach at Pitt St, Stockton. Stockton is handy by ferry but it's 20km away by road. Tent sites are $12/15 a double (unpowered/powered) and on-site cabins start at $40. There are several caravan parks south of Newcastle, around Belmont and on the ocean at Redhead Beach.

Hostels *Backpackers Newcastle* (☎ 4969 3436) occupies a couple of fine old weatherboard houses at 42-44 Denison St, Hamilton. It's clean and friendly and near an interesting part of town. Backpacker accommodation at No 42 has dorm beds for $14 and doubles for $28, while No 44 is more upmarket with doubles for $36. Each house has a communal lounge and kitchen. Use of surfboards is free and one of the owners is a keen surfer who gives lessons. Hamilton is several kilometres from the city centre, but you can phone for a free pick-up from town. Otherwise, any bus heading out of town along Hunter St can drop you off nearby.

Hotels The *Crown & Anchor* (☎ 4929 1027) on the corner of Hunter and Perkins Sts has bright singles/doubles for $28/38 (rates are negotiable if you're in town for a few nights). The *Grand Hotel* (☎ 4929 3489) is an old pub on the corner of Bolton and Church Sts, across from the courthouse, hence the lawyers propping up the front bar. Rooms start at $50 (with TV and en-suite).

Motels The *Northern Star Hotel* (☎ 4961 1087), 112 Beaumont St, has motel-style singles for $40/50 without/with en-suite and doubles with en-suite for $64. There's a string of cheaper motels along the Pacific Highway at Belmont, about 15km south of town.

Places to Eat
During school term, the best deal in town is at *Hunter TAFE College* on Parry St. The cafeteria, operated by the college's catering and hospitality school, offers main courses for $3.50 and desserts for $1.50. Opening times vary. The owners of Backpackers Newcastle can tell you when it's open.

Beaumont St has the greatest concentration and variety of restaurants. If it's Italian you're after, try *Dolomiti Gelato*, *Caffé Giannotti* or *Trieste*. A little way north and around the corner in Maitland Rd (the Pacific Highway) is *Giuseppes*, one of the Hunter region's best Italian restaurants; pizzas and pastas start from $4.70. Back on Beaumont St, the *Anatolia* Turkish restaurant offers top value with most meals under $10.

Newcastle's other main restaurant strip is closer to the city on Darby St, south of King St. The choices include Vietnamese (*Lan's*), Thai (*Al-Oi*), Malaysian (*Rumah Malaysia*) and Indian (*Taj Takeaway*). *Splash* has fish & chips and *Goldberg's Coffee House* serves great cakes and brews a mean coffee.

There are several good places for snacks and meals at the eastern end of town. *Jake's Place* in Pacific St has good coffee, and pasta dishes from $5. *Simon's* on the corner of Bolton and King Sts is a good place for breakfasts, but the coffee's lame.

If you feel like a blow-out, *Alcron* (☎ 4929 2423) at 113 Church St is perhaps the oldest restaurant in Australia and has fine views. Main courses range from $18 to $23.

Entertainment

Newcastle has a busy home-grown music scene, with live bands playing somewhere every night except Monday and Tuesday. There are gig guides in Thursday's *Newcastle Herald* or the weekly *Newcastle Post*, published on Wednesday. The *Cambridge Hotel* is over Wood St from the Regional Museum. It was the home pub of top Aussie bands Screaming Jets and silverchair but was closed for renovations at the time of writing. It may have reopened by the time you read this. The *Hunter on Hunter*, at 417 Hunter St, is a regular live venue and the *Family Hotel*, on the corner of Hunter and Steel Sts, has blues.

The *Kent Hotel* and the *Northern Star Hotel*, both on Beaumont St, have jazz. At 139 Maitland Rd, not far from the end of Beaumont St, is the *Barracks*, an affable pub and Newcastle's main gay venue. South-east of the Barracks, at 61 Maitland Rd, is the *Wickham Park Hotel* – popular with kd lang fans.

The *Hotel Delaney* is a relaxed little pub on the corner of Darby and Council Sts, with music most nights, and the *Brewery* at Queens Wharf is popular and brews its own.

The *Castle*, on the corner of King and Steel Sts, is Newcastle's top dance club, with techno and R&B upstairs and live bands downstairs. It's open Wednesday to Saturday, 8 pm to 3 am (5 am Friday and Saturday nights). The door charge ranges from $3 to $6.

Getting There & Away

Air Aeropelican (☎ 4945 0988) flies several times a day from Sydney to Belmont airport, south of Newcastle. The cheapest one-way fare is $42.

Sydney Harbour Seaplanes (☎ 1800 803 558) flies between Rose Bay in Sydney and Newcastle (pulling up on the harbour between Queens and Merewether St wharves). There are four flights in each direction from Monday to Friday (adults $100/190 single/return, children $50/90). Eastern Australia Airlines (☎ 13 1313) has daily flights to Sydney ($65), while Impulse

flies between Newcastle and Port Macquarie ($153), Coffs Harbour ($201) and Brisbane ($283). Impulse's 14-day advance fares are considerably cheaper: call the airline. Eastern and Impulse use the airport at Williamtown, north of Newcastle.

Bus Between Sydney and Newcastle you're better off taking the train, but heading up the coast from Newcastle buses offer a much better service. Nearly all long-distance buses stop on Watt St near the train station. Cheapish fares from Newcastle include: Sydney $24, Port Macquarie $36, Byron Bay $62, Brisbane $63. Jayes Travel (☎ 4926 2000) at 285 Hunter St, near Darby St, and Tower Travel (☎ 4926 3199) at 245 Hunter St, on the corner of Crown St, can help with bookings.

Train Sydney suburban trains run from Central Station to Newcastle about 20 times a day, taking nearly three hours. The one-way fare is $14.20; an off-peak return is $17.

Other trains heading north on the lines to Armidale and Murwillumbah bypass central Newcastle, stopping at suburban Broadmeadow – just west of Hamilton. Frequent buses run from here to the city centre. An XPT from Central Station to Broadmeadow takes about 2¼ hours and costs $21.

Car Rental As well as the regular places, you can hire used cars from places such as Cheep Heep (☎ 4961 3144) at 107 Tudor St, Hamilton, from $29 a day, including insurance.

Getting Around

To/From the Airport Port Stephens Buses (☎ 4982 2940) stop at Williamtown airport on the run to Nelson Bay. The trip takes 35 minutes and costs $4.20. Local buses Nos 348, 349, 350 or 358 stop outside Belmont airport (one hour, $3.60).

Taxis from Williamtown airport to the city centre cost around $32, from Belmont airport to the city centre around $27.

Bus STA buses cover Newcastle and the eastern side of Lake Macquarie. There are fare deals similar to those on offer in Sydney. An all-day pass costs $6 ($3 concession) and is valid on STA buses and ferries. Most services operate every half-hour. The bus information booth at the west end of the mall, on the corner of Perkins St, has timetables. If it's closed, call the Travel Information Centre (☎ 4961 8933) between 8.30 am and 4.30 pm or pop into the Hamilton bus depot.

Ferry There are ferries to Stockton from Queens Wharf approximately half-hourly, Monday to Thursday from 5.15 am to 11 pm. On Friday and Saturday they run until midnight and on Sunday they stop at 10 pm. The ferry terminus on Queens Wharf has a timetable. Fares cost $1.30/65c adults/children one way.

Bicycle Bike-hire places come and go – the tourist office or the owners of Backpackers Newcastle will know if one is operating.

HUNTER VALLEY

The Hunter Valley has two curiously diverse products – coal and wine. The centre of the valley vineyards is the Pokolbin area near Cessnock and some wineries date from the 1860s. You'll find many of Australia's best-known wine names here.

On the southern side of the valley rise the sandstone ranges of the Wollemi and Goulburn River national parks; the northern side is bordered by the high, rugged ranges leading up to Barrington Tops National Park.

The main road through the Hunter Valley is the New England Highway running north-west from Newcastle and climbing up to the New England tablelands near Murrurundi. The 300km-long Hunter River comes from further west and doesn't meet the highway until Singleton. The valley is wide in the Lower Hunter area, where you'll find most of the wineries. It narrows upstream from Singleton.

There are more than 50 vineyards in the Lower Hunter, and seven more in the Upper Hunter. Generally they're open daily for tastings and sales, with slightly reduced hours

on Sunday. Many have picnic and barbecue facilities.

Organised Tours

Hunter Vineyard Tours (☎ 4991 1659) has daily departures from Newcastle and other Hunter centres for $29 ($45 with lunch). Hunter Valley Day Tours (☎ 4938 5031) runs an award-winning Wine & Cheese Tasting Tour with free hotel pick-ups in the Lower Hunter region for $70. Grapemobile (☎ 4991 2339) offers two-day bike rides through the wineries, with a support bus, accommodation and all meals for $160 per person. It also has day tours and bike hire for $25/15 for a day/half-day. For tours of the Upper Hunter, contact the Scone or Denman information centres.

Lower Hunter Wineries

The valley's wine-growing heartland is the rolling hill country north-west of **Cessnock**. The efficient Cessnock Visitor Information Centre (☎ 4990 4477) is the place to go for maps and brochures before you set out on a winery tour. It's on Aberdare Rd, on the way into town from Sydney, and is open daily from 9 am to 5 pm.

Several wineries run tours, including McWilliams (daily at 11 am and 2 pm, $2 per person); Hunter Estate (daily at 9.30 am); McGuigan Bros (daily at noon); Tyrrells (daily at 1.30 pm) and Rothbury Estate (weekends at 11 am and 2 pm).

Places to Stay Cessnock is the main town and accommodation centre for the vineyards, although there is also pub accommodation in nearby Neath and Bellbird. Almost all places offering accommodation charge more at weekends and you might have to take a package (meals included). Cessnock's information centre can book accommodation.

There are a couple of caravan parks close to Cessnock. The *Valley View* (☎ 4990 2573) on Mount View Rd has tent sites for $5 per person, on-site vans from $25 and cabins from $40. *Cessnock Park* (☎ 4990 5819) off Allandale Rd north of Cessnock has sites for

$12, on-site vans from $30 and cabins from $48.

There is no hostel accommodation in Cessnock, but there are some good deals at the pubs. The *Black Opal Hotel* (☎ 4990 1070) at the southern end of Vincent St, the main shopping street, charges from $20 per person Monday to Thursday, and $25 Friday to Sunday. The *Wentworth Hotel* (☎ 4990 1364) at 36 Vincent St has rooms for $25 per person with breakfast.

Midweek motel prices include $55 to $85 for doubles at the *Cessnock Motel* (☎ 4990 2699) and $55 at the *Hunter Valley Motel* (☎ 4990 1722), both on Allandale Rd. Prices at these and other motels rise steeply at weekends.

There's a lot of accommodation out among the vineyards. Most charge well over $100 a night on weekends, but midweek there are a few places charging around $85 a double, including the *Hunter Country Lodge* (☎ 4938 1744) about 12km north of Cessnock on Branxton Rd, and *Belford Country Cabins* (☎ 6574 7100) on Hermitage Rd north of the Hunter Estate.

Upper Hunter Wineries
The nearest town to the Upper Hunter wineries is **Denman**, a sleepy little place 25km south-west of Muswellbrook.

The Upper Hunter has fewer wineries, but it's worth visiting because the pace is slower and the scenery more beautiful than the Lower Hunter. The area's information centre (☎ 6547 2731) is on Denman's main street at the *Old Carriage Restaurant*, a cafe/restaurant in an old railway carriage. As well as the plentiful accommodation in nearby Muswellbrook and Singleton, there is camping, pub, motel and B&B accommodation in and around Denman.

The New England Highway runs up the Hunter Valley through some old towns and attractive scenery. The **Goulburn River National Park** at the upper end of the valley follows the river as it cuts through sandstone gorges. This was the route used by Aboriginal people travelling from the plains to the sea and the area is rich in cave art and other

sites. You can camp but there are no facilities. Access is from Sandy Hollow (near Denman) or Merriwa (on the Denman to Gulgong road). The Muswellbrook NPWS office (☎ 6541 4144) on the corner of Francis and Maitland Sts has information.

Maitland An old coal-mining centre, Maitland is now a sprawling town with a population of 50,000. Established as a convict settlement in 1818 at one time, along with Sydney and Parramatta, it was among Australia's main settlements. At various times Maitland has been home to politicians (HV 'Doc' Evatt and Cheryl Kernot), theatrical folk (John Bell, Nick Enright and Ruth Cracknell), and a famous boxer (Les Darcy).

The information centre (☎ 4933 2611) on the corner of the New England Highway and High St has a couple of good heritage walk maps. There are frequent trains between Maitland and Newcastle.

High St follows the winding route of the original track through town and part of it is now the **Heritage Mall**. **Brough House** on Church St houses the art gallery, and its neighbour, **Grossman House**, is the local history museum (open weekends).

The renovated *Imperial Hotel* (☎ 4938 6566) at 458 High St has singles/doubles for $32/46 with a self-service breakfast.

Singleton Founded in 1820, the coal-mining town of Singleton (pop 12,500) is one of the oldest towns in the state. The **Singleton Historical Museum** (☎ 4972 1159) in Burdekin Park is housed in the old lock-up (jail), built in 1862. It's open on Sunday and public holidays by appointment. In the centre of town is the southern hemisphere's largest sundial (God knows why!).

The old *Caledonian Hotel* (☎ 6572 1356) on the highway near the town centre has accommodation.

Muswellbrook Like other Hunter Valley towns, Muswellbrook (pop 10,500) was founded early in Australia's white history and has some interesting old buildings, surrounded by spreading residential areas.

Historic *Eatons Hotel* (☎ 6543 2403) on the highway at the northern end of town charges $20/30 a single/double. It may be historic, but the clatter of gaming machines in the front bar and the betting-slip confetti on the floor dampen its appeal.

Scone With over 40 horse studs in the area, Scone dubs itself 'the horse capital of Australia'. Horse Week is held annually in May. You can arrange to visit studs ($3.50 per person) at the information centre (☎ 6545 1526), open daily on the northern-side of town.

There are a few pubs on Kelly St, the main street, offering accommodation, but none are particularly good value. You could try the *Belmore Hotel* (☎ 6545 1526) with singles/doubles for $26/35, or the *Golden Fleece Hotel* (☎ 6545 13577) on the corner of Kelly and Liverpool Sts. *Airlie House Motor Inn* (☎ 6545 1488) has standard motel rooms with singles/doubles starting from $69/79.

Your best bet is the rural *Scone Youth Hostel* (☎ 6545 2072) in the old school house at Segenhoe, 10km east of town. Dorm beds in this historic building are $13, doubles are $28 and family rooms $40. The owners will pick you up from Scone ($2), or you can catch the school bus (50c) at 3.20 pm from the high school.

The butcher opposite the Belmore Hotel in Kelly St sells fantastic meat pies.

At **Burning Mountain**, off the highway 20km north of Scone, a coal seam has been burning for over 5000 years.

Getting There & Around

Trains run from Sydney up the Hunter Valley en route to Armidale and Moree. Batterhams Express (☎ 1800 043 339) runs between Sydney and Tamworth via Cessnock ($22) and Scone ($35) twice a day, Monday to Friday. Rover Motors (☎ 4990 1699) runs between Newcastle and Cessnock ($8.30) frequently on weekdays, less often on Saturday and not at all on Sunday. Sid Fogg's (☎ 1800 045 952) runs up the valley on its route from Newcastle to Dubbo.

There's an interesting back route (with some unsealed roads) between Sydney and the Lower Hunter from Wisemans Ferry, passing through the pretty township of Wollombi, which has a small pub and a couple of accommodation possibilities. A great drive from Sydney to the Upper Hunter is on the Windsor to Singleton road, known as the Putty Road.

You can hire bicycles from Grapemobile (see Organised Tours earlier in this section).

NEWCASTLE TO PORT MACQUARIE
Port Stephens

This huge sheltered bay is about an hour's drive north of Newcastle. The bay, which occupies a submerged valley, stretches more than 20km inland. It's a popular boating and fishing spot, and is well-known for its resident **dolphins**. The bay is surrounded by bushland, and there is a sizeable **koala colony** living at Lemon Tree Passage, on the south side. There is a road to Lemon Tree Passage from the town of Salt Ash.

Development around Port Stephens is confined largely to the Tomaree Peninsula, which forms much of the southern shore. The main town, **Nelson Bay** (pop 7000), has an information centre (☎ 4981 1579, 1800 808 900) near the marina. Nearby, **Shoal Bay** has a long, sheltered beach and is a short walk from surf at Zenith Beach.

Back down the Tomaree Peninsula from Nelson Bay is the small resort town of **Anna Bay**, with good surf beaches nearby. Stockton Bight stretches 35km from Anna Bay to Newcastle, backed by the longest dune in the southern hemisphere.

Opposite Nelson Bay on the northern side of Port Stephens are the small resort settlements of **Tea Gardens** and **Hawks Nest** at the mouth of the Myall River.

Places to Stay There's a YHA hostel in the *Shoal Bay Motel* (☎ 4984 2315) on the beachfront road. Dorm beds are $17 and there are doubles for $36 per person (minimum two people); these rates can rise during school holidays.

The *Seabreeze Hotel* (☎ 4981 1511), just uphill from the information centre, has beds in comfortable, modern dorms for $20. Cooked breakfast is $9.90.

Samurai Beach Bungalows (☎ 4982 1921), just east of Anna Bay on the corner of Frost Rd and Robert Connell Close, offers an opportunity for backpackers to go bush. The bungalows are dotted Asian-style around a covered communal kitchen area. Dorm beds are $15 and doubles $40 to $65. There's free use of surfboards and bicycles. Buses from Newcastle run past the door.

Hawks Nest Beach Caravan Park (☎ 4997 0239) has just a narrow band of bush separating it from a good surf beach. Tent sites are $16 a double and cabins start at $40.

Getting There & Away Port Stephens Coaches (☎ 1800 045 949) has a daily service to Sydney ($22) and there are plenty of buses to Newcastle ($7.60). If you're heading north up the coast, it's easier to backtrack to Newcastle and catch a long-distance bus from there. Great Lakes Coaches (☎ 1800 043 263) has a daily service from Newcastle to Tea Gardens for $13.60.

Getting Around Port Stephens Ferries operates between Nelson Bay and Tea Gardens three times a day (one hour, adults/children $16/9 return).

Barrington Tops National Park
Barrington Tops is a World Heritage wilderness area centred on the rugged Barrington Plateau, which rises to almost 1600m around Mt Barrington and Carey's Peak. The lower reaches of the park are covered by rainforest, while the slopes in-between are dominated by ancient, moss-covered Antarctic beech forest. There are good walking trails, but be prepared for snow in winter and cold snaps at any time. Drinking water must be boiled. Hunter Valley Day Tours (☎ 4938 5031) runs eco-tours to Barrington Tops.

Places to Stay Camping is permitted at a number of sites. The main one is the Gloucester River Camping Area, which is 31km from the Gloucester-Stroud road. The

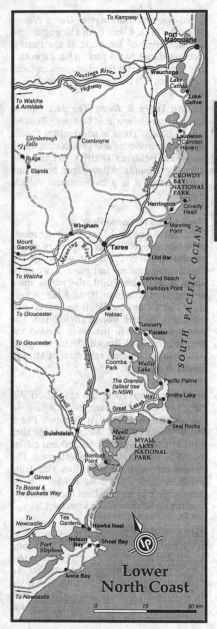

Lower North Coast

award-winning *Barrington Guest House* (☎ 4995 3212), 43km from Dungog on the southern edge of the park, is the nearest accommodation to the park. It has a spectacular setting beneath the plateau escarpment and charges $79 per person with meals.

Getting There & Away The park can be reached from the towns of Dungog, Gloucester and Scone. There is an excellent tourist drive between Scone and Gloucester, which runs past Belltrees (Patrick White's old stamping ground). Allow three hours and don't attempt it in a conventional vehicle after rain.

Myall Lakes National Park

This park is one of the most popular recreation areas in NSW. Its large network of coastal lakes is ideal for water sports. Canoes, windsurfers and runabouts can be hired at **Bombah Point**, the park's main settlement, 11km from Bulahdelah. A car-ferry links Bombah Point to the coastal regions of the park from 8 am to 6 pm. The best beaches are in the north around the township of **Seal Rocks**. There are good walks through coastal rainforest at **Mungo Brush** in the south.

Places to Stay There are several NPWS camp sites around the park, including a good one at Mungo Brush. At Bombah Point, *Myall Shores* (☎ 4997 4495) has tent sites from $18.50, bungalows for $50 and cabins for $70. There's a shop and a restaurant. The owners can organise a minibus ride from Bulahdelah ($5). At Seal Rocks a basic caravan park by an excellent beach has tent sites for $9.50 and on-site vans for $30.

Getting There & Away There is road access to the park from Tea Gardens in the south, from Bulahdelah on the Pacific Highway and from Forster-Tuncurry in the north. You can drive from Tea Gardens to Bulahdelah via the Bombah Point ferry. Seal Rocks is accessible from the Great Lakes Way, a scenic road between Bulahdelah and Forster-

Tuncurry. Great Lakes Coaches (☎ 1800 043 263) services this route.

Forster-Tuncurry (pop 16,000)

Forster-Tuncurry are twin towns on either side of the sea entrance of Wallis Lake. Forster is the larger town and here you'll find the information centre (☎ 6554 8799) on Little St, the lakefront road. As well as the lake there are some excellent sea beaches right in town and many others in the area.

Places to Stay *Forster Beach Caravan Park* (☎ 6554 6269) is right in the centre of town and a short walk from both the lake and the ocean. It has tent sites from $12 to $16 and on-site vans from $33 to $58.

The friendly YHA-affiliated *Dolphin Lodge* (☎ 6555 8155) is at 43 Head St in Forster. Coming from the town centre it's on the left just before the road makes a right-angle turn to the right. It's clean and spacious and has a surf beach virtually at the back door. Dorm beds are $15 and doubles are $34. Boards and bikes are free.

In the off season there are some good deals on motels, with doubles for $35 or less, but around Christmas/January most are expensive – and booked out.

Getting There & Away Forster-Tuncurry is on the Great Lakes Way, which leaves the Pacific Highway near Bulahdelah and rejoins it south of Taree. Great Lakes Coaches (☎ 1800 043 263) runs to Sydney ($38) and Newcastle ($23) daily, while Countrylink operates a combination of bus and train to Sydney twice a day for $41. Greyhound Pioneer (☎ 13 2030) calls in once a day on its Sydney-Brisbane run.

Manning Valley

From Forster-Tuncurry the highway swings inland to **Taree**, a large town serving the farms of the fertile Manning Valley. Further up the valley is the timber town of **Wingham**, where you can visit Wingham Brush, a lovely seven-hectare vestige of the dense rainforest that once covered the valley. Small roads run north from Wingham to

Wauchope, near Port Macquarie, passing through some interesting towns and great scenery around Comboyne.

On the coast near Taree, **Old Bar** is one of several small resorts. **Crowdy Bay National Park** runs up the coast, and there is camping at **Diamond Head** at the northern end of the park. You need to bring your own water.

North of the national park and accessible from the Pacific Highway at Kew, **Camden Haven** is a collection of small towns clustered around the wide sea entrance of Queens Lake. Just north of here the coast road runs past **Lake Cathie** (pronounced cat-eye), both a town and a shallow lake, and then enters the outer suburbs of Port Macquarie.

PORT MACQUARIE (pop 33,700)
One of the larger resorts on the New South Wales north coast, Port Macquarie makes a good stopping point on the journey from Sydney (430km south). It was founded in 1821 and was a convict settlement until 1840.

Port, as it is known, has both a river frontage (the Hastings River enters the sea here) and a series of ocean beaches starting right in the town.

Orientation & Information
The city centre is at the mouth of the Hastings River, and Horton St, the main street, runs down to the water. West of the city centre at the base of the Settlement Point Peninsula is the big Settlement City shopping centre.

The information centre (☎ 1800 025 935) is on Clarence St and is open daily.

Things to See
The **Koala Hospital** is off Lord St about 1km south of the town centre. Convalescent koalas are in outdoor enclosures and you can visit them daily (the best time is from 3 pm, when the koalas are fed). The hospital is in the grounds of **Roto**, a historic homestead open on weekdays from 9 am to 4 pm.

You can meet undamaged koalas and other animals at **Kingfisher Park**, off the Oxley Highway (adults/children $7). **Billabong**

Koala Park is further out, just past the Pacific Highway interchange.

Other than Roto, most surviving old buildings are near the city centre: St Thomas' Church (1828) on William St near Hay St ($1); the Garrison (1830) on the corner of Hay and Clarence Sts; the courthouse (1869) across the road ($2); and the award-winning **museum** (1830) nearby at 22 Clarence St, open Monday to Saturday from 9.30 am to 4.30 pm and Sunday from 1 pm ($4).

An old pilot cottage above Town Beach houses the small **Maritime Museum**, open daily from 10 am to 4 pm ($2). Nearby, a small **observatory** is at the beach end of Lord St. It's open Wednesday and Sunday, at 7.30 pm in winter and 8.15 pm in summer ($2).

Five km south of the town centre on Pacific Drive, **Sea Acres Rainforest Centre** is a 30-hectare flora and fauna reserve protecting a pocket of coastal rainforest. There's an ecology centre with displays and a 1.3km boardwalk. Entry is $8.50 – worth every cent.

A vehicle ferry ($1) operates 24-hours a day across the river at Settlement Point, accessing two roads north. One is a very rough dirt road (4WD required) running along the coast, past Limeburners Creek Nature Reserve to Point Plomer (good surf) and Crescent Head, from where you can rejoin the highway at Kempsey. The second road – slightly better and gravelled – takes a more inland route to meet the Crescent Head-Kempsey road.

Activities
Water sports are top of the activity list. There are some good surf breaks, particularly at Town Beach and Flynns Beach, which is patrolled on weekends and school holidays.

You can hire watercraft at several places on Settlement Point, such as Hastings River Boat Hire (☎ 6583 8811) at Port Marina (powered craft and canoes) and the Settlement Point Boatshed (☎ 6583 6300) next to the ferry departure point. Jordans Boating Centre (☎ 6583 1005) has yachts and windsurfers. Diving is available with Cool 'D' Dive Shop (☎ 6559 7181).

There are plenty of river cruises. The

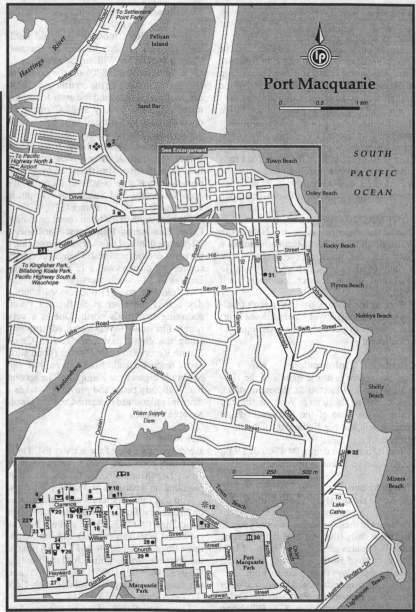

NEW SOUTH WALES

Port Macquarie

To Settlement
Point Ferry

Pelican
Island

Sand Bar

See Enlargement

Town Beach

SOUTH

PACIFIC

OCEAN

Oxley Beach

Rocky Beach

Flynns Beach

Nobbys Beach

Shelly
Beach

Miners
Beach

To
Lake
Cathie

PLACES TO STAY
3   Lindel Port Macquarie Backpackers
6   Port Macquarie Hotel
7   Royal Hotel
9   Sundowner Breakwall Caravan
    Park
11 River Motel
29 Beachside
    Backpackers (YHA)

PLACES TO EAT
10 Toro's Cantina
14 Café Pacific
17 Garrison & Cafes
20 Macquarie Seafoods
22 Fishermen's Co-op
23 Eclipse
26 Yuen Hing

OTHER
1   Settlement City
    Shopping Centre & RSL
2   Port Marina
4   Pilot's Boatshed
5   Post Office
8   Old Courthouse
12 Lookout
13 Observatory
15 Museum
16 Supermarket
18 Information Centre
19 Long-Distance Bus Stop
21 Cruise Departures
24 TC's Nightclub
25 Down Under Nightclub
27 Port Pushbikes
28 Communications Tower
30 Maritime Museum
31 Koala Hospital; Roto Homestead
32 Sea Acres Rainforest Centre

Pelican River Cruise (☎ 018 652 171) puts on a BBQ cruise (Monday to Friday, $28) and a Weekend Explorer cruise (Saturday and Sunday, $15). Both cruises explore the Hastings River and backwaters.

Port Macquarie Camel Safaris (☎ 6583 7650) has beach rides for $22. East Coast Mountain Safaris (☎ 6584 2366) has 4WD tours of the rainforest hinterland, from $35/60 for a half-day/full day.

Places to Stay

Camping The most central caravan park is *Sundowner Breakwall* (☎ 6583 2755) at 1 Munster St, near the river mouth and Town Beach. It has tent sites from $15 and on-site vans from $37. Prices rise sharply during school holidays. There are cheaper places near Flynns Beach and inland along the river or on the Oxley Highway.

Hostels Backpackers have two good hostels to choose from. *Beachside Backpackers* (☎ 6583 5512) is a YHA associate at 40 Church St. Dorm beds are $13. It's clean, friendly and popular and is a short walk from the town centre and the beach. There's free use of bikes and surfboards, and the owners meet the buses. At the time of writing they were constructing family accommodation; call to check their rates.

Lindel Port Macquarie Backpackers (☎ 6583 1791) occupies a beautiful old house beside the Oxley Highway on the way into town. It's clean and well run, with dorm beds for $15 and doubles/twins for $36. They meet buses arriving in town and there are bikes for hire. There's a small pool, and the owner organises regular canoeing and fishing outings.

Hotels & Motels At the northern end of Horton St are the *Port Macquarie Hotel* and the *Royal Hotel*. The reception desk at the Port Macquarie (☎ 6583 1011) handles accommodation for both. The Port Macquarie has singles/doubles for $30/45 with bathroom, $25/40 without. The Royal has motel-style units overlooking the water costing just $40/50 and pub rooms with bathroom for $30/45. Prices rise at peak times.

There are more than 30 motels. The cheapest, not surprisingly, are the ones farthest from the beaches, such as those on Hastings River Drive. In town, the pleasant *River Motel* (☎ 6583 3744) at 5 Clarence St near the corner of School St has off-season doubles for around $45 to $55. Several nearby holiday apartments have similar deals.

Places to Eat

There are dozens of restaurants and cafes around the city centre, with something to suit every budget.

The *Fishermen's Co-op* near the western end of Clarence St sells seafood straight off the boats. If you want your seafood cooked, *Macquarie Seafoods*, on the corner of Clarence and Short Sts, does great fish & chips.

There's a good choice of Asian food. The *Yuen Hing* on Horton St does cheap lunches. *Dang's*, opposite the old courthouse on Hay St, has Malaysian and Vietnamese dishes.

Toro's Cantina on Murray St is a Mexican place with main courses from $9.50. For breakfast, try the *Café Pacific* on Clarence St, where a cooked breakfast costs $7.50, or *Eclipse*, a small place on Short St near the corner of William St.

Margo's Cafe, in the historic Garrison building on the corner of Hay and Clarence Sts, has tables outside and is a pleasant place for coffee and a snack.

Entertainment

There are three nightclubs in town: *Lachlans*, between the Port Macquarie and Royal hotels, *TC's* on William St and *Down Under* around the corner on Short St. The *RSL* club's big new complex at Settlement City has live bands on Friday and Saturday nights.

Getting There & Away

The Oxley Highway runs west from Port Macquarie through Wauchope and eventually reaches the New England tablelands near Walcha. It's a spectacular drive.

Air Eastern Australia (☎ 13 1313) flies to Sydney at least four times a day for $178 one way. Impulse flies to Sydney for the same fare, as well as to Brisbane ($238 one way) via Coffs Harbour and Coolangatta.

Bus Port Macquarie Bus Service (☎ 6583 2161) runs to Wauchope, 19km inland, several times a day for $6.60. This service stops next to the information centre on Clarence St, as do the long-distance services. Greyhound Pioneer (☎ 13 2030) and McCafferty's (☎ 13 1499) stop in town. Kean's (☎ 1800 625 587) runs to Coffs

Harbour ($20), Bellingen ($25) and Dorrigo ($27), Armidale ($40) and Tamworth ($37).

Train The nearest station is at Wauchope. The fare from Sydney to Port Macquarie ($61.50) includes the connecting Countrylink bus between Wauchope and Port (the train pulls into Wauchope at 1.21 pm).

Getting Around

Port Macquarie Bus Service (☎ 6583 2161) runs buses around the town. There are no super-cheap car-rental outfits, only major rental firms. Budget (☎ 6583 5144) is on the corner of William and Short Sts. Port Pushbikes on Hayward St rents ungeared bikes for $8 a half-day, $15 for a day or $25 for a week.

PORT MACQUARIE TO COFFS HARBOUR

Wauchope (pop 4700)

Nineteen km inland from Port Macquarie and on the Hastings River, Wauchope (pronounced 'war hope') is an old timber town. Wauchope's story is told at **Timbertown**, an interesting working replica of an 1880s town. It's open daily from 9.30 am to 3.30 pm ($16).

Wauchope has a range of accommodation including *Rainbow Ridge Hostel* (☎ 6585 6134), a quiet YHA associate, 10km west of town on the Oxley Highway. Dorm beds are $10 or you can camp for $5.

Kempsey Area

North along the Pacific Highway from Wauchope is **Kempsey** (pop 8600), a large town serving the farms of the Macleay Valley and also the home of the Akubra hat. The information centre (☎ 6563 1555) is off the highway at the southern end of town. Next door is the **Macleay River Historical Museum & Cultural Centre** ($2). There is plenty of accommodation in town, but there's no reason to stick around. There are, however, some good spots on the coast.

Crescent Head, a small town 20km from Kempsey, has a quiet front beach and a surf-washed back beach. The *Crescent Head*

Tourist Park (☎ 6566 0261) is right on the beach and has sites from $12 and cabins from $40, rising to $80 in holidays.

There are plenty of holiday apartments and some can be cheaper than cabins at the caravan park – contact either of the two estate agents on the main street (☎ 6566 0500 or 6566 0306). South of town, **Limeburners Creek Nature Reserve** has walking trails and camp sites.

Stretching up the coast from Crescent Head to Smoky Cape is **Hat Head National Park**. Within the park is the quiet township of **Hat Head**, tucked beneath the headland. It has a beautiful sheltered beach, a few shops, a caravan park and holiday flats. There's a basic camp site in the park south of Hat Head and another camp site at the northern end of the park near the **Smoky Cape Lighthouse**. The lighthouse is open to the public on Thursday (and Tuesday in school holidays) from 10 am to 11.45 am and 1 to 2.45 pm.

The pleasant resort town of **South West Rocks** is near the mouth of the Macleay River. Fishing and water sports are the main attractions. **Trial Bay Gaol** is on the headland 3km east of South West Rocks. This imposing edifice was a prison in the late 19th century and housed German internees during WWI. It's now a museum; open daily ($4). Trial Bay is named after the *Trial*, a brig which was stolen from Sydney by convicts in 1816 and wrecked here.

The gaol is part of the **Arakoon State Recreation Area** (☎ 6566 6168), which also manages the bayside camping area next to the gaol. There are sites right on the water for $10, rising to $25 in school holidays.

Getting Around There are buses from Belgrave St in Kempsey to South West Rocks and to Crescent Head. Kean's (☎ 1800 625 587) operates a service to Crescent Head ($5.40) and South West Rocks ($7.80).

Nambucca Heads (pop 6250)
This quiet resort town has a fine setting overlooking the mouth of the Nambucca

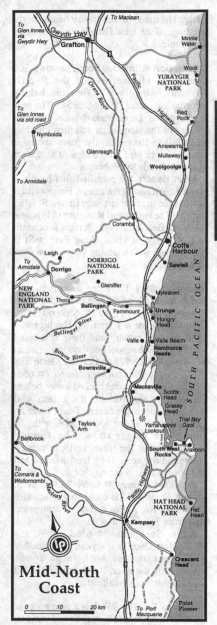

Mid-North Coast

River. The name means 'many bends' in the language of the local Gumbaingeri Aboriginal people.

Orientation & Information The town is a couple of kilometres off the Pacific Highway, where you'll find the helpful information centre (☎ 6568 6954). The road in, Riverside Drive, runs beside the wide estuary of the Nambucca and then climbs a steep hill to Bowra St, the main shopping street. A right turn onto Ridge St at the top of the hill leads to the beaches.

Main Beach, the patrolled surf beach, is about 1.5km east of the centre. Follow Ridge St and take the fork left onto Liston St when it splits. The **Headland Museum** ($1) is near the Main Beach car park. A right fork at the end of Ridge St leads along Parkes St to North Head, with stunning views from **Pilot Lookout**.

Places to Stay There are several caravan parks. As usual, prices rise in holidays. The *Foreshore Caravan Park* (☎ 6568 6014), on Riverside Drive not far from the highway, overlooks the estuary and there is a beach nearby. Outside school holidays tent sites are $11, on-site vans $28 and cabins $36 to $38.

Nambucca Backpackers Hostel (☎ 6568 6360) is a quiet hostel tucked away behind the town at Newman St. It's a 1km walk through bush to the beach. Dorm beds are $15 and doubles are $30 to $38, with discounts for longer stays. The friendly managers meet the buses and can arrange outings in the area. They lend snorkel gear and boogie boards for no charge.

Dunaber House (☎ 6568 9434), at 35 Piggott St, is a B&B close to all facilities. They have two rooms and off-season prices start from $50 for a double.

Scotts Guesthouse (☎ 6568 6386), at 4 Wellington Dve, is a stylish old weatherboard guesthouse with large rooms overlooking the river. It charges $70 to $80 for a double with breakfast.

Places to Eat The *RSL* has a prime site by the river at the foot of Bowra St and turns out some of the cheapest meals in town. The *Golden Sands Hotel* in Bowra St has standard pub meals, and *Midnight Express* behind the pub has a good choice of burgers, including tofu and tempeh burgers. The *V-Wall Tavern* at the end of Wellington Dve serves bistro meals and the views from its balcony over the river-mouth are perfect.

Getting There & Away Most long-distance buses stop on the highway at the Shell service station (southbound) or the Aukaka Caravan Park (northbound). The fare to Sydney with Kirklands is $42, to Byron Bay it's $38.

Newman's (☎ 6568 1296) has four buses a day to Coffs Harbour ($5), while Jessup's (☎ 6653 4552) has a daily bus service on the same route at 7.55 am. Joyce's (☎ 6655 6330) runs from Nambucca to Bellingen ($5). These local services leave from opposite the police station on Bowra St and run only on weekdays.

Nambucca is on the main railway line north from Sydney ($58). The station is about 3km out of town – follow Bowra St north.

Bellingen (pop 2700)
This attractive small town sits on the banks of the Bellinger River just inland from the Pacific Highway about halfway between Nambucca Heads and Coffs Harbour. The turning is north of Urunga. It's a lively country town and a centre for the area's artistic/alternative population. Bellingen Travel (☎ 6655 2055), opposite the post office on the main street, has tourist information.

Things to See & Do The main attraction is the setting in the lush Bellinger Valley. If you have your own transport, there are some great swimming holes to be discovered on the **Never Never River** at the aptly named **Promised Land**, about 10km north of town. Gambaarri Tours (see Coffs Harbour Things to Do) runs a tour of the area.

A huge colony of flying foxes (grey-headed fruit bats) lives on **Bellingen Island**, near the caravan park, from December to March. They're an impressive sight when they head off in their thousands at dusk to feed. The island is a small remnant of subtropical rainforest that once covered the valley. Ridge to Reef (☎ 6655 2382) includes a guided tour of the island in an interesting range of interpretative walks. Platypuses live in the river nearby.

There are plenty of craft shops, including the **Old Butter Factory** on the eastern approach to town. It houses several workshops, a gallery and a cafe. The **Bellingen markets**, held at the park on Church St on the third Saturday of the month, have become a major regional event with more than 250 stalls, live music and other entertainment.

Places to Stay The *Bellingen Caravan Park* (☎ 6655 1338) is across the river – turn onto Wharf St from the main street (the post office is on the corner), cross the bridge and follow the road around to the left, then turn left down Dowle St. You can walk from town.

Bellingen Backpackers (☎ 6655 1116) (also called Belfry Lodge) is a great place to hang out for a few days. It occupies a beautifully renovated weatherboard house overlooking the river on Short St. Dorm beds are $15 and doubles are $32. The pleasant owners will pick you up from Urunga by arrangement. There are bikes for hire ($5 for as long as you stay).

Places to Eat Bellingen has a surprisingly large choice of restaurants for a town of its size. The *Carriageway Cafe*, on the main street, has meals as well as good coffee and cakes. There are several places on Church St, including the *Good Food Shop* with vegetarian takeaways and the laid-back *Cool Creek Cafe* (which also has live music some nights). *Lodge 241*, a cafe cum gallery, at the Dorrigo end of the main street is great for breakfasts and lunches.

Getting There & Away Getting to Bellingen without your own transport can be a bit of a hassle. Kean's (☎ 1800 625 587) stops at

Bellingen on its Port Macquarie-Tamworth run. Jessup's (☎ 6653 4552) operates two services a day to Coffs Harbour – school days only. Buses leave Bellingen at 8 and 9.30 am and Coffs Harbour at 2 and 3.45 pm ($4.50).

Joyce's (☎ 6655 6330) has about three runs a day (fewer in school holidays), weekdays only, between Bellingen and Nambucca Heads ($5). It's difficult to get from Bellingen to Dorrigo without a car, but Joyce's can help get you there on school buses (weekdays only). The bus stop in Bellingen is on the corner of Church St and the main street.

The nearest train station is at Urunga.

Dorrigo (pop 1110)

It's a spectacular drive from Bellingen up to the quiet mountain town of Dorrigo. The road climbs 1000m through dense rainforest, with occasional breaks in the canopy offering great views down the Bellinger Valley to the coast. Dorrigo was one of the last places to be settled in the eastwards push across the New England tablelands. It's a pleasant base for visiting the area's outstanding national parks.

There is an information centre (☎ 6657 2486) at 36 Hickory St, open daily from 10 am to 4 pm.

Things to See & Do A few km north of town on the road to Leigh are the picturesque **Dangar Falls**. The main attraction though is the magnificent subtropical rainforest of **Dorrigo National Park**, 2km east of town. It is the most accessible of Australia's World Heritage rainforests and well worth a visit. The Rainforest Centre (☎ 6657 2309), at the entrance, has information about the park's many walks and is open daily from 9 am to 5 pm. Camping is not allowed in the park. The turn-off to the park is clearly signposted on the Dorrigo-Bellingen road. See the New England section for information on other national parks in this area.

Places to Stay *Dorrigo Mountain Resort* (☎ 6657 2564), a caravan park with some substantial wooden cabins, is just out of town on the road to Bellingen. Sites cost from $10. There are on-site vans ($30) as well as self-contained cabins $44. The *Commercial Hotel/Motel* (☎ 6657 2003) has motel units for $28/36.

Getting There & Away The only bus service is provided by Kean's (☎ 1800 625 587), which uses Dorrigo as a meal stop on its Port Macquarie-Tamworth run. It operates four times a week, going via Coffs Harbour and Armidale. Aussitel in Coffs Harbour and the hostels at Bellingen and Nambucca all organise day trips to the Dorigo National Park.

Urunga & Mylestom

Urunga, about 20km north of Nambucca, is a quiet little town at the mouth of the Bellinger and Kalang rivers. The rivers meet just 200m from the ocean, forming an impressive estuary that is popular for water sports. There is a surf beach just south of town at **Hungry Head**, but the best beach in the area is about 5km south of town at **Third Headland** – signposted off the Pacific Highway along Snapper Beach Rd. The *Ocean View Hotel* (☎ 6655 6221) in Urunga has good singles/doubles for $25/40 with breakfast. The rooms at the front have views over the estuary.

North of Urunga is the turn-off to Mylestom, also called North Beach. This quiet town is in a great location on the banks of the wide Bellinger River and also has ocean beaches. It has a caravan park (☎ 6655 4250) (tent sites $10, on-site vans $20, cabins $25) and a good backpackers hostel, *Riverside Lodge* (☎ 6655 4245), which is on the main street across from the river (the third house on the left as you enter town). The hostel has beds in two-bed 'dorms' for $15 and can organise activities such as white-water rafting and horse riding. There's free use of the lodge's bikes and kayaks. The friendly owners will pick up guests from the train station or bus stop at Urunga; given a day's notice, they can pick you up from Coffs.

COFFS HARBOUR (pop 22,200)

Coffs Harbour is not the most desirable destination on the coast. The town may have veered away from the Gold Coast-style development it seemed hell-bent upon 10 years ago, but the tacky attractions that sprang up in the early days have remained. A string of good beaches stretches north of town, so despite its failings Coffs can be a good base for those keen on outdoor activities and exploring the north-coast hinterland.

Orientation & Information

The Pacific Highway is called Grafton St on its run through town. The city centre is around the junction of Grafton and High Sts. East of Grafton St, High St has been transformed into a rainforest mall. High St resumes on the other side of the mall and becomes the main road to the waterfront jetty area, a couple of kilometres east.

The information centre (☎ 6652 1522, 1800 025 650) is on the corner of Rose Ave and Marcia St.

Beaches

The main beach is **Park Beach**, which is patrolled at weekends and school holidays. There is a good beach at **Korora** and then a string of them up to Woolgoolga. Back in town, **Jetty Beach** is more sheltered and can be good for a swim when the surf is rough.

Other Attractions

The **North Coast Botanic Gardens**, at the end of Hardacre St (off High St), are well worth a visit. It's hard to believe that part of the site was once the town tip. These immaculately maintained gardens contain many endangered species and areas have been planted to re-create the region's different rainforest types. The gardens are also part of the popular **Coffs Creek Walk** that follows the creek upstream from the mouth of Coffs Creek to near the town centre.

Muttonbird Island, linked to the mainland by the harbour's northern breakwater, is home to more than 12,000 pairs of mutton birds (wedge-tailed shearwaters) from late August until April. The island is dotted with

NEW SOUTH WALES

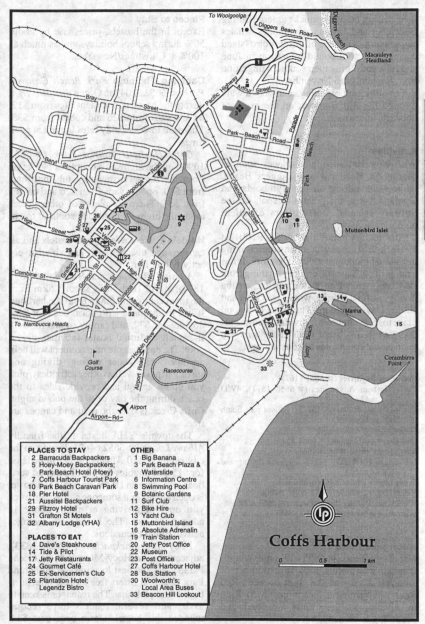

PLACES TO STAY
2 Barracuda Backpackers
5 Hoey-Moey Backpackers;
   Park Beach Hotel (Hoey)
7 Coffs Harbour Tourist Park
10 Park Beach Caravan Park
18 Pier Hotel
21 Aussitel Backpackers
29 Fitzroy Hotel
31 Grafton St Motels
32 Albany Lodge (YHA)

PLACES TO EAT
4 Dave's Steakhouse
14 Tide & Pilot
17 Jetty Restaurants
24 Gourmet Café
25 Ex-Servicemen's Club
26 Plantation Hotel;
   Legendz Bistro

OTHER
1 Big Banana
3 Park Beach Plaza &
   Waterslide
6 Information Centre
8 Swimming Pool
9 Botanic Gardens
11 Surf Club
12 Bike Hire
13 Yacht Club
15 Muttonbird Island
16 Absolute Adrenalin
19 Train Station
20 Jetty Post Office
22 Museum
23 Post Office
27 Coffs Harbour Hotel
28 Bus Station
30 Woolworth's;
   Local Area Buses
33 Beacon Hill Lookout

Coffs Harbour

0   0.5   1 km

their nesting burrows; chicks emerge during December and January. Humpback whales can sometimes be seen off Muttonbird Island during their northbound migration in June and July, and during their southern migration from September to November.

Fans of kitsch big things can take a walk through the **Big Banana**, on the northern outskirts of town.

Activities

With excellent surfing at places such as Macauleys Headland and Diggers Beach, white-water rafting on the Nymboida and Goolang rivers, and great dive spots off the Solitary Islands, Coffs offers excellent outdoor activities.

Absolute Adrenalin (☎ 6651 9100) at 396B High St is a new company representing individual outdoor activity operators. It has a range of packages offering everything from skydiving to white-water rafting, scuba diving, surfing, fishing, whale-watching and Harley Davidson tours. They may be a good place to start, although individual companies may be offering better deals at the time you visit. Some companies to consider are:

Coffs City Skydivers (☎ 6651 1167)
Coffs Harbour Adventures (☎ 6658 1871), 4WD tours and horse riding
Commissioner II (☎ 6651 3271), cruises past South Solitary Island
Dive Quest (☎ 6654 1930)
East Coast Surf School (☎ 6651 5515)
Jetty Dive Centre (☎ 6651 1611)
MV *Laura E* (☎ 6651 1434), deep-sea fishing and whale-spotting
Outer Limits (☎ 6651 4066), abseiling
Valery Trails (☎ 6653 4301), horse riding
Whitewater Rafting Professionals (☎ 6651 4066)
Wildwater Adventures (☎ 6653 4469)

Aboriginal Tours

Gambaarri Tours (☎ 6655 4195) runs recommended interpretive trips to a number of Aboriginal sites on the coast between Red Rock and Nambucca Heads (cost $45). Ring in advance as these tours are conducted according to demand, not schedule.

Places to Stay

Except in the hostels, prices rise by about 50% during school holidays and as much as 100% at Christmas/New Year.

Camping The huge *Park Beach Caravan Park* (☎ 6652 3204) on Ocean Parade is right next to the beach and has tent sites from $12, on-site vans from $26 and cabins from $38. There are lower weekly rates but not at peak times.

Coffs Harbour Tourist Park (☎ 6652 1694), on the highway a couple of blocks on from the Ex-Servicemen's Club, has sites from $10, on-site vans from $26 and cabins from $36. There are plenty of other places along the highway north and south of town.

Hostels There are four good hostels and all can arrange discounts on just about every activity on offer.

Aussitel Backpackers Hostel (☎ 6651 1871), at 312 High St, is about 1.5km from the town centre and 500m from the harbour. It is a lively place with dorm beds for $14, doubles for $32, and family rooms for $40. It has all the usual hostel faciiities plus a pool. The enthusiastic management will help arrange white-water rafting, diving and surfing trips (as well as other activities), pick you up on arrival and provide rides to the beach during the day or to the pub at night. Coffs Creek is over the road and canoes are free.

The town's YHA hostel is the friendly *Albany Lodge* (☎ 6652 6462), 1km from the city centre at 110 Albany St. Dorm beds go for $15 and doubles for $34; bikes and surfboards are free and there's a pool. The hostel is open all day and someone can usually pick you up – if arriving at night, phone in advance to ask. The hostel also arranges activities and excursions.

Hoey-Moey Backpackers (☎ 6652 3833), adjacent to the Hoey-Moey pub on Ocean Parade, has the best location – right behind Park Beach. It offers free bicycle hire, surfboards and pick-ups. The manager is keen to assist and several readers have recommended this hostel. Dorm beds cost $14, singles $25 and doubles $32. Rooms come with en-suite and TV and there are cheap meals for hostel guests at the hotel.

Barracuda Backpackers (☎ 6651 3514) at 19 Arthur St is in a suburban neck of the woods near the Park Beach Plaza Shopping Centre. Several readers have praised their helpfulness. It has the standard facilities and services; dorms cost $13 and doubles $28.

Hotels & Motels The *Fitzroy Hotel* (☎ 6652 3007), on Moonee St, is an old-style neighbourhood pub with singles/doubles for $20/35. Down near the harbour on High St, the *Pier Hotel* (☎ 6652 2110) has a few large, clean rooms for $20 per person, per night.

There's a string of nondescript motels on Grafton St on the southern approach to town, which outside school holiday periods charge around $45-$55 a double. Another group of motels in the Park Beach area has similar rates.

Apartments There is a huge range of holiday apartments and houses. In the off season the cheapest two-bedroom apartments cost around $45 a night (less by the week) and $90 a night in the high season, although many places are only available by the week at this time. The information centre has a booking service (☎ 1800 025 650).

Places to Eat
Some of the best cheap eats can be found in the clubs, such as the *Ex-Servicemen's Club* on the corner of Grafton and Vernon Sts.

There are snack places on the mall, and the pubs in this area have counter meals. The *Gourmet Café*, in the City Boulevard Arcade off the mall, has delicious home-made pies ($1.80) and light meals from around $6. At the Plantation Hotel on Grafton St, *Legendz Bistro* has lunches for $5.50 with a free drink on weekdays.

Dave's Steakhouse, 99 Park Beach Rd, has an all-you-can-eat soup, pasta and salad deal for $11 as well as huge steaks from $18.

In the cluster of restaurants at the jetty end of High St, you'll find the excellent *Tahruah Thai Kitchen*, near the Pier Hotel, with filling

noodle dishes for $7. Most of the neighbours are a few notches upmarket. They include *Peter's Pepermill* (French), the *Royal Viking* (grill), the *Passionfish Brasserie* (multicultural) and a couple of Indian restaurants. There are also pub meals and $5 breakfasts at the *Pier Hotel*.

The harbour is the place to go for seafood. *Coffs Harbour Fishermen's Co-op* has a good takeaway section and a sushi/sashimi bar as well as fresh seafood. The nearby *Yacht Club* has $5 lunches on weekdays and *Tide & Pilot* offers fantastic views while you tuck into dishes like chilli king prawns ($19).

Entertainment
There's something happening every night, although the pickings are fairly slim early in the week. Thursday's edition of the *Coff's Harbour Advocate* has the week's listings.

The *Plantation Hotel* on Grafton St has free local bands from Wednesday to Saturday. Live bands play the *Hoey-Moey* at Park Beach. Big-name touring bands play at the *Sawtell RSL Club*, 5km south of town. The hostels usually organise transport.

Getting There & Away
Greyhound Pioneer (☎ 13 2030) has a booking office by the long-distance bus stop in Moonee St. Coffs Harbour Coaches & Travel (☎ 6652 2877), a few doors away, can fix you up with bus, air and Countrylink tickets.

Air Coffs has a busy airport, on the south edge of town. Ansett (☎ 13 1300) and Eastern Australia (☎ 13 1313) fly to Sydney ($226). Impulse (☎ 13 1381) flies to Brisbane ($216) via Lismore and Coolangatta.

Bus All the long-distance lines on the Sydney to Brisbane route stop at Coffs. The long-distance bus stop is in Moonee St just west of Grafton St.

Fares from Coffs include: Byron Bay $47, Brisbane $49, Nambucca Heads $15, Port Macquarie $32 and Sydney $65.

Local buses stop at the car park next to Woolworths on Park Ave. Ryan's buses

(☎ 6652 3201) run several times daily, except Sunday, to Woolgoolga ($6.50) via beachside towns off the highway. Watson's Woolgoolga Coaches (☎ 6654 1063) connects Coffs Harbour and Grafton on weekdays. The fare to Woolgoologa is $5.50 one way, Grafton $11 (see the Bellingen and Nambucca Heads sections for other local services).

Train The train station (☎ 6651 2757) is near the harbour at the end of High St. The fare to Sydney is $67.

Yacht Coffs is reportedly a good place to pick up a ride along the coast on a yacht or cruiser. Ask around or put a notice in the yacht club at the harbour. Sometimes the hostels know of boat owners who are looking for crew.

Getting Around
A bus service connects the centre, the Jetty and Park Beach but services are infrequent, with none on Sunday.

The Coffs District Taxi Network (☎ 6651 3944) operates a 24-hour service. There's a taxi rank on the corner of High and Gordon Sts.

Bob Wallis World of Wheels (☎ 6652 5102), near the harbour on the corner of Collingwood and Orlando Sts, rents bikes.

COFFS HARBOUR TO BYRON BAY
Woolgoolga (pop 3750)
Twenty-six km north of Coffs, Woolgoolga is a small resort with a fine surf beach. It has a sizeable Indian Sikh population whose *gurdwara* (place of worship), the **Guru Nanak Temple**, is just off the highway at the southern end of town.

The *Woolgoolga Beach Caravan Park* (☎ 6654 1373) has tent sites for $10 and cabins from $34. For Indian food try the *Koh-I-Nor* at the Raj Mahal or *Temple View* near the temple.

North of Woolgoolga is **Arrawarra**, a quiet seaside town with yet another great beach and a pleasant caravan park close to

the water. Sleepy **Red Rock** is on a beautiful little inlet.

Long-distance buses run through Woolgoolga. There are local services to Coffs Harbour, Grafton and nearby beaches. See the Coffs Harbour section for services.

Yuraygir National Park
Yuraygir covers the 60km of coast stretching north from Red Rock to Angourie Point, just south of Yamba. The main attractions are fine beaches and bushwalking in the coastal heath. There are some great camp sites along the coast, including the Illaroo Rest Area at **Minnie Water**. Minnie Water is signposted off the Pacific Highway 10km south of Grafton.

The Solitary Islands
This island group, strung out along the coast from Yuraygir National Park, is a marine reserve at the meeting place of the warmer tropical currents and the more temperate southern currents, with some interesting varieties of fish attracted by the unusual conditions.

Grafton (pop 16,500)
Grafton is a graceful old country town on the banks of the mighty Clarence River. The town is noted for its fine street trees, particularly the spectacular jacarandas which carpet the streets with their mauve flowers at Jacaranda Festival time in late October. The town lies at the heart of a rich agricultural area. The wide Clarence delta is a patchwork of sugar-cane plantations.

On Fitzroy St is **Prentice House** (1880), now an art gallery. The nearby **Schaeffer House** is a historical museum.

The Pacific Highway runs past Grafton, and the Clarence River Tourist Centre (☎ 6642 4677) is on the highway south of the town. The town centre is north of the Clarence River.

Places to Stay The *Rathgar Lodge* (☎ 6642 3181), next to the Caltex service station on the Pacific Highway south of town, has dorm beds for $15.

There's no shortage of motels and many pubs have accommodation. The *Crown Hotel/Motel* (☎ 6642 4000) is a pleasant place overlooking the river on Prince St. Pub rooms are $20/30 for singles/doubles or $30/40 with bathroom. Motel units are $45/55. Another nice old pub in the same area is *Roches* (☎ 6642 2866) at 85 Victoria St, where the spotless rooms are $24/30.

Getting There & Away Long-distance buses stop on the highway in South Grafton, not far from the information centre. Fares include Sydney $52 and Byron Bay $25. Countrylink runs up the Gwydir Highway to Glen Innes four times a week for about $17. Watson's Woolgoolga Coaches (☎ 6654 1063) has three services a day between Grafton and Coffs ($11).

Most local-area buses leave from the Market Square shopping centre in the town centre, not far from the corner of King and Fitzroy Sts.

The train station is on the highway side of the river. The fare to Sydney is $70.

Grafton to Ballina

From Grafton the highway follows the Clarence River north-east, bypassing the pleasant little river port of **Maclean**. Maclean celebrates its Scottish early settlers with a Highland Gathering each Easter.

The fishing town of **Yamba**, at the mouth of the Clarence River, is a growing resort with good beaches. The *Pacific Hotel* (☎ 6646 2466) has a great setting overlooking the main beach on Pilot St. It has backpackers' rooms for $17.50 per person. The Grafton-Yamba Bus Service (☎ 6646 2019) runs five buses a day (three in school holidays) from Grafton to Yamba via Maclean. There are four ferries a day from Yamba to the town of **Iluka**, on the northern bank of the Clarence, for $3.

Just south of Yamba, **Angourie** is one of the coast's top spots for experienced surfers – but beware of the rips.

Iluka is worth a detour off the highway to visit its World Heritage listed **Nature Reserve**, which contains the largest patch of

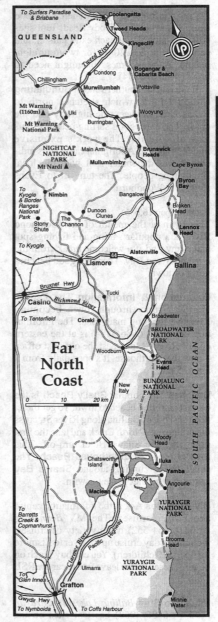

littoral rainforest in NSW. There's a good camp site at nearby Woody Head. Tent sites cost $10, plus $2 for each extra person, and cabins go for $30/40/60 for two/four/eight people. At peak times you might need to book (☎ 6646 6134).

Iluka is at the southern end of **Bundjalung National Park**, which stretches north to Evans Head between the highway and the coast. There are good surfing beaches, plus lots of wildlife. The park's extensive middens and old Aboriginal camp sites indicate it was a popular spot with the local Bundjalung people. The turn-off to Evans Head is at Woodburn.

Ballina (pop 16,056)
This town at the mouth of the Richmond River is a popular sailing and fishing spot and many find it a welcome break from the hype of Byron Bay. There are good beaches north of town.

Orientation & Information The Pacific Highway runs through town, becoming River St, the long main road. The information centre (☎ 6686 3484) is at the eastern end of River St, just past the old post office – now the courthouse. It's open daily from 9 am to 5 pm.

Beaches The popular **Shelly Beach** is the closest patrolled beach to town. To get there, head east out of Ballina along River St, cross the bridge over North Creek and take the first right after the Shaws Hotel turn-off. This road also passes **Lighthouse Beach**. The small beach curving around **Shaws Bay Lagoon** is a quiet place to swim.

River Cruises Ask at the information centre about river cruises. The MV *Bennelong* (☎ 0414 664 552) has a variety of cruises, including a day cruise up the river to Lismore for $55 ($20 children). You can buy lunch on board. These cruises leave from near the RSL Club.

Places to Stay *Ballina Lakeside Caravan Park* (☎ 6686 3953) has tent sites on the edge of Shaws Bay Lagoon for $11 and cabins from $30 to $45. Prices go up sharply during school holidays.

Ballina Travellers Lodge (☎ 6686 6737) is a good, modern YHA hostel at 36-38 Tamar St. Dorm beds are $14 and twins are $32. Bikes, fishing rods and boogie boards can be borrowed for free, and there's a pool. The lodge is also a motel and one of the few in town without highway noise. Doubles are $46 in the low season, rising to $80 around Christmas.

The *Flat Rock Camping Ground* (☎ 6686 4848), just north of Ballina on the coast road to Lennox Head, has tent sites for $5. At Ballina Quays Marina (☎ 6686 4289), off the highway south of the Big Prawn, you can rent houseboats. Prices start at $380 per week. With over 100km of navigable river there's plenty of room to move.

Places to Eat *Shellys on the Beach*, above Shelly Beach, has outdoor tables, good food and wonderful views. It's open from 7.30 am. The huge modern *RSL* has a prime position on the riverbank on the corner of Grant and River Sts. The club's downstairs bistro is great value and has seating on a deck overhanging the water. It's a good place to catch the sunset.

The *Cafe Fresco*, at the Henry Rous Hotel in River St, has a large choice of snacks and light meals as well as good coffee. It's open until midnight every night.

Getting There & Away Most major bus lines stop at the Ballina Transit Centre, on the highway just south of town at the Big Prawn. Countrylink stops on River St near the corner of Cherry St, outside the Jetset Travel agency.

Blanch's (☎ 6686 2144) has six buses a day to Lennox Head ($3.60) and Byron Bay ($6.60), departing from outside Jetset Travel on River St.

Lennox Head (pop 4500)
Lennox Head is a rapidly expanding small town on the coast road halfway between Ballina and Byron Bay. Lennox Head is also

the name of the dramatic headland (a prime hang-gliding site) just south of town. Lennox has some of the best surf on the coast, particularly in winter.

Lake Ainsworth, just back from the beach, is popular for sailing and windsurfing. The water is stained brown by the tannin from the surrounding melaleuca trees. It acts as a water softener and is good for the skin and hair. The Lennox Point Hotel often has bands on weekends.

Places to Stay *Lake Ainsworth Caravan Park* (☎ 6687 7249) has tent sites from $11 and cabins for $34 to $43 (bookings are essential for the high season).

Across the road is *Lennox Beach House Backpackers* (☎ 6687 7636) – purpose-built, very clean and very friendly. Both Lake Ainsworth and the beach are nearby and you can have use of a catamaran and a windsurfer ($5 for as long as you stay). Boards, bikes and other sporting equipment are free. Dorm beds are $15 and there are three doubles for $35.

BYRON BAY (pop 6100)

Byron Bay, a surfing mecca and meeting place for alternative cultures since the 60s, is one of the most popular holiday spots on the east coast. Long-time locals bemoan tourism's impact – understandable when you can't cross the main street for the bumper-to-bumper traffic and you can't hear yourself think for the drone of windchimes. Nonetheless, the beaches are superb, there are good music venues, restaurants and cafes and there's always the lush hinterland to escape to if you just can't stand the congestion and hype any longer.

Orientation & Information

Byron Bay is 6km east of the Pacific Highway. Jonson St, which becomes Bangalow Rd, is the main shopping street.

Tourist information is handled by the Byron Bay Environment Centre in the old cottage outside the train station. Bus timetables are posted up on the wall outside nearby Byron Bay Connections (☎ 6685

5981), along with fares and other information. You can store your bags here for $2 a day as well as buy tickets and book tours.

The local *Echo* newspaper has details on activities in the area and the weekly magazine *Phat* covers the music scene.

Cape Byron

Cape Byron was named by Captain Cook after the poet Byron's grandfather, who had sailed round the world in the 1760s. One spur of the cape is the most easterly point of the Australian mainland. You can drive right up to the picturesque 1901 lighthouse, one of the most powerful in the southern hemisphere. There's a 3.5km walking track right round the cape from the Captain Cook Lookout on Lighthouse Rd. It's circular, so you can leave bikes at the start. You've a good chance of seeing wallabies in the final rainforest stretch.

Humpback whales sometimes pass close by Cape Byron during their northern migration in June/July and the return trip from September to November. Dolphins are frequent visitors all year. The **Byron Bay Whale Centre**, near the lighthouse, is open every day from 9 am to 4.30 pm.

Beaches

The Byron area has a glorious collection of beaches, ranging from 10km stretches of empty sand to secluded little coves. **Main Beach**, immediately in front of the town, is a good swimming beach and sometimes has decent surf. The sand stretches 50km or more, all the way up to the Gold Coast, interrupted only by river or creek entrances and a few small headlands. West of Main Beach is **Belongil Beach**. In 1997 this beach was the setting for a rally in support of nude bathing after complaints from a local resident. The rally listened to reggae in the buff and witnessed enlightening comedy routines. (As yet, there is no designated nude bathing beach in Byron Bay, but most locals are pretty mellow.)

The eastern end of Main Beach, curving away towards Cape Byron, is known as **Clarks Beach** and can be good for surfing.

NEW SOUTH WALES

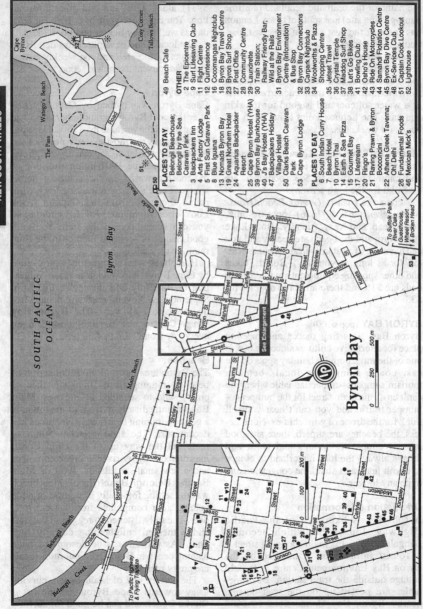

PLACES TO STAY
1 Belongil Beachhouse;
  Belongil by the Sea
  Caravan Park
3 Backpackers Inn
4 Arts Factory Lodge
5 First Sun Caravan Park
8 Blue Iguana
13 Nomads Byron Bay
19 Great Northern Hotel
24 Aquarius Backpacker
  Resort
25 Cape Byron Hostel (YHA)
39 Byron Bay Bunkhouse
40 J's Bay Hostel (YHA)
47 Backpackers Holiday
  Village Hostel
50 Clarks Beach Caravan
  Park
53 Cape Byron Lodge

PLACES TO EAT
6 South Indian Curry House
7 Beach Hotel
10 Byron Thai
14 Earth & Sea Pizza
15 Gourmet Bay
17 Lifestream
20 Ringo's
21 Raving Prawn & Byron
  Bocconcini
22 Athena Greek Taverna;
  Orit Delhi
26 Fundamental Foods
46 Mexican Mick's

49 Beach Cafe

OTHER
2 The Epicentre
9 Surf Lifesaving Club
11 Flight Centre
12 Quintessence
16 Cocomangas Nightclub
18 Byron Bay Travel Centre
23 Byron Surf Shop
27 Post Office
28 Community Centre
29 Laundrette
30 Train Station;
  Railway Friendly Bar;
  Wild at the Rails
31 Byron Bay Environment
  Centre (Information)
  & Bus Stop
32 Byron Bay Connections
33 Carpark Nightclub
34 Woolworths & Plaza
  Shopping Centre
35 Jetset Travel
36 Crystal Temple
37 Maddog Surf Shop
38 Let's Go Bikes
41 Bowling Club
42 Osho's House
43 Ride On Motorcycles
44 Samahdi Flotation Centre
45 Byron Bay Dive Centre
48 Ex-Services Club
51 Captain Cook Lookout
52 Lighthouse

The headland at the end of Clarks is called the Pass and the best surf is off here and at the next beach, **Wategos**. **Little Wategos Beach** is further round, almost at the tip of the cape. Dolphins are quite common, particularly in the surf off Wategos and Little Wategos.

South of Cape Byron, **Tallow Beach** stretches 7km down to a rockier shore around Broken Head, where a succession of small beaches (clothes optional) dot the coast before opening on to **Seven Mile Beach**, which goes all the way to Lennox Head a further 10km south. You can reach Tallow from various points along the Byron Bay-Lennox Head road.

The turn-off to the 'suburb' of **Suffolk Park** (with more good surf, particularly in winter) is 5km from Byron Bay. A further kilometre down the Byron-Lennox road is the turn-off to the Broken Head caravan park.

About 200m before the caravan park, the unsealed Seven Mile Beach Rd turns off south and runs behind the rainforest of the **Broken Head Nature Reserve**. Seven Mile Beach Rd ends after 5km (at the north end of Seven Mile Beach), but several tracks lead down from it through the forest to the Broken Head beaches – two good ones are **Kings Beach** (for which there's a car park 750m down Seven Mile Beach Rd) and **Whites Beach** (reached by a foot track after about 3.25km).

Diving

Diving is popular at Julian Rocks, 3km off shore, a meeting point of cold southerly and warm northerly currents, which attracts a profusion of marine species.

There's cut-throat competition between the growing number of dive operators – ask around to see who has the best deals.

Three operators to consider are Byron Bay Dive Centre (☎ 6685 7149), at 111 Jonson St; Sundive (☎ 6685 7755), in the Cape Byron Hostel complex on Middleton St; and Bayside Scuba (☎ 6685 8333), on the corner of Fletcher and Lawson Sts.

Surfing

Most hostels have free surfboards for guests. The Byron Surf Shop (☎ 6685 7536), on Lawson St near Fletcher St, hires surfboards ($20 a day), boogie boards ($15) and wetsuits ($5). The associated Byron Surf School offers lessons for $20, including board and wetsuit. Let's Go Surfing (☎ 6685 3991) has similar rates for group lessons, or private lessons for $30. North Coast Surfaris (☎ 1800 634 951) offers week-long surfing trips up the coast from Sydney to Byron Bay, stopping at out-of-the-way surf spots. Its bus leaves Sydney every Monday. The price of $249 includes camping and surfing gear and all meals. You'll need a sleeping bag.

Flying

Cape Byron is a great place for hang-gliding. Flight Zone (☎ 6685 8768) and Byron Bay Hang-gliding School (☎ 6685 3917) offer tuition, and tandem flights and tuition. Tandem flights are $65 from Lennox Head. Ring at 10 am to find out if and when there will be flights that day.

Trike flights (ultralight aircraft) are run by Skylimit (☎ 6684 3711) and cost from $55 for 20 minutes. Skylimit also offers tandem hang-gliding. Skydive (☎ 6684 1323) has tandem skydiving. Prices start at $198 for midweek jumps (minimum two people).

Kite-flying is popular and most days around 4 pm you'll see plenty on Main Beach or Tallow Beach, depending on the state of the wind. Byron Kites (☎ 6685 5299) in the Cape Byron Hostel complex will sell you a kite or you can rent one for $20, which includes tuition and five hours flying.

Trapeze

Potential circus stars, both young and old, can head out to the Flying Trapeze (☎ 6685 8000), 3km west of town at the Byron Bay Beach Club. The operators offer the opportunity to make your first catch on a flying trapeze at the end of a two-hour lesson. It gets rave reports and sounds like good value at $20.

Alternative Therapies

There are at least three flotation-tank places: Samadhi (☎ 6685 6905) on Jonson St opposite Woolworths; Osho's House (☎ 6685 692) at 1/30 Carlyle St; and Relax Haven (☎ 6685 8304) at Belongil Beachouse. These places also do massage – at Relax Haven you can get an hour in the tank and an hour-long massage for $40.

Several other places offer massage, acupuncture and other touchy-feely stuff, although some drift into the fuzzier edges of alternative thought. Quintessence Healing Sanctuary (☎ 6685 5533) at 8/11 Fletcher St offers everything from clairvoyance to sports massage.

Organised Tours

Byron Bay to Bush Tours (☎ 6685 6889) and Jim's Alternative Tours (☎ 6685 7720) both run day tours of the spectacular north coast hinterland for $25. Jim's also has trips to The Channon markets on the second Sunday of each month ($10 return) and to Bangalow on the fourth Sunday ($5). Nimbin Tours (☎ 6685 5362) runs to Nimbin from Tuesday to Saturday for $15 return.

Places to Stay

Byron has lots of accommodation, particularly at the budget-end of the market, but beds can still prove hard to find in summer. Prices go up during school holidays and peak around Christmas and Easter.

Camping At peak times you'll be lucky to find a site, and cabins are rented only by the week.

The local council has four caravan parks, all by beaches. *First Sun Caravan Park* (☎ 6685 6544) is on Main Beach close to the town centre. Tent sites start at $13, rising in stages to $22 at peak time. There's a range of cabins, the cheapest going for $50 in the low season and $75 at the peak. *Clarks Beach Caravan Park* (☎ 6685 6496) is off Lighthouse Rd about 1km east of the town centre and has plenty of trees. Sites start at $15 and cabins at $48.

Down at Suffolk Park on Tallow Beach,

Suffolk Park Caravan Park (☎ 6685 3353) is a friendly place with shady sites ($11) and cabins from $38. They can probably squeeze in your tent when everywhere else is full. The small council-run caravan park at Broken Head (☎ 6685 3245) has a superb location overlooking Tallow Beach and is marginally cheaper than the others. There's no shop, so you'll need to bring all your supplies.

Belongil by the Sea (☎ 6685 8111), next to the Belongil Beachouse hostel, has a cluster of cabins dotted around landscaped gardens with a large swimming pool (heated in winter). Prices start at $50 for two people. *Tallow Beach Resort* (☎ 6685 3408, 1800 65 6817) can be found on Tallow Beach and has self-contained cabins from $65.

Hostels The hot competition between the town's numerous hostels is good news for budget travellers. Prices fluctuate depending on demand, peaking around Christmas/January, when you should book. At other times ask about special deals and weekly rates.

Backpackers Holiday Village Hostel (☎ 6685 8888) at 116 Jonson St, close to the bus stop, is a clean, friendly, well-equipped place with a small pool and spa. Dorm beds cost from $14 and doubles from $36. There's one double with bathroom and TV for $43. Well-maintained bicycles, surfboards and boogie boards are free and there are plenty of them.

Backpackers Inn (☎ 6685 8231) at 29 Shirley St is near the beach and half a kilometre from the town centre. It's a modern hostel with a pool and all the usual features, including free bikes and boogie boards. To get to the beach, walk across the lawn, cross the railway line (carefully!) and climb a sand dune. Rates start at $15 for dorms and at $45 for doubles.

The *Cape Byron Lodge* (☎ 6685 6445) is clean, comfortable and well equipped. It's some way from the town centre at 78 Bangalow Rd (the southern end of Jonson St) but only about 10-minutes walk to Tallow Beach. It has a small pool and bikes are free.

This is usually the cheapest hostel in town, with dorm beds starting at $10 and doubles at $30.

Byron Bay has two YHA-affiliated hostels. The impressive *Cape Byron Hostel* (☎ 6685 8788) is close to the town centre and Main Beach, which is on the corner of Byron and Middleton Sts. It's a big building with its own mini shopping centre and a heated pool. Prices (which might rise in summer) are $13 in a 10-person dorm, $14 in a five-person dorm, $36 in a double or twin and $60 for a double with TV, fridge and bathroom.

The other YHA affiliate is the purpose-built *J's Bay Hostel* (☎ 1800 67 8195) on the corner of Carlyle and Middleton Sts. It's a friendly, laid-back place with helpful staff. There's a pool, several pleasant communal areas and a fantastic kitchen. There are facilities for disabled travellers and bikes and boogie boards for hire.

The *Belongil Beachouse* (☎ 6685 7868) is a great place to stay – well-run, relaxed and friendly. It's off Childe St, just over the dunes from Belongil Beach and set amid well-established gardens; bike and boogie-board use is free. The cafe here is a big plus, with excellent, healthy food served between 8 am and 10 pm. There's a nightly half-price special for guests. You can store gear here for $5 a week. Dorm beds start at $13, rising to $17 around Christmas. Singles/doubles with shared bathroom are $33/38, rising to $37/42. There are some upmarket doubles priced from $60, rising to $90.

Aquarius Backpacker Resort (☎ 1800 02 8909) on Lawson St is a well appointed hostel. The small dorms each have their own en-suite, TV and fridge. Dorm beds are $16 and doubles are $45.

Those with an alternative bent and a penchant for late nights will enjoy the atmosphere at the *Arts Factory Lodge* (☎ 6685 7709), with its permaculture gardens and creative furnishings. The huge choice of accommodation ranges from tent sites ($8) to teepees ($14) – not the most secure form of accommodation so don't leave your valuables lying around. Dorm beds are $16 and doubles start at $35. Ideo-logically-sound food is available at the co-owned Piggery Cafe. The Arts Factory is about 10-minutes walk from the town centre and beaches. Staff meet buses and there's free use of bikes as well as regular minibuses to town.

The *Blue Iguana Beach House* (☎ 6685 5298), opposite the surf club on Bay St, has beds in four-person dorms for $15 during the week, rising to $20 at weekends and more at peak times.

The clean and pleasant *Nomads Byron Bay* (☎ 6685 8695) occupies the renovated former council chambers on Lawson St. It charges $15/40 for dorms/doubles. The boisterous *Byron Bay Bunkhouse* (☎ 6685 8311) on Carlyle St has dorm beds for $13 and doubles for $40.

Hotels, Motels & Guesthouses The *Great Northern Hotel* (☎ 6685 6454) on Jonson St has singles/doubles for $30/40 in the low season, rising to $40/50 in the peak season. There are numerous motels lining the southern and western approaches to town.

The *Wheel Resort* (☎ 6685 6139), just south of town on Broken Head Rd, is designed and run by wheelchair users for travellers with disabilities. Rates start at $85 for a cabin for up to three people.

River Oaks Guesthouse (☎ 6685 8679) is a relaxed, gay guesthouse a few kilometres south of the centre at 53-59 Broken Head Rd (lesbians welcome). It has a pool set in pleasant gardens, although Tallow Beach is not far away. Singles/doubles start from $65/75 in the low season.

Apartments Holiday houses and apartments start from around $300 a week in the off season, $500 during school holidays and $900 over Christmas. Letting agents include Elders (☎ 6685 6222) on Jonson St near the train station, which handles bookings for two old cottages at the lighthouse on Cape Byron. There's a two-bedroom cottage for $500 a week (off season), and a three-bedroom cottage for $550. Rents rocket to $1250 and $1350 a week at Christmas.

Places to Eat

There is a wide choice of restaurants, cafes and takeaways serving good food, and vegetarians are particularly well catered for.

Breakfast is served just about everywhere. Overlooking Clarks Beach, the *Beach Cafe* isn't cheap but the views are superb. The *Cafe DOC* at the Cape Byron Hostel complex has breakfast from about $5.50 and good coffee.

The *Beach Hotel* in Bay St has snacks such as burgers from $3.90 and more substantial meals such as grilled fish ($9.50) and steaks (from $13.50). Heading down Jonson St from there, the *South Indian Curry House* is a long-time favourite, with most main courses around $10. It's open nightly for dinner.

South of the roundabout on Jonson St, *Ringo's* is one of Byron's older cafes and has a large menu of snacks and drinks, and meals from around $10. It's open from breakfast ($6.50 for bacon & eggs) until about 8.30 pm. *Lifestream* on Jonson St is a large healthfood cafe with a huge range of goodies. You can put together a decent meal for $5.

Fundamental Foods, next to the post office, has a huge range of goodies as well as organically grown fruit and vegetables. Further along Jonson St is the licensed *Mexican Mick's*, open for dinner Tuesday to Saturday. It's an old favourite and is still reasonably priced, with main courses under $16 and lots of snacks on the big menu. At the Railway Friendly Bar, *Wild at the Rails* opens for lunch and dinner. The food is innovative and not expensive.

Earth & Sea Pizza on Lawson St is a popular pizza place which also has pasta. Over the road is the *Athena Greek Taverna* and the *Oh! Delhi* Indian restaurant and cocktail bar.

The Feros Arcade dog-legs between Lawson and Jonson Sts and has several options: *Byron Bocconcini* is open Monday to Saturday for lunch (simple sandwiches, Lebanese rolls and salads); next door, the *Raving Prawn* has an interesting modern menu with main courses ranging from $14 to $20.

The *Byron Thai*, at the Bay Beach Motel on Lawson St, has an unusually large vegetarian selection.

Entertainment

Byron Bay's nightlife is a major drawcard. The *Railway Friendly Bar*, next to the train station, has live music most nights. The *Beach Hotel* and *Great Northern Hotel* have live bands Thursday to Saturday nights and sometimes on Sunday afternoons. Touring bands play at the latter. *Cocomangas* nightclub in Jonson St opens at 11 pm and the dancing continues until 3 am. The *Carpark* nightclub, in the Plaza Shopping Centre, is more hardcore techno (also open until 3 am).

It's always worth seeing what's on at the *Epicentre*, on Border St just over the railway line. It's *the* place to rave in Byron Bay when the fluro ferals descend from their hinterland retreats. *Phat* magazine is a good source of info on upcoming events, as is the Tuesday entertainment lift-out in the *Echo*.

Getting There & Away

Air The closest airport is at Ballina, but most people use the much larger airport at Coolangatta on the Gold Coast in Queensland. It has frequent direct flights from both Sydney and Melbourne, but you still have to get down to Byron.

Bus Numerous buses run through Byron Bay. Approximate fares are Brisbane $21, Sydney $62, Coffs Harbour $33 and Surfers Paradise $19.

Kirklands' Lismore-Brisbane route passes through Byron Bay and stops at other useful places such as Murwillumbah, Ballina, Tweed Heads and Coolangatta airport. Blanch's (☎ 6686 2144) serves the local area with destinations such as Mullumbimby ($4) and Ballina ($6.60).

Train Byron Bay is on the Sydney to Murwillumbah line, with a daily train in each direction, plus several rail/bus services. From Sydney ($82) the quickest service is the 7.05 am XPT, which reaches Byron Bay at 7.30 pm. This train continues to

Murwillumbah ($6) and connects with a bus to Brisbane ($24 from Byron Bay). The southbound train stops in town at 10 am. To Coffs Harbour the fare is $35.

Car & Motorcycle Rental Earth Car Rentals (☎ 6685 7472) has older cars from $30 a day (including 100 free km), and new cars from $50. Jetset Travel (☎ 6685 6554) rents small current-model cars for $35 a day with 100km free (10c per km over 100km).

Ride on Motorcycles (☎ 6685 6304), on Jonson St opposite Woolworths, hires motorcycles from $35 a day. You need a motorcycle licence, Australian or foreign.

Getting Around
Bicycle The hostels lend bikes of varying quality to guests. Byron Bay Bicycles (☎ 6685 6315) in the Plaza shopping centre on Jonson St has good single-speed bikes for $12 a day, including helmet, and geared bikes for $18 a day. Let's Go Bikes (☎ 6685 6067), nearby on Jonson St, has single-speed bikes at $15 a day.

BYRON BAY TO TWEED HEADS

The Pacific Highway continues north from the Byron Bay turn-off to the Queensland border at Tweed Heads. Just after the Mullumbimby turn-off is **Brunswick Heads**, a river-mouth town with a small fishing fleet, several caravan parks, motels and hotels.

A few kilometres north is the turn-off to the coastal town of **Wooyung**. The coast road from Wooyung to Tweed Heads makes a pleasant alternative to the Pacific Highway. This stretch is known as the Tweed Coast and is much less developed than the Gold Coast to the north.

On the Tweed Coast are the small resorts of **Bogangar-Cabarita** and **Kingscliff**. Cabarita Beach has good surf and there's a good hostel, *Emu Park Backpackers Resort* (☎ 6676 1190). It's one of the cleanest hostels around and the rooms are large. Dorm beds are $15 and there's a 'stay two nights, get the third night free' deal outside school holidays. Doubles cost $33, and the en-suite double with TV is $39. Bikes and

boards are free and the beach is a minute away. The staff will drop you off at Mt Warning and pick you up after your climb for about $45 – not bad among several people. Guests can be picked up from Kingscliff and Coolangatta (Queensland).

Surfside (☎ (07) 5536 7666) has eight buses a day from Tweed Heads to Cabarita Beach ($4.50) on weekdays – five on Saturday and three on Sunday – and frequent services to Kingscliff ($3.10).

Murwillumbah (pop 7650)
Murwillumbah is in a banana and sugar-growing area in the broad Tweed Valley. It's also the main town in this part of the north coast hinterland and there are several communes and 'back to the land' centres in the area. You're also within reach of Mt Warning and the spectacular border ranges. You can cross into Queensland by the Numinbah road through the ranges between the Springbrook and Lamington areas (see the Queensland chapter for more details).

The tourist information centre (☎ 6672 1340) on the Pacific Highway near the train station is due to be transformed into the World Heritage Rainforest Centre. The excellent **Tweed River Regional Art Gallery** is just up the road from the hostel. The **museum** on Queensland Rd opens Wednesday and Friday, 11 am to 4 pm ($2).

Places to Stay & Eat The associate-YHA *Mt Warning Backpackers of Murwillumbah* (☎ 6672 3763) is at 1 Tumbulgum Rd beside the Tweed River – you'll see it on the right as you cross the bridge into town. It's a friendly place with lots of activities, including free canoes and a rowing boat. It can also organise horse rides. Dorm beds are $14, singles $19 and doubles and twins $32.

Several pubs have accommodation, including the solid *Imperial Hotel* (☎ 6672 1036) on the main street across from the post office, with singles/doubles from $20/34 to $39.

Getting There & Away Murwillumbah is served by most buses on the Sydney (about

$60) to Brisbane ($17) coastal run. Except for Kirklands and Greyhound Pioneer (which goes into town), the long-distance buses stop at the train station. Justice Bus Service (☎ 6621 2307) runs to Uki ($4.50), Nimbin ($12) and Lismore ($14). Surfside runs to Tweed Heads ($3.80).

A daily train from Sydney ($88) connects with a bus to the Gold Coast and Brisbane.

TWEED HEADS (pop 37,770)

Sharing a street with the more developed Queensland resort of Coolangatta, Tweed Heads marks the southern end of the Gold Coast strip. The northern side of Boundary St, which runs along a short peninsula to Point Danger above the mouth of the Tweed River, is in Queensland. This end of the Gold Coast is much quieter than the resorts closer to Surfers Paradise.

The Tweed Heads visitor centre (☎ (07) 5536 4244) is at the northern end of Wharf St (the Pacific Highway), just south of the giant Twin Towns Services Club. It's open daily from 9 am to 5 pm (until 3 pm on Saturday and Sunday).

There's also an information kiosk (☎ (07) 5536 7765) in the Beach House complex on the corner of Marine Parade and McLean St in Coolangatta.

Things to See

At Point Danger the towering **Captain Cook Memorial** straddles the state border. The 18m-high monument was completed in 1970 (the bicentenary of Cook's visit) and is topped by a laser-beam lighthouse visible 35km out to sea. The replica of the *Endeavour*'s capstan is made from ballast dumped by Cook after the *Endeavour* ran aground on the Great Barrier Reef and recovered, along with the ship's cannons, in 1968. Point Danger was named by Cook after he nearly ran aground there, too.

There are views over the Tweed Valley and the Gold Coast from the **Razorback Lookout**, 3km from Tweed Heads.

On Kirkwood Rd in South Tweed Heads,

the **Minjungbal Aboriginal Cultural Centre** (☎ (07) 5524 2109) has exhibits on pre-contact history and culture. It's open daily from 10 am to 4 pm. Entry is $6.

Places to Stay

Accommodation in Tweed Heads spills over into Coolangatta and up the Gold Coast, where the choice is more varied. The cheaper motels along Wharf St are feeling the pinch as the highway bypasses Tweed Heads; you'll find doubles advertised for less than $40.

See the Coolangatta section of the Queensland chapter for places to stay across the border.

Places to Eat

The *Tweed Heads Bowls Club* on Wharf St has specials such as weekday roast lunches for under $5; the other clubs are also sources of cheap eats.

The *Fishermans Cove Restaurant* is known for its seafood and has main courses averaging around $19. At Rainbow Bay, on the northern side of Point Danger, *Doyle's on the Beach* has excellent seafood takeaways and a restaurant.

Getting There & Away

All long-distance buses stop at the Coolangatta Transit Centre on the corner of Griffith and Warner Sts. Ticket sales are handled by Golden Gateway Travel (☎ (07) 5536 6600). Coachtrans offers a same-day return to Brisbane for $20, $12 one way. Kirklands goes to Byron Bay for $14.40 and Coffs Harbour for $42.

Surfside (☎ (07) 5536 77666) has frequent services to Murwillumbah ($4.80) and to Kingscliff ($3.10). It also has eight buses a day to Cabarita Beach ($4.50) on weekdays – five on Saturday and three on Sunday. Buses leave from outside the Tweed Heads visitor centre.

There are several car-hire places that will get you moving for $30 a day, such as Tweed Auto Rentals (☎ (07) 5536 8000) at the information centre on Wharf St.

Far North Coast Hinterland

The area stretching 60km or so inland from the Pacific Highway in far northern New South Wales has spectacular forested mountains, and a high population of alternative lifestylers. These settlers, the first of whom were attracted to the area by the Aquarius Festival at Nimbin in 1973, have become a prominent, colourful part of the community.

The country between Lismore and the coast was once known as the Big Scrub, an incredibly inadequate description of a place that must have been close to paradise at the time of European incursion. Much of the 'scrub' was cleared for farming, after loggers had been through and removed the prized red cedar. These days the area is marketed as Rainbow Country.

A web of narrow roads covers the hinterland. If you're planning to explore the area, get the Forestry Commission's Casino area map ($5) – the information centres in Byron Bay and Nimbin are two places that stock it.

Geography

The northern part of the hinterland was formed by volcanic activity (see the Mt Warning entry later in this section) and is essentially a huge bowl almost completely rimmed by mountain ranges, with the spectacular peak of Mt Warning in the centre. The escarpments of the McPherson and Tweed ranges form the north-western rim, with the Razorback Range to the west and the Nightcap Range to the south-west. National parks, some of them World Heritage areas, protect unique and beautiful subtropical rainforests.

The country south of here is a maze of steep hills and beautiful valleys, some still harbouring magnificent stands of rainforest, others cleared for cattle-grazing and plantations – especially macadamia nuts.

Markets & Music

The alternative community can be seen in force at the weekend markets listed below.

The biggest market is at The Channon, between Lismore and Nimbin.

Brunswick Heads
　1st Saturday of the month, behind the Ampol service station
Byron Bay
　1st Sunday, Butler St Reserve
Lismore
　1st and 3rd Sundays, Lismore Shopping Square;
　5th Sunday, Heritage park
Murwillumbah
　1st Sunday, Sunnyside Shopping Centre
Lennox Head
　2nd and 5th Sundays, Lake Ainsworth foreshore
The Channon
　2nd Sunday, Coronation Park
Mullumbimby
　3rd Saturday, Museum
Ballina
　3rd Sunday, Fawcett Park
Uki
　3rd Sunday, Old Buttery
Bangalow
　4th Sunday, Showground
Nimbin
　4th Sunday, Showground

Many accomplished musicians live in the area and they sometimes play at the markets or in the town pub after the market (notably at Uki). Friday's edition of the *Northern Star* includes a guide to the week's gigs and other activities. *Phat* magazine and the Byron *Echo* and Lismore *Echo* newspapers cover most musical and cultural events in the area.

LISMORE (pop 28,400)

Thirty-five km inland from Ballina on the Bruxner Highway to New England, Lismore is the main town of the state's far north. It's on the Wilson River, which forms the north arm of the Richmond River.

The Lismore Visitor & Heritage Centre (☎ 6622 0122) is on the Bruxner Highway – known as Ballina St through town – on the corner of Molesworth St, near the Wilson River. It has a rainforest display ($1) and the Big Scrub Environment Centre (☎ 6621 3278) on Keen St sells topographic maps of the area.

The interesting **Richmond River Historical Society Museum** (☎ 6621 9993) is at

165 Molesworth St and is open weekdays ($2). The **Regional Art Gallery** at 131 Molesworth St is open Tuesday to Sunday (free). **Rotary Park** is an interesting 6-hectare patch of remnant rainforest that has survived while the town has grown around it. The park is dominated by towering hoop pines and giant fig trees. It's just off the Bruxner Highway about 3km east of the information centre. Access is from Rotary Drive.

Tucki Tucki Nature Reserve, 16km south of Lismore on the Woodburn road, is a koala reserve. Initiation ceremonies were held at the Aboriginal **bora ring** nearby.

The Northern Rivers Folk Festival (☎ 6621 7537 for bookings) is held on the October long weekend. The festival features Celtic, indigenous, a capella, African and world music.

The MV *Bennelong* (☎ 0414 664 552) offers a variety of cruises, including a day trip down the river to Ballina for $55 ($20 children).

Places to Stay

Currendina Travellers Lodge (☎ 6621 6118) occupies the old weatherboard Lismore hospital building at 14 Ewing St – Currendina means 'place of healing' in the language of the local Bundjalung Aboriginal people. It's a cosy place close to the city centre with dorms for $15, singles from $20 to $25 and doubles from $39. Smoking and drinking are not permitted. The friendly managers can organise trips to places of interest in the area.

The *Northern Rivers Hotel* (☎ 6621 5797), at the junction of Terania and Bridge Sts on the road out to Nimbin, has good singles/doubles for $20/25.

Places to Eat

The *Northern Rivers Hotel* (see Places to Stay) does unbelievably cheap meals, with roast lunches for $2 and dinners for $3. Opposite the Northern Rivers, philosophically as well as physically, is the vegan *20,000 Cows Cafe* on Bridge St.

Dr Juice on Keen St in the town centre is open during the day for excellent juices and smoothies, plus vegetarian and vegan snacks for around $2. Next door is *Fundamental Health Foods*, a big health-food shop. *Cafe Lisboa*, at the rear of the Civic Hotel at 210 Molesworth St, has good, reasonably priced Portuguese meals.

Getting There & Away

Hazelton (☎ 13 1713) has daily flights to Brisbane and Sydney.

Kirklands (☎ 6622 1499) is based here and runs buses around the immediate area as well as further afield. Destinations include Byron Bay ($10.70), Mullumbimby ($11.20), Murwillumbah ($14.80) and Brisbane ($2.20). There's a handy service to Tenterfield in New England ($21.50) on weekdays. The XPT train from Sydney ($82) stops here.

NIMBIN (pop 320)

The Aquarius Festival of 1973 transformed the declining dairy town of Nimbin into a name synonymous with Australia's 'back to the land' counterculture movement. It remains a friendly and active alternative centre with many communes in the area, yet times have changed. Nowadays, you're just as likely to stumble over a syringe as a joint-but clip as you walk down Cullen St, the main street.

The weird and wonderful **Nimbin Museum** (admission by donation) is on Cullen St near the Rainbow Cafe. It's not your average museum – it's a real hoot. There's a good market on the 4th Sunday of the month and you may catch a local band playing afterwards.

Nimbin Explorer (☎ 6689 1557) has tours of the Nimbin area ($25) and to Border Ranges National Park ($30).

Many people come to the area to visit **Djanbung Gardens** (☎ 6689 1755), a permaculture education centre established by Robyn Francis – a disciple of permaculture guru Bill Mollison. Contact the centre for information about courses. The centre, five-minutes walk from the town centre at 74 Cecil St, is open for information on Tuesday and Thursday from 10 am to 3 pm. Guided tours are run on market days (4th Sunday of the month) at 3 pm, and on Tuesday and Thursday at 10.30 am.

Places to Stay

The council's basic caravan park (☎ 6689 1402) is near the bowling club – go down the road running past the pub. Sites start from $8 and on-site vans from $25.

Granny's Farm (☎ 6689 1333), a YHA-affiliated hostel, is a very relaxed place surrounded by farmland, with platypuses in the nearby creek. It also has a swimming pool. Conventional dorm beds are $13 and doubles $35. Other options are the teepee or 'pleasure dome' for $10 per person, and creekside camping from $6 per person. The friendly managers will sometimes give rides to places of interest. To get there, go north along Cullen St and turn left just before the bridge over the creek.

Grey Gum Lodge (☎ & fax 6689 1713) on the road into town from Lismore is a stylishly renovated weatherboard house. There are six rooms and singles/doubles start from $20/40 with breakfast. There is a pool and the friendly owners serve meals on the verandah given enough notice.

Places to Eat

The *Rainbow Cafe*, in the centre of town on Cullen St, promotes itself as the place where more than a million joints have been smoked, doubtless leading to some serious assaults on the range of delicious cakes (priced from $2.50). There are vegetarian snacks and meals for around $6. It also does breakfast, as does the nearby *Nimbin Rocks Cafe*, the closest thing you'll find to a standard country-town cafe. Across the street, *Choices* has healthy (and not-so-healthy) takeaways and light meals.

At the northern end of Cullen St, *Nimbin Pizza & Trattoria* has pasta from $8.50 and is open daily from 5 pm.

If you have your own transport, try *Calurla Tea Garden* (☎ 6689 7297), 11km from town on the edge of Nightcap National Park. To get there, take Blue Knob Rd north out of Nimbin and turn onto Lillian Rock

Road after 8km. It's open daily from 10 am to 7 pm, and until late on Friday and Saturday nights.

Entertainment

If there's a dance at the town hall, don't miss the opportunity to meet up with the friendly people from the country around Nimbin. There's an annual *Mardi Grass Festival* at the end of April which culminates with the famous *Marijuana Harvest Ball*.

The *Freemasons Hotel* often has music, and the *Bush Theatre & Cafe* at the old butter factory, near the bridge at the northern end of town, has films on Friday and Saturday (7.30 pm), and Sunday (6.30 pm).

Getting There & Away

Free Spirit Tours (☎ 6687 2007) operates a daily service between Byron Bay and Nimbin for $12, as does The Nimbin Shuttle Bus (☎ 6687 2007), also $12. Nimbin Tours (☎ 6685 5362) charges $10 one way between Nimbin and Byron Bay. Justice Bus Service (☎ 6679 5267) runs through Nimbin on its morning school run from Murwillumbah to Lismore and again on the afternoon return. The fare from Murwillumbah is $9.90 and the fare from Lismore is $8.40.

AROUND NIMBIN

The country around Nimbin is superb. The 800m-plus Nightcap Range, originally a flank of the huge Mt Warning volcano, rises north-east of the town and a sealed road leads to one of its highest points, **Mt Nardi**. The range is part of **Nightcap National Park**. The Mt Nardi road gives access to a variety of other vehicle and walking tracks along and across the range, including the historic Nightcap Track, a packhorse trail which was once the main route between Lismore and Murwillumbah. The views from **Pholis Gap** on the Googarna road, towards the western end of the range, are particularly spectacular.

The Tuntable Falls commune, one of the biggest, with its own shop and school and some fine houses, is about 9km east of Nimbin and you can reach it by the public

Tuntable Falls Rd. You can walk to the 123m **Tuntable Falls** themselves, 13km from Nimbin.

The eastern region of the park covers the Terania Creek catchment area. A stunningly beautiful 700m walk leads to **Protesters' Falls**, named after the environmentalists whose 1979 campaign to stop logging was a major factor in the creation of the national park. There is free camping at Terania Creek, but you're supposed to stay only one night. No fires are allowed.

Access to Terania Creek is via **The Channon**, a tiny town off the Nimbin-Lismore road that hosts the biggest of the region's markets on the 2nd Sunday of each month. A dance is sometimes held the night before the market and there's often music afterwards.

The *Channon Teahouse & Craftshop* is a pleasant place for a snack or a light meal and has interesting handicrafts to browse through. It's open daily from 10 am to 5 pm, with dinner on Friday and Saturday nights. The *Channon Village Campsite* (☎ 6688 6321) is basic but pretty and costs $4 per person. Out of town on the road to Terania Creek, *Terania Park Camping Ground* (☎ 6688 6121) has tent sites ($5) and on-site vans ($25).

Nimbin Rocks is an Aboriginal sacred site signposted off along Stony Chute (Kyogle) Rd, which leads west off the Nimbin-Lismore road just south of Nimbin. **Hanging Rock Creek** has falls and a good swimming hole; take the road through Stony Chute for 14km, turn right at the Barker's Vale sign, then left onto Williams Rd; the falls are nearby on the right.

MULLUMBIMBY (pop 2870)

This pleasant little town, known locally as Mullum, is in subtropical countryside 5km off the Pacific Highway, between Bangalow and Brunswick Heads. Perhaps best known for its marijuana – 'Mullumbimby Madness' – it's a centre for the long-established farming community as well as for the alternative folk from nearby areas, although

there's nothing like the cultural frontier mentality of Nimbin here.

West of Mullum in the Whian Whian State Forest, **Minyon Falls** drop 100m into a rainforest gorge. There are good walking tracks around the falls and you can get within a couple of minutes walk by conventional vehicle from Repentance Creek on one of the back roads between Mullum and Lismore. The eastern end of the historic Nightcap Track (see Around Nimbin) emerges at the north of Whian Whian State Forest.

Places to Stay & Eat

There are a couple of motels and, 12km north, *Maca's Main Arm Camping Ground* in Main Arm (☎ 6684 5211) is an idyllic place, under the lee of hills lush with rainforest. It's nothing like a commercial caravan park but the facilities are quite good, with a kitchen, hot showers and a laundry. It costs $6 per person and you can hire tents from $6 a day. To get here, take Main Arm Rd and follow the 'camping' signposts.

The *Popular Cafe* on Burringbar St is a popular place to hang out and *Buon Appetito* on Stuart St has inexpensive pasta (from $5) and pizzas to eat in or take away.

The *Pizza Hive* on Station St has vegetarian meals as well as pizza. *Mullum House* at 103 Stuart St has Chinese mains under $10. *Lu Lu's* on Dalley St brews great coffee and offers snacks like pakoras with coriander sauce for $3.50.

Getting There & Away

Kirklands buses go through Mullum on their Lismore ($11.20) to Brisbane ($21.10) run. The newsagency on the corner of Burringbar and Stuart Sts is the Kirklands agent.

Mullum is on the Sydney ($82) to Murwillumbah railway line.

There are two road routes to Mullum from the Pacific Highway: one turns off just south of Brunswick Heads, and the other is the longer but prettier Coolaman Scenic Drive, which leaves the highway north of Brunswick Heads near the Ocean Shores turn-off.

For a scenic drive to Uki and Mt Warning,

head out to Upper Main Arm, pass Maca's Camping Ground and follow the unsealed road through the Nullum State Forest. Keep to the main road and watch for signposts at a few ambiguous intersections. Watch out for logging trucks and don't try the road after rain – or you stand a good chance of literally sliding off the mountain.

MT WARNING NATIONAL PARK
The dramatic peak of Mt Warning (1160m) dominates the district. It was named by Captain Cook as a landmark for avoiding Point Danger off Tweed Heads. The mountain is the former central magma chamber of a massive volcano formed more than 20 million years ago. It once covered an area of more than 4000 sq km, stretching from Coraki in the south to Beenleigh in the north, and from Kyogle in the west to an eastern rim now covered by the ocean. Erosion has since carved out the deep Tweed and Oxley valleys around Mt Warning, but sections of the flanks survive in the form of the Nightcap Range in the south and parts of the Border Ranges to the north.

The road into the park runs off the Murwillumbah-Uki road. It's about 6km to the car park at the base of the track leading to the summit. Much of the 4.5km walk is through rainforest. The final section is steep (to put it mildly), so allow five hours for a round trip. Take water. If you're on the summit at dawn you'll be the first person on the Australian mainland to see the sun's rays that day! The trail is well marked, but you'll need a torch if you're climbing at night (to reach the summit at dawn).

Even if you don't want to climb Mt Warning it's worth visiting for the superb rainforest in this World Heritage area. There's a short walking track near the car park.

Places to Stay
You can't camp at Mt Warning but the *Wollumbin Wildlife Refuge & Caravan Park* (☎ 6679 5120) on the Mt Warning approach road has tent sites ($10), on-site vans (from $24) and cabins ($35). The vans and cabins cost less if you stay more than one night. There are kitchen facilities and a well-stocked kiosk – and lots of wildlife in the 120-hectare refuge, including koalas. Platypus can be seen at dusk in the adjoining Tweed River.

The *Mt Warning Forest Hideaway* (☎ 6679 7139), 12km south-west of Uki on Byrrill Creek Rd has small units with cooking facilities from $38/45. Another option is the *Mt Warning Backpackers of Murwillumbah* (see that section for details).

Getting There & Away
A Justice's (☎ 6621 2307) school bus runs from Murwillumbah to Uki, Nimbin and Lismore on weekdays. It leaves Knox Park in Murwillumbah at 7 am and can drop you at the start of the 6km Mt Warning approach road. The hostels at Murwillumbah and Cabarita Beach organise trips to the mountain.

BORDER RANGES NATIONAL PARK
The Border Ranges National Park covers the New South Wales side of the McPherson Range along the NSW-Queensland border and some of the range's outlying spurs. The Tweed Range Scenic Drive – gravel but useable in all weather – loops through the park about 100km from Lillian Rock (midway between Uki and Kyogle) to Wiangaree (north of Kyogle on the Woodenbong road). It has some breathtaking lookouts over the Tweed Valley to Mt Warning and the coast. The adrenalin charging walk out to the crag called the **Pinnacle** – about an hour from the road and back – is not for vertigo sufferers! The rainforest along **Brindle Creek** is also breathtaking, and there are several walks from the picnic area here.

There are a couple of camp sites, basic but free, on the Tweed Range Scenic Drive: Forest Tops, high on the range, and Sheepstation Creek, about 6km further west and 15km from the Wiangaree turn-off. There might be tank water but it's best to bring your own.

NEW SOUTH WALES

New England

New England is the area along the Great Dividing Range stretching north from near Newcastle to the Queensland border. It's a vast tableland of sheep and cattle country with many good bushwalking areas and photogenic scenery, and unlike much of the northern-half of Australia, New England has four distinct seasons. If you're travelling along the eastern seaboard, it's worth diverting inland to New England to get a glimpse of the Australian lifestyle away from the coast. There's a lot less tourist hype, for starters.

A diversion is easy enough thanks to the New England Highway, which runs from Hexham, just north of Newcastle, to Brisbane. This route was developed as an inland alternative to the Pacific Highway. It's an excellent road, with far less traffic than on the coast. There is great scenery on the roads linking the New England Highway with the coast, particularly on the Oxley Highway from Bendemeer (just north of Tamworth) to Port Macquarie, and on the Waterfall Way from Armidale to Bellingen via Dorrigo.

National Parks

The eastern side of the tableland tumbles over an escarpment to the coastal plains below, and along this edge is a string of fine national parks. Gorges and waterfalls are a common feature. The NPWS office in Armidale (☎ 6773 7211) has information on all the parks listed below.

Werrikimbe This remote, rugged World Heritage listed park straddles the escarpment north of the Oxley Highway between Walcha and Wauchope. There are two main approaches to the park. The easiest is along the Forbes River road, which turns off the highway at Yarras, 45km west of Wauchope. This leads to the Plateau Beach Rest Area, the launching pad for walks to the gorges of the Forbes and Hastings rivers – recommended for experienced bushwalkers only.

The other approach to the park is along the Kangaroo Flat road, 55km east of Walcha.

Oxley Wild Rivers Consisting of several sections, this park east of Armidale and Walcha is crossed by deep gorges with some spectacular waterfalls – especially after rain. **Wollomombi Falls**, 39km east of Armidale, are among the highest in Australia with a 220m drop; **Apsley Falls** are east of Walcha at the southern end of the park. On the bottom of the gorges is a wilderness area, accessible from Raspberry Rd off the Wollomombi-Kempsey road.

New England & Cathedral Rock New England is a small park with a wide range of ecosystems. There are 20km of walking tracks and, at the bottom of the escarpment, a wilderness area. Access is from near Ebor and there are cabins and camp sites near the entrance at Point Lookout. Book these through the Dorrigo NPWS office (☎ 6657 2309). Cathedral Rock, off the Ebor-Armidale road, has photogenic granite formations.

Dorrigo See the North Coast section for information on this park.

Guy Fawkes River This is gorge country with canoeing and walking. **Ebor Falls**, near the town of Ebor on the road from Armidale to Dorrigo, are spectacular. Access to the park is from Hernani, 15km north-east of Ebor. From here it's 30km to the Chaelundi Rest Area, with camp sites and water.

Gibraltar Range & Washpool Dramatic, forested and wild, these parks lie south and north of the Gwydir Highway between Glen Innes and Grafton. Countrylink buses stop at the visitor centre (the start of a 10km track to the Mulligans Hut camping area in Gibraltar Range) and at the entrance to Washpool (from where it's about 3km to camping areas).

Bald Rock & Boonoo Boonoo Bald Rock is about 30km north of Tenterfield on an unsealed (but deceptively smooth – take it easy) road which continues into Queensland. Bald Rock is a huge granite monolith which has been compared to Uluru. You can walk to the top, and camp near the base. Nearby is Boonoo Boonoo, with a 200m-drop waterfall and basic camping.

Getting There & Away
Airports at Armidale and Tamworth provide daily services to Sydney and Brisbane.

Several bus lines run through New England from Melbourne or Sydney to Brisbane. Kean's (☎ 1800 625 587) runs between Tamworth and Port Macquarie via Coffs Harbour and Armidale; Kirklands (☎ 6622 1499) operates between Lismore and Tenterfield ($21); and Batterhams Express (☎ 1800 043 339) runs between Sydney and Tamworth via the Hunter Valley. Trains run from Sydney to Armidale, from where Countrylink buses run up to Tenterfield.

TAMWORTH (pop 31,865)
Tamworth is the country-music centre of the nation, an antipodean Nashville. The town's population doubles during the 10-day country music festival in January, which culminates with the Australasian country music awards, Golden Guitars, on the Australia Day long weekend.

Guitar-shaped things are all the rage, starting with the information centre (☎ 6766 9422) on the corner of Peel and Murray Sts. Pick up a map of the Heritage Walk or the longer Kamilaroi Walking Track, which begins at the Oxley Scenic Lookout at the northern end of White St.

Country-music memorabilia around town include a collection of photos at the Good Companions Hotel, the **Hands of Fame** near the information centre and, at Tattersalls Hotel on Peel St, **Noses of Fame**!

The **Country Collection**, on the New England Highway in South Tamworth, is hard to miss – out the front is the 12m-high **Golden Guitar**. Inside is a wax museum ($4). Also here is the Longyard Hotel, a major venue during the festival. Recording studios, such as Big Wheel (☎ 6767 9499) and Hadley Records & Yeldah Music (☎ 6765 7813), can be visited by arrangement.

Places to Stay
You'll be lucky to find a bed anywhere during the country-music festival (unless you've booked years in advance).

The *Paradise Caravan Park* (☎ 6766 3120), near the information centre on the corner of East and Peel Sts, has tent sites for $11.50 and on-site vans for $31.

Country Backpackers (☎ 6761 2600) at 169 Marius St (opposite the train station) is basic but clean and perfectly located with helpful managers. Dorms cost $15 with linen and breakfast, and doubles $35.

The *Central Hotel* (☎ 6766 2160), on the corner of Peel and Brisbane Sts in the city centre, has singles/doubles for $25/40 or $32/45 with en suite. Other city-centre pubs include the *Good Companions* (☎ 6766 28 50) on Brisbane St, the *Imperial* (☎ 6766 2613) on the corner of Brisbane and Marius Sts and the *Tamworth* (☎ 6766 2923) on Marius St.

Many motels are enormous but few are cheap. At slow times you might find some charging $45 but don't count on it.

Echo Hills Station (☎ 1800 810 243), about 30km east of town on Mulla Creek Road near Kootingal, offers backpackers a rare opportunity to experience life on a sheep station. It charges $30 per night including meals. Echo Hills also runs week-long courses for would-be jackaroos/jillaroos for about $398. Backpackers can join the activities for $35 a day. They also run a pub crawl by horseback which costs $349 for three days. The owners will pick you up from Tamworth or Sydney by appointment. There are also self-contained cottages from $90.

Getting There & Away
Eastern Australia (☎ 13 1313) and Tamair (☎ 1800 647 878) have daily flights to Sydney for $179 and Impulse (☎ 13 1381) flies to Brisbane for $229. Most of the long-distance buses pull in at the information

centre. Bus fares include $45 to Sydney and $20 to Armidale.

TAMWORTH TO ARMIDALE

The timber town of **Walcha** (pop 1700) is off the New England Highway on the eastern slope of the Great Dividing Range, on the winding and spectacular Oxley Highway route to the coast at Port Macquarie. East of the town is the Apsley Gorge, with magnificent waterfalls; see the National Parks entry earlier in this section.

Back on the highway, the pretty town of **Uralla** (pop 2460) is where bushranger Captain Thunderbolt was buried in 1870. Graffiti-splattered Thunderbolt's Rock, by the highway 7km south of town, was one of his hide-outs. There are several craft shops and the big McCrossin's Mill Museum ($2). A fossicking area is about 5km north-west of Uralla on the Kingstown road. The town of **Gostwyck**, a little piece of England, is 10km south-east of Uralla.

ARMIDALE (pop 21,000)

The regional centre of Armidale is a popular stopping point. The 1000m altitude means it's pleasantly cool in summer and frosty (but often sunny) in winter. The town is famous for its autumn colours, which are at their best in late March and early April.

The Beardy St pedestrian mall and some elegant old buildings make the town centre attractive. It's also a lively town, thanks to the large student population at the University of New England. Education is big business in Armidale; there are also three posh boarding schools, including The Armidale School (TAS), whose imposing buildings and grounds can be seen on the road to Grafton and Dorrigo.

The information centre (☎ 6772 4655, 1800 627 736) is just north of the city centre on the corner of Marsh and Dumaresq Sts. It has walking and driving-tour brochures. The bus station is in the same building.

The **Armidale Folk Museum** is in the city centre on the corner of Faulkner and Rusden Sts and is open daily from 1 to 4 pm (admission donation). The excellent **New England**

Regional Art Museum ($5) is south of the centre on Kentucky St. Just next door you'll find the excellent **Aboriginal Cultural Centre & Keeping Place** which has changing exhibitions; you can visit from 9 am to 5 pm on weekdays or 10 am to 4 pm on weekends ($3).

Saumarez Homestead, on the New England Highway between Armidale and Uralla, is a beautiful, old house that still contains the effects of the rich pastoralists who built it.

The Armidale area is noted for its magnificent gorges and waterfalls – best viewed after rain. The best of them are **Wollomombi Falls**, 39km east of Armidale off the road to Grafton and Dorrigo, and **Dangar's Falls**, 22km south-east of Armidale off the Dangarsleigh road. Both have basic camp sites.

Places to Stay

The *Pembroke Caravan Park* (☎ 6772 6470), about 2km east of town on Grafton Rd, has sites from $12, on-site vans from $20/25 a single/double and cabins between $32/37 and $42/48. It is also an associate-YHA hostel, offering beds in a huge partitioned dorm for $15.50. Families might be offered an en-suite cabin at YHA rates.

Much more convenient is Armidale's 'Pink Pub', the *Wicklow Hotel* (☎ 6772 2421) on the corner of Marsh and Dumaresq Sts just across from the bus station. It has comfortable pub rooms for $18 per person. *Tattersalls Hotel* (☎ 6772 2247) is on the mall so it has little traffic noise. Rooms start at $24/36, more with bathroom attached.

There are more than 20 motels but about the only places with doubles for under $50 are *Rose Villa Motel* (☎ 6772 3872), which charges from $39/45, and *Hideaway Motor Inn* (☎ 6772 5177) which charges from $42/52. Both are on the New England Highway north of town.

Places to Eat

The central streets have a wide variety of eating places. The best place to start is the East Mall. *Tall Paul's* on the corner of Marsh and Beardy Sts has roasts ($8.50), steaks

($11) and less expensive eats such as burgers (from $2.70). *Jean-Pierre's BYO Cafe*, an odd combination of a country town cafe and a French restaurant, has snacks and meals. *Cafe Midale* further along Beardy St has breakfast and light meals from $6.50. *Rumours* has breakfasts from $3.50, burgers from $4.70 and other meals such as nachos and foccacia.

Chinese restaurants include *Mekong* on East Mall, which has weekday smorgasbord lunches for $7 and a smorgasbord dinner on Thursday for $9. *Lee's* next to the hardware store on Beardy St has lunch specials for $4.50 and dinner specials for $11.90.

Getting There & Away
Eastern Australia (☎ 13 1313) and Hazelton (☎ 13 1713) fly to Sydney ($190) and Impulse flies to Brisbane ($243).

Countrylink (☎ 13 2242), McCafferty's (☎ 13 1499) and Greyhound Pioneer (☎ 13 2030) all service Armidale, and Kean's (☎ 1800 625 587) runs down to Coffs Harbour and Port Macquarie, via Dorrigo. Fares from Armidale include Sydney $53, Brisbane $48, Tamworth $20, Glen Innes $25 ($11 with Countrylink), Dorrigo $16, Bellingen $23, Coffs Harbour $24 and Port Macquarie $40.

The train fare from Sydney is $67.

Realistic Car Rentals (☎ 6772 8078) at Armidale Exhaust Centre on the corner of Rusden and Dangar Sts has cars from $45 a day, including insurance and 100 free km.

Getting Around
Armidale Cycle Centre (☎ 6772 3718) at 248 Beardy St (near Allingham St) hires bikes for $4 an hour, $15 a day or $35 a week.

NORTH OF ARMIDALE
Guyra (pop 1800)
Guyra is at an altitude of 1300m, making it one of the highest towns in the state. The **Guyra & District Historical Society Museum** has filled the old council chambers with its collection of pioneering memorabilia. It's open only on Sunday afternoon ($2). **Mother of Ducks** is a waterbird sanc-

tuary on the edge of town. The strange **balancing rock** can be seen by the highway 12km before Glen Innes at Stonehenge.

Glen Innes (pop 6100)
You're still at over 1000m at Glen Innes, a good place to meet bushrangers a century ago. Buses stop at the information centre (☎ 6732 2397) on the New England Highway.

The old hospital on the corner of Ferguson St and West Ave houses **Land of the Beardies History House**, a big folk museum open daily from 2 to 5 pm and also from 10 to noon on weekdays ($4). The main street, Grey St, is worth strolling down for its old buildings. The area was settled by Scots, and Glen Innes regards itself as the Celtic capital of New England – there are bilingual street signs. The impressive **Standing Stones** can be seen on a hill above town.

Black & White (☎ 6732 3687) has a daily bus between Glen Innes and Inverell ($18) Monday to Saturday.

Inverell (pop 9,400)
Inverell is a large country town with some impressive public buildings. The information centre (☎ 6722 1693) is in a converted water tower on Campbell St, a block back from the main shopping street. The **mining museum** is here too – silver was once mined around Inverell and sapphire is still mined. **Inverell Pioneer Village** is open from 2 to 4 pm on Sunday and Monday, and from 10 am to 5 pm the rest of the week ($4, $5 on Sunday, which includes afternoon tea).

You can visit a fully operational sapphire mine at Dejon Sapphire Centre (☎ 6723 2222), 19km east of Inverell on the Gwydir Highway. It has tours at 10.30 am and 3 pm.

The *Empire Hotel* (☎ 6722 1411) is an old pub on Byron St with singles/doubles for $20/35.

Tenterfield (pop 3200)
At the junction of the New England and Bruxner highways, Tenterfield is the last big town before the Queensland border. The information centre (☎ 6736 1082) is on Rouse St, the main street, on the corner of

Miles St. The **Sir Henry Parkes Memorial School of Arts** is where Parkes launched the national federation movement in 1889. The old stone **Saddler's Shop** on High St once belonged to late-Australian entertainer Peter Allen's grandfather (Allen sang about it in the song *Tenterfield Saddler*).

Thunderbolt's Hideout, where bush-ranger Captain Thunderbolt did just that, is 11km out of town. The main attractions in the area are the Bald Rock and Boonoo Boonoo national parks – see the National Parks entry earlier in this section. The information centre can organise tours of these parks with **Woollool Woollool Aboriginal Culture Tours**.

Places to Stay *Tenterfield Lodge* (☎ 6736 1477), a hostel at the western end of Manners St, near the old train station, is a National-Trust-listed former pub built in 1870. Shared rooms are $15 per person, doubles are $35 and family rooms are $45. You can camp out the back for $10 per person and there are on-site vans from $22.

Several pubs have accommodation, such as the *Exchange Hotel* (☎ 6736 1054) on Rouse St with singles/doubles for $14/25.

South Coast

Though much less visited than the coast north of Sydney, the coast south to the Victorian border has many beautiful spots and excellent beaches, good surf and diving, some attractive little fishing towns and forests both lovely and spectacularly wild. The Snowy Mountains are 150km from Sydney.

The Princes Highway runs along the coast from Sydney through Wollongong to the Victorian border. Although a longer and slower route to Melbourne than the Hume Highway, it's much more interesting.

Getting There & Away

Hazelton (☎ 13 1713) flies to Merimbula from Sydney; Kendell (an Ansett subsidiary,

☎ 13 1300, 6922 0100 in Wagga Wagga) flies to Merimbula from Melbourne.

Greyhound Pioneer (☎ 13 2030) travels the Princes Highway. Fares from Sydney include Batemans Bay $34 (six hours), Narooma $42 (seven hours) and Bega $49 (eight hours). Sapphire Coast Express (☎ 4473 5517) runs between Batemans Bay and Melbourne ($61/110 one way/return) twice a week.

A Nowra-based company, Pioneer Motor Service (☎ 4423 5233), runs buses daily between Eden and Sydney ($49), and for short hops between coastal towns it's much cheaper than the big lines. There's also a service between Bega and Canberra. Countrylink (☎ 13 2242) serves Bega on its daily Eden-Canberra run ($35).

Murrays (☎ 9252 3590) has daily buses from Canberra to Batemans Bay ($21.75) and south along the coast to Narooma. Its buses connect with north-bound Pioneer Motor Service buses at Batemans Bay.

The railway from Sydney goes as far south as Bomaderry (Nowra).

WOLLONGONG (pop 219,761)

Only 80km south of Sydney is the state's third-largest city, an industrial centre that includes the biggest steelworks in Australia at nearby Port Kembla. Wollongong also has some superb surf beaches, and the hills behind provide a fine backdrop, great views over the city and coast, and good walks.

The name Illawarra is often applied to Wollongong and its surrounds – it refers specifically to the hills behind the city (the Illawarra Escarpment) and the coastal Lake Illawarra to the south.

Orientation & Information

Crown St is the main commercial street and between Kembla and Keira Sts is a two-block pedestrian mall. Keira St is part of the Princes Highway. Through-traffic bypasses the city on the Southern Freeway.

The tourist information centre (☎ 4228 0300) on the corner of Crown and Kembla Sts opens daily. The post office is on Crown. Wollongong East post office is near the tourist information centre. The SpidrWeb Cafe (☎ 4225 8677), 67 Kembla St, is the Illawarra region's first Internet cafe.

Bushcraft on Stewart St has hiking and camping gear.

Things to See
The fishing fleet is based in the southern part of Wollongong's harbour, **Belmore Basin**, which was cut from solid rock in 1868. There's a fish cooperative (with a fish market, cafe and restaurant) and an 1872 lighthouse.

North Beach, north of the harbour, generally has better surf than the south Wollongong City Beach. The harbour itself has beaches, which are good for children. Other beaches run north up the coast.

The **City Gallery** (☎ 4228 9500) on the corner of Kembla and Burelli Sts opens Tuesday to Friday 10 am to 5 pm, and on weekends from noon to 4 pm. The **Illawarra Museum** (☎ 4228 0158), 11 Market St, contains a reconstruction of the 1902 Mt Kembla town mining disaster and other exhibitions. It's open Wednesday from 10 am to 1 pm, and weekends from 1 to 4 pm ($2, children $1).

The enormous **Nan Tien Buddhist Temple** (☎ 4272 0600), Berkeley Rd, Berkeley, a few kilometres south of the city, is open to visitors.

Places to Stay
You have to go a little way out before you can camp. There are a number of council-run caravan parks: on the beach at Corrimal (☎ 4285 5688), about 6km north of town; near the beach on Farrell Rd in Bulli (☎ 4285 5677), 11km north; and on Fern St (with beach and lake frontage) in Windang (☎ 4297 3166) 15km south, between Lake Illawarra and the sea. All charge about $15 for tent sites (two people) and from $48 for vans or cabins, with prices rising sharply during school and Christmas holidays.

Keiraleagh House (☎ 4228 6765), 60 Kembla St north of Market St, is a large, friendly hostel catering mainly to long-term students but also to short-term visitors. It has

NEW SOUTH WALES

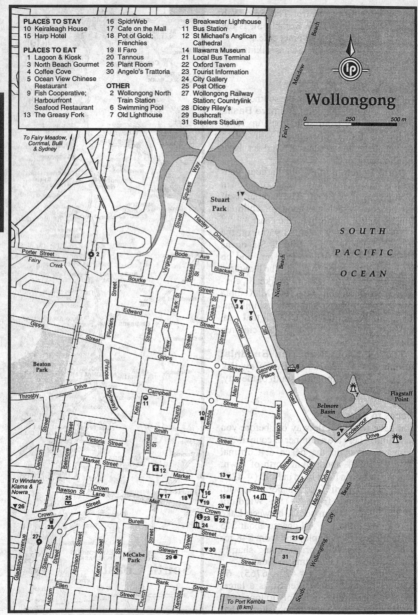

PLACES TO STAY
10 Keiraleagh House
15 Harp Hotel

PLACES TO EAT
1 Lagoon & Kiosk
3 North Beach Gourmet
4 Coffee Cove
5 Ocean View Chinese
  Restaurant
9 Fish Cooperative;
  Harbourfront
  Seafood Restaurant
13 The Greasy Fork

16 SpidrWeb
17 Cafe on the Mall
18 Pot of Gold;
  Frenchies
19 Il Faro
20 Tannous
26 Plant Room
30 Angelo's Trattoria

OTHER
2 Wollongong North
  Train Station
6 Swimming Pool
7 Old Lighthouse

8 Breakwater Lighthouse
11 Bus Station
12 St Michael's Anglican
  Cathedral
14 Illawarra Museum
21 Local Bus Terminal
22 Oxford Tavern
23 Tourist Information
24 City Gallery
25 Post Office
27 Wollongong Railway
  Station; Countrylink
28 Dicey Riley's
29 Bushcraft
31 Steelers Stadium

Wollongong

0   250   500 m

To Fairy Meadow,
Corrimal, Bulli
& Sydney

SOUTH

PACIFIC

OCEAN

Stuart
Park

Fairy
Creek

Porter Street

Beaton
Park

Throsby   Drive

Gipps   Street

To Windang,
Kiama &
Nowra

McCabe
Park

Belmore
Basin

Flagstaff
Point

To Port Kembla
(8 km)

dorms for $15 or singles without/with bath for $20/25.

Several pubs have fairly cheap accommodation, such as the central *Harp Hotel* (☎ 4229 1333), 124 Corrimal St near Crown St, which charges $40/60 for rooms with TV and bathroom (and features bands).

About the only inexpensive motel in the area is the *Cabbage Tree Motel* (☎ 4284 4000), 1 Anama St (behind the Cabbage Tree Hotel) in Fairy Meadow, off the Princes Highway 3.5km north of the city centre. Singles/doubles cost $40/45. Most buses heading north from the Wollongong train station go to Fairy Meadow.

Places to Eat
For good coffee, snacks and meals it's hard to go past *Tannous*, a Lebanese cafe on the corner of Crown and Corrimal Sts. Shish kebabs, felafel and other takeaways are $3.50, or $5.50 if you eat in. Eat-in meals come with large serves of hummus, tabouli and bread.

There are plenty of other places. *Cafe on the Mall* on the corner of Church and Crown Sts opens long hours for snacks and meals. Breakfasts are $6.50. Nearby, in Kembla St, there's the *Pot of Gold*, a Mexican place with mains for $9.90 to $11.90 and, nearby, *Frenchie's Cafe* has good strong coffee and delicious snacks. Across the street is *Il Faro*, with pasta and pizza.

At Belmore Basin, the *Fish Cooperative* is home to the Harbourfront Seafood Restaurant, which opens daily for lunch and dinner with buffets for $17.50 and $25 respectively. More seafood is available at the *Lagoon* (☎ 4226 1766) in Stuart Park behind North Beach. Snapper fillets are $21.50. The restaurant has a great location and opens daily for lunch and dinner. The adjacent *Kiosk* is less expensive.

The *Plant Room*, on Crown St near the corner of Gladstone Ave, up the hill from Wollongong train station, opens during the day for coffee and snacks and at night offers a $15 buffet. It has a relaxed atmosphere, a cosmopolitan menu and live music some evenings.

On Bourke St at North Beach, both *Coffee Cove* and *North Beach Gourmet* are cafes serving breakfast and light meals. There are a few swanky restaurants on Cliff Rd. *Ocean View* is a reasonable Chinese restaurant with a terrace overlooking the water; chicken dishes are around $12.

Entertainment
There are many clubs and pubs with live entertainment. Young bands play at the *Harp Hotel* on Corrimal St and the *Oxford Tavern* on Crown St. *Dicey Riley's*, also on Crown St, has Irish music.

Getting There & Away
Bus The bus station (☎ 4226 1022) is on the corner of Keira and Campbell Sts. Several daily services run to Sydney ($17) and one to Canberra ($28) via Moss Vale and the Southern Highlands. Greyhound Pioneer's Sydney to Melbourne ($64) coastal route runs through Wollongong and direct buses to Brisbane cost $85 (☎ 13 2030). Pioneer Motor Service runs daily to Eden ($47).

Train Many trains run to/from Sydney (about 90 minutes, $6.60 one way; off-peak day-return $7.80) and a fair number continue south to Kiama, Gerringong and Bomaderry (Nowra).

From Port Kembla, Saturday to Tuesday, a tourist train known as the Cockatoo Run (☎ 1800 643 801) heads inland across the Southern Highlands near the Hume Highway and Morton National Park to Moss Vale ($11/20 one way/return).

Getting Around
Two local bus companies service the area: Rutty's (☎ 4271 1322) and John J Hill (☎ 4229 4911). The main stop is on Crown St, where it meets Marine Dve, next to the beach. You can reach most beaches by rail and trains are fairly frequent.

A cycle path runs from the city centre north to Bulli and south to Windang and you can hire bikes in Stuart Park on Sunday and holidays.

AROUND WOLLONGONG

The hills rise dramatically behind Wollongong and there are walking tracks and lookouts on Mt Kembla and Mt Keira less than 10km from the city centre, but no buses go up there. You get spectacular views over the town and coast from **Bulli Scenic Lookout** (pronounced 'bull-eye') high on the escarpment off the Princes Highway, just north of Wollongong.

The country is equally spectacular to the south, inland through the **Macquarie Pass National Park** to Moss Vale or through the Kangaroo Valley. The Fitzroy Falls and other attractions of mountainous **Morton National Park** can be reached by either route.

North of Wollongong there are several excellent beaches. Those with good surf include **Sandon Point**, **Austinmer**, **Headlands** (only for experienced surfers) and **Sharkies**. The pubs at Clifton and Scarborough both have meals, accommodation and spectacular views.

On the road to Otford and Royal National Park, the **Lawrence Hargrave Lookout** at Bald Hill above Stanwell Park is superb for cliff-top viewing. Hargrave, a pioneer aviator, made his first attempts at flying in the area early this century. Hang-gliders fly here today and the Sydney Hang Gliding Centre (☎ 4294 9994) offers courses. South of Wollongong, **Lake Illawarra** is popular for water sports.

WOLLONGONG TO NOWRA

South of Lake Illawarra, **Shellharbour**, a popular holiday resort, is one of the oldest towns along the coast. It was a thriving port back in 1830, but it declined after construction of the railway. There are good beaches on Windang Peninsula north of town and good scuba diving off Bass Point to the south.

Kiama is a pretty seaside town famous for its blowhole, which can spout up to 60m high. Near the blowhole is the heritage Pilot's Cottage Museum. There are also good surf beaches and the scenic Cathedral Rock at Jones Beach. *Blowhole Point Caravan*

Park (☎ 4232 2707) is terrific if it's not too windy, with sites for $12 to $15.

Gerringong, 10km south of Kiama has fine beaches and surf. Pioneer aviator Charles Kingsford-Smith took off in 1933 from Seven Mile Beach – immediately south of Gerringong and now a national park – to fly to New Zealand. *Nesta House* (☎ 4234 1249), an associate YHA hostel on Fern St, is 300m up the hill from Werri Beach. Beds are $13 for members.

The small town of **Berry** was an early settlement, and today it has a number of National Trust classified buildings, a museum and many antique and craft shops. The *Hotel Berry* (☎ 4464 1011) is a pleasant country pub charging $40/50 a single/ double, or $45/60 with bathroom. There are scenic roads from Berry to pretty **Kangaroo Valley**, where there's the Pioneer Farm Settlement (☎ 4465 1306), an old homestead with historic displays, and canoeing on the Shoalhaven and Kangaroo rivers.

Just west of Shoalhaven Heads, **Coolangatta** (no, not the Queensland Coolangatta) has a group of buildings which were constructed by convicts in 1822. They now form part of the Coolangatta Historic Village Resort (☎ 4488 7131), with craft shops, a restaurant and expensive accommodation. The town is also the home of Bigfoot (☎ 4448 7131), a strange vehicle which will carry you to the top of Mt Coolangatta for $10 (children $5) on weekends and school holidays.

SHOALHAVEN

The coastal strip south of Gerringong to Durras Lake, just north of Batemans Bay, is a popular holiday destination known as Shoalhaven, which also stretches 50km inland to include Morton and Budawang national parks. Inland on the Shoalhaven River, the twin towns of **Nowra** and **Bomaderry** form the main population centre. The region is popular for water sports, and white-water rafting is available – phone the Shoalhaven Tourist Centre (☎ 4421 0778) on the highway in Bomaderry. There's also a 24-hour, toll-free number: ☎ 1800 024 261. The NPWS has an office (☎ 4423 9800) at 55 Graham St, Nowra.

Five-km east of Nowra on the northern bank of the Shoalhaven River is **Nowra Animal Park** (☎ 4421 3949). It's a pleasant place to meet some Australian native animals and you can camp in bushland here for $9 ($11 at peak times). *M&M's Guesthouse* (☎ 4422 8006), 1A Scenic Dve, is closer to town, near the bridge on the Nowra side of the river. Dorm beds are $20, double rooms $45; rates include a light breakfast. The associate-YHA *Coach House* (☎ 4421 2084), part of Armstrong's White House at 30 Junction St, has modest dorms with beds for $13 per person.

Inland at Fitzroy Falls, just north of Kangaroo Valley, is the visitor centre (☎ 4887 7270) for **Morton National Park**. South of Morton the line of national parks (Budawang, Deua, Wadbilliga and South East Forests) stretches to the Victorian border. These are outstanding mountain wilderness areas, which are good for rugged bushwalking.

South of Nowra, **Booderee** (an aboriginal word meaning 'bay of plenty'), formerly called Jervis Bay, is quite suburban but **Huskisson**, one of the oldest towns on the bay, is still a pleasant place. There's a fascinating wetlands boardwalk (free) near the Lady Denman Heritage Complex on the Nowra side of Huskisson.

Booderee National Park (☎ 4443 0977) takes up the south-eastern spit of land on Booderee. It has good swimming, surfing and diving on bay and ocean beaches. There are camp sites ($13) at Green Patch and Bristol Point and a more basic camping area at Caves Beach, where there's surf. For all camp sites you have to book. Entry to the park costs $5 per car for a week.

Ulladulla is an area of beautiful lakes, lagoons and beaches. There's good swimming and surfing (try Mollymook beach, just north of town). Or you can take the bushwalk to the top of Pigeon House Mountain (719m) in the impressive Budawang Range.

South Coast Backpackers (☎ 4454 0500),

in Ulladulla at 67 Princes Highway, near the top of the hill north of the shopping centre, is a small place with spacious five-bed dorms and all the usual facilities. Dorm beds cost $15, double rooms $32. They'll take guests to Murramarang National Park or Pigeon House for $15, to Booderee for $4.50.

Fares from Ulladulla with Pioneer Motor Service include Sydney, $23; Nowra, $11; Merry Beach (at the northern end of Murramarang National Park), $6.40; the North Durras turn-off at East Lynne (for Pebbly Beach in Murramarang National Park), $7.80; Batemans Bay, $8.80; and Eden, $29.40.

Murramarang National Park is a beautiful coastal park beginning about 20km south of Ulladulla and running all the way south to Batemans Bay. At lovely Pebbly Beach there's a camp site (☎ 4478 6006), which costs $10 (plus the $7.50 per car entry fee, charges only if you camp). A kiosk operates during school holidays – when tent sites are scarce. Pebbly Beach is about 10km off the highway and there's no public transport.

There's accommodation at settlements within the park. At **Depot Beach** the basic *Moore's Pioneer Park* (☎ 4478 6010) has tent sites for $10 and cabins for $45. As well as the superb beach, **North Durras** is on the inlet to Durras Lake. *Durras Lake North Caravan Park* (☎ 4478 6072) has an on-site van set aside for backpackers ($10 per bed) – ask at the shop.

BATEMANS BAY TO BEGA

The fishing port of **Batemans Bay** is one of the south coast's largest holiday centres. The visitor centre (☎ 4472 6900, 1800 802 528) is on the Princes Highway near the town centre. *Batemans Bay Backpackers* (☎ 4472 4972) is on the Old Princes Highway just south of the town. Beds are $15 a night. Buses run to Canberra ($21.75), Sydney ($34) and Melbourne ($61).

About 60km inland from Batemans Bay on the scenic road to Canberra is **Braidwood**, with its many old buildings and a thriving arts and crafts community. From here there's road access to the superb bushwalking country of the **Budawang Range**.

Moruya, 25km south of Batemans Bay, is a dairy centre, with oyster farming too. There's some fairly unspoiled coast down the side roads south of Moruya. In **Eurobodalla National Park** there are beaches on both sides of a headland at Congo where there's also a basic camp site ($10). Bring your own supplies; you'll need to boil drinking water.

The seaside holiday town of **Narooma** is popular for serious sport fishing in the nearby inlets and lakes. The information centre (☎ 4476 2881) on the beachfront opens daily from 9 am to 5 pm. The NPWS office (☎ 4476 2888) is nearby on the corner of Field St. About 10km off shore is **Montague Island** a nature reserve with a historic lighthouse and many seals and fairy penguins. Tours of the island conducted by NPWS rangers costs $50 (children $35). The clear waters around the island are popular with divers, especially from February to June. The friendly *Bluewater YHA Lodge* (☎ 4476 4440), 11 Riverside Drive near Wagonga Inlet, has dorm beds for $15 and singles/doubles for $25/36.

The delightful, wooden, 19th century town of **Central Tilba**, off the highway 15km south of Narooma, has undergone little change. It perches on the side of **Mt Dromedary** (800m) and you can walk to the top from the nearby town of **Tilba Tilba**. The return walk of 11km takes about five hours, or you could ride up with Mt Dromedary Trail Rides (☎ 4476 3376). Umbarra Cultural Tours (☎ 4473 7232) runs excellent tours to sites of Aboriginal significance, including to Mt Dromedary and in the coastal **Wallaga Lake National Park**.

South of Wallaga Lake and off the Princes Highway, **Bermagui** is a fishing centre made famous 50 years ago by American cowboy-novelist Zane Grey. It's a handy base for visits to both Wallaga Lake and Mimosa Rocks national parks, and for Wadbilliga National Park, inland in the ranges. The main information centre (☎ 6493 4174) is on Cutajo St south of the bridge. The friendly

Blue Pacific (☎ 6493 4921), 77 Murrah St, has backpacker accommodation for $15 as well as regular holiday flats. It's up a hill off the road running along the beach north of the town centre. The turn-off is signposted just north of the fishing-boat wharf. Bega Valley Coaches (☎ 6492 2418) has a weekday service between Bermagui and Bega ($11) and a feeder service connects with Pioneer Motor Service's bus north to Nowra.

More interesting than the inland highway, the largely unsealed coast road between Bermagui and Tathra runs alongside the excellent **Mimosa Rocks National Park**. There are basic camp sites at Aragunnu Beach, Picnic Point and Middle Beach, and a camping area with no facilities at Gillards Beach. Park entry is free, but camping costs $5; bring your own water.

Inland on the Princes Highway is **Cobargo**, another unspoilt, little-changed, old town. The main 2WD access to **Wadbilliga National Park** is near here. It's a rugged wilderness and the thriving animals live in surroundings which haven't changed much in thousands of years.

Bega is a sizeable town near the junction of the Princes and Snowy Mountains highways. The information centre (☎ 6492 2045) is in Gipps St near the corner of Carp St, in a craft shop. The modern, mud-brick *Bega YHA Hostel* (☎ 6492 3103) is on Kirkland Crescent (off Kirkland Ave, which departs the highway about 1km west of the town centre). It's a friendly place where dorm beds cost $13 and doubles $34.

Countrylink's Eden to Canberra service passes through Bega daily (☎ 13 2242). Pioneer Motor Service runs north to Sydney, south to Eden. Greyhound Pioneer (☎ 13 2030) stops here on the run between Sydney and Melbourne, as does Sapphire Coast Express running between Batemans Bay and Melbourne.

SOUTH TO THE VICTORIAN BORDER
The coast here is quite undeveloped, and there are many good beaches and some awe-inspiring forests full of wildlife – and loggers.

Merimbula (pop 4380)

Merimbula is a big holiday resort and retirement town with an impressive 'lake' (actually a large inlet) and ocean beaches. Despite large-scale development, the setting remains beautiful and nearby **Pambula Beach** is quiet in a suburban way.

The tourist information centre (☎ 6495 1250), on the waterfront at the bottom of Market St, opens daily from 9 am to 5 pm. At the wharf on the eastern point is the small **Merimbula Aquarium** (☎ 6495 3227); it opens daily from 10 am to 9 pm ($8, children $5).

Near the surf beach, the spacious *Wandarrah YHA Lodge* (☎ 6495 3503), 8 Marine Parade (follow the signs just south of the bridge), has dorm beds for $15, double rooms for $36. Activities include minibus trips to nearby national parks and rainy day 'mystery tours'.

Eden (pop 3000)

At Eden the road bends away from the coast and into Victoria, running through mighty forests. The town is an old whaling port on Twofold Bay, much less touristy than towns further up the coast. Eden Tourist Centre (☎ 6496 1953) on Imlay St opens weekdays from 9 am to 5 pm and weekends from 9 am to noon.

At the intriguing **Killer Whale Museum** you can learn about the whaler who, in 1891, was swallowed by a whale and regurgitated, unharmed, 15 hours later. Well, almost unharmed. His hair turned white and fell out due to the whale's digestive juices. There's also the skeleton of a killer whale, Old Tom, which led a pack of other killer whales in herding baleen whales into Twofold Bay where they were killed by whalers. The museum opens daily from 10.15 am to 3.45 pm ($4, children $1).

Whales still swim along the coast in October and November. You can book **whale-spotting cruises** ($45, children $30) at Eden Tourist Centre.

The *Australasia Hotel* (☎ 6496 1600) on Imlay St has backpackers' beds for $15, pub

rooms for $25 per person and motel-style rooms for $35 per person.

Boydtown

Boydtown, south of Eden, was founded by Benjamin Boyd, a flamboyant early settler whose landholdings were once second in size only to the Crown's. His grandiose plans included making Boydtown the capital of Australia, but his fortune foundered and so did the town – later he did too, disappearing without trace somewhere in the Pacific. Some of his buildings still stand, and the *Sea Horse Inn* (☎ 6496 1361), a guesthouse built by convict labour, is still in use. You can also camp here for $10.

Ben Boyd National Park & Around

To the north and south of Eden is Ben Boyd National Park – good for walking, camping, swimming and surfing, especially at Long Beach in the north. Edrom Rd is the main access road.

South of Ben Boyd National Park, **Nadgee Nature Reserve** continues down the coast, but it's much less accessible. **Wonboyn**, a small settlement on Wonboyn Lake at the northern end of the reserve, has a small store and *Wonboyn Cabins & Caravan Park* (☎ 6496 9131) with sites for $12. Across the lake from Wonboyn, but with access from Green Cape Rd in Ben Boyd National Park, is *Wonboyn Lake Resort* (☎ 6496 9162), with self-contained cabins from $60 for four people.

Inland from Wonboyn you can follow Imlay Rd (off the Princes Highway) through **South-East Forests National Park**, which extends in pockets north to Wadbilliga National Park and south to the Victorian border.

Snowy Mountains

The Snowy Mountains form part of the Great Dividing Range which straddles the New South Wales-Victoria border. Mt Kosciuszko (pronounced 'kozzyosko' and named after a

Polish hero of the American War of Independence), in New South Wales, has Australia's highest *mainland* summit (2228m). Much of the state's Snowies are within Kosciuszko National Park, an area of year-round interest: skiing in winter, bushwalking and vivid wildflowers in summer. The main ski resorts and the highest country are in the south-centre of the park, west of Jindabyne. Thredbo and the Perisher Valley and Smiggin Holes area are the main downhill skiing areas. Charlottes Pass, Guthega and Mt Blue Cow are smaller downhill areas, as is Mt Selwyn, towards the northern end of the park.

The upper waters of the Murray River form both the state and national-park boundaries in the south-west. The Snowy River, made famous by Banjo Paterson's poem *The Man from Snowy River* and the film based on it, rises just below the summit of Mt Kosciuszko. The Murrumbidgee River also rises in the national park.

You can take white-water rafting trips on the Murray and Snowy rivers in summer when the water is high enough. In summer, horse trail riding is also popular and there are stables near Cooma, Adaminaby, Jindabyne, Tumut and Tumbarumba.

Getting There & Away

Cooma is the eastern gateway to the Snowy Mountains. The most spectacular mountain views are from the Alpine Way (sometimes closed in winter) running between Khancoban, on the western side of the national park, and Jindabyne. There are restrictions on car parking in the national park, particularly in the ski season – check at Cooma or Jindabyne before entering.

Impulse (☎ 13 1381) flies daily to Cooma from Sydney; the standard economy fare is $282. There's no direct flight from Melbourne; Kendell (☎ 13 1300) flies from Melbourne via Sydney but it's very expensive.

Greyhound Pioneer (☎ 13 2030) runs to Cooma ($16 from Canberra, $44 from Sydney) and Jindabyne ($38 from Canberra, $58 from Sydney), with some services continuing on to the resorts. Services are frequent in winter, but less so at other times. Countrylink (☎ 13 2242) runs daily from Sydney, Canberra and Eden.

To Melbourne, V/Line's Capital Link bus (☎ 13 2232) runs from Canberra via Cooma ($47 to Melbourne) to Sale where it connects with a train.

COOMA (pop 7150)

Cooma was the construction centre for the Snowy Mountains Hydroelectric Scheme, built by workers from around the world. The **Avenue of Flags** in Centennial Park, next to Cooma Visitors Centre (☎ 1800 636 525), 119 Sharp St, flies the flags of the 28 nationalities involved. The **Snowy Mountains Information Centre** (☎ 6453 2003, 1800 623 776) on the Monaro Highway 2km north of town opens on weekdays from 8 am to 5 pm and weekends from 8 am to 1 pm.

If you don't have time to take the town walk (maps are available from the visitors centre), at least walk down **Lambie St**, with its historic buildings, and, on Vale St, see the imposing granite **Cooma Courthouse** and nearby **Cooma Gaol Museum** (☎ 6450 1357). Half a kilometre west is the **Southern Cloud Memorial**, which incorporates some of the wreckage of the *Southern Cloud*, an aircraft that crashed in the Snowies in 1931, but only discovered in 1958.

There are several **horse-riding** outfits in the area, including Reynell (☎ 6454 2386) on Bolero Rd (turn off 8km south of Adaminaby) offering mainly accommodation packages, and Yarramba (☎ 6456 7204), off the Snowy Mountains Hwy, midway between Adaminaby and Cooma, offering short rides and one and two-day treks.

Places to Stay

Prices rise in winter, although they are lower here than in Jindabyne or the ski resorts.

The *Mountain View Caravan Park* (☎ 6452 4513), 6km west of Cooma towards Jindabyne, is pleasant with tent sites for $10 ($15 with power) and on-site vans from $25 to $40. Buses on the way to the resorts will stop here by arrangement.

The friendly *Bunkhouse Motel* (☎ 6452 2983) on the corner of Commissioner and Soho Sts has dorm beds for $15 and singles/doubles for $25/40. Each dorm has its own kitchen and en-suite. The *Family Motel* (☎ 6452 1414), 32 Massie St, has shared rooms for $12 ($60 weekly) and singles/doubles from $25/30. In winter it pays to book ahead.

All the pubs have accommodation. The *Australian Hotel* (☎ 6452 1844) on the main street has basic rooms for $20/30, with en-suite rooms also available. The *Royal Hotel* (☎ (6452 2132), on the corner of Sharp and Lambie Sts, is quieter and has clean rooms with shared facilities for $20 per person.

In **Nimmitabel**, a small town on the highway 35km south-east of Cooma, the delightful *Royal Arms* guesthouse (☎ 6454 6422) has rooms for $38/70.

Getting There & Away

All buses except the V/Line service (which stops near Centennial Park) stop at the Snowstop Village on Sharp St a few blocks east of the visitors centre. Snowliner Travel (☎ 6452 1422) on Sharp St opposite the visitors centre handles bus bookings. See also the introductory Getting There & Away section to the Snowy Mountains.

JINDABYNE (pop 4300)

Fifty-six km west of Cooma and a step nearer the mountains, Jindabyne is a modern town on the shore of the artificial Lake Jindabyne, which flooded the old town. In summer you can swim or rent boats. The magnificent, NPWS-operated Snowy Region Visitor Centre (☎ 6450 5600) is in the centre of town on Kosciuszko Rd, the main road in from Cooma. Check the notice board in Nugget's Crossing shopping centre for employment listings, cheap accommodation, car shares and second-hand ski gear.

Paddy Pallin (☎ 6456 2922) and Wilderness Sports (☎ 6456 2966) run guided walks and adventure activities in the Snowies, including mountain biking in summer.

Places to Stay

Winter sees a huge influx of visitors; prices soar, many places are booked out months ahead and overnight accommodation all but disappears. Prices also rise on Friday and Saturday nights throughout the year.

Snowline Caravan Park (☎ 6456 2099) at the intersection of the Alpine Way and Kosciuszko Rd, has tent sites from $12, as well as cabins from $50 a double.

Lazy Harry's Lodge (☎ 6456 1957), fronting Clyde St but accessible from Kosciuszko Rd, is a congenial place with dorm beds for $15 in summer, $25 in winter. Family rooms are also available. A guesthouse with moderate summer prices is the spotless *Sonnblick Lodge* (☎ 6456 2472), 49 Gippsland St, offering B&B for $30/60.

There's a fair range of motel-style places, some converting to longer-term accommodation in winter. *Aspen Hotel/Motel* (☎ 6456 2372), 1 Kosciuszko Rd at the eastern edge of town, has doubles from $60 in summer, $110 in the peak season, which is pretty cheap for this town.

Apartments & Lodges Many places offer ski-season accommodation but they fill up – if possible you should book months in advance. Letting agents include Jindabyne Real Estate (☎ 6456 2216, 1800 020 657). Very approximately, cheaper fully equipped apartments sleeping six cost from around $300 a week in the off season, $600 a week in the high winter season. You can pay a lot more.

KOSCIUSZKO NATIONAL PARK

The 6900 sq km of the state's largest national park include caves, glacial lakes, forest, ski resorts and the highest mountain (2228m) in Australia. Most famous for its snow, the park is also popular in summer when there are excellent bushwalks and marvellous alpine wildflowers. Outside the snow season you can drive to Charlottes Pass, less than 8km from the top of Mt Kosciuszko, from Jindabyne via Kosciuszko Rd. There are other walking trails from Charlottes Pass,

NEW SOUTH WALES

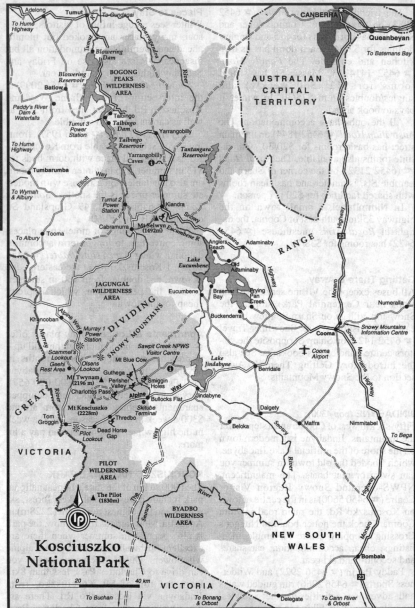

Kosciuszko
National Park

0   20   40 km

including the 20km lakes walk which includes Blue, Albina and Club lakes.

Mt Kosciuszko and the main ski resorts are in the south-centre of the park. From Jindabyne, Kosciuszko Rd leads to the NPWS visitor centre (☎ 6456 2102), about 15km north-west at **Sawpit Creek**, then on to Smiggin Holes, Perisher Valley (33km) and Charlottes Pass, with a turn-off before Perisher Valley to Guthega. The Alpine Way also runs from Jindabyne to Thredbo (33km from Jindabyne) and around to Khancoban on the south-western side of the mountains, with accessibility subject to snow conditions.

Entry to the national park (and that includes all the ski resorts) costs $12 per car, *per day*. This makes the $60 annual pass (giving unlimited entry to all parks in the state and available from NPWS offices) a very good idea. Motorcycles pay $3.50 and bus passengers $4 (children $2; this is usually included in the bus fare).

The CMA's useful *Snowy Kosciuszko* map ($4.95) includes maps of the resorts.

Places to Stay

Bush camping is permitted in most of the park but not in ecologically fragile areas. *Kosciuszko Mountain Retreat* (☎ 6456 2224), up the road from the Sawpit Creek visitor centre, is a pleasant place in bushland. It has tent sites for $19 for two and cabins for $62 a double (plus $7 per extra person). There are no single-night stays in the ski season and around Christmas.

There's plenty of accommodation at the ski resorts, much cheaper in summer, and there's a YHA hostel at Thredbo – see the following sections.

Getting There & Away

Greyhound Pioneer (☎ 13 2020) is the main carrier in this area. There are plenty of services from Sydney and Canberra to Cooma and Jindabyne, from where shuttles will take you to the resorts in winter. From Jindabyne to Smiggin Holes it costs $10 (30 minutes), Perisher $15 (45 minutes), Thredbo $14 (one hour). In summer buses run to Thredbo from Canberra ($38), but not daily.

In winter you can normally drive as far as Perisher Valley, but snow chains must be carried and fitted when directed. The simplest and safest way to get to Perisher/ Smiggins in winter is to take the Skitube (☎ 6456 2010), a tunnel railway up to Perisher Valley and Mt Blue Cow from below the snowline at Bullocks Flat on the Alpine Way. A return trip from Bullocks Flat to either Mt Blue Cow or Perisher costs $22 (children $11) and there are deals on combined Skitube and lift tickets. You can hire skis and equipment at Bullocks Flat, and luggage lockers and overnight parking are also available. The Skitube runs a reduced timetable in summer.

SKIING & SKI RESORTS

Snow skiing in Australia can be a marginal activity. The season is short (July, August and early September) and good snow isn't always likely. Nor are the mountains ideal for downhill skiing – their gently rounded shapes mean that most long runs are relatively easy and the harder runs tend to be short and sharp. Worse, the short seasons mean the operators have to get their returns quickly so costs are high.

The good news is that when the snow's on the ground and the sun's shining, the skiing can be great. You'll find all the fun (not to mention heart-in-the-mouth fear) you could ask for. Further, the open slopes of the Australian Alps are a ski-tourer's paradise – nordic (cross-country or telemark) skiing is becoming increasingly popular. The national park includes some famous trails – Kiandra to Kosciuszko, the Grey Mare Range, Thredbo or Charlottes Pass to Mt Kosciuszko's summit and the Jagungal wilderness. The possibilities for nordic touring are endless, and old cattle-herders' huts may be the only form of accommodation apart from your own tent.

There's also cross-country racing (classic or skating) in Perisher Valley. On the steep slopes of the Main Range near Twynam and Carruthers the cross-country downhill

(XCD) fanatics get their adrenalin rushes. In winter, the cliffs near Blue Lake become a practice ground for alpine climbers.

Snowboarding has taken the High Country by storm. Snowboard hire and lessons are widely available and the major resorts have developed purpose-built runs and bowls.

Australian ski resorts are short of the frenetic nightlife of many European resorts, but compensate with lots of partying among the lodges. Nor is there a great variety of alternative activities apart from toboggan runs. Weekends are crowded because the resorts are so convenient, particularly to Canberra.

Snow Reports

For general snow and road reports ring the various visitor centres or the recorded service (☎ 0055 12370). Two resorts have their own snow-report numbers – Thredbo (☎ 0055 34320) and Perisher Blue (☎ 0055 26664). For cross-country ski reports phone ☎ 0055 26028.

Costs

Lift charges vary – see the following information on the various resorts. Class lessons cost from $30 or can be included in a package with lift tickets from about $60 a day, but much less for five days. Boots, skis and stocks can be hired for around $35 a day, but less for longer and less off the mountain. It's a trade-off whether to hire in the towns risking adjustment problems or at the resort and possibly pay more. There are hire places in towns close to the resorts and many garages hire ski equipment as well as chains. Snow chains must be carried in the mountains during winter even if there's no snow – there are heavy penalties if you haven't got them.

Accommodation

The cheapest (and most fun) way to get out on the slopes is to gather a bunch of friends and rent a lodge or apartment. Costs vary enormously but can be within the bounds of reason. Bring as much food and drink as you can, as supplies in the resorts are expensive.

Many agents (including most travel agents) book accommodation and packages on the snowfields. Specialists include: the *Snowy Mountains Reservation Centre* (☎ 6456 2633, 1800 020 622), aka Ski 'n' Save; *Perisher Blue Snow Holidays* (☎ 6456 1084, 1800 066 177); and *Thredbo Resort Centre* (☎ 6459 4294, 1800 020 589). The *New South Wales Travel Centre* (☎ 13 2077) in Sydney also makes bookings.

Accommodation is cheaper in towns like Jindabyne, and particularly in Cooma, which is some distance below the snow line. Buses shuttle from Jindabyne and Cooma to resorts in the morning and back again in the late afternoon.

Thredbo (1370m)

Thredbo has the longest runs (the longest is 3km through 670m of vertical drop) and the best skiing in Australia. A day ticket costs $58, a five-day pass $250 and a five-day lift and lesson package $305.

In summer Thredbo is still a good place to visit, unlike the other resorts which become ghost towns. It's a popular bushwalking centre with all sorts of excellent and scenic tracks. The chair lift to the top of Mt Crackenback runs right through the summer ($16.50 return). From the top of the chair lift it's a 2km walk or cross-country ski to a lookout point with good views of Mt Kosciuszko, or 7km to the top of the mountain itself. Take adequate clothing and be prepared for all conditions, even in summer.

Places to Stay *Thredbo YHA Lodge* (☎ 6457 6376) costs just $16 a night ($19 per person twin share) outside the ski season and $38/55 per person for a weekday/Saturday night or $225 a six-day week during the ski season. A ballot is held for winter places and you have to enter by April. Most people get the nights they want and even if you aren't in the ballot it's worth checking to see if there are cancellations. In June and at the end of September, when snow might be scanty, there's less pressure on places. There's plenty of room in the off season. The YHA

Tragedy at Thredbo

At 11.40 pm on the night of Wednesday 30 July 1997 a landslide rushed down the hillside from the Alpine Way into the village of Thredbo. It only lasted about 10 seconds, but in that brief time it cut a trail of destruction 30m wide and 60m long. In the process it smashed two ski lodges, Carinya and Bimbadeen, and buried 20 people. Rescue workers soon arrived and, despite the threat of a further landslide and the often below-freezing conditions, they worked round the clock for the next two weeks to clear the debris.

There was only one survivor. Defying the odds, on the Saturday morning, after being buried for over 65 hours, ski instructor Stuart Diver was lifted free and taken to Canberra Hospital.

It's not clear what caused the landslide, but the most likely explanation is excess water run-off. Some observers also claimed that inappropriate development had been a contributing factor. One lodge owner, Loria Palmer, had been told in 1959 by authorities that the site was prone to landslides and had built her lodge elsewhere in Thredbo.

Since the accident things have pretty much returned to normal. However, lodges either side of the accident site have closed and if you're travelling the Alpine Way you'll need to make a detour to get to the village. ■

Travel Centre (☎ 9261 1111) in Sydney is the best place to start making enquiries.

Although prices do drop over summer, there are no spectacular bargains. One of the cheapest is *House of Ullr* (☎ 6457 6210) with doubles for $69 or $79 depending on the view.

There's a pretty but basic free camp site, *Thredbo Diggings*, between Jindabyne and Thredbo, near the Skitube at Bullocks Flat.

Perisher Blue (1680m)

Perisher Blue (☎ 6456 1084, 1800 066 177), which includes Perisher Valley, Smiggin Holes, Mt Blue Cow and Guthega, has 50 lifts, which are accessible with one ticket. It has a great variety of alpine runs, and is a popular cross-country resort with around 1250 hectares of snow-covered terrain. Snowboarding facilities are a high priority, with purpose-designed snowboarding areas and night boarding sessions on the downhill runs.

A day ticket costs $58 (children $30), a one-day combined lesson and lift costs $75 ($50 children). Add an extra $8 ($6 children) for use of the Skitube. One-day lifts and lessons for complete beginners cost $62 ($42 children).

Most accommodation is in Perisher Valley and Smiggin Holes. Peak winter rates at The Lodge (☎ 6457 5012), Smiggin Holes, are around $160 per person including ski hire, dinner and light breakfast.

Charlottes Pass (1780m)

At the base of Mt Kosciuszko, this is the highest and one of the oldest, most isolated resorts in Australia. In winter you have to snowcat the last 8km from Perisher Valley. Five lifts service rather short but uncrowded runs, and this is good ski-touring country.

Mt Selwyn (1492m)

Lying halfway between Tumut and Cooma, this is the only ski resort (☎ 6489 4485) in the north of the national park. It has 12 lifts and is ideal for beginners. One-day lift tickets are $28, and packages that include lift tickets for five days plus lessons are $225. It's a day resort with most accommodation in the **Adaminaby** area.

There are a number of caravan parks near Adaminaby. The *Alpine Tourist Park* (☎ 6454 2438), on the corner of the Snowy Mountains Highway and Letts St, has sites for $12, on-site vans from $29 to $61 a double, cabins $29 to $80. The *Snow Goose Hotel/Motel* (☎ 6454 2202), on Baker St, has hotel rooms for $10 per person, and motel rooms for $35 a double.

Adaminaby Bus Service (☎ 6454 2318) runs between Cooma and Mt Selwyn.

NEW SOUTH WALES

Snowy Mountains Hydroelectric Scheme

This huge project took more than 25 years to build, largely in mountainous terrain that had been barely explored, let alone settled. The scheme was a major source of employment in postwar Australia, and much of the labour was recruited from war-ravaged Europe. Many of those who migrated to Australia to work on the scheme were 'displaced persons' from Eastern Europe. Over 100,000 people worked on the project between 1947 and 1974.

The scheme, however, didn't raise environmental concerns. It was begun at a time when the creation of 17 major dams and the diverting of six rivers was seen as an advance of civilisation rather than the drowning of a wilderness.

Today the scheme provides electricity for Canberra, New South Wales and Victoria and water from the diverted rivers irrigates inland areas. It's estimated that if the electricity produced by the scheme were produced by coal-fired turbines, five million tonnes of carbon dioxide would be released into the atmosphere each year.

Three power stations are open to visitors. Murray 1 station near Khancoban (hourly tours, 10 am to 2 pm) and Tumut 3 station near Talbingo (hourly tours, 10 am to 2 pm) open daily year round and are free. Tumut 2 station near Cabramurra (hourly tours, 11 am to 3 pm) opens daily from September to April and costs $6 (children $4). The Snowy Mountains Information Centre (☎ 6453 2003, 1800 623 776) is in Cooma. ■

THE ALPINE WAY

From the tiny town of **Khancoban** on the western side of the ranges, this spectacular route runs through dense forest around the southern end of Kosciuszko National Park to Thredbo and Jindabyne. Two of the best mountain views are from **Olsens Lookout**, 10km off the Alpine Way on the Geehi Dam road, and **Scammel's Lookout**, just off the Alpine Way.

Khancoban has backpacker accommodation at the basic *Khancoban Backpackers & Fisherman's Lodge*, which has share accommodation for $12 and single/double rooms for $17/25. Each extra person (up to six) costs $6. You need to supply your own bedding and cooking utensils. Book and check in at the nearby Khancoban Alpine Inn (☎ 6076 9471).

There's also backpacker accommodation at the *Snowgum Lodge* (☎ 6076 9522), on Mitchell Ave, for $15. Twin rooms cost $20 per person.

TUMUT AREA

The town of **Tumut** is on the Snowy Mountains Highway outside the north-western side of the national park. Tumut Visitors Centre (☎ 6947 1849) can tell you about visits to the various centres of the Snowy Mountains Hydroelectric Scheme. Australia's largest commercial trout farm is at nearby **Blowering Dam**. For canoeing and rafting, see the friendly people at Adventure Sports (☎ 6947 1531) behind the Old Butter Factory.

Other places to visit are **Tumut 3 Power Station**, 40km south near Talbingo Dam, and the **Yarrangobilly Caves** (☎ 6454 9597), 70km south. You can visit a cave by yourself ($6) or take a tour ($10). There's also a NPWS visitor centre, a thermal pool at a constant and very pleasant 27°C and some beautiful country in the reserve around the caves.

In a fruit-growing area south of Tumut is **Batlow**; picking work is usually available. Near the town is **Hume & Hovell's Lookout** where the two explorers did indeed pause for the view in 1824. **Paddy's River Dam**, about 12km south-east, off the road to Tumbarumba, was built by Chinese gold-miners in the 1850s and there's a trail to the nearby waterfalls.

Continuing south you reach **Tumbarumba**, site of the early exploits of the bushranger Mad Dog Morgan. About 8km west of Tumbarumba, the **Pioneer Women's Hut** (☎ 6921 6565) is an interesting community museum.

South-West & the Murray

This is wide, rolling, sometimes hypnotic country with some of the state's best farming areas and some interesting history. The Murray River forms the boundary between New South Wales and Victoria – most of the larger towns are on the Victorian side. Part of this area is also known as the Riverina because of the meandering Murray and Murrumbidgee rivers and their tributaries.

Getting There & Away
The region is served by a number of airlines, including Ansett (☎ 13 1300), Hazelton (☎ 13 1713) and Kendell (☎ 13 1300).

Several roads run through the south-west – the Hume Highway being the obvious one. There are quieter routes like the Olympic Way running through Cowra, Wagga Wagga and Albury. Routes to Adelaide include the Sturt Highway through Hay and Wentworth and you'll also pass through the south-west if travelling between Brisbane and Melbourne on the Newell Highway. The Melbourne to Sydney bus services run on the Hume and trains run close to it. Fearnes Coaches (☎ 1800 029 918) runs between Sydney and Wagga, Gundagai and Yass (all $39 from Sydney) and Goulburn and Mittagong (both $25).

Countrylink (☎ 13 2242) reaches most other towns in the area. The region is also crisscrossed by major bus routes – from Sydney and Brisbane to both Melbourne and Adelaide.

THE HUME HIGHWAY
The Hume is the main road between Australia's two largest cities. It's the fastest and shortest route and, although it's not the most interesting, there are attractive places and some worthwhile diversions along the way.

One of the simplest diversions is at the Sydney end – take the coastal Princes Highway past Royal National Park to Wollongong. Just after Wollongong take the Illawarra Highway along the picturesque Macquarie Pass to meet the Hume near Moss Vale. Further south you can leave the Hume to visit Canberra or continue beyond Canberra through the Snowy Mountains on the Alpine Way, rejoining the Hume near Albury.

The Hume is a divided freeway from Sydney to beyond Goulburn, but it will be a long time before the whole road is upgraded. There are long stretches of narrow, two-lane road carrying a lot of traffic.

Sydney to Goulburn
The large towns of **Mittagong** and **Bowral** adjoin each other along the Hume Highway. The Southern Highlands Visitors Information Centre (☎ 4871 2888) is in Mittagong. Four km south of town, a winding 65km road leads west to the **Wombeyan Caves** (☎ 4843 5976) with their spectacular limestone formations. The drive up is through superb mountain scenery and there's a pretty camping reserve at the caves. Bowral was where cricketer Sir Donald Bradman, probably Australia's greatest sporting hero, spent

Don Bradman holds the record for the highest ever test-cricket batting average of 99.94 runs

his boyhood. There's a cricket ground and the **Bradman Museum** dedicated to 'the Don', open daily from 10 am to 4 pm. A little further south along the Hume is **Berrima**, a tiny town which was founded in 1829 and has changed remarkably little since then.

South of Berrima are the small town of **Bundanoon** and the large **Morton National Park** (☎ 4887 7270), with the deep gorges and high sandstone plateaus of the **Budawang Range**. There are several entry points to the park: two of the easiest are Fitzroy Falls (on the road between Moss Vale and Nowra) and Bundanoon. The pleasant *Bundanoon YHA Hostel* (☎ 4883 6010) occupies an old Edwardian guesthouse on Railway Ave. It has dorm beds for $14 and doubles for $36. Bundanoon is on the railway line between Sydney ($21) and Canberra (and Melbourne). Countrylink buses (☎ 13 2242) run daily to Wollongong.

Goulburn (pop 21,300)

Goulburn, founded in 1833, is at the heart of a prosperous sheep-grazing district famous for its fine merino wool – hence the three-storey-high **Big Merino** that towers over the Old Hume Highway in town.

Goulburn Visitors Centre (☎ 4823 0492) is on Montague St across from Belmore Park and it has a walking-tour map. There are many fine old buildings, including the impressive **courthouse** on Montague St. The **Old Goulburn Brewery** (☎ 4821 6071), built in 1836, is a large complex down on the river flats. As well as a working brewery, it has accommodation in renovated mews for $36 a person, including breakfast. There's plenty of other accommodation in town, in caravan parks, pubs and motels.

Yass (pop 4840)

Yass is closely connected with the early explorer Hume, after whom the highway is named. On Comur St, next to the tourist information centre (☎ 6226 2557), the **Hamilton Hume Museum** has exhibits relating to him. Near Yass at **Wee Jasper** are Carey's Caves (☎ 6227 9622), open on weekend

afternoons, and you can join the Hume & Hovell Walking Track here.

Just east of Yass the Barton Highway branches off the Hume for Canberra. Trans-border Express (☎ 6226 3788) has several daily buses ($12).

Gundagai (pop 2060)

Gundagai, 386km from Sydney, is one of the more interesting small towns encountered along the Hume. The tourist office (☎ 6944 1341) on Sheridan St opens weekdays from 8 am to 5 pm and on weekends from 9 am to noon and 1 to 5 pm. The tourist office houses **Rusconi's Marble Masterpiece**, a 21,000-piece cathedral model. Is it art? Is it lunacy? Is it worth the $1 entry fee? Probably. You at least get to hear a snatch of the tune, *Along*

Dog on the Tuckerbox

Gundagai features in a number of famous songs, including *Along the Road to Gundagai*, *My Mabel Waits for Me* and *When a Boy from Alabama Meets a Girl from Gundagai*. Its most famous monument, the Dog on the Tuckerbox memorial, is 8km east of town just off the Hume Highway. It's a sculpture of the dog who, in a 19th-century bush ballad (and in a later poem by Jack Moses), 'sat on the tuckerbox, five miles from Gundagai', and refused to help while its owner's bullock team was bogged in the creek. A popular tale claims that in the original version the dog shat, rather than sat, on the tuckerbox. ■

the Road to Gundagai. It was Frank Rusconi who made the Dog on the Tuckerbox memorial (see the aside on the previous page).

The long wooden **Prince Alfred Bridge** (closed to traffic, but you can walk it) crosses the flood plain of the Murrumbidgee River. In 1852, Gundagai suffered Australia's worst flood disaster – 78 deaths were recorded but probably over 100 people drowned. Gold rushes and bushrangers were part of the town's colourful early history. The notorious Captain Moonlight, leader of a gang of gay outlaws, was tried in Gundagai's 1859 **courthouse** on Sheridan St, and is now buried in the town.

Other places of interest include **Gundagai Historical Museum** (☎ 6944 1995) on Homer St, and the **Gabriel Gallery** (☎ 6944 1722) of historic photos on Sheridan St.

Places to Stay The *Gundagai River Caravan Park* (☎ 6944 1702), near the southern end of the Prince Alfred Bridge, has tent sites for $10 and on-site vans for $20. The *Gundagai Caravan Village* (☎ 6944 1057) is in town with sites for $12 and on-site vans for $29. The *Criterion Hotel* (☎ 6944 1048) and the *Royal Hotel* (☎ 6944 1024), both on Sheridan St, have accommodation for $20/35.

Holbrook (pop 1320)

Holbrook, the halfway point between Sydney and Melbourne, was known as Germanton until WWI, during which it was renamed after a British war hero. There's a replica of the submarine in which he won a Victoria Cross, in Holbrook Park. The large **Woolpack Inn Museum** (☎ 6036 2131), opens daily ($3, children $1) and has tourist information.

ALBURY (pop 41,500)

Albury is on the Murray River just below the Hume Weir, across the river from the large town of Wodonga, in Victoria. It's a good base for trips and activities in a variety of terrains: the snowfields and High Country of both Victoria and New South Wales, the vineyards around Rutherglen (Victoria), and the tempestuous upper Murray River, which becomes languid below Albury as it starts its journey to South Australia and the sea. It's also a good place to break the journey between Sydney and Melbourne.

Information

The large Gateway Information Centre (☎ 6041 3875), with information on both New South Wales and Victoria, is on the highway in Wodonga. It opens daily from 9 am to 5 pm. In summer bring insect repellent as there are lots of mosquitoes.

Things to See & Do

In summer you can swim in the Murray River in **Noreuil Park** and you can take river cruises from Wednesday to Sunday on the paddle-steamer *Cumberoona* (☎ 6021 1113) from $8 (children $4.50). **Albury Regional Museum**, Wodonga Place in Noreuil Park, opens daily from 10.30 am to 4.30 pm, and contains material on migration, transport and Aboriginal culture (admission is free). Also in the park is a tree marked by explorer William Hovell when he crossed the Murray on his 1824 expedition with Hume from Sydney to Port Phillip, in Victoria. Charles Sturt departed for his 1838 exploration of the banks of the Murray from here. Albury Backpackers has canoe trips on the Murray for $35 and you don't have to stay there to join one.

Ettamogah Wildlife Sanctuary, 11km north on the highway and open daily ($5, children $2.50), has a collection of Aussie fauna, most of which arrived sick or injured, so this is a genuine sanctuary. A fewe km resnorth, the grotesque **Ettamogah Pub** looms up near the highway – a real-life recreation of a famous Aussie cartoon pub and proof that life (of a sort) follows art, not vice versa.

The good **Jindera Museum**, 16km northwest of Albury in the town of Jindera, opens Tuesday to Sunday, 10 am to 3 pm ($5, $1 students). Jindera is in an area known as **Morgan Country** because of its association with bushranger Mad Dog Morgan. Other pleasant little towns in this area include

Culcairn, west of Holbrook, where the wonderful *Culcairn Hotel* (☎ 6029 8501) has singles/doubles for $28/38.

Places to Stay

Albury Central Caravan Park (☎ 6021 8420), about 2km north of the centre on North St, has tent sites for $10 and cabins from $38.

Albury Backpackers (☎ 6041 1822) on the corner of David and Smollett Sts has dorm beds $14 and a doubles for $30. This is a friendly place which takes care of its guests. It hires out bikes, organises adventure activities and helps you find farm work. There's a great YHA hostel at *Albury Motor Village* (☎ 6040 2999), 372 Wagga Rd (Hume Highway) 4.5km north of the centre of town. Dorm beds cost $14, doubles $36.

Most pubs have beds. *Soden's Australia Hotel* (☎ 6021 2400) on the corner of Wilson and David Sts has rooms for $22/36. Alternatively, there's the *Termo* (☎ 6024 1777), the Terminus Hotel on the corner of Young and Dan Sts, with rooms for $30/40. At both, rooms are basic with shared facilities.

Herb & Horse (☎ 6072 9553) on the Murray River 45km east of Albury-Wodonga is a great place to stay a while. It's an 1890s homestead and farm with home-cooked meals and canoe trips. The horse riding is excellent, with proper equipment and rides of a decent length through beautiful country. There are shared rooms for $20, B&B doubles from $70 and dinner B&B at $65 per person. It can usually arrange free transport from Albury-Wodonga if you ring in advance.

Places to Eat

There are some good places on Dean St west of Kiewa St. *Cafe Gryphon* does good coffee and serves light meals for around $10 until late, while *Pappadums* is good for Indian food. The large *Restaurant 2000*, 639 Dean St, has all-you-can-eat smorgasbords daily for $7.90 at lunch and $12.50 at dinner. *Bahn Thai*, 592 Kiewa St in a beautiful Victorian house, is a good Thai restaurant open nightly.

Getting There & Away

Ansett Express (☎ 13 1300), Kendell (☎ 13 1300) and Hazelton (☎ 13 1713) fly from Albury to Melbourne ($250) and Sydney ($430), with fare reductions on advance purchase tickets.

Buses between Sydney and Melbourne stop at the train station. Most also stop at Viennaworld (a service station/diner) on the highway across from Noreuil Park. Countrylink (☎ 13 2242) runs to Echuca ($31), on the Murray River in Victoria. The one-way fare to Canberra is $25. V/Line (☎ 13 2232) runs to Mildura ($19.10) along the Murray. Mylon Motorways (☎ 6056 3100) has a daylight service to Adelaide ($55).

The nightly Sydney to Melbourne XPT stops in Albury. If you're travelling between the two capital cities it's much cheaper to stop over in Albury on a through ticket than to buy two separate tickets. The same applies to bus tickets.

WAGGA WAGGA (pop 42,850)

Wagga Wagga, on the Murrumbidgee River, is the state's largest inland city. Despite its size, the city retains a relaxed country town feel. The name is pronounced 'wogga' and is usually abbreviated to one word (although there's a literary group called Wagga Wagga Writers Writers).

The long main street is Baylis St, which runs north from the train station, becoming Fitzmaurice St at the northern end. Pick up a driving-tour map from the Wagga Wagga Visitors Centre (☎ 6923 5402) on Tarcutta St. The excellent **Botanic Gardens** are about 1.5km south of the train station. In the gardens is a small zoo with a free-flight aviary of native birds.

The **Wiradjuri Walking Track** begins at the visitors centre and eventually returns there after a 30km tour of the area; it includes some good lookouts. There's a shorter 10km loop past the Wollundry Lagoon. The walks can be done in stages and the visitors centre has maps. From the **beach** near the Tourist Caravan Park you can go swimming and fishing.

On the Olympic Way, about 40km north

of Wagga, the small town of **Junee** has some historic buildings, including the lovely Monte Cristo Homestead ($7/3.50; ☎ 6924 1637) and some splendid pubs. Glass Buslines (☎ 6924 1633) runs a local service from Wagga to Junee on weekdays and picks up along Baylis St.

Places to Stay
The *Tourist Caravan Park* (☎ 6921 2540) is on the river right next to a swimming beach and a couple of blocks from the town centre. Tent sites are $10, on-site vans $32 and cabins $40 to $45.

Several pubs have accommodation, including *Romano's Hotel* (☎ 6921 2013), on Fitzmaurice St, with good rooms for $32/40, some with attached bathrooms. The *Manor* (☎ 6921 5962) is a small, well-restored guesthouse opposite the Memorial Gardens on Morrow St, near Baylis St. Singles/doubles range from $35/60 to $50/100, including breakfast. There are plenty of motels, but none are cheap.

Places to Eat
Baylis/Fitzmaurice St has a surprisingly diverse range of places to eat. At the top of Fitzmaurice St, the *Kebab Place* is an authentic Lebanese takeaway and restaurant. Dick Eyle's *Aussie Cafe* is about the only example of a main-street cafe on Baylis St, but it's good and opens for breakfast. A few doors along is *Family Eating House* which offers all-you-can-eat for $8.50 at lunch and $9.50 at dinner. At the nearby *Saigon Restaurant* most dishes are $7.60 to $10.50. *Bernie's* at the Tourist Hotel is a good vegetarian restaurant.

Getting There & Away
Kendell (☎ 6922 0100) and Hazelton (☎ 13 1713) have services connecting Wagga with Sydney, Melbourne and Brisbane. The standard economy one way/return fare to Sydney is $175/350.

Countrylink buses (☎ 13 2242) leave from the train station but other long-distance services leave from the coach terminal (☎ 6921 1977) on the corner of Gurwood and Trail

Sts, off Fitzmaurice St. You can make bookings here. Wagga is on the railway line between Sydney and Melbourne; the one-way fare to both is $62.

NARRANDERA (pop 4700)
Near the junction of the Newell and Sturt highways, Narrandera is in the Murrumbidgee Irrigation Area (MIA). The tourist information centre (☎ 6959 1766) in Narrandera Park has a walking-tour map.

Lake Talbot is an excellent water sports reserve, partly a long artificial lake and partly a big swimming complex. Bush (including a koala regeneration area) surrounds the lake and a series of walking trails make up the **Bundidgerry Walking Track**.

The **John Lake Centre** at the Inland Fisheries Research Station (☎ 6959 1488) opens weekdays from 9 am to 4 pm and has guided tours (on which you can see a huge Murray cod) at 10.30 am for $5 (children $2.50). To get there, turn off the Sturt Highway 4km south-east of Narrandera.

South of Narrandera on the Newell Highway is **Jerilderie**, immortalised by the bushranger Ned Kelly who held up the whole town for three days in 1879. Kelly relics can be seen in the **Telegraph Office Museum** on Powell St. Close by, the **Willows** (1878), an old house next to Billabong Creek, is part museum, part souvenir shop and part cafe.

Places to Stay & Eat
The *Lake Talbot Caravan Park* (☎ 6959 1302), some way from the town centre at the eastern end of Larmer St, overlooks Lake Talbot and red gum forest. Tent sites are $14, on-site vans cost from $26 and self-contained units $28 to $49.

The *Historic Star Lodge* (☎ 6959 1768), in a fine old hotel on Whitton St opposite the train station, is a B&B that also offers dorm accommodation for $15 to YHA members. There are kitchen facilities. B&B costs from $30/45 a single/double.

Getting There & Away
McCafferty's (☎ 13 1499) and Greyhound Pioneer (☎ 13 2030) have buses to Sydney

($44) and other capital cities, stopping at the old train station.

GRIFFITH (pop 14,200)

Griffith was planned by Walter Burley Griffin, the American architect who designed Canberra, and is the main centre of the Murrumbidgee Irrigation Area (MIA). Griffith Visitors Centre (☎ 6962 4145) is on the corner of Banna Ave (the long main street) and Jondaryan Ave.

Things to See

High on a hill to the north-east of the town centre, **Pioneer Park Museum** (☎ 6962 4196) is a re-creation of an early Riverina village and is worth seeing. It's open daily from 9 am to 5 pm ($5, children $2).

Descendants of the Italian farmers who helped to develop this area make up a large proportion of the population. Although the Hunter Valley is the best-known wine producing area in New South Wales, the Griffith area produces 80% of the state's wine. You can visit 11 **wineries** – the visitors centre has opening times and a map.

Fruit-Picking

Many people come to Griffith looking for fruit-picking work. The grape harvest usually begins around mid-February and lasts six to eight weeks, while the citrus harvest begins in November and runs through to March. Few vineyards and almost none of the other farms have accommodation, or even space to camp, so you'll need your own transport. The Centrelink office (☎ 6969 1100) on Yambil St may be able to help you find work.

Places to Stay

The small *Tourist Caravan Park* (☎ 6962 4537) on Willandra Ave, not far from the bus stop, has tent sites for $15 with power, onsite vans for $36 and cabins from $45. There's a basic camping area at the *showgrounds*, south of the circular western end of the city centre, which has sites for $12 ($50 per week).

Pioneer Park (☎ 6962 4196) has shared accommodation in old shearers' quarters for $10. The rooms are small and basic but there's a good kitchen and lounge. The problem with staying here is that it's a long, steep walk from the city centre and there's no public transport. It's often full at harvest time. The *Area Hotel* (☎ 6962 1322) on Banna Ave has rooms and a continental breakfast for $40.

Places to Eat

Italian food is the region's dominant cuisine. For good coffee and cake or pasta (from $6), try *Caffe Bassano*, 453 Banna Ave. It's also open daily for breakfast. Nearby, down some steps, *La Scala* (☎ 6962 4322) is the best of the Italian restaurants and opens from 6 pm, Tuesday to Sunday. Pastas are $9 to $11. Close by on the other side of Banna Ave, the *Belvedere Restaurant* has more of a cafe atmosphere and it's also a busy takeaway pizzeria.

If you just want a hamburger, *Nibbles* on Banna Ave has good old-fashioned hamburgers ($4 with the lot), which can be taken away or eaten at old-fashioned partitioned tables.

Getting There & Away

Hazelton (☎ 13 1713) flies between Griffith and Sydney daily for $218 one way.

Buses stop at the Griffith Travel & Transit Centre (☎ 6962 7199), 121 Banna Ave in the Mobil service station opposite the visitors centre. Greyhound Pioneer (☎ 13 2030) runs to Sydney ($40), Adelaide ($60) and Canberra ($39). McCafferty's (☎ 13 1499) also runs daily to those cities and is a little cheaper. MIA Intercity Coaches (☎ 6962 3419) runs to Melbourne ($60) three times a week, while Countrylink (☎ 13 2242) runs to Wagga Wagga ($38).

AROUND GRIFFITH

West of Griffith, the last hills of the Great Dividing Range give way to endless plains.

Cocoparra National Park

Cocoparra, just east of Griffith, isn't a large park but its hills and gullies provide some contrasts and there's a fair amount of wild-life. The camping area is on Woolshed Flat in the north of the park, not far from Wool-shed Falls. Bring your own water. Bush camping is permitted away from the roads. Park entry is $7.50 and camping costs $5.

Leeton (pop 6600)
Leeton is the MIA's oldest town (1913) and like Griffith, was designed by Walter Burley Griffin. Although it remains close to the architect's original vision because of early restrictions (now removed) on development, a highway sprawl is developing.

Leeton Visitors Centre (☎ 6953 2832), 8-10 Yanco Ave, opens weekdays from 9 am to 5 pm and on weekends from 9.30 am to 12.30 pm. Ask here about tours of the rice mill and other food-processing plants. Lillypilly Estate (☎ 6953 4069) and Toorak Wines (☎ 6953 2333) are two **wineries** west of Leeton, open Monday to Saturday for tastings and for tours on weekdays – 11.30 am at Toorak Wines, 4 pm at Lillypilly Estate.

Willandra National Park
Willandra, on the plains 160km north-west of Griffith as the crow flies, has been carved from a huge sheep station on a system of lakes, usually dry. The World Heritage listed park's 19,400 hectares represent less than 10% of the area covered by Big Willandra station in its 1870s heyday. The partially restored homestead (1918) was the third to be built on the station.

There are several short walking tracks in the park and the Merton Motor Trail does a loop around the eastern half. The western half has no vehicular access but you can walk here – if you're *very* sure of what you're doing.

There's a camp site ($5) near the home-stead and with permission you can bush camp. Shared accommodation in the 'men's quarters' costs $10.

The main access is off the Hillston to Mossgiel road, around 40km west of Hillston. It takes very little rain to close roads here, so phone the park manager (☎ 6967 8159) or the NPWS office (☎ 6962 7755) at Griffith to check conditions before setting out.

HAY (pop 2900)
In flat, treeless country, Hay is at the junction of the Sturt and Cobb highways and is a substantial town for this part of the world. The Tourist & Amenities Centre (☎ 6993 1003), 407 Moppett St, is just off Lachlan St (the main street). There are some fine swim-ming spots along the Murrumbidgee River, and interesting old buildings like the **Old Hay Gaol** and **Bishops Lodge**, a corru-gated-iron mansion.

There are several caravan parks. The *Bidgee Beach Camping Ground* (☎ 6993 1180) off the Sturt Highway 11km east of Hay is a simple camping area on the banks of the Murrumbidgee. Tent sites are $10 to $15. Most pubs have accommodation, and one of the cheapest is the big *Commercial Hotel* (☎ 6993 1504) with rooms for $15/25. The *New Crown Hotel/Motel* (☎ 6993 1600) charges $35/45.

DENILIQUIN (pop 7820)
Deniliquin is an attractive, bustling country town on a wide bend of the Edward River. Before European settlement, this area was the most densely populated part of Australia.

The Visitors Information Centre (☎ (03) 5881 4150) is inside the **Peppin Heritage Centre** on George St. The heritage centre covers the history of wool-growing in the area; merino sheep breeds developed around here have long been the mainstay of Australia's wool industry. It's open week-days from 9 am to 4 pm and on weekends from 11 am to 2 pm ($3, children $1). The visitors centre at the **Sun Rice Mill**, the largest rice mill in the southern hemisphere, opens weekdays 9 am to noon and 2 to 4 pm, but there are plans to move it to the Peppin Heritage Centre. The **Island Sanctuary** has pleasant walks among the river red gums and lots of animals, including over-friendly emus.

Places to Stay
There are several caravan parks, including

McLean Beach Caravan Park (☎ (03) 5881 2448) at the north-eastern end of Charlotte St, by a good river swimming beach. Tent sites are $12, on-site vans $22 and cabins $45. At the basic but clean *Deniliquin YHA Hostel* (☎ (03) 5881 5025), on the corner of Wood and Macauley Sts about a kilometre south-west of the town centre, YHA members (only) can stay for $7 (children $3.50).

The *Globe Hotel* (☎ (03) 5881 2030) is good value, with rooms at $20 per person, including a cooked breakfast. The *Federal Hotel* (☎ (03) 5881 1260), on the corner of Cressy and Napier Sts, has clean rooms for $25/40 with breakfast.

There are plenty of motels. Trucks roll through town all night, so choose one off the highway, such as the *Riverview Motel* (☎ (03) 5881 2311) at the north-eastern end of Charlotte St. Rooms are $45/55.

Getting There & Away

Long-distance buses stop at the Bus Stop Cafe on Whitelock St. Countrylink (☎ 13 2242) runs to Wagga ($18), from where trains run to Sydney and Melbourne. McCafferty's (☎ 13 1499) stops here on the run between Melbourne ($30) and Brisbane ($119). Victoria's V/Line (☎ 13 2232) also runs daily to Melbourne ($28.40).

ALONG THE MURRAY

Most of the major river towns are on the Victorian side – see the Victoria chapter for more on the river. It's no problem to hop back and forth across the river as in many places roads run along both sides.

The Murray was once an important means of communication, with paddle-steamers splashing upstream and downstream – an antipodean Mississippi. The largest New South Wales town on the river is Albury (see earlier). Downstream from here is **Corowa**, a wine-producing centre – the Lindemans winery has been here since 1860. **Tocumwal** on the Newell Highway is a quiet riverside town with sandy river beaches and a giant fibreglass Murray Cod in the town square. The nearby airport is a gliding centre.

The old river port of **Wentworth** lies at the confluence of the Murray and Darling rivers, 30km north-west of Mildura. The riverboat MV *Loyalty* (☎ (03) 5027 3330) has two-hour cruises to the confluence from Sunday to Friday, leaving the Wentworth & District Services Memorial Club at 1.45 pm. The fare is $12 (children $4). You can see local history in the **Old Wentworth Gaol** ($4.50, children $2.50) and across the road in the **Pioneer World Folk Museum** ($3.50, $1). The **Perry Dunes** are large orange sand dunes 6km north of town, off the road to Broken Hill.

Central West

NSW's central west starts inland from the Blue Mountains and continues for about 400km, gradually changing from rolling agricultural land into the harsh far west. This region has some of the earliest inland towns in Australia. From Sydney, Bathurst is the gateway to the region, and from here you can turn north-west through Orange and Dubbo or south-west through Cowra and West Wyalong.

The Olympic Way, running from Bathurst through Cowra and Wagga to Albury, is an alternative Sydney-Melbourne route. The Newell Highway, the most direct route between Melbourne and Brisbane, also passes through the central west. On long weekends accommodation all along the Newell is booked out.

Getting There & Away

Air The central west is well served by airlines. From Dubbo ($169 from Sydney with Eastern Australia or Hazelton) there are flights to other locations in the centre and far west of the state.

Bus Major lines have services through the region on routes between Sydney and Broken Hill or Adelaide, and from Brisbane to Melbourne or Adelaide. Local companies providing services include Rendell's

Coaches (☎ 1800 023 328). Sid Fogg's (☎ 1800 045 952) runs from Newcastle to Dubbo ($48).

Train Direct trains run from Sydney to Lithgow ($21), Bathurst ($31), Orange ($38) and Dubbo ($55). There are connecting buses from Lithgow station to Cowra ($44 from Sydney), Forbes ($50) and Mudgee ($38).

LITHGOW (pop 11,400)

Lithgow is an industrial town on the western fringe of the Blue Mountains. The Greater Lithgow Visitor Centre (☎ 6353 1859) is on the edge of town in the Old Bowenfels Station, 1 Cooerwull Rd, on the Great Western Highway.

The gracious home, **Eskbank House**, is on Bennett St. It was built in 1841 and now houses a museum. It's open Thursday to Monday between 10 am and 4 pm ($2). There are fine views from **Hassan Walls Lookout**, 5km south of town. A short drive from Lithgow via Inch and Atkinson Sts brings you to the Newnes Plateau. There's a 5km walk from here to a disused railway tunnel, now full of glow-worms.

See the Blue Mountains section earlier in this chapter for information on the nearby Zig Zag Railway and the town of Hartley. **Newnes**, about 50km north of Lithgow, on the edge of the Wollemi National Park, is a ghost town where the pub still functions. The **Gardens of Stone National Park**, 30km north of Lithgow, features Devonian limestone outcrops and Triassic sandstone escarpments. There is an interpretive display and picnic ground at Baal Bone Gap (only accessible by 4WD).

There are frequent trains between Lithgow and Sydney ($21).

BATHURST (pop 26,100)

Bathurst is Australia's oldest inland settlement and it was laid out on a grand scale. The streetscape is relatively intact and there are some impressive Victorian-era buildings, such as the 1880 **courthouse** on Russell St, which houses the **historical museum** ($1).

The information centre (☎ 6332 1444) is on William St.

South-west of the city centre is the 6.2km **Mt Panorama motor racing circuit**. It's the venue for one of Australia's best-known races, the 1000 Touring Car Race, a 1000km race for production cars held in October. You can drive around the circuit (it's a public road) and there's a small **motor racing museum** ($5) at Murray's Corner, open daily from 9 am to 4.30 pm. Also on Mt Panorama are the **Sir Joseph Banks Nature Park** (admission by donation), with a koala and other animals, and the **Bathurst Gold Fields**, a reconstruction of a gold-mining town which is open for tours by appointment ($7). To make an appointment, contact the Bathurst council on ☎ 6332 2022.

Places to Stay & Eat

There are some good pub rooms at the hotels. The cheapest rooms are at the *Railway Hotel* (☎ 6331 2964) on Havana St, where singles/doubles are $20/35 with breakfast. The *Edinboro Castle Hotel* (☎ 6331 5020), in William St, has rooms for $25/40. The *Abercrombie* (☎ 6331 1077) and *Capri* (☎ 6331 2966) motels on Stewart St are the cheapest in town; rates start at $42. For pizza or large servings of pasta (from $8), try *Uncle Joe's Pizza*, opposite the post office on Howick St. *Zeigler's Cafe* on Keppel St has an interesting modern menu and is not too expensive.

AROUND BATHURST

The **Abercrombie Caves** are 72km south of Bathurst. There are several guided tours each day.

There are some interesting old buildings at **Sofala**, 37km north of Bathurst. The fascinating old mining town of **Hill End** is 72km north-west of Bathurst. It was the scene of a gold rush in the 1870s and is classified as an historic site. The visitor centre (☎ 6337 8206) is in the old hospital, which also houses the **museum** ($2). There are three NPWS camping areas. The *Village* and *Glendora* have facilities and charge $10. The *Trough* is more basic and charges $5, while the *Royal Hotel* (☎ 6337 8261) has singles/doubles for $38/60 with breakfast.

Rockley, 34km south of Bathurst, is another classified historic town. North-east of Bathurst is **Rylstone**, where there are sandstone buildings and Aboriginal rock paintings just outside the town (ask at the shire council).

MUDGEE (pop 8200)

Mudgee, about 120km north of both Lithgow and Bathurst, is a fine example of an old country town and is a pleasant place to stay. The information centre (☎ 6372 5875) is on Market St, near the old police station.

Wineries

There are many young wineries run by enthusiastic people, and if you find the Hunter Valley too commercial, you'll enjoy these. Craigmoor can hardly be called a newcomer. It has produced a vintage annually since 1858, making it the second-oldest continually operating winery in Australia. Most of the area's 20 wineries are open daily. In September there's a wine festival.

Places to Stay & Eat

Accommodation tends to fill up on weekends, and several hotels have above-average pub accommodation. The *Woolpack Hotel* (☎ 6372 1908) on Market St charges $15/30 for singles/ doubles, while the *Federal Hotel* (☎ 6372 2150) on Inglis St near the train station charges $17/32 ($20/36 weekends).

Near the wineries to the north of town, *Hithergreen Lodge* (☎ 6372 1022) has motel units for $55/65. A taxi out here costs around $6, or it's a pleasant walk of about 5km.

The best place for a coffee or snack is the *Tramp*; enter through an archway on Market St near the corner of Church St. The *Red Heifer Grill* at the Lawson Park Hotel is recommended for lunch and dinner.

Getting There & Away

Hazelton (☎ 13 1713) flies between Mudgee and Sydney ($176). Countrylink (☎ 13 2242) runs from Sydney to Lithgow from where there are connecting buses to Mudgee ($38 from Sydney). There's also a daily bus to Bathurst.

AROUND MUDGEE

Gulgong (pop 2000)

Gulgong, 30km north-west of Mudgee, is an old gold town once described as 'the hub of the world'. It was the boyhood home of the author Henry Lawson and the **Henry Lawson Centre** on Mayne St houses a collection of 'Lawsonia'; it's open weekdays from 10 am to noon and Saturday till 3 pm ($2).

The information centre (☎ 6374 1202) is in the shire chambers. The huge **Gulgong Pioneer Museum** on Herbert St is one of the best country-town museums in the state ($4). It's open daily from 9 am to 5 pm.

Places to Stay The *Centennial Hotel* (☎ 6374 1241) on Mayne St has singles/doubles with bathroom for $25/35. The *Heritage Centre* on Red Hill is a field-study centre with a dorm for groups. The information centre can tell you if there's room for individuals. A bed costs $6 (no linen).

Other Towns

At **Nagundie**, 11km north of Mudgee, there's a rock that is said to hold water year round – it's an old Aboriginal water hole and you can camp here. Further east, en route to the Goulburn River National Park and the Hunter Valley, **Merriwa** has a number of historic buildings, as has nearby **Cassilis**.

ORANGE (pop 30,700)

This important fruit-growing centre does not grow oranges! Rather, it was named after William of Orange. Pioneer poet Banjo Paterson (who wrote the words of *Waltzing Matilda*) was born here, and the foundations of his birthplace are in Banjo Paterson Park. Orange was considered as a site for the Federal capital before Canberra was eventually selected.

The visitor centre (☎ 6361 5226) is on Byng St. The **museum** on McNamara St includes a 300-year-old tree carved with Aboriginal designs.

The autumn apple-picking season lasts for about six weeks; contact the Commonwealth Employment Service (CES; ☎ 6391 2700) on Anson St.

Australia's first real gold rush took place at **Ophir** 27km north of Orange. The area is now a nature reserve and it's still popular with fossickers – you can buy a licence and hire a gold pan from the Orange visitor centre. **Mt Canobolas** (1395m) is a steep, extinct volcano 20km south-west of Orange. You can drive to the top or there are a couple of walking tracks.

Places to Stay & Eat

The council's *Colour City Showground Caravan Park* (☎ 6362 7254), on Margaret St about 2km north-east of the city centre, has tent sites for $7.50, on-site vans for $25 and cabins for $40.

The renovated *Hotel Canobolas* (☎ 6362 2444), on Summer St on the corner of Lords Place, was once the largest hotel outside Sydney. Most rooms have bathrooms, steam heat, TV and a fridge. Singles/doubles cost $45/70 and rooms with shared bathrooms are $28/45.

The *Keg Country* on the corner of Bathurst Rd and McLachlan St, a few blocks east of the railway line, has mains from $10.

Getting There & Away

Rendell's Coaches (☎ 1800 02 3328) runs to Dubbo ($30) and Sydney ($30) daily. There's also a service to Canberra ($35). Selwood's Coaches (☎ 6362 7963) also runs to Sydney daily ($30).

DUBBO (pop 30,100)

Dubbo is a large agricultural town surrounded by sheep and cattle country. The information centre (☎ 1800 674 443) is at the top end of Macquarie St, the main shopping street, on the corner of Erskine St. You can hire geared bikes for $10 a day at Wheelers (☎ 6882 9899) on the corner of Brisbane and Bultje Sts. The YHA hostel hires bikes to guests for $6 a day.

Things to See & Do

The **Old Dubbo Gaol** ($5), Macquarie St, is open daily from 9 am to 4.30 pm and has 'animatronic' characters telling the story of prison life. Also on Macquarie St is the **museum**, which is open daily from 10 am to 4.30 pm ($5).

Five km south-west of town, the **Western Plains Zoo** (☎ 6882 5888) is the largest open-range zoo in Australia. The Bengal tigers and Asiatic lions alone are worth the price of admission. The zoo's rare black rhinoceroses were flown in from Zimbabwe as part of an international program designed to save these magnificent beasts from extinction.

You're better off walking around the 6km circuit or hiring a bike ($8 for half a day) than joining the crawling line of cars. The zoo is open daily from 9 am to 5 pm ($15/7.50 adults/children).

The slab homestead **Dundullimal** was built by a wealthy grazier in the 1830s. It's 2km beyond the zoo and is open daily ($3).

Places to Stay

The closest caravan park to the town centre is the small *Poplars* (☎ 6882 4067), near the river at the western end of Bultje St. *Dubbo City* (☎ 6882 4820) is also on the river, but on the western bank and a fair distance by road from the centre.

Dubbo Backpackers (☎ 6882 0922) is a pleasant YHA hostel at 87 Brisbane St, north of the railway line. From the bus station head west on Erskine St. Dorm beds are $14 and there are a few twin rooms. Guests get 20% off zoo tickets and the hostel can often arrange a lift out there, or you can hire a bike and ride ($6 a day). The hostel also organises trips to the huge Dubbo stockyards on sale days – an interesting insight into rural life.

Several pubs have accommodation, such as the good *Castlereagh Hotel* (☎ 6882 4877) on the corner of Talbragar and Brisbane Sts, which has singles/doubles from $30/55, including a big cooked breakfast. Also good is the *Western Star* (☎ 6882 4644) on Erskine St; singles/doubles cost $30/50.

The decrepit *John Oxley Motel* (☎ 6882

4622), towards the southern end of Macquarie St, is central and cheap for Dubbo ($40/55) but the rooms are pretty small. There are more than 20 other motels, mostly along Cobra St, although they tend to fill up quickly; book ahead.

For $180 per person, per night you can stay at the Western Plains *Zoofari Lodge*. For that price you get three meals, two-day entry to the zoo, three behind-the-scenes guided tours, bicycle hire and accommodation in luxury tented lodges. For bookings contact Peter Milling Travel (☎ 1800 67 6308), at 105-107 Macquarie St.

Places to Eat

The best value is the bistro at the opulent *Ex-Services Club* on Brisbane St. The *Dubbo Eating House* on Macquarie St, has an all-you-can-eat smorgasbord lunch for $8 and dinner for $9.95.

Scrubbers Steakhouse on Wingewarra St is a small place serving light meals during the day (for around $8) and has $15 steaks at night.

To escape from the mixed-grill menus, head for the southern end of Macquarie St. You'll find good coffee and light meals at *Cafe Monet*, trendy pancakes at *Jule's*

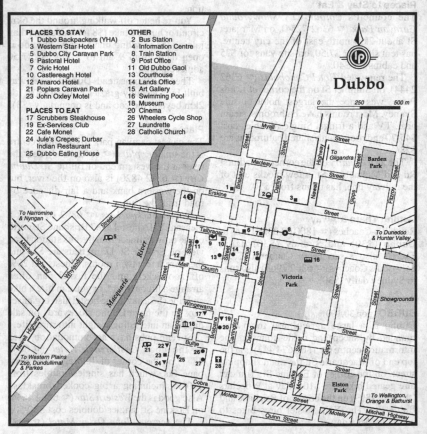

PLACES TO STAY
1 Dubbo Backpackers (YHA)
3 Western Star Hotel
5 Dubbo City Caravan Park
6 Pastoral Hotel
7 Civic Hotel
10 Castlereagh Hotel
12 Amaroo Hotel
21 Poplars Caravan Park
23 John Oxley Motel

PLACES TO EAT
17 Scrubbers Steakhouse
19 Ex-Services Club
22 Cafe Monet
24 Jule's Crepes; Durbar Indian Restaurant
25 Dubbo Eating House

OTHER
2 Bus Station
4 Information Centre
8 Train Station
9 Post Office
11 Old Dubbo Gaol
13 Courthouse
14 Lands Office
15 Art Gallery
16 Swimming Pool
18 Museum
20 Cinema
26 Wheelers Cycle Shop
27 Laundrette
28 Catholic Church

Dubbo

Crepes and exceptional curries at the *Durbar Indian Restaurant*.

Getting There & Away

The air fare from Sydney is $173 with Eastern or Hazelton airlines.

Dubbo is at the junction of the Newell Highway (the main Melbourne-Brisbane route) and the Mitchell Highway (the Sydney-Broken Hill/Adelaide route).

You can buy bus tickets at the bus station (☎ 6884 2411) on Erskine St until late at night. Most of the major bus lines pass through, but the local company, Rendell's (☎ 1800 023 328), often has the cheapest fares. The fare to Sydney is $45. Sid Fogg's buses run to Newcastle three times a week for $48.

The Countrylink bus (☎ 13 2242) to Sydney costs $55.

COWRA (pop 8500)

Cowra is a large country town in the fertile Lachlan Valley. It's best known as the scene of a mass break-out by Japanese prisoners of war during WWII. Nearly 250 prisoners died in the failed 1944 attempt, many by suicide. The strange tale of this impossible escape attempt is told in a book and film, both titled *Die Like the Carp*. The information centre (☎ 6342 4333) is on the highway west of the shopping centre across the bridge.

Things to See & Do

Australian and Japanese **war cemeteries** are 5km south of town and a memorial, 2km south-east of the cemeteries, marks the site of the break-out. Cowra's association with Japan is also commemorated in the superb **Japanese Garden** on Bellevue Hill above the town centre. Large, beautiful and meticulously maintained, it's well worth visiting. The garden and the attached cultural centre open daily from 8.30 am to 5 pm ($6, children $4).

The Lachlan River flows through fertile and pretty farming country to the west of Cowra. The road to Forbes (turn off the Mid-Western Highway about 5km south of

Cowra) runs along the southern bank of the Lachlan and is a pleasant drive.

At Paynters Bridge, about 45km on from the turn-off, cross the Lachlan to **Eugowra**, a town in the shadow of bush-clad hills. Eugowra was held up by the bushranger Ben Hall in 1863 and there's a re-enactment every October.

You can also get here (and to Forbes) via the small town of **Canowindra** (also held up by Ben Hall), on a road running down the northern side of the Lachlan. Canowindra's curving main street, Gaskill St, has a number of old buildings. The **Age of Fishes Museum** (☎ 6344 1008) organises visits to nearby fossil sites, but the town's main attraction is **ballooning**. Several outfits offer flights; Balloon Aloft (☎ 6344 1852, 1800 028 568) charges $175 for a flight and champagne breakfast.

Places to Stay

Cowravan Park (☎ 6342 1058), by the river on Lachlan St south of Kendal St, has sites for $10 and cabins for $40. There are some beautiful old hotels on Kendal St. The *Lachlan Hotel* (☎ 6342 2355) charges $20/30 for singles/doubles, while the *Imperial Hotel* (☎ 6341 2588) and the *Cowra Hotel* (☎ 6342 1925) charge $25/35 with breakfast.

Getting There & Away

Greyhound Pioneer (☎ 13 2030) stops here on its run between Melbourne and Brisbane and Countrylink (☎ 13 22 32) connects Cowra with Bathurst and Cootamundra. Rendell's Coaches (☎ 1800 023 328) runs daily to Canberra.

FORBES (pop 7500)

Forbes is an oddly atmospheric place to wander round. It has wide streets and a number of grand 19th-century buildings reflecting the wealth of its 1860s gold rush. Ben Hall is buried in the town's cemetery – his death is lamented in a bitter folk song, *The Streets of Forbes*. The information centre (☎ 6852 4155), in the old train station off the highway north of town, opens daily from 9 am to 5 pm.

Forbes Museum (☎ 6852 1694), on Cross St, has Ben Hall relics and other memorabilia and opens daily from 3 to 5 pm June to September (2 to 4 pm October to May). One km south beside the Newell Highway, **Lachlan Vintage Village** (☎ 6852 2655), a re-creation of a 19th-century village, opens daily.

There are several caravan parks, pubs and plenty of motels. The old but clean *Vandenberg Hotel* (☎ 6852 2015) on Court St has rooms for $20/30 with breakfast.

Forbes has a lot of long-distance bus traffic, including Greyhound Pioneer (☎ 13 2030) and McCafferty's (☎ 13 1499).

North-West

From Dubbo, roads radiate to various parts of the state. The Newell Highway runs northeast and is the quickest route between Melbourne and Brisbane. The Castlereagh Highway, forking off the Newell 66km from Dubbo at Gilgandra, runs north into the rugged opal country towards the Queensland border (its surfaced section ends soon after Lightning Ridge).

The Mitchell Highway heads north-west to Bourke and Queensland via Nyngan. At Nyngan the Barrier Highway forks off west to Broken Hill.

Getting There & Away
Eastern Australia (☎ 13 1313) and Ansett (☎ 13 1300) fly to several of the main towns. Those on the Newell Highway are served by buses travelling to and from Brisbane, en route to Melbourne or Adelaide. Countrylink trains and/or buses (☎ 13 2242) connect most other towns in the area with Sydney. Fares from Sydney include Gunnedah $55, Coonabarabran $59.40 and Lightning Ridge $75.60.

NEWELL HIGHWAY
Gilgandra is a junction town where the

Newell and Castlereagh highways divide, and a road also cuts across to the Mitchell. It has a small **observatory** with an audiovisual of the moon landing and other space flights, plus a historical display.

Coonabarabran (pop 3000) is an access point for the spectacular granite domes and spires of the rugged **Warrumbungle National Park**, which offers great walking and rock climbing (permit required). There is an NPWS visitor centre (☎ 6825 4364) at the entrance to the park, about 35km west of Coonabarabran. Entry costs $7.50 per car. Camping costs $10 for two people on-site. There's also an NPWS office in Coonabarabran (☎ 6842 1311).

The largest optical telescope in the southern hemisphere is at **Siding Spring**, on the edge of the national park. There's a visitor centre, open daily from 9.30 am to 4 pm. It costs $5 to see the 'Exploring the Universe' display and various hands-on exhibits. If you want to spend $7.50 to look through a telescope, the **Skywatch Observatory** (☎ 6842 2506), on Timor Rd 2km from Coonabarabran, is open nightly. Phone first for viewing times.

Coonabarabran has several motels and caravan parks but during school holidays they can fill up. The *Imperial Hotel* (☎ 6842 1023), a YHA associate, has dorm beds for $14 and singles/doubles for $20/28.

In the country around the national park are a number of places to stay, including *Tibuc* (☎ 6842 1740, evenings best), an organic farm.

Narrabri (pop 6400) is a cotton-growing centre, with the enormous Australia Telescope (actually five linked radio telescope dishes) 25km west on the Yarrie Lake road. The interesting visitor centre is open daily. **Mt Kaputar National Park**, 53km east of Narrabri via a steep, unsealed road, is good for walking, camping and climbing. **Moree** is a large town on the Gwydir River with some reputedly therapeutic hot baths ($3.50).

CASTLEREAGH HIGHWAY
On the edge of the Western Plains is

Coonamble, 98km north of Gilgandra. West of here are the extensive **Macquarie Marshes** with their prolific birdlife. The road continues north to **Walgett**, in dry country near the Grawin and Glengarry opal fields.

A few kilometres off the highway near the Queensland border, **Lightning Ridge** is a huge opal field and the world's only reliable source of black opals. Despite the emphasis on tourism, with underground opal showrooms etc, Lightning Ridge remains a mining community where any battler could strike it rich. The **Moozeum** ($4, children $1) is worth a visit. There are motels (none cheap) and a few caravan parks with on-site vans. The *Tram-o-Tel* (☎ 6829 0448), has self-contained accommodation in old trams and caravans for $20/30.

MITCHELL HIGHWAY

From Dubbo the Mitchell Highway passes through the citrus-growing centre of **Narromine**. **Warren**, further north and off the Mitchell on the Oxley Highway, is an access point for the Macquarie Marshes, as is **Nyngan** where the Mitchell and Barrier highways divide. The huge marshes are breeding grounds for ducks, water hens, swans, pelicans, ibis and herons. Nyngan was the scene of fierce resistance by Aboriginal people to early European encroachment. The highway runs arrow-straight for 206km from Nyngan to Bourke.

Outback

You don't have to travel to central Australia to experience red-soil country, limitless horizons and vast blue skies. The far west of New South Wales is rough, rugged and sparsely populated. It also produces a fair proportion of the state's wealth, particularly from the mines of Broken Hill.

Always seek local advice before travelling on secondary roads west of the Mitchell Highway. You must carry plenty of water, and if you break down *stay with your vehicle*.

BOURKE (pop 2800)

The town of Bourke, about 800km northwest of Sydney, is on the edge of the outback – hence the expression 'back of Bourke' to describe anywhere remote. The area beyond Bourke is flat and featureless as far as the eye can see.

Bourke is on the Darling River as well as the Mitchell Highway and it was once a major river port. Scores of paddle-steamers plied the river and in the 1880s it was possible for wool to be in London just six weeks after leaving Bourke – somewhat quicker than a sea-mail parcel today! The courthouse has a crown on its spire, signifying that its jurisdiction includes maritime cases.

Quite a few famous Australians have passed through Bourke at one time or another. Henry Lawson lived at the Carriers Arms Hotel in 1892 while painting the Great Western Hotel. Fred Hollows, the ophthalmic surgeon whose philanthropic work in third-world countries made him a national hero, chose to be buried here.

Nowadays, the town is less frantic and prosperous than it was in the 1880s. At the time of writing several buildings were boarded up and vandalism seemed to have taken the edge off this fine river town's spirit.

The information centre (☎ 6872 2280) is at the train station on Anson St. Pick up a 'mud map' detailing drives to places like **Mt Gunderbooka**, which has Aboriginal cave art and vivid wildflowers in spring, and **Mt Oxley**.

Brewarrina (usually known as Bree) is 95km east of Bourke. You can see **the Fisheries**, stone fish traps which the Ngemba Aboriginal people used to catch the fish to feed the intertribal gatherings they hosted. 'Brewarrina' means 'good fishing'. Nearby is the **Aboriginal Cultural Museum**.

Places to Stay

There are several caravan parks along the river, including the *Paddlewheel* (☎ 6872 2277) with tent sites at $10, on-site vans ($26 a double) and cabins ($35).

The best of Bourke's hotels is the *Old Royal* (☎ 6872 2544) on Mitchell St between

Sturt and Richard Sts. It has singles/doubles for $31/46. The *Central* (☎ 6872 2151) on the corner of Anson and Richard Sts charges $25/35.

The *Bourke Riverside Motel* (☎ 6872 2539) on Mitchell St has a pleasant setting behind the river. Singles/doubles cost from $35/45.

Outback Accommodation Several stations in the Bourke area (a very large area) offer accommodation. The information centre has details. One of the best is historic *Urisino Station* (☎ 6874 7639), a friendly place which welcomes backpackers (and everyone else). Activities include camel treks (from 10 minutes to two-week safaris) and canoeing on the Paroo River. You can stay in the homestead ($56 per person or $80 with meals and activities) or in backpacker accommodation in old mud-brick cottages ($20 per person). Urisino is 230km west of Bourke, beyond Wanaaring. If you catch the mail truck from Bourke the owners will pick you up from Wanaaring.

Places to Eat
There are several cafes, such as the *Paddleboat Bistro* on Mitchell St. The dining room at the *Old Royal Hotel* is very popular. There is a Chinese restaurant at the Bowling Club and the Ex-Services Club also does meals.

Getting There & Away
Air Link (☎ 9850 6401) has five flights a week from Dubbo to Bourke ($172.50), which connect with Hazelton services from Sydney to Dubbo. Lachlan Travel (☎ 6872 2092) on Oxley St sells tickets.

Countrylink buses (☎ 13 2242) run to Dubbo four times a week and connect with trains to Sydney ($82). It *might* be possible to go along on the bi-weekly mail run to Wanaaring and Brewarrina. The post office (☎ 6872 2017) can put you in touch with the contractors.

The road from Cobar to Bourke is sealed all the way.

BACK OF BOURKE – CORNER COUNTRY
There's no sealed road west of Bourke in New South Wales. If you cared to drive the 713km from Bourke to Broken Hill via Wanaaring and Tibooburra it would be mostly on lonely unsealed roads. The far western corner of the state is a semidesert of red plains, heat, dust and flies, but with interesting physical features and prolific wildlife. Running along the border with Queensland is the Dog Fence, patrolled every day by boundary riders who each look after a 40km section.

Tibooburra
Tiny Tibooburra, the hottest place in the state, is right in the north-western corner and has a number of stone buildings from the 1880s and 90s. The town was once known as the Granites, after the striking granite formations that surround the town. Sturt National Park starts right on the northern edge of town. You can normally reach Tibooburra from Bourke or Broken Hill in a conventional vehicle, except after rain (which is pretty rare!).

The NPWS office (☎ (08) 8091 3308), open daily, also acts as an information centre.

Places to Stay & Eat A basic NPWS camp site is 2km north of town at *Dead Horse Gully*. The camping fee is $5 for two people, plus the $7.50 park entry fee. You'll need to bring drinking water. In town, the *Granites Caravan Park* (☎ (08) 8091 3305) has sites for $10, on-site vans for $24, cabins for $34 and motel units from $40/50.

The two fine old pubs both have rooms. The *Family Hotel* (☎ (08) 8091 3314) has singles/doubles for $20/35, while the *Tibooburra Hotel* (☎ (08) 8091 3310) – known as 'the Two-Storey' – has rooms from $30/40. Both bars are worth a beer: the Family's has a mural by Clifton Pugh, while the Two-Storey's has more than 60 impressively well-worn hats on the wall, left behind when their owners bought new headgear at the pub.

The hotels do good counter meals and

have tables outside where you can sit and watch the occasional 4WD pass by.

Sturt National Park

Sturt National Park occupies the very north-western corner of the state, bordering both South Australia and Queensland. The park has 300km of drivable tracks, camping areas and walks, particularly on the **Jump Up Loop drive** and towards the top of **Mt Wood**. It is recommended that you inform the ranger at Tibooburra where you are heading before venturing into the park. Entry to the park is $7.50 per car and camping costs $5 for two people.

At **Camerons Corner** there's a post to mark the place where Queensland, South Australia and New South Wales meet. It's a favourite goal for visitors and a 4WD is not always necessary to get there. In the Queensland corner, the *Corner Store* (☎ (08) 8091 3872) is known for its home-made pies, cakes, damper and ice cream. Everybody coming by the Corner stops here and the staff can advise on road conditions. You can also buy fuel here.

Milparinka

Milparinka, once a gold town, now consists of little more than a solitary hotel and some old sandstone buildings. In 1845 members of Charles Sturt's expedition from Adelaide, searching for an inland sea, were forced to camp near here for six months. The temperatures were high, the conditions terrible and their supplies inadequate. About 14km north-west of the settlement you can see the grave of James Poole, Sturt's second-in-command, who died of scurvy.

BARRIER HIGHWAY

The Barrier Highway is the main route in the state's west – and just about the only sealed road. It heads west from Nyngan, from where it's 594km to Broken Hill. This provides an alternative route to Adelaide and is the most direct route between Sydney and Western Australia.

Cobar (pop 4500)

Cobar has a modern and highly productive copper mine but it also has an earlier history as evidenced by its old buildings, like the Great Western Hotel with its endless stretch of iron lacework ornamenting the verandah. Pick up a town tour map at the information centre (☎ 6836 2448), which is in the excellent **museum** ($4) at the eastern end of the main street.

Weather balloons are released at 9 am and 3 pm from the meteorological station on the edge of town, off the Louth road.

There are important Aboriginal cave paintings at **Mt Grenfell**, 40km west of Cobar, then another 32km north off the highway. You can't camp here.

The *Cobar Caravan Park* (☎ 6836 2425) has sites for $13, on-site vans for $25 and cabins from $35. Several pubs have accommodation. The *New Occidental* (☎ 6836 2111) charges $15 per person, while the *Great Western* (☎ 6836 2503) has motel-style singles/doubles for $34/44, including breakfast.

Wilcannia (pop 690)

Wilcannia is on the Darling River and was a busy port in the days of paddle-steamers. It's a much quieter place today but you can still see buildings from that era, such as the police station. There are a couple of motels costing around $60 a double. The pubs may provide meals but are best avoided unless you are an experienced bar-room brawler.

White Cliffs (pop 150)

About 100km north-west of Wilcannia is White Cliffs, an opal-mining settlement. For a taste of life in a small outback community it's worth the drive on a dirt road. You can fossick for opals around the old diggings (watch out for unfenced shafts) and there are opal showrooms and underground homes (called dug-outs) open for inspection. The general store has a 'mud map' of the area and information.

As you enter White Cliffs you pass the high-tech dishes of the solar-energy research station, where emus often graze out the front. Tours of the station are held daily at 2 pm.

Places to Stay & Eat The *White Cliffs Hotel* (☎ (08) 8091 6606) has basic rooms, but they have air-con and are good value at $15 per person. A big cooked breakfast costs $8. Across the road from the post office is a small camping area (☎ (08) 8091 6627) where sites cost just $2 per person and showers are $1. There's also a swimming pool.

PJ's Underground (☎ (08) 8091 6626), 1.5km east of the post office on Turley's Hill, has doubles with breakfast for $69. Up on Smiths Hill is the *White Cliffs Underground Motel* (☎ 1800 02 1154). It's surprisingly roomy and the temperature is a constant 22°C, whether there's a heatwave or a frost on the surface. Singles/doubles cost $45/70 and triples $89. There is also an upmarket licensed restaurant.

The *Golf Club*, near the solar station, has Sunday roast lunches for $5.

Mootwingee National Park

This park in the Bynguano Range, 131km north of Broken Hill, teems with wildlife and is a place of exceptional beauty. It is well worth the two-hour drive from Broken Hill on an isolated dirt road. You can also get here from White Cliffs but neither route should be attempted after rain. Entry to the park is $7.50 per car.

In the park is an Aboriginal tribal ground with important rock carvings and cave paintings. The major site is now controlled by the Aboriginal community and is off limits except on ranger-escorted tours on Wednesday and Saturday morning ($5), leaving from the camping area (see below). Tours may not run in the heat of summer. The NPWS office in Broken Hill (☎ (08) 8088 5933) has details.

There are walks through the crumbling sandstone hills to rock pools, which often have enough water for swimming, and rock paintings can be seen in the areas that are not off limits. The *Homestead Creek* camping

area ($10) has bore water. You should book sites, especially during school holidays.

BROKEN HILL (pop 20,950)

Out in the far west, Broken Hill is an oasis in the wilderness. A mining town, it's fascinating not only for its comfortable existence in an extremely unwelcoming environment, but also for the fact that it was once a one-company town that spawned one equally strong union. It has also become a major artistic centre.

There are two working mines in Broken Hill, the deeper being the North Mine, about 1600m deep and incorporating 30km of winding road. At that depth it can reach 60°C and massive refrigeration plants are needed to control the temperature. You can't visit the working mines but there are tours of old mines (see Organised Tours later in this chapter).

History

Broken Hill Proprietary Company (BHP) was formed in 1885 after Charles Rasp, a boundary rider, discovered a silver lode. Miners working on other finds in the area had failed to notice the real wealth. Other mining claims were staked, but BHP was always the 'big mine' and dominated the town. Charles Rasp amassed a personal fortune and BHP, which later diversified into steel production, became Australia's largest company.

Early conditions in the mine were appalling. Hundreds of miners died and many more suffered from lead poisoning and lung disease. This gave rise to the other great force in Broken Hill, the unions. Many miners were immigrants from various countries but all were united in their efforts to improve conditions.

The town's first 35 years saw a militancy rarely matched in Australian industrial relations. Many campaigns were fought, police were called in to break strikes and, though there was a gradual improvement in conditions, the miners lost many confrontations. The turning point was the Big Strike of 1919 and 1920, which lasted for over 18 months.

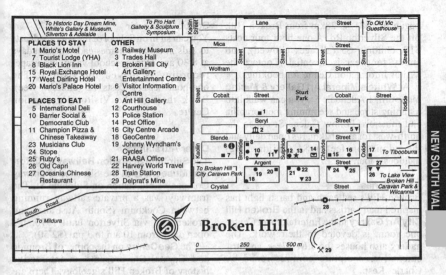

The miners won a 35-hour week and the end of dry drilling, responsible for the dust that afflicted so many of them.

The concept of 'one big union', which had helped to win the strike, was formalised in 1923 with the formation of the Barrier Industrial Council, which still largely runs the town.

Today the world's richest deposits of silver, lead and zinc are still being worked, though zinc is of greatest importance in the Silver City, as Broken Hill is known. There's enough ore left to ensure about another 15 years of mining. Modern technology has greatly reduced the number of jobs but while mining has declined, art has thrived.

Orientation & Information
The city is laid out in a grid and the central area is easy to get around on foot. Argent St is the main street.

The big Visitor Information Centre (☎ (08) 8087 6077) on the corner of Blende and Bromide Sts opens daily. This is also where the buses arrive; there's a bus booking agency and car-rental desk on the premises. Pick up the *Heritage Trails* map ($2).

The NPWS office (☎ (08) 8088 5933) is at 5 Oxide St. The Royal Automobile Association of South Australia (RAASA; ☎ (08) 8088 4999), 261 Argent St, provides reciprocal service to other autoclub members. You can buy your South Australian Desert Parks Pass here (see the Outback section of the South Australia chapter).

There's a laundrette on Argent St just east of the West Darling Hotel.

In many ways Broken Hill is more a part of South Australia than New South Wales. It's 1170km from Sydney but only 509km from Adelaide; clocks are set on Adelaide (central) time, half an hour behind Sydney (eastern) time; and the telephone area code (08) is the same as South Australia's.

Mines
There's an excellent underground tour at **Delprat's Mine** Monday to Saturday, where you don miners' gear and descend 130m for a tour lasting nearly two hours. It costs $23 (children $18). Children under eight years of age are not allowed on the tour. To get there, go up Iodide St, cross the railway tracks and follow the signs – it's about a five-minute drive.

Open daily, **Historic Day Dream Mine**,

begun in 1881, is 28km from Broken Hill, off the Silverton Rd. A one-hour tour costs $10, children $5 (all ages allowed), and sturdy footwear is essential. Contact the Visitor Information Centre for bookings.

At **White's Mineral Art Gallery & Mining Museum**, 1 Allendale St, you can walk into a mining stope and see mining memorabilia and minerals. Follow Galena St out to the north-west for about 2km. It's open daily and the admission fee of $4 (children $2) includes a tour.

Art Galleries

Broken Hill's red earth and harsh light has inspired many artists and in the **Broken Hill City Art Gallery** in the Entertainment Centre one room is devoted to their work. The gallery also houses the *Silver Tree*, an intricate silver sculpture commissioned by Charles Rasp.

There's also a plethora of private galleries, including the **Pro Hart Gallery** (☎ (08) 8087 2441), 108 Wyman St, and **Jack Absalom's Gallery** (☎ (08) 8087 5881), 638 Chapple St. Pro Hart, a former miner, is Broken Hill's best-known artist and a local personality. His kooky gallery is bursting with the fruits of compulsive collecting. Apart from his own work, the gallery displays minor works of major artists (eg Picasso and Dali) and his collection of Australian art is superb. He charges admission ($4, children under 12 free) but many others don't. The **Ant Hill Gallery** (☎ (08) 8087 2441), 24 Bromide St, features local and major Australian artists.

Have a look at the murals inside Mario's Palace Hotel on Argent St.

Royal Flying Doctor Service Base

You can visit the Royal Flying Doctor Service (RFDS; ☎ (08) 8080 1777) base at the airport. The tour ($2, children under 12 free) includes a film, and you can inspect the headquarters, aircraft and the radio room that handles calls from remote towns and stations. Tour times are Monday to Friday at 10.30 am and 3 pm, weekends at 10.30 am. Bookings are made at the Visitor Information Centre or by calling the RFDS.

School of the Air

You can sit in on School of the Air broadcasts to kids in isolated homesteads on weekdays at 8.30 am. During school vacations a tape-recording is played for visitors. The one-hour session costs $2 (children free). Book through the Visitor Information Centre.

Other Attractions

The **Sulphide St Station Railway & Historical Museum** is in the Silverton Tramway Company's old station on Sulphide St. The tramway was a private railway running between Cockburn (South Australia) and Broken Hill via Silverton until 1970. It's open daily from 10 am to 3 pm ($2.50).

The **GeoCentre** on the corner of Bromide and Crystal Sts presents an interactive history of Broken Hill's geology. There are rock and mineral samples, huge and tiny, and displays on mining and metallurgy. It's open weekdays from 10 am to 5 pm and weekends from 1 to 5 pm ($3).

The **Afghani Mosque** on the corner of William and Buck Sts in North Broken Hill is a corrugated-iron building dating from 1891. Afghani cameleers helped open up the outback and the mosque was built on the site of a camel camp. It opens on Sunday from 2.30 to 4.30 pm but no longer functions as a mosque.

The **Sculpture Symposium** was a project by 12 sculptors from several countries who carved sandstone blocks on a hilltop 4km from town. Drive north-west on Kaolin St and keep going on the unsealed road for 2km until you get to the signposted turn-off on the right. From there it's another 2km on a rough road, then a steep walk to the top of the hill. You need to get keys to a gate on the road from the Visitor Information Centre. As well as the sculptures there are excellent views over the plains. This is a good place to watch one of Broken Hill's famous sunsets, as is the **Sundown Nature Trail** 10km north-east of town off the Silver City Highway.

There's a **swimming pool** on McCulloch St north-east of the town centre.

Organised Tours

There are two-hour guided walks of Broken Hill from the Visitor Information Centre at 10 am on Monday, Wednesday, Friday and Saturday. Plenty of companies offer tours of the town and nearby attractions, some going further out to White Cliffs, Mootwingee and other outback destinations. The Visitor Information Centre has information and takes bookings.

Several outfits have longer 4WD tours of the area. Goanna Safaris (☎ (08) 8087 6057) has 4WD outback tours, which get good reviews from travellers.

An interesting way to see some of the country beyond Broken Hill is to go on an outback mail-run. Contact Crittenden Air (☎ (08) 8088 5702) as far in advance as possible – the mail run only takes four people, fewer if there's lots of mail. It departs 6.30 am Saturday and calls at about 14 outback stations, stopping in White Cliffs for a tour and lunch. The cost is $230. Crittenden Air also does other air tours.

Places to Stay

Camping *Broken Hill City Caravan Park* (☎ (08) 8087 3841), on Rakow St (the Barrier Highway) about 3km west of the centre, has sites for $10, on-site vans from $23 and cabins from $30. *Lake View Broken Hill Caravan Park* (☎ (08) 8088 2250), 1 Mann St (the Barrier Highway) 3km north-east, has sites for $10, on-site vans for $26 and cabins from $32.

Hostels The *Tourist Lodge* (☎ (08) 8088 2086), 100 Argent St, is an associate-YHA hostel with dorms for $15 and singles/doubles for $18/30 or $22/36 with air-con.

Hotels & Motels High ceilings, wide corridors and huge verandahs come as standard equipment on pubs in this hot city. All places mentioned here have air-con.

The *Black Lion Inn* (☎ 8087 4801), on the corner of Bromide St and Blende St just across from the bus depot, is a congenial pub with singles/doubles with shared bathroom for $18/28. The elegant old *Royal Exchange Hotel* (☎ (08) 8087 2308), 320 Argent St, has rooms for $24/40 or $34/50 with bathroom, fridge and TV. The price includes a light breakfast. Diagonally opposite, the *Grand Guesthouse* (☎ (08) 8087 5305) has double rooms with shared bathrooms for $54 or $64 with en-suite (both tariffs include breakfast).

Further west on the corner of Sulphide and Argent Sts, *Mario's Palace Hotel* (☎ (08) 8088 1699) is an impressive old pub (1888) covered in murals and featured in *Priscilla Queen of the Desert*. All rooms have fridges, TVs and tea/coffee-making facilities. Singles/doubles are $28/38 or $38/48 with attached bathroom.

Old Vic Guesthouse (☎ (08) 8087 1169), 230 Oxide St, is an airy B&B with rooms for $25/40.

It's hard to understand why anyone would opt for a motel with so many other interesting places to stay. Still, the Visitor Information Centre has a list of them and their prices. The *Sturt Motel* (☎ (08) 8087 3558), 153 Rakow St (Barrier Highway) 4km west of the centre, charges from $37/43 and has cabins for $49/55. Most of the others charge from around $55/65.

Cottages There are some beautiful cottages for rent. *Broken Hill Historic Cottages* (☎ (08) 8087 5305) and *Sue Spicer's Holiday Cottages* (☎ (08) 8087 8488) are both worth checking out. The cottages come complete with everything you could need, sleep up to six people and cost from around $65/350 per night/week.

Places to Eat

The gourmets in Broken Hill are the ones who eat the garnish on their steaks, so don't spend too much time looking for *cuisine minceur* down these dusty streets.

Broken Hill is a club town if ever there was one. The clubs welcome visitors and in most cases you just sign the book at the front door and walk in. Most have reasonably priced, reasonably good and very filling meals. The *Barrier Social & Democratic Club* ('the Demo'), 218 Argent St, has meals including a breakfast (from 6 am, or 7 am weekends) that will keep you going all day. The *Musician's Club*, 267 Crystal St, is slightly cheaper.

There are lots of pubs too – this is a mining town – but you'd be lucky to find them cooking after 8.30 pm or at all on a Sunday. The *Black Lion Inn*, Bromide St, has a $5 counter lunch and main courses in the evening for around $10. The *West Darling Hotel*, on the corner of Oxide and Argent Sts, and many other pubs have counter meals.

On Sulphide St, *Champion Pizza & Chinese Takeaway*, dourly holding its own behind the Pizza Hut, stays open late and does an all-you-can-eat Chinese buffet for $6 after 6 pm. There's a cluster of places at the eastern end of Argent St. The *Oceania Chinese Restaurant* is popular with $7 lunch specials and main courses from around $9.50, and *Old Capri* is a small Italian place boasting home-made pasta.

Stope, on Argent St, is a bakery cafe with good sandwiches and cakes and the best coffee in town. *Ruby's*, 425 Argent St, is OK for light meals and usually has a couple of vegetarian items on the menu.

If you spend too long in the pub and forget all about dinner, you can pick up late-night supplies at the *International Deli*, on Oxide St near Beryl St. It's open until midnight all week and has a good range of cheeses and smallgoods, plus takeaway salads.

Entertainment

Maybe it's because this is a mining town, maybe it's because there are so many nights when it's too hot to sleep, but Broken Hill stays up late. There isn't a lot of formal entertainment but pubs stay open almost until dawn on Thursday, Friday and Saturday nights.

The *Theatre Royal Hotel* on Argent St has a disco, and the *Barrier Social & Democratic Club*, the 'Demo', runs a nightclub on Friday and Saturday nights. The Demo also has live entertainment, but to dig it you will have to be a country cabaret fan. The *Black Lion Inn* is a good pub for a drink. It has a three-page cocktail list and two-for-one deals on some nights.

Two-up (gambling on the fall of two coins) is played at *Burke Ward Hall* on Wills St near the corner of Gypsum St, west of the centre, on Friday and Saturday nights. Broken Hill claims to have retained the atmosphere of a real two-up 'school', unlike the sanitised versions played in casinos.

Getting There & Around

Air Standard one-way fares from Broken Hill include $173 to Adelaide with Kendell (☎ 13 1300), $218 to Melbourne with Southern Australia (Qantas ☎ 13 1313) and $354 to Sydney with Hazelton (☎ 13 1713).

Bus Greyhound Pioneer (☎ 13 2030) runs daily to Adelaide for $56, to Mildura for $37.50 and to Sydney for $99. Most buses depart from the Visitor Information Centre, where you can book seats.

A Victorian V/Line bus runs to Mildura ($37.50) on Wednesday and Friday. Book at the train station.

Train Broken Hill is on the Sydney to Perth railway line so the Indian Pacific passes through. On Sunday and Wednesday it leaves Broken Hill at 3.20 pm and arrives in Sydney at 9.15 am the next day. The economy fare is $86. To Adelaide ($44) and Perth (from $214), it departs Broken Hill on Tuesday and Friday at 9 am.

There's a slightly faster and marginally cheaper daily service to Sydney called Laser, a Countrylink bus (☎ 13 2242) departing Broken Hill daily at 4 am (groan) and connecting with a train at Dubbo, arriving in Sydney at 8.45 pm ($98).

The Countrylink booking office (☎ 13 2242) at the train station opens weekdays.

Car & Motorcycle The Barrier Highway runs east to Wilcannia and Cobar, and west into South Australia. The Silver City

Highway runs south to Wentworth and, mostly unsealed, north to Tibooburra.

The major car-rental companies have offices here but their 'remote region' rates can work out to be expensive. Small cars start at around $75 a day.

Taxi For a taxi call ☎ (08) 8088 1144 or ☎ (08) 8087 2222. There's a taxi office on Chloride St near Argent St.

AROUND BROKEN HILL
Silverton
Silverton, 25km north-west of Broken Hill, is an old silver-mining town, which reached its peak in 1885 when it had a population of 3000 and public buildings designed to last for centuries. In 1889 the mines closed and the population (and many of the houses) moved to Broken Hill.

Today it's an interesting little ghost town, which was used as a setting in the movies *Mad Max II* and *A Town Like Alice*. A number of buildings still stand, including the old gaol (now the museum) and the Silverton Hotel. The hotel is still operating and it displays photographs taken on the film sets. Don't leave here without taking the infamous 'Silverton test'; ask at the bar. There are also a couple of art galleries. The information centre, in the old school, has a walking-tour map.

Bill Canard (☎ (08) 8088 5316) runs a variety of **camel tours** from Silverton. The camels are often hitched up near the hotel or the information centre. You can take a 15-minute tour of the town for $5, a one-hour ride for $20 or a two-hour sunset ride for $40 (children $20). There are also longer treks.

There's accommodation at *Penrose Park* (☎ (08) 8088 5307), signposted to the right as you approach town from Broken Hill. Camp sites cost $2.50 per person, or you can bed down in a choice of 'bunkhouses' – $20 with kitchen, $15 without. There are coin-operated showers and water for washing, but bring or boil drinking-water.

The road beyond Silverton becomes bleak and lonely almost immediately. The **Mundi Mundi Plains** lookout, 5km north of town, gives an idea of just how desolate it gets. Further along, the **Umberumberka Reservoir**, 13km north of Silverton, is a popular picnic spot.

Menindee Lakes
This water storage development on the Darling River, 112km south-east of Broken Hill, offers a variety of water-sport facilities. **Menindee** is the closest town to the area. Burke and Wills stayed at Maidens Hotel on their ill-fated trip north in 1860. The hotel was built in 1854 and still has accommodation (☎ (08) 8091 4208) for around $16 per person including breakfast.

Kinchega National Park is close to town, and the lakes, overflowing from the Darling River, are a haven for birdlife. There are also many kangaroos and other native fauna. The visitor centre is at the site of the old Kinchega Homestead, about 16km from the park entrance, and the shearing shed has been preserved. There's accommodation at the shearer's quarters (book at the Broken Hill NPWS office) and plenty of camp sites along the river.

North of Menindee there are some good, free camp sites around Lakes Wetherell and Pawamaroo, but bone up on minimal impact camping strategies before you set up: this is a water catchment area.

MUNGO NATIONAL PARK
South-east of Menindee and north-east of Mildura is **Lake Mungo**, a dry lake which is the site of the oldest archaeological finds in Australia – human skeletons and artefacts dating back 45,000 years, when Aboriginal people settled on the banks of the once fertile lakes and lived on the plentiful fish, mussels, birds and animals. After 25,000 years the climate changed, the lakes dried up and Aboriginal people adapted to life in a harsh semidesert, with only periodic floods filling the lakes.

A 25km semicircle ('lunette') of huge sand dunes has been created by the never-ending west wind, which continually exposes fabulously ancient remains. The park also includes the dry lake-bed and the

NEW SOUTH WALES

shimmering white cliffs known as the **Walls of China**. Remember, it's illegal in Australia to remove archaeological objects or to disturb human remains.

Mungo is 110km from Mildura and 150km from Balranald on unsealed roads. These towns are the closest places selling fuel. Mallee Outback Experiences (☎ (03) 5021 1621) and Junction Tours (☎ (03) 5027 4309) are two Mildura-based companies offering tours. Mallee Outdoor Experiences charges $45 for a day tour (Wednesday and Saturday).

Information

There's a visitor centre (not always staffed) by the old Mungo woolshed. The NPWS office (☎ (03) 5023 1278) at Buronga near Mildura also has information. A road leads across the dry lake bed to the Walls of China, and you can drive a complete 60km loop of the dunes – but not after rain. Park entry costs $7.50 per car.

Places to Stay

Accommodation fills up during school holidays. There are two camp sites – *Main Camp* is 2km from the visitor centre and *Belah Camp* on the eastern side of the dunes. Camping costs $5 a night. There's also shared accommodation in the old shearers' quarters for $15 per person (children $5) or $25 for a room to yourself. Book through the NPWS office in Buronga.

On the Mildura road about 4km from the visitor centre is *Mungo Lodge* (☎ (03) 5029 7297) where singles/doubles/triples cost from $58/68/78. There's also a restaurant here.

Lord Howe Island

Beautiful Lord Howe is a tiny subtropical island 500km east of Port Macquarie and 770km north-east of Sydney. It's not a budget destination. Unless you've got a boat, you'll have to fly there, and both food and accommodation are expensive. Most visitors take flight and accommodation packages.

The island is listed on the World Heritage Register. It's heavily forested and has beautiful walks, a wide lagoon sheltered by a coral reef and some fine beaches. It's small enough at 11km long and 2.5km wide for you to get around on foot or by bicycle. The southern end is dominated by towering Mt Lidgbird (777m) and Mt Gower (875m). You can climb Mt Gower in around six hours (round trip). There's good diving, snorkelling in the lagoon and you can also inspect the sea life from glass-bottom boats. On the other side of the island there's surf at Blinky Beach.

Information

For information and bookings, try Pacific International Travel (☎ 13 2747) at 91 York St, Sydney or Fastbook Pacific (☎ 9212 5977) at 645 Harris St, Ultimo (Sydney).

Places to Stay

Camping is not permitted on the island. There is plenty of accommodation in lodges and self-contained apartments, but the only way to get a decent deal is to buy a package. Prices are around $600 for five nights or around $800 for a seven-day package, ex-Sydney.

Getting There & Away

Eastern Australia (☎ 13 1313) has frequent flights from Sydney, while Sunstate flies from Brisbane on weekends. Kentia Link (☎ 9212 5977) operates flights from Coffs Harbour and Port Macquarie, as well as to Norfolk Island. Most flights are booked as part of a package deal (see Information).

Getting Around

You can hire bicycles, motorcycles and cars on the island but a bicycle is all you need. There is a 25km/h speed limit throughout the island.

Norfolk Island

Norfolk Island is a green speck in the middle of the Pacific Ocean, 1600km north-east of Sydney and 1000km north-west of the New Zealand city of Auckland. It's the largest of a cluster of three islands emerging from the Norfolk Ridge, which stretches from New Zealand to New Caledonia – the closest landfall almost 700km to the north.

Norfolk is a popular tourist spot, particularly with older Australians and New Zealanders, and tourism is by far the biggest contributor to the local economy. The cost of airfares means it is not a cheap destination and there is no budget accommodation.

Many visitors enjoy Norfolk Island's lush vegetation. The rich volcanic soil and mild subtropical climate provide perfect growing conditions. There are 40-odd plant species that are unique to the island, including the handsome Norfolk Island pine *(Araucaria heterophylla)* which grows everywhere.

History
Little is known about the island's history prior to being sighted by Captain Cook on 10 October 1774 and named after the wife of the ninth Duke of Norfolk. Fifteen convicts were among the first settlers to reach the island on 6 March 1788, founding a penal colony that survived until 1814. The island was abandoned for 11 years before the colonial authorities decided to try again. Governor Darling planned this second penal settlement as 'a place of the extremest punishment short of death'. Under such notorious sadists as commandant John Giles Price, Norfolk became known as 'hell in the Pacific'. The second penal colony lasted until 1855, when the prisoners were shipped off to Van Diemen's Land (Tasmania) and the island was handed over to the descendants of the mutineers from the HMS *Bounty*, who had outgrown their adopted Pitcairn Island. About a third of the present population of 2000 are descended from the 194 Pitcairners who arrived on 8 June 1856.

Visas
The island is a self-governing external territory of Australia; this has important ramifications in terms of passports and visas. Travelling to Norfolk Island from Australia means you will get an exit stamp in your passport and board an international flight. To return to Australia you will need a re-entry visa, or a valid Australian passport. On arrival at Norfolk Island, you will get a 30-day entry permit on presentation of a valid passport.

Orientation & Information
The island measures only 8km by 5km. Vertical cliffs surround much of the coastline, apart from a small area of coastal plain (formerly swamp) around the historic settlement of Kingston. The only settlement of any consequence is the service town of Burnt Pine, at the centre of the island and near the airport. Most of the northern part of the island is within the Norfolk Island National Park.

The Norfolk Islander Visitor Information Centre (☎ 22 147) is next to the post office on the main street in Burnt Pine. The Communications Centre (Norfolk Telecom) is at the edge of town on New Cascade Rd. If you're addressing mail to the island from Australia, the postcode is 2899; the island's international telephone code is 6723.

The Commonwealth Bank and Westpac both have branches in Burnt Pine; the Commonwealth has an ATM. Eftpos is available in most shops.

KINGSTON
The historic settlement of Kingston, built by convicts of the second penal colony, is the island's main attraction. Several of the buildings have been turned into small museums. The finest buildings are those of the colonial administrators along Quality Row, as the settlement's main road is called. The sandstone used for the buildings was quarried from nearby Nepean Island. One place that should not be missed is the convict cemetery, next to the ocean at the far (eastern) end of Quality Row. There are some very poignant epitaphs on the headstones, such as that of

James Saye, who was killed in 1842 during an abortive mutiny:

> Stop Christian, stop and meditate
> On this man's sad and awful fate
> On earth no more he breathes again
> He lived in hope but died in pain

Other Attractions

Just south of Kingston is **Emily Bay**, a good sheltered beach, and there are several operators who will take you out in glass-bottom boats to view the corals in the bay.

St Barnabas Chapel, west of Burnt Pine along Douglas Drive, is a magnificent chapel built by the (Anglican) Melanesian Mission, which was based on the island from 1866 to 1920.

There are various walking tracks in **Norfolk Island National Park**, and good views from Mt Pitt (320m) and Mt Bates (321m). Mt Pitt was the higher of the two before the top was levelled to build a radio transmitter.

Organised Tours

Pinetree Tours (☎ 22 424) and Bounty Excursions (☎ 23 693), both in Burnt Pine, run tours around the island, including half-day introductory tours ($18) taking in all the major points of interest.

Places to Stay

Accommodation is expensive, but the cost is often disguised as most visitors come on package deals, which start at around $600 for a five-night package.

There are lots of places to choose from, but few which make the most of the island's natural attributes. Modern motel-style units predominate, priced from around $90 a double.

The *Highlands Lodge* (☎ 22 741) is a good place nestled on the hillside below the national park with doubles for $142. *Channer's Corner* (☎ 22 532), on the edge of Burnt Pine, has stylish apartments at $95 for two people.

Places to Eat

There are dozens of restaurants offering everything from humble fish & chips to upmarket à la carte. Competition is stiff and prices are quite reasonable, although food in the shops is expensive by Australian standards.

The *Bowling Club* in Burnt Pine has roasts for $8, and the *Workers Club* opposite is equally good value. *Barney Duffy's* is a popular steakhouse in the main shopping area.

Getting There & Away

Norfolk Jet Express flies almost daily from Sydney and three times weekly from Brisbane, and Flight West has four flights a week from Brisbane. Most flights are booked as part of a package. Kentia Link flies to Lord Howe Island (see the Lord Howe Island section). Air New Zealand flies twice a week from Auckland (from around NZ$600 return).

Getting Around

Car hire can be organised at the airport for as little as $9 a day, plus insurance ($3). Petrol is expensive, but you'll struggle to use much. Cows have right of way on the island's roads, and there's a $300 fine for hitting one.

Leaving Norfolk Island

There's a departure tax of $25.

Northern Territory

The fascinating Northern Territory is the most barren and least populated area of Australia (with only 1% of the Australian population living in nearly 20% of the country's area). The populated parts of Australia are predominantly urban and coastal, but it is in the Centre – the Red Heart – that the picture-book, untamed and sometimes surreal Australia exists.

The Centre is not just Uluru (Ayers Rock), bang in the middle of nowhere. There are meteorite craters, eerie canyons, lost valleys of palms, and noisy Alice Springs festivals. Where else is there an annual boat regatta on a dry river bed? The colour red is evident as soon as you arrive – in the soil, the rocks and in Uluru itself. At the other end of the Track – the Stuart Highway, 1500km of bitumen that connects Alice Springs to the north coast – is Darwin, probably Australia's most cosmopolitan city.

Even that long, empty road between Alice Springs and Darwin isn't dull – there are plenty of interesting places along the way. As you travel up or down that single link you'll notice another of the Territory's real surprises – the contrast between the Centre's amazing aridity and the humid, tropical wetness of the Top End in the monsoon season. The wetlands and escarpments of Kakadu National Park are a treasure house of wildlife and Aboriginal rock painting.

The Northern Territory has a small population and a more fragile economy than other parts of Australia, and isn't classified as a state. It was formerly administered by New South Wales and then by South Australia, but it has been controlled by the Federal government since 1911. Since 1978 the Territory has been self-governed, although Canberra still has more say over its internal affairs than over those of the states.

ABORIGINAL PEOPLE
Around 22% of the Territory's population is

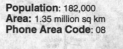

Population: 182,000
Area: 1.35 million sq km
Phone Area Code: 08

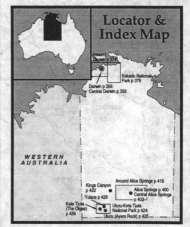

Locator & Index Map

Around Darwin p 374
Kakadu National Park p 378
Darwin p 356
Central Darwin p 358

WESTERN AUSTRALIA

Around Alice Springs p 416
Kings Canyon p 422
Alice Springs p 400
Central Alice Springs
Yulara p 428
Kata Tjuta (The Olgas) p 425
Uluru-Kata Tjuta National Park p 424
Uluru (Ayers Rock) p 425

Highlights
- Taking a boat ride on the wetlands of Kakadu National Park
- Visiting Uluru (Ayers Rock) and Kata Tjuta (the Olgas) at Uluru-Kata Tjuta National Park
- Hiking in the spectacular Kings Canyon, Watarrka National Park
- Fishing for barramundi at Borroloola on the Gulf of Carpentaria
- Paddling a canoe up the Katherine Gorge, Nitmiluk National Park
- Taking an Aboriginal cultural tour at Manyallaluk near Katherine
- Visiting the old gold mines in Tennant Creek
- Trekking the Larapinta Trail in the Western MacDonnell Ranges, near Alice Springs
- Delving into central Australian history at the Old Telegraph Station, Alice Springs

Aboriginal – a higher proportion than in most southern states.

347

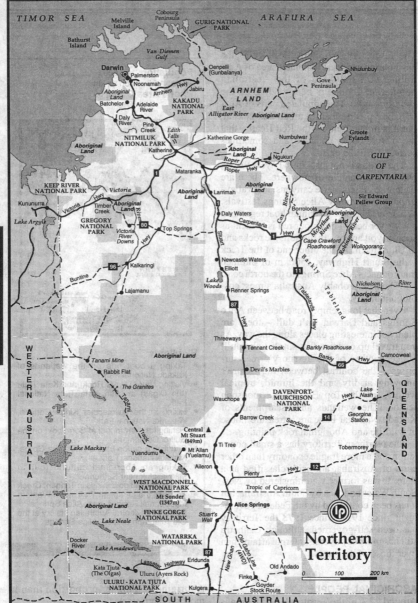

Northern Territory

The process of white settlement in the Northern Territory was just as troubled and violent as elsewhere in Australia, with Aboriginal groups vainly trying to resist the takeover of land on which their way of life depended. By the early 20th century, most Aboriginal people were confined to government reserves or Christian missions. Others lived on cattle stations where they were employed as skilful but poorly paid stockmen or domestic servants, or lived a half-life on the edges of towns, taking on low-paid work and often acquiring an alcohol habit. Only a few – some of those on reserves and cattle stations and in the remote outback – maintained much of their traditional way of life.

During the 1960s, Northern Territory Aboriginal people began to demand more rights. In 1963 the people of Yirrkala on the Gove Peninsula, part of the Arnhem Land reserve, protested against plans for bauxite mining. The Yirrkala people failed to stop the mining, but the way they presented their case (by producing sacred objects and bark paintings that showed their right to the land under Aboriginal custom) was a milestone. In 1966 the Gurindji people on Wave Hill cattle station went on strike and asked that their tribal land, which formed part of the station, be returned to them. Eventually the Gurindji were given 3238sq km in a government-negotiated deal with the station owners.

In 1976 the Aboriginal Land Rights (Northern Territory) Act was passed in Canberra. It handed over all reserves and mission lands in the Territory to Aborigines, and allowed Aboriginal groups to claim government land with which they had traditional ties (unless the land was already leased, or in a town, or set aside for some other special purpose).

Vincent Lingiari & the Wave Hill Stockmen's Strike of 1966

Aboriginal stockmen played a large role in the early days of the pastoral industry in the Northern Territory. Because they were paid such paltry wages (which often never even materialised) a pastoralist could afford to employ many of them, and run his station at a much lower cost. White stockmen received regular and relatively high wages, were given decent food and accommodation, and were able to return to the station homestead every week. By contrast, Aboriginal stockmen received poor food and accommodation, little or no money, and would often spend months in the bush with the cattle.

In the 1960s Vincent Lingiari was a stockman on the huge Wave Hill station, owned by the British Vesteys company. His concern with the way Aboriginal workers were treated led to an appeal to the North Australian Workers' Union (NAWU), which had already applied to the federal court for equal wages for Aboriginal workers. The Federal court approved the granting of equal wages in March 1966, but it was not to take effect until December 1968. The decision led Lingiari to ask the Wave Hill management directly for equal wages. It was refused and, on 23 August 1966, the Aboriginal stockmen walked off the station and camped in nearby Wattie Creek. They were soon joined by others, and before long only stations that gave their Aboriginal workers not only good conditions but also respect, were provided with workers by Lingiari and the other Gurindji elders.

The Wattie Creek camp gained a lot of local support, from both white and Aboriginal people, and it soon developed into a sizable community with housing and a degree of organisation. Having gained the right to equal pay, Lingiari and the Gurindji people felt, perhaps for the first time, that they had some say in the way they were able to live.

This victory led to the hope that perhaps they could achieve something even more important – title to their own land. To this end Lingiari travelled widely in the eastern states campaigning for land rights, and finally made some progress with the Whitlam government. On 16 August 1975, prime minister Gough Whitlam attended a ceremony at Wattie Creek which saw the handing over of 3200sq km of land, now known as Daguragu.

Lingiari was awarded the Order of Australia medal for service to the Aboriginal people, and died at Daguragu in 1988.

The stockmen's strike at Wave Hill was so significant that it is the subject of two songs by well-known but very different Australian songwriters – Ted Egan *(Gurindji Blues)* and Paul Kelly *(From Little Things Big Things Grow)*. ∎

Today Aboriginal people own almost 50% of the Northern Territory. This includes Uluru National Park, which was handed over to its original Pitjantjatjara owners in 1985 and immediately leased back to the Federal government for use as a national park. Minerals on Aboriginal land are still government property – though the landowners' permission for exploration and mining is usually required and has to be paid for.

The Northern Territory land rights laws improved the lot of many Aboriginal people and encouraged the Outstation Movement that started in the 1970s. Aboriginal people began to leave the settlements and return to a more traditional, nomadic lifestyle on their own land. Ironically, equal-pay laws in the 1960s deprived Aboriginal people of a major source of work, as many cattle station owners reacted by employing white stockmen instead.

While white goodwill is on the increase, and more Aboriginal people are able to deal effectively with whites, there are still many yawning gulfs between the cultures. White racism persists, and finding a mode of harmonious coexistence remains a serious and long-term problem. Although the 1993 Native Title Act went some way towards reconciling the two sides, more recent developments over the Wik Decision (see the Government & Politics section in Facts about the Country) demonstrate that there is still a long way to go.

For these and other reasons it's usually hard for short-term visitors to make real contact with Aboriginal people, who often prefer to be left to themselves. For this reason tourism on Aboriginal land is generally restricted. This is gradually changing, however, as more communities feel inclined to share their culture, and are able to do it on their own terms. The benefits to the communities are twofold: the most obvious is the financial gain, the other that introducing Aboriginal culture and customs to non-Aboriginal people helps alleviate the problems caused by the ignorance and mis-

Aboriginal Events & Festivals

There are a number of Aboriginal festivals well worth attending. Although they are usually held on restricted Aboriginal land, permit requirements are generally waived for the festivals. Be aware that alcohol is banned in many communities.

Barunga Wugularr Sports & Cultural Festival

For the four days of the Queen's Birthday long weekend in June, Barunga, 80km south-east of Katherine, becomes a gathering place for Aboriginal people from all over the Territory. There's traditional arts and crafts, as well as dancing and athletics competitions. No accommodation is provided so you'll need your own camping equipment, or visit for the day from Katherine. No permit required.

Merrepen Arts Festival

In June or July, Nauiyu Nambiyu on the banks of the Daly River is the venue for the Merrepen Arts Festival. Several Aboriginal communities from around the district, such as Wadeye, Nauiyu and Peppimenarti, display their arts and crafts. No permit required.

Yuendumu Festival

The Yuendumu community is 270km north-west of Alice Springs, and Aboriginal people from the central and western desert region meet here over a long weekend in early August. There's a mix of traditional and modern sporting and cultural events. BYO camping gear. No permit required.

Oenpelli Open Day

Oenpelli (Gunbalanya) is in Arnhem Land, across the East Alligator River not far from Jabiru. On the first Saturday in August an open day is held where there's a chance to purchase local artefacts and watch sports and dancing events. No permit required.

National Aboriginal Art Award

Every Saturday an exhibition of works entered for this award is held at the Museum & Art Gallery of the Northern Territory in Darwin. It attracts entries from all over the country. ■

understandings of the past. It is important to remember that many Aboriginal people do not appreciate being photographed by strangers, even from a distance.

Permits

You need a permit to enter Aboriginal land, and in general they are only granted if you have friends or relatives working there, or if you're on an organised tour. Wandering at random through Aboriginal land to visit the communities is definitely not on. The exception to this rule is travel along public roads through Aboriginal land – though if you want to stop (other than for fuel or provisions) or deviate, you need a permit. If you stick to the main roads, there's no problem.

Three land councils deal with requests for permits; ask the permits officer of the appropriate council for an application form. The Central Land Council basically deals with all land south of a line drawn between Kununurra (WA) and Mt Isa (QLD), the Northern Land Council is responsible for land north of that line, and the Tiwi Land Council deals with Bathurst and Melville islands.

Permits can take around four to six weeks to be processed, although for Oenpelli they take just half an hour in Jabiru.

Northern Land Council
   9 Rowling St, (PO Box 42921), Casuarina, Darwin, NT 0811 (☎ 8920 5100; fax 8945 2633)
Tiwi Land Council
   Unit 9, Wingate Centre, Sadgrove Crescent, Darwin, NT 0801 (☎ 8981 1633; fax 8941 1016)
Central Land Council
   33 Stuart Highway (PO Box 3321), Alice Springs, NT 0871 (☎ 8951 6211; fax 8953 4343)

Tours on Aboriginal Land

There are a number of tourist operations, some of them Aboriginal-owned, running trips to Aboriginal land and communities. This is the best way to have any meaningful contact with Aboriginal people, even though you may feel that by being on a tour you're not getting the 'real thing'. The fact is that this is the way the Aboriginal owners of the land want tourism to work, so they have some control over who visits what and when.

Arnhem Land offers the most options, mainly because of its proximity to Kakadu. The tours here generally only visit the very western edge of Arnhem Land, and take you to Oenpelli and other places which are normally off limits. Some operators include Umorrduk Safaris and Davidson's Arnhem Land Safaris (see the Arnhem Land and Kakadu sections later for more details).

Other places in the Top End with similar operations include Bathurst and Melville islands, and the Litchfield and Katherine areas, while in the Centre they are in the Alice Springs area and at Uluru. See those sections and Aboriginal Cultural Tours under Darwin for details.

CLIMATE

The climate of the Top End is best described in terms of the Dry and the Wet, rather than winter and summer. Roughly, the Dry lasts from April to September, and the Wet is from October to March, with the heaviest rain falling from January onwards. April, when the rains taper off, and the period from October to December, with it's uncomfortably high humidity and that 'waiting for the rains' feeling (known as the 'build-up'), are transition periods. The Top End is the most thundery part of Australia: Darwin has over 90 'thunderdays' a year, all between September and March.

In the Centre the temperatures are much more variable – plummeting below freezing on winter nights (July to August), and soaring into the high 40s on summer days (December to January). Come prepared for both extremes, and the occasional rainstorm at any time of the year. When it rains, dirt roads quickly become quagmires.

Ask any Territorian when the best time to visit the Territory is and invariably they'll say the wet season. The reasons they'll cite will include that everything is green, there's no dust, the barramundi fishing is at its best, prices drop at many places, there are spectacular electrical storms – and all the tourists have gone home! While it's hard to argue with this sort of logic, the Wet does present problems for the visitor – the humidity is often unbearable unless you're acclimatised, dirt roads are often impassable, swimming in the ocean is impossible because of box jelly-fish (stingers), and some national parks and reserves are either totally or partially closed.

It's also worth remembering that even though the humidity in the Top End is high during the Wet, daytime temperatures remain constant at about 30°C to 33°C. In the southern states at this time of year it is often much hotter, with temperatures into the high 30s and low 40s. In fact, in the summer of 1996-97, Darwin had the lowest maximum temperature of any Australian capital city, including Hobart!

INFORMATION

Surprisingly, the Northern Territory Tourism Commission doesn't have any tourist offices either within the Territory or elsewhere in Australia, although there are regional tourist offices in Darwin, Katherine, Tennant Creek and Alice Springs. See these sections later in this chapter.

If you want any predeparture information, contact the Northern Territory Tourism Commission on ☎ 1800 621 336; ntc@nt.gov.au; www.world.net/Travel/Australia/NTinfo/NTTC.

NATIONAL PARKS

The Northern Territory has some of Australia's best national parks. Most people are aware of the more famous ones, such as Uluru & Kata Tjuta, Kakadu and Nitmiluk (Katherine Gorge), but there are plenty of others that are equally appealing – such as Litchfield, West MacDonnell Ranges and Watarrka (Kings Canyon).

For detailed information on Uluru and Kakadu national parks contact Parks Australia North (☎ 8946 4300; fax 8981 3497) in Smith St, Darwin. You will also find excellent information offices in the parks themselves.

Other parks and natural and historic reserves are run by the Parks & Wildlife Commission of the Northern Territory,

which has offices in Alice Springs, Katherine and Darwin, and information desks in the tourist offices in Darwin and Alice Springs. Parks & Wildlife puts out fact sheets on individual parks, and these are available from the offices or from the parks themselves.

ACTIVITIES
Bushwalking

There are interesting bushwalking trails in the Northern Territory, but take care if you venture off the beaten track. You can climb the ranges surrounding Alice Springs – remember to wear stout shoes, as the spinifex grass and burrs are very sharp. In summer, wear a hat and carry water, even on short walks. In the Top End, walking is best in the Dry, although shorter walks are possible in the Wet when the patches of monsoon rainforest are at their best.

The Larapinta Trail, in the Western Mac-Donnell Ranges near Alice Springs, is well laid out with camp sites and other basic facilities along the way. Trephina Gorge Nature Park, in the Eastern MacDonnells, has a few marked trails, although they are all day-trips or shorter.

At Watarrka there's the excellent Giles Track, a two-day walk along the spectacular George Gill Range.

Gregory National Park, just off the Victoria Highway, also lends itself to extended bushwalks, although there are no marked trails. The same applies to Kakadu.

When undertaking any bushwalks in the Territory parks and reserves it is usually necessary to contact the local ranger for permission. The Darwin Bushwalking Club (☎ 8985 1484) makes weekend expeditions all year-round and welcomes visitors.

Willis's Walkabouts (☎ 8985 2134; fax 8985 2355) is a Darwin-based commercial tour operator offering bushwalks in the Top End, Kimberley and the Centre, ranging from three days to three weeks.

Swimming

Stay out of the sea during the Wet (October to March) because stings from box jellyfish can be fatal. Darwin beaches are popular, however, during the safe months. Beware too, of saltwater crocodiles in both salt and fresh waters in the Top End – though there are quite a few safe, natural swimming holes. Take local advice – and if in doubt, don't take a risk.

It is a good idea to have vinegar with you when swimming in coastal waters in the Territory, as this is the most effective way to treat box jellyfish weals. Don't try to remove the stings.

Fishing

This is good, particularly for barramundi, a perch that often grows over 1m long, puts up a great fight and is great to eat. Barramundi is found both offshore and in estuaries and there are fishing tours for the express purpose of catching it.

Some of the best fishing is found in and around Borroloola in the Gulf country, but Kakadu and Darwin are also OK.

Some of the companies that run fishing tours include Big Barra Fishing Tours (☎ 8932 1473), Fishings Fun (☎ 8981 1444) and Land a Barra Tours (☎ 8932 2543) in and around Darwin and Kakadu, and Croc Spot (☎ 8975 8721) in Borroloola.

There are size and bag limits on barramundi and mud crabs, so be aware of these. For information contact the Fisheries Management Section (☎ 8999 4321) of the Department of Primary Industry & Fisheries in Darwin.

Fossicking

There are many places for the fossicker – check with the Northern Territory Department of Mines & Energy for information on the best places. Good locations for fossicking are around the Harts Range (72km north-east of Alice Springs) for beryl, garnet and quartz; the Eastern MacDonnell Ranges (east of Alice Springs) for beryl and garnet; Tennant Creek for gold and jasper; Anthony Lagoon (215km east of the Stuart Highway, north of Tennant Creek) for ribbonstone; Pine Creek for gold; and Brock's Creek (37km south-west of Adelaide River, south

of Darwin) for topaz, tourmaline, garnet and zircon.

The Department of Mines & Energy publishes *A Guide to Fossicking in the Northern Territory*, available from the offices in Alice Springs (☎ 8951 5658), Tennant Creek (☎ 8962 4477) and Darwin (☎ 8989 5511). A fossicking permit is required, and these are available for $5 per month from the same offices.

GETTING THERE & AWAY

See the Alice Springs, Darwin and Uluru sections for transport into the Northern Territory by bus, train, car and air.

GETTING AROUND
Air

Ansett (☎ 13 1300) and Qantas (☎ 13 1313) service the main centres in the Territory. There's also Airnorth (☎ 1800 627 474) which is affiliated with Ansett and links Darwin, Katherine, Bathurst Island, Jabiru, Oenpelli, Groote Eylandt, Gove Peninsula, Alice Springs and Tennant Creek. The airfares chart details regular fares.

Bus

Within the Territory, fairly good coverage is given by Greyhound Pioneer and McCafferty's. See the relevant Getting There & Away sections for the various towns.

Car

Off the beaten track, 'with care' is the thought to bear in mind, and all the usual precautions apply. You can get up-to-date information on road conditions by phoning the Automobile Association of the Northern Territory (☎ 8953 1322 in Alice Springs, or ☎ 8981 3837 in Darwin). They can also advise you on which roads require a 4WD year-round or just in the Wet.

It's wise to carry a basic kit of spare parts in case of breakdown. It may not be a matter of life or death, but it can save a lot of time, trouble and expense. Carry spare water, and if you do break down off the main roads, remain with the vehicle; you're more likely

NORTHERN TERRITORY

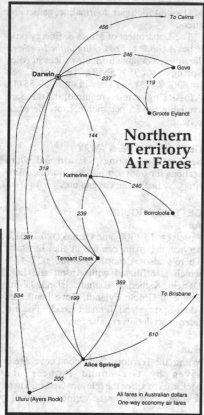

Northern Territory Air Fares

To Cairns
456
246
Darwin
237 — Gove
119
Groote Eylandt
144
319
Katherine
240
239 — Borroloola
381
Tennant Creek
369
To Brisbane
534 199
610
Alice Springs
200
Uluru (Ayers Rock)

All fares in Australian dollars
One-way economy air fares

approaching from the opposite direction on a narrow bitumen road, slow down and pull over – if a road train has to put its wheels off the road to pass you, the shower of stones and rocks that results will not do you or your windscreen any good. On dirt roads it's best to stop altogether, as the dust cloud behind a road train usually blanks your vision completely, if only for a few seconds.

Between sunset and sunrise the Territory's wildlife comes out to play. Hitting a kangaroo is all too easy and the damage to your vehicle, not to mention the kangaroo, can be severe. There are also buffaloes, cattle, wild horses and a number of other driving hazards which you would be wise to avoid. There's really only one sensible way to deal with these road hazards – don't drive at night. If you must drive at night, keep your speed right down, and remember that most animals travel in groups!

An added hazard in the Territory is the fact that there is no speed limit on the open roads, leading to the temptation to travel faster than the road conditions allow.

Hitching

Hitching is generally good, but once away from the main towns lifts can be few and far between. Threeways, where the road to Mt Isa branches off to Alice Springs road, is notorious for long waits for lifts.

Bear in mind, however, that hitching is never entirely safe in any country, and we do not recommend it. Travellers who decide to hitch should understand that they are taking a small but potentially serious risk. People who do choose to hitch will be safer if they travel in pairs and let someone know they are planning to go.

Darwin & the Top End

DARWIN
• *Pop 70,250*

The capital of northern Australia comes as a surprise to many people. Instead of the hard-bitten, rough-and-ready town you might

to be found and you'll have shade and some protection from the elements.

Traffic may be fairly light, but watch out for the two great Northern Territory road hazards – road trains and animals. Road trains are huge trucks (a prime mover plus two or three trailers), which can only be used on the long outback roads of central and northern Australia – they're not allowed into the southern cities. A road train is very long (around 50m) and very big. If you try to overtake one make sure you have plenty of room to complete the manoeuvre – allow about a kilometre. When you see one

expect, Darwin is a lively, modern place with a young population, an easygoing lifestyle and a cosmopolitan atmosphere. However, despite the relative sophistication – you can even get a cafe latte here these days – Darwin is still something of a frontier town, with a fairly transient population.

From the traveller's point of view Darwin is a major stop. It's an obvious base for trips to Kakadu and other Top End natural attractions.

It's a bit of an oasis too – wherever you're travelling, there's a lot of distance to be covered, and having reached Darwin many people rest a bit before leaving.

History

It took a long time to decide on Darwin as the site for the region's centre, and even after the city was established growth was slow and troubled. Early attempts to settle the Top End were mainly due to British fears that the French or Dutch might get a foothold in Australia. Between 1824 and 1829 Fort Dundas on Melville Island and Fort Wellington on the Cobourg Peninsula, 200km north-east of Darwin, were settled and then abandoned. Fort Victoria, settled in 1838 on Cobourg's Port Essington harbour, survived a cyclone and malaria, but was abandoned in 1849.

In 1845 the explorer Leichhardt reached Port Essington overland from Brisbane, arousing prolonged interest in the Top End. The region came under the control of South Australia in 1863, and more ambitious development plans were made. A settlement was established in 1864 at Escape Cliffs on the mouth of the Adelaide River, not too far from Darwin's present location, but this, this was abandoned in 1866. Present-day Darwin was finally founded in 1869. The harbour had been discovered back in 1839 by John Lort Stokes aboard the *Beagle*, who named it Port Darwin after a former shipmate, the evolutionist Charles Darwin. At first the settlement was called Palmerston, but soon became unofficially known as Port Darwin, and in 1911 the name was officially changed.

Darwin's growth was accelerated by the discovery of gold at Pine Creek, about 200km south, in 1871. But once the gold fever had run its course Darwin's development slowed down, due to the harsh, unpredictable climate (including occasional cyclones) and poor communications with other Australian cities.

WWII put Darwin permanently on the

NORTHERN TERRITORY

Darwin: Asian Gateway or Aussie Outpost?

'Down south', Darwin is still seen largely as an outpost – redneck city, a place where male loners and misfits drink themselves silly in sleazy pubs, a place to stop for the night before 'going Bush' again, a place full of dusty jackaroos and beer cans, a cultural black hole.

While 20 years ago this may indeed have been the scenario, Darwin these days is a vastly different place. The city is a melting pot of races, with anywhere between 45 and 60 ethnic groups represented, depending on who you listen to. While some of them, such as the Vietnamese, are recent arrivals, many of the city's Asian residents are fourth generation Australians – and it's probably the only city in Australia to have had a Chinese Lord Mayor (two, in fact).

It comes as a surprise to many visitors that along with the ethnic diversity comes a racial tolerance lacking elsewhere in Australia. There are no ethnic ghettos here. Everyone just gets on with being a Territorian and what you are prepared to do seems to be far more important than where you've come from. (The only blight on this relatively rosy picture is the plight of the city's Aboriginal inhabitants, who suffer the same indignities as in other cities across the country.)

With Australia looking increasingly to Asia for trade, business and tourism opportunities, Darwin sees itself as well placed to become Australia's major link with the region, although it is always going to be an elusive goal with such a small population. As long as it lacks the critical mass, Darwin simply can not support the infrastructure necessary to make it a major Asian gateway city, even though culturally it probably already is. ∎

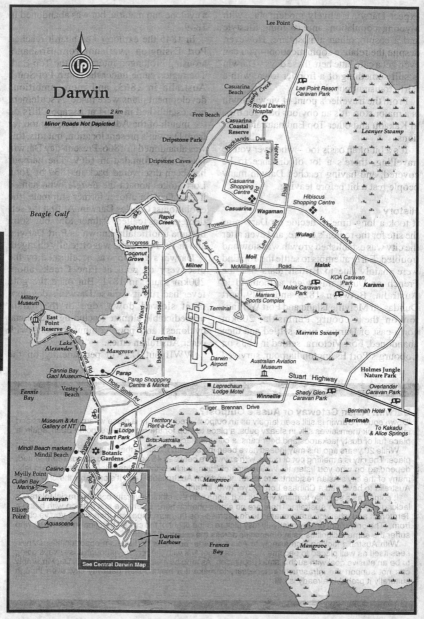

Darwin

```
0        1        2 km
Minor Roads Not Depicted
```

Lee Point

Beagle Gulf

Casuarina Beach
Free Beach
Dripstone Park
Dripstone Caves

Lee Point Resort
Caravan Park

Royal Darwin
Hospital

Casuarina
Coastal
Reserve

Leanyer Swamp

Casuarina
Shopping
Centre

Hibiscus
Shopping
Centre

Rapid
Creek

Nightcliff

Casuarina   Wagaman

Progress Dr

Coconut
Grove

Trower
Rapid Creek

Lee Point Road

Vanderlin Drive

Wulagi

Milner

McMillans   Road

Moil

Malak

Karama

KOA Caravan
Park

Military
Museum

East
Point
Reserve

Lake
Alexander

East

Dick Ward   Drive

Bagot

Road

Marrara
Sports Complex

Malak Caravan
Park

Terminal

Holmes Jungle
Nature Park

Point Rd

Mangrove

Darwin
Airport

Marrara Swamp

Fannie Bay Gaol Museum

Parap

Ross Smith Av

Australian Aviation
Museum

Stuart Highway

Overlander
Caravan Park

Fannie
Bay

Vesteys
Beach

Parap Shoppping
Centre & Market

Leprechaun
Lodge Motel

Shady Glen
Caravan Park

Winnellie

Berrimah Hotel

Museum & Art
Gallery of NT

Park
Lodge

Territory
Rent-a-Car

Tiger Brennan Drive

Berrimah

To Kakadu
& Alice Springs

Mindil Beach markets
Mindil Beach

Casino

Myilly Point

Cullen Bay
Marina

Larrakeyah

Elliott
Point

Aquascene

Stuart Park

Brits Australia

Botanic
Gardens

Glenn Avenue

Gardens Rd

Frances Bay Dv

Mangrove

Darwin
Harbour

Frances
Bay

Mangrove

See Central Darwin Map

map when the town became an important base for Allied action against the Japanese in the Pacific. The road south to the railhead at Alice Springs was surfaced, finally putting the city in direct contact with the rest of the country. Darwin was attacked 64 times during the war and 243 people lost their lives; it was the only place in Australia to suffer prolonged attack.

Modern Darwin has an important role as the front door to Australia's northern region and as a centre for administration and mining. The port facilities have recently had a major upgrade, and there's even talk of the railway line to Alice Springs being completed.

Orientation

Darwin's centre is a fairly compact area at the end of a peninsula. The Stuart Highway does a big loop entering the city and finally heads south to end under the name Daly St. The main shopping area, Smith St and its mall, is about half a kilometre from Daly St.

Most of what you'll want in central Darwin is within two or three blocks of the transit centre or Smith St mall. The suburbs spread a good 12 to 15km away to the north and east, but the airport is conveniently central.

Information

Tourist Offices The Darwin Region Tourism Association (DRTA) Information Centre (☎ 8981 4300) is on the corner of Knuckey and Mitchell Sts. It's open Monday to Friday from 8.30 am to 6 pm, Saturday from 9 am to 3 pm and Sunday from 10 am to 2 pm. It has several decent booklets, displays dozens of brochures and can book just about any tour or accommodation in the Territory. You might also check out the DRTA tourist information desk at the airport (☎ 8945 3386).

There are notice boards in the backpackers' hostels, and these are useful for buying and selling things (like vehicles) or looking for rides.

Foreign Consulates The Indonesian consulate (☎ 8941 0048) is at 18 Harry Chan Ave (PO Box 1953, Darwin 0801) and is open weekdays from 9 am to 1 pm and 2 to 5 pm.

Publications There are a couple of free publications which have some useful detail but they are far from comprehensive. *Darwin & the Top End Today* is published twice-yearly and has information on Darwin and the surrounding area.

Possibly of more use is *This Week in Darwin* as it has listings of what's happening on a weekly basis.

The best source for entertainment listings and gigs is *Pulse*, a free twice-monthly newspaper. You'll find it in the hostels among other places.

Cyclone Tracy

The statistics of this disaster are frightening. Cyclone Tracy built up over Christmas Eve 1974, and by midnight the winds began to reach their full fury. At 3.05 am the airport's anemometer failed, just after it recorded a speed of 217 km/h. It's thought that the peak wind speeds were as high as 280 km/h. Sixty-six lives were lost. Of Darwin's 11,200 houses, 50 to 60% were either totally destroyed or so badly damaged that repair was impossible, and only 400 remained relatively intact.

Much criticism was levelled at the design and construction of Darwin's houses, but plenty of places a century or more old, and built as solidly as you could ask for, also toppled before the awesome winds. The new and rebuilt houses have been cyclone-proofed with steel reinforcements and roofs which are firmly pinned down.

Most people say that next time a cyclone is forecast, they'll jump straight into their cars and head down the Track – and come back afterwards to find out if their houses really were cyclone-proof! Those who stay will probably take advantage of the official cyclone shelter. ■

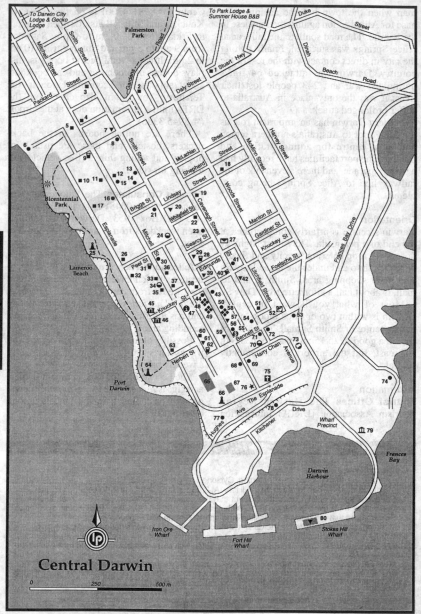

NORTHERN TERRITORY

Central Darwin

PLACES TO STAY
1 Alatai Holiday
2 Metro Inn Darwin
3 Asti Motel
4 Elke's Inner City
5 Banyan View Lodge
  Backpackers
  Apartments
10 Darwin Travelodge
11 Globetrotters Hostel
12 Fawlty Towers
17 Beaufort Towers
18 Frogshollow
  Backpackers
19 Mirrambeena Tourist
  Resort
22 Tiwi Lodge Motel
26 Novotel Atrium
32 Holiday Inn
  Park Suites
33 Darwin City YHA
35 Nomads Darwin
36 Melaleuca Lodge
37 Value Inn
38 Darwin Central Hotel
51 Don Hotel
60 Plaza Hotel Darwin
63 Hotel Darwin

PLACES TO EAT
7 Thai Garden;
  Uncle Sam's
20 Lindsay St Cafe
29 Guiseppe's
39 Swiss Cafe &
  Restaurant

40 Cafe Capri; Hana
  Sushi Bar
42 Pancake Palace
57 Hog's Breath Cafe
59 Victoria Hotel
61 Knife & Fork
  Restaurant
80 The Arcade

OTHER
6 Aquascene
8 Hertz
9 Top End Hotel
13 Thrifty Rent-a-Car
14 Rent-a-Rocket
15 Nifty Rent-a-Car
16 Darwin
  Entertainment
  Centre
21 AANT & Parks
  Australia North
23 International
  Vaccination Clinic
24 McCafferty's
25 Leichhardt Memorial
27 GPO
28 Time
30 Nitemarkets
31 Shennanigans
34 Transit Centre
41 NT General Store
43 Paspalis Centrepoint
44 Indigenous
  Creations
45 Lyons Cottage
46 Admiralty House

47 Darwin Region
  Tourism
  Association
48 Darwin Plaza
49 Galleria
50 Ansett
52 Chinese Temple
53 Dept of Primary
  Industry & Fisheries
54 Garuda
55 Commercial Bank
56 Bookworld
58 Anthony Plaza
62 Petty Sessions
64 ANZAC Memorial
65 Parliament Building
66 Telegraph Cable
  Monument
67 Supreme Court
  Building
68 Old Town Hall
69 Brown's Mart
70 City Bus Terminal
71 Qantas
72 Maps NT
73 Indonesian
  Consulate
74 Deckchair Cinema
75 Christ Church
  Cathedral
76 Police Station & Old
  Courthouse
77 Government House
78 WWII Oil Storage
  Tunnels
79 Indo-Pacific Marine

NORTHERN TERRITORY

Post & Communications The main post office is on the corner of Cavenagh and Edmunds Sts. The poste restante service is efficient. You'll need some form of identification to collect mail.

Useful Organisations Parks Australia North (☎ 8946 4300) is in the MLC building on Smith St near the corner of Briggs St. The Automobile Association of the Northern Territory (☎ 8981 3837) can be found in the same building.

The National Trust (☎ 8981 2848) is at 4 Burnett Place in Myilly Point. Pick up a copy of its Darwin walking-tour leaflet (also available from the tourist office).

Parks & Wildlife (☎ 8999 5511) has its office way out in Palmerston, some 20km from the city centre, which is a real nuisance,

but there's also a desk in the main tourist office in Mitchell St.

The Department of Mines & Energy (☎ 8999 5511) is in the Centrepoint Tower, Smith St mall. For fishing information, the Department of Primary Industry & Fisheries (☎ 8999 5511) has its office in the Harbour View Plaza, Bennett St.

Bookshops Bookworld on Smith St mall is good, as is Angus & Robertson in the Galleria shopping centre, also in the Smith St mall; you'll find all the Lonely Planet guides for travel to Asia here.

For maps, the NT General Store on Cavenagh St has a good range. Other places to try include the Department of Lands, Planning & Environment's Maps NT shop on the corner of Bennett and Cavenagh Sts.

Medical & Emergency Services The Australian Government Health Service runs an International Vaccination Clinic (☎ 8981 7492) at 43 Cavenagh St. The Traveller's Medical & Vaccination Centre (☎ 8981 2907) is at 4 Westralia St, Stuart Park. For emergency medical treatment phone the Royal Darwin Hospital on ☎ 8922 8888.

The Lifeline crisis line is ☎ 13 1114.

Dangers & Annoyances Don't swim in Darwin waters from October to May. Stingers are prevalent, and there are also abundant crocodiles along the coast and rivers. Any 'salties' found in the harbour are removed, and other beaches near the city are patrolled to minimise the risk.

Town Centre
Despite its shaky beginnings and the destruction caused by WWII and Cyclone Tracy, Darwin still has a number of historic buildings. The National Trust produces an interesting booklet titled *A Walk through Historical Darwin*.

Old buildings include the **Victoria Hotel** on Smith St mall, originally built in 1894 and badly damaged by Tracy. On the corner of the mall and Bennett St, the stone **Commercial Bank** dates from 1884. The **old town hall**, a little farther down Smith St, was built in 1883 but was virtually destroyed by Tracy, despite its solid Victorian construction. Today only its walls remain.

Across the road, **Brown's Mart**, a former mining exchange dating from 1885, was badly damaged but now houses a theatre. There's a **Chinese temple**, glossy and new, on the corner of Woods and Bennett Sts.

Christ Church Cathedral, on the Esplanade nearer the harbour, was destroyed by the cyclone. It was originally built in 1902, but all that remained after Tracy was the porch, which had been added in 1944. A new cathedral has been built and the old porch retained.

Darwin Walking Tour

Darwin's tropical climate doesn't lend itself to energetic exertions in the middle of the day, so this walk is most pleasant early in the morning or in the late afternoon.

The best place to start is the very heart of the city, the Smith St Mall. Heading south along Smith St brings you to the historic part of town with the **Old Town Hall**, the former mining exchange (**Brown's Mart**) and, on the corner of the Esplanade, the **former police station and courthouse**.

Turn right along the Esplanade at this corner, and cross to the **Survivors' Lookout**, perched at the top of the cliff and with great views over the harbour. The lookout has some interesting interpretive displays, complete with old WWII photos telling the story of Japanese bombing missions over Darwin.

If the heat's not getting to you, an interesting half-hour diversion is to descend the steps from the lookout down to Kitchener Dve at the base of the cliff and to the **WWII oil storage tunnels**.

Back on the Esplanade, continue on from the Survivor's Lookout and before long you come to **Government House** on the left, nestled in an immaculate tropical garden, and, on the right, the **Submarine Cable Monument** and modern **Supreme Court** and **Parliament House** buildings. If you haven't yet visited Parliament House this is a good opportunity to see the impressive interior, and refresh with a drink from the Speaker's Corner cafe which has great views over the bay.

The Esplanade curves around Parliament House and then runs along the full length of the city centre, with the green expanse of **Bicentennial Park** on the left and a number of **historic buildings** (Hotel Darwin, Admiralty House and Lyons Cottage) on the right. In the park itself are a couple of monuments, and a lookout which gives great sunset views over the bay.

Once at the northern end of the park you can return to Smith St along Daly St, or follow a footpath which leads down to **Doctor's Gully**. This is really only worthwhile when it is fish feeding time at Aquascene, as there is little else to see here, except a signboard with some historic detail and old photos.

From Doctor's Gully a **boardwalk** leads up through a small patch of remnant vegetation, bringing you out on Mitchell St near the Banyan View Lodge. From here it's only a short walk back to the city centre. ■

The 1884 **police station** and **old courthouse** at the corner of Smith St and the Esplanade were badly damaged, but have been restored and are now used as government offices. A little farther south along the Esplanade, **Government House**, built in stages from 1870, was known as the Residency until 1911, and has been damaged by just about every cyclone to hit Darwin. It is once again in fine condition.

Opposite Government House is a **monument** commemorating the submarine telegraph cable which once ran from Darwin to Banyuwangi in Java. This cable put Australia in instant communication with Britain for the first time.

Dominating the streetscape in this corner of the city is the garish **Parliament Building**, opened in 1994 at a cost of $120 million. The inside is fortunately much more appealing and is worth a wander around. It also houses the excellent Northern Territory Library.

Other buildings of interest along the Esplanade include the agreeably tropical **Darwin Hotel**, and **Admiralty House** at the corner of Knuckey St.

Lyons Cottage, across the road at 74 the Esplanade, was the British-Australian Telegraph Residence. Today it is a museum housing displays on pre-1911 north Australian history. It's free and open daily from 10 am to noon and 12.30 to 5 pm. Farther along again is the **Beaufort Darwin Centre**, housing a luxury hotel, a couple of upmarket cafes, and the **Darwin Entertainment Centre** (the latter on Mitchell St).

The Esplanade is fronted by the grassy expanse of **Bicentennial Park**, and a pleasant cliff-top pathway runs along from the Hotel Darwin to Daly St.

Aquascene

At Aquascene, Doctor's Gully, near the corner of Daly St and the Esplanade, fish come in for a feed every day at high tide. Half the stale bread in Darwin gets dispensed to a horde of milkfish, mullet, catfish and batfish. Some are quite big – the milkfish grow to over a metre and will demolish a whole slice of bread in one go. They take it right out of

your hand – it's a great sight and children love it. Feeding times depend on the tides (☎ 8981 7837 for tide times). Admission is $4 ($2.50 children); the bread is free.

Botanic Gardens

The gardens' site north of the city centre was used to grow vegetables during the earliest days of Darwin. Tracy severely damaged the gardens, uprooting three-quarters of the plants. Fortunately, vegetation grows fast in Darwin's climate and the Botanic Gardens, with their noteworthy collection of tropical flora and self-guided Aboriginal Plant Use walk, are well worth a look. There's a coastal section over the road, between Gilruth Ave and Fannie Bay. It's an easy bicycle ride to the gardens from the centre.

Indo-Pacific Marine & Australian Pearling Exhibition

This excellent aquarium is a successful attempt to display living coral and its associated life. Each small tank is a complete ecosystem, with only the occasional extra fish introduced as food for some of the carnivores such as stonefish or angler fish. They sometimes have box jellyfish, as well as more attractive creatures like sea horses, clown fish and butterfly fish. The living coral reef display is especially impressive.

Housed in the same building is the pearling exhibition, which deals with the history of the pearling industry in this area. The exhibition has excellent displays and informative videos.

Both displays are housed in the former Port Authority garage, at the Wharf Precinct, which has been completely renovated and air-conditioned. The Indo-Pacific Marine is open daily from 10 am to 5 pm, and 9 am to 1 pm during the Wet ($12, $4 children) The pearling exhibition hours are weekdays from 10 am to 5 pm, ($6/3).

Wharf Precinct

The Indo-Pacific Marine and Australian Pearling Exhibition are actually part of the Darwin Wharf Precinct, a tourist precinct which has turned what was basically the city's ugly old port facilities into something attractive.

Right at the outer end of the jetty is an old warehouse, now known as the Arcade, which houses a good food centre. The precinct also features the old oil-storage tunnels which were dug into the cliff face during WWII. They are open daily from 9 am to 5 pm ($4).

Myilly Point Historic Precinct

At the northern end of Smith St is this small but important historic precinct of houses built in the 1930s. The buildings were all elevated, and featured asbestos-cement louvres and casement windows, so the ventilation could be regulated according to the weather conditions at the time. Fortunately the houses have survived, although at one stage in the early 1980s it looked as though they would be flattened to make way for the casino. The buildings are now on the Register of the National Estate, and one houses the National Trust (☎ 8981 2848), while another is a gallery and cafe.

Museum & Art Gallery of the Northern Territory

This excellent museum and art gallery is on Conacher St at Fannie Bay, about 4km from the city centre. It's bright, well presented and not too big, but full of interesting displays. A highlight is the Northern Territory Aboriginal art collection. It's particularly strong on carvings and bark paintings from Bathurst and Melville islands and from Arnhem Land.

There's also a good collection on the art of the Pacific and nearby Asian nations, including Indonesian *ikat* (woven cloth) and gamelan instruments, and a sea gypsies' *prahu* (floating home) from Sabah in Malaysia.

Pride of place among the stuffed Northern Territory birds and animals undoubtedly goes to 'Sweetheart', a 5m, 780kg saltwater crocodile, who became quite a Top End personality after numerous encounters with fishing dinghies on the Finniss River south of Darwin. Apparently he had a taste for outboard motors. He died when captured in 1979. You can also see a box jellyfish – safely dead – in a jar.

The museum has a good little bookshop and outside, but under cover, there is an excellent maritime display with a number of vessels, including an old pearling lugger and a Vietnamese refugee boat.

It's open Monday to Friday from 9 am to 5 pm, and Saturday and Sunday from 10 am to 5 pm (admission is free). Bus Nos 4 and 6 go close by, or you can get there on the Tour Tub (see Getting Around later).

Fannie Bay Gaol Museum

Another interesting museum is a little farther out of town at the corner of East Point Rd and Ross Smith Ave. This was Darwin's main jail from 1883 to 1979, after which a new maximum security lockup opened at Berrimah. You can look round the old cells and see the gallows used in the Territory's last hanging in 1952. There are also good displays on Cyclone Tracy, transport, technology and industrial archaeology. The museum is open daily from 10 am to 5 pm (admission is free). Bus Nos 4 and 6 from the city centre go very close to the museum, and it's also on the Tour Tub route.

East Point Reserve

This spit of undeveloped land north of Fannie Bay is good to visit in the late afternoon when wallabies come out to feed, cool breezes spring up and you can watch the sunset across the bay. There are some walking and riding trails as well as a road to the tip of the point.

On the northern side of the point is a series of wartime gun emplacements and the **Military Museum**, devoted to Darwin's WWII activities, open daily from 9.30 am to 5 pm ($5). Bus Nos 4 and 6 will take you 5km from the city centre to the corner of East Point Rd and Ross Smith Ave. From there it's 3km to the tip of the point, or you can take the Tour Tub.

Aviation Heritage Centre

Darwin's aviation museum would be unspectacular were it not for the American

B52 bomber. This truly mammoth aircraft, one of only two displayed outside the USA, dominates the other displays, which include the wreck of a Japanese Zero fighter shot down in 1942. The museum is on the Stuart Highway in Winnellie, about 5km from the centre. It is open daily from 8.30 am to 5 pm ($8). Bus Nos 5 and 8 run along the Stuart Highway.

Crocodylus Park
This wildlife park in Berrimah showcases things crocodilian. It is open daily from 9 am to 5 pm, with feeding at 11 am and 2 pm ($12/6).

Beaches
Darwin has plenty of beaches, but you'd be wise to keep out of the water during the October to May wet season because of the deadly box jellyfish. Popular beaches include **Mindil** and **Vestey's** on Fannie Bay, and **Mandorah**, across the bay from the town (see Around Darwin).

In north Darwin, there's a stinger net protecting part of **Nightcliff** beach off Casuarina Dve, and a stretch of the 7km **Casuarina** beach farther east is an official nude beach. This is a good beach but at low tide it's a long walk to the water's edge.

Scuba Diving
There are some excellent opportunities for scuba diving in Darwin Harbour, largely thanks to the WWII wrecks which provide a habitat for a variety of marine life.

Cullen Bay Dive (☎ 8981 3049; fax 8981 4913) at the Cullen Bay Marina takes divers out to wrecks in the harbour throughout the year. The cost is $54 for one dive including equipment hire, which includes a protective suit to guard against stingers; a second dive is $45. They also do full-day diving trips (two dives) at $128.

Another company which does dives out of Darwin is Coral Divers (☎ 8981 2686) in Stuart Park.

Cycling
Darwin has an excellent series of bicycle

tracks, the main one runs from the northern end of Cavenagh St to Fannie Bay, Coconut Grove, Nightcliff and Casuarina. At Fannie Bay a side track heads out to the East Point Reserve. See the Getting Around section for details of bicycle hire.

Organised Tours
There are many tours in and around Darwin offered by a host of companies. The DRTA information office in Mitchell St is the best place to find out what's available. Many tours go less frequently (if at all) in the wet season. Some of the longer or more adventurous have only a few departures a year; enquire in advance if you're interested.

Aboriginal Cultural Tours If Darwin is your only chance to delve into Aboriginal culture, there are a few options. None of them is particularly cheap as they involve travel out of Darwin, usually by chartered plane. The four-hour Djudian White Crane Dreaming tour, operated by Northern Gateway (☎ 1800 813 288), includes a 25-minute flight to the homelands of the Kuwuma Djudian people and a chance to sample bush tucker. The cost is $388 per person ($175 for children aged three to 12).

The Ngangikurrunggur people at Peppimenarti village south-west of Darwin host day tours operated by Peppi Tours (☎ 1800 811 633) at a cost of $314 fly in or $199 drive in. Tiwi Tours (☎ 1800 811 633) will fly you to Bathurst Island for the day, where you visit the Tiwi people, a pukumani burial site and a local craft outlet. The cost is $240 ($190 children).

City Sights Among the Darwin city tours, Darwin Day Tours' (☎ 8981 8696) five-hour Sunset Tour takes in all the major attractions and finishes with sunset at East Point. The cost is $34 (children $18). Keetleys Tours (☎ 1800 807 868) does similar tours lasting three hours for slightly less.

The Tour Tub (☎ 018 895 982) is an open-sided minibus which tours the various Darwin sights throughout the day (see Getting Around below), and you can either stay on board and do a full circuit or get on and off at the various stops. The cost is $15 ($7.50 children).

Harbour Cruises Darwin Hovercraft Tours (☎ 8941 2233) operates 1¼-hour, 38km hovercraft flights around the harbour from the Frances Bay Dve hoverport for $39 ($29 children), and these can be a lot of fun.

Fishing The Barramundi Fishing Park (☎ 1800 805 627) has afternoon trips to their barra farm, where you can have a go at catch-and-release fishing. The price ($95) includes a barra barbecue dinner.

Darwin Harbour Fishing (☎ 018 895 982) has four-hour afternoon fishing charters from Stokes Hill Wharf for $60 (children $45).

Tours Further Afield A number of operators do trips to the jumping crocodiles at Adelaide River, to the Crocodile Farm and to the Territory Wildlife Park on the Cox Peninsula road. Darwin Day Tours (☎ 8981 8696) does a 5½-hour trip to the Crocodile Farm at 12.50 pm ($56, $40 children), including a visit to the Window on the Wetlands centre at Beatrice Hill; and a marathon 11-hour trip which includes the excellent Territory Wildlife Park ($89). Coo-ee Tours (☎ 1800 670 007) has a popular day-trip which takes in the same attractions.

Special Events
Aside from the **Beer Can Regatta** in July/August, with its sports and contests, there is the **Festival of Darwin** later in August. It's a week of concerts, dances, a picnic in the Botanic Gardens and a parade on the final day. The increasingly popular **Darwin Fringe Festival** is held in the fortnight prior to the Festival of Darwin.

Darwinites are as fond of horse races as other Australians, and two big events at the Fannie Bay track are **St Patrick's Day** (17 March) and the **Darwin Cup Carnival** (July and August). The **Royal Darwin Show** takes place in July, and the **Rodeo & Country Music Concert** are in August.

Darwin is also the starting point for the **Darwin to Ambon Yacht Race**, which kicks off in July/August. The city is abuzz in the days leading up to it.

Places to Stay – bottom end
Camping Camping grounds in Darwin tend to be a long way from the centre, and some of the more conveniently situated caravan parks don't take tent campers.

Shady Glen Caravan Park (☎ 8984 3330)
  10km east of the city, corner of Stuart Highway and Farrell Crescent, Winnellie. Cramped camping, old facilities, minute pool. Camp sites are $16 for two ($19 with power), on-site vans $45 for two.
Lee Point Resort (☎ 8945 0535)
  15km north of the city at Lee Point. Spacious park close to the beach. Facilities are excellent although the shade trees are still a little small and the solar hot water doesn't last too long. Unpowered sites cost $14, ($20 with power), no on-site vans or cabins.
Overlander Caravan Park (☎ 8984 3025)
  13km east of the city at 1064 McMillans Rd, Berrimah. Camp sites at $12 for two ($14 powered), no on-site vans.
Palms Caravan Park (☎ 8932 2891)
  17km south-east of town on the Stuart Highway at Berrimah. Camp sites at $15 for two ($19 with power), on-site vans at $44 and cabins from $70.

Also consider camping at Howard Springs, 26km out, where there are two caravan parks which take campers (see Around Darwin).

Hostels Several of the cheapest places are on or near Mitchell St, conveniently close to the transit centre. Most have guest kitchens, and the showers and toilets are almost always communal. Lonely Planet has received numerous complaints recently about hostel operators pressuring guests to book tours through the hostel. Apparently things get rather ugly if you book elsewhere (they miss out on the commission). They may even ask (demand) that you leave, citing lack of beds or other reasons. If this is the case, you might want to take your business elsewhere anyway.

A popular choice among travellers is *Frogshollow Backpackers* (☎ 1800 068 686) at 27 Lindsay St, a 10-minute walk from the transit centre. It's modern and reasonably clean, and has two spas and a small swimming pool. The charge is $14 a night in a fan-cooled, eight-bed dorm, and there are double rooms for $33 with fan, $38 with air-con or $44 with bath, air-con and TV. It has a well-appointed kitchen, communal area with TV and travel information and, as with other hostels, it does pick-ups from the transit centre (and airport on request).

Globetrotters Hostel (☎ 1800 800 798) at 97 Mitchell St has a pool, two kitchens and frequent barbecues. A bunk is $14 in a four to seven-bed, air-con, self-contained room complete with fridge and TV. Breakfast and dinner is included in the price (we're talking quantity rather than quality here). There's a bar and cheap meals in the evening, and free bicycles for guests to use. Double rooms are available for $44 with attached bath.

Right across the road from Globetrotters, at 88 Mitchell St, is *Fawlty Towers* (☎ 1800 068 886), a friendly, informal hostel in one of the few surviving elevated tropical houses in the city centre. Dorm beds are $14, doubles $38.

The recently refurbished *Darwin City YHA Hostel* (☎ 8981 3995) is at 69A Mitchell St and is part of the transit centre. All the rooms are fan-cooled twins (with air-con at night) and cost $17 per person, or $15 for YHA members. Twin rooms are $17 per person, while singles are $34 and doubles with bath are $48. The building has been extensively renovated, so the facilities are as good as any you'll find in the city, and include a pool, sundeck, modern kitchen and open-air dining area, and the location is great. They also have a comprehensive travel booking service.

Next door to the transit centre is *Nomads Darwin* (☎ 8941 9722) in what was the Youth Hostel some years ago. Beds in four-bed dorms cost $15, twin rooms are $18 per person and doubles are $36. It lacks a pool and other outdoor areas but there are two small spas on the upstairs sundeck.

Across the road from the transit centre is the *Melaleuca Lodge* (☎ 1800 623 543), which is a popular and reasonably well-equipped backpacker hostel. Beds in four to 10-bed rooms are $15, or there are doubles with TV and fridge for $44. All rooms are air-con at night, the kitchen facilities are good and there's a travel desk and swimming pool.

Still on Mitchell St, north of Daly St, is *Elke's Inner City Backpackers* (☎ 1800 808 365) at No 112. It's actually in a couple of recently renovated adjacent houses, and it has much more of a garden feel to it than those right in the heart of the city. There's also a pool and spa between the two buildings. Beds are $15 ($14 VIP members) in four to six-bed dorms, or twin rooms are $38.

The big YWCA *Banyan View Lodge* (☎ 8981 8644) is at 119 Mitchell St. It takes women and men and has no curfew. Rooms have fans and fridges, and are clean and well-kept. There's two TV lounges, a kitchen and an outdoor spa. The charge is $15 per person in a twin-share room; $28/40 singles/doubles, $30/45 with air-con.

Farther north at 151 Mitchell St, about a 10-minute walk from the centre, is the family-run *Darwin City Lodge* (☎ 1800 808 151). Formerly a family home, this place is one of the Cyclone Tracy survivors and it's certainly a bit rough around the edges. However, it's clean, the atmosphere is good, there's a pool and the owners are friendly. It's $14 in a dorm, or there's a separate building nearby which has twin rooms for $38. Most of the rooms have air-con.

In the same area is the *Gecko Lodge* (☎ 1800 811 250) at 146 Mitchell St. This is another smaller hostel in an old house, and there's a pool and a common room. Dorm beds cost $14, or there are twin rooms for $40; all rooms are air-conditioned during the night.

Places to Stay – middle

Guesthouses Darwin has a number of good small guesthouses, and these can make a pleasant change from the hostel scene, especially if you're planning a longer stay. Among those which aren't too far from the centre is the friendly, quiet and airy *Park Lodge* (☎ 8981 5692; fax 8981 3720) at 42

Coronation Dve in Stuart Park, only a short cycle or bus ride from the city centre. All rooms have fan, air-con and fridge; bathrooms, the kitchen, sitting/TV room and laundry are communal. Rooms cost $35/40, and this includes breakfast of toast and jam and tea/coffee. Numerous city buses, including No 10, run to this part of Darwin along the highway; get off near Territory Rent-a-Car.

Close by is the *Summer House B&B* (☎ 8981 8992) at 3 Quarry Crescent, which has two air-con single/double rooms and a couple of two-bedroom apartments, with prices from $60 to $150.

Farther out from the centre at 19 Harcus Crt, Malak, close to the airport, is *Robyn's Nest* (☎ /fax 8927 7400). Two rooms on the ground floor of this family home are let out to guests at $70 per room with attached bath. Both are air-conditioned, with TV, fridge and tea/coffee facilities, and there's a pool and spa.

Also in Malak is the *Parkview Homestay* (☎ 8927 0606), a two-storey place with two air-con rooms (no en-suite bathroom) at $60 including breakfast. There's TV, limited cooking facilities and a pool.

Hotels Good value in this range is the charming *Hotel Darwin* (☎ 8981 9211; fax 8981 9575), right in the heart of the city on the Esplanade. There's a good range of facilities, a pool and a lush garden, which is a rarity for an innercity hotel. The rooms are comfortable, and all have air-con, bath, TV, phone and fridge. Singles/doubles are $95/122, and this includes taxes and a light breakfast.

Also good is the modern *Value Inn* (☎ 8981 4733), in Mitchell St opposite the transit centre. The rooms are comfortable but small, and have fridge, colour TV and bathroom. The price is $164 for up to three people.

The *Don Hotel* (☎ 8981 5311) is also in the centre at 12 Cavenagh St; air-con rooms with TV and fans cost $60/70 including a light breakfast.

Apartments & Holiday Flats Prices in this range often vary between the Dry and the cheaper Wet. Many give discounts if you stay a week or more – usually of the seventh-night-free variety. Typically these places have air-con and swimming pools.

Good value and well-located is the *Peninsular Apartment Hotel* (☎ 1800 808 564; fax 8941 2547) at 115 Smith St, just a short walk from the city centre. Studios have a double and a single bed, and cost $104 ($84 in the Wet), while the two-bedroom apartments accommodate four people and cost $135 ($100).

The *Alatai Holiday Apartments* (☎ 1800 628 833; fax 8981 8887) are modern, self-contained apartments at the northern edge of the city centre on the corner of McMinn and Finniss Sts. Two-bed studio apartments cost $126 ($115 in the Wet), while two-bedroom apartments are $179 ($64). The studios only have a microwave and electric frypan for cooking; the larger apartments also have a stove. The resort has its own pool and an Asian restaurant.

Also in the city centre is the *Mirrambeena Tourist Resort* (☎ 1800 891 100; fax 8981 5116) at 64 Cavenagh St. This large place has 90-odd units, with double rooms at $124, and town houses which sleep up to six people for $151. It has a nice tropical garden complete with pool and spa, and there's a restaurant.

Motels Motels in Darwin tend to be expensive. Conveniently central is the *Asti Motel* (☎ 1800 063 335; fax 8981 8038) on the corner of Smith and Packard Sts just a couple of blocks from the city centre. Rooms cost from $110, and there are some four-bed family rooms for $135.

Also in the centre and reasonably priced is the *Tiwi Lodge Motel* (☎ 8981 6471) on Cavenagh St, where rooms cost $61.

The *Metro Inn Darwin* (☎ 1800 891 128) at 38 Gardens Rd, the continuation of Cavenagh St beyond Daly St, is a comfortable modern motel. Double rooms cost $105, or studio rooms with cooking facilities are $130 (these sleep three people). All rooms have bathroom, fridge and TV. There's also a pool, tennis court and restaurant.

Places to Stay – top end

Darwin's few upmarket hotels are on the Esplanade, making best use of the prime views across the bay. The modern *Beaufort Darwin* (☎ 1800 891 119) is part of the Darwin Entertainment Centre, and has rooms for $280, and suites from $420.

Close by is the *Novotel Atrium* (☎ 8941 0755), which does indeed have an atrium, complete with lush tropical plants, and rooms for $190 and up. Also on the Esplanade is the new *Holiday Inn Park Suites* (☎ 1800 681 686; fax 8943 4388) with rooms from $240/285 for one/two bedroom suites, all with kitchen, balcony and separate living area.

One block back from the Esplanade but still with the fine views is the city's only five-star hotel, the *Plaza Hotel Darwin* (☎ 1800 226 466; fax 8981 1765) at 32 Mitchell St. It has all the facilities you'd expect, including some nonsmoking floors. Rooms here start at $278 for a single/double.

The latest addition to the scene is the new *Darwin Central Hotel* (☎ 8944 9000; fax 8944 9100) on the corner of Smith and Knuckey Sts. Very comfortable and well-furnished rooms cost $215, or $239 with a kitchenette.

Places to Eat

Darwin's proximity to Asia is obvious in its large number of fine Asian eateries, but on the whole eating out is expensive. Takeaway places, a growing number of lunch spots in and around the Smith St mall and the excellent Asian-style markets – held two or three times a week around the city – are the cheapest options.

A number of eateries around town, particularly pubs, offer discount meals for backpackers. Keep an eye out for vouchers at hostels.

Cafes, Pubs & Takeaways Next to the transit centre on Mitchell St there's a small food centre with a couple of reasonably priced stalls and open-air tables. There's a choice of Asian, vegetarian or pasta dishes, which generally cost $5 to $8. At the rear of the arcade is the open-air *Coyote's Cantina*, a very popular licensed Mexican restaurant with very reasonable prices.

A host of snack bars and cafes in the Smith St mall offer lots of choice during the day but they're virtually all closed from about 5 pm on weekdays, Saturday afternoon and all day Sunday.

There's a good collection of fast-food counters in Darwin Plaza towards the Knuckey St end of the mall: *Omar Khayyam* for Middle Eastern and Indian; *La Veg* for health food, lasagne and light meals; *Ozzy Burgers* for, well, burgers; and *Roseland* for yoghurt, fruit salad and ice cream.

The Galleria shopping centre in the mall has a few good places: *Satay King* specialises in Malaysian food and serves that excellent Nonya dish, curry laksa; *Mamma Bella* serves predictable Italian food; *Al Fresco* has gourmet sandwiches and ice cream; and the *Galleria* is a straightforward burger place. There's a good seating area in the centre, although at lunch time it can be difficult to find a table.

Farther up the mall is Anthony Plaza where the *French Bakehouse* is one of the few places you can get a coffee and snack every day. For excellent Malay food head for the no-frills *Rendezvous Cafe*, in the Star Village Arcade, also off the Smith St mall. While the ambitious menu covers the full range of cafe dishes, it's the Malay food that stands out in this excellent little place.

Next door to Anthony Plaza is the *Hog's Breath Cafe*, a very popular American-style grill with good food and occasional live entertainment. Main courses cost around $16.

Opposite Anthony Plaza is the Victoria Arcade where the *Victoria Hotel* has lunch or dinner for around $8 in its Settlers Bar. The lunch-time buffet in the bar upstairs is good value at $7, but it's quantity rather than quality.

Simply Foods at 37 Knuckey St is a busy health-food place. It's a good spot with appealing décor, music and friendly service.

NORTHERN TERRITORY

At 2 Lindsay St there's the very popular open-air *Lindsay St Cafe* in the garden of a typical elevated tropical house. The menu is varied, with a tendency towards Asian cooking. Main courses are around $18.

Cafe Capri on Knuckey St is a chic spot which has a good following. Pasta and salads are the go at lunch time, while in the evening the meals are a bit more sophisticated, featuring dishes such as venison. Main meals are around $20 in the evening, less at lunch time. Almost next door is the BYO *Hana Sushi Bar*, which is open for dinner Monday to Saturday.

In the *Green Room* at the Hotel Darwin you can have a barbecue lunch by the pool for $14; it also has à la carte dishes.

At the end of Stokes Hill Wharf at the Wharf Precinct, the *Arcade* is a small, Asian-style food centre with a number of different shops offering a variety of cuisines. This is a great spot for an al fresco fish & chips lunch washed down with a cool beer, or a cappuccino and cake.

Restaurants The *Pancake Palace* on Cavenagh St near Knuckey St is open daily for lunch and in the evening until 1 am. Conveniently close to many of Darwin's night spots, it has sweet and savoury pancakes from $8.

At 64 Smith St is *Guiseppe's*, one of the few good Italian places in Darwin. Main dishes are in the $10 to $12 range, or there's pizza from $12.

An unusual find is the *Swiss Cafe & Restaurant* tucked away in the Harry Chan Arcade off 58 Smith St. For good, solid European food you can't beat this place, and it's reasonably priced with main dishes around $15. Offering similar fare is the *Knife & Fork Restaurant* on Mitchell St. Here the cuisine is mainly German and Russian, and main courses are in the $17 to $23 range.

Other restaurants include steakhouses, seafood specialists, and French, Greek and Italian cuisine. The numerous Chinese places are generally rather upmarket. An exception being the *Magic Wok* in the post office building on Cavenagh St, where you choose from a buffet selection of game meats and vegetables, and your selection is then stir-fried on the spot by the chef. It's good value at $25.

The *Sizzler* restaurant on Mitchell St is one of an Australia-wide chain. It's amazingly popular, with queues out onto the footpath every night during the Dry. The reason is that it's very good value: for around $16 you can fill your plate from a wide range of dishes, and have dessert too.

On Smith St, just beyond Daly St, the air-con *Thai Garden* serves delicious and reasonably priced Thai food to eat in or take away. There's a takeaway 'Aussie-Chinese' place across the road, and the 24-hour *Uncle Sam's* fast-food joint next door.

Nirvana (☎ 8981 2025) is a licensed restaurant specialising in Indian, Thai and Malaysian food, and it does a pretty good job too. The restaurant is at 6 Dashwood Crescent near Daly St, and is open for dinner (bookings recommended).

Markets The best all-round eating experience in Darwin is the bustling Asian-style market at Mindil Beach on Thursday nights during the dry season. People begin arriving at 5.30 pm, bringing tables, chairs, rugs, grog and kids. They settle under the coconut palms for sunset and then decide which of the tantalising food-stall aromas has the greatest allure. It's difficult to know whether to choose Thai, Sri Lankan, Indian, Chinese, Malaysian, Greek or Portuguese. You'll even find Indonesian black rice pudding. All prices are reasonable – around $3 to $5 for a meal. There are cake stalls, fruit-salad bars, arts and crafts stalls, and sometimes entertainment in the form of a band or street theatre.

Similar food stalls can be found at the Parap market on Saturday morning, the one at Rapid Creek on Sunday morning, and in the Smith St mall in the evening (except Thursday), but Mindil Beach is the best for atmosphere and proximity. It's about 2km from the city centre, off Gilruth Ave. During the Wet, the market transfers to Rapid Creek. Bus Nos 4 and 6 go past Mindil Beach:

No 4 continues on to Rapid Creek, No 6 to Parap.

Entertainment

Darwin is a lively city with bands at several venues and a number of clubs and discos. More sophisticated tastes are also catered for, with theatre, film, concerts and a casino.

The best source of what's on around town is probably the free bimonthly *Pulse* street newspaper.

Bars & Live Music Live bands play upstairs at the *Victoria Hotel*, Wednesday to Saturday from 9 pm. *Rattle and Hum* on the Esplanade is a very popular backpackers hangout with incentives and a courtesy bus to all the hostels.

Right next door to the transit centre is *Shennanigans*, an Irish pub serving draught Guinness and Kilkenny ($4 a pint). It's a popular place with occasional live music and a giant video screen.

The *Don Hotel* is another popular live music venue, and the *Travelodge* also has bands.

The *Billabong Bar* in the Novotel Atrium, on the corner of the Esplanade and Peel St, has live bands on Friday and Saturday nights until 1 am. Take a look at the hotel's spectac-

ular seven-storey, glass-roofed atrium while you're there.

The *Hotel Darwin* is pleasant in the evening for a quiet drink. There's a patio section by the pool. On Friday night its livelier when there's a band in the Green Room, and on Wednesday to Saturday nights the Glasshouse Nightclub specialises in R&B and hip-hop.

The *Jabiru Bar* in the Novotel Atrium is the venue on Wednesday evening for crab races. It's all very light-hearted and there are prizes for the winners.

There's also live music in the evenings at *Sweetheart's Bar* at the MGM Grand Darwin casino.

Nightclubs & Discos The Brewery Bar in the *Top End Hotel* on the corner of Mitchell and Daly Sts is a popular evening venue. The Beachcomber bar at the rear is a popular disco and nightclub (Wednesday to Saturday), while the down-market Sportsmens Bar at the front on Mitchell St is the last bastion of the 'prawn and porn' variety of entertainment – cheap food and strip shows to attract the punters.

Petty Sessions on the corner of Mitchell and Bennett Sts is a combination wine bar,

NORTHERN TERRITORY

An All-Australian Game

The Alice and Darwin casinos offer plenty of opportunities to watch the Australian gambling mania in full flight. You can also observe a part of Australia's cultural heritage, the all-Australian game of two-up.

The essential idea of two-up is to toss two coins and obtain two heads. The players stand around a circular playing area and bet on the coins showing either two heads or two tails when they fall. The 'spinner' uses a 'kip' to toss the coins and the house pays out and takes in as the coins fall – except that nothing happens on 'odd' tosses (one head, one tail) unless they're thrown five times in a row. In this case you lose unless you have also bet on this possibility. The spinner continues tossing until they either throw a pair of tails, throw five odds or throw three pairs of heads. If the spinner manages three pairs of heads then they also win at 7½ to one on any bet placed on that possibility, then start tossing all over again. When the spinner finally loses, the next player in the circle takes over as spinner. ■

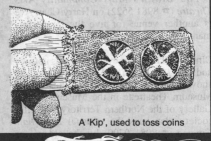

A 'Kip', used to toss coins

nightclub and disco. It's quite a popular place and stays open to 2 am.

On the small street that runs between Smith and Cavenagh Sts one block from Knuckey St is the *Time* disco. It's probably the most popular nightspot in the city, and stays open until the early hours.

Another late-night venue is Mooses nightclub at the *Don Hotel* on Cavenagh St.

Folk & Country Music For something a bit more laid back there's the *Top End Folk Club*, which meets every second Sunday of the month at the Northern Territory University Social Club, the Breezway, at the Casuarina uni campus. Visitors are welcome; call ☎ 8988 1301 for more details.

If you're into country music, the *NT Country Music Association* meets every second Wednesday at the Driver Primary School out in Palmerston. This is the place for bootscooters! Contact ☎ 8932 1030 for details.

Jazz On Sunday afternoons at the casino there's *Jazz on the Lawns*, where you can eat, watch the sunset and listen to some fairly uninspired jazz. There's no charge.

Theatre The *Darwin Entertainment Centre* (☎ 8981 9022) on Mitchell St, opposite McLachlan St, hosts a variety of events, from fashion award nights to plays, rock operas, pantomimes and concerts.

The *Darwin Theatre Company* (☎ 8981 8424) often has play readings and other performances around the city.

The *Brown's Mart Community Arts Theatre* (☎ 8981 5522) on Harry Chan Ave is another venue for live theatre performances.

Cinemas There are several cinemas in town and the *Darwin Film Society* has regular showings of off-beat/artistic films at the Museum Theatrette in the Museum & Art Gallery of the Northern Territory. The film society also runs the unusual *Deckchair Cinema* (☎ 8981 0700) by the old power station near Stokes Hill Wharf. During the

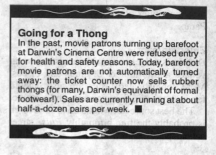

Going for a Thong
In the past, movie patrons turning up barefoot at Darwin's Cinema Centre were refused entry for health and safety reasons. Today, barefoot movie patrons are not automatically turned away: the ticket counter now sells rubber thongs (for many, Darwin's equivalent of formal footwear!). Sales are currently running at about half-a-dozen pairs per week. ■

Dry you can watch a movie under the stars while reclining in a deckchair. Screenings are listed in the newspapers, or on fliers around town.

Casino Finally, there's the *MGM Grand Darwin* casino on Mindil Beach off Gilruth Ave – as long as you're 'properly dressed'. That means no thongs, and men wearing shorts will have to conform to the bizarre Aussie predilection for long socks!

Things to Buy
Aboriginal art is generally cheaper in Alice Springs, but Darwin has greater variety. The Raintree Gallery on Knuckey St is one of a number of places offering a range of art work – bark paintings from Arnhem Land, and interesting carvings by the Tiwi people of Bathurst and Melville islands and by the peoples of central Australia. It is also Aboriginal owned.

Another excellent gallery is Framed, on the Stuart Highway in Stuart Park. There are some fine works here, with prices to match.

T-shirts printed with Aboriginal designs are popular but quality and prices vary. Riji Dij at 38 Smith St has a large range of T-shirts. They are printed by Tiwi Designs and Territoriana, both local companies using Aboriginal designs and, to a large extent, Aboriginal labour. It stocks Tiwi printed fabric and clothing made from fabric printed by central Australian Aboriginal people. Another place worth trying is Indigenous Creations on the Smith St mall and in the transit centre.

The Nitemarkets on the corner of Mitchell and Peel Sts is open nightly from 5 pm and has a range of stalls selling everything from didjeridus to second-hand books. Behind it on Peel St is the backpackers' car market, a popular place to buy and sell second-hand vehicles ($5 per day if you are selling).

You can find Balinese and Indian clothing at Darwin's markets (see Markets in Places to Eat earlier). Local arts and crafts (the market at Parap is said to be the best), jewellery and bric-a-brac are on sale too.

Getting There & Away

Air Darwin is becoming increasingly busy as an international and domestic gateway.

International A popular international route is to and from Indonesia with the Indonesian airlines Merpati or Garuda. Merpati (☎ 1800 060 188) have an office in the new Darwin Central complex on the corner of Smith and Knuckey Sts. Merpati flies twice a week (Wednesday and Saturday) to and from Kupang in Timor ($244/396 one way/return), and on the same days to Ambon ($457/861 via Kupang and Denpasar, where you can have a free stopover).

Garuda (☎ 1800 800 873), on Cavenagh St, has three direct flights a week to Denpasar in Bali ($496/766). Ansett and Qantas also fly this route.

Royal Brunei Airlines (☎ 8941 0966), also on Cavenagh St, flies twice-weekly between Darwin and Bandar Seri Begawan, and on to Manila and Hong Kong.

Singapore Airlines (☎ 8941 1799), in the Paspalis Centrepoint building at the corner of Smith St mall and Knuckey St, also flies to Darwin.

Malaysia Airlines has twice weekly flights to Kuala Lumpur for $689/889. Contact a travel agent for this fare as MAS only give their discounted rates to travel agents.

Domestic Within Australia you can fly to Darwin from other states with Qantas and Ansett.

There are often stops or transfers at Alice Springs, Brisbane or Adelaide on longer flights. Some flights from Queensland stop at Gove or Groote Eylandt. One-way fares include Adelaide $655, Alice Springs $381, Perth $677, Broome $381, Cairns $456, Kununurra $176, Mt Isa $565, Brisbane $680 and Sydney $689. In Darwin, Qantas (☎ 13 1313) is at 16 Bennett St, and Ansett (☎ 13 1300) is at 14 Smith St mall.

For air travel within the Northern Territory see the airfares chart in Getting Around earlier in this chapter. Airnorth's office (☎ 1800 627 474) is at Darwin airport.

Bus You can reach Darwin by bus on three routes – the Western Australian route from Broome, Derby, Port Hedland and Kununurra; the Queensland route through Mt Isa to Threeways and up the Track; or straight up the Track from Alice Springs. Greyhound Pioneer has daily services on all these routes; McCafferty's doesn't operate services in Western Australia. On Queensland services you often have to change buses at Threeways or Tennant Creek, and at Mt Isa. All buses stop at Katherine.

Fares can vary a bit between companies, but if one discounts a fare the other tends to follow quite quickly. Travel times are very similar, but beware of services that schedule long waits for connections in Tennant Creek or Mt Isa. Examples of fares include: around $104 one way to Darwin from Tennant Creek (13 hours), $182 from Mt Isa (21 hours), $259 from Brisbane (51 hours), $97 from Kununurra, $148 from Alice Springs (19 hours), $192 from Broome (22 hours) and $435 from Perth (57 hours). In Darwin, Greyhound Pioneer (☎ 13 2030) operates from the transit centre at 69 Mitchell St; McCafferty's (☎ 13 1499) has its depot close by on the corner of Peel and Smith Sts.

Car Darwin has numerous budget car-rental operators, as well as all the major national and international companies.

Avis
  145 Stuart Highway, Stuart Park (☎ 1800 225 533; fax 8981 3155)

Brits:Australia
    Stuart Highway, Stuart Park (☎ 1800 331 454;
    fax (03) 9416 2933)
Budget
    69 Mitchell St (☎ 13 2727)
Hertz
    Cnr Smith & Daly Sts (☎ 1800 891 112)
Nifty Rent-a-Car
    Mitchell St (☎ 8981 2999; fax 8941 0662)
Territory Rent-a-Car
    64 Stuart Highway, Parap (☎ 1800 891 125; fax
    8981 5247)
Thrifty Rent-a-Car
    Smith St (☎ 1800 652 008)

Rent-a-Rocket (☎ 8941 3733), 7 McLachlan St, offers cheap deals on their mostly 1970s and early 1980s cars. Costs depend on whether you're staying near Darwin, or going further afield. For local trips with Rent-a-Dent you pay around $35 a day, depending on the vehicle. This includes 100 free kilometres, but with these deals you can't go beyond Humpty Doo or Acacia Store (about 70km down the Track). The prices drop for longer rentals.

Nifty Rent-a-Car offers similar deals, but also has newer, air-con vehicles for around $44 per day.

Territory Rent-a-Car is far and away the biggest local operator. Deals to look for include cheaper rates for four or more days hire, weekend specials (three days for roughly the price of two), and one-way hires (to Jabiru, Katherine or Alice Springs).

There are also plenty of 4WD vehicles available in Darwin, but you usually have to book ahead, and fees and deposits can be hefty. The best place to start looking is probably Territory, which has several different models – the cheapest, a Suzuki four-seater, costs around $75 a day including insurance, plus 35c a kilometre over 100km.

Brits:Australia are best for long-term rentals on 4WDs and campervans, and you can do one-way rentals out of the Northern Territory.

Rental companies generally operate a free towing or replacement service if the vehicle breaks down. But (especially with the cheaper operators) check the paperwork to see exactly what you're covered for in terms of damage to vehicles and injuries to passengers. The usual age and insurance requirements apply in Darwin and there may be restrictions on off-bitumen driving, or on the distance you're allowed to go from the city. Even with the big firms the insurance does not cover you when driving off the bitumen, so make sure you know exactly what your liability is in the event of an accident.

Most rental companies are open every day and have agents in the city centre to save you trekking out to the Stuart Highway. Territory, Budget, Hertz and Thrifty all have offices at the airport.

Getting Around

To/From the Airport Darwin's busy airport is only about 6km from the centre of town. The taxi fare into the centre is about $15.

There is an airport shuttle bus (☎ 8941 5000) for $8, which will pick up or drop off almost anywhere in the centre. If you have a confirmed booking at one of the hostels, tell the driver and you get a reduced fare or free trip, depending on the hostel. When leaving Darwin book a day before departure.

Bus Darwin has a fairly good city bus service operating Monday to Friday. However, Saturday services cease around lunch time and on Sunday and holidays they shut down completely. City services start from the small terminal (☎ 8989 6540) on Harry Chan Ave, near the corner of Smith St. Buses enter the city along Mitchell St and leave along Cavenagh St.

Fares are on a zone system – shorter trips are $1 or $1.40, and the longest cost $1.90. Bus No 4 (to Fannie Bay, Nightcliff, Rapid Creek and Casuarina) and No 6 (Fannie Bay, Parap and Stuart Park) are useful for getting to Aquascene, the Botanic Gardens, Mindil Beach, the Museum & Art Gallery, Fannie Bay Gaol Museum and East Point. Bus Nos 5 and 8 go up the Stuart Highway past the airport to Berrimah, from where No 5 goes north to Casuarina and No 8 continues along the highway to Palmerston.

The Tour Tub (☎ 018 895 982) is a private

bus which does a circuit of the city, calling at the major places of interest, and you can hop on or off anywhere. In the city centre it leaves from Knuckey St, at the end of the Smith St mall. The set fare is $15 for the day, and the buses operate hourly from 9 am to 4 pm. Sites visited include Aquascene (only at fish-feeding times), Indo-Pacific Marine and Wharf Precinct, the MGM Grand Darwin casino, the Museum & Art Gallery, Military Museum, Fannie Bay Gaol, Parap markets (Saturday only) and the Botanic Gardens.

Car See Getting There & Away in this section for details on car rental.

Bicycle Darwin has a fairly extensive network of bike tracks. It's a pleasant ride to the Botanic Gardens, Fannie Bay, East Point or even, if you're feeling fit, all the way to Nightcliff and Casuarina. Many of the backpackers' hostels have bicycles, and these are often free for guests to use.

AROUND DARWIN
All the places listed here are within a couple of hours travel from the city.

Howard Springs Nature Park
The springs, with crocodile-free swimming, are 35km east of the city. Turn off to the left 24km down the Stuart Highway, beyond Palmerston. The forest-surrounded swimming hole can get uncomfortably crowded because it's so convenient to the city. Nevertheless on a quiet day it's a pleasant spot for an excursion and there are short walking tracks and lots of bird life.

Places to Stay The *Howard Springs Caravan Park* (☎ 8983 1169) at Whitewood Rd has unpowered ($12) and powered ($18) caravan sites only. The *Coolalinga Caravan Park* (☎ 8983 1026) is on the Stuart Highway, and not as close to the springs. Unpowered sites are $10, with power it's $13.

Arnhem Highway
The Arnhem Highway branches off towards Kakadu, 33km south of Darwin. Only 10km along this road you come to the small town of **Humpty Doo**. Graeme Gow's Reptile World has a big collection of Australian snakes and a knowledgeable owner. It's open daily from 8.30 am to 5.30 pm ($5).

About 15km beyond Humpty Doo is the turn-off to **Fogg Dam Conservation Reserve**, a great place for watching water birds. A farther 8km along the Arnhem Highway is **Adelaide River Crossing** where you can take a 1½-hour river cruise and see saltwater crocodiles jump for bits of meat held out on the end of poles. These trips cost $26 ($15 children) and depart at 9 and 11 am and 1 and 3 pm from May to August, and at 9 and 11 am and 2.30 pm from September to April. The whole thing is a bit of a circus really, but it's fun to see crocs doing something other than sunning themselves on a river bank.

The **Window on the Wetlands** is a modern visitors centre atop Beatrice Hill, a small hill by the Arnhem Highway just a few kilometres past the Fogg Dam turn-off. It's the headquarters for the proposed **Mary**

Saltwater crocodiles, which can grow up to seven metres long, will attack and kill humans

NORTHERN TERRITORY

River National Park, which encompasses important Mary River wetlands. The centre has some excellent 'touchy-feely' displays which give some great detail on the wetland ecosystem, as well as the history of the local Aboriginal people and European pastoral activity. There's also great views out over the Mary River system.

Mary River Crossing, 47km farther on, is popular for barramundi fishing and camping. A reserve here includes lagoons which are a dry-season home for water birds, and granite outcrops which shelter wallabies.

The *Bark Hut Inn* (☎ 8978 8988), 2km beyond Mary River Crossing at **Annaburroo**, is another pleasant place for a halt. There's accommodation here but it's no great shakes. Camping costs $4 per person, or $14 for two with power, or there's basic accommodation at $22/35 for singles/ doubles.

The turn-off to Cooinda (in Kakadu) is 19km beyond the Bark Hut. This is an unsealed road (known as the Jim Jim Rd), often impassable in the Wet; it's easier to continue along the sealed highway. The entrance to Kakadu National Park is a farther 19km along the highway.

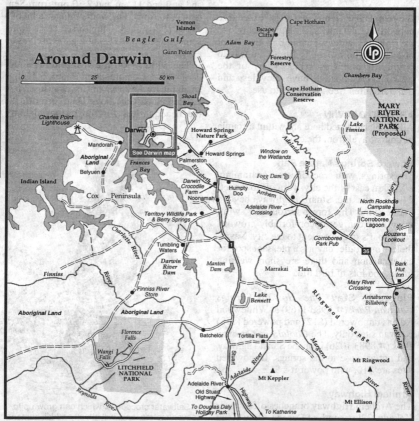

Top End Crocs

There are two types of crocodile in Australia – the freshwater or 'freshie' (Crocodylus johnstoni) and the saltwater or 'saltie' (Crocodylus porosus) – and both are found in the northern part of the country. After a century of being hunted, crocodiles are now protected in the Northern Territory (freshies since 1964 and salties since 1971).

The smaller freshwater crocodile is endemic to Australia and is found in freshwater rivers and billabongs, while the larger saltwater crocodile, found throughout south-east Asia and parts of the Indian Subcontinent, can be found in or near almost any body of water, fresh or salt. Freshwater crocodiles, which have narrower snouts and rarely exceed 3m in length, are harmless to people unless provoked, but saltwater crocodiles, which can grow to 7m or more, can definitely be dangerous.

Ask locally before swimming or even paddling in any rivers or billabongs in the Top End – attacks on humans by salties happen more often than you might think. Warning signs are posted alongside many dangerous stretches of water. The beasts are apparently partial to dogs, and even from some distance can be attracted by the sound of dogs barking.

Crocodiles have become a major tourist attraction (eating the odd tourist certainly helps in this respect) and the Northern Territory is very big on crocodile humour. Darwin's shops have a plentiful supply of crocodile T-shirts and other paraphernalia. ■

There are Greyhound Pioneer bus services along the Arnhem Highway (see the Kakadu National Park Getting There & Around section).

Mary River Wetlands

The Mary River wetlands, which extend north and south of the Arnhem Highway, are scheduled to become the Mary River National Park. For the moment they consist of a number of reserves, including Mary River Crossing Reserve, the Wildman River Reserve, Shady Camp, Mary River Conservation Reserve, Stuart's Tree Historical Reserve and Swim Creek.

This area offers excellent fishing and wildlife spotting opportunities, and because there is not much in the way of infrastructure it is far less visited than nearby, and similar, Kakadu.

There are a couple of private concessions within the park, and these offer both accommodation (see Places to Stay) and trips on the river. From the Point Stuart Wilderness Lodge, 2½-hour wetland tours cost $25/ 12.50, and there are departures at 9 am and 4 pm daily.

At Shady Camp, on the Mary River, about 40km north of the Arnhem Highway, Crocodylus Wildlife Cruises (☎ 8927 0777) run excellent three-hour boat trips over the

fresh and saltwater wetland areas at 6.30 and 10.30 am and 3.30 pm for $45.

Places to Stay There are basic camp sites at North Rockhole and Shady Camp, or you can camp at the *Point Stuart Wilderness Lodge* (☎ 8978 8914) a few kilometres off the main track. There's a good grassy camping area and a swimming pool. It costs $5 to camp, or there are double rooms for $55, and meals are available.

The *Wildman River Wilderness Lodge* (☎ 1800 891 121; fax 8978 8907), also off the main track, charges $100 for a double room. The lodge has a beautiful position on the edge of the flood plains, and has good facilities including a swimming pool and a licensed dining room.

Getting There & Away Access is via the Point Stuart Road, a good dirt road which heads north off the Arnhem Highway 22km east of Annaburroo.

As the popularity of this area increases so does the number of tour operators accessing the park. Already a number of companies operating out of Darwin, such as AKT Holidays (☎ 1800 891 121), combine a trip to Kakadu with a detour to the Mary River wetlands.

Darwin Crocodile Farm

On the Stuart Highway, just a little south of the Arnhem Highway turn-off, this crocodile farm has around 15,000 saltwater and fresh-water crocodiles. This is the residence of many of the crocodiles taken out of Northern Territory waters because they've become a hazard to people. But don't imagine they're here out of human charity. This is a farm, not a rest home, and around 20 of the beasts are killed each day for their skins and meat – you can find crocodile steaks or even crocodile burgers in a number of Darwin eateries.

The farm is open daily from 9 am to 4 pm. Feedings are the most spectacular times to visit and these occur daily at 2 pm, and again on weekends at noon ($9.50/5).

Territory Wildlife Park & Berry Springs

The turn-off to Berry Springs is 48km down the Track from Darwin, then it's 10km along the Cox Peninsula road to the Territory Wild-life Park. Set on 400 hectares of bushland this wildlife park (run by Parks & Wildlife) has some excellent exhibits featuring a wide variety of Australian birds, mammals, rep-tiles and fish, some of which are quite rare. There's a reptile house, superb walk-through aquarium, nocturnal house, aviaries and nature trails. It's well worth the $12 entry fee ($6 children) and you'll need half a day to see it all. The park is open daily from 8.30 am to 4 pm (gates close at 6 pm).

Close by is the **Berry Springs Nature Park**, a great place for a swim and a picnic. There's a thermal waterfall, spring-fed pools ringed with paperbarks and pandanus palms, and abundant bird life. It is open daily from 8 am to 6.30 pm.

A few kilometres farther along the Cox Peninsula road is **Tumbling Waters**, another good picnic and camping area, although there's no swimming due to the presence of 'salties' (saltwater crocodiles). The road con-tinues all the way to **Mandorah**, the last 30km or so being dirt. It's much easier just to catch the ferry from Darwin.

Litchfield National Park

This 650sq-km national park, 140km south of Darwin, encompasses much of the Table-top Range, a wide sandstone plateau mostly surrounded by cliffs. Four waterfalls, which drop off the edge of this plateau, and their surrounding rainforest patches are the park's main attractions. It's well worth a visit, although it's best to avoid weekends as Litchfield is a very popular day-trip destina-tion for locals.

There are two routes to Litchfield Park, both about a two-hour drive from Darwin. One, from the north, involves turning south off the Berry Springs-Cox Peninsula road onto a well-maintained dirt road, which is suitable for conventional vehicles except in the wet season. A second approach is along a bitumen road from Batchelor into the east of the park. The two access roads join up so it's possible to do a loop from the Stuart Highway.

If you enter the park from Batchelor it is 18km from the park boundary to the **Flor-ence Falls** turn-off. The waterfalls lie 5km off the road along a good track. This is an excellent swimming hole in the dry season, as is **Buley Rockhole** a few kilometres away, where you can camp.

Eighteen kilometres beyond the turn-off to Florence Falls is the turn-off to **Tolmer Falls**, which are a 400m walk off the road. There's also a 1.5km walking track here which gives you some excellent views of the area.

It's a farther 7km along the main road to the turn-off for the most popular attraction in Litchfield – **Wangi Falls** (pronounced 'wong-gye'), 2km along a side road. The falls here flow year-round and fill a beautiful swimming hole. There are also extensive picnic and camping areas.

From Wangi it's about 16km to the rangers' station near the park's northern access point.

Bush camping is also allowed at the pretty **Tjaynera (Sandy Creek) Falls**, in a rainfor-est valley in the south of the park (4WD access only). There are several other 4WD tracks in the park, and plenty of bushwalking possibilities.

As usual in the Top End, it's easier to reach

and get around the park from May to October.

River Cruises Excellent wetland cruises on the Reynolds River system are available from the Wangi Kiosk (☎ 8978 2861). These run three times daily and take three hours. As they operate on a working cattle station, they also show you another aspect of the Top End. The tours cost $25.

Organised Tours Plenty of companies offer trips to Litchfield from Darwin. Coo-ee Tours (☎ 1800 670 007) has a popular two-day, 4WD camping trip, which is great value at $120. Day-trips cost $89 (children $65). Aussie Adventure Holidays (☎ 1800 811 633) also does 4WD day-trips from Darwin for $99 (children $66).

Another option is a Darwin to Litchfield and Katherine day-trip. Travel North (☎ 1800 089 103) has these daily (less frequently in off season) at $99 (children $75).

KAKADU NATIONAL PARK

Kakadu National Park is one of the natural marvels not just of the Northern Territory, but of Australia. The longer you stay, the more rewarding it is.

Kakadu stretches more than 200km south from the coast and 100km from east to west, with the main entrance 153km east of Darwin, along a bitumen road. It encompasses a variety of superb landscapes, swarms with wildlife and has some of Australia's best Aboriginal rock art.

Kakadu was proclaimed a national park in three stages. Stage One – the eastern and central part of the park including Ubirr, Nourlangie, Jim Jim Falls, Twin Falls and Yellow Water Billabong – was declared in 1979 and is on the World Heritage List for both its natural and cultural importance (a rare distinction). Stage Two – in the north – was declared in 1984 and won World Heritage listing for its natural importance. Stage Three – in the south – was finally listed in 1991, bringing virtually the whole of the South Alligator River system within the park.

The name Kakadu comes from Gagadju, one of the local Aboriginal languages, and much of Kakadu is Aboriginal land, leased to the government for use as a national park. There are several Aboriginal settlements in the park and about one-third of the park rangers are Aboriginal people. Enclosed by the park, but not part of it, are a few tracts of land designated for other purposes – principally uranium-mining leases in the north-east.

Some of the southern areas are subject to a land claim under the Native Title Act by the Jawoyn people of the Katherine region. Should the claim be successful, the land will be leased back to Parks Australia North for continued use as a national park.

Geography & Vegetation

A straight line on the map separates Kakadu from the Arnhem Land Aboriginal land, which you can't enter without a permit. The circuitous Arnhem Land escarpment, a dramatic 100 to 200m-high sandstone cliff line that forms the natural boundary of the rugged Arnhem Land plateau, winds some 500km through east and south-east Kakadu.

Creeks cut across the rocky plateau and tumble off the escarpment as thundering waterfalls in the wet season. They then flow across the lowlands to swamp the vast flood plains of Kakadu, turning the north of the park into a kind of huge, vegetated lake. From west to east the rivers are the Wildman, the West Alligator, the South Alligator and the East Alligator. Such is the difference between dry and wet seasons that areas on river flood plains which are perfectly dry underfoot in September will be under 3m of water a few months later. As the waters recede in the Dry, some loops of wet-season watercourses become cut off, but don't dry up. These are billabongs – and they're often carpeted with water lilies and are a magnet for water birds.

The coastline has long stretches of mangrove swamp, important for halting erosion and as a breeding ground for marine and bird life. The southern part of the park is dry lowlands with open grassland and eucalypts. Pockets of monsoon rainforest crop up here

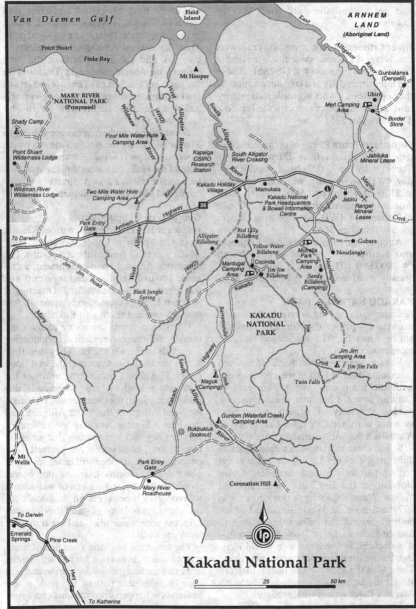

Kakadu National Park

0   25   50 km

as well as in most of the park's other landscapes.

In all, Kakadu has over 1000 plant species, and a number are still used by the local Aboriginal people for food, medicine and other practical purposes.

Climate

The great change between the Dry and the Wet makes a big difference to visitors to Kakadu. Not only is the landscape transformed, but Kakadu's lesser roads often become impassable in the Wet, cutting off some highlights, such as Jim Jim Falls. The local Aboriginal people recognise six seasons in the annual cycle.

The 'build-up' to the Wet (known as *Gunumeleng*) starts in October. Humidity and temperature rises (to 35°C or more) – and the number of mosquitoes, always high near water, rises to near-plague proportions. By November the thunderstorms have started, billabongs start to be replenished and the water birds disperse.

The Wet proper *(Gudjuek)* continues through January, February and March, with violent thunderstorms and an abundance of plant and animal life thriving in the hot, moist conditions. Around 1300mm of rain falls in Kakadu, most of it during this period.

Banggereng, in April, is the season when storms (known as 'knock 'em down' storms) flatten the spear grass, which during the course of the Wet has shot up to 2m in height.

Yekke, from May to mid-June, is the season of mists, when the air starts to dry out. It is quite a good time to visit – there aren't too many other visitors, the wetlands and waterfalls still have a lot of water and most of the tracks are open.

The most comfortable time weatherwise is the late Dry, in July and August – *Wurrgeng* and *Gurrung*. This is when wildlife, especially birds, congregates in big numbers around the shrinking billabongs and watercourses, but it's also when most tourists come to the park.

Wildlife

Kakadu has about 25 species of frog, 60 types of mammal, 51 freshwater fish species, 75 types of reptile, 280 bird species (one-third of all those native to Australia) and at least 4500 kinds of insect. There are frequent additions to the list, and a few of the rarer species are unique to the park. Kakadu's wetlands are on the UN list of Wetlands of International Importance, principally because of their crucial significance to so many types of water bird.

You'll only see a tiny fraction of these creatures in a visit to the park since many are shy, nocturnal or few in numbers. Take advantage of talks and walks led by park rangers – mainly in the Dry – to get to know and see more of the wildlife. Cruises of South Alligator River and Yellow Water Billabong enable you to see the water life.

Reptiles Both Twin and Jim Jim Falls have resident freshwater crocodiles, which are considered harmless, while there are plenty of the dangerous saltwater variety in the park. You're sure to see a few if you take a South Alligator or Yellow Water cruise.

Kakadu's other reptiles include lizards, such as the frilled lizard, and five freshwater turtle species, of which the most common is the northern snake-necked turtle. There are many snakes, including three highly poisonous types, but you're unlikely to see any. Oenpelli pythons, probably unique to the Kakadu escarpment, were only discovered in 1977.

Birds Kakadu's abundant water birds, and their beautiful wetland setting, make a memorable sight. The park is one of the chief refuges in Australia for several species, among them the magpie goose, green pygmy goose and Burdekin duck.

Other fine water birds include pelicans, darters and the Jabiru stork, with its distinctive red legs and long, straight beak.

Herons, egrets, ibis and cormorants are common. You're quite likely to see rainbow bee-eaters and kingfishers (of which there are six types in inland Kakadu). Majestic white-breasted sea eagles are often seen near inland waterways too, and wedge-tailed

Uranium Mining, Aboriginal People and the Environment

Uranium was discovered in the Kakadu region in 1953, and 12 small deposits in the southern reaches of the park were initially worked in the 1960s. However, these were abandoned following the declaration of the Woolwonga Wildlife Sanctuary. Then, in 1970, huge finds were made at Ranger, Nabarlek and Koongarra. The Nabarlek deposit (in Arnhem Land) was mined in the late 1970s and the Ranger Uranium Mine first started producing ore in 1981. The local Aboriginal people were against the mining of uranium on traditional land, but were enticed with the double lure of land title and royalties. In 1973 one of the world's largest high-grade uranium deposits was found at Jabiluka. Now the favoured site for future exploitation, Jabiluka lies 20 km north of Ranger on the edge of the floodplain of the beautiful Magela Creek, a tributary of the East Alligator River.

When the ore body at Ranger was exhausted, mining giant Energy Resources Australia (ERA) was not able to start mining at Jabiluka as the former Labor government had banned the opening of new mines under its three-mines policy. The policy allowed uranium to be minded from only three sites at any one time – Nabarlek, Ranger, and Roxby Downs in South Australia. Before the policy was introduced, Koongarra (discovered by Noranda Australia Ltd in 1970) was close to development, but in 1983 it was also stalled. Lying outside the national park, 30km south of Jabiru and only three km east of Nourlangie, Koongarra is one of the major Aboriginal rock-art sites in Kakadu. The three-mines policy was also partly responsible for the scrapping of Coronation Hill (Guratba), a proposed uranium mine in the south of the park, in 1991. Thus, under Labor, ERA was only able to plan for the opening in 1997 of Ranger 3, adjacent to the present Ranger mine.

With Labor's loss to a coalition of the Liberal and National parties in March 1996, uranium mining in Australia was set to undergo a radical expansion. Green groups have strongly criticised the scrapping of the three-mines policy, pointing out that the contracting world market for uranium will not generate the riches promised and that the ERA has a very poor safety record.

Since 1977 there have been 30 incidents at the Ranger Uranium Mine within Kakadu's boundary. Many of these have allegedly involved contamination of Magela Creek with the release of radioactive waste. Despite this, the prime minister, John Howard, gave the go-ahead to a new mine at Jabiluka in 1998. The traditional owners of the country where the mine is planned, the Mirrar people, have been opposed to uranium mining in the Kakadu area since uranium was first discovered there. They maintain that it threatens their cultural life, poses a threat to their native title, their practice of law and their beliefs and values.■

---

eagles, whistling kites and black kites are common. At night you might hear barking owls calling – they sound just like dogs. The red-tailed black cockatoos are spectacular, you may also catch sight of brolgas and bustards.

Mammals Several types of kangaroo and wallaby inhabit the park, and the shy black wallaroo is more or less unique to Kakadu. You might be lucky enough to see a sugar glider in wooded areas in the daytime. Kakadu is home to 25 bat species and is a key refuge for four endangered varieties.

Water buffalo, which ran wild after being introduced to the Top End from Timor by European settlers in the first half of the 19th century, have been virtually eradicated; an extermination programme was introduced because they were potential carriers of cattle disease and did much damage to the natural environment.

Fish You can't miss the silver barramundi, which creates a distinctive swirl near the water surface. It can grow to well over 1m in length and changes its sex from male to female at the age of five or six years.

Aboriginal Art

Kakadu is an important repository of rock-art collections. There are over 5000 sites, which date from 20,000 years to 10 years old. Two of the finest collections are the galleries at Ubirr and Nourlangie.

The paintings have been classified into three roughly defined periods: Pre-estuarine, which is from the earliest paintings up to around 6000 years ago; Estuarine, which covers the period from 6000 to around 2000 years ago, when the valleys flooded due to the rising sea levels caused by the melting polar ice caps; and Freshwater, from 2000 years ago until the present.

For the local Aboriginal people the rock-art sites are a major source of traditional knowledge, their historical archives if you like, given that they have no written language. The most recent paintings, some executed as recently as the 1980s, connect the local community with the artists, while the older paintings are believed by many Aboriginal people to have been painted by spirit people, and depict stories which connect the people with creation legends and the development of Aboriginal law.

The majority of rock-art sites open to the public are relatively recent, and some visitors feel somewhat cheated when they learn that the paintings were only done in the 1960s. Many people are also surprised to learn that the old paintings they are seeing have actually been touched up by Aboriginal people quite recently. In fact this was not uncommon, although the repainting could only be done by a specific person who had knowledge of the story being depicted. What also comes as a surprise to many people is the way the paintings in a particular site are often layered, with newer paintings being placed right over the top of older ones.

The conservation of the Kakadu rock-art sites is a major part of the park management task. As the paintings are all done with natural, water-soluble ochres, they are very susceptible to water damage from drip lines running across the rock. To prevent this sort of damage small ridges of clear silicon rubber have been made on the rocks above the paintings, so the water flowing down the rock is diverted to either side, or actually drips right off. Buffaloes also damaged the lower paintings as they loved to rub against the walls of the rock shelters. The dust raised by hundreds of tourists tramping past these sites on a daily basis didn't help either. Today most of the accessible sites have boardwalks which not only keep the dust down but also keep people at a suitable distance from the paintings.

Orientation

Where the Arnhem Highway to Kakadu turns east off the Stuart Highway, it's 121km to the park entrance and another 105km to Jabiru. The road is sealed all the way. The Kakadu Highway (also sealed) to Nourlangie, Cooinda and Pine Creek turns south off the Arnhem Highway shortly before Jabiru.

Eight kilometres east of South Alligator a short side road to the south leads to Mamukala, with views over the South Alligator flood plain, an observation building, bird-watching hides and a 3km walking trail.

From Mamukala it's 28km to the turn-off to one of the major sites in the park, Ubirr, 40km away in the northern part of the park near the East Alligator River. This road also gives access to Oenpelli, Arnhem Land and the Cobourg Peninsula, but note that a permit is needed to enter Arnhem Land (apply at the Northern Land Council office in Jabiru).

A turn-off to the north, 20km into the park along the Arnhem Highway, leads to camp sites at Two Mile Hole (8km) and Four Mile Hole (38km) on the Wildman River, which is popular for fishing. The track is not suitable for conventional vehicles except in the Dry, and then only as far as Two Mile Hole.

About 35km further east along the highway, a turn-off to the south, again impassable to conventional vehicles in the Wet, leads to camp sites at Red Lily (35km) and Alligator billabongs (39km), and on to the Jim Jim Road (69km).

Information

The excellent Bowali Information Centre (☎ 8938 1121; fax 8938 1123), on the Kakadu Highway a few kilometres south of the Arnhem Highway turn-off, is open daily from 8 am to 5 pm. Here you'll find informative and interesting displays, including a few to keep the kids happy, a theatrette showing a 25-minute audiovisual presentation on the park (screened on the hour), plenty of leaflets on various aspects of the park, a cafe, gift shop and excellent resource centre with a comprehensive selection of reference books. There is another dozen or so videos featuring various documentaries made about Kakadu in the last few years, and these are also shown throughout the day (on the half hour).

The Warradjan Aboriginal Cultural Centre near Cooinda gives an excellent insight into the culture of the park's traditional owners. The building itself is circular, symbolic of the way Aboriginal people sit in a circle when meeting or talking. The shape is also reminiscent of the *warradjan* (pig-nosed turtle), hence the name of the centre.

In Darwin you can get information on Kakadu from the Parks Australia North office. See Other Information under Darwin earlier in this chapter.

Fuel is available at Kakadu Holiday Village, Border Store (unleaded and diesel only), Jabiru and Cooinda. Jabiru also has a supermarket, post office and a Westpac bank, and the Northern Land Council office here issues permits on the spot for the highly recommended trip to the excellent Injalak arts and crafts outlet in Oenpelli, a half-hour trip across the East Alligator River in Arnhem Land (see the Arnhem Land section later in this chapter).

Entry Fees Entry to the park is $15 (children under 16 free). This entitles you to stay in the park for 14 days. The fee is payable at the park gates as you enter. If there's a few of you and you plan camping in the park, it works out cheaper to get a yearly ticket for $60. This covers one vehicle and all its occupants, as well as camping fees at the Mardugal, Muirella Park, Merl and Gunlom camp sites, which usually cost $7 per person per night.

Ubirr
This spectacular rock-art site lies 40km north of the Arnhem Highway. The turn-off to Ubirr is 100km from the park entrance. The road is sealed but there are several creek crossings which make it impassable for a conventional vehicle for most of the wet season – sometimes for 4WD too. The rock-art site is open daily from 8.30 am until sunset between May and November, 2 pm to sunset the rest of the year.

Shortly before Ubirr you pass the Border Store. Nearby are a couple of **walking trails** close to the East Alligator River, which forms the eastern boundary of the park here. There is a backpackers' hostel and camp site nearby. Aboriginal-guided **Guluyambi River trips** are held on the East Alligator River here. The tours leave daily from the upstream boat ramp at 9 and 11 am, and at 1 and 3 pm ($25, $11 children aged four to 14) and last just under two hours. A free shuttle bus runs between the boat ramp and the Border Store and Merl camping ground. For information and bookings ☎ 1800 089 113.

A path from the Ubirr car park takes you through the main galleries to a lookout with superb views – a 1.5km round trip. There are paintings on numerous rocks along the path, but the highlight is the main gallery with a large array of well-executed and preserved x-ray-style wallabies, possums, goannas, tortoises and fish, plus a couple of *balanda* (white men) with hands on hips. Also of major interest is the Rainbow Serpent painting, and the picture of the Namarkan sisters, shown with string pulled taut between their hands.

The Ubirr paintings are in many different styles. They were painted during the period from over 20,000 years ago to the 20th century.

Jabiru (pop 1700)
The township, originally built to accommodate Ranger Uranium Mine workers, has shops and a public swimming pool. Six kilometres east is Jabiru airport and the Ranger Uranium Mine. There are minibus tours of the mine ($10) available three times a day through Kakadu Parklink (☎ 8979 2411).

Nourlangie
The sight of this looming, mysterious, isolated outlier of the Arnhem Land escarpment makes it easy to understand why it has been important to Aboriginal people for so long. Its long, red, sandstone bulk – striped in places with orange, white and black – slopes up from surrounding woodland to fall away

at one end in sheer, stepped cliffs, at the foot of which is Kakadu's best known collection of rock art.

The name Nourlangie is a corruption of *nawulandja*, an Aboriginal word which refers to an area bigger than the rock itself. The Aboriginal name of the rock is Burrunggui. You reach it at the end of a 12km sealed road which turns east off the Kakadu Highway, 21km south of the Arnhem Highway.

Other interesting spots nearby make it worth spending a whole day in this corner of Kakadu. The last few kilometres of the road are closed from around 5 pm daily.

From the main car park a round-trip walk of about 2km takes you first to the **Anbangbang shelter**, which was used for 20,000 years as a refuge from heat, rain and frequent wet-season thunderstorms. From the gallery you can walk onto a lookout from where you can see the distant Arnhem Land cliff line, which includes Lightning Dreaming (Namarrgon Djadjam), the home of Namarrgon. There's a 12km marked trail all the way round the rock; the park information centre has a leaflet.

Heading back towards the highway you can take turn-offs to three other places of interest. The first, on the left about 1km from the main car park, takes you to **Anbangbang billabong**, with its picnic site and dense carpet of lilies. The second, also on the left, leads to a short walk up to **Nawulandja lookout** with good views back over Nourlangie Rock.

The third turn-off, a dirt track on the right, takes you to another outstanding, although little visited, rock-art gallery, **Nanguluwur**. A farther 6km along this road, and a 3km walk, brings you to **Gubara (Baroalba Springs)**, an area of shaded pools in monsoon forest.

Jim Jim & Twin Falls

These two spectacular waterfalls are along a 4WD dry-season track that turns south off the Kakadu Highway between the Nourlangie and Cooinda turn-offs. It's about 60km to Jim Jim Falls (the last 1km on foot),

---

The Rainbow Serpent
The story of the Rainbow Serpent is found in Aboriginal tradition across Australia, although the story varies from place to place. In Kakadu the serpent is a woman, Kurangali, who painted her image on the rock wall at Ubirr while on a journey through this area. This journey forms a creation path that links the places she visited: Ubirr, Manngarre, the East Alligator River and various places in Arnhem Land.

To the traditional owners of the park, Kurangali is the most powerful spirit, although she spends most of her time resting in billabongs. If disturbed she can be very destructive, causing floods and earthquakes, and one local story has it that she even eats people. ■

---

and 70km to Twin Falls, where the last few hundred metres are through the water up a snaking, forested gorge – great fun on an inflatable air bed.

Jim Jim – a sheer 215m drop – is awesome after the rains, but its waters can shrink to nothing at the end of the Dry. Twin Falls doesn't dry up.

Note that the track to Jim Jim and Twin Falls is often still closed in late May and even into June, so be prepared for that.

Yellow Water & Cooinda

The turn-off to the Cooinda accommodation complex and the superb Yellow Water wetlands, with their big water-bird population, is 52km down the Kakadu Highway from its junction with the Arnhem Highway. It's then about 5km to Cooinda, and a couple more kilometres to the starting point for boat trips on Yellow Water Billabong. These go three times daily (dry season only) and cost $26.50 ($13.50 for children) for two hours. There are also three tours a day (year-round) of 1½ hours for $22.50 ($12.50). This trip is one of the highlights of most people's visit to Kakadu. Early morning is the best time to go as the bird life is most active. You're likely to see a saltwater crocodile or two. It's usually advisable to book your cruise the day before at Cooinda (☎ 8979 0111), particularly for the early departure.

Yellow Water is also an excellent place to watch the sunset, particularly in the Dry when the smoke from the many bushfires which burn in the Top End at this time of year turns bright red in the setting sun. Bring plenty of insect repellent as the mosquitoes are voracious.

Cooinda to Pine Creek

Just south of the Yellow Water and Cooinda turn-off the Kakadu Highway heads south-west for 161km to Pine Creek, out of the park on the Stuart Highway. On the way there is a turn-off to the very scenic falls and plunge pool at **Gunlom (Waterfall Creek)**, which featured in *Crocodile Dundee*. It's 40km along a good dirt road.

Walking

Kakadu is excellent but tough bushwalking country. Many people will be satisfied with the marked trails, which range from 1km to 12km long. For the more adventurous there are infinite possibilities, especially in the drier south and east of the park, but take great care and prepare well. Tell people where you're going and don't go alone. You need a permit from the park information centre to camp outside the established camp sites.

The Darwin Bushwalking Club (☎ 8985 1484) welcomes visitors and may be able to help with information. It has walks most weekends, often in Kakadu. Or you could join a Willis's Walkabouts guided bushwalk (see Organised Tours later in this section). *Kakadu by Foot* is a helpful guide to the marked walking trails in Kakadu. It is published by PAN ($1.95) but seems to be in short supply.

Scenic Flights

Kakadu Air (☎ 8979 2411) does a number of flights over Kakadu. A half-hour flight from Jabiru costs $60, or it's $100 for an hour.

Organised Tours

There are hosts of tours to Kakadu from Darwin and a few that start inside the park.

Two-day tours typically take in Jim Jim Falls, Nourlangie and the Yellow Water cruise, and cost from $220. Companies which seem to be popular include: Hunter Safaris (☎ 8981 2720), $220/320 for two/three days; Kakadu Adventure Safaris (☎ 1800 672 677), $210/320 for two/three days; and Territory Style Tours (☎ 1800 801 991), $240 for two days.

Longer tours usually cover most of the main sights plus a couple of extras. Some combine Kakadu with the Katherine Gorge. One of the popular ones is the Blue Banana (☎ 8945 6800), which charges $150 for transport only and you can get on and off anywhere between Darwin and Katherine as often as you like for three months.

You can take 10-hour 4WD tours to Jim Jim and Twin falls from Jabiru or Cooinda ($120, dry season) with Kakadu Gorge & Waterfall Tours (☎ 8979 2025) or Lord of Kakadu (☎ 8979 2567).

Willis's Walkabouts (☎ 8985 2134) are bushwalks guided by knowledgeable Top End walkers, following your own or preset routes of two days or more. Many of the walks are in Kakadu. Prices vary, but $900 for a two-week trip, including evening meals and return transport from Darwin, is fairly typical.

Into Arnhem Land A couple of outfits offer trips into Arnhem Land from Kakadu. Kakadu Parklink (☎ 8979 2411) has weekday tours from Jabiru or Cooinda into the Mikinj Valley for $140 ($112 children). The trips are usually accompanied by an Aboriginal guide.

Places to Stay & Eat

Prices for accommodation in Kakadu can vary tremendously depending on the season – dry-season prices (given here) can be as much as 50% more than wet-season prices.

Camping Some sites are run by the national parks. Others (with power) are attached to the resorts: *Frontier Kakadu Village*, South Alligator, $10/6 for two with/without power; *Gagadju Lodge Cooinda*, $16/14; and *Fron-*

tier Kakadu Lodge, Jabiru, \$10/6 with/ without power for two people.

A turn-off to the north, 20km into the park along the Arnhem Highway, leads to camp sites at **Two Mile Hole** (8km) and **Four Mile Hole** (38km) on the Wildman River, which is popular for fishing. The track is not suitable for conventional vehicles except in the Dry, and then only as far as Two Mile Hole.

About 35km farther east along the highway, a turn-off to the south, again impassable to conventional vehicles in the Wet, leads to camp sites at **Red Lily** (35km) and **Alligator** billabongs (39km), and on to the Jim Jim Road (69km).

The **South Alligator River Crossing**, with its popular boat ramp and picnic area, is 8km farther along the highway, about 3km past the Kakadu Holiday Village.

The three main national parks camp sites are: *Merl*, near the Border Store; *Muirella Park*, 6km off the Kakadu Highway a few kilometres south of the Nourlangie turn-off; and *Mardugal*, just off the Kakadu Highway 1.5km south of the Cooinda turn-off; Only the Mardugal site is open during the Wet. The camp sites have hot showers, flushing toilets, and drinking water and the fee is \$7 per person (collected on the site).

The national parks provide more basic camp sites in Kakadu, and at these there is no fee. To camp anywhere else you need a permit from the Bowali Information Centre.

South Alligator Just a couple of kilometres west of the South Alligator River on the Arnhem Highway is the *Kakadu Holiday Village* (☎ 1800 818 845), which has twin-bed rooms from \$168. The hotel has a restaurant and a basic shop (7 am to 8 pm), as well as a swimming pool, restaurant and bar.

Jabiru The *Gagadju Crocodile Hotel* (☎ 1800 808 123) is probably most famous for its design – it's set out in the shape of a crocodile, although this is only really apparent from the air. There's nothing very exotic about the hotel itself, although it is comfort-

able enough. Prices start at \$180/200 for a single/double.

The *Frontier Kakadu Lodge* (☎ 8979 2422) has four-bed rooms at \$25 per person, or \$100 for a whole room. The only cooking facilities are a few barbecues, but the pool-side bistro serves reasonable pub-style meals for around \$14.

Apart from the restaurants at the two hotels, there's the *Golden Bowl Restaurant* at the sports club. It does a pretty standard range of Chinese food, and you can eat in or take away.

Lastly there's a cafe in the shopping centre, and a bakery near the fire station.

Ubirr The basic *Hostel Kakadu* (☎ 8979 2232) behind the Border Store is the only place in Kakadu that offers budget accommodation (twin-share) and decent facilities. The budget accommodation at the resort hotels is a bit of an afterthought and there's not much in the way of cooking facilities. The hostel is open year-round (as long as the road remains open) and costs \$14 per person. There's a well-equipped kitchen, lounge room and swimming pool. The Border Store has supplies and snack food and is open daily until 5 pm.

Cooinda This is by far the most popular place to stay, mainly because of the proximity of the Yellow Water wetlands and the early-morning boat cruises. It gets mighty crowded at times, mainly with camping tours. The *Gagadju Lodge Cooinda* (☎ 8979 0145; fax 8979 0148) has some comfortable units for \$110 for up to three people, and much cheaper and more basic air-con 'budget rooms', which are just transportable huts of the type found on many building sites and more commonly known in the Territory as 'demountables' or 'dongas'. For \$19 per person they are quite adequate, if a little cramped (two beds per room). The only cooking facilities are barbecues.

The bistro here serves unexciting and overpriced barbecue meals, which you cook, at around \$15, or there's the more expensive

Mimi Restaurant if you want waiter service and à la carte.

Getting There & Around

Ideally, take your own 4WD. The Arnhem and Kakadu highways are both sealed all the way. Sealed roads lead from the Kakadu Highway to Nourlangie, the Muirella Park camping area and to Ubirr. Other roads are mostly dirt and blocked for varying periods during the Wet and early Dry.

Greyhound Pioneer (☎ 13 2030) run daily buses from Darwin to Cooinda ($33) via Jabiru ($27). The buses stop at the Yellow Water wetland in time for the 1 pm cruise, and wait there for 1½ hours until the cruises finish. The buses leave Darwin at 6.30 am, Jabiru at 10.05 am and arrive at Cooinda at 12.10 pm. Coming back they leave Cooinda at 2.20 pm and Jabiru at 4.15 pm, arriving in Darwin at 7 pm. Jabiru to Cooinda is $7.

Greyhound Pioneer also have a daily service from Jabiru (departing at 10.10 am) to the Border Store (arrives 10.50 am; $16) near Ubirr. The return trip leaves the Border Store at 1.30 pm, makes a 1½ hour stop at Bowali Information Centre, and arrives in Jabiru at 3.50 pm.

It's advisable to check on seat availability in advance.

BATHURST & MELVILLE ISLANDS

These two large, flat islands about 80km north of Darwin are the home of the Tiwi Aboriginal people. You need a permit to visit, and the only realistic option is to take a tour. Tiwi Tours (☎ 1800 811 633), a company which employs many Tiwi among its staff, is the only operator, and its tours are recommended.

The Tiwi people's island homes kept them fairly isolated from mainland developments until this century, and their culture has retained several unique features. Perhaps the best known are the *pukumani* burial poles, carved and painted with symbolic and mythological figures, which are erected around graves. More recently the Tiwi have started producing art for sale – bark painting, textile

screen printing, batik and pottery, using traditional designs and motifs.

The Tiwi had mixed relations with Macassan fisherpeople, who came in search of the trepang, or sea cucumber. A British settlement in the 1820s at Fort Dundas, near Pularumpi on Melville Island, failed partly because of poor relations with the locals. The main settlement on the islands is **Nguiu** in the south-east of Bathurst Island, which was founded in 1911 as a Catholic mission. On Melville Island the settlements are **Pularumpi** and **Milikapiti**.

Most Tiwi live on Bathurst Island and follow a nontraditional lifestyle. Some return to their traditional lands on Melville Island for a few weeks each year. Melville Island also has descendants of the Japanese pearl divers who regularly visited here early this century, and people of mixed Aboriginal and European parentage who were gathered here from around the Territory under government policy half a century ago.

An all-day trip costs $240 and includes the necessary permit, a flight from Darwin to Nguiu, visits to the early Catholic mission buildings, morning tea with Tiwi ladies, swimming at Tomorapi Falls, a trip to a pukumani burial site and the flight back to Darwin from Melville. This tour is available from April to October. Tiwi Tours also offers two-day tours to the islands, staying at a tented camp, for $460.

ARNHEM LAND

The entire eastern half of the Top End is the Arnhem Land Aboriginal Land, which is spectacular, sparsely populated and the source of some good Aboriginal art. Apart from Oenpelli (just across the East Alligator River in Kakadu), the remote Gurig National Park (on the Cobourg Peninsula at the north-west corner) and Gove (the peninsula at the north-east corner), Anhem Land is virtually closed to independent travellers.

Oenpelli

Oenpelli is a fairly nondescript Aboriginal community town, but it is well worth visiting for two reasons: the 17km dirt road from

Kakadu traverses the wildly spectacular East Alligator River flood plain (and is probably as spectacular as anything within Kakadu itself), and Injalak Arts & Crafts has really high quality Aboriginal artefacts at very reasonable prices. Injalak is both a workplace and shopfront for artists and craftspeople who produce traditional paintings on bark and paper, didjeridus, pandanus weavings and baskets, and screenprinted fabrics. All sales benefit the community, and you can also be sure that you are buying authentic pieces. The centre (☎ 8979 0190) is open daily from 9 am to 5 pm, and permits to visit can be obtained on the spot at the Northern Land Council office (☎ 8979 2410) at the Jabiru shopping centre.

Cobourg Peninsula

This remote wilderness includes the Aboriginal-owned **Cobourg Marine Park** and the **Gurig National Park**. Entry to the latter is by permit only.

The ruins of the early British settlement at Victoria can be visited on **Port Essington**, a superb 30km-long natural harbour on the northern side of the peninsula.

At **Black Point** there's a small store open daily except Sunday, but only from 3 to 5 pm. It sells basic provisions, ice, camping gas and fuel (diesel, super, unleaded, outboard mix), and basic mechanical repairs are done. Be warned that credit cards are not accepted here and, as its operation has been erratic in recent years, phone the Black Point ranger station in advance to check its current status.

Permits The track to Cobourg passes through part of Arnhem Land, and as the Aboriginal owners there restrict the number of vehicles going through (15 per week), you're advised to apply up to a year ahead for the necessary permit ($211 per vehicle for seven days). Permit forms are available from the tourist office in Darwin, but all applications should be submitted to the rangers at Gurig, either by fax (☎ 8979 0246) or by mail (Black Point Ranger Station, Gurig National Park, Parks & Wildlife Com-

mission, PO Box 496, Palmerston, NT 0831).

Places to Stay There are 15 shady camp sites about 100m from the shore at the *Smith Point Camping Ground*. It's run by Parks & Wildlife and facilities include a shower and toilet, and barbecues. There's no electricity and generators are banned at night. The charge is $4 per site for three people, plus $1 for each extra person.

The fully equipped, four-bed *Cobourg Cottages* at Smith Point cost $100 for the whole cottage, but you need to bring your own supplies. As with the store, check in advance to see if the cottages are open.

The only other accommodation option is the *Seven Spirit Bay Resort* (☎ 8979 0277), set in secluded wilderness at Vashon Head and accessible only by air or boat. It charges $300 per person for single/double accommodation, but this includes three gourmet meals. Accommodation is in individual open-sided, hexagonal 'habitats', each with semi-outdoor private bathroom! Activities available (at extra cost) include day-trips to Victoria Settlement, guided bushwalks and fishing. Return transfer by air from Darwin costs $250 per person.

Getting There & Away There's an airstrip at Smith Point, just a couple of kilometres or so from the camp site and Black Point, which is serviced by charter flights from Darwin.

The track to Cobourg starts at Oenpelli. It is recommended for 4WD vehicles only, and only take a trailer if you are prepared to have it shaken to bits. The track is also closed in the wet season. The 288km drive to Black Point from the East Alligator River at Cahills Crossing (near Ubirr) takes about six hours and the track is in reasonable condition, the roughest part coming in the hour or so after the turn-off from Murgenella. The trip must be completed in one day as it's not possible to stop overnight on Aboriginal land.

Straight after the Wet, the water level at Cahills Crossing on the East Alligator River can be high, and you can only drive across the ford about an hour either side of the low tide. A tide chart is included with your permit, or the Bowali Information Centre in Kakadu has a list of tide times.

Gove Peninsula

At **Nhulunbuy** (pop 3700) there is a bauxite-mining centre with a deep-water export port. Free tours of the mine are held on Friday mornings (☎ 8987 5345).

The Aboriginal people of nearby **Yirrkala** (pop 520) made an important step in the land rights movement in 1963 when they protested at plans to mine on their traditional land. They failed to stop it, but forced a government enquiry and won compensation, and their case caught the public eye. Buku Larrngay Mulka has an excellent collection of art and artefacts ($2).

Groote Eylandt, a large island off the east Arnhem Land coast, is also Aboriginal land, with a big manganese-mining operation. The main settlement here is **Alyangula** (pop 1230).

Getting There & Away You don't have to have a permit to fly into Nhulunbuy and you can fly there direct from Darwin for $246 or from Cairns for $342 with Qantas or Ansett. Travelling overland through Arnhem Land from Katherine requires a permit; contact the Gove Regional Tourist Association (☎ 8987 1985; fax 8987 2214).

You can hire vehicles in Nhulunbuy to explore the coastline (there are some fine beaches, but beware of crocodiles) and the local area. You need to get a permit to do this from the Northern Land Council in Nhulunbuy (a formality).

Organised Tours

There are a number of tours into Arnhem Land, but these usually only visit the western part.

The Aboriginal-owned and operated Umorrduk Safaris (☎ 8948 1306; fax 8948 1305) has a two-day tour from Darwin to the remote Mudjeegarrdart airstrip in north-western Arnhem Land. The highlight of the trip is a visit to the 20,000-year-old Umorrduk rock-art sites. The cost is $600 per person, plus air transfer of $315 per person, and the trips operate from May through December.

Another operator with a very good reputation is Davidson's Arnhemland Safaris (☎ 8927 5240; fax 8945 0919). Max Davidson has been taking people into Arnhem Land for years and has a concession at Mt Borradaile, north of Oenpelli, where he has set up his safari camp. Close by there's wetlands with excellent fishing and art sites which will knock you out. The camp, which has a very informal and relaxed atmosphere, is open year-round and costs $300 per person per day, which includes accommodation, all meals, guided tours and fishing. Transfers from Darwin can be arranged.

Other trips are available from Jabiru in Kakadu; see the Kakadu National Park section earlier.

Down the Track

It's just under 1500km south from Darwin to Alice Springs, and although at times it can be dreary there is an amazing variety of things to see or do along the road and nearby.

Until WWII the Track really was just that – a dirt track – connecting the Territory's two main towns, Darwin and 'the Alice'. The need to quickly supply Darwin, which was under attack by Japanese aircraft from Timor, led to a rapid upgrading of the road. Although it is now sealed and well maintained, short, sharp floods during the Wet can cut the road and stop all traffic for days at a time.

The Stuart Highway takes its name from John McDouall Stuart, who made the first crossing of Australia from south to north. Twice he turned back due to lack of supplies, ill health and hostile Aboriginal people, but finally completed his epic trek in 1862. Only 10 years later the telegraph line to Darwin was laid along the route he had pioneered, and today the Stuart Highway between Darwin and Alice Springs follows roughly the same path.

DARWIN TO KATHERINE

Some places along the Track south of Darwin (Howard Springs, Darwin Crocodile Farm and Litchfield National Park) are covered in Around Darwin earlier in this chapter.

Batchelor (pop 640)

This small town, 84km down the Track from Darwin, then 13km west, once serviced the now-closed Rum Jungle uranium and copper mine. In recent years it has received a boost from the growing popularity of nearby Litchfield National Park. It has a swimming pool open six days a week and an Aboriginal residential tertiary college.

About an hour's walk away is **Rum Jungle Lake**, where you can canoe or swim.

Places to Stay The *Batchelor Caravillage* (☎ 8976 0166) on Rum Jungle Rd has cabins for $70, or tent sites for $16. The friendly *Banyan Tree Caravan Park* (☎ 8976 0330) is halfway between Batchelor and Litchfield, and has on-site vans at $15 per person, and meals are available.

The *Rum Jungle Motor Inn* (☎ 8976 0123) in Batchelor is expensive at $78/98.

Adelaide River (pop 280)

Not to be confused with Adelaide River Crossing on the Arnhem Highway, this small settlement is on the Stuart Highway 111km south of Darwin. It has a well-kept cemetery for those who died in the 1942-43 Japanese air raids. This stretch of the highway is dotted with WWII airstrips.

Adelaide River has a pub, the *Shady River View Caravan Park* with tent sites for $12, and the *Adelaide River Inn* (☎ 8976 7047) with singles/doubles at $45/75.

About 3.5km from town on Haynes Rd (turn-off opposite the old train station) is *Mt Bundy Station* (☎ 8976 7009), which offers farmstay accommodation in en-suite rooms for $80/120 including breakfast, or there's comfortable backpacker accommodation in the converted stockman's quarters for $18. If you don't have transport ring from Adelaide River to be picked up.

Old Stuart Highway

South of Adelaide River a sealed section of the old Stuart Highway makes a loop to the south before rejoining the main road 52km on. It's a scenic trip without the hustle of the main highway, and it leads to a number of pleasant spots, but access to them is often cut in the Wet.

The beautiful 12m **Robyn Falls** are a short, rocky scramble 17km along this road. The falls, set in a monsoon-forested gorge, dwindle to a trickle in the dry season, but are spectacular in the Wet.

The turn-off to **Daly River** is 14km farther on, and to reach **Douglas Hot Springs Nature Park**, turn south off the old highway just before it rejoins the Stuart Highway and continue for about 35km. The nature park here includes a section of the Douglas River, a pretty camping area and several hot springs – a bit hot for bathing at 40°C, but there are cooler pools.

Butterfly Gorge National Park is about 15km beyond Douglas Hot Springs – you'll need a 4WD to get there. True to its name, butterflies sometimes swarm in the gorge. It's safe to swim in these places, although you may well see 'freshies' (freshwater crocodiles). There are camp sites with toilets and barbecues.

Daly River

Historic Daly River is 109km west of the Stuart Highway. Most of the population are part of the Naniyu Nambiyu Aboriginal community, about 6km away from the rest of the town. Visitors are welcome without a permit, although note that this is a dry community. Also here is Merrepen Arts, a resource centre which is also an outlet for locally made art and crafts. The associated Merrepen Arts Festival is held each year in June/July.

The main activity for visitors is getting out on the river and dangling a line. Boat hire is available at the Mango Farm and Woolianna tourist outfits. At the Mango Farm you can hire a 3.6m dinghy with outboard motor for $36 for two hours, $65 for a half day and $100 for a full day, or take a two-hour river cruise at $20 per person. Woolianna has

NORTHERN TERRITORY

three-person boats at $65/90 for a half/full day and four-person boats for $70/100. Both places operate guided fishing trips on request.

Places to Stay There are a couple of accommodation options here, including the *Woolianna on the Daly Tourist Park* (☎ 8978 2478, tent/van sites), the *Daly River Roadside Inn* (☎ 8978 2418, tent/van sites) and the *Mango Farm* (☎ 8978 2464, tent/van sites and family units).

Pine Creek (pop 520)

This small town, 245km from Darwin, was the scene of a gold rush in the 1870s and some of the old timber and corrugated iron buildings survive. The Kakadu Highway goes north-east from Pine Creek to Kakadu National Park.

The old **train station** has been restored and houses a visitors centre and a display on the Darwin to Pine Creek railway, which opened in 1889 but is now closed. **Pine Creek Museum** ($2) on Railway Parade near the post office has interesting displays on local history. It is usually open weekdays from 10 am to noon and 1 to 5 pm, and on weekends from 10 am to 2 pm. **Ah Toys General Store** is a reminder of the gold-rush days when the Chinese heavily outnumbered Europeans.

Gun Alley Gold Mining (signposted) is an excellent little tourist operation with a demonstration of some historic steam-powered crushing machinery, a talk on the history of gold in Pine Creek, and a chance to find some 'colour' in a pan full of wash, all for $5.

Places to Stay The town has an unattractive caravan park, and there's the *Pine Creek Hotel* (☎ 8976 1288) with air-con singles/doubles at $63/74.

Around Pine Creek

A well-maintained dirt road follows the line of the old railway line east of the highway between Hayes Creek and Pine Creek. This is in fact the original 'north road', which was in use before the 'new road' (now the Old

Stuart Highway!) was built. It's a worthwhile detour to see the 1930s corrugated-iron pub at **Grove Hill** (accommodation and meals available).

About 3km along the Stuart Highway south of Pine Creek is the turn-off to **Umbrawarra Gorge Nature Park**, about 30km west along a dirt road (often impassable in the Wet). There's a camp site with pit toilets and fireplaces, and you can swim in crocodile-free pools 1km from the car park.

Edith Falls

At the 293km mark on the Track you can turn off to the beautiful Edith Falls, 19km east of the road at the western end of the Nitmiluk (Katherine Gorge) National Park. There's a camp site with showers, pit toilets and fireplaces ($5 per person). Swimming is possible in a clear, forest-surrounded plunge pool at the bottom of the falls. You may see freshwater crocodiles (the inoffensive variety), but be careful. There's a good walk up to rapids and more pools above the falls.

KATHERINE (pop 7980)

Apart from Tennant Creek, this is the only town of any size between Darwin and Alice Springs. It's a bustling little place where the Victoria Highway branches off to the Kimberley and Western Australia. The town's population has grown rapidly in recent years, partly because of the establishment of the large Tindal air-force base just south of town.

Katherine has long been an important stopping point, since the river it's built on and named after is the first permanent running water north of Alice Springs. The town includes some historic old buildings, such as the Sportsman's Arms, featured in *We of the Never Never*, Jeannie Gunn's classic novel of turn-of-the-century outback life. The main interest here, however, is the spectacular Katherine Gorge, 30km to the north-east. It's a great place to camp, walk, swim, canoe, take a cruise or simply float along on an air mattress.

In early 1998 the town was devastated by Wet season flooding. The main street was more than 2m under water and the damage bill was in the millions.

Orientation & Information

Katherine's main street, Katherine Tce, is the Stuart Highway as it runs through town. Coming from the north, you cross the Katherine River Bridge just before the town centre. The Victoria Highway to Western Australia branches off 300m on. After another 300m Giles St, the road to Katherine Gorge, branches off in the other direction.

At the end of the town centre is the Katherine Region Tourist Association office (☎ 8972 2650; fax 8972 2969), open Monday to Friday from 8.45 am to 5 pm, Saturday to 3 pm and Sunday from 9.30 am to 4 pm. The bus station is over the road from the tourist office. There's a Parks & Wildlife office (☎ 8973 8888) on Giles St.

Mimi Arts & Crafts on Lindsay St is an Aboriginal-owned and run shop, selling products made over a wide area – from the deserts in the west to the coast in the east. The Framed Gallery on the main street is also worth a look.

Things to See & Do

Katherine's old train station, owned by the National Trust, houses a display on railway history and is open Monday to Friday from 10 am to noon and 1 to 3 pm in the dry season.

The small Katherine Museum is in the old airport terminal building on Gorge Rd, about 1km from the centre of town. There's a good selection of old photos and other bits and pieces of interest, including the original Gypsy Moth biplane flown by Dr Clyde Fenton, the first Flying Doctor. It is open weekdays from 10 am to 4 pm, Saturday from 10 am to 2 pm and Sunday from 2 to 5 pm.

The School of the Air on Giles St offers an opportunity to see how remote outback kids are taught. There are guided tours on weekdays during the school term.

Katherine has a good public swimming pool beside the highway, about 750m south of the bus station. There are also some pleasant thermal pools beside the river, about 3km from town along the Victoria Highway.

The 105-hectare Katherine Low Level Nature Park is 5km from town, just off the Victoria Highway. It's a great spot on the Katherine River, taking in 4km of its shady banks, and the swimming hole by the weir is very popular in the Dry. In the Wet, flash floods can make it dangerous. Facilities provided here include picnic tables, toilets and gas barbecues.

Springvale Homestead, 8km south-west of town (turn right off the Victoria Highway after 3.8km), claims to be the oldest cattle station in the Northern Territory. Today it's also a tourist accommodation centre, and free half-hour tours around the old homestead are given once or twice daily. From May to September, crocodile-spotting cruises ($36 adults, $16 children) are run from here in the evenings, and three nights a week there are fairly touristy Aboriginal corroborees with demonstrations by the local Jawoyn people of fire making, traditional dance and spear throwing ($30.50 including barbecue). There's also horse-riding and cattle mustering.

Organised Tours

Tours are available from Katherine, taking in various combinations of the town and Springvale Homestead attractions, the Gorge, Cutta Cutta Caves, Mataranka and Kakadu. Most accommodation places can book you on these and you'll be picked up from where you're staying – or ask at the tourist office or Travel North in the bus station.

There are excellent Aboriginal tours at Manyallaluk (see that section later for details), and Bill Harney's Jankanginya Tours (☎ 1800 089 103) takes groups on their land, sometimes referred to as Lightning Brothers country. Here you learn about bush tucker, crafts and medicine, and hear some of the nonsecret stories associated with the rock art of the area. Accommodation is in a basic bush camp.

Places to Stay

Camping There are several camping possibilities. One of the nicest is *Springvale*

Homestead (☎ 8972 1355), with shady powered sites for $12. It also has budget units at $39/48 for singles/doubles, and there is a licensed restaurant and a kiosk for snacks. It's 8km out of Katherine; turn right off the Victoria Highway after 4km and follow the signs.

On the road to Springvale, 5km from town, is the Katherine Low Level Caravan Park (☎ 8972 3962), a good place close to the river. Tent sites are $14 for two, or $18 with power. Cabins cost $45. Closer to town, on the Victoria Highway, is the Riverview Caravan Park (☎ 8972 1011), which has reasonably comfortable cabins at $45 and tent sites at $14 ($16 with power). The thermal pools are five minutes walk away.

The Frontier Katherine (☎ 8972 1744), 4km south of town on the Stuart Highway, has powered en-suite camp sites at $20, plus a pool, barbecue area and restaurant. It also has motel rooms for $118.

Hostels Kookaburra Lodge Backpackers (☎ 1800 808 211), on the corner of Lindsay and Third Sts, is just a few minutes walk from the transit centre. It consists of old motel units with between six and 10 beds and costs $13 a night, or there are some twin rooms for $40. With so many people in each unit the bathroom and cooking facilities can get overcrowded at times, but it's a friendly and well-run place.

Just around the corner is the Palm Court Backpackers (☎ 8972 2722), on the corner of Third and Giles Sts. It's in a typically uninspiring old motel building, but the air-con rooms are uncrowded and have their own TV, fridge and bathroom. There's a pool and inadequate communal kitchen. The cost is $12 per person in an eight-bed room, $14 in a four-bed room, or $45 for a double.

The Victoria Lodge (☎ 8972 3464) is at 21 Victoria Highway, not far from the main street. It's a good place with six-bed rooms at $14 per person and doubles at $40.

Motels The Beagle Motor Inn (☎ 8972 3998) at the corner of Lindsay and Fourth Sts

is probably the cheapest, with singles/doubles for $40/50.

Places to Eat
Katherine has one or two of each of the usual types of Aussie eatery. Over the road from the transit centre (BP station), which has a 24-hour cafe, there's a Big Rooster fast-food place. The Katherine Hotel Motel, just up the main street, has counter meals as well as Aussie's Bistro, which is open daily for lunch and dinner and is pretty good value with main courses for around $10. Also here is the more formal Kirby's Restaurant.

Over the road there's the Golden Bowl Chinese restaurant. A block farther up on the corner of Warburton St, the Crossways Hotel does good counter meals for around $7.

Popeye's Pizza on the main street does good pizzas for $13 as well as other meaty main courses for around $10. Next door is Tommo's Bakery with tasty pies, bread and sticky things.

On the corner of Katherine Tce and the Victoria Highway is the Mekhong Thai Cafe & Take-away. This is an unusual find in an outback country town, and it has an extensive menu with entrees at $4 and main courses from $10.

Over on First St there's Annie's Family Restaurant, a bright little place with main courses for around $15, including a self-serve salad bar.

Getting There & Away
Katherine airport is 8km south of town, just off the Stuart Highway. You can fly to Katherine on weekdays from Darwin ($144) and Alice Springs ($369) with Airnorth (☎ 8971 7277).

All buses between Darwin and Alice Springs, Queensland or Western Australia stop at Katherine, which means two or three daily to and from Western Australia, and usually four daily to and from Darwin, Alice Springs and Queensland. See the Darwin section earlier for details. Typical fares from Katherine are Darwin $42, Alice Springs $137, Tennant Creek $68 and Kununurra $54.

NORTHERN TERRITORY

Companies such as Budget (☎ 8971 1333), Hertz (☎ 1800 891 112) and Territory Rent-a-Car (☎ 1800 891 125) all have rental offices/agents in town.

Getting Around

You can rent bicycles at the Kookaburra Lodge, or from Cooper's Cycles (☎ 8972 1213) at 3/16 First St.

Travel North (☎ 1800 089 103) has a bus service six times a day to the Gorge for $15 return (the first at 8 am, the last at 4.15 pm). Departures are from the transit centre, or phone for pick-up from your accommodation.

NITMILUK NATIONAL PARK

Nitmiluk (Katherine Gorge) is 13 gorges, separated from each other by rapids. The gorge walls aren't high, but it is a remote, beautiful place. It is 12km long and has been carved out by the Katherine River, which begins in Arnhem Land. Farther downstream it becomes the Daly River before flowing into the Timor Sea at a point 80km south-west of Darwin. The difference in water levels between the Wet and Dry is staggering. During the dry season the gorge waters are calm, but from November to March they can become a raging torrent.

Swimming in the gorge is safe except when it's in flood. The only crocodiles around are the freshwater variety and they're more often seen in the cooler months. The country surrounding the gorge is excellent for walking.

Information

The visitors centre and car park where the gorge begins and cruises start, is 30km by sealed road from Katherine. The impressive centre (☎ 8972 1886) has displays and information on the national park, which spreads over 1800sq km to include extensive back country and Edith Falls to the north-west, as well as Katherine Gorge. There are details of a wide range of marked walking tracks starting here that go through the picturesque country south of the gorge, descending to the river at various points. Some of the tracks

pass Aboriginal rock paintings up to 7000 years old. The visitors centre, which also has a cafe and souvenir shop, is open daily from 7.30 am to 8 pm.

You can walk to Edith Falls (76km, five days) or places along the way. For the longer or more rugged walks you need a permit from the visitors centre. The Katherine Gorge Canoe Marathon, organised by the Red Cross, takes place in June.

Activities

Canoeing At the river you can rent canoes for one, two or three people (☎ 8972 1253 or call at Travel North in Katherine). These cost $24/36 for a half-day, or $33/49 for a whole day. This is a great way of exploring the gorge. You can also be adventurous and take the canoes out overnight, but you must book in advance as only a limited number of people are allowed to camp in the gorges. You get a map with your canoe showing things of interest along the gorge sides – Aboriginal rock paintings, waterfalls, plant life, and so on.

Gorge Cruise Cruises depart daily. The two-hour run goes to the second gorge and visits rock paintings for $27 ($12 children); it leaves at 9 and 11 am, and at 1 and 3 pm. The four-hour trip goes to the third gorge for $41 ($19), leaving at 9 and 11 am and at 1 pm from April through September and at 9 am only the rest of the year (and only when the water is not too wild). Finally there's an eight-hour trip that takes you to the fifth gorge, and involves walking about 5km. The cost is $69, and it departs daily from April through November at 9 am.

During the Wet there are high-speed jet-boat cruises to the third gorge. They last 45 minutes and cost $32 ($25).

All tickets must be prebooked with Travel North on ☎ 1800 089 103. You can also take light-aircraft ($65 for 30 minutes) and helicopter flights ($65 for 15 minutes) over the gorge.

Aboriginal Guided Bushwalk Every day at 1.30 pm from April through October there's a 2½-hour Aboriginal-guided bushwalk which gives you an opportunity to learn a bit about the Jawoyn people and their traditional way of life. The tours leave from the boat ramp, from where you travel by boat to 17 Mile Creek, where the tour begins. The cost is $19, $10 for children five to 15. Make reservations with Travel North in Katherine (☎ 1800 089 103).

Swimming There's a swimming jetty close to the boat ramp, not far from the visitors centre, although it's not suitable for small children.

Places to Stay
The popular *Gorge Caravan Park* (☎ 8972 1253) has showers, toilets and fireplaces. Wallabies and goannas frequent the camp site. It costs $14 for a site ($18 with power), payable at the visitors centre, and there's plenty of grass and shade.

Getting There & Away
The six-times-daily commuter bus costs $15 return. It operates from the transit centre in Katherine and does accommodation pick-ups.

CUTTA CUTTA CAVES NATURE PARK
Guided tours of these limestone caverns, 24km south-east of Katherine along the Stuart Highway, are held six times a day in the dry season, and cost $7.50 ($3.75 children). Orange horseshoe bats, a rare and endangered species, roost in the main cave, about 15m below the ground. The rock formations outside the caves are impressive.

MANYALLALUK
Manyallaluk is the former 3000sq-km Eva Valley cattle station which abuts the eastern edge of the Nitmiluk National Park. These days it is owned by Top End Aboriginal people, some of whom now organise and lead very highly regarded tours.

The one-day trip includes transport to and from Katherine, lunch, billy tea and damper, and you learn about traditional bush tucker and medicine, spear throwing and playing a didjeridu. The two-day trip adds swimming and rock-art sites. The cost is $95 ($63 children) for the day-trip and $199 ($147) for the two-day trip. For bookings and enquiries phone ☎ 8975 4727, or fax 8975 4724.

The day-trip operates year-round on Monday, Wednesday and Saturday from Katherine, or with your own vehicle you can camp at Manyallaluk ($15 for two) and take the day tour from there, which costs $63. It is possible just to camp without taking the tour, but you are restricted to the camping area. There's a community store with basic supplies and excellent crafts at competitive prices. No permits are needed to visit the community, and alcohol is not permitted.

BARUNGA
Barunga is another Aboriginal community, 13km along the Arnhem Land track beyond the Manyallaluk turn-off. Entry to the community is by permit only, but every year over the Queen's Birthday long weekend in June the settlement really comes alive for the enjoyable Barunga Wugularr Sports & Cultural Festival.

Permits are not required to visit Barunga during the festival, but you will need your own camping gear. Once again, this is a dry community so alcohol is officially not permitted.

KATHERINE TO WESTERN AUSTRALIA
It's 513km on the Victoria Highway from Katherine to Kununurra in Western Australia.

As you approach the Western Australian border you start to see the boab trees found in much of the north-west of Australia. There's a 1½-hour time change when you cross the border. There's also a quarantine inspection post, and all fruit and vegetables must be left here. This only applies when travelling from the Territory to Western Australia.

Flora River Nature Park
This is an interesting and scenic little park that takes in 25km of the Flora River, and includes some limestone tufas (dams) which

create small waterfalls. It is still in the early stages of development, but Parks & Wildlife have just opened an all-weather camp site, complete with an amenities block. A boat ramp and canoe ramps across the tufas are also planned.

The turn-off is 90km south-west of Katherine along the Victoria Highway, and it's then a farther 45km north along a good dirt road.

Victoria River Crossing
The highway is sometimes cut by floods. If you stand on the Victoria River Bridge by the Victoria River Inn at the crossing in the Dry, it's hard to imagine that the wide river far below your feet can actually flow over the top of the bridge!

Timber Creek (pop 560)
From April to October, daily boat trips are made on the river from Timber Creek, farther west. You'll be shown fresh and saltwater crocodiles, fish and turtles being fed – try some billy tea, play the didjeridu and light a fire using fire sticks. The cost of a four-hour morning tour is $35 ($20 children) and bookings can be made at Max's Information Centre in Timber Creek (☎ 8975 0850).

You can see a boab marked by an early explorer at Gregory's Tree Historical Reserve, west of Timber Creek.

Gregory National Park
This little-visited national park to the south-west of Timber Creek covers 10,500sq km and offers good fishing, camping and bushwalking. There's also the 90km 4WD **Bullita Stock Route** which takes eight hours, although it's better to break the journey at one of the three marked camp sites. For more details contact the Parks & Wildlife office in Timber Creek (☎ 8975 0888), or the Bullita ranger (☎ 8975 0833).

Keep River National Park
Bordering Western Australia just off the Victoria Highway, this park is noted for its sandstone landforms and has some excellent walking trails. You can reach the main points

in the park by conventional vehicle during the dry season. Aboriginal art can be seen near the car park at the end of the road.

There's a rangers' station (☎ 9167 8827) 3km into the park from the main road, and there are camp sites with pit toilets at Gurrangalng (15km into the park) and Jarrnarm (28km).

MATARANKA (pop 667)
Mataranka is 103km south-east of Katherine on the Stuart Highway. The attraction is the **Mataranka Thermal Pool**, 7km off the highway just south of the small town. The crystal-clear thermal pool, in a pocket of rainforest, is a great place to wind down after a hot day on the road – though it can get crowded. There's no charge.

The pool is just a short walk from the Mataranka Homestead Resort accommodation area, which includes a backpackers' hostel, camp site, motel rooms and restaurant – it's more relaxed than it sounds since you're a long way from anywhere else.

A couple of hundred metres away is the **Waterhouse River**, where you can walk along the banks, or rent canoes and rowing boats for $5 an hour. Outside the homestead entrance is a replica of the Elsey Station Homestead which was made for the filming of *We of the Never Never* which is set near Mataranka. The replica houses the **Museum of the Never Never** with displays on the history of the Great Northern Railway, bush workshops and WWII, with a number of interesting photographs.

The **Elsey National Park** adjoins the thermal pool reserve and offers some great camping, fishing and walking along the Waterhouse River. It's also far less touristed than the thermal pools.

Places to Stay & Eat
The hostel section at the *Mataranka Homestead Resort* (☎ 8975 4544) is quite comfortable and has some single and twin rooms, though the kitchen is small. It costs $15 per person ($14 with a YHA card). Camping is $14 for a site ($18 with power), and air-con motel rooms with private

NORTHERN TERRITORY

bathroom are $63/75 for singles/doubles. In between there are self-contained cabins which cost $79 for one or two people, $88 for three people. There's a store where you can get basic groceries, a bar with snacks and meals (not cheap), or you can use the camp-site barbecues.

In Mataranka town the *Old Elsey Road-side Inn* (☎ 8975 4512) has a couple of rooms at $45/55, and the *Territory Manor Motel* (☎ 8975 4516) is a more luxurious place with a swimming pool, restaurant and motel rooms at $65/75. Alternatively, you can camp for $18 (with power). Hefty dis-counts are offered during the Wet.

The *12-Mile Yards camp site* in Elsey National Park has good facilities and plenty of grass and shade. Camping costs $5 for adults.

Getting There & Around
Long-distance buses travelling up and down the Stuart Highway call at Mataranka and the Homestead Resort.

MATARANKA TO THREEWAYS
Not far south of the Mataranka Homestead turn-off, the Roper Highway branches east off the Stuart Highway. It leads about 200km to **Roper Bar**, near the Roper River on the southern edge of Arnhem Land, where there's a store with a camp site and a few rooms – mainly visited by fishing enthusi-asts. All but about 20km of the road is sealed.

About 5km south of the Roper junction is the turn-off to the **Elsey Cemetery**, not far from the highway. Here are the graves of characters like 'the Fizzer' who came to life in *We of the Never Never*.

Larrimah (pop 100)
Continuing south from Mataranka you pass through Larrimah – at one time the railway line from Darwin came as far as Birdum, 8km south of here, but it was abandoned after Cyclone Tracy. There's an interesting little museum housed in the former repeater station opposite the pub, and there may be tourist railcar trips to Birdum – ask at the pub.

There are three camping grounds. The one on the highway at the southern end of town, *Green Park Tourist Complex* (☎ 8975 9937), charges $10 per site with power. There's a swimming pool and a few crocodiles in fenced-off ponds.

Daly Waters (pop 50)
Farther south again is Daly Waters, 3km off the highway, an important staging post in the early days of aviation – Amy Johnson landed here. The historic *Daly Waters Pub* (☎ 8975 9925), with air-con motel-type rooms at $45/55, is not surprisingly the focus of local life. It's an atmospheric place, dating from 1893 and said to be the oldest pub in the Territory, and there's good food available. The pub also has a caravan park with tent sites at $7, $12 powered – and there's another WWII airstrip with a restored hangar. The *Hi-Way Inn & Caravan Park* (☎ 8975 9925), on the Stuart Highway, has singles/doubles from $45/55 and powered camp sites at $10.

Daly Waters to Threeways
After Daly Waters, there's the fascinating ghost town of **Newcastle Waters**, a few kilometres west of the highway, and then the cattle town of **Elliott**. As you might expect, the land just gets drier and drier.

Farther south is **Renner Springs**, and this is generally accepted as the dividing line between the seasonally wet Top End and the dry Centre. The actual Renner Springs lie just to the south of the roadhouse, but are hidden in an acacia thicket. These days the water for the roadhouse comes from a bore.

About 50km before Threeways and 4km off the road along a loop of the old Stuart Highway is **Churchill's Head**, a large rock said to look like Britain's wartime prime minister, although it's hard to see any resem-blance whatsoever. Soon after, there's a memorial to Stuart at **Attack Creek**, where the explorer turned back on one of his attempts to cross Australia from south to north, reputedly after his party was attacked by a group of hostile Aboriginal people.

GULF COUNTRY

Just south of Daly Waters the single-lane, sealed Carpentaria Highway heads east to Borroloola, 378km away near the Gulf of Carpentaria and one of the best barramundi fishing spots in the Territory. After 267km the Carpentaria Highway meets the Tablelands Highway, also sealed, at the **Cape Crawford Roadhouse**. The Tablelands Highway runs 404km south to meet the Barkly Highway at **Barkly Roadhouse**; there's no petrol between these two roadhouses.

Borroloola (pop 550)

Borroloola is a small town close to the Gulf of Carpentaria. Tourism and cattle are the mainstays of the economy. The town's colourful past is preserved in the interesting displays housed in the **old police station**, which dates from 1886 and is open Monday to Friday from 10 am to noon. (At other times the key is available from the Holiday Village.) Here you can learn about the Hermit of Borroloola and the Freshwater Admiral, two of the many colourful eccentrics spawned by the local lifestyle and the subject of a David Attenborough documentary in the 1960s.

Borroloola attracts around 10,000 visitors annually, most of them coming for the fishing – the **Borroloola Fishing Classic** held in June each year draws a large number of enthusiasts. Other annual events include the inevitable Rodeo (August) and the Show (July). Croc Spot Tours (☎ 8975 8721) offers a choice of several fishing tours.

Offshore from Borroloola is **Barranyi National Park**, which is well worth a visit if you can arrange it, while 44km along the highway towards Cape Crawford is the picturesque **Caranbirini Waterhole** and **Bukalara Rock Formations**, both right by the road. There's a one-hour walking trail around the base of the eerie formations. Good walking shoes are advised, and watch the spinifex.

Places to Stay & Eat There is little shade at the *McArthur River Caravan Park* (☎ 8975

8734), in the main street, where powered sites cost $14.50 per night (add $2.50 if you're using an air-conditioner). Unpowered sites cost $12 for two adults. Cabins are $65.

The *Borroloola Inn* (☎ 8975 8766) has air-con rooms starting at $50 twin-share. Its bistro restaurant serves a range of sensibly priced and generous meals, and the Sunday-night barbecue is excellent value.

The *Borroloola Holiday Village* (☎ 8975 8742) has air-con units with attached bath, cooking facilities, colour TV and phone (from $92 for a twin room). There are four economy rooms sleeping just one person each ($50), while budget beds in the bunkhouse cost $30.

At North Island in Barranyi National Park, *North Island Paradice Fishing Tours* (☎ 0145 199 084; a satellite phone and fiercely expensive at around $2 per minute!) has accommodation at $165 per person which includes 2½-hour boat transfer, meals and fishing trips.

Getting There & Away Airnorth (☎ 1800 627 474) has three flights a week to Katherine from Darwin ($240).

THREEWAYS

Threeways, 537km north of the Alice, 988km south of Darwin and 643km west of Mt Isa, is basically a bloody long way from anywhere – apart from Tennant Creek, 26km down the Track. This is a classic 'get stuck' point for hitchhikers.

The *Threeways Roadhouse* (☎ 8962 2744) at the junction has air-con rooms at $50, or you can camp for $10 ($15 with power). Just north of the junction is a rather ugly memorial to John Flynn, the founder of the Royal Flying Doctor Service.

TENNANT CREEK (pop 3850)

Apart from Katherine, this is the only town of any size between Darwin and Alice Springs. It's 26km south of Threeways, and 511km north of Alice Springs. A lot of travellers spend a night here, and there are one or two attractions, mainly related to gold mining, to tempt you to stay a bit longer.

To the Warumungu people, Tennant Creek is Jurnkurakurr, the intersection of a number of dreaming tracks.

There's a tale that Tennant Creek was first settled when a wagonload of beer broke down here in the early 1930s and the drivers decided they might as well make themselves comfortable while they consumed the freight. The truth is somewhat more prosaic: the town was established as a result of the small gold rush around the same time. One of the major workings was **Nobles Nob**, 16km east of the town along Peko Rd. It was discovered by a one-eyed man called Jack Noble who formed a surprisingly successful prospecting partnership with the blind William Weaber. This was the biggest open-cut gold mine in the country until mining ceased in 1985. Ore from other local mines is still processed and you can visit the open cut.

Information

The Battery Hill Regional Information Centre (☎ 8962 3388) is in the old Gold Stamp Battery on Peko Rd. It's open weekdays from 9 am to 5 pm, and Saturday from 10 am to noon.

Ngalipanyangu Arts Gallery is an interesting Aboriginal-owned gallery and shop on Irvine St. Most of the items on sale are made locally and prices are lower than in Alice Springs.

Things to See

Along Peko Rd you can visit the old **Gold Stamp Battery**, where gold-bearing ore was crushed and treated. The battery is still in working order and guided tours are given at 9.30 am and 5 pm daily from April to October ($8). There's also an underground tour at 11 am ($8). Along the same road there is the **One Tank Hill lookout**. Nearby is the **Argo mine**, the main operation of the Peko company which used to mine at Warrego, north-west of Tennant Creek.

The small **National Trust Museum**, on Schmidt St near the corner of Windley St, houses six rooms of local memorabilia and reconstructed mining scenes. It's open May to October daily from 4 to 6 pm; admission is $2.

Twelve kilometres north of town are the green-roofed stone buildings of the old **telegraph station**. This is one of only four of the original 11 stations remaining in the Territory (the others are at Barrow Creek, Alice Springs and Powell Creek). The station's telegraph functions ceased in 1935 when a new office opened in the town. Today it is owned by the government and maintained by Parks & Wildlife, and it's worth a wander around.

Organised Tours

Evening tours of the Dot 6 mine close to town make an interesting diversion. You get billy tea and a fireside talk on the history of the mine and Tennant Creek gold mining generally, as well as a tour of the small underground mine. It's amazing to see the lengths people went to find the elusive mineral. The tour includes accommodation pick-up, and costs $14. Book at the transit centre on the main street or phone ☎ 8962 2168.

Norms Gold & Scenic Tours (☎ 0418 891 711) operate in the area and includes tours of the Burnt Shirt Mine ($15), an afternoon prospecting with metal detectors ($20), the Devil's Marbles ($40 including dinner), gold panning and a barbecue ($25).

Places to Stay

Camping The *Outback Caravan Park* (☎ 8962 2459) is 1km east of town along Peko Rd. It has a swimming pool, tent sites at $12 a double ($16 with power) and on-site air-con cabins for $50 a double.

The other choice is the *Tennant Creek Caravan Park* (☎ 8962 2325) on Paterson St (Stuart Highway) on the northern edge of town. It has powered sites at $15, twin 'bunkhouse' rooms at $20 per person, and on-site cabins at $40.

Hostels The *Safari Lodge Motel* (☎ 8962 2207; fax 8962 3188) has a wing of backpacker rooms right next to the Anzac Hill lookout, across the road from its main building on Davidson St. A bed in these air-cooled rooms costs $12, and there are communal cooking facilities.

Another budget alternative is the pleasant little *Tourist Rest Hostel* (☎ 8962 2719), in a shady location on the corner of Leichhardt and Windley Sts. Beds in air-con twin rooms cost $14.

Hotels & Motels Tennant Creek's motels aren't cheap. The *Safari Lodge Motel* (☎ 8962 2207) in the centre of town on Davidson St has singles/doubles for $69/79.

The *Goldfields Hotel Motel* (☎ 8962 2030), just around the corner on the highway, has singles/doubles for $55/65.

At the southern end of town the *Bluestone Motor Inn* (☎ 8962 2617) is the only place in this category with a swimming pool. Units range from $62/67.

Places to Eat
It comes as something of a surprise to find one of the most highly regarded restaurants in the Territory in the local squash centre! The *Dolly Pot Inn* on Davidson St is open daily from 11 am to midnight and offers good-value meals such as steak and salad, and also features home-made waffles.

On the main street there's *Rocky's Pasta & Pizza* (☎ 8962 2049) with, yep, pizzas and pasta, and they also do deliveries. For takeaway snacks and ice cream there's *Priester's Cafe* in the transit centre.

The Memorial Club on Schmidt St welcomes visitors and has good, straight-forward counter meals at its *Memories Bistro*.

The *Bluestone Motor Inn* and the *Eldorado Motor Lodge* both have licensed restaurants.

TENNANT CREEK TO ALICE SPRINGS
About 90km south of Tennant Creek is the **Devil's Marbles Conservation Reserve**, a haphazard pile of giant spherical boulders scattered on both sides of the road. According to Aboriginal mythology they were laid by the Rainbow Serpent. There's also a basic Parks & Wildlife camp site here. At **Wau-**chope**, just to the south of the marbles, there's a pub and caravan park.

After the Devil's Marbles there are only a few places of interest on the trip south to the Alice. Near Barrow Creek the **Stuart Memorial** commemorates John McDouall Stuart. Visible to the east of the highway is Central Mt Stuart.

At **Barrow Creek** itself there is another old post-office telegraph repeater station. It was attacked by Aboriginal people in 1874 and the station master and linesman were killed – their graves are by the road. A great number of Aboriginal people died in the inevitable reprisals.

There's also still a few hundred metres of the original line stretching north from the telegraph station. The pub here is a real outback gem, and the Barrow Creek Races in August are a colourful event which draws people in from all over the area.

The *Barrow Creek Hotel & Caravan Park* (☎ 8956 9753) has singles/doubles for $20/35 and camp sites from $7 ($9 powered).

The road continues through **Ti Tree**, where there's the Gallereaterie, a small cafe and Aboriginal art outlet, usually with artists at work.

Alice Springs

- *Pop 22,500*
The Alice Springs area is the traditional home of the Arrernte Aboriginal people, and to them it is Mparntwe. For them the heart of the area is the junction of the Charles (Anthelke Ulpeye) and Todd (Lhere Mparntwe) rivers, just north of Anzac Hill. All the topographical features of the town were formed by the creative ancestral beings – the Yeperenye, Ntyarlke and Utner-rengatye caterpillars – as they crawled across the landscape from Emily Gap (Anth-werrke), in the MacDonnell Ranges south-east of town. Alice Springs today still has a sizable Aboriginal community with strong links to the area.

The Alice, as it is usually known, was

NORTHERN TERRITORY

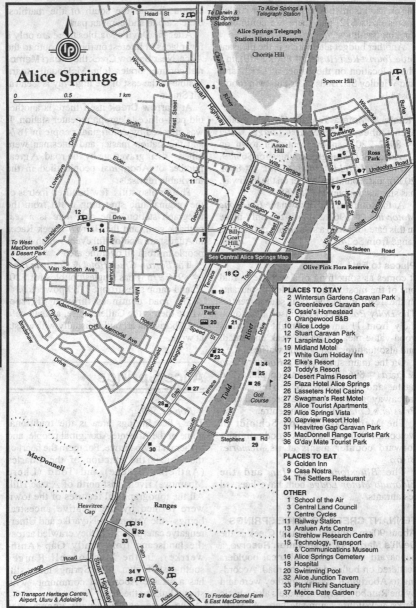

Alice Springs

0   0.5   1 km

PLACES TO STAY
2 Wintersun Gardens Caravan Park
4 Greenleaves Caravan park
5 Ossie's Homestead
6 Orangewood B&B
10 Alice Lodge
12 Stuart Caravan Park
17 Larapinta Lodge
19 Midland Motel
21 White Gum Holiday Inn
22 Elke's Resort
23 Toddy's Resort
24 Desert Palms Resort
25 Plaza Hotel Alice Springs
26 Lasseters Hotel Casino
27 Swagman's Rest Motel
28 Alice Tourist Apartments
29 Alice Springs Vista
30 Gapview Resort Hotel
31 Heavitree Gap Caravan Park
35 MacDonnell Range Tourist Park
36 G'day Mate Tourist Park

PLACES TO EAT
8 Golden Inn
9 Casa Nostra
34 The Settlers Restaurant

OTHER
1 School of the Air
3 Central Land Council
7 Centre Cycles
11 Railway Station
13 Araluen Arts Centre
14 Strehlow Research Centre
15 Technology, Transport
    & Communications Museum
16 Alice Springs Cemetery
18 Hospital
20 Swimming Pool
32 Alice Junction Tavern
33 Pitchi Richi Sanctuary
37 Mecca Date Garden

originally founded in the 1870s as a staging point for the overland telegraph line. A telegraph station was built near a permanent water hole in the bed of the dry Todd River. The river was named after Charles Todd, Superintendent of Telegraphs back in Adelaide, and a spring near the water hole was named after Alice, his wife.

A town, named Stuart, was first established in 1888, a few kilometres south of the telegraph station as a railhead for a proposed railway line. Because the railway didn't materialise immediately, the town developed slowly. Not until 1933 did the town come to be known as Alice Springs.

The Overland Telegraph Line through the Centre was built to connect with the submarine line from Darwin to Java. It was a monumental task, achieved in a remarkably short time.

Alice Springs' growth to its present size has been recent and rapid. When the name was officially changed in 1933 the population had only just reached 200! Even in the 1950s Alice Springs was still a tiny town with a population in the hundreds. Until WWII there was no sealed road to it, and it was only in 1987 that the old road south to

Port Augusta and Adelaide was finally replaced by a new, shorter and fully sealed highway.

Today, Alice Springs is a pleasant, modern town with good shops and restaurants. But while the appearance is modern, the underlying fact is that this is a fairly small rural town in a beautiful but harsh environment a bloody long way from anywhere. The realisation that the outback is only a stone's throw away, as are some of the country's most spectacular natural wonders, do give the town a unique atmosphere which is a major draw for tourists.

Orientation

The centre of Alice Springs is a conveniently compact area just five streets wide, bounded by the dry Todd River on one side and the Stuart Highway on the other. Anzac Hill forms the northern boundary to the central area while Stuart Tce is at the southern end. Many of the places to stay and virtually all of the places to eat are in this central rectangle.

Todd St is the main shopping street; from Wills Tce to Gregory Tce it is a pedestrian mall. The bus centre is centrally located at

---

Alice Events

The Alice has a string of colourful activities, particularly during the cool tourist months from May to August. The **Camel Cup**, a series of extraordinary camel races that gives rise to a frenetic, antipodian Arabia, takes place in mid-July.

The **Alice Springs Agricultural Show** takes place in early July, and the highlight is a fireworks display.

In August there's the **Alice Springs Rodeo**, when for one week the town is full of bow-legged stockmen, swaggering around in 10-gallon hats, cowboy shirts, moleskin jeans and RM Williams Cuban-heeled boots.

Finally in late September there's the event which probably draws the biggest crowds of all – the **Henley-on-Todd Regatta.** Having a series of boat races in the Todd River is slightly complicated by the fact that there is hardly ever any water in the river. Nevertheless, a whole series of races is held for sailing boats, doubles, racing eights and every other boat race class you could think of. The boats are all bottomless, the crews' legs stick out and they simply run down the course!

The **Octoberfest** is held early in October, at the end of the regatta. It's held at the Memorial Club on Gap Rd and there are many frivolous activities including spit the dummy, tug of war, and stein-lifting competitions. For the beer enthusiast there's a range of local and overseas beers and a range of cuisines.

Also through the cooler months there is a string of country **horse races** at Alice Springs and surrounding settlements like Finke, Barrow Creek, Aileron and the Harts Range. They're colourful events and for the communities involved they're the big turnouts of the year. ■

the Melanka Lodge on Todd St, one block south of the mall.

Information

Tourist Office The Central Australian Tourism Industry Association office (CATIA; ☎ 8952 5800) is in the town centre on Gregory Tce near the corner of Leichhardt Tce. The staff are helpful and there's a range of brochures and maps. The office is open weekdays from 9 am to 6 pm, and on weekends from 9 am to 4 pm. This office issues permits to travel on the Mereenie Loop Rd in the Western MacDonnell Ranges.

The *Centralian Advocate* is Alice Springs' twice-weekly newspaper.

Post & Communications The main post office is on Hartley St, and there's a row of public phones outside.

Useful Organisations Parks & Wildlife has a desk at the tourist office, with a comprehensive range of brochures on all the parks and reserves in the Centre. The main office (☎ 8951 8211) is just off the Stuart Highway, about 5km south of town.

The Department of Lands, Planning &

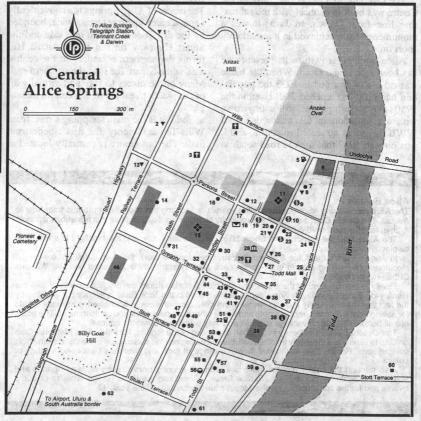

NORTHERN TERRITORY

To Alice Springs
Telegraph Station,
Tennant Creek
& Darwin

Central Alice Springs

0   150   300 m

Anzac Hill

Anzac Oval

Wills Terrace

Undoolya Road

Parsons Street

Stuart Highway

Railway Terrace

Bath Street

Hartley Street

Gregory Terrace

Stott Terrace

Leichhardt Terrace

Todd Mall

Todd River

Pioneer Cemetery

Larapinta Drive

Billy Goat Hill

Telegraph Terrace

Stuart Terrace

Todd St

Stott Terrace

To Airport, Uluru &
South Australia border

Environment office (☎ 8951 5316) on Gregory Tce is a good source for maps, as is the Automobile Association of the Northern Territory (AANT; ☎ 8953 1322), also on Gregory Tce.

Bookshops There are a couple of good bookshops. The Aranta Gallery on Todd St just south of the mall is one, and there's a branch of Angus & Robertson in the Yeperenye shopping centre on Hartley St.

Telegraph Station Historical Reserve

Laying the telegraph line across the dry, harsh centre of Australia was no easy task, as the small museum at the old telegraph station, 4.5km north of town, shows. The original spring, after which the town is named, is also here. The station, one of 12 built along the Overland Telegraph Line in the 1870s, was constructed of local stone from 1871 to 1872 and continued in operation until 1932.

The station is open daily from 8 am to 7 pm in winter, and until 9 pm in summer ($4,

$2 children). From April to October rangers give free guided tours several times a day, and a slide show three evenings a week; at other times you can use the informative brochure issued to all visitors.

The original **Alice Springs** here are a great spot for a cooling dip, and the grassy picnic area by the station has barbecues, tables and some shady gum trees – it's a popular spot on weekends.

It's easy to walk or ride to the station from the Alice – just follow the path on the western side of the riverbed; it takes about half an hour to ride. The main road out to the station is signposted to the right off the Stuart Highway about 2km north of the centre. There's another pleasant circular walk from the station out by the old cemetery and Trig Hill.

Anzac Hill

At the northern end of Todd St you can make the short, sharp ascent to the top of Anzac Hill (or you can drive there). Aboriginal people call the hill Untyeyetweleye, the site

NORTHERN TERRITORY

PLACES TO STAY					
6	Todd Tavern	44	Uncle's Tavern	29	Flynn Church
24	YHA Pioneer Hostel	45	Miss Daisy's	30	Hartley St School
25	Territory Inn	47	Overlander	32	Avis
55	Melanka Lodge		Steakhouse	36	McCafferty's
60	Alice Springs Pacific	54	KFC	37	Department of
	Resort	57	Dingo's Cafe		Lands,
					Planning &
PLACES TO EAT		**OTHER**			Environment
1	Hungry Jack's	3	Anglican Church	38	CATIA (Tourist
2	Red Rooster	4	Catholic Church		Office)
8	Al Fresco	5	Shell Service Station	39	Library & Council
13	McDonalds	7	Cinema Centre		Offices
21	Ristorante Puccini	9	Westpac Bank	40	AANT
26	Red Ochre Grill	10	ANZ Bank	43	Warumpi Arts
27	Scotty's Tavern	11	Alice Plaza	46	K-Mart
31	Pizza Hut	12	Old Courthouse	48	Hertz; Tuncks Store
33	Swingers Cafe	14	Coles (24-hr	49	Panorama Guth
34	Red Dog; Red Rock		Supermarket)	50	Territory Rent-a-Car
	Bakery ; Le	15	Yeperenye Centre	51	Papunya Tula Artists
	Cafetiere	16	Stuart Town Gaol	52	Bojangles
35	Bar Doppio (Cafe	17	The Residency	53	Aboriginal Art &
	Mediterranean);	18	GPO		Cultural Centre
	Camel's Crossing	19	Commonwealth	56	Transit Centre
	Mexican		Bank	58	CAAMA Shop
	Restaurant	20	Ansett	59	Jakurrpa Artists
41	Eranova Cafe	22	Qantas	61	Budget
42	La Casalinga	23	National Bank	62	RFDS Base
		28	Adelaide House		

of the Corkwood Dreaming, the story of a woman who lived alone on the hill. The Two Sisters ancestral beings (Arrweketye therre) are also associated with the hill.

From the top you have a fine view over modern Alice Springs and down to the MacDonnell Ranges that form a southern boundary to the town.

Old Buildings

Along Todd St you can see **Adelaide House**, built in the early 1920s and now preserved as the **John Flynn Memorial Museum**. Originally it was Alice Springs' first hospital. It's open Monday to Friday from 10 am to 4 pm, and Saturday from 10 am to noon. Admission is $3 and includes a cup of tea or coffee. Flynn, who was the founding flying doctor, is also commemorated by the **John Flynn Memorial Church** next door.

There are a number of interesting old buildings along Parsons St including the **Stuart Town Gaol** built from 1907 to 1908. It's open weekdays from 10 am to 12.30 pm, and on Saturday between 10 am and noon. The **Old Courthouse**, which was in use until 1980, is on the corner of Parsons and Hartley Sts, and now houses the fledgling **National Pioneer Women's Hall of Fame**. It is open

daily from 10 am to 2 pm. Across the road on Parsons St is the **Residency** which dates from 1926-27. It's now used for historical exhibits and is open weekdays from 9 am to 4 pm and weekends from 10 am to 4 pm.

Other old buildings include the **Hartley St School**, which now houses the National Trust office and has historical displays, and **Tuncks Store** on the corner of Hartley St and Stott Tce.

Near the corner of Parsons St and Leichhardt Tce, the old **Pioneer Theatre** is a former walk-in (rather than drive-in) cinema dating from 1944. These days it's a YHA hostel.

Museum of Central Australia

Upstairs in the Alice Plaza on the corner of Parsons St and the mall is the Museum of Central Australia. There's an interesting exhibition on meteors and meteorites (Henbury meteorites are on display). There are also exhibits on Aboriginal culture and displays of art of the Centre. It's open from 9 am to 5 pm ($2).

Royal Flying Doctor Service Base

The RFDS base is close to the town centre in Stuart Tce. It's open Monday to Saturday

Alfred Traeger & the Pedal Radio

In the 1920s the severe isolation of outback stations was a major problem. Alfred Traeger, electrical engineer and inventor from Adelaide, had for some years been playing around with radio transmitters, and was invited by the Reverend John Flynn of the Inland Mission to come to the Centre and test out some radio equipment.

Outpost transmitters were set up at Hermannsburg and Arltunga, putting both these places in instant contact with the radio at the Inland Mission in the Alice. Realising that cumbersome equipment that relied on heavy copper-oxide batteries was impractical for use in the bush, Flynn employed Traeger to come up with an alternative. He eventually designed a radio set that used bicycle pedals to drive a generator.

Flynn commissioned Traeger to manufacture 10 of the sets, and these were installed in Queensland with a base at Cloncurry. Within a few years, sets were installed in numerous locations throughout the Territory, still using the Cloncurry base. In April 1939 the Alice Springs station officially began operations.

Traeger's pedal sets revolutionised communications in the outback, and by the late 1930s voice communication (as against the previous Morse only) became the norm. Long after the pedal radio became obsolete, a two-way radio was still referred to as 'the pedal'.

Traeger was made an Officer of the Order of the British Empire in 1944, and died in Adelaide in 1980. ∎

from 9 am to 4 pm, and Sunday from 1 to 4 pm. The tours last half an hour ($3, children $1). There's a small museum, and a souvenir shop.

School of the Air

The School of the Air, which broadcasts lessons to children living on remote outback stations, is on Head St, about 3km north of the centre. During school terms you can hear a live broadcast (depending on class schedules). The school is open Monday to Saturday from 8.30 am to 4.30 pm, and Sunday from 1.30 to 4.30 pm; admission is by donation ($3).

Strehlow Research Centre

This centre, on Larapinta Dve, commemorates the work of Professor Ted Strehlow among the Arrernte people of the district (see the Hermannsburg Mission section later in this chapter). The main function of the building is to house the most comprehensive collection of Aboriginal spirit items in the country. These were entrusted to Strehlow for safekeeping by the local Aboriginal people years ago, when they realised their traditional life was under threat. Because the items are so important, and cannot be viewed by an uninitiated male or *any* female, they are kept in a vault in the centre. There is, however, a very good display on the works of Strehlow, and on the Arrernte people. Strehlow's books about the Arrernte people are still widely read.

The building itself is something of a feature, with its huge rammed-earth wall. The centre is open daily from 10 am to 5 pm ($4; no entry after 4.30 pm).

Araluen Arts Centre

The Araluen Arts Centre on Larapinta Dve has a small gallery full of **Albert Namatjira paintings**, and often other displays as well. The stained-glass windows in the foyer are the centrepiece. It's open weekdays from 10 am to 5 pm ($2).

Alice Springs Cemetery

Adjacent to the technology museum, this

Albert Namatjira (1902-59) successfully captured the essence of the Centre with paintings heavily influenced by European art

cemetery contains a number of interesting graves. The most famous is that of **Albert Namatjira** – it's the sandstone one on the far side. The headstone features a terracotta tile mural of three of Namatjira's dreaming sites in the MacDonnell Ranges. The glazes forming the mural design were painted on by Namatjira's granddaughter, Elaine, and the other work was done by other members of the Hermannsburg Potters.

Other graves in the cemetery include that of Harold Lasseter, who perished in 1931 while trying to relocate the rich gold reef he supposedly found west of Uluru 20 years earlier, and the anthropologist Olive Pink, who spent many years working with the Aboriginal people of the central deserts (see the Olive Pink Flora Reserve later in this section).

Pioneer Cemetery

This is the original Alice Springs cemetery, and today it lies almost forgotten and rarely visited in the light industrial area on the western side of the railway line on George Crescent. The gravestones here tell some of the stories of the original settlers – including that of the young man who died at Temple Bar of 'foul air'.

Panorama Guth

Panorama Guth, at 65 Hartley St in the town centre, is a huge circular panorama which is viewed from an elevated observation point. It depicts almost all the points of interest around the Centre with uncanny realism. Painted by a Dutch artist, Henk Guth, it measures about 60m in circumference ($3, children $1.50). Whether you think it's worth paying money to see a reproduction of what you may see for real is a different question! It's open from Monday to Saturday from 9 am to 5 pm, Sunday from noon to 5 pm.

Olive Pink Flora Reserve

Just across the Todd River from the centre, off Tuncks Rd, the Olive Pink Flora Reserve has a collection of shrubs and trees which are typical of the 200km area around Alice Springs. This arid-zone botanic garden is open from 10 am to 6 pm, and there's a visitors centre open from 10 am to 4 pm. There are some short walks in the reserve, including the climb to the top of Annie Meyer Hill in the Sadadeen Range, from where there's a fine view over the town. The hill is known to the Arrernte people as Tharrarltneme and is a registered sacred site. Looking to the south, in the middle distance is a small ridge running east to west; this is Ntyarlkarle Tyaneme, one of the first sites created by the caterpillar ancestors, and the name relates that this was where the caterpillars crossed the river.

Pitchi Richi Sanctuary

Just south of the Heavitree Gap causeway is Pitchi Richi ('gap in the range'), a miniature folk museum with a collection of sculptures by William Ricketts (you can see more of his interesting work in the William Ricketts Sanctuary in the Dandenongs near Melbourne) and an amazing range of various implements and other household items used by early pioneers. There's also billy tea and damper, and an interesting and lively chat on Arrernte Aboriginal lore and traditions.

The sanctuary itself doesn't look too promising, and at $15 (children $10) it's overpriced but it's still (just) worth a visit. It's open daily from 9 am to 2 pm.

Frontier Camel Farm

A farther 5km south of Pitchi Richi is the Frontier Camel Farm, where you have the chance to ride one of the beasts. These strange 'ships of the desert', guided by their Afghani masters, were the main form of transport before the railways were built. There's a museum with displays about camels, and a guided tour and camel ride is held daily at 10.30 am; 2 pm from April to October. For more details see Camel Rides under Organised Tours later in this chapter.

Also here is the **Arid Australian Reptile House**, which has an excellent collection of snakes and lizards.

The farm is open daily from 9 am to 5 pm. Entry is $5 (children $2.50), including a visit to the reptile house. For the camel tour it's $10 ($5).

Transport Heritage Centre

Transport buffs should like this centre, which features the Old Ghan Museum and the Transport Hall of Fame. It's at the Mac-Donnell Siding, off the Stuart Highway 10km south of Alice Springs. A group of local railway enthusiasts has restored a collection of Ghan locomotives and carriages on a stretch of disused siding from the old narrow-gauge Ghan railway track.

Also here is the Transport Hall of Fame, with a fine collection of old vehicles, including some very early road trains, and other transport memorabilia.

The area is open daily from 9 am to 5 pm and admission is $4 to either museum.

There are also occasional trips on the old Ghan out to Mt Ertiva Siding, 9km south of town. MacDonnell Siding is on the Alice Wanderer bus route (see Getting Around).

Alice Springs Desert Park

The Alice's newest attraction is the impressive Desert Park, 6km west of the centre along Larapinta Dve. Run by Parks & Wildlife, the park is designed to show plants and animals together in a natural setting, and so has separate habitats – currently Desert Rivers, Sand Country and Woodlands (with plans for more in the future). Although it is still new and many of the plants are small, it's well worth a visit. There's also a superb nocturnal house (claimed to be the second largest in the world). The habitats are visited by a 1.5km walking path, but be warned that the only toilets are at the entrance/exit.

The park is open daily from 9 am to 9 pm (last entry 8 pm) and you need to allow three hours for a leisurely wander around. The best time to visit is late or early in the day when the animals are most active. Entry is $12 (family $30).

Camel Rides

Camel treks are another central Australian attraction. You can have a short ride for a few dollars at the Frontier Camel Farm (π 1800 808 499), or take their longer Todd River Ramble, which is a one-hour ride along the bed of the Todd River and also includes a visit to the camel farm ($45; $25 children up to 15). They also do a Spend the Day With a Dromedary tour, which includes lunch at Ooraminna Bush Camp, for $200.

Noel Fullerton's Camel Outback Safaris (π 8956 0925), based at Stuart Well 90km south of Alice Springs, also operates short and extended camel tours (see the South to Uluru section later in this chapter).

Ballooning

Sunrise balloon trips are also popular and cost from $120 ($55 children), which includes breakfast and a 30-minute flight. One-hour flights cost around $170 (children $80).

Balloon operators include Outback Ballooning (π 1800 809 790), Ballooning Downunder (π 8952 8816) and Spinifex Ballooning (π 1800 677 893).

Organised Tours

The tourist office can tell you about all sorts of organised tours from Alice Springs. There are bus tours, 4WD tours, balloon tours, camel tours and a number of combinations which give you, say, a balloon flight and a camel ride for less than if you were to take the two separately.

Note that although many of the tours don't operate daily, there is at least one trip a day to one or more of the major attractions.

Most of the tours follow similar routes and you see much the same on them all, although the level of service and the degree of luxury will determine how much they cost. All the hostels can book tours, and they will also know which company is offering the best deals.

Town Tours AAT Kings (π 1800 334 009) and Tailormade Tours (π 1800 806 641) both do three-hour afternoon town tours for $45.

Aboriginal Culture Tours Rod Steinert Tours (π 8558 8377) operates a variety of tours, including the popular Dreamtime & Bushtucker Tour ($69, $46 children). It's a three-hour trip in which you meet some Warlpiri Aboriginal people and learn a little about their traditional life. You can tag along on the same tour with your own vehicle for $55 ($35).

Oak Valley Tours (π 8956 0959; fax 8956 0965) is an Aboriginal-owned and run organisation that makes day-trips to Ewaninga and Rainbow Valley. These trips also go to Mpwellare and Oak Valley, both on the Hugh River Stock Route and both of cultural significance to the Aboriginal people. The cost is $110 ($80 children) and this includes lunch, and morning and afternoon tea.

Uluru & Kings Canyon Sahara Outback Tours (π 1800 806 240) offers very good daily camping trips to Uluru (Ayers Rock) and elsewhere; these are popular with backpackers. It charges $220 for a two-day trip to the Rock and Kata Tjuta (the Olgas), or you can pay an extra $100 and spend an extra day taking in Kings Canyon – well worthwhile if you have the time.

AKT Holidays (π 1800 891 121), Tracks Outback Expeditions (π 1800 641 100) and Trek-About Tours (π 1800 818 011) are other cheaper operators.

NORTHERN TERRITORY

If your time is really limited you can take a one-day air safari to Uluru and back for $439 ($339 children), which includes a tour around the Rock or climbing it, a trip to Kata Tjuta, buffet lunch and sunset viewing and entry fees. A cheaper option ($338/263) is to travel one way by bus. Contact Airnorth Safaris (☎ 8952 6666).

Other Tours There are plenty of day tours to the other main attractions of the Centre, including the East and West MacDonnells, Palm Valley and Rainbow Valley, Simpsons Gap and Standley Chasm.

Places to Stay – bottom end
Camping There's a number of camping options in Alice Springs:

G'Day Mate Tourist Park (☎ 8952 9589)
Palm Circuit; camp sites ($14, $16 with power) and self-contained cabins which accommodate up to six people ($46 double, $7 each extra adult)
Heavitree Gap Caravan Park (☎ 8952 4866)
Palm Circuit, 4km south of town; camp sites ($12, $15 with power)
MacDonnell Range Tourist Park (☎ 8952 6111)
Palm Place, 5km from town; camp sites ($14.50, $17.50 with power), and on-site cabins ($34 to $76)
Stuart Caravan Park (☎ 8952 2547)
2km west on Larapinta Dve, camp sites ($13, $16 with power), six-bed on-site vans ($35, plus $6 each extra adult) and four-bed cabins ($49, $7)
Wintersun Gardens Caravan Park (☎ 8952 4080)
2.5km north on the Stuart Highway; camp sites ($13, $16 with power), six-bed on-site vans ($36 double, plus $7 each extra adult) and six-bed cabins ($41 to $52 double, $7)

Hostels There are plenty of hostels and guesthouses in Alice Springs. All the places catering to backpackers have the usual facilities and services – pool, courtesy bus, travel desk, bicycle hire etc.

Right in the centre of town, on the corner of Leichhardt Tce and Parsons St in the old Pioneer walk-in cinema, is the YHA *Pioneer Hostel* (☎ 8952 8855; fax 8952 4144). It has beds in air-con dorms: $14 in a four-share room and $15 for a twin; nonmembers pay $2 more. There's a swimming pool, and bicycles for hire.

Also central is the popular *Melanka Lodge* (☎ 1800 815 066; fax 8952 4587) at 94 Todd St, just a couple of steps from the bus station. This is a large place with a variety of air-con rooms, ranging from eight-bed dorms at $12 through to four-bed dorms at $14 and twin-shares at $16 per person. There are also singles/doubles for $30/32, or $55/65 with TV, fridge and bathroom. The communal kitchen is not that well equipped and tends to be pretty grubby. There's a cafeteria, and its Waterhole Bar is the most popular travellers' drinking spot in the Alice.

Over the river and still just a short walk from the centre, is the relaxed *Alice Lodge* (☎ 8953 1975) at 4 Mueller St. This is a small, quiet and friendly hostel with a garden and pool. Nightly rates are $12 in the 10-bed dorm, $14 in a four-bed room, $25 for a single and $16 per person in a double ($1 less for VIP and YHA). There's a small kitchen, pool, barbecue and laundry facilities.

Also on this side of the river at 18 Warburton St is *Ossie's Homestead* (☎ 1800 628 211). B&B in the 12-bed dorm is $12, in a four-bed room $14, and in a double $32 ($1 less for VIP, YHA and Nomads members). There's a swimming pool and the usual facilities, as well as a pet kangaroo. Ossie's also runs trail rides, costing from $60 to $205.

Back on the other side of the river, at 41 Gap Rd, is *Toddy's Resort* (☎ 1800 806 240; fax 8952 1767). This complex has laundry facilities and a communal kitchen (few utensils and not very clean) for those not in the self-contained units. There's a swimming pool, barbecue and small shop on the site. Prices are $10 for six-bed dorms with shared facilities, $12 with TV and bathroom, $34 for doubles ($45 with bathroom). Cheap meals are available and there's also bike hire.

Right next door is *Elke's Resort* (☎ 8952 8134; fax 8952 8143), a new backpackers' in an old apartment building consisting of two-bedroom self-contained units. Beds (six to eight in a unit) cost $13, or doubles are $40.

Places to Stay – middle
Hotels Right by the river at 1 Todd St mall is the *Todd Tavern* (☎ 8952 1255). This pub

gets noisy when there are bands playing on weekends, but it's otherwise quite a reasonable place to stay. Rates are $38 for singles/doubles (some with bathroom) including a light breakfast.

At the southern end of Gap Rd is the *Gapview Resort Hotel* (☎ 1800 896 124; fax 8952 8312). It's about 1km from the centre, and charges from $66 to $95 for double room with bathroom, fridge and TV.

Apartments & Holiday Flats There are very few apartments and flats for rent; in most cases the best you can do is a motel-type room with limited cooking facilities, which usually consists of an electric frypan and a microwave oven.

The *Alice Tourist Apartments* (☎ 1800 806 142; fax 8953 2950) are on Gap Rd. There are one and two-room, self-contained, air-con apartments for $72 for a double, $105 for four and $115 for six people; about $10 less in summer. These places consist of a main room with sleeping, cooking and dining facilities, and the larger flats have a second room with two or four beds. These are a good option for families.

The *White Gum Holiday Inn* (☎ 1800 896 131; fax 8953 2092) at 17 Gap Rd, also has rooms with separate kitchen at $90 for up to four people.

On Barrett Dve, next to the Plaza Hotel Alice Springs, the *Desert Palms Resort* (☎ 1800 678 037; fax 8953 4176) has spacious rooms, each with limited cooking facilities, at $78 for two. There's a large island swimming pool, and nicely landscaped gardens.

Conveniently central is *Larapinta Lodge* (☎ 8952 7255; fax 8952 7101), at 3 Larapinta Dve just over the railway line from the town centre. It has singles/doubles for $67/77, with communal kitchen and laundry, and the obligatory swimming pool.

Motels Alice Springs has a rash of motels, and prices range from around $50 to $100 for a double room. There are often lower prices and special deals during the hot summer months.

At 67 Gap Rd there's the *Swagman's Rest Motel* (☎ 1800 089 612) with singles/doubles for $60/70. The units are self-contained and there's a swimming pool.

At 4 Traeger Ave is the *Midland Motel* (☎ 8952 1588; fax 8952 8280) which charges from $55/65 for its singles/doubles, and there's also a licensed restaurant.

On Leichhardt Tce facing the Todd River is the *Territory Inn* (☎ 1800 089 644; fax 8952 7829), with every available mod-con from $115. There's a licensed restaurant here and meals can be served in your unit.

B&B *Orangewood Alice Springs* (☎ 8952 4114; fax 8952 4664) at 9 McMinn St is a low-key option in a quiet residential street. Rooms with shared facilities cost from $130 to $150 for a double.

A few kilometres north of town, and just off the Stuart Highway, is the very pleasant *Bond Springs Station* (☎ 8952 98988; fax 8953 0963; bondhmst@alice.aust.com). A range of accommodation is offered on this historic working cattle station. All rooms are tastefully furnished, heated and have air-conditioning. The tariff includes breakfast, and evening meals can be taken around the large dining table in the homestead kitchen. The cost is from $50/62 in the budget rooms up to $200 for a suite, or there's an entire cottage for $240 (sleeps five).

Places to Stay – top end
The top-end accommodation is all on the eastern side of the river where there's more room to spread out.

At the top of the range there's the *Plaza Hotel Alice Springs* (☎ 1800 675 212; fax 8952 3822), on Barrett Dve, with rooms from $205 up to $460. The hotel is very well equipped, with facilities including heated pool, spa/sauna and tennis courts.

Almost next door is the *Lasseters Hotel Casino* (☎ 1800 808 975; fax 8953 1680) with double rooms from $150.

Another top-end option is the *Alice Springs Pacific Resort* (☎ 1800 805 055; fax 8953 0995) at 34 Stott Tce right by the Todd River, not far from the centre of town.

Rooms here go for $140/150, and it includes such luxuries as a heated pool.

Lastly there's the *Alice Springs Vista* (☎ 1800 810 664; fax 8952 1988), stuck in the middle of nowhere at the foot of the MacDonnell Ranges on Stephens Rd. The 121 units here go for $120. The resort has a pool, tennis court and barbecue facilities.

Places to Eat
Cafes, Snacks & Fast Food There are numerous places for a sandwich or light snack along the Todd St mall. Many have tables and chairs outside – ideal for breakfast on a cool, sunny morning.

Le Cafetiere is at the southern end of the mall and is open for breakfast, burgers, sandwiches etc. Right next door is the *Red Dog*, a very similar place with tables and umbrellas out on the footpath. Also here is the *Red Rock Bakery*.

The Alice Plaza has a lunch-time cafeteria-style eating place called *Fawlty's* with snacks, light meals, sandwiches and a salad bar. Also here is *Piccolo Puccini*, a pasta joint with dishes from $7; and the *Red Centre Chinese*, a small cafe with eat-in and takeaway food from $5.

In the Yeperenye shopping centre on Hartley St there's the *Boomerang Coffee Shop,* the *Bakery*, another *Fawlty's* outlet and a big Woolworths supermarket.

The closest Alice Springs comes to a New Age cafe is the anonymous *Bar Doppio* (*Cafe Mediterranean*), tucked away in the small Fan Lane off the mall, opposite the Red Dog cafe. It has an excellent range of health-food dishes, and a very relaxed atmosphere. You can BYO and the front window is a good place to check out the notices for what's happening around town. Dishes here cost around $5 to $10.

The *Swingers Cafe* on Gregory Tce has an eclectic menu, with dishes such as focaccia, and foreign treats like curry laksa. It's a good spot, despite the silly name.

Another popular place, especially on Friday evening, is *Uncle's Tavern* on the corner of Gregory Tce and Hartley St. Here you can have a beer or a cappuccino, as well as light meals and snacks.

The *Eranova Cafe*, at 70 Todd St, is one of the busiest eating spots in town and it's a comfortable place, with a good selection of excellent food. It's open for breakfast, lunch and dinner from Monday to Saturday. Meals range from $8 to $15.

Dingo's Cafe on Todd St has a pleasant indoor/outdoor setting, but is not that cheap – a game pie and chips will set you back $7.50.

Alice Springs also has its share of the well-known fast-food outlets.

Pub Meals Far and away the most popular place is the *PubCaf* at the Todd Tavern. The food is tasty and cheap, and there are specials on most nights, when you can get a large meal for $8 to $10.

Scotty's Tavern is a small bar in the mall, and it has substantial main courses, such as barramundi or steak, for $18; other main courses range from $12 to $16.

The noisy *Stuart Arms Hotel* in the Alice Plaza has a fairly unexciting bistro with meals from $9 to $12.

Restaurants At 105 Gregory Tce, *La Casalinga* has been serving up pasta and pizza for many years; it's open from 5 pm to 1 am every night. Meals cost $12 to $16 and it has a bar. You can also get good pasta at the licensed *Al Fresco* at the northern end of the mall. It's open daily from 10 am.

Also in the centre is the licensed *Red Ochre Grill*, opposite Adelaide House. It specialises in modern Australian cuisine, and as well as the usual Territory game meats, there's also a dash of bush tucker, with ingredients such as wattle seeds, yams, warrigal greens and bush tomatoes making an appearance. Lunch is $7 to $14, dinner $12 to $20.

The *Ristorante Puccini* is also on the mall and serves excellent home-made pasta and char-grilled fish, and has Italian-inspired desserts such as marinated fruit with ricotta zabaglione. Expect to pay around $20 for a main course. It's open for lunch on weekdays, and dinner every night.

Across the river from the centre, on the corner of Undoolya Rd and Sturt Tce, *Casa Nostra* is another pizza and pasta specialist.

Of course the Alice has to have a steakhouse, so you can try the *Overlander Steakhouse* at 72 Hartley St. It features 'Territory food' such as beef, buffalo, kangaroo and camel – and the 'Drover's Blowout' ($60 including drinks and accommodation transfers) is a carnivore's delight! It's quite popular, but not that cheap, with main courses in the $20 to $25 range.

Miss Daisy's at the Diplomat Motor Inn on Hartley St features a variety of exotic Territory flora and fauna on its menu – including emu steaks and desert plum sorbet.

Hidden away at the rear of Fan Lane off the mall is the *Camel's Crossing Mexican Restaurant*, which has a varied menu of both vegetarian and meat dishes. It's open nightly except Sunday, and a two-course meal will set you back about $25.

There are a number of Chinese restaurants around the Alice. The *Oriental Gourmet* is on Hartley St, near the corner of Stott Tce. *Chopsticks*, on Hartley St at the Yeperenye shopping centre, is only open in the evenings. Also good is the bright yellow *Golden Inn* on Undoolya Rd, just over the bridge from the centre. Aside from the usual items you can sample some Malaysian and Szechuan dishes. It's open for lunch on weekdays and for dinner every day.

Dining Tours There are a few interesting alternatives which involve taking a ride out of town. One of these is the *Camp Oven Kitchen* (☎ 8953 1411). The meal consists of soup, roast meats and golden syrup dumplings, all cooked in 'camp ovens' – cast-iron pots which are buried in hot coals. The cost is $59 ($45 children), including transfers.

Following a similar theme, but with some bush lore thrown in, are the trips by Tailormade Tours (☎ 1800 806 641), but these cost $75 and require a minimum of 15 people.

Take a Camel to Breakfast/Dinner is another popular dining option. This combines a one-hour camel ride with a meal at the Frontier Camel Farm (☎ 1800 806 499).

The cost is $55 ($35 children aged six to 12) for breakfast and $80 ($60) for dinner.

Entertainment

There's not much. At the Todd Tavern, by the river on the corner of Wills and Leichhardt terraces, there's occasional live bands.

The *Legends Nightclub* in the Alice Plaza is the town's one and only. *Bojangles* is a restaurant and nightclub on Todd St, and the *Alice Junction Tavern* on Palm Circuit has a disco on Friday and Saturday nights.

The *Waterhole Bar* at the Melanka Lodge on Todd St is the place for a beer and to meet other travellers, and there's occasionally live bands as well.

Outback character and raconteur Ted Egan puts on a performance of tall tales and outback songs four nights a week during winter at the *Settlers Restaurant* (☎ 8952 9952). Advance booking is essential.

There are all sorts of events at the *Araluen Arts Centre* on Larapinta Dve, including temporary art exhibits, theatre and music performances and regular films. Bookings can be made at the Araluen booking office (☎ 8952 5022).

On Todd St there's a *cinema centre* which shows standard release movies.

If you want to watch the Australian gambling enthusiasm in a central Australian setting head for *Lasseter's Casino* on Barrett Dve, but dress up.

Things to Buy

Alice Springs has a number of art galleries and craft centres. If you've got an interest in central Australian art or you're looking for a piece to buy, there's a number of Aboriginal-owned places where your money goes directly to the community.

The Aboriginal Art & Cultural Centre at 86 Todd St near the corner of Stott Tce is well worth a look. It is owned and run by the southern Arrernte people, and in addition to selling reasonably priced paintings and artefacts, they also have didjeridu lessons, and boomerang and spear throwing.

The Papunya Tula Artists shop, close by at 78 Todd St just south of the mall, specialises in western desert art, or there's Jukurrpa Artists on the corner of Gap Rd and Leichhardt Tce. At 105 Gregory Tce there's Warumpi Arts, which is owned and run by the Papunya community.

The Central Australian Aboriginal Media Association (CAAMA) shop opposite the transit centre at 101 Todd St is another good place, and prices are not too unreasonable.

This is not to dismiss the outlets which are not Aboriginal owned, it's just that the percentage which actually gets back to the creators of the art is likely to be much smaller. Two of the better ones are Gallery Gondwana and the Australian Aboriginal Dreamtime Gallery, both in the Todd St mall.

Getting There & Away

Air You can fly to Alice Springs with Qantas (☎ 13 1313) or Ansett (☎ 13 1300). The two companies face each other on Todd St at the Parsons St intersection.

Alice Springs to Adelaide costs $402, Uluru $200, Darwin $381, Melbourne $558, Perth $539 and Sydney $560. You can also fly direct to Uluru from Adelaide, Sydney, Perth and Cairns. So if you're planning to fly to the Centre and visit Uluru it would be more economical to fly straight to Uluru, then continue to Alice Springs. See Getting There & Away under the Uluru-Kata Tjuta section for more details.

On the regional routes, Airnorth (☎ 1800

The Ghan

Australia's great railway adventure would have to be the Ghan. The Ghan went through a major change in 1982 and although it's now a rather more modern and comfortable adventure, it's still a great trip.

The Ghan saga started in 1877 when it was decided to build a railway line from Adelaide to Darwin. It took over 50 years to reach Alice Springs, and they're still thinking about the final 1500km to Darwin more than a century later. The basic problem was that they made a big mistake right at the start, a mistake that wasn't finally sorted out until 1980. They built the line in the wrong place.

The grand error was a result of concluding that because all the creek beds north of Marree were bone dry, and because nobody had seen rain, there wasn't going to be rain in the future. In fact they laid the initial stretch of line right across a flood plain and when the rain came the line was simply washed away. In the century or so that the original Ghan line survived it was a regular occurrence for the tracks to be washed away.

The wrong route was only part of the Ghan's problems. At first it was built wide gauge to Marree, then extended narrow gauge to Oodnadatta in 1884. And what a jerry-built line it was – the foundations were flimsy, the sleepers were too light, the grading was too steep and it meandered hopelessly. It was hardly surprising that even in its final days the top speed of the old Ghan was 30km/h!

Early rail travellers went from Adelaide to Marree on the broad-gauge line, changed there to narrow gauge as far as Oodnadatta, then had to make the final journey to Alice Springs by camel train. The Afghani-led camel trains had pioneered transport through the outback and it was from these Afghanis that the Ghan took its name.

Finally in 1929 the line was extended from Oodnadatta to Alice Springs. Though the Ghan was a great adventure, it simply didn't work. At the best of times it was chronically slow and uncomfortable as it bounced and bucked its way down the badly laid line. Worse, it was unreliable and expensive to run. And worst of all, a heavy rainfall could strand it at either end or even in the middle. Parachute drops of supplies to stranded train travellers became part of outback lore and on one occasion the Ghan rolled in 10 days late!

By the early 70s the South Australian state railway system was taken over by the Federal government and a new line to Alice Springs was planned. The $145 million line was to be standard gauge and laid from Tarcoola, north-west of Port Augusta on the transcontinental line, to Alice Springs – and it would be laid where rain would not wash it out. In 1980 the line was completed in circumstances that would be unusual for any major project today – it was ahead of time and on budget.

In 1982 the old Ghan made its last run and the old line was subsequently torn up. One of its last appearances was in the film *Mad Max III*.

Whereas the old train took 140 passengers and, under ideal conditions, made the trip in 50 hours, the new train takes twice as many passengers and does it in 24 hours. It's still the Ghan, but it's not the trip it once was. ∎

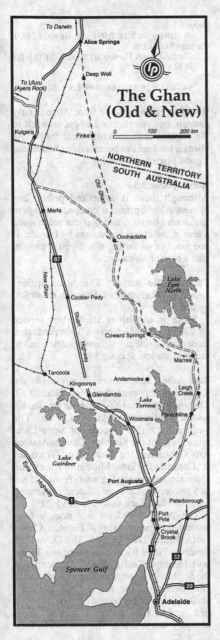

**The Ghan
(Old & New)**

0   100   200 km

627 474) has flights to Uluru twice daily ($200), and daily except Saturday flights to Darwin ($381), Katherine ($369) and Tennant Creek ($199).

Bus Greyhound Pioneer (☎ 13 2030) at the Melanka Lodge on Todd St has daily services from Alice Springs to Yulara ($84), Darwin ($148), Adelaide ($148) and Katherine ($37). It takes about 20 hours from Alice Springs to Darwin (1491km) or Alice Springs to Adelaide (1544km). You can connect to other places at various points up and down the Track – Threeways for Mt Isa and the Queensland coast, Katherine for Western Australia, Erldunda for Uluru, Port Augusta for Perth.

McCafferty's (☎ 13 1499) at 91 Gregory Tce also has daily departures to Adelaide ($135) and Darwin ($145). To Coober Pedy the fare is $69, to Katherine $133 and to Yulara $55.

Train One-way fares on the Ghan between Adelaide and Alice Springs cost $170 in coach class (no sleeper and no meals), $351 in holiday class (a sleeper with shared facilities and no meals) and $539 in 1st class (a self-contained sleeper and meals). Low-season (February through June) fares are slightly less. For bookings phone ☎ 13 2232 during office hours.

The train departs from Adelaide on Monday and Thursday at 2 pm, arriving in Alice Springs the next morning at 9.55 am. From Alice Springs the departures are on Friday and Tuesday at 2 pm, arriving in Adelaide the next day at 10 am.

You can also join the Ghan at Port Augusta, the connecting point on the Sydney to Perth route, and you can transport cars between Alice Springs and Adelaide for $290.

Car The basic thing to remember about getting to Alice Springs is that it's a long way from anywhere, although at least roads to the north and south are sealed. Coming in from Queensland it's 1180km from Mt Isa to Alice Springs or 529km from Threeways (five hours), where the Mt Isa road meets the Darwin to Alice Springs road (the Stuart Highway). Darwin to Alice Springs is 1491km (15 hours), to Yulara it's 443km (4½ hours) and to Kings Canyon 331km (four hours).

These are outback roads, but you're not yet in the *real* outer outback, where a breakdown can mean big trouble. Nevertheless, it's wise to have your vehicle well prepared since getting someone to come out to fix it's likely to be very expensive. While fuel is readily available, make sure you know where the next service station is, and don't cut things too fine.

Similarly, you are unlikely to die of thirst waiting for a vehicle to come by if you do break down, but it's still wise to carry quite a bit of water. Roads can sometimes be made impassable by a short, sharp rainfall and you'll have to wait for the water to recede. It usually won't take long on a sealed road, but you could have to wait rather a long time for a dirt road to dry out and become passable.

Car Rental All the major hire companies have offices in Alice Springs, and Avis, Budget, Hertz and Territory Rent-a-Car also have counters at Alice Springs airport. Avis, Budget, Hertz and Territory all have 4WDs for hire. It's around $95 per day for a Suzuki, including insurance and 100km per day. For a Toyota Landcruiser or similar the price jumps to around $150 per day. Discounts apply for longer rentals (above four to seven days, depending on the company).

Brits:Australia (Koala Campers) has campers and 4WDs for hire, and with country-wide offices one-way rentals become an option. The cost is around $140 per day for unlimited kilometres, plus $20 for insurance, but there is a seven-day minimum rental period.

Avis
    52 Hartley St (☎ 1800 672 099; fax 8953 0087)
Brits:Australia & Koala Camper Rentals
    Cnr Stuart Highway & Power St (☎ 1800 331 454; fax 8953 1441)
Budget
    10 Gap Rd (☎ 8952 8899; fax 8952 5308)

Hertz
    76 Hartley St (☎ 1800 891 112; fax 8952 5493)
Territory Rent-a-Car
    Cnr Stott Tce & Hartley St (☎ 1800 891 125; fax 8952 9797)
Thrifty
    94 Todd St (☎ 1800 634 499; fax 8952 6560)

Hitching Hitching to or from Alice is easy enough, but you do need to get yourself to the edge of town to avoid local traffic. As always, backpacker hostel notice boards are a good place to look for lifts.

Getting Around

Although there is a limited public bus system, Alice Springs is compact enough to get around on foot, and you can reach quite a few of the closer attractions by bicycle. If you want to go farther afield you'll have to take a tour or rent a car.

To/From the Airport The Alice Springs airport is 14km south of the town, about $20 by taxi.

There is an airport shuttle bus service (☎ 8953 0310) which meets flights and takes passengers to all city accommodation and to the train station. It costs $9.

Bus Asbus buses leave from outside the Yeperenye shopping centre on Hartley St. The southern route (No 4) runs along Gap Rd to the southern outskirts of town. The western route (No 1) goes out along Larapinta Dve, for the Strehlow Centre, Araluen Arts Centre and the Technology, Transport & Communications Museum. Buses run approximately every 1½ hours from 7.45 am to 6 pm on weekdays and Saturday morning only. The fare for a short trip is $1.20.

The Alice Wanderer bus does a loop around the major sights – Frontier Camel Farm, Mecca Date Garden, The Olive Pink Reserve, Pitchi Richi Sanctuary, the Transport Heritage Centre, Flying Doctor Base, the Strehlow Centre, Panorama Guth, Anzac Hill, School of the Air and the telegraph station. You can get on and off wherever you like, and it runs every 70 minutes from around 9 am to 3 pm. The cost is $18 for a

NORTHERN TERRITORY

full day (or $50 including entry fees), and if you phone ahead (☎ 8952 2111), you can be picked up from your accommodation prior to the 9 am departure. The most convenient pick-up point is the Melanka Lodge.

Car See Getting There & Away earlier for details on car rental.

Bicycle Alice Springs has a number of bicycle tracks and a bike is a great way to get around town and out to the closer attractions, particularly in winter. The best place to rent a bike is from the hostel you're staying at. Typical rates are $10 per day.

Centre Cycles (☎ 8953 2966) at 14 Lindsay Ave east of the town centre has 15-speed mountain bikes for $12 per day, or $45 per week. It's advisable to book ahead in winter.

The MacDonnell Ranges

Outside Alice Springs there are a great number of places you can visit within a day or with overnight stops thrown in. Generally they're found by heading east or west along the roads running parallel to the MacDonnell Ranges, which are directly south of Alice Springs.

Places farther south are usually visited on the way to Uluru.

The scenery in the ranges is superb. There are many gorges that cut through the rocky cliffs and their sheer walls are spectacular. In the shaded gorges there are rocky water holes, a great deal of wildlife (which can be seen if you're quiet and observant) and wildflowers in the spring.

You can get out to these gorges on group tours or with your own transport. Some of the closer ones are accessible by bicycle or on foot. By yourself, the Centre's eerie emptiness and peace can touch you in a way that is impossible in a big group.

Getting There & Away
Unfortunately, and somewhat surprisingly, there is no scheduled transport to either the Eastern or Western Macs, so without your own transport you're stuck with taking a tour. Virtually all places are covered by tours from the Alice, so it's a matter of looking around to find one which suits.

EASTERN MACDONNELL RANGES
Heading south from Alice Springs and just through the Heavitree Gap, there is a sign for the Ross Highway. The highway is sealed all the way to the Trephina Gorge turn-off, about 75km from Alice Springs. It's in pretty good condition most of the way to Arltunga, about 100km from Alice Springs. From here the road bends back north and west to rejoin the Stuart Highway 50km north of Alice Springs, but this section is a much rougher road and sometimes requires a 4WD.

Emily & Jessie Gaps Nature Park
Emily Gap, 16km out of town, is the next gap through the ranges east of the Heavitree Gap – it's narrow and often has water running through it. Known to the Arrernte as Anthwerrke, this is one of the most important Aboriginal sites in the Alice Springs area as it was from here that the caterpillar ancestral beings of Mparntwe (Alice Springs) originated.

The gap is registered as a sacred site and there are some well-preserved paintings on the eastern wall, although it often involves a swim to get to them.

Jessie Gap is only 8km farther on and, like the previous gap, is a popular picnic and barbecue spot.

The two gaps are important to the Eastern Arrernte people as they are associated with the Caterpillar Dreaming trail.

Corroboree Rock Conservation Reserve
Shortly after Jessie Gap there's the Undoolya Gap, another pass through the range, then the road continues 43km to Corroboree Rock. There are many strangely shaped outcrops of rocks in the range and this one is said to have been used by Aboriginal people as a storehouse for sacred objects. It is a registered

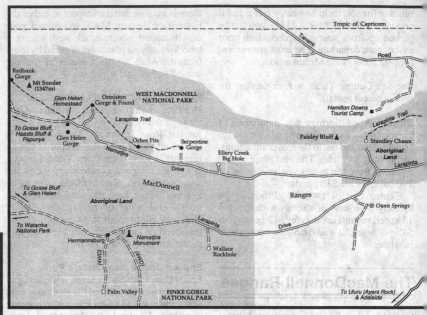

sacred site and is listed on the National Estate. Despite the name, it is doubtful if the rock was ever used as a corroboree area, due to the lack of water in the vicinity.

Trephina Gorge Nature Park

About 60km out, and a few kilometres north of the road, is Trephina Gorge. It's wider and longer than the other gaps in the range – here you are well north of the main MacDonnell Ranges and in a new ridge. There's a good walk along the edge of the gorge, and the trail then drops down to the sandy creek bed and loops back to the starting point.

Keen walkers can follow a longer trail (about five hours), which continues to the delightful **John Hayes Rockhole**, a few kilometres west of Trephina Gorge. Here the sheltered section of a deep gorge provides a series of water holes which retain water long after the more exposed places have dried up. You can clamber around the rockholes or follow the 90-minute Chain of Ponds marked

trail which takes you up to a lookout above the gorge and then back through the gorge – perhaps you'll see why it is also called the Valley of the Eagles.

There's an excellent camp site at the gorge, and a smaller one (only two sites) at John Hayes Rockhole. There's a fee of $1 per adult for camping.

Ross River Homestead

From Trephina Gorge it's 10km south-east to the *Ross River Homestead* (☎ 1800 241 711; fax 8956 9823). It's much favoured by coach tours, but is equally good for independent visitors. It's a friendly sort of place and there's lots to do, including walks in the spectacular surrounding countryside, excursions to other attractions, short camel rides or safaris and horse-riding. Or simply lazing around with a cold one.

Air-con cabins with en-suite cost $107 for two; four-bed dorms are $13 per person; or you can camp for $12 for two ($16 powered).

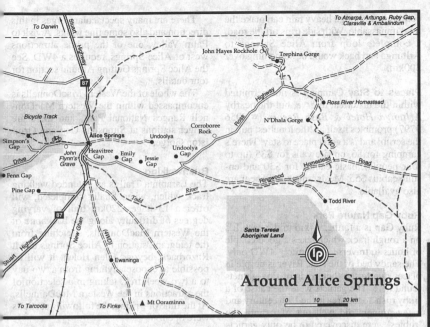

Around Alice Springs

(Map labels:)
To Darwin
Stuart Highway
John Hayes Rockhole
Trephina Gorge
To Atnarpa, Arltunga, Ruby Gap, Claraville & Ambalindum
Ross River Homestead
Ross Highway
Bicycle Track
N'Dhala Gorge
Corroboree Rock
Simpson's Gap
Drive
Alice Springs
Undoolya
Undoolya Gap
Heavitree Gap
John Flynn's Grave
Emily Gap
Jessie Gap
Homestead Road
Fenn Gap
Pine Gap
Todd River
Ringwood
Todd River
Stuart Highway
New Ghan
Santa Teresa Aboriginal Land
Ewaninga
0 10 20 km
To Tarcoola
To Finke
Mt Ooraminna

There's also a restaurant, which has good food, and a very popular bar.

N'Dhala Gorge Nature Park

N'Dhala Gorge is about 10km south of Ross River Homestead and has around 6000 ancient Aboriginal rock carvings, although they're generally not easy to spot. You may see rock wallabies. The track into N'Dhala from Ross River is sandy and requires 4WD. It's possible to turn off before the gorge and loop around it to return to Alice Springs by the Ringwood Homestead road, but this also requires a 4WD.

There's a small camp site here with a toilet, but you need to bring your own water and firewood. The flies are friendly, too.

Arltunga Historical Reserve

At the eastern end of the MacDonnell Ranges, 110km north-east of Alice Springs, Arltunga is a gold-mining ghost town. Gold was discovered here in 1887 and 10 years

later reef gold was discovered, but by 1912 the mining activity had petered out. Old buildings, a couple of cemeteries and the many deserted mine sites are all that remain. Alluvial (surface) gold has been completely worked out in the Arltunga Reserve, but there may still be gold further afield in the area, and in fact mining has recommenced in recent years (although it's some distance from the old town). There are plenty of signs to explain things and some old mine shafts you can safely descend and explore a little way. The reserve has an excellent visitors centre, with many old photographs and some displays. There's a ranger-guided tour of one of the mines on Sunday afternoon at 2.30 pm, and during school holidays in June and September the old gold battery at the visitors centre is fired up on Tuesday, Thursday and Sunday at 11 am.

The 40km section of road between Arltunga and the turn-off just before Ross River Homestead is unsealed but in good condition, although heavy rain can make the road impassable. With side trips off the road, a complete loop from Alice Springs to Arltunga and back would be something over 300km.

Places to Stay Camping is not permitted within the historical reserve, but the nearby *Arltunga Hotel & Bush Resort* (☎ 8956 9797) promotes itself as 'the loneliest pub in the scrub' and is a good place to stay. There's camping for $6, on-site vans for $35 (up to four people), basic cabins for $30 and en-suite cabins $55. Meals, snacks and beer are also available.

Ruby Gap Nature Park
Ruby Gap is a farther 44km to the east. It's on a rough track which takes a good couple of hours to traverse – definitely 4WD only. The sandy bed of the Hale River is purple in places due to the thousands of tiny garnets found here. The garnets were the cause of a 'ruby rush' to the area in the 19th century and a few miners did well out of it until the 'rubies' were discovered to be only garnets and virtually worthless. It's a remote and evocative place, and is well worth the effort involved in reaching it.

There's excellent bush camping along the riverbank in the park, and there are some beautiful spots. However, this is a remote area and you need to be well equipped – and bring your own water and collect firewood on the way in.

Lakers Outback Scenic Tours (☎ 8953 3131) has two-day trips from Alice Springs (departing Saturday) for $240, with accommodation at Ross River Homestead.

WESTERN MACDONNELL RANGES
Heading west from the Alice, Larapinta Dve divides just beyond Standley Chasm: Namatjira Dve continues slightly north-west and is sealed all the way to Glen Helen, 132km from town. Beyond there the road continues to Haasts Bluff and Papunya, in Aboriginal land. From the fork near Standley Chasm, Larapinta Dve continues south-west to Hermannsburg and beyond.

There are many spectacular gorges in this direction and also some fine walks. A visit to Palm Valley, one of the prime attractions west of Alice Springs, requires a 4WD. See the Alice Springs Getting Around section for tour details.

The whole of the Western MacDonnells is encompassed within the Western MacDonnell Ranges National Park, and there are ranger stations at Simpsons Gap and Ormiston Gorge.

Bushwalking
The Larapinta Trail is an extended walking track which, when finally completed, will offer a 13-stage, 220km trail of varying degrees of difficulty along the backbone of the Western MacDonnells, stretching from the telegraph station in Alice Springs to Mt Razorback, beyond Glen Helen. It will be possible to choose anything from a two-day to a two-week trek, taking in a selection of the attractions in the Western MacDonnells. At the time of writing, the following sections were open:

Section 1: Alice Springs Telegraph Station to Simpsons Gap (24km)
Section 2: Simpsons Gap to Jay Creek (23km)
Section 3: Jay Creek to Standley Chasm (14km)
Section 8: Serpentine Gorge to Ochre Pits (18km)
Section 9: Ochre Pits to Ormiston Gorge (29km)
Section 10: Ormiston Gorge to Glen Helen (12.5km)
Section 11: Glen Helen to Redbank Gorge (27km)
Section 12: Redbank Gorge to Mt Sonder (16km return)

Detailed trail notes and maps ($1 per section) are available from the Parks & Wildlife desk at the tourist office in Alice Springs, or contact the Parks & Wildlife office (☎ 8951 8211) for further details.

Simpsons Gap
Westbound from Alice Springs on Larapinta Dve you soon come to the **Desert Wildlife Park & Botanic Gardens** (see section under Alice Springs) and **John Flynn's Grave**. The flying doctor's final resting place is topped by one of the Devils Marbles,

brought down the Track from near Tennant Creek.

A little farther on is the picturesque Simpsons Gap, 22km out. Like the other gaps it is an awesome example of nature's power and patience – for a river to cut a path through solid rock is amazing, but for a river that rarely ever runs to cut such a path is positively mind-boggling. There are often rock wallabies in the jumble of rocks on either side of the gap.

Standley Chasm

Standley Chasm is 51km out and is probably the most spectacular gap around Alice Springs. It is incredibly narrow – the near-vertical walls almost meet above you. Only for a scant 15 minutes each day does the late morning sun illuminate the bottom of the gorge – and this is obviously the time that most tourists visit; early or late in the day it is much more peaceful. The chasm is on Aboriginal land and entry is $3.

Namatjira Drive

Not far beyond Standley Chasm you can choose the northerly Namatjira Dve or the more southerly Larapinta Dve. West along Namatjira Dve another series of gorges and gaps in the range awaits you. **Ellery Creek Big Hole** is 93km from Alice Springs and has a large permanent water hole – just the place for a cooling dip, and there's a basic camp site close by. It's only 13km farther to **Serpentine Gorge**, a narrow gorge with a pleasant water hole at the entrance.

The **Ochre Pits**, just off the road 11km west of Serpentine, were a source of painting material for the Aboriginal people. The various coloured ochres are weathered limestone, and the colouring is actually iron-oxide stains.

The large and rugged **Ormiston Gorge** also has a water hole and it leads to the enclosed valley of **Ormiston Pound**. When the water holes of the Pound dry up, the fish burrow into the sand, going into a sort of suspended animation and reappearing after rain. There's some good, short walking trails around here.

Only a couple of kilometres farther is the turn-off to the scenic **Glen Helen Gorge**, where the Finke River cuts through the Mac-Donnells. The road is gravel beyond this point, but if you continue west you'll reach the red-walled **Redbank Gorge**, which has permanent water, 161km from Alice Springs. Also out this way is **Mt Sonder**. At 1347m, it's the highest point in the Northern Territory.

Places to Stay & Eat There's no accommodation in the Western MacDonnells. There are, however, camp sites at Ellery Creek Big Hole, Ormiston Gorge and Redbank Gorge.

Larapinta Drive

Taking the alternative road to the south from Standley Chasm, Larapinta Dve crosses the Hugh River, and then Ellery Creek before reaching the turn-off for **Wallace Rockhole**, 17km off the main road and 117km from Alice Springs. This is an Arrernte Aboriginal community (☎ 8956 7415) which offers camping ($8, on-site vans $40, cabins $95) and rock-art tours daily on demand ($8). Alcohol is prohibited here.

Back on Larapinta Dve, shortly before Hermannsburg, is the **Namatjira Monument**. Today the artistic skills of the central Australian Aboriginal people are widely known and appreciated. This certainly wasn't the case when Albert Namatjira started to paint his central Australian landscapes in 1934.

In 1957 Namatjira was the first Aboriginal person to be granted Australian citizenship. Because of his fame, he was allowed to buy alcohol at a time when this was otherwise illegal for Aboriginal people, but in 1958 he was jailed for six months for supplying alcohol to members of his family. He died the following year, aged only 57. (For further information on Namatjira see the Aboriginal art section in Facts about the Country.)

Hermannsburg (pop 440)

Only 8km beyond the Namatjira monument you reach the Hermannsburg Aboriginal settlement, 125km from Alice Springs. The

NORTHERN TERRITORY

NORTHERN TERRITORY

Hermannsburg Mission was established by German Lutheran missionaries in the middle of the last century. Many of the buildings are intact, and it's well worth a stroll through.

Although the town is restricted Aboriginal land, permits are not required to visit the mission or store, or to travel through. The Kata-Anga Tea Rooms serve excellent home-made pastries, and you can also get fuel (no credit cards) and basic provisions at the community store. The staff at the tea rooms also issue permits for travel on the Mereenie Loop Road (see below).

Hermannsburg's most famous resident was Professor Ted Strehlow (see Strehlow Research Centre under Alice Springs).

Finke Gorge National Park

From Hermannsburg a 4WD trail follows the Finke River south to the Finke Gorge National Park, only 12km farther on.

Palm Valley, in the park, is a gorge filled with a variety of palm tree unique to this part of the MacDonnells – the central Australian cabbage palm (*Livistona mariae*). This strangely tropical find in the dry Centre makes Palm Valley a popular day-trip.

The track to the park crosses the sandy bed of the Finke a number of times and you need a 4WD to get through, not so much because of the risk of getting bogged, but because of the high ground clearance needed to negotiate the numerous bars of rock on the track to the gorge.

There's a beautiful shady camping area ($10) with some long-drop toilets, and a couple of signposted walks.

If you are travelling by 4WD there's a track that traverses the full length of the picturesque Finke Gorge, much of the time along the bed of the (usually) dry Finke River. It's a rough but worthwhile trip, and the camp sites at Boggy Hole, about 2½ hours from Hermannsburg, make an excellent overnight stop. If you are in a hurry you can get from Palm Valley all the way to Watarrka (Kings Canyon) National Park in less than eight hours via this route. Ask the rangers at Palm Valley or Kings Canyon for details.

Mereenie Loop Road

From Hermannsburg you can continue west to the Areyonga turn-off (no visitors), and then take the Mereenie Loop Road to Kings Canyon. This dirt road is suitable for robust conventional vehicles and offers an excellent alternative to the Ernest Giles Road as a way of reaching Kings Canyon.

To travel the loop road you need a permit from the Central Land Council as it passes through Aboriginal land. The permit includes the informative *Mereenie Tour Pass* booklet, which provides details about the local Aboriginal culture and has a route map. Permits are issued on the spot by the tourist office in Alice Springs, the service station at the Kings Canyon Resort and at the Kata-Anga Tea Rooms at Hermannsburg.

South to Uluru

You can make some interesting diversions off the road south from Alice Springs. There are also a number of attractions to the east of the Stuart Highway, but these mostly require a 4WD.

RAINBOW VALLEY NATURE PARK

The eerie sandstone bluffs of the James Range are the main attraction of this small park, which lies 22km off the Stuart Highway along an unsignposted 4WD track 75km south of Alice Springs. There's a basic camp site but you will need to bring your own firewood and water.

CAMEL OUTBACK SAFARIS

This camel farm, 90km south of Alice at **Stuart's Well**, is run by Noel Fullerton, the 'camel king', who started the annual Camel Cup and has won it four times. For a few dollars you can try your hand at camel riding and there are extended safaris into Rainbow Valley and the outback. The farm exports camels to places around the world, including the Arab nations of the Gulf and the Sahara.

It has been estimated that the central deserts are home to about 15,000 wild

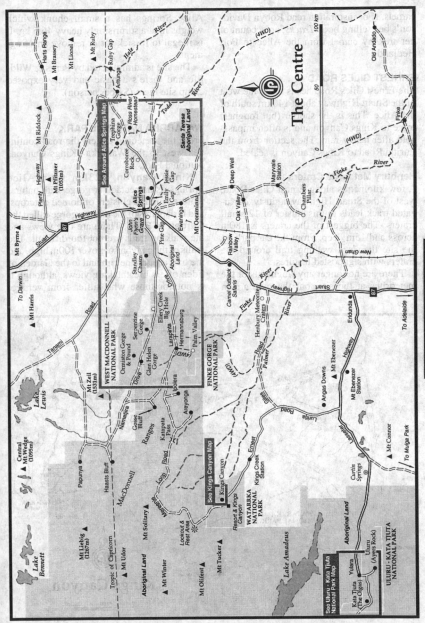

camels. (For inspiration read Robyn Davidson's bestselling book *Tracks*, an account of her trek by camel from the Alice to Port Hedland.)

ERNEST GILES ROAD

The Ernest Giles Road heads off to the west of the Stuart Highway about 140km south of the Alice. This is the shorter (but rougher) route to Kings Canyon and is often impassable after heavy rain. The section from the Luritja Road to Kings Canyon is sealed.

Henbury Meteorite Craters

A few kilometres along Ernest Giles Road, west of the Stuart Highway, a dusty, corrugated track leads to this cluster of 12 small craters. The biggest of the craters is 180m across and 15m deep. From the car park by the site there's a walking trail around the craters with signposted features.

There are no longer any fragments of the meteorites at the site, but the museum in Alice Springs has a small chunk which weighs in at a surprisingly heavy 46.5 kg. It is illegal to fossick for or remove any fragments.

The site is administered by Parks & Wildlife and there's a basic and very exposed camp site there ($1 per person).

WATARRKA NATIONAL PARK

From the meteorite craters the road continues west to the Watarrka (Kings Canyon) National Park.

Kings Canyon, 323km from Alice Springs, is a spectacular gorge with natural features such as clusters of domed outcrops, and lush palms of the narrow gorge called the **Garden of Eden**. There are fine views and the walking trails are not too difficult. The walls of the canyon soar over 100m high, and the trail around the rim and to the Garden of Eden offers breathtaking views, although it is not for those who suffer from vertigo.

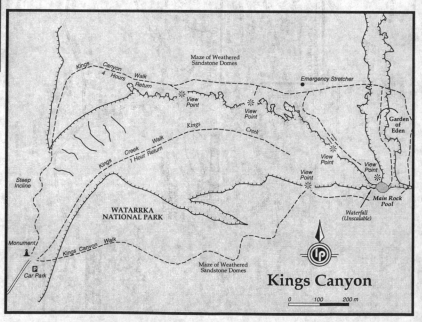

Kings Canyon

There's a ranger station (☎ 8956 7460) 22km east of the canyon.

The Giles Track is a 22km walking track along the ridge to between the gorge and Kathleen Springs, 2.5km from the ranger station. It takes two days to walk, and you need to register with the rangers.

Fifteen-minute helicopter flights are available from the resort (☎ 8956 7873), or from Kings Creek Station (see Places to Stay). They cost $140 for 35 minutes.

Places to Stay & Eat

The closest accommodation available is at the *Kings Canyon Resort* (☎ 1800 891 101; fax 8956 7410), 6km west of the canyon. Camp sites cost $20, $25 with power. There's a backpackers' bunk house with beds in four-bed rooms at a hefty $33 each ($75 double), or more luxurious motel-type accommodation for $291. The resort has a swimming pool, bar, cafe, restaurant, shop and (expensive) fuel.

Otherwise, there's the basic but friendly *Kings Creek Station Camping Ground* (☎ 8956 7474), on Ernest Giles Road just outside the national park's eastern boundary and about 35km from the canyon. The very pleasant camp site is set among large desert oaks and camping costs $8 per person plus $1 per site for power. Fuel, ice and limited stores are available seven days a week at the shop.

THE OLD GHAN ROAD

Following the 'old south road' which runs close to the old Ghan railway line, it's only 35km from Alice Springs to **Ewaninga**, with its prehistoric Aboriginal rock carvings. The carvings found here and at N'Dhala Gorge are thought to have been made by Aboriginal tribes who lived here earlier than the current tribes of the Centre.

The eerie, sandstone **Chambers Pillar** is carved with the names and visit dates of early explorers – and, unfortunately, some much less worthy modern-day graffitists. To the Aboriginal people of the area, Chambers Pillar is the remains of Itirkawara, a gecko ancestor of great strength. It's 160km from

Alice Springs and a 4WD is required for the last 44km from the turn-off at Maryvale station. There's a basic camp site but you need to bring water and firewood.

Back on the main track south, you eventually arrive at **Finke**, a small Apatula Aboriginal settlement 230km south of Alice Springs. When the old Ghan was running, Finke was a thriving little town; these days it seems to have drifted into a permanent torpor. There's a basic community store, which is also the outlet for the Apatula Arts Centre, and fuel is available on weekdays. Alcohol is prohibited.

From Finke you can turn west to join the Stuart Highway at Kulgera (150km), or east to Old Andado station on the edge of the Simpson Desert (120km). Just 21km west of Finke, and 12km north of the road along a signposted track, is the **Lambert Centre**. Here stands a 5m-high replica of the flagpole found on top of Parliament House in Canberra. The reason? This point has been determined as Australia's centre of gravity!

Uluru-Kata Tjuta National Park

ULURU (AYERS ROCK)

Australia's biggest drawcard, the world famous Uluru (Ayers Rock), is 3.6km long and rises a towering 348m from the surrounding sandy scrubland. It's believed that two-thirds of the Rock lies beneath the sand. Everybody knows how its colour changes as the setting sun turns it a series of deeper and darker reds before it fades into grey. A performance in reverse, with fewer spectators, is given at dawn.

The mighty Rock offers much more than pretty colours – the entire area is of deep cultural significance to the local Anangu Aboriginal people, and there are opportunities to delve into their culture. To Anangu it is known as Uluru – the name given to the Rock and the national park which surrounds it. The Aboriginal people own the national

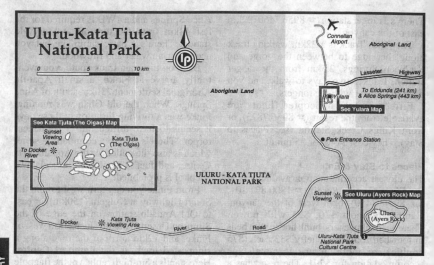

Uluru-Kata Tjuta National Park

park, although it is leased permanently to, and administered by, Parks Australia North (the Federal government's national parks body) in conjunction with the traditional owners.

There are plenty of walks and other activities around Uluru and the township of Yulara, and it is not at all difficult to spend several days here.

Information

The superb Uluru-Kata Tjuta National Park Cultural Centre (☎ 8956 3138; fax 8956 3139) is 1km before the Rock on the road from Yulara. There are some excellent dynamic displays here, as well as original art on the walls. Also here is the Maruku Arts & Crafts outlet where you can see artists at work. This is about the cheapest place in the Centre to buy souvenirs (carvings etc) and you're buying direct from the artists. There's also the Aboriginal-run Ininti Store, which sells snacks and souvenirs, the Anangu Tours booking desk, and a picnic area with free gas barbecues. The centre is open daily from 7 am to 5.30 pm from April through October, (to 6 pm the rest of the year), and photography is not permitted. Free 1½ hour tours of

the centre are conducted from Monday to Wednesday at 3.15 pm.

Entry to the national park costs $15 (free for children under 16) and this is good for a five-day visit. Entry permits can be bought from the visitors centre at Yulara (see below), or from the park entrance on the road between Yulara and Uluru.

The park is open daily from half an hour before sunrise to sunset.

Walks Around Uluru

There are walking trails around Uluru, and guided walks delving into the plants, wildlife, geology and mythology of the area. All the walks are flat and are suitable for wheelchairs.

Base Walk (10km) It can take five hours to walk around the base of Uluru at a leisurely pace, looking at the caves and paintings on the way, and often you'll have it pretty much to yourself. Full details of the Mala and Kuniya walks (see below) are given in the self-guided walks brochure available from the rangers' station for $1.

Note that there are several Aboriginal sacred sites around the base of Uluru.

They're fenced off and clearly signposted and to enter these areas is a grave offence, not just for non-Aboriginal people but for 'ineligible' Aboriginal people as well.

Mala Walk (2km return) This walk starts from the base of the climbing point and takes about 1½ hours at a very leisurely pace. The *tjukurpa* (traditional law) of the Mala (hare-wallaby people) is of great importance to the Anangu. You can do this walk on your own, or there are guided walks daily at 10 am from the car park (8 am October through April; no booking necessary).

Liru Walk (2km one way) This starts from the Cultural Centre and goes to the base of Uluru, linking up with the Base Walk track.

Mutitjulu Walk (1km return) Mutitjulu is a permanent water hole on the southern side of Uluru. The tjukurpa tells of the clash between two ancestral snakes, Kuniya and Liru (see the Rainbow Serpent aside in the Top End section). The water hole is a short walk from the car park on the southern side.

Aboriginal Cultural Tours
Anangu Tours offer a couple of tours around the base. These are excellent, it's just a pity they are out of reach of the budget traveller. Bookings are essential as there is a limit of 20 people on each tour.

Liru Tour This gives an insight into the way the local Anangu people made use of the area's shrubs and bush materials. It is a two-hour guided walk, and it operates daily at 8.30 am from the Culture Centre; the cost is $39 ($29 children) and bookings are essential (☎ 8956 2123). With transfers from Yulara and breakfast at the Cultural Centre restaurant the cost is $78 ($63).

Kuniya Tour This teaches you about the Kuniya tjukurpa, and also about food and medicine plants found at Mutitjulu. Tours start from the Mutitjulu car park at 4 pm (5 pm October through March), and cost $39 ($29). With transfers the cost is $65 ($49).

Climbing Uluru
Those climbing Uluru should take care – numerous people have met their maker doing so, usually by having a heart attack, but some

NORTHERN TERRITORY

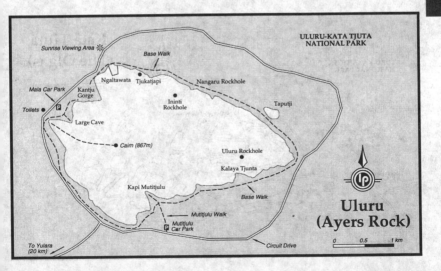

ULURU-KATA TJUTA NATIONAL PARK

Sunrise Viewing Area

Base Walk

Ngaltawata Tjukatjapi

Nangaru Rockhole

Mala Car Park

Kantju Gorge

Toilets

Large Cave

Ininti Rockhole

Taputji

Cairn (867m)

Uluru Rockhole

Kalaya Tjunta

Kapi Mutitjulu

Base Walk

Mutitjulu Walk

Mutitjulu Car Park

To Yulara (20 km)

Circuit Drive

0   0.5   1 km

Uluru (Ayers Rock)

NORTHERN TERRITORY

'We Don't Climb'

'If you worry about Aboriginal law, then leave it, don't climb it. The chain is still there if you want to climb it. You should think about Tjukurpa and stay on the ground. Please don't climb.'

These are the words of Barbara Tjikatu, one of the traditional owners of Uluru.

It's important to note that it goes against Aboriginal spiritual beliefs to climb Uluru, and the Anangu (local Aboriginal) people would very much prefer you didn't. One reason for this is that the route taken by visitors is associated closely with the Mala tjukurpa, the traditional law of the hare-wallaby people. Another is that Anangu feel responsible for all people on the Rock, and are greatly saddened when a visitor to their land is injured or dies there. We strongly urge you to respect the Anangu's wishes and refrain from climbing. ■

by taking a fatal tumble. Avoid climbing in the heat of the day during the hot season. There is an emergency phone at the car park at the base of the climb, and another at the top of the chain, about halfway up the climbing route. The climb is actually closed between 10 am and 4 pm on days

when the forecast temperature is more than 38°C.

The climb is 1.6km and takes about two hours up and back with a good rest at the top. The first part of the walk is by far the steepest and most arduous, and there's a chain to hold on to. It's often extremely windy at the top, even when it's not at the base, so make sure hats are well tied on.

KATA TJUTA (THE OLGAS)

Kata Tjuta (the Olgas), a collection of smaller, more rounded rocks, stands about 30km to the west of Uluru. Though less well-known, the monoliths are equally impressive – indeed many people find them more captivating. Meaning 'many heads', Kata Tjuta is of tjukurpa significance.

The tallest rock, **Mt Olga**, at 546m, is about 200m higher than Uluru. There are a couple of walking trails, the main one being to the **Valley of the Winds**, a 7km circuit track (2½ to four hours). It's not particularly arduous, but be prepared with water, and sun protection. There is also a short (2km return) signposted trail into the pretty Olga Gorge (Tatintjawiya).

There's a picnic and sunset viewing area

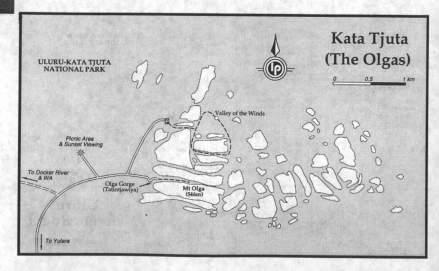

Kata Tjuta (The Olgas)

ULURU-KATA TJUTA NATIONAL PARK

0   0.5   1 km

Valley of the Winds

Picnic Area & Sunset Viewing

To Docker River & WA

Olga Gorge (Tatintjawiya)

Mt Olga (546m)

To Yulara

with toilet facilities just off the access road a few kilometres west of the base of Kata Tjuta.

A lonely sign at the western end of the access road points out that there is a hell of a lot of nothing if you travel west – although, if suitably equipped, you can travel all the way to Kalgoorlie and on to Perth in Western Australia. It's 200km to Docker River, an Aboriginal settlement on the road west, and about 1500km to Kalgoorlie. See the Warburton Road information in the Getting Around chapter.

YULARA (pop 2750)

Yulara, the service village for the national park, has effectively turned one of the world's least hospitable regions into an easy and comfortable place to visit. Lying just outside the national park, 20km from Uluru and 53km from Kata Tjuta, the complex, administered by the Northern Territory government's Ayers Rock Corporation, makes an excellent and surprisingly democratic base for exploring the area's renowned attractions. Opened in 1984, it supplies the only accommodation, food outlets and other services available in the region. The village incorporates the Ayers Rock Resort, and it combines flair with low, earth-toned buildings, fitting unobtrusively into the dunes.

By the 1970s it was clear that planning was required for the development of the area. Between 1931 and 1946 only 22 people were known to have climbed Uluru. In 1969 about 23,000 people visited the area. Ten years later the figure was 65,000 and now the annual rate is approaching 400,000!

Orientation & Information

In the spacious village area, where everything is within 15 minutes walk of the centre, there is a visitors centre, four hotels, apartments, a backpackers' lodge, two camp sites, a bank, post office, petrol station, newsagency, restaurants, a Royal Flying Doctor Service medical centre, supermarket, craft gallery, bistro and even a pink police station!

The Tour & Information Centre (☎ 8956 2240; fax 8956 2403) in the shopping square

is open daily from 8.30 am to 8.30 pm and it's the place to book tours as all operators have desks here. There's also a central desk which can provide general information about the park itself.

Also in the resort, near the Desert Gardens Hotel, is the Visitor Centre (☎ 8957 7377) which contains good displays on the geography, flora, fauna and history of the region. The centre is open daily from 8.30 am to 5 pm.

The shopping-square complex includes a supermarket, newsagency, post office and travel agency. You can get colour film processed at Territory Colour's same-day service. The only bank at Yulara is ANZ, but you can also use the EFTPOS facilities at the supermarket and the Mobil service station. There's a childcare centre in the village for children aged between three months and eight years, which operates daily from 8 am to 5.30 pm. The cost is $16.50 for half a day or $27.50 for a full day. Bookings can be made on ☎ 8956 2097.

Activities

There are a number of activities in the resort, some conducted by the rangers and others organised by the resort.

The Uluru – Heart of Australia **slide show and talk** takes place daily at 1 pm in the auditorium behind the visitors centre. It's free and you don't need to book.

The **Garden Walk** is a guided tour through the native garden of the Sails in the Desert Hotel. It takes place on weekdays at 7.30 am

---

Grog

Please be aware that alcohol (grog) is a problem among some of the local Mutitjulu Aboriginal people living near Uluru. Their community is a 'dry' one and, at the request of its Aboriginal leaders, the liquor outlet in Yulara does not sell alcohol to Aboriginal people. You may be approached at Yulara by Aborigines wanting you to buy them grog. The community leaders appeal to you not to do so. ■

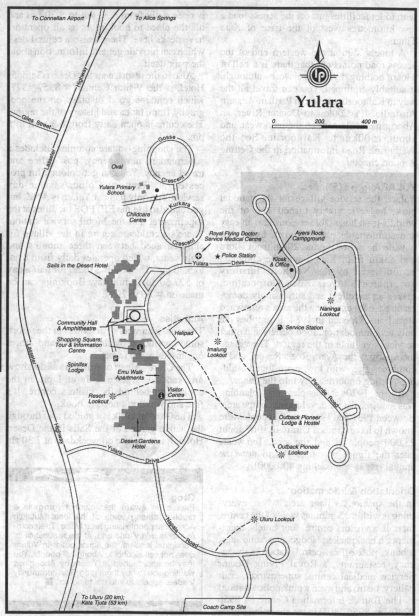

Yulara

0   200   400 m

To Connellan Airport

To Alice Springs

Giles Street

Lasseter Highway

Gosse

Crescent

Oval

Yulara Primary School

Childcare Centre

Kurkara

Crescent

Royal Flying Doctor Service Medical Centre

Police Station

Yulara Drive

Ayers Rock Campground

Kiosk & Office

Naninga Lookout

Sails in the Desert Hotel

Community Hall & Amphitheatre

Shopping Square; Tour & Information Centre

Spinifex Lodge

Emu Walk Apartments

Resort Lookout

Visitor Centre

Desert Gardens Hotel

Yulara Drive

Helipad

Imalung Lookout

Service Station

Perentie Road

Outback Pioneer Lodge & Hostel

Outback Pioneer Lookout

Uluru Lookout

Napala Road

Lasseter Highway

To Uluru (20 km); Kata Tjuta (53 km)

Coach Camp Site

and is led by the hotel's resident gardener. This tour is also free and there's no need to book.

Each evening there's the **Night Sky Show**, which is an informative look into local astrological legends, with the use of telescopes and binoculars (slide show on cloudy nights). The 1½ hour trips are at 8.30, 9.30 and 10.15 pm, and bookings are required (☎ 1800 803 174). The cost is $21 (children $12) and you are picked up from your accommodation.

Frontier Camel Tours from Alice Springs also have camel rides at Yulara. Their base is at the coach camp site and can be reached by way of the resort shuttle. Short rides operate on demand from 10.30 am to 2 pm ($5), or you can do a longer morning or evening ride over the dunes away from the resort (and get good views of Uluru), for $65 including champagne and nibbles (evening) or billy tea and damper (morning) and transfers. Book at your accommodation or the Tour & Information Centre.

Flights While the enjoyment of those on the ground may be diminished by the constant buzz of light aircraft and helicopters overhead, for those actually up there it's an unforgettable – and very popular – trip.

Three companies operate the trips and they collect you from wherever you're staying.

Rockayer (☎ 8956 2345) charges $65 ($55 children aged four to 14) for a 30-minute flight over the Rock and Kata Tjuta, or $175 for a 110-minute flight, which includes Lake Amadeus and Kings Canyon. Airnorth Safaris (☎ 8952 6666) offer the same trips for $65 and $160 respectively.

Ayers Rock Helicopters (☎ 8956 2077) charges $80 for the 15-minute Uluru flight, and $152 for the 30-minute Uluru and Kata Tjuta flight. There are no child concessions on any helicopter flights, which make them an expensive proposition for families.

Organised Tours
From Yulara Three companies operate tours out of Yulara. If you arrive here from anywhere other than Alice Springs without a tour booked then you're pretty much limited to these three.

Uluru Experience Several possibilities are available with Uluru Experience (☎ 1800 803 174). The five-hour Uluru Walk includes the base walk and breakfast for $69 ($54 children aged six to 15); Spirit of Uluru is a four-hour vehicle tour around the base of the rock, also including breakfast, for $69 ($54); and the Olgas & Dunes Tour includes the

NORTHERN TERRITORY

Lasseter's Lost Reef

Gold prospector Lewis Hubert (Harold Bell) Lasseter (1880?-1931) is immortalised as one of Australia's great hopefuls. We still know of him today because of Ion Idriess's romantic account *Lasseter's Last Ride* (1931); otherwise he would probably have faded into the red dust of the Petermann Range. Sometime between 1897 and 1911 Lasseter claimed to have found 'a vast gold-bearing reef' in central Australia, some 23km in length. The diminutive Lasseter had supposedly been looking for rubies when he stumbled upon gold as thick as 'plums in a pudding'. It was in the remote, arid Petermann Range in central Australia on the Northern Territory-South Australia border.

In 1930 the Central Australian Gold Exploration Company was formed, with Lasseter as a guide. The expedition was well equipped with an aeroplane, trucks and wireless. But things started to go wrong: the aircraft crashed near Uluru and Fred Blakeley, the expedition leader, abandoned it. Lasseter, after an argument with another hopeful prospector, Paul Johns, headed out alone to look for the reef.

Lasseter died of starvation in January 1931 near Shaws Creek. His diaries were retrieved and in them he claimed to have pegged the reef. Idriess used these diaries to write his book.

Subsequent attempts to find Lasseter's lost reef have been unsuccessful. His name is perpetuated in the Lasseter Highway, which runs from the Stuart Highway near Erldunda to Uluru. ∎

walk into Olga Gorge and sunset at the Olgas for $51 ($41). The Uluru Experience Pass lets you choose any two of the above tours, and includes breakfast, for $107 ($83), and gives you a discount on the Night Sky Show. These tours are really only worth considering if you don't have your own transport.

AAT-Kings This company (☎ 1800 334 009) has a Rock Pass which includes guided base tour, sunset, climb, sunrise and Kata Tjuta tours for $142 ($71 children under 15). The pass is valid for three days, and includes the $15 national park entry fee. The 24 Hour Pass ($110/87) gives you almost the same but you have to complete the lot within 24 hours, which is a tall order.

All these activities are also available in various combinations on a one-off basis: base tour ($36/18 adults/children), sunrise tour ($33/17), climb ($33/17), sunset ($23/12), base and sunset ($52/26), sunrise and climb ($55/28), climb and base ($60/30), sunrise and base ($55/28), sunrise, climb and base ($74/37), Kata Tjuta and Uluru sunset ($62/31). These prices do not include the park entry fee.

AAT-Kings also offers the Olgas Sunset & Dinner Tour, on which you can do the three-hour Valley of the Winds walk, then enjoy a barbecue with the sunset on the Olgas for $95 ($48).

Anangu Tours This tour company (☎ 8956 2123) is owned and operated by Anangu from the Mutitjulu community. Their tour desk is at the Cultural Centre inside the park, but they also arrange transfers from Yulara. The Anangu tours are led by two Anangu guides and one interpreter, and they offer a unique chance to meet and talk with Anangu. The tours currently offer walks in the Uluru vicinity (see Aboriginal Cultural Tours under Uluru for details), and instruct visitors on elements of Anangu culture.

From Alice Springs All-inclusive tours to Uluru by private operators start as low as about $245 for a three-day camping trip which includes Kings Canyon, although

around $300 is the average. Companies such as AKT Holidays (☎ 1800 891 121) and Sahara Tours (☎ 1800 806 240) are popular with the budget conscious.

Things to check for when shopping around for tours include the time it takes to get to the Rock and Kata Tjuta, and whether the return is done early or late in the day. Prices can vary with the season and demand, and sometimes there may be cheaper 'standby' fares available. Bus-pass travellers should note that the bus services to the Rock are often heavily booked – if your schedule is tight it's best to plan ahead.

Tours which include accommodation other than camping are generally much more expensive, starting at around $320 for two days.

Another option is the passes offered by Greyhound Pioneer and McCafferty's. These are good value as they give you return transport to Yulara, the base tour, climb, Kata Tjuta and sunrise and sunset tours, and include the park entry fee. See the Getting There & Away section for more details.

Places to Stay
Yulara has something for every budget, from a camp sites to a five-star hotel. With the popularity of the place, however, it is advisable to book all accommodation in advance, especially during school holidays.

All accommodation, with the exception of the camping ground, should be booked through the central reservation office in Sydney (☎ 1800 089 622). There is also a 5% Northern Territory Bed Tax to be added.

Camping With over 400 camp sites, the large *Ayers Rock Campground* (☎ 8956 2055) costs $20 for two people on an unpowered site ($32 with power). There are 15 new six-bed cabins for $92 for up to four adults, and $10 for each additional adult. Most of the camp sites have beautifully manicured patches of green grass, while the spaces for vans and caravans are gravel. The camping ground is set among native gardens, and there's quite a bit of shade. There's also a swimming pool, free gas barbecues and the reception kiosk sells basic food supplies.

Dormitory & Budget Accommodation For backpackers the place to head for is the well-equipped *Outback Pioneer Lodge* (☎ 8956 2170), on the far side of the village from the shopping centre, about a 10-minute walk across the dunes. A bed in a 20-bed dorm costs $19 ($17 for YHA members). There's decent communal cooking facilities, and baggage storage lockers are available for a small fee. The only problem is that check-in is not until 1 pm, which is a real bore if you've arrived at sparrow's fart on the overnight Greyhound Pioneer bus from Adelaide. There are also cabin-type rooms with either two bunk beds or a double bed and one bunk, costing $116 for up to four people, including bedding. The rooms have fridges, TV and tea/coffee-making facilities, but bathrooms and cooking facilities are communal.

Part of the same complex is known as the *Outback Pioneer Hotel* and this has expensive en-suite rooms, some with limited cooking facilities, for $256. All buildings have air-con and heating, and there's a swimming pool. Out the back is a good lookout point for sunset views of Uluru.

Next up is the *Spinifex Lodge* (☎ 8956 2131) near the visitors centre. It has 68 one-bedroom units which accommodate from two to four people at a cost of $103 for a double. These are quite good value, the main drawbacks being that the cooking facilities are limited to a microwave, an electric frypan and a toaster, and the bathrooms are communal.

Apartments Probably the best deal at Yulara, especially for families, is offered by the *Emu Walk Apartments* (☎ 8956 2000). There are one and two-bedroom flats which accommodate from four to eight people. They have a lounge with TV, a fully equipped kitchen and there's a communal laundry. They are also very central, being right between the visitors centre and the shopping square. The cost ranges from $261 to $323.

Hotels The two remaining options are both top-end hotels. The *Desert Gardens Hotel* (☎ 8956 2100) has 160 rooms with TV, phone, minibar and room service. The 2nd floor rooms in the newer part of the hotel have limited views of Uluru from the balcony. The cost ranges from $286 for a standard double to $329 for a Deluxe Rock View double, and the hotel has a pool and a restaurant.

At the top of the range is the *Sails in the Desert Hotel* (☎ 8956 2200), which has all the facilities you'd expect in a top hotel, including in-house movies, 24-hour room service, spa (also in some rooms) and tennis court. The 228 rooms start at $351 for a double and go all the way up to $630 for the deluxe suite.

Places to Eat
The range of eating options is equally varied. At the shopping centre the *Yulara Take-Away* does pretty reasonable fast food which you can take away or eat at the tables in the shopping area. It's open daily from 9 am to 8 pm. Also in the shopping centre is a bakery (open daily from 9 am to 7 pm) and an ice-cream parlour (daily from 11 am to 5 pm).

The Outback Pioneer Lodge also has a couple of choices. The *Pioneer Kitchen* offers light meals and snacks and is open from early morning until early evening. One of the best deals at Yulara is the 'Self-Cook Barbecue' which takes place at the noisy bar here every night. For $12 to $17 you get meat (beef, chicken, sausages, hamburger or fish) which you then barbecue yourself, and there's a range of salads. There's also a cheaper vegetarian dish, or you can just have the salads. It's a popular place to eat, probably made more so by the fact that 'exotic' meats such as kangaroo, buffalo and crocodile are often available. For more conventional dining the hotel also has the *Bough House* by the pool. The roast dinner buffet is good value at $10, while other meals are in the $11 to $15 range. The lodge sells the only take-away liquor at Yulara (noon to 7 pm only).

NORTHERN TERRITORY

Gecko's Cafe in the shopping square is a smart casual licensed restaurant, open daily from 8.30 am to 11 pm. Main courses, such as pizza or pasta are $16, fish (from where?) or steak are more expensive at $26, which is a bit steep really.

The Desert Gardens Hotel has the *Bunya Bar* restaurant for casual dining and the more formal *White Gums*, which has breakfast at $17, a buffet dinner for $37, or two-course à la carte for $39.

Finally the Sails in the Desert Hotel has the *Rockpool* poolside restaurant (lunch only), the *Winikiku*, which features buffet meals and is open from 6 am to 11 pm, and the more sophisticated *Kunia Room* for upmarket dining. The focus here is modern Australian cuisine.

Entertainment

Each evening (at 9 pm from September-April and 8 pm May-August) at the *Amphitheatre* there's the Nukanya Dreaming Aboriginal dance performance. Also featured are traditional songs and music. The cost is $15 ($7 children) and bookings should be made at hotel desks or the Tour & Information Centre.

All the hotels have at least one bar, and if you are really bored you could see a movie at the *Auditorium* behind the visitors centre. Recent releases are screened from Friday to Sunday and cost $6 ($3 children). For listings see the notice board outside the visitors centre.

Getting There & Away

Air Connellan airport is about 5km from Yulara. You can fly direct from various major centres as well as from Alice Springs. Ansett has at least three flights daily for the 45-minute, $200 hop from Alice to the Rock.

The numerous flights direct to Uluru can be money savers. If, for example, you were intending to fly into the Centre from Adelaide, it makes a lot more sense to travel Adelaide-Uluru-Alice Springs rather than Adelaide-Alice Springs-Uluru-Alice Springs. You can fly direct between Uluru and Perth ($506 one way), Adelaide ($570),

Cairns ($522), Sydney ($507) and Darwin ($534) with Qantas or Ansett.

Airnorth (☎ 1800 627 474) also has daily direct flights between Uluru and Alice Springs ($200).

Day-trips to Uluru by air from Alice Springs cost from about $440, or $340 if you go one way by bus.

Bus Apart from hitching, the cheapest way to get to the Rock is to take a bus or tour. Greyhound Pioneer and McCafferty's both have daily services between Alice Springs and Uluru. The 441km trip takes about 5½ hours.

The fare for one-way travel with McCafferty's is $77 (specials of $55 are common) from Alice Springs to Yulara, $60 from Erldunda on the Stuart Highway. With Greyhound Pioneer it's $84 from the Alice.

Bus Passes McCafferty's has a Rock Pass which is valid for three days and includes return transport from Alice Springs. Then at the Rock itself you join the following AAT-Kings tours: guided base tour, Kata Tjuta and sunset tour, Uluru climb, Uluru sunrise and sunset. The pass includes the park entry fee and costs $222. The only condition is that you must stay for two nights, and this is at your own expense.

With Greyhound Pioneer you can take a two-day accommodated package (Ayers Rock Experience) from Alice Springs, which includes the company's own morning Ayers Rock climb and base tour and the afternoon Olgas and sunset tour. The price depends on the level of accommodation you want; in the dorms at the Outback Pioneer it's $170, or $258 in the standard units. Adding an extra day to include Kings Canyon costs $220/363. If you already have a Greyhound Pioneer pass (see the Getting Around chapter) which gets you to Yulara, then the tours are already included.

There are also direct services between Adelaide and Uluru, although this actually means connecting with another bus at Erldunda, the turn-off from the Stuart

Highway. Adelaide to Uluru takes about 22 hours for the 1720km trip and costs $159.

Car Hertz (☎ 8956 2244) and Avis (☎ 8956 2266) both have desks at the airport, and Territory Rent-a-Car (☎ 8956 2030) is at the Outback Pioneer Hotel.

Renting a car in Alice Springs to go down to Uluru and back can be worthwhile if there's a group of you. You're looking at $70 to $100 a day for a car from the big operators; this only includes 100km a day, each extra kilometre costing $0.25. Deals on offer include up to 300 free kilometres per day which is a much more realistic option. On one of these deals if you spent four days and covered 1200km – the minimum if you want to include a visit to Kings Canyon – you'd be up for around $600 (including insurance and petrol) which is cheaper than the Alice Springs to Yulara return bus fare alone for four people. A three-day rental (without Kings Canyon) would be about $500.

The road from the Alice to Yulara is sealed and there are regular food and petrol stops along the way. Yulara is 443km from Alice Springs, 244km west of Erldunda on the Stuart Highway, and the whole journey takes about 4½

hours. The stretch of road leading to Kings Canyon (304km) is also sealed and takes about 3½ hours.

Getting Around

The resort sprawls a bit, but it's not too large to get around on foot, and there's a free shuttle bus which runs between all accommodation points daily, every 15 minutes from 10.30 am to 2.30 pm and from 6.30 pm to 12.30 am. Walking trails lead across the dunes to little lookouts over the village and surrounding terrain.

A free shuttle bus operated by AAT-Kings meets all flights and drops at all accommodation points around the resort.

The National Park Without your own transport the options are to take inclusive tours or to use the share-taxi arrangement offered by Sunworth (☎ 8956 2152). They offer transport-only fares of $20 return to Uluru (with or without sunset), $25 including sunrise, and $15 for sunset only. All you need to do is phone to arrange a pick-up from Yulara, then organise with the drivers as to what you want to do at the Rock itself. To Kata Tjuta it's $35 for a morning, $40 for the afternoon, including Uluru sunset viewing.

Queensland

Population: 3.34 million
Area: 1,727,000 sq km
Phone Area Code: 07

Locator & Map Index

- Cape Tribulation Area p 577
- Cooktown p 582
- Port Douglas p 573
- Kuranda p 567
- Around Cairns p 566
- Central Cairns p 557
- Magnetic Island p 541
- Townsville p 535
- Airlie Beach p 525
- Mt Isa p 597
- Charters Towers p 545
- Whitsunday Coast p 530
- Mackay p 520
- Great Keppel Island p 514
- Rockhampton p 511
- Fraser Island p 499
- Hervey Bay pp 496-7
- Noosa p 483
- Sunshine Coast p 480
- Brisbane p 444
- Moreton Bay p 465
- Central Brisbane pp 450-1
- Gold Coast p 470
- Surfers Paradise p 472

Highlights

- Diving and snorkelling on the incomparable Great Barrier Reef
- Taking a 4WD trip around beautiful Fraser Island
- Cruising the Whitsunday Islands
- Visiting Australia's northern tip – the rugged Cape York Peninsula
- Partying at the great nightlife centres of Cairns, Surfers Paradise and Brisbane
- Joining a whale-watching tour at Hervey Bay and spotting a platypus in the wild at the Eungella National Park

Queensland is Australia's holiday state. Whether you prefer neon-lit Surfers Paradise, a deserted beach, an island resort or excellent diving on the Great Barrier Reef, rainforest treks, the wide expanse of the outback or remote national parks, you're certain to find something to suit your taste. Brisbane, the state capital, is a lively city. In the north, Cairns is a busy travellers' centre and base for a whole range of side trips and activities. Between Brisbane and Cairns there are strings of towns and islands, offering virtually every pastime you can imagine connected with the sea. Inland, several spectacular national parks are scattered over the ranges and between the isolated towns and cattle stations. In the far south-west corner of the state you'll find one of the most isolated towns of all, Birdsville, on the famous Birdsville Track.

North of Cairns, the Cape York Peninsula remains a wilderness against which people still test themselves. You can get an easy taste of this frontier in Cooktown, Australia's first British settlement and once a riotous gold-rush town. Just inland from Cairns is the lush Atherton Tableland with countless beautiful waterfalls and scenic spots. Further inland, on the main route across Queensland to the Northern Territory, is the outback mining town of Mt Isa and, south-east of here, the town of Longreach with its Stockman's Hall of Fame.

HISTORY

Queensland started as yet another penal colony in 1824. As usual, the free settlers soon followed and Queensland became a separate colony independent of New South Wales in 1859. Its early white settlers indulged in one of the greatest land grabs of all time and encountered fierce Aboriginal opposition. For much of the 19th century, what amounted to a guerrilla war took place along the frontiers of the white advance. To find out about the aboriginal resistance to European expansion, get hold of *The Other Side of the Frontier*, by historian Henry Reynolds. It's a fascinating read. For a different angle on the subject, Glenville Pike's *Queensland Frontier*, recounts some of the incredible experiences of the Queensland pioneers.

Traditionally, agriculture and mining have been the backbone of the Queensland economy: the state contains a substantial chunk of Australia's mineral wealth. More recently, vast amounts of money have been invested in tourism, which is on the verge of becoming the state's leading money earner.

ABORIGINAL PEOPLE & KANAKAS

By the turn of the century, the Aboriginal people of Queensland had been comprehensively run off their lands, and the white authorities had set up reserves around the state for the survivors. A few of these reserves were places where Aboriginal people could live a self-sufficient life; others were strife-ridden places with people from different areas and cultures thrown unhappily together under unsympathetic rule.

It wasn't until the 1980s that control of the reserves was transferred to their residents, and that the reserves became known as 'communities'. These freehold grants, known as Deeds of Grant in Trust, are subject to right of access for prospecting, exploration or mining. This falls well short of the freehold ownership that Aboriginal people have in other parts of Australia, such as the Northern Territory.

Visitor interest has prompted opportunities to have some contact with Aboriginal culture – in addition to rock-art sites at various locations, you can visit a number of communities, including the Yarrabah community south of Cairns and the Hopevale community north of Cooktown, and take tours with Aboriginal content, such as at Mission Beach and Mossman. The award-winning Tjapukai Dance Theatre, an Aboriginal dance group based in Cairns, performs most days for tourists. Perhaps the most exciting event is the Laura Aboriginal Dance & Cultural Festival, held every second year in June on the Cape York Peninsula.

Another people on the fringes of Queensland society – though less so – are the Kanakas, descendants of Pacific Islanders brought in during the 19th century to work, mainly on sugar plantations, under virtual slave conditions. The business of collecting, transporting and delivering them was called blackbirding. The first Kanakas were brought over in 1863 for Robert Towns, the man whose money got Townsville going, and about 60,000 more followed until blackbirding stopped in 1905. You'll come across quite a few Kanakas in the coastal area north of Rockhampton.

GEOGRAPHY

Queensland has a series of distinct regions, generally running parallel to the coast. First there's the coastal strip – the basis for the booming tourist trade. Along this strip there are beaches, bays, islands and, of course, the Great Barrier Reef. Much of the coastal region is green and productive with lush rainforests, endless fields of sugar cane and stunning national parks.

Next comes the Great Dividing Range, the mountain range that continues down through New South Wales and Victoria. The mountains come closest to the coast in Queensland and are most spectacular in the far north, near Cairns, and in the far south.

Then there are the tablelands – areas of flat agricultural land that run to the west. These fertile areas extend farthest west in the south where the Darling Downs have some of the most productive grain-growing land in Australia.

Finally, there's the vast inland area, the barren outback fading into the Northern Territory. Rain can temporarily make this desert bloom but basically it's an area of long, empty roads and tiny settlements.

There are a couple of variations from these basic divisions. In the far northern Gulf Country and Cape York Peninsula there are huge empty regions cut by countless dry riverbeds that can become swollen torrents in the wet season. The whole area is a network of waterways, sometimes bringing road transport to a complete halt.

The Tropic of Capricorn crosses Queensland about a quarter of the way up, running

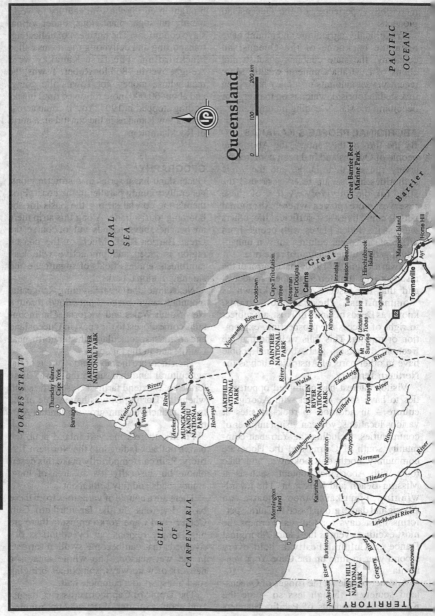

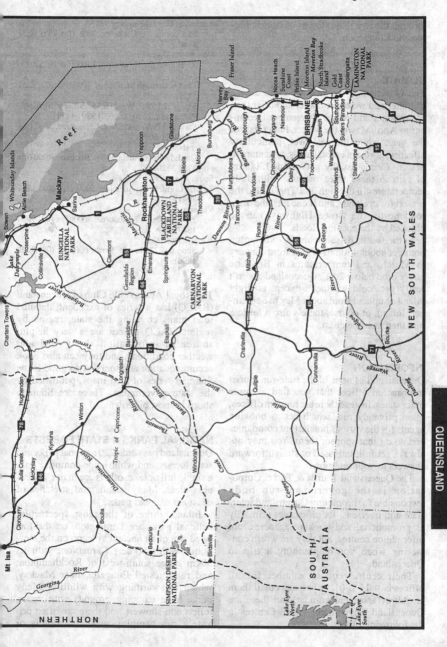

through the two major towns of Rockhampton and Longreach.

CLIMATE

The Queensland seasons are more a case of hotter and wetter or cooler and drier than of summer and winter. November/December to April/May is the wetter, hotter half of the year, while the real Wet, particularly affecting northern coastal areas, is January to March. Cairns usually gets about 1300mm of rain in these three months, with daily temperatures in the high 30s. This is also the season for cyclones, and if one hits, the main road north, the Bruce Highway, can be blocked by the ensuing floods.

In the south, Brisbane and Rockhampton both get about 450mm of rain from January to March, and temperatures in Brisbane rarely drop below 20°C. Queensland doesn't really get 'cold weather', except at night inland or upland from about May to September. Inland, of course, there's also a lot less rain than near the coast.

INFORMATION

Queensland has none of the state-run tourist information offices that you find in some other states. Instead there are tourism offices, often privately run, which act as booking agents for the various hotels, tour companies and so on that sponsor them. You may not always get full, unbiased or straightforward answers to your questions.

The Queensland Tourist & Travel Corporation is the government-run body responsible for promoting Queensland interstate and overseas. Its offices act primarily as promotional and booking agencies, not information centres, but they are worth contacting when you're planning a trip to Queensland.

Their central contact number for all offices is ☎ 13 1801, or you can email them at qldtravl@ozemail.com.au, and there are Queensland Government Travel Centres in the following places:

Australian Capital Territory
   25 Garema St, Canberra, 2601 (fax (02) 6257 4160)
New South Wales
   97 Hunter St, Newcastle, 2300 (fax (02) 4926 2800)
   156 Castlereagh St, Sydney, 2000 (fax (02) 9231 5153)
   Shop 2159, Westfield Shoppingtown, Parramatta, 2150 (fax (02) 9891 1159)
   Shop 2, 376 Victoria Ave, Chatswood, 2067 (fax (02) 9411 6079)
Queensland
   Cnr Edward & Adelaide Sts, Brisbane, 4000 (fax 3221 5320)
South Australia
   10 Grenfell St, Adelaide, 5000 (fax (08) 8211 8841)
Victoria
   257 Collins St, Melbourne, 3000 (fax (03) 9654 1847)
Western Australia
   Shop 6, 777 Hay St, Perth, 6000 (☎ (08) 9322 1800)

The Royal Automobile Club of Queensland (RACQ) has a series of excellent, detailed road maps covering the state, region by region. RACQ offices are a very helpful source of information about road and weather conditions, and they can also book accommodation and tours. Also good is the Sunmap series of area maps, published by the state government. There are Sunmap shops in most big towns.

NATIONAL PARKS & STATE FORESTS

Queensland has some 220 national parks and state forests, and while some comprise only a single hill or lake, others are major wilderness areas. Many islands and stretches of coast are national parks.

Inland, three of the most spectacular national parks are Lamington, on the forested rim of an ancient volcano on the New South Wales border; Carnarvon, with its 30km gorge south-west of Rockhampton; and rainforested Eungella, near Mackay, which is swarming with wildlife. Many parks have camping grounds with water, toilets and showers and there are often privately run camping grounds, motels or lodges on the park fringes. Sizeable parks usually have a network of walking tracks.

The Queensland Department of Environment operates five main information centres. You can also get information from the Queensland National Parks & Wildlife Service (QNPWS, part of the Department of Environment & Heritage) offices in most major towns, and from the park rangers. The Department of Environment information centres are at:

Brisbane
    160 Ann St (☎ 3227 8186)
Toowoomba
    158 Hume St (☎ 4639 4599)
Rockhampton
    Yeppoon Rd (☎ 4936 0511)
Townsville
    Great Barrier Reef Wonderland (☎ 4721 2399)
Cairns
    10 McLeod St (☎ 4052 3096)

To camp in a national park – whether in a fixed camping ground or in the bush – you need a permit, available in advance either by writing to or calling in at the appropriate QNPWS or Department of Environment office, or from a ranger at the park itself. Camping in national parks costs $3.50 per person per night, in state forests it's $2. Some camping grounds fill up at holiday times, so you may need to book well ahead; you can usually book sites six to 12 weeks ahead by writing to the appropriate office. Lists of camping grounds are available from QNPWS offices.

The handy *Discover National Parks* booklets ($2.50) also have useful information about Queensland's national parks and state forests, including things to do, camping details and how to get there. These booklets are available from bookshops and QNPWS offices. Also useful is the *Camping in Queensland* booklet ($5) which lists camp sites and facilities at all the national parks and state forests throughout Queensland.

ACTIVITIES
Bushwalking
This is a popular activity year-round. There are excellent bushwalking possibilities in many parts of the state, including several of the larger coastal islands such as Fraser and Hinchinbrook. National parks and state forests often have marked walking trails. Favourite bushwalkers' national parks on the mainland include Lamington in the southern Border Ranges, Main Range in the Great Divide, Cooloola just north of the Sunshine Coast, and Bellenden Ker south of Cairns, which contains Queensland's highest peak, Mt Bartle Frere (1657m). You can get full information from national park and state forest offices.

There are bushwalking clubs around the state and several useful guidebooks. Lonely Planet's *Bushwalking in Australia* includes three walks in Queensland, which range between two and five days in length.

Water Sports
Diving & Snorkelling The Great Barrier Reef provides some of the world's best diving and there's ample opportunity to learn and pursue this activity. The Queensland coast is probably the world's cheapest place to learn to scuba dive in tropical water – a five-day course leading to a recognised open water certificate usually costs between $300 and $500 and you almost always do a good part of your learning out on the Barrier Reef itself. These courses are very popular and nearly every town along the coast has one or more dive schools. The three most popular places are Airlie Beach, Townsville and Cairns.

Important factors to consider when choosing a course include the school's reputation, the relative amounts of time spent on pool/classroom training and out in the ocean, and whether your open-water time is spent on the outer reef as opposed to reefs around islands or even just off the mainland (the outer reef is usually more spectacular). Normally you have to show you can tread water for 10 minutes, and swim 200m, before you can start a course. Most schools also require a medical, which usually costs extra (around $50).

For certified divers, trips and equipment

hire are available just about everywhere. You usually have to show evidence of qualifications. You can snorkel almost everywhere too. There are coral reefs off some mainland beaches and around several of the islands, and many day trips out to the Barrier Reef provide snorkelling gear free.

During the wet season, which is usually January to March, floods can wash a lot of mud out into the ocean and visibility for divers and snorkellers is sometimes affected.

The Pisces *Diving & Snorkelling Guide to Australia (Coral Sea & Great Barrier Reef)* is an excellent guide to all the dives available on the reef.

White-Water Rafting & Canoeing The

Tully and North Johnstone rivers between Townsville and Cairns are the big ones for white-water rafting. You can do day trips for about $120, or longer expeditions.

Coastal Queensland is full of waterways and lakes so there's no shortage of canoeing territory. You can hire canoes or join canoe tours in several places, including Noosa, Townsville and Cairns.

Swimming & Surfing Popular surfing and

swimming beaches are south of Brisbane on the Gold Coast and north on the Sunshine Coast. North of Fraser Island the beaches are sheltered by the Great Barrier Reef so they're great for swimming but no good for surf. The clear, sheltered waters of the reef hardly need to be mentioned. There are also innumerable good, freshwater swimming spots around the state.

Other Water Sports Sailing enthusiasts will

find many places that hire out boats, both along the coast and inland. Airlie Beach and the Whitsunday Islands are possibly the biggest centres and you can find almost any type of boating or sailing you want there.

Fishing is one of Queensland's most popular sports and you can hire fishing gear or boats in many places. Sailboards can also be hired in many spots along the coast.

Warning From around November to April,

avoid swimming on unprotected northern beaches where deadly box jellyfish may lurk. If in any doubt, check with locals. If you're still in doubt, don't swim. Great Keppel Island is usually the most northerly safe place in the box jellyfish season. Also in northern waters, saltwater crocodiles are a hazard. They may be found close to the shore in the open sea or near creeks and rivers – especially tidal ones – sometimes at surprising distances inland.

Fossicking

There are lots of good fossicking areas in Queensland; see the *Gem Field* brochure published by the Queensland Tourist & Travel Corporation. It lists the places where you'll have a fair chance of finding gems and the types you might find. You'll need a 'miners right' before you set out.

GETTING THERE & AWAY

See the Brisbane Getting There & Away section for details on transport to Queensland.

GETTING AROUND

The peak tourist seasons are from mid-December to late January, 10 days either side of Easter, and mid-June to mid-October. The low season is February and March.

Air

Ansett (☎ 13 1300) and Qantas (☎ 13 1313) both fly to Queensland's major cities, connecting them to the southern states and across to the Northern Territory. There's also a multitude of smaller airlines operating up and down the coast, across the Cape York Peninsula and into the outback. During the wet season, such flights are often the only means of getting around the Gulf of Carpentaria or the Cape York Peninsula. These smaller airlines include Sunstate (book through Qantas) and Flight West (☎ 13 2392 within Queensland or ☎ 1800 777 879 from elsewhere in Australia, or book through Ansett).

Bus

Greyhound Pioneer Australia (☎ 13 2030) and McCafferty's (☎ 13 1499) have the most comprehensive bus networks throughout Queensland and cover all the major destinations. The busiest route is the coastal run up the Bruce Hwy from Brisbane to Cairns – both companies offer various passes, which cover all or part of this route. Greyhound Pioneer has the six-month Whitsunday Pass for travel between Brisbane and Airlie Beach ($116) and the three month Sunseeker, which takes you between Cairns and Sydney ($205). An Aussie Kilometre Pass for Brisbane to Cairns costs $176.

McCafferty's has a number of passes which include Queensland, but none for travel only in Queensland. See the general Getting Around chapter for more details of passes.

Oz Experience has a number of tours which take in the Queensland coast, such as the six-month Strewth pass, which allows travel between Byron Bay and Cairns for $180.

The other major bus routes are the inland routes from Brisbane to Mt Isa (continuing into the Northern Territory); from Townsville to Mt Isa; and from Rockhampton to Longreach (McCafferty's only). Prices are fairly similar, although McCafferty's tends to be a dollar or two cheaper.

Train

The main railway line is the Brisbane to Cairns run. There are also inland services from Brisbane to Charleville, from Rockhampton to Longreach, and from Townsville to Mt Isa. Local services include the *Gulflander* and the *Savannahlander* – see the Gulf Savannah section for details.

Queensland trains are slower than buses but are similarly priced if you travel economy class. They're almost all air-con and you can get sleeping berths on most trains for $30 a night in economy, or $50 in 1st class. You can break your journey on most services for no extra cost provided you complete the trip within 14 days. The only

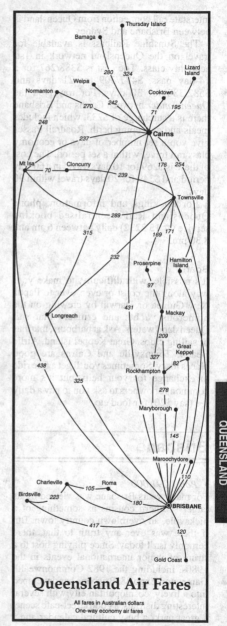

Queensland Air Fares

All fares in Australian dollars
One-way economy air fares

QUEENSLAND

interstate rail connection from Queensland is between Brisbane and Sydney.

The Sunshine Railpass is available for travel on the Queensland network in 1st/economy class. The cost is $388/267 for a 14-day pass, $477/309 for 21 days and $582/388 for 30 days. For travel on the *Queenslander* between Cairns and Brisbane there is a surcharge of $233, which includes meals and a sleeping berth. Roadrail Passes give you a set number of days of economy class rail travel within a set period. The cost of these is $269 for 10 days travel in a 60-day period and $349 for 20 days travel within 90 days.

For bookings and information, phone Queensland Rail's centralised booking service (☎ 13 2232) daily between 6 am and 8.30 pm.

Boat

It's possible, with difficulty, to make your way along the coast or even over to Papua New Guinea or Darwin by crewing on the numerous yachts and cruisers that sail Queensland waters. Ask at harbours, marinas or sailing clubs. Great Keppel Island, Airlie Beach, Townsville and Cairns are good places to try. Sometimes you'll get a free ride in exchange for your help, but it's more common for owners to ask you to pay a daily fee (say $20) for food etc.

Brisbane

• *Pop 1,291,000*

For many years Brisbane was viewed by its larger southern cousins as something of a hicksville, an overblown country town. But if there was ever any truth to that, there certainly isn't today. Since playing host to a string of major international events in the 1980s, including the 1982 Commonwealth Games and Expo 88, Brisbane has developed into a lively, cosmopolitan city with several interesting districts, a good street-cafe scene, a great park, a busy cultural calendar and a

decent nightlife – though you'll need to do some work to find it.

The city began as a dumping ground for the more recalcitrant convicts the colony of New South Wales wanted as far away as possible. The tropical country to the north seemed a good place to banish them to. Accordingly, in 1824, a penal settlement was established at Redcliffe on Moreton Bay but it was soon abandoned due to lack of water and hostile Aboriginal people. The settlement was moved south and inland to the present site of Brisbane where a town grew up.

Although the penal settlement was abandoned in 1839, Brisbane's future was assured when the area was thrown open to free settlers in 1842. As Queensland's huge agricultural potential and mineral riches were developed, so Brisbane grew. Today, it's the third-largest city in Australia.

Although close to the coast, Brisbane is very much a river city. It's a scenic place, surrounded by hills and fine lookouts, with several impressive bridges spanning the Brisbane River. It also enjoys an excellent climate.

Several of Queensland's major attractions can be reached on day trips from Brisbane. The Gold and Sunshine coasts and their mountainous hinterlands are short bus rides from the city, and you can also visit the islands of Moreton Bay or head inland towards the Great Dividing Range and the Darling Downs.

Orientation

Brisbane is built along and between the looping meanders of the Brisbane River, about 25km upstream from the river mouth. The Brisbane transit centre, where you'll arrive if you're coming by bus, train or airport shuttle, is on Roma St about 500m west of the city centre – which is focused on the Queen St Mall.

Most of the city's accommodation and eating options are clustered in the inner suburbs surrounding the city. Immediately north is Spring Hill, with some good mid-range options, while west of the centre is

Brisbane Walking Tour

As good a place as any to start is at the classically-styled **City Hall** where you should take the lift up to the top of the bell tower for the **view** – this will give some idea of the layout of the central part of the city.

On leaving turn right out of the entrance, cross Adelaide St and head straight down Albert St to the **Queen St Mall**. This is the city's main shopping thoroughfare and it's nothing you're going to be writing home about, but swing right and look up to the left at some of the facades – the former Carlton Hotel, the former Telegraph Building, the former York Hotel. Turn around and head down the mall to **Hoyts Regent Theatre,** which will be on your right, and pass through the foyer into the former booking hall, built in the days when movie houses were designed as temples to the glamour of the screen.

Retrace your steps back along the mall to the junction with Albert St and head downhill, past the information kiosk. This time keep your eyes on the ground and look for the bronze plaques set in the paving; these form part of a **literary trail** down Albert St, each plaque featuring a quote about Brisbane extracted from the work of one of the 32 featured writers. Albert St has a couple of good cafes and one of the better city pubs, Gilhooley's.

Take a left after Gilhooley's onto Charlotte St and continue across Edward St (notice the pattern in the street names: east-west are all women, north-south men) and after about 150m there's an entrance into the grounds of **St Stephen's Cathedral**. While the cathedral isn't particularly significant, pass around it and out onto Elizabeth St – then turn around for a great photo of the twin Gothic spires against a background of mirrored-glass office blocks.

Opposite the cathedral on the north side of Elizabeth St is an arched opening; follow it through. This runs alongside the **post office**, built in the 1870s, which has a beautiful facade where you emerge on Queen St. (The newsagency you pass in the alleyway has Brisbane's best selection of overseas newspapers.) Next door and to the left of the post office (as seen from Queen St) is an amazingly imposing building, complete with carved gargoyles, which looks like it was lifted from a movie set in Gotham City – it only lacks Batman perched on top. During WWII this building, now known as **MacArthur Chambers**, was used as the headquarters of the commander-in-chief of the South-West Pacific area, General MacArthur.

Walk on past the chambers, crossing Creek St and on into the heart of Brisbane's central business district (CBD). At the junction with Wharf St, turning right would take you up to the upmarket dining complexes of **Riverside** and **Eagle St Pier** (bizarrely, in the case of the latter, it's visually dominated by a McDonald's) but, instead, turn left and walk two blocks up to Ann St. There are two choices here: a left will take you past the Victorian-era **Central Station** and, opposite, the Greek Classical **Shrine of Remembrance**, from where it's 300m back to City Hall. Alternatively, off to the right Ann St runs straight through the heart of Fortitude Valley, just over half a kilometre away.

Fortitude Valley is well worth exploring. Before the Valley you'll first pass **St John's Cathedral,** begun in 1901 and still under construction (this fact is proudly proclaimed on a billboard out front but is it really something to boast about?) and then the **Orient Hotel**, one of the city's oldest pubs and still a popular gig venue. Once you cross the slip road for the Story bridge you're in the Valley's modest **Chinatown**. One block after the dragon gateway of the Chinatown mall is the **Brunswick St Mall** with several good cafes, a decent bar and, at the bottom, **McWhirters**, an eclectic shopping emporium.

To return to the city catch almost any of the buses from the stop on Ann St just before the Story Bridge road junction. ∎

Petrie Terrace, with several budget hostels, and Paddington, an attractive residential suburb with good cafes and restaurants. North-east from the city, along Ann St, is Fortitude Valley, a fairly trendy area incorporating a small Chinatown and lots of cafes, restaurants and clubs. East beyond the Valley is New Farm, an upwardly mobile district of pricey eat-and-be-seen places.

South across the Victoria Bridge is South Brisbane, with the Queensland Cultural Centre and the South Bank Parklands; further south are Highgate Hill and the hip West End.

Information

Tourist Offices At the transit centre, on level 3, is the privately-run Brisbane Visitors Accommodation Service desk (☎ 3236 2020), which offers a booking and information service for backpackers. It operates weekdays from 7 am to 6 pm and weekends from 8 am to 5 pm. There's also an information desk on level 2.

The Queen St Mall information centre (☎ 3229 5918), on the corner of Queen and Albert Sts, is good on things to see and do around town; it's open Monday to Thursday from 9 am to 5.30 pm, Friday to 9 pm, Saturday to 4 pm and Sunday from 10 am to 4 pm.

There's also the less useful Tourism Brisbane information desk (☎ 3221 8411) in the City Hall, on King George Square and a Queensland Travel & Tourism Corporation centre (☎ 13 1801), on the corner of Adelaide and Edward Sts, which is more a booking office than an information centre but they may be able to answer some queries.

Post & Communications The main post office is in Queen St and it's open weekdays from 7 am to 6 pm. At weekends there's a Post Shop, which performs the function of a post office, on the 2nd level of the Myer Centre off the Queen St Mall; it's open from 10 am to 4 pm Saturday and Sunday.

Email The Central City Library in the basement of the City Plaza complex behind City

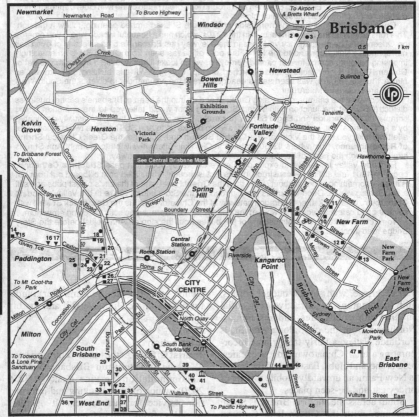

Hall has Internet stations for hire at $4 per hour. It's open 10 am to 6 pm weekdays and 10 am to 3 pm at weekends. *The Hub* (☎ 3229 1119) is an Internet cafe at 125 Margaret St in the city centre, and at the corner of Brunswick and Ann Sts down in the Valley there's *Cafe Scene* (☎ 3216 0624).

Useful Organisations The RACQ (☎ 3361 2444) is beside the main post office at 261 Queen St. For information on national parks, the Naturally Queensland office (☎ 3227 8186) at 160 Ann St is open on weekdays from 8.30 am to 5 pm.

The city council produces a series of brochures on Brisbane for the disabled, which should be available from the BCC Customer Services Centre at City Plaza behind the City Hall, or call the Disability Services Unit on ☎ 3403 5769.

Bookshops The city's best is the Mary Ryan Bookshop on Queen St Mall, one of a small family-run chain (others are in Paddington

and New Farm). Angus & Robertson Bookworld are on Post Office Square in Adelaide St and at the south-west end of the Queen St Mall. The largest range of travel guides and maps is to be found at World Wide Maps & Guides at 187 George St (100m south of the Queen St Mall).

For second-hand titles try Archives Fine Books, spread over three shops at 40-42 Charlotte St in the city centre, or Emma's Bookshop, a small but densely crammed place at 82A Vulture St in the West End.

Medical Services The Travellers' Medical & Vaccination Centre (☎ 3221 9066), on the 6th floor of the Qantas building at 247 Adelaide St, can handle all vaccinations and medical advice for travellers. There's also a 24-hour Travellers' Medical Service (☎ 3211 3611), on the 1st floor at 245 Albert St above McDonald's, which offers travel vaccinations, women's health care and first aid kits. The Brisbane Sexual Health Clinic (☎ 3227 7091) is at 484 Adelaide St.

PLACES TO STAY		47	Courtney Place	3	Newstead House
5	Red Hot Chilli Packers' Hostel; Brunswick Hotel		Backpackers	4	The Valley Swimming Pool
6	Globetrekkers' Hostel	**PLACES TO EAT**		7	New Farm Mountain Bikes
8	The Bowen Terrace	1	Breakfast Creek Hotel	9	Village Twin Cinemas
10	The Homestead	15	King Tut's Wa Wa Hut	18	Brisbane Arts Theatre
11	Atoa House Travellers' Hostel	16	Jakarta Indonesian Restaurant	22	Caxton Hotel
12	Allender Apartments	17	Sultan's Kitchen	23	Crazies Comedy Restaurant;
13	Edward Lodge	21	Irish Connection		Casablanca
14	Waverley B&B	29	Three Monkeys Coffee House	24	The Underground Nightclub
19	Aussie Way Backpackers	30	Wok On Inn	25	La Boite Theatre
20	Banana Benders Backpackers	31	Qan Heng's Restaurant	28	Castlemaine Perkins XXXX Brewery
26	Brisbane City YHA; City Backpackers Hostel	32	Cafe Babylon	33	Emma's Bookshop
		34	Caffe Tempo; Cafe Nouveau	41	Queensland Maritime Museum
27	Yellow Submarine Backpackers	36	Khan's Kitchen; Kim Thanh; Mogul Room	42	The Capitol
35	Brisbane Resort			43	The Cliffs Rock-Climbing Area
37	Swagman's Rest	39	Captain Snapper		
38	Somewhere to Stay	40	Ship Inn	48	Brisbane Cricket Ground (The Gabba)
44	Paramount Apartments	**OTHER**			
45	Kangaroo Motel	2	Breakfast Creek Wharf		
46	A1 Motel				

QUEENSLAND

City Centre

Brisbane's **City Hall**, on the corner of Adelaide and Albert Sts, has gradually been surrounded by skyscrapers but the observation platform still provides a great view across the city – a free lift runs weekdays from 8.30 am to 4.30 pm and Saturday from 10 am to 4.30 pm. There's also a free art gallery on the ground floor, open daily from 10 am to 5 pm.

There are a great many other attractive **historical buildings** dotted around the centre and Brisbane City Council publishes a series of *Heritage Trail* brochures that guide you around some of the most interesting. One worth taking a look at is the old **Treasury Building**, near the Victoria bridge on George St, which is now Brisbane's 24-hour casino.

Just a little way south at 110 George St is the **Sciencentre**, a hands-on science museum with interactive displays, optical illusions, a perception tunnel and a regular 20-minute show in the theatre. It's open daily from 10 am to 5 pm ($7).

Continuing south on George St brings you to **Parliament House**, dating from 1868 and built in French Renaissance style. Free tours are given Monday to Friday five times a day (except when Parliament is sitting). To the east, the parliament building overlooks Brisbane's **Botanic Gardens** which occupy 18 hectares at the southern end of the city centre, contained in a loop of the river. The gardens are popular with in-line skaters, joggers, picnickers and lunching office workers, and they're open 24 hours a day (and lit at night). There are free guided tours of the gardens leaving from the rotunda just south of the Albert St entrance every day except Monday at 11 am and 1 pm.

Queensland Cultural Centre

This is an extensive cultural complex just across Victoria Bridge from the city centre and includes the city's main art gallery, museum and theatre complex.

The **Queensland Museum** contains a fairly lively and diverse set of collections, all of which are in some way relevant to Queensland – that includes a dinosaur garden, exhibitions on whales, the history of photography and natural history, and an extensive collection of Melanesian artefacts. There's also a small aviation section with the *Avian Cirrus*, in which Queensland's Bert Hinkler made the first England to Australia solo flight in 1928. The museum is open daily from 9 am to 5 pm. Admission is free.

The **Queensland Art Gallery** has an impressive permanent collection of Australian artists and also features visiting exhibitions. It's open daily from 10 am to 5 pm and admission is free. There are free guided tours during the week at 11 am and 1 and 2 pm, and on weekends at 11 am and 2 and 3 pm.

South Bank Parklands

Brisbane's South Bank, formerly the site of Expo 88, has been extensively redeveloped and is now an excellent landscaped, riverside park with grassy areas, streams and a fantastic open-air **swimming pool** designed to resemble a lagoon, complete with a crescent of white sandy beach. There are also numerous cafes and restaurants and a weekend market. It's always worth wandering down here at weekends during summer as there's usually some kind of performance, fair or food festival taking place.

In the plaza in the centre of the parkland, the **Butterfly & Insect House** is a tropical conservatorium which is home to hundreds of freely-fluttering Australian butterflies, as well as a securely glass-encased collection of insects and spiders. It's open daily from 8.30 am to 5 pm ($8, children $4.50).

The South Bank visitor information centre (☎ 3867 2051) is located on the central Stanley St Plaza and is open daily from 8 am to 8 pm. You can also phone ☎ 3867 2020 for a recorded message with details of the current entertainment program.

Other Museums

The **Queensland Maritime Museum**, just south of South Bank, has a wide range of displays including an 1881 dry dock, an impressive collection of model ships, relics from old wrecks, and numerous boats such as the WWII frigate HMAS *Diamantina*. It's open from 9.30 am to 5 pm daily ($5, children $2.50).

Markets

The **Crafts Village** at South Bank is a handicraft market which sets up on Friday evenings, and Saturday and Sunday until 5 pm. Over at the **Eagle St Pier** there's a similar Sunday morning market also devoted to handicrafts. The two can be easily visited together using the City Cat. On Saturday, the **Fortitude Valley Market** in the Brunswick St Mall is a small affair comprising artsy-craftsy, hippy stalls. There's usually live entertainment and plenty of streetside cafes in which to kick back and observe.

Mt Coot-tha Park

Located 8km west of the city centre, Mt Coot-tha has a great **lookout point** with views out over Brisbane to the bay and over to Moreton and Stradbroke islands, the Glass House Mountains to the north and the mountains in the Gold Coast hinterland to the south. If you want to linger over the views, there's a good cafe and restaurant open every day for lunch and dinner.

There are some good walks around Mt Coot-tha and its foothills, like the one to JC Slaughter Falls on Simpsons Rd. There's also an **Aboriginal Art Trail**, a 1.5km walking trail which takes you past eight art sites with work by local Aboriginal artists including tree carvings, rock paintings and a dance pit.

The very beautiful **Mt Coot-tha Botanic Gardens**, at the foot of the mountain, covers 52 hectares and includes over 20,000 species of plants, an enclosed tropical dome, an arid zone, rainforests and a Japanese garden. It's open daily from 8.30 am to 5.30 pm. There are free guided walks through the gardens at 11 am and 1 pm daily except Sunday.

Also within the gardens is the **Sir Thomas Brisbane Planetarium** (also known as the Cosmic Skydome), the largest planetarium in Australia. There are 45-minute shows at 3.30 and 7.30 pm from Wednesday to Friday;

1.30, 3.30 and 7.30 pm on Saturday; and 1.30 and 3.30 pm on Sunday ($8, children $4.50).

To get to the botanic gardens take bus No 37A ($2) which departs at 13 minutes past each hour from Ann St close to King George Square. The ride takes about 15 minutes and the bus drops you off in the car park. The lookout is 3km from the botanic gardens – turn left out of the car park and start climbing. It's a tough walk. There is a bus directly to the lookout, No 10C from Adelaide St, but at the time of writing it departed twice a day only at 8.50 am and 2.10 pm – call ☎ 13 1230 to check current times.

Brisbane Forest Park

The Brisbane Forest Park is a 26,500 hectare natural bushland reserve stretching from the outskirts of Brisbane for more than 50km to the north and west. There's an **information centre** (☎ 3300 4855) in the Gap, at the start of the park, which is open weekdays from 8.30 am to 4.30 pm and on weekends 10 am to 5 pm. The rangers run regular guided bushwalks and tours – ring for details.

In the same spot is **Walk-About Creek**, a freshwater study centre where you can see fish, lizards, pythons and turtles at close quarters. It's open daily from 9 am to 4.30 pm (weekends from 10 am; $3.50). Upstairs, there's a good cafe/restaurant.

To get to the park from the city, follow Musgrave, Waterworks and Mt Nebo roads. You can take a bus to the Gap – it's about a 700m walk to the information centre. Note that the walking trails start elsewhere in the park and you'll need transport to reach them.

Wildlife Sanctuaries

The **Alma Park Zoo** at Kallangur, 28km north of the city centre, is an excellent zoo in a spacious garden setting. It has a large collection of Australian wildlife including koalas, kangaroos, emus, dingoes, and exotic animals such as Malaysian sun bears, leopards and monkeys. It's open daily from 9 am to 5 pm ($15, children $8). A daily 'zoo train' departs from the transit centre at 9 am (Caboolture line); get off at

QUEENSLAND

Brisbane From the Cat

Easily the best way to view Brisbane is from the river and the best way of getting about the river is on a City Cat. These large, blue catamaran ferries glide up and downstream all day from around 6 am until after 11 pm. A $3 ticket will allow you travel the whole route (from Bretts Wharf to the University of Queensland and back takes two hours) but if you step off you'll have to buy a new ticket. Alternatively, buy a saver card (see the Getting Around section) for as little as $4 and you can hop on and off wherever you like.

Upriver From Riverside Riverside is the CBD stop at the north end of Elizabeth St, next to the Eagle St Pier complex. Heading upstream, the cliffs of Kangaroo Point are off to the left, while over to the right the river is fringed by mangroves. As the City Cat passes under the Captain Cook Bridge, over to the left is the Maritime Museum. **QUT Gardens Point** is the place to get off to visit the Parliament Building and the City Botanic Gardens, after which there's a zigzag sprint across the river to **South Bank** for the parklands and back across to **North Quay** for the Casino and the Queen St Mall.

Upstream from North Quay is the longest uninterrupted stretch of the route, passing under three bridges and then cruising along with the riverside suburb of Auchenflower on the right and the grassy banks of South Brisbane over on the left. The lighthouse-like structure passed on the left is actually a scriving tower for the local gasworks. South Brisbane gives way to Orleigh Park, one of the city's most fashionable addresses.

Both **Guyatt Park** and **West End** service residential areas and there's nothing to get off for, but on the next bend is the City Cats' upstream terminus, **University of Queensland**, a place well worth spending a few hours. It's an attractive campus with some good museums, excellent sporting facilities, a bookshop, the Schonell Cinema and a good cheap cafe. There's a helpful information office in a small building beside the main entrance.

Downriver from Riverside Heading downstream the City Cat immediately passes under the Story Bridge, built in 1934-40 and sharing some of the same design engineers as the Sydney Harbour Bridge. The river continues to loop around the peninsula of Kangaroo Point, a former shipbuilding area now the site of a major, upmarket residential development. Across the river, on the left, is the suburb of New Farm serviced by **Sydney St**. The City Cat then shuttles over to **Mowbray Park**, the stop for East Brisbane, and then back to **New Farm Park** – a large and quite beautiful park with a good kiosk cafe in the middle.

Just past the park the route passes through the old wharf area with huge brick warehouses lining the river to the left. The two stops on this stretch, **Hawthorne** and **Bulimba**, are for residential districts. After leaving Bulimba you can see over on the far bank a small, wooded park headland; hidden within the trees is Newstead House, one of Brisbane's oldest residences, now a small museum. Across the creek from Newstead is the Breakfast Creek Hotel, an excellent place for lunch. The downriver terminus of the City Cat is **Bretts Wharf**. As you approach look up to the left where on the hillside are the white-painted verandahs of what is perhaps Brisbane's most beautiful Queenslander house. From Bretts Wharf it's just a short walk to trendy, cafe-laden Racecourse Rd, or 1km back to Breakfast Creek.

The University of Queensland, Guyatt Park, North Quay, South bank and Hawthorne stops all have disabled access. ■

Dakabin (50 minutes) where there'll be a courtesy bus for the zoo.

Just a 35 minute, $2.60 bus ride from the city centre, the **Lone Pine Koala Sanctuary** is also an easy half-day trip. The sanctuary is set in attractive parklands beside the river and is home to a wide variety of Australian wildlife of which the star attractions are the 130 or so koalas. They are undeniably cute

and can be held. You can also picnic in a field of tame kangaroos. Talks about the animals are given throughout the day. Lone Pine is open from 8 am to 5 pm daily ($12.50, or $9 with a VIP or YHA card, children $6.50). Cityxpress bus No 581 leaves at 35 minutes past the hour from the Koala platform at the Queen St Mall underground bus station. Alternatively, the MV *Mirimar* (☎ 3221

Northern Territory
Top: With no rail link to the south, road trains are the freight carriers
Bottom: Colourful mail boxes in the outback

Northern Territory
Top: Kings Canyon, Watarrka National Park
Middle: The Ghan
Bottom: Billabongs at Kakadu National Park

0300) cruises up the Brisbane River to the sanctuary, costing $15 return for adults and $8 for children (Lone Pine admission not included). It departs daily at 10 am from North Quay, next to Victoria Bridge, at the end of the Queen St Mall.

Activities

The Cliffs, on the south bank of the Brisbane River in Kangaroo Point, is an excellent **rock climbing** venue which is floodlit until midnight or later. Several operators offer climbing and abseiling instruction here, including Jane Clarkson's Outdoor Adventures (☎ 0411 554 079). For beginners, there are Saturday morning abseiling sessions (three to four hours; $30), and introductory rock climbing on Wednesday nights ($10 per person); she also organises abseiling and climbing trips out of Brisbane.

Skatebiz (☎ 3220 0157) at 101 Albert St hires out **in-line skates** from $10 for two hours.

Kayak Escapes (☎ 3359 3486) runs **kayaking** trips up the Upper Brisbane River, with day trips on Thursday ($75) and two-day expeditions on Tuesday and Saturday ($175 to $225 including meals and camping gear). Jane Clarkson's Outdoor Adventures also does one-day kayaking trips for $65.

For bicycle hire see the Getting Around section.

Good **Swimming Pools** include the Valley Pool (☎ 3852 1231), open daily from 5.30 am (from 7.30 am on Sunday, on the corner of Wickham and East Sts in Fortitude Valley; the old Spring Hill Baths (☎ 3831 7881) in Torrington St; and the Olympic-sized Centenary Pool (☎ 3831 2665) nearby on Gregory Tce. Plus, of course, there's the 'lagoon' at the South Bank Parklands.

Organised Tours & Cruises

City Tours The open-sided City Sights trambus shuttles around 18 of the city's major landmarks (including the South Bank Parklands, CBD and the Valley & Chinatown), departing every 40 minutes between 9 am and 4.20 pm from Post Office Square in Queen St – you can get off and on when-

ever and wherever you want. One-day tickets cost $15 for adults – get them from City Hall or the tourist information kiosk on Queen St Mall. There's also a good, council-run two-hour City Heights tour, which goes up to Mt Coot-tha Lookout and Botanic Gardens. It departs daily at 2 pm from the City Hall City Sights bus stop on Adelaide St and costs $7.

Brewery Tours From Monday to Wednesday at 11 am, 1.30, 4.30 and 7 pm there are guided tours of the Castlemaine-Perkins XXXX brewery (☎ 3361 7597) on Milton Rd. Most hostels organise trips or you can go along on your own but you must book. The tour lasts about an hour, costs $5 and you get four free beers at the end. The brewery is 1.5km west of the transit centre or take an Ipswich train (departing the transit centre and Central Station every 15 minutes; $1.40) to Milton Rd station, right outside the brewery.

The Carlton Brewhouse (VB and Fosters) (☎ 3826 5858) also conducts tours of its premises, which are a half-hour south of the city centre. A bus departs the transit centre at 9.15 and 11.15 am and 1.15 pm daily and the cost is $10 including beer, lunch and transfers.

River Cruises The *Kookaburra Queen I & II* (☎ 3221 1300) are restored wooden paddle-steamers that cruise the Brisbane River. There are 1½ hour cruises at 10 am and 12.45 pm ($20), an additional Sunday afternoon cruise at 3.30 pm ($20), and 2½ hour daily dinner cruises at 7.30 pm (Sunday at 6.30 pm) for $40 with buffet. The cruises depart from the Eagle St Pier, next to the Riverside Centre.

The *Brisbane Star* (☎ 018 190 604) does a four-hour Sunday cruise from the city to the Brisbane River mouth and back, departing at 1 pm from the Edward St Pier. Cost per person is $10.

Other Tours Run by a former backpacking globetrotter, Rob's Rainforest Tours (☎ 019 496 607) offers several different daytrips out of Brisbane, taking travellers to the

QUEENSLAND

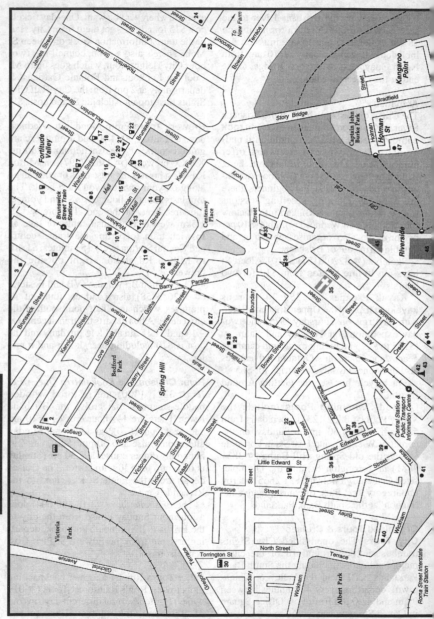

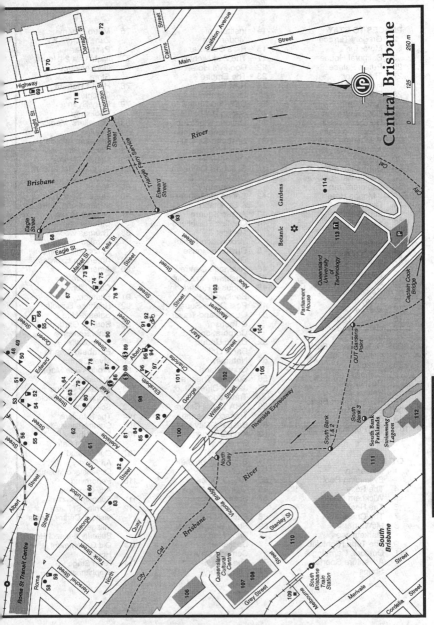

Central Brisbane

PLACES TO STAY
2 Gregory Terrace Motor Inn
3 Balmoral House
25 Pete's Palace
27 Thornbury House B&B
28 Dahrl Court Apartments
29 Kookaburra Inn
36 Dorchester Self-Contained Units
37 Yale Inner-City Inn
38 Annie's Shandon Inn
39 Astor Motel
40 Soho Club Motel
53 Palace Backpackers
60 Explorers' Inn
70 Il Mondo Hotel
71 Ryan's on the River
109 Sly Fox Hotel

PLACES TO EAT
10 Vietnamese Restaurant
12 Universal Noodle Restaurant
13 Enjoy Inn
16 Mellino's
18 Lucky's Trattoria
19 Cafe Scene Internet Cafe
20 Cafe Europ & Bitch
21 California Cafe
50 Mekong Chinese Restaurant
54 Palace Cafe
76 Hungry Heart Bistro
94 Pane e Vino
96 Govinda's
103 The Hub Internet Cafe

OTHER
1 Centenary Swimming Pool
4 The Roxy
5 Wickham Hotel
6 The Healer
7 The Chelsea
8 McWhirters Marketplace
9 The Tube Nightclub
11 Outdoor, Camping & Adventure Sports Shops

14 Institute of Modern Art
15 Ric's Cafe-Bar
17 The Zoo Nightclub
22 Dooley's Hotel
23 The Empire
24 New Farm Laundromat
26 CES Job Centre
30 Spring Hill Baths
31 Options Nightclub
32 Sportsman's Hotel
33 Brisbane Sexual Health Centre
34 Orient Hotel
35 St John's Cathedral
41 Old Windmill & Observatory
42 Shrine of Memories & Cenotaph
43 Anzac Square
44 Qantas; Traveller's Medical & Vaccination Clinic
45 Customs House Gallery
46 Riverside Centre
47 Brisbane Jazz Club
48 Angus & Robertson Bookworld
49 Post Office Square
51 Queensland Travel & Tourism Corporation
52 Down Under Bar & Grill
55 Naturally Queensland
56 Suncorp Theatre
57 Jazz & Blues Club; Travelodge
58 YHA Travel Centre
59 Transcontinental
61 Brisbane City Hall
62 King George Square
63 STA Travel
64 Broadway on the Mall
65 RACQ Office
66 Main Post Office
67 St Stephen's Cathedral
68 Eagle St Pier
69 Story Bridge Hotel
72 Snug Harbour Dockside; Comedy Cafe
73 The Gig
74 The Victory

75 Metro Cinema; Zane's Caffe & Pasta Bar
77 Night Owl 24Hour Convenience Store
78 Hoyt's Regent Cinema
79 Mary Ryan Bookshop
80 Travellers' Medical Service
81 Brisbane Arcade
82 Central City Library
83 Dendy Cinema
84 Angus & Robertson Bookworld
85 Ansett
86 Queen St Mal Information Centre
87 Greater Union Cinema
88 Thomas Cook Foreign Exchange Centre
89 American Express
90 American Bookstore; Caffe Libri
91 Skatebiz
92 Brisbane Bicycle Sales & Hire
93 Botanic Gardens Main Entrance
95 Gilhooley's
97 Elizabeth Arcade
98 Myer Centre
99 World Wide Maps &Guides
100 Treasury Casino
101 Archives Fine Books
102 Sciencentre
104 The Mansions
105 Commissariat Stores
106 State Library; Riverfront Cafe
107 Queensland Art Gallery
108 Queensland Museum
110 Performing Arts Complex
111 Suncorp Piazza
112 Stanley St Plaza Visitors' Centre; Crafts Village; Butterfly & Insect House
113 Old Government House
114 River Stage Amphitheatre

QUEENSLAND

rainforests at Mount Glorious, Kondalilla Falls and the Glasshouse Mountains, and Lamington National Park. Several Lonely Planet readers have written in with high praise for the tours. The price per person is $35, which includes morning tea, a barbecue lunch and pick-up and return to your hostel.

There are several other operators running similar hinterland trips but in general their prices are considerably higher than Rob's.

Something a little more unusual that also offers good value is Araucaria Ecotours' (☎ 5544 1283; ecotoura@eisnet.au) three-day wilderness trip into the Mt Barney National Park area. The tour picks up in Brisbane every Wednesday morning (usually at South Brisbane station but also at the transit centre by arrangement) and involves trekking through various forest types with halts for examining flora and fauna, including a creek where a platypus often puts in an appearance. There are also possibilities to swim and snorkel in a creek, and maybe do some boating too. However, the accent is firmly on the educational – the tours are led by Ronda Green, a qualified research wildlife ecologist who really knows her stuff. The cost is $160 including accommodation but not meals.

For a day trip to the Gold Coast, the High Roller bus (☎ 3222 4067) to Conrad Jupiters Casino is good value. It leaves from the Roma St transit centre daily at 9 am and costs $10 return, which includes a $5 meal voucher and a $5 gaming voucher.

Special Events

The major event on the arts calendar is the annual Brisbane Festival held every August/September. The other big event is the Ekka or Royal National Agricultural Show held at the exhibition grounds in early August. There's also a 10-day international film festival in August and a three-day Writers' Festival in September. Also in September is Livid, an annual one-day alternative rock festival. After Spring, April would seem to be the other big festival month containing an international comedy festival, the Streets of Brisbane festival, the Queens-

land Heritage Week and the Brisbane Travel Show at the South Bank Exhibition Centre.

Places to Stay

Brisbane has plenty of hostels and backpackers' places, and there are also quite a few well-priced hotels, motels and self-contained apartment blocks within easy reach of the centre.

Camping The closest park to the city centre is *Newmarket Gardens Caravan Park* (☎ 33 56 1458), just 4km to the north at 199 Ashgrove Ave, in Ashgrove. Several bus routes connect it with town and there's a train station nearby. Powered sites for two people are $16, and on-site vans go for $29 for a double or $34 for three people. Otherwise, you can try the following:

Aspley Acres Caravan Park (☎ 3263 2668), 13km north, 1420 Gympie Rd, Aspley; tent sites from $10, on-site vans from $32, cabins at $40
Dress Circle Village (☎ 3341 6133), 14km south, 10 Holmead Rd, Eight Mile Plain; tent sites from $10, on-site cabins from $50
Gateway Junction Village (☎ 3341 6333) and *Sheldon Caravan Park* (☎ 3341 6166); both 19km south, in School Rd, Roachdale

Hostels The Brisbane Visitors Accommodation Service (☎ 3236 2020), on the 3rd level of the transit centre, is a free booking service open on weekdays from 7 am to 6 pm and weekends from 8 am to 5 pm. This place has brochures and information on all the hostels and other budget options, and once you have decided where to stay they'll ring the hostel and arrange for someone to pick you up.

Brisbane's hostels are concentrated in three main areas: Petrie Terrace & Paddington, just west of the city centre; Fortitude Valley and New Farm, north-east of the city; and south of the city in South & East Brisbane and West End.

City There's only one hostel in the City, the *Palace Backpackers* (☎ 1800 676 340), but it's probably Brisbane's best. Located at the corner of Ann and Edward Sts it's as central as you can get and just five-minutes walk from the transit centre. It occupies a Heritage-listed, former Salvation Army headquarters, which has been extensively modernised – facilities include a huge communal kitchen, TV lounges, laundries, a tour desk, a job finders club and a rooftop sundeck. Downstairs is the city's most popular backpackers' bar, Down Under (see Entertainment). The only drawback is that the partying has a tendency to spill over into the hostel corridors, and nights at the Palace can be far from quiet. Dorm beds are from $15 (five to seven per room) to $17 (three or four per room), singles without/with air-con are $22/25, doubles are $34/38.

Spring Hill The *Kookaburra Inn* (☎ /fax 3832 1303) at 41 Phillips St is an old converted Queenslander with communal kitchens, bathrooms and laundry facilities. It's well located in a quiet, leafy street, not too far out of the city centre, and is especially popular with Japanese travellers. There are no dorms; singles/doubles cost $30/40 with cheaper weekly rates.

Petrie Terrace & Paddington Petrie Tce isn't the most exciting of areas but it is close to the transit centre and neighbouring Caxton St has plenty of good cafes, restaurants and bars.

There are three adjacent hostels on Upper Roma St, the first of which is the pink-painted *City Backpackers' Hostel* (☎ 3211 3221) at 380 Upper Roma St, a newish and fairly charmless two-storey, 76-bed hostel. A bed in a four to six-bunk dorm costs $13, twins and doubles cost $32. The *Roma St Hostel*, right next door, is not recommended. A little further along at 392 Upper Roma St is the *Brisbane City YHA* (☎ 3236 1004) with excellent facilities including a good on-site cafe, a tour booking desk and provision for the disabled. The cost for non-YHA members is $19 per person in a four to six-bed dorm (no mixed dorms) or $42 for a twin room. There are also twins, doubles and triples with air-con and en-suite for a little more.

One block south of Upper Roma is *Yellow*

Submarine Backpackers (☎ 3211 3424) at 66 Quay St, occupying a brightly painted – yellow, naturally – old house. It's very homely and friendly with a pool, small garden terraces and BBQ grills. They'll also help you find work here. Dorms (three or six beds to a room) are $13 per night, twins and singles $30.

Banana Benders Backpackers (☎ 3367 1157) is a short walk north, on the corner of Petrie Tce and Jessie St. The outside is painted bright yellow and blue, so you can't miss it. It's a small place in two sections with the usual facilities, and it has good views over to the west. The dorms are mostly four-share and cost $14 a night; doubles are $32. The only hassle here is that Petrie Tce can get noisy during peak hours.

Down the side street past Banana Benders is the small *Aussie Way Backpackers* (☎ 3369 0711) at 34 Cricket St. It's a recently renovated, beautiful two-storey timber house with a front balcony – very clean, quiet and well set up. A bed in one of the three to five-bunk dorms costs $14 a night; there are also two single rooms at $27 and one double at $32.

Fortitude Valley & New Farm The YHA-associated *Balmoral House* (☎ 3252 1397) at 33 Amelia St in the Valley has been renovated in recent years and good facilities include a laundry and large kitchen. The place is well located for nightlife in the Valley – that said it's a fairly quiet establishment and definitely not a party place. A bed in a three or four-bed dorm is $13, singles/doubles with shared bathrooms cost $28/32.

All the rest of the hostels are out in New Farm, most of them a 10-minute walk from the Valley – itself a 15 minute walk from the city centre – but two regular bus services run along Brunswick St and down into town.

Pete's Palace (☎ 3254 1984) at 515 Brunswick St is popular with long-termers and feels very much like a student house. Dorm beds (four to a room) are from $11 and a very basic double goes for $30.

One block further, the *Red Hot Chilli Packers'* (☎ 3392 0137) at 569 Brunswick

St is housed above the Brunswick Hotel. It's a bit grubby but, again, it's popular with semi-settled travellers and has a job club to help newcomers find work. Dorm beds are $12 (or $70 per week), doubles are $30 ($180 a week).

Three blocks further and a right into Balfour St, the *Globetrekkers' Hostel* (☎ 3358 1251), is a renovated 100 year-old timber house. It's small and tranquil and very friendly. A bed in a five-bunk dorm costs $12 (there's a women's dorm), twins are $28 and doubles are $30. This place also allows travellers with mobile homes to park up out the back and use the hostel facilities for $5 a night.

The *Bowen Terrace* (☎ 3254 1575) at 365 Bowen Tce, like the Globetrekkers, is family run and as such is well maintained, orderly and quiet. Singles are from $18 to $23, while a large, well-furnished double with fridge and TV goes for $35.

The *Homestead* (☎ 3358 3538) at 57 Annie St is a large, modern place with reasonable facilities and a party attitude. It offers free use of bikes and free trips to Mt Coot-tha lookout. A bed in a six or eight-bed dorm costs $12 while doubles and twins with shared facilities cost $32.

Further down Annie St at No 95 is the long-running *Atoa House Travellers' Hostel* (☎ 3358 4507), which occupies three adjacent Queenslander-style houses. Dorm beds cost $14 a night, singles/doubles are $25/32. The hostel has a spacious backyard with plenty of grass and shady trees, and if you have your own tent you can camp out the back for $7 a night. It's a bit of a trek from here up to Brunswick St and the bus stop.

South & East Brisbane & West End The
Sly Fox (☎ 3844 0022), on the corner of Melbourne and Hope Sts in South Brisbane, occupies the top three storeys of an old pub. The location is good – it's a short walk from South Bank and the city – but the place is a bit shabby, the kitchen is tiny and the pub has live music, so it tends to be noisy. Dorm beds cost $11 and $12, twins and doubles $35.

A further 10-minute walk south is the

Brisbane Resort (☎ 3844 9956) at 110 Vulture St, West End, a purpose-built backpackers' complex. Rooms have a TV, fridge and en-suite bathrooms, and there are five kitchens, a games room, a pool, a bar, and a cafe serving cheap food. However, the place has an authoritarian air and is very soulless. Dorms are $12 or $15 depending on the number of beds in the room, while singles go for $30 and doubles $45. The *Swagman's Rest*, over the road at 145 Vulture St, is run by the same people as the Resort and shares the same reception.

Somewhere to Stay (☎ 3846 2858) at 45 Brighton Rd is 100m south of Vulture Rd and the Resort. It's a huge, rambling, wooden house with a small pool and a nice tree-shaded deck adjacent to a cheap cafe open for breakfast, lunch and evening meals. Dorm beds range from $12 to $15, with the newer rooms having a TV, fridge, private bathroom and balcony. Singles cost $20 to $25, doubles and twins $30 to $45.

Over in East Brisbane, in a quiet suburban street is *Courtney Place Backpackers* (☎ 3891 5166) at 50 Geelong St, a very clean, comfortable and quiet, non-partying place. A bed in an eight-bed dorm costs $14, singles are $25 and good doubles are $30. Although the Courtney Place is some way from the centre by road, the Mowbray Park City Cat stop is only three-minutes walk away.

Guesthouses & B&Bs If you can stomach the kewpie dolls and cuteness, *Annie's Shandon Inn* (☎ 3831 8684) at 405 Upper Edward St in Spring Hill is a friendly guesthouse with immaculate singles/doubles at $40/50 including a light breakfast. Four rooms with private bathroom go for $50/60. The *Yale Inner-City Inn* (☎ 3832 1663), next to Annie's at 413 Upper Edward St, has singles/doubles at $35/45 and a few rooms with private bathrooms at $55. The tariff includes a light breakfast. Rooms are small and the facilities are quite old, but the place is clean.

Still in Spring Hill, *Thornbury House B&B* (☎ 3832 5985) at 1 Thornbury St is a

QUEENSLAND

charming two-storey timber Queenslander built in 1886 and attractively renovated in heritage style. There are four excellent double rooms for $90 and five smaller, attic-style single rooms for $55.

About 2km west of the centre, in Padding-ton, the *Waverley B&B* (☎ 3369 8973) at 5 Latrobe Tce is also a renovated two-storey Queenslander, with a family home upstairs and two guestrooms and two excellent guest units at the rear with their own entrance. Rates are $65/90.

Over in New Farm, the *Edward Lodge* (☎ 3254 1078) at 75 Sydney St is an excel-lent two-storey guesthouse catering exclusively to gays and lesbians, with eight immaculate double rooms each with their own en-suite. There's an attractive breakfast courtyard and a spa pool. The tariff is $65/75 for singles/doubles, including breakfast.

Self-Contained Apartments Not far north of the centre in Spring Hill, the *Dorchester Self-Contained Units* (☎ 3831 2967; fax 3832 2932) at 484 Upper Edward St is a two-storey block of self-contained one-bedroom units costing $60/70/80 for singles/doubles/triples.

About 500m further north-east, the *Dahrl Court Apartments* (☎ 3832 3458; fax 3839 2591) at 45 Phillips St have been recom-mended by several travellers. One-bedroom apartments here have a separate kitchen (with a small breakfast provided) and cost $65/75 for singles/doubles and $100 for four people. There's also a large basement apart-ment that sleeps groups of up to 12 people at $25 a head.

On the corner of Brunswick St and Moreton St in New Farm, the *Allender Apartments* (☎ 3358 5832) is a two-storey block of old cream-brick flats that have recently been refurbished. The studio units are beautiful – large and sumptuously fur-nished with a generous king-sized bed – and offer excellent value at $55 for a standard or $75 for deluxe. It's too far to walk from here to the centre so you need to be prepared to take buses or, better still, have your own transport.

Motels The main motel drags are Wickham/Gregory Tce on the northern edge of the city, and Main St – especially the Kangaroo Point stretch – which is the link road to the southern Gold Coast Hwy.

At 397 Gregory Tce, the four-star *Gregory Terrace Motor Inn* (☎ 3832 1769; fax 3832 2640) overlooks Victoria Park and is just across from the Centenary Swimming Pool. Motel units cost $88 a double, and there are a couple of two-bedroom apartments that sleep up to eight people and cost $120 for two plus $10 for each extra person.

Closer to the city in Wickham Tce, the *Astor Motel* (☎ 3831 9522; fax 3831 7360), near the junction with Upper Edward Street, charges $89/95 for comfortable singles/doubles. A few minutes walk west at 333 Wickham Tce, the *Soho Club Motel* (☎ 3831 7722; fax 3831 8050) charges $49/58 for far more basic singles/doubles.

At Kangaroo Point, the *Kangaroo Motel* (☎ 3391 1145) at 624 Main St has singles/doubles for $48/53, while the *Paramount Apartments* (☎ 3393 1444) at 649 Main St and the *A1 Motel* (☎ 3391 6222) at No 646 both charge $60 for self-contained units.

Hotels One of the best accommodation deals in Brisbane is the *Explorers' Inn* (☎ 3211 3488; fax 3211 3499), a modern three-star hotel in an old building at 63 Turbot St on the edge of the city centre, just a few minutes walk from the transit centre. The facilities are good and the rooms, though a little cabin-like, are immaculate and excellent value at $64 for a double or twin.

In north Kangaroo Point, *Ryan's On The River* (☎ 3391 1011; fax 3391 1824) at 269 Main St is very close to the landing stage for the city ferry. All rooms have some sort of river view and most go for $99.

Il Mondo (☎ 3392 0111; fax 3392 0544) at 25 Rotherham St is housed in a quirky post-modern building with a very attractive, semi-open air cafe/restaurant on the ground floor. It has no river views but is still only a few minutes walk from the city ferry. Singles range from $59 to $70, doubles from $59 to $79.

Places to Eat – cafes & budget dining

Brisbane's cafe scene has blossomed in recent years. There's no shortage of good budget eateries in the city and surrounding areas.

City For breakfast, the best deal for the hungry is at the *Pane e Vino*, on the corner of Albert and Charlotte Sts. The breakfast special here is an enormous plate of sausage, bacon, mushrooms, toast and two eggs (easily enough for two) plus coffee and juice for $7.50.

There's also the *Palace Cafe* on Ann St which offers a variety of breakfasts for $5 and under.

There's an abundance of cheap lunch time eateries in the city centre catering for the hordes of office workers and shoppers. Probably the best variety and value is offered in the food courts found in the shopping malls – try *Eatz* in the basement of the Broadway centre and the *Eatery* in the basement of the Myer centre, both off the Queen St Mall.

Another office favourite, the *Hungry Heart Bistro* has a variety of pastas, rice casseroles, noodles and the like served in generous portions for under $5. It's open weekdays only from 7 am to 4 pm and is at 102-104 Edward St opposite the Metro cinema.

For a big feed, the *Mekong Chinese Restaurant*, on Adelaide St just north of Edward St, does an all-you-can-eat lunch and dinner for $6.90, while the Hare Krishna-run *Govinda's Restaurant*, upstairs at 99 Elizabeth St, offers all-you-can-eat vegetarian meals for $5. It's open weekdays for lunch and Friday and Sunday for dinner.

The *Down Under Bar & Grill* also has cheap lunches and evening meals served from 6 pm (see Entertainment later in this section).

Petrie Terrace & Paddington Probably the best place for a decent, reasonably priced meal round here is the *City YHA hostel cafe* – you don't have to be staying at the hostel to eat there. Alternatively, the *Paddo Tavern*

on Given Tce, about 1km east of Petrie Tce, does $1.95 lunches during the week.

At 28 Caxton St the *Irish Connection* is a bar/restaurant with a fairly limited menu but what's there is good. Soups start at $4, while the Guinness & beef pie at $10 comes in a serving sufficient for two people. It's open for lunch and dinner.

Fortitude Valley There's a good produce market and an international foodhall inside *McWhirters Marketplace* on the corner of Brunswick and Wickham Sts. Of the many Chinese, Vietnamese etc joints, an excellent budget option is the *Universal Noodle Restaurant* at 145 Wickham St. It's a cheap 'n' cheerful cafeteria-style eatery with a huge range of dishes in the $5.50 to $6.80 range; it's open daily from 11 am until late.

There's a cluster of eateries at the east end of the Brunswick St Mall, most of which have pavement seating. Of these *Mellino's* at No 330, a casual cafe that's open 24 hours a day, is the most reasonably priced – you can get a cooked breakfast for $4, pastas for $8.90 and a pizza for two for under $10. The best breakfast deal is the *California*, on the corner of Brunswick and McLachlan Sts, a cafe that opened in 1951 and retains many of the original fittings. The breakfasts are good and huge – order one to share.

West End Like the Valley, the West End has a fairly cosmopolitan range of cafes and restaurants, including quite a few budget places.

Three Monkeys Coffee House, at 58 Mollison St just west of the roundabout, is a relaxed place with seductive pseudo-Moroccan decor, good coffee and cakes, and a wide range of food in the $6 to $10 range. It is open daily from 10.30 am until midnight.

South on Boundary St are at least half a dozen trendy cafes all of which do food of some sort. They include *Caffe Tempo*, a hip little streetfront eatery at No 181; two doors south at No 185 is *Cafe Nouveau*, an attractive Italian-style place with an outrageously pretentious menu featuring items such as 'Ming Dynasty fillet of pork' and 'Rebirth of

QUEENSLAND

Venus salad'; *Cafe Babylon*, across the road at No 142, is very New Agey with ethnic decor, astrology evenings and tarot readers. Its noticeboard is the place to look should you find yourself in need of a psychic or some brushing up on your African dance techniques. One door up, the *Green Grocer* is a good health-food shop with a wide range of organic fruit and vegies, juices, wheat and gluten-free breads.

For something more down-to-earth, *Qan Heng's* at 151 Boundary St offers good Chinese and Vietnamese meals from $5.50 to $9, and has an all-you-can-eat lunch for $6.50. The *Wok On Inn* at No 94 is a good noodle bar at which you choose the noodle type, cooking style (Chinese, Malay or Thai) and the ingredients. Servings are large and cost from $7.50 to $10.50. It's open from 11.30 am to 2 pm and again from 5.30 pm until late.

Over on Hardgrave Rd, the small *Khan's Kitchen* serves cheap traditional Pakistani dishes. The most expensive dish here is $9 and there's a lot on the menu that's cheaper. *Kim Thanh* at No 93 is a large and noisy Chinese and Vietnamese BYO with main courses from $7 to $9 and a good value Vietnamese banquet menu.

Places to Eat – restaurants

Many of Brisbane's restaurants take advantage of the balmy climate by providing outdoor eating areas.

City There are precious few restaurants in the City as it tends to empty out at night with the homeward migration of its office and shop workers.

Gilhooley's, the Irish pub on Albert St, serves very good basic fare like stews and Guinness & beef pie for around $8, plus other pricey dishes like steaks for about $16.

Zane's Caffe & Pasta Bar, underneath the Metro cinema on Edward St, has artful pasta creations in the $9 to $12 range; it's open from noon to 9 pm Tuesday and Thursday and until 11 pm Thursday and Friday.

The city's premier dining spot is the Eagle St Pier complex and adjacent Riverside Centre. Both are home to several upmarket, credit-card crimping establishments of the kind best visited when somebody else is footing the bill. The two that are constantly talked about and always seem busy are *Il Centro*, an impressive Italian joint, and *Pier Nine*, a sophisticated oyster bar and seafood restaurant.

South Bank There are about a dozen restaurants and cafes in the South Bank Parklands. However, having something of a captive audience they don't have to try too hard and a lot of the food available here is second rate and overpriced. A popular exception would seem to be *Captain Snapper*, a large seafood and steak restaurant that is constantly crowded. The food here is unadventurous but wholesome and the prices are reasonable.

On the southern edge of South Bank, the *Ship Inn* has reasonably priced bistro meals like fettuccine carbonara ($7), ploughman's platters ($8) and T-bone steaks ($9.90). One of the best value eateries on the riverfront is the simple *Riverfront Cafe* at the State Library. It has great rolls and sandwiches, coffee and snacks, and the tables on the outdoor courtyard overlook the river.

Petrie Terrace & Paddington The *Sultan's Kitchen* (☎ 3368 2194) at 163 Given Tce is an excellent Indian restaurant (BYO) with great curries. It's open for lunch and dinner daily (except Saturday lunch), but it's pretty popular so book on weekends. The lunch time smorgasbord is $12.95, and at dinner mains are around $14.

At 215 Given Tce, the *Jakarta Indonesian Restaurant* is a reasonably priced restaurant with an evocative all-bamboo decor. Rice, noodle and vegetarian dishes are $7 to $12, and seafood and meat dishes are from $10 to $13. It's open from 6 pm Tuesday to Sunday.

A little further on is the very popular *King Tut's Wa Wa Hut*, an outdoor cafe with good salads, pastas, burgers, juices and sandwiches, all reasonably priced. Just up from King Tut's at 283 Given Tce, *Le Scoops* is another popular eatery, featuring an outdoor crêperie serving up sweet and savoury crêpes and pancakes. It opens for breakfast, lunch and dinner – the Sunday brunch is especially good.

Fortitude Valley The Valley is one of the best eating areas to explore, especially on Friday evening and Saturday when it's bustling with crowds of people wandering the streets, eating at outdoor tables and spilling out of the various pubs and bars.

Duncan St, between Ann and Wickham Sts, is Brisbane's Chinatown, home to a large number of Asian restaurants. The *Enjoy Inn*, on the corner of Wickham and Duncan Sts, is widely regarded as serving the best Cantonese food in town. During the week it's a little quiet and formal but at weekends it gets really lively. Main courses are in the $8 to $16 range, and it's open daily from noon till 3 pm and 5 pm to midnight.

Over the road at 194 Wickham St, the licensed *Vietnamese Restaurant* is also highly recommended. It's smart but casual, with a menu that offers some interesting variations on standard Asian cuisine. The food is excellent and very reasonably priced (main dishes $8 to $12), and consequently the place is busy most evenings.

If you want really good Italian cooking we highly recommend *Lucky's Trattoria*, a BYO at 683 Ann St. The pasta dishes here are fantastic – some of the best we've ever had, anywhere. It gets busy at weekends and you may have to wait for a table; no reservations are taken. Mains start at around $9.

At 360 Brunswick St, the hip and arty *Cafe Europe* BYO is extremely popular. As the name suggests, it has a very European feel, with timber booths topped with butcher's paper inside and a row of tables out on the footpath. The home-made pastas ($10 to $13) are good and mains hover around the $15 mark.

Dooley's Hotel, the big Irish pub on the corner of Brunswick St and McLachlan St, also has a couple of eating options.

West End On Hardgrave Rd, 400m west of Boundary, there's a strip of more than 10 cafes and restaurants, all within 150m of each other. The northernmost cluster are housed in the former Rialto theatre, including the excellent *Mogul Room*. It has an extensive menu but on weekday lunch times go for the smorgasbord: rice, naan, papadums, raita, daal, three curries, pickles and a sweet will cost you $11. The restaurant opens at 11.30 am for lunch and then again at 6 pm for dinner; it's closed on Monday.

A few blocks further south at 166 Hardgrave Rd is the *Soup Kitchen*, a trendy eatery fronted by an open-air courtyard. It's a cafe by day and a restaurant by night. It specialises in soups ($6 to $8) and pastas ($9.50 to $13.50), and also has interesting daily specials ($11.50 to $13.50). Around the corner in Dornoch Tce is *Caravanserai*, a former pawnbroker's shop converted into an attractive Turkish restaurant with an open kitchen in the centre. Main dishes range from $9.50 to $11. The place features belly dancing on Saturday nights.

Breakfast Creek On the north side of a bend in the Brisbane River, the famous *Breakfast Creek Hotel*, a great rambling building dating from 1889, is a real Brisbane institution. It's long been an ALP and trade union hang-out. In the public bar the beer is still drawn from a wooden keg. The pub's open-air Spanish Garden Steak House is renowned for its steaks and spare ribs, and a huge feed will set you back between $12 and $18; there are daily specials for about $6. It's open daily from noon to 3 pm and 5 to 9 pm. To get there take bus No 117 from Queen St or a City Cat to Bretts Wharf and then walk back along the river for about 1km.

Entertainment

The free entertainment papers – *Time Off*, *Rave* and the *Scene* (pick them up at record stores and some cafes) – have comprehensive listings of gigs, pubs, clubs and theatre. For what's on at the cinema, pick up the daily *Courier Mail*.

Backpacker Venues The backpacker bar scene in Brisbane is extremely limited – to the extent that there's really only one

QUEENSLAND

contender. Luckily it's a good one. The *Down Under* at the top of Edward St in the city, underneath the Palace Backpackers, is full-on seven nights a week, with cheap beer and promotions most nights, and loud, loud music. Dancing on the tables is encouraged and things keep going until the early hours. On Monday nights there's an alternative in the form of the long-running 'Monday Madness' at the Bomb Shelter, part of the *Story Bridge Hotel* in Kangaroo Point. It's a good party night with all the various hostels putting up teams to compete in beer races etc.

Pubs & Live Music Since the early 1990s cafes have very much taken over as the places to drink at, especially in the more fashionable parts of town like Fortitude Valley and West End. This has resulted in the appearance of some curious hybrid bar/cafes like New Farm's *Bitch* on Brunswick St and *Ric's Cafe-Bar*, well worth visiting for the retro-chic lounge decor, 100m down the road in the mall. More conventionally, *Dooley's*, also on Brunswick St in the Valley, is a large and excellent Irish pub with a great number of pool tables in the upstairs bar.

Dooley's is just one of a growing number of Irish bars – there's also *Kelly's* at 521 Stanley St in South Brisbane and the very popular *Gilhooley's* on Albert St, which is just about the best place for a drink in the city. Most of the other city pubs can be pretty rough and tend to have unwelcoming door policies.

Plenty of pubs, bars and clubs feature live music, with cover charges from $6 for local acts but much more for touring bands. According to our source at *Time Off* listings magazine, the best gig venues in town are the *Zoo* (☎ 3854 1381) at 711 Ann St in the Valley (more than one band, apparently, has rated this place as the best small venue in Australia), the *Chelsea* (☎ 3257 0619) at 25 Warner St (also in the Valley), the *Capitol* (☎ 3255 1091) at 588 Stanley St in South Brisbane, and the *Orient Hotel* at the top of Ann and Queen Sts in the City. All of these places host different kinds of music on dif-

ferent nights of the week; check the free press for details.

Nightclubs Brisbane has a lively nightclub scene, if you know where to look. Mainstream clubs are mostly based in and around the city, and the alternative scene is centred in Fortitude Valley.

The city nightclubs attract a sort of hair-down office crowd and play a lot of soul and dance; they include the *Gig* at 22 Market St, *City Rowers* at the Eagle St Pier, and *Friday's* at 123 Eagle St. Probably the best of the mainstream clubs is the *Underground* at 61 Petrie Tce.

Over in the Valley, a great night out is indie music-driven *Superdeluxe*, upstairs at the Empire on the corner of Brunswick and Ann Sts, which takes place every Friday and Saturday night from 9 pm to 5 am. Monkey Business, Thursday and Saturday at the *Brunswick Hotel* in the Valley, is another good one, and the *Tube* at 210 Wickham St in the Valley has some good nights, too.

Gay & Lesbian Scene Brisbane has a lively gay and lesbian scene, covered by the free fortnightly *BrotherSister*. One of the city's busiest venues is the *Wickham Hotel* at 308 Wickham St in the Valley, which provides entertainment (drag shows, strippers, promotions and great dance music) seven nights a week. The *Sportsman's Hotel* at 130 Leichhardt St in Spring Hill is another mainstay of the scene with drag acts, talent quests and promotions. *Options* at 18 Little Edward St, also in Spring Hill, is a popular nightclub with live shows upstairs and a dance club downstairs.

The *Sandpit* has an occasional women-only night held at the Melbourne Hotel in West End; for information on dates call ☎ 0411 724 897

Jazz & Blues The *Jazz & Blues Club*, which is on the ground floor of the Travelodge (next to the transit centre), is the city's major venue for this kind of music with good local and international acts on stage from Tuesday to Saturday. The *Brisbane Jazz Club* down by the riverside at 1 Annie St, Kangaroo Point is where the jazz purists head on Saturday (trad and Dixie) and Sunday (big band) nights. For a Sunday afternoon jazz fix, check out the *Story Bridge Hotel* or *Snug Harbour Dockside*, both in Kangaroo Point.

For R&B, check the *Healer* (☎ 3852 2575) at 27 Warner St in the Valley, a small venue in a converted church.

Theatre The *Performing Arts Complex* (☎ 3846 4444) in the Queensland Cultural Centre in South Brisbane features concerts, plays, dance performances and film screenings in its three venues.

Brisbane's other main theatre spaces include the *Suncorp Theatre* (☎ 3221 5177) at 179 Turbot St (performances by the Queensland Ballet and Queensland Theatre companies); the *Brisbane Arts Theatre* (☎ 3369 2344) at 210 Petrie Tce (amateur theatre); and the *La Boite Repertory Theatre* (☎ 3369 1622) at 57 Hale St, off Petrie Tce.

Cinemas The big, multi-screen, city centre cinemas are *Hoyts Regent* on the Queen St Mall, *Hoyts Myer Centre* in the basement of the Myer shopping mall, and *Greater Union* with five screens on Albert St, just south of the mall. They all show mainstream releases and tickets are $12 ($9 before 6 pm) or $6 all day Tuesday.

The *Dendy* at 346 George St in the city centre, the *Classic* at 963 Stanley St, East Brisbane, and the *Metro* at 109 Edward St also in the city centre, all specialise in art-house and independent films. The Metro, in particular, is a beautiful little cinema and offers a good two-films-for-$5 deal on Sunday nights.

There's also the *Village Twin* at 701 Brunswick St in New Farm, which screens a combination of art-house and mainstream releases. Tickets here are discounted on Tuesday, Wednesday and Thursday nights.

Spectator Sport You can see interstate cricket matches and international Test cricket at the Brisbane Cricket Ground (the Gabba) in Woolloongabba, just south of Kangaroo Point. The cricket season runs from October to March.

During the other half of the year, rugby league is the big spectator sport. Local heroes, the Brisbane Broncos, play their home games at the ANZ Stadium in Upper Mt Gravatt. Brisbane also has an Australian Football League club, the Brisbane Lions, based at the Gabba. Brisbane's major horse-racing tracks are at Doomben and Eagle Farm.

Getting There & Away

Brisbane's transit centre, on Roma St about 500m west of the centre, is the main terminus for all long-distance buses and trains (bookings also). The centre has shops, banks, a post office, plenty of places to eat and drink, an accommodation booking service on the 3rd level and an information office on the 2nd level. Left-luggage lockers are on the 3rd level ($4 a day); there's also a cloakroom where you can store items longer term.

The easiest way to book all domestic flights and bus tickets is to use the Backpackers Travel Centre (☎ 3221 2225) located on the upper floor of the Brisbane Arcade off the Queen St Mall. Debbie's manned the desk for more than 10 years and is well up on the cheapest ways to get from A to B and back again.

Air Qantas has its travel centre (☎ 13 1313 for domestic flights, 13 1211 for international) at 247 Adelaide St in the city centre. Ansett (☎ 13 1300) has an office on the corner of Queen and George Sts. Both have frequent flights to the southern capitals and to the main Queensland centres.

Standard one-way fares from Brisbane include Sydney ($303), Melbourne ($441), Adelaide ($535) and Perth ($730). Within Queensland, one-way fares include Townsville ($363), Rockhampton ($273), Mackay ($327), Proserpine ($329), Cairns ($428) and Mt Isa ($438, Ansett only).

The little outback airline Flight West (☎ 13 2392) goes to Roma ($180 one way), Charleville ($240), Quilpie and Barcaldine

($306), Blackall ($283), Longreach ($334), Winton and Windorah ($339) and Birdsville ($417).

Bus The bus companies all have booking desks on the 3rd level of the transit centre but if you're shopping around for fare deals, see the Backpackers Travel Centre mentioned earlier in this section.

Greyhound Pioneer and McCafferty's both run from Sydney to Brisbane. The coastal run along the Pacific Highway takes about 17 hours; the inland New England Highway trip takes a couple of hours less. The usual fare is between $69 and $75, but Premier Pioneer Motor Services (☎ 1300 368 100) often has cheaper deals.

Between Brisbane and Melbourne, the most direct route is the Newell Highway, which takes about 24 hours. Again, Greyhound Pioneer and McCafferty's travel this route daily. The fare between Brisbane and Melbourne is about $108.

To Adelaide, the shortest route (via Dubbo) takes about 31 hours and costs about $148.

North to Cairns, Greyhound Pioneer and McCafferty's run five buses a day. The approximate fares and journey times to places along the coast are as follows:

Destination	Time	Cost
Noosa Heads	2 hours	$14
Hervey Bay	4½ hours	$32-$38
Rockhampton	9 hours	$61
Mackay	13 hours	$91
Townsville	19 hours	$119
Cairns	24 hours	$139

McCafferty's and Greyhound Pioneer also run daily services to the Northern Territory – it's a 46-hour trip to Darwin ($246) via Longreach (17 hours, $80) and Mt Isa (24 hours, $120).

Train Countrylink has a daily XTP service between Brisbane and Sydney. The north-bound train runs overnight and the southbound train runs during the day. The trip takes 13½ hours and costs $98/142 in economy/1st class, and $224.50 in a sleeper.

North from Brisbane, the *Spirit of Capricorn* runs the 639km to Rockhampton daily (9½ hours; $67 economy only). The *Sunlander* departs three days a week for the 1631km journey to Cairns (30 hours; $253 1st-class sleeper, $165 economy sleeper, $135 economy seat), via Mackay and Townsville. The *Spirit of the Tropics* is an all-economy train (ie no sleeping berths) that covers the same route twice a week.

The luxurious *Queenslander* does the Brisbane to Cairns run weekly. All passengers travel 1st class, with sleeping berths and all meals included in the fares. Sectors and fares include Brisbane-Mackay (16 hours, $300), Brisbane-Townsville (21 hours, $344) and Brisbane-Cairns (29 hours, $389). For another $270, you can take your car with you from Brisbane to Cairns.

The *Westlander* runs on the inland route to Charleville via Roma twice a week; the trip takes 16½ hours and costs $77 for an economy seat, $172 for a 1st-class sleeper.

For reservations, telephone Queensland Rail (☎ 13 2232) or call into its Railway Travel Centre (☎ 3235 1323) beside Central Station at 305 Edward St.

Car Hire If you have a car, beware of the two-hour parking limit in the city and inner suburbs – there are no signs, and the parking inspectors are merciless.

The big rental firms all have offices in Brisbane and there are a number of smaller operators. One budget operator that we've received good reports on is Integra Car Rentals (☎ 3252 5752) at 79 McLachlan St, Fortitude Valley. It does one-way rentals (Cairns, Sydney, Melbourne) and also has good value campervans. Others that might be worth checking include Cheap Rate Rentals (☎ 3252 3803), Car-azy Rentals (☎ 3257 1104), Ideal (☎ 3260 2307) and National (☎ 3854 1499).

Getting Around

For all city bus, train and ferry information,

ring the Trans-Info Service (☎ 13 1230); it operates daily from 6 am to 10 pm. There's a train information office at Central Station, and bus and ferry information is also available at the Queen St information centre and in the bus station information centre under the Queen St Mall.

To/From the Airport Brisbane's airport is north-east of the city, with the new international/domestic terminal about 15km away. Coachtrans runs the Skytrans (☎ 3236 1000) shuttle bus between the transit centre and the airport, with services about every half-hour between 5 am and 8.30 pm. The fare is $6.50. Coachtrans also operates the Airporter (☎ 5588 8777) direct services from the airport to the Gold Coast ($29), while Suncoast Pacific (☎ 3236 1901) has a direct service to the Sunshine Coast.

A taxi to the city centre costs about $20.

Bus The red City Circle bus No 333 does a clockwise loop round the area along George, Adelaide, Wharf, Eagle, Mary, Albert and Alice Sts every five minutes on weekdays between 8 am and 5.45 pm; rides are $1.40.

In addition to the normal city buses, there are Cityxpress buses that run between the suburbs and the city centre, and Rockets, which are fast peak-hour commuter buses. From the transit centre you need to walk into the city centre to pick up some buses. Most above-ground bus stops in the city are colour-coded to help you find the right one. The underground bus station beneath the Myer Centre is used mainly by Cityxpresses and buses to/from the south of the city.

In the city centre, buses cost $1.40 a trip. If you're going to be using public transport a lot on any single day, it's worth getting an Off-Peak Saver card for $4 which gives unlimited travel on buses, ferries and City Cats between 9 am and 3.30 pm and after 7 pm, or all day Saturday and Sunday. Alternatively, the Day Rover card at $6 gives the same thing but without the time limitations.

Buses run every 10 to 20 minutes Monday to Friday till about 6 pm, and on Saturday morning. Services are less frequent on weekday evenings, Saturday afternoon and evening, and Sunday. Buses cease at 7 pm on Sunday, and 11 pm on other days.

Train The fast Citytrain network has seven lines: to Ipswich, Beenleigh and Cleveland in the south and Pinkenba, Shorncliffe, Caboolture and Ferny Grove in the north. All trains go through Roma St, Central and Brunswick St stations and a journey in the central area is $1.40.

Boat Brisbane has an excellent fast and efficient ferry service along and across the Brisbane River in the form of the City Cats. The City Cats are large blue catamarans that zip along the river between Queensland University in the west and Bretts Wharf in the east, stopping en route at North Quay (for the Queen St Mall), South Bank, Riverside (for the CBD) and New Farm Park. They run every 20 minutes from 6 am until around 10.30 pm weekdays, and until midnight on Friday and Saturday, and 8.30 pm on Sunday. City Cats are also wheelchair accessible.

In addition, there are three cross-river ferries, the most useful being between Eagle St and Kangaroo Point and Riverside and Kangaroo Point.

Fares range from $1.40 for cross river trips to $3 for the whole length of the route. Off-Peak and Day Rover cards are valid on ferries and City Cats.

Bicycle Brisbane has some excellent bike tracks, particularly around the Brisbane River. Pick up a copy of the city council's *Safe Bikeways* brochure from information centres, which includes good bike route maps.

A good way to spend a day is to ride the riverside bicycle track from the city Botanic Gardens out to the University of Queensland. It's about 7km one way and you can stop for a beer at the Regatta pub in Toowong.

There are several places that hire out bikes. Backpackers Mountain Bike Hire (☎ 1800 635 286) charges $16 a day, including free helmet, maps and delivery and pick-up of bikes. Brisbane Bicycle Sales (☎ 3229 2433) at 87 Albert St in the city centre hires out mountain bikes for $9 an hour or $20 a day.

Bicycles are allowed on city trains, except on weekdays during peak hours (7 to 9 am and 3 to 6.30 pm). You can also take bikes on City Cats and ferries for free.

Moreton Bay

Moreton Bay, at the mouth of the Brisbane River, is reckoned to have some 365 islands. Of these, the two that most people head for are Moreton Island, in particular to participate in the dolphin feeding at the Tangalooma resort, and North Stradbroke for its great beaches and surfing. Manly, a mainland coastal suburb, is also a good spot to kick back for a few days – there's a good hostel and free yachting on Wednesday.

THE BAYSIDE
Redcliffe, 35km north of Brisbane, was the first white settlement in Queensland.

The local Aboriginal people called the place Humpybong, or 'Dead Houses', and the name is still applied to the peninsula. Redcliffe is now an outer suburb of Brisbane and a popular retirement place. South of Redcliffe, **Sandgate** is another long-running seaside resort, now also more of an outer suburb.

Coastal towns south of the Brisbane River mouth include Wynnum, Manly, Cleveland and Redland Bay. **Manly** is an attractive seaside suburb with the largest marina in the southern hemisphere after Fremantle. Every Wednesday there are yacht races out in the bay and quite a few of the captains are happy to take guests on board free of charge. Enquire at one of the yacht clubs along the waterfront or at *Nomads Moreton Bay Lodge* (☎ 3396 3020) in the heart of Manly Village at 45 Cambridge Pde, which is a well set up backpackers' hostel surrounded by cafes and restaurants and across the road from a pub. Dorms cost $14 and doubles from $35. The hostel can also arrange sailing trips and two-day tours to Moreton Island, and help to find work in the area.

Cleveland is the main access point for North Stradbroke Island (see Getting There & Away later in this section). There's an 1864 lighthouse at Cleveland Point as well as an 1853 courthouse which is now a restaurant.

SOUTH & NORTH STRADBROKE ISLANDS
The two Stradbroke Islands used to be one, but in 1896 a storm cut the sand spit that joined them. Today, South Stradbroke is virtually uninhabited but it's a popular day trip from the Gold Coast.

North Stradbroke – or 'Straddie' – is a larger island with a permanent population and, although it is a popular escape from Brisbane, it's still relatively unspoilt (that said, the Christmas and Easter holidays can get pretty hectic). It's a sand island and, despite some heavy sand-mining operations, there's plenty of vegetation and beautiful scenery, especially in the north.

Dunwich, Amity Point and Point Lookout, the three small centres on the island, are all in the north and connected by sealed roads. Most of the southern part of the island is closed to visitors due to the mining and the only road into this swampier, more remote area is a private mining company road.

The Stradbroke Island visitor information centre (☎ 3409 9555) is near the ferry terminal in Dunwich; it's open from 8.45 am to 4 pm weekdays and until 3 pm at weekends.

Activities
Beaches & Water Sports Straddie's best beaches are around Point Lookout, where there's a series of points and bays around the headland and endless stretches of white sand.

There are some excellent surfing breaks here, and you can hire surfboards and boogie boards from various places. You can also sandboard – surf down dunes just behind Main Beach. It's great fun and costs $25 for two hours – call ☎ 3409 8082 or 3409 8696 for information and booking. The same

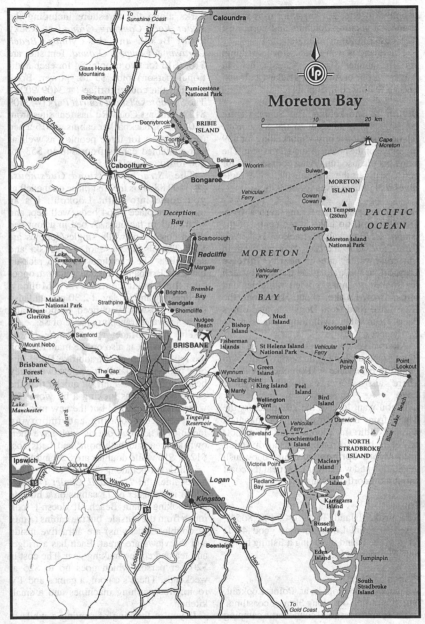

people also offer sea kayaking trips with a chance of spotting dolphins and porpoises; they cost $35 for three hours.

The island is also famous for its fishing, and the annual Straddie Classic, held in August, is one of Australia's richest and best-known fishing competitions.

Diving & Snorkelling The Scuba Centre (☎ 3409 8715) adjacent to the Stradbroke Island Guesthouse offers snorkelling for $39 inclusive of the boat trip and all the gear. The same people also run diving courses, and for certified divers they have all-inclusive single dives and double dives for $63/98.

Hiking A sealed road runs across from Dunwich to **Blue Lake** in the centre of the island; a 2.7km walking track will take you from the road to the lake. You can swim in the freshwater lake or nearby **Tortoise Lagoon**, or walk along the track and watch for snakes, goannas, golden wallabies and birds. **Brown Lake**, about 3km along the Blue Lake road from Dunwich, also offers deep freshwater swimming and is more easily accessible.

Alternatively, you could walk south from Point Lookout along Main Beach then 2.5km inland to Blue Lake – 11km one way in all. There's also a shorter beach walk to **Keyhole Lake**.

If you want to hike the 20km across the island from Dunwich to Point Lookout, a number of dirt track loops break the monotony of the bitumen road. A pleasant diversion is to **Myora Springs**, surrounded by lush vegetation and walking tracks, near the coast about 4km north of Dunwich.

Tours
Stradbroke Island Tours (☎ 3409 8051), based in Point Lookout, runs good 4WD tours of the island including a fishing trip or half-day tour ($28).

Places to Stay
All accommodation is at Point Lookout, which is strung out along 3km of coastline.

There are some good council-run camping parks along the foreshore including the *Adder Rock Camping Ground* at Rocky Point Beach and the *Cylinder Beach Caravan & Camping Ground*. Tent sites are $10, ($13 for two people; $4 for each additional person) plus $5 for power. Book through the council office (☎ 3409 9025). The *Stradbroke Island Tourist Park* (☎ 3409 8127) on East Coast Rd has tent sites from $10 to $15, backpacker cabins at $15 a bed (or $10 each for three people), as well as self-contained cabins from $48 to $53 (or $60 for four people).

The *Stradbroke Island Guesthouse* (☎ 3409 8888) is the first place on the left as you come into Point Lookout. It's an impressive place of 64 beds, well kept and with modern facilities. A bed in a four-bed dorm costs $16, while singles/doubles are $38. There's free use of a surf ski and sandsailer. The guesthouse runs a pick-up bus from Brisbane, which leaves from opposite the transit centre every Monday, Wednesday and Friday at 2.30 pm, and also stops at hostels; you need to book, and there's a water transport charge of $8.

The next place, the *Straddie Hostel* (☎ 3409 8679), is also on the main road, on the left just after the Stradbroke Hotel (the only pub on the island). It's a neat two-storey beach-house that's a fair bit quieter than the guesthouse. It was looking a bit worse for wear when we visited but the new management are redecorating and improving facilities. The large dorms each have their own kitchen and bathroom, and beds cost $12 or $15 while doubles are $28 and $30.

A little further along the road on the right-hand side, the *Headland Chalet* (☎ 3409 8252) is a cluster of 11 cabins on a hillside overlooking Main Beach. It doesn't look much from the outside, but the cabins (a mix of doubles and twins) are attractive inside and the views are great. Each has a fridge, and tea and coffee-making gear. The cost is $20 per person which goes up to $25 at weekends. There's a pool, a games and TV room, free washing machines and a small kitchen.

If you're thinking of staying a while, a

holiday flat or house can be good value, especially outside the holiday seasons. There are several real estate agents, including the *Accommodation Centre* (☎ 3409 8255), which is behind the Laughing Buddha Cafe in the Point Lookout Shopping Village.

Places to Eat

There are a couple of general stores selling groceries in Point Lookout, but it's worth bringing basic supplies as the price mark-up on the island is significant. Otherwise, the two best eateries are the *Stradbroke Hotel* and the *Laughing Buddha Cafe*. The hotel has a bistro, open for lunch and dinner, with a fairly extensive menu in the $6 to $15 range, and there's a pleasant dining terrace out the back overlooking Cylinder Beach. The cafe, part of the Point Lookout Shopping Village complex, is a good place for breakfast (plenty of filled focaccia and similar snacks) though it's also open for dinner from 6 to 8 pm.

Getting There & Away

To get to Straddie you need to take a bus or train to Cleveland to connect with the ferry. Stradbroke Island Coaches (☎ 3807 4205) depart from bay 24 of Brisbane's Roma St Transit Centre at 8 and 9.15 am and 12.30, 4 and 5 pm Monday to Friday. The single fare to Cleveland is $4 ($8 return). Alternatively, you can catch a Citylink train from any of Brisbane's central stations to Cleveland (one hour; departures every half-hour from 5 am onwards) for $3.10. A courtesy bus departs from Cleveland train station to the ferry terminal 15 minutes before every sailing.

At Cleveland, two water-taxi companies shuttle across to Dunwich: Stradbroke Ferries (☎ 3286 2666) and the *Stradbroke Flyer* (☎ 3286 1964). Both companies have sailings roughly hourly between 5 am and 6 pm, seven days a week (sailings start later on Sunday). Fares are $6 one way, $10 return. It's preferable to take the Stradbroke Ferries boat as this is met on the island by a connecting bus to Point Lookout – the Stradbroke Flyer docks at One Mile Jetty, 1.5km north

of central Dunwich and it's difficult to pick up public transport from here.

Stradbroke Ferries also runs a vehicle ferry from Cleveland to Dunwich about 12 times a day. It costs $63 return for a vehicle plus passengers.

People staying at the Stradbroke Island Guesthouse can also take advantage of their courtesy bus – see Places to Stay above.

Getting Around

Stradbroke Island Coaches (☎ 3807 4205) runs 10 services a day between the three main centres; Dunwich to Point Lookout costs $4 ($7 return).

MORETON ISLAND (pop 120)

North of Stradbroke, Moreton Island is less visited and still almost a wilderness. Apart from a few rocky headlands it's all sand, with Mt Tempest – towering to 280m – the highest coastal sandhill in the world. It's a strange landscape, alternating between bare sand, forest, lakes and swamps, with a 30km surf beach along the eastern side. The island's birdlife is prolific, and at its northern tip is a **lighthouse**, built in 1857. Sand-mining leases on the island have been cancelled and 96% of the island is now a national park.

Moreton Island has no sealed roads but 4WD vehicles can travel along beaches and a few cross-island tracks – seek local advice about tides and creek crossings. The QNPWS publishes a map of the island, which you can get from the QNPWS office at False Patch Wrecks between Cowan Cowan and Tangalooma.

Tangalooma, halfway down the western side of the island, is a popular tourist resort sited at an old whaling station. The main attraction at Tangalooma is the wild dolphin feeding which takes place each evening – usually about eight or nine dolphins swim in from the ocean and take fish from the hands of volunteer feeders. The feeding is carefully regulated and accompanied by commentary. The dolphin feeding is free but you must be an overnight guest of the resort – there is nothing, however, stopping campers coming to watch. Call the Dolphin Education Centre

(☎ 3408 2666) between 1 and 5 pm for more details.

The only other settlements, all on the west coast, are **Bulwer** near the north-west tip, **Cowan Cowan** between Bulwer and Tangalooma, and **Kooringal** near the southern tip. The shops at Kooringal and Bulwer are expensive, so bring what you can from the mainland.

Without your own vehicle, walking is the only way to get around, and you'll need several days to explore the island. There are some trails around the resort area, and there are quite a few decommissioned 4WD roads with good walks. It's about 14km from Tangalooma or the Ben-Ewa camping ground on the west side to Eagers Creek camping ground on the east, then 7km up the beach to Blue Lagoon and another 6km to Cape Moreton at the north-eastern tip. There's a strenuous track to the summit of **Mt Tempest**, about 3km inland from Eagers Creek; the views at the top are worth the effort.

About 3km south and inland from Tangalooma is an area of bare sand known as the **Desert**, while the **Big Sandhills** and the **Little Sandhills** are towards the narrow southern end of the island. The biggest lakes and some swamps are in the north-east, and the west coast from Cowan Cowan past Bulwer is also swampy.

Organised Tours
Sunrover Expeditions (☎ 3203 4241) has good 4WD day tours ($100 with lunch) three times a week from Brisbane, and three-day camping trips ($300 all inclusive), which go once or twice a month or four times a month from January to March. You can also use the *Tangalooma Flyer* (see the Getting There & Away section) for day trips but, unfortunately, the return boat departs the island before dolphin feeding time.

Places to Stay
QNPWS camp sites, with water, toilets and cold showers are at Ben-Ewa and False Patch Wrecks, both between Cowan Cowan and Tangalooma, and at Eagers Creek and Blue

Lagoon on the island's east coast. Sites cost $3.50 per person per night. For information and camping permits, contact the QNPWS (☎ 3227 8186) at 160 Ann St in Brisbane, or the ranger at False Patch Wrecks (☎ 3408 2710).

There are a few holiday flats or houses for rent at Kooringal, Cowan Cowan and Bulwer. A twin room at the *Tangalooma Resort* (☎ 3268 6333) costs from $145 per night.

Getting There & Away
The *Tangalooma Flyer* (☎ 3268 6333), a fast catamaran operated by the Tangalooma resort, leaves from a dock at Holt St, off Kingsford-Smith Dve, every day at 10am (a courtesy bus departs Brisbane's transit centre for the wharf at 9.15am). You can use it for a day trip or for camping drop-offs; the return fare is $30 and you have to book.

The *Moreton Venture* (☎ 3895 1000) is a vehicular ferry which runs six days a week from Whyte Island (at the southern side of the Brisbane River mouth) to Tangalooma or to Reeder Point. The return fare is $125 for a 4WD (including passengers); pedestrians are charged $20 return.

Another ferry to the island is the *Combie Trader* (☎ 3203 6399), with daily services between Scarborough and Bulwer (except Tuesday). Return fares are also $125 for a 4WD and four people, and $20 for pedestrians. The ferry also does day trips on Monday, Wednesday, Saturday and Sunday for $20 return.

ST HELENA ISLAND
Little St Helena Island, which is only 6km from the mouth of the Brisbane River, was a high-security prison from 1867 to 1932 and is now a national park. There are remains of several prison buildings and the first passenger tramway in Brisbane which, when built in 1884, had horse-drawn cars. Sandy beaches and mangroves alternate around the coast.

St Helena Island Guided Tours (☎ 3260 7944) runs day trips ($35 including lunch or $28 BYO) from the BP Marina on Kingsford-

Smith Dve, Breakfast Creek, every Sunday and two or three other days a week, leaving at 9 am and returning at 5 pm. St Helena Ferries (☎ 3396 3994) runs two to three trips a week on its *Cat o' Nine Tails* catamaran, leaving from Manly Harbour. The $30 return fare includes a one-hour tour and entry to the national park. You can reach Manly from central Brisbane in about 35 minutes by train (Cleveland Line).

OTHER ISLANDS
Coochie Island
Coochiemudlo Island is a 10-minute ferry ride from Victoria Point on the southern Bayside. It's a popular outing from the mainland, having good beaches, but it is more built-up than most other Moreton Bay islands you can visit. You can hire bicycles, boats, catamarans and surf skis on the island. The ferry runs continuously on weekends and holidays from 8 am to 5.30 or 6 pm, less often on other days.

Bay Isles
Russell, **Lamb**, **Karragarra** and **Macleay** islands, known as the Bay Isles, are between the southern end of North Stradbroke and the mainland. Russell is the largest (about 7km long), and the interesting Green Dragon Museum is in the north-west of the island. Bay Islands Ferries (☎ 3286 2666), operating from the Banana St ramp in Redland Bay, does a loop around the isles three or four times a day.

Bribie Island
Bribie Island, at the northern end of Moreton Bay, is 31km long but apart from the southern end, where there are a couple of small towns, the island is largely untouched.

There's a bridge across Pumicestone Passage from the mainland to Bellara on the south-west coast. Bongaree, just south of Bellara, is the main town. Buses run there from Caboolture and Brisbane. Bongaree and Bellara, and Woorim on the south-east coast, have a few motels and holiday flats.

Gold Coast

• *Pop 274,000*

The Gold Coast is a 35km strip of beaches running north from the NSW/Queensland border. It's the most thoroughly commercialised area in Australia and is virtually one continuous development culminating in the high-rise crassness of the Surfers Paradise resort.

This coast has been a holiday spot since the 1880s, but developers only started taking serious notice of Surfers after WWII. These days more than two million visitors a year come to the Gold Coast. Accommodation ranges from backpackers' hostels to resort hotels, and there's quite a range of things to do – good surf beaches, excellent eating and entertainment possibilities and a hinterland with some fine natural features. There's also a huge variety of artificial 'attractions' and theme parks, although most are very commercial and fairly expensive.

Orientation
The whole coast from Tweed Heads in New South Wales up to Main Beach, to the north of Surfers Paradise, is developed, but most of the real action is around Surfers itself. Tweed Heads and Coolangatta at the southern end are older, quieter, cheaper resorts. Moving north from there you pass through Kirra, Bilinga, Tugun, Currumbin, Palm Beach, Burleigh Heads, Miami, Nobby Beach, Mermaid Beach and Broadbeach – all lower-key resorts.

Southport, the oldest town in the area, is north and just inland from Surfers, behind the sheltered expanse of the Broadwater, which is fed by the Nerang and Coomera rivers. The Gold Coast Hwy runs right along the coastal strip, leaving the Pacific Highway just north of Coolangatta and rejoining it inland from Southport.

The Gold Coast airport is at Coolangatta. Most buses to the Gold Coast travel the full length of the strip.

QUEENSLAND

Information

The Gold Coast Tourism Bureau (☎ 5538 4419) on the Cavill Ave Mall in Surfers Paradise is open weekdays from 8 am to 5 pm, Saturday from 9 am to 5 pm and Sunday from 9 am to 3.30 pm.

In Coolangatta, there's a tourist information booth (☎ 5536 7765) at the Beach House Plaza on Marine Pde, open weekdays from 8 am to 2 pm and 3 to 4 pm, and Saturday from 8 am to 3 pm. Nearby can be found the Tweed visitors centre (☎ 5536 4244) on the corner of Wharf and Bay Sts in Tweed Heads, open weekdays from 9 am to 5 pm, Saturday from 9 am to 3 pm and Sunday from 10 am to 3 pm.

For information on the area's national parks, flora and fauna, there's a QNPWS information centre (☎ 5535 3032) by the Burleigh Heads National Park entrance on the Gold Coast Hwy, open from 9 am to 4 pm daily.

Email can be sent and received at the Sugar Shack Internet Cafe (☎ 5532 4495) on the Southport Mall beside the Australia Fair shopping centre. It's open daily from 9 am to 9 pm.

Southport & Main Beach

Sheltered from the ocean by the Spit, Southport was the original town on the Gold Coast but it's now modern, residential and rather nondescript. There is little to see or do in Southport but it makes a pleasant, quiet base from which to explore.

Between Southport and Surfers is Main Beach, and north of that the Spit – a narrow, 3km-long tongue of sand dividing the ocean from the Broadwater. On the Broadwater side of the Spit are three adjacent waterside complexes – **Fisherman's Wharf** is the departure point for most pleasure cruises, and has a pub, restaurant, swimming pool and shops.

Immediately south of Fisherman's Wharf are the **Marina Mirage**, an upmarket shopping and dining complex, and **Mariners' Cove**, a collection of cheaper eating places. Further north on the Spit is **Sea World** (see Theme Parks later this section). The beach at the northern end of the Spit is not developed and is good for relatively secluded sunbathing.

Surfers Paradise

Surfers has come a long way since 1936 when there was just the then brand-new Surfers Paradise Hotel, a little hideaway 9km from Southport. The hotel has now been swallowed up by a shopping/eating complex called the Paradise Centre, just one of several such developments that constitute the highly commercialised centre of what's now a vibrant if tacky beachside resort. The popu-

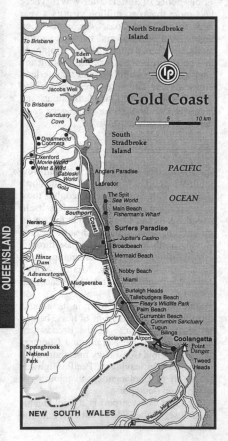

Gold Coast

larity of Surfers these days rests not so much on the sand and surf (which is better down the coast) but on the shopping and nightlife and its proximity to attractions like the Gold Coast theme parks.

For backpackers it's probably the most partying place in Queensland after Cairns, and hostel staff work hard to whip guests up into a goodtime groove on virtually every night of the week. Despite all this, at most times of the year you may not have to go very far north or south to find a relatively open, blissful stretch of white sand.

The town is extremely small and at its heart consists only of two or three streets; Cavill Ave, with a pedestrian mall at its beach end, is the main thoroughfare, while Orchid Ave, one block in from the seafront Esplanade, is the nightclub and bar strip.

Southern Gold Coast

Just south of Surfers at Broadbeach, the **Conrad Jupiters Casino** is a Gold Coast landmark – it was Queensland's first legal casino (see Entertainment later in this section). The **Burleigh Heads National Park**, on the north side of the mouth of Tallebudgera Creek, is a small but diverse forest reserve with walking trails around and through the rocky headland, as well as a lookout and picnic area. On the northern side is one of Australia's most famous surfing point breaks.

There are three excellent wildlife sanctuaries in this area but if you're going to visit only one we recommend making it the **Currumbin Sanctuary** (☎ 5598 1645). It's a large bushland park flocked by technicoloured lorikeets and other birds, with tree kangaroos, koalas, emus and lots more Australian fauna. The sanctuary is off the Gold Coast Hwy half a kilometre south of Currumbin Creek; it is open daily from 8 am to 5 pm ($16). If you're travelling by the Surfside bus, get off at stop No 20.

Fleays Wildlife Park (☎ 5576 2411), 2km inland along the Tallebudgera Creek in West Burleigh, also has a fine collection of native wildlife and 4km of walking tracks through mangroves and rainforest. The platypus was

first bred in captivity here. It's open daily from 9 am to 5 pm and costs $9.50. About 9km inland from the coast, **Olson's Bird Gardens** (☎ 5533 0208) is another attractive sub-tropical garden with a collection of over 1000 exotic birds in enclosures. The gardens are open every day from 9 am to 5 pm ($9).

The twin towns of **Coolangatta** and **Tweed Heads** mark the southern end of the Gold Coast. Tweed Heads is in New South Wales but the two places merge into each other. At **Point Danger**, the headland at the end of the state border, there are good views from the Captain Cook memorial.

Theme Parks

The Gold Coast's theme parks are a major drawcard for tourists. While they are generally quite expensive, the ticket price usually covers all rides and shows, so for a full day's entertainment they can be worthwhile and good fun.

Sea World (☎ 5588 2222) on the Spit in Main Beach is the longest-running of the Gold Coast theme parks. The main draws are the animal performances, which include twice daily dolphin and sea lion shows, and shark-feeding. In addition to these there are rides including a corkscrew rollercoaster, a monorail, a pirate ship, a water park with slides and an adventure ride called the Bermuda Triangle. Sea World is open daily from 9.30 am to 5 pm ($39/24 for adults/children).

Movie World (☎ 5573 8485), otherwise known as 'Hollywood on the Gold Coast', is a re-creation of the Warner Brothers film studio in Hollywood, and claims to be Australia's number one tourist attraction. Warner Bros cartoon characters wander round keeping the kids happy and there are stunt shows, movie sets, a Batman ride and the newest attraction, the Lethal Weapon ride, an inverted, suspended rollercoaster which has you spending most of the 105 second ride upside down. The place is open every day from 9.30 am to 5.30 pm ($39/24 for adults/children).

Wet 'n' Wild, (☎ 5573 2255) just south of Movie World, is a fun water sports park –

probably the country's best. It has a couple of great raft slides, a twister (in which you pelt down a water-sprayed enclosed, tightly spiralled tube), a speed slide on which people have clocked up 70km/h and a 1m-wave pool. Wet 'n' Wild also screens 'Dive-In

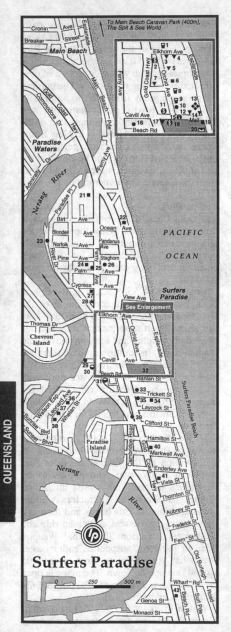

Surfers Paradise

0   250   500 m

PLACES TO STAY
6   Diamonds Resort
21   Marriott
22   Surf & Sun Backpackers
24   Cheers Backpackers
27   Delilah Motel
34   Trickett Gardens Holiday Apartments
36   Surfers Central Backpackers
37   Sleeping Inn Surfers
38   Couple O' Days Accommodation
40   Silver Sands Motel
41   Admiral Motor Inn
42   Surfers Paradise Backpackers Resort

PLACES TO EAT
3   The Latin Quarter
4   Beachside Cafe
5   Costa Dora; Happy House
7   New Seoul
12   Gold Star
14   McDonald's
17   Hard Rock Cafe

OTHER
1   Paddy Og's
2   Currency Exchange Bureau
8   Cocktails & Dreams; The Party; Shooters Bar
9   Bourbon Bar
10   Aquabus Booking Kiosk
11   American Express
13   Raptis Plaza
15   Gold Coast Tourism Bureau
16   Ansett; Queensland Rail Office
18   Thomas Cook Foreign Exchange
19   Surfers Beach Hut Beach Hire
20   Post Office
23   Budd's Beach Water Sportz
25   South Pacific Rentals
26   Bungee, Bungee Rocket & Flycoaster
28   Police Station
29   Tiki Village Wharf
30   Bus Stop for Southport
31   Surfers Paradise Transit Centre
32   Paradise Centre
33   24 Hour Convenience Store
35   Qantas
39   Hoyts Cinema Centre

Movies' every Saturday night from September to April (and every night during January) – you get to watch a film while floating on a rubber tube in the wave pool. Wet 'n' Wild is open every day from 10 am to 4 pm in winter, 5 pm in summer and 9 pm in late December and January ($21/15 for adults/ children).

Dreamworld (☎ 5588 1111), a couple of kilometres north at Coomera, is a Disneyland-style creation with 11 different theme areas, a wildlife sanctuary, and various thrill rides including the newest, the Tower of Terror, on which you plummet from a height of 38 storeys reaching a speed of 160km/h. It's open daily from 10 am to 5 pm and costs $34/29 for adults/kids. At **Cableski World** (☎ 5537 6300), 12km north of Surfers near Sanctuary Cove, you can water-ski by being towed around a large network of lakes by overhead cables; day passes are $30, night passes $17.

Activities

Water Sports & Surfing Aussie Bob's (☎ 5591 7577) at the Marina Mirage in Main Beach, Budd's Beach Water Sportz (☎ 5592 0644) on River Dve at Surfers, and Surfers Beach Hut Beach Hire at the beach end of the Cavill Ave Mall, rent a wide range of gear including jet skis, fishing boats and sailboards, and can take you parasailing, water-skiing and more. Prices for jet skiing are about $50 to $60 per half hour (jet skis normally take two, so that's $30 per person) and for parasailing $50 per person, and you're usually up for about 10 to 15 minutes.

XTSea Charters (☎ 5532 4299), at Fishermans Wharf, offers all the above plus speed boat canal tours, jet boats and Oz Ducks, which are like motorised inflated tyres.

You can also sea kayak from the north end of the Spit to South Stradbroke Island, possibly encountering dolphins en route. Trips depart at 8.30 am and last about three hours; the price of $29 includes pick-ups. Call ☎ 5527 5785 for bookings.

Bungee-Jumping At Bungee Down Under (☎ 5531 1103), on the Spit by Sea World,

first-time jumpers pay $69, while for experienced jumpers it's $50. Backpackers pay $49 on Monday. In Surfers, a former car park just off Ferny Ave is home to a bungee rocket ($68), which is basically a giant catapult in which you take the place of the projectile ($25 per person), and something called a flycoaster in which you get to play Peter Pan, swung from a hoist 20m up ($29).

Horse Riding Numinbah Valley Adventure Trails (☎ 5533 4137) has three-hour horse-riding treks through beautiful rainforest and river scenery in the Numinbah Valley 30km south of Nerang, costing $40 per person or $45 with pick-ups from the coast.

Gum Nuts Horse Riding Resort (☎ 5543 0191), on Nerang-Broadbeach Rd in Carrara, also has half-day riding for $35 ($40 in the afternoon) and a full day with lunch for $60. The price includes Gold Coast pick-ups.

Other Activities Off The Edge (☎ 5592 6406) offers downhill mountain biking out in the hinterland forests. There are a variety of routes from those for the timid to slopes for those with a deathwish – and to cut out the tiresome bit a van takes you back uphill each time. The cost is $30 for backpackers including pick-ups. The same company also offers a 'triple challenge' which begins with some trail biking, moves on to powerboating and then peaks with your choice of a bungee jump, jet ski or parasail. The all-in cost is $130, including a free meal and a beer.

Clifftop Adventures Co (☎ 018 752 510) offers forward abseiling from $40, or you can rap jump (☎ 5526 9986) from the top of a 20-floor building for $55.

Organised Tours & Cruises

The Aquabus (☎ 5539 0222) is good; it's a semi-aquatic vehicle that departs five times daily from Cavill Ave in Surfers and makes a 75-minute tour up Main Beach and the Spit and sails back on the Broadwater. The fare is $22 and you can book from the kiosk on Cavill Ave.

Hinterland Trips We've had plenty of good feedback for Off The Edge (☎ 5592 6406), which does an excellent daytrip out to the Springbrook Plateau taking in some hiking, walks behind waterfalls, swimming and a BBQ lunch with wine – the price, including pick-ups is excellent value at $29 for backpackers.

Doug Robbins' Off The Beaten Track tours (☎ 5533 5366) offers overnight trips from the Gold Coast to the Springbrook Plateau, which are also great value at $40 per person, including return transport, accommodation, a meal, and a half to full-day bushwalk. Doug will pick you up in the morning and drop you back on the coast in the following morning.

Cruises During the summer months, cruises on offer from Surfers include two-hour harbour and canal trips (about $22) and cruises to South Stradbroke Island (about $45 including lunch). Boats depart from Marina Mirage or Fisherman's Wharf on the Spit, or from the Tiki Village Wharf down at the river end of Cavill Ave. Operators change from season to season, so ask at your accommodation what's available and what they've had good word on.

Special Events

Various life-saving carnivals and ironman and ironwoman events are held on the coast during summer and there's also the Surfers Paradise International Triathalon each April. June sees the Gold Coast International Jazz and Blues Festival held over two days at the Gold Coast International Hotel, and the Gold Coast International Marathon is run in July. In mid-October (in 1998 it's 15 to 17 October) the whole town comes to a standstill for the IndyCar motor race between the high rises of Surfers. There's a four-day carnival to coincide with the event but if you want access to the race it will cost from $25 to $45 for a day pass.

Places to Stay

Backpacker hostels aside, all accommodation rates are seasonal; tariffs given here rise by as much as 50% during the school holidays and 100% at Christmas time.

Camping There are caravan/camping parks all the way along the Gold Coast from Main Beach to Coolangatta. Most of the foreshore parks are run by the local council and are quite good. The closest to Surfers is the *Main Beach Caravan Park* (☎ 5581 7722) on Main Beach Pde (near the southern end of the Spit), with tent sites from $16. The riverside *Broadwater Tourist Park* (☎ 5581 7733), just off the Gold Coast Hwy in Southport, has tent sites from $15. Neither has any on-site accommodation.

In Burleigh Heads, the *Burleigh Beach Tourist Park* (☎ 5581 7755), just back from the beach, has sites from $16. Further south in Coolangatta/Tweed Heads, the *Border Caravan Park* (☎ 5536 3134) on Boundary St has tent sites from $11 to $18 and on-site vans from $27 to $60.

Hostels Most people choose to stay as close to the centre of Surfers as possible, but some of the hostels a bit further out run regular courtesy buses to/from Surfers.

Southport Trekkers (☎ 5591 5616) at 22 White St, about 1km south of Southport's transit centre, is a strong candidate for southeast Queensland's best hostel. It's clean, well cared for and has a comfortable, homely feel. Accommodation is in three or four-bed dorms, or twins with their own TV. The staff organise trips to nightclubs in Surfers every evening. Beds are $15, while twins are $32 for the room.

Over on Main Beach in the Mariners' Cove complex, the YHA-affiliated *British Arms Hostel* (☎ 5571 1776) is a fairly new place right on the wharfside. It's a little bit spartan but the management are working hard to liven things up with free beers on check-in, twice weekly barbecues and various other activities. Dorms go for $14 to $18 while doubles are $36.

Surfers Paradise Surfers has several decent hostel options. The one we like best is the

100-bed *Cheers Backpackers* (☎ 5531 6539) at 8 Pine Ave. It's well set up with a decent pool, and an excellent bar area and large barbecue courtyard. Beds in dorms of either two, four or six beds cost $12 or $14. Cheers is very party-oriented with video nights, karaoke evenings and vouchers for the nightclubs, many of which are within staggering distance of here.

Another partyin' place, *Surf & Sun* (☎ 5592 2363) just north of the centre at 3323 Gold Coast Hwy looks very barrack-like from the outside but inside it's comfortable and all rooms have TV and ensuite. It's $13 a night in a four-bed dorm or $18 each in a double.

For facilities the *Surfers Paradise Backpackers Resort* (☎ 5592 4677), at 2835 Gold Coast Hwy, is unbeatable – a decent-sized pool, a small gym and sauna, a pool room, tennis court, free-use laundry and basement parking. The only drawback is that the hostel is some way south of the centre; there is, however, a courtesy bus. A dorm or unit bed costs $14, doubles are $36.

Just south of the transit centre on Whelan St there's a string of three hostels. *Surfers Central Backpackers* at No 40 is badly in need of renovation and until that happens we recommend giving it a miss. *Sleeping Inn Surfers* (☎ 5592 4455) at 26 Whelan St is modern, well-furnished and clean, and good for anyone who wants privacy and comfort. Dorms are $15, doubles are $40. We've had mixed reports on a *Couple O' Days Accommodation* (☎ 5592 4200) at 18 Whelan St and we suggest you check your room and make sure that you're happy with it before paying as the reception displays conspicuous 'no refund' notices. Dorm beds are $14.

Coolangatta The *Sunset Strip Budget Resort* (☎ 5599 5517) at 199-203 Boundary St has motel-style singles/doubles/triples for $30/40/60 all with shared bathrooms. There's a TV lounge, kitchen and dining area and a large pool. Guests also have free use of surf and boogie boards.

The *Coolangatta YHA* (☎ 5536 7644) is at 230 Coolangatta Rd, Bilinga, just north of

the airport and about 3km from central Coolangatta. For nonmembers, a bed in a six or eight-bed dorm costs $17 and doubles are $38. It's a newish building, with good facilities including a pool, but it's not convenient for anything except planespotting.

Motels & Holiday Apartments Budget motels line the highway and advertise cheap deals in flashing neon signs. Holiday apartments can be excellent value, especially for a group of three or four. Many of the apartments have a two-night minimum stay, and a seven-night minimum during the peak holiday seasons.

Surfers Paradise At 2985 Gold Coast Hwy, the *Silver Sands Motel* (☎ 5538 6041) has attractively refurbished units and a small pool, with doubles starting at $55. Close by at No 2965, the *Admiral Motor Inn* (☎ 5539 8759) has rooms starting from $50, while the *Delilah Motel* (☎ 5538 1722) on the corner of Ferny and Cypress Aves has rooms from $65.

At 24-30 Trickett St, the *Trickett Gardens Holiday Apartments* (☎ 5539 0988) is a low-rise block of good one and two-bedroom apartments that range from $92 to $116 for two people, $132 to $178 for four.

Diamonds Resort (☎ 5570 1011) is a small budget resort in the heart of Surfers at 19 Orchid Ave, with motel units and apartments from $70 to $90.

There are quite a few cheap motels just south of Surfers along the Gold Coast Hwy at Mermaid Beach. The *Red Emu Motel* (☎ 5575 2748) at No 2583 has doubles from $35, while the *Mermaid Beach Motel* (☎ 5575 1577) at No 2395 has clean units from $25.

Southern Gold Coast In Burleigh Heads, the *Hillhaven Holiday Apartments* (☎ 5535 1055) at 2 Goodwin Tce have the prime position in Burleigh, with great views along the coast. Oldish but comfy apartments start from $110 for two bedrooms and $150 for three bedrooms.

In Coolangatta, *At the Beach Motel*

QUEENSLAND

(☎ 5536 3599) on the corner of Musgrave St and Winston St has motel units ranging from $45 to $80 a night, as well as self-contained one-bedroom units from $60 to $120 and two-bedroom units from $90. *On the Beach Holiday Units* (☎ 5536 3624) at 118 Marine Pde is a complex of older-style units on the foreshore. The place is a little shabby but some of the units are extremely roomy and the location, across from the beach, is excellent. Beach view doubles are $60, those at the back $50.

Places to Eat

Surfers Paradise There are plenty of choices in and around the Cavill Ave Mall. If you just want to fill up cheaply then there are a couple of all-you-can-eat Chinese including *Gold Star*, just east of the junction with Orchid Ave, which charges $5.90 at lunch and dinner. There are more good budget eateries in the Raptis Plaza Arcade including Thai and Vietnamese, a carvery and bakery, and an excellent Japanese place, *Sumo*, which does cheap takeaways.

At the northern end of Orchid Ave, *Costa Dora* and *Happy House* are neighbouring, pavement restaurants, which serve up very reasonably priced Italian and Chinese respectively – you can eat well for under $10 and both places are licensed.

Around the corner in Elkhorn Ave, the *Latin Quarter* is a great little BYO Italian bistro with pasta from $10 and other mains from $15 – good for a splurge. Further along, the *Beachside Cafe* is open 24 hours daily and has breakfast deals at $5.50 for orange juice, cereal, bacon and eggs, tea or coffee.

A particular favourite of ours is the *New Seoul*, a Korean place at the Gold Coast Hwy end of the Centre Arcade. It does a lunchtime special of a main meal, rice and kimchi for $8. It gets very busy in the evenings.

Southern Gold Coast In Burleigh Heads, the *Pagoda Buffet* on the Gold Coast Hwy in the centre of town has all-you-can-eat Asian buffets at $6.50 for lunch and $8.50 for dinner. *Tim's Malaysian Hut*, upstairs in the Old Burleigh Theatre Arcade on Goodwin

Tce, has good hawker-style noodles, vegetables, seafood and meat dishes in the $7 to $12 range. It's BYO and opens nightly for dinner and for yum-cha-style lunches from Friday to Sunday. *Montezuma's* is a licensed Mexican eatery with mains from $8 to $12. There are also a couple of good streetfront cafes fronting the arcade.

In Coolangatta the most pleasant places to eat are the two Surf Life Saving Clubs, one at Greenmount Beach, the other at Rainbow Bay. They both serve well-priced lunches and dinners and you can eat out on the deck overlooking the beach. The huge *Twin Towns Services Club* has a snack bar on the 2nd floor which has good meals for $6 to $8 and $4.50 lunches on weekdays.

Entertainment

Nightclubs Orchid Ave in Surfers is the Gold Coast's main bar and nightclub strip. Many of the backpackers' hostels organise nights out at the clubs, usually with free admission and cheap drinks and food. The starting place most nights is *Bourbon Bar*, a fairly gloomy basement bar popular for its cut-price beer and especially busy on Thursday, which is karaoke night. *Shooters* is an American-style saloon with pool tables, big-screen videos and occasional live entertainment. It gets particularly busy on Sunday when they offer a free meal and free pool to groups from hostels – otherwise it's $5 to get in.

The other two major backpacker-friendly places are *Cocktails & Dreams* and the *Party*, two nightclubs, one above the other, linked by an internal staircase. They have different themes most week nights; party games on Monday, flares, funksters and 70s music on Tuesday, toga parties and slave auctions on Wednesday, and 'man-o-man/babe-o-babe' contests on Thursday.

Paddy Og's, on Elkhorn Ave, is a large Irish bar which attracts an older, more sedate crowd.

Cinemas Cinemas include *Hoyts* (☎ 5570 3355), on the corner of the Gold Coast Hwy and Clifford St, a six-screen complex buried within the Pacific Fair shopping centre at Broadbeach, the *Mermaid 5* (☎ 11 621), 2514 Gold Coast Hwy at Mermaid Beach, and the *Coolangatta Cinema Centre* (☎ 5536 8900), on level two at the Beach House Plaza.

Casino Conrad Jupiters Casino, just off the Gold Coast Hwy at Broadbeach, is open 24 hours a day and has more than 100 gaming tables, including blackjack, roulette, two-up and craps, as well as hundreds of poker machines. Admission is free but you have to be over 18 years of age. There's a dress code of 'neat casual' – basically, long socks if you're wearing shorts, no sleeveless T-shirts and no ripped jeans.

Getting There & Away
Air Coolangatta's Bilinga airport is the seventh busiest in Australia. Ansett and Qantas fly direct from the major cities including Sydney ($306), Melbourne ($441), Adelaide ($471) and Perth ($730).

Bus The Surfers Paradise transit centre on the corner of Beach and Cambridge Rds is where you'll arrive if you're coming by bus. Inside are the booking desks of the bus companies, a cafeteria, left-luggage lockers ($4 a day) and the In Transit (☎ 5592 2911) backpackers' accommodation booking desk.

McCafferty's, Greyhound Pioneer and Coachtrans all have frequent services to Brisbane ($12 or $14), Byron Bay ($18 or $19) and Sydney ($66 to $79); Greyhound also has one service a day to Noosa ($28), changing at Brisbane.

The trip to Brisbane takes about 1½ hours from Surfers and just over two hours from Coolangatta.

Train The Gold Coast is served by Helensvale and the newly-opened Nerang stations, which have direct links to Brisbane's Roma St and Central stations. Neither Helensvale or Nerang are particularly close to any of the main Gold Coast centres but Surfside buses run regular shuttles from the train stations down to Surfers

and beyond and to the theme parks. The one-way Brisbane-Helensvale (65 minutes) fare is $7.20, while the Surfside shuttle to/from Surfers Paradise is $3.30.

There's a Queensland Rail booking office (☎ 5539 9088) in the Cavill Park Building on Beach Rd opposite the transit centre.

Getting Around
To/From the Airport Coachtrans (☎ 5588 8747) meets every flight into Coolangatta airport (Qantas and Ansett) with transfers to Coolangatta ($7 one-way), Burleigh Heads ($8), Surfers ($9) and Main Beach ($10).

Bus Surfside Buslines (☎ 5536 7666) runs a frequent service 24 hours a day up and down the Gold Coast Hwy between Southport and Tweed Heads and beyond. You can buy individual fares, get a Day Rover ticket for $8, or a weekly one for $26.

Car, Bicycle & Moped There are dozens of car-rental firms around with flyers in every hostel, motel and hotel. A few of the cheaper ones are Red Back Rentals (☎ 5592 1655) and Costless (☎ 5592 4499), both in the transit centre at Surfers, and Rent-A-Bomb (☎ 5538 8222) at 8 Beach Rd.

South Pacific Rentals (☎ 5592 5878) at 102 Ferny Avenue across from the bungee-jumping, hires out mopeds at $35 for two hours or $60 a day.

Red Back Rentals also has bikes for $15 a day, Surfers Beach Hut Beach Hire at the beach end of the Cavill Ave Mall has them for $15 a half day or $20 for a full day, or Green Bicycle Rentals (☎ 018 766 880) has good mountain bikes for $18 a day and will deliver.

GOLD COAST HINTERLAND
The mountains of the **McPherson Range**, about 20km inland from Coolangatta and stretching about 60km back along the NSW border to meet the Great Dividing Range, are a paradise for walkers. The great views and beautiful natural features are easily accessible if you have a car, and there are plenty of wonderfully scenic drives. Otherwise, there

are several places offering tours and day trips from the coast. Expect a lot of rain in the mountains from December to March, and winter nights can be cold.

Tamborine Mountain
Just 45km north-west of the Gold Coast, this 600m-high plateau is on a northern spur of the McPherson Range. Patches of the area's original forests remain in nine small national parks. There are gorges, spectacular waterfalls including Witches Falls and Cedar Creek Falls, walking tracks and great views inland or over the coast. However, because of its proximity to the coast, this area is more developed and commercialised than the ranges further south.

The main access roads are from Oxenford on the Pacific Hwy or via Nerang from the coast. There's an information centre (☎ 5545 1171) in North Tamborine. Some of the best lookouts are in **Witches Falls National Park**, south-west of North Tamborine, and at **Cameron Falls**, north-west of North Tamborine. **Macrozamia Grove National Park**, near Mt Tamborine township, has some extremely old macrozamia palms.

Springbrook National Park
This forested 900m-high plateau is, like the rest of the McPherson Range, a remnant of the huge volcano once centred on Mt Warning in New South Wales. It's a lovely drive from the Gold Coast, reached by a sealed road via Mudgeeraba.

There are three sections of the national park: Springbrook, Mt Cougal and Natural Bridge. The vegetation is cool-temperate rainforest and eucalypt forest, with gorges, cliffs, forests, waterfalls, an extensive network of walking tracks and several picnic areas.

At the **Gwongorella picnic area**, just off the Springbrook road, the lovely Purling Brook Falls drop 109m into rainforest. Downstream, Waringa Pool is a beautiful summer swimming hole. There's a good camping ground beside the picnic area.

The **Natural Bridge section**, off the Nerang to Murwillumbah road, has a 1km walking circuit leading to a rock arch spanning a water-formed cave that is home to a huge colony of glow-worms.

There are rangers' offices and information centres at Natural Bridge and Springbrook where you can pick up a copy of the national park's walking tracks leaflet. Camping permits for Gwongorella are available from the ranger at Springbrook (☎ 5533 5147, weekdays only, between 3 and 4 pm). Springbrook township itself has a general store, tearooms and craft shops, and several guesthouses. See Organised Tours & Cruises earlier in the Gold Coast section for details of trips to Springbrook from the coast.

Lamington National Park
West of Springbrook, this 200 sq km park covers more of the McPherson Range and adjoins the Border Ranges National Park in NSW. It includes thickly wooded valleys, 1100m-high ranges, plus most of the Lamington Plateau. Much of the vegetation is subtropical rainforest. There are beautiful gorges, caves, superb views, waterfalls and pools, and lots of wildlife. Bower birds are quite common and pademelons, a type of small wallaby, can be seen late in the afternoon.

The two most popular and accessible sections, **Binna Burra** and **Green Mountains**, can both be reached via sealed roads from Canungra. The 24km Border Trail walk links the two.

The park has 160km of walking tracks ranging from a 'senses trail' for blind people at Binna Burra to a tree-top canopy walk along a series of suspension bridges at Green Mountains. Walking trail maps and brochures are available from the QNPWS offices at Binna Burra (☎ 5533 3584) and Green Mountains (☎ 5544 0634), both open weekdays only from 1 to 3.30 pm.

Places to Stay The *Binna Burra Camp Ground* (☎ 5533 3758) has a great setting and good facilities; tent and van sites cost $7 per person, while on-site tents cost $36 a night for two. The *Binna Burra Mountain Lodge* (☎ 5533 3622) is a good mountain retreat with three types of rustic log cabins which cost from $99 to $149 per person per night, which includes all meals, free hiking and climbing gear, and activities like guided walks, bus trips and abseiling.

O'Reilly's Guesthouse (☎ 5544 0644) at Green Mountains is a fantastic place to splash out on if you can afford it. It was built in the 1930s and retains much period charm, plus it's smack in the middle of the national park. Beds are from $114 per person per night, inclusive of all meals and activities like bushwalks and 4WD bus trips. There's also a kiosk, and a National Parks camping ground about 600m away with sites for $3.50 per person per night.

You can bush camp in Lamington but only a limited number of permits are issued. You can get information from the QNPWS offices at Burleigh Heads or Brisbane, but camping permits must be obtained from the ranger at Green Mountains.

Getting There & Away The Binna Burra bus service (☎ 5533 3622) operates daily between Surfers and Binna Burra (one hour, $16 one way), departing from Surfers at 1.15 pm and from Binna Burra at 10.30 am – book ahead.

Allstate Scenic Tours (☎ 3285 1777) has services daily (except Saturday) departing Brisbane at 9.30 am for O'Reilly's (three hours, $20 or $35 for a return day trip), returning at 3.30 pm.

Mountain Coach Company (☎ 5524 4249) has a daily Green Mountains service picking up along the Gold Coast ($35 return).

Mt Lindesay Highway
This road runs south from Brisbane, across the Great Dividing Range west of Lamington and into New South Wales at Woodenbong. **Beaudesert**, in cattle country 66km from Brisbane and 20km south-west of Tamborine Mountain, has a pioneer museum, a tourist centre on Jane St, and several motels.

West of Beaudesert is the stretch of the Great Dividing Range known as the **Scenic Rim** (see the Darling Downs section later in

this chapter). Further south, **Mt Barney National Park** is undeveloped but popular with bushwalkers and climbers. It's in the Great Dividing Range just north of the state border. You reach it from the Rathdowney to Boonah road. There's a tourist office (☎ 5544 1222) on the highway at Rathdowney.

Sunshine Coast

The stretch of coast from the top of Bribie Island to Noosa is known as the Sunshine Coast. It's a popular holiday area, renowned for fine beaches, good surfing and fishing. Although it doesn't have the high-rise jungle and neon-lit strips of the Gold Coast, the coast is still quite commercial and has been heavily developed.

Noosa is the most fashionable and exclusive town on the coast, but it also has a good range of budget accommodation, an excellent national park and great beaches. Maroochydore is also quite popular. North of Noosa is the Cooloola National Park and Rainbow Beach, an access point for Fraser Island.

Getting There & Away
Bus Greyhound Pioneer and McCafferty's buses travel along the Bruce Hwy, but both have only one service a day each way from Brisbane to Noosa and Maroochydore. The main Sunshine Coast operator is Suncoast Pacific (☎ 3236 1901). It runs frequent direct services from the Brisbane transit centre and Brisbane airport to Noosa (three hours, $19) via Maroochydore (two hours, $16).

From Cooroy and Nambour on the highway, Tewantin Bus Services (☎ 5449 7422) runs regular buses across to Noosa, continuing to Maroochydore, while Sunshine Coast Coaches (☎ 5443 4555) has daily services south from Maroochydore and inland across to Landsborough and Nambour.

Train The most convenient stations for the

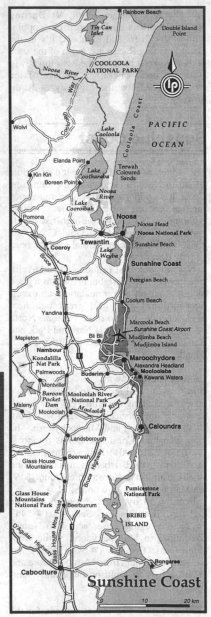

Sunshine Coast are Nambour and Cooroy. There are services daily to these places from Brisbane and from the north.

CABOOLTURE (pop 17,600)

This region, 49km north of Brisbane, once had a large Aboriginal population. Nowadays it's a prosperous dairy centre.

It also has two interesting attractions. Seven km east (signposted off the road to Bribie Island), the **Abbey Museum** is a world social history museum with a small but well-presented collection of ancient artefacts, weaponry, pottery and costumes. The collection was previously housed in the UK, Cyprus, Egypt and Sri Lanka. It's open Tuesday, Thursday, Friday and Saturday from 10 am to 4 pm; entry is $4.

The **Caboolture Historical Village** on Beerburrum Rd, 2km north of the town, has about 30 early Australian buildings in a bush setting. It is open daily from 10 am to 3 pm and entry is $5.

GLASS HOUSE MOUNTAINS

About 20km north of Caboolture, the Glass House Mountains are a dramatic visual starting point for the Sunshine Coast. They're a bizarre series of volcanic crags rising abruptly out of the plain to a height of around 300m. They were named by Captain Cook and, depending on whose story you believe, he either noted the reflections of the glass-smooth rock sides of the mountains, or he thought they looked like the glass furnaces in his native Yorkshire.

The mountains are great for scenic drives, bushwalking and rock climbing. The main access is via the Forest Drive, a 22km-long series of sealed and unsealed roads that wind through the ranges from Beerburrum to the Glass House Mountains township, with several spectacular lookout points en route.

There are four small national parks within the range, and each has walking/climbing trails of varying levels of difficulty: Mt Ngungun is an easy two-hour walk to the summit; Mt Beerwah and Mt Tibrogargan are steep and difficult three-hour climbs; and Mt Coonowrin is popular with experienced

RICHARD I'ANSON

GADI FARFOUR

Queensland
Top: Egg Rock seen from Bellbird Lookout, Lamington National Park
Bottom: The Lagoon, South Bank Parklands, Brisbane

MARK ARMSTRONG

JOHN CHAPMAN

MARK ARMSTRONG

Queensland
Top: Barron River, near Cairns
Middle: Mt Warning, Lamington National Park
Bottom: Sandy beach, Fraser Island

rock climbers. Contact the ranger (☎ 5494 6630) at Beerwah for more information.

Mt Tibrogargan Relaxapark (☎ 5496 0151) 1.5km north of Beerburrum has a shop, walking trails, and information on walks and wildlife; tent sites are $11, on-site vans $22 to $241 and self-contained units from $45.

CALOUNDRA (pop 28,500)

At the southern end of the Sunshine Coast, Caloundra has some decent beaches and excellent fishing, but compared with places further north, it's a bit faded these days. It's still a popular holiday town with families, and has numerous caravan parks and holiday flats, but no backpackers' hostel. Bulcock Beach, good for windsurfing, is just down from the main street, overlooking the northern end of Bribie Island.

Points of interest include the **Queensland Air Museum** (☎ 5492 5930) at Caloundra aerodrome, which is open Wednesday, Saturday and Sunday from 10 am to 4 pm ($4), and **Aussie World & the Ettamogah Pub** on the Bruce Highway, just north of the Caloundra turn-off.

There's a tourist office (☎ 5491 0202) on Caloundra Rd, 2km west of the town centre.

Places to Stay

The *Hibiscus Holiday Park* (☎ 5491 1564) on the corner of Bowman and Landsborough Park Rds is close to the beach and the centre; tent sites are from $12, on-site vans from $25 and cabins from $32. Opposite the bus terminal, the *Dolphins Motel* (☎ 5491 2511) at 6 Cooma Tce has good units ranging seasonally from $48 to $75 for doubles.

MOOLOOLABA, ALEXANDRA HEADLAND & MAROOCHYDORE (pop 36,000)

North from Caloundra, the coast is built-up most of the way to the triple towns of Mooloolaba, Alexandra Headland and Maroochydore, which sprawl together to form the Sunshine Coast's biggest and most heavily developed urban conglomeration.

Maroochydore, the main town, is a busy commercial centre and popular tourist spot, with both an ocean beach and the Maroochy River, which has lots of pelicans and a few islands. Alexandra Headland has a pleasant beach and good surfing off a rocky point. Mooloolaba has the brightest atmosphere and the best beach and a strip of shops along the beachfront, including cafes, restaurants and the odd nightspot. Also at Mooloolaba is the **Wharf**, a riverfront development with shops, eateries, a tavern, a marina and the excellent **Underwater World**, a large oceanarium with a transparent tunnel leading underneath and performing-seal shows. It's open daily from 9 am to 6 pm ($16.90).

Information

The Maroochy tourist information centre (☎ 5479 1566) is near the corner of Aerodrome Rd (the main road connecting Maroochydore and Mooloolaba) and Sixth Ave; it's open weekdays from 9 to 5 pm and weekends 9 to 4 pm.

Activities

As in Caloundra, the main attractions here are the excellent beaches. There are numerous surf shops along the coast where you can hire surf and boogie boards, and in-line skates and bicycles (both $15 a half-day, $20 a day) can be hired from Maroochy Skate Biz (☎ 5443 6111) on the foreshore at 174 Alexandria Pde in Alexandra Headland.

Places to Stay

The best caravan/camping parks are the foreshore parks run by the local council. They include *Cotton Tree Caravan Park* (☎ 5443 1253) on the Esplanade and the *Seabreeze Caravan Park* (☎ 5443 1167) behind the information centre. Tent sites are from $12, and powered sites from $14 (no on-site vans).

There are three hostels in Maroochydore – ring from the bus stop for a pick-up. The best is possibly the *Cotton Tree Beachouse* (☎ 5443 1755), a comfortable, rambling old timber guesthouse overlooking the river. There are free surfboards and boogie boards and free jet skiing sessions twice a week.

QUEENSLAND

Dorm beds are $14, singles $30, doubles and twins $32. It's at 15 the Esplanade, just five-minutes walk from the bus station.

At 50 Parker St, the *Suncoast Back-packers' Lodge* (☎ 5443 7544) is a modern, purpose-built hostel with free bikes, surf-boards and boogie boards, and dorms at $14 and doubles at $34. *Maroochydore YHA Backpackers* (☎ 5443 3151) is at 24 Schir-mann Dve, buried in a residential estate a couple of turns off Bradman Ave. It's a bit institutional and has mainly six to eight-bed dorms from $16 a night with a few doubles at $36.

There are dozens of motels and holiday units but generally they are expensive. *Tallows Lodge Motel* (☎ 5443 2981) at 10 Memorial Ave is close to the beach and has self-contained units from $45 to $70. Alter-natively, there's a batch of cheap motels on Brisbane Rd, the main road south out of Mooloolaba.

Places to Eat
For cheap eating, about the best option is the *food court* at the Sunshine Plaza shopping centre where there must be about 20 outlets offering a huge variety of different food types at budget prices. Alternatively, over at the Wharf, *Friday's* is a popular tavern/bar and eatery with a great deal on T-bone steaks – from $7.95. There's also a branch of the *Hog's Breath Cafe* at the Wharf. For good cafes and places where you can get a decent salad or pasta, try the extension of Alexandra Pde, east of the junction with Brisbane Rd.

Back in Maroochydore, *Hathi Indian Res-taurant* at 25 Aerodrome Rd has all-you-can-eat Indian smorgasbords for $14 a head and main courses in the $8 to $10 range. *Lefty's BYO* is an intimate little BYO that specialises in very good Greek, Italian and Mexican food, with mains in the $14 to $18 range. It's open Tuesday to Saturday for dinner.

Getting There & Away
Long-distance buses stop at the Suncoast Pacific Bus Terminal (☎ 5443 1011) on First Ave in Maroochydore, just off Aerodrome Rd (near KFC).

NOOSA
Despite being a surfers' mecca since the early 1960s, Noosa has so far managed to avoid the blitzkreig development that has afflicted the Gold Coast. It remains a low-key resort for the fashionable, as well as a popular stop-off for travellers moving up or down the coast. It has good beaches, some fine cafes and restaurants, a very accessible national park nestling next door and just a little to the north, the walks, waterways and beaches of the Cooloola National Park.

Orientation
Noosa is actually a string of small, linked centres stretching back from the mouth of the Noosa River and along its maze of tributary creeks and lakes. The most popular resort area and the liveliest part of town is Noosa Heads, centred on the trendy shopping and dining zone of Hastings St. Three km west – inland along the Noosa River – is Noosaville, which is where most of the river tours depart from. The river at this point is seawater and fringed with occasional sandy beaches. Gympie Tce, which runs along the river shore, has a string of eating and drinking places and is quite lively most evenings.

A kilometre south of Noosa Heads, up the hill, is Noosa Junction, another shopping and eating area, from where a main road leads east to Sunshine Beach, the quietest and most residential of the four main areas, but also the place with the best beaches and surf.

Information
The tourist information centre (☎ 5447 4988) is in Hastings St and it's open daily from 9 am to 5 pm. There are also several less useful, privately run tourist information offices, which double as booking agents for accommodation, trips and tours.

The best bookshop in the area is Written Dimensions, next to the cinema on Sunshine Beach Rd in Noosa Junction. A few doors away, at the back of a small arcade, is the Book Exchange, a second-hand place. Down

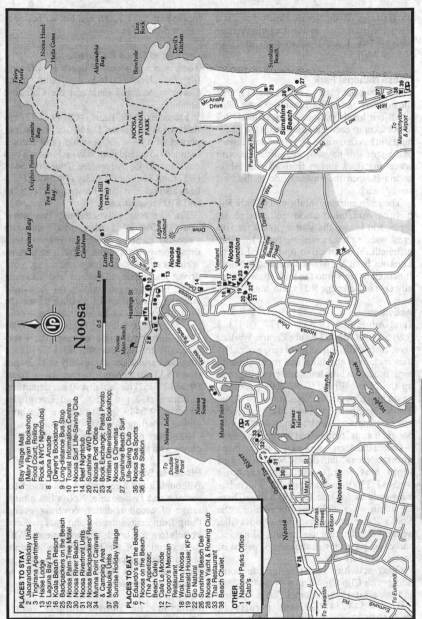

PLACES TO STAY
2 Jacaranda Holiday Units
3 Tingirana Apartments
13 Halse Lodge
15 Laguna Bay Inn
16 Koala Beach Resort
25 Backpackers on the Beach
29 Noosa Palm Tree Motel
30 Noosa River Beach
31 Noosa Riverfront Units
32 Noosa Backpackers' Resort
34 Munna Point Caravan
     & Camping Area
37 Melaluka Units
39 Sunrise Holiday Village

PLACES TO EAT
6 Eduardo's on the Beach
7 Noosa on the Beach
     (The Appetizer;
     Beach Cafe)
12 Cafe Le Monde
17 Topopo's Mexican
     Restaurant
18 Wok Inn Noosa
19 Emerald House; KFC
22 Go Natural
26 Sunshine Beach Deli
28 Noosa Yacht & Rowing Club
33 Thai Restaurant
38 Beach Chalet

OTHER
1 National Parks Office
4 Cato's
5 Bay Village Mall
     (Mary Ryan Bookshop;
     Food Court; Rolling
     Rock & NYC Nightclubs)
8 Laguna Arcade
     (Dwyer's Bookstore)
9 Long-distance Bus Stop
10 Tourist Information Centre
11 Noosa Surf Life-Saving Club
14 Reef Nightclub
20 Sunshine 4WD Rentals
21 Noosa Post Office
23 Book Exchange; Pasta Pronto
24 Written Dimensions Bookshop;
     Noosa 5 Cinemas
27 Sunshine Beach Surf
     Life-Saving Club
35 Noosa Sea Sports
36 Police Station

on Hastings St in Noosa Heads there's a Dwyer's Bookstore in the Laguna Arcade and a Mary Ryan Bookshop in the Bay Village Mall.

Noosa National Park

The spectacular cape at Noosa Head marks the northern end of the Sunshine Coast. This small but lovely national park extends for about 2km in each direction from the headland and has fine walks, great coastal scenery and a string of bays on the north side with waves that draw surfers from all over. Alexandria Bay on the eastern side is the best sandy beach.

The main entrance, at the end of Park Rd, has a car park, information centre and picnic areas, and is also the starting point for five great walking tracks ranging from 1 to 4km in length. You can drive up to the Laguna Lookout from Viewland Dve in the Noosa Junction, or walk into the park from McAnally Dve or Parkedge Rd in Sunshine Beach.

Activities

Total Adventures (☎ 5474 0177, 018 148 609) based at Noosa Leisure Centre, Wallace Dve, Noosaville runs a good range of activities including abseiling and rock climbing trips, mountain bike tours and canoeing trips up the Noosa River. They also offer sea-kayaking trips from September to June. Noosa Sea Sports (☎ 5447 3426) in Noosa Sound shopping centre rents surfboards, boogie boards, fishing and snorkelling gear.

Catamarans and surf skis can be hired from the Noosa Main Beach. Most of the surf shops rent boards, including Ozmosis (☎ 5447 3300) in Hastings St, which has mini-malibus for hire for $30 a day. There are about seven different places along the Noosa River in Gympie Tce, Noosaville, where you can rent out fishing dinghies, barbecue pontoons, catamarans, jet skis, canoes and surf skis.

Other activities on offer include horse riding with Clip Clop Treks (☎ 5449 1254) and camel safaris with Camel Company Australia (☎ 5442 4402), and paraflying (☎ 5449 9630), joy flights in the Red Baron

biplane (☎ 5474 1200) and hot-air ballooning (☎ 5495 6714).

Organised Tours & Cruises

There are a number of operators offering trips from Noosa up to Fraser Island via the Cooloola National Park and the Coloured Sands.

Fraser Explorer Tours (☎ 5449 8647) has daily trips to Fraser Island for a cost per person of $90 – it's possible (and recommended) to extend your stay on Fraser to two days for $145. Adventure Tours (☎ 5447 6957) and Sunlover Holidays (☎ 5474 0777) both also operate daily Fraser tours for $115 and $105 respectively.

For the more adventurous, Trailblazer Tours (☎ 5449 8151) offers good value with three-day camping safaris to Fraser Island departing twice a week ($165 per person, which covers everything including your driver and guide, all meals and camping gear). For more information on the island and alternative ways of visiting it, see the Fraser Coast section later in this chapter.

Several companies run boats up the Noosa River into the Everglades area: the Everglades Water Bus Co (☎ 5447 1838) has a four-hour cruise departing daily at 12.30 pm (from $43 per person); Noosa River Tours (☎ 5449 7362) has a daily 10 am departure, returning at 3 pm ($50); and Everglades Express (☎ 5449 9422) offers a 3½ hour cruise, departing twice daily ($38).

There are plenty of other tours on offer – check with the tourist centre.

Places to Stay

Although it has a reputation as a resort for the rich and fashionable, Noosa has a huge range of accommodation covering everything from caravan parks and backpackers' hostels to resort hotels and apartments. With the exception of the backpackers' hostels, accommodation prices can rise by 50% in busy times and by 100% in the December to January peak season.

Camping The *Sunrise Holiday Village* (☎ 5447 3294) on David Low Way overlooking Sunshine Beach has tent sites from $12 to $15, on-site vans from $30 to $45, and cabins from $30 to $55. Unfortunately facilities and maintenance are not what they might be. Better is the *Munna Point Caravan & Camping Area* (☎ 5449 7050) beside the river in Russell St, Noosaville, with tent sites from $11.

Hostels All of Noosa's hostels have courtesy buses and do pick-ups from the bus stop – all, that is, except the *Halse Lodge* (☎ 1800 242 567) which doesn't need to, being only 100m away. It's a fine, 100-year-old heritage-listed building with polished wooden floors, a colonial-type dining room and big verandahs. The only drawback is that the place is a little austere – no partying here. Dorms go for $16 (six-bed) and $18 (four-bed), but the spartan doubles are way overpriced at $44.

A 10-minute walk uphill from the beach, *Koala Beach Resort* (☎ 5447 3355) at Noosa Junction is the place to go for noise and beery evenings. It's a converted motel with good facilities including a pool and bar. A place in a six-bed dorm costs $14 and doubles are $30, or motel units go for $50 for a double plus $7.50 for extras (they sleep five or six).

The *Noosa Backpackers' Resort* (☎ 5449 8151) at 9 William St over in Noosaville is a relaxed place with a good seated courtyard area, a pool and a small bar. Like the above two places there are cheap meals available, free boogie and surf boards, and a variety of trips and tours on offer. Dorm beds are $15, doubles $32.

Over in Sunshine Beach, *Backpackers on the Beach* (☎ 5447 4739) at 26 Stevens St is a little remote but it is almost on top of Noosa's best stretch of beach. Beds cost $14 a night. Also at Sunshine Beach, the *Melaluka Units* (☎ 5447 3663) at 7 Selene St benefit from being right by the beach. It has two and three-bedroom holiday units with beds costing $16 per person, plus a one-bedroom unit for $40.

Motels & Holiday Units The best places to stay are those along the beachfront around Hastings St – they're also the most expensive. Cheapest of the bunch are the *Tingirana Apartments* (☎ 5447 3274) at 25 Hastings St, with motel units ranging from $65 to $95 and one-bedroom apartments for four from $95 to $130, and the *Jacaranda Holiday Units* (☎ 5447 4011) across the road, with motel-style units that sleep up to three ranging from $70 to $105 a night, and self-contained one-bedroom units sleeping up to five costing from $90 to $150.

About 1km back, the *Laguna Bay Inn* (☎ 5449 2873) at 2 Viewland Dve, Noosa Junction, is a good option with four comfortable self-contained units in a shady garden setting, with a pool and barbecue area. The units sleep up to six and range from $60 to $100 a night.

One of the best areas for cheaper accommodation is along Gympie Tce, the main road through Noosaville. *Noosa Riverfront Units* (☎ 5449 7595) at 277 Gympie Tce has good budget units from $40 for a studio unit or from $80 for two bedrooms. At No 281, *Noosa River Beach* (☎ 5449 7873) has old-fashioned budget units from $40 to $100 a night. Further along at No 233, the *Noosa Palm Tree Motel* (☎ 5449 7311) has eight motel style units and eight self-contained units that range from $50/55 to $55/90 for singles/doubles in the low/high season.

Places to Eat
Budget For a cheap lunch on Hastings St, the *Bay Village food court* has a pizza & pasta bar, a bakery, a Chinese kitchen, a fish bar and a deli. You can eat well here for around $5.

In the Noosa On The Beach complex, just west of the tourist information centre, the *Appetizer*, a greasy, stand-up type place, does Aussie brekkie for $5 and snacks like burgers and fish & chips from around $4. It's open from 7 am to 8 pm. In the same complex but on the beachfront, the *Beach Cafe* is a good spot for breakfast with a menu including muesli with fresh fruit ($5.70) or bacon & eggs ($6.50). They also do pastas, salads and other various meals from $8.50.

At Noosa Junction, a few doors past KFC,

the *Emerald House* is a cheap Chinese restaurant with most dishes on the menu at about $7. It's open daily from 11.30 am to 2 pm for lunch (except Monday) and 5 to 9 pm for dinner.

Hastings St Possibly the best value restaurant on Hastings St remains the ever-popular *Cafe Le Monde*, east of the roundabout. Dining is out front in a large covered courtyard with a large menu that attempts to please everyone. We tried Thai, Italian and Aussie dishes and all were excellent, served in enormous portions and at pretty good prices – $12 to $16 for our mains.

Eduardo's on the Beach, at the end of an arcade at 25 Hastings St, has about the best setting in town. It's a relaxed BYO with beachy decor and a small beachfront deck, and opens every day for breakfast, lunch and dinner. For lunch, meals such as pastas, seafood curries or reef fish with lime and ginger sauce range from $12 to $14. The dinner menu mains are around $18. Eduardo's is very popular and it's a good idea to book ahead – ask for a table on the deck.

Noosa Junction *Pasta Pronto*, at 2/25 Sunshine Beach Rd, down toward the cinema, has excellent homemade pastas ranging from bolognese at $10.50 to marinara at $17. At lunch time (11.30 am to 2.30 pm) it has daily specials for $7.50. It's open for dinner Monday to Saturday from 5.30 to 9 pm.

Back on the roundabout at the junction, *Wok Inn Noosa* is a cheerful noodle bar where you create your own dishes. It's open from 11 am until late. A couple of doors away up the hill *Topopo's Mexican Restaurant* is a colourful cantina with main courses for around $10 combo dishes for around $13, as well as margaritas and sangria by the glass or jug – drink prices tend to be kept pretty low to attract the crowds from Koala over the road.

Back on Sunshine Rd, *Go Natural* is a health-food shop with plenty of sandwich and salad-type lunch options.

Noosaville In front of the Noosa Backpackers' Resort in William St, the *Thai Restaurant* is very good with competitive prices to appeal to the budget conscious lodged in the dorms behind. It's BYO and opens nightly for dinner.

On Gympie Tce, just before you cross the river, the *Noosa Yacht & Rowing Club* is a new two-storey riverfront building which opens every day for lunch and dinner and on Sunday for breakfast. The food here is cheap and hearty with most meals around the $8 to $10 mark.

Sunshine Beach If you're staying in Sunshine Beach, there's a general store, a fruit and vegie shop, and a couple of eateries in the small shopping centre in Duke St – of these the *Sunshine Beach Deli* is a decent gourmet deli with vegetarian dishes, homemade pastries and burgers and hot sandwiches. Down at the beach, the *Sunshine Beach Surf Life-Saving Club* serves bistro meals and has a courtyard overlooking the ocean.

Entertainment
The bar and club scene in Noosa is not particularly great. If you are staying at *Koala Beach Resort* then you're sorted as that's pretty much the liveliest place most evenings. Alternatively, downstairs at the Noosa Reef Hotel on Noosa Dve, the *Reef Nightclub* opens from Thursday to Sunday nights till late, while the pub also has occasional live bands and Sunday afternoon sessions. Otherwise most folks tend to sip in cafe-bars like *Cato's* on Hastings.

Noosa's main nightclub is the *Rolling Rock*, upstairs in the Bay Village plaza off Hastings St. It's open every night until around 3 am, with a 'smart casual' dress code and cover charges between $5 and $7. Nearby and run by the same operator, the *NYC* is a quieter, more sophisticated cocktail bar with an outdoor courtyard.

At 1 Tingira Cres in Sunshine Beach, the *Beach Chalet* is a good live music venue, bar and eatery that features everything from world music, reggae and African soul music to jazz and rock 'n' roll. It currently opens on Monday, Friday and Saturday.

The *Noosa 5 Cinemas* (☎ 5447 5300) at Noosa Junction, is a plush, comfortable place that screens latest release movies. Tickets are cheaper before 6 pm and Tuesday is budget day. The cinema also has a special 'movie mania' deal on Sunday evenings with three current release films for $10.

Getting There & Around

Long-distance buses stop at the bus terminal near the corner of Noosa Dve and Noosa Pde, just back from Hastings St. Advance tickets are available from the booking desk inside the Avis office across the road from the bus stop.

Tewantin Bus Services (☎ 5449 7422) runs frequent daily services up and down the coast between Noosa and Maroochydore, and has local services linking Noosa Heads, Noosaville, Noosa Junction, etc. It also runs a special service on Saturday to the Eumundi Markets – see the Sunshine Coast Hinterland section for times.

If you want to drive up the Cooloola Coast beach to the Teewah Coloured Sands, Double Island Point, Rainbow Beach or Fraser Island, Sunshine 4WD Rentals (☎ 5447 3702), beside the Noosa Junction post office, rents four-seater Suzuki Sierras from $80 a day and seven-seater Nissan Patrols from $135 a day.

Bicycle Hire Bikes can be hired from a number of places, including Sierra Mountain Bike Hire (☎ 5474 8277) based in the Budget Rent-a-Car office in Bay Village, Hastings St, which charges $12 per day and Koala Bike Hire (☎ 5474 2733), which has mountain bikes from $10 a day.

COOLOOLA COAST

Stretching for 50km between Noosa and Rainbow Beach, the Cooloola Coast is a remote strip of long sandy beaches backed by the Cooloola National Park. Although this stretch is undeveloped, at times it is so popular with campers you might be excused for thinking otherwise.

The Cooloola Way, a gravel road, runs from Tewantin all the way up to Rainbow Beach (via Boreen Point and the national park). From Tewantin, the Noosa River Ferry operates daily from 6 am to 10 pm (Friday and Saturday until midnight) and costs $4 per car. On the other side are Lake Cooroibah and the beaches of Laguna Bay, and if you have a 4WD at low tide you can continue right up the beach to Rainbow Beach and Wide Bay passing the Teewah Coloured Sands and the rusting *Cherry Venture*, a 3000 tonne freighter swept ashore by a cyclone in 1973.

Lake Cooroibah

There are several good camping grounds between Lake Cooroibah and the coast, including the low-key *Lake Cooroibah Resort* (☎ 5447 1225), with a bar/restaurant, tennis courts, horse riding, tent sites, on-site tents and cabins. Also based here is the *Camel Company Australia* (☎ 5442 4402) offering two-hour camel treks for $30 or half-day treks (Thursday only) for $45, overnight safaris ($125) and six-day safaris to Fraser Island ($720 all-inclusive).

Boreen Point

On the western shores of Lake Cootharaba, Boreen Point is a relaxed little place with a caravan park, a motel and a few holiday units. The historic *Apollonian Hotel* (☎ 5485 3100) has a garden setting, shady verandahs, meals and simple double rooms from $30. The *Jetty* restaurant (☎ 5485 3167), with a lovely setting overlooking the lake, has lunches daily and dinners on Friday and Saturday.

Cooloola National Park

North of Noosa, the Cooloola National Park covers over 54,000 hectares, with the Noosa River running through the centre. It's a varied wilderness area with long sandy beaches, mangrove-lined waterways, forest, heaths and lakes, all of it featuring plentiful birdlife and lots of wildflowers in spring.

You can drive through the park, although the best way to see Cooloola is from a boat.

QUEENSLAND

Boats can be hired from Tewantin and Noosaville, or there are various operators offering cruises from Noosa – see Organised Tours & Cruises.

Five km north of Boreen Point at Elanda Point there's a lakeside camping ground and a rangers' office (☎ 5449 7364). Several walking trails start here including the 46km Cooloola Wilderness Trail and a 7km trail to the QNPWS visitor centre (☎ 5449 7364) on Kinaba Island.

Places to Stay *Gagaju* (☎ 5474 3522) is an unconventional and totally laidback riverside wilderness camp in forest bordering the Cooloola National Park. It's run by two former travellers who have built the place (furniture and bunks included) from scavenged timber. Possible activities include free canoeing and mountain biking, bushwalking and, in season, cane toad golf – cruel it may sound but we're assured that it's totally environmentally friendly. There's just one communal dorm with beds at $10 a night or you can pitch your own tent for $6. Shower and toilet facilities are basic and bring your own food.

There are also about 10 camping grounds in the park, many of them alongside the river. The main ones are *Fig Tree Point* at the north of Lake Cootharaba, and *Harry's Hut*, about 4km upstream. *Freshwater* is the main camp on the coast; it's about 6km south of Double Island Point.

SUNSHINE COAST HINTERLAND
The mountains of the **Blackall Range** rise just in from the coast, and this scenic hinterland area has mountain towns, guesthouses and B&Bs, national parks with rainforests and waterfalls, art and craft galleries, and lots of tourists.

Nambour is the main commercial centre for the region. It's an attractive town but it has little of interest for travellers. Six km south, the **Big Pineapple** is one of Queensland's kitschy 'big things'. As well as the 15m-high fibreglass fruit there's a train ride through a plantation, a macadamia orchard tour and a themed boat ride which together

cost $13.50 for adults – all very tacky but also very popular.

Further north, thousands flock to the **Eumundi Village Market** every Saturday morning. Eumundi is a charming little rural centre and the original home of Eumundi Lager (now brewed on the Gold Coast). Buses run from Noosa to Eumundi roughly every half-hour on Saturday morning. West of town, you can fossick for thunder eggs at **Thunder Egg Farm**.

The scenic Mapleton to Maleny road runs right along the ridge line of the Blackall Range. **Mapleton Falls National Park** is 4km west of Mapleton and **Kondalilla National Park** is 3km off the Mapleton to Montville stretch of the road. Both have rainforest. At Mapleton Falls, Pencil Creek plunges 120m, while the Kondalilla Falls drop 80m into a rainforest valley. This is a great area for exploring – there's lots of birdlife and several walking tracks in the parks.

Midway between Mapleton and Maleny, **Montville** is a very popular tourist spot, with lots of craft shops and restaurants.

The Big Pineapple exemplifies the Australian penchant for building very large, kitsch objects

The **Maleny Folk Festival**, held annually over the five days leading up to New Year's Eve, is the closest thing Australia has to Woodstock (☎ 3846 7055 for information).

SOUTH BURNETT REGION

Further inland, the South Burnett region includes Australia's most important peanut-growing area. The thing to do here is visit the **Bunya Mountains National Park**. The Bunyas are isolated outliers of the Great Dividing Range, which rise abruptly to over 1000m, and are accessible by sealed road from Dalby or Kingaroy. They are covered with a variety of vegetation from rainforest to heathland and if you haven't already seen wallabies in the wild then this is where to go for guaranteed sightings. There are three camping grounds, plus a network of walking tracks to numerous waterfalls and lookouts. The ranger (☎ 4668 3127) is at Dandabah at the entrance to the park.

Darling Downs

West of the Great Dividing Range in southern Queensland stretch the rolling plains of the Darling Downs, some of the most fertile agricultural land in Australia. Towns such as Toowoomba and Warwick are among the most historic in the state. South of Warwick, the scenic Granite Belt region has Queensland's only wine-growing district and some fine national parks. Other regional attractions include the historic Jondaryan Woolshed west of Toowoomba and the Miles Historical Village.

West of the Darling Downs, the population becomes more scattered as the crop-producing areas give way to sheep and cattle country.

Getting There & Away

Air Flight West (☎ 13 2392) flies daily from Brisbane to Roma ($180) and Charleville ($241).

Bus McCafferty's operates the following

Appropriated from Aboriginal people in the 1840s, the Darling Downs soon became the colony's richest cattle and sheep farming areas

bus services that pass through the Darling: from Brisbane to Longreach (17 hours, $77) along the Warrego Highway via Ipswich, Toowoomba (two hours, $15), Miles (5½ hours, $28), Roma (seven hours, $37) and Charleville (10 hours, $44); and inland from Brisbane via Toowoomba and Goondiwindi (five hours, $34) to Melbourne.

McCafferty's also has an inland service from Brisbane to Sydney that goes along the New England Highway via Warwick (2¾ hours, $23) and Stanthorpe (3½ hours, $29). There are also McCafferty's buses between Toowoomba and the Gold Coast ($20), and between Brisbane and Rockhampton via Toowoomba and Miles.

Train The *Westlander* runs twice a week from Brisbane to Charleville via Ipswich, Toowoomba and Roma. One-way fares are $77 for an economy seat, $107 for an economy sleeper and $172 for a 1st-class sleeper. There are connecting bus services from Charleville to Quilpie and Cunnamulla.

IPSWICH TO WARWICK

Virtually an outer suburb of Brisbane, now Ipswich was a convict settlement as early as 1827 and an important early Queensland town. It still contains many fine old houses and public buildings, and these are described

QUEENSLAND

in the excellent *Ipswich City Heritage Trails* leaflet available from the tourist office (☎ 3281 0555) on the corner of D'Arcy Place and Brisbane St.

South-west of Ipswich, the Cunningham Highway to Warwick crosses the Great Dividing Range at **Cunningham's Gap**, with 1100m mountains rising either side of the road. **Main Range National Park**, which covers the Great Dividing Range for about 20km north and south of Cunningham's Gap, is great walking country, with a variety of walks starting from the car park at the crest of the gap. Much of the range is covered in rainforest. There's a camping ground and information office by the road on the western side of the gap; contact the ranger (☎ 4666 1133) for permits.

WARWICK (pop 11,000)

Warwick, 162km south-west of Brisbane, is the oldest town in Queensland after the capital. It's a busy farming centre noted for its roses, numerous historic buildings built of local sandstone, and its rodeo (held over the last weekend in October).

The Warwick tourist information centre (☎ 4661 3122) at 49 Albion St is a good one with plenty of material on the neighbouring South Downs towns too; it's open 9 am to 5 pm weekdays, 10 am to 3 pm Saturday, and 10 am to 2 pm Sunday.

Warwick's major attraction is **Pringle Cottage & Museum** on Dragon St, dating from 1863. It is open daily except Tuesday and entry costs $3.50.

The *Warwick Tourist Park* (☎ 4661 8335) at 18 Palmer Ave, off the New England Hwy on the northern outskirts of town, has unpowered/powered sites at $10/13 and dormitory accommodation at $10 per person. The *Criterion Hotel* (☎ 4661 1042) at 84 Palmerin St is a huge old country pub with clean and simple rooms opening up onto a broad front verandah costing $20 per person, including a cooked breakfast. Of the dozen or so motels in town the *Centre Point Mid-City Motor Inn* (☎ 4661 3488) at 32 Albion St is the most central; it charges $54 a double.

STANTHORPE & THE GRANITE BELT

South of Warwick is the Granite Belt, an elevated plateau of the Great Dividing Range 800 to 950m above sea level. It's known for fruit and vegetable production and wine making, and there are around 20 wineries in the area, most of which are open to visitors.

Stanthorpe is the main centre for the region and it has a good range of accommodation, a historical museum and an art gallery. It celebrates its standing as Queensland's coolest town with a Brass Monkey Festival every July. The tourist information office (☎ 4681 2057) is in the Civic Centre on the corner of Marsh and Lock Sts, open on weekdays from 8.45 am to 5 pm and Saturday 10 am to 1 pm.

The *Central Hotel* (☎ 4681 2044) on the corner of High and Victoria Sts has good singles/doubles from $25/40, while 12km north at Thulimbah on the New England Hwy, the *Summit Lodge Backpackers* (☎ 4683 2599) specialises in finding fruit and vegetable-picking work for travellers and has dorm beds for $12.50 a night – ring ahead to see what's available.

From the highway 26km south of Stanthorpe, a sealed road leads 9km east up to **Girraween National Park**, an area of 1000m-high hills, huge granite outcrops, and valleys. The park has a visitor centre (☎ 4684 5157), two camping grounds with hot showers, and several walking tracks of varying length. Girraween adjoins Bald Rock National Park over the border in New South Wales. It can fall below freezing on winter nights up here, but summer days are warm.

GOONDIWINDI (pop 4,400)

West of Warwick, Goondiwindi is on the New South Wales border and the Macintyre River. Known as the home of the great race-horse, Gunsynd, it's an attractive small town and a popular stop on the Newell Hwy between Melbourne and Brisbane. There's a small museum in the old customs house and a wildlife sanctuary at the Boobera Lagoon. The municipal tourist office (☎ 4671 2653) is in the base of a concrete water tower on

McLean St, 50m north of the junction with Marshall, the town's main drag. It's open Monday to Friday from 9 am to 5 pm.

If you plan on staying the night here the best value is *O'Shea's Royal Hotel-Motel* (☎ 4671 1877), which has motel-style singles/doubles at $39/46 and some cheaper hotel rooms.

TOOWOOMBA (pop 83,000)

On the edge of the Great Dividing Range and the Darling Downs, 138km inland from Brisbane, Toowoomba is a gracious city with pleasant parks, tree-lined streets and many early buildings. The local tourist information centre (☎ 4639 3797) is inconveniently located some 1.5km south-east of the centre on James St, at the junction with Kitchener St. It's open weekdays from 8.30 am to 5 pm and weekends from 9.30 am to 3 pm.

It's odds on that the staff at the centre will direct you to visit sights such as: the **Cobb & Co Museum**, at 27 Lindsay St, which has a large collection of old horse-drawn carriages and buggies and is open 9 am to 4 pm daily ($4); the **Toowoomba Regional Art Gallery** at 531 Ruthven St; and the **Ju Raku En Japanese Garden**, a beautiful spot but several kilometres south of the centre at the University of Southern Queensland in West St – you need a car to get there.

Near the train station at 70 Russell St, the *Hotel Norville* (☎ 4639 2954) has clean upstairs rooms from $20 per person, while *Jeffery's Rainforest Motel-Caravan Park* (☎ 4635 5999) at 864 Ruthven St a couple of kilometres south of the centre has excellent, modern self-contained units from $41/43.

TOOWOOMBA TO ROMA

At **Jondaryan**, 45km west of Toowoomba, you can visit the 1859 Jondaryan Woolshed (☎ 4692 2229), a historic tourist complex with rustic old buildings and daily shearing and blacksmithing demonstrations ($10). There's also a YHA-associated youth hostel here in authentically spartan shearers' quarters, with beds for $9 and camping sites for $8.

At Miles, 167km further west, the **Miles**

Historical Village is also worth a visit; it's open daily from 8 am to 5 pm ($9). There's also an information centre at the village with the same opening hours.

There are two caravan parks in town, a pub, the *Hotel Australia* (☎ 4627 1106) and four motels, the most central of which is the *Golden West Motor Inn* (☎ 4627 1688) at 50 Murilla St with singles/doubles from $54/64.

ROMA (pop 6,000)

An early Queensland settlement and now the centre for a huge sheep and cattle-raising district, Roma also has some curious small industries. There's enough oil in the area to support a small refinery, which produces just enough petroleum for local use. Gas deposits are much larger, and Roma supplies Brisbane through a 450km pipeline. The local information centre (☎ 4622 4355) sits in the shadow of the Historic Oil Rig, an authentic drilling rig from the 1920s, at the eastern entrance to town. It's open 9 am to 5 pm daily.

Fraser Coast

The focal point of this stretch of coast is the majestic Fraser Island – at 120km long it's the world's largest sand island. Hervey Bay, the major access point for the island, has grown into a busy tourist centre, while the southern access point is the sleepy and attractive Rainbow Beach.

Along the Bruce Highway are the rural centres of Gympie, the turn-off for Rainbow Beach, and Maryborough, the turn-off for Hervey Bay. Further north, Bundaberg is the largest town in the area and mostly famous as the home of the distinctive Bundaberg rum.

GYMPIE (pop 11,000)

Gympie came about as the result of an 1867 gold rush and became one of Queensland's richest goldfields, mined right up until 1920. A week-long Gold Rush Festival is held in

Gympie every October. The Country Music Muster in August is also pretty big.

There's a tourist office (☎ 5482 5444) beside the Bruce Hwy on the southern outskirts of town, open daily from 8.30 am to 3.30 pm. It also incorporates a QNPWS office where you can get permits and information for Fraser Island and the Cooloola National Park.

Nearby is the interesting and extensive **Gympie & District Historical & Mining Museum**, open daily from 9 am to 5 pm ($6). A few kilometres north of the town on Fraser Rd is the **Woodworks Forestry & Timber Museum**, open weekdays from 9 am to 4 pm ($2.50).

Gympie has several motels and caravan parks, and it's on the main bus and train routes north from Brisbane.

RAINBOW BEACH (pop 830)

This little settlement on Wide Bay, 70km north-east of Gympie, is the southern access point for Fraser Island and the northern access point for the Cooloola National Park. The centre of town, which is little more than a cluster of shops, a post office and a caravan park, is on Rainbow Beach road at the point where it stops dead on the clifftops. Down below are kilometres of good beach with few people around, while 1km south-east is the 120m-high **Carlo Sandblow** and beyond it

the coloured sand cliffs which gave the town its name.

The privately run Rainbow Beach tourist information centre (☎ 5486 3227) at 8 Rainbow Beach Rd has a list of other walks in the area. In a 4WD it's possible to drive to Noosa, 70km south, along the beach most of the way. See the Cooloola National Park section in the Sunshine Coast chapter for more details.

From Rainbow Beach it's a 13km drive north along the beach to Inskip Point, where ferries leave for Fraser Island (see the Fraser Island section for details of services).

The place for information on Fraser Island and Cooloola National Park is the Rainbow Beach information centre, actually the QNPWS office (☎ 5486 3160), situated off to the right of the main road as you enter Rainbow Beach. This is also the place to get vehicle and camping permits. It's open daily from 7 am to 4 pm.

Organised Tours

Rainbow Beach Backpackers runs a free trip south down the beach every morning for guests. It also organises day trips to Fraser Island for about $95 per head. Surf & Sand Safaris (☎ 5486 3131) runs four-hour 4WD trips south down the beach taking in Double Island Point, the wreck of the *Cherry Venture* and the Coloured Sands for $40 a head. Sun Safari Tours (☎ 5486 3154) offers day trips

The wreck of the *Cherry Venture* at Rainbow Beach

to Fraser Island costing $60 for adults and also a half-day tour south to Double Island Point for $30.

Places to Stay
Rainbow Beach Backpackers (☎ 5486 3288) at 66 Rainbow Beach Rd (the first place on the left as you enter town) charges from $12 per person in a dorm or $30 for a double, though rooms are sparse and facilities are poor. Camping sites out back are $12.

The *Rainbow Beach Holiday Village & Caravan Park* (☎ 5486 3222) on Rainbow Beach Rd is a good foreshore camping and caravan park that has a backpackers' section with three-bed cabin-tents for $10 per person. Tent sites start from $12, powered sites from $14, on-site vans from $25 and cabins cost from $45 to $60.

Getting There & Away
Polley's Coaches (☎ 5482 2700) in Gympie runs bus services between Gympie and Rainbow Beach every weekday. Buses leave Gympie at 6 am and 2 pm, and Rainbow Beach at 7.45 am and 4 pm.

Another way to Rainbow Beach is to hitch along the beaches up from Noosa or on to Fraser Island. If you have a 4WD vehicle you can drive this way too.

MARYBOROUGH (pop 21,000)
Maryborough's early importance as an industrial centre and port on the Mary River led to the construction of a series of imposing Victorian buildings. The greatest concentration of these is along Wharf St, and includes the impressive **post office** (1869).

Maryborough's most interesting feature is the National Trust classified **Brennan & Geraghty's Store** at 64 Lennox St. This historic store was run by the same family for 100 years and has been preserved intact with original stock, trading records and other fascinating stuff – well worth a look. It is open daily from 10 am to 3 pm ($3).

There are several motels and caravan parks in the town, plus budget accommodation in some of the old hotels.

HERVEY BAY (pop 32,000)
The once-sleepy settlement of Hervey Bay has grown at an astronomical rate in the last decade, and is now a major stopover on the backpacker circuit. The main attractions are Fraser Island, for which Hervey Bay is the main access point, and whale-watching trips in the bay.

The town is made up of five small settlements strung along a north-facing 10km stretch of coast. Of the five areas, Pialba is the main business and shopping centre but Torquay is where most of the accommodation and eating places are.

Fraser Island is 12km across the Great Sandy Strait from Urangan, with Woody Island in between. River Heads, the departure point for the main Fraser Island ferries, is 15km south of Urangan – although the Kingfisher foot passenger ferry goes from Urangan harbour, as do the whale-watching boats.

Information
There are numerous privately run information centres and tour booking offices, the most helpful of which is the **Hervey Bay Tourist & Visitor Centre** (☎ 1800 649 926; bookitere@cyberlink.com.au) at 63 Old Maryborough Rd in Pialba, open daily from 7.30 am to 5 pm. The owner, Pete Reeve, organises various aboriginal activities and tours (see later in this section) and this is also the best place to come if you need help with accommodation. For whale-watching bookings etc there's also the Hervey Bay Central Booking Office (☎ 4124 1300) at 363 Charlton Esplanade.

Things to See
Hervey Bay Nature World, near the corner of Maryborough Rd and Fairway Dve in Pialba, has native fauna including wedge-tailed eagles and koalas, as well as introduced species such as camels and water buffaloes. It's open daily from 9 am to 5.30 pm ($7).

Vic Hislop's Great White Shark Expo, on the corner of Charlton Esplanade and Elizabeth St in Urangan, has a collection of

The Whales of Hervey Bay

Up to 3000 humpbacks enter the waters of Hervey Bay every year on the return leg of their annual migration, during which they swim some 5000km from Antarctic waters up to the warmer waters off eastern Australia. They come in clusters of two or three (known as pods) with the numbers usually peaking in early September.

No-one is quite sure why the whales make the diversion from their homeward leg into the Bay, but one theory is that it might be a kind of pit stop that gives the whales a chance to rest up after a stressed period of birthing and mating. A few weeks in the calm, warm waters may also give the new calves more time to develop the protective layers of blubber necessary for survival in the icy Antarctic waters.

The R&R theory certainly seems to be borne out by the behaviour of the whales who are positively playful some days. It's not uncommon for the animals to swim up to boats and cruise alongside within touching distance of the excited camera-wielding whale-spotters on board. Often one great eye will be clear of the water, raising the question of who is actually watching whom? ■

photos, newspaper articles, jaw bones and three Great White sharks kept in a freezer with viewing portals. It also continuously screens a couple of shark documentaries. The centre is open daily from 8.30 am to 6 pm ($10 or $8 for backpackers).

Urangan Pier, a little further along Charlton Esplanade, is 1.4km long. Once used for sugar and oil handling, it's now a popular fishing spot.

One km east of the pier at Dayman Point is **Neptune's Reef World**, a small and old-fashioned aquarium with coral displays, fish, seals, turtles and a shark. There are touch tanks where turtles and stingrays can be petted and seal displays at 10.30 am and 3 pm. It is open every day from 9.30 am ($8). From the point itself, there are good views over to Woody and Fraser islands.

Organised Tours

Whale Watching Boat tours to watch the humpback whales on their annual migration operate out of Hervey Bay every day, weather permitting, between mid-July and late October. There are 17 licensed operators out of Hervey Bay and which boat you go with depends on what kind of experience you want. The smaller boats take between 32 and 50 passengers and tend to go out twice a day for four hours each time, once in the early morning and once in the afternoon. Whale-wise the time of the day doesn't matter, but the sea tends to be calmer in the first part of the day. Prices for half day tours are $55 to $60 with substantial reductions for children. From personal experience we recommend the MV *Seaspray* (☎ 4125 3586), smallest and fastest of all the whale-watching boats.

The larger boats run full-day trips. This doesn't necessarily mean more time spent with the whales as some of these boats can take two or three hours or more to cruise out to Platypus Bay where the whales swim. Amenities are better though, with most boats including a lunch of some kind and all having a licensed bar. The boat that was most often recommended to us was the MV *Bay Runner* (☎ 4125 3188) which charges $58 for a seven-hour trip.

Bookings for boats can be made through your accommodation or one of the information centres.

Aboriginal Tours Pete Reeve of the Hervey Bay Tourist & Visitors Centre (see Information) can organise two-hour walks in the Hervey Bay area, led by an Aboriginal guide, highlighting the craft of collecting naturally occurring foods and medicines. The walk also includes a demonstration of spear and boomerang throwing.

Fraser Island Trips For information on tours to Fraser, see under Visiting Fraser Island later in this section.

Places to Stay
Camping & Caravans There are at least a dozen caravan parks in Hervey Bay. Some of the best are the council-run parks along the Esplanade at Pialba (☎ 4128 1399), Scarness (☎ 4128 1274) and Torquay (☎ 4125 1578). All of these places charge the same rates – tent sites start from $12, powered sites from $14, and on-site vans from $30 a double. These prices increase during the holiday season.

Hostels Hervey Bay has a growing number of backpackers' hostels, spread between Scarness and Urangan. All do pick-ups from the main bus stop, and most organise trips to Fraser Island as well as booking whale-watching tours and other activities.

The best organised are the attractively laid out *Koala Backpackers* (☎ 4125 3601) at 408 Charlton Esplanade, Torquay, across the road from the beach, and the far less appealing *Beaches Hervey Bay Backpackers* (☎ 4124 1322) at 195 Torquay Tce. Both have pools and bars and are partying places with games and entertainment most nights. Rooms at both are no more than adequate – Koala has six-bed dorms at $14 per person or doubles and twins at $30; Beaches charges $15 for a place in a six-bed dorm.

The *Friendly Hostel* (☎ 4124 4107) at 182 Torquay Rd, Scarness, is a small, quiet place with three separate units, each with three bedrooms, a TV lounge, kitchen and bathroom. The place is immaculately clean and comfortable and certainly lives up to its name. Beds are $12 per person.

The *Colonial Backpackers' Resort* (☎ 4125 1844), on the corner of Boatharbour Dve and Pulgul St, is set in 4.5 hectares of bushland, near the marina where the whale-watching and some Fraser Island boats depart from. Accommodation is in wooden cabins: dorms contain three beds for $13 per person, twins are $14 per person (both shared facilities), while doubles have en-suite and kitchen and go for $32. There are also self-contained cabins, which will take up to six people for $45. Facilities include an on-site restaurant/bar, two tennis courts, a volleyball court and one of Queensland's few hostel pools large enough to actually swim in.

The other place that we'd recommend is *Boomerang Backpackers* (☎ 4124 3970) at 335 Charlton Esplanade, Scarness. It specialises in doubles and twins with two bedrooms to a unit and each unit has its own kitchen, bathroom and lounge. Rates are $26 per double, or there are some private units where you get the whole thing to yourself for $35 a double. Boomerang also has about 20 dorm beds from $11 a night.

QUEENSLAND

Other options include *Fraser Magic Backpackers* (☎ 4124 3488) at 369 Charlton Esplanade, which despite being relatively new, is already fairly rundown and has a very gloomy atmosphere (dorms $14, doubles $30) and *Olympus Backpackers Villas* (☎ 4124 5331) at 184 Torquay Rd, Scarness, a purpose-built hostel with eight separate two storey apartments, each with bathroom, kitchen and TV lounge (dorms $13, twins and doubles $28).

Motels & Holiday Units Some of these places offer fantastic value and can work out much cheaper than a hostel, particularly if there's a group of you. *Beachcomber Holiday Units* (☎ 4124 2152) at 384 Charlton Esplanade has very comfortable self-contained units consisting of a double bedroom, bathroom, kitchen and living room with fold-out double bed for $40.

The nearby *Bay View Motel* (☎ 4128 1134) at 399 Charlton Esplanade offers similar for the same price but is a little less homely.

Places to Eat

The *Colonial*, *Koala* and *Beaches* hostels

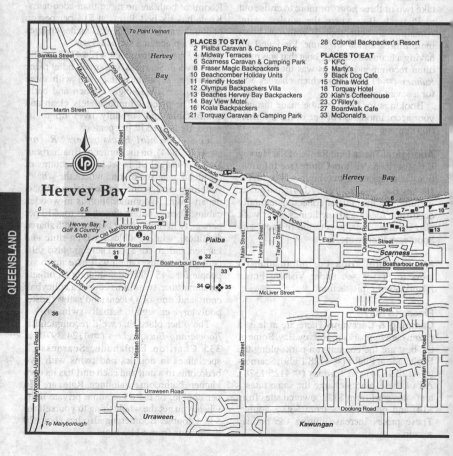

PLACES TO STAY
2   Pialba Caravan & Camping Park
4   Midway Terraces
6   Scarness Caravan & Camping Park
8   Fraser Magic Backpackers
10 Beachcomber Holiday Units
11 Friendly Hostel
12 Olympus Backpackers Villa
13 Beaches Hervey Bay Backpackers
14 Bay View Motel
16 Koala Backpackers
21 Torquay Caravan & Camping Park

28 Colonial Backpacker's Resort

PLACES TO EAT
3   KFC
5   Marty's
9   Black Dog Cafe
15 China World
18 Torquay Hotel
20 Kiah's Coffeehouse
23 O'Riley's
27 Boardwalk Cafe
33 McDonald's

Hervey Bay

have their own cheap restaurants, and in the case of the latter at least, non-residents are welcome to eat there. Otherwise, Charlton Esplanade in Torquay is the food focus in Hervey Bay.

The cheapest deal has to be at *Marty's*, a pub on the corner of the Esplanade and Queens Road: it does a special of a T-bone steak, chips and salad, plus a pot of beer for $6.50. Other meals are served, all in the $6.50 to $8.50 range.

China World at 402 Charlton Esplanade on the corner of Tavistock St has an all-you-can-eat deal for $7 at lunch and $9 in the

evening. Dishes on the standard menu are also very good, most of which are in the $8 to $10 range. It's open until 9 pm only.

O'Riley's on the corner of the Esplanade and Macks Rd is a relaxed BYO pancake, pizza and pasta joint with savoury crepes and pasta under $9, pizzas in the $10 to $12 range (enough for two) and a range of dessert pancakes from $4 to $6. It's open 5 to 9.30 pm daily, 10.30 pm on Friday and Saturday.

The *Black Dog Cafe* on the corner of the Esplanade and Denman Camp Rd also has some interesting dishes centred on sushi ($4 to $5), teriyaki and noodles ($7 to $8). It's

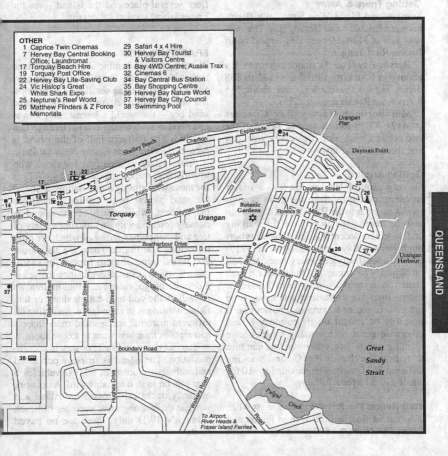

OTHER
1 Caprice Twin Cinemas
7 Hervey Bay Central Booking Office; Laundromat
17 Torquay Beach Hire
19 Torquay Post Office
22 Hervey Bay Life-Saving Club
24 Vic Hislop's Great White Shark Expo
25 Neptune's Reef World
26 Matthew Flinders & Z Force Memorials
29 Safari 4 x 4 Hire
30 Hervey Bay Tourist & Visitors Centre
31 Bay 4WD Centre; Aussie Trax
32 Cinemas 6
34 Bay Central Bus Station
35 Bay Shopping Centre
36 Hervey Bay Nature World
37 Hervey Bay City Council
38 Swimming Pool

QUEENSLAND

open daily from 9.30 am to 10 pm (closed Tuesday).

For atmospheric dining try the *Boardwalk Cafe* overlooking the Urangan marina. It does good lunches of pasta, quiche and filled pastries for $5.50 to $7 and dinners in the $12 to $15 range. It's open 6.30 am to late Tuesday to Saturday and 6.30 am to 6.30 pm Sunday and Monday.

For good breakfasts try *Kiah's Coffee-house* on the corner of Bideford and Truro Sts. It also has plenty of vegetarian options for lunches.

Getting There & Away

Sunstate and Flight West have daily flights between Brisbane and Hervey Bay. The one-way fare is $124. Hervey Bay airport is off Booral Rd, Urangan.

Hervey Bay is on the major bus route. It's about 4½ hours from Brisbane ($32 to $38 depending on the carrier), and about 5½ hours from Rockhampton ($55).

Maryborough-Hervey Bay Coaches (☎ 4121 3719) runs a service between the two centres, with nine trips every weekday and three on Saturday.

Getting Around

Getting around Hervey Bay is a major problem. Distances from the main accommodation areas to the Bay Central bus station and the marina are prohibitive for walking and there's no decent bus service – Maryborough-Hervey Bay Coaches (☎ 4121 3719) does run local services every weekday and on Saturday mornings but the buses on each route run at intervals of up to two hours or more. Taxis are expensive and have to be ordered. If you're staying in a hostel you'll probably be reliant on its courtesy buses, otherwise get a bike – many hostels have them for guests' use, otherwise you can hire them from the Hervey Bay Central Booking Office at 363 Charlton Esplanade for $10 for a half day, $15 for a full day.

4WD Rental The Bay 4WD Centre (☎ 4128 2981) at 54 Boatharbour Dve in Pialba and Safari 4X4 Hire (☎ 1800 689 819) at 55 Old Maryborough Rd have good, reliable vehicles ranging from about $90 a day for a Suzuki Sierra to $125 for a Toyota Landcruiser, which usually involves a two-day minimum.

Aussie Trax (☎ 1800 062 275) at 56 Boatharbour Dve, Pialba, has old ex-army jeeps from $85 a day as well as Suzuki Sierras and Landrover Defender Wagons at $130 a day.

A $500 deposit is generally required – this can be made on a credit card if you have one – and drivers must be over 21. All the above hire operators also give 4WD instruction to first time drivers. You can also hire 4WD from several places on the island – see the Fraser Island section for details.

FRASER ISLAND

The thing to keep in mind about Fraser Island is that it's all sand. There's no soil, no clay and only two or three small rocky outcrops. It's one gigantic, 120km by 15km foliated sand bar – the world's largest, and it was inscribed as such on the World Heritage List in 1993. The northern half of the island is protected as the Great Sandy National Park.

Fraser Island is a delight for those who love fishing, walking, exploring by 4WD or for those who simply enjoy nature. Some of the sand blows (large drifting dunes) are magnificent, while much of the island is densely forested with an amazing variety of tree and plant types, many of which are only to be found on Fraser. There are also about 200 lakes, some of them superb for swimming – which is just as well since the sea is a definite no-go; there are lethal undertows as well as the odd man-eating shark or ten. Other wildlife is in abundance, including 40 different mammal species and more insects and reptiles than you want to know about.

You can camp on Fraser or stay in accommodation. The island is sparsely populated and although more than 20,000 vehicles a year pile on to it, it remains wild. A network of sandy tracks crisscrosses the island and you can drive along great stretches of beach – but it's 4WD only; there are no paved roads.

History

The island takes its name from the captain of a ship which was wrecked further north in 1836. Making their way south to look for help, a group from the ship fell among Aborigines on Fraser Island. Some of the group died during their two-month wait for rescue, but others, including Fraser, survived with Aboriginal help.

To the Butchulla Aborigines, the island was known as K'gari (which translates as 'Paradise') after a spirit who helped the great god Beeral create the earth and other worlds. K'gari loved earth so much she asked Beeral to let her live there and so he changed her into a beautiful island with trees and animals for company and limpid lakes for eyes through which she could gaze up at the heavens, her former home. The Aborigines were driven off their K'gari onto missions when timber cutters moved on to the island in the 1860s. The cutters were after satinay, a rainforest tree, which only grows on Fraser, highly resistant to the marine life which normally rots timber. Satinay was used to line the Suez Canal. It was not until 1991 that logging on the island ceased.

In the mid-1970s, Fraser Island was the subject of a bitter struggle between conservationists and industry – in this case a sand-mining company. The decision went to the conservationists.

Information

There's a visitor centre on the east coast of the island at Eurong (☎ 4127 9128), and ranger's offices at Dundubara and Waddy Point. These places all have plenty of leaflets detailing walking trails and the flora and fauna found on the island.

At Central Station (the old forestry depot) there's a small display on the history of exploration and logging on the island.

General supplies are available from stores at Eurong, Happy Valley and Cathedral Beach, but as you might expect, prices are high. There are also public telephones at these sites.

Permits You'll need a permit to take a

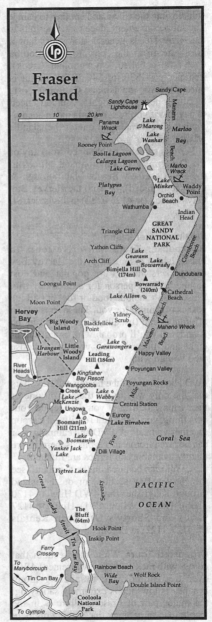

Fraser Island

vehicle onto the island and another to camp. The most convenient place to get permits is the River Heads general store, just half a kilometre from the ferry to Wanggoolba Creek (also called Woongoolber Creek). Vehicles cost $30, or $40 if the permit is purchased on the island. Camping costs $3.50 per person per night – you don't need to pay this if you're staying in cabin accommodation or camping in one of the island's private camping grounds.

Permits can also be obtained from any of the Department of Environment offices in the area (Rainbow Beach, Maryborough & Gympie included), or from the Hervey Bay City Council (☎ 4125 0222) in Tavistock St, Torquay.

Visiting Fraser Island
Backpacker Tours Self-drive tours to Fraser Island organised by the Hervey Bay backpackers' hostels are popular and cost around $95 per person for a three-day trip. This doesn't include food or fuel but all the gear is organised for you. These trips are an affordable and (usually) fun way to see the island, but you'll probably be in a group of eight and, like relatives, you can't choose who you go with.

4WD Hire Some of the hostels tell travellers that the only way to get there is on one of their trips. Not true. If you'd rather do your own thing, you could quite easily get a group together yourself. A 4WD and camping gear can be hired from various places, permits are readily available and ferries are frequent.

A 4WD can be hired on the mainland (see the Hervey Bay section) or on the island through Kingfisher Bay 4WD Hire (☎ 4120 3366), Happy Valley 4WD Hire (☎ 4127 9260) and Shorty's Off Road Rentals (☎ 4127 9122) at Eurong.

Organised Tours While the freedom that comes with racking your own (rented) 4WD over tree stumps and thundering along beaches at low tide is extremely satisfying, the major part of Fraser's allure is in the whole load of geology that's going on there

and in the island's plantlife and the things that flap, pad and crawl about in it. It takes someone who knows their stuff to bring it to life. Several operators offer one, two or three-day tours led by well-informed guides. (See also Noosa and Rainbow Beach for tours from those places.)

Top Tours (☎ 1800 063 933) and Fraser Venture Day Tours (☎ 4125 4444) do day trips to Fraser for $65. Kingfisher Bay (☎ 1800 072 555) is slightly more expensive at $75 for adults and $40 for children. Each outfit follows a different route but a typical tour, conducted in a hulking 4WD bus with a ranger guide, might take in a trip up the east coast to the *Maheno* wreck and the Cathedrals, plus Central Station and a couple of the lakes in the centre of the island. Most day tours to Fraser Island allow you to split the trip and stay a few days on the island before coming back.

Air Fraser Island (☎ 4125 3600) flies out of Hervey Bay airport and lands on the island's east coast beach. You can do a day trip for $35 per person (once down you're left to amuse yourself for the day until it's time to fly back), or for $85 per person a day's hire of a 4WD is included; there are also two-day tours for around $150 per person which includes return flights, a tent and one day's 4WD hire.

Top Tours has a two-day trip for $150 including a night's accommodation at Happy Valley. Fraser Venture Tours offers similar with an overnight at the Eurong Beach Resort for $145. In both cases accommodation is quad share and a sleeping bag is required.

Kingfisher Bay also has a three-day 'Wilderness Adventure'. This is the one that we tried out and we can wholeheartedly recommend it. It takes in all the island's major sites and includes opportunities for bush walking, swimming and snorkelling. The $225 package also includes three meals a day (the breakfast is fantastic), twin or quad accommodation and use of all facilities at the luxury Kingfisher Bay Resort.

Driving on the Island
The only thing stopping you taking a con-

ventional (non-4WD) vehicle onto the island is the fact that you probably won't get more than half a kilometre before you get bogged in sand. Small 4WD sedans are OK, but you may have ground-clearance problems on some of the inland tracks – a 'proper' 4WD gives maximum mobility.

Driving on the island requires a good deal of care, to protect not only yourself but the fragile environment. Plan your trip reckoning on covering roughly 20km an hour on inland tracks and 50km an hour on the eastern beach.

Driving Tips During the period we were in south-east Queensland researching this part of the book no fewer than five serious accidents were reported in the local press involving inexperienced drivers rolling 4WDs on Fraser. In two cases injured passengers had to be airlifted off the island. If you've never driven a 4WD before, and are going to be doing so on Fraser, consider following these basic rules:

- Don't rush. Braking can be unpredictable in soft sand. The best way to cope with uneven surfaces and obstacles is to maintain a slow but steady speed.
- When driving on the island's tracks you should have 4WD engaged at all times, not so much because of the danger of getting stuck, but because your wheels are less likely to spin and damage the sandy tracks.
- Apart from the beaches, where you are free to drive at will, all tracks are obvious and you must stick to them.
- The tracks are only wide enough to accommodate one vehicle. When meeting an oncoming vehicle the 'I'm Bigger Than You' rule applies. Pull over to allow buses and trucks to pass.
- When driving on the beaches the speed limit is 80km/h. Keep an eye out for washouts at the many creek outlets, especially after heavy rain – cross creeks as close to the ocean as possible and never stop in a creek as the sand under your wheels will be washed away.
- Driving on the eastern beach, the island's 'main highway' is fairly straightforward but the western beach is treacherous and has swamps and holes – avoid it.
- Make sure you know the tide times. Two hours either side of low tide is the best time to travel as large expanses of smooth, hard sand are exposed.

At high tide it is much more difficult and quite slow going.
- Do not drive at speed through shallow salt water – it causes rust and the sand could be quickly washed from under your wheels bogging down the vehicle.
- Use your indicators to show oncoming vehicles which side you intend passing on.
- Drive slowly on the beach when passing walkers and people fishing as they probably won't hear you coming above the roar of the surf.

Around the Island
Starting from the south at Hook Point, you cross a number of creeks and get to Dilli Village, the former sand-mining centre. After the settlements of Eurong and Happy Valley, you cross **Eli Creek**, the largest stream on the east coast. Wooden boardwalks go 400m back up the creek and it's pleasant to enter the water up here and drift back down to the beach. About 65km from Hook Point are the remains of the *Maheno*, a former passenger liner blown ashore here by a typhoon in 1935 as it was being towed to a Japanese scrapyard.

Four km beyond Eurong is a signposted walking trail to the beautiful **Lake Wabby**, possibly the highlight of the island. The deepest of Fraser's lakes, it's surrounded on three sides by eucalypt forest while on the other is a massive sandblow whose steep bow crashes into the lake. From the beach, Wabby is a 45-minute walk (rewarded by a swim in the lake), or you can drive a further 2.6km north along the beach to take a scenic route up to a lookout on the inland side of the lake – this is well worth doing as the lake seen from the lookout is spectacular.

A popular inland area for visitors is the south-central lake and rainforest country around Central Station and McKenzie, Jennings, Birrabeen and Boomanjin lakes. **Lake McKenzie** is unbelievably clear. Known as a 'window' lake, the water here is actually part of the water table, and so has not flowed anywhere over land. It's a wildly disorienting experience to snorkel here, to look down through a face mask and then suddenly have the bottom drop precipitously away to a depth of 15m where it is still visible.

Two signposted vehicle tracks lead inland

from Happy Valley: one goes to **Lake Gar-awongera**, then south to the beach again at Poyungan Valley (15km); the other heads to **Yidney Scrub** and a number of lakes before returning to the ocean beach north of the wreck of the *Maheno* (45km). The latter route will take you to some fine lakes and good lookout points among the highest dunes on the island.

Not far north of Happy Valley you enter the national park and pass the *Maheno* and the **Cathedrals**, 25km of coloured sand cliffs. Dundubara has a ranger's hut and probably the best camping ground on the island. Then there's a 20km stretch of beach before you come to the rock outcrop of **Indian Head**, the best vantage point on the island. Climb up onto the headland and scan the waters below for sharks, manta rays, dolphins and, in season, whales further out.

Beyond Indian Head are Middle Rocks and Waddy Point and then **Orchid Beach**, and it's a further 30km of beach up to **Sandy Cape**, the northern tip, with its lighthouse a few more kilometres to the west.

Places to Stay & Eat

Come well equipped since supplies on the island are limited and only available in a few places. And be prepared for mosquitoes and horseflies.

Camping The QNPWS and Forestry Department operate 11 camping grounds on the island, some accessible only by boat or on foot. Those in the north at Dundubara, Waddy Point and Wathumba and in the south at Central Station, Lake Boomanjin and Lake McKenzie have toilets and showers. You can also camp on some stretches of beach. To camp in any of these public areas you need a permit.

There's also the privately run *Cathedral Beach Resort & Camping Park* (☎ 4127 9177), 34km north of Eurong. Tent sites cost $14 and cabins cost $75 for up to four people – note that they don't take backpacker groups here.

Other Accommodation The *Dilli Village*

Recreation Camp (☎ 4127 9130) is 200m from the east coast and 24km from Hook Point. A four-bed cabin with shower and kitchen costs $45 per night or there are cabins without kitchens or bathrooms at $10 per person. You can also camp here for $4 per person.

The *Eurong Beach Resort* (☎ 4127 9122), 35km north of Hook Point on the east coast, has cabins containing four bunks at $12 per bed or A-frame cottages at $90 for four people plus $5 per extra person (maximum eight). There are also more expensive motel units and two-bedroom apartments.

Just south of Happy Valley, the low-key *Yidney Rocks Cabins* (☎ 4127 9167) are right on the edge of the beach. They're old but comfortable; the nightly rate is $65 for up to six people or $80 for up to eight. The *Fraser Island Retreat Happy Valley Resort* (☎ 4127 9144) has good self-contained timber lodges for $160/175 a night for doubles/triples.

The impressive and luxurious *Kingfisher Bay Resort* (☎ 1800 072 555) on the west coast has what are called 'Wilderness Cabins' which contain a kitchen, dining area, bathrooms and two four-bed dorms plus two twins all at $30 per person. There are also hotel rooms from $220 per double, two-bedroom villas suitable for four/five people from $690 for three nights, and three-bedroom villas suitable for six from $960 for three nights. The resort has restaurants, bars and shops and, architecturally, it's worth a look even if you're not staying here. There's also a day-trippers' section near the jetty, with the *Sandbar* bar and brassiere.

Getting There & Away

Vehicle ferries (known locally as barges) operate to the southern end of Fraser Island from Inskip Point north of Rainbow Beach, and to the west coast of the island from River Heads, south of Urangan. The *Rainbow Venture* (☎ 5486 3154) makes the 10-minute crossing from Inskip Point to Hook Point on Fraser Island regularly from about 7 am to 4.30 pm daily. The price is $45 return for a vehicle and passengers, and you can get tickets on board the ferry. Walk-on passengers pay $5.

The *Fraser Venture* (☎ 4125 4444) makes the 30-minute crossing from River Heads to Wanggoolba Creek on the west coast of Fraser Island. It departs daily from River Heads at 9 and 10.15 am and 3.30 pm. It returns from the island at 9.30 am, 2.30 and 4 pm. On Saturday there is also a 7 am service from River Heads, which returns at 7.30 am from the island. The barge takes 27 vehicles but it's still advisable to book. The return fare for vehicle and driver is $55, plus $3 for each extra passenger. Walk-on passengers pay $10 return.

The Kingfisher Bay Resort (☎ 4125 5155) also operates two boats. The *Fraser II* does the 45-minute crossing from River Heads to Kingfisher Bay daily. Departures from River Heads are at 7 and 11 am and 2 pm, and from the island at 9.45 am, 12.45 and 4.30 pm. The return fare is $60 for a vehicle and driver, plus $4 for extras.

The *Kingfisher 3* is a passenger catamaran that crosses from the Urangan Boat Harbour to Kingfisher Bay five times a day (first departure 8.30 am) for a return fare of $30 for adults and $15 for children.

There's also a ferry, the *Fraser Dawn*, from Urangan to Moon Point on the island, but this is an inconvenient place to land as it's a long drive across to the other side.

CHILDERS (pop 1500)

Childers, a historic township on the Bruce Highway, has quite a few pretty Victorian-era buildings. The town is also the turn-off for the lovely **Woodgate Beach** and **Woodgate National Park**.

The *Palace Backpackers' Hostel* (☎ 4126 2244) right in the centre of Childers at 72 Churchill St is a converted historic two-storey pub. It's a workers' hostel geared to fruit picking and the management will find guests work. The facilities are very good, with a big communal kitchen, walk-in fridge, big TV room, games and clean showers. All beds cost $14 per night or $90 per week, including transport to and from work.

BUNDABERG (pop 41,000)

Bundaberg attracts a steady stream of travellers looking for harvest work, picking everything from avocados to zucchinis, and the hostels here can often help you find work – but ring before you come to check on the work situation. It's a reasonably attractive town 15km inland from the coast, most famous for its Bundaberg rum and as the southernmost access point for the Great Barrier Reef and departure point for Lady Elliot and Lady Musgrave islands.

Orientation & Information

The excellent Bundaberg tourist information centre (☎ 1800 060 499) is on Bourbong St, the town's main drag, about 1km west of the centre. It's open daily from 9 am to 5 pm.

Things to See

The main thing everybody does here is take a tour of the **Bundaberg Rum Distillery** (☎ 4152 4077) on Avenue St in East Bundaberg, about 2km east from the centre of town. Tours are run weekdays between 10 am and 3 pm and weekends between 10 am and 2 pm and cost $5, which includes a sample of the product.

Bundaberg's attractive **Botanic Gardens** are 2km north of the centre on Gin Gin Rd. Within the gardens reserve are rose gardens, walking paths, a historical museum and **Hinkler House Museum**, dedicated to the life of the aviator Bert Hinkler who was born in Bundaberg and in 1928 made the first solo flight between England and Australia. Hinkler's former home was transported here from Southampton, England, and rebuilt to house a collection of memorabilia and information on the aviation pioneer. Nearby is the **Bundaberg & District Historical Museum**. Both museums are open daily from 10 am to 4 pm, and both charge $2.50 admission.

Activities

Salty's (☎ 4151 6422) at 200 Bourbong St, and Bundaberg Aqua Scuba (☎ 4153 5761) on Targo St next to the bus station, both offer what must be the cheapest PADI open water

Mon Repos Turtle Rookery

Australia's most accessible turtle rookery is at Mon Repos Beach, 15km north-east of Bundaberg. Four types of turtle – loggerhead, green, flatback and leatherback – have been known to nest here, but it's predominantly the loggerhead that lays its eggs here. The rookery is unusual, since turtles generally prefer sandy islands off the coast. The nesting season runs from early November through to the end of March, and you're most likely to see the turtles laying their eggs at about midnight when the tide is high. From mid-January to March, the young begin to emerge and make their way quickly to the sea. Observation of the turtles is controlled by the QNPWS Information Centre (☎ 4159 2628), which is open daily during the season from 7 pm to 6 am; entry costs $4.

During the season, the QNPWS operates a 24-hour hotline (☎ 4159 1652) with recorded information about the turtles. There are no local bus services to Mon Repos, but Lady Musgrave Bus Services (☎ 018 988 280) runs bus tours from Bundaberg to Mon Repos during the turtle season. The $15 return trip includes entry to the rookery, and the driver will pick you up from wherever you're staying. ■

courses in Queensland – $149, which includes a dive off Lady Musgrave Island.

Places to Stay & Eat

All of Bundaberg's hostels specialise in finding harvesting work for travellers.

The *Bundaberg Backpackers & Travellers Lodge* (☎ 4152 2080) is diagonally opposite the bus terminal, on the corner of Targo and Crofton Sts. It's clean and modern with a friendly atmosphere; a bed in a four-bed dorm costs $15 a night, which includes transport to and from work.

City Centre Backpackers (☎ 4151 3501), in the former Grosvenor Hotel at 216 Bourbong St, has two sections: two to eight-bed bunk rooms upstairs, and six-bed motel units out the back. Bunk beds cost $13 or a bed in one of the motel units costs $15. They also have three doubles at $30.

Across the road is *Federal Backpackers* (☎ 4153 3711) at 221 Bourbong St, in a big old wooden building leased from the pub downstairs. While it has plenty of character it's also extremely dirty and facilities are poor. Dorms in a room with 10 beds are $14 or $15 in a room with four beds.

The *Lyelta Lodge & Motel* (☎ 4151 3344) at 8 Maryborough St has motel-style rooms at $34 and a guesthouse section with singles/doubles with shared bathrooms for $25/30.

For a cheap pub feed, head for the *Grand Hotel* on the corner of Bourbong and Targo

Sts or the *Club Hotel* on the corner of Bourbong and Tanotitha Sts which has a small garden dining area round the side entered off Tanotitha. Both places do basic dishes like roasts and chops for under $5, served noon to 2 pm.

Numero Uno at 163 Bourbong St is a popular Italian bistro with good pastas under $12, pizzas under $10 and mains from $12 to $15.

Getting There & Away

Air services are by Sunstate (from Brisbane, Gladstone, Rockhampton, Mackay and Townsville daily) and Flight West (daily from Brisbane and Gladstone). The one-way Brisbane-Bundaberg fare is $186.

The main bus stop is Stewart's coach terminal (☎ 4153 2646) at 66 Targo St. One-way bus fares from Bundaberg include Brisbane ($46), Hervey Bay ($22), Rockhampton ($42) and Gladstone ($38).

Bundaberg is also a stop for trains between Brisbane and Rockhampton or Cairns.

Capricorn Coast

This central coastal area of Queensland takes its name from its position straddling the Tropic of Capricorn. Rockhampton is the major population centre in the area, and just off the coast lies Great Keppel Island, a popular getaway. Offshore from Gladstone are the Southern Reef Islands, the southernmost part of the Great Barrier Reef, while south of Gladstone are the laid-back townships of Seventeen Seventy and Agnes Water, the state's northernmost surf beach.

Inland, the Capricorn Hinterland has the fascinating gem fields region and the spectacular Carnarvon and Blackdown Tableland national parks.

SOUTHERN REEF ISLANDS

The southernmost part of the Great Barrier Reef, known as the Capricornia section,

begins 80km north-east of Bundaberg around Lady Elliot Island. The coral reefs and cays in this group dot the ocean for about 140km up to Tryon Island east of Rockhampton.

Several cays in this part of the reef are excellent for snorkelling, diving and just getting back to nature – though reaching them is generally more expensive than reaching islands nearer the coast. Access is from Bundaberg, Gladstone or Rosslyn Bay near Rockhampton. A few islands are important breeding grounds for turtles and sea birds.

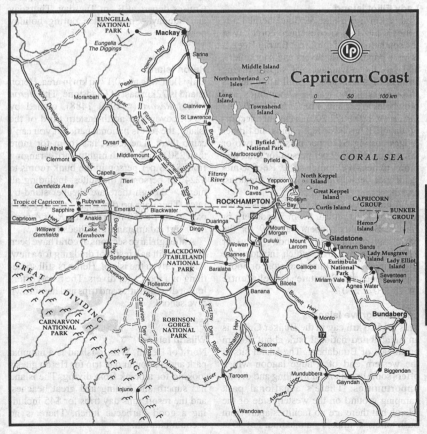

QUEENSLAND

On the four national park islands where camping is allowed (Lady Musgrave, Masthead, Tryon and North West), campers must be totally self-sufficient. Numbers of campers are limited so it's advisable to apply well ahead for a camping permit. You can book six months ahead for these islands instead of the usual six to 12 weeks for other Queensland national parks. Contact the QNPWS (☎ 4972 6055) in Gladstone. If you get a permit you'll also receive information on any rules, such as restrictions on the use of generators, and on how to avoid harming the wildlife.

Lady Elliot Island

Eighty km north-east of Bundaberg, Lady Elliot is a 0.4 sq km vegetated coral cay at the southern end of the Great Barrier Reef. It is very popular with divers and snorkellers, and has the advantages of superb diving straight off the beach, as well as numerous shipwrecks, coral gardens, bommies and blowholes to explore. The *Lady Elliot Island Resort* (☎ 1800 072 200) is the only accommodation. It has basic tent-cabins and timber lodges costing $115 per person for two or three people or $99 per person for four, and more expensive motel-style Reef Units ($150 per person). Costs include breakfast and dinner.

Whitaker Air Charters flies guests to the resort for $130 return. From Bundaberg or Hervey Bay, day-trippers pay $99 for the basic day-return flight (standby only) or $130 for the day trip, which includes the flight, lunch, snorkelling gear etc. For bookings phone the Sunstate Travel Centre (☎ 1800 072 200).

Lady Musgrave Island

This 0.15 sq km cay in the Bunker Group is an uninhabited national park about 100km north-east of Bundaberg. The island sits at the western end of a huge lagoon which offers some excellent snorkelling and diving opportunities. There's a national park camping ground on the western side of the island, but there are no facilities apart from bush toilets. Campers – a maximum of 50 at any one time – must be totally self-sufficient. You'll need to bring your own drinking water and a gas or fuel stove.

The MV *Lady Musgrave* (☎ 4152 9011) operates day trips from Bundaberg on Tuesday, Thursday, Saturday and Sunday at 8.30 am. The cost is $96 which includes lunch, snorkelling gear and a glass-bottomed boat ride. The trip takes 2½ hours and you have about four hours on the island. The MV *Spirit of 1770* (☎ 4974 9077) has day trips to Lady Musgrave Island out of Seventeen Seventy (85 minutes to get there, six hours on the island) costing $105 for adults, with lunch, snorkelling and fishing gear included. Cruises depart at 8 am Tuesday, Thursday and Sunday – more often during holiday periods.

Heron Island

Only 1km long and 0.17 sq km in area, Heron Island is 72km east of Gladstone. The *Heron Island Resort* (☎ 4978 1488), owned by P&O, covers the north-eastern third of the island; the rest is national park but you can't camp there. The resort has room for more than 250 people, with nightly tariffs ranging from $158 per person in the bunk rooms to $224 per person in the suites, including all meals – though there are cheaper stand-by rates. There are no day trips – resort guests pay another $150 return in the *Reef Adventurer* fast catamaran from Gladstone.

Although large sections of coral have been killed by silt as a result of dredging for a new, longer jetty at the island, Heron is still something of a mecca for divers. The resort offers lots of dive facilities and trips and has its own dive school.

Wilson Island

North of Heron, Wilson Island is a national park and a popular day trip for Heron guests looking for a break from diving. The island has superb snorkelling and great beaches, and the resort runs day trips for $45 including a good barbecue lunch. There is no accommodation.

QUEENSLAND

North West Island

At 0.9 sq km, North West Island is the biggest cay on the Barrier Reef. It's all national park, and it is one of the major nesting sites for green turtles, with nesting occurring between November and February. It's a popular destination for campers, but there's a limit of 150 people and you must be totally self-sufficient (including a fuel stove). Book with the Department of Environment office (☎ 4972 6055) in Gladstone.

There are no day trips to the island, but a couple of operators offer camping drop-offs. From Seventeen Seventy, the MV *Spirit of 1770* (☎ 4974 9077) will do drop-offs for $100 per person each way; they also have camping gear and dinghies available for hire.

Tryon Island

Immediately north of North West Island, this tiny, beautiful six hectare national park island is another important nesting area for sea birds and green turtles. There is a camping ground but the island is currently closed to visitors to allow for revegetation. Check with the Department of Environment office in Gladstone (☎ 4972 6055) for the latest.

AGNES WATER & SEVENTEEN SEVENTY (pop 250 & 200)

These two coastal towns are among the state's less commercialised seaside destinations, with Seventeen Seventy being perhaps the most beautiful and tranquil spot on the whole south-east Queensland coast. There are few shops here, just one pub, a couple of caravan parks and a few cabins and B&Bs. Most people come here for the fishing or boating or to visit the neighbouring national parks. Things do get a little hectic at Christmas and Easter time and you'll need to book ahead to secure accommodation at these times.

Access is from Miriam Vale on the Bruce Hwy along a 57km road, one third of which is unsealed. There are no bus or train services.

The office of 1770 Environmental Tours, at the marina on Captain Cook Dve, serves as an information centre (☎ 4974 9422) for the immediate area and it can help with booking activities and finding accommodation. It's open Monday to Saturday from 9 am to 5 pm, Sunday 1 to 5 pm.

The LARC *Sir Joseph Banks* (☎ 4974 9422), a large amphibious vehicle, does full-day environmental tours of Round Hill Creek, Bustard Head and Eurimbula National Park. Tours operate on Wednesday and Saturday (more often during the peak season) and cost $70.

Places to Stay

The *Agnes Water Caravan Park* (☎ 4974 9193), on the foreshore in Jeffery Crt, has tent sites from $8 and cabins from $30, while the *Seventeen Seventy Camping Ground* (☎ 4974 9286) has sites for $10 and on-site vans at $30 a double. The *Captain Cook Holiday Village* (☎ 4974 9219) is another excellent camping and caravan park in a great bush setting, 300m from the beach. Nightly costs are $10 for tent sites, $15 for a bed in a backpackers' bungalow and $20 for an on-site van. There are also self-contained timber bungalows and cabins that sleep up to seven people.

Four km inland from Agnes Water, just off the main access road, *Hoban's Hideaway* (☎ 4974 9144) is a friendly, well-run B&B in an attractive, colonial-style timber homestead with a guests' section containing three immaculately presented double bedrooms with en-suites, a lounge room and dining room, an outdoor patio and a barbecue area. The tariff for singles/doubles is $70/86 including breakfast.

GLADSTONE (pop 26,500)

Twenty km off the Bruce Hwy, Gladstone is one of the busiest ports in Australia, handling agricultural, mineral and coal exports from central Queensland. From a visitor's point of view though, it's a pretty dull place. The town's otherwise attractive estuary setting is marred by a scattering of scenically-challenged industrial plants.

Gladstone's marina is the main departure

QUEENSLAND

point for boats to Heron, Masthead and Wilson islands on the Barrier Reef.

The Gladstone visitor information centre (☎ 4972 9922) at the marina is open on weekdays from 8.30 am to 5 pm and on weekends from 9 am to 5 pm. The Department of Environment office (☎ 4972 6055) is a good source of information. It's open for

The Great Barrier Reef

Facts & Figures The Great Barrier Reef is 2000km in length. It starts slightly south of the Tropic of Capricorn, somewhere out from Bundaberg or Gladstone, and ends in Torres Strait, just south of Papua New Guinea. It is not only the most extensive reef system in the world, but the biggest structure made by living organisms. At its southern end the reef is up to 300km from the mainland, while at the northern end it runs nearer the coast, is much less broken and can be up to 80km wide.

In the 'lagoon' between the outer reef and the coast, the waters are dotted with smaller reefs, cays and islands. Drilling on the reef has indicated that the coral may be more than 500m thick. Most of the reef is about two million years old, but there are sections dating back 18 million years.

What is It? Coral is formed by a small, primitive animal, a marine polyp of the family *Coelenterata*. Some polyps, known as hard corals, form a hard surface by excreting lime. When they die, the hard 'skeletons' remain and these gradually build up the reef. New polyps grow on their dead predecessors and continually add to the reef. The skeletons of hard corals are white; the colours of reefs come from living polyps.

Coral needs a number of preconditions for healthy growth. The water temperature must not drop below 17.5˚C – thus the Barrier Reef does not continue farther south into cooler waters. The water must be clear to allow sunlight to penetrate, and it must be salty. Coral will not grow below a depth of 30m because sunlight does not penetrate sufficiently. Nor does it grow around river mouths: the Barrier Reef ends near Papua New Guinea because the Fly River's enormous water flow is both fresh and muddy.

One of the most spectacular sights of the Barrier Reef occurs for a few nights after a full moon in late spring or early summer when vast numbers of corals spawn at the same time. The tiny bundles of sperm and eggs are visible to the naked eye and the event has been likened to a gigantic underwater snowstorm.

Reef Types What's known as the Great Barrier Reef is not one reef but about 2600 separate ones. Basically, reefs are either fringing or barrier. You will find fringing reefs off sloping sides of islands or the mainland coast. Barrier reefs are farther out to sea: the 'real' Great Barrier Reef, or outer reef, is at the edge of the Australian continental shelf, and the channel between the reef and the coast can be 60m deep. In places, the reef rises straight up from that depth. This raises the question of how the reef built up when coral cannot survive below 30m. One theory is that it gradually grew as the sea bed subsided. Another theory is that the sea level gradually rose, and the coral growth was able to keep pace.

Reef Inhabitants There are about 400 different types of coral on the Barrier Reef. Equally colourful are the many clams that appear to be embedded in the coral. Other reef inhabitants include about 1500 species of fish, 4000 types of mollusc (clams, snails etc), 350 echinoderms (sea urchins, starfish, sea cucumbers etc, all with a five-arm body plan), and countless thousands of species of sponge, worm and crustacean (crabs, shrimps etc).

Reef waters are also home to dugong (the sea cows believed to have given rise to the mermaid myth) and are breeding grounds for humpback whales, which migrate every winter from Antarctica. The reef's islands form important nesting colonies for many types of sea bird, and six of the world's seven species of sea turtle lay eggs on the islands' sandy beaches in spring or summer.

Crown-of-Thorns Starfish One reef inhabitant that has enjoyed enormous publicity is the crown-of-thorns starfish, notorious because it appears to be chewing through large areas of the reef. It's thought that the crown-of-thorns develop a taste for coral when the reef ecology is upset; for example, when the supply of bivalves (oysters, clams), which comprise its normal diet, is diminished.

QUEENSLAND

business in Park Lane Plaza on the corner of Goondoon and Tank Sts.

Gladstone Backpackers (☎ 4972 5744) at 12 Rollo St is a small, extremely friendly place close to both the marina and the town's main street. The owner, Bob, is the local QNPWS snake catcher and he usually has a reptile or two in the garage. Dorms have

Dangerous Creatures Hungry sharks are the usual idea of an aquatic nasty, but the Barrier Reef's most unpleasant creatures are generally less dramatic. For a start, there are scorpion fish with highly venomous spines. The butterfly cod is a very beautiful scorpion fish and relies on its colourful, slow-moving appearance to warn off possible enemies. In contrast, the stonefish lies hidden on the bottom, looking just like a rock, and is very dangerous to step on.

Stinging jellyfish are a danger only in coastal waters and only in certain seasons. The deadly 'sea wasp' is, in fact, a box jellyfish (see the Warning at the beginning of this chapter). As for sharks, there has been no recorded case of a visitor to the reef islands meeting a hungry one.

Viewing the Reef The best way of seeing the reef is by diving or snorkelling in it. Otherwise you can view it through the floor of glass-bottom boats or the windows of semi-submersibles, or descend below the ocean surface inside 'underwater observatories'. You can also see a living coral reef and its accompanying life forms without leaving dry land, at the Great Barrier Reef Wonderland aquarium in Townsville.

Innumerable tour operators run day trips to the outer reef and to coral-fringed islands from towns on the Queensland coast. The cost depends on how much reef-viewing paraphernalia is used, how far the reef is from the coast, how luxurious the vessel is that takes you there, and whether lunch is included. Usually, free use of snorkelling gear is part of the package. Some islands also have good reefs and are usually cheaper to reach; you can stay on quite a few of them.

The Great Barrier Reef Marine Park Authority (GBRMPA) is the body looking after the welfare of most of the reef. Its address is PO Box 1379, Townsville, Queensland 4810 (☎ 4750 0700). It has an office in the Great Barrier Reef Wonderland complex in Townsville.

Islands There are three types of island off the Queensland coast. In the south, before you reach the Barrier Reef, are several large vegetated sand islands, including North Stradbroke, Moreton and Fraser islands. These are interesting to visit, although not for coral. Strung along the whole coast, mostly close inshore, are continental islands, such as Great Keppel, most of the Whitsundays, Hinchinbrook and Dunk. At one time, these would have been the peaks of coastal ranges, but rising sea levels submerged the mountains. The islands' vegetation is similar to that of the adjacent mainland.

The true coral islands, or cays, are on the outer reef or isolated between it and the mainland. Green Island near Cairns, the Low Isles near Port Douglas, and Heron Island off Gladstone, are all cays. Cays are formed when a reef is above sea level, even at high tide. Dead coral is ground down by water action to form sand and, in some cases, vegetation eventually takes root. Coral cays are low-lying, unlike the often hilly islands closer to the coast. There are about 300 cays on the reef, and 69 are vegetated.

The islands are extremely variable so don't let the catchword 'reef island' suck you in. Most of the popular resort islands are actually continental islands and some are well south of the Barrier Reef. Many continental islands have fringing reefs as well as other attractions for which a tiny dot-on-the-map coral cay is simply too small; there may be hills to climb, bushwalks to explore and secluded beaches.

The islands also vary considerably in their accessibility. For example, Lady Elliot is a $135 return flight, whereas others cost only a few dollars by ferry. If you want to stay on an island rather than make a day trip from the mainland, this too can vary widely in cost. Accommodation is generally in the form of expensive resorts, where most visitors will be on an all-inclusive package holiday. But there are a few exceptions to this rule, and on many islands it's possible to camp. A few islands have proper camping areas with toilets and fresh water on tap; on others you'll even have to take drinking water with you.

For more information on individual islands, see the Capricorn Coast, Whitsunday Coast, North Coast and Far North Queensland sections of this chapter. Also good is Lonely Planet's *Islands of Australia's Great Barrier Reef.* ∎

QUEENSLAND

three or four beds which go for $15 a night; doubles are $32. The hostel offers free use of bicycles and will pick guests up from the bus drop-off.

Most coast buses stop at Gladstone and it's on the Brisbane to Rockhampton rail route. You can also fly there with Sunstate or Flight West.

ROCKHAMPTON (pop 57,500)

Australia's 'beef capital' sits astride the Tropic of Capricorn. First settled by Europeans in 1855, Rockhampton had a relatively small, early gold rush but cattle soon became the big industry.

Rockhampton is the administrative and commercial centre of central Queensland. It has a few tourist attractions, including a good art gallery, an Aboriginal cultural centre and excellent parks and gardens, but it is mainly an access point for Great Keppel and other islands – boats leave from Rosslyn Bay about 50km away. Also near Rocky are the spectacular limestone caves in the Berserker Range to the north, the old gold-mining town of Mt Morgan (38km south-west), the Koorana Crocodile Farm near Emu Park, and the very popular Myella Farm Stay (see the Capricorn Hinterland section).

Orientation

Rockhampton is about 40km from the coast, straddling the Fitzroy River. The long Fitzroy Bridge connects the old central part of Rockhampton with the newer suburbs to the north.

The Bruce Highway skirts the town centre and crosses the river upstream from the Fitzroy Bridge.

Information

The Capricorn Information Centre (☎ 4927 2055) is on the highway 3km south of the centre, beside the Tropic of Capricorn marker. More convenient is the helpful Riverside Information Centre (☎ 4922 5339) on Quay St, which is open weekdays from 8.30 am to 4.30 pm and weekends from 9 am to 4 pm. There's a Department of Environment office (☎ 4936 0511) 7km north-west of the centre, near the turn-off to Yeppoon.

Things to See

There are many fine buildings in the town, particularly on **Quay St**, which has a number of grand buildings that date to the gold-rush days. You can pick up tourist leaflets and magazines that map out town walking trails.

The **Rockhampton City Art Gallery** on Victoria Pde is open on weekdays from 10 am to 4 pm and on Sunday from 2 to 4 pm (free). On the Bruce Highway, 6km north of the centre, is the **Dreamtime Cultural Centre** (☎ 4936 1655), an Aboriginal heritage display centre. It's open daily from 10 am to 3.30 pm and tours are run daily at 11 am and 2 pm ($11/5 adults/children). The impressive **Botanic Gardens** at the end of Spencer St in the south of the city were established in 1869 and have an excellent tropical collection and a small and rather nasty zoo (free). North of the centre the **Cliff Kershaw Gardens** is an excellent botanical park dedicated to Australian native plants.

Places to Stay

Camping The small *Municipal Riverside Caravan Park* (☎ 4922 3779) in Reaney St, just across the bridge from the city centre, has tent sites for $9 but no on-site vans. The *Southside Holiday Village* (☎ 4927 3013), across the Bruce Highway from the Capricorn Information Centre, is a well-kept place with tent sites from $13.50 and on-site cabins from $35.50.

Hostels The *Rockhampton City YHA* (☎ 4927 5288) at 60 MacFarlane St is spacious and friendly, with good facilities, dorms at $15, twin rooms at $34 and family rooms for $44; nonmembers pay $3 extra per night. Evening meals are available for $5. It's a 20-minute walk north of the centre or you can get there on a High St bus, except on weekends. The hostel is five-minutes walk from McCafferty's terminal, and the other bus companies will drop you nearby on request. This is a good place to organise trips to Great Keppel Island and to book the popular YHA hostel there.

Duthies Leichhardt Hotel (☎ 4927 6733) on the corner of Denham and Bolsover Sts has recently refurbished two and three-bed motel-type rooms at $15 per person, which is good value, although these may not be available if the hotel is close to full.

Hotels & Motels On Quay St beside the Fitzroy Bridge, the *Criterion Hotel* (☎ 4922 1225) is one of Rockhampton's most magnificent old buildings. Budget rooms with shared bathrooms are $20/30 for singles/

doubles and renovated period-style suites are $45/50 with air-con. *Duthies Leichhardt Hotel* (☎ 4927 6733), on the corner of Denham and Bolsover Sts has motel rooms from $50/60. *Porky's Motel* (☎ 4927 8100) is quite central at 141 George St and, despite the dodgy name, has respectable rooms at $39/44, plus $8 for each extra adult. You'll find dozens of other motels on the Bruce Highway as you come into Rockhampton from either the north or south.

Places to Eat

The *Swagman Cafe* at 8 Denham St does

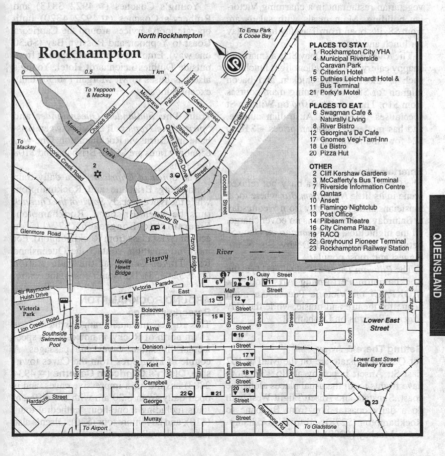

PLACES TO STAY
1 Rockhampton City YHA
4 Municipal Riverside Caravan Park
5 Criterion Hotel
15 Duthies Leichhardt Hotel & Bus Terminal
21 Porky's Motel

PLACES TO EAT
6 Swagman Cafe & Naturally Living
8 River Bistro
12 Georgina's De Cafe
17 Gnomes Vegi-Tarri-Inn
18 Le Bistro
20 Pizza Hut

OTHER
2 Cliff Kershaw Gardens
3 McCafferty's Bus Terminal
7 Riverside Information Centre
9 Qantas
10 Ansett
11 Flamingo Nightclub
13 Post Office
14 Pilbeam Theatre
16 City Cinema Plaza
19 RACQ
22 Greyhound Pioneer Terminal
23 Rockhampton Railway Station

QUEENSLAND

cooked breakfasts from $5 as well as the usual burgers, sangers etc, and two shops farther north *Natural Living* has healthy lunches and salads. The *Criterion Hotel* has hearty and excellent-value bar meals from $7.50 to $9 and the Bush Inn Steakhouse with steak and seafood from $8 to $10.

Georgina's De Cafe at 171 Bolsover St is a trendy cafe-eatery with a good range of gourmet tucker – pasta, focaccia, salads and delicious cakes. Evening meals, such as Cajun chicken, cost $14 to $16.

On the corner of William St and Denison Lane, *Gnomes Vegi-Tarri-Inn* is a very good vegetarian restaurant in a charming Victorian building. Main meals with salads are from $8; it's open from Tuesday to Saturday for lunch and dinner.

The *River Bistro* on Quay St is a smart and snappy eatery, with excellent light lunches – such as the delicious chicken and bacon mignon for $8 – and evening main courses from $16. The cosy *Le Bistro* on William St specialises in Modern Australian cuisine, and has modern Australian prices – $18 to $24 for a main course.

Entertainment

The Criterion Hotel has a busy but relaxed scene in its little *Newsroom Bar* where local musicians and groups play from Wednesday to Saturday nights; there is no cover charge. Of the nightclubs, the *Flamingo* on Quay St between William and Derby Sts is the biggest and most popular.

The *Pilbeam Theatre* (☎ 4927 4111) at the Rockhampton Performing Arts Complex (ROKPAC) on Victoria Pde is the main venue for theatre and music, while the *City Cinema Plaza* is on Denham St.

Getting There & Away

Air Qantas/Sunstate are on the Mall at 107 East St; Ansett is nearby at No 137. Both have flights to all the usual places along the coast. Sunstate and Ansett/Flight West both do a daily coastal hop from Brisbane to Rockhampton ($278) and from Rockhampton to Mackay ($209).

Bus The McCafferty's terminal (☎ 4927 2844) is just north of the bridge off Queen Elizabeth Dve; the Greyhound Pioneer terminal is at the Mobil roadhouse in George St, near the corner of Fitzroy St, although they also stop at the Mobil station close to McCafferty's north of the river. Both companies stop in Rocky on their major coastal runs. Destinations include Mackay (four hours, $43), Cairns (16 hours, $98) and Brisbane (10½ hours, $67). McCafferty's also runs to Emerald ($28) twice daily, and has services to Longreach ($51) three times a week.

Young's Coaches (☎ 4922 3813) and Rothery's Coaches (☎ 4922 4320) both operate loop services around the Capricorn Coast to Yeppoon and Rosslyn Bay ($6.30 one way), Emu Park and back, leaving from outside Duthies Leichhardt Hotel. Young's also has buses to Mt Morgan ($6.30) daily except Sunday.

Train The *Sunlander, Queenslander* and *Spirit of the Tropics* all travel between Brisbane and Cairns via Rockhampton. One-way economy fares are $67 to Brisbane and $108 to Cairns.

The *Spirit of Capricorn* is a daily train connecting Brisbane and Rockhampton, while the twice-weekly *Spirit of the Outback* runs between Brisbane, Rockhampton, Emerald and Longreach ($72/115 in economy/1st class from Rockhampton). For more information, contact the Queensland Rail Travel Centre at the train station (☎ 4932 0453), 1km south-east of the centre.

AROUND ROCKHAMPTON
Berserker Range

This rugged mountain range, which starts 26km north of Rocky, is noted for its spectacular limestone caves and passages. A couple of kilometres from the Caves township, **Olsen's Capricorn Caverns** (☎ 4934 2883) has the most impressive caves, and is open daily from 8.30 am with six different tours including a one-hour 'cathedral tour' ($10), and adventure tour ($30). Olsen's also has a pool, walking trails and barbecue areas.

Nearby, the family-run **Cammoo Caves** has self-guided tours daily from 8.30 am to 4.30 pm ($7).

Mt Morgan (pop 2500)
The open-cut gold and copper mine at Mt Morgan, 38km south-west of Rockhampton on the Burnett Highway, was worked (off and on) from the 1880s until 1981. Mt Morgan is a registered heritage town with a well-preserved collection of turn-of-the-century buildings. The tourist office (☎ 4938 2312) is housed in a lovely old train station.

The interesting **Mt Morgan Historical Museum** on the corner of Morgan and East Sts is open daily from 10 am to 1 pm (Sunday until 4 pm); entry is $2. Silver Wattle Tours (☎ 4938 1081) runs 2½-hour tours that take in the town sights, the mine, and a cave with dinosaur footprints on its ceiling, departing daily at 9.30 am and 1 pm ($18.50).

There's a good caravan park on the southern outskirts, and a couple of the old pubs offer budget accommodation. The *Miners' Rest Motel Units* (☎ 4938 2350) 1km south of the centre has good cottages from $40 a double.

Young's Bus Service (☎ 4922 3813) has regular buses from Rockhampton to Mt Morgan from Monday to Saturday; the fare is $6.30 one way. McCafferty's also passes through here on its inland Rockhampton-Brisbane run.

YEPPOON (pop 9000)
Yeppoon is a relaxed seaside township 43km north-east of Rockhampton. It's the main centre on the Capricorn Coast, and although Great Keppel Island is the area's main attraction, Yeppoon itself has quite good beaches and is a reasonably popular holiday town. Boats to Great Keppel leave from Rosslyn Bay, 7km south.

The Capricorn Coast Information Centre (☎ 1800 675 785) is at the Ross Creek Roundabout at the entrance to the town.

If you have transport, it's an interesting drive from Yeppoon up to the tiny town of Byfield, 40km north. The road passes through various state forest parks with good

picnic and camping grounds, and you can visit a pottery and a historic homestead en route.

Places to Stay
Up on the hill behind the town, the *Barrier Reef Backpackers* (☎ 4939 4702) at 30 Queen St is a relaxed place in a comfortable old timber house. It has all the usual facilities, a large backyard and good views of the town. Four-bed dorms cost $15 per person ($14 VIP/YHA members), doubles $33, and they offer free pick-ups from Rocky and will drop you at Rosslyn Bay if you're going to Great Keppel.

There are numerous motels and holiday flats. The *Como Holiday Units* (☎ 4939 1594) opposite the beach at 32 Anzac Pde has self-contained one and two-bedroom units at $50 a double, plus $8 for each extra adult.

YEPPOON TO EMU PARK
There are beaches dotted all along the 19km coast from Yeppoon south to Emu Park. At **Cooee Bay**, a couple of kilometres from Yeppoon, the World & Australian Cooeeing Contest & Carnival is held each August.

Rosslyn Bay Boat Harbour, about 7km south of Yeppoon, is the departure point for ferries to Great Keppel Island and other Keppel Bay islands. There's a free day-car park at the harbour, or the Kempsea lock-up car park (on the main road near the harbour turn-off) charges $4.50 a day ($6 under cover; $3 for motorbikes).

South of Rosslyn Bay are three fine headlands with good views – **Double Head, Bluff Point** and **Pinnacle Point**. After Pinnacle Point the road crosses **Causeway Lake**, a saltwater inlet where you can rent canoes and sailboards. Further south at **Emu Park** there are more good views and the 'Singing Ship' – a series of drilled tubes and pipes that emit whistling or moaning sounds when there's a breeze blowing. It's a memorial to Captain Cook.

Koorana Crocodile Farm is 5km off the Emu Park to Rockhampton road. The turn-off is 15km from Emu Park. The farm has hundreds of crocs and is open daily from 11.30 am, with 1½-hour tours daily at 1 pm ($10/5).

Most towns along this stretch of coast have caravan and camping parks, and there are numerous motels and holiday flats.

GREAT KEPPEL ISLAND

Although it's not actually on the reef, Great Keppel is the equal of most islands up the coast. Known as 'wappaburra' (resting place) to the local Aboriginal people, the island is 13km offshore, and although it's too big for you to see it all in an afternoon, it's small enough to explore over a few days. It covers 14 sq km and boasts 18km of very fine white-sand beaches.

The Great! Keppel Island Resort, owned by Qantas, is beyond the reach of the average shoestring traveller, but the good news about Great Keppel is that, unlike many of the resort islands, there are some good budget accommodation alternatives, and it's also one of the cheapest and easiest Queensland islands to reach. Day-trippers to the island have access to a pool, bar and restaurant at the resort, and they can hire all sorts of water sports gear.

QUEENSLAND

Great Keppel Island

1 Keppel Reef Scuba Adventures
2 Keppel Haven
3 Keppel Kamp Out
4 Ferry Arrivals
5 Great Keppel YHA; Island Pizza
6 Keppel Lodge
7 Shell House
8 Keppel Watersports
9 Daytrippers' Facilities
10 Great! Keppel Island Resort

0   1   2 km

Things to See & Do

Great Keppel's beaches are among the best of any on the resort islands. The main **Fisherman's** and **Putney** beaches are very pleasant, or you can walk around the island and find your own deserted stretch of white sand. The water is clear and warm and there is good coral at many points around the island, especially between Great Keppel and Humpy Island to the south. A 30-minute walk/scramble around the headland south of the resort brings you to **Monkey Beach** where there's good snorkelling.

There are a number of bushwalking tracks. The longest, and one of the more difficult, goes across to the lighthouse near **Bald Rock Point** on the far side of the island (2½ hours one way). Some beaches, such as **Red Beach** near the lighthouse, are only accessible by boat.

There's an **underwater observatory** by Middle Island, close to Great Keppel. A confiscated Taiwanese fishing junk was sunk next to the observatory to provide a haven for fish.

The Beach Shed on Putney Beach and Keppel Watersports on Fisherman's Beach both hire out water sports gear including sailboards, catamarans, motorboats and snorkelling gear, and can take you waterskiing or parasailing. Keppel Reef Scuba Adventures (☎ 4939 5022) on Putney Beach has introductory dives ($80) or, if you're certified, two dives with all gear supplied for $100. Five-day diving courses cost $420.

Organised Cruises

Keppel Tourist Services (☎ 4933 6744) runs various cruises aboard the *Reefcat*. Its island cruise departs daily from Rosslyn Bay at 9.15 am and from Fisherman's Beach at 10 am, and continues to the pontoon moored off the northern tip of the island where you stay for around three hours before returning. The cruise includes boom netting, snorkelling, glass-bottom boat trip and lunch. The cruise costs $70 from Rosslyn Bay, or $65 if you are already on the island. At 12.15 pm each day there is a cruise to the underwater observatory from Fisherman's Beach ($10).

Places to Stay

The *Great Keppel YHA Hostel* (☎ 4927 5288) is pretty basic but still very popular, with 16-bed dorms at $16 and eight-bed cabins with bathrooms at $17; nonmembers pay $3 extra. They hire out snorkelling gear and organise bushwalks and other activities. Book through the Rockhampton Youth Hostel or the YHA head office in Brisbane (☎ 3236 1680). Their $79 deal ($89 non-members) is good value: you get one night in Rocky, two nights on the island and bus and boat transfers.

Keppel Haven (☎ 4939 1907) has semi-permanent safari tents that sleep up to four people at $25 per person (bedding not supplied); communal facilities include fridges, barbecues and basic kitchen equipment. There are also 12 self-contained six-bed cabins at $110 a double, plus $30 for each extra person.

Next door to Keppel Haven is *Keppel Kamp Out* (☎ 4939 2131), which is geared to the 18 to 35 age bracket, and has organised activities. The cost of $69 per person per day ($49 stand-by usually available) includes twin-share tents, three meals and activities such as water sports, parties and video nights.

Keppel Lodge (☎ 4939 4251) has four good motel-style units that sleep up to five and cost from $90 a double plus $30 for extras; there's a large communal lounge and kitchen and a barbecue area.

The *Great! Keppel Island Resort* is particularly popular with young people and promotes itself as 'the active resort'. All-inclusive daily costs start at $270 for a double, but Qantas has package deals which include airfares, and these work out much cheaper.

Places to Eat

If you want to cook it's best to bring a few basic supplies. Fruit, vegetables, groceries and dairy foods are sold at the reasonably pricey kiosk at *Keppel Haven*. Next door, the *Bar & Bistro* does lunches and evening meals (burgers $7, grills $15), but the resort *cafe* is cheaper. Near the YHA, the friendly

QUEENSLAND

Island Pizza makes good pizzas ($10 to $26), pasta and submarines. It's open Wednesday to Sunday.

In the resort day-trippers' area, the *Keppel Cafe* does burgers ($5), fish & chips ($7) etc, and the *Anchorage Char Grill* has grilled steak or fish with salad and chips for $12. The *Shell House* does excellent Devonshire teas. The friendly owner has lived on Keppel for many years, and his tropical garden offers a pleasant break from the sun.

Getting There & Away

Air Qantas flies at least twice daily between Rockhampton and Great Keppel ($82 one way).

Boat Ferries for Great Keppel leave from Rosslyn Bay Harbour on the Capricorn Coast. Keppel Tourist Services (☎ 4933 6744) operates two boats, the *Reefcat* and the *Spirit of Keppel*. The *Reefcat* leaves Rosslyn Bay at 9.15 am and returns from Great Keppel at 4.30 pm, and costs $70 return including an island tour ($25 without the tour). The *Spirit of Keppel* leaves Rosslyn Bay at 11.30 am and 3.30 pm, and returns from Great Keppel at 2 and 4.30 pm ($25 return).

OTHER KEPPEL BAY ISLANDS

Great Keppel is only the biggest of the 18 continental islands dotted around Keppel Bay, all within 20km of the coast. You may get to visit **Middle Island**, with its underwater observatory, or **Halfway** or **Humpy** islands if you're staying on Great Keppel. Most of the islands have clean white beaches and several (notably Halfway) have excellent fringing coral reefs. Some, including Middle and **Miall**, are national parks where you can maroon yourself for a few days' camping. To camp on a national park island, you need to take all your own supplies, including water. Numbers of campers on each island are restricted – for example, 18 at a time on Middle and six on Miall. You can get information and permits from the Department of Environment regional office in Rockhampton (☎ 4936 0511) or the QNPWS rangers' office at Rosslyn Bay Harbour (☎ 4933 6595).

North Keppel is the second-largest of the group and one of the most northerly. It covers 6.3 sq km and is a national park. The most popular camping spot is Considine Beach on the north-west coast, which has well water for washing, and toilets. Take drinking water, insect repellent and a fuel stove.

Just south of North Keppel, tiny **Pumpkin Island** has five cabins (☎ 4939 2431) that accommodate either five or six people each at a cost of $130 per cabin. There's water and solar electricity, and each cabin has a stove, fridge and a bathroom with shower. Bedding is provided. Camping costs $12 per person.

The Keppel Bay Marina (☎ 4933 6244) can organise a water taxi for camping drop-off services from Rosslyn Bay to the islands; prices start from $300 return for up to four people, plus $40 for each extra person.

CAPRICORN HINTERLAND

The Capricorn Highway runs inland, virtually along the Tropic of Capricorn, across the central Queensland highlands to Barcaldine, from where you can continue west and north-west along the Landsborough Highway to meet the Townsville to Mt Isa road.

The area was first opened up by miners looking for gold and copper around Emerald and sapphires around Anakie, but cattle, grain crops and coal provide its main living today. Carnarvon National Park, south of Emerald, is one of Queensland's most spectacular.

Getting There & Away

McCafferty's has a Rockhampton to Longreach service three times a week, which calls at all towns along the Capricorn Highway. The twice-weekly *Spirit of the Outback* train follows the same route.

Baralaba

About 25km south-west of Rockhampton and 22km east of Baralaba is *Myella Farm Stay* (☎ 4998 1290), a working cattle station. It's owned by a hospitable family and offers the 'City Slickers' experience – horse riding, cattle mustering, helping out with the fence repairs etc – and has received good reports from travellers. You stay in a recently renovated timber farmhouse; the cost is around $70 per person per day, which includes all meals and activities. Ring for directions.

Blackdown Tableland National Park

The Blackdown Tableland is a spectacular 600m sandstone plateau that rises suddenly out of the flat plains of central Queensland. It's definitely worth a visit, with stunning panoramas, great bushwalks to waterfalls and lookout points, Aboriginal rock art, plus some unique wildlife and plant species.

There's a self-registration camping area at **South Mimosa Creek**, about 10km into the park. Bookings (advisable during school holidays) can be made with the ranger at Dingo (☎ 4986 1964). Bring water, and a gas stove for cooking.

The turn-off to the tableland is 12km west of **Dingo** and 35km east of the coal-mining centre of **Blackwater**. The 25km gravel road can be unsafe in wet weather and isn't suitable for caravans at any time – the last 7km are incredibly steep and slippery.

Coal Mines

Several of the massive open-cut Queensland coal mines in this region offer free tours lasting about 1½ hours; book ahead. The Blackwater mine tour (☎ 4986 0666), 20km south of Blackwater, leaves the mine office on Wednesday at 10 am. For the Peak Downs (☎ 4968 8233) mine near Moranbah, buses depart Moranbah town square at 10 am on Thursday, and the tour takes about 2½ hours. Tours of Blair Athol mine (☎ 4983 1866) near Clermont start on Tuesday at 9 am.

Gem Fields

West of Emerald, about 270km inland from Rockhampton, the gem fields around Anakie, Sapphire and Rubyvale and the Willows gem field are known for sapphires, zircons, amethysts, rubies, topaz, jasper, and even diamonds and gold. To go fossicking, you need a 'fossicking licence', sold from the Emerald courthouse or on the gem field.

If you're just passing through, you can buy a bucket of 'wash' (dirt) from one of the fossicking parks and hand-sieve and wash it ($4). There are also a couple of tourist mines that you can visit and explore, including the excellent **Silk 'n' Sapphire Mine** 1.5km north of Rubyvale, with adventurous hands-on underground tours from $30 for two hours.

Anakie, 42km west of Emerald just off the Capricorn Highway, has a pub, a caravan park and an information centre (☎ 4985 4525). **Sapphire** is 10km north of Anakie on a sealed road, with **Rubyvale**, the main town for the fields, 7km further north. Rubyvale has a pub, a general store, a post office and a few gem shops and galleries.

At Sapphire, *Sunrise Cabins & Camping* (☎ 4985 4281), about 1km out of town on the road to Rubyvale, has camp sites at $10 or rustic stone cabins with communal kitchen facilities from $12/26, plus $2 for each extra person (maximum six). You can get information, licences and maps, and hire fossicking gear here.

Ramboda Homestead (☎ 4985 4154), on the highway near the turn-off to Sapphire, is a farmstay with dinner B&B from $35/80, and it does pick-ups from Anakie. There are also caravan/camping parks at Anakie, Rubyvale and Willows Gemfield.

Clermont (pop 2400)

North of Emerald is Clermont, with the huge Blair Athol open-cut coal mine. Clermont is Queensland's oldest tropical inland town, founded on copper, gold, sheep and cattle. It was the scene of goldfield race riots in the 1880s, and there was a military takeover of the town in 1891 after a confrontation between striking sheep shearers and non-union labour. The town has a couple of pubs and a caravan park with on-site vans.

Springsure (pop 950)

Springsure, 66km south of Emerald, has an attractive setting with a backdrop of granite mountains and surrounding sunflower fields. There's a small **historical museum** by the windmill as you enter town from the south.

The **Virgin Rock**, an outcrop of Mt Zamia on the northern outskirts, was named after early settlers claimed to have seen the image of the Virgin Mary in the rock face.

Ten km south-west, at Burnside, is the **Old Rainworth Fort**, built following the Wills Massacre of 1861 when Aboriginal people killed 19 whites on Cullin-La-Ringo Station north-west of Springsure.

For accommodation you have the choice of a motel or a caravan park.

Carnarvon National Park

Rugged Carnarvon National Park, in the middle of the Great Dividing Range, features dramatic gorge scenery and many Aboriginal rock paintings and carvings. The national park has several sections, but the impressive Carnarvon Gorge is all that most people see as the rest is pretty inaccessible.

Carnarvon Gorge is stunning partly because it's an oasis surrounded by drier plains and partly because of the variety of its scenery, which includes sandstone cliffs, moss gardens, deep pools, and rare palms and ferns. There's also lots of wildlife. Aboriginal art can be viewed at two main sites – the **Art Gallery** and **Cathedral Cave**.

From Rolleston to Carnarvon Gorge, the road is bitumen for 20km and unsealed for 75km. From Roma via Injune and Wyseby, the road is good bitumen for about 200km, then unsealed and fairly rough for the last 45km. After rain, both roads are impassable.

Three km into the Carnarvon Gorge section there's an information centre and a scenic camping ground. The main walking track starts beside the information centre and follows Carnarvon Creek through the gorge, with detours to various points of interest such as the Moss Garden (3.6km from the camping ground), Ward's Canyon (4.8km), the Art Gallery (5.6km) and Cathedral Cave (9.3km). You should allow at least half a day for a visit here, and bring lunch and water with you as there are no shops.

To get into the more westerly and rugged Mt Moffatt section of the park, there are two unsealed roads from Injune: one through Womblebank station, the other via West-grove station. There are no through roads from Mt Moffatt to Carnarvon Gorge or to the third and fourth remote sections of the park – Salvator Rosa and Ka Ka Mundi. Mt Moffatt has some beautiful scenery, diverse vegetation and wildlife, and **Kenniff Cave**, an important Aboriginal archaeological site. It's believed Aboriginal people lived here as long as 20,000 years ago.

Places to Stay The *Oasis Lodge* (☎ 4984 4503), near the entrance to the Carnarvon Gorge section of the park, offers 'safari cabins' from $150 a night per person, including full board and organised activities ($80 from December to March, without activities). There's a general store with fuel.

You need a permit to camp at the national park camping ground, and it's advisable (essential during school holidays) to book by phoning the Carnarvon Gorge rangers (☎ 4984 4505). Sites cost $3.50 per person per night or you can bush camp for $2 per night. Wood for cooking is scarce, so bring your own gas stove.

You can also camp at Big Ben camping area, 500m upstream from Cathedral Cave – a 12km walk up the gorge. Again, permits are required, and you must carry a fuel stove. If you camp here, you can explore the side gorges unhurriedly.

In the Mt Moffatt section, camping with a permit is allowed at four sites but you need to be completely self-sufficient, and a 4WD is advisable; phone the Mt Moffatt rangers for details (☎ 4626 3581).

Whitsunday Coast

The Whitsunday Islands, which lie just off the coast between Mackay and Bowen, are famous for their clear, aqua-blue waters and forested islands. This is one of the most beautiful parts of the coast, and there's an extensive range of activities to choose from, including dive courses, cruises to and around the islands, snorkelling, fishing and sailing.

Mackay is a major regional centre, while

A Sweet Success

Sugar is easily the most visible crop from Mackay, north past Cairns and up the Queensland coast. Sugar was a success almost from the day it was introduced to the region in 1865, but its early days had a distinctly unsavoury air as the plantations were worked by Pacific Islander people, referred to as Kanakas, who were often forced from their homes to work on Australian cane fields. 'Blackbirding', as this virtual slave trading was known, was not stamped out until 1905.

Today, cane growing is a highly mechanised business and visitors can inspect crushing plants during the harvesting season (roughly July to October). The most spectacular part of the operation is the firing of the cane fields, when rubbish is burnt off by night fires. Mechanical harvesters cut and gather the cane, which is then transported to the sugar mills, often on narrow-gauge railway lines laid through the cane fields. The cane is shredded and passed through a series of crushers. The extracted juice is heated and cleaned of impurities and then evaporated to form a syrup. Next, the syrup is reduced to molasses and low-grade sugar. Further refining stages end with the sugar loaded into bulk containers for export.

Sugar production is a remarkably efficient process. The crushed fibres, known as bagasse, are burnt as fuel; impurities separated from the juice are used as fertilisers; and the molasses is used either to produce ethanol or as stock feed. ■

the main access point for the islands is Airlie Beach, which is a very popular travellers' hangout, mainly because many companies offering dive courses and boat trips to the islands operate from here.

MACKAY (pop 44,800)

Mackay is surrounded by sugar cane and processes a third of Australia's sugar crop. The sugar, loaded at the world's largest sugar-loading terminal, at Port Mackay, has been grown here since 1865.

Mackay is nothing special, yet its town centre is attractively planted and there are some good beaches a bus ride away. It's also an access point for the national parks at Eungella and Cape Hillsborough, and for the Great Barrier Reef. There are some interesting islands only an hour or two away.

Orientation

Mackay is split into two halves by the broad Pioneer River, with the compact city centre laid out in a simple grid on the south side of the river. Victoria St, the main street, is an attractive thoroughfare with a central plantation. The bus terminal is a few hundred metres west of the centre on Milton St; the train station and airport are both about 3km south of the centre. The harbour is 6km

north, and the best beaches are about 15km north.

Information

Mackay's tourist office (☎ 4952 2677), in a replica of the old Richmond Sugar Mill, is about 3km south of the centre on Nebo Rd (the Bruce Hwy). It's open weekdays from 8.30 am to 5 pm and weekends from 9 am to 4 pm. While you're here, pick up a copy of the very handy *Things to See & Do in Mackay* brochure. The RACQ (☎ 4957 2918) is at 214 Victoria St, and the Department of Environment office (☎ 4951 8788) is on the corner of Wood and River Sts.

Things to See & Do

Despite the effects of several major cyclones, Mackay still has some interesting old buildings – the tourist office's *A Heritage Walk in Mackay* brochure guides you around 21 historic sites. There are botanic gardens and an orchid house in **Queens Park**, towards the eastern end of Gordon St, and good views over the harbour from **Mt Basset**, and at **Rotary Lookout** on Mt Oscar in North Mackay.

The **Town Beach**, 2km from the centre at the eastern end of Shakespeare St, is generally shallow and muddy; **Illawong Beach**, a couple of kilometres further south, is only slightly better. A better option is the sandy **Harbour Beach**, 6km north and just south of the harbour, although the best beaches are about 16km north of Mackay at Blacks Beach, Eimeo and Bucasia.

In the cane-crushing season (July to December) the **Farleigh Sugar Mill** (☎ 4957 4727), 12km north-west of Mackay, has two-hour tours on weekdays at 1 pm ($10). You can also do two-hour farm tours of the **Polstone Sugar Farm** (☎ 4959 7298), about 6km west, on Monday, Wednesday and Friday at 1.30 pm ($12).

The **Illawong Fauna Sanctuary** (☎ 4959 1777), an excellent private fauna park at Mirani, in the Pioneer Valley on the road to Eungella, has kangaroos, birds, crocodiles (fed at 2.30 pm) and koalas (3.30 pm); it's open daily and costs $10 ($5 children). There's also a children's playground, a swimming pool and homestay accommodation. A day tour from Mackay is $40/20.

Organised Tours & Cruises

Roylen's Cruises (☎ 4955 3066) runs fast catamaran trips from Mackay Harbour to Credlin Reef on the outer reef, where Roylen's has a pontoon with an underwater observatory. Trips depart on Monday, Wednesday and Friday ($100 including lunch and a semi-submersible ride); you can hire snorkelling or diving gear. Roylen's also has good cruises to Brampton Island daily ($50 including lunch at the resort). On weekends only, its catamarans continue on to Hamilton Island and Lindeman Island ($35 one way, $95 return including lunch) in the Whitsundays.

Reeforest Tours (☎ 4953 1000) has day trips to Eungella National Park for $45 ($20 to $30 for children).

The Illawong Fauna Sanctuary (see under Things to See & Do earlier) has extended outback tours to the gem fields around Sapphire. The cost is $275 for three days.

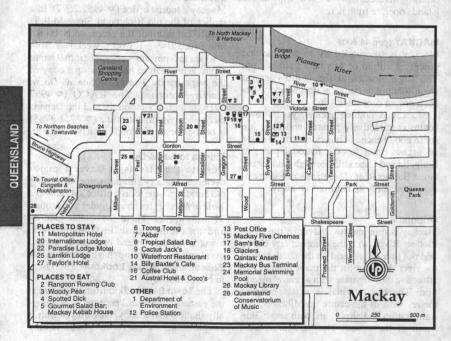

PLACES TO STAY
11 Metropolitan Hotel
20 International Lodge
22 Paradise Lodge Motel
25 Larrikin Lodge
27 Taylor's Hotel

PLACES TO EAT
2 Rangoon Rowing Club
3 Woody Pear
4 Spotted Dick
5 Gourmet Salad Bar;
   Mackay Kebab House

6 Toong Toong
7 Akbar
8 Tropical Salad Bar
9 Cactus Jack's
10 Waterfront Restaurant
14 Billy Baxter's Cafe
16 Coffee Club
21 Austral Hotel & Coco's

OTHER
1 Department of
   Environment
12 Police Station

13 Post Office
15 Mackay Five Cinemas
17 Sam's Bar
18 Glaciers
19 Qantas; Ansett
23 Mackay Bus Terminal
24 Memorial Swimming
   Pool
26 Mackay Library
28 Queensland
   Conservatorium
   of Music

Mackay

0   250   500 m

Places to Stay
Camping The modern *Beach Tourist Park* (☎ 4957 4021), on Petrie St at Illawong Beach about 4km south of the centre, has tent sites at $13, camp-o-tels (permanent tents with beds and lighting) at $18 and on-site cabins from $40.

The *Central Tourist Park* (☎ 4957 6141), at 15 Malcomson St in North Mackay, has tent sites from $10 and cabins from $25 a double.

Hostels *Larrikin Lodge* (☎ 4951 3728) at 32 Peel St is a small associate-YHA hostel in an airy timber house, with a small pool. The hostel is fairly straightforward, but it's well-run and has a friendly atmosphere. Dorm beds cost $14 and doubles $30; there's also a family room at $40 and units in the backyard with twins for $30.

Pubs & Motels *Taylor's Hotel* (☎ 4957 2500) on the corner of Wood and Alfred Sts has single rooms (only) for $20. The *Metropolitan Hotel* (☎ 4957 2802) on the corner of Gordon and Carlyle Sts has en-suite singles/doubles for $40/50 including a light breakfast.

The friendly *International Lodge* (☎ 4951 1022) at 40 Macalister St is quite central and has good budget motel rooms from $38/44. The *Paradise Lodge Motel* (☎ 4951 3644), in the street behind the bus station at 19 Peel St, has units at $46/52. There are about a thousand motels strung along Nebo Rd (the Bruce Hwy) south of the centre. The closest of these, the *Cool Palms Motel* (☎ 4957 5477) at 4 Nebo Rd, has budget rooms from $38/40.

Places to Eat
At 23 Wood St, the narrow and popular *Gourmet Salad Bar* is a lunchtime bargain with rolls and sandwiches from $2 as well as very cheap salads and cakes. Nearby, the *Mackay Kebab House* has chicken and lamb kebabs, and felafels.

The *Tropical Salad Bar*, on the corner of Victoria and Sydney Sts, has breakfast specials, fresh juices, smoothies, sandwiches and salads.

Mackay seems to have a pub on every corner in the city centre, so finding a counter meal is not a problem. *Wilkinson's Hotel* on the corner of Victoria and Gregory Sts has the trendy Rangoon Rowing Club upstairs, with pasta around $10 and other mains $18 to $20.

The friendly *Austral Hotel* on the corner of Victoria and Peel Sts has the tropical-style Coco's with mains in the $10 to $16 range and cheap meals in the corner bar.

On Sydney St the *Spotted Dick* is a very groovy renovated pub, complete with polished floors and red-felt pool tables. The menu is interesting without being too adventurous, and includes pizzas ($10), light meals such as deep-fried camembert ($8) and other mains ($10 to $13).

The *Coffee Club* on Wood St is another hip licensed bar, with meals such as fillet mignon ($18) and kebabs ($8).

The *Woody Pear* on Wood St is a cosy little BYO restaurant, open for dinner Tuesday to Saturday. At 10 Sydney St, *Toong Tong* is a well presented Thai restaurant with mains from $10 to $14, and *Akbar*, across the road at No 27, has good Indian curries at similar prices.

Billy Baxter's Cafe, next to the post office on the corner of Gordon and Sydney Sts, has bacon and eggs on pancakes ($7) and good coffee – it's open day and night. The lively *Cactus Jack's* on Victoria St has Mexican meals from $10 to $13, and it's licensed.

Mackay's best and most impressive eatery is the *Waterfront Restaurant & Espresso Bar* at 8 River St, with a covered decking area overlooking the river. It's licensed, lunchtime mains range from $14 to $18, at dinner it's $16 to $25.

Entertainment
The popular *Sam's Bar*, upstairs in the former Australian Hotel on the corner of Wood and Victoria Sts, is a laid-back meeting place, with pool tables and balconies overlooking the street. Other nightclubs

include the *Saloon Bar*, at 99 Victoria St, and *Glaciers* upstairs at 85 Victoria St.

The *Austral Hotel* has live music on weekends.

The *Queensland Conservatorium of Music* (☎ 4957 3727) at 418 Shakespeare St has jazz and classical performances – call to find out what's on. The *Mackay Five Cinemas* is at 30 Gordon St.

Getting There & Away
Air Ansett's office is on the corner of Victoria and Macalister Sts; Qantas is nearby at 105 Victoria St. Both airlines have direct flights to/from Brisbane ($327), Townsville ($204) and Rockhampton ($209), and connecting flights to other state capitals.

Flight West flies to/from Cairns ($253), and Sunstate/Qantas flies to/from Proserpine ($97). Helijet (☎ 4957 7400) has a range of flights from Mackay to Hamilton Island ($95 one way, $130 same-day return).

Bus Greyhound Pioneer and McCafferty's buses on the Bruce Highway runs stop at the Mackay Bus Terminal (☎ 4951 3088) on Milton St. Major stops along the coast include Cairns (11 hours, $72), Townsville (eight hours, $47), Airlie Beach (two hours, $24) and Brisbane (15 hours, $91).

Train The *Sunlander* and *Queenslander* (both from Brisbane to Cairns) stop at Mackay. A sleeper to/from Brisbane on the *Sunlander* costs $130/199 in economy/1st; to/from Cairns it's 102/172. The *Queenslander* has only 1st class at $300 to/from Brisbane. The train station is at Paget, about 3km south of the centre.

Getting Around
It costs about $10 for a taxi from Mackay airport to the city. Avis, Budget and Hertz have counters at the airport.

Local bus services are operated by Mackay Transit Coaches (☎ 4957 3330). The Taxi Transit Service (☎ 1800 815 559) takes people to the northern beaches for $3.60 one way.

AROUND MACKAY
Brampton & Carlisle Islands
These two mountainous national park islands are in the Cumberland Group, 32km north-east of Mackay. Both are about five sq km in area, and are joined by a sand bank which you can walk across at low tide. Carlisle's highest point is 389m Skiddaw Peak, and Brampton's is 219m Brampton Peak. Both islands have forested slopes, sandy beaches, good walks and fringing coral reefs with good snorkelling.

The Qantas-owned *Brampton Island Resort* (☎ 13 1415) is a good mid-range family resort which costs from $140 per person per day twin share, including breakfast, tennis, golf and water sports; there is also a restaurant and a cafe. **Brampton** is also a popular day trip destination, with its good beaches, walking trails and water sports gear for hire.

Carlisle Island is uninhabited, and there's a QNPWS camp site across from the resort. There are no facilities so you must be totally self-sufficient (although you could always pop across to the resort for a beer or a bite).

Roylen's Cruises (☎ 4955 3066) has daily cruises from Mackay Harbour to Brampton; the return fare of $50 includes a smorgasbord lunch at the resort. You can also fly daily from Mackay ($80 one way with Sunstate).

Most other islands in the Cumberland Group and the Sir James Smith Group to the north are also national parks; if you fancy a spot of Robinson Crusoeing and can afford to charter a boat or a seaplane, Goldsmith and Scawfell are good bets. Contact the Department of Environment offices in Mackay (☎ 4951 8788) or the QNPWS Seaforth office (☎ 4959 0410) for all camping permits and information.

Newry & Rabbit Islands
The Newry Island Group is a cluster of rocky, wild-looking continental islands just off the coast about 40km north-west of Mackay. **Newry Island**, 1km long, has a small and very low-key resort (☎ 4959 0214) where camping is $7 per site, a bunk is $8, and cabins, which sleep up to five and have

their own bathrooms and cooking facilities, cost $20 per person (maximum charge $60). The resort has a restaurant and bar, and will pick up guests from Victor Creek, 4km west of Seaforth, for $15 return.

Rabbit Island, the largest of the group at 4.5 sq km, has a national park camping ground with toilets and a rainwater tank, which might be empty in dry times. It also has the only sandy beaches in the group. From November to January sea turtles nest here. Contact the Mackay Department of Environment office (☎ 4951 8788) or the QNPWS Seaforth office (☎ 4959 0410) for permits and information.

Eungella National Park

Most days of the year you can be pretty sure of seeing platypuses close to the Broken River bridge and camping ground in this large national park, 84km west of Mackay. The best times to see the creatures are immediately after dawn and at dusk; you must remain patiently still and silent.

Eungella (pronounced '*young*-gulla', meaning 'Land of Clouds') covers nearly 500 sq km of the Clarke Range, climbing to 1280m at Mt Dalrymple. The area has been cut off from other rainforest areas for roughly 30,000 years and it has at least six life forms that exist nowhere else: the Eungella honeyeater (a bird), the orange-sided skink (a lizard), the Mackay tulip oak (a tall buttressed rainforest tree) and three species of frog of which one – the Eungella gastric brooding frog – has the unusual ability to incubate its eggs in its stomach and give birth by spitting out the tadpoles!

The main access road from Mackay takes you through the long and narrow **Pioneer Valley**, with a turn-off near Finch Hatton township to **Finch Hatton Gorge**. The last section of the 12km drive to the gorge is quite rough and involves several creek crossings. At the gorge, there's a swimming hole, picnic areas and a 1.6km walking trail to the spectacular Araluen Falls.

Eungella, 28km past Finch Hatton, is a sleepy mountain township with a guesthouse and a couple of tearooms. At **Broken River**, 5km south of Eungella, there's a rangers' office, a camping ground, picnic area, swimming hole and kiosk. Several excellent walking tracks start from around the Broken River picnic area. There's a platypus-viewing platform near the bridge, and colourful birds are prolific. At night, the rufous bettong, a small kangaroo, is quite common. You might also see two types of brushtail possum and two species of glider. Park rangers sometimes lead wildlife watching sessions, or night spotlighting trips to pick out nocturnal animals.

Places to Stay A couple of kilometres from the Finch Hatton Gorge is the *Platypus Bush Camp* (☎ 4958 3204), a simple bush retreat with a lovely forest setting by a creek. You can camp ($5 per person) or sleep in a slab-timber hut ($45 for up to three people); there are communal cooking shelters, hot showers and toilets. Bring your own food and linen. If you phone from Finch Hatton village, someone will pick you up.

In Eungella township, the old *Eungella Chalet* (☎ 4958 4509) is an old-fashioned guesthouse perched on the edge of the mountain. It's fairly basic but it has spectacular views, a pool, a bar and restaurant, and a hang-gliding platform. In the guesthouse section, backpacker beds are $15, singles/doubles are $30/45 and rooms with private bathroom are $65. Out the back are timber cabins from $80.

There's a good QNPWS camping ground ($3.50 per person per night) at Broken River; for bookings and permits contact the ranger on ☎ 4958 4552 (bookings recommended during school holidays). Also beside the bridge here, the *Broken River Mountain Retreat* (☎ 4958 4528) has motel-style timber cabins from $55 and four-bed self-contained units from $75 a double ($10 extra adults).

Getting There & Away There are no buses to Eungella, but Reeforest runs day trips from Mackay and will do camping drop-offs – see the Mackay Organised Tours & Cruises section for details.

Cape Hillsborough National Park

This small coastal park, 54km north of Mackay, takes in the rocky Cape Hillsborough (300m high), and nearby Andrews Point and Wedge Island, which are joined by a causeway at low tide. There are beaches and some good short walking tracks, and the scenery ranges from cliffs, rocky coast, dunes and scrub to rainforest and woodland. Kangaroos hang out on the beaches here and wallabies, sugar gliders and turtles are also quite common. There's a rangers' office and information centre (☎ 4959 0410) on the foreshore, and a good picnic and barbecue area nearby.

Places to Stay At the end of the Cape Hillsborough road, the *Cape Hillsborough Resort* (☎ 4959 0152) has tent sites from $10, cabins from $30 to $45, and motel-type rooms from $49.

There's a small QNPWS self-registration camping ground ($8 per site) at Smalleys Beach. Facilities include toilets, water and picnic shelters.

AIRLIE BEACH (pop 3000)

Airlie Beach, 25km north-west of Proserpine off the Bruce Highway, is the gateway to the Whitsunday Islands. It's a small but lively centre that has grown phenomenally since the mid-1980s. The whole town revolves around tourism and pleasure boating, and it attracts a diverse bunch of boaties, backpackers and other tourists. It has an excellent range of budget to mid-range accommodation, plenty of good eateries and a lively nightlife.

Airlie Beach also has a reputation as a centre for learning to scuba dive. A wide assortment of travel agents and tour operators are based here, and most boats to the islands leave from Shute Harbour, 8km east of Airlie Beach, or from the Abel Point Marina, 1km west. Whale watching boat trips, between July and September, are another attraction. Despite all of the recent development, Airlie Beach is still a small place that has managed to retain something of its relaxed air.

Information

There's a tourist office (☎ 4945 3711) on the Bruce Highway at Proserpine, near the turnoff to Airlie Beach.

In Airlie Beach nearly everything of importance is on the main road, Shute Harbour Rd. There are numerous privately run 'information centres' (ie booking agencies) along Shute Harbour Rd, including Destination Whitsunday (☎ 1800 644 563) and the Airlie Beach Tourist Information Centre (☎ 4946 6665).

The Department of Environment office (☎ 4946 7022) is 3km past Airlie Beach towards Shute Harbour, and is open weekdays from 8 am to 5 pm and at varying weekend hours. This office deals with camping bookings and permits for the Conway and Whitsunday Islands national parks.

Things to See & Do

The **Wildlife Park** has a large collection of Australian animals, birds and reptiles, with various daily shows including crocodile feeding; it's open daily from 8.30 am to 5 pm ($15). The park is 8km west of town – a courtesy bus does pick-ups from Airlie Beach. Also here is a bungee set-up ($49) and a pool with waterslides ($5 all day).

The beaches at Airlie aren't great, but there are two places where you can hire catamarans, windsurfers and other water sports gear. There's a good 25m pool at the Coral Sea Resort on Ocean View; non-guests can visit for $5.

Brandy Creek Trail Rides (☎ 4946 6665) offers three-hour rides through a nearby forest ($37) and will pick you up from your accommodation. Whitsunday 4WD Tours and Fawlty's 4WD Tropical Tours both offer half-day rainforest tours ($38).

Other possibilities include tandem skydiving ($239), paintball wars ($49), sea kayaking ($58) and parasailing ($40) – you can book these through your accommodation or one of the agents in Airlie Beach.

Diving Four outfits in and around Airlie Beach offer five to seven-day scuba-diving certificate courses. Standard costs vary from $250 to $500; with the cheaper courses you spend most of your time in a pool or classroom, whereas the better courses combine tuition on the mainland with three or four days diving on the Great Barrier Reef. All the firms also offer diving trips for certified divers. Book where you are staying or at one of the agencies on the main road in Airlie Beach.

The companies include: Oceania Dive (☎ 1800 075 035), Pro-Dive (☎ 1800 075 120), True Blue (☎ 1800 635 889) and Kelly Dive (☎ 1800 063 454), all with offices/shops in the centre of Airlie Beach.

Special Events

Airlie Beach is the centre of activities during the Whitsunday Fun Race (for cruising yachts) each September. The festivities include a Miss Figurehead competition where the contestants traditionally compete topless.

Places to Stay

Camping There are four good caravan parks along the road between Airlie Beach and Shute Harbour. The closest of these, the *Island Gateway Holiday Resort* (☎ 4946 6228), is about 1.5km east of Airlie Beach. There's also the *Shute Harbour Gardens Caravan Park* (☎ 4946 6483), 2.5km east, and the *Flame Tree Tourist Village* (☎ 1800 069 388), 6km east. All have good facilities including a pool, and tent sites from $12, on-site vans from $30 and cabins from $40.

You can also camp at the central *Koala Beach Resort* (see Hostels) for $8/12 for one/two people, but only if you don't have a car.

Hostels Airlie is a major stopover on the backpackers' circuit and has a good range of hostels. The competition can be quite fierce, and at the main bus stop there's a row of booths where the hostel reps tout for trade when the buses arrive. All the places out of

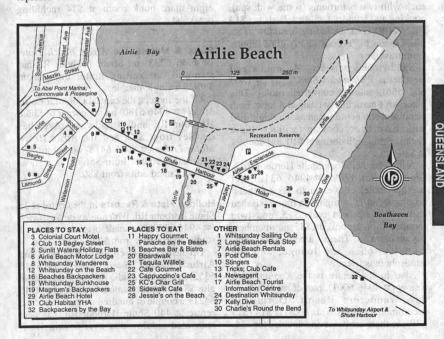

PLACES TO STAY	PLACES TO EAT	OTHER
3 Colonial Court Motel	11 Happy Gourmet;	1 Whitsunday Sailing Club
4 Club 13 Begley Street	Panache on the Beach	2 Long-distance Bus Stop
5 Sunlit Waters Holiday Flats	15 Beaches Bar & Bistro	7 Airlie Beach Rentals
6 Airlie Beach Motor Lodge	20 Boardwalk	9 Post Office
8 Whitsunday Wanderers	21 Tequila Willie's	10 Stingers
12 Whitsunday on the Beach	22 Cafe Gourmet	13 Tricks; Club Cafe
16 Beaches Backpackers	23 Cappuccino's Cafe	14 Newsagent
18 Whitsunday Bunkhouse	25 KC's Char Grill	17 Airlie Beach Tourist
19 Magnum's Backpackers	26 Sidewalk Cafe	Information Centre
29 Airlie Beach Hotel	28 Jessie's on the Beach	24 Destination Whitsunday
31 Club Habitat YHA		27 Kelly Dive
32 Backpackers by the Bay		30 Charlie's Round the Bend

QUEENSLAND

the centre run courtesy buses to and from Airlie Beach. It's quite common for hostels to charge around $8 for the first night if you are prepared to pay for two nights up front.

Right in the centre, *Magnum's Backpackers* (☎ 4946 6266) is a huge place, set out in a very pleasant tropical garden with two pools. The emphasis here is on partying – there's a bar/eatery next door with activities each night. The cheapest dorms are the eight-share units at $12 a night; four-share is $14.

Also in the centre is *Beaches Backpackers* (☎ 4946 6244), another big place with a party attitude and its own bar and restaurant. The rooms and facilities in this converted motel are good, with six-bed (not bunk) units with their own bathroom and balcony, TV and air-con, a pool and a good kitchen. Beds cost $14 a night ($13 VIP).

Club 13 Begley St (☎ 4946 7376) has great views over the bay from the hill just above the centre. This modern multilevel place consists of five three-bedroom apartments, each with two bathrooms (some with spa), cooking and laundry facilities. Beds are $14 ($13 VIP/YHA), including breakfast. This place seems to get consistently good reports from travellers.

Sandwiched between Magnum's and Beaches is *Whitsunday Bunkhouse* (☎ 1800 683 566), another converted motel. This place isn't particularly flash, and lacks both a pool and other outdoor areas. The eight-bed units have basic cooking facilities. It's a cheap option with dorms at $10 and doubles at $30.

A little further along Shute Harbour Rd is *Club Habitat YHA* (☎ 4946 6312), yet another motel converted to backpackers' accommodation. A night in a four to six-bed unit with bathroom costs $15, and twin rooms with bathroom cost $35; nonmembers pay an extra $3. There's a pool, good communal kitchen and lounge, and the atmosphere is friendly.

Also in the centre is the *Koala Beach Resort* (☎ 4946 6001), part of the Whitsunday Wanderers Resort. Dormitory accommodation (up to six beds) is $14 ($13 VIP), or there are twins and doubles for $36.

The units sleep up to six people, are air-con and fully self-contained.

A couple of hundred metres out of town towards Shute Harbour is *Backpackers by the Bay* (☎ 4946 7267) at Lot 5, Hermitage Dve. It's a small, relaxed hostel with a good atmosphere, and is generally quieter than those in the centre. It's recently been thoroughly renovated and so boasts excellent facilities. The nightly cost in a small four-bed dorm is $13 and doubles are $30.

The *Bush Village Backpackers' Resort* (☎ 4946 6177), 1.5km west of Airlie Beach in St Martin's Lane, Cannonvale, is a small place with a bar, pool, a pleasant garden setting and comfy four-bed cabins, each with cooking facilities, fridge, bathroom and TV. Bunks range from $10 to $16, twins are $34 and doubles $34 to $44, and the price includes breakfast.

The *Reef Oceania Village* (☎ 4946 6137), in Cannonvale 3km west of Airlie, has a backpacker section with a bed in a six to eight-share bunk room at $14 including breakfast.

Pubs & Motels The *Airlie Beach Hotel* (☎ 4946 6233) on Shute Harbour Rd has standard, unexciting motel units from $39/49 a single/double.

Of the motels, the central *Colonial Court Motel* (☎ 4946 6180) on the corner of Shute Harbour Rd and Broadwater Ave, has doubles from $50, and the *Airlie Beach Motor Lodge* (☎ 4946 6418) on Lamond St has double rooms from $56/62 as well as self-contained units from $80.

Holiday Flats & Resorts In the centre at 26 Shute Harbour Rd, *Whitsunday on the Beach* (☎ 4946 6359) has small, brightly renovated studio apartments from $75 to $85.

Up the hill on the corner of Begley St and Airlie Crescent, *Sunlit Waters* (☎ 4946 6352) has budget studio flats at $40 a double plus $8 for extras. *Boathaven Lodge* (☎ 4946 6421), a couple of hundred metres east of the centre at 440 Shute Harbour Rd, has neat renovated studio units overlooking Boathaven Bay from $50 a double plus $10 for extra adults.

Of the numerous resorts, *Whitsunday Wanderers* (☎ 4946 6446) on Shute Harbour Rd has four pools, two spas, tennis courts, landscaped gardens, a bar and restaurant, and Melanesian-style units for $38 to $54 per person, depending on the season.

Club Crocodile (☎ 1800 075 125) at Cannonvale, 2km west of Airlie Beach, has modern units around a central courtyard, two swimming pools, gym, tennis courts and heated spa, and costs $55 per person including 'tropical' breakfast. The *Coral Sea Resort* (☎ 1800 075 061) at 25 Ocean View Ave overlooks the ocean from a low headland and has double units from $130 ($165 with ocean views).

Places to Eat

Most of the eating possibilities are on, or just off, Shute Harbour Rd in Airlie Beach. If you're preparing your own food there's a small supermarket on the main street near the car park entrance, and a large shopping centre at Canonvale.

Beaches Bar & Bistro is almost always crowded with both travellers and locals, and has salads, pasta and burgers ($5 to $6), roasts, chicken and seafood ($6 to $8) and steak ($12). *Magnum's Bar & Grill* is also popular and has a similar set-up, with pool tables and a video screen. Meals start at $6.

The *Happy Gourmet* at 263 Shute Harbour Rd is a great place for lunch, with delicious filled rolls and sandwiches and home-made cakes. *Cafe Gourmet* at No 289 also has good rolls and sandwiches plus smoothies and juices.

Cappuccino's Cafe in a breezy arcade has focaccias ($6), pasta ($10 to $12) and serious coffee. The *Sidewalk Cafe* on Airlie Esplanade has great fish & chips ($4) while *Jessie's on the Beach* does good breakfast deals for $3.65. The *Club Cafe* is a modern licensed place open all day, with an Asian inspired menu – laksa ($9), tempura ($9) and noodle dishes ($9 to $12). It's just a pity there isn't more outside seating.

The open-air *Boardwalk*, next to

Magnum's, is popular in the evenings, and the pizzas ($10 to $13) are good value. *Panache on the Beach* is a very pleasant open-air place with pasta from $12 to $14 and other mains $18 to $22.

If you must have Mexican, *Tequila Willie's* is open for lunch and dinner and is good value at $9 for main courses, $13 to $18 for grills.

Entertainment

The *Airlie Beach Hotel* has toad races on Tuesday and Thursday nights at 7.30 pm. You can buy a steed for $3 and there are good prizes for the winners (usually boat cruises), and the whole evening is a rowdy, fun event. The pub also has live rock music in the back bar on weekends. Several of the bars and cafes, including *KC's Char Grill* and *Charlie's Round the Bend*, have live music most nights.

There are a couple of nightclubs on Shute Harbour Rd: *Tricks*, upstairs next to the newsagency, and *Stingers* upstairs in an arcade near the post office.

Getting There & Away

Air The closest major airports are at Proserpine and Hamilton Island (Ansett only).

There are a few operators based at the Whitsunday airport, a small airfield about 6km past Airlie Beach towards Shute Harbour. Island Air Taxis (☎ 4946 9933) flies to Hamilton ($45) and Lindeman ($55) islands. Heli Reef (☎ 4946 9102), Coral Air Whitsunday (☎ 4946 9111) and Island Air Taxis do joy flights out over the reef.

Bus Most Greyhound Pioneer and McCafferty's buses make the detour from the highway to Airlie Beach, stopping in the main car park between the shops and beach. Buses run to/from all the main centres along the coast, including Brisbane (18 hours, $103), Mackay (two hours, $24), Townsville (4½ hours, $35) and Cairns (11 hours, $59).

Sampson's (☎ 4945 2377) runs local bus services from Proserpine to Airlie Beach ($6.50) and Shute Harbour ($8.40); buses operate daily from 6 am to 7 pm. Sampson's also meets all flights at Proserpine airport and goes to Airlie Beach ($11) and Shute Harbour ($13).

Boat The sailing club is at the end of Airlie Esplanade. There are notice boards at the Abel Point Marina showing when rides or crewing are available. Ask around Airlie Beach or Shute Harbour.

Getting Around
Several car rental agencies operate locally; Avis, Budget and National all have agencies on Shute Harbour Rd. Airlie Beach Rentals (☎ 4946 6110), on the corner of Begley St and Waterson Rd, has cars from $45 a day and scooters from $30 a day. Whitsunday Taxis can be booked on ☎ 1800 811 388.

CONWAY NATIONAL PARK
The road between Airlie Beach and Shute Harbour passes through Conway National Park, which stretches away north and south along the coast. The southern end of the park separates the Whitsunday Passage from Repulse Bay, named by Captain Cook who strayed into it thinking it was the main passage.

Most of the park comprises rugged ranges and valleys covered in rainforest, but there are a few walking tracks in the surrounding area. The 2.4km walk up to **Mt Rooper lookout**, north of the road, gives good views of the Whitsunday Passage and islands. Another pleasant walk is along Mandalay Rd, about 3km east of Airlie Beach, up to **Mandalay Point** (actually outside the national park).

To reach the beautiful **Cedar Creek Falls**, turn off the Proserpine-Airlie Beach road on to Conway Rd, 8km from Proserpine. It's then about 15km to the falls – the roads are well signposted. At the end of Conway Rd, 27km from the turn-off, is the small settlement of **Conway**, with a beach and a caravan park.

WHITSUNDAY ISLANDS
The 74 Whitsunday Islands are probably the best-known Queensland islands, and one of Australia's pleasure-boating capitals. The group was named by Captain Cook who sailed through here on 3 July 1770. The islands are scattered on both sides of the Whitsunday Passage and are all within 50km of Shute Harbour. The Whitsundays are mostly continental islands – the tips of underwater mountains – but many of them have fringing coral reefs. The actual Great Barrier Reef is at least 60km out from Shute Harbour; Hook Reef is the nearest part of it.

The islands – mostly hilly and wooded – and the passages between them are certainly beautiful, and while a few are developed with tourist resorts, most are uninhabited and several offer the chance of some back-to-nature beach camping and bushwalking. All but four of the Whitsundays are either predominantly or completely national park. The exceptions are Dent Island, and the resort islands of Hamilton, Daydream and Hayman. The other main resorts are on South Molle, Lindeman, Long and Hook islands.

Most people staying in the resorts are on package holidays and, with the exception of the cabins on Hook Island, resort accommodation is beyond the reach of the shoestring traveller. All the resorts offer low-season discounts and standby rates – check with the booking agencies in Airlie Beach.

Camping on the Islands
Although accommodation in the island resorts is mostly expensive, it's possible to camp on several islands. Hook Island has a privately run camping ground and a QNPWS site, and on North Molle, South Molle, Tancred, Whitsunday (three camping areas), Henning, Long, South Repulse, Planton, Lindeman, Thomas and Hook islands you can camp cheaply at QNPWS sites. Self-sufficiency is the key to camping in these sites; some have toilets, but only a few have drinking water, and then not always year-round. You're advised to take five litres of water per person per day, plus three days extra supply in case you get stuck. You must also have a fuel stove as wood fires are banned. The Department of Environment

office (see the Airlie Beach Information section earlier) publishes a leaflet that describes the various sites, and provides detailed information on what to take and do. You can book sites and get camping permits ($3.50 per person per night) here, and the rangers can advise you on the best spots and how to get to them.

Getting There & Away

For information on boat transport to/from the islands, talk to the rangers or contact one of the many booking agencies in Airlie Beach. Island Camping Connection (☎ 4946 5255) will drop you off at Long, North Molle, South Molle, Planton or Tancred Island for $35 return (minimum of two people). Alternatively, for $50 to $65 return per person, a number of the regular day-trip boats will drop you off at the end of a cruise and pick you up again on an agreed date.

Long Island

The closest resort island to the coast, Long Island has three resorts and is nearly all national park. The island is about 11km long but no more than 1.5km wide, and it has lots of rainforest, 13km of walking tracks and some fine lookouts.

At Happy Bay in the north, the *Club Crocodile Resort* (☎ 1800 075 125) is a modern mid-range resort fronting a long expanse of genuine tropical island beach. The resort has two pools, a café, a restaurant, tennis courts, water sports and so on, as well as the obligatory disco. There are three levels of rooms ranging from $50 a double (including transfers) to $190 a double. The cheaper rooms have communal facilities and no air-con, but are about the cheapest resort option.

Two km south, the small *Long Island Palm Bay Hideaway* (☎ 4946 9233) is a low-key, old-fashioned resort with Melanesian style *bures* (cabins), all with verandahs, kitchenettes and bathrooms. The resort is a pleasant reminder of days gone by, and so offers a simple, relaxing stay. Prices are very contemporary, however, with doubles starting at $146/224. Breakfast is $10, lunch $17 and dinner $19.

Whitsundays

Curiously, the Whitsundays are misnamed – Captain Cook didn't really sail through them on Whit Sunday. When he returned to England, it was found that his meticulously kept log was a day out because he had not allowed for crossing the international date line! As he sailed through the Whitsundays and further north, Cook was unaware of the existence of the Great Barrier Reef, although he realised that something to the east of his ship was making the water unusually calm. It wasn't until he ran aground on the Endeavour Reef, near Cooktown, that he finally found out about the reef. ∎

At the southern end of the island is *Whitsunday Wilderness Lodge* (☎ 4946 97 77), a low-key, eco-friendly resort with eight comfortable beachfront cabins. The cost is $1290 per person, per week, including transfers and daily guided boat and walking trips.

Hook Island

Second-largest of the Whitsundays, Hook Island is 53 sq km and rises to a relatively high 450m at Hook Peak. There are a number of beaches dotted around the island. It's mainly national park, with a camping area at Maureens Cove.

The *Hook Island Wilderness Resort* (☎ 4946 9380) is the only true budget resort in the Whitsundays. It's a simple and basic lodge with 12 adjoining bunk units; a bunk costs $14 a night, and doubles are $55. They also have tent sites at $9 per person, and there's a casual restaurant serving cheap breakfasts, lunches and dinners, as well as communal cooking and bathroom facilities.

The island also has an unimpressive underwater observatory ($5). The launch trip to the resort is $25 per person.

The beautiful, fjord-like Nara Inlet on Hook Island is a very popular deep-water anchorage for visiting yachts.

Daydream Island

Tiny Daydream Island, about 1km long and a few hundred metres wide, is the nearest

QUEENSLAND

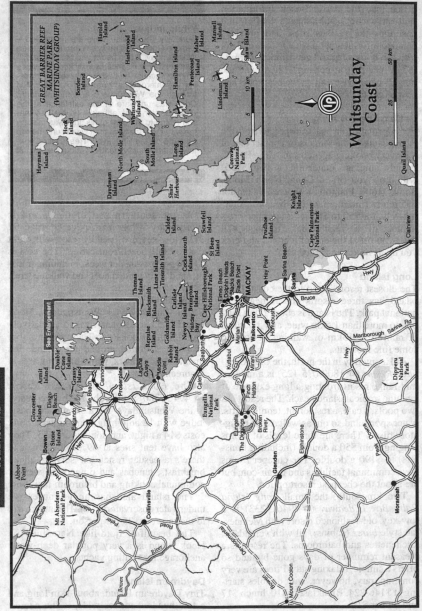

QUEENSLAND

resort island to Shute Harbour. At the northern end is the 300-room *Daydream Island Travelodge Resort* (☎ 1800 075 040), a modern resort catering mainly for families. Rooms start at $123 per person including meals, transfers, use of tennis courts, a gym, pools, water sports gear etc.

Daydream has a good day-trippers' section at the southern end, with a pool, bar and cafe, and water sports gear for hire. The return trip from Shute Harbour costs $22.

South Molle Island

At 4 sq km, South Molle is the largest of the Molle group of islands and it is virtually joined to Mid Molle and North Molle. It has long stretches of beach and is crisscrossed by walking tracks. The highest point is 198m Mt Jeffreys, but the climb up Spion Kop is also worthwhile. You can spend a day walking on the island for the cost of the $22 ferry trip.

Most of South Molle is national park but there's the *South Molle Island Resort* (☎ 1300 363 300) in the north, where the boats come in. It's one of the older resorts, with straightforward motel-style rooms, a small golf course, a gym, tennis courts and water sports gear. Nightly costs range from $310 to $370 per person (single or double), which includes all meals and activities. Dozens of rainbow lorikeets fly in to feed every day at 3 pm.

Hamilton Island (pop 1500)

The most heavily developed resort island in the Whitsundays, Hamilton is about 5 sq km and rises to 200m at Passage Peak. It is more like a town than a resort, having its own airport, a 200-boat marina, shops, restaurants and bars, and accommodation for more than 2000 people, including three high-rise tower blocks. Not surprisingly, the range of entertainment is extensive (and expensive): helicopter joy rides, game fishing, parasailing, cruising, scuba diving, nine restaurants, squash courts and a hill-top fauna reserve with wombats, crocodiles and koalas. The cheapest double room costs $130/160 a night, ranging up to $1200 a night for your own private villa. Meals cost $15 for breakfast, $45 for breakfast and dinner. For reservations phone ☎ 1800 075 110.

Hamilton can make an interesting day trip from Shute Harbour ($36 return for the launch only), and you can use all of the resort facilities.

The airport is used mainly by people jetting between resort islands, with launches and helicopters laid on to whisk them off to their chosen spots. Ansett flies non-stop between Hamilton and Brisbane ($322 one way), Cairns ($254), Melbourne ($540) and Sydney ($453).

Hayman Island

The most northerly of the Whitsundays, Hayman is 4 sq km, and rises to 250m above sea level. It has forested hills, valleys and beaches. Owned by Ansett, Hayman has become such an exclusive resort that day trips no longer call there. The nearest you'll probably get is some of the reefs or small islands nearby such as Black Island (also called Bali Hai) or Arkhurst, Langford or Bird islands.

The *Hayman Island Resort* (☎ 1800 075 175), fronted by a wide, shallow reef that emerges from the water at low tide, is a luxurious five-star hotel dripping with style. Rooms range from $460 for Palm Garden rooms to $1500 a night for a suite, all including breakfast.

Lindeman Island

One of the most southerly of the Whitsundays, Lindeman covers 8 sq km, most of which is national park. The island has 20km of walking trails and the highest point is 210m Mt Oldfield. Lindeman has plenty of little beaches and secluded bays, and there are also a lot of small islands dotted around, some of which are easy to get across to.

The *Club Med Resort* (☎ 1800 807 973) in the south has a pool, several restaurants, a bar, a golf course, tennis and lots of water-based activities. Nightly tariffs range from $199 plus a one-off $50 membership, including all meals and most activities. The internationally famous Club Med style is

Workers' Hostels

With casual labour and seasonal work being very much part of the working holiday scene in Queensland, there are a number of hostels, principally along the coast, which attract itinerant workers – and backpackers – in search of a job.

Most of these hostels are OK, if a little seedy, and the owners are usually helpful in finding work for people and are often involved in the industries themselves.

Unfortunately some of the hostels are run by people who exploit the fact that the people staying with them are often low on cash and may be desperate for work. Be wary of accepting accommodation or other services free in advance,' as we have received many letters from travellers complaining that they are paid minimal wages and can basically only work for their food and board and don't actually get to save anything.

In addition to this problem it also seems that some hostel owners are not averse to using threats to intimidate travellers into staying almost against their will – 'a cross between Basil Fawlty and Charles Manson' was a description we received from a disgruntled backpacker about one overbearing hostel owner.

The best bet is to try and talk to other travellers who have stayed at a place, and not to accept accommodation, transport or other services in lieu of pay. ■

very evident here, with a heavy emphasis on fun, fun, fun.

There is a QNPWS camp site at Boat Port.

Day trips to Lindeman cost $108 from Shute Harbour, but this is a *long* day with many hours spent on the boat getting to and from. You can also fly there with Island Air Taxis ($55 one way, $65 day return) from Whitsunday airport on the mainland, or with Helijet from Mackay ($95).

Whitsunday Island

The largest of the Whitsundays, this island covers 109 sq km and rises to 438m at Whitsunday Peak. There's no resort, but 6km-long Whitehaven Beach on the south-east coast is the longest and finest beach in the group (some say in the country!), with good snorkelling off its southern end. There are QNPWS camping areas at Dugong, Sawmill and Joe's beaches, all on the west side of the island.

Getting Around

Air Hamilton and Lindeman islands are the only islands with airports. See the Airlie Beach Getting There & Away section for details of flights from the mainland.

Boat There's a bamboozling array of boat trips heading out to the islands. Fantasea

Cruises (☎ 4946 5111) and Whitsunday Allover (☎ 4946 6900) are the two major operators for transfers to the islands – most of their boats depart from Shute Harbour. Island transfers cost between $20 and $35 return depending on the distance involved; you can also buy tickets that combine visits to two or more islands.

In addition, there are literally dozens of different cruises and pleasure trips heading out to the islands and reefs; these depart from either Shute Harbour or the Abel Point Marina near Airlie Beach.

Depending on how much time and money you have, you can choose from the following: day trips to the islands or reefs from $50 to $120; overnight cruises from $120; two-night/three-day trips from $250; or self-skippered charter yachts from about $275 for three days (sailing experience required).

All of the boats and trips are different, so it's worth speaking to a couple of the booking agents to find out which trip will suit you. There are leisurely sailing cruises to uninhabited islands, high-speed diving trips to outer reefs, fishing expeditions, and cruises that take in several destinations. Most trips include activities such as snorkelling and boom netting, with scuba diving as an optional extra. It's worth asking how many people will be on your boat.

Most of the cruise operators do bus pick-ups from Airlie Beach. You can bus to Shute Harbour or you can leave your car in the Shute Harbour car park for $7 for 24 hours. There's a lock-up car park a few hundred metres back along the road by the Shell service station, costing $5 from 8 am to 5 pm or $8 for 24 hours.

Roylen's Cruises has weekend trips from Mackay to Hamilton and Lindeman islands – see the earlier Mackay section for details.

BOWEN (pop 8900)

Bowen, founded in 1861, was the first coastal settlement north of Rockhampton. Although soon overshadowed by Mackay to the south and Townsville to the north, Bowen survived, and today it is a thriving fruit and vegetable-growing centre. It isn't much of a tourist town, but lots of travellers come here looking for seasonal picking work.

The Bowen Historical Museum at 22 Gordon St has displays relating to the town's early history. It's open weekdays and Sunday morning. Just north of Bowen, a string of sandy beaches, some of them quite secluded, dot the coast around the cape.

There's a helpful tourist office at 34 Williams St.

Places to Stay

There are three 'workers hostels' in Bowen that specialise in finding seasonal picking (mainly tomatoes) for travellers. All three are fairly basic, and have buses that do pick-ups and run workers to and from work (sometimes free, Barnacles is $4). It's a competitive scene, and it's worth ringing around before you come, to find out what's available.

Barnacles Backpackers (☎ 4786 4400) at 16 Gordon St, has two sections, with dorm beds at $12 and doubles $28. It can get quite crowded however, and the kitchen facilities are woefully inadequate. As it is essentially a workers hostel, you may not feel comfortable here if you are just passing through.

The long-running *Bowen Backpackers* (☎ 4786 3433) is nearby at 56 Herbert St (the main road). It has a good reputation for finding fruit-picking work, although the owners may get very annoyed if, after finding you work, you move elsewhere, such as the (cheaper) caravan park. The nightly cost is $13 in four to eight-bed dorms.

The latest hostel to open here is *Trinity's Backpackers* (☎ 4786 4199) at 93 Horseshoe Bay Rd. It has five or 10-share self-contained units at $11 a night. Once again, help is given to find work.

Getting There & Away

The long-distance bus stop is outside the Traveland travel agency (☎ 4786 2835) on William St, near the centre. There are buses along the coast to Rockhampton (7½ hours, $74), Airlie Beach (one hour, $21) and Townsville (2½ hours, $31). The *Sunlander* and *Queenslander* trains also stop at Bowen (at Bootooloo Siding, 3km south of the centre). The economy fare from Brisbane is $139 in a sleeper.

North Coast

AYR TO TOWNSVILLE

Ayr (pop 8700) is on the delta of one of the biggest rivers in Queensland, the Burdekin, and it is the major commercial centre for the rich farmlands and cane fields of the Burdekin Valley. On Wilmington St, the Ayr Nature Display has exhibits of preserved butterflies, moths and beetles; it's open daily from 8 am to 5 pm ($2.50). South across the Burdekin River is **Home Hill**, where you can visit the bizarre Ashworth's Fantastic Tourist Attraction with its tacky souvenir shop, pottery gallery and collection of fossils, gemstones and rocks ($2).

Between Ayr and Townsville is the turn-off to the Australian Institute of Marine Science on Cape Ferguson. You can visit it on weekdays from 9 am to 3 pm, and between March and November there are free guided tours every Friday at 10 am.

About 60km north-west of Ayr and 86km south of Townsville there's another turn-off from the Bruce Highway to the **Bowling**

Green Bay National Park. It's 6km from the highway to the park, where there's a good camping ground (firewood provided) and a ranger station (☎ 4778 8203) near Alligator Creek. There are two long walking trails (17 and 8km return) and the creek has good swimming holes. Alligator Creek tumbles down between two rugged ranges that rise steeply from the coastal plains. The taller range peaks in Mt Elliot (1234m), whose higher slopes harbour some of Queensland's most southerly tropical rainforest. There's no public transport to the park, and the main gate is closed between sundown and 6.30 am.

TOWNSVILLE (pop 109,900)

The fourth-largest city in Queensland, Townsville is the port city for the agricultural and mining production of the vast inland region of northern Queensland. Founded in 1864 through the efforts of a Scot, John Melton Black, and the money of Robert Towns, a Sydney-based sea captain and financier, Townsville developed mainly on the back of Chinese and Kanaka labour.

Today Townsville is a working city, a major armed forces base, and the site of James Cook University. It's the start of the main highway from Queensland all the way across to the Northern Territory. It's the only departure point for Magnetic Island (20 minutes away by ferry), and the Barrier Reef is about 1¾ hours away by fast catamaran.

From a travellers' point of view, Townsville hasn't really got a lot going for it. The city's main attractions are the excellent aquarium at the Great Barrier Reef Wonderland, and as an access point for Magnetic Island.

In recent years redevelopment of the Flinders St East and Palmer St heritage areas on opposite sides of Ross Creek has given the Townsville city centre a real lift.

Orientation

Townsville centres on Ross Creek and is dominated by 290m-high Castle Hill, which has a lookout perched on top. The city sprawls a long way, but the centre is a fairly compact area that you can easily get around on foot.

The transit centre, the arrival and departure point for long-distance buses, is on Palmer St, just south of Ross Creek. The city centre is immediately to the north of the creek, over the Dean St bridge. Flinders St Mall stretches to the left from the northern side of the bridge, towards the train station. To the right of the bridge is the Flinders St East area, which contains many of the town's oldest buildings, plus cafes, restaurants, the Great Barrier Reef Wonderland and the ferry terminal.

Information

Townsville Enterprises' main tourist information office (☎ 4778 3555) is on the Bruce Highway, 8km south of the city centre. There's also a more convenient information booth (☎ 4721 3660) in the middle of Flinders St Mall, between Stokes and Denham Sts. It's open Monday to Saturday from 9 am to 5 pm and Sunday to 12.30 pm. The RACQ (☎ 4721 4888) is at 635 Sturt St close to the city centre. The main post office can be found on the corner of Flinders St Mall and Denham St. There's also a Department of Environment information office (☎ 4721 2399) at the Wonderland, open from Monday to Friday from 9 am to 5 pm, and Saturday from 1 to 5 pm.

The Mary Who bookshop on Stanley St has Internet/email access ($5 per half hour), as does the Transit Centre Backpackers ($2 per five minutes).

Great Barrier Reef Wonderland

Townsville's top attraction is at the end of Flinders St East beside Ross Creek. Although its impressive aquarium is the highlight, there are several other sections including a theatre, a museum, shops and the Great Barrier Reef Marine Park Authority office.

Aquarium The huge main tank has a living coral reef and hundreds of reef fish, sharks, rays and other marine life, and you can walk beneath the tank through a clear domed

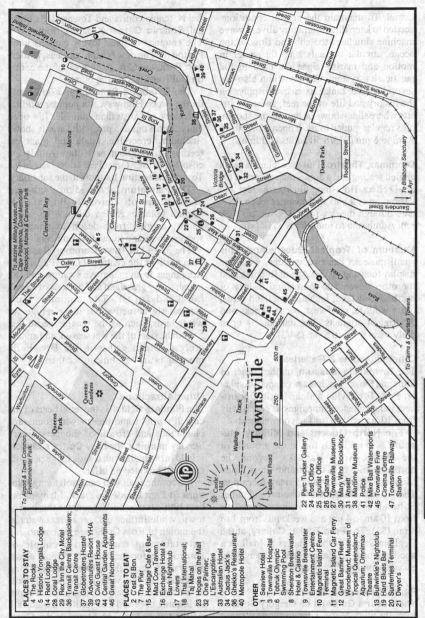

Townsville

PLACES TO STAY
4 The Rocks
5 Historic Yongala Lodge
14 Reef Lodge
28 Coral Lodge
29 Rex Inn the City Motel
36 Transit Centre Backpackers;
   Transit Centre
37 Globetrotters Hostel
39 Adventurers Resort YHA
43 Civic Guest House
44 Central Garden Apartments
46 Great Northern Hotel

PLACES TO EAT
2 C'est Si Bon
7 The Pier
15 Heritage Cafe & Bar;
   Mad Cow Tavern
16 Exchange Hotel &
   Bank Nightclub
17 Lovers
18 Thai International;
   Taj Mahal
23 Hoges on the Mall
32 One Palmer;
   L'Escargotière
33 Australian Hotel
34 Cactus Jack's
36 Ghekko's Restaurant
40 Metropole Hotel

OTHER
1 Seaview Hotel
3 Townsville Hospital
6 Tobruk Olympic
   Swimming Pool
8 Sheraton Breakwater
   Hotel & Casino
9 Townsville Breakwater
   Entertainment Centre
10 Magnetic Island Ferry
   Terminal
11 Magnetic Island Car Ferry
12 Great Barrier Reef
   Wonderland; Museum of
   Tropical Queensland;
   Aquarium; Omnimax
   Theatre
13 Bullwinkle's Nightclub
19 Hard Blues Bar
20 Sunferries Terminal
21 Dwyer's
22 Perc Tucker Gallery
24 Post Office
25 Tourist Office
26 Qantas
27 Townsville Museum
30 Mary Who Bookshop
31 Ansett
38 Maritime Museum
41 Police
42 Mike Ball Watersports
45 Townsville Five
   Cinema Centre
47 Townsville Railway
   Station

QUEENSLAND

tunnel. To maintain the natural conditions needed to keep this community alive, a wave machine simulates the ebb and flow of the ocean, circular currents keep the water in motion and marine algae are used in the purification system. The aquarium also has several smaller tanks, extensive displays on the history and life of the reef, and a theatrette where slide-shows on the reef are shown, plus regular guided tours. It opens daily from 9 am to 5 pm ($13/6.50 adults/children).

Omnimax Theatre This is a cinema with angled seating and a dome-shaped screen for a 3-D effect. Hour-long films on the reef and various other topics such as outer space alternate through the day from 9.30 am till 4.30 pm. Admission to one film is $11.50/6.

Museum of Tropical Queensland This small museum has two sections, with one display focusing on the 'Age of Reptiles' and the other devoted to the natural history of north Queensland, including wetland birds, other wildlife, rainforest, ocean wrecks and Aboriginal artefacts. The museum is open daily from 9 am to 5 pm ($4/2).

Other Museums & Galleries
The **Townsville Museum**, on the corner of Sturt and Stokes Sts, has a permanent display on early Townsville and the North Queensland independence campaigns. It's open daily from 10 am to 3 pm (to 1 pm on weekends).

The **North Queensland Military Museum** is in an 1890s fort in the grounds of the Jezzine Army Barracks, beyond the northern end of The Strand; it is open Monday, Wednesday and Friday mornings. There's also a **Maritime Museum** on Palmer St beside Ross Creek; it is open weekdays from 10 am to 4 pm and weekends from 1 to 4 pm ($3). The **Perc Tucker Gallery**, at the Denham St end of the Flinders St Mall, is a good regional art gallery that is open daily except Monday (free entry).

Parks, Gardens & Sanctuaries
The **Queens Gardens** on Gregory St, 1km from the town centre, contain sports playing fields, tennis courts and Townsville's original **Botanic Gardens**, dating from 1878. The entrance to these lovely gardens is on Paxton St. The new botanic gardens, **Anderson Park**, are 6km south-west of the centre on Gulliver St, Mundingburra.

The **Billabong Sanctuary**, 17km south on the Bruce Highway, is a popular wildlife sanctuary of Australian animals. It's open daily from 8 am to 5 pm, with various shows (including crocodile, koala and giant eel feeding) throughout each day. Admission costs $18/9. See Organised Tours later in the Townsville section for tours to the sanctuary.

The **Palmetum**, about 15km south-west of the centre off University Rd, is a 25-hectare botanic garden devoted to native palms, ranging from desert to rainforest species, in their natural environments.

The 32 sq km **Town Common Reserve**, 5km north of the centre off Cape Pallarenda Rd, ranges from mangrove swamps and salt marsh to dry grassland and pockets of woodland and forest. The common isn't particularly attractive but it's a refuge for water birds, such as the magpie geese that herald the start of the wet season, and stately brolgas, which gather in the Dry. Early morning is the best time to see them.

Other Attractions
The **Flinders St Mall** is the retail heart of the city. It's bright and breezy with fountains, plantations and crowds of shoppers. Every Sunday morning, the busy **Cotter's Market** is held in the mall, with a wide range of crafts and local produce on offer.

East of the mall you can stroll along **Flinders St East** beside the creek. Many of the best 19th-century buildings are in this part of town, while further out, on a breakwater at the mouth of Ross Creek, are the casino, the entertainment centre and a couple of upmarket seafood restaurants. A more pleasant walk is north along **The Strand**, a long beachfront drive with a marina, gardens, some awesome banyan trees, the Tobruk swimming pool and a big artificial waterfall. At the top end of The Strand is the **Coral**

Memorial Rockpool, a large artificial swimming pool on the edge of the ocean.

Activities
Diving Townsville has four or five diving schools, including one of Australia's best – Mike Ball Watersports (☎ 4772 3022) at 252 Walker St. Five-day certificate courses start twice a week and cost either $395 with two separate day trips to the reef or alternatively $480 with two days/three nights on the reef, staying on board their boat *Watersport*. You have to take a $50 medical before you start the course.

Pro-Dive (☎ 4721 1760), another well-regarded dive school, has an office in the Great Barrier Reef Wonderland. Pro-Dive's weekly five-day certificate course costs $480 and also includes two nights and three days on the reef, with a total of eight dives.

You can get cheap or free accommodation at some hostels if you book a dive course from that hostel.

For experienced divers, the wreck of the *Yongala*, a passenger liner that sank off Cape Bowling Green in 1911 with 122 lives lost, is more of an attraction than the John Brewer Reef, which is the destination for many day trips. The *Yongala* has huge numbers of fish and other marine life, including turtles and rays. John Brewer Reef has been damaged by the crown-of-thorns starfish and cyclones, and parts of the reef have little live coral. Mike Ball and Pro-Dive both run trips out to the *Yongala* (from $165).

Other Activities Risky Business (☎ 4725 4571) has abseiling ($54) and skyseiling (like a huge flying fox, $79), and Coral Sea Skydivers (☎ 4725 6780) will let you throw yourself out of a plane for $197 (tandem dive); freefall courses cost $390.

Tour de Townsville Bicycle Tours (☎ 4721 2026) has a variety of cycling tours ($25 to $29) as well as bikes for hire.

Organised Tours
Pure Pleasure Cruises (☎ 4721 3555) has five trips a week out to Kelso Reef on the outer reef. The cost of $130 (children $65) includes lunch and snorkelling gear; scuba dives are an optional extra.

Detours (☎ 4721 5977) offers a variety of tours in and around Townsville, including a city sights tour (weekdays, two hours, $22), tours to the Billabong Sanctuary (daily, 3½ hours, $29), or Charters Towers (Monday and Wednesday, eight hours, $67), and cruises to Dunk and Bedarra Islands (Thursday and Sunday, $98).

Places to Stay
Camping There are two caravan parks which are only about 3km from the centre. The better choice is the *Rowes Bay Caravan Park* (☎ 4771 3576), opposite the beach on Heatley Pde in Rowes Bay. Tent sites are $13 and on-site cabins start from $38. The *Town & Country Caravan Park* (☎ 4772 1487) at 16 Kings Rd, West End, has tent sites for $10, on-site vans from $25 and cabins from $45.

Hostels Townsville's hostel scene is probably the best example of large operators jumping on the budget accommodation bandwagon. Two huge hostels in Townsville is at least one too many, and the resulting oversupply of beds means that the general standard of hostels here is not as good as in many other towns along the coast.

On the south side of Ross Creek there are at least three hostels that are conveniently close to the transit centre but a bit isolated from the town centre. The huge *Adventurers Resort YHA* (☎ 4721 1522) at 79 Palmer St is a multilevel complex with over 300 beds, a shop and a swimming pool. The facilities are quite good, but because of its size it tends to feel impersonal. Accommodation in a four-bunk dorm costs $14 for YHA members, singles/doubles cost $24/32. Non-members pay an extra $3 per person.

Townsville's other huge offering is the *Transit Centre Backpackers* (☎ 1800 628 836), which is upstairs on top of the transit centre. It's big, clean and charmless, but if you really want to stay on top of a bus station they have dorm beds for $14 and singles/doubles for $25/32. Their free evening city tour is popular.

QUEENSLAND

Between these two places is the smaller *Globetrotters Hostel* (☎ 4771 3242), behind a house at 45 Palmer St. It's a relaxed, old-style hostel with all the usual facilities – kitchen area, lounge, pool, laundry – and it is clean and well-run. Six-bed dorms cost $13 per night, singles cost $26, and a twin room is $32.

The other hostels are on the north side of Ross Creek, in and around the city centre. The pick of this bunch is the *Civic Guest House* (☎ 4771 5381) at 262 Walker St. This clean and easy-going hostel has three or four-bed dorms for $14, six-bed dorms with bathroom and air-con for $16, and pleasant singles/doubles from $28/33, or $48 with air-con and private bathroom. Their courtesy bus does pick-ups and there's a free barbecue on Friday night.

The *Reef Lodge* (☎ 4721 1112) at 4 Wickham St is another small, old-fashioned but fairly clean place with a variety of rooms in several buildings. Dorm beds start at $12 and singles/doubles at $28/32. Most rooms have coin-in-the-slot air-con.

Pubs & Guesthouses The *Great Northern Hotel* (☎ 4771 6191), across the road from the train station at 500 Flinders St, is a good old-fashioned pub with clean, simple rooms at $20/30, and a few doubles with private bathrooms at $40; the food downstairs is good. At 32 Hale St, the *Coral Lodge* (☎ 4771 5512) is a neat, friendly guesthouse in a renovated Queenslander building, with air-con rooms from $38/48 as well as self-contained units from $48, including a light breakfast.

The *Rocks* (☎ 4771 5700) at 20 Cleveland Tce is a superb, renovated historic home with great views over the bay. All the rooms have period furnishings and are great value at $78/88 including breakfast. Evening meals are available on request.

Motels & Holiday Units Cheaper motels include the *Tropical Hideaway Motel* (☎ 4771 4355) at 74 The Strand, with doubles from $55; the central *Rex Inn the City* (☎ 4771 6048) at 143 Wills St, with

rooms from $70; and the *Beach House Motel* (☎ 4721 1333) at 66 The Strand, with rooms at $59/65.

The *Historic Yongala Lodge* (☎ 4772 4633) at 11 Fryer St has modern motel units and self-contained rooms from $69/79 and heritage-style units from $80, as well as a good Greek restaurant at the front (see Places to Eat).

The *Townsville Seaside Apartments* (☎ 4721 3155) at 105 The Strand has renovated 1960s-style air-con one-bedroom apartments from $55 a double or two-bedroom from $90.

The high-rise *Aquarius on the Beach* (☎ 4772 4255) at 75 The Strand has excellent self-contained suites (only), complete with great views, from $110 for two.

Places to Eat
Flinders St East is the main area for eateries, and it offers plenty of choice. The *Heritage Cafe & Bar* is a modern, cosy place with light meals (pasta etc) from $8 to $10, other mains are slightly more.

The *Thai International Restaurant*, upstairs at No 235, has fine soups for $6, a good range of vegetarian dishes from $6 to $9 and other mains from $10 to $14. Downstairs is the *Taj Mahal*, an Indian and Persian restaurant with vegetarian dishes from $11 to $14, others are $15 to $18.

On the same street is *Lovers*, a trendy cafe/restaurant with a downstairs licensed cafe section (main courses $12 to $15) and a slightly more formal upstairs section ($17 to $20). The Exchange Hotel has the pleasant *Thai Exchange* upstairs on the balcony (mains $9 to $14) and the casual *Portraits Wine Bar* with bistro-type meals.

Still in Flinders St, but on the Mall, is *Hoges on the Mall*, a family restaurant with main meals at $13 to $16, and breakfast from $6.

The *casino* has amazingly cheap (and low glam) meals for the punters – $6 gets you a roast and vegies.

Many of the pubs also do decent counter meals. The *Great Northern Hotel*, on the corner of Flinders and Blackwood Sts, has an excellent bistro with mains from $10 to $12 and good bar meals from $5 to $8. The *Seaview Hotel*, on the corner of The Strand and Gregory St, is another popular pub, and it has a pleasant beer garden.

C'est Si Bon, on Eyre St near the Gregory St corner, is a good little gourmet deli with salads, sandwiches and other home-made goodies.

South of the river, Palmer St also has some good pubs and eateries. *One Palmer*, on the corner of Palmer and Dean Sts, is a modern licensed cafe (mains $14 to $18), while next door is *L'Escargotiére*, a simple BYO French restaurant.

Further along, in front of the transit centre, is *Ghekko's*, a training restaurant staffed by catering students. The full works here, including silver service and starched linen, costs just $9 for main courses. It's open for lunch Wednesday to Friday, for dinner Wednesday to Sunday.

At No 21 is *Cactus Jack's Bar & Grill* (☎ 4721 1478), a lively licensed Mexican place with main courses in the $10 to $14 range; you'll need to book on weekends. The *Metropole Hotel*, next to the YHA, has good bistro meals in the rear beer garden, or there's more formal dining in its *La Met* restaurant.

The *Historic Yongala Lodge* is fronted by a Greek restaurant in a lovely 19th-century building with period furnishings, memorabilia and finds from the *Yongala* shipwreck. Main meals are in the $18 to $25 range. The *Pier*, on the breakwater on Sir Leslie Thiess Dve, is an upmarket seafood restaurant with lunchtime mains at $20 and evening meals from $20 to $25.

Entertainment

Townsville's lively nightlife also centres on Flinders St East. The *Hard Blues Bar* at No 237 is the main venue for live music, and has a different theme each night. *Portraits Wine Bar*, at the Exchange Hotel at No 151, attracts an older, more sophisticated crowd. Nearby at No 169 is the *Bank*, the city's most upmarket nightclub; it's open nightly till late, with a small cover charge and dress regulations. *Bullwinkle's Cabaret & Bar*, on the corner of Flinders St East and Wickham St, is another popular nightclub.

The *Mad Cow Tavern* is a new bar on Flinders St East, and close by is *Dwyer's*, an Irish bar with live music Wednesday to Saturday – and Guinness, of course.

Along The Strand, the popular *Seaview Hotel*, on the corner of Gregory St, has live music in the beer garden, as well as the Arizona Bar and Breezes (an over-28s nightclub) upstairs with occasional rock and roll bands.

The *Townsville Five Cinema Centre*, on the corner of Sturt and Blackwood Sts, shows mainstream current releases. The impressive *Townsville Breakwater Entertainment Centre* (☎ 4771 4000) is the main venue for concerts, the performing arts and other cultural events.

If you have the right clothes and fancy trying your luck on the spin of the wheel, the *Sheraton Breakwater Casino* is at the end of Sir Leslie Thiess Dve, beyond Flinders St East.

Getting There & Away

Air Ansett and Qantas have daily flights between Townsville and all the major cities, including Cairns ($176), Brisbane ($363) and Alice Springs ($431). Ansett and Qantas both have offices in the Flinders St Mall.

Sunstate/Qantas has flights within Queensland to Dunk Island ($129), Mackay ($204), Proserpine ($169), Rockhampton ($291), Gladstone and Bundaberg, while Flight West flies to Mt Isa ($289), often with stops at smaller places on the way, plus Mackay ($204) and Rockhampton ($291).

Bus All long-distance buses operate from the transit centre on Palmer St. Both Greyhound Pioneer and McCafferty's have frequent services up and down the coastal Bruce Highway. Fares and travel times from Townsville include Brisbane (20 hours, $119), Rockhampton (nine hours, $73), Mackay (4½ hours, $47), Airlie Beach (four hours, $35), Mission Beach (3½ hours, $33) and Cairns (six hours, $37). There are also daily services inland to Mt Isa (12 hours,

QUEENSLAND

$81) via Charters Towers (1¾ hours, $14), continuing on to the Northern Territory.

Train The Brisbane-Cairns *Sunlander* travels through Townsville three times a week. From Brisbane to Townsville takes 22 hours ($148 for an economy sleeper, $226 for a 1st-class sleeper). From Townsville, Proserpine ($36/57 economy/1st class seat) is a four-hour journey, Rockhampton is 11 hours ($77/122) and Cairns is 7½ hours ($41/65). The faster and more luxurious *Queenslander* does the Brisbane-Cairns run once a week – the Brisbane-Townsville fare is $344 which includes all meals and a sleeping compartment.

The *Inlander* heads inland twice-weekly from Townsville to Mt Isa (18 hours, $125/192 in economy/1st-class sleeper) via Charters Towers (three hours, $20/32).

Car Rental The larger car-rental agencies are all represented in Townsville. Smaller operators include Rent-a-Rocket (☎ 4772 1442), 14 Dean St, South Townsville; Sunrunner Moke Hire (☎ 4721 5038) at 11 Anthony St, South Townsville; and Townsville Car Rentals (☎ 4772 1093) at 12 Palmer St (near the transit centre).

Getting Around
To/From the Airport Townsville airport is 5km north-west of the city at Garbutt; a taxi to the centre costs $10. The Airport Shuttle (☎ 4775 5544) services all main arrivals and departures. The shuttle costs $5/8 one-way/return and will drop you off or pick you up almost anywhere fairly central.

Bus Sunbus runs local bus services around Townsville. Route maps and timetables are available in the Transit Mall (near the Flinders St Mall tourist office).

Taxi For a taxi in Townsville, call Standard White Cabs (☎ 13 1008).

MAGNETIC ISLAND (pop 2100)
Tourists first came to Magnetic Island from the mainland more than 100 years ago,

making it one of Queensland's oldest resort islands. Although popular, it remains a somewhat old-fashioned resort island, with the main attractions being its fine beaches, excellent bushwalks, abundant wildlife as well as laid-back atmosphere. It's also cheap and easy to get to, being only 8km offshore from Townsville (15 minutes by ferry).

Magnetic Island was named by Captain Cook, who thought his ship's compass went funny when he sailed by in 1770. It's dominated by 494m Mt Cook.

Magnetic is one of the larger reef islands (52 sq km) and about half of it is national park. The island is surrounded by the Great Barrier Reef Marine Park, and so there are restrictions on fishing and collecting in some areas of the island.

There are several small towns along the coast and the island has quite a different atmosphere to the purely resort islands along the reef – it's almost an outer suburb of Townsville, with many of the 2500 residents commuting to the mainland by ferry.

Orientation & Information
Magnetic Island is roughly triangular in shape. Picnic Bay, the main town and ferry pier, is at the southern corner. There's a road up the eastern side of the island to Horseshoe Bay and there's a rough track along the west coast. Along the north coast it's walking only.

The Island Travel Centre (☎ 4778 5155) has an information centre and booking office between the end of the pier and the mall in Picnic Bay. You can book local tours and accommodation here, and organise domestic and international travel arrangements. There's a Department of Environment office (☎ 4778 5378) on Hurst St in Picnic Bay.

Picnic Bay
Picnic Bay is the main settlement, and the stop for the ferries. The mall along the waterfront has a good selection of shops and eateries, and you can hire bikes, cars, scooters and mokes here. Picnic Bay also has quite a few places to stay, and the main beach has

a stinger-free enclosure and is patrolled by a life-saving club.

There's a lookout above the town and just to the west of Picnic Bay is **Cockle Bay** with the wreck of the *City of Adelaide*. Heading around the coast in the other direction is **Rocky Bay** where there's a short, steep walk down to its beautiful beach. The popular **Picnic Bay Golf Course** is open to the public.

Nelly Bay

Next up the coast is Nelly Bay, which has a good beach with shade and a reef at low tide. At the far end of the bay there are some pioneer graves. The north end of the bay is marred by the half-finished marina project which was abandoned some years ago after the developers went broke.

Arcadia

Around the headland is **Geoffrey Bay**, with an interesting 400m low-tide reef walk over the fringing coral reef from the southern end of the beach; a board indicates the start of the trail.

Overlooking the bay is the town of Arcadia, with shops, more places to stay and the Arcadia Hotel Resort (where there are live bands at weekends and a pool that is open to the public). Just around the next headland is the very pleasant **Alma Bay beach**.

Radical Bay & the Forts

The road runs back from the coast until you reach the junction of the road to Radical Bay. You can go straight to Horseshoe Bay, take the central track via the Forts, or turn right to Radical Bay (rough vehicle track), with walking tracks leading off it to secluded Arthur and Florence bays, and the old **Searchlight Station** on the headland between the two bays.

From Radical Bay you can walk across the headland to beautiful **Balding Bay** (an unof-

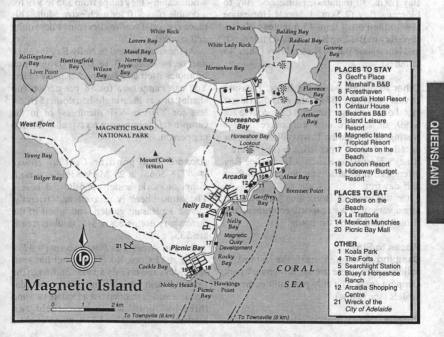

Magnetic Island

PLACES TO STAY
3 Geoff's Place
7 Marshall's B&B
8 Foresthaven
10 Arcadia Hotel Resort
11 Centaur House
13 Beaches B&B
15 Island Leisure Resort
16 Magnetic Island Tropical Resort
17 Coconuts on the Beach
18 Dunoon Resort
19 Hideaway Budget Resort

PLACES TO EAT
2 Cotters on the Beach
9 La Trattoria
14 Mexican Munchies
20 Picnic Bay Mall

OTHER
1 Koala Park
4 The Forts
5 Searchlight Station
6 Bluey's Horseshoe Ranch
12 Arcadia Shopping Centre
21 Wreck of the City of Adelaide

QUEENSLAND

ficial nude bathing beach) and **Horseshoe Bay**.

Horseshoe Bay

Horseshoe Bay, on the north coast of the island, has a few shops, accommodation and a long stretch of beach. There's a fairly desolate **Koala Park**, which is quite a long drive off the main road, and a **mango plantation**, signposted off the main road, which you can visit. At the beach there are boats, sailboards and canoes for hire. From the beach you can walk to Maud Bay, around to the west, or over to Radical Bay.

Activities

Bushwalking The Department of Environment produces a leaflet for Magnetic Island's excellent bushwalking tracks. Possible walks, with distances and one-way travel times, include: Nelly Bay to Arcadia (6km, 2 hours); Picnic Bay to West Point (8km, 2½ hours); Horseshoe Bay road to Arthur Bay (2km, 30 minutes); Horseshoe Bay to Florence Bay (2.5km, 1 hour); Horseshoe Bay to the Forts (2km, 45 minutes); Horseshoe Bay to Balding Bay (3km, 45 minutes); and Horseshoe Bay to Radical Bay (3km, 45 minutes).

Other Activities Magnetic Island Pleasure Divers (☎ 4778 5788) at the Arcadia Resort Hotel offers a basic five-day dive course for $199, or a more comprehensive course costing $295. (See the Townsville section for details of dive operators based there.) Bluey's Horseshoe Ranch at Horseshoe Bay offers trail rides at $18 an hour or $45 for a half-day trot.

On the beach at Horseshoe Bay you can hire a variety of water sports equipment and fishing dinghies by the hour.

Places to Stay

Camping Although half the island is national park, there are no designated park camping areas. The only possibilities are the hostels (see below).

Hostels There's a good selection of back-

packers' hostels on the island and it's a competitive scene, with several hostels sending vehicles to meet the ferries at Picnic Bay. There are also package deals on accommodation and transport (see Getting There & Away in this section).

Picnic Bay Only a minute's walk from the Picnic Bay ferry pier, the *Hideaway Budget Resort* (☎ 4778 5110) at 32 Picnic St is a clean, renovated place with a small kitchen, pool, a TV room and laundry facilities. A bed in a twin or double room costs $14 per person, or there are self-contained cabins at $45.

Nelly Bay The *Magnetic Island Tropical Resort* (☎ 4778 5955) on Yates St, just off the main road, is a very good budget resort with a swimming pool, an inexpensive restaurant and a pleasant garden setting. A bed in a four to six-bed timber cabin with attached bath costs $16, or you can rent a whole cabin – they range from $45 to $79 for a double plus $10 for each extra adult. This place is good if you're after somewhere quiet and relaxed.

At the southern end of Nelly Bay is *Coconuts on the Beach* (☎ 1800 065 696), which promotes itself as a backpacker party place. You can camp here for $8 per person (no shade), or stay in an eight-bed dorm ($16, $1 less for YHA or VIP members) or in the camp-o-tels (permanent tents), also for $16 per person.

Arcadia The popular *Centaur House* (☎ 4778 5668) at 27 Marine Pde is a rambling, old-style hostel opposite the beach. The atmosphere is relaxed and friendly, there's a pleasant garden, and a bed in the downstairs dorms costs $15; double rooms are $35.

Also in Arcadia is *Foresthaven* (☎ 4778 5153) at 11 Cook Rd. This hostel has seen better days and is fairly spartan, although the peaceful bush setting is nice. Accommodation is in old-fashioned but adequate two and three-bed units which have their own kitchen; dorm beds cost $14, twins/doubles cost $34, or there are self-contained rooms from $25 per person. It's a friendly place and the owners speak German and French.

Horseshoe Bay *Geoff's Place* (☎ 4778 5577) is one of the island's most popular places for young travellers, although maintenance and service are suffering these days. There are extensive grounds and you can camp for $6 per person or share a four or eight-bed A-frame cedar cabin for $14 (eight-bed cabins have their own bathroom). There's a communal kitchen, a bar and basic meals cost around $5. The hostel's courtesy bus shuttles between here and Picnic Bay to meet the ferries.

Other Accommodation There are plenty of pubs, motels, holiday flats and even a couple of B&Bs. Rates for these places vary seasonally, and in the school holiday periods you'll probably need to book.

In Picnic Bay, the *Picnic Bay Hotel* (☎ 4778 5166) on the Esplanade has air-con motel rooms from $50. The *Dunoon Resort* (☎ 4778 5161) on the corner of Granite St and the Esplanade has self-contained units from $76.

The impressive *Island Leisure Resort* (☎ 4778 5511) at 4 Kelly St in Nelly Bay has a pool, tennis court and gym, and units from $94. In Arcadia, the *Arcadia Hotel Resort* (☎ 4778 5177) has motel units from $60/70.

There are also two B&Bs in Arcadia. The friendly *Marshall's B&B* (☎ 4778 5112) at 3 Endeavour Rd is a relaxed place with singles/doubles from $35/50. *Beaches B&B* (☎ 4778 5303) is a stylish timber cottage with a pool and separate guest wing. Rooms cost $60 a double.

Places to Eat
Picnic Bay The Picnic Bay Mall, along the waterfront, has a good selection of eating places plus a supermarket. The *Picnic Bay Pub* has decent counter meals. Further along, the *Green Frog Cafe* is good for breakfasts or light lunches.

The licensed *Maxine's*, at the far end of the Esplanade, is a bit more upmarket and has

steaks, and Thai and Malaysian mains from $17 to $25.

Nelly Bay *Mexican Munchies* runs the gamut from enchiladas to tacos, and is open daily from 6 pm. Main courses are $12 to $14, and you need to book in advance (☎ 4778 5658). In the small shopping centre on the main road are *Possums Cafe* and a supermarket.

Arcadia The *Arcadia Hotel Resort* has bistro meals from $10 to $12 and sometimes puts on special deals for backpackers; there's also a more expensive restaurant section. Across the road at Alma Bay, the BYO *La Trattoria* has a great setting overlooking a pretty little bay, and does pizzas, pasta and seafood at very reasonable prices. Close by is *Alla Capri*, a licensed open-air place which has all-you-can-eat pasta deals on Tuesday for $7.50.

In the small shopping centre on Hayles Ave, the BYO *Blue Waters Cafe & Restaurant* has a pleasant little courtyard and some of the best food on the island. It's a burger-bar by day; at night mains range from $14 to $17 and they have three-course deals for $15. Nearby, the *Bakehouse* is open early and is a good place for a breakfast of coffee and croissants. Next door is *Banister's Seafood*, which is a good fish & chips place with an open-air dining area; it's BYO.

Horseshoe Bay *Cotters on the Beach* is a relaxed licensed restaurant with lunches from $5 to $9 and steak, chicken and seafood dinners from $10 to $17. Next door, the *Bounty Snack Bar* has takeaways and there's a small general store where you can buy groceries.

Getting There & Away
Two companies operate passenger ferries between Townsville and Magnetic.

Sunferries (☎ 4771 3855) operates about 10 services a day between 6.20 am and 7.15 pm from its terminal on Flinders St East. The trip takes about 20 minutes and costs $7/13 one-way/return. The only inconvenience is that there is not much in the way of car parking in the Flinders St area.

Magnetic Island Ferries (☎ 4772 7122) runs a similar service from its terminal at the breakwater on Sir Leslie Thiess Dve near the casino. The first ferry leaves Townsville daily at 6 am; the last to the island is at 6.15, 7, 10.30 or 11.30 pm, depending on the day of the week. The trip takes about 15 minutes and the return fare is $14 ($11 for students).

You can also buy package deals which include return ferry tickets and accommodation; one-night packages start at $29. Check with the hostels in Townsville for deals.

The Capricorn Barge Company (☎ 4772 5422) runs a vehicular ferry to Arcadia from the south side of Ross Creek four times a day during the week and twice a day on weekends. It's $96 return for a car and up to six passengers, $31 return for a motorbike and $12 return for walk-on passengers.

Bicycles are carried free on all ferries.

Getting Around
Bus The Magnetic Island Bus Service operates between Picnic Bay and Horseshoe Bay 11 to 20 times a day, meeting all ferries and dropping off at all accommodation places. Some bus trips include Radical Bay, others the Koala Park. You can get individual tickets ($1.50 to $3.50) or a full-day pass ($9).

Car, Moke & Moped Rental Moke Magnetic (☎ 4778 5377), in an arcade off the Picnic Bay Mall, and Holiday Moke Hire (☎ 4778 5703), based in the Jetty Cafe in the Picnic Bay Mall, have Mokes from $33 a day ($30 if you're over 25) plus 30c per km. Both companies also have Suzuki Sierras, Mazda 121s and other vehicles.

Roadrunner Scooter Hire (☎ 4778 5222) has an office in an arcade off the Picnic Bay Mall. Day hire of mopeds is $25, half-day hire $19, and 24-hour hire $30.

Bicycle Magnetic Island is ideal for cycling, and mountain bikes are available for rent at several places, including the Esplanade in Picnic Bay, Foresthaven in Arcadia and on

the waterfront in Horseshoe Bay. Bikes cost $10 for a day, and $6 for half a day.

NORTH COAST HINTERLAND
The Flinders Highway heads inland from Townsville and runs due west for almost 800km to Cloncurry, via the gold-mining town of Charters Towers.

Ravenswood (pop 200)
At Mingela, 83km from Townsville, a sealed road leads 40km south to Ravenswood, a living ghost town which dates back to the gold-rush days. Although many of the buildings were demolished or fell down years ago, some interesting **old buildings** linger amid the scattered red-earth hills, including the old post office, two historic pubs and the restored courthouse, police station and cell block compound, which houses a fascinating mining and historical museum (open 10 am to 3 pm), staffed by the gregarious Woody.

In recent years a couple of companies have recommenced mining operations here, breathing new life back into the town.

The impressive *Imperial Hotel* (☎ 4770 2131), built in the flamboyant style known as 'goldfields brash', has a great public bar, a dining room with home-cooked meals, and B&B from $35/45, or $50 for an air-con double. There's also a free council camping ground, and another pub with rooms.

Eighty km on down the road past Ravenswood, the big **Burdekin Falls Dam**, completed in 1987, holds back more than 200 sq km of water.

Charters Towers (pop 9000)
This busy town, 130km inland from Townsville, was fabulously rich during the gold rush. Many old houses with classic verandahs and wrought-iron lacework, imposing public buildings and mining structures remain. It's possible to make a day trip here from Townsville and get a glimpse of outback Queensland on the way.

The gleam of gold was first spotted in 1871, in a creek bed at the foot of Towers Hill by an Aboriginal boy, Jupiter Mosman. Within a few years, the surrounding area was peppered with diggings and a large town had grown. In its heyday (around the turn of the century), Charters Towers had almost 100 mines and a population of 30,000, and it even had its own stock exchange. It attracted wealth seekers from far and wide and came to be known as 'The World'. Mosman St, the main street in those days, had 25 pubs.

When the gold ran out in the 1920s, the city shrank, but it survived as a centre for the beef industry. Since the mid-1980s, Charters Towers has seen a bit of a gold revival as modern processes enable companies to work those deposits found in previously uneconomical areas. The town is very proud of its history, gold heritage and historic buildings, and even the local police station was renovated in heritage style following lobbying by concerned residents.

Information The helpful tourist office (☎ 4752 0314), in the renovated Queensland Bank building sandwiched between the historic City Hall and Stock Exchange buildings, is open daily from 9 am to 5 pm. Pick up the free *Guide to Charters Towers* booklet and a copy of the National Trust's walking tour leaflet.

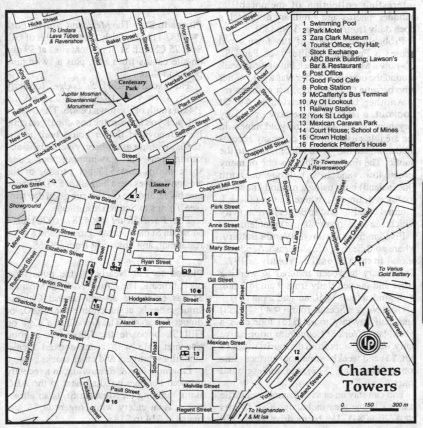

1 Swimming Pool
2 Park Motel
3 Zara Clark Museum
4 Tourist Office; City Hall; Stock Exchange
5 ABC Bank Building; Lawson's Bar & Restaurant
6 Post Office
7 Good Food Cafe
8 Police Station
9 McCafferty's Bus Terminal
10 Ay Ot Lookout
11 Railway Station
12 York St Lodge
13 Mexican Caravan Park
14 Court House; School of Mines
15 Crown Hotel
16 Frederick Pfeiffer's House

Charters Towers

0   150   300 m

QUEENSLAND

The National Trust of Queensland (☎ 47 87 2374) has an office in the Stock Exchange Arcade on Mosman St.

Things to See & Do On Mosman St a few metres up the hill from the corner of Gill St, is the picturesque **Stock Exchange Arcade**, built in 1887 and restored in 1972. At the end of the arcade opposite the information office is the interesting **Assay Room & Mining Museum** ($1). Further up Mosman St, the recently restored **ABC Bank Building** (1891) is now the World Theatre.

At 62 Mosman St, the **Zara Clark Museum** is well worth a visit to see an interesting collection of memorabilia, antiques, photos and a military display. It's open daily from 10 am to 3 pm ($3).

Probably the finest of the town's old houses is Frederick Pfeiffer's, on Paull St. It's now a Mormon chapel, but you can walk around the outside. Pfeiffer was a gold miner who became Queensland's first millionaire.

Another fine old mansion is **Ay Ot Lookout**, a restored house now owned by Leyshon Mining, one of the gold miners in the area. It's used for VIP company accommodation, but the ground floor is open to the public. The timber building is one of many around town (and, in fact, throughout north Queensland) built using a method known as 'balloon framing', where the walls lack external cladding and so do not have a cavity which can lead to vermin (rat) problems.

Five km from town is the **Venus Battery**, where gold-bearing ore was crushed and processed from 1872 until as recently as 1972. The battery has been restored to working order and is open daily from 9 am to 3 pm, with guided tours at 10 am and 2 pm ($3).

Gold Nugget Scenic Tours (☎ 4787 1568) runs half-day city tours ($15) four days a week. Ian at York St Lodge runs informative daily walking tours from the tourist office (1 pm, $5) and weekly three-hour surface mine tours (Thursday, $12) and underground tours.

You can stay on or visit a number of cattle stations in the area including: *Bluff Downs* (☎ 4770 4084), 1½ hours drive away, $70 double including dinner and breakfast; *Powlathanga* (☎ 4787 4957), 34km to the west; *Wambiana* (☎ 4787 6689), dorm accommodation, 69km; and *Virginia Park* (☎ 4770 3125), between Charters and Townsville.

Special Events During the Australia Day weekend in late January, more than 100 cricket teams and their supporters converge on Charters Towers for a competition known as the Goldfield Ashes. The town also hosts one of Australia's biggest annual country music festivals, on the May Day weekend, and has a major rodeo every Easter.

Places to Stay The *Mexican Caravan Park* (☎ 4787 1161) is fairly central, south of Gill St at 75 Church St. It has tent sites at $9 and on-site cabins from $43, plus a swimming pool and store.

The excellent *York St Lodge*, formerly Scotty's, (☎ 4787 1028) is at 58 York St, 1.4km south of the town centre. The owners will pick you up from the bus stop if you ring. It's a renovated timber house built in the 1880s, with pleasant breezy verandahs and sitting areas, and a swimming pool. Four-share dorms cost $15 per person, or the air-con doubles are a bargain at $38. You can hire bikes, and the owners run good day trips (see Things to See & Do earlier).

The *Park Motel* (☎ 4787 1022) at 1 Mosman St has pleasant grounds and a good restaurant, and units cost from $60/68.

Places to Eat Nearly all the pubs have decent meals. The *Crown Hotel* in Mosman St has extensive all-you-can-eat Chinese smorgasbords at lunchtime for $5.90, or dinner for $6.40. The *Good Food Cafe* on Gill St, opposite the library, is a good gourmet cafe with home-cooked meals, smoothies, burgers and other snacks.

Lawson's Bar & Restaurant, in a recently restored heritage building next to the ABC Bank building on Mosman St, is an attractive, casual eatery with burgers at $8 and mains at $14 to $18.

Getting There & Away McCafferty's have daily services from Townsville to Charters Towers (1¾ hours, $14), continuing on to Mt Isa (10 hours, $79). Buses arrive and depart at the Caltex service station at 105 Gill St. Greyhound Pioneer buses don't stop in Charters Towers.

The train station is on Enterprise Rd, 1.5km east of the centre. The twice-weekly *Inlander* also runs from Townsville to Charters Towers (three hours, $20/32 in economy/1st class) and continues on to Mt Isa (17 hours, $115/177 in an economy/1st class sleeper).

TOWNSVILLE TO MISSION BEACH
Paluma Range National Park

The Mt Spec – Big Crystal Creek section of this national park, which straddles the 1000m-plus Paluma Range west of the Bruce Highway, has Australia's most southerly pocket of tropical rainforest.

To get there, turn-off the Bruce Highway 62km north of Townsville (47km south of Ingham). There are two access routes. The southern route is a narrow and spectacular road that winds up along the southern edge of the park, passing **Little Crystal Creek** (with a waterfall and good swimming beside a stone bridge) and **McClelland's Lookout** (three good walking trails) on the way to the sleepy mountain village of **Paluma** (18km). The northern route leads to **Big Crystal Creek** (4km), which has good swimming, a barbecue area, plus a camp site – to book (compulsory, as key must be collected and deposit paid), contact the Department of Environment's Ingham office (☎ 4776 1700). Bower birds are relatively common in the park.

The **Jourama Falls section** of the park, which contains the Seaview Range, is six unsealed kilometres off the highway, 90km north of Townsville (19km south of Ingham). It is centred on the Waterview Creek, and has good swimming holes, several lookouts, a picnic area and a self-registration camping ground (bookings from the Jourama Falls ranger on ☎ 4777 3112). There are walking trails to the waterfalls (600m) and the falls lookout (1.2km).

Ingham (pop 5000)

Ingham, a major sugar-producing town, celebrates its Italian heritage with the Australian-Italian Festival each May.

There's a good tourist centre (☎ 4776 5211) on the corner of Lannercost St and Townsville Rd. The Department of Environment office (☎ 4776 1700), at the end of an arcade at 11 Lannercost St, deals with information for Paluma Range, Lumholtz (Wallaman Falls) and Hinchinbrook and Orpheus islands. The *Hotel Hinchinbrook* (☎ 4776 2227) at 83 Lannercost St offers beds to backpackers at $15 each in a twin room, or $25 for the whole room, and has good bistro meals with mains from $6 to $9.

Around Ingham

There are a number of places to visit around Ingham. At the Wallaman Falls section of the **Lumholtz National Park**, 50km west of Ingham on a tributary of the Herbert River, the Wallaman Falls cascade for 305m – the longest single drop in Australia. The falls are most spectacular in the wet season. You can usually reach them by conventional vehicle along an unsealed road; there's a QNPWS camping area with a swimming hole nearby.

Only 7km east of Ingham is the **Victoria Mill**, the largest sugar mill in the southern hemisphere. Free tours are given in the crushing season (about July to December). **Lucinda**, a port town 24km from Ingham, is the access point for the southern end of Hinchinbrook Island. It also has a 6km jetty used for shipping the sugar.

Orpheus Island

Lying off the coast between Townsville and Ingham, Orpheus is a narrow 13-sq-km granite island surrounded by coral reefs. The second largest of the Palm group, it's a quiet, secluded island that is good for camping, snorkelling and diving. Orpheus is mostly national park and is heavily forested, with lots of birdlife; turtles also nest here. Bush camping is allowed in two places (permits

QUEENSLAND

obtainable from Cardwell) but take your own water and fuel stove. Also on the island are a giant-clam research station and a small resort with rooms at $400-plus per person.

Campers can get there by charter boat from Dungeness (north of Lucinda) for about $120 return per person – contact the MV *Scuba Doo* (☎ 4777 8220) for details.

Cardwell (pop 1400)

Cardwell is one of north Queensland's very earliest towns, dating from 1864, and it is the only town on the highway between Brisbane and Cairns that is actually on the coast. It's more or less a one-street place.

Information The Department of Environment's Rainforest & Reef Information Centre (☎ 4066 8115), beside the main jetty at 142 Victoria St, has information and permits for Hinchinbrook and other national parks in the area. It's open weekdays from 8 am to 5 pm and at varying times on weekends.

If you are travelling south from Cardwell, there is a fruit fly inspection point between here and Ingham, and most fruit and a number of vegetables must be surrendered to the officers here, who also have the right to search your vehicle.

Things to See & Do Cardwell is mainly the departure point for Hinchinbrook and other islands, but there are also numerous points of interest around town. The **Cardwell Forest Drive** starts from the centre of town and is a 26km round trip, taking you to some excellent lookouts, swimming holes, walking tracks and picnic areas.

Most of the coastal forest north of Cardwell is protected as the **Edmund Kennedy National Park**. There's a walking track at the southern end of the park, although the boardwalk seems to have fallen into disrepair. The creeks here are home to estuarine crocodiles, so swimming isn't advised.

The **Murray Falls**, which have fine rock pools for swimming and a walking track and barbecue area, are signposted 22km west of the highway, about 27km north of Cardwell.

Between Cardwell and Ingham the Bruce

Highway briefly climbs high above the coast with tremendous views down across the winding, mangrove-lined waterways known as the Everglades, which separate Hinchinbrook Island from the coast.

Places to Stay The well set up *Kookaburra Holiday Park* (☎ 4066 8648), which includes the YHA *Hinchinbrook Hostel*, is 800m north of the centre at 175 Bruce Highway. The hostel has dorm beds at $13 and doubles at $30 ($1 more for nonmembers), camp sites at $7 per person, and on-site vans, cabins and units starting from $30. The facilities include a pool, free mountain bikes and fishing gear. This place is a good source of information about Hinchinbrook and other attractions in the area.

Further north at 178 Bowen St (behind the 'big crab'), the *Cardwell Backpackers' Hostel* (☎ 4066 8014) has dorm beds and double rooms, but it's a pretty seedy workers' hostel. Cardwell also has several other caravan parks, a pub, motels and holiday units.

Getting There & Away All buses between Townsville and Cairns stop at Cardwell. The fare is about $20 from either place. Cardwell is also on the main Brisbane to Cairns railway.

Hinchinbrook Island

This island is a spectacular and unspoiled wilderness area, with granite mountains rising dramatically from the sea and a varied terrain of lush tropical forest on the mainland side and thick mangroves lining the shores, towering mountains in the middle, and long sandy beaches and secluded bays on the eastern side. All 399 sq km of the island is a national park and rugged Mt Bowen, at 1121m, is the highest peak. There's plenty of wildlife, especially pretty-faced wallabies and the iridescent-blue Ulysses butterfly.

Hinchinbrook is very popular with bushwalkers and naturalists and has some excellent walking tracks. The highlight is the **Thorsborne Trail** (also known as the East Coast Trail), a 32km walking track from

Ramsay Bay to Zoe Bay and on to George Point at the southern tip. It's a three to five-day walk, although you can walk shorter sections if you don't have that much time. Zoe Bay, with its beautiful waterfall, is one of the most scenic spots on the island. Walkers are warned to take plenty of insect repellent; the sandflies and mosquitoes on Hinchinbrook can be a real pest. You'll also have to learn how to protect your food from the native bush rats, and there are estuarine crocodiles in the mangroves!

There's a low-key resort (☎ 4066 8585) on the northern peninsula, Cape Richards, with rooms for 60 people, but it's not cheap at $265-plus per person including meals.

There are seven QNPWS camping grounds along the Thorsborne Trail, plus others at Macushla and Scraggy Point in the north. Fires are banned so you'll need a fuel stove, and all rubbish must be carried out for disposal on the mainland. There is a limit of 40 people allowed on the main trail at any one time, so it's necessary to book ahead, especially for holiday periods. The Department of Environment produces the informative *Thorsborne Trail* and *Hinchinbrook to Dunk Island* leaflets. To book permits and for detailed trail information, contact the Department of Environment Rainforest & Reef Centre in Cardwell (☎ 4066 8601).

Getting There & Away Hinchinbrook Island Ferries (☎ 1800 682 702) at 131 Bruce Hwy has a ferry departing at 9 am returning around 4.30 pm (return fare $69). This service operates daily from June through November, and three times a week December through May. If you want to walk the Thorsborne Trail the one-way cost from Cardwell to the northern end is $45 with Hinchinbrook Island Ferries. You also need to arrange your southern boat pick-up with Hinchinbrook Wilderness Safaris (☎ 4777 8307). The cost is also $45, which includes transport back to Cardwell.

Tully (pop 2500)
The wettest place in Australia gets a drench-ing average of over 4000mm a year, and the Tully River is the setting for white-water rafting trips. There's a tourist office on the highway, and the very basic *Tully Backpackers Hostel* (☎ 4068 2820) costs $14 a bed; they sometimes find fruit-picking work for travellers. There's also a caravan park and a motel, although nearby Mission Beach is a much more appealing place to stay.

MISSION BEACH (pop 1000)
This small stretch of coast is a very popular stopover on the backpacker circuit. The name Mission Beach actually covers a string of small settlements – Mission, Wongaling and South Mission beaches, Bingil Bay and Garners Beach – dotted along a 14km coastal strip east of Tully.

This is a good base for visits to Dunk Island and the Barrier Reef, white-water rafting trips on the Tully River, boat trips out to the reef and walks through the rainforest.

Mission Beach is named after an Aboriginal mission that was founded here in 1914 but destroyed by a cyclone in 1918. Tam O'Shanter Point, beyond South Mission Beach, was the starting point for the ill-fated 1848 overland expedition to Cape York led by 30-year-old Edmund Kennedy. All but three of the party's 13 members died, including Kennedy, who was killed by Aboriginal people. There's a memorial to the expedition at Tam O'Shanter Point.

Information
There's a tourist centre (☎ 4068 7099) on Porters Promenade in Mission Beach. It's open daily from 9 am to 5 pm (Sunday to 4 pm). Next door is the Wet Tropics Visitor Centre (☎ 4068 7179), with information on the local environment and conservation of cassowaries (open 10 am to 4 pm daily).

Zola's Books, in the cluster of shops at Mission Beach, has email facilities in addition to new and second-hand books.

Activities
Walks The rainforest around Mission Beach is a haunt of cassowaries but unfortunately the population of these large flightless birds

has been depleted by road accidents and the destruction of rainforest by logging and cyclones. The rainforest comes right down to the coast in places and there are some impressive walks, including the Licuala Walking Track (two hours), Lacey's Creek Walk (30 minutes), the Bicton Hill Lookout (1½ hours) and the Edmund Kennedy Walking Track (three hours).

Mission Beach Rainforest Treks (☎ 4058 7137) runs guided walks through the forests. The four-hour morning walk costs $28 and the 2½-hour night walk is $18.

The Girramay Walkabout (☎ 4068 8676) is an Aboriginal cultural walking tour through the rainforest. They are good fun, and cost $50 (minimum age 12).

White-Water Rafting & Sea Kayaking
Raging Thunder (☎ 4031 1466) and R'n'R (☎ 1800 079 039) charge $118 from Mission Beach for trips on the Tully River. These are the same as the trips on offer in Cairns, but you'll save about $10 and several hours travel time by doing them from here.

Raging Thunder also offers sea-kayaking day trips to the Family Islands for $90. Sunbird Adventures (☎ 4068 8229) has morning sea kayaking and snorkelling trips for $32.

Other Activities
Jump the Beach (☎ 4050 0671) offers tandem skydives for $228, or there's water sports gear for hire on the beach at Castaways.

Organised Cruises
There are three cruise companies based at the Clump Point jetty just north of Mission Beach. Friendship Cruises takes day trips out to the reef with snorkelling and a ride in a glass-bottom boat ($59). On the *Quick Cat* you can do a reef trip ($122), or a day trip to Dunk Island ($22). The MV *Lawrence Kavanagh* also does day trips to Dunk ($22) and a combined Dunk-Bedarra trip with a barbecue lunch ($44).

Places to Stay
Camping In Mission Beach, there's a

council-run camping ground on the foreshore with sites for $8, or the well equipped *Hideaway Holiday Village* (☎ 4068 7104) opposite has tent sites from $3 and on-site cabins from $40. At South Mission Beach, the *Beachcomber Coconut Village* (☎ 4068 8129) has tent sites from $15.50, camp-o-tels from $24 and on-site cabins from $43.

Hostels All three hostels have courtesy buses and do pick-ups from both bus stops.

The *Treehouse* (☎ 4068 7137), an associate YHA hostel, is at Bingil Bay, 6km north of Mission Beach. This popular and very laid-back hostel is in an impressive timber stilt house surrounded by rainforest, with a pool, bikes for hire and good views over the forest and the coast. A bed in a six-bed dorm costs $16, doubles are $40, or you can pitch your tent on the lawns for $10.

The other hostels are both at Wongaling Beach, 5km south of Mission Beach. *Scotty's Mission Beach House* (☎ 4068 8676), opposite the beach at 167 Reid Rd, is friendly and fun-oriented and has a good pool. There are dorm beds at $15 ($14 VIP) and doubles cost $35 or $40, with the more expensive rooms having their own bathrooms and air-con. At the front of the hostel is the bar & grill, which specialises in steaks and has seafood, roasts, curries and vego dishes from $5 to $20.

Mission Beach Backpackers Lodge (☎ 4068 8317) at 28 Wongaling Beach Rd is a modern, well-equipped place with a pool and garden. There are two buildings, one with spacious dorms at $15 a bed ($14 VIP), the other with very good double rooms from $32 to $38. This easy-going hostel is a five-minute walk from the beach.

Motels & Holiday Units There's a scattering of motels, holiday units and resorts along the coast. The *Waters Edge* (☎ 4068 8890) at 32 Reid Rd, Wongaling Beach, has oldish but clean self-contained holiday units on the waterfront that sleep up to eight and cost from $60 a double plus $10 for each extra person.

The *Clump Point Eco Village* (☎ 4068 7534), on the foreshore a few kilometres north of Mission Beach, has good timber bungalows that sleep up to five and start at $98 a night. With its lush gardens, this place has a great tropical feel.

If you're feeling flush, the *Point Resort* (☎ 1800 079 090) at South Mission Beach is a very stylish resort with rooms from $160 a double.

Places to Eat

Mission Beach proper has a good selection of eateries. The tiny *Port 'o Call Cafe*, beside the bus stop, has breakfasts, home-made meals and good coffee. In the arcade just across Campbell St, *On the Bite* has good fish & chips and burgers. Close by is the *Beach Terraces Cafe*, with an interesting, varied menu, main courses around $15 and some vegetarian dishes.

There are more eateries across the road: *Butterflies* is a friendly Mexican place with entrées from $8 and mains from $11 to $15. Next door is *Food*, a modern brasserie with mains around $15 and vegetarian dishes, such as lasagna, at $12. The cosy *Friends* is a popular open-air BYO with mains for about $17, and further down David St is an Italian bistro called *Piccolo Paradiso*, with pizzas and pasta from $7 to $10 and other mains at $14 to $16.

The *Mission Beach Hotel* in Wongaling Beach has a bistro and cheap bar meals. If you're preparing your own food, there are supermarkets in Mission Beach and Wongaling Beach.

Getting There & Around

McCafferty's buses stop outside the Port 'o Call Cafe in Mission Beach, while Greyhound Pioneer stops at the Mission Beach Resort in Wongaling Beach. The average fare is $15 from Cairns and $39 from Townsville.

Australia Coach does five runs a day between Mission Beach and Cairns ($25, or $15 to/from Innisfail). Advance bookings are required (☎ 4031 3555).

Mission Beach Bus Service does regular runs from Bingil Bay to South Mission

between 8.30 am and 5 pm, with limited evening services. The maximum fare is $4.

Moke & Moped Hire (☎ 4068 7783) has mokes for $40 per day and scooters for $30.

DUNK ISLAND & THE FAMILY ISLANDS

Dunk Island is an easy and affordable day trip from Mission Beach. It's 4.5km off the coast and has walking tracks through rainforest, and good beaches.

The Qantas-owned *Dunk Island Resort* (☎ 13 1415) at Brammo Bay on the northern end of the island has rooms from $170 per person. There's also a QNPWS camping ground close to the resort, as well as a takeaway food kiosk and a water sports place that hires out catamarans, sailboards and snorkelling gear. Camping permits ($3.50 per person) can be booked through the resort's water sports office (☎ 4068 8199). Dunk is noted for prolific birdlife (nearly 150 species) and many butterflies. There are superb views over the entrances to the Hinchinbrook Channel from the top of 271m Mt Kootaloo. Thirteen km of walking tracks lead from the camping ground area to headlands and beaches.

South of Dunk are the seven tiny Family Islands. One of them, Bedarra, has a very exclusive resort, which costs a mere $1000/1290 a day all-inclusive. Five of the other Family Islands are national parks and you can bush camp on Wheeler and Combe (permits available at Cardwell; take your own water).

Getting There & Away

Dowd's Water Taxis (☎ 4068 8310) has seven daily services from Wongaling Beach to Dunk and back ($22 return).

You can fly to Dunk with Sunstate/Qantas from Townsville ($130) or Cairns ($130).

MISSION BEACH TO CAIRNS
Mission Beach to Innisfail

Eight km north of **El Arish**, you can turn off the Bruce Highway and take an interesting alternative route to Innisfail via the sugarcane townships of **Silkwood** and **Mena Creek**, 20km south-west of Innisfail. At

Mena Creek, Paronella Park (☎ 4065 3225) is a rambling tropical garden set among the ruins of a Spanish castle built in the 1930s. This place is quite bizarre and well worth a visit – it's open daily from 9 am to 5 pm and costs $8. They also have a caravan park next door with sites from $11 and on-site cabins from $28.

At **Mourilyan**, 7km south of Innisfail, there's the Australian Sugar Museum, open daily from 9 am to 4.30 pm, and the Innisfail tourist office (☎ 4063 2000). An export terminal on the coast east of Mourilyan handles the sugar produced in Innisfail, Tully and Mourilyan.

Innisfail (pop 8980)

At the junction of the North and South Johnstone rivers, this solid and prosperous sugar city has a large Italian population. The Italians arrived early this century to work the cane fields, and in the 1930s there was even a local 'mafia' called the Black Hand.

There's a tourist office at Mourilyan (see earlier section). Points of interest include a **Chinese Joss House** on Owen St, the **Historical Society Museum** at 11 Edith St, and the **Johnstone River Crocodile Farm** 4km east on the Flying Fish Point road ($10).

The *River Drive Van Park* (☎ 4061 2515) is on River Ave, and there are numerous pubs and motels.

The *Endeavour* (☎ 4061 6610) at 31 Gladys St and *Backpackers Innisfail* (☎ 4061 2284) at 73 Rankin St both have dorm beds for $15 and are predominantly workers' hostels.

The *Codge Lodge*, also on Rankin St, is a new hostel in a renovated house and is very well equipped with facilities such as washing machines and driers. There's also a pool and views of the river from the back balcony. Dorm beds are $15, singles/doubles are $17/34. The owner may be able to help with finding banana-picking work.

The Palmerston Highway winds up to the Atherton Tableland, passing through the rainforest of the **Wooroonooran (Palmerston) National Park**, which has a number of

creeks, waterfalls, scenic walking tracks and a self-registration camping ground at Henrietta Creek, just off the road.

Innisfail to Cairns

About 22km north of Innisfail there's a turning to **Josephine Falls**, a popular picnic spot 8km inland. There are waterfalls, natural waterslides and swimming holes, although you need to take care as the rocks can be very slippery and the whirlpools treacherous – heed the warning signs. The falls are at the foot of the Bellenden Ker range, which includes Queensland's highest peak, **Mt Bartle Frere** (1657m).

The Mt Bartle Frere Hiking Track leads from the car park to the Bartle Frere summit. The ascent is for fit and experienced walkers – it's a 15km, two-day return trip, and rain and cloud can close in suddenly.

Over on the coast at **Bramston Beach**, the *Plantation Village Resort* (☎ 4067 4133) is a good budget resort with camp sites ($12), motel units (from $39) and self-contained cabins (from $49), plus a restaurant, pool and tennis courts.

Seven km inland from Babinda, **Babinda Boulders** is a good picnic place with a huge swimming hole, barbecues and walking trails.

Nearby, *Bowenia Lodge* (☎ 4067 1631) has basic accommodation at $20 per person. From the boulders you can walk the **Goldfield Track**, which leads 10km to the **Goldsborough Valley State Forest Park**, across a saddle in the Bellenden Ker range.

Gordonvale, 33km north of Babinda, has two Sikh *gurdwaras* (places of worship). The winding Gillies Highway leads from here up onto the Atherton Tableland. During the cutting season (July to October), there are tours ($6) of the Mulgrave Sugar Mill (☎ 40 56 3300).

Four km north is a turn-off to the **Yarrabah Aboriginal Community**, where the Menmuny Museum is open weekdays from 8.30 am to 4 pm ($6). On the way you can detour to the Cairns Crocodile Farm ($10, feeding at 1.45 pm).

Far North Queensland

Queensland's far north is one of the most popular tourist destinations in Australia, especially in winter when sun-starved southerners flock here in droves.

Cairns, with its international airport, is the major centre for the region. It's a place where most travellers spend a few days before heading off: north to the superb rainforests of Daintree and Cape Tribulation and the historic town of Cooktown; west to the cool air of the Atherton Tableland; or east to the islands and the Great Barrier Reef.

CAIRNS (pop 92,000)

The 'capital' of the far north, Cairns is firmly established as one of Australia's top travellers' destinations. It is a centre for a whole host of activities – not only reef trips and scuba diving but white-water rafting, canoeing, horse riding, bungee-jumping and sky diving. On the down side, Cairns' rapid tourist growth has destroyed much of the city's laid-back tropical atmosphere. It also lacks a beach, but there are some good ones not far north.

Cairns marks the end of the Bruce Highway and the railway line from Brisbane, and is at its climatic best – and busiest – from May to October; in summer the high humidity can be draining.

History

The town began in 1876, a beachhead among mangroves, intended as a port for the Hodgkinson River goldfield 100km inland. Initially it struggled under rivalry from Smithfield 12km north, a rowdy frontier town that was washed away by a flood in 1879 (it's now an outer suburb of Cairns), and then there was competition from Port Douglas, founded in 1877 after Christie Palmerston discovered an easier route from there to the goldfield. What saved Cairns was the Atherton Tableland 'tin rush' in 1880. Cairns became the starting point for the railway line to the tableland, which was built a few years later.

Orientation

The centre of Cairns is a relatively compact area running back from the Esplanade. Off Wharf St (the southern continuation of the Esplanade), you'll find Great Adventures Wharf, Marlin Jetty and the Pier – the main departure points for reef trips. Further around is Trinity Wharf (a cruise-liner dock with shops and cafes) and the transit centre, where long-distance buses arrive and depart.

Back from the waterfront is City Place, a pedestrian mall at the meeting of Shields and Lake Sts.

Cairns is surrounded by mangrove swamps to the south and north. The sea in front of the town is shallow and at low tide it becomes a long sweep of mud, with lots of interesting water birds.

Information

Tourist Offices The Wet Tropics Information Centre, on the Esplanade across from the Shields St corner, combines information with displays on the environment and rainforests of the far north. It's open daily from 9.30 am to 5.30 pm. For phone queries, call the Far North Queensland Promotion Bureau (☎ 4051 3588).

There are literally dozens of privately run 'information centres' in Cairns, and these places are basically tour-booking agencies. Most of the backpackers hostels also have helpful tour-booking desks. Note that each booking agent will be pushing different tours, depending on the commission deal they have with the tour companies, so shop around.

The Community Information Service (☎ 4051 4953) in Tropical Arcade off Shields St, half a block back from the Esplanade, has more offbeat information like where you can play croquet or do tai chi, details on foreign consulates and health services etc.

Other Information The RACQ office (☎ 40 33 6433) at 520 Mulgrave Rd, Earlville, is a

PLACES TO STAY
1 Costa Blanca Apartments
2 181 The Esplanade
3 Floriana Guesthouse
4 JJ's Backpackers
5 Captain Cook's Backpackers
6 Calypso Inn
9 Castaways
10 Pacific Cay Holiday Units
11 Concord Holiday Units
12 Castle Holiday Flats
13 Bel-Air Hostel
14 Rosie's Backpackers
15 Silver Palm Guesthouse
16 Caravella's 149
18 Tracks Hostel
19 Inn the Tropics
20 U2 Hostel
21 Poinsettia Motel
22 Parkview Backpackers
26 Leo's
39 YHA On The Esplanade;
     Chapel Bar

40 Hostel 89
41 Bellview
42 Jimmy's On The Esplanade
43 Caravella's 77 Hostel
44 International Hostel
60 Aussie II Hostel
69 Macleod St YHA Hostel
72 Gone Walkabout House
73 Dreamtime Travellers' Rest
74 Ryan's Rest Guesthouse

PLACES TO EAT
7 Cock & Bull Tavern
25 Old Ambulance Cafe Bistro
34 Silver Dragon Chinese
     Restaurant;
     Willie's Seaside Cafe
38 The Meeting Place
59 Cafe Zuzu
61 Paris Croissant
62 Sawasdee
63 La Fettucine; Gypsy Dee's
64 Red Ochre Grill
66 Mozart Pastry
68 John & Diana's Breakfast &
     Burger House
76 Tiny's Juice Bar
77 Yama's Japanese Restaurant;
     Cyclone Cafe

OTHER
8 Hospital
17 Cheap car rental companies
23 Cairns Civic Centre
24 Jolly Frog Car Rentals
27 Taka II Dive
28 Cairns Library

29 Cairns Five Cinemas
30 Cairns Museum
31 City Place Amphitheatre
32 Qantas & Sunstate Airlines
33 Walker's Bookshop
35 Wool Shed; Cairns
     Curry House
36 Cairns Dive Centre
37 Beach Nightclub
45 Air Niugini
46 Johno's Blues Bar
47 Wet Tropics Information Centre
48 Cairns Regional Gallery
49 Pro Dive
50 Great Adventures Booking Office
51 Trinity Wharf; Transit Centre
52 Reef Casino
53 Ansett
54 Thomas Cook
55 Orchid Plaza; Australia
     Post Shop; American
     Express
56 Lake St Transit Centre
57 STA Travel
58 Central Arcade;
     Tropo's Nightclub
65 Rusty's Bazaar
67 Rusty's Pub
70 Department of Environment
71 Railway Station
75 Police
78 Sports Bar
79 Samuel's Saloon; Court
     Jester Bar; Playpen
     Nightclub
80 Post Office
81 Far North Queensland
     Promotion Bureau

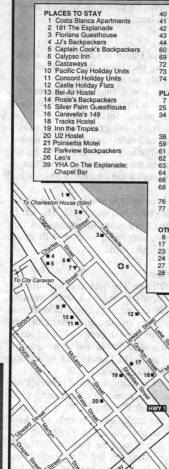

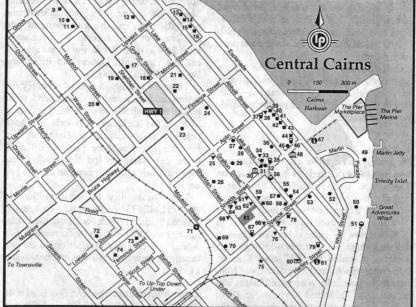

Central Cairns

0   150   300 m

Cairns
Harbour

The Pier
Marketplace

The Pier
Marina

Cairns Inlet

Marlin Jetty

Trinity Inlet

Great
Adventures
Wharf

To Charleston House (50m)

To City Caravan

To Townsville

To Up-Top Down
Under

good place to get maps and information on road conditions, especially if you're driving up to Cooktown or the Cape York Peninsula, or across to the Gulf.

The Department of Environment office (☎ 4052 3096) at 10 McLeod St is open on weekdays from 8.30 am to 4.30 pm; it deals with camping permits and information for the region's national parks, including islands.

Post & Communications The main post office, on the corner of Grafton and Hartley Sts, has a poste restante service. For general business (stamps etc), there's also an Australia Post shop in the Orchid Plaza on Lake St.

There's email/Internet access at the Memphis Bar in the Pier complex, and at the Calypso Inn hostel.

Bookshops Proudmans, in the Pier complex, and Walker's Bookshop, at 96 Lake St, both sell a good range of reading material. For maps, try Northern Disposals at 47 Sheridan St.

Things to See & Do

Cairns' main attraction is as a base for getting to the places that surround it, but there are a few places in town worth visiting. The impressive **Cairns Regional Gallery** is housed in a cleverly restored historic building on the corner of Abbott and Shields Sts, and features theme exhibitions, works by local artists and loans from major galleries. It is open daily from 10 am to 6 pm ($5/2 adults/students).

Most of Cairns' older buildings have been engulfed by the booming developments of the 1980s and 90s. The oldest part of town is the **Trinity Wharf** area, but even this has been redeveloped. There are still some imposing neoclassical buildings from the 1920s on Abbott St, and the frontages around the corner of Spence and Lake Sts date from 1909 to 1926. A walk along the **Esplanade Walking Trail**, with views over to rainforested mountains across the estuary and cool breezes in the evening is very agreeable.

Housed in the 1907 School of Arts building on the corner of Lake and Shields Sts, the **Cairns Museum** has some interesting historic displays on the far north including Aboriginal artefacts, a display on the construction of the Cairns to Kuranda railway, and exhibits on the old Palmer River and Hodgkinson goldfields. It's open daily (except Sunday) from 10 am to 4 pm ($3).

The colourful markets at **Rusty's Bazaar**, on Sheridan St between Spence and Shields Sts, are great for people-watching and for browsing among the dozens of stalls which sell fruit and vegies, arts and crafts, clothes and more. The markets are held on Friday night and Saturday and Sunday mornings; Saturday is the busiest and best time.

The **Pier Marketplace** is a glossy shopping plaza with expensive boutiques, souvenir shops, a foodhall, cafes and restaurants. On weekends the **Mud Markets** are held here, with a wide range of stalls selling food and local arts and crafts. Also here is the impressive **Undersea World** aquarium, which is open daily from 8 am to 8 pm; entry is steep at $10 but there are often 20% discount vouchers available from the various hostels. The best time to visit is when the sharks are being fed (four times daily).

Three km north-west of town are the **Flecker Botanic Gardens** on Collins Ave in Edge Hill. Over the road from the gardens, a boardwalk leads through a patch of rainforest to **Saltwater Creek** and the two small **Centenary Lakes**. Collins Ave turns west off Sheridan St (the Cook Hwy) 3km from the centre of Cairns. The gardens are 700m from the turning. Near the gardens is the entrance to the **Whitfield Range Environmental Park**, one of the last remnants of rainforest around Cairns – two long walking tracks give good views over the city and coast. You can get there with Sunbus or the Cairns Explorer.

Also in Edge Hill, the **Royal Flying Doctor Service** visitor centre and regional office, at 1 Junction St, is open to visitors daily from 8.30 am to 5 pm weekdays and 9 am to 4.30 pm on weekends ($5).

The **Tjapukai Dance Theatre**, an award-winning Aboriginal dance troupe, has a theatre complex beside the Skyrail terminal at Smithfield, just off the Captain Cook Highway about 15km north of the centre. This multi-million dollar complex incorporates four sections – a cultural village, a 'creation theatre', an audio-visual show, and a traditional dance theatre. Performances include a re-enactment of a traditional corroboree, boomerang and spear-throwing and the telling of Dreamtime stories. The complex is open daily from 9 am to 5 pm; entry costs $24 ($12 children), or $36 ($18) with return bus transfers from Cairns. Allow at least two hours.

Activities

Diving & Snorkelling Cairns is one of the scuba-diving capitals of the Barrier Reef, which is closer to the coast here than it is further south.

Most people look for a course that takes them to the outer Barrier Reef rather than the reefs around Green or Fitzroy islands. Some places give you more time on the reef than others but you may prefer an extra day in the pool and classroom before venturing out. A chat with people who have already done a course can tell you some of the pros and cons. A good teacher can make all the difference to your confidence and the amount of fun you have. Another factor is how big the groups are – the smaller the better if you want personal attention.

The main schools include: Deep Sea Divers Den (☎ 4031 2223), 319 Draper St; Pro-Dive (☎ 4031 5255), Marlin Jetty; Down Under Dive (☎ 4031 1288), 155 Sheridan St; Cairns Dive Centre (☎ 1800 642 591), 135 Abbott St; Tusa Dive (☎ 4031 1248), 93 the Esplanade; and Taka II Dive (☎ 4051 8722), 131 Lake St. Most of these places can be booked through the hostels.

Prices differ quite a bit between schools but usually one or other of them has a discount going. Expect to pay about $350 to $450 for a five-day course of two days in the pool and classroom, a day trip to the reef and back, and two more days on the reef with an overnight stay on board.

If you want to learn about the reef before you dive, Reef Teach offers an entertaining and educational lecture at Boland's Centre, 14 Spence St, every night (except Sunday) from 6.15 to 8.30 pm. The lectures are well worth attending and get good reports from travellers. The cost is $10 – for more details phone ☎ 4051 6882.

White-Water Rafting, Kayaking & Canoeing Three of the rivers flowing down from the Atherton Tableland make for some excellent white-water rafting. Most popular is a day in the rainforested gorges of the Tully River, 150km south of Cairns. So many people do this trip that there can be 20 or more craft on the river at once, meaning you may have to queue up to shoot each section of rapids – yet despite this, most people are exhilarated at the end of the day. The Tully day trips leave daily year-round. Two companies running them from Cairns are: Raging Thunder (☎ 4030 7990), 97 Hartley St; and R 'n' R (☎ 1800 079 039), 74 Abbott St. Day trips on the Tully cost about $128 from Cairns. There are cheaper half-day trips on the Barron River ($66), not far inland from Cairns, or you can make two-day ($350) or five-day ($770) expeditions on the remote North Johnstone River which rises near Malanda and enters the sea at Innisfail.

Foaming Fury (☎ 4032 1460), 21 Berry St, offers white-water rafting ($118) on the Russell River south of Bellenden Ker National Park, half-day trips on the Barron River ($66) and day trips on the Johnston River ($123).

The Adventure Company (☎ 4051 4777) has one-day wilderness canoe paddles on the Musgrave River ($89) and three-day sea-kayaking tours out of Mission Beach ($498).

Other Activities At Smithfield, 15km north, you can bungee-jump with AJ Hackett (☎ 4057 7188) from a steel tower with sensational views ($95 including transfers).

Blazing Saddles and Springmount Station

(☎ 4093 4493) both offer half-day horse trail rides for about $65, including pick-ups from Cairns. Dan's Tours (☎ 4033 0128) has full day mountain bike tours to the Daintree ($95). Skydive Cairns (☎ 4035 9667) has tandem skydiving, or for air travel at a more leisurely pace there are three ballooning outfits with half-hour ($105) and one-hour flights ($170), including transfers and breakfast. Contact Raging Thunder (☎ 4030 7990), Hot Air (☎ 1800 800 829) or Champagne Balloon Flights (☎ 1800 677 444).

Northern Air Adventures (☎ 4035 9156) has half-hour flights out over Green Island and Arlington and Upton Reefs ($50), or one-hour flights which also include Batt Reef ($90).

Organised Tours & Cruises

There are literally hundreds of tours available out of Cairns, some of which are specially aimed at backpackers and are very good value. You can make bookings through your accommodation or at one of the many booking agencies in town.

Cairns Half-day trips around the city sights, or two-hour cruises from Marlin Jetty up along Trinity Inlet and around Admiralty Island, start from around $20.

Atherton Tableland The 'conventional' bus tour companies run day trips to the Atherton Tableland, which usually include the waterfalls and lakes circuit and the Kuranda markets, and range from $66 to $85. Jungle Tours (☎ 1800 817 234) has smaller group trips for backpackers for about $45 to $50. Uncle Brian's quirky tours (☎ 4050 0615) have received good reports from travellers and a day trip is $55.

Daintree & Cape Tribulation Cape Trib is one of the most popular day-trip destinations, and there are dozens of operators offering tours. Even though the road is almost all bitumen and easily negotiable by car, most operators still use 4WD vehicles and often mislead people into thinking they are going on an off-road adventure which

they couldn't do in their car – it's not, so don't be fooled.

Jungle Tours (☎ 1800 817 234) offers fun-oriented trips up to Cape Trib, usually with a cruise on the Daintree River thrown in, for $82 (no lunch). If you have time, you'd be better off taking one of their overnight or longer packages – $78 for two days and $89 for three days, which includes accommodation at Crocodylus Village and/or PK's Jungle Village. Dan's Tours has mountain bike trips to Cape Trib – see Other Activities earlier in this section.

Cooktown Strikie's Safaris (☎ 1800 809 999) runs good 4WD trips to Cooktown from Cairns and Port Douglas, visiting places such as Black Mountain and the Lion's Den Hotel along the way. A day trip costs $85, two-day trips $220 (meals and accommodation not included).

Barrier Reef & Islands There are dozens of options available for day trips to the reef. It's worth asking a few questions before you book, such as how many passengers the boat takes, what's included in the price and how much the 'extras' (such as wetsuit hire and introductory dives) cost, and exactly where the boat is going. Some companies employ a dubious definition of 'outer reef'; as a general rule, the further out you go, the better the diving.

Great Adventures (☎ 1800 079 080) is the major operator with the biggest boats and a wide range of combination cruises, including a day trip to either Norman or Moore Reef. You get about three hours on a pontoon at the reef itself, lunch, snorkelling gear, and a semi-submersible and glass-bottom boat ride thrown in.

Compass (☎ 1800 815 811) and Noah's Ark Cruises (☎ 4051 5666) have popular day trips to Hastings Reef and Michaelmas Cay for $55, including boom netting, snorkelling gear and lunch. Certified divers can take two dives for an extra $45.

Falla (☎ 4031 3488), *Seahorse* (☎ 4031 4692) and *Passions of Paradise* (☎ 4050 0676) are all ocean-going yachts that 'sail' out to Upolo Cay, Green Island and Paradise Reef daily for about $50, which includes lunch and snorkelling gear.

There are many, many other boats and operators, so shop around.

Undara Lava Tubes Australian Pacific (☎ 13 1304) and Undara Experience (☎ 4031 7933) have two-day trips out to the Undara Lava Tubes for $297 including accommodation, meals and the tour of the remarkable lava tubes.

Cape York See the Cape York section later in this chapter for details of tours from Cairns to Cape York.

Places to Stay

Cairns has a huge range of tourist accommodation catering for everybody from budget-conscious backpackers to deep-pocketed tourists. There are plenty of hostels, as well as cheap guesthouses and holiday flats. Prices go up and down with the seasons, and lower weekly rates are par for the course. Prices given here for the more expensive places can rise 30% or 40% in the peak season, and some of the hostels will charge a dollar or two less in the quiet times.

Camping There are about a dozen caravan parks in and around Cairns, but none are really central. Almost without exception they take campers as well as caravans. The closest to the centre is the *City Caravan Park* (☎ 4051 1467), about 2km north-west on the corner of Little and James Sts, with tent sites from $14, and on-site vans from $44.

Out on the Bruce Highway, about 8km south of the centre, is the *Cairns Coconut Caravan Village* (☎ 4054 6644) with camp sites from $18.50, on-site cabins from $49 and units from $75. If you want to camp by the beach, the *Yorkeys Knob Beachfront Van Park* (☎ 4055 7201), about 20km north, has tent sites and on-site vans.

Hostels Cairns is the backpacking capital of Queensland and has more than 20 hostels, ranging from the huge pack-'em-in type to

the smaller, quieter owner-operated places. Most have fan-cooled bunk rooms with shared bathrooms, kitchens and laundries, lounge and TV rooms, and a swimming pool, and many also offer private rooms with their own facilities. Nightly costs for dorms range from about $14 to $18. Unfortunately, you have to beware of theft in some places – use lock-up rooms and safes if they're available.

You have a choice of staying in or around the Esplanade, which has the greatest concentration of hostels, or in one of the places further out. The Esplanade hostels tend to have little outdoor space and to be more cramped, but they are in the thick of the action. The hostels away from the centre offer a bit more breathing space and are generally quieter, and the inconvenience of being out of the centre is minimal as there are courtesy buses that make regular runs into town.

Esplanade Starting from the corner of Shields St and heading along the Esplanade, the *International Hostel* (☎ 4031 1424) at No 67 is a big, old multi-level place with about 200 beds and plenty of atmosphere. Fan-cooled four, six and eight-bed dorms are $12, twin rooms are $28 and doubles range from $28 to $36 with either air-con and TV or a private bathroom. Guests also get a free meal at the Rattle 'n' Hum pub next door.

Caravella's Hostel 77 (☎ 4051 2159) at No 77 is another big, rambling place. It's one of the longest established Cairns hostels and has old-fashioned but clean rooms, all with air-con. The cost in four to six-bunk dorms is $16 and singles/doubles range from $22/30 to $26/34, or $40 with private bathroom. All these prices include an evening meal, and there's also free luggage storage.

Jimmy's on the Esplanade (☎ 4031 6884) at No 83 is a reasonably modern place with 46 beds in six-bed air-con units with their own bathrooms. There's a pool and kitchen; dorms cost $15, doubles are $36 or $50 with your own bathroom.

Next door, the *Bellview* (☎ 4031 4377) is a good quiet hostel with clean and comfortable four-bed dorms at $16 and singles/twins from $27/36; all rooms have air-con. The kitchen is good and there's a small pool, a laundry, and a good, cheap cafe. They also have motel-style units from $49.

Hostel 89 (☎ 1800 061 712) at No 89 is one of the better Esplanade hostels. It's a smallish and helpful place, with twin and double rooms and a few three ($18) or four-bed ($17) dorms, all air-conditioned. Singles/doubles are from $36/44. Security is good, with a locked grille at the street entrance.

At No 93 is *YHA on the Esplanade* (☎ 4031 1919). There are two blocks, one with spacious, airy five-bed dorms with their own bathroom, the other with small twins and doubles. Some rooms have air-con. Dorm beds cost $17 and doubles $38; nonmembers pay an extra $3.

Three blocks further along the Esplanade is another cluster of hostels. At No 149 is the large *Caravella's 149* (☎ 4031 5680), which can get somewhat crowded. You pay $16 in a six-share dorm with air-con, or $15 in a four-share dorm with fan. Doubles cost $30 ($32 air-con), and all prices include an evening meal.

Rosie's Backpackers (☎ 4051 0235) at No 155 has several buildings with spacious dorms or six-bed flats; dorm beds are $15 and there are a couple of doubles at $35. This place is helpful, well-run and has a small pool. Next door at No 157, the *Bel-Air Hostel* (☎ 4031 4790) is a renovated two-storey Queenslander with doubles and twins downstairs for $30 and four-bunk dorms upstairs at $16; all rooms have air-con, the price includes breakfast, and there's a pool.

Around Town Three blocks back from the Esplanade, *Parkview Backpackers* (☎ 4051 3700) is at 174 Grafton St. This is a friendly and laid-back place where you can relax by the pool and listen to music. It's in a rambling old timber building with a large tropical garden; four to eight-bed dorms are $14 and twins and doubles $30.

Tracks Hostel (☎ 4031 1474), nearby on the corner of Grafton and Minnie Sts, spans three old timber houses that look a little run-down, but many people like the atmosphere. Dorm beds are $14 and doubles $28, all including an evening meal.

JJ's Backpackers (☎ 4051 7642) at 11 Charles St is a small block of apartments converted into a hostel with dorm beds for $14 and doubles for $32, plus a small pool. It's a bit far from the centre to be really convenient and it's not as clean as it could be.

Captain Cook Backpackers Hostel (☎ 4051 6811) at 204 Sheridan St is a huge converted motel with lots of beds, two pools, a bar and a restaurant. This place has been recently renovated and offers modern facilities and good value for money. Dorm beds are $15, doubles are $48, and each unit has its own cooking facilities. Evening meals are available for $5 (free if you buy a jug of beer or wine).

At 207 Sheridan St is *Castaways* (☎ 4051 1238), a somewhat tatty and cramped smallish place with dorms ($15) as well as single/double rooms ($27/32). All rooms are fan-cooled and have a fridge, and there's a pool and free barbecues three nights a week.

At 72 Grafton St, the *Aussie II Hostel* (☎ 4051 7620) is a basic old-style hostel with about 60 beds. It's a bit of a crash pad, but it's central and cheap at $10 a night.

The YHA *McLeod St Youth Hostel* (☎ 4051 0772) at 20-24 McLeod St has dorm beds for $16 and singles/doubles for $26/36. Nonmembers pay $3 extra. The facilities are good and the hostel has car parking spaces.

Two blocks west of the station at 274 Draper St, *Gone Walkabout Hostel* (☎ 4051 6160) is small, popular and well-run with a friendly atmosphere. Set in two breezy old houses, it has a few four-bed dorms at $12 and mostly twins/doubles at $25, plus a tiny pool. It's not a place for late partying.

The *Up-Top Down Under* (☎ 4051 3636) at 164-170 Spence St, 1.5km from the town centre, is a spacious and quiet place with a large, well-equipped kitchen, two TV lounges (smoking and non) and a pool. Dorm beds are $15 and singles/doubles $28/32, all with shared bathroom.

The *U2 Hostel* (☎ 4031 4077), 77 McLeod

St is a restored Queenslander divided into five flats, and has a pool, dorms at $13 and singles/doubles at $26/30, although most rooms lack windows.

The *Calypso Inn* (☎ 1800 815 628), on Digger St behind the Cock & Bull tavern, is a friendly, low-key hostel in a renovated Queenslander. The downstairs area has a pool, bar and restaurant in a tropical garden. Dorm beds are $14 and singles/doubles $25/30.

Inn The Tropics (☎ 4031 1088) at 141 Sheridan St has a good pool and a small guests' kitchen. Dorm beds are $15, motel-style rooms are $28/36 with shared bathroom or $38/46 with en-suite.

Guesthouses A number of guesthouse-type places cater for budget travellers, with an emphasis on rooms rather than dorms. These places are generally quieter, smaller and a bit more personalised than the hostels.

Dreamtime Travellers' Rest (☎ 4031 6753) at 4 Terminus St is a small guesthouse run by a friendly and enthusiastic young couple. It's in a brightly renovated timber Queenslander and has a good pool, double rooms from $35 and three or four-bed (no bunks) rooms at $15 per person.

Another good guesthouse with a similar set-up is *Ryan's Rest* (☎ 4051 4734), down the road at 18 Terminus St. It's a cosy and quiet family-run place with three good double rooms upstairs at $35, twins/doubles at $25 and a four-bed dorm at $15 per person.

The Art-Deco *Floriana Guesthouse* (☎ 4051 7886) at 183 the Esplanade has four self-contained units with polished timber floors, TVs, en suites and kitchenettes. This place is excellent value at $55 to $70 for up to four. The old building next door has 24 simple rooms with communal facilities at $28 to $42 for doubles, some with air-con, or $48 with appealing ocean views (book ahead).

At 8 McKenzie St, *Charleston House* (☎ 4051 6317) is an old Queenslander also renovated in Art-Deco style. It's divided into eight comfortable flats and costs $112/150. *Leo's* (☎ 1800 636 626) at 100 Sheridan St is a recently renovated place where bright single/double rooms with fridge and share bathroom are $35/40, or with sink and air-con it's $45/48.

At 153 the Esplanade, the *Silver Palm Guesthouse* (☎ 4031 6099) is a quiet little place with singles/doubles from $33/38 ($48 for an en-suite double), including use of a kitchen, laundry, pool and TV room.

18-24 James (☎ 1800 621 824) at, funnily enough, 18-24 James St, is an exclusively gay and lesbian hotel with four-share rooms at $50 per person or singles/doubles at $95/109, all including a tropical breakfast.

Motels & Holiday Flats There are a few budget motels around the centre: the *Poinsettia Motel* (☎ 4051 2144) at 169 Lake St has decent budget rooms from $46/50.

Holiday flats are well worth considering, especially for a group of three or four people who are staying a few days or more. Expect pools, air-con and laundry facilities in this category. Holiday flats generally supply all bedding, cooking utensils etc.

At 209 Lake St, the *Castle Holiday Flats* (☎ 4031 2229) is one of the cheapest places, and it has a small pool. Self-contained one-bedroom flats cost from $40 per night and two-bedroom flats from $60.

On the waterfront at 241 the Esplanade, the *Costa Blanca Apartments* (☎ 4051 3114) aren't particularly flashy, but they're clean and comfortable enough, and sleep up to four people. They range from $85 a double plus $5 for extras. There's a guest laundry and a big pool.

There's a string of motels and holiday units along Sheridan St – these include the *Pacific Cay* (☎ 4051 0151) at No 193, with one-bedroom units from $55 and two-bedroom units from $65, and the *Concord Holiday Units* (☎ 4031 4522) at No 183, with one-bedroom units at $47/57 single/double.

181 The Esplanade (☎ 4052 6888) is a 10-storey complex of modern one to three-bedroom apartments which cost from $180 to $280.

Places to Eat

Cairns has an abundance of eateries, so you shouldn't have too much trouble finding somewhere to satisfy your particular gastronomic craving and/or your budget.

Cafes & Delis The Esplanade, between Shields and Aplin Sts, is basically wall-to-wall eateries with plenty of variety – Italian and Chinese food, burgers, kebabs, pizzas, seafood and ice cream – open all hours. The *Night Markets*, in the thick of it, is a modern and somewhat stark and soulless hawker-style food court but with plenty of choices. Better is the *Meeting Place* around the corner in Aplin St. The stalls here include Japanese, Thai, Chinese, steak and seafood; meals are in the $7 to $14 range, there's a bar and a few tables out on the pavement.

Mozart Pastry, on the corner of Grafton and Spence Sts, is good for a breakfast croissant and coffee, and for pastries, cakes and sandwiches. *Paris Croissant* is another good breakfast bet, with croissants from $2. The somewhat downmarket *John & Diana's Breakfast & Burger House* at 35 Sheridan St also has cooked breakfasts for $5 or less.

The very popular *Tiny's Juice Bar*, on Grafton St near the Spence St corner, has a great range of fruit and vegetable juices as well as filled rolls and lentil and tofu burgers at good prices. Close by is the cosy little *Cafe Cyclone*.

Willie's Seaside Cafe is a bright and airy (if misnamed) cafe right by City Square and so is good for catching the lunch time performances given in the amphitheatre there. A *de riguer* focaccia and cafe latte lunch costs $6.50.

Just around the corner and tucked away in an arcade is the *Cairns Curry House*, with good value curries from $6.50.

On the corner of Grafton and Aplin Sts, the *Old Ambulance Cafe Bistro* is a chic new place in, as the name suggests, the old ambulance station. It's a popular place and has great coffee and filled croissants.

Restaurants *La Fettucini* is a narrow bistro at 43 Shields St. It has great home-made

pasta at $12 and Italian mains for about $16; it's BYO. Next door is the dim and exotic *Gypsy Dee's*, with a bar, live acoustic music nightly and mains in the $12 to $18 range. On the corner of Shields and Sheridan Sts, the *Red Ochre Grill* is a stylish restaurant with innovative Aussie bush tucker, but it's not cheap with mains ranging from $17 to $25.

The *Silver Dragon* Chinese restaurant at 102 Lake St has a good buffet lunch deal for $4.90.

The friendly *Sawasdee* at 89 Grafton St is a tiny BYO Thai restaurant with lunch specials from $7.50 and dinner mains from $11 to $16. Across the road, the *Cafe ZuZu* is a narrow and groovy eatery with pasta from $8 and other mains from $8 to $12.

For Japanese food, try *Yama* on the corner of Spence and Grafton Sts – it has good-value lunches and dinners.

The Pier Marketplace has a couple of good eating options, including a good international food hall and *Johnny Rocket's*, an American-style burger joint. On the 1st floor is *Donnini's*, a smart licensed restaurant with some of the best Italian food in town; gourmet pizzas from $9 to $16, pasta from $12 to $16 and Italian mains about $17.

Nightclubs & Pubs Most of the hostels have give-away vouchers for cheap (or free) meals at various nightclubs, pubs and bars around town. *Samuel's Saloon*, near the corner of Hartley and Lake Sts, is one of the most popular places, with cheap roasts, pasta and stews. They even have a bus that picks up hungry travellers from the hostels.

On the Esplanade, next to the International Hostel, *Rattle 'n' Hum* is a new place where you can get traditional English/Irish pub grub for around $10 in a lively but relaxed atmosphere.

The *Beach* on the corner of Abbott and Aplin Sts is another popular nightclub with cheap meal (and drink) deals. The *Wool Shed*, on Shields St in the mall, has meals in the $5 to $10 range and a Sunday barbecue (50c).

On the corner of Digger and Grove Sts, the

Cock & Bull Tavern is an excellent English-style tavern with draught beers and 'hearty' (of course!), stodgy tucker in the $8 to $10 range – just the spot for homesick Poms, and far enough from the touristy centre of town to have the atmosphere of a 'local'.

Entertainment

The free and widely available mag *Son of Barfly* covers music gigs, movies, pubs and clubs – and it's quite an entertaining read in itself.

Pubs & Live Music Free lunchtime concerts are held daily at the *City Place Amphitheatre*, in the mall on the corner of Lake and Shields St.

The long-running *Johno's Blues Bar*, above McDonald's on the corner of Shields St and the Esplanade, has blues, rock and R&B bands every night until late; the cover charge is about $5.

Quite a few pubs in Cairns have regular live bands, including the *Fox & Firkin*, on the corner of Spence and Lake Sts, the *Crown Hotel* on the corner of Shields and Grafton Sts, and the *Pier Tavern* overlooking the bay from the Pier Marketplace – their Sunday arvo sessions are all the go.

In Shields St, *Gypsy Dee's* has live acoustic, jazz and blues music at night (see Places to Eat).

Chapel is a low-key bar with live acoustic music on some nights. It's on the 1st floor close to the YHA On the Esplanade hostel.

Nightclubs & Bars Cairns' nightclub scene is notoriously wild and promiscuous, especially in the early hours of the morning – it has been said that if you can't get lucky here you may as well stop trying! The huge complex on the corner of Lake and Hartley Sts houses three places: *Samuel's Saloon*, a backpacker bar and eatery; the *Playpen International*, a huge nightclub that often has big-name bands; and the more upmarket *Court Jester Bar*.

On Shields St in the mall, the phenomenally popular *Wool Shed* is a hectic backpackers' bar with party games, theme nights and other wild stuff, while the *Beach* nightclub, on the corner of Abbott and Aplin Sts, has a huge video screen, low lighting, loud music, happy hours and competition nights such as Mr Backpacker.

Rusty's Pub on the corner of Spence and Sheridan Sts has a gay night with a floor show on Saturday nights.

Cinemas & Theatre The *Cairns Five Cinemas* at 108 Grafton St screen mainstream releases, or there's the *Coral Drive-in* on the Bruce Highway on the southern edge of town. The *Cairns Civic Theatre* (☎ 4050 1777) is the main venue for theatre and concerts – ring to see what's on.

Casino Cairns' big *Reef Casino* is on the block bordered by the Esplanade, and Wharf, Abbott and Spence Sts. Inside it's thoroughly characterless, the decor is glitzy and tacky and the place lacks any atmosphere at all – basically a big, gaudy, poker machine venue.

Things to Buy

Many artists live in the Cairns region, so there's a wide range of local handicrafts available at the various markets, including the weekend Mud Markets at the Pier Marketplace and Rusty's Bazaar (mainly food), and the stalls in the rear of the Night Markets food hall on the Esplanade.

Harris Brothers, on the corner of Shields and Sheridan Sts, has a good range of Aussie clothing, boots and Akubra hats.

Getting There & Away

Air Qantas and Sunstate (☎ 13 1313) have an office on the corner of Shields and Lake Sts; Ansett (☎ 13 1300) is at 13 Spence St.

Domestic Flights Ansett and Qantas have daily flights between Cairns and all the major destinations including Melbourne ($660 one way), Sydney ($587), Brisbane ($428), Townsville ($176), Darwin ($456), Alice Springs ($417), Perth ($691) and Adelaide ($642).

Shorter hops within Queensland are

shared between a number of smaller airlines. Sunstate flies to Bamaga ($280), Lizard Island ($195) and Thursday Island ($324). Ansett flies to Weipa ($242) and Mt Isa ($237). Flight West flies to Cooktown ($75) and operates a service through the Gulf, the Cape York Peninsula and to Bamaga and the Torres Strait Islands. Hinterland Aviation (☎ 4035 9323) has flights to Cow Bay, south of Cape Tribulation, for $83.

International Flights Cairns airport has regular flights to and from North America, Papua New Guinea and Asia. Air Niugini (☎ 4051 4177) is at 4 Shields St; the Port Moresby flight costs $390 one way and goes at least once daily. Qantas also flies to Port Moresby (daily except Wednesday and Sunday), as well as Singapore (daily except Thursday, from $839) and Hong Kong (Thursday, from $839).

Bus All the bus companies operate from the transit centre at Trinity Wharf. Most backpackers' hostels have courtesy buses that meet the arriving buses.

Greyhound Pioneer (☎ 13 2030) and McCafferty's (☎ 13 1499) both run at least five buses a day up the coast from Brisbane and Townsville to Cairns. Journey times and fares are: Brisbane, 27 hours, $148; Rockhampton, 15 hours, $98; Mackay, 11 hours, $78; and Townsville, six hours, $42.

Coral Coaches (☎ 4031 7577) has daily buses to Port Douglas ($16), Cape Tribulation ($28) and Cooktown via either the inland road ($47) or the coastal road ($52). It also operates a weekly service to and from Weipa ($125).

White Car Coaches (☎ 4091 1855) has services to Kuranda and the Atherton Tableland, and Cairns-Karumba Coachline (☎ 4031 5448) has services to Karumba ($122) in the Gulf, via the Undara Lava Tubes ($42).

Train Three trains run between Cairns and Brisbane – the *Sunlander* (three times a week), the *Queenslander* and the *Spirit of the Tropics* (both weekly). The 1631km trip

from Brisbane takes 32 hours. The luxurious *Queenslander* leaves Brisbane on Sunday and Cairns on Tuesday; the fare is $389 including sleeping berth and all meals (1st class only). For another $270 you can put your car on the train too. The economy/1st class fare for a sleeper on the *Sunlander* or *Spirit of the Tropics* is $165/253. Call Queensland Rail for bookings and enquiries (☎ 13 2232)

Car, 4WD & Motorcycle Rental It's well worth considering renting a vehicle. There's plenty to see and do on land around Cairns, whether it's doing the beach crawl up to Port Douglas and Cape Trib or exploring the Atherton Tableland. The major rental firms have desks at the airport and offices in town, and there are dozens of smaller local operators offering good deals – shop around, but watch out for hidden costs such as insurance and per-km charges. Generally, small cars are about $45 per day with 300km free.

Note that most Cairns rental firms specifically prohibit you from taking their cars on the road to Cooktown, to Chillagoe or up the Cape Tribulation road. If you ignore this prohibition and get caught, you'll lose your deposit and/or be up for a hefty fine, so if you're planning to tackle one of these routes you'll need to hire a 4WD. These are widely available, but they cost about $95 a day with up to 300km free. See the Cape York section for details of some operators who rent 4WDs for Cape York trips.

Jolly Frog Rentals at 149 Lake St rents off-road motorbikes from $65 a day (200km free) and road bikes up to 1100cc from $120. They also have mopeds (motorcycle licence not required) for $29.

Boat The daily *Quicksilver* (☎ 4099 5500) fast-catamaran service links Cairns with Port Douglas. The trip takes 1½ hours and costs $20 one way, and $30 return.

Getting Around
To/From the Airport The approach road to the Cairns airport (domestic and international flights) leaves the main highway about

3.5km north of the centre. The old Cairns airport (local flights) is reached from a second turning about 1.5km further north.

The Australia Coach shuttle bus (☎ 4031 3555) meets all incoming flights and runs a regular pick-up and drop-off service between the airport and town; the one-way fare is $4.50. A taxi is about $11.

Bus Sunbus runs the local bus services in and around Cairns. Schedules for most of them are posted at the main city stop (known as the Lake St transit centre) in City Place. There is 24-hour service on the main routes, including up to Yorkeys Knob and Holloways Beach (service No 1C), to Trinity and Clifton beaches and to Palm Cove (1, 1A, 1Z). To Machans Beach, service No 4 runs between 6 am and 11 pm. Heading south, bus No 1B goes as far as the Coconut Resort on the Bruce Highway, and it also operates 24 hours.

The Cairns Explorer (☎ 4055 1240) is an air-con service that plies a circular route around the city, and you can get on or off at any of the eight stops. It departs daily every hour from 9 am to 4 pm (Monday to Saturday from October to April) from the Lake St transit centre, and a day ticket costs $25. Stops include the Pier Marketplace, the mangrove boardwalk near the airport, the botanic gardens and the Royal Flying Doctor Service complex.

Bicycle Most of the hostels and car-hire firms, plus quite a few other places, have bikes for hire so you'll have no trouble tracking one down. Expect to pay about $10 a day.

ISLANDS OFF CAIRNS

Off the coast from Cairns are Green Island and Fitzroy Island. Both attract hordes of day-trippers (some say too many), and both have resorts owned by the cruise company Great Adventures, which in turn is owned by the Japanese corporation Daikyo.

South of Cairns, the Frankland Islands Group is a cluster of undeveloped national park islands. You can do day trips to these islands or camp overnight or longer.

Green Island

Green Island, 27km north-east of Cairns, is a coral cay 660m long by 260m wide. The island and its surrounding reef are all national park, although a multi-million dollar tourist resort takes up a substantial proportion of the island. Nevertheless, a 10-minute stroll from the resort to the far end of the island will remind you that the beach is beautiful, the water fine, the snorkelling good and the fish prolific.

The resort has a separate and somewhat crowded section for day-trippers, with impressive facilities, including a pool, a bar, several eateries and water sports gear for hire. Marineland Melanesia is worth a visit ($7), with its aquarium of fish, turtles, sting-rays and crocs, and a bizarre collection of Melanesian artefacts.

The five-star *Green Island Reef Resort* (☎ 1800 673 366) has room for 92 guests who each pay $250-plus a night.

Getting There & Away Great Adventures (☎ 4051 0455) has two services to Green Island: by launch ($30 return) or by fast catamaran ($50 return). Other operators include the Big Cat (☎ 4051 0444) with a day cruise for $42 (lunch $8).

Fitzroy Island

Six km off the coast and 29km south-east of Cairns, Fitzroy is a continental island with coral-covered beaches which are good for snorkelling but not ideal for swimming and sunbaking, although Nudey Beach (1.2km and 45 minutes return) is quite pleasant. Snorkellers will find good coral only 50m off the beach in the resort area, and the island has its own dive school. There are some fine walks, including one to the island's high point.

The *Fitzroy Island Resort* (☎ 1800 079 080) has hostel-style bunk rooms with shared kitchen, bathroom and laundry facilities at $28 per person including linen, and 'villa units' at $240/340 for singles/doubles including activities, breakfast and dinner. There's also a council camping ground (permits and bookings are advisable, available through Department of Environment in Cairns). Sites cost $15 a night for up to five people but only one tent per site, and campers can use most of the resort's facilities. Day-trippers have access to the resort facilities, which include a pool, snack bar, a bar, a couple of shops and a laundrette.

Getting There & Away Great Adventures (☎ 1800 079 080) and Sunlover Cruises (☎ 1800 810 512) both have return trips for $30.

Frankland Islands
Frankland Island Cruise & Dive (☎ 1800 079 039) has day trips to these untouched national park islands, costing $125 including lunch and snorkelling gear. If you like the idea of camping on a remote tropical island, they also do camping drop-offs for $140 per person (permit required).

ATHERTON TABLELAND
Inland from the coast between Innisfail and Cairns, the land rises sharply then rolls gently across the lush Atherton Tableland towards the Great Dividing Range. The tableland's altitude, more than 900m in places, tempers the tropical heat, and the abundant rainfall and rich volcanic soil combine to make this one of the greenest places in Queensland. In the south are the state's two highest mountains – Bartle Frere (1657m) and Bellenden Ker (1591m).

Little more than a century ago, this peaceful, pastoral region was still wild jungle. The first pioneers came in the 1870s, looking for a repeat of the Palmer River gold rush, further north. As elsewhere in Queensland, the Aboriginal population opposed the intrusion but was soon overrun. Some gold was found and rather more tin, but although mining spurred the development of roads and railways through the rugged, difficult land of the plateau, farming and timber soon became the chief activities.

Getting There & Around
The historic train ride and the Skyrail cableway from Cairns to Kuranda are major

attractions, and there are bus services to the main towns from Cairns, although having your own vehicle is the ideal way to get around. There are also some good tours on offer from Cairns.

From south to north, the three major roads from the coast are: the Palmerston Highway from Innisfail to Millaa Millaa; the Gillies Highway from Yungaburra to Gordonvale and Atherton; and the Kennedy Highway from Cairns to Kuranda and Mareeba. The Peninsula Developmental Road heads north from Mareeba towards Cooktown, with a turning at Mt Molloy to Mossman.

Kuranda (pop 660)
Famed for its markets, this mountain town is surrounded by spectacular tropical scenery. Unfortunately, Kuranda's charms have long since been discovered by the masses, and the place is flooded with tourists on market days. Many of the stalls and shops sell mainly trashy souvenirs, although there are still quite a few good arts, craft and produce stalls.

Things to See & Do The Kuranda Markets are held every Wednesday, Thursday, Friday and Sunday, although things quieten after about 2 pm. On other days, Kuranda reverts to its normal sleepy character.

Within the market area, Birdworld ($7) is a large canopied garden with lake, waterfalls and over 30 species of birds; it's open daily from 9 am to 4 pm. Also within the market is Kuranda Bungy ($60).

The **Australian Butterfly Sanctuary** ($10) is open daily from 10 am to 3 pm and has regular guided tours. On Coondoo St, the **Kuranda Wildlife Noctarium** ($9), where you can see nocturnal rainforest animals such as gliders, fruit bats and echidnas, is open daily from 10 am to 4 pm.

Over the footbridge behind the train station, Kuranda Riverboat & Rainforest Tours (☎ 4093 7476) runs 45-minute riverboat cruises ($10), and has one-hour guided rainforest walks daily at 11.45 am ($10).

There are several picturesque walks starting with short signed tracks down through

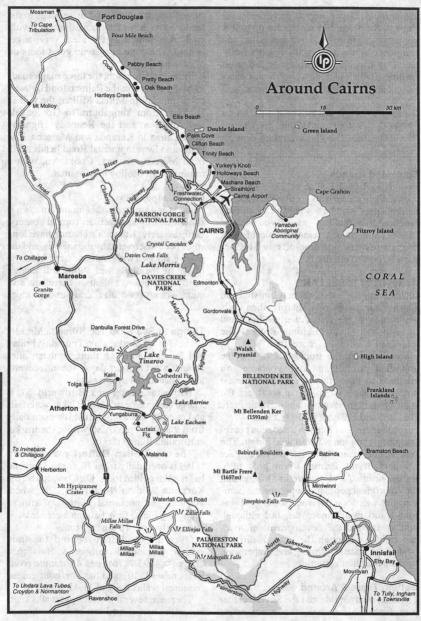

Around Cairns

0   15   30 km

Mossman

To Cape
Tribulation

Port Douglas

Four Mile Beach

Cook

Pebbly Beach

Pretty Beach
Oak Beach

Hartleys Creek

Mt Molloy

Ellis Beach

Double Island

Palm Cove

Clifton Beach

Trinity Beach

Yorkey's Knob

Holloways Beach

Kuranda

Machans Beach

Strathlord

Freshwater
Connection

Cairns Airport

Green Island

Cape Grafton

BARRON GORGE
NATIONAL PARK

CAIRNS

Fitzroy Island

Yarrabah
Aboriginal
Community

Crystal Cascades

Davies Creek Falls

To Chillagoe

Lake Morris

Mareeba

DAVIES CREEK
NATIONAL
PARK

Edmonton

CORAL
SEA

Granite
Gorge

Gordonvale

Danbulla Forest Drive

High Island

Tinaroo Falls

Lake
Tinaroo

Walsh
Pyramid

Kairi

Tolga

Cathedral Fig

Gillies

BELLENDEN KER
NATIONAL PARK

Frankland
Islands

Atherton

Yungaburra

Lake Barrine

Lake Eacham

Curtain
Fig

Peeramon

Mt Bellenden Ker
(1591m)

To Irvinebank
& Chillagoe

Malanda

Babinda Boulders

Babinda

Bramston Beach

Herberton

Mt Hypipamee
Crater

Mt Bartle Frere
(1657m)

Mirriwinni

Waterfall Circuit Road

Josephine Falls

Zillie Falls

Millaa Millaa
Falls

Ellinjaa Falls

North Johnstone River

Innisfail

Millaa
Millaa

Millaa Millaa

PALMERSTON
NATIONAL PARK

Mungalli Falls

Etty Bay

Mourilyan

To Undara Lava Tubes,
Croydon & Normanton

Ravenshoe

Palmerston Highway

To Tully, Ingham
& Townsville

QUEENSLAND

the market. **Jumrum Creek Environmental Park**, off the Barron Falls road, 700m from the bottom of Thongon St, has a short walking track and a big population of fruit bats. Further down, the Barron Falls road divides: the left fork takes you to a lookout over the falls, while a further 1.5km along the right fork brings you to Wrights Lookout where you can see back down the Barron Gorge to Cairns.

Places to Stay The leafy *Kuranda Van Park* (☎ 4093 7316) is a few kilometres out of town, up the road directly opposite the Kuranda turn-off on the Kennedy Highway. It has camp sites for $13 and on-site cabins from $35.

The agreeably rustic *Kuranda Hostel* (☎ 4093 7355), also known as *Mrs Miller's*, is at 6 Arara St, near the train station. It's a big, rambling old timber building with a huge garden, a small saltwater pool, spacious lounge/TV rooms and an enlightening graf-

fiti room. It's a quiet and relaxing place to stay, with dorm beds at $13 and doubles are $32 (VIP/YHA $1 less).

Tentative Nests (☎ 4093 9555), at 26 Barron Falls Rd about 2km from town, offers unusual accommodation in tented platforms in the rainforest. The cost is $50 per person, or $60 with breakfast and $88 with full board. Transfers to or from Cairns cost $5.

The *Bottom Pub/Kuranda Hotel* (☎ 4093 7206) at the corner of Coondoo and Arara Sts remains doggedly downmarket and has a pool and 12 very basic motel-style rooms with ceiling fans from $39/49.

A couple of kilometres out of town, back on the Kennedy Highway towards Mareeba, the upmarket *Kuranda Rainforest Resort* (☎ 4093 7555) has a bar, restaurant, swimming pool and tennis courts. En-suite two-bedroom cabins (some with cooking facilities) cost $120/138 plus $30 for extra adults.

Places to Eat Some of the best food is found

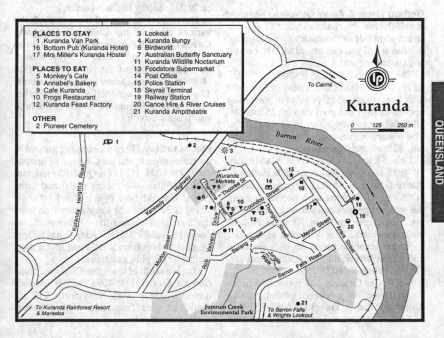

PLACES TO STAY
1 Kuranda Van Park
16 Bottom Pub (Kuranda Hotel)
17 Mrs Miller's Kuranda Hostel

PLACES TO EAT
5 Monkey's Cafe
8 Annabel's Bakery
9 Cafe Kuranda
10 Frogs Restaurant
12 Kuranda Feast Factory

OTHER
2 Pioneer Cemetery

3 Lookout
4 Kuranda Bungy
6 Birdworld
7 Australian Butterfly Sanctuary
11 Kuranda Wildlife Noctarium
13 Foodstore Supermarket
14 Post Office
15 Police Station
18 Skyrail Terminal
19 Railway Station
20 Canoe Hire & River Cruises
21 Kuranda Ampitheatre

To Cairns

Kuranda

0   125   250 m

Barron River

To Kuranda Rainforest Resort & Mareeba

Jumrum Creek Environmental Park

To Barron Falls & Wrights Lookout

QUEENSLAND

in the market's food stalls – fresh juices, Thai stir-fries, Indian curries etc – just follow your nose! There's a supermarket in Coondoo St if you're self-catering.

Both pubs do counter meals. The Bottom Pub has the very pleasant *Garden Bar & Grill* in its backyard, with a swimming pool, shady lawns and burgers for $5 and other grills from about $8.

Monkey's Cafe/Restaurant, down at the bottom end of Therwine St near the markets, is a good earthy BYO cafe serving breakfast, lunch and dinner. *Frogs Restaurant* on Coondoo St is another good local eatery. There's live music here on Sunday nights.

The *Feast Factory* is a large place with balconies looking right into the rainforest, and buffet meals for $11.

Cafe Kuranda, on the corner of Coondoo and Therwine Sts, does sandwiches, snacks and takeaways, and a few doors up on Therwine St, *Annabel's Bakery* has a large range of pies, pastries and more.

Getting There & Away Getting to Kuranda is half the fun. You have a choice of a scenic steam-train ride or the cableway through the rainforests. If you can afford to, take one up and the other back.

The Kuranda Scenic Railway (☎ 4052 6249) winds 34km from Cairns to Kuranda. This line, which took five years to build, was opened in 1891 and goes through 15 tunnels, climbing more than 300m in the last 21km. The historic steam trains operate daily and cost $25/40 one way/return.

The Skyrail Rainforest Cableway (☎ 4038 1555) is a 7.5km gondola cableway that runs from Smithfield, a northern suburb of Cairns, to Kuranda with two stops along the way. It operates daily from 8 am to 3.30 pm (last departure from Kuranda at 2.30 pm); fares are $27/45. A number of day tour packages combine travel on both the train and the cableway, and these cost from $66 (Tropic Wings ☎ 4035 3555).

White Car Coaches has buses five times daily (twice on weekends) from outside Tropical Paradise Travel (☎ 4051 9533) at 51 Spence St, Cairns. The fare is $7 one way.

Mareeba (pop 7000)
From Kuranda, the Kennedy Highway runs west across the tableland to Mareeba, the centre of a tobacco and rice-growing area, then continues south to Atherton in the centre of the tableland. Mareeba has a wide range of accommodation and in July hosts one of Australia's biggest rodeos.

The new Information Centre & Museum (☎ 4092 5674) near the Kuranda turn-off is open daily from 10 am to 4 pm.

Chillagoe (pop 500)
From Mareeba, you can continue 140km west to the old mining township of Chillagoe, and get a glimpse of the outback. All but the last 34km of the route is along sealed roads, and although the last section is pretty bumpy, it won't present a problem for conventional vehicles during the dry season. At Chillagoe you can visit impressive limestone caves and rock pinnacles, Aboriginal rock-art galleries, ruins of smelters from early this century and a museum.

The rangers run guided tours through the various caves of the **Chillagoe-Mungana Caves National Park**, leaving daily at 9 and 11 am and 1.30 pm ($5 to $7.50) – contact the Department of Environment office (☎ 4094 7163) on Queen St for more details. The rangers can also tell you about other caves with self-guiding trails, for which you'll need a torch.

Places to Stay There's a camping ground in the national park, and the *Chillagoe Caravan Park* (☎ 4094 7177) on Queen St has tent sites ($10), on-site cabins ($40) and units ($50). The old *Post Office Hotel* (☎ 4094 7119) at 37 Queen St has narrow iron beds upstairs for $15, and the *Chillagoe Caves Lodge* (☎ 4094 7106) at 7 King St has budget singles/doubles from $20/25 and motel units from $40/45, plus a restaurant.

One km north of town, the *Chillagoe Bush Camp & Ecolodge* (☎ 4094 7155) is a former miners' village with beds from $12.50, doubles/triples from $45/50 and home-cooked meals.

Getting There & Away White Car Coaches (☎ 4091 1855) has bus services from Cairns to Chillagoe ($39) three times a week, with a change at Mareeba ($12 one way). There are day tours from Cairns for about $100.

Atherton (pop 5700)

Although it's a pleasant, prosperous town, Atherton has little of interest in its own right. Railco (☎ 4791 4871) is a local volunteer organisation which from Wednesday to Sunday runs steam train trips to Herberton (1½ hours each way, $25 return).

Atherton Backpackers (☎ 4091 3552) at 37 Alice St, not far from the centre of town, is quite a good place and has dorm beds from $12 and doubles for $29.

Lake Tinaroo

From Atherton or nearby Tolga it's a short drive to this large lake created for the Barron River hydroelectric power scheme. It's open year-round for barramundi fishing. Tinaroo Falls, at the north-western corner of the lake, has a motel and the *Lake Tinaroo Holiday Park* (☎ 4095 8232) with tent sites ($11) and on-site cabins (from $34/38). Just out of town overlooking the dam wall, *Cafe Pensini's Deckbar & Bistro* is a good spot for a snack.

The road continues over the dam as a gravel track that does a 31km circuit of the lake through the **Danbulla State Forest**, finally emerging on the Gillies Highway 4km north-east of Lake Barrine. This is called the **Danbulla Forest Drive** and it's a pleasant trip – though sometimes impassable for conventional vehicles after heavy rain. It passes several self-registration lakeside camping grounds, run by the Department of Natural Resources (☎ 4095 8459). **Lake Euramoo**, about halfway along, is in a double volcanic crater; there's a short botanical walk around the lake. There is another crater at **Mobo Creek**, a short walk off the drive. Then, 25km from the dam, it's a short walk to the **Cathedral Fig**, a truly gigantic strangler fig tree.

Yungaburra (pop 985)

This pretty village is 13km east of Atherton along the Gillies Highway. It's right in the centre of the tableland, has some good restaurants and accommodation and, if you have transport, it's a good base from which to explore the lakes, waterfalls and national parks nearby. The central streets of the town have been classified by the National Trust and are quite atmospheric.

Three km out of Yungaburra on the Malanda road is the strangler fig known as the **Curtain Fig** for its aerial roots, which form a 15m-high hanging screen.

Places to Stay & Eat *On the Wallaby* (☎ 4095 2013), 37 Eacham Rd, is a small backpackers' hostel with double and twin rooms upstairs and good living areas downstairs. The cost is $15 per person, or you can camp in the backyard for $8. They have a good $55 package which includes return bus from Cairns, accommodation and canoe trips.

The *Lake Eacham Hotel* (☎ 4095 3515) is a fine old timber pub with a magnificent dining room and comfy rooms upstairs at $30/35. Or there's the (non-smoking) *Kookaburra Lodge* (☎ 4095 3222) on the corner of Oak St and Eacham Rd, with bright modern units from $65 a double. There's a pool and tiny dining room with three-course meals for $20.

Gumtree Getaway (☎ 4095 3105) is a B&B farm just outside town on the Atherton road with accommodation at $88 for a double.

There are three good restaurants: the chalet-style *Nick's Swiss-Italian Restaurant* with occasional live piano playing; the charming little *Burra Inn* opposite the pub, which has excellent country-style mains for about $18; and *Snibbles BYO* with light lunches from $6, dinner mains from $15 and a two-course dinner Wednesday to Saturday for $15.

Lakes Eacham & Barrine

These two lovely crater lakes are off the Gillies Highway east of Yungaburra. Both are reached by sealed roads and are great swimming spots. There are rainforest walking tracks around their perimeters – 6.5km around Lake Barrine, and 4km around Lake Eacham.

The *Lake Barrine Teahouse* (☎ 4095 3847) serves Devonshire teas and snacks, and you can take a 45-minute cruise ($7) daily at 10.15 am, 12 noon and 3.15 pm. Lake Eacham is quieter and more beautiful – an excellent place for a picnic or a swim, and there's a small floating pool for kids.

Both lakes are national parks and camping is not allowed. However, there are camp sites at *Lake Eacham Tourist Park* (☎ 4095 3730), 2km down the Malanda road from Lake Eacham. *Chambers Wildlife Rainforest Apartments* (☎ 4095 3754) has a number of self-contained one-bedroom apartments sleeping one to four people at $80 for two.

Malanda (pop 950)
About 15km south of Lake Eacham is Malanda, a busy dairy centre that claims to have the longest milk run in Australia, since it supplies milk all the way to Darwin and the north of Western Australia. On the Atherton road on the outskirts, the **Malanda Falls** drop into a big old swimming pool, with picnic facilities and a short walking trail nearby.

Places to Stay There's a caravan park beside the falls, and the huge old *Malanda Hotel* (☎ 4096 5101) has pub rooms at $16/32 and good bistro meals – the Friday and Saturday night smorgasbords are particularly popular.

The *Honeyflow Country Guesthouse* (☎ 4096 8173) is 7km from town on the Gordonvale road. It is a heritage homestead set in beautiful gardens, and costs $160 for a double including dinner and breakfast.

Fairdale Farmstay (☎ 4096 6599) is a working dairy farm 3km south of town with a six-bed cottage at $100, or $65/85 for rooms in the homestead (including breakfast).

Millaa Millaa (pop 320)
The 16km 'waterfall circuit' road near this small town, 24km south of Malanda, passes some of the most picturesque falls on the tableland. You enter the circuit by taking Theresa Creek Rd 1km east of Millaa Millaa on the Palmerston Highway. **Millaa Millaa Falls**, the first falls you reach, are the most spectacular and have the best swimming hole.

Continuing around the circuit, you reach **Zillie Falls** and then **Ellinjaa Falls** before returning to the Palmerston Highway just 2.5km out of Millaa Millaa. A further 5.5km down the Palmerston Highway there's a turning to **Mungalli Falls**, 5km off the highway, where the *Mungalli Falls Outpost* (☎ 4031 1144) has cabins ($40 double, shared cooking and toilet facilities), a teahouse and horse trail rides.

Millaa Millaa itself has a pub and a caravan park, and the Eacham Historical Society Museum is on the main street.

Mt Hypipamee National Park
The Kennedy Highway between Atherton and Ravenshoe passes the eerie Mt Hypipamee crater. It's a scenic 800m (return) walk from the picnic area, past **Dinner Falls**, to this narrow, 138m-deep crater with its spooky, evil-looking lake far below.

Herberton (pop 990)
On a slightly longer alternative route between Atherton and Ravenshoe is this old tin-mining town, which holds the colourful Tin Festival each September. On Holdcroft Dve is the Herberton Historical Village, with about 30 old buildings that have been transported here from around the tableland.

Ravenshoe (pop 900)
Ravenshoe is on the western edge of the tableland, at an altitude of 915m. It was once a thriving timber town, but things are pretty quiet around here nowadays. It has an excellent Visitor Centre (☎ 4097 7700), a caravan park, a couple of pubs and a motel.

On weekends at 2.30 pm, you can take a 7km ride on the Millstream Express, a historic steam train ($10). The **Little Mill-stream Falls** are 2km south of Ravenshoe on the Tully Gorge road. Six km past Ravenshoe and 1km off the road are the **Millstream Falls**, the widest in Australia although only 13m high (no swimming).

Kennedy Highway

Beyond Ravenshoe, the small mining town of **Mt Garnet**, 47km west, comes alive one weekend every May when it hosts one of Queensland's top outback race meetings. If you're heading west there is a staffed fruit fly quarantine inspection post 4km from town; all fruit and some vegetables must be deposited here, and vehicles may be searched.

About 60km past Mt Garnet, the Kennedy Highway (Australia's Highway 1) passes through **Forty Mile Scrub National Park**, where the semi-evergreen vine thicket is a descendant of the vegetation that covered much of the Gondwana super-continent 300 million years ago – before Australia, South America, India, Africa and Antarctica drifted apart. Just past the park is the turn-off to **Undara Lava Tubes** (a must-see) and the Gulf region; see the Gulf Savannah section later in this chapter for details of the area west of here.

CAIRNS TO PORT DOUGLAS

The Bruce Highway, which runs nearly 2000km north from Brisbane, ends in Cairns, but the sealed coastal road continues another 110km north to Mossman and Daintree. This final stretch, the Cook Highway, is a treat because it often runs right along the shore and there are some superb beaches.

Heading out of Cairns, towards the airport, you'll find an interesting and informative elevated **mangrove boardwalk** 200m before you reach the airport. There are explanatory signs at regular intervals, and these give some insight into the surprising ecological complexities of swamp vegetation. There's a small observation platform.

Kamerunga Rd, off the Cook Highway just north of the airport turning, leads inland to the **Freshwater Connection**, a railway

museum complex where you can also catch the Kuranda Scenic Railway. It's 10km from the centre of town. Just beyond Freshwater is the turning south along Redlynch Intake Rd to **Crystal Cascades**, a popular outing 22km from Cairns, with waterfalls and swimming holes.

North along the Cook Highway are the Cairns northern beaches, which are really a string of suburbs. In order, these are Machans, Holloways, Yorkeys Knob, Trinity, Kewarra and Clifton beaches and Palm Cove. **Holloways Beach** has a good foreshore caravan park. **Trinity Beach** is perhaps the best for a short trip from Cairns, with pleasant beaches, a pub and a cluster of eateries and upmarket resorts along the beachfront. Backpackers can share a four-bed room at the *Sundowner Motel* (☎ 4055 6194) on the Esplanade for $15 a night.

Further north, **Palm Cove** is an exclusive little resort town with fancy hotels, expensive boutiques and restaurants; the very good council-run *Palm Cove Camping Area* on the foreshore has tent sites from $8. On the highway, Wild World has lots of crocodiles and snakes, tame kangaroos and Australian birds; there are shows daily.

Around the headland past Palm Cove and Double Island, **Ellis Beach** is a lovely spot. Its southern end is an unofficial nude bathing beach and in the central part of the beach is the *Ellis Beach Leisure Park* (☎ 4055 3538), which has a good camping ground and a restaurant/bar complex with live music most Sunday afternoons.

Soon after Ellis Beach is Hartleys Creek Crocodile Farm, with a collection of Australian wildlife. Most of the enclosures are a bit shoddy, but skill and spectacle make it an interesting 'animal place'. When they feed Charlie the crocodile in the 'Crocodile Attack Show' (3 pm) you know for certain why it's not wise to get bitten by one! The park is open daily ($13).

The secluded *Turtle Cove Resort* (☎ 4059 1800), 45km north of Cairns, is a popular gay resort. Prices start from $105 for a double including breakfast.

Shortly before Mossman there's a turn-off

QUEENSLAND

to fashionable Port Douglas. The turn-off to Cape Tribulation is just before Daintree village. From Cape Tribulation it's possible to continue up to historic Cooktown by 4WD along the controversial Bloomfield Track (see the aside in the Cape Tribulation Area section). Alternatively, there's the partly surfaced inland road from Cairns, but both roads to Cooktown can be impassable after periods of heavy rain.

PORT DOUGLAS (pop 3600)

In the early days of far north Queensland's development, Port Douglas was a rival for Cairns, but when Cairns eventually got the upper hand, Port Douglas became a sleepy little backwater. In the mid-1980s, however, people began to realise what a delightful place it was, and up went a couple of multi-million dollar resorts. These were quickly followed by a golf course, fast catamaran services from Cairns, a marina and shopping complex, and an avenue of palms lining the road from the Cook Highway to Port Douglas – all the ingredients of a retreat for the rich and fashionable. Yet, despite all this development, Port, as it's known locally, has managed to keep a good deal of its original charm and there is cheap accommodation available.

The little town has a couple of good central pubs with outdoor sitting areas, and a string of interesting shops and restaurants to wander around when the beach, the boats and the lookout get dull. You can make trips to the Low Isles, the Great Barrier Reef, the Mossman Gorge and Cape Tribulation.

Orientation & Information

It's 6km from the highway along a long, low spit of land to Port Douglas. The Sheraton Mirage resort occupies a long stretch of Four Mile Beach. The main road in, Davidson St, ends in a T-intersection with Macrossan St; the beach is to the right, and to the left is the town centre with most of the shops and restaurants. There's a fine view over the coastline and sea from Flagstaff Hill lookout.

There are several tour booking agents, including the helpful Port Douglas Tourist Information Centre (☎ 4099 5599) at 23 Macrossan St and the Paradise Information & Booking Centre (☎ 4099 4144) at 30 Wharf St.

Things to See

On the pier off Anzac Park, **Ben Cropp's Shipwreck Museum** is quite interesting and open daily from 9 am to 5 pm ($5). At the **Rainforest Habitat**, where the Port Douglas road leaves the main highway, an enclosed canopy houses an artificial rainforest with elevated timber boardwalks, with at least 30 bird and butterfly species. It's a good introduction to the rainforest, although it's not cheap at $16 per person.

Port's **Sunday Markets**, held in Anzac Park at the northern end of Macrossan St, feature dozens of different stalls and tents, selling fruit and vegies, clothing, crafts and more.

Diving

Several companies offer learn-to-dive courses here. The Port Douglas Dive Centre (☎ 4099 5327), with a shop near the public wharf, has a four-day course at $530; Aussie Dive (☎ 1800 646 548) is the cheapest at $350 for a PADI course. Quicksilver (☎ 4099 5050), based at the Marina, has a five-day course at $439. Most of the boats heading out to the reef offer dives for certified divers – see the following sections.

Organised Tours

Reef Trips Quicksilver's huge fast cats do daily trips to Agincourt Reef on the outer reef for $130, which includes snorkelling gear, a semi-submersible ride, underwater observatory viewing and lunch. For certified divers, two 40-minute dives will cost an extra $90 with all gear provided. If you'd rather go in a smaller group, there are quite a few smaller boats, including *Wavelength*, *Poseidon* and *MV Freestyle*, which offer similar but much more personalised reef, snorkelling and diving trips starting at about $90.

Low Isles There are also cruises out to the Low Isles, a fine little coral cay surrounded by a lagoon and topped by an old lighthouse. Several of the smaller boats, such as *Sail Away*, *Willow* and *Shaolin*, offer good day trips from $85 to $100, which generally include lunch, snorkelling gear and boom netting. Quicksilver also runs trips to the Low Isles for $89. All boats operate from the Marina, and you can book with one of the agents on Macrossan St.

Other Tours There are numerous operators offering day trips to Cape Tribulation, some via Mossman Gorge, from about $90. A two-day 4WD Cooktown loop – up via the

Bloomfield Track, back via the inland road – with Strikies Safaris (☎ 4099 5599) is $220, not including meals and accommodation. Amber Dahlberg's Eco Cruises offers birdwatching tours of the mangroves and wetlands of Dickson Inlet (two hours, $35). Many of the tours out of Cairns also do pick-ups from Port Douglas. Bookings can be made with any of the agencies in town.

Bike N Hike does excellent mountain bike day trips to the Mowbray Valley for $45.

Places to Stay

Port Douglas has three caravan parks. The

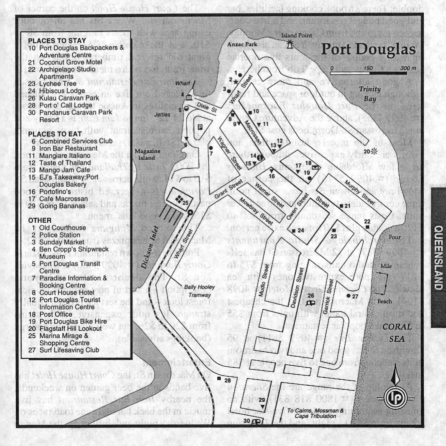

PLACES TO STAY
10 Port Douglas Backpackers & Adventure Centre
21 Coconut Grove Motel
22 Archipelago Studio Apartments
23 Lychee Tree
24 Hibiscus Lodge
26 Kulau Caravan Park
28 Port o' Call Lodge
30 Pandanus Caravan Park Resort

PLACES TO EAT
6 Combined Services Club
9 Iron Bar Restaurant
11 Mangiare Italiano
12 Taste of Thailand
13 Mango Jam Cafe
15 EJ's Takeaway; Port Douglas Bakery
16 Portofino's
17 Cafe Macrossan
29 Going Bananas

OTHER
1 Old Courthouse
2 Police Station
3 Sunday Market
4 Ben Cropp's Shipwreck Museum
5 Port Douglas Transit Centre
7 Paradise Information & Booking Centre
8 Court House Hotel
12 Port Douglas Tourist Information Centre
18 Post Office
19 Port Douglas Bike Hire
20 Flagstaff Hill Lookout
25 Marina Mirage & Shopping Centre
27 Surf Lifesaving Club

Port Douglas

Island Point

Anzac Park

Trinity Bay

Wharf

Dixie St

Jetties

Magazine Island

Wharf Street

Macrossan Street

Wagner Street

Grant Street

Warner Street

Mowbray Street

Owen Street

Murphy Street

Dickson Inlet

Bally Hooley Tramway

Mudlo Street

Davidson Street

Garrick Street

Four Mile Beach

CORAL SEA

To Cairns, Mossman & Cape Tribulation

QUEENSLAND

Kulau Caravan Park (☎ 4099 5449) at 24 Davidson St is the closest to the centre and a short walk from the beach. It has tent sites from $14 and on-site cabins from $50. About a kilometre further out, the *Pandanus Van Park* (☎ 4099 5944) at 111 Davidson St has tent sites from $13 and on-site cabins from $45.

The *Port o' Call Lodge* (☎ 4099 5422) in Wharf St, about 1km south of the centre, just off Davidson St, is a YHA-associate and has modern four-bed units with private bathrooms at $17 per person ($18 for nonmembers). It also has air-con motel units that range seasonally from about $72 a double. There's a pool, cooking facilities, bar and good budget restaurant, and a free courtesy coach to and from Cairns every Monday, Wednesday and Saturday. You can also hook up with a couple of the tours that operate between Cairns and Cape Trib from here.

A good alternative and more central, although lacking in outdoor space and facilities, is the *Port Douglas Backpackers* (☎ 4099 4883), above the Adventure Centre at 8 Macrossan St. Dorm beds cost $15.

Most of the motels, holiday flats and resorts are fairly expensive, although there are a few affordable exceptions. *Hibiscus Lodge* (☎ 4099 5315) on the corner of Mowbray and Owen Sts has a small pool, three comfy older-style units and three newer units. Costs range seasonally from $60 to $120 a double plus $10 for each extra person.

The *Archipelago Studio Apartments* (☎ 4099 5387) at 72 Macrossan St has self-contained studio units ranging from $75 to $145 (the more expensive ones with sea views). The *Coconut Grove Motel* (☎ 4098 5124), at 58 Macrossan St, is the cheapest and most central motel with units from $55 to $75 and a popular restaurant.

The *Lychee Tree* (☎ 4099 5811) at 95 Davidson St has good one and two-bedroom units sleeping from one to five people at $85 to $105.

At the top of the range are the *Sheraton Mirage Resort* (☎ 1800 818 831), with an amazing swimming pool and five-star hotel rooms from $430 a night, and the *Torresian Resort* (☎ 4099 5577), with hotel rooms starting from $155 a night and villas from $175.

Places to Eat

Port Douglas has a great range of cafes and restaurants, mostly along Macrossan St, although not too many places cater for budget travellers.

EJ's Takeaway, with fish & chips and burgers, and the *Port Douglas Bakery* on Grant St are a good place to start. *Cafe Macrossan* at 42 Macrossan St is a breakfast place, but also has good snacks. Next door is the trendy and popular *Salsa Bar & Grill*.

The *Court House Hotel* on the corner of Macrossan and Wharf Sts has an outdoor eating area with meals ranging from $8 to $10, and the *Combined Services Club*, a great old tin and timber building on the waterfront, has bistro meals from $7 to $10.

The *Iron Bar Restaurant* at 5 Macrossan St is decked out like an outback woolshed and specialises in Aussie tucker, and across at No 24 the *Mango Jam Cafe* is a lively and popular bar/restaurant with tasty gourmet pizzas ($10), pasta, salads and lots more.

On Grant St near the Macrossan St corner, the BYO *Taste of Thailand* has mains from $10 to $14, while across at 31 Macrossan St, *Portofinos* is a licensed bistro with good pasta, curries, pizzas and salads from $10 to $15, and a good kids' menu.

The relaxed *Mangiare Italiano* at 18 Macrossan St has pizzas from $10 to $12.

Port's best-known restaurant is the bizarre *Going Bananas* (☎ 4099 5400) at 87 Davidson St. The décor is almost beyond description – a sort of post-cyclone tropical forest look – and the service is often equally strange. It's quite expensive, with mains from $20 to $26, but well worth the splurge (bookings advisable).

Entertainment

On Macrossan St, the *Court House Hotel* has live bands in the beer garden on weekends, the nearby *Iron Bar Restaurant* has live music in the back bar and cane toad races on Wednesday night and, further up, the *Mango*

Jam Cafe has live music on Tuesday and Friday. The *Coconut Grove Motel* on Macrossan St has live music on weekends and is popular with locals.

Upstairs in the Marina complex are *FJ's Nightclub* and the *Waterfront Bar*, with three bars and live bands three nights a week.

The bar at *Going Bananas* is a popular watering hole, or you could always pop into the *Sheraton Mirage Resort* for a drink – it's worth a look.

Getting There & Away

Bus The Port Douglas transit centre (☎ 4099 5351) is just off Wharf St. Coral Coaches (☎ 4098 2600) covers the Cairns to Cooktown coastal route via Port Douglas, Mossman, Daintree, Cape Tribulation and Bloomfield. It rus about eight buses a day between Cairns and Port Douglas (1½ hours, $16), about 13 buses a day from Port Douglas to Mossman ($6), twice-daily buses to Daintree village ($12) and Cape Tribulation (2½ hours, $20), and buses to Cooktown via the (coastal) Bloomfield Track on Tuesday, Thursday and Saturday (about six hours, $45). Every Wednesday, Friday and Sunday, they go from Cairns to Cooktown via the inland road (about 5½ hours, $47), and on Friday to Weipa (12½ hours, $220).

Coral Coaches usually lets you stop over as often as you like along the route, so it can be as good as any tour.

Boat The daily *Quicksilver* (4099 5500) fast catamaran service between Cairns and the Marina at Port Douglas costs $20/30 one way/return.

Getting Around

Avis, National and Budget all have offices on Macrossan St. Cheaper local operators include Network (☎ 4099 5111) and Crocodile Car Rentals (☎ 4099 555), who specialise in 4WD hire.

Port is very compact, and the best way to get around is by bike. Port Douglas Bike Hire (☎ 4099 5799) at 40 Macrossan St and the Port o' Call Lodge both hire out good bikes for $10 a day. Call ☎ 4099 5345 for a taxi.

MOSSMAN (pop 1900)

Mossman, Australia's most northerly sugar town and a centre for tropical fruit-growing, has a couple of accommodation places but is of little interest. At beautiful **Mossman Gorge**, 5km west, there are some excellent swimming holes and rapids and a 3km circuit walking track through rainforest. Coral Coaches runs buses up to the gorge from Mossman and Port Douglas.

Places to Stay & Eat

You can't camp at the Gorge, but there's a creekside caravan park next to the swimming pool in Mossman. The old green and cream *Exchange Hotel* in the centre of town has basic but clean pub rooms at $17/32. The *Demi-View Motel* (☎ 4098 1277) at 41 Front St has budget rooms at $50/60, and the *White Cockatoo Cabins* (☎ 4098 2222), 1km south of the centre, has good self-contained cabins from $60 a double.

The most convenient eatery is the *Palms Cafe* opposite the Exchange Hotel.

DAINTREE

The highway continues 36km beyond Mossman to the quaint village of Daintree, passing the turn-off to the Daintree River ferry after 24km.

Originally established as a logging town, with timber cutters concentrating on the prized red cedars that were so common in this area, Daintree is now known as a centre for river cruises along the beautiful Daintree River. It's a fairly quiet little backwater, with a couple of shops and cafes and several good B&Bs. The Timber Museum, Gallery & Shop is worth a look, although the pieces for sale carry astronomical price tags.

Daintree River Tours

There are at least half a dozen operators offering river trips on the Daintree from various points between the ferry and Daintree village. It's certainly a worthwhile activity. Birdlife is prolific, and in the cooler months (April-September) croc sightings are common, especially on sunny days when the tide is low, as they love to sun themselves on the exposed banks.

The larger commercial operators include the Daintree Rainforest River Trains (☎ 1800 808 309), based beside the ferry crossing, with one-hour cruises for $12 and 1½ hour cruises for $20, and the more low-key Daintree River & Cruise Centre (4km beyond the ferry turn-off on the Mossman to Daintree road), with one-hour cruises for $10 and 1½ hour cruises for $15. These operators can take about 50 to 60 passengers in their boats and mainly cater for people on packaged tours, but they will also take passing travellers along.

There are several operators that offer more personalised tours for smaller groups. Chris Dahlberg's Specialised River Tours (☎ 4098 6169), based at the Red Mill B&B in Daintree village, takes groups of up to 12 people, and Chris is an enthusiastic birdwatcher and knowledgeable guide. His two-hour trips depart at 6.30 am in winter and 6 am in summer and cost $25. Electric Boat Cruises (☎ 1800 686 103) take groups of 12 people in very quiet electric-powered boats for 1½-hour cruises at $25 including breakfast, or one-hour cruises throughout the day ($15). Far North River Safaris (☎ 4098 6120) takes only four passengers, as does On the Daintree (☎ 4090 7638). This latter company does 2½-hour early morning cruises from the crossing for $25, and at other times on demand.

Places to Stay

The Daintree Riverview Caravan Park (☎ 4098 6119) has tent sites for $12 and on-site vans from $35.

There are several B&Bs in Daintree. The excellent Red Mill House (☎ 4098 6169) in the centre of town has three comfortable rooms, lovely spacious gardens and a pool. The cost is from $25/55 for singles/doubles, which includes a delicious breakfast on the balcony. This place is not suitable for young children. Weroona Cottage (☎ 4098 6198) at 2 Douglas St is a small cabin which costs $65

for a double with breakfast. Also here is Daintree Cottage, a fully furnished cottage which can sleep up to five people, and the cost is $75.

There's also the impressive Daintree Eco Lodge (☎ 4098 6100), with classy timber lodges starting at $308/330 for singles/doubles.

Kenadon Homestead Cabins (☎ 4098 6142) on Dagmar St have also been recommended. The cost is $60 for a double plus $10 for each extra person (maximum of five).

Places to Eat

In Daintree village, Jacanas Restaurant is a casual cafe with sandwiches, burgers and main meals from $10, while across the road the Big Barramundi has an outdoor eating area with light snacks and meals such as tasty barbecued barramundi with salad ($12). There's also the excellent Baaru House restaurant at the Daintree Eco Lodge.

CAPE TRIBULATION AREA

After crossing the Daintree River by ferry, there's another 34km of (mostly sealed) road, with a few hills and creek crossings, to Cape Tribulation. The road is quite good and, unless there has been exceptionally heavy rain, conventional vehicles can make it easily, with care, to Cape Trib.

Cape Tribulation was named by Captain Cook; it was a little north of here that trouble started when his ship ran onto the Endeavour Reef. Mt Sorrow was also named by Cook.

In the 1970s, much of this coast was a seldom-visited hippie outpost, with settlements like Cedar Bay, north of Cape Trib between Bloomfield and Cooktown. These days, Cape Tribulation is much more accessible and there's a steady stream of operators ferrying tourists up from Port Douglas and Cairns. It's no longer quite so isolated, but it's still an incredibly beautiful stretch of coast, and it is one of the few places in Australia where tropical rainforest meets the sea.

Remember, however, that this is rainforest – you'll need to bring mosquito repellent.

TONY WHEELER

TONY WHEELER

TONY WHEELER

TONY WHEELER

TONY WHEELER

Queensland
A: Hinchinbrook Island
B: Pisonias, Lady Musgrave Island
C: Heron Island
D: Watson's Bay, Lizard Island
E: South Molle Island

HUGH FINLAY

HUGH FINLAY

Queensland
Top: The archetypal north Queensland pub
Bottom: Sugar cane fields near Cairns

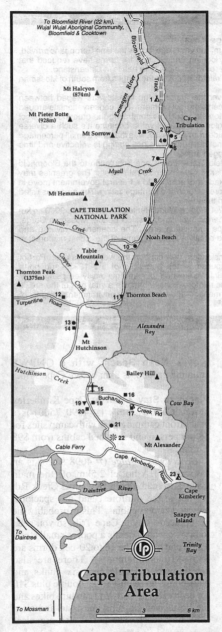

Cape Tribulation Area

Approaching Cape Trib from the south, the last bank is at Mossman. You can get fuel at two or three places between Mossman and Cooktown along this coastal route.

Note that accommodation at Cape Trib is limited and often booked out during peak holiday periods – ring in advance to make sure there will be a bed for you when you arrive.

Getting There & Away

See the Cairns and Port Douglas sections for details of the buses between those places and Cape Trib. There are also some excellent deals for tours out of Cairns and Port Douglas that include accommodation at the Cape Trib hostels; for example, $78 including one night's accommodation or $89 including two nights. See Organised Tours & Cruises in the Cairns section for more details.

It's quite easy to hitch because, beyond the Daintree ferry, all vehicles have to head to Cape Trib – there's nowhere else to go!

PLACES TO STAY
1. Pilgrim Sands Holiday Park
3. Cape Trib Retreat
6. PK's Jungle Village
8. Coconut Beach Rainforest Resort
9. Noah Beach Camping Area
12. Heritage Lodge
14. Lync-Haven
16. Crocodylus Village
18. Rainforest Retreat
20. Cow Bay Hotel
23. Club Daintree

PLACES TO EAT
11. Thornton Beach Kiosk
19. Latitudes 16.12°

OTHER
2. Cape Tribulation Parking Area
4. Bat House
5. Ranger Station
7. Cape Trib Store
10. Marrdja Botanical Walk
13. Wundu Trailrides
15. Cow Bay Airstrip
17. Matt Lock's Service Station & General Store
21. Daintree Rainforest Environmental Centre
22. Alexandra Range Lookout

QUEENSLAND

Queensland's Wet Tropics World Heritage Area

Nearly all of Australia was covered in rainforest 50 million years ago, but by the time Europeans arrived, only about 1% of the rainforest was left. Today, logging and clearing for farms have reduced that amount to less than 0.3% – about 20,000 sq km – of which more than half is in Queensland.

The biggest area of surviving virgin wet tropical rainforest covers the ranges from south of Mossman up to Cooktown. It's called the Greater Daintree.

Throughout the 1980s, a series of battles over the future of the forests was waged between conservationists, the timber industry and the Queensland government. The conservationists argued that apart from the usual reasons for saving rainforests – such as combating the greenhouse effect and preserving species' habitats – this forest region has special value because it's such a diverse genetic storehouse. The timber industry's case, aside from job losses, was that only a small percentage of the rainforest was used for timber – and then not destructively, since cutting is selective and time is left for the forest to regenerate before being logged again.

The 1983 fight over the controversial Bloomfield Track, from Cape Tribulation to the Bloomfield River, drew international attention to the fight to save Queensland's rainforests. The greenies may have lost that battle but the exposure of the blockade indirectly led to a Federal government move in 1987 to nominate Queensland's wet tropical rainforests for World Heritage listing. The area was listed in 1988, with a total ban on commercial logging in the area.

Stretching from Townsville to Cooktown, the Wet Tropics World Heritage Area covers 9000 sq km of the coast and hinterland, and includes the Atherton Tableland, Mission Beach, Mossman Gorge, Jourama Falls, Mt Spec and the Daintree-Cape Tribulation area. The scenery is diverse and spectacular, ranging from coastal mangroves and eucalypt forest to some of the oldest rainforest in the world.

A 1993 survey found that 80% of north Queenslanders now support the wet tropics area. Part of the reason for the turnaround has been ecotourism – the buzzword of the 1990s and north Queensland's green gold mine. With reef and rainforest-related tourism now easily eclipsing sugar production as the Far North's biggest industry, the rainforests have become a vital part of the area's livelihood. The challenge now is to learn how to manage and minimise the environmental impact of the enormous growth in tourism and population. ■

Daintree River to Cape Tribulation

The Daintree River ferry is the gateway to Cape Trib. Ferries operate every few minutes from 6 am to midnight and cost $6 for a car, $3 for a motorbike and $1 for a pedestrian.

Three km beyond the ferry, Cape Kimberley Rd leads down to Cape Kimberley beach, 5km away. About 9km from the ferry, just after you cross the spectacular Heights of Alexandra range (and lookout), is the **Daintree Rainforest Environmental Centre** – an excellent information centre with rainforest displays, a self-guided forest boardwalk and an audiovisual show. It's open daily from 9 am to 5 pm ($8).

About 12km from the ferry you reach Buchanan Creek Rd, which is the turn-off for **Cow Bay** (5.5km) and Crocodylus Village.

Further on, the road strikes the shore at **Thornton Beach**. The **Marrdja Botanical Walk**, at Noah Creek, is an interesting 800m boardwalk through rainforest and mangroves. **Noah Beach**, with a QNPWS camping ground, is 8km before Cape Trib.

Places to Stay & Eat At Cape Kimberley beach, *Club Daintree* (☎ 4090 7500) is a beachfront camping park with camp sites for $8 per person and four-bed cabins from $98 a night.

Crocodylus Village (☎ 4098 9166) is an associate-YHA hostel 2.5km off the main Cape Trib road, down Buchanan Creek Rd. It's set in the rainforest and has spacious, elevated canvas cabins. This is probably the best place to stay at Cape Trib, so you need to book ahead. There's a pool, a small store, a cafe and a bar. The 16 to 20-bed dorms are $15 ($16 nonmembers). There are also cabins with a double bed, six bunks and bathrooms; these cost $50 a double plus $10 for each extra person. You can hire bikes and the hostel vehicle runs guests to and from Cow Bay beach. The hostel also organises

QUEENSLAND

quite a few activities, including informative guided walks through the forests each morning and evening, half-day horse rides ($39), a three-hour sunrise paddletrek ($35) and a two-day sea-kayaking trip to Snapper Island ($159 with everything supplied).

Back on the Cape Trib road near the turn-off, the *Cow Bay Hotel* (☎ 4098 9011) has bistro meals and motel units at $60/65. Across the road there's the *Rainforest Retreat* (☎ 4098 9101), with self-contained motel units from $70 and a 20-bed bunk-house at $15 per person. There's also a pool and a restaurant. Next door, *Latitudes 16.12°* is an open-fronted restaurant with everything from burgers and curries to coral trout and barramundi.

About 5km north of the Cow Bay turning is *Lync-Haven* (☎ 4098 9155), a 16-hectare property with walking trails, plenty of wild-life, a cafe/restaurant, tent sites at $5 per person and a self-contained, six-berth cabin at $85 a double plus $10 for each extra person.

On the Turpentine Rd, which runs inland along the left bank of the Coopers Creek near Thornton Beach, the secluded *Heritage Lodge* (☎ 4098 9138) is a small, low-key resort with its own classy restaurant, a great swimming hole and motel-style units from $155 a double including breakfast.

At Thornton Beach, the *Cafe on Sea Kiosk*

is a laid-back beachfront eatery, with take-aways and a bar/cafe with good meals from $5 to $12. Further north on the beachfront is the self-registration *Noah Beach Camping Area*, with 16 shady sites, toilets and water – permits can be booked through the rangers at Cape Trib (☎ 4098 0052).

Cape Tribulation

Cape Tribulation is famed for its superb scenery, with long beaches stretching north and south from the low, forest-covered cape. If you want to do more than relax on the beach, there is a good range of activities which can be booked directly or through wherever you're staying. Paul Mason's Cape Trib Guided Rainforest Walks (☎ 4098 0070) has four-hour daytime walks and 2½-hour night walks ($20 each walk). The boats *Rum Runner* (☎ 1800 686 444) and *Taipan Lady* (☎ 4031 1588) both offer cruises out to the reef (from $59 including lunch and snorkelling gear), and Wundu Trailrides (☎ 4098 9156) offers three-hour horse rides ($39).

The **Bat House**, opposite PK's, is a small rainforest information and education centre, open daily from 10 am to 4 pm.

Places to Stay & Eat *PK's Jungle Village* (☎ 4098 0040) is a very well set up backpackers' hostel with comfortable log

---

Ferals in the Forests

Ferals, the alternative lifestylers who live deep in the dark rainforests of Far North Queensland, are the hippies of the 1990s – with a couple of fundamental differences. The long hair, flares, tie-dyed clothes and peace signs of the 1960s and 70s have been replaced by shaven or dreadlocked hair, ragged rainbow-coloured clothes, bare feet or heavy work boots, and body piercing galore. And instead of peace, love and understanding, ferals espouse radical environmentalism.

Ideologically, ferals reject contemporary culture and see city life as the ultimate urban nightmare. They consider the mass-production, mass-consumption doctrines that drive modern society to be totally unsustainable in the long term. Rather than seeing themselves as dropouts, ferals consider their lifestyle to be the way of the future, and that their rejection of materialism is the only way modern society will ever progress to a point where life on earth is sustainable.

Ferals live in communal, semi-nomadic tribal groups. Most of them are vegetarians who live off unemployment benefits and avoid using mass produced goods or fossil fuels, and they see themselves at the protectors of the forests they live in. You'll often see them wandering barefoot around places like Cairns and Mossman, where they come to collect supplies and their unemployment benefits. ■

cabins, a pool, a bar, and a restaurant with cheap meals. The nightly cost in an eight-bed cabin is $17 per person, cabins are $50 a double, or you can camp in the grounds for $8. PK's has a strong party atmosphere, so if you're looking for peace and quiet you'll be better off down at Crocodylus Village or elsewhere. There's a cheap restaurant and a bar here, and they offer similar tours to Crocodylus.

At 19 Nicola Dve, signposted from PK's, is the *Cape Trib Retreat* (☎ 4098 0037), a casual B&B place with rainforest literally in the backyard. The elevated timber home has cathedral ceilings and features rainforest timbers. The cost is $45/65, or $85 for an en-suite double.

Three km north of PK's, the *Pilgrim Sands Holiday Park* (☎ 4098 0030) is set in the thick of the forest, with a short walk down to a secluded beach. Tent sites are $13 for two and two-bedroom units (five beds) are $53 a double ($9.50 for extra adults), or with bathroom $72 a double ($12).

Three km south of the cape, the *Coconut Beach Rainforest Resort* (☎ 4098 0033) has stylish units with all the mod-cons from $215 a double and villas from $315 a night.

CAPE TRIBULATION TO COOKTOWN

Heading north from Cape Tribulation, the spectacular Bloomfield Track (4WD only) continues through the forest as far as the **Wujal Wujal Aboriginal community** 22km north, on the far side of the Bloomfield River crossing. Even for 4WD vehicles, a number of amazingly steep sections of the Bloomfield Track can be impassable after heavy rain.

From Wujal Wujal another dirt road – rough but usually passable in a conventional vehicle in the Dry – heads 46km north through the tiny settlements of **Bloomfield**, **Rossville** and **Helenvale** to meet the main Cooktown road (also dirt) 28km before Cooktown.

Places to Stay & Eat

Bloomfield Beach Camping (☎ 4060 8207), 11km north of the Bloomfield River cross-

ing, has a pleasant setting and tent sites for $6 per person and on-site tents at $15 per person (bedding supplied), plus a bar and restaurant. It also offers tours and river cruises. The *Bloomfield Wilderness Lodge* (☎ 4035 9166) is close to the mouth of the Bloomfield River and aims to make holes in fat wallets, with package deals from $658 per person twin-share for three nights, including air transfers, meals and activities.

Signposted 33km north of the Bloomfield River, the simple *Home Rule Rainforest Lodge* (☎ 4060 3925) has a lovely, peaceful setting, with a bar, good cooking facilities and/or cheap meals. They have bunk rooms at $15 per person and camping at $6 per person. There's a two-hour walk to a nearby waterfall, and horse riding is available. Ring from Rossville for a pick-up.

Nine km north at Helenvale, the *Lion's Den Hotel* (☎ 4060 3911) is a colourful, 1875 bush pub with corrugated tin walls and a slab-timber bar. It has cheap meals and you can camp out the back by the river ($4) or – if the boss thinks you're up to scratch – stay in the spartan rooms for $18/25.

CAIRNS TO COOKTOWN – THE INLAND ROAD

The 'main' road up from Cairns loops through Kuranda, Mareeba, Mt Molloy, the tungsten mining town of Mt Carbine, Palmer River and Lakeland, where the road up to Cape York Peninsula splits off. Most of the second half of this 341km road is unsealed and often corrugated.

In **Mt Molloy**, the *National Hotel* (☎ 4094 1133) has cheap accommodation. James Venture Mulligan, the man who started both the Palmer River and Hodgkinson River gold rushes, is buried in the Mt Molloy cemetery. At the **Palmer River** crossing there's a cafe/petrol station and a camping ground. The 1873 to 1883 Palmer River gold rush occurred in very remote country about 70km west of here. Its main towns were Palmerville and Maytown, of which very little are left today.

Shortly before Cooktown, the road passes **Black Mountain**, a pile of thousands of granite boulders. It's said that between the huge rocks there are ways which will take you under the hill from one side to the other, but people have died trying to find them. Black Mountain is known to Aboriginal people as Kalcajagga – 'Place of the Spears'. The colour comes not from the rocks, but from lichen growing on them.

COOKTOWN (pop 1400)

Cooktown can claim to have been Australia's first British settlement. From June to August 1770, Captain Cook beached his barque *Endeavour* here, and during that time, Joseph Banks, the chief naturalist, took the chance to study Australian flora and fauna along the banks of the Endeavour River. Banks collected 186 plant species and wrote the first European description of a kangaroo. The north side of the river has scarcely changed since then.

The British explorers had amicable contacts with the local Aboriginal people, but race relations in the area turned sour a century later when Cooktown was founded as the unruly port for the 1873 to 1883 Palmer River gold rush 140km south-west. Hell's Gate, a narrow pass on the track between Cooktown and the Palmer River, was the scene of frequent ambushes as Aboriginal people tried to stop their lands being overrun. Battle Camp, about 60km inland from Cooktown, was the site of a major battle between whites and Cape York Aboriginal people.

In 1874, before Cairns was even thought of, Cooktown was the second-biggest town in Queensland. At its peak there were no less than 94 pubs, almost as many brothels, and the population was over 30,000! As many as half of the inhabitants were Chinese, and their industrious presence led to some wild race riots.

After the gold rush ended, cyclones and a WWII evacuation came close to killing Cooktown. The opening of the excellent James Cook Historical Museum in 1970 started to bring in some visitor dollars, although Cooktown's population is still only around 1300 and only three pubs remain.

The effort of getting to Cooktown is rewarded not only by the atmosphere but by some fascinating reminders of the area's past. With a vehicle, you can use the town as a base for visiting the Quinkan rock art galleries near Laura or even Lakefield National Park.

Orientation & Information

Cooktown is on the inland side of a headland sheltering the mouth of the Endeavour River. Charlotte St runs south from the wharf, and along it are the three pubs, a post office, a bank, several cafes and a restaurant.

The Cooktown Tourist Information Centre (☎ 4069 6100) is in O'Connor Arcade on Charlotte St, between the Cooktown Hotel and Westcoast Hotel.

Things to See

Charlotte St has a number of interesting monuments, including one to the tragic Mary Watson (see the Lizard Island section) opposite the Sovereign Resort. A little further towards the wharf are memorials to the equally tragic explorer, Edmund Kennedy, and to Captain Cook. Behind these is a cannon, which was sent from Brisbane in 1885 along with three cannonballs, two rifles and one officer in response to Cooktown's plea for defences against a feared Russian invasion! Right by the waterside, a stone with an inscription marks the spot where the *Endeavour* was careened.

The **James Cook Historical Museum**, in a handsome 1880s convent on Helen St, near the corner of Furneaux St, has some fascinating displays relating to all aspects of Cooktown's past: Aboriginal people, Cook's voyages, the Palmer River gold rush and the Chinese community. The museum is open daily from 9.30 am to 4 pm and costs $5. The **Cooktown Museum** a block away on Walker St isn't really worth the admission price – it's more of a souvenir shop.

On Charlotte St the **Jackey Jackey** has a window display of interesting historical photos, and across the road is the **School of Arts Gallery**.

The **Cooktown Cemetery** on the McIvor

River-Cooktown Rd is worth a visit. There are many interesting graves, including those of Mary Watson and the 'Normanby Woman' – thought to have been a north European who survived a shipwreck as a child and lived with Aboriginal people for years until 'rescued' by whites. She died soon after.

The old **powder magazine**, a short walk around the northern tip of the headland, dates back to 1874, making it the oldest brick building in far north Queensland.

There are spectacular views from the lookout up on **Grassy Hill**. The very pleasant **Botanic Gardens**, off Walker St, were first planted in 1886 and restoration started in 1984. Walking trails lead from the gardens to the beaches at Cherry Tree and Finch bays.

Organised Tours

An interesting range of tours from Cooktown is on offer; these can be booked directly or through the tourist office.

Cooktown Cruises (☎ 4069 5712) has a two-hour scenic cruise up to the head of the Endeavour River and back via a mangrove creek ($18), departing daily at 2 pm.

Cooktown Tours (☎ 4069 5125) offers 1½-hour town tours ($16) and full-day 4WD

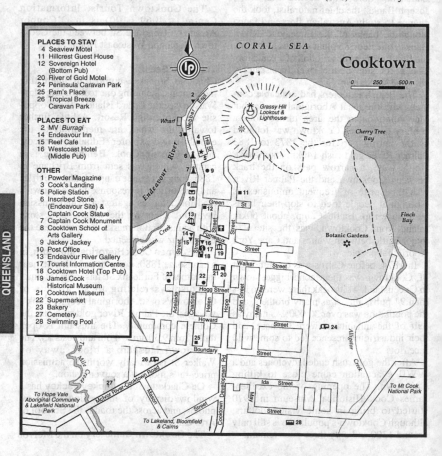

PLACES TO STAY
4 Seaview Motel
11 Hillcrest Guest House
12 Sovereign Hotel (Bottom Pub)
20 River of Gold Motel
24 Peninsula Caravan Park
25 Pam's Place
26 Tropical Breeze Caravan Park

PLACES TO EAT
2 MV *Burragi*
14 Endeavour Inn
15 Reef Cafe
16 Westcoast Hotel (Middle Pub)

OTHER
1 Powder Magazine
3 Cook's Landing
5 Police Station
6 Inscribed Stone (Endeavour Site) & Captain Cook Statue
7 Captain Cook Monument
8 Cooktown School of Arts Gallery
9 Jackey Jackey
10 Post Office
13 Endeavour River Gallery
17 Tourist Information Centre
18 Cooktown Hotel (Top Pub)
19 James Cook Historical Museum
21 Cooktown Museum
22 Supermarket
23 Bakery
27 Cemetery
28 Swimming Pool

CORAL SEA

Cooktown

0   250   500 m

Grassy Hill Lookout & Lighthouse

Cherry Tree Bay

Finch Bay

Botanic Gardens

Wharf

Webber Esp

Hill St

Endeavour River

Chinaman Creek

Green St

Furneaux Street

Adelaide Street

Charlotte Street

Helen Street

Hope Street

John Street

May Street

Walker Street

Hogg Street

Howard Street

Boundary Street

Two Mile Creek

Alligator Creek

Ida Street

Cooktown Development Rd

Mason Street

McIvor River-Cooktown Road

To Hope Vale Aboriginal Community & Lakefield National Park

To Lakeland, Bloomfield & Cairns

To Mt Cook National Park

QUEENSLAND

trips to Black Mountain and the Lion's Den Hotel ($99); both depart daily at 9 am.

Reel River Sportsfishing (☎ 4069 5346) offers lure-fishing trips on weekends and during school holidays (from $60/100 per person for a half/full day).

Munbah Aboriginal Cultural Tours has day trips to various sights around town including the Coloured Sands and Cape Bedford ($99 including lunch), and you can take an interesting trip on the local bus out to the Hope Vale Aboriginal Community ($20 return, departures on weekdays at 7.30 am and 3 pm). For bookings contact the Tourist Information Centre.

Places to Stay

There are two good caravan parks: the *Tropical Breeze Caravan Park* (☎ 4069 5417) on the McIvor River-Cooktown Rd, and the *Peninsula Caravan Park* (☎ 4069 5407) in the bush at the end of Howard St. Both have tent sites, on-site vans and units.

Pam's Place (☎ 4069 5166), on the corner of Charlotte and Boundary Sts, is a comfortable, well-equipped, associate-YHA hostel with a pool, good kitchen, and TV lounge. Bunks are $15 a night, and singles/doubles are $20 per person (nonmembers pay $1 extra). The *Hillcrest Guest House* (☎ 4069 5305) on Hope St is a friendly old place with singles/doubles with shared facilities from $30/45 including breakfast.

The impressive *Sovereign Resort* (☎ 4069 5400), on the corner of Charlotte and Green Sts, has a superb pool and well-appointed single/double rooms at $95/105, and two-bedroom apartments at $135. The *Seaview Motel* (☎ 4069 5377) on Charlotte St has good units from $60/70 a single/double, and the modern *River of Gold Motel* (☎ 4069 5222) on the corner of Hope and Walker Sts has singles/doubles from $60/68.

Places to Eat

The *Reef Cafe*, on the main street, is a decent takeaway place with good fish & chips. The *China Dina Cafe*, hidden in the arcade between the Cooktown and Westcoast hotels, is the spot for pizzas and vaguely Chinese food.

The *Cooktown Hotel* has a great beer garden with decent bistro meals from $8 to $12 (probably the best value in town), or the *Sovereign Resort* has an excellent balcony restaurant upstairs with tables overlooking the river and mains for about $14 at lunch time and from $19 to $23 at dinner.

The *Endeavour Inn*, on the corner of Charlotte and Furneaux Sts, is a relaxed colonial-style restaurant with a small bar, a courtyard dining area and live entertainment some weekends. They have a good reputation for their food – mains range from $17 to $19.

For something different, eat aboard the MV *Burragi*, a small former Sydney Harbour ferry now permanently moored near the jetty. It's both licensed and BYO, and mains cost around $18.

Getting There & Away

Air Flight West has daily flights between Cairns and Cooktown for $71.

Bus Coral Coaches (☎ 4098 2600) travels from Cairns to Cooktown via the inland road on Wednesday, Friday and Sunday (6½ hours, $47) and via the Bloomfield Track on Tuesday, Thursday and Saturday (8½ hours, $52).

Getting Around

Endeavour Car Hire (☎ 4069 6100) is the only vehicle rental agency in town. For a taxi phone ☎ 4069 5387.

LIZARD ISLAND

Lizard Island, the farthest north of the Barrier Reef resort islands, is about 100km from Cooktown. It was named by Joseph Banks after the numerous lizards he saw there. He and Cook spent a day on the island, trying to find a way out through the reef to the open sea.

A tragedy occurred on the island in 1881 when a settler's wife, Mary Watson, took to sea in a large metal pot with her son and a Chinese servant, after Aboriginal people killed her other servant while her husband was away fishing. The three eventually died of thirst on a barren island to the north, Mary leaving a diary of their terrible last days. Their tragic story is told at the Cooktown museum. Lizard is dry, rocky and mountainous, with superb beaches, great swimming and snorkelling, the remains of the Watsons' cottage, a pricey resort and a camping ground. There are plenty of bushwalks and birdlife, and great views from Cook's Look, the highest point on the island, from where Captain Cook surveyed the area.

Places to Stay

There's a small QNPWS camping ground at Watson's Bay. It has a fireplace, pit toilet, picnic table and a hand-pumped water supply 250m away. Camping permits are available from the Department of Environment (☎ 4052 3096) in Cairns, and you must take all supplies. You'll also need charcoal: fires are banned and all wood on the island, including driftwood, is protected; light planes are prohibited from carrying stove fuels.

At the exclusive *Lizard Island Resort* (☎ 4060 3999), singles/doubles cost from $860/1040 per day, including all meals and use of the facilities. Because of its isolation, the resort has been a favourite retreat for celebrities, and a popular stop for yachties, for many years.

Getting There & Away

Sunstate Airlines flies from Cairns for $195 one way, and Aussie Airways (☎ 1800 620 022) has a good day trip from Cairns for $299 per person including lunch and snorkelling gear. Marineair Seaplanes (☎ 4069 5860) has day trips from Cooktown for $195 and does camping drop-offs costing $400 each way for up to four people – worth considering if you're staying a few days.

Cape York Peninsula

The Cape York Peninsula is one of the wildest and least populated parts of Australia. The Tip, as it is called, is the most northerly point on the mainland of Australia,

and islands dot the Torres Strait between here and Papua New Guinea, only 150km away.

Getting up to the Tip along the rough and rugged Peninsula Developmental Road is still one of Australia's great road adventures. It's a trip for the tough and experienced since the roads are all dirt, and even at the height of the Dry there are some difficult river crossings. Several tour operators offer this adventure to those who can't or don't want to go it alone.

Of the numerous books on the Cape, Ron and Viv Moon's *Cape York – An Adventurer's Guide* is the most comprehensive. Lonely Planet's *Outback Australia* and *Queensland* guides have extensive information for travellers to Cape York.

Information & Permits

Visits to the RACQ, the Far North Queensland Promotion Bureau and the Department of Environment offices in Cairns are well worthwhile before you head north. You don't need a permit to visit Aboriginal or Torres Strait Islander communities, but you do to camp on Aboriginal land (which is effectively most of the land north of the Dulhunty River). Designated camping grounds are provided in a number of areas, including Seisia, Umagico, Pajinka and Punsand Bay. Camping elsewhere in the area requires a permit from the Injinoo Community Council (☎ 4069 3252) or Pajinka Wilderness Lodge. You can write to the Injinoo Community Council, PO Box 7757, Cairns, Qld 4870. Apart from Bamaga, most of the mainland Aboriginal communities are well off the main track north, and do not have any facilities or accommodation for travellers.

Getting There & Away

Air Sunstate/Qantas flies daily from Cairns to Bamaga ($324), Lizard Island ($195) and Thursday Island ($324). Ansett flies to Weipa ($242). Flight West also operates a daily service through the Peninsula and to the Torres Strait Islands.

Cape York Air (☎ 4035 9399) operates the Peninsula Mail Run, claimed to be the longest in the world. It flies to remote cattle

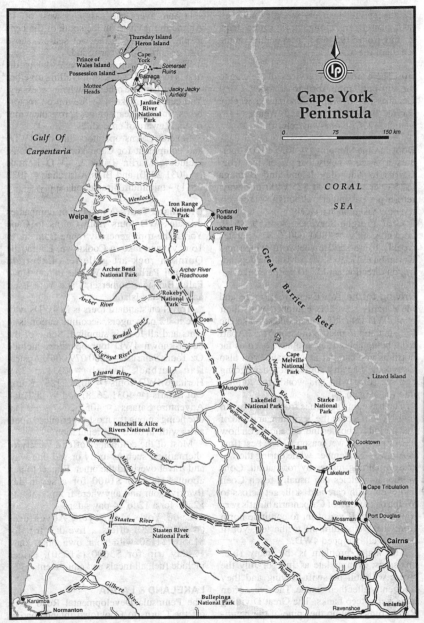

Cape York Peninsula

Gulf Of
Carpentaria

CORAL

SEA

Great Barrier Reef

Thursday Island
Heron Island
Prince of
Wales Island
Possession Island
Cape
York
Somerset
Ruins
Bamaga
Mottee
Heads
Jacky Jacky
Airfield
Jardine River
National Park

Wenlock
Iron Range
National Park
Portland
Roads
Lockhart River
Weipa

Archer Bend
National Park
Archer River
Roadhouse
Archer River
Rokeby
National Park
Kendall River
Coen
Holroyd River
Edward River
Cape Melville
National Park
Lizard Island
Musgrave
Lakefield
National Park
Starke
National Park
Mitchell & Alice
Rivers National Park
Kowanyama
Peninsula Dev Road
Alice River
Laura
Cooktown
Mitchell River
Lakeland
Cape Tribulation
Daintree
Mossman
Port Douglas
Staaten River
Staaten River
National Park
Cairns
Gilbert River
Burke Dev Road
Mareeba
Karumba
Bullepinga
National Park
Ravenshoe
Innisfail
Normanton

0   75   150 km

stations and towns every weekday and will take passengers along, with round trips costing from $195 to $390 depending on the length of the trip.

Bus There are no bus services all the way to the top but, from April to October, Coral Coaches (☎ 4098 2600) operates a weekly service between Cairns and Weipa (13½ hours, $125/235 one-way/return).

Boat Jardine Shipping (☎ 4035 1900) operates a twice weekly barge service from Cairns to Thursday Island and Bamaga ($750 per vehicle and $250/400 one-way/return per passenger), although passengers are only taken once a week.

Gulf Freight Services (☎ 4069 8619; bookings only ☎ 1800 640 079) operates weekly barge services between Weipa and Karumba ($275 to $370 per vehicle depending on direction, and $210 per passenger).

Driving to the Top Every year, more and more hardy travellers equipped with their own 4WD vehicles or trail bikes, make the long haul up to the top of Cape York. Apart from being able to say you have been as far north as you can get in Australia, you also test yourself against some pretty hard going and see some wild and wonderful country into the bargain.

The travelling season is from mid-May to mid-November but the beginning and end of that period are borderline, depending on how late or early the wet season is. The best time is August – September, while during the wet season nothing moves by road at all. Conventional vehicles can usually reach Coen and even, with care and skill, get across to Weipa on the Gulf of Carpentaria but it's *very* rough going. If you want to continue north from the Weipa turn-off to the top, you'll need a well-equipped 4WD.

The major problem is the many river crossings; even as late as June or July the rivers will still be swift-flowing and they frequently alter their course. The rivers often have very steep banks. The Great Dividing Range runs right up the spine of the penin-

sula and rivers run east and west off it. Although the rivers in the south of the peninsula flow only in the wet season, those further north flow year-round.

The ideal set-up for a Cape York expedition is two 4WD vehicles travelling together – one can haul the other out where necessary. You can also make it to the top on motorbikes, floating the machines across the wider rivers. Beware of crocodiles!

Several Cairns operators hire out 4WDs and equipment for Cape York expeditions, including Marlin Truck & 4WD Rentals (☎ 4031 2360) and Brits:Australia (☎ 4032 2611) – minimum hire periods apply.

Organised Tours A number of companies operate 4WD tours from Cairns to Cape York. The trips generally range from six to 16 days, and take in Cooktown, Laura, the Quinkan rock-art galleries, Lakefield National Park, Coen, Weipa, Indian Head Falls, Bamaga, Somerset, Cape York itself and Thursday Island.

Travel on standard tours is in 4WDs with five to 12 passengers, accommodation is in tents and all food is supplied. Some of the better-known 4WD tour operators include Oz Tours Safaris (☎ 1800 079 006), Australian Outback Travel (☎ 4031 5833), Heritage 4WD Tours (☎ 4038 2186), Kamp Out Safaris (☎ 4031 2628) and Wild Track Adventure Safaris (☎ 4055 2247), the last one being among the most experienced operators with an excellent reputation.

Most of the companies offer a variety of alternatives, such as to fly or sail one way, and travel overland the other. Expect to pay about $1000 to $1400 for a seven-day fly/drive tour and anywhere from $1500 to $2500 for a 12 to 14-day safari.

Cape York Motorcycle Adventures (☎ 4059 0220) offers a five-day trip for $1550 ($1150 with your own bike) or a 12-day trip for $3600 ($1950). Prices include fuel, all meals and equipment.

LAKELAND & LAURA
The Peninsula Developmental Road turns off the Cairns to Cooktown inland road at

Lakeland. Facilities here include a general store with food, petrol and diesel, a small caravan/camping park and a hotel-motel. From Lakeland it's 734km to Bamaga, almost at the top of the peninsula. The first stretch to Laura is not too bad, just some corrugations, potholes, grids and causeways – the creek crossings are bridged. It gets worse.

About 48km from Lakeland is the turn-off to the **Quinkan Aboriginal rock-art galleries** at Split Rock, located in spectacular sandstone country. The art was executed by Aboriginal tribes whose descendants were decimated during the Palmer River gold rush of the 1870s. The galleries contain some superb examples of well preserved rock paintings dating back 14,000 years. Entry to the park costs $3 per person (honesty box).

Laura, 12km north of Split Rock, has a general store with food and fuel, a place for minor mechanical repairs, a post office, a Commonwealth Bank agency, a pleasant pub and an airstrip.

At Jowalbinna Bush Camp (☎ 4060 3236), 40km west of Laura by 4WD, the Trezise Bush Guide Service (☎ 4055 1865) offers excellent guided day walks to some of the magnificent rock-art sites in the area ($60 per adult). Visitors can stay overnight at the bush camp ($5 per person to camp or $30 in a cabin). You can also get to the camp using Coral Coaches' (☎ 4098 2600) weekly Cairns to Weipa bus service. It also has a package for $355, which includes return bus travel from Cairns, two nights at Jowalbinna, meals and guide services.

The major event is the Laura Aboriginal Dance & Cultural Festival, held every second year (odd numbers) on the last weekend of June. All the Cape York Aboriginal communities assemble for this festival, which is a great opportunity for outsiders to witness living Aboriginal culture.

Lakefield National Park

The main turn-off to Lakefield National Park is just past Laura and it's only about a 45-minute drive from Laura into the park. Conventional vehicles can get as far as the ranger station at New Laura, and possibly well into the northern section of the park during the dry season.

Lakefield is the second-largest national park in Queensland and the most accessible of those on the Cape York Peninsula. It's best known for its wetlands and associated wildlife. The park's extensive river system drains into Princess Charlotte Bay on its northern perimeter. This is the only national park on the peninsula where fishing is permitted, and a canoe is a good way to investigate the park. Watch out for the crocs! For camping permits see the rangers at New Laura (☎ 4060 3260) or Lakefield (☎ 4060 3271), further north in the park. The *Lotus Bird Lodge* (☎ 1800 674 974) on Violet Vale Station offers exclusive accommodation in individual cottages at $165 per person for full board.

The wide sweep of Princess Charlotte Bay, which includes the coastal section of Lakefield National Park, is the site of some of Australia's biggest rock-art galleries. Unfortunately, this stretch of coast is extremely hard to reach except from the sea.

LAURA TO ARCHER RIVER ROADHOUSE

North from Laura, there's the Hann River crossing and the *Hann River Roadhouse* (☎ 4060 3242) at the 75km mark. Another 62km on is **Musgrave** with its historic *Musgrave Telegraph Station* (☎ 4060 3229), built in 1887. The station has accommodation at $20/30 for singles/doubles as well as camp sites, a payphone, a cafe and an airstrip, and you can get petrol, diesel, food and beer here.

Coen, 108km north of Musgrave, is virtually the capital of the peninsula with a pub, two general stores, a hospital, school and police station. You can get mechanical repairs done here. Coen has an airstrip and a racecourse where picnic races are held in August. The whole peninsula closes down for this event. The *Exchange Hotel* (☎ 4060 1133) has pub rooms at $25/35 and units at $35/45, and the delightful Mrs Taylor's *Homestead Guest House* (☎ 4060 1157) has

QUEENSLAND

singles/doubles at $30/50 and home-cooked meals.

Beside the Archer River, 65km north of Coen, the *Archer River Roadhouse* (☎ 4060 3266) has great burgers as well as beer, fuel and groceries, and can handle minor mechanical repairs. There are camp sites, or units at $30/40.

Northern National Parks

Three national parks can be reached from the main track north of Coen. To stay at any of them you must be totally self-sufficient. Only a few kilometres north of Coen, before Archer River Roadhouse, you can turn west to **Mungkan Kandju National Park** – the ranger station (☎ 4060 3256) is in Rokeby, about 70km off the main track. Access is for 4WD only. This little-visited park covers a large area including the McIlwraith Range and the junction of the Coen and Archer rivers. There are no facilities but bush camping is permitted at a number of river sites. These parks are best explored by bushwalkers. Contact the Department of Environment office in Coen (☎ 4060 1137) for more information.

Around 21km north of the Archer River Roadhouse is the turn-off to Portland Roads, the Lockhart River Aboriginal community and **Iron Range National Park**. The 135km road into the tiny coastal settlement of Portland Roads passes through the national park. Although still pretty rough, this track has been improved. If you visit the national park, register with the ranger (☎ 4060 7170) on arrival. It has the rugged hills of the Janet and Tozer ranges, beautiful coastal scenery as well as Australia's largest area of lowland rainforest, plus some animals which are also found in New Guinea but no further south in Australia. Bush camping is permitted.

The fourth of the northern national parks is the **Jardine River National Park**.

WEIPA (pop 2200)

Weipa is 135km from the main track. The southern turn-off to it is 47km north of the Archer River crossing. You can also get to Weipa from Batavia Downs, which is 48km

further up the main track and has a 19th-century homestead. The two approaches converge about halfway along.

Weipa is a modern mining town that works the world's largest deposits of bauxite (the ore from which aluminium is processed). The mining company, Comalco, runs regular tours of its operations from May to December. The town has a wide range of facilities including a motel, a hotel and a camping ground.

In the vicinity, there's interesting country to explore, good fishing and some pleasant camping sites.

NORTH TO THE JARDINE

Back on the main track, after Batavia Downs, there is almost 200km of rough road and numerous river crossings (the Wenlock and the Dulhunty being the two major ones) before you reach the Jardine River ferry crossing. Between the Wenlock River and the Jardine ferry there are two possible routes: the more direct but rougher old route (Telegraph Track, 155km), and the more circuitous but quicker new route (193km), which branches off the old route about 40km north of the Wenlock River. Don't miss **Indian Head Falls**, one of the most popular camping and swimming spots on the Cape.

The Jardine River ferry, operated by the Injinoo Community Council, operates daily from 8 am to 5 pm. A fee is charged for the ferry ($80 return), and this includes a permit and camping fees.

Stretching east to the coast from the main track is the **Jardine River National Park**. The Jardine River spills more fresh water into the sea than any other river in Australia. It's wild impenetrable country.

THE TIP

The first settlement north of the Jardine River is **Bamaga**, the Cape's largest Torres Strait Islander community. The town has postal facilities, a hospital, a Commonwealth Bank agency, a supermarket, mechanical repairs and fuel. It's only about 40km from Bamaga to the very northern tip. **Seisia**, on the coast 5km north-west, has a good camping ground with units.

North-east of Bamaga, off the Cape York track and about 11km south-east of the cape, is **Somerset**, which was established in 1863 as a haven for shipwrecked sailors and a signal to the rest of the world that this was British territory. It was hoped at one time that it might become a major trading centre, a sort of Singapore of north Queensland, but it was closed in 1879 when its functions were moved to Thursday Island, which was also thought more suitable for a pearling industry. There's nothing much left at Somerset now, but the fishing is good and there are lovely views.

At **Cape York** itself are two resorts. *Pajinka Wilderness Lodge* (☎ 4062 2100), 400m from the Tip, is a luxury resort with cabin-style rooms ranging from $230 to $270 per person, including all meals. It also has a small camping ground with a kiosk, toilets and showers. Camping costs $8 per person. The scenic *Punsand Bay Private Reserve* (☎ 4069 1722) on the western side of the cape provides more modest accommodation. There are cabins and permanent tents or you can pitch your own in the camping ground. Sites cost $8 per person; cabins and permanent tents are from $95 to $135 per person, including meals.

TORRES STRAIT ISLANDS

The Torres Strait Islands have been a part of Queensland since 1879, the best-known of them being Thursday Island. The 70 other islands are sprinkled from Cape York in the south almost to New Guinea in the north, but only 17 are inhabited and all but three are set aside for islanders.

Torres Strait Islanders came from Melanesia and Polynesia about 2000 years ago, bringing with them a more material culture than that of the mainland Aboriginal people.

It was a claim by a Torres Strait Islander, Eddie Mabo, to traditional ownership of Murray Island that eventually led to the High Court handing down its ground-breaking Mabo ruling. The court's decision in turn became the basis for the Federal government's 1993 Native Title legislation (see Government in the Facts about the Country chapter).

Thursday Island is hilly and just over 3 sq km in area. At one time it was a major pearling centre and the cemeteries tell the hard tale of what a dangerous occupation it was. Some pearls are still produced here from seeded 'culture farms', which don't offer much employment to the locals.

Thursday Island is a rough-and-ready but generally easy-going place and its main appeal is its cultural mix – Asians, Europeans and Pacific Islanders have all contributed to its history.

Places to Stay
Options include the *Jumula Dubbins Hostel* (☎ 4069 2122) at $19 a single (if there's space – ring ahead); the *Federal Hotel* (☎ 4069 1569) from $45/65 a single/double; and the *Jardine Motel* (☎ 4069 2555) at $130/160. Accommodation is also available on Horn Island at the *Gateway Torres Strait Motel* (☎ 4069 1092) for $96/122, and at the *Wongai Hotel* (☎ 40 69 1683).

Getting There & Around
Sunstate/Qantas and Flight West fly daily between Cairns and Thursday Island. The airport is actually on nearby Horn Island – a ferry links the two islands (hourly, $5). Several smaller airlines operate flights around the other islands in the strait.

Peddell's Ferry & Tour Bus Service (☎ 4069 1551) operates ferry services from Seisia, Pajinka and Punsand Bay on the mainland to Thursday Island daily except Sunday.

Gulf Savannah

The Gulf Savannah is a vast, flat and sparsely populated landscape of bushland, saltpans and savannah grasslands, all cut by a huge number of tidal creeks and rivers that feed into the Gulf of Carpentaria. During the Wet, the dirt roads turn to mud and even the sealed roads can be flooded, so June to September is the safest time to visit this area.

Two of the settlements in the region, Burketown and Normanton, were founded in the 1860s, before better-known places on the Pacific coast such as Cairns and Cooktown. Europeans settled the area as sheep and cattle country, also in the hope of providing a western port for produce from further east and south in Queensland.

Today the Gulf is mainly cattle country. It's a remote, hot, tough region with excellent fishing and a large crocodile population.

This remote area's main attraction is the superb Riversleigh fossil field, which is part of Lawn Hill National Park, north of Mt Isa.

For tourist information, advice on road conditions and general enquiries, contact the Gulf Local Authorities Development Association, 55 McLeod St, Cairns (☎ 4031 1631).

Savannah Guides

The Savannah Guides are a network of professionals who staff guide posts at strategic locations throughout the Gulf. They are people with good local knowledge, and they have access to points of interest, many of which are on private property and would be difficult to visit unaccompanied. Contact the Gulf Savannah Tourist Association (☎ 4031 1631) in Cairns for more information on the guides.

Getting There & Around

Air Trans State Airlines (☎ 1800 677 566) flies a few times a week between Cairns and various places in the Gulf, including Normanton ($270), Karumba ($294), Burketown ($356) and Mornington Island ($367).

Bus Cairns-Karumba Coachline (☎ 4031 5448) has a service three times a week between Cairns and Karumba (12 hours, $122) via Undara ($42), Georgetown ($64), Croydon ($87) and Normanton ($110). Campbell's Coaches (☎ 4743 2006) has a weekly bus service from Mt Isa to Normanton ($69) and Karumba ($75).

Train Although there are no train services into the Gulf, there are two very popular

Once or twice a year livestock are 'mustered' into yards for sale or to check on their welfare

QUEENSLAND

short services within the Gulf. The famous *Gulflander* (☎ 4745 1391), a weird-looking, snub-nosed vintage train, travels the 153km between Croydon and Normanton (four hours, $35), leaving Normanton every Wednesday and returning from Croydon every Thursday. The newer *Savannahlander* runs twice-weekly between Mt Surprise and Forsayth (120km, five hours, $35), leaving Mt Surprise every Monday and Thursday and returning from Forsayth every Tuesday and Friday.

There are bus services from Cairns that connect with both trains.

Car & Motorcycle There are two main roads into the Gulf region. The Gulf Developmental Road takes you from the Kennedy Highway, south of the Atherton Tablelands, across to Normanton (450km, about 300km of which is sealed), while the Burke Developmental Road runs north from Cloncurry to Normanton (378km, sealed all the way) via the Burke & Wills Roadhouse. There is also a sealed road between Julia Creek and the Burke & Wills Roadhouse.

Other roads through the region are unsealed. If you're driving on any of these roads, make sure you seek advice on road conditions and fuel stops, and carry plenty of water with you.

GULF DEVELOPMENTAL ROAD
Undara Volcanic National Park
The massive volcanic tubes here were formed around 190,000 years ago after the eruption of a single shield volcano. Huge lava flows drained towards the sea, forming a surface crust as they cooled. Meanwhile, molten lava continued to flow through the centre of the tubes, eventually leaving these hollow basalt chambers. They are the largest lava tube system in the world, are unique in Australia and a must-see if you are in the region.

The *Undara Lava Lodge's* (☎ 4097 1411) resident guides run full-day tours ($85 including lunch) and half-day tours ($66 including lunch, $55 without) and 1½-hour introductory tours ($21). The lodge also has three accommodation options: camping/caravan sites ($16 per person); semipermanent tents ($18 per person or $58 with breakfast and dinner); and charmingly restored old railway carriages ($98 per person including breakfast and dinner). There's a restaurant and bar but no shops here so, if you're self-catering, you'll need to bring supplies. There's good barbecue and cooking facilities in the camping area.

The turn-off to Undara is 17km past the start of the Gulf Developmental Road and from there it's another 15km of good dirt road to the lodge. If you're travelling by bus, the lodge will pick you up from the turn-off.

Undara to Croydon
Mt Surprise, 39km past the Undara turn-off, is the starting point for the *Savannahlander* train. The town has a curiosity museum, a caravan park, two roadhouses and the *Mt Surprise Hotel* (☎ 4062 3118), which has basic rooms for $20.

The **Elizabeth Creek** gem field, 42km north-west of Mt Surprise and accessible by conventional vehicle in the Dry, is Australia's best topaz field. Information on the field is available at the Mt Surprise service station (☎ 4062 3153).

South and west of Mt Surprise are the old mining townships of Einasleigh and Forsayth, which you can visit on the *Savannahlander*. If you're driving, there's also a (poorly marked) road off the highway midway between Mt Surprise and Georgetown – it's a slow and bumpy 150km loop through the towns and back to the highway.

Einasleigh is a ramshackle little place with a collection of mostly derelict tin buildings. **Forsayth** isn't much bigger, although it is perhaps a little more alive, and the *Goldfields Hotel* (☎ 4062 5374) has air-con rooms at $50 per person including breakfast and dinner. Forty-five km south of Forsayth is the scenic **Cobbold Gorge**, where the *Cobbold Camping Village* (☎ 4062 5470) offers budget tours (three hours, $25) and half-day tours ($50). Camping is $5.

Back on the highway midway between Mt Surprise and Georgetown, you can soak

QUEENSLAND

yourself in the **Tallaroo Hot Springs** ($8, Easter to September only).

Croydon (pop 220)

Connected to Normanton by the *Gulflander* train, this old gold-mining town was once the biggest in the Gulf. It's reckoned that at one time there were 5000 gold mines in the area and reminders of them are scattered all around the countryside.

By the end of WWI the gold had run out and the town became little more than a ghost town, but there are still a few interesting historic buildings here, including the old **shire hall**, the **courthouse**, the **mining warden's office** and the **Club Hotel**.

The *Club Hotel* (☎ 4745 6184) has backpacker beds on the upstairs verandah for $15, pub rooms at $28/40 and motel units at $35/50; meals are available.

Normanton (pop 1300)

Normanton was first set up as a port for the Cloncurry copper fields but then became Croydon's gold-rush port, its population peaking at 3000 in 1891. Today it's the Gulf's major town, a bustling little centre with good barramundi fishing and a handful of historic buildings. These include the train station, a lovely Victorian-era building that houses the *Gulflander* train when it's not travelling to Croydon and back.

Accommodation includes a caravan park, the *Albion Hotel* (☎ 4745 1218) with beds in miners' huts at $20 (often booked out) or motel-style units at $45/50, and the *Gulfland Motel* (☎ 4745 1290), which has good singles/doubles at $60/72.

Karumba (pop 1050)

Karumba, 69km from Normanton by sealed road and actually on the Gulf at the mangrove-fringed mouth of the **Norman River**, is a prawn, barramundi and crab-fishing centre. It's possible to hire boats to undertake fishing trips from here, and there's a regular vehicular barge between Karumba and Weipa.

The town quite has an interesting history. At one time it was a refuelling station for the Qantas flying boats that used to connect Sydney and the UK. The RAAF also had Catalina flying boats based here.

Most of the accommodation places cater for fishing enthusiasts. The *Karumba Lodge Hotel* (☎ 4745 9143) charges $55/65 for singles/doubles, and the *Gulf Country Caravan Park* (☎ 4745 9148) has on-site cabins ($28/40).

NORMANTON TO CLONCURRY

South of Normanton, the flat plains are interrupted by a solitary hill beside the road – Bang Bang Jump-up. The *Burke & Wills Roadhouse* (☎ 4742 5909), 195km south of Normanton, has four air-con rooms at $30/40 and a few camping sites at $4 per person. **Quamby**, 43km north of Cloncurry, was originally a Cobb & Co coach stop. The historic *Quamby Hotel* (☎ 4742 5952) has air-con rooms at $25/45 per person, and a pool.

NORMANTON TO THE NORTHERN TERRITORY BORDER

The historic Gulf Track stretches from Normanton across to Roper Bar in the Northern Territory. Although the entire route is along unsealed roads, a 4WD vehicle isn't normally required during the dry season.

Camp 119, the northernmost camp of the Burke and Wills expedition of 1861, is signposted 37km west of Normanton. Also of interest are the spectacular **Leichhardt Falls** and **Floraville Station**, both about 160km west of Normanton.

With a population of about 230, **Burketown** is probably best known for its isolation. It's in the centre of a cattle-raising area, close to the Albert River and about 25km south of the Gulf. Some of Nevil Shute's novel *A Town Like Alice* is set here.

Burketown is an excellent place for birdwatching, and is also one of the places where you can view the phenomenon known as 'Morning Glory' – weird tubular cloud formations extending the full length of the horizon, which roll out of the Gulf in the early morning, often in lines of three or four. This only happens from September to November.

The town's focal point is the *Burketown Pub* (☎ 4745 5104), a great old pub housed in the former customs house, with pub rooms upstairs from $35/55 and motel-style units from $65/95. There's also a caravan park (no on-site vans).

Escott Lodge (☎ 4748 5577), 17km northwest of Burketown, is a working cattle station and fishing resort with camp sites and singles/doubles from $45/70; meals and tours are available.

The *Hell's Gate Roadhouse* (☎ 4745 8258), 175km west of Burketown, has meals, camp sites, 4WD tours (groups of five or more) and four air-con rooms with B&B from $25 per person.

BURKETOWN TO CAMOOWEAL

This road is the most direct route to Lawn Hill National Park, although for conventional vehicles the mostly sealed route via the Burke & Wills Roadhouse provides much easier access to the park.

The *Gregory Downs Hotel* (☎ 4748 5566), 117km south of Burketown, is the main turn-off to Lawn Hill. The pub sells fuel and has motel units at $50/60 or you can camp out the back on the river bank. There's a great swimming hole here, and every Labour Day in May the pub hosts the Gregory River Canoe Races – great fun if you're in the area.

Lawn Hill National Park

Amid arid country 100km west of Gregory Downs, the Lawn Hill Gorge is an oasis of gorges, creeks, ponds and tropical vegetation that the Aboriginal people have enjoyed for perhaps 30,000 years. Their paintings and old camping sites abound. Two rock-art sites have been made accessible to visitors. There are freshwater crocodiles – the inoffensive variety – in the creek.

In the southern part of the park is the amazing World Heritage listed **Riversleigh fossil field**. The field contains fossils ranging from 15 million to a mere 50,000 years old, making it one of the world's pre-

eminent fossil sites. The fossils include everything from giant snakes to carnivorous kangaroos to small rodents. The Riversleigh Fossils Interpretive Centre in Mt Isa has fossils on display and is well worth a look if you can't get out to the park.

There are 20km of walking tracks, a camping ground with showers and toilets at Lawn Hill; it's very popular and sites must be booked well in advance (especially March to September) with the park rangers (☎ 4748 5572) or the Department of Environment office in Mt Isa (☎ 4743 2055). *Adel's Grove Kiosk* (☎ 4748 5502), 10km east of the park entrance, sells fuel and basic food supplies. It also has a camping ground and canoes for hire. There's also accommodation at *Bowthorn Homestead* (☎ 4745 8132), about 30km north of Adel's Grove on a track to Doomadgee, at $75 per person including all meals, or you can camp by the waterhole for $6.

Getting to the park poses a few problems simply because it is a long way from anywhere. The last 230km or so from Mt Isa – after you leave the Barkly Highway – are unsealed and often impassable after rain. A 4WD vehicle is recommended, though it is not always necessary in the dry season.

Outback

Heading west from the Queensland coast across the Great Dividing Range, the land soon starts to become drier, and the towns smaller and further apart.

The outback, although sparsely settled, is well serviced by major roads. The Flinders Highway connects northern Queensland with the Northern Territory, and despite its importance as Australia's Highway 1, it is in many places a narrow and badly deteriorated strip of bitumen. West of Cloncurry it becomes the Barkly Highway. The Capricorn Highway runs along the Tropic of Capricorn from Rockhampton to Longreach; and the Landsborough and Mitchell highways run from the New South Wales border south of Cunnamulla right up to Mt Isa.

Once off these major arteries, however, road conditions deteriorate rapidly, services are far apart and you need to be fully self-sufficient, carrying spare parts, fuel and water. With the correct preparation, it's possible to make the great outback journeys down the tracks that connect Queensland with South Australia (the Strzelecki and

Waterpumps, providing artesian water for stock, punctuate the outback landscape

Birdsville tracks) and the Northern Territory (the Plenty and Sandover highways).

Getting There & Away

Air The major towns of the outback are serviced by Flight West Airlines. Ansett also has flights to Mt Isa from Cairns ($337) and Brisbane ($438), while Augusta Airways (☎ (08) 8642 3100) flies on Saturday from Port Augusta (South Australia) to Birdsville ($255 one way), Bedourie and Boulia.

Bus McCafferty's (☎ 13 1499) operates three major bus routes through the outback: from Townsville to Mt Isa (and on to the Northern Territory), from Rockhampton to Longreach, and from Brisbane to Mt Isa (via Longreach). Greyhound Pioneer (☎ 13 2030) also does the Townsville to the Northern Territory run.

Train Similarly, there are three train services heading inland from the coast, all running twice weekly: the *Spirit of the Outback* from Brisbane to Longreach (via Rockhampton), the *Westlander* from Brisbane to Charleville (with connecting buses to Cunnamulla and Quilpie), and the *Inlander* from Townsville to Mt Isa.

CHARTERS TOWERS TO CLONCURRY

As a scenic drive, the Flinders Highway is probably the most boring route in Queensland, although there are a few points of interest along the way to break the monotony. The highway was originally a Cobb & Co coach run, and along its length are a series of small towns that were established as stopovers for the coaches. **Pentland**, 105km west of Charters Towers, and **Torrens Creek**, 50km further on, both have pubs, fuel and camping grounds. At **Prairie**, 200km west of Charters Towers, the friendly and historic *Prairie Hotel* (☎ 4741 5121) has cheap accommodation and camping.

Hughenden, a busy commercial centre on the banks of the Flinders River, bills itself as 'the home of beauty and the beast'. The 'beast' is imprisoned in the **Dinosaur Display Centre** on Gray St – a replica of the skeleton of *Muttaburrasaurus*, one of the largest and most complete dinosaur skeletons found in Australia.

The 'beauty' is the **Porcupine Gorge National Park**, an oasis in the dry country north of Hughenden. It's about 70km along the mostly unsealed, often corrugated Kennedy Developmental Road to **Pyramid Lookout**. You can camp here and it's an easy 30-minute walk down into the gorge, with some fine rock formations and a permanent creek. Few people come here and there's a fair bit of wildlife. The Kennedy Developmental Road eventually takes you to Undara and the Atherton Tableland, and it is a scenic if at times rough trip.

Back in town, the *Allan Terry Caravan Park* (☎ 4741 1190) opposite the train station has sites for $8 and on-site vans from $23, and the town swimming pool is next door. The *Grand Hotel* (☎ 4741 1588), on the corner of Gray and Stanfield Sts, has timber-lined pub rooms at $16/32, more with air-con.

Keep your eyes open for wild emus and brolgas on the Hughenden to Cloncurry stretch. **Richmond**, 112km from Hughenden, and **Julia Creek**, 144km further on, are both small towns with motels and caravan/camping parks. From Julia Creek, the (bitumen) Wills Developmental Road turns off north to Normanton (420km) and Karumba (494km) on the Gulf of Carpentaria. You can also reach Burketown (467km) this way; see the Gulf Savannah section for more information on these towns.

CLONCURRY (pop 2500)

The centre for a copper boom in the last century, 'the Curry' was the largest copper producer in the British Empire in 1916. Today it's a pastoral centre, and the town's major claim to fame is as the birthplace of the Royal Flying Doctor Service.

The **John Flynn Place** museum and art gallery in Daintree St houses interesting exhibits on mining, the Royal Flying Doctor Service and the School of the Air. It is open weekdays from 7 am to 4 pm, and weekends from 9 am to 3 pm ($5).

Cloncurry's **Mary Kathleen Park & Museum**, on the east side of town, is partly housed in buildings transported from the town of Mary Kathleen and includes relics of the Burke and Wills expedition and a big collection of local rocks and minerals. The Burke Developmental Road, north from Cloncurry, is sealed all the way to Normanton (375km) and Karumba (446km).

Places to Stay

You can camp in the *Cloncurry Caravan Park* (☎ 4742 1313) opposite the museum, or there's the *Wagon Wheel Motel* (☎ 4742 1866) at 54 Ramsay St with budget singles/doubles from $35/45. On the eastern edge of town are the *Gilbert Park Cabins* (☎ 4742 2300), with modern self-contained units from $55.

CLONCURRY TO MT ISA

This 124km stretch of the Flinders Highway has a number of interesting stops. At **Corella River**, 43km west of Cloncurry, there's a memorial cairn to the Burke and Wills expedition, which passed here in 1861. Another kilometre down the road is the **Kalkadoon and Mitakoodi Memorial**, which marks an old Aboriginal tribal boundary (see the aside on the Kalkadoons).

The turning to **Lake Julius**, Mt Isa's reserve water supply, is 36km beyond Mary Kathleen. It's 90km of unsealed and bumpy road north to the lake, which is a popular spot for fishing, canoeing, sailing and other water sports. The *Lake Julius Recreation Camp* (☎ 4742 5998) has camp sites ($2 per person), dorm beds ($5.50 per person) and there are self-contained units ($32.60 for up to four).

Battle Mountain, north of the Lake Julius dam wall, was the scene of the last stand of the Kalkadoon people in 1884. About 30km north-east of the lake is the tiny township of **Kajabbi**, where the historic *Kalkadoon Hotel* (☎ 4742 5979) has Trevor (the guitar-playing publican), Saturday night barbecues, annual yabbie races (April) and budget accommodation.

QUEENSLAND

Last Stand of the Kalkadoons

Before the coming of the Europeans, the arid and rocky hill country to the north-west of Mt Isa was home to the Kalkadoons, one of the fiercest and most warlike of the Aboriginal tribes. They were one of the last tribes to resist white settlement, and from the mid-1870s they conducted a guerilla-type war, frequently ambushing settlers and police.

In 1884 the authorities sent Frederick Urquhart, the Sub-Inspector of Police, to the region to take command. In September of that year, Urquhart gathered his troops and, heavily armed, they rode to the rocky hill that came to be known as Battle Mountain. The Kalkadoons, with only their spears for weapons, stood no chance against the carbines of the troopers and were all but wiped out in a bloody massacre that marked the end of Aboriginal resistance in the region.

A memorial beside the Barkly Highway, 42 km west of Cloncurry, is inscribed with the words:

You who pass by are now entering the ancient tribal lands of the Kalkadoon/Mitakoodi, dispossessed by the European. Honour their name, be brother and sister to their descendants. ■

MT ISA (pop 21,750)

The mining town of Mt Isa owes its existence to an immensely rich copper, silver, lead and zinc mine. The skyline is dominated by the massive 270m-high exhaust stack from the lead smelter. 'The Isa', as the town is known locally, is a rough and ready but prosperous town, and the job opportunities here have attracted people from about 60 different ethnic groups. There's plenty to see in town and you can tour the mine.

The first Mt Isa deposits were discovered in 1923 by the prospector, John Campbell Miles, who gave Mt Isa its name – a corruption of Mt Ida, a goldfield in Western Australia. Since the ore deposits were large and low-grade, working them required the sort of investment only a company could make. Mt Isa Mines was founded in 1924 but it was during and after WWII that Mt Isa really took off, and today it's the Western world's biggest silver and lead producer. The ore is transported 900km to Townsville by rail.

Orientation & Information

The town centre, a fairly compact area, is immediately east of the Leichhardt River, which separates it from the mining area.

The Riversleigh Fossils Interpretive Centre & Tourist Office (☎ 4749 1555), in Centenary Park on Marian St, is open week-days from 8 am to 4.30 pm, and on weekends from 9 am to 2 pm. There's also a laundromat here, and Greyhound Pioneer has an office and depot here.

The QBD Bookshop, in an arcade at 27 Simpson St, is the best bookshop between Townsville and Darwin.

The Mine

The mine is the major attraction and there are two tours available.

The four-hour underground tour, for which you don a hard hat and miner's suit, takes you down into some of the 4600km of tunnels. Tours leave Monday to Friday at 7.30 and 11.30 am and cost $35. Book ahead on ☎ 4744 2104 – there's a maximum of nine on each tour, and you must be over 16 years of age.

The two-hour surface tours (by bus) are run by Campbell's Coaches (☎ 4743 2006). Drivers pick up from various places on request and the tour costs $13. It's well worth the money, especially as the bus takes you right through the major workshops and mine site, and the price includes a visit to the visitors centre (see below). The tours depart weekdays at 9 am (and 1 pm on demand). Mt Isa Mines also runs the **John Middlin Mining Display & Visitor Centre** on Church St, with audio-visuals, photographic displays and a 'simulated underground

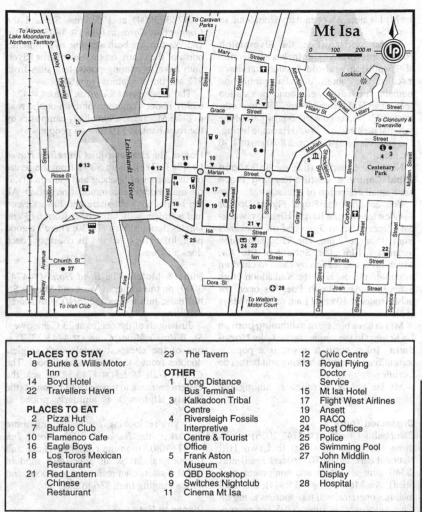

Mt Isa

0   100   200 m

PLACES TO STAY			23	The Tavern		12	Civic Centre
8	Burke & Wills Motor Inn			**OTHER**		13	Royal Flying Doctor Service
14	Boyd Hotel		1	Long Distance Bus Terminal		15	Mt Isa Hotel
22	Travellers Haven		3	Kalkadoon Tribal Centre		17	Flight West Airlines
PLACES TO EAT			4	Riversleigh Fossils Interpretive Centre & Tourist Office		19	Ansett
2	Pizza Hut					20	RACQ
7	Buffalo Club					24	Post Office
10	Flamenco Cafe		5	Frank Aston Museum		25	Police
16	Eagle Boys		6	QBD Bookshop		26	Swimming Pool
18	Los Toros Mexican Restaurant		9	Switches Nightclub		27	John Middlin Mining Display
21	Red Lantern Chinese Restaurant		11	Cinema Mt Isa		28	Hospital

experience'. It's open weekdays from 9 am to 4 pm and weekends from 9 am to 2 pm (shorter hours during summer); entry costs $4.

Other Attractions

The **Frank Aston Museum** is a partly under-ground complex on a hill at the corner of Shackleton and Marina Sts. This rambling place has a diverse collection ranging from old mining gear to ageing flying doctor radios, and displays on the Lardil Aboriginal people of Mornington Island in the Gulf of Carpentaria and the Kalkadoon people from the Mt Isa area. It's open daily from 9 am to 4 pm ($4).

At the tourist office, the **Riversleigh Fossils Interpretive Centre** has a collection of 15-million-year-old fossils that have revealed much about Australia's prehistoric animals. The fossils were found on a station near Lawn Hill National Park, 250km northwest of Mt Isa, and the site is now part of the national park and has World Heritage listing. The centre is open daily from 8.30 am to 4.30 pm ($5).

Next to the tourist office, the **Kalkadoon Tribal Centre & Culture-Keeping Place** has a small collection of artefacts.

You can visit the **Royal Flying Doctor Service** base on the Barkly Highway, weekdays from 9 am to 5 pm and on weekends from 10 am to 2 pm. The $2.50 admission includes a film. The **School of the Air**, which brings education by radio to children in remote places, is at the Kalkadoon High School on Abel Smith Pde. It's open for public tours at 10 and 11 am on school days ($2).

Mt Isa has a big, clean **swimming pool** on Isa St, next to the tennis courts. **Lake Moondarra**, 16km north of town, is a popular recreational area with boating and barbecue facilities.

Mt Isa's August rodeo is among the biggest in Australia.

Organised Tours
Campbell's Coaches (☎ 4743 2006) runs a three-day camping safari to Lawn Hill National Park and the Riversleigh fossil sites ($340 with all meals and equipment supplied). Air Mt Isa (☎ 4743 2844), the local mail run operator, will take tourists along on their twice-weekly runs ($195 per person, bookings required). It also does a day tour of Riversleigh for $315.

Look-About Trips (☎ 4743 9523) does day tours to Kajabbi and Lake Julius ($60), a night town tour ($10) and a half-day town tour ($15).

Places to Stay
Camping The *Riverside Tourist Park*

(☎ 4743 3904) at 195 West St, and the *Copper City Caravan Park* (☎ 4743 4676) at 185 West St, are both a couple of kilometres north of the centre on the Leichhardt River; both have swimming pools, tent sites from $12 and on-site cabins from $40.

The *Moondarra Caravan Park* (☎ 4743 9780), about 4km north of town on the road to Lake Moondarra, has shady camp sites by the river bank at $10 for two people.

Hostel The clean and quiet *Travellers Haven* (☎ 4743 0313), about 500m from the centre on the corner of Spencer and Pamela Sts, is the main budget accommodation option. All the rooms are twin-share and have air-con and a fridge, with bunk beds from $13 and singles/doubles from $26/30. There's a good pool, bikes for hire, and its courtesy coach does pick-ups.

Pubs & Motels The *Boyd Hotel* (☎ 4743 3000) on the corner of West and Marian Sts has basic pub rooms at $25/40 with shared facilities.

Just south of the centre at 23 Camooweal St, *Walton's Motor Court* (☎ 4743 2377) is one of the cheapest motels with singles/doubles from $45/56 and a small pool. The *Copper Gate Motel* (☎ 4743 3233), near the eastern entrance to town at 97 Marian St (the Barkly Highway), is similarly priced at $47/56.

If you're looking for something more upmarket, the *Burke & Wills Motor Inn* (☎ 4743 8000) on the corner of Grace and Camooweal Sts is an impressive modern motel with its own restaurant and pool, and rooms ranging from $86 to $95.

Places to Eat
Mt Isa's clubs are among the best places to eat. The *Irish Club*, 2km south of the centre on the corner of Buckley and Nineteenth Aves is excellent value, with smorgasbords at $8 for lunch and $13 for dinner, and bistro meals from $6 to $12. On the corner of Camooweal and Grace Sts, the *Buffalo Club* also has good meals ranging from $8 to $14. Visitors to the clubs sign in as honorary

buffaloes or Irish persons, and dress regulations apply.

The *Tavern*, on Isa St, has good pub food with cheap counter meals in the public bar, and bistro meals from $10. The *Flamenco Cafe* on Marian St also has burgers, sandwiches and 20 flavours of ice cream.

For pizzas (take-away or home delivery) there's *Eagle Boys* (☎ 13 14330) on West St.

The very popular *Los Toros Mexican Restaurant* is a lively cantina-style eatery with main courses in the $12 to $16 range. It's licensed and open every night except Monday.

For Chinese food try the *Red Lantern* on the corner of Isa and Simpson Sts.

Entertainment

Switches Nightclub on Miles St is a big upmarket nightclub, open Wednesday to Saturday until 3 am; there's a $5 cover charge and dress regulations apply.

There are live bands in the *Boyd Hotel* most weekends. Also popular are the *Kave* nightclub in the Mt Isa Hotel and the *Buffalo Club* on Grace St. The *Irish Club* (☎ 4743 2577) has a good entertainment program, with free video nights on Monday and Tuesday and a mixture of live music, a disco and karaoke on weekends – ring to find out what's on.

The *Cinema Mt Isa* (☎ 4743 2043) on Marian St screens latest releases.

Getting There & Away

Air Ansett has an office at 8 Miles St and Flight West Airlines (☎ 13 2392) is at 14 Miles St.

Ansett has direct flights daily to Brisbane ($438) and Cairns ($281).

Flight West also flies to Cairns, as well as to Normanton ($248), Karumba ($243) and various other places in the Gulf.

Bus The Campbell's Coaches terminal (☎ 4743 3685) at 27 Barkly Highway is the main depot for McCafferty's buses, while Greyhound Pioneer buses stop at the rear of

the Riversleigh Fossil Centre & Tourist Office on Marian St.

Both companies have daily services between Townsville and Mt Isa (9½ hours, $84), continuing on from Mt Isa to Tennant Creek in the Northern Territory (7½ hours, $75). From Tennant Creek you can head north to Darwin ($158 from Mt Isa) or south to Alice Springs ($138). McCafferty's also has daily buses south to Brisbane (24 hours, $112) by the inland route through Winton ($52) and Longreach ($59).

Campbell's Coaches (☎ 4743 2006) goes to Normanton ($69) and Karumba ($75) once a week.

Train The air-con *Inlander* operates twice-weekly between Townsville and Mt Isa, via Charters Towers, Hughenden and Cloncurry. The full journey takes about 18 hours and costs $192/125 in a 1st-class/economy sleeper.

MT ISA TO THREEWAYS

Camooweal, 188km from Mt Isa and 13km east of the Northern Territory border, was established in 1884 as a service centre for the vast cattle stations of the Barkly Tablelands. It has a couple of historic buildings – in particular, **Freckleton's General Store** is worth a visit – as well as a pub and a couple of roadhouses (with extremely expensive fuel).

From Camooweal, you can head north to the Lawn Hill National Park and Burketown (see the earlier Gulf Savannah section for details). Eight km south of town is the **Camooweal Caves National Park**, where there is a network of unusual caves and caverns with sinkhole openings. This can be a dangerous place to wander around – there are no facilities, and the road in is rough and unsealed.

There's nothing much for the whole 460km to the Threeways junction in the Northern Territory. The next petrol station west of Camooweal is 270km along at *Barkly Homestead* (☎ (08) 8964 4549). You can camp here for $4 per person. Motel rooms are $62/68.

MT ISA TO LONGREACH

Fourteen km east of Cloncurry, the narrow Landsborough Highway turns off south-east to McKinlay (91km), Kynuna (165km), Winton (328km) and Longreach (501km).

McKinlay is a tiny settlement that probably would have been doomed to eternal insignificance were it not for the fact that it is the location of the *Walkabout Creek Hotel* (☎ 4746 8424) which featured in the amazingly successful movie *Crocodile Dundee*. Photos from the film and other memorabilia clutter the walls of the pub. If you want to hang around there are air-con rooms at $38/46 and tent sites from $10.

Kynuna, another 74km south-east, isn't much bigger than McKinlay. The *Blue Heeler Hotel* (☎ 4746 8650) is another renowned old outback pub, which for some reason has its own surf life-saving club! It's a good spot for a feed and there are pub rooms from $30, motel-style units from $50/60 and tent sites at the *Never Never Caravan Park* from $12. The nearest beach may be almost 1000km away, but every year in September the pub hosts a surf life-saving carnival, complete with surfboard relays, a tug of war and a beach party at night.

The turn-off to the **Combo Waterhole**, which Banjo Patterson is said to have visited in 1895 before he wrote *Waltzing Matilda*, is signposted off the highway about 12km east of Kynuna.

Winton (pop 1100)

Winton is a sheep-raising centre and also the railhead from which cattle are transported after being brought from the Channel Country by road train. It's a friendly, laid-back place with some interesting attractions and characters, and if you're not in a hurry it's a good place for a stopover.

On Elderslie St, beside the post office, is the **Qantilda Museum**, which commemorates two local claims to fame: the founding of Qantas at Winton in 1920 and the poetry of Banjo Patterson. The museum houses an interesting collection of memorabilia and is open daily from 9 am to 4 pm ($5). Across the road are the **Jolly Swagman** statue – a

tribute to Banjo Patterson and the unknown swagmen who lie in unmarked graves in the area – and the **Winton Swimming Pool**.

The **Royal Theatre**, out the back of the Stopover Cafe in the centre of town, is a wonderful open-air theatre with canvas-slung chairs, corrugated tin walls and a star-studded ceiling. Films are screened every Saturday night and, from April to September, on Wednesday night as well.

There are a couple of operators offering tours from Winton – see the following South of Winton section.

The Gift & Gem Centre (☎ 4657 1296) on Elderslie St acts as the local information office. Winton's major festival is the nine-day Outback Festival, held every second year (odd numbers) during the September school holidays.

Places to Stay & Eat The *Matilda Country Caravan Park* (☎ 4657 1607) at 43 Chirnside St has tent sites from $10, on-site vans and cabins from $25 to $50.

At 67 Elderslie St in the centre of town, the *North Gregory Hotel* (☎ 4657 1375) has clean budget rooms with air-con at $25 a head. Opposite the Qantilda Museum, the *Matilda Motel* (☎ 4657 1433) has units from $45/50.

The *North Gregory Hotel* has good bistro meals and a beer garden with a char-grill out the back. You can also have a meal in the Qantas Board Room Lounge at the *Winton Club*, where the fledgling airline's first meeting was held back in 1921. The club is one block back from the centre on the corner of Oondooroo and Vindex Sts.

Getting There & Away Winton is on McCafferty's Brisbane to Mt Isa bus route. There are also connecting bus services between Winton and Longreach that meet up with the *Spirit of the Outback* train.

South of Winton

Carisbrooke Station (☎ 4657 3984), 85km south-west of Winton, has a wildlife sanctuary, Aboriginal paintings and bora rings (circular ceremonial grounds). The station offers day tours (with advance notice) from Winton ($85 per person, minimum of four) or from the homestead ($60), and has a self-contained unit at $50, shearer's quarters at $20 per person and camping for $5.

At **Lark Quarry Environmental Park**, 115km south-west of Winton, dinosaur footprints 100 million years old have been perfectly preserved in limestone. It takes about two hours to drive from Winton to Lark Quarry in a conventional vehicle but the dirt road is impassable in wet weather – you can get directions at the Winton Shire Council offices (☎ 4657 1188) at 78 Vindex St. Alternatively, Diamantina Outback Tours (☎ 4657 1514) runs day trips from Winton to Lark Quarry for $75 per person (minimum of four).

LONGREACH (pop 3750)

This prosperous outback town was the home of the Queensland & Northern Territory Aerial Service – better known as Qantas – earlier this century, but these days it's just as famous for the Australian Stockman's Hall of Fame & Outback Heritage Centre, one of the biggest attractions in outback Queensland.

Longreach's human population is vastly outnumbered by the sheep population, which numbers over a million; there are a fair few cattle too.

The tourist office (☎ 4658 3555), itself a replica of the first Qantas booking office, is on the corner of Duck and Eagle Sts. It is usually open daily from 9 am to 5 pm (Sunday to 1 pm).

Stockman's Hall of Fame & Outback Heritage Centre

The centre is housed in a beautifully conceived building, 2km east of town along the road to Barcaldine. The excellent displays are divided into periods from the first white settlement through to today, and these deal with all aspects of the pioneering pastoral days. The Hall was built as a tribute to the early explorers and stockmen, and also commemorates the crucial roles played by the pioneer women and Aboriginal stockmen, although the section on the latter is pathetically brief.

It's well worth visiting the Hall of Fame, as it gives a fascinating insight into this side of the development of outback Australia. Allow yourself half a day to take it all in. Admission is $15 ($10 students), which is valid for two days, and the centre is open daily from 9 am to 5 pm.

It's a pleasant half-hour walk to the Hall of Fame, or a taxi will cost you about $6.

Qantas Founders Outback Museum

The original Qantas hangar, which still stands at Longreach airport (almost opposite the Hall of Fame), was also the first aircraft 'factory' in Australia – six DH-50 biplanes were assembled here in 1926. The hangar is home to Stage 1 of this new aviation museum which features, among other exhibits, a full-scale replica of the first aircraft owned by the airline, an Avro 504K. It is open daily from 9 am to 5 pm ($6).

Organised Tours

The Outback Travel Centre (☎ 4658 1776) at 115 Eagle St offers a variety of tours including a full-day tour that takes in the Hall of Fame, an outback station and a dinner cruise along the Thomson River for $49.

There are also a couple of operators offering popular sunset dinner cruises along the Thomson River for $25. Book with Yellow-

---

Captain Starlight

Longreach was the starting point for one of Queensland's most colourful early crimes when, in 1870, Harry Redford and two accomplices stole 1000 head of cattle and trotted them 2400km to South Australia, where they were sold. Redford's exploit opened up a new stock route south, and when he was finally brought to justice in 1873 he was found not guilty by an adoring public. Ralph Bolderwood's classic Australian novel *Robbery Under Arms* later immortalised Redford as 'Captain Starlight'. ■

QUEENSLAND

The Origins of Qantas

Qantas, the Queensland & Northern Territory Aerial Service, had humble beginnings as a joy flight and air taxi service in Queensland's outback – and at times it seems like every second town in the outback has claims to being the birthplace of Australia's major airline.

The idea to establish the airline came about when two former Flying Corps airmen, Hudson Fysh and Paul McGuinness, travelled through outback Queensland to prepare the route for the famous London to Melbourne Air Race. Together they saw the potential for an air service to link the remote outback centres, and with the financial backing of a number of local pastoralists, they established an airline.

The fledgling company was registered for business at Winton on 16 November 1920, and the first official meeting was held in the Winton Club. Soon after, it was decided to move the company headquarters to Longreach, where the first office was opened in Duck St. Qantas' first regular air service, begun on 22 November 1922, was between Cloncurry and Charleville; Longreach remained the headquarters of the airline until it was moved to Brisbane in 1930. ■

belly Express on ☎ 4658 2360 or Billabong Boat Cruises on ☎ 4658 1776.

Queensland Helicopters offers scenic flights from the Longreach Aerodrome from $25 per person; book through the tourist office.

Places to Stay & Eat

There is no backpacker accommodation in Longreach. The cheapest options are the pubs, with at least four to choose from on Eagle St. Best value are the *Royal* (☎ 4658 2118) and the *Central* (☎ 4658 2263), with basic air-con pub rooms for $20/35. The *Lyceum Hotel* (☎ 4658 1036) at 131 has also been recommended, with air-con rooms from $15.

The *Gunnadoo Caravan Park* (☎ 4658 1781), east of town on the corner of the highway and Thrush Rd, has tent sites at $12 as well as self-contained cabins from $48. *Aussie Betta Cabins* (☎ 4658 2322), on the highway about halfway to the Hall of Fame, has modern self-contained cabins from $55 a double plus $5 for extra persons.

Hallview Lodge B&B (☎ 4658 3777) is a comfortable, renovated, air-con timber house on the corner of Womproo and Thrush Rds. It has singles/doubles with en-suite and breakfast for $45/62 and does pick-ups from the train and bus terminals.

For a group or family, the *Old Time Cottage* (☎ 4658 3557) at 158 Crane St is a fully self-contained old-style cottage with established garden. It has air-con, sleeps six and costs $55 a double or $65 for a family.

Motels are not cheap. The *Longreach Motor Inn* (☎ 4658 2322) at 84 Galah St has good motel rooms from $62/72.

There's a cafe out at the Hall of Fame, and there are also several cafes, takeaways and a bakery on Eagle St in the centre of town.

The pub meals are about as dreary as you'll find – this is what Australian food used to be like everywhere! Best is perhaps *Starlight's Hideout Tavern*, also on Eagle St, with bistro meals of a sort.

On the corner of Galah and Swan Sts, the *Bush Verandah Restaurant* is a little BYO with rustic décor and country-style cooking (mains $16 to $20, open Wednesday to Saturday).

Getting There & Away

Flight West has daily flights from Longreach to Brisbane ($326), and also flies twice a week to Winton ($94) and Townsville ($233).

McCafferty's buses stop out the back of Longreach Travel World (☎ 4658 1155) at 113 Eagle St. There are daily services to Winton (two hours, $22), Mt Isa (7½ hours, $59), Brisbane (17 hours, $83) and three times a week to Rockhampton (nine hours, $65).

The *Spirit of the Outback* train runs twice a

week between Longreach and Rockhampton (14 hours, $165/102 in a 1st-class/ economy sleeper); there are connecting bus services between Longreach and Winton ($26).

LONGREACH TO WINDORAH
The Thomson Developmental Road is the most direct route for people wanting to cut across towards Birdsville from Longreach. The first half of the trip is a narrow sealed road to **Stonehenge**, a tiny settlement in a dry and rocky landscape with half a dozen tin houses and a pub. The *Stonehenge Hotel* (☎ 4658 5944) sells fuel and has doubles at $50 including evening meal and breakfast.

The second half of the route is over unsealed roads of dirt, gravel and sand. **Jundah**, 65km south of Stonehenge, is a neat little administrative centre with a pub and a general store.

LONGREACH TO CHARLEVILLE
Ilfracombe (pop 340)
This small town 28km east of Longreach modestly calls itself 'the Hub of the West' and boasts a train station, a general store, a swimming pool, a golf course and a pub. Along the highway you'll see the **Ilfracombe Folk Museum**, a scattered collection of historic buildings, farming equipment and carts and buggies. The charming little *Wellshot Hotel* (☎ 4658 2106) is well worth a visit and has cheap meals and clean rooms from $25/40.

Barcaldine (pop 1600)
Barcaldine (pronounced 'bar-*call*-din'), at the junction of the Landsborough and Capricorn highways 108km east of Longreach, gained a place in Australian history in 1891 when it became the headquarters of a major shearers' strike. The confrontation saw the troops called in, and led to the formation of the Australian Workers' Party, the forerunner of today's Australian Labor Party. The **Tree of Knowledge**, a ghost gum near the train station, was the meeting place of the organisers and still stands as a monument to workers and their rights. There's a tourist office (☎ 4651 1724) beside the train station.

Barcaldine's **Australian Workers Heritage Centre**, built to commemorate the role of workers in the formation of Australian social, political and industrial movements, is one of the most impressive attractions in the outback. Set in landscaped gardens, its excellent displays include a circular theatre-tent, an old one-teacher schoolhouse and a replica of Queensland's Legislative Assembly. It's open daily from 9 am to 5 pm (from 10 am on Sunday); entry costs $5.

The **Barcaldine & District Folk Museum** on the corner of Gidyea and Beech Sts has an eclectic collection of memorabilia and is open daily ($2). On the corner of Pine and Bauhinia Sts is the **Beta Farm Outback Heritage & Wildlife Centre**, a ramshackle farmlet with historic buildings, a fauna park, art studios, and billy tea and damper. It's open most days from April to September ($7).

Places to Stay & Eat The *Homestead Caravan Park* (☎ 4651 1308) on Box St has tent sites, on-site vans and cabins, and the owners run a couple of good day trips. The *Commercial Hotel* (☎ 4651 1242) at 67 Oak St has singles/doubles from $20/35 and good bistro meals, and *Charley's Coffee Lounge* next door has home-cooked meals.

The *Landsborough Lodge Motel* (☎ 4651 1100) on the corner of Box and Boree Sts is the best of the four motels, with doubles from $68.

Blackall (pop 1400)
South of Barcaldine is Blackall, supposedly the site of the mythical Black Stump. Four km north-east is the **Blackall Woolscour**, the only steam-driven scour (wool cleaner) left in Queensland. Built in 1908, it operated up until 1978. Although the machinery is not actually operating (yet), the woolscour is open for personalised tours daily from 8 am to 4 pm ($5).

In town, the **Jackie Howe Memorial Statue** is a tribute to the legendary shearer from Warwick.

The Art of the Drive-By Wave

Driving along those long, remote roads of the outback certainly gives you plenty of time to contemplate life, loneliness and the transient nature of contemporary existence. In the days of yore, when the pace of the world was much gentler, travellers would have the time to stop and chat with those riding or walking the other way and exchange news and information, such as which inns had the softest beds, the best meals, the coldest beer etc. Nowadays all of this has been compressed into a split-second greeting as we zoom past each other on smooth black-topped highways, encased in our metal contraptions, at collective speeds of over 200 km/h.

The incidence of the drive-by wave rises in direct proportion to the remoteness of the road being travelled. Closer to the coast and larger cities, hardly anyone acknowledges other drivers, but as you head into the outback you'll start to notice passing drivers waving at you. At first you might think all these waves are identical, but a closer study will reveal subtle but significant variations in the wave.

The most common method is the four-finger version, in which the thumb remains hooked around the steering wheel while the four fingers of the right hand are raised in an abrupt, Nazi-style salute. This is widely recognised as the state-of-the-art drive-by wave. Variations include the nonchalant one (index) or two-finger wave – this is usually practiced by seasoned outback travellers, although an imitative version is often employed by novices attempting to be incredibly cool. At the other extreme is the full-hand wave, where the right hand actually leaves the steering wheel. ■

CHARLEVILLE (pop 3300)

At the junction of the Mitchell and Warrego highways, Charleville is a major outback centre. The town was an important centre for early explorers and, being on the Warrego River, it is something of an oasis.

There's a tourist office (☎ 4654 3057) on Sturt St on the southern edge of town. Almost opposite is CDEP, an Aboriginal workshop with limited artefacts and an expert didjeridu player.

The **Historic House Museum** is housed in the 1880 Queensland National Bank building at 91 Albert St. South-east of the centre on Park St, the Department of Environment operates a captive breeding program where you can see several endangered species, including the yellow-footed rock wallaby and the bilby.

You can also visit the **Royal Flying Doctor Service** base, the **School of the Air** and the **Skywatch** observatory at the meteorological bureau, which has high-powered telescopes through which you can study the heavens on any cloudless night from March to November ($8). Book through the tourist office or accommodation.

Places to Stay & Eat There are a couple of caravan parks and three motels, but the best place to stay is at *Corones Hotel* (☎ 4654 1022), a grand old country pub on the corner of Wills and Galatea Sts. Basic pub rooms go for $10 per person twin share, while restored heritage-style rooms are great value at $35/45. Next to the pub, *Poppa's Caffe* has excellent food.

CUNNAMULLA (pop 1450)

The southernmost town in western Queensland, Cunnamulla is on the Warrego River 120km north of the Queensland-NSW border. It's another sheep-raising centre, noted for its wildflowers. Accommodation options include a caravan park, a pub and a motel.

THE CHANNEL COUNTRY

The remote and sparsely populated southwest corner of Queensland, bordering the Northern Territory, South Australia and NSW, takes its name from the myriad channels that crisscross the area. In this inhospitable region it hardly ever rains, but water from the summer monsoon farther north pours into the Channel Country along the Georgina, Hamilton and Diamantina rivers and along Cooper Creek. Flooding towards the great depression of Lake Eyre in South Australia, the mass of water arrives on this huge plain, eventually drying up in water holes or salt pans.

Only on rare occasions (the early 70s and 1989 during this century) does the vast amount of water actually reach Lake Eyre and fill it. For a short period after each wet season, however, the Channel Country does become fertile, and cattle are grazed here.

Getting There & Around

Some roads from the east and north to the fringes of the Channel Country are sealed, but during the October to May wet season even these can be cut, and the dirt roads become quagmires. In addition, the summer heat is unbearable, so a visit is best made in the cooler winter, from May to September. Visiting this area requires a sturdy vehicle (4WD if you want to get off the beaten track) and some experience of outback driving. Always carry plenty of drinking water and petrol, and if you're heading off the main roads notify the police, so that if you don't turn up at the next town, the necessary steps can be taken.

The main road through the Channel Country is the **Diamantina Developmental Road**. It runs south from Mt Isa through Boulia to Bedourie and then turns east through Windorah and Quilpie to Charleville. In all, it's a long and lonely 1340km, a little over half of which is sealed.

Mt Isa to Birdsville

It's 295km south from Mt Isa to Boulia, and the only facilities along the route are at **Dajarra**, which has a pub and a roadhouse.

Boulia, with a shire population of 600, is the 'capital' of the Channel Country. Burke and Wills passed through here on their long trek, and there's a museum in a restored 1888 stone house in the little town. Near Boulia, the mysterious Min Min Light, a sort of earthbound UFO, is sometimes seen. It's said to resemble the headlights of a car and can hover a metre or two above the ground before vanishing and reappearing in a different place. The *Australian Hotel-Motel* (☎ 4746 3144) has singles/doubles at $30/35, or $45/55 with private bathroom.

There's also a caravan park (no on-site vans) and a decent new motel, opened in 1997, the *Boulia Desert Sands Motel* (☎ 4746 3000) with rooms at $60/65.

If you're heading east from Boulia, the sealed Kennedy Developmental Road runs 360km to Winton. The *Middleton Hotel* (☎ 4657 3980), 192km west, is the only fuel stop along the way. They offer accommodation in caravans at $15 per person.

It's 200 unsealed kilometres south from Boulia to **Bedourie**, the administrative centre for the huge Diamantina Shire Council. The town's *Royal Hotel* (☎ 4746 1201) hasn't changed much since it was built in 1880; it has budget accommodation. The new *Simpson Desert Roadhouse* (☎ 4746 1291) has a general store, a restaurant, motel units for $52/64 and a caravan park.

Twenty-three km south of Bedourie is the intersection of the Diamantina Developmental Road (which turns east towards Windorah, 400km away) and the Eyre Developmental Road, which takes you 170km south to Birdsville.

Birdsville (pop 100)

This tiny settlement is the most remote place in Queensland and possesses one of Australia's most famous pubs – the Birdsville Hotel.

Birdsville, only 12km from the South Australian border, is the northern end of the 481km Birdsville Track, which leads down to Marree in South Australia. In the late 19th century Birdsville was quite a busy place as cattle were driven south to South Australia and a customs charge was made on each head of cattle leaving Queensland. With Federation, the charge was abolished and Birdsville became almost ghost-like, although in recent years the growing tourism industry has revitalised the town. Its big moment today is the annual Birdsville Races on the first weekend in September, when as many as 6000 racing and boozing enthusiasts make the trip to Birdsville.

Birdsville gets its water from a 1219m deep artesian well, which delivers the water at over 100°C.

Don't miss the **Birdsville Working Museum**. Inside this big tin shed is one of the most impressive private museums in Australia, with a fascinating collection of drover's gear, shearing equipment, wool presses and much more. It's open daily and private tours cost $5.

Birdsville's facilities include a couple of roadhouses, a general store, a hospital and a caravan park. The *Birdsville Hotel* (☎ 4656 3244) dates from 1884 but it has been impressively renovated, and has modern motel-style units out the back at $45/70 for singles/doubles.

Birdsville Track

To the south, the Birdsville Track passes between the Simpson Desert to the west and Sturt's Stony Desert to the east. The first stretch from Birdsville has two alternative routes. Ask for local advice about which is better. The Inner Track – marked 'not recommended' on most maps – crosses the Goyder Lagoon (the 'end' of the Diamantina River) and a big Wet will sometimes cut this route. The longer, more easterly Outside Track crosses sandy country at the edge of the desert where it is sometimes difficult to find the track. You can contact the Birdsville police (☎ 4656 3220) for advice on road conditions.

Simpson Desert National Park

West of Birdsville, the waterless Simpson Desert National Park is Queensland's biggest at 5000 sq km. Conventional cars can tackle the Birdsville Track quite easily but the Simpson requires a 4WD and far more preparation. Official advice is that crossings should only be tackled by parties of at least two 4WD vehicles and that you should have a radio to call for help if necessary. Permits are required before you can traverse the park. They are available from the police station in Birdsville (☎ 4656 3220) or QNPWS offices. For more information, contact the QNPWS offices in Longreach (☎ 4658 1761) or Charleville (☎ 4654 1255).

Birdsville to Charleville

The Birdsville Developmental Road heads east from Birdsville, meeting up with the Diamantina Developmental Road after 275km of rough gravel and sand – watch out for cattle grids and sudden dips at the many dry creek crossings. Betoota, the sole 'town' between Birdsville and Windorah, closed down in late 1997 and now motorists have to carry enough fuel to take them safely over the 384km distance.

Windorah is either very dry or very wet. The town's general store sells fuel and groceries, the *Western Star Hotel* (☎ 4656 3166) has air-con rooms at $30/35, and there's a caravan park (of sorts).

Quilpie is an opal-mining town and the railhead from which cattle are transported to the coast. It has a good range of facilities, including two pubs, a motel and several service stations. From here it's another 210km to Charleville.

South of Quilpie and west of Cunnamulla are the remote **Yowah Opal Fields** and the town of **Eulo**, which hosts the World Lizard Racing Championships in late August/early September. **Thargomindah**, 130km west of Eulo, has a pub and a motel. From here camel trains used to cross to Bourke in New South Wales. **Noccundra**, another 145km farther west, was once a busy little community. It now has only a hotel and a population of eight. If you have a 4WD you can continue west to Innamincka on the Strzelecki Track in South Australia, via the site of the **Dig Tree**, where Burke and Wills camped on their ill-fated 1860-61 expedition (see Innamincka in the Outback section of the South Australia chapter).

South Australia

South Australia is the driest state – not even Western Australia has such a large proportion of semidesert. It is also the most urbanised. Adelaide, the capital, once had a reputation as the wowsers' capital and is often referred to as 'the city of churches'. Although the churches are still there, times have changed. Today the city's cultural spirit is epitomised by the biennial Adelaide Festival of Arts, while the death of wowserism is nowhere better seen than in the Barossa Valley Vintage Festival, also held every two years. Another example of South Australia's relatively liberal attitude is that it was the first Australian state to have a legal nudist beach – Maşlin Beach, just a short drive south of Adelaide.

South Australia is renowned for its vineyards and wineries. The Barossa Valley just north of Adelaide is probably Australia's best-known wine-producing area, but there are also the fine Clare Valley, Coonawarra and McLaren Vale districts.

Further north, the rugged Flinders Ranges offer spectacular scenery and superb bushwalking, while the vast outback has some of the most inhospitable yet fascinating semidesert country in Australia. The long drive west across the Nullarbor Plain runs close to dramatic cliffs along the Great Australian Bight, with whale-watching at Head of Bight.

That still leaves the mighty Murray River, the wild south-east coast, laid-back Kangaroo Island and the diverse Eyre, Yorke and Fleurieu peninsulas. All have plenty to offer the visitor.

Colonel William Light landed at Holdfast Bay (today Glenelg) in 1836, proclaimed the area a British colony and chose a site about 10km inland for the capital. Light designed and surveyed the city, and the colony's first governor, Captain John Hindmarsh, named it after the wife of the then reigning British monarch, William IV. At first, progress in the independently managed colony was slow

Population: 1.47 million
Area: 984,277 sq km
Phone Area Code: 08

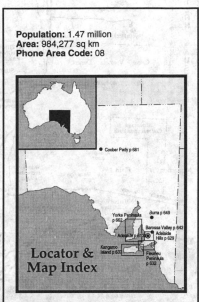

Coober Pedy p 681

Yorke Peninsula p 662

Burra p 649

Barossa Valley p 643

Adelaide p 613

Adelaide Hills p 629

Kangaroo Island p 637

Fleurieu Peninsula p 632

Locator & Map Index

Highlights

- Soaking up the cosmopolitan atmosphere of Rundle Street's lively cafe scene
- Watching southern right whales from the cliffs at Victor Harbor or Head of Bight
- Canoeing the quiet backwaters of the Murray River National Park
- Sampling the wines on a tour of the Barossa and Clare valleys
- Listening to the night silence from a lonely sand ridge by the Oodnadatta Track
- Experiencing the lunar landscapes and frontier atmosphere of Coober Pedy and Andamooka
- Exploring the rugged ramparts of the northern Flinders Ranges

and only British government funds saved it from bankruptcy. The colony was self-supporting by the mid-1840s and self-governing by 1856.

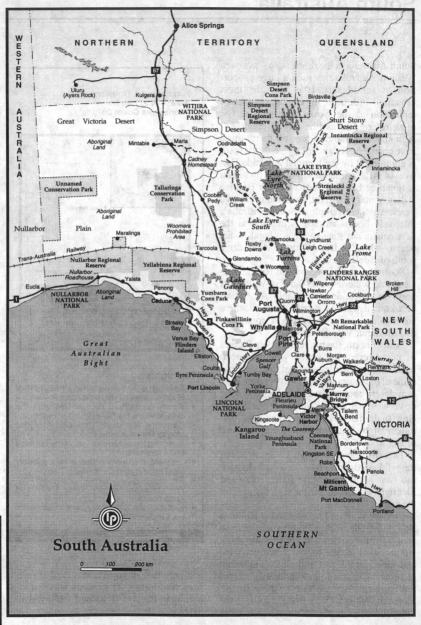

South Australia

RICHARD I'ANSON

NEXT 96 km

RICHARD NEBESKY

South Australia
Top: Adelaide and the Torrens River, after a storm
Bottom: Sign on the Eyre Highway, Nullarbor Plain

RICHARD I'ANSON

RICHARD I'ANSON

South Australia
Top: Vineyards in late afternoon, McLaren Vale
Bottom: Gums, dry creek bed & ranges, Flinders Ranges National Park

ABORIGINAL PEOPLE

It is estimated that there were 12,000 Aboriginal people in South Australia at the beginning of the 19th century. In the decades following white settlement, many were either killed by the settlers or died from starvation and introduced diseases. Except in the north-west, which was mainly unsuitable for pastoral development, they were usually forcibly dispossessed of their traditional lands. As a result, there was a general movement to missions and other centres where they could find safety and obtain food rations.

Today, most of the state's 16,000 Aboriginal people live in urban centres such as Adelaide and Port Augusta. In 1966 South Australia became the first state to grant Aboriginal people title to their land. The early 1980s saw most of the land lying west of the Stuart Highway and north of the railway to Perth being transferred to Aboriginal ownership.

Survival in Our Own Land, edited by Christobel Mattingley & Ken Hampton, has been exhaustively researched and has beautifully written individual and historical accounts by Nungas (South Australian Aboriginal people). It is available from good bookshops in Adelaide.

GEOGRAPHY

South Australia is sparsely settled, with over 80% of its population living in Adelaide and a handful of major rural centres. The state's productive agricultural regions are found in the south: the Fleurieu Peninsula near Adelaide, the Mid-North, the Eyre and Yorke peninsulas, the South-East and the Murray River irrigation centres. As you travel further north or west the terrain becomes increasingly drier and more inhospitable; the outback, which takes up over three-quarters of the state's area, is largely semidesert with scattered dry salt lakes.

The state's topography mainly consists of vast plains and low relief. Over 80% of the land area is less than 300m above sea level, and few points rise above 700m. The only hills of any real significance are the Mt Lofty and Flinders ranges, which form a continuous spine running 800km from south-east of Adelaide into the interior.

South Australia's most important watercourse by far is the Murray River, which rises in the Australian Alps and meets the sea at Lake Alexandrina. The state's low and unreliable rainfall has resulted in water from the Murray being piped over long distances to ensure the survival of many communities, including Adelaide. In fact, around 90% of South Australians depend either wholly or partly on the river for their water supply. The continuing deterioration of the Murray's water quality and flow rates is thus a major concern to the state.

INFORMATION

The South Australian Tourism Commission (SATC) and regional tourism associations produce an excellent range of regional brochures and newspapers. These are available from SATC travel centres, which can also supply tour and accommodation costs and so on, and make bookings. SATC travel centres are at:

South Australia
  1 King William St, Adelaide (☎ 1300 366 770; sthaustour@tourism.sa.gov.au; www.tourism.sa.gov.au)
New South Wales
  247 Pitt St, Sydney 2000 (☎ (02) 9264 3375; 1800 805 153)
Victoria
  455 Bourke St, Melbourne 3000 (☎ (03) 9606 0222; 1800 804 008)
Western Australia
  1st Floor, Wesley Centre, 93 William St, Perth 6000 (☎ (08) 9481 1268)
Queensland
  Level 1, 245 Albert St, Brisbane 4000 (☎ (07) 3229 8533)

The State Information Centre (☎ 8204 1900) at 77 Grenfell St Adelaide, is a handy resource centre with brochures and other publications covering a vast range of topics from museums, industries and legislation to cycling and trekking routes. It's open weekdays only, from 9 am to 5 pm.

NATIONAL PARKS

For general information on national parks and conservation reserves, contact the Department of Environment & Natural Resources Information Centre (☎ 8204 1910); fax 8204 1919), 77 Grenfell St. It's open weekdays only from 9 am to 5 pm.

If you intend visiting the state's conservation areas you should enquire about the Holiday Parks Pass ($15). It covers entry and camping permits to a number of the most popular parks, excluding the desert parks, and is valid for four weeks. The information centre can tell you where to purchase one.

ACTIVITIES
Bushwalking

Close to Adelaide there are many walks in the Mt Lofty Ranges, including those at Belair National Park, Cleland and Morialta conservation parks and the Para Wirra recreation park.

In the Flinders Ranges there are excellent walks in the Mt Remarkable and Flinders Ranges national parks, and farther north in the Gammon Ranges National Park and adjoining Arkaroola-Mt Painter Wildlife Sanctuary. The 1500km **Heysen Trail** winds south from near Blinman, in the central Flinders Ranges, to Cape Jervis on the southern tip of the Fleurieu Peninsula.

Several bushwalking clubs in the Adelaide area organise weekend walks in the Mt Lofty and Flinders ranges. Information can be obtained from outdoor shops such as Paddy Pallin and Thor Adventure Equipment (☎ 8232 3155), which share a shop at 228 Rundle St, Adelaide. They hire gear, too.

Women of the Wilderness (☎ 8340 2422) are at the YWCA, 320 Port Rd, Hindmarsh. They run courses and organise outdoor activities for women such as bushwalking, canoeing and surfing. A good general guide to bushwalks in South Australia is Tyrone T Thomas' *Fifty Walks in South Australia*.

Water Sports

Canoeing & Sailing The Murray River and the Coorong (south of Murray Bridge) are popular for canoeing trips. Visitors can hire equipment and join trips organised by canoeing associations. There is good sailing all along Adelaide's shoreline in the Gulf St Vincent, and there are numerous sailing clubs.

Scuba Diving There are some good diving possibilities around Adelaide. Off Glenelg

---

Heysen Trail

One of the world's great long-distance walks, the Heysen Trail extends over 1500km from Cape Jervis at the tip of the Fleurieu Peninsula to Parachilna Gorge in the northern Flinders Ranges. En route it travels along the Mt Lofty Ranges, through the Barossa Valley wine region and the fascinating old copper town of Burra in the mid-north, and into the Flinders Ranges, scaling Mt Remarkable and Mt Brown, then on to Wilpena Pound.

The trail was named in honour of Sir Hans Heysen (1877-1968), South Australia's best-known landscape artist. Sir Hans emigrated to Adelaide from Germany at the age of seven, and sold his first painting nine years later. Unlike many artists he became famous in his own lifetime, winning a number of prestigious awards. His favourite subjects were the Australian gum tree and the rural landscapes of the Mt Lofty and Flinders ranges.

The Heysen Trail presents a remarkable challenge, but it is also possible to follow short sections of the trail on day trips or over a few days. Due to fire restrictions, the trail is closed between November and April. Unfortunately, a recent decision to halt funding for maintenance has placed its future under a cloud.

Good maps detailing each section (there are 15) are available for $5.50 each from the Department of Recreation & Sport, PO Box 219, Brooklyn Park, SA 5032 (☎ 8416 6677). You can also get them from any good map shop, the Environment & Natural Resources Information Centre at 77 Grenfell St in Adelaide, and various outlets along the trail. ■

there's an artificial reef centred on a sunken barge; at Port Noarlunga (18km south) you can shore dive on the Marine Reserve or boat dive on the *HA Lum*, a sunken fishing boat.

Despite the effects of stormwater run-off, the reefs off Snapper Point and Aldinga (42 and 43km south respectively) are still good. You can snorkel at Snapper Point, but the Aldinga Reef is better for scuba diving.

At Second Valley (65km south of Adelaide) the water is generally clear and the caves are accessible, while 23km farther on at Rapid Bay you can dive from the jetty and see abundant marine life. Other good areas include most jetties around the Yorke Peninsula, the reefs off Port Lincoln and the reefs, wrecks and drop-offs around Kangaroo Island. Any of the scuba-gear shops in Adelaide will be able to give you pointers on places to dive around the state.

Swimming & Surfing There are fine swimming beaches right along the South Australian coast. The Adelaide suburbs of Seacliff, Brighton, Somerton, Glenelg, West Beach, Henley Beach, Grange, West Lakes, Semaphore, Glanville and Largs Bay all have popular city beaches. Further south there are several beaches with reasonable surf in the right conditions – Seaford and Southport have reliable if small waves. Skinny-dipping is permitted at Maslin Beach, 40km south of the city.

You have to get over to Pondalowie Bay on the Yorke Peninsula for the state's most reliable

waves, and there are more powerful breaks nearby. Other worthwhile surfing spots can be found along the Eyre Peninsula between Port Lincoln and the Ceduna area; Cactus Beach, near Penong west of Ceduna, is world-famous for its surf. Closer to Adelaide, and near Victor Harbor on the Fleurieu Peninsula, there's often good surf at Waitpinga Beach, Middleton and Port Elliot.

GETTING THERE & AWAY
See the Adelaide Getting There & Away section for details on transport to South Australia. If you are travelling to Western Australia you can't take honey, plants, fruit or vegetables past the Australia quarantine checkpoint at Border Village; there's a similar checkpoint at Ceduna for those heading east. If you're travelling to or from Victoria there are checkpoints on the Mallee Highway at Pinnaroo and on the Sturt Highway between Mildura and Renmark. There's another at Oodla-Wirra, on the Barrier Highway from Broken Hill.

GETTING AROUND
Air
Kendell Airlines (book through Ansett on ☎ 13 1300) is by far the main regional operator with flights from Adelaide to Mt Gambier, Kangaroo Island, Port Lincoln, Ceduna, Coober Pedy and Broken Hill (in New South Wales). See the South Australian airfares chart for prices.

Bus
As well as the major interstate companies, services within the state include Stateliner (the main operator) and Premier (☎ 8415 5555 for both) and a number of smaller local companies.

South Australian Air Fares
All fares in Australian dollars
One-way economy air fares

Train
Apart from suburban trains and a couple of tourist steam trains, South Australia does not have any intrastate passenger trains. You can, however, get on and off the *Indian Pacific* (Sydney to Perth), the *Ghan* (Alice Springs to Adelaide) and the *Overland* (Adelaide to Melbourne) at various points along the line (see the Getting Around chapter earlier in this book and the Getting There and Away section under Adelaide later in this chapter).

Adelaide

- *Pop 978,000*

Adelaide is a solid, even gracious, city: when the early colonists built they generally built with stone. The solidity goes further than architecture, however, as Adelaide is still very much an 'old money' place.

It's also civilised and calm in a way no other Australian capital city can match. What's more, it has a superb setting, for the city centre is surrounded by green parkland and the metropolitan area is bounded by the hills of the Mt Lofty Ranges, which crowd it against the sea.

Orientation
The city centre is laid out on a grid and has several squares. The main street is King William St, with Victoria Square at the geographical centre of the city. Most cross streets change their name at King William St.

Rundle Mall is a colourful hive of activity and most of the big shops are here. Just across King William St, Rundle Mall becomes Hindley St. Here there are plenty of reasonably priced restaurants and snack bars, and a number of glitzy bars and dance clubs.

These days, however, Hindley St is looking decidedly weary and Rundle St (the eastern extension of Rundle Mall) has become Adelaide's cosmopolitan heart and avant-garde artists' quarter. Here you'll find the best in al fresco dining, retro clothing and *haute grunge*.

The next street north of Hindley St is North Tce, with the casino and suburban train station just to the west of King William St, and a string of magnificent public buildings, including the art gallery, museum, state library and university, to the east.

Continue north and you're in the North Parkland, with its Festival Centre; King William Rd then crosses the Torrens River into North Adelaide.

Maps Mapland (☎ 8226 4946) at the Department of Environment & Natural Resources, 300 Richmond Rd, Netley, has an excellent range of maps. Maps are also sold at the department's Land Information Centre, which is in the Colonel Light Centre at 25 Pirie St.

Information
Tourist Offices The SATC travel centre (☎ 8212 1505; 1300 366 770) is at 1 King William St on the corner of North Tce. It's open from 8.45 am to 5 pm weekdays, and 9 am to 2 pm weekends and public holidays. The centre has a wide range of information specific to tourism, including regional brochures.

Women Travellers The Women's Information Service (☎ 8303 0590), Station Arcade, 136 North Tce (opposite the train station), operates from 8 am to 6 pm weekdays and 9 am to 5 pm on Saturday. It can advise on just about anything, or direct you to someone who can.

Gay & Lesbian Travellers Gayline (☎ 8362 3223) operates nightly between 7 and 10 pm, and on weekends from 2 to 5 pm. It offers a counselling and general information service, including information on social activities and accommodation.

Adelaide Gay Times (☎ 8232 1544) publishes *Adelaide gt*, a fortnightly newspaper that is an excellent all-round reference for travelling gays and lesbians. Call them to get details of outlets near you. They also publish the useful *Lesbian & Gay Adelaide Map*,

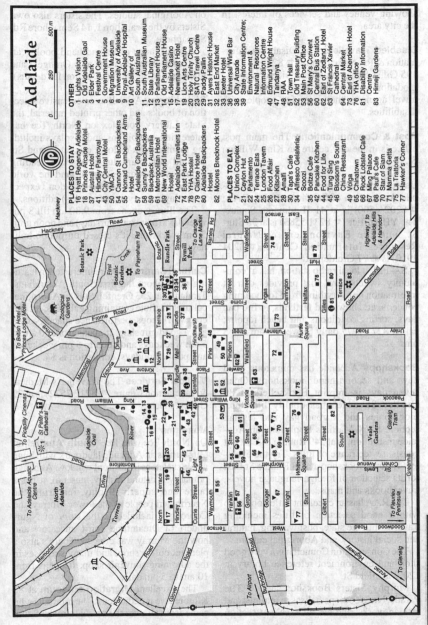

Adelaide

0   250   500 m

PLACES TO STAY
16 Hyatt Regency Adelaide
18 Princes Arcade Motel
37 Austral Hotel
41 Hindley Parkroyal
43 City Central Motel
50 YMCA
54 Cannon St Backpackers
55 Nomad Cumberland Arms Hotel
57 Adelaide City Backpackers
58 Sunny's Backpackers
59 Backpack Australia
61 Metropolitan Hotel
69 New World International Hostel
72 Adelaide Travellers Inn
74 East Park Lodge
78 YHA Hostel
79 Clarice Hotel
80 Adelaide Backpackers Hostel
82 Moores Brecknock Hotel

PLACES TO EAT
7 Union Complex
21 Peylon Hut
22 Parliamente
24 Terrace Eats
25 Leonardo's
26 Food Affair
27 Kitschen
30 Tapa's Cafe
34 Alfresco Gelateria; Scoozi
35 Boltze Cafe
42 Pancake Kitchen
44 Food for Life
45 Tung Sing
46 Blossom's South China Restaurant
49 Volga
66 Rock Lobster Cafe
67 Ming Palace
68 Saul's Safe
70 Stuf S Sun
71 Mamma Getta
75 La Trattoria
77 Hawker's Corner

OTHER
1 Lights Vision
2 Old Adelaide Gaol
3 Elder Park
4 Festival Centre
5 Government House
6 Migration Museum
8 University of Adelaide
9 Royal Adelaide Hospital
10 Art Gallery of South Australia
11 South Australian Museum
12 State Library
13 Parliament House
14 Old Parliament House
15 Adelaide Casino
17 Newmarket Hotel
19 Lion Arts Centre
20 Holy Trinity Church
23 SATC Travel Centre
29 Paddy Pallin
31 Ayers Historic House
32 East End Market
33 Exeter Hotel
36 Universal Wine Bar
38 City Arcade
39 State Information Centre; Environment & Natural Resources Information Centre
40 Edmund Wright House
47 Tandanya
48 RAA
51 Town Hall
52 Old Treasury Building
53 Main Post Office
56 St Mary's Convent
60 Central Bus Station
62 Earl of Zedland Hotel
63 St Francis Xavier Cathedral
64 Central Market
73 Earl of Aberdeen Hotel
76 YHA office
81 Disability Information Centre
83 Himeji Gardens

SOUTH AUSTRALIA

showing venues and services of interest in the city area.

Disabled Travellers The Disability Information & Resource Centre (☎ 8223 7522) at 195 Gilles St can provide advice on accommodation venues, tourist destinations and travel agencies that cater for people with disabilities.

Post & Communications The main post office is in the city centre on King William St.

Useful Organisations The Royal Automobile Association of South Australia (RAA; ☎ 8202 4500) is at 41 Hindmarsh Square. The YHA office (☎ 8231 5583) is at 38 Sturt St, and the Environment & Natural Resources Information Centre (☎ 8204 1910) is at 77 Grenfell St.

SA-FM, a local radio station, has a 'community switchboard' that provides current information on everything from forthcoming concerts, art shows and festivals, to fire ban days, surfing conditions and beach reports; call ☎ 8271 1277 daily between 9 am and 5 pm.

Bookshops Adelaide has numerous good new and second-hand bookshops. Open seven days is Imprint Booksellers at 80 Hindley St, which has quality literature, biographies and a good gay and lesbian section. Mary Martin's Bookshop, an Adelaide institution, is at 249 Rundle St East – it boasts a wide range of titles. Try the excellent Europa Bookshop at 238 Rundle St East for its selection of foreign-language novels, travel books and maps.

The RAA has an excellent little bookshop with a good selection of titles including travel within the state, bushwalking, natural and social history, and Aboriginal culture.

The Conservation Council has a very good shop and environment reference library at 120 Wakefield St.

Murphy Sisters Bookshop at 240 The Parade, Norwood, specialises in feminist and lesbian works, and has an excellent section

on Aboriginal studies. The sisters also own Sisters by the Sea, Shop 1, 14 Semaphore Rd, Semaphore.

A good range of second-hand books can be found at the Central and Orange Lane markets (see the Markets section for details).

State Library As well as an extensive selection of books and other printed material, the State Library complex on North Tce has interesting exhibitions and displays including memorabilia of local cricket legend Sir Donald Bradman. Its newspaper reading room has newspapers from around the world – these come by surface mail, so don't expect yesterday's (or even last week's) editions.

The library opens from 9.30 am till 8 pm weekdays (5 pm on Thursday) and noon until 5 pm weekends. It's closed on public holidays.

Cultural Centre If you're interested in learning more about the first South Australians, Tandanya at 253 Grenfell St is an Aboriginal cultural institute containing galleries, art and craft workshops, performance spaces, a cafe and a good gift shop. It opens from 10 am to 5 pm weekdays and noon to 5 pm weekends and public holidays; admission is $4.

Medical Services The Traveller's Medical & Vaccination Centre (☎ 8212 7522) is at 29 Gilbert Place.

Museums
On North Tce, the free **South Australian Museum** is an Adelaide landmark with huge whale skeletons in the front window. Although primarily a natural history museum, it has a large and superb display featuring the Ngarrindjeri people of the lower Murray and Coorong – included is the story of Ngurunderi (a Dreamtime spirit ancestor) and how the Murray was created. There's also a pleasant coffee shop, and many surprises in the adjoining souvenir shop. It opens from 10 am to 5 pm daily.

The excellent **Migration Museum** at 82 Kintore Ave is dedicated to the migrants who came from all over the world to make South

Adelaide Walking Tour

There are several good walks in and around the city centre. This tour, of about 4km, takes you on a loop starting at the intersection of King William Rd and North Terrace. It includes solidly evocative reminders of Adelaide's more halcyon past, as well as the botanical gardens and attractive parkland along the River Torrens. Most places mentioned here are described in more detail elsewhere in this chapter. Allow a full day for more than just a quick look.

One of the city's major thoroughfares, **North Terrace** is a broad boulevard lined with some of South Australia's finest public buildings. The earliest were constructed during the 1830s, but most are a legacy of the copper, wheat and wool booms that took place from the early 1840s through to around 1880.

Right on the corner with King William Rd, and outside the wrought-iron gates of **Government House** (1838), is the **South African War Memorial** with its impressive statue. Heading east from here you'll see the stone wall surrounding the grounds of Government House on your left; on the right, the **London Tavern** is a great place to enjoy a refreshing drink at the end of the tour.

On the near corner with Kintore Ave is the **National War Memorial**. The **Institute Building** on the opposite corner dates from 1836, which makes it the oldest on North Terrace; it now houses major art exhibitions. It's a few steps down the avenue to the **State Library** and a few more to the excellent **Migration Museum**.

Continuing along North Terrace, the **South Australian Museum** has fine Aboriginal and natural history displays; if you're tired already there's a very pleasant coffee shop here. Next door is the **Art Gallery of SA**, where you'll have no trouble filling a couple of hours admiring its many magnificent exhibits.

Keep walking east and you pass the imposing facade of the **University of Adelaide**, founded in 1874 with a grant made from the profits of copper mining. It was the first university in Australia to admit women to degree courses. The much smaller **University of South Australia** is next door on the corner with leafy Frome Rd. If you want, you can shorten the tour here by turning left (north) on Frome Rd to the **Zoological Gardens**.

A little further along and across the terrace is **Ayer's House** (1846). The elegant bluestone home of early premier Sir Henry Ayers is now part museum, part restaurant. Continue on this southern side to the grand old **Botanic Hotel** at the corner with East Terrace. If it's a market day (Friday, weekends and most public holidays), a short detour up this street to the **East End Market** would be worthwhile

The main gates to the 20-hectare **Adelaide Botanic Garden** are on North Terrace, directly opposite the Botanic Hotel. From here, a network of paths links various highlights including a **tropical rainforest conservatory** and a **historic palm house** (1877). There's also a good kiosk where you can grab a drink and sandwich.

Head generally north through the botanic garden to **Plane Tree Dve**, then turn left. Leave the road at the elbow bend and continue straight ahead (west) to Frome Rd, where you turn right. The **zoo entrance** is just in front by the River Torrens.

From the zoo, pleasant walks meander through the parks and gardens that line both banks of the river as far as **King William Rd**. Having reached this busy thoroughfare you turn left (south) past the Festival Centre to North Terrace, and the end of this tour. ■

Australia their home. Many fascinating displays, including some that will horrify you, explain how the state's rich multicultural society has evolved. It opens from 10 am to 5 pm weekdays, and 1 to 5 pm weekends and public holidays; admission is by donation, and tours ($4.50) are available.

The free **Museum of Classical Archaeology** on the 1st floor of the Mitchell Building (in the University of Adelaide grounds on North Tce) has a small but representative collection of antiquities dating from the 3rd millennium BC (Egypt and Mesopotamia) to the European Middle Ages. It opens noon to 3 pm weekdays with a short recess in summer. The **Maritime Museum**, 126 Lipson St, Port Adelaide, has several old ships, including the *Nelcebee*, the third-oldest ship on Lloyd's register. There's also an old lighthouse and a computer register of early migrants. It opens from 10 am to 5 pm daily; admission is $8.50. Bus Nos 151 or 153 will get you there from North Tce, or you can take the train.

Next door is the **Port Dock Station Railway Museum**, which features a huge collection of railway memorabilia. It opens from 10 am to 5 pm daily; admission is $6.

The fascinating **Investigator Science & Technology Centre** ($7.50) is close to the city at the Wayville Showgrounds off Goodwood Rd. It takes an entertaining look at science and is usually open from 10 am to 5 pm daily. The museum may be closed while exhibitions are changed, so check first on ☎ 8410 1115. To get there, take bus No 212, 214, 216, 296 or 297 from King William St.

Also interesting is the **Old Adelaide Gaol** (1841-1988) at Gaol Rd, Thebarton. On weekdays you can do self-guided tours ($5) between 11 am and 4 pm; guided tours ($6) are conducted on Sunday and public holidays between 11.30 am and 3.30 pm. Features include the hanging tower and various gaol artefacts.

Art Galleries

On North Tce, next to the museum, the **Art Gallery of South Australia** has a wide selection of contemporary Australian and overseas works, including a fine collection of Asian ceramics. It opens from 10 am to 5 pm daily, admission is free and you can do general guided tours (weekdays at 11 am and 2 pm and weekends at 11 am and 3 pm, leaving from the North Tce entrance). There is a good art bookshop on the premises.

The gallery of the **Royal South Australian Society of the Arts** in the Institute Building on the corner of North Tce and Kintore Ave has some wonderful exhibitions; it opens from 11 am to 5 pm weekdays and 2 to 5 pm weekends; admission is free.

Grand City Buildings

Close to the city centre, 288 North Tce, **Ayers Historic House** (1846) was the residence of Sir Henry Ayers, seven times South Australia's premier. The elegant bluestone mansion opens from 10 am to 4 pm Tuesday to Friday, and 1 to 4 pm weekends and public holidays. Admission is $5 and there are tours (bookings ☎ 8223 1234).

At 59 King William St, **Edmund Wright**

The Three Shades (1880) is one of 20 bronze sculptures by master French sculptor Auguste Rodin acquired in 1996 by the Art Gallery of South Australia

House (1876) was originally constructed in an elaborate Renaissance style with intricate decoration for the Bank of South Australia. It opens from 9 am to 4.30 pm daily and admission is free, but you can't really see much apart from the old banking chamber. You'll also find the State History Centre here, with good information on state historical societies.

The imposing **Adelaide Town Hall**, built between 1863 and 1866 in 16th-century Renaissance style, looks out onto King William St between Flinders and Pirie Sts. The faces of Queen Victoria and Prince Albert are carved into the facade. There are free tours on Tuesday, Wednesday and Thursday (bookings ☎ 8203 7442). The **main post office** building across the road is almost as impressive.

Government House, on North Tce, was built between 1838 and 1840, with further additions in 1855. The earliest section is one of the oldest buildings in Adelaide. **Parliament House** has a facade with 10 marble Corinthian columns. Building commenced in 1883 but was not completed until 1939.

Holy Trinity Church, also on North Tce,

was the first Anglican church in the state; it was built in 1838. Other early churches are **St Francis Xavier Cathedral** on Wakefield St (around 1856) and **St Peter's Cathedral** in Pennington Tce, North Adelaide (1869-76).

St Francis Xavier Cathedral is beside Victoria Square, where you will also find a number of other important early buildings: the **Magistrate's Court** (1847-50); the **Supreme Court** (1869); and the old **Treasury building** (1839), which has a small museum.

Festival Centre

The Adelaide Festival Centre (☎ 8216 8600) is on King William St close to the Torrens River. Looking vaguely like a squared-off version of the Sydney Opera House, it performs a similar function, with a variety of auditoriums and theatres but a far greater range of activities.

While the centre is visually uninspiring, it does have a marvellous riverside setting; people picnic on the grass in front of the theatre and there are several places to eat. You can hire pedal boats nearby, or enjoy free concerts (see the Entertainment section) and exhibitions.

Botanic Gardens & Other Parks

The central city is completely surrounded by green parkland. The Torrens River, itself bordered by park, separates Adelaide from North Adelaide, also surrounded by parkland.

On North Tce, the 20-hectare **Adelaide Botanic Garden** has pleasant artificial lakes and is only a short stroll from the city centre. The gardens open weekdays from 8 am to sunset, and on weekends and public holidays from 9 am to sunset. Free guided tours taking about 1½ hours leave from the kiosk on Tuesday, Friday and Sunday at 10.30 am. Open 10 am to 4 pm daily, a stunning conservatory ($2.50) recreates a tropical rainforest environment.

Rymill Park in the East Parkland has a boating lake and a 600m-long jogging track. The South Parkland contains the **Veale**

Gardens, with streams and flowerbeds, and the Japanese **Himeji Gardens**. To the west are a number of sports grounds, while the **North Parkland** borders the Torrens and surrounds North Adelaide. The **Adelaide Oval**, the site of interstate and international cricket matches, is north of the Torrens River in this part of the park.

Light's Vision

On Montefiore Hill, north of the city centre across the Torrens River, is a statue of Colonel William Light, Adelaide's founder. He's said to have stood here and mapped out his visionary plan. In the afternoon there's a nice view of the city's gleaming office towers rising above the trees, with the Adelaide Hills making a scenic backdrop.

Adelaide Zoo

On Frome Rd, the zoo holds about 1500 exotic and native mammals, birds and reptiles, and also has a children's zoo. Its Southeast Asian rainforest exhibit is a major drawcard.

The zoo opens daily (including Christmas Day) from 9.30 am to 5 pm; admission is $10. A different way of getting there is to take a cruise on the *Popeye* ($5), which departs daily (weather permitting) from Elder Park in front of the Festival Centre. You can also catch bus No 272 or 273 from Grenfell St (get off at stop 2), or take a pleasant walk along the Torrens from Elder Park.

Markets

Close to the centre of town, the **Central Market**, off Victoria Square between Grote and Gouger Sts, is a great place for selfcatering travellers. You can buy fresh produce direct from the producer, so things are generally quite a bit cheaper than in the shops. It's open Tuesday (7 am to 5.30 pm), Thursday (11 am to 5.30 pm), Friday (7 am to 9 pm) and Saturday (7 am to 3 pm). The best time to get there for real bargains is just after lunch on Saturday, when unsold produce is disposed of at give-away prices.

The very popular and trendy **East End Market** off the east end of Rundle St is open

Monday, Friday, weekends and most public holidays from 10 am to 5 pm. There's a huge market bazaar with about 200 variety stalls and a food court selling everything from Asian fare to French bread and Italian gelati. You can also buy fresh produce here.

The much smaller **Orange Lane Market** in Norwood is more casual and will appeal to alternative lifestylers – it's the place to go for Indian fabrics, second-hand clothing, massage, tarot readings, palmistry, remedies, bric-a-brac and junk. You'll find it on the corner of Edward St and Orange Lane (off Norwood Pde) on weekends and public holidays from 10 am to 6 pm.

Suburban Historic Buildings

In Jetty St, Grange (west of the city centre), is **Sturt's Cottage**, the home of the early Australian explorer. It opens from 1 to 5 pm (4 pm in winter) Friday to Sunday and public holidays ($3). Take bus No 130 or 137 from Grenfell St and get off at stop 29A.

North-west of the city centre in Semaphore there's **Fort Glanville** at 359 Military Rd Semaphore Park. The fort was built in 1878, when Australia was suffering a phase of Russophobia as a result of the Crimean War. It opens from 1 to 5 pm on the third Sunday of each month between September and May ($3.50).

In Springfield (7km south-east of the city), magnificent **Carrick Hill** at 46 Carrick Hill Dve is built in the style of an Elizabethan manor house set in an English-style garden. It opens from 10 am to 5 pm Wednesday to Sunday and public holidays ($8), and there are free guided tours at 11 am and 2 pm. Catch bus No 171 from King William St and get off at stop 16.

Mother Mary MacKillop Sites

The Australian saint-to-be lived in Adelaide for 16 years and there are a number of sites associated with her. They include **St Mary's Convent** at 253 Franklin St, Adelaide, where she was excommunicated, and **St Ignatius Church** on Queen St, Norwood, where she assisted at mass during her excommunication period.

Another is **St Joseph's Convent** at 286 Portrush Rd, Kensington where you find the **Mary MacKillop Centre**. The centre has historic photos and artefacts, as well as a leaflet describing eight significant pilgrimage sites. It opens from 10 am to 4 pm weekdays (except Wednesday) and 1 to 4 pm Sunday.

Glenelg

Glenelg has Adelaide's most popular beach, and is one of the state's favourite summer seaside holiday destinations. For this reason there's a large choice of accommodation, including a couple of backpacker hostels.

The first South Australian colonists actually landed in Glenelg so there are several places of historic interest. A vintage tram runs from Victoria Square in the city centre right to Glenelg Beach, taking about 30 minutes (see the following Getting Around section for details).

There's a small tourist centre behind the town hall, close to the jetty. In the same premises, Beach Hire (☎ 8294 1477) hires deckchairs, umbrellas, wave skis and body boards. It's open from September to April only; the opening times vary, but if it's sunny, it'll be open.

On MacFarlane St, the **Old Gum Tree** marks the spot where the proclamation of South Australia was read in 1836. Governor Hindmarsh and the first colonists landed on the beach nearby.

The boat harbour has Glenelg's premier attraction: a full-size replica of **HMS Buffalo**, the original settlers' conveyance. The original *Buffalo* was built in 1813 in India and wrecked off New Zealand in 1840. On board, you'll find one of Adelaide's best seafood restaurants, as well as an interesting museum featuring the ship's voyage from England to South Australia; it opens from 10.30 am to 5 pm daily (noon to 5 pm Saturday) and entry is $2.50.

Ice Skating & Indoor Skiing

Adelaide's ice-skating rink at 23 East Tce, Thebarton, is open daily. There are two ice rinks and a 150m-long slope surfaced with artificial snow – you can also ski, toboggan and snowboard here. Take bus Nos 151 or 153 from North Tce and get off at stop 2.

Organised Tours

There is a huge variety of tours available in and around Adelaide; the SATC has details. Most of the hostels have travel or tour agencies specialising in backpacker deals.

For $22 you can get a day pass on the Adelaide Explorer (☎ 8364 1933), a road-registered tram replica, which does a continuous circuit of a number of attractions, including Glenelg. The tour takes 2¾ hours and you can get on and off en route; daily departures are at 9 and 10.15 am, and 12.15, 1.30 and 3 pm, and they leave from 14 King William St.

Premier (☎ 8415 5555) has a range of half-day tours including the city sights ($24), Hahndorf in the Adelaide Hills ($25), or the Mt Lofty Ranges and the Cleland Wildlife Park ($25). They also have reasonably priced day tours, including the Barossa ($32 including lunch and four wineries).

Tour Delights (☎ 8262 6900) has a very good daily Barossa winery tour ($47), including lunch and a visit to six wineries. Busway (same ☎) does a Barossa day tour for $35, including lunch, three wineries and sightseeing; and an Adelaide Hills tour ($40) including lunch at Hahndorf's wonderful Hofbrauhaus.

Prime Mini Tours (☎ 8293 4900) also does a good Barossa day tour (three wineries and sightseeing) and goes three times a week to the Adelaide Hills. Both trips cost $36 including lunch.

Bound-Away Tours (☎ 8371 3147) offers a day tour of the Adelaide Hills and Fleurieu Peninsula for $39, not including lunch. Among other highlights, you visit Hahndorf and a McLaren Vale winery. They also do a full-day trip to the Murray including a six-hour houseboat cruise with barbecue lunch ($72).

Kangaroo Island Air & Sea Adventures (☎ 8231 1744) has a range of two-day packages ex-Adelaide to Kangaroo Island starting at $160. Also try Kangaroo Island Ferry Connections (☎ 8553 1233) for their two-day

packages. If you're short on time, Kangaroo Island Sealink (☎ 13 1301) has day tours from $140 including the Seal Bay seal colony. These options include the bus run to Cape Jervis and the ferry across to Penneshaw, and return.

There are several tours to the Flinders Ranges. Wallaby Tracks Adventure Tours (☎ 8648 6655; 1800 639 933) does a three-day package for $250 ex-Adelaide including bush camping, visits to Aboriginal sites and a Wilpena Pound bushwalk. Also try Stateliner (☎ 8415 5555) as they've offered backpacker specials in the past.

Special Events

The Adelaide Festival of the Arts is one of Australia's premier cultural events and takes place in February and/or March of even-numbered years. The three-week festival attracts culture vultures from all over Australia to drama, dance, music (including a world-music event, WOMAD), and other live performances. It also has a writers' week, art exhibitions, poetry readings and other activities with guest speakers and international performers. For information phone the Festival Centre on ☎ 8226 8111.

The Fringe Festival, which takes place at the same time, features alternative contemporary performance art, music and more; phone ☎ 8231 7760 for details.

Places to Stay

Many caravan park, hostel, motel and hotel prices rise between Christmas and the end of January, when accommodation is extremely scarce – some also put their prices up in other school holiday periods. Unless otherwise stated, all prices given here are off-peak.

Places to Stay – bottom end

Camping There are quite a few caravan parks around Adelaide. The following are within 10km of the city centre – check the tourist office for others. All prices given are for two people.

Adelaide Caravan Park (☎ 8363 1566), 2km north-east at Bruton St, Hackney; on-site vans from $38, cabins $57 and camp sites $19

Windsor Gardens Caravan Park (☎ 8261 1091), 7km north-east at 78 Windsor Grove, Windsor Gardens; camp sites from $10 and cabins for $35 ($50 for three or four adults).

West Beach Caravan Park (☎ 8356 7654), 8km west at Military Rd, West Beach; camp sites from $14, on-site vans $36 and cabins from $52. This park is close to the beach and only a couple of kilometres from Glenelg.

Marine Land Holiday Village (☎ 8353 2655), also on Military Rd, West Beach; two-bedroom villas for $90, two-bedroom holiday units for $67, self-contained cabins for $54 and caravans, that have external toilets ,for $49. There are no camp sites.

Hostels – city There are a number of back-packer hostels, with the standard varying from excellent to ordinary. Competition is fierce, and as a result all sorts of freebies (free tours, free breakfasts, free apple pie, free coffee and so forth) are offered to tempt you through the door, particularly in the winter off season. Almost all can book tours for you.

Most hostels offer a free pick up/drop off service from the airport, bus station or train station. Several are within easy walking distance of the bus station on Franklin St.

When you leave the terminal, turn left onto Franklin St and on the next corner you'll find the friendly and much-improved *Sunny's Backpackers Hostel* (☎ 8231 2430). Dorm beds are priced from $13 and twin share/doubles are $15 per person; off-street parking is available. There's a licensed travel agent on the premises (open at 6 am).

At 11 Cannon St, a lane running off Franklin St opposite the bus station, the large and somewhat cavernous *Cannon St Backpackers* (☎ 8410 1218) has bunk beds for $11 and singles/doubles for $21/28. It isn't what you'd call intimate, but it's clean and has good facilities, including undercover parking, cheap meals, a popular bar and a licensed travel agency. You can hire bicycles for $12 a day.

Backpack Australia (☎ 8231 0639) is at 128 Grote St, opposite the Central Market. Beds cost from $10 to $15, but facilities are cramped. Also on offer are a bar, cheap meals and a small camping space on the roof. By all accounts it has some memorable parties.

New World International Hostel (☎ 8212 6888) at 29-31 Compton St is also handy to the Central Market. Dorm beds in light, airy rooms cost $12.

The attractive *Nomad's Cumberland Arms Hotel* (☎ 1800 819 883) at 205 Waymouth St has a variety of rooms, from $11 in an eight-bed dorm to $16 per person in a double. There is no kitchen (one is planned) but cheap meals are available in the public bar downstairs.

Nearby, at 239 Franklin St, *Adelaide City Backpackers* (☎ 8212 2668) is in a lovely old two-storey house. The dorms are reasonably spacious, if gloomy, with bunk beds from $13; private rooms cost from $18/33 for singles/doubles. It has an appealing bar, but note that parties are not encouraged. You can also get cheap meals, and there's a pleasant outdoor area to eat them in.

Most of the other hostels are clustered in the south-eastern corner of the city centre. You can get there on bus No 191 or 192 from Pulteney St or take any bus going to the South Tce area (Nos 171 and 172 to Hutt St; 201 to 203 to the King William St and South Tce corner), although it's not really that far to walk.

The very pleasant and well-appointed *Adelaide YHA Hostel* (☎ 8223 6007) is at 290 Gilles St. Beds for members cost $13, and there's a free phone to YHA Travel. The reception is closed between 11.30 am and 4 pm daily. In terms of facilities and standards it's one of the best – if not *the* best – of Adelaide's hostels.

Nearby is the *Adelaide Backpackers Hostel* (☎ 8223 5680) at 263 Gilles St where dorm beds cost from $12, and double rooms are $28. Bicycles are for hire at $8 for half a day.

Next door, at 257 Gilles St, *Rucksackers Riders International* (☎ 8232 0823) is very popular with motorcycle and bicycle travellers. The rooms in this attractive 110-year-old bluestone villa are heated day and night in winter; dorm beds cost $10, and a twin room with en suite is $12 per person. Margaret, the manager, has a reputation for being extremely helpful.

Two streets closer to the city centre at 118 Carrington St is the *Adelaide Travellers Inn* (☎ 8232 5330). Dorm beds are $10 and doubles are $26 in reasonable-size bedrooms, but other facilities are cramped. There's some off-street parking.

The *Adelaide Backpackers Inn* (☎ 8223 6635), next door at 112 Carrington St, is a converted pub with dorm beds from $15. Their annexe across the road at No 109 is more upmarket, with a good kitchen, and small but comfortable rooms for $25/44/45. There's a licensed travel agent on the premises.

At the eastern end of Angas St, the three-storey *East Park Lodge* (☎ 8223 1228) at No 341 was built 85 years ago as a Salvation Army hostel for young country ladies. The building is labyrinthine, but it has good facilities and enjoys the nicest location of any of Adelaide's hostels, with the leafy East Parkland just a few steps away. Dorm beds cost $13 and single/double rooms are $19/32.

The large and basic *YMCA* (☎ 8223 1611) at 76 Flinders St is more central and takes guests of either sex. Dorms cost $15 and singles/twins are $25/35, with a 10% discount for members. There are gyms and squash courts on the premises, and you can book into the hostel 24 hours.

Hostels – Glenelg In a grand old apartment building at 7 Moseley St, the friendly and well-maintained *Glenelg Backpackers Resort* (☎ 8376 0007; 1800 066 422) is just around the corner from the tram terminus. It offers comfortable beds (not bunks) from $12 in dorms and $22/32 in private rooms with fridges. The kitchen is very pokey, but there's a cheap licensed cafe on the premises. It's a good place if you like entertainment, what with its public bar, live bands (Friday and Saturday nights), karaoke (Wednesday night) and games area.

Albert Hall (☎ 1800 060 488; 8376 0488) is a little further south of the tram line, in a great location on the beach at 16 South Esplanade. This is an impressive mansion with a spectacular ballroom, but many of its rooms are disappointingly shabby. Dorm beds cost from $13 and there are ultrabasic private rooms from $20/30.

Hotels Unless otherwise stated, the following provide basic pub-style accommodation with common facilities.

The *Metropolitan Hotel* (☎ 8231 5471) at 46 Grote St is opposite the Central Market. It has singles/doubles for $20/35. At 205 Rundle St, the *Austral Hotel* (☎ 8223 4660) has rooms for $25/35. There's a trendy bar downstairs, and it's a short walk to several good restaurants, cafes and bars.

Moore's Brecknock Hotel (☎ 8231 5467) at 410 King William St has rooms for $30/45, including a light breakfast. This is a popular Irish pub, and Irish folk groups play on Friday nights.

The popular *St Vincent Hotel* (☎ 8294 4377) at 28 Jetty Rd, close to the tram stop in Glenelg, has basic single/twin rooms from $33/55, and self-contained singles/doubles for $45/65 – all with a light breakfast.

Holiday Flats & Apartments There are many holiday flats and serviced apartments; most quote weekly rather than daily rates.

The *Glenelg Seaway Apartments* (☎ 8295 8503) at 18 Durham St – about a minute's walk from the tram stop – offers shared accommodation with kitchen for backpackers at $15 year-round; its self-contained apartments are $50 off-peak ($60 peak) for a couple. This place is good value and the owner, Vladimir, is very friendly and helpful. Off-street parking is available.

Colleges At Adelaide University, *St Ann's College* (☎ 8267 1478) operates as a hostel from the second week in December to the end of January; beds are $16 ($20 if you need linen). At other colleges, accommodation generally includes meals and is much more expensive.

Places to Stay – middle
Hotels & Motels The *City Central Motel*

(☎ 8231 4049) at 23 Hindley St has small rooms, but they're clean and comfortable. Singles/doubles cost $52/59. Off-street parking can be arranged.

At 262-266 Hindley St, the *Princes Arcade Motel* (☎ 8231 9524) has motel rooms from $45/50, and off-street parking is available.

The *Clarice Motel* (☎ 8223 3560) is at 220 Hutt St. There are basic twin single rooms with shared facilities for $28/45, and motel rooms for $49/59/69. All tariffs include a light breakfast.

The *Princes Lodge Motel* (☎ 8267 5566), in an elegant two-storey old house at 73 Lefevre Tce, North Adelaide, has pleasant singles/doubles with a light breakfast from $30/58. It's within walking distance of the city, and handy to the restaurants and cafes on O'Connell and Melbourne Sts.

Festival Lodge (☎ 8212 7877) at 140 North Tce is opposite the casino and has rooms from $68/80. There's no on-site parking, but the motel negotiates reduced rates with a nearby car park.

Although there are motels all over Adelaide, it's worth noting that there's a 'motel alley' along Glen Osmond Rd, leading into the city centre from the south-east. This is quite a busy road so some places are noisy. Worth mentioning is *Powell's Court* (☎ 8271 7033), 2km out at 2 Glen Osmond Rd, Parkside. One-bedroom units cost $48/52/60/68, and there's a three-bedroom unit sleeping up to nine – it costs $102 for the first six and $5 per extra adult. All units have kitchens.

Places to Stay – top end

Hotels These offer various different rates depending on such factors as the view; weekend room-only rates are cheaper (these are the ones indicated) – make sure to check their weekend packages. All rates are for one or two persons.

The *Hindley Parkroyal* (☎ 8231 5552), 65 Hindley St, offers luxury accommodation from $150. Opposite the casino, and with panoramic views from above the 7th floor, the *Stamford Plaza* (☎ 8461 1111), 150 North Tce, has luxuriously appointed rooms from $135. With a handsome pile of chips from the casino you could indulge yourself at the *Hyatt Regency Adelaide* (☎ 8231 1234), North Tce, where rooms start at $240.

Places to Eat

With around 700 restaurants and the huge variety of cuisines on offer, dining out in Adelaide is a culinary adventure. A high proportion of restaurants is licensed.

The *Advertiser* newspaper generally publishes a useful reference to the constantly changing food scene. Check their front counter at 121 King William St, and larger newsagencies.

Rundle St At the eastern extension of Rundle Mall, Rundle St has evolved into Adelaide's bohemian quarter, with shops specialising in Art Deco artefacts and alternative clothing, and a swag of restaurants and cafes.

In the mall itself, *Tce Eats* is a large, casual dining area in the basement of the Myer Centre, between the mall and North Tce. Its numerous eateries include Mexican, Asian, Italian and English, and there's access through to the evocative *London Tavern* at the North Tce end, which does pub-style meals.

The *City Cross Arcade*, between Rundle Mall and Grenfell St, also has a variety of European and Asian eateries.

Amalfi at 29 Frome St, just off Rundle St, has excellent Italian cuisine and a great menu. It's often difficult to get into, but hang around as it's worth the wait.

Tapas Cafe at 242 Rundle St is a wonderful Spanish bar and restaurant. Imagine tucking into treats such as 'kid goat braised in Moroccan spices with an apricot and walnut infused couscous'.

For something even spicier, *Taj Tandoor* at No 253 is one of Adelaide's best Indian restaurants. Main courses are $9 to $16.

Just up the street is 'little Italy'. The *Alfresco Gelateria* at No 260 is a good place for a gelato, cappuccino or a variety of sweets. *Scoozi* at No 272 is a huge cosmopolitan cafe noted for its wood-oven pizzas.

In between is *Piatto*, with more pasta and pizza. The tables on the sidewalk outside these places are popular on balmy nights.

The *Red Ochre Grill* at Ebenezer Place, opposite the Alfresco Gelataria, is Australian bush tucker gone gourmet. It's open for lunch and dinner, and the menu reads like an internal memo from the National Parks & Wildlife Service (NPWS). It's meals are superb, and you may never again get to sample emu or wallaby, followed by wattle-seed pavlova. It's not cheap – an average of $19 for a main course – but worth the splurge.

At 286 is *Boltz Cafe*, another al fresco place. It specialises in modern Australian fare with Asian and Mediterranean influences. The upstairs bar has stand-up comics on Thursday nights.

Hindley St An epicentre of Adelaide nightlife, Hindley St has gone to seed in recent years. However, there are still many good eateries to be found among the glittery bars and discos.

On Gilbert Place, which dog-legs between Hindley and King William Sts, the *Pancake Kitchen* is open 24 hours a day and has main-course specials from $7. Next door, the *Penang Chinese Restaurant* is open Monday to Saturday from 11 am until 10 pm and is a little cheaper.

Cafe Boulevard at 15 Hindley is a pleasant coffee lounge with hot meals for under $8 and cheap and delicious sweets.

The *Ceylon Hut*, just off Hindley St at 27 Bank St, has tasty curries from $12.

Oli's in the Hindley Parkroyal has an imaginative dinner menu with main courses from $17. For lunch there's a choice of buffet ($25) or a la carte (from $10).

Abdul and Jamil's friendly *Quiet Waters* in the basement at No 75 is a pleasant Lebanese coffee lounge serving predominantly vegetarian dishes. Takeaways are available and if you want to eat in it's BYO. There's a belly dancer on Wednesday night.

On the 1st floor at No 79, *Food for Life*, a Hare Krishna restaurant, has vegetarian food (all you can eat) for $5, including dessert. It's open Monday to Saturday from noon to 3 pm (8 pm Friday).

Tung Sing at No 147 is open every day from 5.30 pm. Traditional Chinese dishes are between $8 and $13. Still on Hindley St but across Morphett St, *Blossom's South China Restaurant* at No 167 serves dishes from $4.50, with vegetarian featuring prominently.

North Terrace The *Pullman Adelaide Casino Restaurant* has a very good smorgasbord, with lunch at $22 ($24 on weekends) and dinner from $27 ($29 on weekends). It's closed Monday and Tuesday.

Parlamento at No 140 on the corner of Bank St is one of the city's better pasta places and has a great atmosphere. Main courses start under $9.

At No 150, the popular *Pasta Hound* in the Fox & Hounds Pub (part of the Stamford Plaza Hotel) is similarly priced. The pub has live jazz from Monday to Thursday from 7 pm.

Food Affair at the Gallerie Shopping Centre, which runs from North Tce through to Gawler Place and John Martins on Rundle Mall, has numerous international eateries.

Kitschen at No 225 on the corner of Austin St is good for coffee and lunches – try their home-made soup. It's a popular hangout for university students.

Gouger St This is another street of many restaurants, many of which have become local institutions.

Tacked on to the western end of Central Market is *Chinatown*, which has a large collection of mainly Asian-style eateries; one group of kitchens shares a busy communal eating area.

The very popular *Mamma Getta Restaurant* at No 55 is an authentic Italian place with most dishes around $7.

At No 67 the *Star of Siam* serves delicious Thai food. Main courses for lunch start at $7 and dinner at $10.

Paul's at No 79 serves some of the best fish & chips in town, while across the road at No 76 is the award-winning fish restaurant

Stanley's; both are reasonably priced. The nearby *Rock Lobster Cafe* at No 108 is even better, but you pay more.

Ming Palace at No 201 serves good Chinese food, with Peking duck a specialty. It's open daily.

Around Town There are a number of good restaurants and cafes on O'Connell St in North Adelaide. *Himeiji* at No 73 is a Japanese restaurant with one of the best sushi bars in town. It's rather expensive, but worth it.

The trendy *Equinox Bistro* at Adelaide University is in the Union Complex, above the Cloisters off Victoria Dve. It's open weekdays from 10 am to 10 pm (8 pm in university holiday periods) and has main courses from just $5. The *Union Cafeteria* on the ground floor is even cheaper.

Also good value is *Hawker's Corner* on the corner of West Tce and Wright St. It's open daily, except Monday, for lunch and dinner and has Chinese, Vietnamese, Thai and Indian food. It's popular with overseas students – in fact, there's a student hostel on the premises.

The *Volga*, upstairs at 116 Flinders St, is Adelaide's only Russian restaurant. It's a friendly place, with Roma (Gypsy) violinists (Friday and Saturday nights) and beluga caviar for those with expensive palates. Main meals (without the caviar) range from $10 to $21.

At 346 King William St, *La Trattoria* is an Adelaide institution for pizza and pasta. Mains cost from $10, and there are lunchtime specials for around $7.

Adelaide is very well supplied with hotels offering counter meals, particularly at lunchtime. Just look for the telltale blackboards outside. You won't have to search for long to find one with meals around $5, particularly now that most have poker machines – many offer good-sized meals at ridiculous prices to get people through the door.

In North Adelaide, the *British* at 58 Finniss St has a great beer garden where you can grill the food yourself at the barbecue. Large steak meals are about $14 ($2 to $3 less if you cook your own).

Entertainment

Bookings for performances at the Festival Centre and other Adelaide venues can be made through Bass on ☎ 13 1246. There are numerous Bass outlets around town, including one at the centre (open Monday to Saturday from 9 am to 8 pm) and another on the 5th floor of the Myer department store in Rundle Mall – look in the *White Pages* telephone book for others.

Cinemas Adelaide has several commercial cinemas; call ☎ 0055 14632 for a recorded listing of films showing around town.

The major venue for alternative films is *Palace East End Cinemas* (☎ 8232 3434) at 274 Rundle St. It's open daily and shows Australian, foreign-language, classic and art-house films on its four screens – Monday is cheap night ($7 tickets). Also worth checking is the *Nova Cinema* (☎ 8223 6333) almost across the road at No 251.

Pubs & Music There are lots of pubs with entertainment. Check *The Guide* in Thursday's *Advertiser* newspaper or phone the radio station SA-FM (☎ 8272 1990) for a recorded rundown of who's playing what, and where. The free music paper *Rip it Up* is worth picking up for its listings. For theatre and gallery reviews check the free monthly *Adelaide Review*. You'll find both publications at record shops, hotels, cafes and night spots around town.

The only pub brewing its own beer is the *Port Dock Brewery Hotel* at 10 Todd St in Port Adelaide. It produces four distinctive beers – overseen by a German brewing specialist – and an alcoholic lemonade.

At 57 Flinders St, the *Earl of Zetland Hotel* claims to have the world's largest collection of malt whiskies, with over 275 varieties available by the nip.

There's the usual rock pub circuit. The *Earl of Aberdeen* on Carrington St at Hurtle Square is a very nice, very trendy place with lots of character and usually a rock band on Wednesday, Friday and Saturday nights, and Sunday afternoon. It's close to the backpackers hostels in the south-east of the city centre.

On Rundle St, the *Austral* and the *Exeter* at Nos 205 and 246 respectively often have bands and DJs. They're popular with business folk and office workers during the day (both pubs have interesting lunchtime menus), while at night they're university student hang-outs. Try them if you're looking for a place for a drink before heading out to eat. Nearby, at No 242, *Tapas* has a jazz band on Friday night and flamenco on Saturday night.

Also good for a pre-dinner drink is the *Universal Wine Bar* at 285 Rundle St; it's got a great atmosphere, with plenty of iron filigree, and the doors fold back on summer nights so you can catch the breeze.

The most popular Adelaide club is the Heaven Nightclub, in the grand old *Newmarket Hotel* on the corner of West and North Tces. Open every night, it has DJs between Wednesday and Saturday nights. The pub also has Joplins Nightclub, which has live bands nightly and is popular with the older set.

Others worth mentioning in the city centre are *The Planet*, with three dance clubs at 77 Pirie St, and the *Rio International Nightclub* at 111 Hindley St. Both are open nightly. The *Mars Bar* at 120 Gouger St is a popular dance club for gays and lesbians. It opens nightly at 10 am.

The *UniBar* (☎ 8303 5401) in the Union Complex at Adelaide University often features big-name and up-coming rock bands during lunchtime, afternoons and evenings – usually Friday. The bar is also an excellent venue for avant-garde performances and social activities. The complex is off Victoria Drive and above the Cloisters, and visitors are welcome.

There are often free concerts in the amphitheatre at the *Festival Centre* on alternate Sundays during summer, and in the centre's foyer every Sunday during winter. On Saturday nights between 10 pm and 1 am, the *Fezbah*, also at the centre, is a good jazz and rock venue; admission is $7.

Every Friday night the *Irish Club* at 11 Carrington St has live music from 8 pm until late. You don't have to be Irish to get in.

Casino The *Adelaide Casino* is housed in the grand old train station on North Tce and boasts a magnificent foyer – some visitors find this the best part of the place. Apart from a wide range of gambling facilities (including a two-up game, naturally) there are three bars and two restaurants. It opens from 10 am to 4 am daily (6 am from Friday to Sunday and on public holidays). Smart casual dress is required.

Things to Buy

Rundle St is a good place for retro clothes and boutiques; the East End and Orange Lane markets are worth checking for second-hand and alternative clothing (see the earlier Markets section for details).

Tandanya at 253 Grenfell St has a range of Aboriginal arts and crafts; it's open daily.

High-quality craftwork is produced and sold at the Jam Factory Craft & Design Centre, in the Lion Arts Centre on the corner of Morphett St and North Tce. It also has a shop at 74 Gawler Place in the city centre.

Getting There & Away

Air Adelaide is connected by regular air services to all Australian capitals. Many flights from Melbourne and Sydney to the Northern Territory go via Adelaide, and the Darwin route is often heavily booked. Qantas (☎ 13 1313) can be found at 144 North Tce and Ansett (☎ 13 1300) is at 142 North Tce.

Standard one-way fares from Adelaide include: Brisbane $535, Sydney $372, Melbourne $260, Perth $557, Alice Springs $402 and Darwin $685. Remember that there are almost always cheaper fares available.

For airfares within the state, refer to the airfares chart in the introductory Getting Around section in this chapter.

Bus Most interstate and intrastate services go from Adelaide's central bus station at 101-111 Franklin St. The major carriers – Greyhound Pioneer, Stateliner and McCafferty's – have their offices here. Left-luggage lockers are available.

Greyhound Pioneer (☎ 13 2030) has services between Adelaide and all major cities.

SOUTH AUSTRALIA

The fare to Melbourne is $56 (11 hours), Sydney $99 (22 hours), Perth $214 (34 hours) and Alice Springs $148 (20 hours). There's a 10% discount for backpackers.

McCafferty's (☎ 13 1499) also offers backpackers a 10% discount. Fares include Melbourne $40, Sydney $85 via Melbourne and $96 direct, Alice Springs $135, Darwin $252, Brisbane $150 and Cairns $280.

The Victorian government's V/Line bus (☎ 8231 7620) runs between Adelaide and Bendigo daily – from Bendigo you catch the train to Melbourne. The fare from Adelaide to Melbourne is $49, and the bus departs Adelaide from 296 Hindley St.

Firefly Express (☎ 8231 1488) is at 110 Franklin St opposite the central bus station. It runs to Melbourne every evening at 8.30 pm ($40) and on to Sydney for $75 ex-Adelaide.

Another alternative to the major bus lines between Adelaide and Melbourne is to spend three days and two nights on the trip with the Wayward Bus Company (☎ 8232 6646; 1800 882 823). Its minibuses deviate from the main highways, taking in Victoria's spectacular Great Ocean Road and several national parks, including the Twelve Apostles and the Coorong. The $170 fare includes lunches but not accommodation or other meals. Trips depart from both ends on Wednesday and Saturday; enquire about longer trips in summer.

Wayward has a similar eight-day Adelaide to Alice Springs trip. Departures are weekly, and take in the Clare Valley, the Flinders Ranges, the Oodnadatta Track, Coober Pedy, Uluru (Ayers Rock) and Kings Canyon. The $640 cost includes admission to all national parks, all meals, and camping or bunk-house accommodation en route.

An operator associated with Wayward does a 10-day trip Adelaide to Perth for $700, departing weekly from both ends (contact Wayward for details).

Stateliner, Premier Roadlines (☎ 8415 5555 for both) and other South Australian operators are at the central bus station. Stateliner has services to Wilpena Pound, Port Lincoln, Ceduna, Roxby Downs, Coober Pedy and Renmark, and Loxton in the Riverland area. Premier goes to Goolwa, Victor Harbor and Moonta. See the appropriate Getting There & Away sections in this chapter for details.

A number of smaller operators provide regional services from Adelaide – details are given in the regional sections later in this chapter.

Train There are two stations in Adelaide: the one on North Tce, for suburban trains; and the interstate terminal (13 2232 for bookings and enquiries) on Railway Tce, Keswick, just south-west of the city centre. It's wise to book ahead, particularly on the very popular *Ghan*. You have to ask about discounts, which usually aren't advertised.

To Melbourne the nightly *Overland* takes about 12 hours and costs $58 economy, $116 in 1st class and $182 with sleeper.

You can travel daily between Sydney and Adelaide via Melbourne on the *Melbourne Express* (Sydney to Melbourne), and twice weekly via Broken Hill on the *Indian Pacific* (Sydney to Perth). Via Melbourne it's $149 economy, $242 for a 1st-class seat and $403 for a 1st-class sleeper. The connection is poor in Melbourne – you will need to spend the day there. Via Broken Hill it's $152 economy, $303 for a holiday-class economy sleeper and $456 for a 1st-class sleeper.

There's also the Speedlink – a daily bus and train connection that is not only cheaper but five or six hours faster. You travel from Sydney to Albury on the XPT train, and then from Albury to Adelaide on a V/Line bus. The travel time is under 20 hours. An economy/1st-class seat is $103/156.

Between Adelaide and Perth there is the *Indian Pacific*, which runs twice weekly (Tuesday and Friday). The trip takes about 36 hours. Fares are $248 for an economy seat, $520 for a holiday-class sleeper (no meals), and $805 for a 1st-class sleeper with meals.

The *Ghan* between Adelaide and Alice Springs runs weekly throughout the year (departing Monday), with a second departure from Adelaide on Monday and Alice Springs on Tuesday, from April through

November. The fare is $150 in economy, $319 in a holiday-class sleeper (no meals) and $524 in a 1st-class sleeper with meals.

Boat Kangaroo Island Express Ferries runs a passenger ferry service from Glenelg to Kingscote; see the Kangaroo Island section for details.

Car & Motorcycle Rental The *Yellow Pages* lists over 30 vehicle rental companies in Adelaide, including all the major national companies.

Those with cheaper rates include:

Access Rent-a-Car	☎ 1800 812 580
Action Rent-a-Car	☎ 8352 7044
Airport Rent-a-Car	☎ 8343 8855
Delta	☎ 13 1390
Rent-a-Bug	☎ 8234 0911
Smile Rent-a-Car	☎ 8234 0655

Show & Go (☎ 8376 0333) at 236 Brighton Rd, Brighton has motor scooters for $49 per day (driver's licence required) and motorcycles from 250cc ($59) to 1000cc (from $89). A full motorcycle licence is required for all bikes.

Getting Around

To/From the Airport Adelaide's international airport is 7km west of the city centre. An airport bus service (☎ 8381 5311) operates between city hotels and some hostels at least half-hourly from around 7 am to 9.30 pm on weekdays, and hourly on weekends and public holidays for $6. From Victoria Square to the domestic terminal takes about 30 minutes; slightly less to the international terminal. If you're catching a flight on one of the smaller regional airlines let the driver know, as the drop-off point is different. You don't have to be staying at the hotel to catch the bus.

Remember, too, that most of the hostels will pick you up and drop you off if you're staying with them. A taxi costs about $15 from the city centre.

Budget, Hertz, Avis and Thrifty have hire-car desks at the airport.

To/From the Train Station The airport to city bus service calls into the interstate train station at Keswick on its regular run; it costs $3 from the station to the city centre. See To/From the Airport (above) for details.

Public Transport Adelaide has an integrated local transport system operated by TransAdelaide (TA; ☎ 8210 1000). The TA Information Bureau, where you can get timetables and free guides and brochures on services, is on the corner of King William and Currie Sts.

The system covers metropolitan buses and trains, as well as the Glenelg tram and the O-Bahn Busway, which runs on concrete tracks between the city centre and Tea Tree Plaza, home of the huge Westfield Shopping Centre.

Tickets purchased on board the buses are $2.70 before 9 am, after 3 pm and on weekends, and $1.60 between 9 am and 3 pm weekdays. They are valid for two hours from the commencement of the first journey. (Tickets cannot be purchased on board some trains.)

For travellers, the best deal is the day-trip ticket, which permits unlimited travel for the whole day and costs $5.10. They can be prepurchased from any post office.

There are two free Bee Line bus services. No 99B runs in a loop from the Glenelg tram terminus at Victoria Square, down King William St and around the corner to the train station. It leaves the square every five to eight minutes weekdays from 7.47 am to 5.52 pm, and every 15 minutes on Friday to 9.20 pm and on Saturday from 8.37 am to 5.37 pm.

The No 99C bus service runs around the margins of the city centre from the train station, passing the Central and East End markets en route. It leaves the station every 15 minutes on weekdays between 7.54 am and 5.54 pm (9.09 pm Friday) and every 30 minutes on Saturday between 8.39 am and 5.09 pm.

Vintage trams rattle their way along a single line out to the Glenelg beach from Victoria Square in the city.

Bicycle Adelaide is a relatively cyclist-friendly city, with good cycling tracks and bicycle lanes on many streets. Bicycle SA (☎ 8410 1406) can give advice on the local cycling scene.

Linear Park Mountain Bike Hire (☎ 0411 596 065) is at Elder Park, near the Popeye landing just below the Festival Theatre; it's on the Linear Park Bike & Walking Track, a 40km sealed path that wends its way mainly along the Torrens River from the beach to the foot of the Adelaide Hills. Bicycles are $8 per hour or $20 for the day, including helmets – groups of four or more get a 25% discount.

Velodrome Cycles (☎ 8223 6678) at 43 Rundle Mall rents mountain bikes from $20 per day or $70 for a week, including helmet. Flinders Outdoor Leisure (☎ 8359 3344) at 235 Pirie St has a similar deal except day hire is $15.

Some hostels hire out mountain bikes.

Adelaide Hills

Only 30 minutes drive from the city centre and you're in the scenic Adelaide Hills, part of the Mt Lofty Ranges and a popular day-trip destination from Adelaide. Apart from the gentle beauty of the hills themselves, with their huge gum trees and landscapes, there's great bushwalking (over 1000km of trails), several forested conservation parks, and historic townships such as Hahndorf and Strathalbyn. There are also several good wineries.

The Adelaide Hills Visitor Centre (☎ 8388 1185; 1800 353 323; fax 8388 1319) is at 41 Main St in Hahndorf; it opens from 10 am to 4 pm daily.

NATIONAL PARKS & SCENIC DRIVES

To visit the northern hills area, leave the city via North Tce, Botanic Rd and then Payneham Rd and continue on to Torrens Gorge Rd. This scenic route takes you through Birdwood and north to the Barossa Valley. However, you might prefer to head

south at Birdwood and travel through Hahndorf, returning to Adelaide via the South Eastern Freeway. Alternatively, leave Payneham Rd and take McGill Rd through **Morialta Conservation Park**, near Rostrevor, which has walking trails, waterfalls and a rugged gorge.

Continue south via Norton Summit and Summertown to the popular **Cleland Wildlife Park**. It has numerous species of Australian fauna and you can have your photo taken with a koala (2 to 4 pm daily; $8). The park opens from 9.30 am to 5 pm daily and entry is $7. Take bus No 822 from Grenfell St in Adelaide or visit on one of the day tours that operate from the city.

From the wildlife park you can walk through the bush (2km) or drive up to **Mt Lofty Summit** (727m), which has a good restaurant and beautiful views over the city. From here continue south for 1.5km to the stunning **Mt Lofty Botanical Gardens** (open from 8 am to 4 pm weekdays, and 10 am to 5 pm weekends).

Farther south is Crafers, from where you can head back to the city via the freeway. Alternatively, head west to **Belair National Park**, which has more walking trails and picnic facilities. The grand lifestyle of South Australia's colonial gentry is also here on display at **Old Government House**, built in 1859 as the governor's summer residence. The park opens daily from 8.30 am to sunset and entry costs $5 per car. You can get here from Adelaide on bus No 195 from King William St (get off at stop 27) or take the train to Belair station on the edge of the park.

The **Warrawong Sanctuary** (☎ 8370 9422) on Stock Rd, near Mylor, has a variety of native wildlife, including some rare species. Dawn and sunset guided walks must be booked and cost $15 ($12 if you're in a group of four); there are also day walks for $10. To reach the sanctuary from Adelaide, turn off the freeway at Stirling and follow the signs from the Stirling roundabout.

Places to Stay

There are 'limited access' YHA hostels (for members only) in the Mt Lofty Ranges at

Para Wirra, Norton Summit, Mt Lofty, Mylor and Kuitpo. These hostels are all on the Heysen Trail (see Activities in the introduction to this chapter) and cost between $6 and $10. You must book in advance and obtain a key from the YHA office (☎ 8231 5583) in Adelaide.

Fuzzies Farm (☎ 8390 1111) at Norton Summit 15km east of the city is a unique opportunity to learn practical skills in a friendly farm environment. You can join in a wide variety of activities such as animal care, organic gardening, land management, building construction and wood

crafts. Like the setting, their cafe and self-contained bushland cabins are great; the daily rate for helpers is $10 including city transfers, all meals and laundry. Stays of at least one week are preferred, and bookings are essential. Budget package tours are also available.

Getting There & Away
Public transport is limited to a couple of bus runs operating from the central bus station in Adelaide. For details see the various town sections.

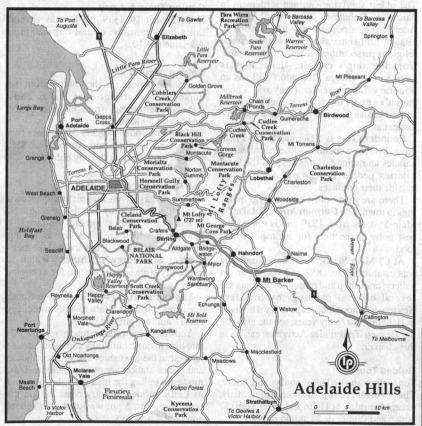

Adelaide Hills

0   5   10 km

BIRDWOOD (pop 1100)
The **National Motor Museum** in the historic Birdwood Mill has Australia's largest collection of vintage and classic cars and motorcycles. It opens from 9 am to 5 pm daily and admission is $8.50.

You can get to Birdwood (50km east of Adelaide) either via Gumeracha or via Lobethal, passing through the scenic **Torrens River Gorge** en route.

ABM Coachlines (☎ 8347 3336) runs from Adelaide to Birdwood on weekdays for $7.30.

HAHNDORF (pop 1750)
The oldest surviving German settlement in Australia, Hahndorf, 29km south-east of Adelaide, is a popular day trip. Settled in 1839 by Lutherans who left Prussia to escape religious persecution, the town took its name from the ship's captain, Hahn; *dorf* is German for 'village'. Hahndorf still has an honorary *Burgermeister* (mayor). These days it's a major tourist attraction, with more stuffed koalas than you can shake a eucalyptus leaf at.

Founders Day is a German festival held on a March weekend – there are street parades and wine tastings, and all the local eateries peddle their wares from tables outside their premises.

There are many old German-style buildings in town. The **German Arms Hotel** at 50 Main St dates from 1839 and is one of the best pubs in the hills for atmosphere and food.

At 68 Main St, the **Hahndorf Academy** was established in 1857 and houses an art gallery, craft shop and museum – you can see several original paintings by Sir Hans Heysen, a famous landscape artist who lived in Hahndorf for many years; see the aside on the Heysen Trail under Activities earlier in this chapter.

Guided Tours
Tours through Sir Hans' studio and house, The Cedars (1858), are conducted daily, except Saturday, at 11 am and 1 and 3 pm ($7 house and studio; or $4 studio only).

Places to Stay & Eat
The *Hahndorf Resort* (☎ 8388 7921) is 1.5km out of town on Main St. Camp sites start at $10, cabins cost $46 and motel rooms are from $69 for singles/doubles. The only other alternatives are a couple of fairly expensive motels.

Hahndorf has many good restaurants and several feature German food. They include the *German Arms Hotel* as well as the *German Cake Shop*, both on Main St. *Karl's German Coffee House* at 17 Main St is recommended by locals for authentic German cuisine.

Getting There & Away
Hills Transit (☎ 8339 1191) runs several times daily from the central bus station in Adelaide ($4.10).

Getting Around
A pleasant way to see the town is from the horse-drawn carriage that leaves daily (weather permitting) from in front of the Institute at 59 Main St.

Hahndorf Tours (☎ 8388 3325) does two to four-hour minibus tours costing from $15, but you have to book the day before.

STRATHALBYN (pop 2900)
On the Angas River, this picturesque town was settled in 1839 by Scottish immigrants. It has many interesting old buildings, a number of which are classified as having heritage significance. They include the magnificent **St Andrew's Church**, which is unusually large and decorative for a country town.

The tourist office (☎ 8536 3212) on South Tce is open from 9.30 am to 4 pm weekdays and 11 am to 4 pm weekends.

You can buy a walking-tour pamphlet ($2) that lists historic buildings and other sites of interest in the township. The old courthouse and police station are now a National Trust **museum** telling the history of the town and its Celtic influence; entry costs $2 and it's open from 2 to 5 pm weekends and school and public holidays.

Places to Stay

The council caravan park (☎ 8536 3681) in the showgrounds on Coronation Rd has grassed camp sites for $10 and on-site vans from $22.

The *Terminus Hotel* (☎ 8536 2026) on Rankine St has singles/doubles for $25/45, including a light breakfast, while the *Robin Hood Hotel* (☎ 8536 2608) on High St charges $28/45, also with breakfast.

Getting There & Away

Hills Transit (☎ 8339 1191) runs from Adelaide to Strathalbyn (changing at Mt Barker) on weekdays for $6.

SteamRanger (☎ 8391 1223) runs a tourist train on alternate Sundays from Mt Barker to Strathalbyn and return for $16, spending around 2½ hours in the town.

Fleurieu Peninsula

South of Adelaide is the Fleurieu Peninsula, with attractions close enough to be visited on day trips from the city. The coast has a number of excellent swimming and surfing beaches, while inland there's rolling farmland, a handful of conservation areas and the vineyards of the McLaren Vale area.

There are also several small historic towns such as Port Elliott, Goolwa and Willunga.

The peninsula was named by Frenchman Nicholas Baudin after Napoleon's minister for the navy, who financed Baudin's expedition to Australia. In the early days, settlers on the peninsula ran a smuggling business. In 1837 a whaling station was established at Encounter Bay and this became the colony's first successful industry.

GULF ST VINCENT BEACHES

There's a series of fine swimming beaches along the Gulf St Vincent coast of the peninsula. They extend all the way from **Christie's Beach** through **Port Noarlunga**, **Seaford Beach** and **Moana Beach** to **Maslin Beach**. Farther south, beyond **Aldinga Beach** and **Sellicks Beach**, the coastline is rockier but there are still good beaches at **Carrickalinga** and **Normanville**.

Yankalilla, just in from the coast near Normanville, has gained recent fame thanks to the image of Jesus and the Virgin Mary that has mysteriously appeared on a wall of the Anglican church. This picturesque little town also has the first **schoolhouse** established by Mother Mary MacKillop (1867).

The coast road ends at **Cape Jervis** at the tip of the peninsula, where vehicle ferries travel back and forth across Backstairs Passage to Kangaroo Island, 13km away. There's a good swimming beach here if you're early for the ferry – the beach is 2km by road to the north of the ferry.

Along the south coast near Cape Jervis is the **Deep Creek Conservation Park**, with walking tracks including the Heysen Trail, and bush camping areas.

Inman Valley on the main road between Yankalilla and Victor Harbor is a pretty spot in a prime dairy and grazing area. It's an access point for the Heysen Trail.

Places to Stay

On the main road about 3.5km before the ferry landing, the friendly *Old Cape Jervis Station Homestead* (☎ 8598 0233) has a range of accommodation from $17.50 per person – this gets you a bed in the historic shearers' quarters, with use of the kitchen. Alternatively, the *Cape Jervis Tavern* (☎ 8598 0276) in town has self-contained rooms for $45/55.

There are *caravan parks* in Normanville, Second Valley and the Wirrina Resort, all of which have camp sites, on-site vans and cabins.

The *Old School House* (☎ 8558 8376) in Inman Valley 16km west of Victor Harbor is in an attractive setting but there's no public transport. Bunks are $12 and maps of the Heysen Trail are available from the hostel manager.

Getting There & Away

A public bus service (bookings ☎ 8231 1744) runs once daily to Cape Jervis from

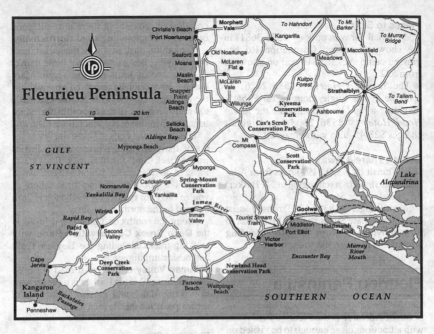

Adelaide. The fare to Yankalilla is $12 and to Cape Jervis $14.

SOUTHERN VALES

Adelaide has sprawled so far that the small town of **Morphett Vale** is now an outer suburb. Among its historic buildings is St Mary's (1846), the first Roman Catholic church in the state. **Old Noarlunga** is a tiny old historic township only 10 minutes drive from McLaren Vale.

Interesting **heritage walks** (☎ 8384 7918) are conducted on various days in Morphett Vale, Old Noarlunga, Port Noarlunga and Reynella. They take 1½ to two hours and cost $9; times are flexible. The McLaren Vale & Fleurieu Visitor Centre (☎ 8323 9455; rhand@mclarenvale.aust.com) on Main Rd at the northern end of McLaren Vale is open from 10 am to 5 pm daily.

Wineries

The peninsula has a string of wineries around McLaren Vale (pop 2300), as well as Reynella, Willunga and Langhorne Creek. The area is particularly well-suited to red wines, but a trend towards white wine consumption in the 1970s prompted growers to diversify.

There are around two dozen wineries with cellar-door sales in the McLaren Vale area and about 50 in the whole region. The first winery was established in Reynella in 1838 – some existing wineries date to the last century and have fine old buildings. Most are open from 10 am to 5 pm daily.

Each winery has its own appeal, whether it be a superb setting or just a good, full-bodied drop of the home product. The following are suggestions to help with your explorations.

Chapel Hill, Chapei Hill Rd, McLaren Vale south, has a magnificent hill-top location with views over the Gulf St Vincent. This is a small vineyard producing sophisticated whites and reds.

SOUTH AUSTRALIA

Noon's, Rifle Range Rd, McLaren Vale south, specialises in full-bodied reds. This winery is in a pleasant rural setting beside a small creek, and there are barbecue facilities.

d'Arenberg, Osborne Rd, McLaren Vale, has produced consistently good wines since 1928. There is nothing highbrow about this place – the tasting room is very informal and the staff are friendly and helpful.

Woodstock, Douglas Gully Rd, McLaren Flat, is a small winery with a restaurant and tranquil garden setting.

The McLaren Vale **Wine Bushing Festival** takes place over a week in late October and/or early November each year. It's a busy time of wine tastings and tours, and the whole thing is topped by a grand feast. During the festival, you can sample offerings from the McLaren Vale wineries on the winery bus service, which picks up and drops off imbibers en route.

The **Sea & Vines Festival** in June and the **Continuous Picnic** in October are weekend-long celebrations of food, wine and music.

A great way to visit a few wineries is on a camel with the Outback Camel Co (☎ 8543 2280). Several tours are available, including a one-day trek for $80 – they don't operate in winter. Alternatively, Sea & Vine Tours (☎ 8384 5151) will take you in their private hire car to various wineries for $70 per person, including lunch.

The only other option is to walk or cycle. There's a walking/bicycle track along the old railway line from McLaren Vale to Willunga, 6km to the south.

Willunga in the south of the Southern Vales winery area is a lovely old town with numerous interesting buildings from the colonial era. It's a major centre for Australian almond growing, and hosts the **Almond Blossom Festival** in July.

There are fine views, kangaroos and walks in the **Mt Magnificent Conservation Park**, 12km east of Willunga. This is another access point for the Heysen Trail.

Places to Stay & Eat
The friendly *McLaren Vale Lakeside*

Caravan Park (☎ 8323 9255), set amid vineyards on Field St, has camp sites ($13), on-site vans (from $32) and luxury cabins ($48).

In Willunga, to the south of McLaren Vale, the *Willunga Hotel* (☎ 8556 2135) has pub rooms from $20/35 for singles/doubles. It's also one of the best places in town for meals.

The *Emu Adventure Farm Stay* (☎ 8363 1583) is in a rich farming area halfway between Willunga and Aldinga Beach. It offers backpacker beds for $20 including a substantial breakfast, and there is access to good bushwalking.

There are several good restaurants in McLaren Vale. *Magnum's* in the Hotel McLaren is recommended for a top feed, as is *The Barn* bistro. Both are on Main Rd. Perhaps best of all is the historic *Salopian Inn*, just out of town on the Willunga Rd; it has a fascinating menu featuring fresh local produce, but is expensive (main courses start at $20). You'll need to book (☎ 8323 8769) as it's small and popular.

Several wineries have restaurants, and wine-tasters' lunches can be good value.

Getting There & Away
Premier (☎ 8415 5555) has up to three buses a day from Adelaide to McLaren Vale ($5).

VICTOR HARBOR (pop 7300)
The main town on the peninsula, and 84km south of Adelaide, Victor Harbor looks out onto Encounter Bay, where the British and French explorers Flinders and Baudin, had their historic meeting in 1802. There's a memorial to the 'encounter' up on the headland known as the Bluff. It's a steep climb for fine views.

Victor Harbor was founded early as a sealing and whaling centre. The first whaling station was established here at Rosetta Harbor, below the Bluff, in 1837 and another followed soon after on Granite Island. Operations ceased in 1864 due to a dramatic decline in whale numbers.

Information
The tourist office (☎ 8552 5738) at 10

Railway Tce is open from 10 am to 4 pm daily (9 am to 5 pm in summer).

Things to See

Historic buildings include **St Augustine's Church of England** (1869), the **Telegraph Station** (1869), the **Fountain Inn** (1840) and the **Old Station Master's Residence** (1866).

Victor Harbor is protected from the angry Southern Ocean by **Granite Island**, which is connected to the mainland by a causeway. You can ride out there on a double-decker tram pulled by Clydesdale draught horses ($4 return). It's an easy climb to the top of the hill, from where there are good views across the bay.

Granite Island is a rookery for little penguins. The **Penguin Interpretive Centre** (☎ 8552 7555) on the island has excellent audio-visual displays. It also operates one-hour **guided walks** every evening to watch the penguins come home from fishing. Walks cost $5 and leave from the centre at dusk.

Between June and October you might be lucky enough to see a **southern right whale** swimming near the causeway. Victor Harbor is on the migratory path of these splendid animals and you can observe them from several points around the bay, including the Bluff. You'll need binoculars with a magnification power of seven or more.

If you want to learn more about whales, the **South Australian Whale Centre** at the causeway end of Railway Tce is the place to go. It operates a 'whale information network' that covers sightings and strandings on the South Australian coast. It is open from 9 am to 5 pm daily (often later in summer) and entry costs $5 (see the boxed aside for further details).

On Flinders Pde, opposite the end of the causeway, the new **Encounter Coast Discovery Centre** explores the history of the southern Fleurieu from before European settlement to 1900. It has interesting displays and is open from 1 to 4 pm Wednesday to Sunday ($4).

Places to Stay

There are a number of caravan parks, hotels, motels and B&Bs in and around Victor Harbor; details are available from the tourist office.

The *Victor Harbor Beachfront Caravan Park* (☎ 8552 1111) on the foreshore at 114 Victoria St has camp sites from $12, basic cabins from $40 and self-contained cabins from $50.

The *Anchorage Guest House* (☎ 8552 5970) at 21 Flinders Pde has bunk beds in upmarket backpacker dorms for $17.50 including YHA discount. It also has rooms in a heritage-listed guesthouse from $35/60.

The *Grosvenor Hotel* (☎ 8552 1011), a

Southern Right Whales

Southern right whales are so called because they were considered by whalers to be the 'right' whales to hunt – large quantities of oil and fine whalebone meant a tidy profit from each carcass. Southern rights once roamed the seas in prolific numbers, but unrestrained slaughter last century reduced the population from 100,000 to an estimated 3000 today. Although considered an endangered species, they appear to be fighting back. During recent years, southern right whales have appeared in Encounter Bay, off Victor Harbor, from June to October during their annual breeding migration to warmer coastal waters.

The South Australian Whale Centre operates a whale information network from its information and interpretive centre on Railway Terrace in Victor Harbor. To report a sighting, call ☎8552 5644; or for current information on where the whales are, call ☎0055 31223.

The centre has an informative booklet (gold-coin donation) that tells you all about whale-watching, including useful tips on how to avoid damaging the fragile coastal environment. For more information, you can write to the centre at PO Box 950, Victor Harbor, SA 5211. ■

block away on Ocean St, has backpacker accommodation for $20 and pub rooms for $25/49. The most central of the motels is the *City Motel* (☎ 8552 2455), next to the post office on Ocean St, which has singles/doubles from $55/65.

Places to Eat

The *Original Fish & Chip Shop* in the town centre on Ocean St is popular, but best of the local seafood takeaways is *Pa's Place*, next to the Yilki Store – it's along the coast about 3km south of the town centre. Both also have sit-down meals.

The atmosphere at the *Grosvenor* is nothing flash but you can get a decent cheap feed there. For more formal dining the *Hotel Victor* is best.

Also worth trying is the *Anchorage Guesthouse* complex, which has a good licensed cafe with live entertainment most weekends.

For a different eating experience, *Klaus's Wurst Haus*, run by the ebullient Klaus himself, claims to sell the best German hot dogs in Australia. You'll find his tiny van in the park on the causeway end of Railway Tce; it's open weekends only.

Getting There & Away

SteamRanger (☎ 8391 1223) runs a tourist train on alternate Sundays from Mt Barker (in the Adelaide Hills) to Victor Harbor via Strathalbyn and Goolwa and return for $32 – the locomotives are diesel in summer and steam in winter. It spends about three hours in town before making the return journey.

Every Sunday, and daily over summer school holidays and Easter, the steam Cockle Train travels the scenic Encounter Coast between Goolwa and Victor Harbor. The return fare is $14, and tickets can be purchased at the station in Victor Harbor.

Premier (☎ 8415 5555) has two to three services daily from Adelaide for $11.60.

At the time of writing, a 23km sealed cycle path was being constructed along the coast from Victor Harbor to the Murray Mouth.

Getting Around

Motor scooters can be hired from Victor

Leisure (☎ 8552 1875) at the Shell service station, 105 Victoria St, for $25 per hour; day rates on application.

PORT ELLIOT (pop 1400)

Port Elliot, established in 1854 as the seaport for Murray River trade, is on Horseshoe Bay, a smaller part of Encounter Bay. **Horseshoe Bay** has a safe swimming beach and a nice cliff-top walk. Nearby surf beaches include **Boomer Beach** on the western edge of town and **Middleton Beach**, to the east. The Southern Surf Shop, a few doors west from the Royal Family Hotel, rents surfing gear and can provide information on surfing conditions.

Places to Stay & Eat

You can camp ($12) or stay in cabins (from $48 for four people) at the *Port Elliot Caravan Park* (☎ 8554 2134) on Horseshoe Bay.

The *Royal Family Hotel* (☎ 8554 2219) at 32 North Tce has rooms for $20/30; counter meals start at $5, and there's an excellent bakery across the road.

Getting There & Away

Premier (☎ 8415 5555) has up to three services daily from Adelaide to Port Elliot ($11.60).

GOOLWA (pop 3700)

On Lake Alexandrina near the mouth of the Murray River, Goolwa initially grew with the developing trade along the river. When the Murray mouth silted up and large ships were unable to get up to Goolwa, a railway line (the first in the state) was built from Goolwa to nearby Port Elliot. In the 1870s a new railway line to Adelaide from Murray Bridge spelt the end for Goolwa as a port town.

The tourist office (☎ 8555 1144; fax 8555 3810), open from 9 am to 5 pm daily, is in the centre of Goolwa in the **Signal Point River Murray Interpretive Centre**. On the waterfront, the centre contains interesting exhibits on the early history of life on the river ($5). Walking-tour pamphlets of Goolwa are available.

The **museum** on Porter St ($2) is open every afternoon except Monday and Friday. It's well worth a visit for its displays on early settlement and farming.

The **Sir Richard Peninsula** is a long stretch of beach leading to the mouth of the Murray. You can drive along it (4WD only), but there's no way across to the Coorong beach on the other side.

There are a variety of cruises on the lower Murray on the MV *Aroona* or PS *Mundoo* from $12. More amusing is a trip with the Coorong Pirate (☎ 018 812 000), a large and irredeemably ocker gentleman who runs fun trips from $6. His tours leave on the hour from 10 am to 3 pm (October to April only).

A free vehicle ferry from Goolwa to **Hindmarsh Island** operates 24 hours a day. The construction of a proposed bridge is dependent on the outcome of a legal challenge arising from claims by local Aboriginal people that it would damage sacred sites.

Places to Stay

The closest caravan park to town is the *Goolwa Camping & Tourist Park* (☎ 8555 2144) on Kessell Rd, which has camp sites from $10, on-site vans from $25 and cabins from $45.

Right on the river about 1km out, the *South Lakes Motel* (☎ 8555 2194) has rooms with kitchens from $45/49.

In the middle of town, the *Corio Hotel* (☎ 8555 1136) on Railway Tce has rooms for $25/50, including a light breakfast.

Graham's Castle (☎ 8555 2182), a rambling home built in 1868, is on Castle St about 2km out and 500m from the beach. They have basic twin-share rooms for $12/24, and there's a swimming pool, games room, bar and licensed cafe. They'll pick you up from the town centre if you give them a ring on arrival. They also run ecologically oriented boat expeditions into the Coorong National Park from $22, and minibus tours of the area.

On Hindmarsh Island, *Narnu Farm*

(☎ 8555 2002) has rustic cottages from $70 for singles and doubles and $8 for each extra adult. This is a pioneer farm and guests are encouraged to take part in farm activities, such as feeding the animals and hand-milking the cows.

Getting There & Away

Premier (☎ 8415 5555) has daily buses to Adelaide for $11.60. See the earlier Victor Harbor section for details of steam trains that pass through Goolwa.

Kangaroo Island

Separated from the mainland about 9500 years ago, Kangaroo Island is Australia's third-largest island (after Tasmania, and Melville Island off Darwin). About 150km long and 30km wide, the island offers peaceful scenery, a varied coastline including towering cliffs, swimming and surf beaches, lots of native wildlife and good fishing. There are also a number of shipwrecks off the coast, many of which are of interest to scuba divers.

The island was unoccupied by Aboriginal people at the time of European settlement; stone implements have been discovered, however, and these suggest human occupation more than 11,000 years ago. Archaeologists are uncertain as to what caused the demise of these early inhabitants, but it's thought they disappeared about 2250 years ago.

Kangaroo Island has a rough-and-ready early European history with sealers, whalers and escaped convicts all playing their often ruthless part. Many of the place names on the island are French – the first thorough survey of its coast was carried out by the French explorer Nicholas Baudin on two visits in 1802 and 1803. The island was named by Matthew Flinders in 1802 after his crew slaughtered many kangaroos here and enjoyed a welcome feast of fresh meat.

Kangaroo Island's geographical isolation from the mainland has been a boon to its native wildlife: it is free of dingoes, rabbits and foxes. Because of this, a number of threatened native Australian animals, such as the koala and platypus, have been introduced to ensure their survival.

Information

The Kangaroo Island Gateway Visitor Information Centre (☎ 8553 1185; tourki @ozemail.com.au) is on the Kingscote road just outside the little township of Penneshaw. It opens weekdays from 9 am to 5 pm and weekends and public holidays from 10 am to 4 pm.

The main National Parks & Wildlife Service (NPWS) office is at 37 Dauncey St in Kingscote (☎ 8553 2381). It is open from 8.45 am to 5 pm weekdays.

The Island Parks Pass ($20), which can be purchased only on the island, covers all NPWS entry and camping fees on the island. It also entitles holders to free NPWS tours (see under Organised Tours). Permits and passes can be obtained from any of the island's seven National Parks offices; contact the Kingscote office for details.

During summer, and into April, fire restrictions are in force. Only gas fires may be lit in national parks, and on days of total fire ban, no fires may be lit (including gas fires). Penalties for lighting a fire illegally are severe. Contact district council offices, the Country Fire Service or park rangers for further information.

Organised Tours

The NPWS operates a range of economical guided tours and walks for visitors to areas of conservation and historical significance, and these are free for Island Parks Pass holders. Note that the Pass does not cover the penguin walks at Kingscote and Penneshaw.

At **Seal Bay**, 55km south-west of Kingscote, guided tours to the sea-lion colony are conducted daily every 45 minutes between 9 am and 4.15 pm (later in summer). Tours at the **Kelly Hill Caves Conservation Park**, 79km from Kingscote, take place daily between 10 am and 4 pm (3 pm in winter).

Rangers also conduct tours of the historic lighthouses at **Cape Borda**, 103km from Kingscote on the western extremity of the island, and **Cape Willoughby**, 28km south-east of Penneshaw at the island's eastern end; see the sections on Flinders Chase and Penneshaw for times.

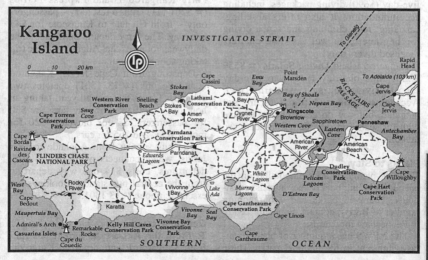

SOUTH AUSTRALIA

Bookings are only required if you are part of a large group.

Package Tours The island ferry companies (see below under Getting There & Away) and many tour operators on the island offer packages ex-Adelaide. Competition is fierce, so if you shop around you should pick up a good deal. Don't forget to check the hostels in Adelaide.

Bus Tours Tours designed for backpackers and other budget travellers are run by the Penneshaw Youth Hostel (☎ 8553 1284; 1800 018 258), Adelaide Sightseeing (☎ 8231 4144) and Kangaroo Island Ferry Connections (☎ 8553 1233; 1800 018 484). You can expect to pay anywhere between $65 and $80 for a day tour that includes lunch and a visit to Seal Bay and Flinders Chase.

There are also more personalised 4WD tours, fishing charters and tours, walking tours, and visits to such places as a eucalyptus oil distillery and a sheep's milk dairy.

Scuba Diving Tours Adventureland Diving (☎ 8553 1072), 10km from Penneshaw on the Kingscote road, runs one-day ($95) to five-day ($690) diving packages, including accommodation. It also offers abseiling, canoeing, rock climbing and scuba diving for beginners, as well as dive charters (licensed divers only).

Kangaroo Island Diving Safaris (☎ 8559 3225) runs one-day ($150) to five-day ($650) diving tours at Western River. Accommodation and transfers are not included, but you do get a chance to dive with fur seals and see 30cm-long leafy sea dragons.

Places to Stay
There is plenty of accommodation on the island, including backpacker hostels, guesthouses, caravan parks and a burgeoning number of B&Bs; contact the visitor centre in Penneshaw for details.

The NPWS has a number of historic cottages for rent in the national parks. These range from basic huts ($10 per person) to the more upmarket lightkeeper's cottages ($90 minimum per cottage) at Cape Willoughby and Cape du Couedic.

Kangaroo Island Ferry Connections (☎ 8553 1233; 1800 018 484) in Penneshaw has a range of combined accommodation and car-hire packages. Staff can book selfcontained properties around the island starting at $50 for a double (car hire extra). In addition to those at the main townships, small and mainly basic caravan parks are located at Emu Bay, Stokes Bay, Vivonne Bay and near Rocky River.

Getting There & Away
Air Kendell Airlines (☎ 13 1300) services Kingscote from Adelaide for $82 one way or has an advance-purchase Saver fare for $55.

Albatross Airlines (☎ 8553 2296) in Kingscote flies from Adelaide to Kingscote three times daily ($60). Its free courtesy bus transfers passengers between the airport and Kingscote.

Emu Air (☎ 8234 3711; 1800 182 353) has a twice-daily service to Kingscote from Adelaide; the fare is $70 one way.

Ferry Kangaroo Island Express Ferries (☎ 8261 1111) runs a fast ferry – passengers only – from Glenelg to Kingscote for $43 one way. The ferry departs both ends once daily year-round except August, with the trip taking about 2½ hours.

Departing from Cape Jervis, Kangaroo Island Sealink (☎ 13 1301) operates two vehicular ferries that run all year, taking an hour to Penneshaw. One-way fares are $30 for passengers, $5 for bicycles, $20 for motorcycles and $65 for cars.

The bus service from Adelaide to Port Jervis, which connects with Sealink ferry departures, costs $14 one way departing from the central bus station. Bookings are essential; phone ☎ 13 1301.

Getting Around
To/From the Airport An airport bus runs from Kangaroo Island airport to Kingscote

for $10. The airport is 14km from the town centre.

To/From the Ferry Landings The Sealink Shuttle (☎ 13 1301) connects with most ferries and links Penneshaw with Kingscote ($11) and American River ($6.50). You have to book.

Car & Motorcycle Most of the island's rural roads are unsealed. Many are narrow, and have loose gravel surfaces and sharp corners, not to mention dust and wandering wildlife, so drive slowly.

Car Rental There are four car-hire companies, all based at Kingscote: Excel (☎ 8553 3255), Hertz/Kangaroo Island Rental Cars (☎ 8553 2390; 1800 088 296) and Budget (☎ 8553 3133).

Very few of Adelaide's car-rental outlets will allow their vehicles to be taken across to Kangaroo Island. Two exceptions are Smile Rent-a-Car (☎ 8234 0655) and Access Rent-a-Car (☎ 8223 7466) – with the latter, a $10 per day Kangaroo Island surcharge applies.

Scooter/Motorcycle Rental In Kingscote you can hire scooters from: the Country Cottage Shop (☎ 8553 2148) at 6 Centenary Ave, for $45 for a day; and at Servo Plus (☎ 8553 2787) next to the hostel at 21 Murray St for $35. You can't take them on unsealed roads.

Bicycle Hire The number of unsealed roads and the relatively long distances between settlements can make cycling hard work. If you're still game, bicycles (including tandems) can be hired from Servo Plus for $18 a day.

KINGSCOTE (pop 1500)

Kingscote, the main town on the island, was the first white settlement in South Australia. Although Europeans had been on the island for many years, Kingscote was only formally settled in 1836. It was all but abandoned just a few years later, when most settlers had moved to the mainland.

There are branches of the ANZ and BankSA in town, but no ATMs. However, there are plenty of EFTPOS outlets, some of which will let you withdraw cash – one is at Servo Plus, next to the backpackers' hostel at 21 Murray St.

Things to See & Do

The **tidal pool** about 500m south of the jetty is the best place in town to swim. Most locals head out to **Emu Bay**, 18km away.

Hope Cottage on Centenary Ave was built in 1857. It is now a good museum ($2.50), with a variety of colonial implements and memorabilia. There's an old lighthouse and eucalyptus-oil distillery in the grounds. It's open from 2 to 4 pm daily.

Pelican feeding takes place every evening at 4 pm at the wharf near the town centre. A number of these wonderful beaked battleships usually turn up for the free tucker, as well as a Pacific gull or two. A donation of $2 is requested.

Each evening at 7.30 and 8.30 pm (8.30 and 9.30 pm during daylight saving) rangers take visitors on a **Discovering Penguins walk**. They leave from the Penguin Burrow at the Ozone Hotel on the Esplanade and cost $5 – wear sturdy footwear and leave your camera flash behind.

Places to Stay & Eat

The *Kangaroo Island Caravan Park* (☎ 85 53 2325) is on the Esplanade close to the town centre. It has camp sites from $12, on-site vans from $30, self-contained cabins from $45 and flats from $55 – the rates are for up to four people. They also operate the caravan park at Emu Bay.

On the foreshore at Brownlow, about 3km west of the town centre, the *Kingscote Nepean Bay Tourist Park* (☎ 8553 2394) has camp sites from $11, on-site vans from $28 and cabins from $33.

The friendly *Kangaroo Island Central Backpackers Hostel* (☎ 8553 2787) at 19 Murray St has dorm beds ($14) and twin and double rooms for $37 (extra persons $18). While the facilities are well maintained, the kitchen is minuscule and the dorms are crowded.

On Chapman Tce overlooking the tidal pool is *Nomads Ellson's Seaview Guesthouse* (☎ 8553 2030). This old-style guesthouse has luxurious budget rooms where dorm beds are $18 and singles/doubles are $20/36 (take $2 off per person for subsequent nights). There is no kitchen, but it's only a short walk to the handful of cafes and takeaways in the town centre.

The *Queenscliffe Family Hotel* (☎ 8553 2254) and the *Ozone Hotel* (☎ 8553 2011) are both in the town centre and charge upwards of $60/70. Otherwise there are several motels.

AMERICAN RIVER (pop 300)

Between Kingscote and Penneshaw, this small settlement takes its name from the American sealers who built a boat here in 1804. The town is on a small peninsula and shelters an inner bay, named **Pelican Lagoon** by Flinders, and now a bird sanctuary. Every afternoon at 4.30 pm down on the wharf you can watch the **pelican-feeding**.

Places to Stay & Eat

Linnetts Island Club (☎ 8553 7053) has rooms with share facilities from $28/56 and hostel beds for $12 ($17 with linen). It also manages the *American River Caravan Park* next door, where camp sites cost from $15.

At *Casuarina Holiday Units* (☎ 8553 7020), next to the post office, basic self-contained units sleeping up to five cost from $38 for two people and $6 for extra adults.

PENNESHAW (pop 300)

Looking across Backstairs Passage to the Fleurieu Peninsula, Penneshaw is a quiet little resort town with a white sandy beach at **Hog's Bay**. It's the arrival point for ferries from Cape Jervis.

The visitor centre issues camping permits for Chapmans River, Antechamber Bay, Browns Beach and American River.

There's no bank in town, but Sharpys has an ANZ agency, Servwel has the BankSA agency and the post office is an agent for the Commonwealth Bank. All have EFTPOS cash withdrawal facilities.

Things to See & Do

In the evenings rangers take visitors to view the penguins that nest in the sand dunes and cliffs near the township – you'll generally see more penguins here than at Kingscote. Tours ($25) depart from the 'Penguin Rookery' on the foreshore near the ferry terminal, leaving at 8.30 and 9.30 pm in summer (7 and 8 pm in winter). Take sturdy shoes and leave your camera flash behind.

The **Penneshaw Maritime & Folk Museum** has some interesting memorabilia on local history. It opens Monday, Wednesday and Saturday from 10 am to noon and 3 to 5 pm ($2).

Penneshaw is situated on Dudley Peninsula, a knob of land at the eastern end of the island. The peninsula has several points of interest outside the town itself: **Pennington Bay** has surf; the sheltered waters of **Chapman River** are popular for canoeing; and the **Cape Willoughby Lighthouse**, the oldest lighthouse in the state (first operated in 1852) has half-hour tours every 30 minutes between 10 am and 4 pm daily.

Places to Stay

The basic *Penneshaw Youth Hostel* (☎ 8553 1284) on North Tce has dorm beds for $14, or twin rooms for $16 per person. It has a cafe on the premises.

The *Penguin Walk Hostel* (☎ 8553 1233) charges the same rates, but there the similarity ends. Its dorms (maximum six beds) are quite pleasant and spacious; each has its own bathroom and cooking facilities. The twin rooms have share facilities and there's a communal kitchen. The hostel is right by the ferry landing and a stone's throw from the swimming beach.

Alternatively, the *Penneshaw Caravan Park* (☎ 8553 1075) has shady camp sites and on-site caravans next to the beach.

NORTH COAST

There are several fine, sheltered beaches along the north coast. Near Kingscote, **Emu**

Bay has a beautiful, long sweep of sand. Other good beaches include **Stokes Bay**, **Snelling Beach** and **Western River Cove**.

FLINDERS CHASE NATIONAL PARK

Occupying the western end of the island, Flinders Chase is one of South Australia's most significant national parks. There is plenty of mallee scrub, but also beautiful tall forests with koalas, echidnas and possums; the kangaroos and emus have become so fearless they'll brazenly badger you for food – the picnic and barbecue area at Rocky River Homestead is fenced off to protect visitors from these freeloaders.

On the north-western corner of the island, **Cape Borda** has a lighthouse built in 1858. There are guided tours on weekdays from 11 am to 3.15 pm (2 pm in winter and 4.15 pm in the summer school holidays). At nearby **Harvey's Return** is a small, poignant cemetery on the cliff top.

Just south of Cape Borda is the **Ravine des Casoars**, with one of the island's most pleasant walking trails (8km return). This lovely spot was named by Baudin after the dwarf emus he saw there – the species became extinct soon after European settlement.

In the south-eastern corner of the park, **Cape du Couedic** is wild and remote, with towering cliffs. A picturesque lighthouse built in 1906 tops the cape; you can follow the path from the car park down to **Admirals Arch** – a large natural archway formed by pounding seas. New Zealand fur seals are often seen here.

At Kirkpatrick Point, a couple of kilometres east of Cape du Couedic, the **Remarkable Rocks** are a cluster of large, weather-sculpted granite boulders on a huge dome swooping 75m down to the sea.

Places to Stay

In Flinders Chase you can camp at the Rocky River park headquarters and in other designated areas with a permit. Watch out for the kangaroos: they get into tents looking for food and can cause a lot of damage.

There are a very limited number of hot showers in the park, but facilities are better at the *Western KI Caravan Park* (☎ 8559 7201) on the South Coast Rd just a few minutes drive east from Rocky River. There are plenty of wild koalas here as well.

There are a number of historic cottages available for hire in the park; see Places to Stay at the beginning of this section.

SOUTH COAST

The south coast is rough and wave-swept compared with the north. At **Hanson Bay**, close to Cape du Couedic, there's a colony of fairy penguins. A little farther east you come to **Kelly Hill Caves**, a series of limestone caves 'discovered' in the 1880s by a horse named Kelly, which fell into them through a hole in the ground; see Organised Tours at the start of this section.

Vivonne Bay has a long and beautiful beach. There is excellent fishing but bathers should take great care; the undertows are fierce and swimmers are advised to stick close to the jetty or the river mouth. **Seal Bay** is another sweeping beach, with a large colony of Australian sea lions; see Organised Tours at the start of this section.

Near Seal Bay and close to the south coast road is **Little Sahara**, a series of enormous, white sand dunes.

Places to Eat

Historic *Kaiwarra Cottage* on the South Coast Rd near the Seal Bay turn-off has light meals and Devonshire teas.

Barossa Valley

This famous area, about 55km north-east of Adelaide, is Australia's best-known wine-producing district – it crushes about a quarter of the Australian vintage of 500,000 tonnes. The valley is gently sloping and measures about 40km long and five to 11km wide.

The Barossa still has a German flavour from its early days, which started with the original settlement in 1842. Fleeing religious persecution in Prussia and Silesia, the first settlers weren't wine makers, but fortunately someone soon came along and recognised the valley's potential. The name is actually a misspelling of Barrosa in Spain, close to where Spanish sherry comes from. Prior to WWI, place names in the Barossa probably sounded even more Germanic, but during the war many names were patriotically anglicised. When the fervour died down some were changed back.

You must get off the main road to begin to appreciate the Barossa Valley. Take the scenic drive between Angaston and Tanunda, the palm-fringed road to Seppeltsfield and Marananga, or wander through the sleepy historic hamlet of Bethany.

Information

The Barossa Wine & Visitor Centre (☎ 1800 812 662; bwta@dove.net.au; www.dove.net.au/bwta/welcome.html) at 66-68 Murray St in Tanunda opens weekdays from 9 am to 5 pm and weekends and public holidays from 10 am to 4 pm. It includes an interpretive centre ($2) designed to educate visitors about wine.

Wineries

The Barossa has over 50 wineries; almost all are open to the public and offer free wine tastings. Get a copy of the regional tourist guide for full details of locations and opening hours.

The following are some well-known – and some not so well-known – wineries.

Chateau Yaldara at Lyndoch was established in 1947 in the ruins of a 19th-century winery and flour mill. It has a notable antique collection which can be seen on conducted tours ($2).

St Hallett at Tanunda is a small winery, well known for its top quality wines. There is a keg factory opposite where you can watch kegs being made.

Orlando at Rowland Flat, between Lyndoch and Tanunda, was established in 1847 and is one of the oldest wineries in the valley.

Saltram Wine Estate in Angaston is another old winery. Established in 1859, it has friendly and informative staff, and is set in beautiful gardens.

Seppelts in Seppeltsfield was founded in 1852; the old bluestone buildings are surrounded by gardens and date palms. The extensive complex includes a picnic area with gas barbecues. There is also a family mausoleum. Daily tours cost $3.

Wolf Blass out beyond Nuriootpa was only founded in 1973, but quickly became one of the better known wine labels in Australia. There's an interesting heritage museum at the winery.

Yalumba in Angaston was founded way back in 1849. The blue-marble winery, topped by a clock tower and surrounded by gardens, is the largest family-owned winery in Australia.

Bethany Wines, Bethany Rd, Bethany, is a small family-operated winery in a scenic location. Its white port is highly recommended.

Grant Burge Wines, Jacobs Creek, Barossa Valley Highway, Tanunda, is a relative newcomer but has earned a reputation for consistently good wines. The winery boasts a beautifully restored tasting room.

Special Events

The colourful **Vintage Festival** is the Barossa's big event, taking place over seven days starting on Easter Monday in odd-numbered years. It features processions, brass bands, tug-of-war contests between the wineries, traditional dinners and, of course, a lot of wine tasting.

However, the **Classic Gourmet Weekend** held in August or September is considered by many to be more fun. It has a carnival atmosphere and features fine food, wine and music. In September or October there's the two-week **International Barossa Music Festival** featuring jazz and classical music. **Barossa Under the Stars**, held in January or February, has night picnics and top entertainment (in 1996 the main drawcard was Shirley Bassey).

Other festive occasions include the **Oom Pah Fest** in January, the **Hot-Air Balloon Regatta** in May and a **Brass Band Competition** in November.

Events in the Barossa revolve around the grape-growing seasons. It takes four to five years for grape vines to reach maturity after they are first planted in September and October. Their useful life is usually around 40 years. The vines are pruned heavily from July to August and grow and produce fruit over summer. The busiest months are from

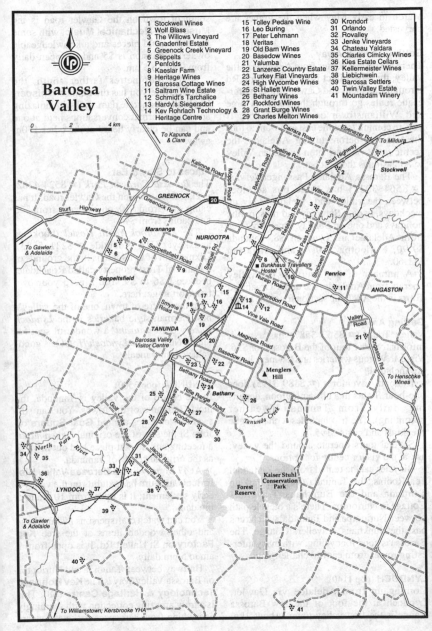

Barossa Valley

1 Stockwell Wines	15 Tolley Pedare Wine	30 Krondorf
2 Wolf Blass	16 Leo Buring	31 Orlando
3 The Willows Vineyard	17 Peter Lehmann	32 Rovalley
4 Gnadenfrei Estate	18 Veritas	33 Jenke Vineyards
5 Greenock Creek Vineyard	19 Old Barn Wines	34 Chateau Yaldara
6 Seppelts	20 Basedow Wines	35 Charles Cimicky Wines
7 Penfolds	21 Yalumba	36 Kies Estate Cellars
8 Kaeslar Farm	22 Lanzerac Country Estate	37 Kellermeister Wines
9 Heritage Wines	23 Turkey Flat Vineyards	38 Liebichwein
10 Barossa Cottage Wines	24 High Wycombe Wines	39 Barossa Settlers
11 Saltram Wine Estate	25 St Hallett Wines	40 Twin Valley Estate
12 Schmidt's Tarchalice	26 Bethany Wines	41 Mountadam Winery
13 Hardy's Siegersdorf	27 Rockford Wines	
14 Kev Rohrlach Technology & Heritage Centre	28 Grant Burge Wines	
	29 Charles Melton Wines	

March to early May when the grapes are harvested.

Getting There & Away

There are several routes from Adelaide to the valley; the most direct is via Main North Rd through Elizabeth and Gawler. More picturesque routes go through the Torrens Gorge and Williamstown or via Birdwood. If you're coming from the east and want to tour the wineries before hitting Adelaide, the scenic route via Springton and Eden Valley to Angaston is the best bet.

The Barossa Adelaide Passenger Service (☎ 8564 3022) has three bus services between the valley and Adelaide daily on weekdays, two on Saturday and most public holidays and one on Sunday. One-way fares from Adelaide are Lyndoch $8, Tanunda $9.90, Nuriootpa $10.70 and Angaston $11.60.

A number of day tours to the valley operate from Adelaide; see under Organised Tours in the Adelaide section for some ideas.

Getting Around

Valley Tours (☎ 8563 3587) has a good, informative day tour of the Barossa for $36. Visits to various wineries and a winery lunch are included.

Balloon Adventures (☎ 8389 3195) does one-hour flights in a hot-air balloon, departing daily from Tanunda (weather permitting). The trip includes a champagne breakfast and costs $195.

Several tours operate around the valley; ask at the visitor centre for options.

Bicycles can be rented from the Zinfandel Tea Rooms, the Tanunda Caravan Park in Tanunda and the Bunkhaus Travellers Cottage in Nuriootpa. There's a bicycle path between Nuriootpa and Tanunda, which runs past the Bunkhaus Travellers Cottage. The Barossa is good for cycling, with many interesting routes from easy to challenging.

LYNDOCH (pop 1140)

Coming up from Adelaide via Gawler, Lyndoch at the foot of the low Barossa Range is the first valley town. About 1km south of town on the Gawler road is the **Museum of Mechanical Music**, with some fascinating old pieces and a knowledgeable owner; admission is $5 and it's open daily from 9 am to 5 pm.

A few kilometres farther south, the Barossa Reservoir has the famous **Whispering Wall**, a concrete dam wall with amazing acoustics; normal conversations held at one end can be clearly heard at the other 150m away.

Places to Stay & Eat

The *Barossa Caravan Park* (☎ 8524 4262) is 2km from town on the Gawler road. It has camp sites from $10, on-site vans from $25 and cabins from $45.

The *Kersbrook Youth Hostel* (bookings and key: YHA Adelaide ☎ 8231 5583), 20km south of Lyndoch, is in the grounds of a National Trust property called Roachdale; beds cost $6 to $9. You'll need your own transport to get here.

In the centre of town, one of the valley's best German-style bakeries is the *Lyndoch Bakery & Restaurant*, a wonderful spot for lunch. Nearby, the *Lyndoch Hotel* has good-value counter meals.

TANUNDA (pop 3500)

In the centre of the valley is Tanunda, the most Germanic of the towns. You can still see early cottages around **Goat Square** on John St the site of the original *ziegenmarkt*, a meeting and market place laid out in 1842 as the original centre of Tanunda.

At 47 Murray St the **Barossa Valley Historical Museum** has exhibits on the valley's early settlement; it is open from 10 am to 5 pm daily.

You can watch craftspersons making kegs and other wooden items at the free **Keg Factory** on St Hallett Rd. It is open from 9 am to 5 pm daily.

Halfway between Tanunda and Nuriootpa on Barossa Valley Way is The **Kev Rohrlach Technology & Heritage Centre** ($8). This is a truly amazing collection with seemingly everything from aerospace rockets to steam

Norm's Coolies travel in style to their shows at Breezy Gully Farm

engines. It's open from 11 am to 4 pm daily (10 am to 5 pm Sunday).

Three kilometres from Tanunda on the Gomersal road, **Norm's Coolies**, trained sheepdogs, go through their paces at the Breezy Gully Farm on Monday, Wednesday and Saturday at 2 pm ($6). The performance is worth seeing.

There are fine old Lutheran churches in all the valley towns but Tanunda has some of the most interesting. The **Tabor Church** dates from 1849; the 1868 Lutheran **St John's Church** has life-size wooden statues of Christ, Moses, and the apostles Peter, Paul and John.

From Tanunda, turn off the main road and take the scenic drive through Bethany and via Menglers Hill to Angaston. It runs through beautiful, rural country featuring large gums; the view over the valley from Menglers Hill is superb as long as you can ignore the dreadful statues in the foreground.

Places to Stay & Eat
The *Tanunda Caravan Park* (☎ 8563 2784) on the Barossa Valley Highway has camp sites for $11, on-site vans from $27 and cabins from $35. There's also the reasonable *Tanunda Hotel* (☎ 8563 2030) at 51 Murray St with singles/doubles with share facilities for $44/50 and self-contained rooms for $54/60. Otherwise there are two or three expensive motels and several B&Bs.

The *Zinfandel Tea Rooms* at 58 Murray St has delicious light lunches and also does breakfast. For real value it's hard to beat the *Tanunda Club* at 45 MacDonnell St, which sells hearty dinners for $6.

NURIOOTPA (pop 3500)
At the northern end of the valley is its commercial centre, Nuriootpa. There are several pleasant picnic areas along the Para River, as well as some nice river walks close to the town centre.

Places to Stay
The *Barossa Valley Tourist Park* (☎ 8562 1404) on Penrice Rd in Nuriootpa has camp sites from $12 and cabins from $30.

The *Bunkhaus Travellers Cottage* (☎ 85 62 2260) is set on a family vineyard, 1km outside Nuriootpa on the Barossa Valley Highway to Tanunda (look for the keg on the corner). It's a very pleasant and welcoming place with dorm beds from $12 plus a cottage for four people (a double bed costs from $35). Mountain bikes can be hired here and Jan, the very friendly proprietor, will be pleased to help you plan your day.

The *Angas Park Hotel* (☎ 8562 1050) at 22 Murray St has basic rooms for $15.

ANGASTON (pop 1850)
On the eastern side of the valley, this town was named after George Fife Angas, one of

the area's pioneers. Magnificent **Collingrove Homestead**, built by his son in 1856, is owned by the National Trust; it opens weekdays from 1 to 4.30 pm and during festivals from 11 am to 4.30 pm (entry $4; see the following Places to Stay entry).

The **Bethany Art Gallery** at 12 Washington St is worth visiting for its arts and crafts.

Places to Stay

Angaston has the *Barossa Valley Hotel* (☎ 8564 2014) at 41 Murray St, a reasonable hotel with B&B rates of $20 per person. Just down the street at No 59 is the *Angaston Hotel* (☎ 8564 2428). Rooms are $25 per person for B&B.

Good for a splurge is the historic *Collingrove Homestead* (☎ 8564 2061), about 7km from town on the Eden Valley road. The five rooms are part of the old servants' quarters and cost $160 per double including a cooked breakfast.

BETHANY & AROUND

South-east of Tanunda, **Bethany** was the first German settlement in the valley. Old cottages still stand around the Bethany reserve; the *Landhaus* claims to be the world's smallest licensed restaurant – it seats 12 and bookings are essential.

Just south-east of the Barossa in the Eden Valley is **Springton** and the Herbig Tree – a hollow gum tree that was home to a pioneer family from 1855 to 1860.

Mid-North

The area between Adelaide and Port Augusta is generally known as the Mid-North. It includes some of the most productive farming land in the state, and is noted for its wheat and fine wool. Good wines are produced in the Clare Valley, and there are a number of small historic towns, such as Auburn, Burra, Kapunda and Mintaro, whose streetscapes have changed little over the past 100 years.

Two main routes run north from Adelaide

through the area. One runs to Gawler where you can turn east to the Barossa Valley and the Riverland area, or continue north through Burra to Peterborough. From there you can head west to Port Augusta, north-west to the Flinders Ranges or continue on the Barrier Highway to Broken Hill in New South Wales.

The second route heads through Port Wakefield and on to Port Pirie and Port Augusta on Spencer Gulf. You can then travel north-east to the Flinders Ranges, south-west to the Eyre Peninsula, north to Alice Springs or head west towards the Nullarbor and Western Australia.

KAPUNDA (pop 2200)

About 80km north of Adelaide and a little north of the Barossa Valley, historic Kapunda is off the main roads that head north. However, you can take a pleasant back route from the valley through the town and join the Barrier Highway a little farther north.

Copper was found at Kapunda in 1842 and it became the first mining town in Australia. At its peak in 1861 it had 11 hotels and was the colony's major commercial centre outside Adelaide. Large-scale operations ceased in 1878 and the mines closed altogether in 1912.

The Kapunda & Light Information Centre (☎ 8566 2902) on Main St opens daily from 10 am to 4 pm.

On the edge of town, a **lookout** offers views over the old open-cut mines and mine chimneys. There's a 1.5km interpretive walking track through the old mining area.

On Hill St in the town centre, the **Mining Interpretive Centre** ($2) has interesting displays and is open from 1 to 4 pm from Saturday to Thursday. Next door in the big old Baptist church the **Kapunda Museum** ($3) is one of the state's best folk museums. It's open the same hours.

An 8m-high bronze statue entitled 'Map Kernow' (or 'Son of Cornwall' in old Cornish) stands at the Adelaide end of town as a tribute to pioneer miners.

The *Sir John Franklin Hotel* (☎ 8566

3233) in Main St has counter meals from $5, and rooms costing $20/40 for singles/ doubles.

The attractive *Dutton Park Caravan Park* (☎ 8566 2094) has camp sites from $11 and self-contained cabins for $40.

AUBURN (pop 300)

The township of Auburn, 24km south of Clare, has some beautifully preserved historic buildings, particularly on St Vincent St. Auburn was the birthplace of CJ Dennis, one of Australia's best-known colonial authors.

The **Auburn Gallery** on Main North Rd in the middle of town has some fine local work and interesting crafts. It's open from Monday to Thursday.

CLARE (pop 2800)

At the heart of the Clare Valley wine region, this attractive town 135km north of Adelaide has eschewed many of the tourist trappings characteristic of the Barossa Valley. It was settled in 1842 and named after County Clare in Ireland.

The Clare Valley Tourist Information Centre (☎ 8842 2131; fax 8842 1117) in the town hall on Main North Rd, is open from 9 am to 5 pm daily (10 am to 4 pm Sunday and public holidays). Half-day tours of the district can be arranged here ($15).

Clare itself has a number of interesting buildings, including an impressive Catholic church. The police station and courthouse date from 1850 and are preserved as a **National Trust museum**; it opens weekends and public holidays from 10 am to noon and 2 to 4 pm ($2).

Established in 1851 by Jesuit priests, **Sevenhill Cellars**, at Sevenhill about 7km south of Clare, was the valley's first winery. It still produces communion wine, as well as a very good verdelho. The marvellous **St Aloysius Church** adjoins the winery and dates from 1875.

There are many other wineries in the valley, including the Leasingham Winery (1894) on Clare's southern outskirts. Opening times vary, but the regional guide,

available at the tourist centre, has all the relevant details.

Special Events

The Clare Valley's major event is the **Clare Valley Gourmet Weekend**, a festival of wine, food and music put on by local wineries over the Adelaide Cup weekend in May.

Another not to be missed is the **Clare Valley Spring Festival**, featuring good musicians and a carnival atmosphere – not to mention fine wine and food, of course. It's held on a weekend in early November.

Places to Stay

The attractive and friendly *Clare Caravan Park* (☎ 8842 2724) on Main North Rd, 4km south of the Clare GPO, is the closest camping ground to town. It has sites from $11 (or $8 if you're travelling solo), on-site vans for $30 and cabins from $40.

On Main St, the *Taminga Hotel* (☎ 8842 2808) has basic singles/doubles for $16/32.

The *Clare Hotel* (☎ 8842 2816) on Main North Rd – an extension of Main St – has single pub rooms for $19 and motel rooms for $40/45.

Bentley's Hotel/Motel (☎ 8842 2815) also on Main North Rd has spartan backpacker beds in twin rooms for $10, self-contained hotel rooms for $45/55 and motel rooms for $55 (singles and doubles).

Bungaree Station (☎ 8842 2677) 12km north of Clare has accommodation in the shearers' quarters for $15 a bed. This working farm has many historical exhibits. If you're staying here, self-conducted cassette tours are possible between 9 am and sundown ($8 including morning or afternoon tea).

Geralka Farm (☎ 8845 8081) on the Spalding road 25km north of Clare is another working farm that caters for visitors. You can camp ($14 for a powered site) or stay in on-site vans (from $28).

In **Mintaro**, a small heritage town 18km south-east of Clare, the historic *Martindale Hall* (☎ 8843 9088) is an imposing mansion that offers B&B for $65 per person.

SOUTH AUSTRALIA

Getting There & Away

Bute Buses (☎ 8826 2346) go daily except Saturday to Clare from Adelaide for $15.

Getting Around

You can wander on foot or by bike past some of the district's finest wineries on the **Riesling Trail**, which meanders through the valley from Auburn to Clare (it was due for completion in 1998).

Clare Valley Cycle Hire (☎ 8842 2782) at 32 Victoria Rd in Clare has bicycles for $16 a day including helmet.

BURRA (pop 1000)

This pretty little town is bursting at the seams with historic sites. It was a copper-mining centre from 1847 to 1877, with various British ethnic groups forming their own distinctive communities (the Cornish being the most numerous).

The district, Burra Burra, takes its name from the Hindi word for 'great' by one account, and from the Aboriginal name of the creek by another.

Information

The Burra District Tourist Information Centre (☎ 8892 2154; fax 8892 2555) on Market Square is open daily from 9 am to 5 pm.

Here you can purchase the *Discovering Historic Burra* booklet ($5), which describes numerous sites on a 11km heritage trail. The booklet and keys to eight sites are included in the *Burra Passport*, which costs $20 for a car containing two adults ($5 for each extra adult) – you also get reduced-price entry to the Enginehouse and Bon Accord museums.

Things to See & Do

Burra has many substantial stone buildings, tiny Cornish cottages and numerous other reminders of the mining days. The tourist centre can arrange tours of the town – a two-hour tour costs $20 per person ($15 if there's four or more in your group).

The **Market Square Museum** ($2) is across from the tourist office and features a shop, post office and house as they might

have looked between 1880 and 1930. It's open from 1 to 3 pm Friday, weekends and public holidays.

The 33 cottages at **Paxton Square** were built for Cornish miners in the 1850s. One of the cottages, **Malowen Lowarth**, has been furnished in 1850s style. It opens on Saturday from 1 to 3 pm and Sunday and public holidays from 10.30 am to 12.30 pm ($3). The other cottages are available for accommodation (see Places to Stay & Eat).

In Burra's early days nearly 1500 people lived in **dugouts** by the creek and a couple of these have been preserved. Other interesting old buildings include **Redruth Gaol**, Tregony St, and more **Cornish cottages** on Truro St, North Burra.

The **Burra Mine and Enginehouse Museum** are on the site of an original mine and are extremely well presented, with plenty of information – the Enginehouse Museum ($3) is open daily from 11 am to 2 pm, but you can wander elsewhere around the mine site at any time.

The **Bon Accord Complex** ($3) near the old train station in North Burra was a Scottish mining enterprise; however, instead of ore, an underground water source was discovered. Not to be deterred, the canny Scots sold the site to the town, and the property supplied Burra's water until 1966. The site is now a historical interpretive centre, open daily from 12.30 to 2.30 pm.

Places to Stay & Eat

You can stay at the historic *Paxton Square Cottages* (☎ 8892 2622) from $25/35 (linen extra).

Several historic hotels offer basic pub-style accommodation. Typical is the once-grand *Burra Hotel* (☎ 8892 2389) on Market Square, which has singles/doubles with ceiling fans for $30/50, including a cooked breakfast.

The *Burra Motor Inn* (☎ 8892 2777) on Market St has large rooms overlooking the creek. Singles and doubles cost $60. Alternatively, there are numerous B&B places from $75 for two persons – the tourist office can supply all details.

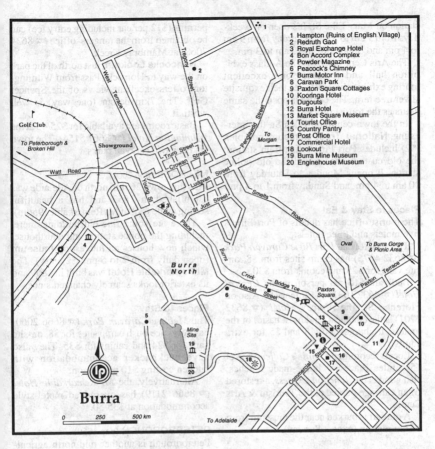

1 Hampton (Ruins of English Village)
2 Redruth Gaol
3 Royal Exchange Hotel
4 Bon Accord Complex
5 Powder Magazine
6 Peacock's Chimney
7 Burra Motor Inn
8 Caravan Park
9 Paxton Square Cottages
10 Kooringa Hotel
11 Dugouts
12 Burra Hotel
13 Market Square Museum
14 Tourist Office
15 Country Pantry
16 Post Office
17 Commercial Hotel
18 Lookout
19 Burra Mine Museum
20 Enginehouse Museum

Burra

Down by peaceful Burra Creek on Bridge Tce is the town's caravan park (☎ 8892 2442), which has shaded camp sites from $10.

Most of the hotels sell good counter meals and have more formal dining rooms. Alternatively, the *Country Pantry* on Commercial St near the tourist centre is good for lunches.

Getting There & Away
Greyhound Pioneer's Adelaide to Sydney service passes through Burra daily, and it's $18 to Adelaide – the tourist centre is the agency. Bute Buses (☎ 8826 2346) has a

service three times weekly, which passes through Burra ($16.80) on its Adelaide to Orroroo run.

Ask at the Burra tourist centre about back-packer packages (day or longer) from Adelaide.

PORT PIRIE (pop 13,600)
Port Pirie, 84km south of Port Augusta, is an industrial centre with a huge lead-smelting complex that handles the output from Broken Hill.

The tourist office (☎ 8633 0439) is at the **Tourism & Arts Centre** in the former train station on Mary Ellie St. It's open on week-days from 9 am to 5 pm, Saturday from 9 am to 4 pm and Sunday from 10 am to 3 pm.

The Arts Centre here has an A-class exhibition hall and receives some excellent touring exhibitions; ask to see their exquisite silver tree fern. The centre is open the same hours as the tourist office.

In the town centre on Ellen St, the interesting **National Trust museum** complex ($2) includes Port Pirie's first train station, the old customs house and the old police station. It opens Monday to Saturday from 10 am to 4 pm, and Sunday from 1 to 4 pm.

Places to Stay & Eat
The tourist office has details of Port Pirie's five motels and three hotels.

The very formal *Port Pirie Caravan Park* (☎ 8632 4275) has camp sites from $8, on-site vans for $25 and cabins from $30.

Beds are $15 per person in the *Central Hotel* (☎ 8632 1031) on Florence St. Also on Florence St, the *Abaccy Motel* (☎ 8632 3701) is the cheapest (and most basic) of the motels. It charges $40/45 and $5 for extra adults.

Locals recommend *Annie's Coffee Shop* at 15 Jubilee Place for home-made lunches; also good is the *Junction Express*, a restored Ghan carriage parked at the Tourism & Arts Centre.

A pie cart is parked near the museum from 10 pm nightly (except Sunday).

MT REMARKABLE NATIONAL PARK
North of Port Pirie, between Melrose and Wilmington and on the southern edge of the Flinders Ranges, is the Mt Remarkable National Park (see the Flinders Ranges section later in this chapter). From **Wilmington** (pop 260) you can drive into the park and enjoy some nice bushwalks. These include a walk through colourful **Alligator Gorge**, its walls only 2m apart in places.

The entry fee to the Alligator Gorge area is $5 per car. There's no vehicle-based camping here, but there is a large and attractive camping area at Mambray Creek on the other (western) side of the range. Camping

permits ($12 per car including entry fee) can be obtained from the rangers' office (☎ 8634 7068) at Mambray Creek.

Hancocks Lookout, just north of the park on the way to Horrocks Pass from Wilmington, offers excellent views of the Spencer Gulf. The 7km detour (one way) is well worth it.

Basic rooms are available for $25/45 at the *Wilmington Hotel* (☎ 8667 5154). The town also has two caravan parks.

MELROSE (pop 200)
This tiny town 265km north of Adelaide was established in 1853 and has a beautiful setting at the foot of Mt Remarkable (956m).

There are some fine old buildings here, including the police station and courthouse, which now houses an interesting **museum** (open daily from 2 to 5 pm; $2 entry). The **Mt Remarkable Hotel** was built in 1859 and its exterior looks scarcely changed since.

Places to Stay
The *Melrose Caravan Park* (☎ 8666 2060) has very nice bush camp sites for $8, on-site vans for $24 and cabins for $35. They also have backpacker accommodation with kitchen costing $10 per person.

Alternatively, the *Mt Remarkable Hotel* (☎ 8666 2119) has overpriced motel-style accommodation at $35/50.

PETERBOROUGH (pop 1850)
Peterborough is another mid-north agricultural service town. There are several worthwhile attractions, mostly of a historic nature.

The tourist office (☎ 8651 2708) in the old railway carriage near the town hall is open daily from 9 am to 4 pm.

Steamtown at the western end of Main St is a working railway museum. On holiday weekends between April and October, steam trains run between Peterborough and Orroroo ($22 return) or Eurelia ($29 return); call ☎ 8651 3566 for details.

Tiny **Terowie** (pop 200), 23km south of Peterborough, is worth the short detour off the Barrier Highway. The town was originally linked by broad-gauge train line to Adelaide and by narrow-gauge line to Peterborough – the railway yards provided hundreds of jobs, as goods had to be transferred from carriages on one line to the other. At its peak, the population exceeded 2000 people. In 1967 the broad-gauge line was extended to Peterborough, sounding the death knell for Terowie. The town is worth a visit as much for its lingering air of a bygone age, as for its wonderful, though sadly deteriorating, historic streetscape.

Places to Stay

The *Budget Travellers' Hostel* (☎ 8651 2711) in Railway Tce behind the train station has beds from $12; its clean, homely facilities and dedicated management make this good value.

Alternatively, the friendly *Peterborough Caravan Park* (☎ 8651 2545) on Grove St has grassy camp sites from $10, on-site vans for $25 and cabins from $32.

OTHER MID-NORTH TOWNS

Other towns include **Carrieton**, where a major rodeo is held towards the end of December each year. **Bruce** and **Hammond** are old railheads, which have virtually faded away to ghost towns – the latter has *Molly Brown's Kitchen*, a good restaurant.

Orroroo, an agricultural centre, has the fascinating Yesteryear Costume Gallery, a restored settlers cottage, and Aboriginal rock carvings at Pekina Creek.

Heading south from Melrose you come to tiny **Murraytown**, where there's a pub and very little else.

Continuing on, you can turn west through the scenic Germein Gorge to **Port Germein**. Here you will find the very friendly *Casual Affair* (☎ 8634 5242), a pleasant coffee shop, gallery and craft centre, with some backpackers' accommodation. Dorm beds are in a tranquil, Japanese-style room, and cost $10. Cheap meals are available, and you can hire bicycles.

Alternatively, go straight ahead from Murraytown to **Wirrabara**. On the outskirts of the nearby Wirrabara Forest is a *YHA*

youth hostel (☎ 8668 4158) with beds costing $8 for YHA members – $11 if you're a nonmember. There are some nice walks in the forest, which is on the Heysen Trail.

South-East

The Dukes Highway provides the most direct route between Adelaide and Melbourne (729km), but you wouldn't take it if you wanted to see interesting country – although there are some worthwhile detours.

The Princes Highway runs close to the coast and has greater appeal. Along here you can visit the Coorong (an extensive coastal lagoon system), call in at quiet fishing and holiday towns, detour into the Coonawarra wine belt and see the crater lakes around Mt Gambier.

Getting There & Away

Air Kendell Airlines and O'Connors Air Services (☎ 8723 0666) have daily return flights from Mt Gambier to Adelaide and Melbourne. One-way fares to both cities are $150 (seven-day advance purchase $114).

Bus Stateliner (☎ 8415 5555) runs from the central bus station in Adelaide to Mt Gambier daily for $39. You can travel either along the coast via the Coorong, stopping at Meningie ($19), Kingston SE ($30) and Robe ($34); or inland via Bordertown ($29), Naracoorte ($36) and Penola ($37).

THE COORONG NATIONAL PARK

The Coorong is a narrow lagoon curving along the coast for 145km from Lake Alexandrina to near Kingston SE. A complex series of salt pans, it is separated from the sea by the huge sand dunes of the Younghusband Peninsula. There is vehicle access through the dunes and onto the surf beach in several places.

This magnificent area is home to vast numbers of water birds. *Storm Boy*, a film about a young boy's friendship with a pelican, and based on a novel of the same name by Colin Thiele, was shot on the Coorong. These wonderful birds are very evident in the park, as are ducks, waders and swans.

Coorong Nature Tours (☎ 8574 0037) has a good reputation for its nature-based trips. Tours ex-Meningie start at $50 for a half day and $100 for a full day – pick-ups in A'delaide can be arranged.

Places to Stay

The park has plenty of bush camp sites, but you need a permit ($5 per vehicle per night). These can be purchased from numerous outlets in the area including both roadhouses at Salt Creek and the NPWS office (☎ 8575 1200) on the Princes Highway in Meningie. General park information can also be obtained here.

Camp Coorong (☎ 8575 1557), on the highway 10km south of Meningie, is run by the Ngarrindjeri Lands & Progress Association. The Cultural Museum here has information about the Ngarrindjeri Aboriginal people. There are several tours on which you can learn about traditional lifestyles and visit a midden site. Self-contained units and bunk-house beds are available, but you have to book.

Alternatively there are several caravan parks and motels scattered along the Princes Highway between Meningie and Salt Creek.

KINGSTON SE (pop 1450)

Near the southern end of the Coorong, Kingston is a small holiday and fishing port. It is a centre for rock-lobster fishing, and the annual **Lobsterfest**, held in the second week of January, is celebrated with live bands and exhibitions.

The Australian obsession with gigantic fauna and flora is apparent in **Larry the Big Lobster**, which looms over the highway on the Adelaide approach to town. Larry fronts a tourist information centre and cafe. You can buy freshly cooked rock lobster at the jetty during the lobster season (October through April).

From Kingston conventional vehicles can drive 16km along the beach to the **Granites**,

while with a 4WD you can – depending on the tides – continue on past the Coorong to the Murray Mouth.

Places to Stay & Eat

The friendly *Kingston Caravan Park* (☎ 8767 2050) on Marine Pde has camp sites from $10, on-site vans for $26 and cabins from $30.

The small and homely *Backpackers Hostel* (☎ 8767 2107) is in a house at 21 Holland St. It has good facilities and Mrs Derr, the manager, charges $11 for dorm bunks including use of her kitchen.

Clean but basic singles/doubles without private facilities are available at the *Crown Inn Hotel* (☎ 8767 2005) on Agnes St for $16/28, and at the *Royal Mail Hotel* on Hansen St for $20/30. Both pubs sell counter meals.

ROBE (pop 750)

Robe, a charming holiday and fishing port dating from 1845, was one of the state's first settlements. Its citizens made a fortune in the late 1850s when the Victorian government instituted a £10-per-head tax on Chinese gold miners. Many Chinese circumvented the tax by getting to Victoria via Robe; 10,000 arrived in 1857 alone. The **Chinamen's Wells** in the region are a reminder of that time.

The tourist office (☎ 8768 2465) is in the public library at the Smillie and Victoria Sts intersection.

There are numerous interesting old stone buildings in Robe, including the 1863 **customs house** on Royal Circus, which is now a nautical museum. The tourist office has a leaflet ($1) that takes you on a walk around many of them.

There's a safe swimming beach opposite the town centre. About 2km from town off the Kingston road, **Long Beach** is good for windsurfing and board surfing.

Wilsons of Robe is an excellent **arts and crafts shop** on the main street.

Places to Stay

Robe is a hugely popular summer holiday

destination. There's plenty of accommodation, but you'll be lucky to find any vacancies in peak periods.

About 1km out of town on the Kingston road, the *Lakeside Tourist Park* (☎ 8768 2193) is in a beautiful setting with resident ducks and peacocks. Camp sites are from $12, on-site vans are from $28 and cabins are from $45.

A little further out, and on the Nora Creina road, the aptly named *Bushland Cabins* (☎ 8768 2386) is very peaceful and has lots of wildlife. It has limited backpacker beds for $13, bush camp sites for $10 and basic self-contained cabins for $36 – the cabins sleep up to six ($6 for each extra person).

At the southern end of Long Beach, the *Long Beach Caravan Park* (☎ 8768 2237) has backpacker cabins for $20/28 ($4 for extra persons up to a total of six). The wonderful *Caledonian Inn* (☎ 8768 2029) on Victoria St has basic rooms for $30/50 with a light breakfast, and self contained cottages within a stone's throw of the beach for $70/90. Its restaurant is one of the best in Robe.

BEACHPORT (pop 440)

If you have a yen for peace and solitude, you'll love this quiet little seaside town south of Robe with its long jetty, aquamarine sea and historic buildings. It's a lobster-fishing port, and during the season you can buy freshly cooked lobsters at the jetty.

The **Old Wool & Grain Store Museum** ($2) is in a National Trust building on the main street. It has relics of Beachport's whaling days and rooms furnished in 1870s style. The free **Aboriginal Artefacts Museum** on McCourt St has an extensive collection. Ask at the council office for keys to both buildings.

There's good board surfing at the local surf beach, and windsurfing is popular at **Lake George**, 5km north of the township. The hypersaline **Pool of Salome** is a pretty swimming lake among sand hills on the outskirts of town.

Places to Stay & Eat

The *Beachport Caravan Park* (☎ 8735 8128) is very ordinary but in a great location near the beach. Much nicer is the *Southern Ocean Tourist Park* (☎ 8735 8153), which has camp sites for $12 and cabins from $45.

Right on the beach and near the jetty, the friendly *Beachport Backpackers* (☎ 8735 8197) is in the historic harbourmaster's house (1880). It's clean and comfortable, with a cosy log fire on winter evenings, and there's a spacious kitchen. Dorm beds cost from $12 – this includes breakfast, which usually features Sarah's delicious homemade bread. Mountain bikes and surf boards are available for guests' use.

Pub-style accommodation is available at the *Beachport Hotel* (☎ 8735 8003) for $22/40. *Bompa's* (☎ 8735 8333) near the jetty has delightful rooms with share facilities from $50 for doubles, with a light breakfast.

MILLICENT (pop 4700)

At Millicent, 50km north-west of Mt Gambier, the 'Alternative 1' route through Robe and Beachport rejoins the main road.

At the Mt Gambier end of George St, the tourist centre (☎ 8733 3205) is open daily from 9.30 am to 4.30 pm. It has a good quality **craft shop** and there's an excellent National Trust **museum** ($4) in the complex with many interesting displays. Millicent is also home to the **Millicent Shell Garden**.

The **Canunda National Park** with its giant sand dunes and rugged coastal scenery is 13km west of town. It features 4WD tracks (in summer you can drive all the way from Southend to Carpenter's Rocks) and pleasant walks. You can camp near Southend – contact the ranger at Southend (☎ 8735 6053) for details and permits.

In **Tantanoola**, 21km to the south-east, the stuffed 'Tantanoola tiger' is on display at the Tantanoola Tiger Hotel. This beast, actually an Assyrian wolf, was shot in 1895 after a lot of publicity. It was presumed to have escaped from a shipwreck, but why a ship would have a wolf on board is not quite clear!

The **Tantanoola Caves** are on the Princes Highway 8km away. The visitor centre (☎ 8734 4153) runs tours ($6) of the show

A tribute to kitsch, the Millicent Shell Garden (open mid-August to mid-June) is well worth a visit

cave every hour from 9.15 am to 4 pm daily (more often in the summer school holidays and over Easter). They're the only caves in South Australia with wheelchair access.

MT GAMBIER (pop 22,000)
The major town and commercial centre of the South-East, Mt Gambier is 486km from Adelaide. It is built on the slopes of the extinct volcano from which the town takes its name.

Information
For details on local attractions contact the large Lady Nelson Tourist Information & Interpretive Centre (☎ 8724 9750; 1800 087 187; fax 8723 2833) on Jubilee Highway East. It's open daily from 9 am to 5 pm.

Allow at least an hour to look through the interpretive centre ($6), which features a replica, complete with sound effects and taped commentary, of the historic brig *Lady Nelson*. It also has a good audio-visual which acknowledges the devastating impact of European settlement on local Aboriginal people.

Things to See & Do
There are three craters, two of which have lakes. The beautiful **Blue Lake** is the best-known, although from about March to November the lake is more grey than blue – in November it mysteriously changes back to blue again. In March, the **Blue Lake Festival** is celebrated with exhibitions, concerts and food and wine tasting.

Blue Lake is about 85m deep at its deepest point and there's a 5km scenic drive around it. The lakes are a popular recreation spot and have been developed with boardwalks (over Valley Lake), a wildlife park, picnic areas and walking trails.

In the evenings you can visit the floodlit sunken gardens in the **Umpherston Sinkhole** and watch the possums feeding. You can also do daily tours ($4) down to the water table in the **Engelbrecht Cave**, a popular cave-diving spot. Both are in the town area and the tourist office can provide details.

Places to Stay & Eat
Mt Gambier has six caravan parks and all offer camp sites, on-site vans and cabins. You can get details from the tourist office.

The *Blue Lake Motel* (☎ 8725 5211) at 1 Kennedy Ave just off the highway has dorm rooms and good facilities, including a kitchen, for $12 per person.

The *Mount View Motel* (☎ 8725 8478) on Davison St charges $33 for singles and $38/40 for doubles/twins in its standard rooms. Few other motels in town come anywhere near these prices.

There are a number of grand old hotels in the town's busy centre and all offer accommodation and meals. On Commercial St, the *Federal Hotel* (☎ 8723 1099) has singles/doubles for $17/30 while the *South Australia Hotel* (☎ 8725 2404) charges $20/30.

Also on Commercial St, the *Commercial*

Hotel (☎ 8725 3006) charges $17/30 for its pub rooms and $10 per person in its backpacker rooms.

Other than the pubs, the best value in town for a big feed is the *Barn Steakhouse*, about 2km out on Nelson Rd. It serves huge meals, as does *Charlies Family Diner* in the Western Tavern on Jubilee Highway West – several cuisines are available here.

Getting There & Away
Stateliner buses depart daily for Adelaide (six hours; $39).

PORT MACDONNELL (pop 660)
South of Mt Gambier, this rock-lobster fishing centre was once the second most important port in the state, hence the surprisingly large and handsome 1863 **customs house**. There's a **Maritime Museum**, and colonial poet Adam Lindsay Gordon's home, **Dingley Dell**, is now a museum ($4); there are guided tours on Sunday, long weekends and school holidays.

The area has some fine walks, including the path to the top of **Mt Schank**, an extinct volcano. Closer to town, the rugged coastline to the west is worth a visit.

NARACOORTE (pop 4700)
Settled in the 1840s, Naracoorte is one of the oldest towns in the state and one of the largest in the south-east.

The tourist office (☎ 8762 1518) is at the award-winning **Sheep's Back Museum** on MacDonnell St. The museum, which is housed in an old flour mill, has interesting displays on the wool industry. It's open daily from 10 am to 4 pm and entry is $5.

On Jenkins Tce, the **Naracoorte Museum & Snake Pit** ($6.50) has an eclectic and interesting collection, including local venomous snakes – there are daily feeding demonstrations between October and April. It's closed from mid-July to the end of August; check at the tourist office for other times.

The **Naracoorte Caves Conservation Park** (open daily) is 12km south-east of Naracoorte off the Penola road. Its limestone

caves featured in David Attenborough's *Life on Earth* series, and have earned World Heritage listing thanks to the Pleistocene fossil deposits in **Victoria Fossil Cave**.

There are four show caves: the fossil cave, **Alexandra Cave** (the main attraction), **Blanche Cave** and the **Wet Cave**. The Wet Cave can be seen on a self-guided tour. For the others, guided tours run from 9.30 am to 3.30 pm ($5).

The **Bat Cave**, from which bats make a spectacular departure on summer evenings, isn't open to the public, but infra-red TV cameras allow you to view the goings-on inside ($7.50).

Adventure tours to undeveloped caves in the area (wear sneakers or sandshoes and old clothes) start at $15 for novices and $30 for advanced explorers; you can hire overalls and kneepads for $5.

There are some 155 bird species (79 are waterbirds) at the **Bool Lagoon Game Reserve**, 24km to the south, which, with the adjoining **Hacks Lagoon Conservation Park**, is the region's largest surviving wetland. Self-guided walks and pleasant camp sites are available – sites cost $12 per car including the $5 entry fee. A spectacular time to visit is the ibis nesting season (September to January), when you can watch the action from bird hides.

Places to Stay & Eat
The attractive *Naracoorte Caravan Park* (☎ 8762 2128) at 81 Park Tce close to the town centre has camp sites from $10, on-site vans for $33 and cabins from $38.

The *Naracoorte Caves* has a basic camping area with a free laundry next to the kiosk; sites cost $12 per car.

Naracoorte's three hotels all have good-value meals.

COONAWARRA & PENOLA
The compact (25 sq km) wine-producing area of Coonawarra, which is renowned for its reds, is 10km north of Penola. Over 20 wineries offer cellar-door sales, most on a daily basis.

There are numerous heritage buildings in

historic **Penola** (pop 1200), which has won fame for its association with the Sisters of St Joseph of the Sacred Heart. This was the order co-founded in 1866 by Mother Mary MacKillop, who is to be canonised as Australia's first saint. Penola has been named as a significant MacKillop pilgrimage site.

The tourist centre (☎ 8737 2855) on Arthur St is open from 9 am to 5 pm weekdays and 10 am to 4 pm weekends and public holidays.

The **Woods-MacKillop Schoolhouse**, built in 1867, has memorabilia associated with Mary MacKillop and Father Julian Tenison Woods, who co-founded it. It was the first in Australia to welcome children from lower socio-economic backgrounds. It's open daily from 10 am to 4 pm and admission is a gold-coin 'donation'. At the time of writing, an interpretive centre was due to open next door.

Places to Stay

Backpacker beds are available for $10 at *Whiskas Woolshed* (☎ 8737 2428; 018 854 505), 12km south-west of Penola and off the Millicent road. Rooms in the old woolshed sleep up to nine people and each has oil heating. It also has a large recreation room, kitchen and laundry.

At 38 Riddoch St in the centre of town, *Nomads McKay's Trek Inn* (☎ 1800 626 844) has clean and comfortable backpacker bunks for $16 including linen and a light breakfast. Gary, the manager, is a friendly fellow who can advise you on adventure activities in the area – you get a free night's accommodation if you break the record around the hostel's rock-climbing circuit. Mountain bikes can be hired for $15 a day.

Alternatively, over 20 restored historic cottages in the Penola district offer accommodation, with prices starting at $60 for twin share. For more details, or to make a reservation, contact the tourist information centre.

Penola also has two hotels and a caravan park.

Getting There & Away

Stateliner buses (☎ 8415 5555) depart daily for Adelaide ($37) and Mt Gambier ($8) from the Penola Supermarket in Church St.

THE DUKES HIGHWAY

The last town on the South Australian side of the border is **Bordertown** (pop 2350). The town is the birthplace of former Australian prime minister Bob Hawke, and there's a bust of Bob outside the town hall. On the left as you enter from Victoria there is a wildlife park, with various species of Australian fauna, including rare white kangaroos, behind a wire fence.

Keith (pop 1100) has the vast Ngarkat group of conservation parks 16km north. Also worth visiting is the **Padthaway** wine-growing area, 62km south of Keith on the Naracoorte road – there are cellar-door sales at the historic Padthaway Homestead.

Murray River

Australia's greatest river starts in the Snowy Mountains in the Australian Alps and for most of its length forms the boundary between New South Wales and Victoria. It meanders for 650km through South Australia, first heading west to Morgan and then turning south towards Lake Alexandrina.

En route, the river is tapped to provide domestic water for Adelaide as well as country towns as far away as Whyalla and Woomera. Between the Victorian border and Waikerie, irrigation has turned previously unproductive land into an important wine-making and fruit-growing region. This section is generally known as the Riverland.

The Murray has a fascinating history. Before the advent of railways, it was Australia's Mississippi, with paddle-steamers carrying trade from the interior down to the coast. Several of these shallow-draught vessels have been restored and you can relive the past on cruises of a few hours or several days. They include the huge stern-wheeler PS *Murray River Princess*, which regularly makes its stately passage up and down the river from Mannum.

Accommodation

There's plenty of conventional accommodation along the Murray, including a hostel in Berri. Alternatively, you can rent a fully self-contained houseboat and set off to explore the river.

Houseboats can be hired in most towns. However, they're very popular from October to April, so for these months it's wise to book well ahead. The Houseboat Hirers Association (☎ 8395 0999) in Adelaide can give advice and arrange a boat for you, or ask at any tourist office. Prices vary hugely, but in the high season you can expect to pay around $25 per person per night depending on such factors as size of boat and duration of hire. Prices are usually considerably cheaper in winter.

Alternatively, there are numerous bush camp sites among huge river red gums scattered along the river, particularly east of Morgan.

Getting There & Away

Air Southern Australia Airlines flights can be booked through Qantas (☎ 13 1313). They fly daily from Adelaide to Renmark ($116) and Mildura ($78 ex-Renmark).

Bus Stateliner (☎ 8415 5555) has daily services from Adelaide to the Riverland towns. The fare to Berri, Loxton and Renmark is $28.

Greyhound Pioneer runs daily through the Riverland en route to Sydney but can't drop off until past Renmark. Its fare to Sydney from Renmark is $83.

RENMARK (pop 4350)

In the centre of the Riverland irrigation area and 254km from Adelaide, Renmark was the first of the river towns and a starting point for the great irrigation projects that revolutionised the area.

The tourist office (☎ /fax 8586 6704) is on Murray Ave, beside the river. It's open from 9 am to 5 pm weekdays, 9 am to 4 pm

Saturday and noon to 4 pm Sunday. Attached is an interpretive centre which includes the recommissioned 1911 paddle-steamer *Industry* ($2).

Renmark River Cruises (☎ 8595 1862) offers cruises for $15 on the MV *River Rambler* departing from the town wharf daily at 2 pm. Ask at the tourist office about 4WD, fishing and dinghy tours in the area.

Wineries, such as Angoves on Bookmark Rd and Renmano on Industry Rd, have cellar-door sales and tastings.

Upstream from town, the huge **Chowilla Regional Reserve** (part of the sprawling Bookmark Biosphere Reserve) is great for bush camping, canoeing and bushwalking – access is along the north bank from Renmark. For details contact the NPWS office (☎ 8695 2111) on Vaughan Tce in Berri.

Places to Stay & Eat

Idyllically situated on the river about 1km east of town is the *Renmark Caravan Park* (☎ 8586 6315). Camp sites cost from $9, on-site vans are $27 and cabins are from $43. It rents out canoes from $5 for an hour.

Further along the river beside the Paringa Bridge, the *Riverbend Caravan Park* (☎ 8595 5131) has camp sites from $9, on-site vans for $24 and cabins from $32. It also hires canoes ($5 per hour).

The tastefully renovated *Renmark Hotel/Motel* (☎ 8586 6755) on Murray Ave has hotel rooms at $40/45 for singles/doubles. It has counter meals, a bistro and dining room; the *Renmark Club*, across from the hotel, also does good-value meals.

Camping in the *Chowilla Regional Reserve* costs $5 per car per night – contact the NPWS office in Berri for a permit.

BERRI (pop 3900)

At one time a refuelling stop for the wood-burning paddle-steamers, the town takes its name from the Aboriginal *berri berri*, meaning 'big bend in the river'.

The tourist office (☎ 8582 1655; fax 8582 3201) on Vaughan Tce opens weekdays from 9 am to 5 pm (Saturday to 11.30 am).

The lookout on the corner of Vaughan Tce and Fiedler St has good views over the town and river. Near the Berri Hotel/Motel on Riverside Ave is a **monument** to Jimmy James, a famous Aboriginal tracker.

The **Willabalangaloo Reserve** ($4) is a flora and fauna reserve with walking trails and a historic homestead. It's open Thursday to Monday from 10 am to 4 pm (daily during school holidays).

Berri Estates winery at Glossop, 7km west of Berri, is one of the biggest in Australia, if not the southern hemisphere. It's open for tastings and cellar-door sales Monday to Saturday from 9 am to 5 pm.

Road access to the beautiful Katarapko Creek section of the **Murray River National Park** is through Berri or Winkie (near Glossop). This is another great area for bush camping, canoeing and bird-watching – for details contact the NPWS office (☎ 8695 2111) on Vaughan Tce.

You can hire one and two-person canoes from Lyons Motors (☎ 8582 1449; after hours 8582 1859) on Riverview Dve from $5 per hour and $25 per day; transport can be arranged.

Places to Stay

The *Berri Riverside Caravan Park* on Riverview Rd (☎ 8582 3723) has camp sites from $10, on-site vans from $31 and cabins from $38.

Berri Backpackers (☎ 8582 3144) on the Sturt Highway on the Barmera side of town is one of the best-equipped hostels you'll find anywhere in the state – but it's only for international visitors. Among other things it has a swimming pool, sauna, tennis court and volleyball court, as well as bicycles and canoes for guests' use. The manager has excellent contacts if you want seasonal work in local orchards and vineyards. Beds are $13 ($85 per week).

At the *Berri Hotel/Motel* (☎ 8582 1411) on Riverview Dve singles/doubles with own shower cost from $48/53 in the pub.

Bush camping in the *Katarapko Creek* area costs $5 per car per night – contact the NPWS office for a permit.

The *Berri Club* across from Berri Backpackers has great-value meals from Thursday to Sunday nights.

LOXTON (pop 3300)

From Berri the Murray makes a large loop south of the Sturt Highway, with Loxton at its base. From here you can canoe across to the Katarapko Creek section of the Murray River National Park, which occupies much of the area within the loop (see the Berri section, above, for more details).

The tourist office (☎ 8584 7919) at the roundabout on Bookpurnong Tce is open from 9 am to 5 pm weekdays, 9.30 am to 12.30 pm Saturday and 1 to 4 pm Sunday and public holidays.

Loxton's major attraction is the **Historical Village**, with over 30 fully furnished buildings. It's open daily from 10 am to 4 pm (weekends 5 pm); admission is $5.

The **Australian Vintage winery** is open daily except Sunday for tastings.

Riverland Canoeing Adventures (☎ 8584 1494) on Alamein Ave, towards Renmark, rents one-person kayaks for $15 per day and double kayaks and canoes for $25 a day. Transport, maps and camping equipment can also be hired.

Places to Stay & Eat

The *Loxton Riverfront Caravan Park* (☎ 8584 7862) is 2km from town. It has camp sites from $10, on-site vans for $25, cabins from $32 and you can hire canoes ($7.50 for an hour or $25 for a day).

The *Loxton Hotel/Motel* (☎ 8584 7266) on East Tce has shabby pub singles/doubles for $20/25 and more upmarket rooms from $41/46. It has a very good bistro plus counter meals. Next door, the Aussie whopper burgers at the *Spring Leaf* takeaway are just that – whopping.

BARMERA (pop 1800)

On the shores of Lake Bonney, Barmera was on the old overland stock route from New South Wales. The ruins of **Napper's Old Accommodation House**, built in 1850 at the mouth of Chambers Creek, are a reminder of that era, as is the **Overland Corner Hotel** on the Morgan road, 19km north-west of town. Built in 1859, it's now owned by the National Trust and has a small museum and walking trails. You can also stay here – see Places to Stay.

The tourist office (☎ 8588 2289; brmtrvl @www.murray.net.au) is at the top of the main street next to the roundabout, and is open weekdays from 9 am to 5.30 pm and Saturday until noon.

Lake Bonney, which has sandy beaches, is popular for swimming and water sports. There's a nudist beach at **Pelican Point**.

You'll find a game reserve at **Moorook** and another across the river from **Kingston-on-Murray** – the latter backs onto the Overland Corner Hotel. Both reserves have nature trails and are good spots for birdwatching and canoeing. For camping permits, contact the Berri NPWS office (☎ 8695 2111).

Riverland Safaris (☎ 8588 3270) offers various guided tours, including winery visits and fishing and yabbying trips.

Places to Stay
There are several caravan parks in the area, with the closest to the town centre being the *Lake Bonney Holiday Park* (☎ 8588 2234) on the lake shore. It has camp sites from $12, cabins from $25 and self-contained cottages from $45.

The comfortable *Barmera Hotel/Motel* (☎ 8588 2111) has budget singles for $20 and self-contained rooms for $35. Out at the historic *Overland Corner Hotel* (☎ 8588 7021), double rooms cost $36/50, including a cooked breakfast.

WAIKERIE (pop 1800)
A citrus-growing centre, the town takes its name from the Aboriginal word for 'anything that flies', after the teeming birdlife on the nearby lagoons and river. It also has the most active gliding centre in Australia (☎ 8541 2644).

For tourist information go to the **Orange Tree** (☎ 8541 2332) on the Sturt Highway on the Barmera side of town – look out for its large, green fibreglass sphere with red spots. It sells a comprehensive range of local fruit and nut products and is open daily from 9 am to 5.30 pm.

Places to Stay
The *Waikerie Hotel/Motel* (☎ 8541 2999) on McCoy St in the town centre has self-contained pub rooms at $35/45 for singles/ doubles, and you can eat in the front bar or bistro.

Down by the river on the west side of town, the *Waikerie Caravan Park* (☎ 8541 2651) has camp sites for $10 and cabins from $32.

Reasonably priced bush camping is available at *Eremophila Park* (☎ 8589 3023), a private nature park off the Sturt Highway 33km east of town – there's no power, but other amenities are available.

MORGAN (pop 1350)
In its prime this was the busiest river port in Australia, with wharves towering 12m high. There's a car ferry across the Murray here. Most businesses around town will sell you a leaflet detailing a heritage walk (50c), while the **Port of Morgan Historic Museum**, by the river below the town centre just upstream from the ferry, has exhibits on the paddle-steamer trade; it opens according to demand.

Places to Stay
Down by the ferry landing, the *Morgan Riverside Caravan Park* (☎ 8540 2207) has camp sites from $9, on-site vans for $27 and cabins from $35. It also rents out canoes for $6 an hour and $20 a day.

Opposite each other on Railway Tce, the *Commercial Hotel* (☎ 8540 2107) and *Terminus Hotel/Motel* (☎ 8540 2006) both have basic pub rooms for $15 per person.

SWAN REACH (pop 250)
This sleepy old town, 70km south-west of Waikerie, has picturesque river scenery but not many swans – there are lots of pelicans, however. Just downstream the Murray makes a tight meander known as **Big Bend**; the lookout beside the Walker Flat road 9km

from town gives you a great view of its towering yellow cliffs.

MANNUM (pop 2000)

The *Mary Ann*, Australia's first riverboat, was built here and made the first paddle-steamer trip up the Murray in 1853. There are many relics of the pioneering days, including the fully restored 1897 paddle-steamer *Marion*, now a floating museum ($3) moored near the tourist centre (☎ 8569 1303). Both open daily, 9 am to 4 pm.

The **Purnong Rd Bird Sanctuary** is a great spot to see water birds; it starts at the Mannum Caravan Park and you drive along it for several kilometres on the main road to Purnong. **Cascade Waterfalls**, 9km from Mannum on Reedy Creek, are worth a visit. Although the falls only flow during winter, the rugged scenery and large river red gums can be enjoyed at any time.

River Cruises

The grand paddle-steamer *Murray River Princess* operates from Mannum and does three and five-night and some weekend cruises. Contact Captain Cook Cruises (☎ 1800 804 843) for times and prices – their weekend cruises start at around $340 per person twin-share.

The PS *Marion* often does short cruises on weekends; check at the tourist centre for an operating schedule.

The MV *Lady Mannum* also does short cruises; check times with Lady Mannum Cruises (☎ 8569 1438) in the main street.

Places to Stay

The *Mannum Caravan Park* (☎ 8569 1402) on the town side of the ferry crossing has camp sites from $10, cabins from $42, and a bunkhouse with kitchen for $12. You can camp for free on the other side of the river near the ferry and use the shower facilities ($2.50) at the caravan park.

Getting There & Away

ABM Coachlines (☎ 8347 3336) runs to Mannum from Adelaide via Birdwood on weekdays for $11.20 one way.

MURRAY BRIDGE (pop 13,000)

South Australia's largest river town, only 82km south-east of Adelaide, is named for its 1km-long bridge; built in 1879, it was the first to span the Murray. It's a popular area for fishing, swimming, water-skiing and bar-becues.

The tourist office (☎ 8532 6660; fax 8532 5288) on South Tce is open from 8.30 am to 4.30 pm weekdays, 10 am to 3.45 pm on Saturday, and 10 am to 2 pm on Sunday and public holidays.

Things to See & Do

Butterfly House ($7) is 4km out on the Wellington road. Open 10 am to 5 pm daily, its tropical hot house has numerous species of gorgeous butterflies that flutter about your ears as you observe and photograph them.

On 1000 hectares 20km west of town, the open-range **Monarto Zoological Park** has Australian and international exhibits, including herds of zebras and giraffes. It's open from 10 am to 5 pm daily and entry costs $10, including a bus ride through the park (departing 10.30 am to 3.30 pm daily).

River Cruises

The MV *Barrangul* has a restaurant on board and irregularly operates day cruises – check at the tourist office for times.

The PS *Proud Mary* departs from Murray Bridge on two, three and five-night cruises. Contact Proud Australia Holidays (☎ 8231 9472) in Adelaide for times and prices.

Places to Stay & Eat

The *Avoca Dell Caravan Park* (☎ 8532 2095), across the river from town and north of the bridge, has camp sites from $12 and cabins from $32.

In the centre of town at 12 Sixth St the pleasant *Balcony B&B Guest House* (☎ 8531 1411) has basic backpacker rooms for $16/30 ($20 per person standard rate). If you want to go more upmarket, they have rooms with four-poster beds and share facilities for $29/45. These prices include a continental breakfast, which you can eat on the balcony.

They also hire canoes ($6 for an hour and $20 for a day).

The *Murray Bridge Community Club* and the *Happy Gathering* Chinese restaurant, both at the junction of First and Seventh Sts in the town centre, are recommended for good-value meals. It's a fair way out, but the *Italian Club* on Lincoln Rd is worth trying, particularly on Thursday night – all the pasta you can eat costs $7.

Getting There & Away

Buses to Adelaide cost $11 with the Murray Bridge Passenger Service (☎ 8532 6660); they leave daily from outside the tourist office, where tickets can be purchased. If you are travelling from Adelaide, bookings need to be made with Premier on ☎ 8415 5555.

Tickets to Mt Gambier ($39) with Stateliner (☎ 8415 5555) must be booked at the central bus station in Adelaide. You can pick up a Greyhound Pioneer bus to Melbourne ($56) and Sydney ($114 via Melbourne) daily.

TAILEM BEND (pop 1500)

Tailem Bend's major attraction is **Old Tailem Town**, a fascinating re-creation of a pioneer village with many old buildings; it opens daily from 10 am to 5 pm and entry costs $7.50. You can take a ferry across the Murray to Jervois from where it's 11km to the pretty hamlet of **Wellington**, near where the river enters Lake Alexandrina. Here you'll find the **Old Wellington Court House Museum** (open daily) and the historic Wellington Hotel, where you can sit on the lawn and watch the river go by. Aboriginal middens can be seen 2km south-east of the township. Tailem Bend has two hotels, a motel and two caravan parks.

Yorke Peninsula

The Yorke Peninsula is a popular holiday area within easy driving distance of Adelaide. There are pleasant beaches along both sides, while Innes National Park on the tip

has good fishing, surfing and diving. The economy was originally based on the so-called 'Copper Triangle' centred on Kadina. As the copper mines declined, agriculture developed and most of the land now grows barley and other grains.

The main tourist office for Yorke Peninsula is in the old train station in Moonta (☎ 8825 1891; fax 8825 2930) and is open from 9 am to 5 pm daily.

Getting There & Away

Premier (☎ 8415 5555) operates a daily bus from Adelaide to Kadina, Wallaroo, Moonta, Port Hughes and Moonta Bay. It takes about three hours to Moonta and costs $11.30.

The Yorke Peninsula Passenger Service (☎ 8391 2977) runs from Adelaide's central bus station to Yorketown daily except Saturday. The route alternates between the east coast and down the centre of the peninsula. Fares from Adelaide are: Ardrossan $18.50, Port Vincent $24, and Edithburgh and Warooka (both $25).

WEST COAST

The west coast, facing onto the Spencer Gulf, has several quiet swimming beaches and small resorts. These are off the main road from Wallaroo, which runs inland through small farming communities.

The west coast of the 'foot' (from Corny Point down to Innes National Park) has some good surfing breaks, fine coastal scenery and a couple of bush camping areas.

In the early 1860s, copper was discovered in the Moonta-Kadina-Wallaroo area and soon a full-scale mining rush was on. Most miners were from Cornwall in England, and the area still has a strong Cornish flavour – it was often referred to as **Little Cornwall**. The boom peaked around the turn of the century, but in the early 1920s a slump in copper prices and rising labour costs closed all the peninsula's mines. The lack of development since then has largely preserved the historic streetscapes.

In celebration of its Cornish heritage, the

Kernewek Lowender Festival is held here over several days in May of odd-numbered years. It's a chance to try Cornish pasties or watch a wheelbarrow race, and if you drink enough traditional beer you may see a piskey – a mischievous sprite believed, by the Cornish people, to bring good fortune.

Kadina (pop 3500)

The largest town on the peninsula, Kadina was once the main copper-mining centre. A booklet available from the Moonta tourist office takes you on a tour of the town's numerous historic sites.

The **Kadina Heritage Museum** ($3) features Matta House (1863), the restored home of the Matta Matta mine manager. There's also the Matta Matta mine, old farming machinery and a blacksmith's shop, among other displays. It opens Wednesday and weekends from 2 to 4.30 pm (from 10 am on public and school holidays).

The **Wallaroo Mines** are 1km west of the

There is no shortage of shops selling delicious Cornish pasties in Kadina

town on the Wallaroo road. It takes half an hour to stroll around the area, which includes numerous deep shafts and the impressive ruin of a stone engine house.

Also interesting is the **Banking & Currency Museum** ($3) in an old bank on Graves St. It is open from 10 am to 5 pm daily except Friday and Saturday (closed during June).

Places to Stay & Eat The *Kadina Caravan Park* (☎ 8821 2259) has camp sites from $12 and on-site vans for $32.

The *Wombat Hotel* (☎ 8821 1108) on Taylor St charges $19 per person, while the *Kadina Hotel* (☎ 8821 1008), a block away, has singles/doubles with private bathroom for $35/50. Both include a light breakfast.

Cornish pasties are sold in several shops, but the most popular are those produced by *Prices Bakery* on Goyder St. *Sarah's Place* nearby is particularly good for pancakes and lunches. The *Dynasty Room*, a Chinese place also on Goyder St, has lunch specials, as do the pubs.

Wallaroo (pop 2500)

This port town was a major centre during the copper boom. The 'big stack', one of the great chimneys from the copper smelters (built in 1861), still stands, but today the

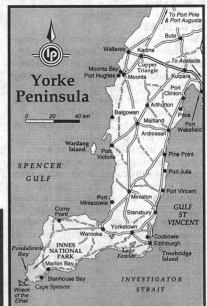

Yorke Peninsula

0   20   40 km

To Port Pirie
& Port Augusta

Bute

Wallaroo   Kadina

To Adelaide

Moonta Bay   Copper
Port Hughes   Triangle
              Moonta   Kulpara

Port
Clinton

Balgowan   Arthurton   Price

Maitland   Port
            Wakefield
Ardrossan

Wardang
Island   Port
          Victoria   Pine Point

SPENCER
GULF   Port Julia

Port   Minlaton   Port Vincent
Minlacowie

Corny   Stansbury   GULF
Point   ST
        Yorketown   VINCENT

Warooka   Coobowie
           Edithburgh
Pondalowie   INNES   Troubridge
Bay   NATIONAL   Lake   Island
       PARK   Fowler
Marion Bay

Stenhouse Bay   INVESTIGATOR
Cape Spencer   STRAIT
Wreck
of the
Ethel

port's main function is exporting agricultural products.

In the old post office on Jetty Rd there's the fascinating **Heritage & Nautical Museum** ($3), open on Wednesday, weekends and public and school holidays. It tells about the square-rigged sailing ships that serviced this area from England, and has a detailed history of Caroline Carleton, who wrote the words to 'Song of Australia'.

A booklet detailing a town heritage walk can be obtained from the tourist desk (☎ 8823 2020) in the new post office on the corner of Irwin St and Owen Tce.

Places to Stay & Eat On the beach near the jetty, the *Office Beach Caravan Park* (☎ 8823 2722) has camp sites from $12, on-site vans for $27, cabins from $32 and self-contained units from $45.

The *Weerona Hotel* (☎ 8823 2008) on John Tce has singles/doubles for $22/34. Alternatively, the *Sonbern Lodge Motel* (☎ 8823 2291), to the south-east on John Tce two blocks away, charges $24/38 for basic rooms and $35/55 for self-contained rooms in its charming, older lodge section.

The town's five hotels have counter meals and there are several takeaways, a bakery and tea rooms.

Moonta (pop 2900)

In the late 19th century the copper mine at Moonta, 18km south of Wallaroo, was the richest mine in Australia. The town grew so large that its school had 1100 students.

The wonderful old school building now houses an excellent folk museum ($3) featuring displays on the Cornish miners' lifestyles; it's open from 1 to 4 pm daily except Sunday. The museum is part of the **Moonta Heritage Site** on the eastern outskirts of town, which you can explore with a self-guiding booklet from the tourist office. Nearby is a fully restored **miner's cottage** and garden.

A tourist train ($2.50) runs around the adjoining **Moonta Mines** area on weekends and public and school holidays. A section of the old underground workings at the **Wheal Hughes** mine was to be opened to the public in 1998 – see the tourist office for details.

Places to Stay Right on the beach 3km from town, the *Moonta Bay Top Tourist Park* (☎ 8825 2406) has camp sites from $12 and cabins from $47.

The *Cornwall Hotel* (☎ 8825 2304) on Ryan St has singles/doubles for $25/50; at the nearby *Royal Hotel* (☎ 8825 2108) they're $25/40, including a light breakfast.

There are numerous places to eat. Recommended is the *Cornish Kitchen* on Ellen St, a great place for homemade Cornish pasties and lunches.

EAST COAST

The east-coast road from the top of Gulf St Vincent down to Stenhouse Bay near Cape Spencer is generally within 1km or two of the sea. En route, tracks and roads lead to sandy beaches and secluded coves.

Ardrossan is the largest port on this coast. It has an interesting National Trust folk museum featuring the famous stump-jump plough (open from 2.30 to 4 pm Sunday and public holidays) on Fifth St.

Continuing south, in the next 50km the road runs through several small seaside resorts, including tranquil **Port Vincent**. Here you find the *Tuckerway Youth Hostel* (☎ 8853 7285), with good facilities and beds from $9.

Further south, **Edithburgh** has a tidal swimming pool in a small cove; from the cliff-tops you can look across to **Troubridge Island** and its prominent lighthouse. A 2½-hour tour, including a historical commentary, can be taken to the island, where overnight stays are also available in the old lighthouse keeper's cottage (☎ 8852 6290).

Near Marion Bay on the coast road is *Hillocks Drive* (☎ 8854 4002), a large farm where you can enjoy some wonderful coastal scenery, native wildlife and wildflowers (July to November). Bush camping is $5, and on-site vans are from $22. For day visitors there's a $3 entry fee.

Yorketown (pop 700) is the district's business and administrative centre. It's a

SOUTH AUSTRALIA

pleasant, friendly place and you'll probably find accommodation here when the seaside resorts are full over summer.

INNES NATIONAL PARK

The southern tip of the peninsula, marked by Cape Spencer, is part of the Innes National Park. There's a $5 entry fee per vehicle. **Stenhouse Bay**, just outside the park, and **Pondalowie Bay**, within the park, are the principal settlements. The park has spectacular coastal scenery as well as good fishing, reef diving and surfing. You'll go a long way to find quieter emus!

Pondalowie Bay is the base for a large lobster-fishing fleet and also has a fine surf beach. All other beaches, except for Browns Beach, are dangerous for swimming.

In the park is the wreck of the steel barque *Ethel*, a 711-tonne ship which ran aground in 1904. All that remains are the ribs of the hull rising forlornly from the sands. Her anchor is mounted in a memorial on the cliff top above the beach. Just past the Cape Spencer turn-off, a sign on the right directs you to the ruins of the **Inneston Historic Site**. Inneston was a gypsum-mining community abandoned in 1930.

Places to Stay

With a permit (from $5 to $15 per car per night, depending on facilities), you can camp in a number of places in the park, or stay in basic huts (from $22 per hut). The NPWS office in Stenhouse Bay (☎ 8854 4040) can provide details.

Getting There & Away

There is no public transport to the end of the peninsula. The Yorke Peninsula Passenger Service will take you to Warooka or Yorketown, from where you could try to hitch.

Eyre Peninsula

The wide, triangular Eyre Peninsula points south between Spencer Gulf and the Great Australian Bight. It's bordered in the north by the Eyre Highway from Port Augusta to Ceduna. The coastal run is in two parts: the Lincoln Highway south-west from Port Augusta to Port Lincoln; and the Flinders Highway north-west to Ceduna. It's 468km from Port Augusta direct to Ceduna via the Eyre Highway; via the coast road it's 763km.

The coast is an extremely popular summer holiday area with many good beaches, sheltered bays and pleasant little port towns. On the wild western side are superb surf beaches, spectacular coastal scenery and important breeding grounds for the southern right whale, the Australian sea lion and the great white shark – some scenes for *Jaws* were filmed here.

Eyre Peninsula is also a major agricultural region, while the iron-ore deposits at Iron Knob and Iron Baron are processed and shipped from the busy port of Whyalla. The peninsula takes its name from Edward John Eyre, the hardy explorer who, in 1841, made the first recorded overland crossing between Adelaide and Albany, WA.

Getting There & Away

Air Kendell Airlines (☎ 13 1300) flies daily from Adelaide to Port Lincoln ($121) and Whyalla ($120), and daily except Saturday to Ceduna ($206).

Lincoln Airlines (☎ 1800 018 234) flies between Port Lincoln and Adelaide for $95 four times daily.

Whyalla Airlines (☎ 1800 088 858) has daily services from Adelaide to Cleve ($85), Wudinna ($100) and Whyalla ($90).

Bus Stateliner (☎ 8415 5555) has daily services from Adelaide to Port Augusta ($29), Whyalla ($33), Port Lincoln ($58), Ceduna ($68) and Streaky Bay ($61).

PORT AUGUSTA (pop 14,000)

Matthew Flinders was the first European to set foot in the area, but the town of Port Augusta was not established until 1854. Today, this busy city is the gateway to the outback region of South Australia. It's also a major crossroads for travellers.

From here, roads head west across the

Nullarbor to Western Australia, north to Alice Springs in the Northern Territory, south to Adelaide and east to Broken Hill in New South Wales. The railway line between the east and west coasts and the Adelaide to Alice Springs route both pass through Port Augusta.

Information

The tourist information centre (☎ 8641 0793; fax 8642 4288) is in the Wadlata Outback Centre at 41 Flinders Tce – this is the major information source for the Flinders Ranges and the outback, but also has a good selection of material on the Eyre Peninsula. It's open from 9 am to 5.30 pm weekdays and 10 am to 4 pm weekends.

Open the same hours, the Wadlata Outback Centre is an interesting interpretive centre ($6.50), with numerous exhibits tracing the Aboriginal and European history of the Flinders Ranges and the outback. It's well worth the price.

Things to See & Do

There are tours ($2) of the **School of the Air** at 59 Power Crescent on weekdays at 10 am. You can also tour the **Royal Flying Doctor Service** at 4 Vincent St on weekdays between 10 am and 3 pm; admission is by donation.

Another good educational tour takes you around the huge **Northern Power Station** (☎ 8641 1633) – it has the added advantage of being free. Tours of the complex depart at 11 am and 1 pm; closed footwear, long trousers and long-sleeved shirts are essential.

Off the Stuart Highway, the **Australian Arid Lands Botanic Garden** covers 200 hectares on the northern edge of town. There are several walks and an interesting information centre.

Other attractions include the **Curdnatta Art & Pottery Gallery** in Port Augusta's first train station, 101 Commercial rd near the Wadlata Outback Centre. The **Homestead Park Pioneer Museum** ($2.50) features an original log-cabin homestead from the Flinders Ranges. It's on Elsie St and is open from 10 am to 5 pm daily.

Places to Stay

There are plenty of places to stay in Port Augusta; the tourist centre has details.

The efficient *Port Augusta Holiday Park* (☎ 8642 2974) at the junction of the Stuart and Eyre Hwys has camp sites for $14, on-site vans for $35 and cabins from $41. It also has a four-bed bunk house for backpackers ($12) with an adjacent campers' kitchen.

Port Augusta Backpackers (☎ 8641 1063) at 17 Trent Rd has beds for $12. You can arrange Flinders Ranges tours here. The hostel is just off Highway 1, and if you ask the bus drivers they'll let you off nearby.

The *Flinders Hotel/Motel* (☎ 8642 2544) at 39 Commercial Rd has backpacker beds for $14 and self-contained rooms for $42/55.

Getting There & Away

Air Augusta Airways (☎ 8642 3100; bookings ☎ 13 1300) flies weekdays to Adelaide ($115), Leigh Creek and Woomera (both $100).

On Saturday (returning Sunday) you can take the mail plane to Boulia in outback Queensland, stopping at Innamincka and Birdsville on the way; for details check with Augusta Airways. Twin-share packages are $965 ex-Adelaide and $720 ex-Port Augusta.

Bus The bus station for Stateliner and Greyhound Pioneer is at 23 McKay St.

Stateliner (☎ 8642 5055) runs to Adelaide ($29), Coober Pedy ($62), Wilpena Pound ($25), Whyalla ($12), Port Lincoln ($41), Ceduna ($54) and other places on the Eyre Peninsula.

Greyhound Pioneer (☎ 13 2030) travels to Perth ($214), Alice Springs ($147) and Sydney ($132).

McCafferty's (☎ 13 1499) travels to Alice Springs ($135) and Sydney ($111) from the Shell Meteor service station (☎ 8642 6488) on Highway 1 on the Adelaide side of town.

Train From Port Augusta you can get to all mainland capitals except Darwin by train. For bookings and enquiries call ☎ 3 2232.

Sydney is 32 hours away. A standard

economy ticket costs $185, while an economy/1st-class sleeper is $362/545.

It takes 33 hours to Perth; an economy seat is $224 and an economy/1st-class sleeper is $467/704.

To Alice Springs takes 16 hours and costs $136 economy and $295/500 economy/first-class sleeper.

It's four hours to Adelaide ($33).

WHYALLA (pop 23,400)

The largest city in the state after Adelaide, Whyalla is a major steel-producing centre with a busy deep-water port.

Information

The tourist centre (☎ 8645 7900) on the Lincoln Highway on the northern side of town is open weekdays from 8.45 am to 5.10 pm, Saturday from 9 am to 4 pm and Sunday from 10 am to 4 pm.

Things to See & Do

There are interesting tours of the **BHP steel works** on Monday, Wednesday and Saturday at 9.30 am. They start from the tourist centre and cost $8. Long trousers, long-sleeved shirts and closed footwear are essential.

Next door to the tourist centre is the **Maritime Museum**, featuring the 650-tonne, WWII corvette HMAS *Whyalla*; admission is $5 and it's open from 10 am to 4 pm daily.

Iron ore comes to Whyalla from the open-cut mines of Iron Knob, Iron Monarch, Iron Baron and Iron Duke. **Iron Knob** was the first iron-ore deposit in Australia to be exploited; there are tours ($3) of the mine on weekdays at 10 am and 2 pm and the Iron Knob tourist office (☎ 8646 2129) can give details. Enclosed footwear is essential.

The **Whyalla Wildlife & Reptile Sanctuary** ($5) on the Lincoln Highway near the airport is definitely worth a visit; it opens daily at 10 am and there are many exhibits.

On Ekblom St, there are historical exhibits in the **Mt Laura Homestead Museum** ($2). It's open from 2 to 4 pm Sunday, Monday and Wednesday and 10 am to noon Friday.

Places to Stay & Eat

The *Whyalla Foreshore Caravan Park* (☎ 8645 7474) on Broadbent Tce has camp sites for $10, on-site vans for $24 and cabins from $28. Prices for camp sites and on-site vans are similar at the friendly *Hillview Caravan Park* (☎ 8645 9357), off the Lincoln Highway 5km south of town, except their cabins cost from $43.

Hotels in the city centre have basic rooms from $25/40 for singles/doubles – the tourist office can provide all details.

The *Oriental Inn* on Essington Lewis Ave is said to be the best Chinese restaurant in town. Almost next door is the very popular *Bogart's Caffé*, which offers fancier meals than the pubs but still at a reasonable price.

COWELL (pop 750)

Cowell is a pleasant little town near a large jade deposit. The various mines have closed down as a result of marketing difficulties, but you can purchase a wide range of jade products from the Jade Motel on the Lincoln Highway at the northern end of town. Oysters are farmed locally, and you can buy them from several outlets for as little as $5 a dozen.

Places to Stay

Close to the town centre, the *Cowell Foreshore Caravan Park* (☎ 8629 2307) charges $11 for camp sites, from $30 for on-site vans and from $35 for cabins.

Alternatively, the lovely old *Franklin Harbour Hotel* (☎ 8629 2015) on Main St in the town centre has rooms for $15/25, while the impressive *Commercial Hotel* (☎ 8629 2181) nearby charges $20/30.

Schultz Farm (☎ 8629 2194), run by kindly Mr and Mrs Schultz, has spacious rooms for $25/45, including a cooked breakfast. It's about 1km south-west of town.

COWELL TO PORT LINCOLN

The first township on the road south from Cowell is **Elbow Hill** (15km down the Lincoln Highway). There's not much here, but the beaches at nearby **Point Gibbon**

(6km) are magnificent with huge, white sand dunes behind a beautiful coastline.

The very hospitable *Elbow Hill Inn* (☎ 8628 5012) provides light lunches and dinners. It also has two rooms with en-suites (from $70 for doubles), and a pool.

Back on the coast, **Arno Bay** is another small beach resort with a pub and caravan park.

South again is **Port Neill**, a pleasant little seaside town with a vintage vehicle museum. Farther south is **Tumby Bay**, with its long, curving white-sand beach, a National Trust museum and a number of old buildings around the town. Hales Mini Mart (☎ 8688 2584) has tourist information and also hires out tandem bicycles ($5 per hour).

The **Sir Joseph Banks Islands**, 15km offshore, form a marine conservation park. A couple of islands in this group have sea-lion colonies, and there are many attractive bays and reefs plus a wide variety of sea birds, including Cape Barren Geese. Cruises and boat hire can be arranged; contact Hales Mini Mart in Tumby Bay or the tourist office in Port Lincoln.

PORT LINCOLN (pop 11,500)

Port Lincoln, at the southern end of the Eyre Peninsula, is 662km from Adelaide by road but only 250km as the crow flies. The first settlers arrived in 1839 and the town has grown to become the tuna-fishing capital of Australia. The annual **Tunarama Festival**, held over the Australia Day weekend in January, signals the start of the tuna-fishing season with boisterous merriment. There's tuna and wheat-sheaf tossing, keg rolling, slippery pole climbing, a boat-building race, stalls and bands.

Information

The Port Lincoln Visitor Information Centre (☎ 1800 629 911; fax 8683 3544) is at 66 Tasman Tce (the foreshore). It's open from 9 am to 5.30 pm daily.

Contact the NPWS office (☎ 8688 3177) at 75 Liverpool St for information on Lincoln National Park and Coffin Bay National Park.

There are some good surfing and diving spots near the town. For information about the best areas, contact the Port Lincoln Skin-Diving & Surfing Centre (☎ 8682 4428) at 1 King St. Licensed divers can also hire scuba-diving equipment.

Things to See & Do

Port Lincoln is well situated on Boston Bay. There are a number of historic buildings, including the **Old Mill** on Dorset Place, which has a lookout affording good views over the bay.

The **Lincoln Hotel** at 20 Tasman Tce in the town centre dates from 1840, making it the oldest hotel on the peninsula. On the Flinders Highway, **Mill Cottage** ($2 with guided tour) is a historic homestead built in 1866; it's open from 2 to 4.30 pm daily except Monday.

Thirty-one km offshore is **Dangerous Reef**, a major breeding area for the white pointer shark. Cruises to the reef can be arranged from October to April through the tourist office or Westward Ho Holiday Units (☎ 8682 2425) – sightings of sharks are rare, but you'll probably see plenty of sea lions. Prices start at $55, which includes a visit to an underwater viewing platform at a tuna farm moored near Boston Island.

For tours, contact the Visitor Information Centre for details. Tours available include a town tour ($20), a day tour of the town and Whalers Way ($60) and a day tour incorporating the lower Eyre Peninsula and Coffin Bay ($60). A 3½-hour yacht cruise ($25) takes you around Boston Bay and out to the tuna farms. If money is no object, and you've plenty of time, you can go **cage diving** and (hopefully) observe white pointers at Dangerous Reef.

Places to Stay & Eat

There are a number of hotels, motels and holiday flats in and around town; the tourist office has details.

The popular *Kirton Point Caravan Park* (☎ 8682 2537) is 3km east of the town centre, and has camp sites from $10 and cabins from $23.

Cheapest of the five hotels in the city centre is the historic *Lincoln Hotel* (☎ 8682 1277). Singles/doubles with shared facilities are $20/35 and $25/45 with private bathroom. Close behind is the *Great Northern Hotel* (☎ 8682 3350) at $20/38.

Westward Ho Holiday Units (☎ 8682 2425) has flats from $50 for doubles. If there's six of you and you have your own bedding, you can get a flat for $58 outside holiday periods.

There are plenty of eating establishments in the city centre. One of the most popular is *Bugs Restaurant* on Eyre St, which has delicious pasta from $9 to $12. They also make wonderful soups.

AROUND PORT LINCOLN

Cape Carnot, better known as Whalers Way, is 32km south of Port Lincoln and features beautiful and rugged coastal scenery. Although it is privately owned, it is possible to visit by obtaining a permit ($15 plus key deposit). Valid for 24 hours, this enables you to camp at Redbanks or Groper Bay. Permits can be obtained from most petrol stations or the tourist office in Port Lincoln.

You can also buy permits ($8) to visit **Mikkira Koala Sanctuary** (closed November to February) from most petrol stations in Port Lincoln or at the tourist office. However, you shouldn't expect too much!

Sleaford Bay's beautiful beaches are a 3km detour off the road to Whalers Way.

Also south of Port Lincoln is the **Lincoln National Park**, again with a magnificent coastline including quiet coves and pounding surf beaches. Entry to the park costs $5 per car, and it'll cost another $5 per night if you're going to camp – you can obtain permits at the entry station. Most of the park's vehicle tracks are suitable for conventional vehicles but you will need a 4WD to visit tranquil **Memory Cove** – there's a $10 key deposit for this area.

PORT LINCOLN TO STREAKY BAY
Coffin Bay

Ominous-sounding Coffin Bay (it was named by Matthew Flinders to honour Sir Isaac Coffin) is a sheltered stretch of water with many quiet beaches and good fishing. The main centre is the holidayville of Coffin Bay (usual population 200). From here you can visit wild coastal scenery along the ocean side of **Coffin Bay Peninsula**, which is entirely taken up by a national park. Access for conventional vehicles is limited within the park – you can get to scenic **Point Avoid** quite easily, but otherwise you need a 4WD. Entry to the park costs $5 per car.

Birdlife, including some unusual migratory species, is a feature of the **Kellidie Bay Conservation Park**, just outside Coffin Bay township.

Places to Stay The *Coffin Bay Caravan Park* (☎ 8685 4170) is the only place in town where you can camp ($10 for couples); it also has on-site vans ($25) and basic cabins ($35). The pub does counter meals (from $6) and there's a couple of takeaways.

Bush camping (generally with difficult access) is allowed at several places on the peninsula and permits cost $5 per car. Contact the ranger at the park entry station (☎ 8685 4047) near Coffin Bay township.

Coffin Bay to Point Labatt

Just past **Coulta**, 40km north of Coffin Bay, there's good surfing at **Greenly Beach**. **Locks Well**, about 15km south of **Elliston** (a small resort and fishing town on peaceful Waterloo Bay), is one of several good salmon-fishing spots along this wild coast. Elliston itself has two caravan parks, a pub and a motel.

Just north of Elliston, take the 7km detour to **Anxious Bay** and **Salmon Point** for some great ocean scenery – en route you pass **Blackfellows**, which has some of the strongest waves on the west coast. From here you can see distant **Flinders Island**, where there's a sheep station and tourist accommodation.

At **Venus Bay** are quiet beaches, plenty of pelicans and a small caravan park. Alternatively, you can camp in the bush ($5 per car) at the **Venus Bay Conservation Park**, which has fine coastal scenery, plenty of wildlife and fishing.

Shortly before Streaky Bay, the turn-off to **Point Labatt** takes you to one of the few permanent colonies of sea lions on the Australian mainland. You can view them from the cliff top, 50m above.

STREAKY BAY (pop 1000)

This attractive little town takes its name from the 'streaky' water, caused by seaweed in the bay. The main tourist information outlet is in the Shell Auto Mart (☎ 8626 1126) at 15 Alfred Tce; it's open from 8 am to 6 pm daily.

A museum ($2) on Montgomerie Tce containing the **Kelsh Pioneer Hut** and other exhibits is open from 2 to 4 pm Tuesday and Friday, and at other times by prior arrangement. Open the same hours, the **Powerhouse Museum** opposite the Shell Auto Mart on Alfred Tce has a large collection of restored engines.

Curious granite outcrops known as inselbergs are found at numerous places around the Eyre Peninsula. One of the most impressive is a group known as **Murphy's Haystacks**, near the highway about 20km south-east of Streaky Bay. **Back Beach**, 4km west of Streaky Bay, is good for surfing; there's some grand cliff scenery around the coast here.

There are oyster farms here and further along the coast at sleepy **Smoky Bay**. You can get fresh oysters from as little as $5 for a dozen from several outlets.

Places to Stay & Eat

About 1km west of town, the *Foreshore Tourist Park* (☎ 8626 1666) has ungrassed camp sites from $11 and cabins from $34. The adjoining kiosk does good takeaways.

Dorm-style beds are $10 in *Labatt House* (☎ 8626 1126) on Alfred Tce across from the Shell Auto Mart. It's said to be quite friendly, and its kitchen, dining room and lounge are spacious and clean. You can get good cheap meals at the Auto Mart, and the town bakery is also recommended.

Just up the road in the centre of town, the comfortable *Streaky Bay Community Hotel/*

Motel (☎ 8626 1008) has basic rooms for $25/30 and rooms with TV and private bathroom for $48/57, both in the pub section.

The friendly *Smoky Bay Caravan Park* (☎ 8625 7030) has camp sites from $8 and basic cabins from $18 for doubles.

CEDUNA (pop 2600)

Just past the junction of the Eyre and Flinders highways, Ceduna marks the end of the Eyre Peninsula and the start of the long, lonely highway across the Nullarbor Plain into Western Australia. The town was founded in 1896, although there had been a **whaling station** on St Peter Island, off nearby Cape Thevenard, back in 1850.

The tourist office is in the Ceduna Travel Centre (☎ 8625 2780) at 58 Poynton St (the main street); it's open from 9 am to 5 pm weekdays and 9 to 11.30 am Saturday. After a few days fruitlessly waiting for a lift you might find yourself paying it a visit to buy a bus ticket to Western Australia. Greyhound Pioneer charges $166 to Norseman and $214 to Perth.

The **Old Schoolhouse Museum** on Park Tce has pioneer exhibits, but what's really interesting are the artefacts and newspaper clippings from the British atomic weapons program at Maralinga. Entry costs $2 and it's open daily except Sunday – check at the tourist office for times.

There are many beaches and sheltered coves around Ceduna, with good surfing and fishing. **Laura Bay Conservation Park**, off the road to Smoky Bay 20km south-west of Ceduna, has mangroves and tidal flats that attract many species of seabirds and waders.

Turn off the highway at **Penong**, about 75km west of Ceduna, and a 20km dirt track gets you to Point Sinclair. Here you'll find famous (to surfers) **Cactus Beach**, which has some of Australia's best surfing breaks. The area is private property but you can camp for $5; bring your own drinking water. You can also do overnight **camel safaris** for $80 per person per day all-inclusive – ring ☎ 8625 1093 for details.

Farther west is **Head of Bight**, where southern right whales come in close to shore during the breeding season from June to October. Between 20 and 30 calves are born here each year, and you'll usually see several adults swimming along the cliffs. There are excellent lookout points, but it's best if you have binoculars.

Head of Bight is on Aboriginal land, but you can get permits ($7) and information from the Yalata Roadhouse and the Nullarbor Hotel/Motel, both on the Eyre Highway. The turn-off to the viewing area is 78km past Yalata, heading west.

Places to Stay
The best of the four caravan parks here is the *Ceduna Foreshore Caravan Park* (☎ 8625 2290) near the town centre. It's quite attractive and has camp sites from $13 and cabins from $34 (extra adults $3). We've had good reports about the friendly and helpful management of *Greenacres Backpackers* (☎ 017 165 346) at 12 Khulmann St near the Greyhound Pioneer bus station. Beds in dorms and private rooms – a couple have fans – cost $15, including dinner.

The *Ceduna Community Hotel/Motel* (☎ 8625 2008) has basic rooms for $25/29 and self-contained rooms for $35/37, both are in the pub section. Don't leave any valuables in your car if it's parked in the street overnight – not that you should do this anywhere else, either.

Farther west on the Eyre Hwy there are basic caravan parks at the Nundroo Hotel/Motel Inn (☎ 8625 6120), Yalata Roadhouse (☎ 8625 6807), Nullarbor Hotel/Motel Inn (☎ 8625 6271) and Border Village (☎ 9039 3474).

Flinders Ranges

Rising from the northern end of Gulf St Vincent and running north for 400km into the arid outback, the Flinders Ranges offer some of the most spectacular and rugged scenery in South Australia. It's a superb area for bushwalks, wildlife or taking in the ever-changing colours of the outback. In the far north, the ranges are hemmed in by sand ridges and barren salt lakes.

As in many other dry regions of Australia, the vegetation here is surprisingly diverse and colourful. In the early spring, after good rains, the country is carpeted with wildflowers. In summer the days can be searingly hot but the nights usually cool down to a pleasant temperature. Winter and early spring are probably the best times to visit, although there are attractions at any time of the year.

In 1802, when Flinders set foot on the coast near Port Augusta, there were several Aboriginal tribes in the region. You can visit some of their sites: the cave paintings at Yourambulla (near Hawker) and Arkaroo (near Wilpena); and the rock carvings at Sacred Canyon (near Wilpena) and Chambers Gorge.

Bushwalking is one of the main attractions of the area, but this is wild, rugged country and care should be taken before setting out. Wilpena Pound, the Arkaroola-Mt Painter Wildlife Sanctuary and Mt Remarkable National Park all have excellent walks, many of them along marked trails. The Heysen Trail starts in Parachilna Gorge, near Blinman, and winds south through the ranges from there.

Information
Flinders Ranges & Outback South Australia Tourism (☎ 8373 3430; 1800 633 060; flinders.ranges@adelaide.on.net; www.outback.aus.com) has its head office at 142 Gawler Place in Adelaide. They're open from 8.30 am to 5 pm weekdays.

Otherwise the main tourist information outlet is in the Wadlata Outback Centre at 41 Flinders Tce, Port Augusta (see the earlier section on the Eyre Peninsula).

The NPWS head office for the Flinders Ranges is in Hawker (☎ 8648 4244), in the same building as the post office. The visitor centre at Wilpena (☎ 8648 0048) has information on display and is open from 8 am to 5 pm daily.

You'll need a good map of the area as there are many back roads and a variety of road surfaces. According to local experts, the

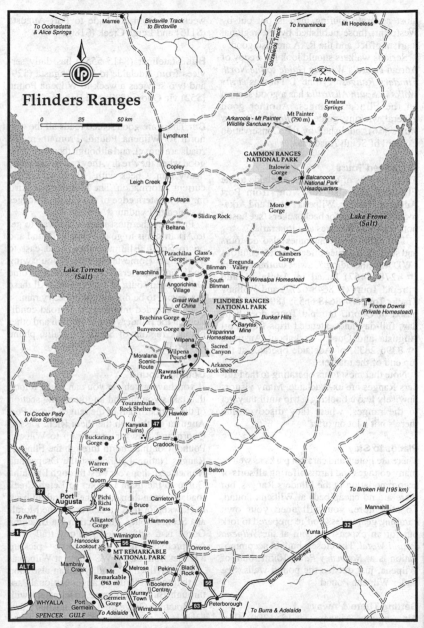

most accurate touring map is put out by Westprint; those published by the regional tourism office and the RAA are also good.

Serious walkers should look for a copy of Adrian Heard's *Walking Guide to the North Flinders Ranges*. Tyrone T Thomas' *Fifty Walks in South Australia* has a good section on the Flinders Ranges. Another good general walking guide is *Flinders Ranges Walks* ($6), published by the Conservation Council of South Australia.

Organised Tours
There are lots of tours from Adelaide to the Flinders and also tours out from Port Augusta, Hawker, Wilpena Pound and Arkaroola. Some cater for backpackers (see hostel notice boards for fares and itineraries).

The major bus companies also do tours and some companies offer more adventurous 4WD trips including: Gawler Outback Tours (☎ 8278 4467) based in Adelaide, and Intrepid Tours (☎ 8648 6277) and Wallaby Tracks Tours (☎ 8648 6655; 1800 639 933) based in Quorn. Intrepid Tours does half-day, full-day and extended trips from Port Augusta and Quorn. Trekabout Australia (☎ 8396 2833) of Adelaide operates at the top end of the market.

Note that most tours operating to the Flinders Ranges are ex-Adelaide. Many visitors unwisely leave booking a trip until they get to the ranges, where they discover that there's not a lot on offer.

Places to Stay
There are hotels and caravan parks as well as many cottages and farms offering all sorts of accommodation in the Flinders Ranges, but there are no cheap beds at Wilpena Pound. To stay here, you will need your own camping gear unless you're prepared to fork out for an expensive room at the *Wilpena Pound Motel*. The closest budget accommodation is at *Rawnsley Park*, 10km south of Wilpena, just outside the pound walls. See under Wilpena Pound.

Getting There & Away
Air Augusta Airways (☎ 13 1300) flies weekdays from Adelaide to Port Augusta ($115) and Leigh Creek ($180).

Bus Stateliner (8415 5555) has daily services from Adelaide to Port Augusta ($29) and two services a week to Wilpena Pound ($52) via Quorn ($37) and Hawker ($46).

Car There are good sealed roads all the way north to Wilpena Pound. From there the roads are gravel, and although these are quite good when they're dry, they can be closed by heavy rain. Check with NPWS offices for current information. The Marree road skirting the western edge of the Flinders Ranges is sealed to Lyndhurst.

Probably the most interesting way to get to Arkaroola is to go to Wilpena Pound and on to South Blinman, then head east to Wirrealpa Homestead, where you swing north via Chambers Gorge to meet the Frome Downs road south of Balcanoona. All these roads tend to be difficult after heavy rain.

For recorded information on road conditions in the Flinders Ranges region and other outback regions of South Australia, phone ☎ 11 633.

Getting Around
If you have a vehicle you can make a loop that takes you around an interesting section of the southern part of the ranges. From Port Augusta go through the Pichi Richi Pass to Quorn and Hawker and on up to Wilpena Pound. Continue north through the Flinders Ranges National Park past the Oraparinna Homestead, then veer west through Brachina Gorge to the main Hawker to Leigh Creek road. You can then either head straight back to Hawker, or make a detour via the Moralana Scenic Route. The section via Brachina Gorge is a self-guided geology trail, with interpretive signs posted en route – pick up a leaflet from the NPWS office at Wilpena.

From Wilpena Pound, you can also loop north into the Flinders Ranges National Park through Bunyeroo Gorge, meeting up with the Brachina Gorge road. You can then either head back to Wilpena via the Oraparinna

Homestead, or head west to the Hawker to Leigh Creek road through Brachina Gorge.

QUORN (pop 1000)

The picturesque 'gateway to the Flinders' is about 330km north of Adelaide and 41km north-east of Port Augusta. It became an important railway town after the completion of the Great Northern Railway in 1878, and it still retains the atmosphere of its pioneering days.

The tourist office (☎ 8648 6419) next to the council chambers in Seventh St is usually open from 10 am to 4 pm weekends and public holidays, but is unreliable at other times – if it's closed, ask at the council chambers or the caravan park.

The railway was closed in 1957, but part of the line to Port Augusta has reopened as a tourism venture. A vintage train – often pulled by a steam engine – makes a 32km round trip from Quorn to the scenic **Pichi Richi Pass** for $22. During school holiday periods the train runs fairly frequently, otherwise it operates every second and fourth Sunday and on public holidays between early March and late November (enquiries ☎ 8276 6232; recorded information ☎ 8395 2566).

Ask at the train station about tours ($5) of the **railway workshop** – usually conducted on train days. Here you'll find a large and fascinating collection of locomotives, carriages, freight wagons, brake vans and sundry items.

The town has a couple of interesting art galleries. The **Junction Art Gallery**, on a farm off the Yarah Vale Gorge road about 16km north of town, is a very friendly place with high-quality arts and crafts, and walking trails. A little further out on the same road, **Warren Gorge** has good rock climbing and pleasant picnic sites.

There are several good walks in Pitchi Richi Pass out on the Port Augusta road, including the **Waukerie Creek Trail** and the Heysen Trail. Closer to town are walks at **Dutchman's Stern** and **Devil's Peak** – these are both within easy cycling distance.

Places to Stay & Eat

The *Quorn Caravan Park* (☎ 8648 6206) on Silo Rd just behind the old train station has camp sites from $10, on-site vans without air-con for $28 and cabins with air-con for $44. It also has magnificent gum trees, although the screeching corellas in them aren't so inspiring first thing in the morning.

In the old hospital at 12 First St, *Andu Lodge* (☎ 1800 639 933) is a very good hostel with excellent facilities and a quiet, comfortable atmosphere. Beds in spacious dorms cost $14, and there are doubles for $32. You can hire mountain bikes ($12 for a day) and Mick, the owner, will tell you about the bushwalks and rides around town. He also does backpacker-friendly tours. Transfers to and from Port Augusta can be arranged for $6 each way.

The *Transcontinental Hotel* (☎ 8648 6076) on Railway Tce is the pick of the town's four hotels for accommodation. It's a friendly place with standard rooms (no air-con) at $29/49, including breakfast.

Quorn's four pubs sell counter and dining-room meals, usually starting at about $6. There's a very good restaurant in the *Quorn Mill Motel* at the west end of Railway Tce and another at the old *Willows Brewery* in Pitchi Richi Pass about 10km south on the Port Augusta road.

KANYAKA

About 40km north of Quorn, on the way to Hawker, are the impressive ruins of the old Kanyaka settlement, founded in 1851. Up to 70 families lived here, tending the settlement's 50,000 sheep, but it was finally abandoned in 1888 as a result of drought and overgrazing.

From the homestead ruins, you can drive along the creek to the old woolshed, then walk about 1.5km to picturesque **Kanyaka Waterhole**, which is overlooked by the so-called **Death Rock**.

If you're coming from Wilpena Pound, don't be confused by the sign that indicates the old Kanyaka town site – the clearly marked turn-off for the ruins is about 4km further on.

HAWKER (pop 300)

Hawker is 55km south of Wilpena Pound. For tourist information, chat with the helpful staff at Hawker Motors (the Mobil service station) on the corner of Wilpena Rd and Cradock Rd.

There are Aboriginal rock paintings 12km west of Hawker at the **Yourambulla Rock Shelter**, a hollow in the rocks high up on the side of Yourambulla Peak, a half-hour walk from the car park. The **Jarvis Hill Lookout** is about 6km south-west of Hawker and affords good views over Hawker and north to Wilpena Pound.

The **Moralana Scenic Route** is a round-trip drive from Hawker, taking in the magnificent scenery between the Elders and Wilpena ranges. It is 24km to the Moralana turn-off, then 28km along an unsealed road that joins up with the sealed Hawker to Leigh Creek road. From here it's 43km back to Hawker.

Places to Stay

The *Hawker Caravan Park* (☎ 8648 4006) on the northern outskirts of town on the Wilpena road has lawned camp sites for $11, on-site vans for $30 and deluxe cabins for $55 – all units have air-con. About 1km north-west of town on the Leigh Creek road, the *Flinders Ranges Caravan Park* (☎ 8648 4266) has camp sites and on-site vans for almost identical prices.

The *Hawker Hotel/Motel* (☎ 8648 4102) on Elder Tce has pub-style rooms (some with air-con) for $25/35 and motel units for $50/60. The *Outback Motel* (☎ 8648 4100) charges $55/65.

The *Sight-Seers Cafe* on Elder Tce has reasonably priced meals and takeaways, as does the *Hawker Shopping Centre* on the Wilpena road, which has a well-stocked grocery section. Alternatively, the *Hawker Hotel/Motel* normally has good counter meals.

WILPENA POUND

The best-known feature of the ranges and the main attraction in the 94,500-hectare **Flinders Ranges National Park**, is the large natural basin known as Wilpena Pound. Covering about 80 sq km, it is ringed by cliffs and is accessible only by the narrow gap through which Wilpena Creek exits the pound. On the outside, the Wilpena Wall soars almost sheer for 500m; inside, the basin slopes relatively gently away from the peaks.

There is plenty of wildlife in the park, particularly euros (wallaroos), red and grey kangaroos, and birds – everything from rosellas, galahs and budgerigars to emus and wedge-tailed eagles. You may even see beautiful yellow-footed rock-wallabies, whose numbers are increasing now that foxes and rabbits are being controlled. **Brachina Gorge** is a good spot for wallabies.

Sacred Canyon, with its many petroglyphs (rock carvings), is to the east. To the north and still within the national park are striking scenic attractions, such as **Bunyeroo Creek**, Brachina Gorge and the **Aroona Valley**. There are several attractive bush-camping areas, all accessible by conventional vehicle. The 20km **Brachina Gorge Geological Trail** (you follow it in your car) features an outstanding geological sequence of exposed sedimentary rock.

Entry to the park costs $5 per car (you don't need to buy an entry permit if you're camping); pay at the visitor centre in the Wilpena tourist village, near the pound entrance.

Bushwalks

If you're planning to walk for more than about three hours, fill in the log book at the visitor centre – and don't forget to 'sign off' when you return. Searches are no longer initiated by the rangers, so make sure someone responsible knows the details of your walk.

There is a series of clearly marked walking trails (sections that incorporate parts of the Heysen Trail are indicated by red markers) and these are listed in the leaflet *Bushwalking in the Flinders Ranges National Park*, issued by the NPWS ($1). Topographical maps (scale 1:50,000) are available for $7.50 from the visitor centre.

Flinders Ranges Dreaming

The almost palpable 'spirit of place' of the Flinders Ranges has inspired a rich heritage of dreaming stories. Wilpena Pound was an important ceremonial site, known by the Adnyamathanha ('hill people') as Ikara. A lot of the legends – many secret, but some related by Adnyamathanha elders – explain creation, the extraordinary geological features of the pound, and the native birds and animals that inhabit it.

One Adnyamathanha story describes Akurra, a giant snake that carved out gorges in his quest to find water. The rumblings from his giant belly can be heard resounding around the walls of Ikara.

Another story relates that the walls of the pound are the bodies of two Akurra, who coiled around Ikara during an initiation ceremony, creating a whirlwind, and devoured most of the participants.

In another story the bossy eagle Wildu, seeking revenge on his nephews who had tried to kill him, built a great fire. All the birds were caught in the flames and, originally white, they emerged blackened and burnt. The magpies and willie wagtails were partially blackened, but the crows were entirely blackened and have remained so until this day. ■

Solo walks are not recommended and you must be adequately equipped – particularly with drinking water and sun protection, especially during the summer months.

Most of the walks start from the visitor centre, which is near the main camp site. The St Marys Peak walk is probably the most interesting, but there are plenty of others worth considering. They vary from short walks suitable for people with small children, to longer ones taking more than a day.

You should allow a day for the walk to **St Marys Peak** and back, whether you do it as an up-and-down or a round-trip. Up and back, it's faster and more interesting to take the route outside Wilpena Pound as the scenery this way is much more spectacular.

The final climb up to the **Tanderra Saddle** is fairly steep and the final stretch from there to the summit is a real scramble. However, the views are some of the best in South Australia, with the white glimmer of **Lake Torrens** off to the west, the beautiful Aroona Valley to the north, and the pound spread out below your feet.

Descending from the peak you can either head back down on the same direct route or take the longer round-trip walk through Wilpena Pound. This is the same track you take to get to **Edeowie Gorge**. Alternatively, you can take your time and stay at the **Cooinda** bush-camping area within the Pound.

Arkaroo Rock is at the base of the Wilpena Range, about 10km south of Wilpena off the Hawker road. It takes about half an hour to walk from the car park to the rock shelter, where there are well-preserved Aboriginal paintings. The walk itself is worth the effort.

Organised Tours

The following tours can be booked through the Wilpena Pound Motel (☎ 1800 805 802).

Aboriginal stockman Ron Coulthard takes trail rides in the Wilpena area. There isn't a set program, but you'll certainly learn something of the bush and Aboriginal culture. Prices range from $40 for two hours to $100 for a day trek.

You can take a scenic flight from Wilpena for $45 (20 minutes) or $55 (30 minutes). Costs increase if there are less than three people on the flight.

Nearby **Arkaba** station can be explored on a 4WD tour for $50 (four hours) or $70 (full day including a barbecue/vegetarian lunch). You see some spectacular country on these trips.

Places to Stay & Eat

Unless you've got a tent there is no cheap accommodation at Wilpena. The main camping ground has sites from $11; it's close to the visitor centre, which has a well-stocked store – this is where you pay all fees.

Bush camping within the park itself costs $5 per car per night, and you can pick up a permit at the visitor centre.

Otherwise, the *Wilpena Pound Motel* (☎ 1800 805 802) has all mod cons including a swimming pool and rooms from $85/93. Rates may fall significantly during December and January (they'd want to!).

You can get groceries and last-minute camping requirements at the store in the visitor centre. Counter lunches are available in the motel bar, and there's also a very good restaurant.

Off the Hawker road, about 20km south of Wilpena and close to the Pound's outer edge, the friendly owners of *Rawnsley Park* (☎ 8648 0030) have camp sites from $10, on-site vans for $36 and cabins with air-con for $58. There are several good bushwalks on offer, and you can also do trail rides and 4WD tours ($50 for a half-day and $80 for a full day).

BLINMAN (pop 30)

From the 1860s to the 1890s this was a busy copper town but today it's just a quaint hamlet on the circular route around the Flinders Ranges National Park. It's a useful starting point for visits to many of the scenic attractions in the area. You can also do camel treks ranging from two days ($285) to eight days ($885) through remote station country; phone ☎ 8543 2280 or 8541 4123 for details.

About 1km to the north is the historic **Blinman copper mine**, with walking trails and interpretive signs.

The delightful *Blinman Hotel* (☎ 8648 4867) has a real outback pub flavour – rooms cost $25 per person or $30 with bathroom. Next door, the dusty *Blinman Caravan Park* (ask at the pub) has camp sites for $5 and powered sites for $10.

AROUND BLINMAN

Dramatic **Mt Chambers Gorge**, 64km to the north-east of Blinman towards Arkaroola, features a striking gallery of Aboriginal rock carvings. From Mt Chambers you can see over Lake Frome to the east and all the way

along the Flinders Ranges from Mt Painter in the north to Wilpena Pound in the south.

The beautiful **Aroona Valley** and the **Aroona Homestead** ruins, to the south of Blinman in the Flinders Ranges National Park, are reached from **Brachina Gorge** further south. An inspiring scenic drive links Blinman with Parachilna, to the west. This route takes you through **Parachilna Gorge**, where there are some lovely picnic and camping spots – this is the northern end of the Heysen Trail.

North of Parachilna, on the Marree road, you turn east at the Beltana Roadhouse to get to historic **Beltana** (8km). This small settlement almost became a ghost town, but is now inhabited by interesting people seeking to escape the rat race. It's a fascinating spot and the roadhouse (☎ 8675 2744) has information on the area.

Places to Stay & Eat

Angorichina Tourist Village (☎ 8648 4842), about halfway between Blinman and Parachilna in the Parachilna Gorge, boasts a magnificent setting with steep hills all around. It has camp sites from $8, on-site vans for $30 and units from $45.

A number of stations in the area offer accommodation. *Gum Creek Station* (☎ 8648 4883) 15km south of Blinman has shearers' quarters for $10 per adult, but there's a minimum charge of $50 per night. It's closed during summer.

At tiny Parachilna there's the *Prairie Hotel* (☎ 8648 4895), which has camp sites from $10, basic cabins from $40 and very nice rooms with private bathroom for $55/70. The pub has a great menu featuring Australian bush tucker, and offers a real gourmet experience: its emu pâté on damper is delicious. Almost next door, the *Old Schoolhouse* (☎ 8648 4676) has bunks and cooking facilities for $12 per person (camping $5 per person). Ask at the pub or hostel about camel rides and treks, scenic flights and 4WD trips.

LEIGH CREEK (pop 2000)

North of Beltana, Leigh Creek's huge open-cut coal mine supplies the Port Augusta power station. The present town of Leigh Creek was developed in 1980 when its predecessor was demolished to make way for mining. Landscaping has created a very pleasant, leafy environment in dramatic contrast to the stark surroundings.

The *Leigh Creek Caravan Park* (☎ 8675 2025) on Acacia Rd near the town centre has good amenities but the ground is like concrete. Optima Energy offers free tours of the mining operations lasting up to 2½ hours. For an update on schedules ring ☎ 8675 4316.

From Leigh Creek, you can visit the **Aroona Dam** (10km to the south-west), **Gammon Ranges National Park** and **Arkaroola** (respectively 100 and 130km to the east). For information on the Gammon Ranges National Park contact the ranger at Balcanoona on ☎ 8648 4829, or the NPWS office in Hawker.

ARKAROOLA
The Arkaroola tourist village, in the northern part of the Flinders Ranges, was established in 1968. It's a privately operated wildlife reserve (the Arkaroola-Mt Painter Wildlife Sanctuary) in rugged and spectacular country, with many wonderful examples of the outback environment.

Arkaroola has a garage which sells fuel and can do mechanical repairs.

From the village you can take the highly recommended, half-day **Ridgetop Tour** (by 4WD; $50) through amazing mountain scenery. Another excellent tour ($20) allows you to view the heavens through a high-powered telescope at the **Arkaroola Astronomical Observatory**.

This was a mining area and old tracks lead to rock pools at the **Barraranna Gorge** and **Echo Camp**, and to water holes at Arkaroola and **Nooldoonooldoona**. Farther on are the **Bolla Bollana Springs** and the ruins of a copper smelter. You can take a guided or tag-along tour, or do your own thing on most of the sanctuary's 100km of graded tracks. Most places of interest are accessible to con-

ventional vehicles, with some hiking involved.

Mt Painter is a magnificent landmark and you pass close to it on the ridge-top tour. There are fine views from **Freeling Heights** across Yudnamutana Gorge and from **Siller's Lookout** over the salt flats of Lake Frome. **Paralana Hot Springs** is the 'last hurrah' of Australia's geyser activity. It's geologically interesting but otherwise not worth a special trip.

Places to Stay & Eat
The resort (☎ 8648 4848) has a good range of accommodation. Camp sites in the dusty caravan park and down along the creek (much nicer) cost $10, as do bunk beds. Cabins without air-con cost from $29 twin share and motel units with air-con cost from $49 a double. There's a small shop where you can buy basic supplies, and a good restaurant.

Outback

The area north of Eyre Peninsula and the Flinders Ranges stretches into the vast, empty outback that is South Australia's far north. Although sparsely populated and often difficult to travel through, it has much of interest. However, without 4WD or camels it's often not possible to stray far from the few main roads. Entry permits are required for large parts of the north-west (which are either Aboriginal land or the Woomera Prohibited Area).

Information
Flinders Ranges & Outback South Australia Tourism (☎ 8373 3430; 1800 633 060; flinders.ranges@adelaide.on.net; www.outback.aus.com) has its head office at 142 Gawler Place in Adelaide. It's open from 8.30 am to 5 pm weekdays.

Otherwise the main tourist information outlet is in the Wadlata Outback Centre at 41 Flinders Tce, Port Augusta (see the earlier section on the Eyre Peninsula).

SOUTH AUSTRALIA

For information on national parks, and an update on the entry/camping permit system, contact the NPWS office (☎ 8648 5310) at 9 MacKay St in Port Augusta.

National Park Permits To visit most of the outback's conservation areas you need a Desert Parks Pass, which costs $60 per vehicle. It's valid for a year and includes an excellent information book and detailed route and area maps.

Desert Parks Passes are available in many centres including: all state NPWS regional offices; Adelaide (RAA and the Environment & Natural Resources Information Centre), Alice Springs (Shell Todd service station), Birdsville (Birdsville Auto, near the service station), Coober Pedy (Underground Books), Hawker (Hawker Motors), Innamincka (Trading Post), Marree (Marree General Store), Mt Dare Homestead, Oodnadatta (Pink Roadhouse), Port Augusta (Wadlata Outback Centre), William Creek (William Creek Hotel) and the NPWS office at Wilpena.

The NPWS office in Port Augusta can advise on further outlets.

However, if you just want to visit Cooper Creek in the Innamincka Regional Reserve, Lake Eyre in the Lake Eyre National Park or Dalhousie Springs in the Witjira National Park, you need only buy a day/night permit for $15 per vehicle. These are available from Mt Dare Homestead, the Pink Roadhouse in Oodnadatta, the William Creek Hotel, the Marree General Store and the rangers at Innamincka and Dalhousie Springs.

ROUTES NORTH

The Stuart Highway is sealed all the way from Port Augusta to Darwin. It's a long, boring drive and the temptation to get it over with quickly has resulted in many high-speed collisions between cars and cattle, sheep, kangaroos and wedge-tailed eagles. Take care, particularly at night.

For those who want to travel to the Northern Territory by a more adventurous route there's the **Oodnadatta Track**. This often lonely road runs from Port Augusta through the Flinders Ranges to Leigh Creek, Lyndhurst, Marree and Oodnadatta before joining the Stuart Highway at Marla, about 180km south of the Territory border. For most of the way it runs close to the defunct 'Old Ghan' train line.

The Track is sealed as far as Lyndhurst, after which it's a rough, dusty outback road all the way to Marla. There are several routes across to the Stuart Highway: from Lake Eyre south via Roxby Downs to Pimba; from William Creek west to Coober Pedy; and from Oodnadatta south to Coober Pedy or west to Cadney Homestead (a roadhouse on the Stuart Highway). With a 4WD you can keep going up the old railway line from Oodnadatta to Alice Springs, visiting Witjira National Park and Old Andado on the way.

The two other routes of interest in the far north are the **Birdsville** and **Strzelecki** tracks (see the relevant sections later in this chapter). These days the tracks have been so much improved that during the winter it's usually quite feasible to do them in any car that's in good condition and has reasonable ground clearance.

For more information on these roads check with the state automobile associations. *Outback Central & South Australia*, published by the South Australian Department of Lands, is an excellent tourist map with a lot of interesting information. Westprint does a good *Simpson Desert South-Lake Eyre* map that covers all three tracks. For more detail on outback travel, see Lonely Planet's *Outback Australia*.

The South Australian outback includes much of the **Simpson Desert** and the harsh, rocky landscape of the **Sturt Stony Desert**. There are also huge salt lakes that fill with water every once in a long while. **Lake Eyre**, used by Donald Campbell for his attempt on the world's land-speed record in the 60s, filled up for a time in the 70s. It was full again in 1989, only the third occasion since Europeans settled this area over 130 years ago.

When soaking rain does fall on this usually dry land the effect is amazing – flowers bloom and plants grow at a breakneck pace in order to complete their life cycles before the drought returns. There is even a species of frog that goes into suspended animation, remaining in the ground for years on end, only to pop up when the rains come again.

On a much more mundane level, roads can either be washed out or turned into glue-like mud. Venture into the wrong place after heavy rain and you may be stuck for days – or even weeks.

Note that repair facilities and spare parts are often extremely limited, so be prepared in case of breakdown.

WOOMERA (pop 1350)
During the 50s and 60s Woomera was used to launch experimental British rockets and conduct tests in an abortive European project to send a satellite into orbit. The Woomera Prohibited Area, into which rockets are still fired, occupies a vast stretch of land in the centre of the state.

Woomera is now an 'open town', but it is just a shadow of its former self. While rocket research still goes on, these days its main role is to service the mostly US personnel working at the Joint Facility at Nurrungar, a short distance south.

A small **heritage centre** (☎ 8673 7042) in the middle of town has interesting displays that tell you about Woomera's past and present roles, and what may happen in the future. Outside is a collection of old military aircraft, rockets and missiles. The centre is open from 9 am to 5 pm daily (10 am to 2 pm summer).

Ask at the heritage centre about tours of the rocket range.

Places to Stay & Eat
The *Woomera Travellers' Village* (☎ 8673 7800), near the town entrance, has backpacker accommodation ($15/20 for singles/doubles with ceiling fans and $17/24 with air-con), grassed camp sites ($5 per person), on-site vans with air-con (from $25), self-contained cabins ($60) and budget motel units ($45). There is a camper's kitchen, but it's small and basic.

The only alternative is the *Eldo Hotel*

(☎ 8673 7867) on Kotara Ave. It has rooms with air-con from $33/60 without a private bathroom.

The small shopping centre has a coffee lounge and snack bar with the usual takeaway fare. For something better you'll have to try the *Eldo Hotel*. It serves counter meals from about $8 and restaurant meals averaging $12 for a main course.

Getting There & Away
Air Augusta Airways (☎ 13 1300) flies from Adelaide to Woomera for $180.

Bus Woomera is 7km off the Stuart Highway from the scruffy little settlement of Pimba, 175km north of Port Augusta. Stateliner and the long-distance bus lines pass through Woomera daily. With Stateliner it's $50 to Adelaide and $40 to Coober Pedy.

ANDAMOOKA (pop 500)
Off the Stuart Highway, 110km north of Woomera on a good sealed road, Andamooka is a rough-and-ready opal-mining town with a strong frontier flavour. However, the local residents are friendly and welcoming. For general information call in to the post office in the centre of town – it's by Duke's Bottle House. There are various tours, including a guided walk ($5) around local points of interest.

Olympic Dam is a huge uranium, gold, silver and copper mine on Roxby Downs Station near Andamooka. Except from November through March there are daily tours of the mine (surface only), metallurgical plant and town. They take 2½ hours, cost $19.50, and leave at 9.45 am from the Olympic Dam Tours office (☎ 8671 0788), next to the BP service station in **Roxby Downs** township.

Places to Stay & Eat
Andamooka You can camp (from $14) or stay in an on-site van or cabin without air-con (both $30) at the dusty *Andamooka Caravan Park* (☎ 8672 7117), 94 Government Rd in the town centre. There's not

much shade here – not that there is anywhere else, for that matter.

Duke's Bottlehouse (☎ 8672 7007), 275 Opal Creek Blvd, has a self-contained room with air-con sleeping three for $25 per person, as well as more upmarket motel rooms for $46/60. Alternatively, the *Andamooka Opal Hotel/Motel* (☎ 8672 7078), on the corner of Watkins Ave and Chicago Sq, has self-contained rooms from $55/65.

The best place in town to eat is the *Tuckerbox Restaurant*, next to the Duke's Bottlehouse, which sells hearty meals for reasonable prices.

Roxby Downs The *Roxby Downs Caravan Park* (☎ 8671 1000), Pioneer Dve near the town centre, has grassed camp sites for $11 and on-site vans with air-con for $34, otherwise you'll have to stay at the expensive motel. You can get reasonably priced bistro and counter meals at the *tavern* across from the motel.

Getting There & Away
Stateliner has buses daily except Saturday to Roxby Downs ($63).

GLENDAMBO (pop 30)
Glendambo is 113km north of Pimba and 252km south of Coober Pedy. It was created in 1982 as a service centre on the new Stuart Highway to replace the township of Kingoonya, which was bypassed. Glendambo has a good pub, motel, two roadhouses and a caravan park. The Mobil Roadhouse, which closes at midnight, is the RAA agent and generally has the best-value meals.

The *Glendambo Tourist Centre* (☎ 8672 1030) has bars, a restaurant, a 12-bed bunk house ($12 per bed) and motel rooms each sleeping up to five people (singles/doubles go for $65/70 plus $12 for each extra person).

Right next door is the *BP Roadhouse & Caravan Park* (☎ 8672 1035), which has grassy tent sites for $10. Its on-site vans (no air-con) cost $25 plus $5 for each additional person.

If you're heading north remember that there are no refuelling stops between here and Coober Pedy.

COOBER PEDY (pop 2700)
On the Stuart Highway, 535km north of Port Augusta, Coober Pedy is one of Australia's best-known outback towns. It is very cosmopolitan – about 40 nationalities are represented. The name 'Coober Pedy' is Aboriginal and is said to mean 'white fellow's hole in the ground'. This aptly describes the place, as about half the population lives in dugouts to shelter from the extreme climate: daytime summer temperatures can soar to over 50°C and the winter nights are freezing cold. Apart from the dugouts, there are over 250,000 mine shafts in the area! Keep your eyes open when you're walking around.

Coober Pedy is in an extremely inhospitable area and the town reflects this; water is expensive and the rainfall scanty, so even in the middle of winter it looks dried out and dusty, with piles of rusting junk scattered here and there. It's not as ramshackle as it used to be, but even so you could never describe it as attractive. In fact, the town looks a bit like the end of the world – which is probably why much of *Mad Max III* was filmed here.

There are plenty of opal shops, but banking facilities are limited: there's an EFTPOS cash-withdrawal facility at Fast Photo, a Westpac branch with ATM, and a Commonwealth Bank agency in the post office. All are in the main street (Hutchison St).

Coober Pedy has a reputation for being pretty volatile: since 1987 the police station has been bombed twice and the courthouse once, the most successful restaurant was demolished by a blast and hundreds of thousands of dollars worth of mining equipment has gone the same way. More recently, two police cars were blown up!

But for visitors Coober Pedy is by and large a friendly place. It would, however, be unwise for lone females to accept invitations

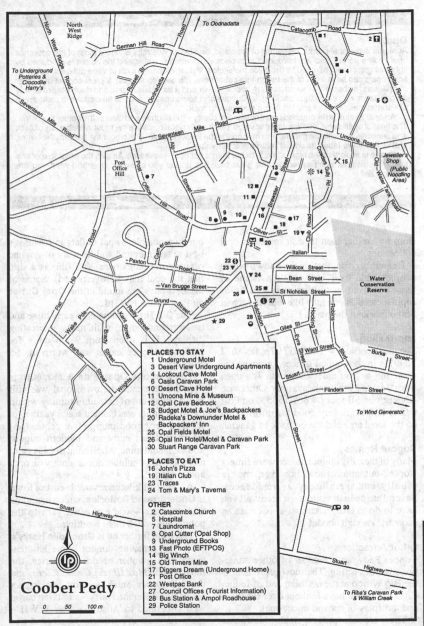

PLACES TO STAY
1 Underground Motel
3 Desert View Underground Apartments
4 Lookout Cave Motel
6 Oasis Caravan Park
10 Desert Cave Hotel
11 Umoona Mine & Museum
12 Opal Cave Bedrock
18 Budget Motel & Joe's Backpackers
20 Radeka's Downunder Motel &
   Backpackers' Inn
25 Opal Fields Motel
26 Opal Inn Hotel/Motel & Caravan Park
30 Stuart Range Caravan Park

PLACES TO EAT
16 John's Pizza
19 Italian Club
23 Traces
24 Tom & Mary's Taverna

OTHER
2 Catacombs Church
5 Hospital
7 Laundromat
8 Opal Cutter (Opal Shop)
9 Underground Books
13 Fast Photo (EFTPOS)
14 Big Winch
15 Old Timers Mine
17 Diggers Dream (Underground Home)
21 Post Office
22 Westpac Bank
27 Council Offices (Tourist Information)
28 Bus Station & Ampol Roadhouse
29 Police Station

Coober Pedy

0   50   100 m

SOUTH AUSTRALIA

Opals

Australia is the opal-producing centre of the world, and South Australia is where most of the country's opals come from. Opals are hardened from silica suspended in water, and the colour is produced by light being split and reflected by the silica molecules. Valuable opals are cut in three different fashions: solid opals can be cut out of the rough into cabochons (domed-top stones); triplets consist of a layer of opal sandwiched between an opaque backing layer and a transparent cap; and doublets are simply an opal layer with an opaque backing. In Queensland some opals are found embedded in rock; these are sometimes polished and left in the surrounding rock.

An opal's value is determined by its colour and clarity – the brighter and clearer the colour the better. The type of opal is also a determinant of value: black and crystal opals are the most valuable, semiblack and semicrystal are in the middle, and milk opal is the least valuable. The bigger the pattern, the better, and visible flaws (such as cracks) also affect the value.

Shape is important – a high dome is better than a flat opal – as is size. As with the purchase of any sort of gemstone, don't expect to find great bargains unless you clearly understand what you are buying. ■

from unfamiliar men to visit mines or opal collections.

Remember, too, that this is a town where people value their individuality. Some of those involved in tourism may not be as sophisticated as you may like, but this is part of the fabric of the place.

Information

The tourist office (☎ 1800 637 076; fax 8672 5699) is in the council offices, opposite the Opal Inn as you enter the town. It's open from 9 am to 5 pm weekdays only. Otherwise Underground Books (☎ 8672 5558) on Post Office Hill Rd is very good for information on the local area and the outback in general.

Dugout Homes

Many of the early dugout homes were simply worked-out mines; now, however, they're usually cut specifically as residences. Several are open to visitors – it seems all you have to do to charge admission is create an eccentric enough abode!

Other Attractions

Coober Pedy has a number of other attractions worth visiting. The most prominent is the **Big Winch** at the northern end of Italian Club Rd, which has a lookout over the town and a display of cut and uncut opal.

There are numerous reputable – and some not so reputable – opal outlets in town; it's best to shop around and be wary of anyone offering discounts over 30% (this is a sign that the opal may be overpriced). Some of the best buys are found at the **Opal Cutter** on Post Office Hill Rd.

The **Old Timers Mine** is an early mine and underground home, with many interesting displays. It is open from 9 am daily for self-guided tours and is well worth the $5 entry fee.

The **Umoona Opal Mine & Museum** is right in the centre of town; opal was still being pulled out of here until mining within the town limits was banned some years ago. It has a very good interpretive centre ($5) which includes early and modern dugout homes, an old mine, Aboriginal displays and an excellent 18-minute documentary on opal and mining.

A couple of kilometres north-east of town is **Underground Potteries**, which has some fine products – you can often yarn to the potters and watch them working.

Three km further on is **Crocodile Harry's** ($2). This amazing dugout home has featured in a number of documentaries, the movies *Mad Max III* and *Ground Zero*, and the mini-series *Stark*, so you can expect something different. Harry – a Latvian baron who emigrated to Australia after WWII – spent 13 years in northern Queensland and the Northern Territory hunting crocodiles. He's one of the town's great characters, and on a good day is a charming fellow.

Opal Mining

The town survives on opals, which were first discovered here by a teenage boy in 1915. Keen fossickers can have a go themselves, the safest area being the **Jeweller's Shop** opal field in the north-east corner of town – fossicking through the mullock, or waste, dumps is known as noodling.

There are literally hundreds of working mines around Coober Pedy but there are no big operators. When somebody makes a find, dozens of miners home in like bees around a honey pot. Looking at all the vacant ground between the various 'fields' makes you wonder just how much opal is still down there!

Organised Tours

There are several sightseeing tours of around four hours that take you into an opal mine, underground home and various other places in and around town. The tours offered by Radeka's Downunder Motel and Joe's Backpackers (both $25) are popular with backpackers; the Desert Cave Hotel has a couple of good tours, one of which concentrates on the mining aspect.

The Opal Quest tour (ask at Underground Books) is the only one to enter a working mine and give hands-on mining experience. This interesting two-hour tour costs $25.

Also good is an informative 'star tour' ($12) where you explore the heavens from the Moon Plain – an appropriate venue. Book at Radeka's for this one.

On Monday and Thursday you can travel with the mail truck along 600km of dirt roads as it does the round trip from Coober Pedy to Oodnadatta and William Creek. This is a great way to get off the beaten track and visit small, remote outback communities. The backpackers' special price is $60, which doesn't include lunch. For details, call ☎ 1800 069 911 or contact Underground Books.

Places to Stay

Camping There are three caravan parks in town and another farther out. None are visually inspiring – there's no lawn but plenty of dust, and the ground is as hard as nails. Showers are usually extra (typically 20c per minute).

Reasonably central to the action are the new *Opal Inn Caravan Park* (☎ 8672 5054), which has camp sites for $9, and the *Oasis Caravan Park* (☎ 8672 5169) on Seventeen Mile Rd, a short walk from the town centre, which has the best shade and shelter. Camp sites here cost $5.50 per person. The Oasis also has basic twin rooms with air-con for $20/25, and an undercover swimming pool in a big old storage tank.

The *Stuart Range Caravan Park* (☎ 8672 5179) is the largest and has the best facilities; its cabins are more like motel rooms. The park is about 1km from town, near the main entrance off the Stuart Highway.

Friendliest (and most basic) of all is *Riba's* (☎ 8672 5614) on the William Creek road 5km from town. It has above-ground sites costing $4.50 per person – you can camp underground for $8 – and showers are free. They also have an interesting one-hour evening mine tour for $10, which includes the above-ground camping fee if you're staying there.

Hostels The underground *Joe's Backpackers* (☎ 8672 5163) attached to the *Budget Motel* on Oliver St near the town centre has two-bedroom, apartment-style bunkhouses, each sleeping up to 10. Beds cost $14 including linen and showers, but there's no laundry (the laundromat is a short walk away on Post Office Hill Rd). They do free transfers from the bus station and airport.

Opposite Joe's, the *Backpackers' Inn* at Radeka's Downunder Motel (☎ 8672 5223) offers underground bunks in open alcoves for $14, including linen and showers. If you want privacy, their renovated twins and doubles (from $35) with share facilities are quite pleasant. It has a communal kitchen and laundry. You can book in between 7.30 am and 1 am, and they also do free transfers.

The very basic *Opal Cave Bedrock* (☎ 8672 5028) on Hutchison St in the town centre has 13 four-bed alcoves opening off a wide central passageway – curtains provide a measure of privacy here. Beds cost $12 including linen and showers, and it's a fair hike to the toilets and showers out the front, particularly for the males. Kitchen facilities are limited.

The underground *Umoona Opal Mine* (☎ 8672 5288) on Hutchison St in the town centre has beds in basic, two-bunk private rooms for $10 each, including shower (linen is $5 extra). There are only limited kitchen facilities.

Hotels & Motels There are a number of hotels and motels, some underground and some with big air-cons. Most are expensive! Listed here are the cheaper places.

The *Opal Inn Hotel/Motel* (☎ 8672 5054) on Hutchison St in the town centre has basic pub rooms with air-con for $25/35 and motel rooms from $40/45/50 for singles/doubles/ triples.

Radeka's Downunder Motel (☎ 8672 5223) has an underground family room sleeping six for $90; their motel units are very good and cost $50/70/75. The above-ground *Budget Motel* (☎ 8672 5163) opposite was being renovated at the time of writing.

Dug into a hill on the north-west outskirts of town, the *Desert View Underground Apartments* (☎ 8672 3330) has three-bedroom units with kitchen sleeping up to nine for $65/80 and $20 for each extra person.

Places to Eat
Cheap eats are not that easy to come by, but you can get reasonably priced counter meals in the saloon bar of the *Opal Inn* – Thursday and Friday are 'specials' nights ($6). The *Italian Club* on Italian Club Rd has similarly priced specials on Wednesday and Saturday nights.

There are a couple of Greek places: *Tom & Mary's Taverna* and *Traces* on Hutchison St in the town centre. Both are popular in the evenings and Traces stays open until late. Both do platters which make an economical meal for three or four people.

The *Breakaways Cafe*, under Traces, is popular for lunches.

Otherwise there are more expensive restaurants as well as several takeaways and coffee lounges in the main street.

Getting Around
The Opal Cave (next to the Opal Cave Bedrock) rents out mountain bikes for $8 a day, while the Desert Cave Hotel (☎ 8672 5688) has an agency for Territory Rent-a-Car – local hire and one-way rentals can be arranged.

Getting There & Away
Air Kendell Airlines (book through Ansett on ☎ 13 1300) flies from Adelaide to Coober Pedy most days of the week ($262). The Desert Cave Hotel handles reservations and operates the airport shuttle bus ($5 one-way). Most hostels will meet you if you ring ahead.

Bus It's 413km from Coober Pedy to Kulgera, just across the border into the Northern Territory, and from there it's another 275km to Alice Springs.

Stateliner charges $82 from Adelaide to Coober Pedy. With Greyhound Pioneer it's $87 from Adelaide, $70 from Alice Springs and $66 from Yulara near Uluru (Ayers Rock).

The bus station for Stateliner and Greyhound is in the Ampol roadhouse, on the main road into town from the Stuart Highway.

McCafferty's stops at John's Pizza in the main street. It charges $69 to Alice Springs.

AROUND COOBER PEDY
Breakaways Reserve
The Breakaways Reserve is a colourfully stark area of mesa hills and scarps about 35km north of Coober Pedy. Here you find the white-and-yellow formation known as the **Castle**, which featured in the films *Mad Max III* and *Priscilla, Queen of the Desert*. Entry is subject to a permit ($2 per person)

which you can get from the tourist office or Underground Books.

You can make an interesting loop (70km of mainly unsealed road) from Coober Pedy taking in the Breakaways before following the Dog Fence along the Dog Fence track back to the Oodnadatta road. (The fence is supposed to keep dingoes to the north, away from the sheep.) Underground Books has a leaflet and 'mud map' ($1) – the route is generally OK for conventional vehicles.

MARLA (pop 250)

In the mulga scrub about 180km south of the Northern Territory border, Marla replaced Oodnadatta as the official regional centre when the Ghan railway line was re-routed in 1980. The rough-and-ready **Mintabie** opal field is on Aboriginal land 35km west – you need a permit ($5 from the Marla police station) to visit.

Fuel and provisions are available in Marla 24 hours a day; there's also an EFTPOS cash-withdrawal facility.

The *Marla Travellers Rest* (☎ 8670 7001) has camp sites for $5 per person (power $5 extra), basic air-con cabins sleeping two for $19/28 and spacious motel rooms from $59/65. There's a choice of takeaway, à la carte and restaurant meals.

On the Stuart Highway 85km south of Marla, *Cadney Homestead* (☎ 8670 7994) has camp sites for $6 per (power $5 extra), cabins without air-con sleeping two for $25 (linen extra) and motel rooms at $70/77.

If you're heading for Oodnadatta, turning off the highway at Cadney gives you a shorter run on dirt roads than the routes via Marla or Coober Pedy. You pass through the aptly named **Painted Desert** on the way – there are camp sites and cabins at *Copper Hills* homestead (☎ 8670 7995) about 32km east of Cadney. You can visit this interesting area weekdays on a day tour operated by the station. It costs $60 per person, lunch included, and requires a minimum of four people.

MARREE (pop 100)

On the rugged alternative road north through Oodnadatta, sleepy Marree was a staging post for the Afghani-led camel trains of the last century. There are still a couple of old date palms here, and an incongruously large pub.

Marree is at the southern end of the Birdsville Track, and has a good range of services including EFTPOS (in both minimarkets). The place really fires up during the **Marree Australian Camel Cup**, held on the first Saturday in July of odd-numbered years.

Ask at the Oasis Cafe about scenic flights over **Lake Eyre**.

Places to Stay

The *Oasis Caravan Park* (☎ 8675 8352) in the town centre has lawned camp sites from $5 per person, and self-contained cabins with air-con for $20 per person. Outside town at the turn-off to Birdsville, the somewhat dustier *Marree Tourist & Campers Park* (☎ 8675 8371) has camp sites from $5 per person, on-site vans for $25, a bunkhouse (no air-con) for $10 per person, and twin rooms with air-con for $12/20. There's a campers' kitchen, and you can get fuel here.

Alternatively, the grand old *Great Northern Hotel* (☎ 8675 8344) in the town centre has old-style pub rooms ranging from $25 for a single room to $80 for a family room. It has counter meals from $10.

WILLIAM CREEK (pop 10)

On the Oodnadatta Track about halfway between Oodnadatta and Marree, the quaint **William Creek Hotel** is a real old outback pub, with more character than you'll find in a host of Adelaide hotels. Ask here about scenic flights over nearby Lake Eyre.

The pub sells fuel and meals, and has rooms costing $30 per person with air-con and $12 without. Dusty camp sites cost $5 per person.

At **Coward Springs**, about 150km west of Marree (70km south of William Creek), is a small, very basic camp site with toilets and showers. You can do camel treks here in the cooler months, and there's a warm-water spa.

SOUTH AUSTRALIA

OODNADATTA (pop 150)

The tiny town of Oodnadatta (like Marree, it lost much of its population when the Old Ghan Railway closed down) is at the point where the road and the old railway line diverged.

One of the town's most distinctive features is the **Pink Roadhouse**, an excellent place to ask advice about track conditions and attractions in any direction. The owners, Adam and Lynnie Plate, have spent a great deal of time and effort putting in road signs and kilometre pegs over a huge area in this district – even in the Simpson Desert you'll come across signs erected by this dedicated pair! They have no doubt saved many a 4WD traveller hours of searching for the right track. The roadhouse is also the place to buy a permit if you intend camping at Dalhousie Springs.

The old train station has been converted into an interesting little **museum**. It is kept locked but pick up the key from the pub, store or roadhouse.

The local Aboriginal community owns the town's only pub and the general store.

Places to Stay

The *Oodnadatta Caravan Park* (☎ 8670 7822) attached to the Pink Roadhouse has plenty of accommodation including camp sites from $13, a self-contained backpacker cabin sleeping seven for $9 each, and basic motel-style rooms for $40. All units have air-con. The *Transcontinental Hotel* (☎ 86 70 78 04) has air-con singles/doubles with share facilities for $30/55. You can get meals at the pub (dinner only) and roadhouse.

BIRDSVILLE TRACK

Years ago cattle from the south-west of Queensland were walked down the Birdsville Track to Marree where they were loaded onto trains. Motor transport took over from the drovers in the 1960s and these days the cattle are trucked out in road trains. It's 520km between Marree and Birdsville, just across the border.

Although conventional vehicles can usually manage the track without difficulty, it's worth bearing in mind that traffic is anything but heavy – particularly in summer. Petrol, diesel and minor mechanical repairs are available at the **Mungeranie Roadhouse** (☎ 8675 8317), about 205km from Marree (315km from Birdsville). It also has camping, rooms and meals.

The track is more or less at the meeting point between the sand dunes of the Simpson Desert to the west and the desolate wastes of Sturt Stony Desert to the east. There are ruins of a couple of homesteads along the track and artesian bores gush out boiling-hot salty water at many places.

At Clifton Hill, about 200km south of Birdsville, the track splits with the main route going around the eastern side of Goyders Lagoon.

The last travellers to die on the track were a family of five. They took a wrong turning, got lost, ran out of petrol and perished from thirst.

STRZELECKI TRACK

These days the Strzelecki Track can be handled by conventional vehicles. It starts at Lyndhurst, about 80km south of Marree, and runs 460km to the tiny outpost of Innamincka. The discovery of natural gas deposits near Moomba has brought a great deal of development and improvement to the track, although the amount of heavy transport means the surface is often rough.

The new Moomba-Strzelecki Track is better kept but longer and less interesting than the old track, which follows the Strzelecki Creek. Accommodation, provisions and fuel are available at Lyndhurst and Innamincka, but there's nothing in between.

INNAMINCKA (pop 15)

At the northern end of the Strzelecki Track, Innamincka is on Cooper Creek, where the Burke and Wills expedition of 1860 came to its tragic and hopeless end. Near here is the famous **Dig Tree**, as well as the memorials and markers where Burke and Wills died and where King, the sole survivor, was found.

There is also a memorial where Howitt, who led the rescue party, set up his depot on the creek. The dig tree is actually across the border in Queensland. The word 'dig' is no longer visible, but the expedition's camp number can still be made out.

Cooper Creek flows only after heavy soaking rains fall over central Queensland, but there are permanent water holes. The area had a large Aboriginal population prior to white settlement, and relics such as middens and grinding stones are common.

Westprint's *Innamincka-Coongie Lakes* map is a good source of information on the Innamincka area. For a moving account of the Burke and Wills expedition, read Alan Moorehead's *Cooper's Creek*.

You can get fuel and provisions at the Innamincka Trading Post. The old **Australian Inland Mission hospital** now houses the NPWS ranger's office (☎ 8675 9909) and interpretive displays on the surrounding **Innamincka Regional Reserve**.

Places to Stay & Eat

The *Innamincka Hotel* (☎ 8675 9901) has motel-style rooms sleeping five for $40/60 (extra persons $10 each). It does takeaways and has counter meals in the evenings – its Wednesday night 'Beef-and-Creek' and Sunday night roasts are both good value at $10 for all you can eat.

The *Innamincka Trading Post* (☎ 8675 9900) has three very modest two-bedroom cabins sleeping up to four for $40/60/85/100.

There are plenty of good places to camp among the coolabahs along Cooper Creek, but there are no facilities whatsoever – see the ranger for a permit if you want to camp within the Innamincka Regional Reserve. For a donation to the Flying Doctor you can use the shower, toilet and laundry facilities (sorry, no washing machines here) outside the trading post.

THE GHAN

See the Northern Territory chapter for details of the famous Ghan railway line from Adelaide to Alice Springs.

Tasmania

Population: 474,600
Area: 67,800 sq km
Phone Area Code: ☎ 03

Locator &
Map Index

Launceston p 731
Central Launceston p 732

Devonport
p 744

North-West
p 749

Around Launceston
p 738

East Coast
p 723

The West
p 754

Hobart p 699
Central Hobart p 702

Tasman
Peninsula
p 718

South-East
Coast p 714

Highlights

- Trekking through Cradle Mountain-Lake St Clair – the world's last temperate wilderness area
- Exploring convict history among the ruins of Port Arthur
- Strolling along Hobart's waterfront and sipping a coffee at Salamanca Place
- Enjoying the hospitality and history of the sandstone garrison towns along the Midland Highway
- Dipping a toe in Wineglass Bay on the very beautiful Freycinet Peninsula
- Climbing the Nut and finding a fossil on Tassie's 'top end'

Tasmania is Australia's only island state and this has been a major influence on its historical, cultural and geographical development. Being an island, it was considered an ideal location for penal settlements, and convicts who re-offended on the Australian mainland were shipped here. Its isolation has also helped preserve its rich colonial heritage, and ensured that most of the state's wilderness areas (with a few notable exceptions) have remained relatively unspoiled.

The first European to see Tasmania was the Dutch navigator Abel Tasman, who arrived in 1642 and named it Van Diemen's Land, after the governor of the Dutch East Indies. In the 18th century, Tasmania was sighted and visited by a series of European sailors, including captains Tobias Furneaux, James Cook and William Bligh, all of whom believed it to be part of the Australian mainland.

European contact with the Tasmanian coast became more frequent after the soldiers and convicts of the First Fleet settled at Sydney Cove in 1788, mainly because ships heading to the colony of New South Wales from the west had to sail around the island.

In 1798 Lieutenant Matthew Flinders circumnavigated Van Diemen's Land, proving it to be an island. He named the rough stretch of sea between the island and the mainland Bass Strait, after George Bass, the ship's surgeon. The discovery of Bass Strait shortened the journey to Sydney from India or the Cape of Good Hope by a week.

In the late 1790s Governor King of New South Wales decided to establish a second colony in Australia, south of Sydney Cove. Port Phillip Bay in Victoria was considered, but a site on the Derwent River in Tasmania was finally chosen, and in 1804 Hobart Town was established. Although convicts were sent with the first settlers, penal settlements were not built until later: at Macquarie Harbour in 1821, at Maria Island in 1825 and at Port Arthur in 1832. For more than three decades, Van Diemen's Land was the most feared destination for British convicts.

In 1856 transportation to Van Diemen's Land was abolished and its first parliament was elected. Also in 1856, in an effort to escape the stigma of its dreadful penal reputation, Van Diemen's Land became officially known as Tasmania, after its first European visitor.

Reminders of the island's convict days and early colonial history are everywhere. There are the penal settlement ruins at Port Arthur, many convict-built bridges, a host of beautifully preserved Georgian sandstone buildings and more than 20 historic towns and villages classified by the National Trust.

Tasmania is also renowned world wide for its pristine wilderness areas and, during the last 20 or so years, for the pivotal role it has played in world environmental and conservation issues.

In the 1989 state elections, Tasmania's Green Independents gained 18% of the vote and held the balance of power in parliament until the 1992 election. Elections in 1996 resulted in a hung parliament, with the balance of power once again being held by the Greens. In 1997 parliament was debating the merits and methods of abolishing the outdated, non-democratic upper house, which is seen by many as a conservative-controlled handbrake on Tasmania's progress.

For background on the development of Tasmania's green movement as documented by many of the major players, read *The Rest of the World is Watching – Tasmania and the Greens*, edited by C Pybus & R Flanagan.

Hand colored lithograph;
Rex Nan Kivell collection, National Library of Australia

An example of 19th century colonial propaganda. The title of the illustration is incorrect: the proclamation was actually issued in 1829 by Governor Arthur. At this time soldiers were given the right to shoot on sight any Aboriginal person found in an area of European settlement.

ABORIGINAL PEOPLE

Since European settlement the story of Australia's Aboriginal people has not been a happy one, and nowhere has it been more tragic than in Tasmania.

Tasmania's Aboriginal people became separated from the mainland over 10,000 years ago when rising ocean levels, caused by the thawing of the last ice age, cut the area off from the rest of the continent. From that time on, their culture diverged from that of the mainland population, where the Aboriginal people developed more specialised tools for throwing, such as boomerangs, and spear-holders. In Tasmania the only throwing tools that were developed were a simple spear, a wooden waddie and stones. The Tasmanian Aboriginal people lived by hunting, fishing and gathering, sheltered in bark lean-tos and, despite Tasmania's cold weather, went naked apart from a coating of grease and charcoal. Their society was based on sharing and exchange – a concept with which the European invaders failed to come to terms.

European settlers found Tasmania fertile

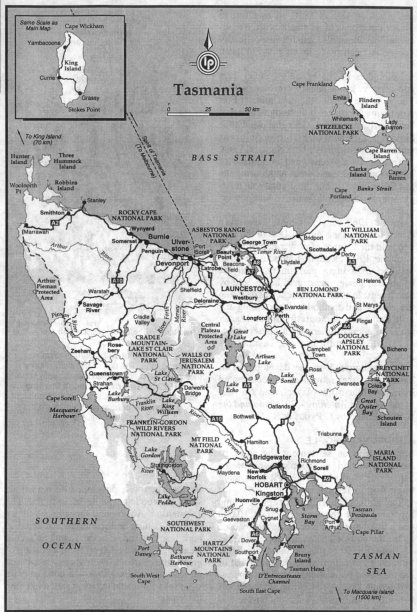

Same Scale as
Main Map
Cape Wickham

Yambacoona

King
Island

Currie

Grassy

Stokes Point

Tasmania

0   25   50 km

To King Island
(70 km)

Hunter
Island

Three
Hummock
Island

Woolnorth
Pt

Robbins
Island

Stanley

Smithton

Marrawah

A2

ROCKY CAPE
NATIONAL PARK

Wynyard

Somerset

Burnie

Penguin   Ulver-
            stone

Devonport

Latrobe

Port
Sorell

Beauty
Point

Beaconsfield

ASBESTOS RANGE
NATIONAL PARK

George Town

Tamar River

Bridport

Scottsdale

Lilydale

Derby

A3

MT WILLIAM
NATIONAL
PARK

Arthur

River

Waratah

Savage
River

Arthur
Pieman
Protected
Area

Pieman

River

Rosebery

Zeehan

Queenstown

Strahan

Lake
Burbury

Cape Sorell

Macquarie
Harbour

A10

Sheffield

Forth

River

Mersey

River

Cradle
Valley

CRADLE
MOUNTAIN-
LAKE ST CLAIR
NATIONAL
PARK

Lake
St Clair

Deloraine

A8

A7

LAUNCESTON

Westbury

Longford

Perth

Evandale

Central
Plateau
Protected
Area

Great
Lake

WALLS OF
JERUSALEM
NATIONAL
PARK

Arthurs
Lake

South Esk

Fingal

A4

Campbell
Town

St Helens

St Marys

BEN LOMOND
NATIONAL PARK

DOUGLAS
APSLEY
NATIONAL
PARK

Bicheno

Lake
Sorell

Macquarie

River

Ross

Lake
Echo

A5

Derwent
Bridge

Lake
King
William

Franklin
River

River

FRANKLIN-GORDON
WILD RIVERS
NATIONAL PARK

Lake
Gordon

Strathgordon

Gordon

River

Lake
Pedder

Bothwell

A10

Oatlands

Hamilton

MT FIELD
NATIONAL
PARK

Derwent

River

Maydena

New
Norfolk

Bridgewater

Richmond

Sorell

Triabunna

A3

Swansea

Coles
Bay

FREYCINET
NATIONAL
PARK

Great
Oyster
Bay

Schouten
Island

MARIA
ISLAND
NATIONAL
PARK

HOBART

Kingston

Huonville

Huon

River

Snug

Geeveston

Cygnet

Storm
Bay

A9

Port
Arthur

Tasman
Peninsula

Cape Pillar

SOUTHERN

OCEAN

A6

Dover

Southport

Alonnah

Bruny
Island

Tasman Head

SOUTHWEST
NATIONAL
PARK

HARTZ
MOUNTAINS
NATIONAL
PARK

Port
Davey

Bathurst
Harbour

South West
Cape

D'Entrecasteaux
Channel

South East Cape

*TASMAN
SEA*

To Macquarie Island
(1500 km)

BASS   STRAIT

Spirit of Tasmania
(To Melbourne)

Cape Frankland

Emita

Flinders
Island

Whitemark

Lady
Barron

STRZELECKI
NATIONAL PARK

Cape Barren
Island

Clarke
Island

Cape
Barren

Cape
Portland

Banks Strait

and fenced it off to make farms. As the Aboriginal people lost more and more of their traditional hunting grounds, they realised that the Europeans had come to steal their land, not share it, and began to fight for what was rightfully theirs. By 1806 the killing on both sides was out of control. Aboriginal people speared shepherds and their stock, and, in turn, were hunted and shot. Europeans abducted Aboriginal children to use as forced labour, raped and tortured Aboriginal women, gave poisoned flour to friendly tribes, and laid steel traps in the bush.

In 1828 martial law was proclaimed by Governor Arthur, giving soldiers the right to arrest or shoot on sight any Aboriginal person found in an area of European settlement. Finally, in an attempt to flush out all Aboriginal people and corner them on the Tasman Peninsula, a human chain known as the Black Line was formed by the settlers. This moved for three weeks through the settled region of the state and although it failed to round up the remaining aboriginal people it succeeded in driving the tribes from the settled districts and their traditional homeland.

Between 1829 and 1834 the remnants of this once proud and peaceful race were collected from all over the island and resettled in a reserve on Flinders Island – to be 'civilised' and Christianised. Most of them died of despair, homesickness, poor food or respiratory disease. Of the 135 who went to the island, only 47 survived to be transferred to Oyster Cove in 1847. It's hard to believe, but during those first 35 years of European settlement, 183 Europeans and nearly 4000 Aboriginal people were killed.

European sealers had been working in Bass Strait since 1798 and although they occasionally raided tribes along the coast, their contact with Aboriginal people was mainly based on trade. Aboriginal women were also traded and many sealers settled on the Bass Strait islands with these women and had families.

By 1847 a new Aboriginal community, with a lifestyle based on both Aboriginal and

Truganini, the last remaining full-blooded Tasmanian Aborigine, died in 1876 at Oyster Cove, an Aboriginal settlement where movement was restricted and rations insufficient.

European ways, had emerged on the Furneaux group of islands, saving the Tasmanian Aboriginal people from total extinction. Today there are more than 6500 of their descendants still living in Tasmania.

GEOGRAPHY
Although Tasmania is a small state, its geographical diversity ensures that it has something for everyone.

Tasmania's population is concentrated mainly on the north and south-east coasts, where the undulating countryside is rich and fertile. The coast and its bays are accessible and inviting, with attractive coves and beaches. In winter, the midlands region looks like a re-creation of the green England so beloved of early settlers, and the sparsely populated lakes country in the central highlands is serenely beautiful.

By contrast, the south-west and west coasts are amazingly wild and virtually untouched. For much of the year raging seas batter the the west coast and rainfall is high. Inland, the rich and divrse forests and the mountains of Tasmania's west and southwest form one of the world's last great wilderness areas, almost all of it made up of national parks, which have been listed as World Heritage regions.

INFORMATION
Tourist Offices
There are privately run Tasmanian Travel & Information Centres in Hobart, Launceston, Devonport and Burnie. On the mainland there are government-run Travel Centres in:

Australian Capital Territory
    165 City Walk, Canberra 2601 (☎ (02) 6209 2133)
New South Wales
    149 King St, Sydney 2000 (☎ (02) 9202 2022)
Queensland
    40 Queen St, Brisbane 4000 (☎ (07) 3405 4122)
South Australia
    32 King William St, Adelaide 5000 (☎ (08) 8400 5533)
Victoria
    256 Collins St, Melbourne 3000 (☎ (03) 9206 7933)

These travel centres have information on just about everything you need to know about Tasmania and are also able to book accommodation, tours and even airline, boat and bus tickets. The Department of Tourism publishes an invaluable free newspaper called *Tasmanian Travelways* which, along with feature articles, has comprehensive statewide listings of accommodation, activities, public transport, connecting transport facilities and vehicle hire, all with an indication of current costs.

The travel centres also stock a host of free tourist literature, including the monthly magazines *This Week in Tasmania* and *Treasure Islander* and the excellent *Let's Talk About...* leaflets, which provide in-depth information about particular towns and regions. The annual *Tasmania Visitors Guide*, which has a good fold-out touring map of Tasmania, is also free and particularly useful.

One of the best maps of the island is produced by the Royal Automobile Club of Tasmania (RACT) and costs $2. It's available from any Tasmanian Travel & Information Centre or RACT office.

Money
Automatic teller machines (ATMs) are not all that common outside Hobart, Launceston and major towns across the north coast, however many businesses across the state have EFTPOS, where you can pay for transactions directly from your bank account or credit card, and you can usually make cash withdrawals with the proviso that you also purchase something.

Accommodation
There's a good range of accommodation available in Tasmania, including youth hostels in most of the major towns and plenty of caravan parks, most of which have camp sites as well as on-site vans and en-suite cabins. Tasmania also has a wide selection of colonial accommodation – that is, places built prior to 1901 and decorated in a colonial style. Although a bit pricey ($70 to $100 for a double B&B), colonial accommodation is a great way to savour Tasmania's history, and can be a real treat for a couple of nights.

Despite the variety of places to stay, Tasmania's major tourist centres are often fully booked in summer, so it's wise to make reservations. While camping grounds, hostels and smaller hotels usually don't vary their prices significantly according to season, B&B and motel accommodation is at its most expensive in summer (principally the January holiday period) and most will have stand-by rates at other times of the year. Even if stand-by rates are not advertised, put your bargaining skills to use.

NATIONAL PARKS
Tasmania has set aside a greater percentage of its land as national park or scenic reserve than any other Australian state. In 1982, Tasmania's three largest national parks, Cradle Mountain-Lake St Clair, Franklin-Gordon Wild Rivers and South-West, along with much of the Central Plateau were placed on the UNESCO World Heritage List. This listing acknowledged that these parks comprise one of the last great temperate wilderness areas left in the world. Today, about 20% of Tasmania is World Heritage Area

protected from logging, hydroelectric power schemes and, with a few simple rules, ourselves.

An entry fee is charged for all of Tassie's national parks; a pass is needed whether there is a collection booth or not. There are a number of passes available. A one-day pass to any number of parks costs $9 per car or $3 per person. The best value for most will be the holiday pass which costs $30 per vehicle, or $12 per person for bushwalkers, cyclists and motorcyclists. This is valid for two months from the date of issue and provides entry into all parks. An annual pass ($42) for cars only is available at park entrances, from many bus and tour operators and from the national parks head office (☎ 6233 8011) at 134 Macquarie St, Hobart.

ACTIVITIES
Bushwalking
Tasmania, with its many national parks, has some of the finest bushwalks in Australia, the most well-known of which is the superb Cradle Mountain-Lake St Clair Overland Track. (See the Cradle Mountain-Lake St Clair section for more detail on this walk.)

Good books on the subject include *100 Walks in Tasmania* by Tyrone T Thomas, *South West Tasmania* by John Chapman, *Cradle Mountain Lake St Clair* by John Chapman & John Siseman, and Lonely Planet's *Bushwalking in Australia*, which has a large section on some of Tasmania's best walks.

On long walks, it's important to remember that in any season a fine day can quickly deteriorate into a blizzard become cold and stormy, so warm clothing, waterproof gear, a tent and compass are vital. The Department of Parks, Wildlife & Heritage publishes a booklet called *Welcome to the Wilderness – Bushwalking Trip Planner for Tasmania's World Heritage Area*, which has sections on planning, minimal-impact bushwalking and wilderness survival. Also included is a very useful equipment check list which is essential reading for bushwalkers who are unfamiliar with Tasmania's notoriously changeable weather.

If you write to the department at Main Post Office Box 44A, Hobart, or call ☎ 6233 6191, you'll be sent this booklet and other leaflets free of charge. You can also pick up all the department's literature from its head office at 134 Macquarie St, Hobart; from its northern regional office at Prospect Offices, Bass Highway, South Launceston; or from any rangers' office in the national parks.

The department also produces and sells an excellent series of maps; again, these can be sent for, or picked up, at outdoor-equipment stores, Wilderness Society shops and news-agencies throughout the state. The Tasmap Centre (☎ 6233 3382) is on the ground floor of the department's head office.

As bushwalking is so popular in Tasmania, there are many excellent shops selling bush gear, as well as several youth hostels which hire out equipment or take bushwalking tours. In the former category, Paddy Pallin in Hobart and Launceston, Allgoods in Launceston and the Backpackers' Barn in Devonport all have a very good range of bushwalking gear and plenty of invaluable advice (see the relevant sections for details).

See the sections on individual national parks for more information on Tasmania's walks.

Water Sports
Swimming The north and east coasts have many sheltered white-sand beaches which are excellent for swimming. On the west coast, however, there's some pretty ferocious surf and the beaches are unpatrolled.

Although there are some pleasant beaches near Hobart, such as Bellerive and Sandy Bay, these tend to be polluted so it's better to head towards Kingston, Blackmans Bay or Seven Mile Beach for safe swimming.

Surfing Tasmania has plenty of good surf beaches. Close to Hobart, the best spots are Clifton Beach and the surf beach en route to South Arm. The southern beaches of Bruny Island, particularly Cloudy Bay, are also good. The east coast from Bicheno north to St Helens has good surf when conditions are favourable. The greatest spot of all is

Marrawah on the west coast, though you'll need your own transport to get there.

Scuba Diving On the east coast and around King and Flinders islands there are some excellent scuba-diving opportunities. Equipment can be rented in Hobart, Launceston or on the east coast, and dive courses in Tasmania are considerably cheaper than those on the mainland.

Rafting & Canoeing Rafting, rowing and canoeing are all popular pastimes. The most challenging of rivers to raft is the Franklin (see the Franklin-Gordon Wild Rivers National Park section), although rafting trips are also organised on the Picton, upper Huon, Weld and Leven rivers. To book with a tour operator contact a Tasmanian Travel Centre, or to book direct see the *Tasmanian Travelways* outdoor adventure listings.

Fishing Fishing is another popular activity. Many of the rivers offer superb trout fishing, and the coastal waters are also good. A licence is required to fish in Tasmania's inland waters, and there are bag, season and size limits on a number of fish. Licences cost $40 for the full season, $22 for 14 days, $13 for three days and $8 for one day. They are available from many sports stores, post offices, and Tasmanian Travel & Information Centres and there are child and pensioner concessions.

In general, inland waters open for fishing on the Saturday closest to 1 August and close on the Sunday nearest 30 April. Different dates apply to some places: you can fish at the Great Lake until early June, while around Bradys Lake there is a very short season from November to March. There are many such exceptions and they are detailed in the *Fishing Code* brochure (see below). The lakes in the centre of the state – Arthurs Lake, Great Lake, Little Pine Lagoon (fly-fishing only), Western Lakes (including Lake St Clair), Lake Sorell and Lake Pedder – are the best-known spots for both brown and rainbow trout.

Saltwater fishing is allowed all year

without a permit although size restrictions and bag limits apply. For more information contact the Tasmanian Inland Fisheries Commission (☎ 6223 6622), 127 Davey St, Hobart and ask for a current *Fishing Code* brochure.

Caving

Tasmania's caves are regarded as being some of the most impressive in Australia. The caves at Mole Creek and Hastings are open daily to the public but gems such as the Kubla Khan and Croesus caves (near Mole Creek) and the extremely large Exit Cave are only accessible to experienced cavers. Most caves are locked; to enter them you must apply for a permit through your speleological club or association .

Skiing

There are two minor ski resorts in Tasmania: Ben Lomond, 60km from Launceston; and Mt Mawson, in Mt Field National Park. Both offer cheaper, although less-developed, ski facilities than the major resorts in Victoria and New South Wales, but despite the state's southerly latitude, snowfalls tend to be fairly light and unreliable. For more information see the sections on the Ben Lomond and Mt Field national parks.

GETTING THERE & AWAY
Air

The airlines that fly to Tassie are Ansett (☎ 13 1300), Qantas and its subsidiary Southern Australia Airlines (☎ 13 1313), Kendell (☎ 13 1300), Island Airlines (☎ 1800 818 455), Aus-Air (☎ 9580 6166, Melbourne; ☎ 1800 331 256, Tasmania), King Island Airlines (☎ 9580 3777) and Phillip Island Air Services (☎ 5956 7316).

International flights also operate direct from Christchurch in New Zealand to Hobart. Both Qantas and Air New Zealand operate this route with return fares ranging from $576 to $1042 depending on the season and booking conditions.

Ansett and Qantas have flights to Tasmania from most Australian state capitals, while the other airlines operate from various airports in

Victoria. Most flights are to Hobart, Launceston, Devonport, Wynyard (Burnie), Smithton, Flinders Island or King Island.

Air fares to Tasmania are constantly changing, but because of the number of operators, prices are competitive and you can get some good deals – especially if you book well in advance or if you are planning a trip in the winter months. In addition, students under 25 years can get some good discounts on fares with the larger airlines.

To/From Hobart The standard one-way economy fare from Melbourne is $226 with Ansett and Qantas, although much cheaper fares are often available (about $240 return, or even less depending on the flight). From Sydney the standard one-way fare is $327 (rock-bottom return $269) and from Brisbane $443 (rock-bottom return $409).

To/From Launceston Ansett and Qantas fly from Melbourne for $196 one way, but it's around $220 return if you book well in advance. The smaller airlines flying out of Melbourne generally use the city's second-string airports (Essendon and Moorabbin) and have lower base rates but offer fewer discounts. Island Airlines and Aus-Air fly from Traralgon to Launceston via Flinders Island for $184 and $175, respectively. If you wanted to stay on Flinders for a few days you would need to pay for the individual sectors which, depending on the season and type of ticket, could cost substantially more.

To/From Devonport & Wynyard (Burnie) There are flights from Melbourne to Devonport and Burnie with Kendell Airlines ($192 and $178 respectively) and Aus-Air ($165 and $154). Phillip Island Air Services flies to Burnie for $105 one way.

To/From Other Destinations Aus-Air and Kendell Airlines fly to King Island. Aus-Air and Island Airlines also fly to Flinders Island. Fewer discounts are available to these destinations and, as you will need accommodation, the best deal is to buy a fly-drive package (which includes accommodation).

See the Bass Strait Islands section at the end of this chapter for details.

Bus
From most parts of central and eastern Australia, McCafferty's (☎ 13 1499) can get you to Melbourne, organise transfer to the ferry and the ferry booking, as well as the Tassie Wilderness Pass which uses Redline and Tasmanian Wilderness Travel buses.

Boat
The *Spirit of Tasmania*, which operates between Melbourne and Devonport, can accommodate 1300 passengers and over 600 vehicles. It has nine decks and, with its swimming pool, saunas, restaurant, gaming machines and bars, is more like a floating hotel than a ferry. The public areas of the ship have been designed to cater for wheelchair access, and four cabins have been specially designed for this purpose.

It departs from the TT-Line terminal (☎ 13 2010) at Melbourne's Station Pier on Monday, Wednesday and Friday at 6 pm and from the terminal on the Esplanade in Devonport on Saturday, Tuesday and Thursday at 6 pm, arriving 14½ hours later, at 8.30 am. An additional sailing is scheduled for the December/January holiday period: it leaves Melbourne on Sunday at 9 am and Devonport on Monday at 2 am. There is also a slight adjustment to the usual timetable to fit in the extra sailing.

Fares depend on whether you're travelling in the peak holiday (roughly December-January), shoulder (February-April and October-November) or off peak (May to September) season. Contact TT-Line for precise dates. One-way fares range from $103 ($132 peak season) in hostel-style accommodation (20-bed cabins) up to $225 for suites ($308 peak season). Student, pensioner and child discounts apply to cabins but not to hostel-style accommodation. All fares include an evening buffet dinner and continental breakfast, but you can also choose to eat (and pay) at the more formal restaurant.

The cost for accompanied vehicles

depends on the size of the vehicle and is currently subsidised by a federal government rebate. The minimum one-way rate is $30 ($40 peak season) for cars, while motorcycles cost $25 ($30) and bicycles $20 ($25).

Devil Cat, a large wave-piercing catamaran, started operating in the summer of 1997-98 and the plan is for this to be a permanent summer service. The details here are subject to alteration so contact the Tasmanian Travel Information Centre in Melbourne (☎ 9206 7933) or TT-Line (☎ 132 0101) for the latest information. The peak season is from 17 December to 24 January when a one-way fare costs $150, car $40 and bicycle $25. The shoulder season is from 25 January to 18 April when the one-way fare will be $136, car $30 and bicycle $20. The cat departs from Station Pier in Port Melbourne on Tuesday, Thursday and Saturday at 1 pm, arriving at George Town at about 7 pm. The return voyages leave George Town on Wednesday, Friday and Sunday, again at 1 pm arriving about 7 pm.

GETTING AROUND
Air
Tas Air (☎ 6248 5577)) and Par Avion

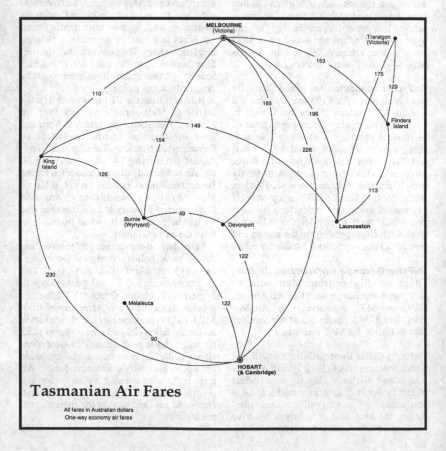

Tasmanian Air Fares

All fares in Australian dollars
One-way economy air fares

(☎ 6248 5390), based at Cambridge airport about 15km east of the city centre, operate passenger and charter flights between most rural centres. Tas Air flies regularly between Hobart and Burnie, and Devonport and King Island (see the air fare chart). Par Avion flies bushwalkers to Melaleuca, or a group of five can charter a twin engine to Launceston for $490.

Bus

Tasmania has a good bus network connecting all major towns and centres, but weekend services are infrequent and this can be inconvenient for the traveller with only a limited amount of time in the state. There are more buses in summer than in winter.

The main bus companies are Tasmanian Redline Coaches (☎ 1300 360 000), Hobart Coaches (☎ 1800 030 620), and Tasmanian Wilderness Travel/Tigerline(☎ 1300 300 520, or 6334 4442), and they cover most of the state between them. All three have depots in the major centres of Hobart, Launceston and Devonport as well as agents in the stopover towns.

The companies have their own special passes; you can't use a Greyhound Pioneer Aussie Pass in Tasmania, but McCafferty's (see Getting There & Away – Bus) can organise the Tassie Wilderness Pass as long as you book at least one sector of its mainland service. Redline, in conjunction with Tasmanian Wilderness Travel, also has the Tassie Wilderness Pass, for seven, 14 or 30 days, which gives you unrestricted travel on all its routes for $99, $149 or $199 respectively. The number of days refers to travel days only and the pass is valid for a slightly longer period. Also, extra travel days can be bought for about $10 per day.

If you are considering buying any of these passes, don't forget to check the weekend timetables. You will need to plan your trip carefully to make these passes worthwhile. *Tasmanian Travelways* has details of timetables and fares for major routes. These passes can also be bought in advance on the mainland from Tasmanian Travel Centres or in Tasmania at information centres, bus depots and agencies. To give you some idea of the costs, a one-way trip between Hobart and Launceston costs about $19, between Hobart and Queenstown $35 and between Launceston and Bicheno $21.

Train

There are no passenger rail services in Tasmania, which probably accounts for the number of railway models, displays and exhibitions in the state!

Car & Campervan

Although you can bring cars from the mainland to Tasmania, it might work out cheaper to rent one for your visit, particularly if your stay is a short one. Tasmania has a wide range of national and local car-rental agencies, and the rates (along with parking fines) are considerably lower than on the mainland.

Tasmanian Travelways lists many of the rental options, but before you decide on a company, don't forget to ask about any kilometre limitations and find out what the insurance covers. Also ensure that there are no hidden seasonal adjustments. It is, however, quite normal for smaller rental companies to ask for a bond of around $200.

Large national firms such as Avis, Budget and Autorent-Hertz have standard rates for cars, from about $60 per day. By booking in advance and choosing smaller cars, rates can be as low as $40 per day for one-week hire (outside holiday season). In summer, daily rates are generally higher at around $50 to $60 for multi-day hire of a small car.

Small local firms such as Advance Car Rentals, which has offices in Hobart, Launceston, Devonport and St Helens, charge from $32 a day, but with varied conditions. Tasmania also has a number of companies renting older cars such as VW beetles from $25 a day. In this bracket Rent-a-Bug, with offices in Hobart and Devonport, has a good reputation. See the individual Getting There & Away entries for specific locations for more information. The larger firms have offices at the airports and docks; if you book in advance, most smaller companies can arrange for you to collect your car at point of arrival.

Tasmanian Travelways also has a listing of campervan rental companies. Of the larger national firms only Autorent-Hertz has campervans, starting at about $700 a week. Savings can be made by going to the smaller operators but must be weighed against the rental conditions and general condition of the vehicle – make sure you are familiar and confident with both before you sign.

Warning While driving around the state watch out for the wildlife, which all too often ends up flattened on the roadside. If possible, avoid driving between dusk and dawn as this is when marsupials are most active. Also be wary of 'black ice', an invisible layer of ice over the bitumen, especially on the shaded side of mountain passes. A startlingly high number of single vehicle accidents occur every year due, in part, to the large number of international and interstate drivers not familiar with Tasmanian driving conditions.

Hitching
Travel by thumb in Tassie is generally good, but wrap up in winter and keep a raincoat handy. A good number of the state's roads are still unsurfaced and the traffic can be very light, so although these roads often lead to interesting places, you normally have to give them a miss if you're hitching.

Bicycle
Tasmania is a good size for exploring by bicycle and you can hire bikes throughout the state. If you plan to cycle between Hobart and Launceston via either coast, count on it taking around 10 to 14 days. For a full circuit of the island, you should allow 14 to 28 days. Get a copy of *Bicycling Tasmania* by Ian Terry & Rob Beedham to help plan your trip.

Rent-a-Cycle at the Launceston City Youth Hostel has a good variety of touring and mountain bikes plus all the equipment you'll need for short or long trips. You should be able to hire a bike for between $12 and $16 a day or $65 and $95 a week. If you're planning an extended ride it's worth considering buying a bike and selling it at the end.

If you bring a bike over on the *Spirit of Tasmania* it will cost you $20 to $25 each way, depending on the season. By air, Ansett and Qantas charge $10 to carry a bicycle one way to Hobart or Launceston. It's easier to get your bike over to Tassie on flights to Hobart or Launceston than on those to smaller airports such as Burnie or Devonport.

Hobart

• *Pop 126,000*

Hobart is Australia's second-oldest city and its southernmost capital. Straddling the mouth of the Derwent River and backed by towering Mt Wellington, which offers fine views over the city, Hobart has managed to combine the benefits of a modern city with a rich colonial heritage and a serene natural beauty. The beautiful Georgian buildings, the busy harbour and the easy-going atmosphere all make Hobart one of the most enjoyable and engaging of Australia's cities.

The first inhabitants of the area were the Aboriginal Mouheneer tribe who lived a semi-nomadic lifestyle. The first European colony in Tasmania was founded in 1803 at Risdon Cove, but a year later Lieutenant-Colonel David Collins, governor of the new settlement in Van Diemen's Land, sailed down the Derwent River and decided that a cove about 10km below Risdon and on the opposite shore was a better place to settle. This became the site of Tasmania's future capital city and began as a village of tents and wattle-and-daub huts with a population of 262 (178 of whom were convicts).

Hobart Town, as it was known until 1881, was proclaimed a city in 1842. Very important to its development was the Derwent River estuary, one of the world's finest deepwater harbours, and many merchants made their fortunes from the whaling trade, shipbuilding and the export of products such as merino wool and corn.

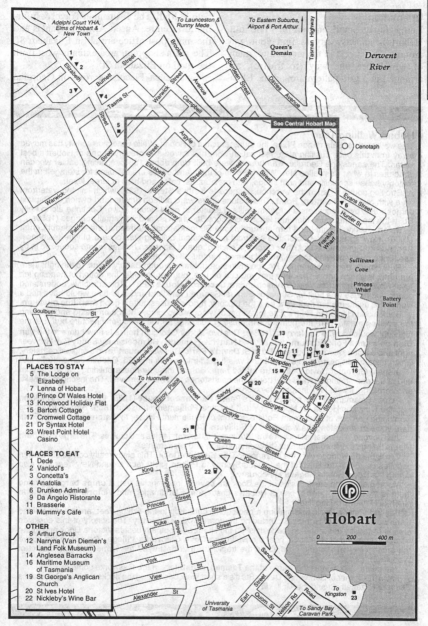

See Central Hobart Map

Cenotaph

Derwent River

Queen's Domain

To Launceston & Runny Mede

To Eastern Suburbs, Airport & Port Arthur

Adelphi Court YHA, Elms of Hobart & New Town

Sullivans Cove

Princes Wharf

Battery Point

To Huonville

To Kingston

To Sandy Bay Caravan Park

University of Tasmania

Hobart

0   200   400 m

PLACES TO STAY
5   The Lodge on Elizabeth
7   Lenna of Hobart
10 Prince Of Wales Hotel
13 Knopwood Holiday Flat
15 Barton Cottage
17 Cromwell Cottage
21 Dr Syntax Hotel
23 Wrest Point Hotel Casino

PLACES TO EAT
1   Dede
2   Vanidol's
3   Concetta's
4   Anatolia
6   Drunken Admiral
9   Da Angelo Ristorante
11 Brasserie
18 Mummy's Cafe

OTHER
8   Arthur Circus
12 Narryna (Van Diemen's Land Folk Museum)
14 Anglesea Barracks
16 Maritime Museum of Tasmania
19 St George's Anglican Church
20 St Ives Hotel
22 Nickleby's Wine Bar

Orientation

Being fairly small and simply laid out, Hobart is an easy city to find your way around. The streets in the city centre, many of which are one way (to traffic), are arranged in a grid pattern around the Eliza-beth St Mall. The Tasmanian Travel & Information Centre, Ansett Airlines, Qantas and the main post office are all in Elizabeth St. The main shopping area extends west from the mall on Elizabeth St.

Salamanca Place, the row of Georgian

Hobart Walking Tour

This walk starts at **Salamanca Place**, the tourist precinct of Hobart. While waterside activity has moved away from this once bustling area, restoration work has saved and preserved one of Hobart's best vistas. The sandstone Georgian warehouses were built from about 1835, replacing earlier wooden structures in what was called New Wharf. Some of the warehouses are still used for storage but the majority house speciality and craft shops, with restaurants, cafes and bars at street level.

Strolling south, a gap in the warehouses leads to **Kelly's Steps** (1839), which link the waterfront area with residential **Battery Point**. These stone stairs were built on private land owned by Captain James Kelly, by all accounts a larger-than-life character in early Hobart Town. Continue along Kelly St, at the top of the stairs, then turn left at McGregor St, which is lined with small cottages (1850s).

Before making a right-hand turn at Runnymede St, look across the road at the wonderful **Lenna** (1880). Now an upmarket hotel, this splendid neoclassical building was once a private residence. Continue up Runnymede to **Arthur Circus**, a circle of quaint Georgian houses (some squeezed in by sacrificing plenty of living space) around a small, central village green.

Runnymede ends at Hampden Rd, the main thoroughfare through Battery Point. To the right there are antique shops and restaurants that you can peruse, but first consider the option of heading left and following narrow Secheron Rd which ends at **Secheron House** (1831). This attractive, understated sandstone house was built for Surveyor General George Frankland and in its time would have had a wonderful, uninterrupted river view from the balcony. It now houses quite a good **maritime museum.**

Back along Hampden Rd it's time for a spot of window shopping, antique browsing and planning the evening meal. There are numerous interesting buildings for the period-architecture buff, but the highlight would have to be **Narryna** (1834). This two-storey Georgian house is now home to the **Van Diemen's Land Folk Museum**. Just beyond Narryna, Hampden Rd meets busy Sandy Bay Rd; veer right and continue along Sandy Bay Rd to **St David's Park.** This was Hobart Town's original cemetery, which became an overgrown eyesore and was turned into a park in 1926. Captain James Kelly and Lieutenant Governor David Collins are buried here. Behind the courthouse buildings, at the bottom end of the park, retaining walls now house the headstones that were removed. The inscriptions make an interesting, if sobering, insight into colonial life.

Across Salamanca Place from St David's Park is **Parliament House** (1835). Originally, this building was the Customs House for Hobart Town. It became Parliament House in 1856. Stroll through the manicured gardens of Parliament Square, in front of Parliament House, to **Waterman's Dock**. From here you can walk along the waterfront of **Sullivans Cove.**

Just beyond Waterman's Dock are the terminals for harbour ferries and cruises. The large **Elizabeth Pier** is being converted to upmarket accommodation and restaurants.

Cross the drawbridge over the entrance to **Constitution Dock**. This place really comes alive when yachties celebrate the finish of the famous Sydney to Hobart yacht race around New Year and also during the Royal Hobart Regatta in February.

Moored along the eastern side of the dock are several inexpensive **fish & chips barges**, behind them is **Mures Fish Centre**, one of Hobart's gastronomic landmarks, and **Victoria Dock**, home to much of Hobart's fishing fleet.

Beyond Victoria Dock, and making a photogenic backdrop to the fishing fleet, are the dilapidated warehouses (1836) of **Hunter St**, including the former IXL jam factory. The history of this dockside area is pictorially described on 'pedestals' on the Hunter St footpath beside Victoria Dock and at the north-eastern end of Hunter St, near the **Sullivans Cove Gasworks Village.** You can stand above the archaeological site and read about the tragic fire that destroyed the former red-light district of Wapping.

You might also sample the wares at the **Tasmania Distillery** in the Gasworks complex.

From the corner of Hunter and Davey Sts it's a short walk back along the docks to either Salamanca Place or Elizabeth St and the Mall. ∎

warehouses, is along the waterfront, while just south of this is Battery Point, Hobart's delightful, well-preserved early colonial district. If you follow the river around from Battery Point you'll come to Sandy Bay, the site of Hobart's university and the Wrest Point Hotel Casino – one of Hobart's main landmarks.

The northern side of the centre is bounded by the recreation area known locally as the Domain (short for the Queen's Domain), which includes the Royal Tasmanian Botanical Gardens and the Derwent River. From here the Tasman Bridge crosses the river to the eastern suburbs and the airport.

Maps For road maps of the state and Hobart go to the Travel & Information Centre on the corner of Elizabeth and Davey Sts. For more specific needs, such as topographic maps or marine charts, try the Tasmap Centre in the Lands Building at 134 Macquarie St or the Tasmanian Map Centre at 96 Elizabeth St.

Information

Tourist Office The Tasmanian Travel & Information Centre (☎ 6230 8233) on the corner of Davey and Elizabeth Sts is open weekdays from 8.30 am to 5.15 pm, from 9 am to 4 pm on Saturday and public holidays, and from 9 am to 1 pm on Sunday.

If you have an FM radio, you can pick up tourist information broadcast on 88 MHz within a 6km radius of the city centre.

Post The main post office is in the centre of the city, on the corner of Elizabeth and Macquarie Sts.

Other Services The Tasmanian YHA office (☎ 6234 9617) is at 28 Criterion St and is open Monday to Friday from 9 am to 5 pm. The Royal Automobile Club of Tasmania (RACT; ☎ 13 1111) is on the corner of Murray and Patrick Sts.

The Wilderness Society's head office (☎ 6234 9366) is at 130 Davey St and its shop is in the Galleria, Salamanca Place; the National Trust shop is in the same arcade.

For information about national parks go to the Lands Information Bureau Sales Centre at 134 Macquarie St. If your travel pack is haemorrhaging, or you're having trouble with your zipper, go to Luggage Repairs at 149a Liverpool St.

Bookshops Angus & Robinson in the Elizabeth St mall will cover general needs. The Tasmanian Map Centre specialises in guide books and travel literature. Recent publications relating to green issues can be found at the Wilderness Society's shop (see Other Services); and if you're after a first edition of an old classic or an out-of-print book on Tasmania go to Astrolabe Books at 81 Salamanca Place.

Historic Buildings

One of the things that makes Hobart so unusual among Australian cities is its wealth of old and remarkably well-preserved buildings. There are more than 90 buildings in Hobart that are classified by the National Trust and 60 of these, featuring some of Hobart's best Georgian architecture, are in Macquarie and Davey Sts. An excellent booklet on both new and old buildings, *An Architectural Guide to the City of Hobart*, is available from the National Trust for $3.20.

Close to the city centre is **St David's Park**, which was the site of the budding colony's cemetery. After years of neglect it was 'recycled' and gravestones dating from the earliest days of the colony were mounted into retaining walls. The inscriptions provide a powerful reminder of the harshness of colonial life. In Murray St is **Parliament House**, which was originally a customs house. Hobart's prestigious **Theatre Royal** at 29 Campbell St was built in 1837 and is the oldest theatre in Australia.

There's a **royal tennis court** in Davey St, one of only three in the southern hemisphere, which you can look into on the National Trust's Saturday morning tour – see the following Organised Tours & Cruises section for details. (Royal or 'real' tennis is an ancient form of tennis played in a four-walled indoor court.) The historic **Penitentiary Chapel & Criminal Courts** are at 28 Campbell St; the National Trust runs daily tours of the buildings between 10 am and 2 pm ($6/3 adults/children) and there are ghost tours at 8 pm ($7/4).

Runnymede, 61 Bay Rd, New Town, is a gracious colonial residence dating from the early 1830s. It was built for Robert Pitcairn, the first lawyer to qualify in Tasmania and a leading advocate for the abolition of transportation of convicts. Now managed by the National Trust, it is open daily from 10 am to 4.30 pm ($5). To get there take bus No 15

or 16 from the corner of Argyle and Macquarie Sts.

Salamanca Place
The row of beautiful sandstone warehouses on the harbour front at Salamanca Place is a prime example of Australian colonial architecture. Dating back to the whaling days of the 1830s, these warehouses were the centre of Hobart Town's trade and commerce. Today they have been tastefully developed to house galleries, restaurants, nightspots and shops selling everything from vegetables to antiques. Every Saturday morning a

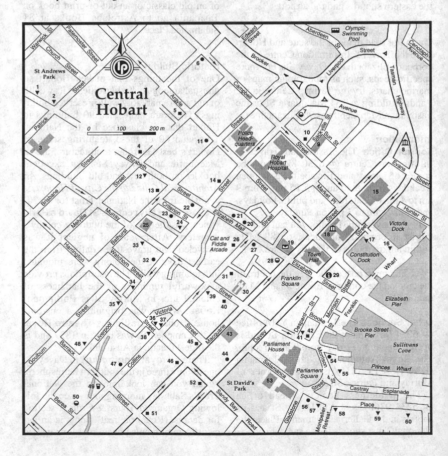

popular open-air **market** is held at Salamanca Place.

Battery Point

Behind Princes Wharf is the historic core of Hobart, the old port area known as Battery Point. Its name comes from the gun battery that stood on the promontory by the guardhouse (1818). During colonial times this area was a colourful maritime village, home to master mariners, shipwrights, sailors, fishermen, coopers and merchants.

Don't miss **Arthur Circus** – a small circle of quaint cottages built around a village green – or **St George's Anglican Church**. To help you navigate, pick up a copy of the *Battery Point and Sullivans Cove Tourist Trail* ($1) from the visitor centre.

Van Diemen's Land Folk Museum The oldest folk museum in Australia is housed in

Narryna, a fine Georgian home at 103 Hampden Rd, Battery Point. Dating from 1836, it stands in beautiful grounds and has a large and fascinating collection of relics from Tasmania's early pioneering days. It's open Tuesday to Friday from 10 am to 5 pm and at weekends from 2 to 5 pm ($5/2).

Maritime Museum of Tasmania Secheron House in Secheron Rd Battery Point, was built in 1831 and is classified by the National Trust. It now houses the fascinating Maritime Museum, which has an extensive collection of photos, paintings, models and relics depicting Tasmania's, and particularly Hobart's, colourful shipping history. It's open daily from 10 am to 4.30 pm ($4).

Tasmanian Museum & Art Gallery
The excellent Tasmanian Museum & Art Gallery at 5 Argyle St (enter via Macquarie

PLACES TO STAY		
4	Black Prince Hotel	
5	Ocean Child Hotel	
10	Theatre Royal Hotel	
15	Hotel Grand Chancellor	
13	New Sydney Hotel	
14	Brunswick Hotel	
26	Ship Hotel	
31	Central City Backpackers	
40	Country Comfort Hadleys Hotel	
42	Customs House Hotel	
45	Astor Private Hotel	
46	Hobart Macquarie Motor Inn	
51	Duke Backpackers and Hotel	
52	Freemasons Hotel	

PLACES TO EAT		
1	Kaos Cafe	
2	Trattoria Casablanca	
12	Golden Bamboo	
16	Mures Fish Centre	
17	Floating Seafood Stalls	
24	Kafe Kara	
33	Tatts	
34	Hara Cafe	
35	Shamrock Hotel	

36	Cafe Toulouse	
37	Orient Express; Seoul Korean Restaurant	
38	Little Bali; Little Salama	
39	Little Italy	
41	Areeba! Mexican Restaurant	
48	Cafe Who	
55	Sisco's on the Pier	
57	Retro Cafe	
58	Maldini; Knopwood's Retreat Bar	
59	Mr Wooby's	
60	Ball & Chain Grill; Mikaku; Panache Restaurants	

OTHER		
3	RACT	
6	National Trust; Penitentiary Chapel & Criminal Courts	
7	Hobart Coaches	
8	Sullivan's Cove Gasworks Village	
9	Theatre Royal	
11	Tasmanian Map Centre	

18	Tasmanian Museum & Art Gallery	
19	Post Office	
20	Ansett	
21	Qantas	
22	Paddy Pallin	
23	Tasmanian YHA Office	
25	State Library	
27	Angus & Robertson Bookshop	
28	Metro City Bus Station	
29	Travel & Information Centre	
30	St David's Cathedral	
32	Luggage Repairs	
43	Tasmap & National Parks Offices	
44	Royal Tennis Court	
47	Village Cinema	
49	Cornish Mount Tavern	
50	Redline Coaches; Transit Centre Backpackers	
53	Supreme Court	
54	Harley Tours of Hobart	
56	Galleria & National Trust Shop	

St) incorporates Hobart's oldest building, the Commissariat Store (1808). The museum section features a Tasmanian Aboriginal display and relics from the state's colonial heritage, while the gallery has a good collection of Tasmanian colonial art. Entry is free and it's open daily from 10 am to 5 pm. There are free guided tours of the museum Wednesday to Sunday at 2.30 pm.

Anglesea Barracks

Built in 1811, this is the oldest military establishment in Australia still used by the army. The entrance is off Davey St. On Tuesday at 11 am there is a guided tour of the Military Museum of Tasmania and the grounds ($2). In summer there is an additional tour on Saturday at 1.30 pm.

Cascade Brewery

Australia's oldest brewery, on Cascade Rd close to the city centre, is still in use and produces some of the finest beer in the country – although no doubt others would argue differently! There are two-hour tours daily at 9.30 am and 1 pm ($7); bookings are essential (☎ 6224 1144). The brewery is on the south-western edge of the city centre; bus Nos 44, 46 and 49 go right by it – alight at stop 18.

Risdon Cove

This is the site of the first European settlement in Tasmania and is definitely worth a visit. It's on the eastern shore of the Derwent about 10km from the city. To get there take a No 68 bus from the Eastlands Shopping Centre, Rosny Park; entry is free.

Other Attractions

The **Allport Library & Museum of Fine Arts** is based in the State Library at 91 Murray St. It has a collection of rare books on Australasia and the Pacific region and you can visit on weekdays from 9.30 am to 5 pm (free).

Other museums include the **John Elliott Classics Museum** at the University of Tasmania (open weekdays only from February to November; free) and the **Tasmanian**

Transport Museum in Glenorchy (weekends only, 1 to 4 pm; $3). Australia's first public museum, the **Lady Franklin Gallery**, is in Lenah Valley Rd (weekends only, 1.30 to 4.30 pm; free).

Just by the Tasman Bridge are the **Royal Tasmanian Botanical Gardens**, which are open from 8 am to 4.45 pm daily; free. They are very pleasant and definitely worth a visit, as is the nearby bushland reserve called the **Queen's Domain**.

Hobart is dominated by 1270m-high **Mt Wellington** which has many fine views and interesting walking tracks. The *Mt Wellington Walks* map has all details. To get there (without taking a tour), take bus No 48 or 49 from Franklin Square in Elizabeth St; it will take you to Fern Tree at the base of the mountain, but from there it's a 13km walk to the top!

There are also good views from the **Old Signal Station** on Mt Nelson, above Sandy Bay.

Organised Tours & Cruises

Several boat cruise companies operate from the Brooke St Pier and Franklin Wharf and offer a variety of cruises in and around the harbour. One of the most popular is the four-hour Cadbury's Cruise, run by the Cruise Company (☎ 6234 9294), which costs $33 (children $16). Leaving at 10 am on weekdays you do a slow return cruise to the Cadbury Schweppes factory in Claremont where you disembark and tour the premises (this is a good place to stock up on chocolate if you are planning any bushwalking).

Cruise timetables are pretty changeable as they depend on tides and seasons so it is best to book. Harbour cruises are also available and vary from one to three hours. The daily lunch cruise ($20) is good value.

There's a Saturday morning walking tour concentrating on the historic Battery Point area and departing from the wishing well in Franklin Square at 9.30 am ($5) – you don't have to book, just turn up. During summer, twilight walks are held along the waterfront starting at 6.30 pm ($8.50). You must book earlier in the day at the information centre in Elizabeth St.

Day and half-day bus tours in and around Hobart are operated by Redline and Tigerline. Typical half-day tours include trips to Richmond ($20), the City Sights and Mt Wellington ($23). Full-day tour destinations include Port Arthur ($40), the Huon Valley ($45) and Maria Island ($43). Tasmanian Wilderness Travel also runs day and two-day excursions to places such as Mt Field National Park ($39) and Cradle Mountain ($75).

For something different try Harley Tours of Hobart (☎ 6224 1565) offering a ride around Hobart in a Harley Davidson sidecar. They operate from the waterfront and rides start from $15.

Scenic flights are run by Par Avion (☎ 6248 5390) and Tas Air (☎ 6248 5577) from Cambridge airport, 15km from the city. Flight prices start from $60 per person for 30 minutes. Par Avion offers tours to the South West: half-day tours ($140) include return flight, boat tour and morning or afternoon tea; full day tours ($240) include return flight, boat and walking tours and a gourmet lunch.

Special Events

Hobart's premier festival is the Hobart Summer Festival (28 December to 31 January), featuring Taste of Tasmania, a Tasmanian food and wine extravaganza on the waterfront. The grazing, quaffing and entertainment lasts from 28 December to 3 January, coinciding with the party atmosphere generated by the spectators and celebrating yachties at the finish of the annual Sydney to Hobart Yacht Race.

The Royal Hobart Regatta, in early February, is a major four-day aquatic carnival with boat races and other activities. The last day of the carnival, a Monday, is a public holiday and almost the entire town closes down.

Places to Stay

Camping The handiest camping ground is the *Sandy Bay Caravan Park* (☎ 6225 1264),

less than 3km from the city at 1 Peel St, Sandy Bay. It charges $12 a double for a camp site, while on-site vans are $32 a double and cabins $50. To get there, take Metro bus No 54, 55 or 56 from stop D in Elizabeth St near the main post office. There are also parks a little further out at Elwick and Berriedale (north of the city) and at Mornington (in the eastern suburbs).

Hostels Right in the centre of town is the *Central City Backpackers* (☎ 6224 2404) at 138 Collins St. It's a rambling place with excellent facilities and friendly staff. There are spacious communal areas including a bar, as well as a laundry and individual safe-deposit boxes. The cost is $14 for a bed in a six-bed dorm, $16 in a three or four-bed dorm, $19 per person in a twin-share or double room, and $30 for a single room. Security is good here and it's clean and quiet.

At the Redline bus depot at 199 Collins St is the *Transit Centre Backpackers* (☎ 6231 2400). It has beds for $12 per night and all facilities. The communal area is very large and it's a quiet place. It is open from 9 am to 11 pm (later if Redline informs them of a delayed bus); just press the buzzer at the front door which is kept locked for security.

A number of hotels in the city centre offer backpacker accommodation. They can be noisy and smoky depending on the bar scene downstairs. The *New Sydney Hotel* (☎ 6234 4516) is at 87 Bathurst St, the *Ship Hotel* (☎ 6234 4419) is at 73 Collins St, near the mall, and the *Ocean Child Hotel* can be found on the corner of Argyle and Melville Sts. All charge $12 for basic facilities and bed linen costs extra.

Hobart's YHA hostel, *Adelphi Court* (☎ 6228 4829), is 2.5km from the city at 17 Stoke St, New Town. It's an excellent hostel with good facilities and charges $13 for a dorm bed, or $18 per person for a twin room. To get there, take Metro bus No 15 or 16 from Argyle St to stop 8A, or any one of bus Nos 25 to 42, 100, or 105 to 128 to stop 13. Redline also provides a drop-off and pick-up service on the airport bus.

The *Woodlands Hostel* (☎ 6228 6720) at

7 Woodlands Ave, New Town, is a superb building and one of New Town's original homes, but it is only used as an overflow hostel when Adelphi Court is full. It's best to turn up at nearby Adelphi first and if there isn't any room you'll be directed here.

Guesthouses In addition to its hostel, *Adelphi Court* (☎ 6228 4829) also has guesthouse accommodation from $45 (single and double) including a cooked breakfast.

In Sandy Bay there's *Red Chapel House* (☎ 6225 2273) at 27 Red Chapel Ave, past the casino. Singles/doubles in this smoke-free establishment cost $60/85 including cooked breakfast, and the place has a friendly, family-run atmosphere.

If you have the money, Battery Point has some beautiful colonial guesthouses and cottages. *Barton Cottage* (☎ 6224 1606) at 72 Hampden Rd is a two-storey building which dates back to 1837 and is classified by the National Trust. B&B accommodation costs $80/110. Another worth considering is *Cromwell Cottage* (☎ 6223 6734) at 6 Cromwell St. This two-storey townhouse dates from the late 1880s and is in a beautiful position overlooking the Derwent River. Rooms start at $85/110 for B&B.

Another area for B&B accommodation, and about as close to town as Battery Point, is North Hobart. The *Lodge on Elizabeth* (☎ 6231 3830) at 249 Elizabeth St is an old mansion full of antiques and charges $90/115. A bit further up the road, the *Elms of Hobart* (☎ 6231 3277) at 452 Elizabeth St is more luxurious. A National Trust classified mansion, the rate here with breakfast is $104/118.

An interesting option is the *Signalman's Cottage* (☎ 6223 1215) on the top of Mt Nelson at 685 Nelson Rd. There's just the single self-contained one-bedroom unit and the cost is $65/75. You'd need your own transport for this place to be convenient.

Hotels There are numerous public hotels offering basic accommodation, usually share facilities and a continental breakfast. Look at a few before deciding as standards can drop

dramatically and prices don't always reflect the standard of the rooms. At 67 Liverpool St, near the mall, the *Brunswick Hotel* (☎ 6234 4981) is pretty central and has average singles/doubles costing $30/50 with a continental breakfast. Across the road at 72 Liverpool St the *Alabama Hotel* (☎ 6234 3737) is a little more comfortable and charges $27/44. Two blocks up from the mall at 145 Elizabeth St is the *Black Prince* (☎ 6234 3501), which has large, modern rooms with bathroom and TV for $40/50.

If you want to stay near the docks, the *Customs House Hotel* (☎ 6234 6645) at 1 Murray St has good views of the waterfront and charges $45/65 ($70 for en-suite double) with a continental breakfast. The *Prince of Wales Hotel* (☎ 6223 6355) in Hampden Rd, Battery Point, provides basic accommodation with private facilities for $55/65 including breakfast.

There are also a couple of moderately priced hotels in Sandy Bay. The *Dr Syntax Hotel* (☎ 6223 6258) at 139 Sandy Bay Rd is very close to Battery Point. It has comfortable singles/doubles with TV for $39/55 (breakfast extra).

The *Beach House Hotel* (☎ 6225 1161) at 646 Sandy Bay Rd is 2km past the casino and has good rooms with TV and continental breakfast for $45/55.

More upmarket is the charming *Astor Private Hotel* (☎ 6234 6611) at 157 Macquarie St. Singles/doubles with a continental breakfast cost $50/65. *Country Comfort Hadleys Hotel* (☎ 6223 4355) at 34 Murray St is one of Hobart's best older-style hotels. Rooms start at $85.

Top-end, international-standard accommodation is available at the *Hotel Grand Chancellor* (☎ 6235 4535), the all too dominating brick block in the heart of the city at 1 Davey St, which charges from $135/150; or the *Wrest Point Hotel Casino* (☎ 6225 0112) at 410 Sandy Bay Rd, 5km south of the city centre. Rooms start at $100 in the motel and $198 in the tower.

If none of these appeal, there's always the wonderful *Lenna of Hobart* (☎ 6232 3900), an old mansion at 20 Runnymede St, Battery

Point, which is steeped in history and luxury and charges from $140 for a room.

Motels & Holiday Flats There are plenty of motels in Hobart but some are rather a long way out. The cheapest include the *Shoreline Motor Hotel* (☎ 6247 9504) on the corner of Rokeby Rd and Shoreline Drive, Howrah, which charges $50/60 with continental breakfast; the *Marina Motel* (☎ 6228 4748) at 153 Risdon Rd, Lutana, where singles/doubles cost from $39/49; and the *Hobart Tower Motel* (☎ 6228 0166) at 300 Park St, New Town, which charges from $54/58. Closer to the city centre, the *Mayfair Motel* (☎ 6231 1188) at 17 Cavell St, West Hobart, has rooms starting at $75/85.

Hobart has a number of self-contained holiday flats with fully equipped kitchens. Fairly close to town, the *Domain View Holiday Flats* (☎ 6234 1181) at 352 Argyle St, North Hobart, charges $60 a double and $5 for each extra person, with a one-night surcharge. The *Knopwood Holiday Flat* (☎ 6223 2290) at 6 Knopwood St, Battery Point is a three-bedroom upstairs flat overlooking Salamanca Place. It costs $70 a double and $20 for each extra person, and has a one-night surcharge.

Places to Eat

Cafes & Light Meals Good espresso is not too hard to find in Hobart. There are plenty of street cafes in the central business district, the tourist precinct around Salamanca Place, and in the thriving restaurant scene in Elizabeth St, North Hobart.

A good lunch-time cafe is *Cafe Toulouse* at 79 Harrington St. There's a good selection of croissants and quiches and you can get a quick, light meal for around $8. *Kafe Kara* at 119 Liverpool St offers similarly priced light meals as well as cakes and good coffee.

Popular with greens and new-agers is *Retro Cafe* on the corner of Salamanca Place and Montpelier Retreat; it's so popular that you often can't get a table. It opens at 8 am and serves great breakfasts and continues with good food through the day. It closes at 6 pm except Friday, when the doors stay

open until midnight. Go alone to *Maldini*, nearby on Salamanca Place, the tiramisu cake – yes, a cake version of the dessert – is simply too good to share.

If you're looking for a snack late at night, or you just happen to be rubbernecking in Battery Point and need to rest your legs, drop in to *Mummy's Cafe* at 38 Waterloo Crescent, just off Hampden Rd. Cakes of various types are the speciality and it's popular for after-theatre snacks. It's open Sunday to Thursday from 10 am to midnight, and Friday and Saturday from 10 am to 2 am.

Another good place for quality snacks is the *Cove* buffet in the Hotel Grand Chancellor. Prices are reasonable with light meals at $7 to $14. For a late-night treat try the dessert and cheese selection; for $12.50 you can eat all you like from the buffet.

Approaching North Hobart on Elizabeth St, *Kaos Cafe* at No 273 enjoys a good reputation. It's open from noon to midnight daily except Sunday, when it closes at 10 pm.

A little more difficult to get to, but well worth the effort, is the historic *Mount Nelson Signal Station Tea House*, on the summit of Mt Nelson, which has spectacular panoramic views of Hobart and the surrounding area.

Takeaways Constitution Dock has a number of floating takeaway seafood stalls (you can't miss them) such as *Mako Quality Seafoods* and *Flippers*.

For more exotic takeaways try the tiny *Little Bali* at 84A Harrington St. The dishes are excellent value at around $5. It's open from 11 am to 3 pm weekdays and every evening from 5 to 9.30 pm. Next door is the even smaller *Little Salama* offering Mediterranean and Asian food to go. If pasta is more to your liking, the *Little Italy* at 152 Collins St serves excellent, cheap pasta and is open from 8.30 am to 8 pm or later on weekdays.

Pub Meals You can get fed for under $5 at the *Cornish Mount Tavern* on the corner of Barrack and Liverpool Sts. Many other hotels serve good counter meals in the $8 to $14 range, including the *New Sydney Hotel* at 87 Bathurst St; the *Shamrock*, with fine

Guinness and Beamish on tap, on the corner of Harrington and Liverpool Sts; and the *Aberfeldy Hotel* on the corner of Davey and Molle Sts.

The Customs House Hotel, 1 Murray St, serves excellent bar meals for under $10, and there is also a reputable restaurant on the premises.

Restaurants The licensed *Hara Cafe* at 181 Liverpool St has an extensive range of mouth-watering vegetarian and vegan dishes and is open Monday to Saturday from 10 am until late evening.

At the intersection of Harrington and Collins Street there are a number of small, inexpensive Asian restaurants. At 147a Collins St is the informal *Orient Express* and upstairs at 149c Collins St is *Seoul Korean Restaurant*.

Elizabeth St in North Hobart has a reputation for good-value, ethnic cuisine. At No 321 is *Anatolia*, a popular BYO Turkish restaurant. For good-value pasta and Italian dishes try *Concetta's* at No 340 or *Trattoria Casablanca* at No 213, which is open every evening until after midnight.

North Hobart also has plenty of Asian restaurants. *Vanidols* at 353 Elizabeth St is an often crowded BYO restaurant successfully producing Thai, Indian and Indonesian cuisine under the one roof. Main courses are a reasonable $10 to $15; it's open Tuesday to Sunday. Just up the street at No 369 is another BYO Asian restaurant, *Dede*, which is comfortable and has Indonesian and Thai dishes. For Chinese food fans the *Golden Bamboo* at 116 Elizabeth St has been recommended by a reader.

Understandably, Salamanca Place boasts a few swish eateries. Excellent Italian cuisine can be found at *Maldini*. *Mr Wooby's*, tucked away in a side lane, is a pleasant licensed eatery where you can get excellent meals; it's open until quite late. Nearby, at 87 Salamanca Place, is the licensed *Ball & Chain Grill*, which has a good reputation for grilled steaks; main courses are around $15. At No 89 there's *Panache*, a licensed cafe/restaurant which has an outdoor eating

area by the adjoining rock walls. For excellent Japanese food, try the licensed *Mikaku* at No 85.

Right behind the Customs House Hotel at 7 Despard St is *Areeba!* Mexican restaurant and bar. Innovative Mexican and Santa Fe style cuisine distinguish this place from run-of-the-mill Mexican nosheries.

At 31 Campbell St there's the *Theatre Royal Hotel*, with a highly acclaimed bistro.

In Hampden Rd, Battery Point, is the very popular *Brasserie*, which has a reputation for excellent food at moderate prices. Also in Hampden Rd, at No 47, is the popular *Da Angelo Ristorante* (☎ 6223 7011), which serves pasta and pizza for $10. Come early or book as it's often full.

For seafood, head down to the docks. At *Mures Fish Centre*, Victoria Dock, the Upper Deck is licensed and has spectacular harbour views and consistently good seafood. Downstairs, at the less formal bistro or Lower Deck, you can get fish & chips and other fishy fare, or an ice cream. There is also a sushi bar on the ground floor.

Over at 1 Murray St Pier *Sisco's on the Pier* prepares local seafood with modern Mediterranean flair. Also on the waterfront, the licensed *Drunken Admiral* at 17 Hunter St is open every evening and has good seafood and a great atmosphere.

Entertainment

The *Mercury* newspaper has details on most of Hobart's entertainment in its Friday insert, Pulse.

The *New Sydney Hotel* at 87 Bathurst St is Hobart's Irish pub and there is live music there most nights. *Tatts*, 112 Murray St, is a large cafe/bar with live bands on Friday and Saturday nights.

For jazz, blues and rock & roll, both the *St Ives Hotel* at 86 Sandy Bay Rd and the *Travellers Rest*, 394 Sandy Bay Rd, have bands Wednesday to Sunday nights.

Round Midnight is a nightclub at 39 Salamanca Place, on the top floor of the building, which also houses the *Knopwood's Retreat* bar. It is open Tuesday to Saturday until 4 am.

Nickleby's Wine Bar at 217 Sandy Bay Rd is a popular late-night venue. In the early evening it is a reasonable restaurant, and later live music lasts until the early hours. A similar place is the trendy *Cafe Who*, 251 Liverpool St, which serves meals until 10 pm and has live jazz most nights. There are four restaurants, five bars, live entertainment and excellent odds to lose some money at the *Wrest Point Hotel Casino*. The casino disco is on every night with a cover charge on Friday and Saturday only.

At 375 Elizabeth St, North Hobart, you'll find the *State Cinema* (☎ 6234 6318), which screens art house and independent films, while at 181 Collins St there's a large *Village* complex which shows mainstream releases.

Things to Buy

Bushwalking Needs Northwest of the mall on Elizabeth St, Mountain Design (No 74), Paddy Pallin (No 76), Jolly Swagman (No 107) and Country Comfort (No 104) sell outdoor apparel and camping equipment. Goshawk Gear, on the corner of Barrack and Goulburn Sts, buys and sells second-hand gear.

Tasmaniana The noble Huon pine, a prized timber for boat building and cabinet making, is heavily featured in Tasmanian souvenir shops. Its fine grain, oily texture and aroma are unmistakable features of this valuable wood. Nowadays, the tourist dollar provides the incentive for the production of all manner of decorative and sometimes useful objects – fruit, eggs, bowls, pepper grinders etc – from Huon pine and other native timbers such as sassafras, myrtle and blackwood. The Salamanca Place art and craft stores show what a lathe and a fertile imagination can produce, and even more wood turning permutations can be found at the Saturday morning open-air market.

Getting There & Away

Air For information on international and domestic flights to and from Hobart see the Getting There & Away section at the beginning of this chapter. Ansett (☎ 13 1300) has

an office in the Elizabeth St Mall, as does Qantas (☎ 13 1313).

Bus The main bus companies operating from Hobart are Tasmanian Redline Coaches (☎ 1300 360 000) and Tasmanian Wilderness Travel/Tigerline (☎ 1300 300 520, 6334 4442) both at the Transit Centre, 199 Collins St; and Hobart Coaches (☎ 1800 030 620) at 4 Liverpool St. Hobart Coaches' destinations include New Norfolk ($4.10), Woodbridge ($5.40), Cygnet ($6.80), Geeveston ($9.10), Dover ($12) and Port Arthur ($11.50).

Redline and Tasmanian Wilderness Travel/Tigerline run to Bicheno ($19.60), Swansea ($16), St Marys ($34.70; Redline only) and St Helens ($28). Redline also runs to Oatlands ($10.60), Launceston ($19), Deloraine ($25.70), Devonport ($29), Burnie ($36.90), Wynyard ($39.40), Stanley ($47.30) and Smithton ($47.30). Tasmanian Wilderness Travel/Tigerline services the west coast: Derwent Bridge ($23.80), Queenstown ($35.60) and Strahan ($40.40).

Tasmanian Wilderness Travel also provides smaller buses, personal service and more interesting destinations off the main roads such as Cockle Creek and Scotts Peak Dam in the south-west. For a comprehensive list of destinations, pick up a timetable from their desk at the Transit Centre, or from the visitor centre.

Car Rental There are more than 20 car-rental firms in Hobart. Some of the cheaper ones include Rent-a-Bug (☎ 6231 0300) at 105 Murray St; Selective (☎ 6234 3311) at 132 Argyle St, Advance Car Rentals (☎ 6224 0822) at 277 Macquarie St; Bargain Car Rentals (☎ 6234 6959) at 189A Harrington St; and Statewide Rent-a-Car (☎ 6225 1204) at 388 Sandy Bay Rd, Sandy Bay.

Hitching To start hitching north, first take a Bridgewater or Brighton bus from opposite the main post office in Elizabeth St. To hitch along the east coast, take a bus to Sorell first.

Getting Around

To/From the Airport The airport is in

Hobart's eastern suburbs, 16km from the city centre. Redline runs a pick-up and drop-off shuttle service between the city centre (via Adelphi YHA and some other accommodation places on request) and the airport for $6.60. By taxi it costs about $20 to get into the city.

Bus The local bus service is run by Metro. The main office (☎ 13 2201) is at 18 Elizabeth St, opposite the main post office. Most buses leave from this area of Elizabeth St, known as the Metro City bus station. If you're planning to bus around Hobart it's worth buying Metro's user-friendly timetable (60c). For $3.10 you can get a Day Rover ticket which can be used all day at weekends and between 9 am and 4.30 pm and after 6 pm on weekdays. There's also the City Explorer, which stops at several sights around the city, and the ticket is valid all day; get details from the Metro office.

Bicycle Transit Centre Backpackers has a limited number of mountain bikes for hire. Brake Out (☎ 6234 7632) hires bicycles from the Wrest Point Casino and, in summer, bikes can be hired from a mobile operation which sets up in the parklands near the cenotaph.

Boat On weekdays the ferry *Wrest Point Wanderer* operates between Franklin Wharf and Bellerive Wharf and is a very pleasant way to cross the Derwent River. It departs from Franklin Wharf at 7.45 and 8.15 am and at 4.35 and 5.15 pm. From Bellerive there are services at 8 and 8.35 am and at 4.55 and 5.35 pm. A one-way ticket costs $2. There is no weekend service.

Around Hobart

TAROONA
Ten km from Hobart, on the Channel Highway, is Taroona's **Shot Tower**, completed in 1870. From the top of the 48m-high

tower there are fine views over the Derwent River estuary. Lead shot was once produced in high towers like this by dropping molten lead from the top which, on its way down, formed a perfect sphere.

The tower, small museum, craft shop and beautiful grounds are open daily from 9 am to 5.30 pm ($3/1.80). There is also a tearoom which advertises 'convictshire' teas. Take bus No 60 from Franklin Square near Elizabeth St and get off at stop 45.

From Taroona Beach you can walk around to Kingston Beach (4.5km) along the **Alum Cliffs Track**; at some points the track runs close to rock cliffs and you get good views of the Derwent across to Opossum Bay.

KINGSTON (pop 13,750)
The town of Kingston, 11km south of Hobart, is the headquarters of the **Commonwealth Antarctic Division**. The centre is open weekdays from 9 am to 5 pm and admission to its fine display is free. There's a pleasant picnic area beside Browns River at the eastern end of Kingston Beach.

Close by there are also some pleasant beaches, including **Blackmans Bay**, which has a blowhole; **Tinderbox**, where you can go snorkelling along an underwater trail marked with submerged information plates; and **Howden**. There are views across to Bruny Island from Piersons Point, near Tinderbox.

PONTVILLE (pop 1425)
Further north, on the Midland Highway, is the historic town of Pontville, which has a number of interesting buildings dating from the 1830s. Much of the freestone used in Tasmania's early buildings was supplied from quarries at Pontville. The **barracks** beside the river and **St Marks Anglican Church** on top of the hill are worth a visit.

In nearby Brighton, on Briggs Rd 3km off the highway, is the very good **Bonorong Park Wildlife Centre**, which is open daily from 9 am to 5 pm ($5).

NEW NORFOLK (pop 5280)
Set in the lush, rolling countryside of the

Derwent Valley, New Norfolk is an interesting historical town. It was first settled in 1803 and became an important hop-growing centre, which is why the area is dotted with old oast houses used for drying hops. Also distinctive are the rows of tall poplars planted to protect crops from the wind.

Originally called Elizabeth Town, New Norfolk was renamed after the arrival of settlers (1807 onwards) from the abandoned Pacific Ocean colony on Norfolk Island.

Things to See & Do

The **Visitors Historical & Information Centre**, next to the council chambers in Circle St, has an interesting display of photographs and other memorabilia. The key to the centre can be obtained from the council office during working hours.

The **Oast House** on Hobart Rd is a museum devoted to the history of the hop industry, with a tearoom and a fine-arts gallery. It's open daily from 10 am to 5 pm ($3.50). The building itself has been classified by the National Trust and is worth seeing from the outside, even if you don't go in.

Also interesting to visit are **St Matthew's Church of England**, built in 1823, which is Tasmania's oldest existing church, and the **Bush Inn**, claimed to be the oldest continuously licensed hotel in Australia. The **Old Colony Inn** at 21 Montagu St is a wonderful museum of colonial furnishings and artefacts; there's also a tearoom where you can get some great home-made snacks and sit in the award-winning garden. The inn is open from 9 am to 5 pm ($1.50).

Australian Newsprint Mills (☎ 6261 0433) is one of the area's major industries and tours can be arranged Tuesday to Friday if you give at least 24 hours notice.

For $40 (children $20) you can also take a **jet-boat ride** on the Derwent River rapids. The 30-minute ride can be booked at the Devil Jet office (☎ 6261 3460), which is behind the Bush Inn.

In 1864, rainbow and brown trout were bred, for the first time in the southern hemisphere, in the **salmon ponds** at Plenty, 11km west of New Norfolk. The ponds and

museum on Lower Bushy Park Rd are open daily ($3.50). You can also sit in the restaurant which serves fine food and watch the fish being fed without paying an entry fee.

Places to Stay

Camp sites ($8), on-site vans ($25) and cabins ($40) are available at *New Norfolk Caravan Park* (☎ 6261 1268) on the Esplanade, 1.5km north of town. It's a great place if you want to fish in the river.

The hotel choices here are pretty limited. The *Bush Inn* (☎ 6261 2011), Montagu St, was built in 1815 and has plain singles/doubles from $28/48 including a cooked breakfast, but there's a one-night surcharge. The *Old Colony Inn* (☎ 6261 2731), also in Montagu St, has just one double room – for short people only – for $70 (watch the doors!). On the other side of the river from the main town, *Rosie's Inn* at 5 Oast St provides B&B for $80 a double.

The nicest (but most expensive) place is *Tynwald* (☎ 6261 2667), overlooking the river by the Oast House. It's a three-storey house dating back to the 1830s and oozing with character. The rooms are well furnished, and it has a heated swimming pool and a tennis court for the energetic. Rooms cost from $110, which includes a light breakfast.

Getting There & Away

Hobart Coaches (☎ 1800 030 620) is the main operator between Hobart and New Norfolk ($4.10) and on weekdays there are usually six buses in both directions. On weekends there's a limited service. In New Norfolk, the buses leave from the Fairview Newsagency in Station St.

MT FIELD NATIONAL PARK

Mt Field, 80km from Hobart, was declared a national park in 1916, which makes it one of Australia's oldest. The park is well known for its spectacular mountain scenery, alpine moorland, dense rainforest, lakes, abundant wildlife and spectacular waterfalls. To get to the magnificent 40m **Russell Falls** it's an easy 15-minute walk (the path is suitable for wheelchairs), and there are also easy walks to Lady Barron, Horseshoe and Marriotts falls as well as eight-hour bushwalks. With sufficient snow, there's cross-country and limited downhill skiing at **Mt Mawson**.

Places to Stay

Lake Dobson Cabins, 15km into the park, are three very basic six-bunk cabins. The cost per cabin is $20 a night, plus $10 for each extra adult, and you must book at the rangers' office (☎ 6288 1149). There's also a camping ground managed by the park kiosk (no bookings are taken); a site (for two) costs $10 and a park entry permit is required.

The *Mt Field National Park Youth Hostel* (☎ 6288 1369) is 200m past the turn-off to the park and charges $12 a night; YHA members only. The nearby *Russell Falls Holiday Cottages* (☎ 6288 1198) consists of four one or two-bedroom fully equipped cottages which cost $50 a double, plus $10 for each extra person.

Getting There & Away

Tasmanian Wilderness Travel/Tigerline has a daily service to the park during summer (December to March; $35 return). For the rest of the year there are services on Tuesday, Thursday and Saturday. Tigerline and Redline run day tours to the park, some are self-guided and timetables vary so pick up copies of the tour timetables from the Hobart Tourist & Information Centre.

RICHMOND (pop 770)

Richmond is just 24km from Hobart and, with more than 50 buildings dating from the 19th century, is Tasmania's premier historic town. Straddling the Coal River, on the old route between Hobart and Port Arthur, Richmond was once a strategic military post and convict station. The much-photographed **Richmond Bridge**, built by convicts in 1823, is the oldest road bridge in Australia.

With the completion of the Sorell Causeway in 1872, traffic travelling to the Tasman Peninsula and the east coast bypassed Richmond. For over 100 years the town lay dormant until the recent tourist boom.

Things to See & Do

The northern wing of **Richmond Gaol** was built in 1825, five years before the settlement at Port Arthur, and is the best preserved convict jail in Australia. It is open daily from 10 am to 5 pm ($4/1.50).

Other places of interest include **St John's Church** (1836), the oldest Catholic church in Australia; **St Luke's Church of England** (1834); the **courthouse** (1825); the **old post office** (1826); the **Bridge Inn** (1817); the **granary** (1829); and the **Richmond Arms Hotel** (1888). There's also a model village (designed from original plans) of Hobart Town as it was in the 1820s. It's open daily from 9 am to 5 pm ($5/2.50). The maze, on the main street, is fun but is made of wooden divides, not hedges ($3.50/2.50).

Places to Stay & Eat

Accommodation in Richmond is mostly of the 'colonial cottage' type and is not particularly cheap. Cheapest of all is the *Richmond Cabin & Tourist Park* (☎ 6260 2192) on Middle Tea Tree Rd opposite Prospect House. It has camp sites ($12 for two people), on-site vans ($32) and cabins ($48).

The cheapest B&B is the *Richmond Country Bed & Breakfast* (☎ 6260 4238) on Prossers Rd, 4km north of town, which charges $45/70 for singles/doubles. Everything else is rather expensive, such as the *Red Brier Cottage* (☎ 6260 2349) in Bridge St, which charges from $95 for a double.

Prospect House (☎ 6260 2207) is a superb two-storey Georgian country mansion set in 10 hectares of grounds. It's just outside Richmond, on the Hobart road. Accommodation costs $94/104 and breakfast costs extra.

You can get something to eat and drink at the *Richmond Wine Centre* on Bridge Rd. This new building is set back from the street and is a good place for breakfast and lunch. There are also several tearooms with light meals; try *Ma Foosies* in the main street for some country service. The town also has a bakery hidden behind the saddlery building.

Getting There & Away

If you have your own car, Richmond is an

easy day trip from Hobart. If not, both Redline and Tigerline have bus tours most days to Richmond. Hobart Coaches runs four regular buses a day on weekdays to and from Richmond ($3.90 one way); there are no scheduled weekend services.

South-East Coast

South of Hobart are the scenic fruit-growing and timber areas of the Huon Peninsula, D'Entrecasteaux Channel and Esperance, as well as beautiful Bruny Island and the Hartz Mountains National Park. Once mainly an apple-growing region, the area has now diversified and produces a range of other fruits, Atlantic salmon and wines as well as catering to the growing tourism industry. With the abundance of fresh local produce, some of the hotels turn out fabulous meals.

Around the end of February and during March there is fruit-picking work, but competition for jobs is stiff.

KETTERING (pop 310)
The small port of Kettering, on a sheltered bay 34km south of Hobart, is the terminal for the Bruny Island car ferry. The nearby town of **Snug** has a walking track to Snug Falls (one hour return).

If you are after a good meal try the excellent food at the *Oyster Cove Inn* for a high-standard pub meal. Singles/doubles upstairs cost $25/60.

The nearby *Herons Rise Vineyard* (☎ 6267 4339) has private, luxury accommodation for $90 a double.

On weekdays, Hobart Coaches has four buses a day to Woodbridge via Kingston, Margate, Snug and continuing on to Kettering. A single service runs on Saturday morning from Kettering to Hobart with the return service in the afternoon. There are no Sunday services.

The excellent Bruny D'Entrecasteaux Visitor Centre (☎ 6267 4494) is located at the Bruny Island ferry terminal. As well as purchasing ferry tickets you can get all the latest information on accommodation and services on the island.

BRUNY ISLAND (pop 520)
Bruny Island is almost two islands, joined by an isthmus where mutton birds and other waterfowl breed. It is a peaceful and beautiful retreat. The sparsely populated island has several nature reserves and is renowned for its varied wildlife, including fairy penguins and many reptile species.

The island's coastal scenery is superb and there are plenty of fine swimming and surf beaches, as well as good sea and freshwater fishing. There are a number of signposted walking tracks within the reserves and the proposed South Bruny National Park, especially on the Labillardiere Peninsula and at Fluted Cape.

The island was sighted by Abel Tasman in 1642 and later visited by Furneaux, Cook, Bligh and Cox between 1770 and 1790, but was named after Rear-Admiral Bruni D'Entrecasteaux, who explored and surveyed the area in 1792. Initially the Aboriginal people were friendly towards the Europeans, but relations deteriorated after the sealers and whalers arrived. The island itself remained little changed until the car ferry started in 1954.

Tourism has now become an important part of the island's economy but it is still fairly low-key. There are no massive resorts, just interesting cottages and guesthouses, most of which are self-contained. Supplies can be bought at Adventure Bay, and there are a few small shops at the other settlements, but it's best to stock up on food before boarding the ferry. Also, it is wise to book accommodation in advance as managers often don't live next door to their rental cottages. The Bruny D'Entrecasteaux Visitors Centre is the central booking office for all accommodation on Bruny Island. A car is necessary to get around the island, unless you travel on the daily mail bus (see Getting There & Away later in this section). Drive slowly as most roads are gravel.

The island's history is recorded in the **Bligh Museum of Pacific Exploration** at

Adventure Bay, South Bruny ($2.50). Also of historical interest is South Bruny's **lighthouse**, which was built in 1836 and is the second oldest in Australia. The lighthouse reserve is open to the public.

Places to Stay & Eat

Adventure Bay on the southern part of the island is the main accommodation area, but there are places dotted throughout the island. Alonnah is the other main settlement.

The *Adventure Bay Caravan Park* (☎ 6293 1270) has camp sites for $10, on-site vans for $30 and cosy three-bed cabins

for $45. Meals can be arranged if notice is given. The *Captain James Cook Caravan Park* (☎ 6293 1128) is closer to town and has camp sites for $7, on-site vans for $32. The *Penguin Tea Room* at Adventure Bay has good meals.

There are free bush camp sites in a couple of the reserves. The one at Jetty Beach near the lighthouse on the south of the island is on a beautiful sheltered cove. Other sites are near the isthmus and at Cloudy Bay.

The only other cheap accommodation is the *Lumeah Hostel* (☎ 6293 1265) in Adventure Bay, which has dormitory beds for $13

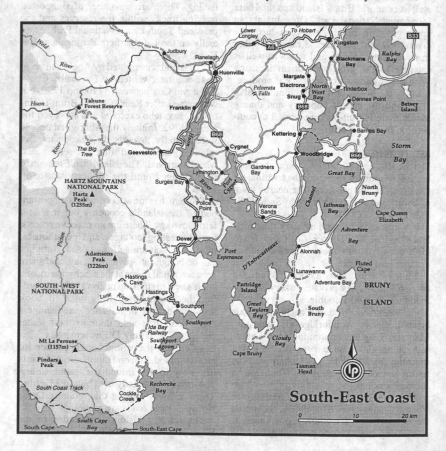

South-East Coast

0   10   20 km

($20 for nonmembers). The *Bruny Hotel* (☎ 6293 1148) at Allonah has singles/doubles for $35/50, and standard pub meals.

Cottages can be rented from $60 a double. Near Adventure Bay are *Rosebud Cottage* (☎ 6293 1325), *Mavista Cottage* (☎ 6293 1347) and *Seaside Cottages* (☎ 6293 1403). If you want your own house then rent the *Christopher Lumsden Cottage* for $55 a double plus $10 for each extra adult. A minimum stay of two nights applies.

Getting There & Away
On weekdays there are nine ferry services daily between Kettering and Roberts Point on Bruny Island. On Friday there is an extra crossing, and the weekend schedule can vary, so check the times in the Friday edition of the *Mercury* newspaper. There's no charge for foot passengers, but if you have a car it costs $18 return weekdays and $23 on weekends and public holidays. Bicycles cost $3. Hobart Coaches' Kettering bus service normally connects with the ferry.

If you don't have your own transport, for $5 you can catch the 9.30 am mail bus from Kettering, which visits most settlements on the island and returns to Kettering at 8.35 am the following day. Enquire at the Bruny D'Entrecasteaux Visitor Centre.

CYGNET (pop 850)
Named 'Port de Cygne Noir' (Port of the Black Swan) by Rear-Admiral D'Entrecasteaux after the many swans seen on the bay, this town is now known as Cygnet. The surrounding area has many orchards with a wide variety of fruit including apples, stone fruits and berries. The region also offers some excellent fishing, bushwalking and good beaches with safe swimming conditions, particularly at **Verona Sands** on the southern end of the peninsula.

Close to Cygnet is the **Talune Wildlife Park & Koala Garden** ($6/2), the **Hartzview Vineyard** with wine tastings, and the **Deepings wood-turning workshop**.

Places to Stay
Balfes Hill Youth Hostel (☎ 6295 1551) is on the Channel Highway, about 5km north of the town. It charges $12 a night ($15 for nonmembers) and can get crowded during the fruit-picking season. From December to April the manager organises walks twice weekly to beautiful South Cape Bay, the most southern beach in Tasmania. A package with two nights accommodation costs around $90. Mountain bikes are available for rent from the hostel for $12 per day.

The *Cygnet Hotel* (☎ 6295 1267) has singles/doubles for $25/50 with a cooked breakfast. There's also a basic camping ground opposite the hotel; it charges a bargain $7 per camp site. If you are fruit picking, many of the hotels in Cygnet will rent you a room at a reasonable weekly rate. Most other accommodation is well out of town on farms and costs $70 to $90 a double.

Getting There & Away
Hobart Coaches has a daily weekday service from Hobart to Cygnet via Snug at 5.15 pm. The return service leaves at 6.55 am.

HUONVILLE (pop 1720)
Named after Huon de Kermadec, who was second in command to D'Entrecasteaux, this small, busy town on the picturesque Huon River is another apple-growing centre. The valuable softwood, Huon pine, was also first discovered here. For the visitor, one of the main attractions these days is a jet-boat ride on the river ($35/20 adults/children). You can also hire pedal boats and aqua bikes from the office (☎ 6264 1838) on the esplanade. In the nearby hills are Horseback Wilderness Tours (☎ 018 128 405), and a trout farm (☎ 6266 0243) where you are guaranteed to catch a fish.

There is little accommodation in the town. The *Huonville Grand Hotel* (☎ 6264 1004), near the river, is an old pub with rooms for $25/35. See the following section for information on transport to Huonville.

GEEVESTON (pop 780)
This town was founded by the Geeves family and their descendants still live here. It is an important base for the timber industry as well

as the gateway to the Hartz Mountains National Park.

The town's main attraction is the **Esperance Forest & Heritage Centre**, in the main street, which is open daily from 10 am to 4 pm ($4/2.50). It has comprehensive displays on all aspects of forestry. The centre also incorporates the South-West Visitor Centre (☎ 6297 1836).

If you have your own transport, head out of town to the **Tahune Forest Reserve**, but first pick up a copy of the map and information brochure from the Esperance Forest & Heritage Centre. There are several lookouts and walks along the way with a good picnic ground and Huon pine walk at the reserve on the banks of the Huon River. On the way back to Geeveston take the one-way Arve Loop Rd to see the Big Tree, indeed a very large *Eucalyptus regnans*.

Tasmanian Wilderness Travel/Tigerline runs five buses each weekday (one on Sunday) between Hobart and Geeveston ($9.10) via Huonville.

HARTZ MOUNTAINS NATIONAL PARK

This national park, classified as part of the World Heritage Area, is very popular with weekend walkers and day-trippers as it's only 84km from Hobart. The park is renowned for its rugged mountains, glacial lakes, gorges, alpine moorlands and dense rainforest. The area is subject to rapid changes in weather, so even on a day walk take waterproof gear and warm clothing. The usual park entry fee applies.

There are some great views from the **Waratah Lookout** (24km from Geeveston) – look for the jagged peaks of the Snowy Range and the Devils Backbone. There are good walks in the park, including tracks to Hartz Peak (five to six hours), and Lakes Osborne and Perry (two hours).

DOVER (pop 480)

This picturesque fishing port, 21km south of Geeveston on the Huon Highway, has some fine beaches and excellent bushwalks. The three small islands in the bay are known as Faith, Hope and Charity. Last century, the

processing and exporting of Huon pine was Dover's major industry, and sleepers made here and in the nearby timber towns of Strathblane and Raminea were shipped to China, India and Germany. If you have your own car and are heading further south, it's a good idea to buy petrol and food supplies here.

Places to Stay

The *Dover Beachside Caravan Park* (☎ 6298 1301) on Kent Beach Rd has camp sites ($10), on-site vans ($30) and en-suite cabins ($50). The *Dover Hotel* (☎ 6298 1210) on the Huon Highway has hotel rooms for $30 per person with breakfast, or more expensive motel rooms ($60 plus extra for breakfast).

For something more comfortable try *Annes Old Rectory* (☎ 6298 1222). This is beside the road as you enter the town. It has good old-fashioned service, and charges $48/60 for singles/doubles.

Getting There & Away

Hobart Coaches runs one bus a day from Hobart to Dover ($12) on weekdays in the late afternoon, returning in the morning (7 am). On school days a second bus operates.

HASTINGS

The spectacular **Hastings Cave & Thermal Pool** attracts visitors to this once-thriving logging and wharf town, 21km south of Dover. The cave is found among the lush vegetation of the **Hastings Caves State Reserve**, 10km inland from Hastings and well signposted from the Huon Highway. Daily tours of the cave ($8/4/) leave promptly at 15 minutes past the hour between 10.15 am and 4.15 pm, with extra tours daily from December to April. Allow 10 minutes drive then five minutes walk through rainforest to the cave entrance. For the more energetic, a short track continues past the cave to a viewpoint overlooking the forest.

About 5km before the cave is a thermal swimming pool ($2.50/1.50/), filled daily with warm water from a thermal spring. Near the pool there's a kiosk and a restaurant. The 10 minute sensory walk near the pool is suitable for blind people and well worth doing.

For those interested in a more adventurous exploration of the caves, Exit Cave Adventure Tours (☎ 6243 0546) runs a trip which is suitable for beginners. It leaves Hobart at 8 am and bookings are essential.

LUNE RIVER

A few kilometres south-west of Hastings is Lune River, a haven for gem collectors and the site of Australia's most southerly post office and youth hostel. From here you can also take a scenic 6km ride on the **Ida Bay Railway** to the lovely beach at Deep Hole Bay. The train runs on Sunday year-round at noon, 1.30 and 3 pm. In the warmer months extra services run on Saturday and Wednesday. The ride costs $10/5).

The most southerly drive you can make in Australia is along the secondary gravel road from Lune River to **Cockle Creek** and beautiful **Recherche Bay**. This is an area of spectacular mountain peaks and endless beaches – ideal for camping and bushwalking. This is also the start (or end) of the challenging South Coast Track which, with the right preparation and a week or so to spare, will take you all the way to Port Davey in the south-west. See Lonely Planet's *Bushwalking in Australia* for track notes.

Places to Stay

The *Lune River Youth Hostel* (☎ 6298 3163), also known as the Doing Place, charges $10 a night ($12 nonmembers). It's a cosy hostel and there's certainly plenty to do – ask the managers about hiring mountain bikes or kayaks, or about bushwalking, fishing and caving. Don't forget to bring plenty of food with you as the hostel only has basic supplies. The hostel runs a shuttle bus connecting with the Hobart Coaches Dover service; bookings are essential.

Getting There & Away

Apart from the hostel bus, the only other service is that run by Tasmanian Wilderness Travel (☎ 1300 300 520). The bus runs on Monday, Wednesday and Friday in summer all the way to the end of the road at Cockle Creek for a flat fee of $42 one way or $80 return.

Tasman Peninsula

The Arthur Highway runs from Hobart through Sorell and Copping to Port Arthur, 100km away. As there is no bank on the Tasman Peninsula and the supermarkets are quite expensive, it's a good idea to take advantage of facilities at Sorell. And to get you into the convict mood, at Copping there's an excellent **colonial convict exhibition** ($6/2.50) which features many objects once used at Port Arthur.

PORT ARTHUR

In 1830, Governor Arthur chose the Tasman Peninsula as the place to confine prisoners who had committed further crimes in the colony. He called the peninsula a 'natural penitentiary' because it was only connected to the mainland by a narrow strip of land less than 100m wide, called Eaglehawk Neck. To deter convicts from escaping, ferocious guard dogs were chained in a line across the isthmus and a rumour circulated that waters on either side were infested with sharks.

Between 1830 and 1877, about 12,500 convicts served sentences at Port Arthur, and for some of them it was a living hell. In reality, those who behaved often lived in better conditions than they had endured back home in England and Ireland.

The historic township of Port Arthur became the centre of a network of penal stations on the peninsula and was, itself, much more than just a prison town. It had fine buildings and thriving industries including timber milling, shipbuilding, coal mining, brick and nail production and shoemaking.

Australia's first railway literally 'ran' the 7km between Norfolk Bay and Long Bay: convicts pushed the carriages along the tracks. A semaphore telegraph system allowed instant communication between Port Arthur, the penal outstations and Hobart. Convict farms provided fresh vegetables, a boys' prison was built at Point Puer to reform and educate juvenile convicts, and a church (today one of the most readily recognised tourist sights in Tasmania) was erected.

The well-presented historic site of Port Arthur is Tasmania's premier tourist attraction. At the time of writing, the entrance and reception area was undergoing major refurbishment as part of the management and local community's restitution efforts following the tragic shootings on 28 April 1996.

For $13/6.50 you can visit all the restored buildings, including the Lunatic Asylum (now a museum) and the Model Prison. The ticket is valid for 48 hours and entitles you to admission to the museum, a guided tour of the settlement and a cruise on the harbour circumnavigating, but not stopping at, the **Isle of the Dead**.

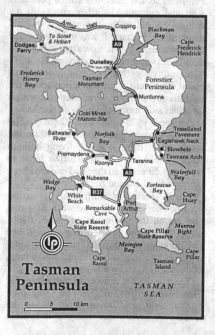

The site is open daily from 9 am to 5 pm, but there's nothing to stop you from wandering around outside those hours without paying the entry fee, although the museum and tours are closed.

Organised Tours
The guided tours (included in the site entry fee) are well worthwhile and leave hourly from the car park in front of the information office (☎ 6250 2363) between 9.30 am and 3.30 pm. A guided walk around the Isle of the Dead costs $5.

Ghostly apparitions, poltergeists and unexplained happenings have been recorded since the 1870s, and nightly lantern-lit walking 'ghost tours' of the buildings and ruins are fun, but also pretty spooky. Two-hour ghost tours leave from outside the information office at 6.30 and 9.30 pm (an hour later during summer daylight-saving) and are well worth the $10/7.50.

For a fun and different outlook on Port Arthur and the surrounding coast, Baidarka Experience (☎ 6250 2612) runs two-hour and half-day sea kayak tours.

Places to Stay
The *Port Arthur Caravan Park* (☎ 6250 2340) is 2km before Port Arthur at Garden Point. It costs $11 to camp, $13 for the hostel and $50 a double for a cabin. You can pay historic site entry fees at the reception office and follow a track around the shoreline from here to Port Arthur.

The *Port Arthur Youth Hostel* (☎ 6250 2311) is very well positioned on the edge of the historic site and charges $11 a night ($14 for nonmembers). To get there, continue half a kilometre past the Port Arthur turn-off and turn left at the sign for the hostel and the Port Arthur Motor Inn. You can buy your historic-site entry ticket at the hostel.

If you don't mind staying some distance from the town, there are some pleasant farm-style B&Bs. *Anderton's Accommodation* (☎ 6250 2378), 2½km south of Port Arthur, and the *Norfolk Bay Convict Station* (☎ 6250 3487) at Tarrana both provide friendly service for around $70 a double.

Apart from this, most of Port Arthur's accommodation is pricey. The *Port Arthur Motor Inn* (☎ 6250 2101) overlooks the site and has rooms from $100. In this same area, but without views of the ruins, are the *Port Arthur Villas* (☎ 6250 2239); self-contained units sleep four to six people and cost from $70 a double plus $12 for each extra adult.

Places to Eat

The licensed restaurant *Langfords*, in the restored policemen's quarters inside the settlement, is a good place for a cuppa or for a light lunch (the servings of delicious cake are large and come with lashings of cream), and is open from 10 am to 3.30 pm. The *Port Arthur Motor Inn*, next to the youth hostel, offers more formal dining but often has cheap specials on the menu. For fast food, the cafe is next to the information office and is open from 9 am to 6 pm (5 pm in the low season).

Entertainment

There is some unique entertainment at Port Arthur. The classic 1926 silent movie *For the Term of His Natural Life* is screened in the museum daily (there's no extra fee). This film, based on the Marcus Clarke novel about convict life, was filmed on location in Port Arthur. The book was written in 1874 and is Australia's best known colonial novel. Ask at the information centre about screening times.

Getting There & Away

If you don't have your own transport, the easiest way to visit Port Arthur on a day trip from Hobart is on an organised tour. During the summer season you can often use Tigerline or Redline. Check timetables at the Transit Centre or the visitor centre in Hobart. Hobart Coaches has a single weekday service which travels via most towns on the Tasman Peninsula for $11.50.

AROUND THE TASMAN PENINSULA

The Tasman Peninsula has many bushwalks, superb scenery, delightful stretches of beach and beautiful bays. Near Eaglehawk Neck

there are the incredible coastal formations of the **Tessellated Pavement**, the **Blowhole**, the **Devils Kitchen**, **Tasmans Arch** and **Waterfall Bay**.

South of Port Arthur is **Remarkable Cave**, which you can walk through when the tide is out. Around the peninsula are some spectacular walks to Mt Brown (four to five hours), Cape Raoul (1½ hours to the lookout, five hours to the cape) and Cape Huay (five hours). The pocket-sized guide *Tasman Tracks* provides detailed notes. It's available from bookshops and walking shops, such as Paddy Pallin, in Hobart.

You can also visit the remains of the penal outstations at **Koonya**, **Premaydena** and **Saltwater River**, and the ruins of the dreaded **Coal Mines Station**. The **Tasmanian Devil Park** at Taranna is open daily ($10/5). The **Bush Mill**, on the Arthur Highway, features a steam railway and pioneer settlement ($12/6).

Organised Tours

If you want to go on a guided walk contact the Storeys at Tasman Trails (☎ 6250 3329). They take bookings up until the walk starts at 9 am and charge $33 for a day's outing including basic gear and lunch.

Places to Stay & Eat

At Eaglehawk Neck, 20km before the penal settlement, is the *Eaglehawk Neck Backpackers* (☎ 6250 3248) on Old Jetty Rd (the side road heading west from the north side of the isthmus). It's a small and friendly hostel charging $12 a night, and a good base from which to explore the Eaglehawk Neck area.

At the pleasant seaside town of Nubeena, 11km beyond Port Arthur, the *White Beach Caravan Park* (☎ 6250 2142) has camp sites ($12), on-site vans ($30) and cabins ($45). Also worth checking out is *Parker's Holiday Cottages* (☎ 6250 2138) – self-contained five-bed units cost $50 for a double and $10 for each additional person. The *Nubeena Tavern* does good counter meals.

Near Koonya is the *Seaview Lodge Host Farm* (☎ 6250 2766), which offers bunk beds for $15 or private doubles for $40. You can also stay in town at the *Cascades* for $90 a double.

There are free, but very basic, camping facilities at Lime Bay and White Beach run by the Department of Parks, Wildlife & Heritage. At Fortescue Bay there is a camping ground at Mill Creek run by the Forestry Commission of Tasmania (☎ 6250 2433). There's no power, but cold showers and firewood are available. The charge is $6 per person.

Midlands

Tasmania's midlands region has a definite English feel due to the diligent efforts of early settlers who planted English trees and hedgerows. The agricultural potential of the area contributed to Tasmania's rapid settlement, and coach stations, garrison towns, stone villages and pastoral properties soon sprang up as convict gangs constructed the main road between Hobart and Launceston. Fine wool, beef cattle and timber milling put the midlands on the map and these, along with tourism, are still the main industries.

The course of the Midland Highway has changed slightly from its original route and many of the historic towns are now bypassed, but it's definitely worth making a few detours to see them.

Getting There & Away
Redline has several services daily up and down the Midland Highway, which can drop you off at any of the towns along the way. Fares from Hobart include Oatlands $10.60, Ross $14.20, Campbell Town $17.10 and Launceston $19.

OATLANDS (pop 540)
With the largest collection of Georgian architecture in Australia, and the largest number of buildings dating from before 1837, Oatlands is not to be missed. In the main street alone, there are 87 historic buildings and the oldest is the 1829 convict-built

courthouse. Much of the sandstone for these early buildings came from the shores of **Lake Dulverton**, now a wildlife sanctuary, which is beside the town.

One of Oatlands' main attractions is **Callington Mill**, the restoration of which was Tasmania's main Bicentennial project. The mill features a faithfully restored cap with a fantail attachment that would turn its sails (if it had any) into the wind. You can walk around the grounds for free.

An unusual way of seeing Oatlands' sights is to go on one of Peter Fielding's (☎ 6254 1135) ghost tours. The tours start at 8 pm (9 pm in summer); $8/4, candles supplied.

Places to Stay & Eat
There's plenty of accommodation in Oatlands, although much of it is of the more expensive colonial type. The *Oatlands Youth Hostel* (☎ 6254 1320) at 9 Wellington St is a couple of hundred metres off the main street and charges $10 a night, $13 for nonmembers. The *Midlands Hotel* (☎ 6254 1103) at 91 High St charges $35/45 for singles/ doubles with continental breakfast. The *Oatlands Lodge* (☎ 6254 1444), nearby at 92 High St, has rooms from $65/95 a double including breakfast. *Blossom's of Oatlands*, on the main street, is a good place for meals.

ROSS (pop 280)
This ex-garrison town, 120km from Hobart, is steeped in colonial charm and history. It was established in 1812 to protect travellers on the main north-south road and was an important coach staging post.

Things to See
The town is known for its convict-built **Ross Bridge**, the third-oldest bridge in Australia. Daniel Herbert, a convict stonemason, was granted a pardon for his detailed work on the 184 panels which decorate the arches.

In the heart of town is a crossroads which can lead you in one of four directions: 'temptation' (represented by the Man-O-Ross Hotel); 'salvation' (the Catholic church); 'recreation' (the town hall); and 'damnation' (the old jail).

The intricate carvings decorating the arches on Ross Bridge were completed by a convicted highwayman, David Herbert. He was granted his freedom in exchange for the work.

Historic buildings include the **Scotch Thistle Inn**; the **old barracks**, restored by the National Trust; the **Uniting Church** (1885); **St John's Church of England** (1868); and the **post office** (1896).

The **Tasmanian Wool Centre**, a museum and craft shop in Church St, is open daily from 9.30 am to 5.30 pm ($4/2).

Places to Stay & Eat

Adjacent to the Ross Bridge is the *Ross Caravan Park* (☎ 6381 5462), which has cheap camp sites ($8) and cheap stone cabins ($15/25). The *Man-O-Ross Hotel* (☎ 6381 5240) in Church St has singles/doubles for $35/55.

By far the best place to stay is the *Ross Bakery Inn* (☎ 6281 5246) in the main street (Church St). The cost is $55/89, which includes breakfast lovingly baked in the 100-year-old wood-fired oven in the adjacent bakery.

For lunch try the *Ross Village Bakery* next to the Ross Bakery Inn. The only place for dinner is the hotel; the counter meals are fairly ordinary.

CAMPBELL TOWN (pop 820)

Twelve km north of Ross is Campbell Town, another former garrison settlement which boasts more examples of early colonial architecture. These include the convict-built **Red Bridge** (1836), the **Grange** (1847), St Luke's **Church of England** (1835), the **Campbell Town Inn** (1840), the building known as the **Foxhunters Return** (1829), and the **old school** (1878).

There's a secondary road from Campbell Town to Swansea on the east coast; the daily Redline bus from Hobart to Bicheno travels this route. Another highway, the A4, runs from Conara Junction, 11km north of Campbell Town, east to St Marys. Buses running from Launceston to Bicheno follow the A4.

LAKE COUNTRY

The sparsely populated Lake Country on Tasmania's Central Plateau is a region of breathtaking scenery with steep mountains, hundreds of glacial lakes, crystal-clear streams, waterfalls and a good variety of wildlife. It's also known for its fine trout fishing, and for its ambitious hydroelectric schemes which have seen the damming of rivers, the creation of artificial lakes, the building of power stations (both above and below ground) as well as the construction of massive pipelines.

Tasmania has the largest hydroelectric power system in Australia. The first dam was constructed on Great Lake in 1911. Subsequently, the Derwent, Mersey, South Esk, Forth, Gordon, King, Anthony and Pieman rivers were also dammed. If you want to inspect the developments, go along to the Tungatinah, Tarraleah and Liapootah power stations on the extensive Derwent scheme between Queenstown and Hobart.

On the eastern edge of the Central Plateau is the **Walls of Jerusalem National Park**, which is a focal point for mountaineers, bushwalkers and cross-country skiers. There's excellent fishing at **Lake King William**, on the Derwent River, south of the Lyell Highway, as well as at **Lake Sorell**, **Lake Crescent**, **Arthurs Lake** and **Little Pine Lagoon**.

At Waddamana, on the road which loops off the Lake Highway between Bothwell and Great Lake, there's the **Waddamana Power Museum**. It has an interesting display of the state's early hydro history, and is open daily from 10 am to 4 pm (free).

Getting There & Away

Public transport to this area is not good (and neither is hitching). Redline runs a daily service between Bothwell and Hobart. This leaves Bothwell at 7 am and Hobart at 4 pm for the return journey. There is no connecting service between Bothwell and Great Lake.

Tasmanian Wilderness Travel's services between Lake St Clair and Launceston or Devonport go via Bronte Park and Miena. This service runs daily (except Friday and Sunday) during the summer, and only once a week in autumn, winter and spring. Booking is essential.

BOTHWELL (pop 360)

Bothwell, in the beautiful Clyde River valley, is a charming and historic town, with 53 buildings recognised or classified by the National Trust. Places of particular interest include the beautifully restored **Slate Cottage** of 1835; a **bootmaker's shop**, fitted out as it would have been in the 1890s; **Thorpe Mill**, a flour mill from the 1820s; the delightful **St Luke's Church** (1830); and the **Castle Hotel**, first licensed in 1821.

Although Bothwell is probably best known for its great trout fishing, it also has Australia's oldest golf course. This is still in use today and is open to members of any golf club. There is also the **Australasian** (no less!) **Golf Museum** which resides within

the Visitor Information Centre in the **Old School House** (1887).

Places to Stay

Accommodation in Bothwell can be expensive, but *Mrs Wood's Farmhouse* (☎ 6259 5612) at Dennistoun, 8km from town, is highly recommended with singles/doubles from $20/40. You can also try *Bothwell Grange* (☎ 6259 5556), at $58/70 for B&B, which is in town.

At Swan Bay, near Miena, the *Great Lake Hotel* (☎ 6259 8163) has singles/doubles for $50/65 including a continental breakfast, and cabins for the same price plus $10 for each extra person.

East Coast

Tasmania's scenic east coast, with its long sandy beaches, fine fishing and rare peacefulness, is known as the 'sun coast' because of its mild and often sunny climate.

Exploration and settlement of the region, which was found to be most suitable for grazing, proceeded rapidly after the establishment of Hobart in 1803. Offshore fishing, and particularly whaling, also became important industries, as did tin mining and timber cutting. Many of the convicts who served out their terms in the area stayed on to help the settlers lay the foundations of the fishing, wool, beef and grain industries which are still significant in the region today.

The best features are the major national parks of Maria Island and Freycinet. The spectacular scenery around Coles Bay is not to be missed, and Bicheno, Swansea and Triabunna are pleasant seaside towns in which to spend a few restful days.

Banking facilities on the east coast are limited and in some towns the banks are only open one or two days a week. There are agencies for the Commonwealth Bank at all post offices. There are also EFTPOS facilities in the main coastal towns and at Coles Bay and St Marys.

Getting There & Around

Redline and Tasmanian Wilderness Travel/Tigerline are the main bus companies operating, but a couple of smaller ones – Peakes Coach Service (☎ 6372 2390) and Bicheno Coach Services (☎ 6257 0293) – also do runs between Swansea, Coles Bay, Bicheno and St Marys. With all of these you can buy your tickets when boarding.

Bus services are limited at weekends (but you can get in and out of Coles Bay – see that section later), so it might take a little longer than anticipated to travel between towns.

BUCKLAND

This tiny township, 61km from Hobart, was once a staging post for coaches. Ye Olde Buckland Inn, at 5 Kent St, welcomed coach drivers and travellers a century ago and today offers a good counter lunch every day and dinner on Friday and Saturday nights. The new roadhouse offers light meals and snacks.

The stone **Church of St John the Baptist**, dating from 1846, is worth a visit. It has a stained-glass window which was rescued from a 14th-century abbey in England just before Cromwell sacked the building.

ORFORD (pop 460)

Orford is a popular little seaside resort on the Prosser River (named after an escaped prisoner who was caught on its banks). The area has good fishing, swimming and some excellent walks.

Places to Stay

There's plenty of accommodation in Orford, although no real backpacker places. *Sea Breeze Holiday Cabins* (☎ 6257 1375), on the corner of Rudd Ave and Walpole St, charges $45 a double. On the Tasman Highway, the *Blue Waters Motor Hotel* (☎ 6257 1102) has singles/doubles for $35/45, while the *Island View Motel* (☎ 6257 1114) has them for $50/60.

More lavish, and expensive, is the *Eastcoaster Resort*, on Louisville Point Rd,

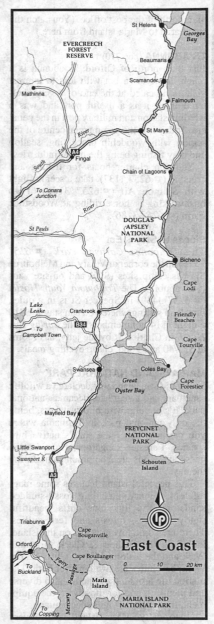

East Coast

4km north of the post office. (You catch the catamaran to Maria Island from here.)

TRIABUNNA (pop 770)

Just 8km north of Orford, Triabunna is a much larger town but with less to interest visitors. Located at the end of a very sheltered inlet, it is a useful port and was a whaling station and military port in the penal era. Today it is the commercial centre of the region with woodchip processing, scallop and cray fishing being the major industries.

You can charter boats for fishing and cruising (☎ 6257 1137), take a scenic flight with Salmon Air (☎ 6257 3186) or go bushwalking or horse riding at Woodstock Farm (☎ 6257 3186).

Places to Stay & Eat

The *Triabunna Caravan Park* (☎ 6257 3575) on the corner of Vicary and Melbourne Sts has camp sites ($10) and on-site vans ($25 double). The *Triabunna Youth Hostel* (☎ 6257 3439) in Spencer St is in a quiet, farmland setting where you can stay for $10 a night ($14 nonmembers). The *Spring Bay Hotel*, in Charles St by the jetty, has rooms at $25/40 and good, cheap evening meals.

MARIA ISLAND NATIONAL PARK

In 1971 Maria Island was declared a wildlife sanctuary and a year later became a national park. It's popular with bird-watchers, being the only national park in Tasmania where you can see 11 of the state's native bird species. Forester kangaroos, Cape Barren geese and emus are a common sight during the day.

This peaceful island features some magnificent scenery, including fossil-studded sandstone and limestone cliffs, beautiful sandy beaches, forests and fern gullies. There are some lovely walks on the island, including the Bishop & Clerk Mountain Walk and the historical Fossil Cliffs Nature Walk; brochures are available for both. The marine life around the island is also diverse and plentiful, and for those with the equipment, the scuba diving is spectacular.

Historically, Maria Island is also very interesting – from 1825 to 1832 the settlement of **Darlington** was Tasmania's second penal colony (the first was Sarah Island near Strahan). The remains of the penal village, including the commissariat store (1825) and the mill house (1846), are remarkably well preserved and easy to visit; in fact, you'll probably end up staying in one of the old buildings. There are no shops on the island so don't forget to bring your own supplies. A current national park pass is required.

Places to Stay

The rooms in the penitentiary at Darlington and some of the other buildings have been converted into bunkhouses for visitors. These are called the *Parks, Wildlife & Heritage Penitentiary Units* (☎ 6257 1420) and cost $8 a night, but it's wise to book as the beds are sometimes taken by school groups. There is also a camping ground at Darlington for $6 per adult.

Getting There & Away

The *Eastcoaster Express* (☎ 6257 1589) is operated by the Eastcoaster Resort, Louisville Point Rd, 4km north of the Orford post office. It has three services a day between the resort and Maria Island, with an extra service daily from December to April. The return fare is $17 for day visitors ($10 children) and $20 ($13) for campers.

SWANSEA (pop 495)

On the shores of Great Oyster Bay, with superb views across to the Freycinet Peninsula, Swansea is a popular place for camping, boating, fishing and surfing. It was first settled in the 1820s and is the administrative centre for Glamorgan, Australia's oldest rural municipality.

Swansea has a number of interesting historic buildings, including the original **council chambers**, which are still in use, and the lovely red-brick **Morris' General Store**, built in 1838. The community centre dates from 1860 and houses a **museum of local history** and the only oversized billiard table in Australia. The museum is open Monday to Saturday ($4).

The **Swansea Bark Mill & East Coast Museum** at 96 Tasman Highway is also worth a look. The restored mill displays working models of equipment used in the processing of black-wattle bark, a basic ingredient used in the tanning of heavy leathers. The adjoining museum features displays of Swansea's early history, including some superb old photographs. It's open daily from 9 am to 5 pm ($5/2.75).

Places to Stay & Eat

The *Swansea Caravan Park* (☎ 6257 8177) in Shaw St, just by the beach, is very clean and has good services. Camp sites cost $10 and cabins are $50 to $70 a double.

The *Swansea Youth Hostel* (☎ 6257 8367) at 5 Franklin St is in a lovely spot near the sea, although it's not a particularly attractive building. It charges $12 ($15 nonmembers), and in the busy summer season priority is given to YHA members.

Also in Franklin St, almost opposite the youth hostel, is the *Oyster Bay Guest House* (☎ 6257 8110), which was built in 1836 and offers friendly colonial accommodation at $55/95 with a cooked breakfast. *Freycinet Waters Beachside Cottage* (☎ 6257 8080) is a bright and breezy B&B with definite seaside ambience charging $65/80.

Just Maggies at 26 Franklin St, has coffee, cakes and light lunches. For something special try the licensed *Shy Albatross Restaurant* in the Oyster Bay Guest House.

Getting There & Away

Tasmanian Wilderness Travel/Tigerline has an afternoon service on weekdays from Hobart to Swansea ($16) and a morning service on Wednesday, Friday and Sunday that continues to Bicheno ($19.60) and St Helens ($28.50). There's also an afternoon service on weekdays. During January and February, there's an additional morning service on Saturday.

Redline operates an afternoon service on weekdays from Hobart and Launceston to Swansea and Bicheno. On weekdays, Peakes Coach Service runs a daily bus between Swansea and St Marys for $8 (via Bicheno).

COLES BAY & FREYCINET NATIONAL PARK

The small township of Coles Bay is dominated by the spectacular 300m-high, pink granite mountains known as the **Hazards**. The town is the gateway to many white-sand beaches, secluded coves, rocky cliffs and excellent bushwalks in the **Freycinet National Park**.

The park, incorporating Freycinet Peninsula, beautiful Schouten Island and the Friendly Beaches (on the east coast north of Coles Bay), is noted for its coastal heaths, orchids and other wildflowers and for its wildlife, including black cockatoos, yellow wattlebirds, honeyeaters and Bennetts wallabies. Walks include a 27km circuit of the peninsula plus many other shorter tracks, one of the most beautiful being the return walk to **Wineglass Bay** (2½ to three hours). On any walk remember to sign in (and sign out) at the registration booth at the car park. A current national parks pass is also required.

On the road in to Coles Bay, look for **Moulting Lagoon Game Reserve**, which is a breeding ground for black swans and wild ducks.

Information

The post office/store/information centre is open daily and sells groceries, basic supplies and petrol. It also has a newsagency and boat hire. The Iluka Holiday Centre has its own minisupermarket, takeaway food, bistro and petrol.

Places to Stay

Coles Bay offers a variety of accommodation to suit all travel budgets.

The national park camping ground (☎ 6257 0101) stretches along Richardsons Beach and has sites for $10 for two people. Bookings can be made at the rangers' office, but during peak periods, such as school holidays, it is essential to book well in advance. Facilities are basic – pit toilets and cold water – there are no hot showers!

The *Coles Bay Caravan Park* (☎ 6257 0100) is 3km by road from Coles Bay at the western end of Muir's Beach. Sites cost $11 for two and on-site vans are $30.

Freycinet Backpackers (☎ 6257 0100), part of the aforementioned caravan park, has dormitory-style accommodation for $14 per person. *Iluka Backpackers* is the year-round YHA hostel in Coles Bay and is in the Iluka Holiday Centre (see next entry). Clean and pleasant dorm accommodation costs $13 ($15 for nonmembers) and linen can be hired.

The *Iluka Holiday Centre* (☎ 6257 0115) on Muir's Beach has the cheapest accommodation in Coles Bay itself. There are camp sites ($10), on-site vans ($30) and cabins ($50).

The *Coles Bay Youth Hostel*, actually in the national park, is mainly used by groups and must be booked at the YHA head office in Hobart (☎ 6234 9617). Keys are obtained from the Iluka Holiday Centre.

There are a number of private shacks and cabins for rent, and these are probably the best deal for a group. *Pine Lodge Cabins* (☎ 6257 0113) in Harold St charges from $55 per cabin, and *Jessie's Cottage* (☎ 6257 0143), on the Esplanade by the general store, from $80 a double and $20 for each extra person.

Surrounded by the national park is *Freycinet Lodge* (☎ 6257 0101) at the southern end of Richardsons Beach. Rooms cost $150 a double, and there are some with disabled access. Park entry fees for guests are paid by the lodge.

The scenery at the free camp sites of Wineglass Bay (one to 1½ hours), Hazards Beach (two to three hours) and Cooks Beach (about 4½ hours) is well worth the walk. There's little reliable drinking water at any of these sites, and little elsewhere on the peninsula, so you'll normally need to carry your own.

Places to Eat

Eating options are limited. There's the *Iluka Tavern & Bistro* for pub meals, *Madge Malloys* licensed seafood restaurant next to the general store, *Seashells* seafood takeaway opposite the general store, and the *Iluka Bakery* which has pizza at nights as well as the usual cakes and pies and sandwiches during the day.

More expensive is the *Freycinet* restaurant at the Freycinet Lodge, but the views are superb. Other than that it's a matter of putting your own food together. The general store and the Iluka supermarket are pretty well stocked.

Getting There & Away

Redline and Tasmanian Wilderness Travel/Tigerline can drop you at the Coles Bay turn-off en route to Bicheno and you can hitch the 28km from there but, depending on the season, traffic may be light. Bicheno Coach Services (☎ 6257 0293) runs at least two buses each day between Coles Bay and Bicheno. In Bicheno, buses depart from the takeaway in Burgess St, and in Coles Bay from the general store/post office; tickets are $5 per person and $2.50 for a bicycle.

It is more than 5km from the town to the national park's car park (where the walking tracks start), and Bicheno Coach Services has a weekday shuttle bus. You must book however. The cost is $2 return. It leaves the general store at 9.40 am, and departs from the car park for the return trip at 10 am.

BICHENO (pop 700)

In the early 1800s, whalers and sealers used Bicheno's narrow harbour, called the Gulch, to shelter their boats. They also built lookouts in the hills to watch for passing whales. These days, fishing is still one of the town's major occupations, and if you are down at the Gulch around lunch time, when all the fishing boats return, you can buy fresh crayfish, abalone, oysters or anything else caught that night straight from the boats.

Tourism is also very important to Bicheno and it has a very good information centre in the main street at which you can book tours (penguins, glass-bottom boat, fishing etc) and hire bikes ($15 a day). Bicheno has beautiful beaches and is a lovely spot to visit for a few days.

Things to See & Do

An interesting 3km **foreshore walk** from

Redbill Point to the blowhole continues south around the beach to Courlands Bay. You can also walk up to the **Whalers Lookout** and the **Freycinet Lookout** for good views.

At nightfall you may be lucky enough to see the fairy penguins at the northern end of Redbill Beach, but if you want to avoid overly disturbing the birds and learn a little about their habits, go on the tour organised at the information centre. At low tide you can walk out to **Diamond Island**, opposite the youth hostel.

The Dive Centre (☎ 6375 1138) opposite the Sea Life Centre on the foreshore runs courses, which are cheaper than those in warmer waters off the mainland, and you can also hire or buy diving equipment from its shop.

The **Sealife Centre** is open daily from 9 am to 5 pm and features Tasmanian marine life swimming behind glass windows. There's also a restored trading ketch, but at $4 for admission, the centre is rather over-priced and a bit depressing. Seven km north of town is the 32-hectare **East Coast Birdlife & Animal Park**, which is open daily from 9 am to 5 pm ($6.50).

Just a couple of kilometres north of the animal park is the turn off to the **Douglas-Apsley National Park**. The park was proclaimed in 1989 and protects a large and undisturbed sclerophyll forest. It has a number of waterfalls and gorges, and birds and animals are prolific. There's road access to the **Apsley Gorge** in the south of the park, where there's a water hole with excellent swimming. You can walk the north-south trail through the park in a couple of days.

Places to Stay

The *Bicheno Cabin & Tourist Park* (☎ 6375 1117) in Champ St has camp sites ($10.50) and on-site vans from $30. The *Bicheno Caravan Park* (☎ 6375 1280) on the corner of Burgess and Tribe Sts charges $7 a double for a camp site and $25 a double for an on-site van.

A more comfortable option is the *Bicheno Hostel* in Morrison St charging $13 per person. It is centrally located and much newer than the youth hostel. Also new is the *Waubs Harbour Backpackers* (☎ 6375 1117) at 4 Champ St where a dorm bed costs $14. *Camp Seaview* (☎ 6375 1247) also has back-packer accommodation for $13. The *Bicheno Youth Hostel* (☎ 6375 1293) is in a lovely location 3km north of town on the beach opposite Diamond Island, but this is its only redeeming feature. It's $11 a night ($14 for nonmembers). Bookings during the summer period are recommended.

The *Silver Sands Resort* (☎ 6375 1266) at the end of Burgess St has singles/doubles starting at $30/60, but you'll definitely pay more than this for rooms overlooking the bay.

Places to Eat

In the main shopping centre there's the *Galleon Cafe & Takeaway*, which has the usual takeaway meals as well as pizza. Nearby is *Rose's Coffee Lounge*, which is open daily from 8.30 am. It serves reasonably priced breakfasts as well as light meals, cake and coffee. The bakery also has a coffee shop.

The *Silver Sands Resort* restaurant has seafood and grills from $10. Also in Burgess St is *Cyrano* restaurant which specialises in seafood and French cuisine. On the Tasman Highway, the *Longboat Tavern* has good counter meals, and *Waubs Bay Seafood* has a great seafood pizza.

Getting There & Away

Redline has an afternoon service from Hobart ($30.70) and Launceston ($21.10) each weekday and on Sunday. The return trips are in the morning. Tasmanian Wilderness Travel/Tigerline runs buses to/from Hobart on Wednesday, Friday and Sunday.

ST MARYS (pop 590)

St Marys is a charming little town, 10km inland from the coast, near the Mt Nicholas range. There's not much to do except enjoy the peacefulness of the countryside, visit a number of waterfalls in the area, and take walks in the state forest.

Places to Stay & Eat

The *Seaview Farm Hostel* (☎ 6372 2341), on a working sheep farm, is surrounded by state forest. It's at the end of a dirt track, 8km from St Marys on German Town Rd, and commands magnificent views of the coast, ocean and mountains. Singles/doubles cost $22/37.

The *St Marys Hotel* (☎ 6372 2181), has singles/doubles at $28/52. The pub also serves counter meals. South of St Marys, beside the highway in Elephant Pass, is the *Mt Elephant Pancake Barn*, a road-side eatery that has so greatly impressed some travellers that they have written to us about it.

Getting There & Away

Peakes Coaches operates between St Marys and Swansea ($8) and Bicheno ($4). Redline has one service from Launceston and another from Hobart every day except Saturday – both continue to St Helens.

North-East

The north-east corner of the state is worth a visit as it's off the normal tourist route. It can be very scenic and quiet with long beach and bush walks around St Helens and in the Mt William National Park. There are also some attractions to visit, such as the Tin Mine Centre in Derby, Pipers Brook vineyard and the Lavender Farm in Nabowla. The main centres are Bridport on the north coast, Scottsdale inland and St Helens on the east coast.

SCAMANDER (pop 435)

Scamander township is stretched along some of the loveliest, white-sand beaches on the east coast and these are protected in a coastal reserve. You can take walks along the beach or hire a dinghy and go fishing in the river.

Places to Stay & Eat

The *Kookaburra Caravan & Camping Ground* (☎ 6372 5121), 1.5km north of the river, is very reasonably priced with sites for

$10 for two people and on-site vans for $25. It's only a short walk to the beach. The *Scamander Beach Resort Hotel* (☎ 6372 5255) is an imposing, three-storey building with good views and charges $75 a double.

There are not too many places to eat. Try the *Beach Cafe* at the Shell garage for afternoon teas and snacks, the hotel, or *Bensons* in nearby Beaumaris for restaurant meals; otherwise bring your own food.

ST HELENS (pop 1770)

St Helens, on Georges Bay, is the largest town on the east coast. First settled in 1830, this old whaling town has an interesting and varied history, which is recorded in the **history room** at 59 Cecilia St, adjacent to the town's library. It's open weekdays from 9 am to 4 pm ($4).

Today, St Helens is Tasmania's largest fishing port, with a big fleet based in the bay. Visitors can charter boats for offshore game fishing or just take a lazy cruise.

While the beaches in town are not particularly good for swimming, there are excellent scenic beaches at **Binalong Bay** (10km from St Helens), **Sloop Rock** (12km) and **Stieglitz** (7km), as well as at St Helens and Humbug points. You can also visit **St Columba Falls**, near Pyengana, 24km away.

There are three banks in town and EFTPOS facilities are available at the service stations and supermarkets.

Places to Stay & Eat

The *St Helens Caravan Park* (☎ 6376 1290) is just out of town, south of the bridge on Penelope St. For two people, camp sites are $12, on-site vans $30 and cabins cost from $40.

The *St Helens Youth Hostel* (☎ 6376 1661) at 5 Cameron St is in a lovely, quiet spot by the beach and charges $12 a night. The *Artnor Lodge* (☎ 6376 1234) in Cecilia St is a comfortable guesthouse charging $45/60 with breakfast. For self-catering accommodation, try *Queechy Cottages* (☎ 6376 1321) on the highway about 1km south of the centre. Units for four to six people, with ocean views, cost $50 a double, $10 each extra person.

In the main street, *St Helens Bakery* does breakfast from 7 am and has the usual sandwiches, pies and cakes for lunch. You can eat in or take away. *Trimboli's Pizza* in Circassian St has good pizza and pasta. *Jim's Italian* in Cecilia St is a little cheaper.

Getting There & Away

Tasmanian Wilderness Travel/Tigerline runs a winter service on Wednesday, Friday and Sunday from Hobart to St Helens and operates more frequently in summer ($28.50), but not on Tuesday. Redline has daily (except Saturday) connections to Launceston ($18.80). The Redline agent in St Helens is the newsagency in Cecilia St. During the week you can get to St Marys or Derby (to connect with the Redline bus to Launceston) with the Suncoast Bus Service (ask at the post office).

WELDBOROUGH

The Weldborough Pass, with its mountain scenery and dense rainforests, is quite spectacular. During the tin-mining boom last century, hundreds of Chinese migrated to Tasmania and many made Weldborough their base. The joss house now in Launceston's Queen Victoria Museum & Art Gallery was built in Weldborough.

The *Weldborough Hotel*, the town's only pub, also calls itself the 'worst little pub in Tassie' and has, among other things, 'leprechaun pee soup' and 'leeches and cream' on the menu, but don't be put off – it's quite a nice place to stop for a drink.

GLADSTONE

About 25km off the Tasman Highway, between St Helens and Scottsdale, is the tiny town of Gladstone. It was one of the last tin-mining centres in north-eastern Tasmania, until the mine closed in 1982. The area also had a number of mining communities and a large Chinese population. Today, many old mining settlements are just ghost towns, and Gladstone shows signs of heading in the same direction.

Twelve km from Gladstone is the popular **Mt William National Park**, where you can see many Forester kangaroos, the Tasmanian subspecies of the eastern grey kangaroo. The park also has some excellent beaches – Picnic Rocks is a good surf beach – and there are good bushwalks along beaches and fire trails. The return walk to the summit of Mt William is around 3km. It's a gentle climb and takes about 1½ hours. There are several bush camp sites with pit toilets and bore water, but you'll need to carry drinking water. The **Eddystone Lighthouse**, built in 1887, is within the park boundary. For more information, call the rangers' office (☎ 6357 2108). National park entry fees apply.

DERBY

In 1874, tin was discovered in Derby and, due mainly to the Briseis Tin Mine, this little township flourished throughout the late 19th century. Today Derby is a classified historic town and some of the old mine buildings are now part of the excellent **Tin Mine Centre**, which features a mine museum of old photographs and mining implements, and a re-creation of an old mining shanty town. The centre opens 10 am to 4 pm ($4/1.50).

Derby comes alive in late October when several thousand people arrive for the annual Derby River Derby, a 5km course for all sorts of inflatable craft.

Places to Stay & Eat

The *Dorset Hotel* (☎ 6354 2360) has singles/doubles for $35/55 with breakfast, and also does good counter meals. The *Crib Shed Tea Rooms* (part of the mine museum) serves delicious scones.

Six km from Winnaleah, near Derby, is the peaceful *Merlinkei Farm Hostel* (☎ 6354 2152), which charges $12 a night ($14 nonmembers). You can ring from Winnaleah and the manager will pick you up. Being a dairy farm, it has an unlimited supply of fresh milk.

Getting There & Away

Redline has two services every weekday from Launceston to Derby via Scottsdale

($12.60). There's only one service on Sunday, and none on Saturday. The Redline agent is the general store in Derby's main street. On weekdays you can get to St Helens and Winnaleah with the Suncoast Bus Service.

SCOTTSDALE (pop 1920)

Scottsdale, the major town in the north-east, serves some of Tasmania's richest agricultural and forestry country, and its setting is quite beautiful. A camp site at the nearby *Scottsdale Camping Ground* (☎ 6352 2017) costs $10 for two people. Of the two hotels in town, accommodation is cheaper ($20/30 a single/double) at *Lords Hotel* (☎ 6352 2319), 2 King St. For bus services to Scottsdale, see the Getting There & Away section for Derby.

AROUND SCOTTSDALE

At Nabowla, 21km west of Scottsdale, is the **Bridestowe Lavender Farm**. It's open daily during the spectacular flowering season from mid-December to late January ($3). At other times it's open weekdays only and entry is free. Twenty-one km north of Scottsdale is the popular beach resort of **Bridport**, where there's plenty of accommodation. From there it's another 45km to the unspoiled beaches and great diving and snorkelling at **Tomahawk**.

To get to Bridport, you can take a local bus from Scottsdale; buses depart twice daily on weekdays from the Redline stop in Scottsdale. You'll need your own transport to visit Tomahawk. Travelling west from Bridport on the B82 brings you to the **Pipers Brook** and **Pipers River** wine producing region. There are several wineries with free tastings and cellar-door sales.

Launceston

- *Pop 67,800*

Officially founded by Lieutenant-Colonel William Paterson in 1805, Launceston is Australia's third-oldest city and the commercial centre of northern Tasmania.

The Tamar River estuary was explored in 1798 by Bass and Flinders, who were attempting to circumnavigate Van Diemen's Land to prove there was no land connection with the rest of Australia. Launceston was the third attempt at a settlement on the river and was originally called Patersonia, after its founder.

In 1907 the city was renamed in honour of Governor King, who was born in Launceston, England, a town settled 1000 years before on the Tamar River in the county of Cornwall.

Orientation

The city centre is arranged in a grid pattern around the Brisbane St Mall, between Charles and St John Sts. Two blocks north, in Cameron St, there's another pedestrian mall called Civic Square. To the east is Yorktown Square, a charming and lively area of restored buildings which have been turned into shops and restaurants. Launceston's main attractions are all within walking distance of the centre.

Information

The Tasmanian Travel & Information Centre (☎ 6336 3133) on the corner of St John and Paterson Sts is open weekdays from 9 am to 5 pm, and Saturday and public holidays (and Sunday during the high season) from 9 am to 3 pm. Information is also available on the radio at 99.3 FM.

For road maps and motoring information go to the RACT office on the corner of George and York Sts. For bushwalking maps and camping gear go to Paddy Pallin at 110 George St, or Allgoods on the corner of York and St John Sts.

The Wilderness Society's shop at 174 Charles St has information relevant to conservation issues as well as loads of 'green' paraphernalia for sale – proceeds of which go towards protecting Tasmania's wilderness. There's a craft market in Yorktown Square every Sunday.

Cataract Gorge

Only a 10-minute walk from the city centre is the magnificent Cataract Gorge. Here, almost vertical cliffs line the banks of the South Esk River as it enters the Tamar. The area around the gorge has been made a wildlife reserve and is one of Launceston's most popular tourist attractions.

Two walking tracks, one on either side of the gorge, lead up to **First Basin**, which is filled with water from the South Esk River. The walk takes about 30 minutes; the northern trail is the easier. The waters of First Basin are very cold and deep, so you may feel safer swimming in the concrete pool. The landscaped area around the basin features picnic spots, the Gorge Restaurant, a cafe and lots of peacocks. The gorge is worth visiting at night when it's lit up.

There's also a chair lift which crosses the basin to the reserve on the other side; a six-minute ride costs $5 one way or return. A good walking track leads further up the gorge to **Second Basin** and Duck Reach, 45 minutes each way. A little further on is the Trevallyn Dam quarry where you can do 'simulated' hang-gliding for $10 (open

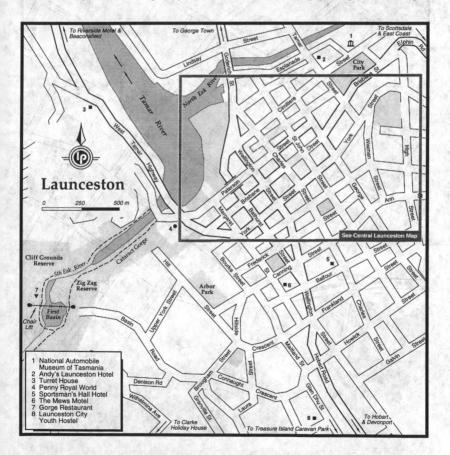

1 National Automobile
   Museum of Tasmania
2 Andy's Launceston Hotel
3 Turret House
4 Penny Royal World
5 Sportsman's Hall Hotel
6 The Mews Motel
7 Gorge Restaurant
8 Launceston City
   Youth Hostel

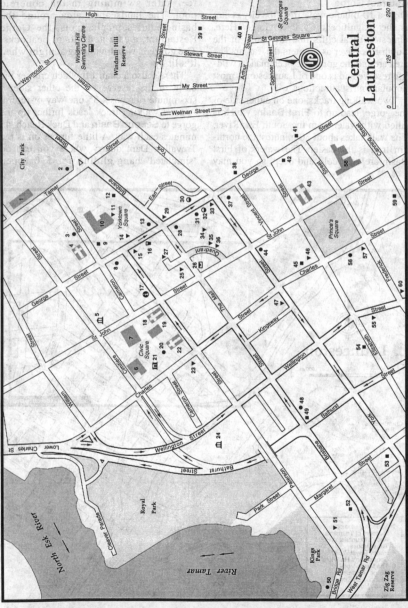

Central Launceston

daily in summer; weekends and holidays in winter).

Penny Royal World

The Penny Royal entertainment complex has exhibits including working 19th-century water mills and windmills, gunpowder mills and model boats. You can take a ride on a barge or a restored city tram or take a 45-minute cruise part-way up the gorge on the *Lady Stelfox* paddle-steamer. Although some parts of the Penny Royal complex are interesting, overall it's not worth the $19.50 ($9.50 children) admission. You can, however, just pay for one of the attractions; the cruise, for instance, costs $6.50 ($3.50 children) or visiting the windmill and corn mill is $4 ($2).

Queen Victoria Museum & Art Gallery

The Queen Victoria Museum & Art Gallery was built late last century and displays the splendour of the period both inside and out.

It has a collection of Tasmanian fauna, Aboriginal artefacts and colonial paintings. A major attraction is the splendid joss house, donated by the descendants of Chinese settlers. The centre is open Monday to Saturday from 10 am to 5 pm and Sunday from 2 to 5 pm. The gallery and museum are free. The planetarium is popular ($1.50) with one show Tuesday to Friday at 3 pm and two shows on Saturday at 2 and 3 pm.

The historic Johnstone & Wilmot warehouse, on the corner of Cimitiere and St John Sts, dates from 1842. It houses the **Community History** branch of the museum and operates a genealogical service. It is open Monday to Saturday from 10 am to 4 pm and Sunday from 2 to 4 pm.

Historic Buildings

In Civic Square is **Macquarie House**, built in 1830 as a warehouse but later used as a military barracks and office building. It now occasionally houses special theme exhibitions

---

PLACES TO STAY
9 Batman Fawkner Inn
10 Novotel Launceston Hotel
12 The Maldon
38 Fiona's B&B
39 Windmill Hill Tourist Lodge
40 Ashton Gate Guest House
41 Launceston City Backpackers
42 Colonial Motor Inn
45 Hotel Tasmania & Saloon
49 Irish Murphys
52 Rose Lodge
53 Old Bakery Inn
54 YHA summer hostel
59 Canning Cottage

PLACES TO EAT
11 Tairyo Japanese Restaurant & Sushi Bar
14 La Cantina
15 Shrimps
23 Arpar's Thai Restaurant
25 Banjo's
27 Croplines Coffee

29 Konditorei Manfred
33 O'Keefes Hotel
34 Muffin Kitchen
35 Crows Nest Coffee Shoppe
36 Pasta Resistance Too
46 Canton
47 Hari's Curry
51 Owl's Nest
55 Calabrisella Pizza
57 Fee & Me
60 Pizza Pub

OTHER
1 Albert Hall
2 Design Centre of Tasmania
3 Advnace Car Rentals
4 Holy Trinity Church
5 Community History Museum
6 Police Station
7 Town Hall
8 Old Umbrella Shop
13 Ansett
16 Royal Hotel
17 Travel & Information Centre
18 St Andrews Church

19 Library
20 Tasmap Centre
21 Macquarie House
22 Pilgrim Uniting Church
24 Queen Victoria Museum & Art Gallery
26 Post Office & Commonwealth Bank
28 Qantas
30 Tasmanian Wilderness Travel
31 Paddy Pallin
32 Tasmanian Redline Coaches
37 RACT
43 St Johns Church
44 Allgoods
48 Tamar Valley Coaches
50 Ritchies Mill Art Centre; Ripples Restaurant
56 The Wilderness Society Shop
58 St Andrews Hospital

of the Queen Victoria Museum & Art Gallery.

The **Old Umbrella Shop** at 60 George St was built in the 1860s and still houses a selection of umbrellas. Classified by the National Trust, it is the last genuine period shop in the state. The interior is lined with Tasmanian blackwood timber, and a good range of National Trust items are on sale. It's open from 9 am to 5 pm on weekdays and from 9 am to noon on Saturday.

On weekdays at 9.45 am there's a highly recommended one-hour guided historic walk around the city centre and former waterfront. The tours leave from the Tasmanian Travel & Information Centre and cost $10. At the centre you can also pick up a copy of the *Launceston – a walk through history* brochure and do it without the tour.

On the Midland Highway, 6km south of the city, is **Franklin House**, one of Launceston's most attractive Georgian homes. It was built in 1838 and has been beautifully restored and furnished by the National Trust. The house is open daily from 9 am to 5 pm (4 pm in winter); $6.

Parks & Gardens

Launceston is sometimes referred to as 'the garden city', and with so many beautiful public squares, parks and reserves, it's easy to see why.

The 13-hectare **City Park** is a fine example of a Victorian garden and features an elegant fountain, a bandstand, a monkey enclosure, a radio museum, a conservatory and a very old wisteria (behind the radio museum). **Prince's Square**, between Charles and St John Sts, features a bronze fountain bought at the 1858 Paris Exhibition, and a disconcerting statue of William Russ Pugh, credited with the first use of ether for surgical purposes in the southern hemisphere, descending stairs into the park.

Other public parks and gardens include **Royal Park**, near the junction between the North Esk and Tamar rivers; the **Punchbowl Reserve**, with its magnificent rhododendron garden; **Windmill Hill Reserve**; the **Trevallyn Recreation Area** and the Cataract Gorge (see earlier).

Other Attractions

The **National Automobile Museum of Tasmania** is on the corner of Cimitiere and Willis Sts. It's open from 9 am to 5 pm daily, but at $7.50 admission it is strictly for the enthusiast. The **Design Centre of Tasmania**, on the corner of Brisbane and Tamar Sts, is a retail outlet displaying work by the state's top artists and craftspeople.

For textile buffs, **Waverley Woollen Mills** was established in 1874 and is the oldest operating woollen mill in Australia. It is on Waverley Rd, 5km from the city centre, and is open weekdays from 9 am to 4 pm ($3). **Tamar Knitting Mills**, founded in 1926, is at 21 Hobart Rd and can also be inspected. It is open daily from 9 am to 4 pm; a self-guided tour is free.

Organised Tours

For further enquires about the following and other tours ask at the Travel & Information Centre. The Coach Tram Tour Company (☎ 6336 3133) has a comprehensive three-hour tour of the city sights for $23. Tasmanian Redline Coaches (☎ 6331 3233) in George St has half and full-day tours of city sights and the Tamar Valley ($33), the north-west coast ($35), the north-east ($40) and Cradle Mountain ($39). Tasmanian Wilderness Travel (☎ 6334 4442) has tours to Evandale Market on Sunday ($25), Tamar Valley ($35) and Cradle Mountain ($45).

At Home Point in Royal Park, Tamar River Cruises (☎ 6334 9900) offers four-hour river cruises from $46/23). There is also a seaplane (☎ 6334 9922) based here offering scenic flights costing from $50 for 20 minutes.

Places to Stay

Camping The *Treasure Island Caravan Park* (☎ 6344 2600) is in Glen Dhu St, 1km south of the city beside the expressway. It has camp sites ($13 a double), on-site vans ($32) and en-suite cabins with linen ($48). As this is the only caravan park in Launceston, it can get crowded at times, and being right next to the highway is quite noisy.

Hostels The smoke-free and friendly *Launceston City Backpackers* (☎ 6334 2327) at 173 George St is in the centre of town. It's an old, thoughtfully renovated house costing $14 per person in four-bed rooms.

Andy's Launceston Hotel (☎ 6331 4513), 1 Tamar St, has backpacker accommodation for $12. There's cheap meals, entertainment and even an Internet cafe. *Irish Murphys* (☎ 6331 4440), 211 Brisbane St, charges $14 for backpacker accommodation. It can get pretty noisy here.

The independent *Launceston City Youth Hostel* (☎ 6344 9779) is at 36 Thistle St, 2km from the centre of town. It has dorm beds and family rooms for $12 per person a night. The building dates from the 1940s and used to be the canteen for the Coats Patons woollen mill. The hostel has mountain and touring bikes as well as a comprehensive selection of bushwalking gear for hire.

At present the YHA runs a summer-only hostel (☎ 6334 4505) at 132 Elizabeth St; advance bookings can be made through the Hobart YHA office.

Guesthouses The *Rose Lodge* (☎ 6334 0120), 270 Brisbane St, provides friendly service and small but comfortable singles/ doubles with a cooked breakfast for $50/65.

The *Mews Motel* (☎ 6331 2861), 89 Margaret St, is closer to a guesthouse than a motel and is also reasonably priced at $55/ 63. Set back from George St, *Fiona's B&B* (☎ 6334 5965) offers delightful rooms for $55/70.

On the other side of the city, the *Windmill Hill Tourist Lodge* (☎ 6331 9337) at 22 High St charges $60/70. The lodge also has self-contained holiday flats at $75 a double.

If you can afford it, there are some great guesthouses offering rather luxurious heritage accommodation, such as the cosy *Turret House* (☎ 6334 7033), 41 West Tamar Rd, at $65/95 including a cooked breakfast. It's

north of Cataract Gorge, which makes for a delightful early morning walk.

Ashton Gate Guest House (☎ 6331 6180), on top of the hill at 32 High St, has rooms for $65/85 with a continental breakfast. A bit closer to town at 32 Brisbane St, the *Maldon* (☎ 6331 3211) provides good rooms in a grand Victorian building for $65/75.

Another place with a bit of history is the *Old Bakery Inn* (☎ 6331 7900) on the corner of York and Margaret Sts. It dates back to 1870 and charges $75/80.

For something really different, you could try renting your own fully furnished two-bedroom colonial cottage. The *Canning Cottage* (☎ 63314876) is actually two separate cottages at 26-28 Canning St. Both are very cosy and there are lots of steep steps and narrow doorways. The cost is a very reasonable $85 for a double with breakfast provisions.

Hotels Launceston has a good selection of hotels for a town of its size. One of the cheapest and quietest is the *Sportsman's Hall Hotel* (☎ 6331 3968) at 252 Charles St where singles/doubles cost $30/45, including a cooked breakfast.

Close by at 191 Charles St is the *Hotel Tasmania* (☎ 6331 7355), better known as the Saloon. The rooms have a fridge and telephone and cost $45/55, including continental breakfast.

Andy's Launceston Hotel (☎ 6331 4513), 1 Tamar St, has cheap B&B for $25/35. The rambling but mostly comfortable *Batman Fawkner Inn* (☎ 6331 7222) at 35 Cameron St has a range of single rooms from $25 to $46 and doubles at $65. The $25 rooms are small and dingy.

If you really want to be pampered then try the *Country Club Casino* (☎ 6444 8855) at Prospect Vale, 5km south of the city. Rooms are $219 a double ($115 during the week in the non-holiday periods).

Motels & Holiday Flats The *Riverside Motel* (☎ 6327 2522), 407 West Tamar Rd, is a little out of town near Cataract Gorge and charges $75 a double with breakfast. An attractive but pricey place in town is the *Colonial Motor Inn*, with rooms from $94 a double.

Although a little difficult to find, *Clarke Holiday House* (☎ 6334 2237) at 19 Neika Ave, about 1km out of town, is good value with rooms at $35 a double.

Places to Eat

Croplines Coffee at 1 Brisbane Court is worth the effort to find – it has the best coffee in town. *Banjo's* bakes all its own bread, pizza and cakes, and has two shops in town, one in Yorktown Square and one at 98 Brisbane St; both are open daily from 6 am to 6 pm. At Yorktown Square, *Molly York's Coffee Shoppe* is another fine place for breakfast and lunch.

For lunch there are some good-value places around the Quadrant in the city. The best bargain has to be *Pasta Resistance Too* with serves at $4.50 to $7. It's a tiny place packed full of customers. In a side lane, the *Muffin Kitchen* provides some interesting light meals. For somewhere more peaceful try the nearby 1st-floor *Crows Nest Coffee Shoppe*. Cooked meals are about $8, sandwiches about $3.50.

Konditorei Manfred, a German patisserie and cafe, has delicious, inexpensive homemade German rolls and pastries. It's at 95 George St, near the Redline depot, and is a good place to sit while waiting for a bus.

Ripples Restaurant, in the Ritchies Mill Art Centre opposite Penny Royal, specialises in light meals such as crêpes and pancakes, and there's a lovely view of the boats on the Tamar River from the outdoor tables.

Most of Launceston's many hotels have filling, reasonably priced counter meals ranging from $8 to $14. *O'Keefes Hotel* at 124 George St is a popular pub for meals starting at $5.50. The *Pizza Pub* on the corner of Wellington and Frederick Sts has OK pizzas for the cheap prices. The *South Charles Cafe* at the Sportsman's Hall Hotel (see Places to Stay) has restaurant-quality meals at reasonable prices.

There are a few good restaurants in

Launceston charging $10 to $16 for a main course. One of the most popular is *Calabrisella Pizza* (☎ 6331 1958), 56 Wellington St, which serves excellent Italian food and is often packed, so bookings are advisable. It opens daily (except Tuesday) at 5 pm and usually closes at midnight. You can also get takeaway pizza.

La Cantina in George St beside Yorktown Square is a popular licensed restaurant with Italian dishes from $10 to $18. *Arpar's Thai Restaurant* on the corner of Charles and Paterson Sts is well worth a visit; main courses cost around $12.

For Chinese food try the *Canton* at 201 Charles St; it's one of the best moderately priced Chinese restaurants in town. *Hari's Curry* at 152 York St has cheap and OK Indian takeaway and dining in.

Next to the Penny Royal complex, and with a good selection of Tasmanian wines and excellent meals, is the *Owl's Nest* at 147 Paterson St. The *Gorge Restaurant* at Cataract Gorge has fairly good food and undoubtedly the best setting in Launceston with main courses from $15 to $20.

For upmarket seafood and an intimate atmosphere go to *Shrimps* at 72 George St. *Fee & Me* offers elaborate fine dining at 190 Charles St. *Tairyo* on Yorktown Square is Launceston's Japanese restaurant; mains cost from $14 to $22.

Entertainment

There's quite a good range of evening entertainment in Launceston, most of which is advertised either in the free *Launceston Week* newspaper or in *This Week in Tasmania*.

The *Pavilion Tavern* in Yorktown Square has music from Tuesday to Saturday nights and a cabaret-style nightclub. The *Saloon* at 191 Charles St provides dancing in a trendy wild-west setting. The *Royal Hotel* in George St is another popular venue for live bands Wednesday to Saturday nights. *O'Keefes Hotel* at 124 George St has live bands on Friday, Saturday and Sunday after 10 pm. *Irish Murphys*, 211 Brisbane St, has bands Thursday, Friday and Saturday nights and seems to attract half of Launceston.

If you want to risk a few dollars, or just observe how the rich play, check out the *Launceston Federal Country Club Casino* at Prospect, 10km from the city centre. Most big-name bands touring from the mainland usually perform here. You don't have to pay to get in and about the only article of clothing disapproved of these days is track shoes. The disco at the casino, *Regines*, is free.

Getting There & Away

Air For information on domestic flights to and from Launceston, see the Getting There & Away section at the beginning of this chapter. Ansett is at 54 Brisbane St and Qantas is on the corner of Brisbane and George Sts.

Bus The main bus companies operating out of Launceston are Redline (☎ 1300 360 000, 6331 3233), 112 George St; Tasmanian Wilderness Travel/Tigerline (☎ 1300 300 520, 6334 4442), 101 George St; and Tamar Valley Coaches (☎ 6334 0828), 26 Wellington St.

Both Redline and Tasmanian Wilderness Travel/Tigerline run buses to Deloraine ($6.70), and Devonport ($13.30). Redline also has services to Hobart ($19), Burnie ($17.90), Wynyard ($20.40), Stanley ($27.30), Smithton ($27.30), George Town ($7), St Marys ($15.10), St Helens ($18.80), Bicheno ($21.10) and Swansea ($18). Tasmanian Wilderness Travel/Tigerline also has services to the west coast, including Cradle Mountain ($40) and Cynthia Bay ($49), as well as to Ben Lomond during the ski season ($29 return).

Car Rental There are plenty of car-rental firms in Launceston. Among the cheapest are Advance Car Rentals (☎ 6344 2164), 32 Cameron St, and Aberdeen Car Rentals (☎ 6344 5811), 35 Punchbowl Rd. Prices range from $25 to over $100 for a single hire day, less for longer rentals.

Getting Around

To/From the Airport Redline operates an airport shuttle service which meets all incoming flights and picks up passengers an hour or so before all departures. The fare is $7. A taxi costs about $18 to the city.

Bus The local bus service is run by Metro, and the main departure points are the two blocks in St John St between Paterson and York Sts. For $3.10 you can buy an unlimited travel Day Rover ticket which can be used all day at weekends and between 9 am and 4.30 pm and after 6 pm on weekdays. Most routes, however, do not operate in the evenings, and Sunday services are limited.

Bicycle Rent-a-Cycle, at the Launceston City Youth Hostel (☎ 6344 9779), has a good range of 10-speed tourers and mountain bikes. The tourers cost $12 a day or $65 a week, including helmet and panniers; mountain bikes cost $16 a day or $95 a week. There's a reducing rate for each additional week, and a bond applies to all rentals.

Around Launceston

HADSPEN (pop 1730)

Eighteen km from Launceston and just west of Hadspen is **Entally House**, one of Tasmania's best-known historic homes. It was built in 1819 by Thomas Haydock Reibey but is now owned by the National Trust. Set in beautiful grounds, it creates a vivid picture of what life must have been like for the well-to-do on an early farming property. The home, its stables, church, coach house and grounds are open daily from 10 am to 5 pm ($6/4).

On the roadside 2km west of Hadspen is **Carrick Mill**, a lovely, ivy-covered bluestone mill which dates from 1810. It has been well restored and now houses a restaurant that's open for lunch and dinner. On the side road near the mill and beside the dramatic ruins of the burnt-out Archers Folly, is the **Copper Art Gallery**. The art is unusual, entry is free and all works are for sale.

TASMANIA

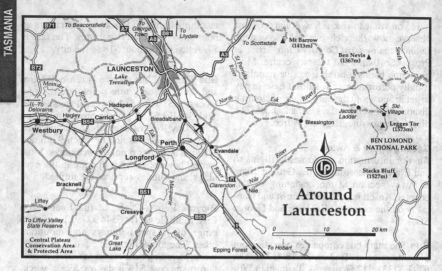

Places to Stay & Eat

In Hadspen, on the corner of the Bass Highway and Main Rd, is the *Launceston Cabin & Tourist Park* (☎ 6393 6391). The park has good facilities and charges $12 for a camp site and $45 a double in well-equipped cabins. The *Red Feather Inn* (☎ 6393 6331), built in 1844, has a good restaurant with main meals for around $15.

WESTBURY (pop 1280)

The historic town of Westbury, 28km west of Launceston, is best known for its **White House**, a property built in 1841. The house features colonial furnishings, vintage cars and a collection of 19th-century toys, and is open every day except Monday from 10 am to 4 pm ($6).

The **Westbury Gemstone, Mineral & Mural Display** and **Pearn's Steam World** are next door neighbours on the Bass Highway. They are open daily ($3 each). The town has a rare village green where a Maypole festival is held every November.

There are a couple of bakeries in town, but try the small range of quality goods baked in the wood-fired oven at the *Whitehouse*. The *Westbury Hotel* has basic singles/doubles for

$30/60, while *Fitzpatricks Inn* (☎ 6393 1153) has good value B&B for $30/60.

Redline (☎ 1300 360 000) runs at least three services each weekday from Launceston, stopping at Westbury before continuing on to Deloraine and Mole Creek or Devonport. Bookings are essential. Tasmanian Wilderness Travel/Tigerline (☎ 1300 300 520; 6334 3600 in Launceston) also runs buses daily along the main highway from Launceston to Devonport.

LIFFEY VALLEY

The Liffey Valley State Reserve protects the very beautiful rainforested valley at the foot of the Great Western Tiers and features the impressive **Liffey Valley Falls**. It's a popular destination for fishing and bushwalking, and day-trippers are also attracted by an amazing fernery.

The fernery, tearooms and gallery were built from wattle and pine. You can sit in the tearooms, enjoy freshly made scones and take in the view of Drys Bluff which, at 1297m, is the highest peak in the Great Western Tiers. The fernery and tearooms are open Wednesday to Sunday from 11 am to 5 pm but are closed during July. Liffey is 34km south of Carrick, via Bracknell, and is a good day trip from Launceston.

LONGFORD (pop 2820)
Longford, a National Trust classified town, is 27km from Launceston, in the rich pastoral area watered by the South Esk and Macquarie rivers.

One of the best ways to explore this historic town is to follow the free *Longford Village* brochure, which will guide you past many colonial buildings. Car racing fans must visit the Country Club Hotel which is full of Australian Grand Prix memorabilia from the 1950s and 60s.

If you want to stay overnight, the *Riverside Caravan Park* (☎ 6391 1470), on the banks of the Macquarie River, has camp sites ($9) and on-site vans ($30). The *Country Club Hotel* has bargain singles/doubles for $25/35 with a cooked breakfast. There are also a variety of B&B places around town for $80 to $120 a double.

EVANDALE (pop 1030)
Evandale, 19km south of Launceston in the South Esk Valley, is another town classified by the National Trust. Many of its 19th-century buildings are in excellent condition. In keeping with its old-world atmosphere, Evandale hosts the National Penny Farthing Championships in February each year, attracting national and international competitors. A market is held here every Sunday morning.

If you have your own transport and you've made an early start from Launceston, you'll be disappointed to find the Tourism & History Centre (on your left as you enter town) doesn't open till 11 am (closes 3 pm). Continue into town and head for Browns Village Store for a friendly informed chat and a cup of tea or coffee.

Eleven km south of Evandale is the National Trust property of **Clarendon**, which was completed in 1838 and is one of the grandest Georgian mansions in Australià. The house and its formal gardens are open daily from 10 am to 5 pm (closing an hour earlier in winter); $6/3.

The **Clarendon Arms Hotel** has been licensed since 1847 and there are some interesting murals in the hall depicting the area's history.

Places to Stay & Eat
For light meals and to stock up on groceries head to *Browns Village Store* in Russell St. The old *Clarendon Arms Hotel* (☎ 6391 8181) also in Russell St has rooms from $30/40; breakfast is extra. Much more interesting is *Greg & Gill's Place* (☎ 6391 8248) in a quiet corner of town and a lovely garden setting. The cost is $50/75 for a double including a light breakfast.

There are a number of the ubiquitous tea-rooms-cum-galleries, such as *Russells Restaurant*, opposite the old bakery in Russell St. Meals here cost $10 to $14. The pubs around town provide the usual counter meals.

LILYDALE (pop 340)
The small town of Lilydale, 27km from Launceston, stands at the foot of Mt Arthur. Three km from the town is the **Lilydale Falls Reserve**, which has camping facilities and two easily accessible waterfalls. At the nearby town of Lalla, there's the century-old **rhododendron gardens**, which are spectacular in spring; entry is $2 per vehicle.

BEN LOMOND NATIONAL PARK
This 165-sq-km park, 50km south-east of Launceston, includes the entire Ben Lomond Range and is best known for its good snow coverage and skiing facilities. During the ski season, a kiosk, tavern and restaurant are open in the alpine village and there's accommodation at the *Creek Inn* (☎ 6372 2444). Backpacker accommodation costs $15/30 shoulder/peak season and units which sleep four adults are $95/180 including breakfast. Lift tickets and equipment-hire cost about half what they do on the mainland: skis, boots and poles are around $34/20 a day for adults/children and lift passes about $30 per day and cheaper on weekdays. The scenery at Ben Lomond is magnificent all year round and the park is particularly noted for its

alpine wildflowers which run riot in spring and summer. The park's highest point is Legges Tor (1573m), which is also the second-highest peak in Tasmania. It can be reached via a good walking track from Carr Villa, on the slopes of Ben Lomond.

Getting There & Away
During the ski season, Tasmanian Wilderness Travel (☎ 1300 300 520) has a daily return service ($29) between the ski fields and Launceston. It also runs a shuttle service from the bottom of Jacobs Ladder to the alpine village ($6 one way). The ladder is a very steep climb on an unsealed road with six hairpin bends and no safety barriers – parking below it is advised.

Tamar Valley & North Coast

The northern plains are actually gently rolling hills and farmlands which extend from the Tamar Valley north of Launceston and west to the Great Western Tiers. There are some interesting towns and scenic spots and the best way to explore this area is to leave the highways and follow the quiet minor roads through the small towns. Most roads in this region are sealed.

The Tamar River separates the east and west Tamar districts and links Launceston with its ocean port of Bell Bay. Crossing the river near Deviot is Batman Bridge, the only bridge on the lower reaches of the Tamar. The river is tidal for the 64km to Launceston and wends its way through some lovely orchards, pastures, forests and vineyards. Black swans inhabit the area.

The Tamar Valley and nearby Pipers River (see the North East section) are among Tasmania's main wine-producing areas and the dry, premium wines produced here have achieved wide recognition.

European history in the region dates from 1798, when Bass and Flinders discovered the estuary and settlement commenced in 1804.

Slowly the valley developed, despite resistance from the Aboriginal people, first as a port of call for sailors and sealers from the Bass Strait islands and then as a sanctuary for some of the desperate characters who took to the bush during the convict days. By the 1830s the Aboriginal people had been driven out of their former hunting grounds.

In the late 1870s, gold was discovered at Cabbage Tree Hill – now Beaconsfield – and the fortunes of the valley took a new turn. The region boomed and for a time this was the third-largest town in Tasmania, before the mines closed in 1914.

Getting There & Away
On weekdays, Tamar Valley Coaches (☎ 6334 0828) has at least one bus a day along the West Tamar Highway, but there are no weekend services.

On most weekdays Redline has three buses a day up the East Tamar Valley between Launceston and George Town. The service extends to Low Head if advance bookings are made. On Sunday, there is a single service each way in the evenings. There are no Saturday services.

ROSEVEARS
This is a tiny riverside settlement on a side road off the West Tamar Highway. The main attraction is the **Waterbird Haven Trust**, a sanctuary for marine birds ($4). B&B is available beside the haven for $30/50 singles/doubles, but you'd have to be very fond of waterfowl to stay here. The *Rosevears Waterfront Tavern* has pub meals but no accommodation.

The other feature here is the **Strathblynn Wine Centre**. This is an outlet for Pipers Brook and tastings are free. Light lunches are also available at the centre.

BEACONSFIELD (pop 1010)
The once-thriving gold-mining town of Beaconsfield is still dominated by the ruins of its three original mine buildings. Two of these house the **Grubb Shaft Museum** complex, which is open daily from 10 am to 4 pm; entry is $4 (children 50c). It is staffed

by volunteers and is worth the visit. It is a must see if you're travelling with children as there are hands-on interactive exhibits including a noisy waterwheel-powered battery which is sure to please. A free display opposite the mine buildings has a reconstruction of a miner's cottage and old school. Beaconsfield Gold has opened up the old Hart shaft next to the museum, and with today's technology is hoping to strike some of the town's still plentiful gold reserves.

The town has two bakeries and an unusual takeaway counter hidden in the back of the supermarket. Of the two hotels in town only the *Club Hotel* offers accommodation but, at the time of writing, the mining company had booked all the rooms for the foreseeable future.

AROUND BEACONSFIELD

Further north is picturesque **Beauty Point**, the site of the Australian Maritime College. The *Redbill Point Van Park* provides tent sites ($8 a double), on-site vans ($25) and cabins ($42). Down by the wharf, the *Beauty Point Motor Hotel* has singles/doubles for $45/55 and a restaurant with waterfront views. You may see signs by the road advertising a vehicular ferry to George Town – at the time of writing that particular operation had ceased.

At the mouth of the Tamar River, the quiet holiday and fishing resorts of **Greens Beach** and **Kelso** have good beaches and caravan parks.

GEORGE TOWN (pop 4500)

George Town is on the eastern shore of the Tamar River close to the heads. It is best known as the site where Colonel Paterson landed in 1804, leading to the settlement of northern Tasmania. Although these days the town gets relatively few visitors, there are some interesting attractions in George Town and the surrounding area.

Just north of the town is Low Head which provides the navigation aids for ships to enter the river. The **pilot station** at Low Head, dating from 1835, is the oldest in Australia and houses an interesting **mari-**time museum, and a good cafe which is open daily; admission is $2. There are several navigational lead lights (miniature lighthouses) around town which date from 1881. Penguins return to their burrows near the lighthouse daily at dusk. There is good surf at **East Beach** on Bass Strait, and safe swimming in the river.

In Cimitiere St, the **Grove** is a very lovely Georgian stone residence built in the 1830s which has been classified by the National Trust. It's open daily from 10.30 am to 4 pm and admission is $4. Refreshments are available and lunch is served by staff in period costume.

The **old watch house** in Macquarie St dates from 1843 and has been turned into a Community Arts Centre; it's open on weekdays and costs nothing to look around. Also of interest is the **St Mary Magdalen Anglican Church** in Anne St.

Places to Stay

The *Travellers Lodge* (☎ 6382 3261) at 4 Elizabeth St is a YHA hostel in a restored house which dates back to 1891. It has beds for $12 ($14 for nonmembers) and family rooms for $40.

The *Pier Hotel Motel* (☎ 6382 1300), 3 Elizabeth St, has singles doubles at $40/50 and motel rooms from $99 a double. *Gray's Hotel* (☎ 6382 2655), 77 Macquarie St, charges $60/65.

If you have transport the *Beach Pines Holiday Village* (☎ 6382 2602), well out of town close to Low Head but right by the sea, has camp sites at $12 a double and cabins for $50.

Getting There & Away

George Town is the point of arrival and departure for the summer only *Devil Cat* service to Melbourne (see the main getting There & Away section).

HILLWOOD

South of Georgetown is the attractive rural area of Hillwood, where you can pick your own strawberries, raspberries and apples in season and sample Tasmanian fruit wines and cheese all year at the **Hillwood Straw-berry Farm** (☎ 6394 8180). The village is also noted for its fishing and lovely river views.

DELORAINE (pop 2170)

Deloraine is Tasmania's largest inland town and, with its lovely riverside picnic area, superb setting at the foot of the Great Western Tiers and good amenities, makes a great base from which to explore the surrounding area. Being so close to the Cradle Mountain area, and even closer to a number of impressive waterfalls and shorter walking tracks, Deloraine is fast becoming a major bushwalking centre. You'll find the visitor information centre near the roundabout at the top of the main street.

The town itself has a lot of charm, as many of its Georgian and Victorian buildings have been faithfully restored. Places of interest include the **folk museum** ($1) and **St Mark's Church of England**. Two km east of the town is the **Bowerbank Mill**, which is classified by the National Trust; these days it's a gallery and offers accommodation starting at $95/120.

Places to Stay & Eat

For camping there's the *Apex Caravan Park* (☎ 6362 2345) in West Parade, 500m from the town centre, where camp sites are $8/10 for unpowered/powered sites. There are no on-site vans or cabins available.

The *Highview Lodge Youth Hostel* (☎ 6362 2996) perched on the hillside at 8 Blake St has magnificent views of the Great Western Tiers and charges $12 ($15 nonmembers). The managers organise some reasonably priced and well-equipped trips to Cradle Mountain, the Walls of Jerusalem and other destinations, and mountain bikes and touring bikes are available for rent. This hostel receives excellent reports from many travellers. *Kev's Kumphy Korner* (☎ 6362 3267), is a backpackers' hostel at 24 Lake Highway, across the river from the main part of town. It's clean, modern and charges $10 a night but is only open in summer.

Almost opposite Kev's is the *Bush Inn*

(☎ 6362 2365), which offers hotel accommodation with a continental breakfast for $20/40. Back over the river at the bottom of the town is the *Deloraine Hotel* also charging $20/40.

Next door to the Deloraine Hotel is *Bonneys Inn* (☎ 6362 2974), which charges $40/70 for B&B in friendly colonial accommodation. The already attractive rates are negotiable outside the summer holiday season.

One of the best places to eat in Deloraine is *Emu Bay Brasserie* in the main street which is open daily from 8 am onwards. The atmosphere is relaxed and the range of very reasonably priced dishes is excellent.

Getting There & Away

Redline (☎ 1300 360 000) runs five services each weekday from Launceston through Westbury to Deloraine. Most buses continue to Devonport and bookings are essential. Tasmanian Wilderness Travel/Tigerline (☎ 1300 300 520) also runs regular buses daily along the main highway from Launceston through Deloraine to Devonport. There are also special services through Deloraine from Launceston, Devonport, the Walls of Jerusalem and Cynthia Bay at the southern end of the Overland Track. During summer these services operate daily, while in the cooler seasons there are about three services a week.

MOLE CREEK (pop 260)

About 25km west of Deloraine is Mole Creek, in the vicinity of which you'll find spectacular limestone caves, leatherwood honey and one of Tasmania's best wildlife parks.

Marakoopa Cave, from the Aboriginal word meaning 'handsome', is a wet cave 15km from Mole Creek which features two underground streams and an incredible glow-worm display. **King Solomon Cave** is a dry cave with amazing calcite crystals that reflect light; it has very few steps in it, making it the better cave for the less energetic. There are at least five tours in each cave daily. A visit to one cave costs $8/4, or you can visit both for $12/6. Current tour times are prominently displayed on access roads, or ring the ranger (☎ 6363 5182).

The leatherwood tree only grows in the damp western part of Tasmania, so honey made from its flower is unique to this state. From January to April, when the honey is being extracted, you can visit the **Stephens Leatherwood Honey Factory** and learn all about this fascinating industry. The factory is open during weekdays, and admission is free.

Two km from Chudleigh, east of Mole Creek, is the **Trowunna Wildlife Park**, which is worth a visit. It's open daily from 9 am to 5 pm ($7.50/3.50).

Places to Stay

Two km west of town, at the turn-off to the caves and Cradle Mountain, is the *Mole Creek Camping Ground* (☎ 6363 1150). It has basic facilities and charges $5.

The *Mole Creek Hotel* (☎ 6363 1102), in the main street, has rooms for $25/55 and counter meals daily. The *Mole Creek Guest House* (☎ 6363 1313), also in the main street, is a small place with B&B from $30/50.

SHEFFIELD (pop 1020)

Sheffield is either referred to as 'the town of murals' or 'the outdoor art gallery'. Since 1986, 25 murals depicting the history of the area have been painted in and around this little town, with a further 10 in the surrounding district, and these have become a major tourist attraction.

The Visitor Information Centre is in pioneer crescent behind Flo's Country Kitchen.

At the **Diversity Murals Theatrette**, at the western end of the main street, you can see an interesting documentary explaining the history and meaning of the individual paintings. The theatrette is open all day Monday to Saturday, and Sunday afternoons; admission is free with an optional donation.

The scenery around Sheffield is also impressive, with **Mt Roland** (1231m) domi-

nating the peaceful farmlands, thick forests, and rivers brimming with fish. Nearby is beautiful **Lake Barrington**, part of the Mersey-Forth hydroelectric scheme and a major rowing venue and state recreation reserve.

Places to Stay & Eat

The cheapest accommodation in the area is 16km out of town at Gowrie Park, at the base of Mt Roland. *Gowrie Park Backpackers* (☎ 6491 1385) costs only $8.50 a night for bunkhouse-style rooms. Linen hire is extra. Meals are available here at the *Weindorfers* restaurant but as reports from travellers vary about the food we recommend bringing your own supplies. This is an excellent base for walks to Mt Roland.

In town itself, the *Sheffield Caravan Park* (☎ 6491 1366) is tucked in behind the town hall. Facilities are basic and it costs $8 to pitch your tent and $25 for an on-site van. The *Roland Rock Motel & Hostel* (☎ 6491 1821) has backpacker accommodation for $15 as well as motel rooms for $35/45.

The *Sheffield Hotel* (☎ 6491 1130) has rooms for $30/40 with a light breakfast. The town also has a motor inn, and several host farms and cottages in the surrounding hills with accommodation at higher prices (the visitor centre has listings).

The *Red Rose Cafe* in Main St is a welcome reprieve from pub meals and takeaways. The menu is varied and caters for a range of budgets, and the food is good. For curiosity value alone *Flo's Country Kitchen* (Or is it *Flo's Pumpkin Scone Shoppe*?). This is run by Flo Bjelke-Peterson, a former senator and wife of the former Queensland premier, Joh Bjelke-Peterson; the speciality is pumpkin scones.

DEVONPORT (pop 22,300)

Nestled behind the dramatic lighthouse-topped Mersey Bluff, Devonport is the terminal for the *Spirit of Tasmania*, the vehicular ferry that runs between Victoria and Tasmania.

The Bluff Lighthouse was built in 1889 to direct the colony's rapidly growing sea traffic, and its light can be seen from up to 27km out to sea. Today, the port is still important and handles much of the export produce from the rich agricultural areas of northern Tasmania.

Devonport tries hard to attract tourists but its visitors are usually arriving or departing rather than actually staying. Indeed, the city is often referred to as the 'gateway to Tasmania'.

Information

For any information about Devonport and Tasmania in general, head for the Backpacker's Barn (☎ 6424 3628) at 12 Edward St. The Barn is open daily from 9 am to 6 pm, and the friendly staff can arrange transport (including minibus charter), car rental, help organise itineraries and look after your backpack. It has a cafe, an excellent bushwalking shop, a fax service, a rest room with showers which travellers can use for $2, and backpacker accommodation.

The Devonport Showcase (☎ 6424 8176) at 5 Best St also has a complete range of tourist information with displays and workshop demonstrations of arts and crafts. The centre is the official information centre and is open daily from 9 am to 5 pm. You can also listen to the tourist radio on 99.3 FM.

Tiagarra

The **Tasmanian Aboriginal Culture & Art Centre** is at Mersey Bluff, on the road to the lighthouse. It's known as Tiagarra, which is the Tasmanian Aboriginal word for 'keep', and was set up to preserve the art and culture of the Tasmanian Aboriginal people. The

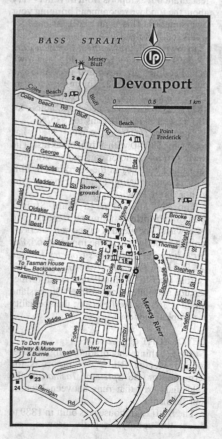

PLACES TO STAY
3   Mersey Bluff Caravan Park
5   River View Lodge
6   Elimatta Motor Inn
7   Abel Tasman Caravan Park
10 Tamahere Hotel
12 Edgewater Hotel & Motor Inn
18 Alexander & Formby Hotels
20 Macfie Manor
22 Argosy Motor Inn
24 MacWright House (YHA)

PLACES TO EAT
8   Renusha's & Rialto Restaurants
9   Klaas's Bakehouse
16 Laksa House
21 Dangerous Liaisons

OTHER
1   Bluff Lighthouse
2   Tiagarra
4   Maritime & Folk Musuem
11 Devonport Showcase
13 *Spirit of Tasmania* Ferry Terminal
14 Post Office
15 Taswegia
17 Devonport Gallery & Art Centre
19 Backpacker's Barn & Our House
23 Home Hill

centre has a rare collection of more than 250 rock engravings, and is open daily from 9 am to 5 pm; it's well worth the $3 ($2 concession) admission which includes a guided tour.

Museums
The **Tasmanian Maritime & Folk Museum**, halfway to Mersey Bluff near the foreshore, has a display of model sailing ships based on the vessels which visited Tasmania in the early days. It's open Tuesday to Sunday from 10 am to 4.30 pm ($2).

Taswegia in the lovely old building at 55-57 Formby Rd is a commercial printing house with an interesting printing museum. It's open daily from 10 am to 5 pm ($2).

The **Don River Railway & Museum** 4km out of town on the Bass Highway towards Ulverstone features a collection of steam locomotives and passenger carriages, and you can take a ride on a vintage train along the banks of the Don River. It's open most days from 10 am to 4 pm; admission to the site costs $4 which is refunded if you pay for a steam train ride ($7, children $4).

Other Attractions
The **Devonport Gallery** at 45-47 Stewart St is open Monday to Friday from 10 am to 5 pm, and Sunday afternoons (free).

At 77 Middle Rd, not far from the YHA hostel, is **Home Hill**, which used to be the residence of Joseph and Dame Enid Lyons and is now administered by the National Trust. Joseph Lyons is the only Australian to have been both the premier of his state and prime minister of Australia, and Dame Enid Lyons was the first woman to become a member of the House of Representatives. Home Hill is open Tuesday to Thursday and at weekends from 2 to 4 pm ($6).

Organised Tours
Most of the tours operating out of Devonport travel to Tasmania's wilderness areas and they vary from one-day trips to four-day tours. The two main operators are Tasmanian Wilderness Travel (book at the Backpacker's Barn or at the counter at the ferry terminal)

and Maxwell's Charter Tour Coach & Taxi Service (☎ 6492 1431). Tasman Bush Tours (☎ 6423 2335) operates over 20 tours from the Tasman House Backpackers.

Places to Stay
East Devonport has two caravan parks, both of which are close to the beach and have good reputations. The *Abel Tasman Caravan Park* (☎ 6427 8794) at 6 Wright St has camp sites ($7), on-site vans ($32) and cabins ($50). *Devonport's Vacation Village* (☎ 64 27 8886) in North Caroline St (1km east of Abel Tasman) has camp sites ($14) and single/double cabins ($25/40).

The *Mersey Bluff Caravan Park* (☎ 6424 8655) is 2.5km from town, near Tiagarra. It's a pleasant place with some good beaches nearby. It has camp sites ($14 a double), vans ($40) and cabins ($50).

The *Tamahere Hotel* (☎ 6424 1898) provides backpacker accommodation for $10 and singles/doubles for $30/50; en-suite rooms cost $35/55. The other budget accommodation is *Tasman House Backpackers* (☎ 6423 2335) at 169 Steele St. Rooms vary from bunkhouse to motel style. A dorm costs $10 per person, twin $12 per person, double $25 and en-suite double $30. It's a 15-minute walk from town and transport can be arranged when booking.

MacWright House (☎ 6424 5696), 400m past Home Hill at 115 Middle Rd, is Devonport's YHA hostel; it charges $10 a night ($12 nonmembers) and is a 40-minute walk from the town centre. A Tasmanian Wilderness Travel bus can transport you from the ferry terminal or airport right to the hostel.

The friendly *River View Lodge* (☎ 6424 7357) at 18 Victoria Parade on the foreshore charges $55/68 for singles/doubles, which includes an excellent cooked breakfast; it has a wheelchair-friendly room and is deservedly popular with travellers.

Macfie Manor (☎ 6424 1719) at 44 Macfie St is a beautiful two-storey Federation brick building. Completely renovated, it charges $65/85 for singles/doubles including a cooked breakfast.

TASMANIA

Two good hotels close to the centre of town are the *Alexander Hotel* (☎ 6424 2252) at 78 Formby Rd, which charges $30/40 for comfortable clean rooms and a continental breakfast; and the *Formby Hotel* (☎ 6424 1601) at 82 Formby Rd, where rooms cost $35/45 with a cooked breakfast; en-suite rooms are $15/20 dearer.

There are quite a number of motels in the city centre and East Devonport. The *Edgewater Hotel & Motor Inn* (☎ 6427 8441) at 2 Thomas St in East Devonport is not very attractive from the outside, but is close to the ferry terminal and charges from $40/45 for singles/doubles. The *Argosy Motor Inn* (☎ 6427 8872) in Tarleton St, East Devonport charges $69/74. North of the city centre at 15 Victoria Parade, the *Elimatta Motor Inn* (☎ 6424 6555) charges from $50/55.

Places to Eat

Our House, the cafe at the front of the Backpacker's Barn, 12 Edward St, is open daily from 9 am to 4 pm. The *Old Devonport Town Coffee Shop* in the Devonport Showcase is also open daily and is good for a drink or a snack. *Klaas's Bakehouse*, 11 Oldaker St, is only open on weekdays but has excellent cakes and pastries.

Most hotels have good counter meals for around $8 to $15; try the *Tamahere* at 34 Best St, the *Alexander* at 78 Formby Rd, or the *Formby* at 82 Formby Rd. In East Devonport, the *Edgewater Hotel* at 2 Thomas St has cheap counter meals.

Devonport has a good selection of moderately priced restaurants. *Dangerous Liaisons* at 28 Forbes St is open Tuesday to Friday for good value lunch and dinner (dinner only on Saturday). If you prefer pasta try the *Rialto Restaurant* at 159 Rooke St. While the pasta is not fancy, service is prompt. It's open Monday to Friday for lunch and every evening for dinner until late. Next door is *Renusha's* Indian restaurant.

For Chinese food, try the *Silky Apple* at 33 King St, near the post office, and for Malaysian and Chinese, *Laksa House* is opposite the Backpacker's Barn in Edward St. These restaurants are open every evening and also serve takeaway.

Entertainment

Check the *Advocate* newspaper for Devonport's entertainment details. The *Warehouse Nightclub* and *Spurs Saloon* are in King St. The *Elimatta Motor Inn* at 15 Victoria Parade occasionally has weekend bands, and on Wednesday, Friday and Saturday nights there's a nightclub called *Steps*. The *Tamahere Hotel* has entertainment on Friday and Saturday nights.

Getting There & Away

Air For information on domestic flights to and from Devonport, see the Getting There & Away section at the beginning of this chapter.

Bus Redline and Tasmanian Wilderness Travel have counters at the ferry terminal. All buses stop at the ferry terminal. The Redline depot is at 9 Edward St. Redline has daily buses from Devonport to Hobart ($32.30), Launceston ($13.30), Burnie ($7.10) and Smithton ($17.50).

Tasmanian Wilderness Travel/Tigerline has daily buses to Launceston ($12.50), Burnie ($6.50), Queenstown ($29.10) and Strahan ($34.50).

During the summer, Tasmanian Wilderness Travel buses depart daily from Devonport to Sheffield and to Cradle Mountain ($38) and Lake St Clair. There's a twice-weekly bus to the Walls of Jerusalem. Departure points are the Devonport Showcase and the Redline Depot.

If there is a group of you, or you can organise a group of five to eight like-minded people on the way over on the ferry, and none of the scheduled services suit your particular needs, you can charter a minibus from Cradle Mountain Transport; ask at the Backpacker's Barn. For example, a bus from Devonport to Cradle Mountain costs $130.

Car Rental There are plenty of cheap car-rental firms such as Range/Rent-a-Bug (☎ 6427 9034) at 5 Murray St, East

Devonport. The major companies all have desks at the *Spirit of Tasmania* terminal or just opposite it.

Boat See the Getting There & Away section at the beginning of this chapter for details on the *Spirit of Tasmania* ferry service between Melbourne and Devonport. The TT Line terminal (☎ 13 2010) is on the Esplanade, East Devonport. When you get off the boat look for the Redline bus with the sign 'Devonport City'. This will deliver you to the Redline terminal and the Backpacker's Barn in Edward St.

Getting Around
There's a shuttle bus that meets every flight at the airport and takes you into town for $5. The taxi fare into town is about $15.

Mersey Bus & Coach Service operates the local bus service. Devonport Showcase has the timetable and list of destinations.

There's also a Mersey River ferry service linking central Devonport with East Devonport, which operates seven days a week. The one-way adult fare is $1.50 and bicycles cost 50c. Enquire about hire bicycles at the Backpackers' Barn.

AROUND DEVONPORT
Formerly a farm, the **Asbestos Range National Park** was declared a national park in 1976 and named after the mineral once found in the area (there hasn't been any mining for over 80 years and the area is quite safe!). It's 25km east of Devonport. Animals and birds are prolific, and there are a number of signed walking tracks through the park. The **Springlawn Nature Walk** takes about an hour from the car park and includes a boardwalk over a wetland to a bird hide.

There are four camp sites in the park with pit toilets, bore water and firewood provided. For more information, contact the park ranger on ☎ 6428 6277.

ULVERSTONE (pop 9,792)
Ulverstone, at the mouth of the Leven River, is a pleasant town with some fine beaches and good amenities; it's a good base from which to explore the surrounding area.

The **local history museum**, 50 Main St, focuses on European pioneers and their activities in the region ($2/1).

Just 30km south is the **Gunns Plains Cave Reserve**; daily guided tours of the spectacular wet cave leave hourly from 10 am to 4 pm ($8/4). Also at Gunns Plains, *Wings Farm Park* (☎ 6429 1335) has backpacker accommodation ($10), doubles ($15) and a cabin which sleeps four ($45). Nearby is **Leven Canyon**, a magnificent gorge with a number of walking tracks.

If you're driving from Ulverstone to Penguin, consider taking the old Bass Highway, which runs closer to the coast than the new one and offers some fine views of three small islands known as the **Three Sisters**. As you approach Penguin the countryside takes on a 'Thomas the Tank Engine' feel as cottage gardens, small-gauge railway track and the seaside somehow all fit into the model-like vista.

Places to Stay & Eat
The *Ulverstone Caravan Park* (☎ 6425 2624) in Water St is close to town and has camp sites ($10), on-site vans ($32 for a double), en-suite cabins ($42) and units with linen ($52).

The rather majestic *Furner's Hotel* (☎ 6425 1488) has very comfortable en-suite singles/doubles for $40/65 including a cooked breakfast. This is stylish accommodation and there is no noisy public bar downstairs. There is a very good bistro, however, featuring Tasmanian highland beef and cheesecakes that would stand proud in New York.

For a friendly guesthouse in a great location try the *Ocean View Guest House* (☎ 6425 5401) at 1 Victoria St, 100m from the beach. It's a lovely old house where singles/doubles with a continental breakfast cost from $45/65. If you prefer a motel try the *Ulverstone Motor Lodge*, just across the river from town, at $45 for a single or double.

Pedro the Fisherman, down by the wharf, does extremely cheap, but filling, takeaway fish & chips. Around the back, overlooking the water is *Pedro's the Restaurant*, an upmarket seafood place.

In Reibey St there's *Sam's Pizza Bar* for takeaway, and the *Jade Willow* Chinese restaurant.

Getting There & Away

See the Burnie Getting There & Away section for details of transport to and from Ulverstone.

North-West

Tasmania's magnificent north-west coast is a land as rich in history as it is diverse in scenery. Its story goes back 37,000 years to a time when giant kangaroos and wombats roamed the area. Aboriginal tribes once took shelter in the caves along the coast, leaving a legacy of rock engravings and middens.

Europeans quickly realised the potential of the region and settlers moved farther and farther west, building towns along the coast and inland on the many rivers. The area was soon transformed into a vital part of the young colony's developing economy.

BURNIE (pop 19,130)

Although Burnie sits on the shores of Emu Bay and is backed by rich farming land, it is factory smoke, not the views, which usually welcomes the visitor to Tasmania's fourth-largest city. One of Burnie's main assets is its deep-water port, which makes cargo shipping an important industry. Another major employer, Amcor, owns Associated Pulp & Paper Mills, which began producing paper in 1938.

The town (named after William Burnie, a director of the Van Diemen's Land Company) started life quietly, growing mainly potatoes for the first 40 years, until the discovery of tin at Mt Bischoff in Waratah. In 1878, the Van Diemen's Land Company opened a wooden tramway between the mine at Waratah and the port of Burnie. This was the humble beginning of the important Emu

Bay Railway which, in the 1900s, linked the port of Burnie to the rich silver fields of Zeehan and Rosebery. The Emu Bay Railway, which travels through some wild and impressive country, still operates today but does not carry passengers.

The Tasmanian Travel & Information Centre in High St, attached to the Pioneer Village Museum, is a good source of information on Tasmania's north-west. Pick up a copy of the *Walk Through Burnie* brochure for a self-guided walking tour of the town centre.

Things to See & Do

The **Pioneer Village Museum**, in High St, next to the Civic Plaza, has an authentic blacksmith's shop, printer and boot shop. This impressive museum is open Monday to Friday from 9 am to 5 pm, and weekends from 1.30 to 4.30 pm ($4.50/1.50).

Burnie Park is quite pleasant and features an animal sanctuary and the oldest building in town, the Burnie Inn. The inn was built in 1847 and moved from its original site to the park in 1973. It's classified by the National Trust and is open on weekends.

From Monday to Friday at 2 pm you can take a free tour of the Amcor complex. The Lactos cheese factory on Old Surrey Rd is open daily and you can taste and purchase the products. The **Burnie Regional Art Gallery** in Wilmot St is open daily and is also worth a look.

There are a number of waterfalls and viewpoints in the Burnie area, including **Roundhill Lookout** and **Fern Glade**, just 3km from the centre, and the impressive **Guide Falls** at Ridgley, 16km away. The impressive **Emu Valley Rhododendron Gardens**, 8km south of Burnie, are open daily between September and March ($3).

Places to Stay

Burnie is not overly endowed with budget accommodation (much of the accommodation is pretty expensive and aimed at the business traveller) and most recreational travellers will be passing through and spending the night elsewhere. At Cooee, 3km west

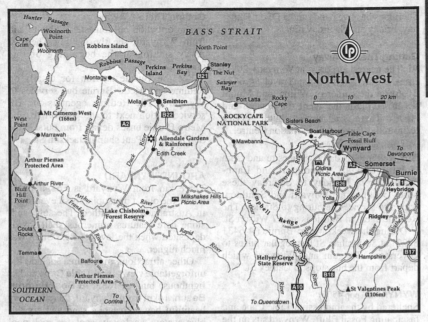

North-West

BASS STRAIT

Hunter Passage
Woolnorth Point
Cape Grim
Woolnorth
Robbins Island
North Point
Robbins Passage
Perkins Island
Perkins Bay
Stanley
The Nut
B21
Montagu
Sawyer Bay
Mella
Smithton
Port Latta
Rocky Cape
B22
ROCKY CAPE NATIONAL PARK
Sisters Beach
Mt Cameron West (168m)
A2
Boat Harbour
Table Cape
Fossil Bluff
Wynyard
To Devonport
West Point
Marrawah
Allendale Gardens & Rainforest
Edith Creek
Mawbanna
Oldina Picnic Area
A2
Somerset
Burnie
Arthur Pieman Protected Area
Heybridge
Bluff Hill Point
Arthur River
Milkshakes Hills Picnic Area
Yolla
B26
Couta Rocks
Lake Chisholm Forest Reserve
Rapid River
Ridgley
Temma
Balfour
Hellyer Gorge State Reserve
Hampshire
B17
Arthur Pieman Protected Area
SOUTHERN OCEAN
To Corinna
To Queenstown
A10
A18
St Valentines Peak (1106m)

0   10   20 km

of Burnie on the Bass Highway, the *Treasure Island Caravan Park* (☎ 6431 1925) has camp sites ($10 a double), on-site vans ($36) and cabins ($52). It also has hostel accommodation for $15 per person.

Cheapest of the hotels is the *Regent* (☎ 6431 1933) at 26 North Terrace, which charges $30/35 for singles/doubles. *Glen Osborne House* (☎ 6431 9866) at 9 Aileen Crescent, about 1km from the town centre, is a beautiful period house with large en-suite rooms for $75/99 including breakfast.

Closer to the town centre is the *Burnie Town House* (☎ 6431 4455) at 139 Wilson St, which charges $95 for en-suite rooms. For accommodation with a bit of character, *Apartments Down Town* (☎ 6432 3219), 52 Alexander St, has Art Deco rooms from $79/90.

Places to Eat

There are plenty of cafes in the town centre. For cheap lunches try *Buccachino's* in Wilmot St or the *Napoli* cafe above the Harris Scarfe department store on the corner of Wilson and Cattley Sts.

Most hotels have reasonably priced counter meals from Monday to Saturday.

The *Beach Hotel* at 1 Wilson St, on the waterfront, always has a good spread.

Ladbrooke St, between Mount and Wilson Sts, is the area to go when you're hungry. The *Kasbah Pizza Bar* is open until late, and opposite is *Li Yin*, which has an all-you-can-eat Chinese buffet for $13.80.

Not far away, at 104 Wilson St, is the more upmarket *Flannery's Restaurant* (☎ 6431 9393) which has good service and mouth-watering meals for around $19.

Entertainment

Check the *Advocate* newspaper for entertainment listings. On Friday and Saturday nights there is a disco at the *Bay View Hotel*.

On Friday nights the *Beach Hotel* is a popular place for a drink.

Sheridans has live bands and a DJ on Thursday, Friday and Saturday nights.

Getting There & Away

Air The nearest airport is at Wynyard, 20km from Burnie. North West Travel (☎ 6431 2166) on the corner of Wilmot and Mount Sts in Burnie is the agent for Kendell and Ansett. There is an airport shuttle service to/from the Travel & Information Centre.

Bus Redline has daily services to and from Hobart ($36.90), Devonport and Launceston. From Monday to Saturday these buses continue to Wynyard and Smithton, with two services detouring to Stanley. The Redline agent in Burnie is at 117 Wilson St.

During the week, Metro Burnie (☎ 6431 3822) at 30 Strahan St has regular buses to Ulverstone, Penguin and Wynyard which depart from the bus stops in Cattley St.

WYNYARD (pop 4500)

Sheltered by the impressive Table Cape and fascinating Fossil Bluff, Wynyard sits on the seafront and the banks of the Inglis River. The town is surrounded by beautiful patchwork farmland which is best appreciated by flying into Wynyard airport.

Although there's not much to see in the town itself, Wynyard is a good base from which to explore the many attractions in the area. There is a Visitor Information Centre in Goldie St, not far from the wharves.

Places to Stay & Eat

Close to town, on the Esplanade, *Wynyard Caravan Park* (☎ 6442 1998) has camp sites ($10), on-site vans ($33) and cabins ($52).

The *Wynyard Youth Hostel* (☎ 6442 2013) is at 36 Dodgin St, one block south of the main street, and has rooms for $11 ($14 nonmembers). If you've arrived by air, it's only a five-minute walk from the airport.

The *Federal Hotel* (☎ 6442 2056) at 82 Goldie St in the middle of town charges $30/50 for B&B and also has good counter lunches daily and dinner Monday to Saturday.

Getting There & Away

For information on domestic flights to and from Wynyard, see the Getting There & Away section at the beginning of this chapter.

See the Burnie section for details on Redline and Metro Burnie bus services to Wynyard. The Redline agent is the BP service station next to the post office, and Metro Burnie buses depart from outside the St Vincent de Paul shop in Jackson St.

AROUND WYNYARD

Three km from Wynyard is **Fossil Bluff**, where the oldest marsupial fossil ever found in Australia was unearthed. The soft sandstone here features numerous shell fossils deposited when the level of Bass Strait was much higher.

Other attractions in the area include the unforgettable views from **Table Cape** and its lighthouse built in 1885. At **Boat Harbour Beach**, 14km from Wynyard, there is a very beautiful bay with white sand and crystal-blue water – a lovely spot for rock-pool exploring and snorkelling. If you want to stay the night, the *Boat Harbour Beach Backpackers* (☎ 6445 1273) in Strawberry Lane not far from the beach charges $14 per person. The secluded location and spectacular views are worth the trouble to get there. The owner can pick you up from the highway at the Boat Harbour turn-off. The town also has a caravan park, motel and cottage accommodation.

Nearby, in the **Rocky Cape National Park**, is Sisters Beach, an 8km expanse of glistening white sand with safe swimming and good fishing. Also in the park is the 10-hectare **Birdland Native Gardens**, which has information on many native bird species. You can also visit a number of waterfalls, including **Detention Falls**, 3km south of Myalla, and **Dip Falls**, near Mawbanna.

Unless you have your own transport, you will have to hitch to get to most of these places. Redline Coaches will drop you at the turn-off to Boat Harbour (3km) and Sisters Beach (8km).

STANLEY (pop 540)

Nestled at the foot of the extraordinary Circular Head (better known as the Nut), Stanley is a very appealing historic village which has changed little since its early days. In 1826 it became the headquarters of the London-based Van Diemen's Land Company, which was granted a charter to settle and cultivate Circular Head and the north-western tip of Tasmania.

The area prospered when it began shipping large quantities of mutton, beef and potatoes to Victoria's goldfields, and continued to prosper when settlers discovered rich dairying land behind Sisters Hills and tin reserves at Mt Bischoff.

Today, Stanley is a charming fishing village with many historic buildings and great seascapes. To better appreciate Stanley's charm, pick up a walking-tour map from De Jonge's Souvenirs or the Discovery Centre, both in Church St.

The Nut

This striking 152m-high volcanic rock formation, thought to be 12.5 million years old, can be seen for many kilometres around Stanley. It's a steep 20-minute climb to the top, but the view is definitely worth it. For the less energetic, a chair lift operates, weather permitting, from 9.30 am to 4.30 pm; rides cost $6 (children $4, family $15). At the top you can take a leisurely stroll from one lookout to the next or catch the Nut Buggy ($5, children under 10 free).

Other Attractions

The old bluestone building on the seafront is the **Van Diemen's Land Company Store**, designed by colonial architect John Lee Archer and dating from 1844. The company's headquarters were at **Highfield**, 2km north of Stanley. This historic site has recently been restored and is open daily ($2 entry to outbuildings and grounds, $5 entry to full site including house interior).

Near the wharf in Stanley is a particularly fine old bluestone building which used to be a grain store (now a restaurant). It was built in 1843 from stones brought to Stanley as ship's ballast.

The little folk museum called the **Discovery Centre**, in Church St, is open daily from 10 am to 4.30 pm ($3). Next door, the **Plough Inn** (1840) has been fully restored and houses the Stanley Craft Centre.

Other buildings of historical interest include **Lyons Cottage** in Church St, which was the birthplace of former prime minister Joseph Lyons (open from 10 am to 4 pm, admission by donation); the **Union Hotel**, also in Church St, which dates from 1849; and the **Presbyterian church**, which was probably Australia's first prefabricated building, bought in England and transported to Stanley in 1853.

Places to Stay

The *Stanley Youth Hostel* (☎ 6458 1266) in Wharf Rd is part of the *Stanley Caravan Park* and charges $12 a night ($14 nonmembers). The caravan park has camp sites ($9.50), on-site vans ($30) and en-suite cabins ($52).

Pol & Pen (☎ 6458 1334) is a pair of two-bedroom self-contained cottages, which are good value at $65 a double. The *Union Hotel* (☎ 6458 1161) in Church St has basic rooms for $25/40 a single/double, breakfast extra. There are many B&B cottages dotted around Stanley; prices range from $70 to $120 a double in the holiday season – bargain hard at other times, though many will be closed in winter.

Places to Eat

Hursey Seafoods at 2 Alexander Terrace sells live fish from the tanks in the shop, as well as takeaways. Next door is *Kermie's Cafe*, where you get to sit down and eat the same food at higher prices. Upstairs is *Julie & Patrick's Seafood Restaurant* where the best of the fish and crayfish are served in the evenings. All three businesses are run by the same people; the cafe and shop close at 6 pm when the restaurant opens for the evening.

Sullivans, a licensed restaurant at 25 Church St, is open daily and serves light lunches, teas and dinner. The *Union Hotel* has quite good counter meals, and at the Nut there is the *Nut Rock Cafe*.

Getting There & Away

Redline has two services a day on weekdays running from Hobart to Smithton via Stanley, and three running via Stanley in the other direction. The Redline agent is the BP service station on the corner of Wharf Rd and Marine Esplanade.

AROUND STANLEY

Twenty-two km from Stanley, **Smithton** serves one of Tasmania's largest forestry areas and is also the administrative centre for Circular Head. There's not much to see or do in the town itself, but the airport makes it an arrival point for some light aircraft flights from the mainland.

Allendale Gardens, on the B22 road to Edith Creek, are a good place to walk around or relax; the two-hectare property includes impressive botanical gardens, a rainforest walk, a wildflower section and a cafe serving Devonshire teas. The centre is open daily from 9 am to 6 pm (closed June to August); $5/2.50.

Temperate rainforest and button-grass moorland can be found at **Milkshake Forest Reserve**, 45km south of Smithton. A further 26km south-west of the reserve, set in lovely rainforest, is tranquil **Lake Chisholm**.

MARRAWAH

Marrawah, at the end of the Bass Highway, is where the wild Indian Ocean occasionally throws up the remains of ships wrecked on the dangerous and rugged west coast. To visit Marrawah, the most westerly town in Tasmania, it is best to have your own vehicle, but from Monday to Saturday you can get a lift with the mail run from Smithton.

The area has seen minimal disturbance from European development and was once popular with the Tasmanian Aboriginal people. Many signs of these people remain, and particular areas have been proclaimed reserves to protect the remaining relics, including rock carvings, middens and hut depressions. The main Aboriginal sites are at **Mt Cameron West**, near Green Point, **West Point** and **Sundown Point**.

The township of Marrawah consists of a hotel serving daily counter meals, and a general store selling petrol and supplies. The hotel has no accommodation, but there is a basic camp site at Green Point, 2km from Marrawah. This region is good for fishing, canoeing, camping and bushwalking, or just for getting away from it all. Marrawah's main attraction, however, is its enormous surf – the state's surfing championships are held here every year around Easter.

ARTHUR RIVER

The sleepy town of Arthur River, 14km south of Marrawah, is mainly a collection of holiday houses belonging to people who come here to fish. There is one kiosk with basic supplies, no public transport and, apart from a camp site with basic facilities, only one place to stay. The *Arthur River Holiday Units* (☎ 6457 1288) in Gardiner St has doubles for $60 to $70.

Apart from the fishing, visitors come here to explore the **Arthur Pieman Protected Area** and to take a cruise on the Arthur River. The attractions of the protected area include magnificent ocean beaches, Rebecca Lagoon, Temma Harbour, waterfalls on the Nelson Bay River, the old mining town of Balfour, the Pieman River and the Norfolk Ranges.

Arthur River Cruise

Scenic day cruises on the Arthur River (☎ 6457 1158) depart at 10.15 am and return around 3 pm. You sail up the river to the confluence of the Arthur and Frankland rivers. The cruise runs daily in summer; book at any Tasmanian Travel & Information Centre. The cost is $40 each ($20 children).

HELLYER GORGE

Seven km from Burnie is the small town of Somerset, at the junction of the Murchison and Bass highways. Hellyer Gorge is about 40km south of Somerset on the banks of the Hellyer River. The highway winds its way through the impressive gorge. At the picnic area by the river, there are two very short walks which provide a welcome break from driving. From Burnie to the Waratah area there is an alternative road which is faster but less scenic. It passes through Ridgley and Hampshire on road B18 and avoids the winding road through the Hellyer Gorge. This has diverted some traffic away from the peaceful reserves in the gorge.

About 40km south of Hellyer Gorge, is the turn off to Cradle Mountain. This is a major road linking the west coast (via the northern end of Cradle Mountain National Park) with the region south of Devonport.

The West

Nature at its most awe-inspiring is the attraction of Tasmania's rugged and magnificent west coast. Formidable mountains, button grass plains, ancient rivers, tranquil lakes, dense rainforests and a treacherous coast are all features of this compelling and beautiful region, some of which is now World Heritage Area.

Many centuries before the arrival of Europeans, this part of Tasmania was home to many of the state's Aboriginal people, and plenty of archaeological evidence, some of it more than 20,000 years old, has been found of these original inhabitants.

Prior to 1932, when the road from Hobart to Queenstown was built, the only way into the area was by sea, through the dangerously narrow Hells Gates into Macquarie Harbour. Despite such inaccessibility, early European settlement brought explorers, convicts, soldiers, loggers, prospectors, railway gangs and fishermen, while the 20th century has brought outdoor adventurers, naturalists and environmental crusaders.

It was over the wild rivers, beautiful lakes and tranquil valleys of Tasmania's southwest that battles between environmentalists and big business raged. The proposed damming of the Franklin and Lower Gordon rivers caused the greatest and longest-running environmental debate in Australia's history in the 1980s and has subsequently seen the boom of ecotourism in Strahan.

While debate continues on questions of wilderness versus electricity, and World Heritage Area versus woodchipping, nature herself has begun to reclaim what is hers. The hills around Queenstown, left barren from the mining era, are now beginning to show signs of regeneration.

CORINNA

Corinna, 28km south-west of Savage River, was once a thriving gold-mining settlement but is now little more than a ghost town. These days it's the scenery and the Pieman River Cruises (☎ 6446 1170) that attract visitors. The cruise passes impressive forests of eucalypts, ferns and Huon pines to Pieman Heads. Costing $30 (children $15), which includes morning tea, the tours on the MV *Arcadia II* depart daily at 10.30 am and return at 2.30 pm. It's definitely wise to book during the summer months.

The only accommodation is at the *Pieman Retreat Cabins* (☎ 6446 1170). Cabins can sleep up to six people and cost $60 a double and $10 for each extra person. The cabins are self-contained and linen is available at extra cost.

The Pieman River Barge operates daily from 9 am to 5 pm ($10).

ROSEBERY (pop 1440)

Gold was discovered in Rosebery in the late 1800s and mining began early in the next century with the completion of the Emu Bay Railway between Burnie and Zeehan. However, when the Zeehan lead smelters closed in 1913 operations also closed in Rosebery. The Electrolytic Zinc Company then bought and reopened the mine in 1936 and it has operated ever since.

Eight km south of town, at the abandoned mining town of Williamsford, is the start of an excellent walk to the impressive **Montezuma Falls**.

There's not much to see in Rosebery, but if you want to stay overnight the *Mount Black Lodge* (☎ 6473 1039) has hostel accommodation for $15 and singles/doubles for $35/60. The *Plandome Hotel* (☎ 6473 1351) has counter meals and accommodation for $25/38, and there's a caravan park with camping ($8), on-site vans ($28), cabins ($45) and a hostel ($12).

ZEEHAN (pop 1120)

In 1882 rich deposits of silver and lead were discovered in the quiet little town of Zeehan, and by the turn of the century it had become a booming mining centre, known as Silver City, with a population that peaked at nearly 10,000. In its heyday Zeehan had 26 hotels,

and its Gaiety Theatre seated 1000 people. In 1908, however, the mines began to fail and the town declined.

With the reopening and expansion of the Renison Tin Mine at Renison Bell, Zeehan experienced a revival in the late 1960s, becoming the housing base for Renison Ltd.

Things to See

Buildings that remain from the early boom days include the once-famous **Grand Hotel** encompassing the **Gaiety Theatre**, the **post office**, the **bank** and **St Luke's Church**.

For an excellent insight into the workings

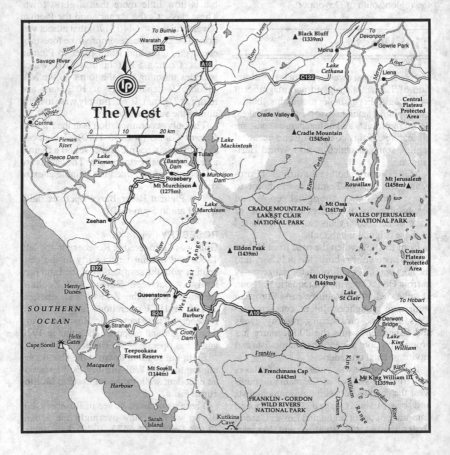

of a mine, visit the **West Coast Pioneers' Memorial Museum** in Main St. It's open daily from 8.30 am to 5 pm ($3/1). The museum also features an interesting mineral collection and an exhibit of early west-coast railways.

Places to Stay

At the *Treasure Island West Coast Caravan Park* (☎ 6471 6633) in Hurst St there are camp sites ($12), on-site vans ($35) and cabins ($45). The *Heemskirk Motor Hotel* (☎ 6471 6107) in Main St has singles/doubles for $66/72 and a holiday unit for $100 a double.

The old *Hotel Cecil* (☎ 6471 6221) in Main St has singles/doubles for $40/50 and self-contained holiday units that sleep four for $90 a double and $8 for each extra person.

Getting There & Away

Tasmanian Wilderness Travel/Tigerline runs a service between Burnie and Strahan (both directions) via Zeehan on Tuesday and Thursday, as well as Saturday in summer. The agent in Zeehan is Bassetts Hardware in Main St. The service between Strahan and Launceston/Devonport operates on Tuesday and Saturday all year and also stops in Zeehan.

QUEENSTOWN (pop 2630)

The final, winding descent into Queenstown from the Lyell Highway is an unforgettable experience. With deep, eroded gullies and naked, multicoloured hills, there is no escaping the fact that this is a mining town and that the destruction of the surrounding area is a direct result of this industry.

The discovery of alluvial gold in the Queen River valley in 1881 first brought prospectors to the area. Two years later, mining began on the rich Mt Lyell deposits and for nearly a decade miners extracted a few ounces of gold a day ignoring the mountain's rich copper reserves. In 1891, however, the Mt Lyell Mining Company began to concentrate on copper, which soon

became the most profitable mineral on the west coast.

After 20 years of mining, the rainforested hills around Queenstown had been stripped bare – three million tonnes of timber had been felled to feed the furnaces. By 1900, uncontrolled pollution from the copper smelters was killing any vegetation that had not already been cut down, and bushfires – fuelled by the sulphur-impregnated soils and dead stumps – raged through the hills every summer. The West's high rainfall then washed away all the top soil, preventing revegetation for many years. The smelters closed in 1969 and in recent years a tinge of green from the odd hardy bush has reappeared across the hills.

The Mt Lyell mine closed temporarily in late 1994, although there is still some small-scale mining in the area. It seems Queenstown's future rests with the tourism industry.

Things to See

The **Galley Museum** started life as the Imperial Hotel (1898) and was the first brick hotel in Queenstown. The museum features a good collection of old photographs of the history of Queenstown, as well as a display from the town's pioneering days. The museum is open Monday to Friday from 10 am to 4.30 pm, and weekends from 1.30 to 4.30 pm ($3). Opposite the museum, the **Miner's Siding** is a public park featuring a restored ABT steam locomotive and a rock sculpture telling the history of the Queenstown to Strahan railway.

There are good views from **Spion Kop Lookout**, in the centre of town (follow Bowes St). If you look at the football oval you will notice that it is cream instead of green, Queenstown's footy team is tough – they play on gravel, not grass.

Queenstown has a good *Historic Walk* brochure which guides you around the town from the Galley Museum to Spion Kop Lookout. You can pick up the leaflet and map in most shops or hotels and it is an excellent way to see all the sights.

There is a **chair lift** which rises 369m, giving good views of the stark hills ($4/2).

Places to Stay & Eat

The *Queenstown Cabin & Tourist Park* (☎ 6471 1332) at 17 Grafton St, about 500m from the town centre, has below-average bunkhouse accommodation for $10 plus $6 for each extra person. There are also on-site vans ($30) and cabins ($45).

At 1 Penghana Rd, just over the bridge on the way to Strahan, is the *Mountain View Holiday Lodge* (☎ 6471 1163), which is the old single men's quarters for the Mt Lyell Mining Company. The hostel section is pretty basic, but for $10 a night you get your own room and there are cooking facilities. Many of the rooms have been renovated as motel-style units and cost $55 a double.

The *Empire Hotel* (☎ 6471 1699) at 2 Orr St is a lovely old hotel with an imposing staircase classified by the National Trust. Clean and pleasant singles/doubles cost from $20/35; breakfast costs extra.

The *Mount Lyell Motor Inn* (☎ 6471 1888) at 1 Orr St has motel suites from $35/45.

Apart from counter meals, which are pretty good at the *Mount Lyell Motor Inn*, Queenstown has little to offer in the way of places to eat. In Orr St, *Axel's* has good cakes and light snacks, and nearby you'll find the usual takeaways.

Getting There & Away

Tasmanian Wilderness Travel/Tigerline has a bus service between Hobart and Strahan (both directions) via Queenstown on Wednesday, Friday and Sunday, as well as Monday in summer. There is a service between Burnie and Strahan via Queenstown on Tuesday and Thursday, as well as Saturday in Summer, and there is a daily service to Strahan ($5.40). The agent is Gumleys Newsagency.

STRAHAN (pop 700)

Strahan, 37km from Queenstown on Macquarie Harbour, is the only town on this rugged and dangerous coast. Though only a shadow of its former self, the town is rich in convict, logging and mining history.

Treacherous seas, the lack of natural harbours and high rainfall discouraged early settlement of the region until Macquarie Harbour was discovered by sailors searching for the source of the Huon pine that frequently washed up on the southern beaches.

In those days, the area was totally inaccessible by land and very difficult to reach by sea, and in 1821 these dubious assets prompted the establishment of a penal settlement on **Sarah Island**, in the middle of the harbour. Its main function was to isolate the worst of the colony's convicts and to use their muscle to harvest the huge stands of Huon pine. The convicts worked upriver 12 hours a day, often in leg irons, felling the pines and rafting them back to the island's saw-pits where they were used to build ships and furniture.

Sarah Island appeared in Marcus Clarke's graphic novel about convict life *For the Term of his Natural Life*. In 1834, however, after the establishment of the 'escape-proof' penal settlement at Port Arthur, Sarah Island was abandoned.

As the port for Queenstown, Strahan reached its peak of prosperity with the west-coast mining boom, and the completion of the Mt Lyell Mining Company's railway line in the late 1890s. Steamers operated regularly between Strahan and Hobart, and Launceston and Melbourne carrying copper, gold, silver, lead, timber and passengers. The closure of some of the mines and the opening

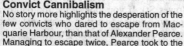

Convict Cannibalism

No story more highlights the desperation of the few convicts who dared to escape from Macquarie Harbour, than that of Alexander Pearce. Managing to escape twice, Pearce took to the grisly habit of eating his fellow escapees. Upon his capture after a second attempt he confessed to his crime and, to prove it, produced a bloody morsel of his mate from his pocket! ■

of the Emu Bay Railway from Zeehan to Burnie led to the decline of Strahan as a port.

These days, Strahan is a charming seaside town in danger of becoming a garishly folksy tourist trap. It draws droves of visitors, longing for a wilderness-in-Reeboks experience aboard the Gordon River cruises.

Information

The architecturally innovative **Strahan Wharf Centre** (☎ 6471 7488) is a tourist attraction in its own right. Beyond the Huon pine reception desk you enter the well laid out and informative displays which present all aspects of the history of the south-west. The centre is open daily from 10 am to 6 pm (8 pm in summer); entry to the museum section is $4.50 (children $3, family $9).

There is an office of the Department of Parks, Wildlife & Heritage in the old customs house building close to the town centre. This building also houses the post office. For banking, the post office is a Commonwealth agent, the newsagent handles ANZ accounts, and even the YHA does Commonwealth Bank EFTPOS.

Things to See

The **Union Steamship Building** (1894) and the **Customs House** are two imposing solid reminders of Strahan's former glory. The walk to **Hogarth Falls** starts east of the town centre at Peoples Park; allow one hour return.

The **lighthouse** at Cape Sorell, on the south head of the harbour, is the third-largest in Tasmania. Opposite the caravan park is a small **gemstone & mineral museum**.

Six km from the town is the impressive 33km **Ocean Beach**, where the sunsets have to be seen to be believed. In October, when the birds return from their winter migration, the beach is also a mutton-bird rookery. About 14km along the road from Strahan to Zeehan are the **Henty Dunes**, some spectacular sand dunes, many of which are more than 30m in height.

Organised Tours & Cruises

Gordon River Cruise The traditional way

of experiencing the beauty of the Gordon River is on one of the cruises which operate out of Strahan.

Gordon River Cruises (☎ 6471 7187) has half-day trips (9 am to 2 pm) for $44 ($24 children) including morning tea, or full-day trips (9 am to 3.30 pm) for $62 ($30 children) including a smorgasbord lunch.

World Heritage Tours (☎ 6471 7174) has the MV *Heritage Wanderer II*, which costs $42 ($18 children) for a trip from 9 am to 3.30 pm; a smorgasbord lunch is available on board ($8).

All cruises include a visit to Sarah Island, a Heritage Rainforest Walk and views of Hells Gates (the narrow entrance to Macquarie Harbour).

West Coast Yacht Charters (☎ 6471 7422) offers various fishing and sightseeing cruises including a two day/two night cruise which costs $320 (children $160); everything is included in the price.

Seaplane Tour A highly recommended way to see the river and surrounding World Heritage Area is on a seaplane tour with Wilderness Air (☎ 6471 7280). The planes take off from Strahan's wharf about every 1½ hours from 9 am onwards and fly up the river to Sir John Falls, where they land so that you can take a walk in the rainforest before flying back via Sarah Island and Ocean Beach. The 80-minute flight is well worth the $99. Demand for flights is heavy, so book ahead.

Another company, Seair (☎ 6471 2777) operates in the summer months only.

Jet-Boat Ride Wild Rivers Jet (☎ 6471 7174; book at Strahan wharf) offers 50-minute jet-boat rides up the King River for $36 ($22 children); the rides operate daily from 9 am to 5 pm.

Places to Stay

Although Strahan has a range of accommodation, places are often full in summer and closed in winter, so it's best to book.

The *West Strahan Caravan Park* (☎ 6471 7239) charges $12 for a camp site for two,

Wild Winds on the Westcoaster

The Westcoaster yacht race starts in Melbourne and heads down Tasmania's wild and windy west coast. With few harbours for shelter, it is indeed one of the toughest yachting events around. The race concludes over the same days as its more famous counterpart, the Sydney to Hobart yacht race. Constitution Dock in Hobart is definitely the place to be around New Year, when yachts fill the harbour and there is much celebrating. ∎

and there's also a camping ground with basic facilities 15km away at Macquarie Heads.

At $13 ($15 for nonmembers), the *Strahan Youth Hostel* (☎ 6471 7255) in Harvey St has the cheapest accommodation in town. It also has serviced cabins at $46 a double. It is about a 10-minute walk from the town centre.

You can overnight on board a sailing boat, the *Stormbreaker*, moored at the wharf. B&B costs $30 per person, but you have to disembark before 8 am when the cruising starts.

Three km from town on Ocean Beach Rd is the historic *Strahan Wilderness Lodge* (☎ 6471 7142), where singles/doubles with continental breakfast cost $30/40. Unless you have your own transport, it may be a bit inconvenient.

Hamer's Hotel (☎ 6471 7191) is opposite the wharf and has basic rooms for $48/65, including a continental breakfast. It also has a group of somewhat twee, self-contained cottages built in various colonial styles, and these are also on the waterfront. The cost is $99 to $149 a double.

For a memorable stay you could try the historic *Franklin Manor* (☎ 6471 7311), on the Esplanade just around the bay from the town centre. It costs from $135/145 to stay in a self-contained suite including breakfast.

Places to Eat

At the magnificent *Franklin Manor* (☎ 6471 7311) you can get an excellent three-course meal, but it's best to book. *Hamer's Hotel* and *Regatta Point Tavern*, on the Esplanade,

and the *Strahan Inn*, in Jolly St, have good restaurants; the Regatta Point Tavern is the cheapest.

The *Strahan Bakery* has salad rolls and cakes and at night doubles as a pizza shop. The *Fish Cafe* has OK seafood takeaways.

Getting There & Away

Tasmanian Wilderness Travel/Tigerline has a bus service between Hobart and Strahan (both directions, $40.40) on Wednesday, Friday and Sunday, as well as Monday in summer. There is a service between Burnie and Strahan ($35.60) on Tuesday and Thursday, as well as Saturday in summer. The agent is King Billy Teas opposite the wharf.

There are also services to/from Launceston ($49) and Devonport ($43) via Cradle Mountain on Tuesday and Saturday.

FRANKLIN-GORDON WILD RIVERS NATIONAL PARK

This World Heritage listed park includes the catchment areas of the Franklin and Olga rivers and part of the Gordon River, as well as the excellent bushwalking region known as **Frenchmans Cap**. It has a number of unique plant species and a major Aboriginal archaeological site at **Kutikina Cave**.

Much of the park is impenetrable rainforest, but the Lyell Highway traverses its northern end and there are a few short walks which start from the road. These include hikes to **Donaghys Hill**, from which you can see the Franklin River and the magnificent white quartzite dome of Frenchmans Cap, and a walk to **Nelson Falls**.

The walk to Frenchmans Cap takes three to five days and is the park's best-known bushwalk. The best way to see this magnificent park, however, is not to cross the Franklin River but to raft down it.

Rafting the Franklin

The Franklin is a very wild river and rafting it can be a hazardous journey. Experienced rafters can tackle it if they are fully equipped and prepared, or there are tour companies which offer complete rafting packages. Whether you go with an independent group or a tour operator, you should contact the Department of Parks, Wildlife & Heritage (☎ 6233 6391) for the latest information on permits and regulations.

All expeditions should register at the booth at the junction between the Lyell Highway and the Collingwood River, 49km west of Derwent Bridge. The trip, starting at Collingwood River and ending at Heritage Landing on the Franklin, takes about 14 days (you can do a shorter eight-day one). From the exit point (the same for both trips), you can be picked up by a Wilderness Air seaplane, or 22km further down the river by a Gordon River cruise boat.

Tour companies that arrange complete rafting packages include Peregrine Adventures (☎ 6231 0977) at 282 Murray St, Hobart; Rafting Tasmania (☎ 6239 1080), 675 Summerleas Rd, Fern Tree; and Tasmanian Expeditions (☎ 6334 3477), 110 George St Launceston. An all-inclusive rafting package, including transport, costs around $180 a day. Departures are mainly from December to March.

CRADLE MOUNTAIN-LAKE ST CLAIR

Tasmania's best-known national park is the superb 1262-sq-km World Heritage Area of Cradle Mountain-Lake St Clair. The spectacular mountain peaks, deep gorges, lakes, tarns, wild open moorlands, and the reserve's incredible variety of wildlife, extend from the Great Western Tiers in Tasmania's north to Derwent Bridge on the Lyell Highway in the south. It is one of the most glaciated areas in Australia and includes Mt Ossa (1617m), Tasmania's highest mountain, and Lake St Clair, Australia's deepest natural freshwater lake.

The preservation of this region as a national park is due, in part, to Gustav Weindorfer, an Austrian who fell in love with the area and proclaimed 'This must be a national park for all time. It is magnificent. Everyone should know about it, and come and enjoy it'. In 1912 he built a chalet out of King Billy pine, called it *Waldheim* (German for Forest Home) and, from 1916, lived there permanently. Today, eight bushwalkers' huts

have been constructed near his original chalet at the northern end of the park, and the area is named Waldheim, after his chalet.

There are plenty of day walks in both the Cradle Valley and Cynthia Bay (Lake St Clair) regions, but it is the spectacular 80km walk between the two that has turned this park into a bushwalkers' mecca. The Overland Track is one of the finest bushwalks in Australia, and in summer up to 100 people a day can set off on it. The track can be walked in either direction, but most people walk from Cradle Valley to Cynthia Bay.

Cradle Valley

At the northern park boundary, and built on the verge of an amazing rainforest, the visitor centre (☎ 6492 1110) and rangers' station (☎ 6492 1133) is open year-round from 8 am to 5 pm. The centre is staffed by rangers who can advise you about weather conditions, walking gear, maximum and minimum walking groups, bush safety, and bush etiquette.

For visitors in wheelchairs, or with youngsters in prams, the centre also features an easy, but quite spectacular, 500m circular boardwalk through the adjacent rainforest called the **Rainforest-Pencil Pine Falls Walking Track**.

Seair (☎ 6492 1132), which operates from the Cradle View Restaurant, offers a much less energetic way to see all the sights. A 25-minute flight to see Cradle Mountain and Barn Bluff costs $70 per person; a 50-minute flight for the above plus Lake St Clair and Walls of Jerusalem costs $100; a 65-minute flight for the above plus Frenchmans cap and Mt Lyell costs $140.

Whatever time of the year you visit, be prepared for cold, wet weather in the Cradle Valley area – on average it rains on seven days out of 10, is cloudy eight days in 10, the sun shines all day only one day in 10, and it snows on 54 days each year!

Lake St Clair

Cynthia Bay, near the southern park boundary, also has an informative rangers' station (☎ 6289 1172) where you register to walk the Overland Track in the opposite direction. At the nearby kiosk (☎ 6289 1137) you can book a seat on the small *Idaclair!* ferry. The boat does a one-way ($15) or return ($20) trip to Narcissus Hut at the northern end of Lake St Clair ($25 if you break the trip for a couple of hours, $30 if you return on a different day) departing at 9 am and 12.30 and 3 pm. The boat is available for charter. From the same kiosk you can also hire dinghies for a spot of fishing or relaxing on the lake, but don't fall in – it's freezing!

The Overland Track

The best time to walk the Overland Track is during summer, when the flowering plants are most prolific, although spring and autumn also have their attractions. You can walk the track in winter, but only if you're very experienced.

The trail is well marked for its entire length and, at an easy pace, takes around five or six days to walk. En route, however, there are many secondary paths leading up to mountains such as Mt Ossa or other natural features, so the length of time you take is only limited by the amount of supplies you can carry. There are 12 unattended huts along the track which you can use for overnight accommodation, but in summer they can get full so make sure you carry a tent. Camp fires are banned so you must carry a fuel stove.

The most dangerous part of the walk is the exposed high plateau between Waldheim and Pelion Creek, near Mt Pelion West. The south-west wind that blows across here can be bitterly cold and sometimes strong enough to knock you off your feet.

If you are walking from Cradle Valley to Cynthia Bay, you have the option of radioing from Narcissus Hut for the *Idaclair!* ferry to come and pick you up, saving a 5½-hour walk.

A detailed description of the walk is given in Lonely Planet's *Bushwalking in Australia*.

Places to Stay & Eat
Cradle Valley Region The cheapest place in this area is the *Cradle Mountain Camping Ground* (☎ 6492 1395), 2.5km outside the national park. It costs $14 a double to camp here in summer or $20 per person to stay in the bunkhouse. Huts cost $28 a double and en-suite cabins $72 a double. Bedding is hired out at exorbitant rates so bring a warm sleeping bag.

At Waldheim, 5km into the national park, there are eight basic huts, all containing gas stoves, cooking utensils and wood heaters but no bedding. The minimum fees for these cabins are $55 to $75. Check-in and bookings for the huts are handled by the Cradle Mountain Visitor Centre.

Just on the national park boundary is the luxurious *Cradle Mountain Lodge* (☎ 6492 1303), where singles or doubles in the main chalet cost $92 and basic self-contained cabins are $160 a double. The lodge has good facilities for its guests and anyone is welcome to eat at the excellent restaurant (make sure you book first), visit the Tavern Bar or buy basic groceries and unleaded petrol at the lodge's general store. Expect prices to be higher (in some cases considerably) than in other parts of the state; if that's a problem, bring everything with you.

Cradle Mountain Highlanders (☎ 6492 1116) has achieved luxury with rustic appeal in its en-suite cabins. The experience costs $130 a double including full breakfast provisions. It is easy to miss the entrance, which is on your right soon after passing the Cradle View Restaurant and airfield as you approach the park.

The *Cradle View Restaurant*, near the camping ground, serves reasonably priced home-made meals; you can also buy petrol and diesel from outside the restaurant. Don't rely on it being open on weekdays or petrol being available from June to September.

On the way to Cradle Mountain from Devonport, near the crossroads at Moina, there is a turn-off to a luxurious mountain retreat, *Lemonthyme Lodge* (☎ 6492 1112). Accommodation ranges from $85 a double in the lodge to $175 a double in a spa cabin. It's a long drive in on a dirt road so make sure you book first.

Lake St Clair At the southern end of Lake St

Clair, *Lakeside St Clair Wilderness Holidays* (☎ 6289 1137) has several huts, plenty of camp sites and a kiosk that sells basic food supplies. It costs $15 for two to camp and $20 per person to stay in the bunkhouse. Cabins cost from $148 a double.

At Derwent Bridge, 5km away, there's accommodation at the wooden chalet-style *Derwent Bridge Wilderness Hotel* (☎ 6289 1144). Rooms in huts cost $20 per person, and rooms in the hotel are $45/65 including a continental breakfast. The hotel does good, hearty meals at normal prices and, with its open fire and friendly staff, is a good place to spend an evening (especially if you've just come in from doing the 'overland'). You can also buy food, basic supplies and maps, and rent fishing or bushwalking gear here.

Just off the Lyell Highway at Bronte Park, the *Bronte Park Highland Village* (☎ 6289 1126) has singles/doubles for $45/60 and cabins at $65 to $110 a double. There are also camp sites for $10 a double, and hostel beds for $15. The hotel also has good meals at reasonable prices. The only other accommodation is at the *Derwent Bridge Chalets* (☎ 6289 1125), which charges $108 a double in summer.

Getting There & Away

Cradle Valley Region Transport to/from this area was once a big problem but the construction of the link road to the west coast has meant that the park is now only a short diversion from the Murchison or Midland highways. Tasmanian Wilderness Travel/ Tigerline buses to/from Devonport ($22.70) and Burnie ($29.20) stop in Cradle Valley on their way to/from Strahan every Tuesday and Thursday, as well as Saturday in summer.

During summer, Tasmanian Wilderness Travel has buses every day from Hobart ($48.60) Launceston ($40) and Devonport ($38); during winter the buses run only on Tuesday, Thursday and Saturday. On Tuesday and Saturday the bus continues to Strahan ($38) and returns on the same day.

Lake St Clair Tasmanian Wilderness Travel/Tigerline has services between Hobart and Strahan via Derwent Bridge on Wednesday, Friday and Sunday, as well as Monday in summer. A one-way fare from Hobart to Derwent Bridge is $23.80, and from there to Strahan is $18.10. The agent is the Road House on the Lyell Highway. Enquire about connections to Lake St Clair.

There are also return trips to Lake St Clair from Devonport ($49) and Launceston ($45; Saturday, as well as Monday, Tuesday and Thursday in summer) and Hobart ($40; Sunday, as well as Thursday in summer).

Getting Around

Cradle Valley Region During summer, a Tasmanian Wilderness Travel bus will take you from the camping ground to Lake Dove for $5. Maxwell's (☎ 6492 1431) also runs a shuttle bus on demand for $5 per person.

Cynthia Bay Region Maxwell's also runs an informal taxi to and from Cynthia Bay and Derwent Bridge for $5, operating daily on demand (bookings essential). This meets the regular Tigerline bus along the highway.

South-West

SOUTH-WEST NATIONAL PARK

There are few places left in the world as isolated and untouched as Tasmania's south-west wilderness, the state's largest national park. It is the home of some of the world's last tracts of virgin temperate rainforest, and

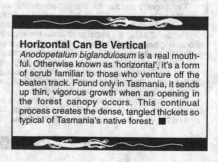

Horizontal Can Be Vertical

Anodopetalum biglandulosum is a real mouthful. Otherwise known as 'horizontal', it's a form of scrub familiar to those who venture off the beaten track. Found only in Tasmania, it sends up thin, vigorous growth when an opening in the forest canopy occurs. This continual process creates the dense, tangled thickets so typical of Tasmania's native forest. ∎

these contribute much to the grandeur and extraordinary diversity of this ancient area.

The south-west is the habitat of the endemic Huon pine, which lives for more than 3000 years, and of the swamp gum, the world's tallest hardwood and flowering plant. About 300 species of lichen, moss and fern, some rare and endangered, dapple the rainforest in as many shades of green; glacial tarns with mirror reflections are drops of silver on the jagged mountains; and in summer, the alpine meadows are picture-perfect with wildflowers and flowering shrubs. Through it all run the wild rivers, with rapids tearing through deep gorges and waterfalls plunging over cliffs.

Each year more and more people venture into the heart of this incredible part of Tasmania's World Heritage Area, seeking the peace, isolation and challenge of a region as old as the last ice age.

The best-known walk in the park is the **South Coast Track** between Port Davey and Cockle Creek, near Recherche Bay. This takes about 10 days and should only be tackled by experienced hikers, well prepared for the often vicious weather conditions. Light planes are used to airlift bushwalkers into the south-west and there is vehicle access to Cockle Creek. Detailed notes to some of the walks in this region are available in Lonely Planet's *Bushwalking in Australia*.

A whole range of escorted wilderness adventures are possible, involving flying, hiking, rafting, canoeing, mountaineering, caving and camping. More information on these can be obtained from the Department of Parks & Wildlife (☎ 6233 6191). Entry fees apply even if you're just driving on the road through the park.

LAKE PEDDER
At the edge of the south-west wilderness lies Lake Pedder, once a spectacularly beautiful natural lake considered the crown jewel of the region. In 1972, however, it was flooded to become part of the Gordon River power development. Together with nearby Lake Gordon, Pedder now holds 27 times the volume of water in Sydney Harbour and is

---

Pedder 2000

While travelling around Tasmania you may come across a framed picture of Lake Pedder in a restaurant, cafe or craft shop. The image of this serene lake with its gently sloping beach surrounded by glacier-carved mountain ranges surely epitomises the gentle beauty and rugged grandeur of the Tasmanian wilderness. Unfortunately, the lake is no more, having been drowned in an artificial impoundment in 1972. The image is now a sign of hope and a symbol of the awakening of the environmental movement in Tasmania.

The battle to stop construction of the impoundment failed in its primary aim, but all was not lost. The skills and professionalism of the Tasmanian environment movement, now recognised as a world leader, were developed and honed at Lake Pedder, and the hope that one day the impoundment would be drained has never been lost.

The primary reason for the impoundment was electricity generation. However, the electricity generated is surplus to Tasmania's needs and while the biggest growth industry in the last twenty years has been tourism one of Tasmania's greatest attractions lies shrouded from view.

Pedder 2000 is a campaign to drain the impoundment and restore the lake to its former glory. A Federal government inquiry in 1995 found that draining of the impoundment was feasible, and a scientific study revealed that the natural features of the former lake were intact, under a thin layer of silt. The major sticking points to 'pulling the plug' were the expense and the lack of political will on the part of the Tasmanian government. The latter's largely economic arguments are disputed by the folks at Pedder 2000 who also believe that the Federal government has the power, and indeed the obligation, to act through its world heritage legislation.

It seems action will only occur when there is a sufficient ground swell of public opinion to sway political will. If you're interested in this campaign, contact Pedder 2000 at 130 Davey St, Hobart 7000 or visit the web site at pedder.csse.swin.edu.au. ∎

the largest inland freshwater catchment in Australia. The underground Gordon power station is the largest in Tasmania and on most days tours are available for $5. The visitors centre at the dam site has plenty of information about the scheme.

The hydroelectric scheme was built in controversial circumstances, and today many people would like Lake Pedder to be drained and restored to its original condition (see the Pedder 2000 aside in this section).

STRATHGORDON

Built to service HEC employees, the township of Strathgordon is the base from which to visit Lakes Pedder and Gordon, the Gordon Dam and the power station. Strathgordon is also becoming a popular bushwalking, trout fishing, boating and water-skiing resort. There's a camping ground, and accommodation is available at the *Lake Pedder Motor Inn* (☎ 6280 1166), where singles/doubles cost from $50. Meals are also available from the restaurant at standard hotel prices.

Bass Strait Islands

Tasmania has two groups of islands, the Hunter and Furneaux groups, at the western and eastern entrances to Bass Strait respectively. Once the transient homes of sealers, sailors and prospectors, today these islands are inhabited by rural communities and are rich in wildlife and natural beauty.

KING ISLAND (pop 2000)

At the western end of Bass Strait in the Hunter Group, this small island has beautiful beaches and quiet lagoons. Discovered in 1798, King Island quickly gained a reputation as a breeding ground for seals and sea elephants. Just as quickly, however, these animals were hunted close to extinction by brutal sealers and sailors known as the Straitsmen.

Over the years, the stormy seas of Bass Strait have claimed many ships and there are

several wrecks around the island. The worst occurred in 1845 when the *Cataraqui*, an immigrant ship, went down with 399 people aboard.

King Island is best known for its dairy produce, although kelp and large crayfish are other valuable exports.

Things to See & Do

King Island's four lighthouses guard against its treacherous seas. The one at Currie, built in 1880, is open in the afternoon on weekends (or by appointment) for $3. The Cape Wickham lighthouse is the tallest in the southern hemisphere and is worth visiting for the view of the surrounding coastal scenery.

Currie Museum, originally the lighthouse keeper's cottage, is open from 2 to 4 pm on weekends. It features many maritime and local history displays and entry is $2. Kelp Industries Pty Ltd is the only kelp processing plant in Australia. From the roadside you can see kelp drying on racks.

The **King Island Dairy** is a must for visitors. It is open all day on weekdays and on Sunday from 12.30 to 4 pm, although times are liable to change. Swimming at deserted beaches or in freshwater lakes, scuba diving among exotic marine life and shipwrecks, surfing and fishing are all popular.

If you're interested in a drier pastime, try bushwalking; there is abundant wildlife, including a small colony of fairy penguins at Grassy.

Organised Tours

King Island Coach Tours (☎ 6462 1138) and Top Tours (☎ 6462 1245) offer half-day trips from $27 and full-day trips from $52.

King Island Dive Charters (☎ 6461 1133) has single dives for $45 or day trips for $90 including equipment hire and lunch. It also offers fishing charters for $540 a day for up to six people all inclusive.

Places to Stay

Near Currie, the *Bass Caravan Park* (☎ 6462 1260) has on-site vans for $35/45 single/double and self-contained units for $70 a double. The *King Island Colonial*

TASMANIA

King Island is famous for its superb dairy
produce, cheeses in particular

Lodge (☎ 6462 1245) has moderate B&B for
$45/65 singles/doubles. The *Boomerang
Motel* (☎ 6462 1288) has rooms with superb
ocean views for $80/90, and it's only a short
walk into town.

There are a couple of host farms on the
island, such as *Pegarah* (☎ 6461 12480),
which charge about $60 a double for B&B.

Places to Eat

Currie has many fine eating places within
walking distance of most of the accommodation. The *Coffee Shop*, open daily, serves
light meals, while the *Bakery* has home-
made pies.

The *Fishbowl Restaurant* (☎ 6462 1288)
at the Boomerang Motel features local
produce and has spectacular ocean views;
bookings are essential. The *Cataraqui Restaurant* at Parers Hotel offers a similar menu
and the hotel also has a bistro.

On the other side of the island in Naracoopa, the *Golden Spoon Restaurant*
(☎ 6461 1103) provides lunch and afternoon
tea. For dinner it is essential to book.

Getting There & Away

Aus-Air (☎ 1800 331 256), Kendell Airlines
(☎ 1800 338 894) as well as King Island
Airlines (☎ (03) 9580 3777) fly to the island.

Regular flights are available from Melbourne ($110-$146 one way), Launceston
($149) and Burnie ($126). Package deals are
often the best value with two nights accommodation plus a hire car for $230 per person
from Melbourne. Similar deals are available
from Launceston.

Getting Around

There is no public transport on the island and
most roads are gravel, so drive carefully.
Kendell Airlines can arrange airport transfers to Currie for $7 per person each way and
to Naracoopa for $28 per person each way.
Hire-car companies will meet you at the
airport and should be booked.

Howell's Auto Rent (☎ 6462 1282) has
cars from around $65 a day with insurance.

FLINDERS ISLAND (pop 1010)

Flinders Island is the largest of the 52 islands
which comprise the Furneaux Group. First
charted in 1798 by the British explorer Matthew Flinders, the Furneaux Group became
a base for the Straitsmen, who not only
slaughtered seals in their tens cf thousands
but also indulged in piracy.

The most tragic part of Flinders Island's
history, however, was its role in the virtual
annihilation of Tasmania's Aboriginal
people between 1829 and 1834. Of the 135
survivors who were transported to Wybalenna (an Aboriginal word meaning Black
Man's House) to be 'civilised', only 47 survived to make their final journey to Oyster
Cove near Hobart in 1847.

On a brighter note, Flinders Island has
many attractions, including beautiful
beaches, good fishing and scuba diving.

The island's main industries are farming,
fishing and seasonal mutton-birding. Its
administrative centre is Whitemark, and
Lady Barron in the south is the main fishing
area and deep-water port. Petrol is available
in Whitemark and Lady Barron only.

Things to See & Do

Today all that remains of the unfortunate
settlement at **Wybalenna** is the cemetery and

the chapel, restored by the National Trust and open to visitors.

Nearby, the **Emita Museum** displays a variety of Aboriginal artefacts as well as old sealing and sailing relics. It's open weekends from 1 to 4 pm and during summer from 1 to 5 pm on weekdays as well ($2).

Bushwalking is very popular, and many visitors climb **Mt Strezlecki**. The walk commences about 10km south of Whitemark, is well signposted and takes three to five hours return. The island supports a wide variety of wildlife, including many bird species, the most well known being the Cape Barren goose (now protected) and the mutton bird. Mutton birds are readily seen at dusk, and Flinders Island Adventures (☎ 6359 4507) runs evening tours from December to March from Lady Barron.

Mountain bicycles are available for hire from Flinders Island Bike Hire (☎ 6359 2000) at Whitemark police station. Bikes cost $10 per day and can be collected at the airport on arrival if sufficient notice is given.

Scuba divers can visit several locations on the northern and western coasts. In many places you can enter from the beach or shelving rocks. There are shipwrecks around the island, some clearly visible from shore.

Rock and beach fishing are popular all year. Fishing tackle and bait can be purchased from many stores, however you need to bring your own rod. A more unusual pastime is fossicking for 'diamonds' (which are actually fragments of topaz) on the beach and creek at Killiecrankie Bay.

Jimmy's Island Tours (☎ 6359 2112) runs day-long coach tours for around $62 per person as well as a three-day package coach tour including accommodation and airfares for around $500.

Places to Stay

Flinders Island Cabin Park (☎ 6359 2188) is 5km north of Whitemark, next to the airport. It has self-contained cabins for $27/37 a single/double. The *Interstate Hotel* (☎ 6359 2114), in the centre of Whitemark, has singles/doubles starting at $26/47; ensuite rooms are $42/67.

There are also a variety of holiday homes around the island, including *Echo Hills Holiday Units* (☎ 6359 6509) and *Seaview Cottage* (☎ 6359 2011), both charging around $65 a double.

The *Flinders Island Lodge* (☎ 6359 3521), at Lady Barron overlooking the picturesque Furneaux Sound has singles/doubles from $65/98. Rooms are spacious and the service is friendly. Picnic lunch baskets can be ordered here.

Places to Eat

The *Bakery* at Whitemark sells pies, bread and cold drinks on weekdays. It's also the local pizza place on Friday nights. *Jimmy's Fast Food* store in Whitemark is open daily and serves grills and other takeaway meals.

The *Interstate Hotel* in Whitemark serves a range of reasonably priced counter meals from Monday to Saturday. The *Whitemark Sports Club* has a cosy restaurant with a quality menu. Meals are also available in the bistro throughout the week in summer. Bookings for the restaurant are necessary.

Patterson's Store in Lady Barron is open daily and also acts as a post office and a Commonwealth Bank agency. The *Shearwater Restaurant* at the Flinders Island Lodge in Lady Barron has a fine selection of bistro meals every day. The *General Store* at Killiecrankie provides snacks and drinks.

Getting There & Away

Aus-Air (1800 331 256) and Island Airlines (☎ 1800 818 455) fly to the island. There are flights most days from Melbourne ($110 to $153) and Launceston ($113). The cheapest way to see the island is by using one of the many package deals. These provide return airfares, accommodation for two or more nights and car hire with unlimited mileage. Costs vary according to season, but packages start at around $220 from Launceston and $270 from Melbourne.

Getting Around

In Whitemark, there are a number of companies offering cars for hire. These include Bowman Transport (☎ 6359 2388), Flinders Island Car Rentals (☎ 6359 2168) and Flinders Island Transport Services (☎ 6359 2060). All operations charge around $50 a day.

Victoria

In the early 1800s there was great interest from Europe in the new continent of Australia. The French sent ships to explore the south coast, and in 1803, hoping to forestall a French settlement, Britain hurriedly sent an expedition to establish a colony at Sorrento on Port Phillip Bay. This first settlement on the bay lasted less than a year and, unable to find a permanent supply of fresh water, the settlers set sail for Tasmania.

It wasn't until 1835 that the first permanent European settlement was made at the present site of Melbourne, although whalers and sealers had used the Victorian coast for a number of years. The earliest settlers, John Batman and John Pascoe Fawkner, came to Melbourne in search of the land they had been unable to obtain in Tasmania. Not until 1837, by which time several hundred settlers had moved in, was the town named Melbourne and given an official seal of approval.

The new settlement's free-enterprise spirit led to clashes with the staid powers of Sydney. The settlers were not interested in the convict system, for example, and on a number of occasions turned convict ships away. The settlers wanted to form a breakaway colony, and their PR efforts included naming it after the Queen and the capital city after her prime minister, Lord Melbourne.

Finally, in 1851, the colony of Victoria was formed. At about the same time gold was discovered, and the population doubled. Many diggers made or lost their fortunes and returned to their homelands, but many more stayed to establish new settlements and work the land.

Victoria is Australia's smallest mainland state but features some of the country's most diverse landscapes and some of its most impressive national parks. Melbourne is Australia's second-largest city and lays claim to being the fashion, food and cultural capital of Australia. For years it was also considered to be Australia's financial and

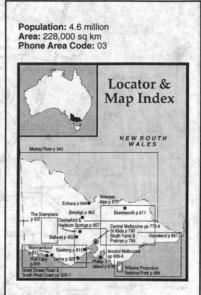

Population: 4.6 million
Area: 228,000 sq km
Phone Area Code: 03

Locator & Map Index

NEW SOUTH WALES

Murray River p 843

Victorian Alps p 875

Echuca p 849
Bendigo p 862
Beechworth p 871

The Grampians p 837
Daylesford & Hepburn Springs p 857

Central Melbourne pp 775-9
St Kilda p 790
South Yarra & Prahran p 788
Gippsland p 881

Ballarat p 852

Warrnambool p 831
Geelong p 811
Around Melbourne pp 808-9

Port Fairy p 833
Lorne p 829

Great Ocean Road & South West Coast pp 820-1
Phillip Island p 816
Wilsons Promontory National Park p 884

Highlights

- Driving the spectacular Great Ocean Road from Anglesea to the Port Campbell National Park
- Enjoying adventure activities, including skiing, bushwalking, hang-gliding and fly-fishing in the High Country
- Taking a leisurely cycling tour around the wineries of the Rutherglen area
- Visiting the re-created 1860s gold-mining town of Sovereign Hill, Ballarat
- Soaking up the history of the port of Echuca on the Murray River, with its evocative reminders of the paddle-steamer era
- Bushwalking among the wildflowers, wildlife and mystical beauty of the Grampians National Park
- Visiting Melbourne in spring – for the gardens, the Melbourne Cup, the Aussie Rules Grand Final, and the Melbourne International Festival

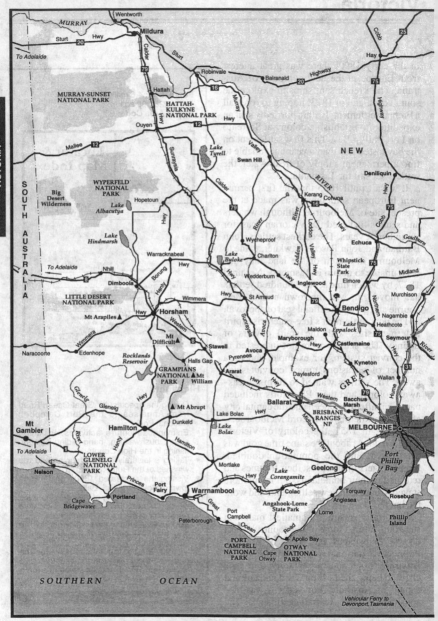

MURRAY

Wentworth

Sturt   Hwy   20

Mildura

To Adelaide

Calder   79

Robinvale

Hattah   16

Hattah

MURRAY-SUNSET
NATIONAL PARK

HATTAH-
KULKYNE
NATIONAL PARK

Murray   Hwy

Ouyen   12

Balranald   20   Highway

Hay   75   Highway

Cobb   25

Mallee   12

Lake
Tyrell

Valley   Hwy

Swan Hill

N E W

Deniliquin

SOUTH   AUSTRALIA

Big
Desert
Wilderness

WYPERFELD
NATIONAL
PARK

Lake
Albacutya

Hopetoun

Sunraysia   Hwy

Calder   79

RIVER

Kerang   16   Cohuna

Echuca   75

Goulburn

Midland

Lake
Hindmarsh

Warracknabeal

Wycheproof

River

Loddon   Valley   Hwy

Loddon

Whipstick
State
Park

Elmore

Murchison

To Adelaide   Nhill   8

Dimboola

Borung   Hwy

Hwy   Charlton

Lake
Buloke

Wedderburn

Inglewood

Bendigo

Nagambie

Heathcote

LITTLE DESERT
NATIONAL PARK

Henty   Hwy

Wimmera   Hwy

Horsham

Hwy   St Arnaud   79

Maldon   Lake
Eppalock

Maryborough   Hwy   Castlemaine   75   Seymour

River

Naracoorte   Edenhope

Mt Arapiles

Mt
Difficult   8   Stawell

Western   Hwy

Wimmera   Hwy

Halls Gap

Avoca   Pyrenees

Ararat

Sunraysia   Hwy

Avoca   River

Kyneton   Wallan

GREAT   31

Hume   Hwy

Rocklands
Reservoir

GRAMPIANS
NATIONAL   Mt
PARK   William

Daylesford

Western   Hwy   79   Bacchus
Marsh

Ballarat   BRISBANE
RANGES
NP   8   Fwy

Mt Gambier

Glenelg

Hamilton

Mt Abrupt

Dunkeld

Lake Bolac

Lake
Bolac

Midland   Hwy

MELBOURNE

Henty   Hwy

Hamilton   Hwy

Hwy   Hwy

Port
Phillip
Bay

To Adelaide   1

Nelson

LOWER
GLENELG
NATIONAL
PARK

River

Princes   Port
Fairy

Mortlake   Hwy

Lake
Corangamite

Geelong

Torquay   Rosebud

Anglesea

Phillip
Island

Cape
Bridgewater   Portland

Warrnambool   1   Colac

Angahook-Lorne
State Park

Lorne

Peterborough

Great   Port
Campbell

Ocean

PORT
CAMPBELL
NATIONAL
PARK   Cape
Otway

Road   Apollo Bay

OTWAY
NATIONAL
PARK

SOUTHERN   OCEAN

Vehicular Ferry to
Devonport, Tasmania

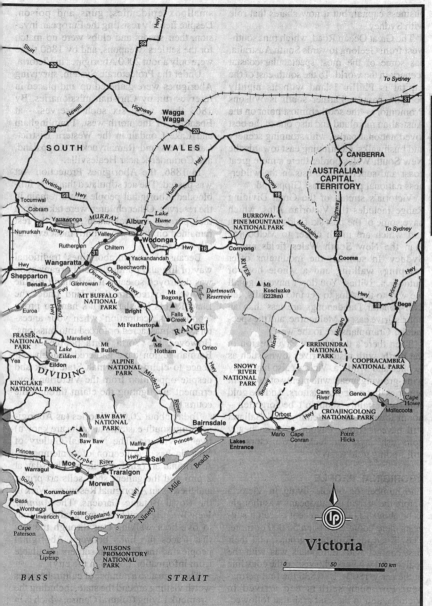

VICTORIA

Victoria

business capital, but it now shares that role with Sydney.

The Great Ocean Road, which runs southwest from Geelong towards South Australia, has some of the most spectacular coastal scenery in the world. To the south-east of the capital is Phillip Island with its nightly penguin parade. Farther south is Wilsons Promontory – the southernmost point on the Australian mainland and also one of the best loved national parks, with stunning scenery and bushwalks. Continuing east towards the New South Wales border there's more great coast and superb rainforests in the wilderness national parks of East Gippsland.

Victoria's stretch of the Great Dividing Range includes the Victorian Alps, which have some of the best ski fields in Australia and which are much closer to Melbourne than the New South Wales fields are to Sydney. In summer the mountains offer camping, walking and a whole host of outdoor activities. You don't have to go all the way to the Alps to get into the hills; the ever-popular Dandenongs are less than an hour's drive east of Melbourne, and the spectacular Grampians are to the west.

Then there's the Murray River region in the north, with historic river towns such as Echuca and Mildura. Victoria also has many wine-growing areas, with plenty of excellent wineries that welcome visitors. And the gold country certainly shouldn't be forgotten – boom towns such as Bendigo and Ballarat still have a strong flavour of those heady gold-rush days, and lucky prospectors are still finding gold today.

ABORIGINAL PEOPLE

The number of people living in Victoria before the arrival of Europeans was thought to be about 12,000, but recent research suggests there could have been 50,000 or more. They lived in 38 distinct groups, and their first contact with Europeans was with the sealers and whalers who visited the coastline in the early 1800s. By 1835 the first permanent European settlers had arrived in Victoria, and in the land grab that followed, the Aborigines were all but wiped out – by smallpox epidemics, guns and poison. Despite fiercely resisting the European invasion, their spears and clubs were no match for the settlers' weapons, and by 1860 there were only about 2000 Aborigines in Victoria.

Under the Protectorate System, surviving Aborigines were gathered up and placed in reserves run by Christian missionaries. By 1863 there were six such reserves – at Ebenezer in the north-west, Framlingham and Lake Condah in the Western District, Lake Tyers and Ramahyuck in Gippsland, and Coranderrk near Healesville.

In 1886, the Aborigines Protection Act was passed. The act stipulated that only full-blooded Aboriginal people could remain in the reserves. Other children were taken from their parents and 'relocated', while the rest remained on the reserves until most eventually died out.

Because Victorian aborigines' traditional way of life and political/social organisation was destroyed so early it is difficult for the survivors to reclaim their land under the Land Rights legislation. It's hard to prove 'continuous occupation' when your ancestors were massacred or forced into missions. However, the Yorta Yorta people of the Barmah region have gathered enough evidence to claim the Barmah State Park and despite opposition from the Victorian government are fighting the claim through the courts.

Today about 20,000 Koories (as Aborigines from south-eastern Australia are known) live in Victoria. The National Gallery of Victoria has a collection of contemporary Aboriginal art (guided tours on Thursday at 2 pm) and the gallery shop sells art prints, and there is an Aboriginal Resources Walk in the Royal Botanic Gardens. The *Another View Walking Trail* brochure detailing a four to five-hour walking tour through the city that traces the links between Aboriginal people and the European settlers (available from information booths in the city).

There are also a number of cultural centres worth visiting around the state, including the Brambuk Living Cultural Centre, which is in the Grampians National Park and the

Dharnya Centre in the Barmah State Park north-east of Echuca.

GEOGRAPHY

Victoria's geography is very diverse, containing much the same elements as New South Wales and Queensland but in a much smaller area. It includes a long coastline, the final stretch of the Great Dividing Range and associated outcrops plus flatter country to the west.

The Victorian coast is particularly varied. On the eastern side is the mountain-backed Gippsland region, with a large system of lakes, while to the west is spectacular coastline running to South Australia. The sea pounding Victoria's coast is Bass Strait and unlike the Indian and Pacific oceans (which surround much of Australia) it is quite cold in winter.

The Great Dividing Range reaches its greatest altitude across the Victoria-New South Wales border. The mountains run south-west, then bend around to run more directly west as the range crosses north of Melbourne and finally fades out before the South Australian border.

The north-west of the state, beyond the Great Dividing Range, is flat plains. Much of the plains were created over the aeons by the floods and meanderings of the mighty Murray River. For most of the length of the border between New South Wales and Victoria, the Murray forms the actual boundary. It is especially dry and empty in the extreme north-west of the state, where you'll find the eerie semidesert of the Sunset Country.

CLIMATE

Statistically, the weather in Victoria and Melbourne is not too bad; average temperatures in summer or winter are only a few degrees less than Sydney's and Melbourne is certainly far less humid than Sydney or Brisbane. The annual rainfall is also less than in either of those damp cities. The trouble with Melbourne's climate is that it's totally unpredictable (especially in spring); hence the old joke that if you don't like the weather, just wait a minute. Expect the unexpected.

Although the weather is basically somewhat cooler in Melbourne than elsewhere in continental Australia, you'll rarely need more than a light overcoat or jacket, even during winter. Inland, however, in places like Ballarat or in the Alps, it can get really cold. North of the Great Dividing Range winter nights can be frosty but the days are often clear and warm.

In summer the whole state heats up and January and February heat waves in Victoria can mean temperatures in the 40°Cs. Melbourne has higher summer maximum temperatures than Sydney or Brisbane, but a run of hot days is broken by temperatures cooler than in either of those cities.

Basically, Victoria is worth visiting at any time of year but to miss the really gloomy weather, avoid the south of the state in June, July and August.

INFORMATION

Tourism Victoria operates two interstate information offices:

New South Wales
    403 George St, Sydney 2000 (☎ (02) 9299 2288)
South Australia
    16 Grenfell St, Adelaide 5000 (☎ (08) 8231 4129)

Remarkably, Tourism Victoria doesn't have an office in Melbourne. Tourist information is handled by the RACV's Victorian Information Centre & Booking Service (☎ 9790 2121; toll-free 1800 337 743) in the town hall on the corner of Swanston Walk and Little Collins St in the city.

The government-run bookshop, Information Victoria (☎ 1300 366 365) is at 356 Collins St. You can pick up free maps of national parks or buy more detailed topographic maps.

NATIONAL & STATE PARKS

Victoria has 34 national parks, 40 state parks and a wide range of other protected areas, including coastal and marine reserves and historic areas. These parks are managed by Parks Victoria, which has

VICTORIA

The Major Mitchell Trail

The Major Mitchell Trail is a 1700km 'cultural trail' which follows as closely as possible the route taken by the New South Wales surveyor general on his exploratory trip through Victoria in 1836.

Mitchell entered Victoria near present-day Swan Hill, and travelled south to the coast before returning to New South Wales through Hamilton, Castlemaine, Benalla and Wodonga. On his trip he named many places, including the Grampians, Mt Alexander, Mt Macedon and the Loddon, Glenelg and Wimmera rivers, and explored some previously little-known areas.

Mitchell was so pleasantly surprised by the verdant lushness of the land, in comparison with the dry expanses of New South Wales, that he named the area *Australia Felix* (Australia Fair).

The route today covers many backroads and is well signposted with distinctive small brown and blue signs. An excellent descriptive handbook is available from Parks Victoria and local tourist offices for $12.95. ∎

offices in Melbourne and throughout the state and also publishes leaflets about virtually every park in Victoria.

Parks Victoria (☎ 13 1963) has a good information centre at Vault 11, Banana Alley, 383 Flinders St. It's open from 8 am to 6 pm on weekdays but you can phone for information seven days a week, even after business hours. The Natural Resources & Environment office (☎ 9412 4795), 240 Victoria Pde in East Melbourne, also provides a good range of information on parks and state forests, and sells some excellent posters.

Parks Victoria also has offices in some of the larger regional towns (as well as offices in the parks themselves), usually still called by the old name, DC&NR.

ACTIVITIES
Bushwalking

Victoria has some great bushwalking areas and a number of active clubs. Check the outdoor-gear shops around Hardware and Little Bourke Sts in Melbourne for local club news and magazines. For more information about bushwalking in Victoria look for the handy walking guides *50 Bush Walks in Victoria* by Sandra Bardwell and *120 Walks in Victoria* by Tyrone T Thomas. Lonely Planet's *Bushwalking in Australia* is also useful.

Walking areas close to the city include the You Yangs, 56km to the south-west, with a wide variety of bird life; and the Dandenongs, right on the eastern edge of the metropolitan area. Wilsons Promontory is to the south-east in Gippsland. 'The Prom' has many marked trails from Tidal River and from Telegraph Bay – walks that can take from a few hours to a couple of days. The Australian Alps Walking Track traverses the High Country from Walhalla, east of Melbourne, to the outskirts of Canberra. The track runs through national parks and wilderness areas for almost all of its 655km length, and for much of it you're a long way from a road, let alone a town. There are popular marked trails in the Bright and Mt Buffalo areas of the Alps.

The Grampians, 250km to the west, are where Victoria's only remaining red kangaroos hang out. The Croajingolong National

Park near Mallacoota in East Gippsland is equally rugged inland but the coastal walks are easier.

You can have backpacks and camping equipment repaired by Remote Repairs at 377 Little Bourke St, above the Mountain Designs shop.

Rock Climbing

Again, the Hardware St outdoor-gear shops are good information sources. Mt Arapiles, in the Western District 330km north-west of Melbourne near Natimuk, is famous among rock climbers from around the world as it has a huge variety of climbs for all levels of skill.

If you just want to scramble around in rather crowded conditions there is Hanging Rock (of *Picnic at Hanging Rock* fame), 72km north-west of Melbourne. Sugarloaf and Jawbones are 112km north-east of Melbourne in the Cathedral Range State Park, a popular weekend spot. The Grampians, 250km west of Melbourne, have a wide variety of climbs. At Mt Buffalo, 369km north in the alpine area, the hardest climb is Buffalo Gorge.

Swimming & Surfing

Melbourne's Port Phillip Bay doesn't have great beaches, although there is reasonably good swimming on the eastern side of the bay. Along the Mornington Peninsula you have the choice between sheltered bay beaches on one side and the ocean beaches on the other side.

Outside of the bay, however, the Victorian coastline features some truly spectacular and lovely ocean beaches, many of which have good surf – when the conditions are right, of course. A good surfing reference is the booklet *Where to Look for Surf in Victoria* ($19.95), which covers the coastline from Cape Otway to Wilsons Prom.

The coast along the Great Ocean Road features dramatic contrasts between sandy beaches at places such as Anglesea, Apollo Bay and Discovery Bay and rugged cliffs and gorges along the Port Campbell National Park. There are also fine beaches all along the eastern coastline, including those at

Victoria provides a large variety of climbs for all skill levels

Phillip Island, Wilsons Promontory, Lakes Entrance and Mallacoota.

Scuba Diving

Flinders, Portland, Kilcunda, Torquay, Anglesea, Lorne, Apollo Bay, Mallacoota, Portsea, Sorrento and Wilsons Prom are all good diving areas. In Melbourne there are clubs and organisations renting equipment, and many larger coastal towns have dive shops. Companies offering courses and diving trips include the Melbourne Diving School (☎ 9459 4111). Queenscliff Dive Centre (☎ 5258 1188) offers a one-day course that counts towards a certificate course which can be continued there or at other locations around Australia – handy if you're travelling around quickly.

Boating & Sailing

There are many sailing clubs in Melbourne around Port Phillip Bay. Other boating areas around the state include the large Gippsland

Lakes system, Lake Eildon, and Mallacoota Inlet in East Gippsland. At all of these places you can hire yachts and launches, which work out to be quite economical among a group of people.

Houseboat holidays can be arranged on Lake Eildon and on the Murray River at Echuca and Mildura.

White-Water Rafting

Operators including Peregrine Adventures (☎ 9662 2700) and Snowy River Expeditions (☎ 5155 0220) run white-water rafting trips on various rivers in the Victorian Alps. Trips operate year-round, although the best times are during the snow melts from about August to December. Costs are around $125 for one day to $550 for five-day expeditions.

Skiing

See the section on the Alps for the Victorian ski fields.

Cycling

Victoria is a great place for cycling. Melbourne has some good bike tracks, and in the country you'll find hundreds of kilometres of good roads that carry little traffic. Especially appealing is the fact that in many areas you'll ride a very long way without encountering a hill. Wine regions such as Rutherglen are popular areas for cycling tours and the High Country is much favoured by mountain bikers.

Contact the helpful Bicycle Victoria (☎ 9328 3000) at 19 O'Connell St in North Melbourne for more information; ask about their regular tours and events such as the Great Victorian Bike Ride (every November) and the Easter Bike Ride. The book *Bicycling Around Victoria* ($19.95) by Ray Peace details 50 different bike rides. *Discovering Victoria's Bike Paths* ($15.95) is also good.

ORGANISED TOURS

A growing number of companies offer fun and inexpensive tours aimed at independent travellers, from day trips to several-day expeditions. Most tours operate out of Melbourne; hostels have details and most take bookings. The Great Ocean Road, the Grampians and Phillip Island are the main destinations, but some outfits will take you farther afield.

For buses such as the Wayward Bus, which take you on a tour en route to another city, see the Getting There & Away chapter at the front of the book (see also Organised Tours in the Great Ocean Road and Phillip Island sections, later in this chapter).

Well-known outfits include Mac's Backpacker Bus (☎ 5241 3180) and Autopia Tours (☎ 9326 5536).

Some interesting smaller tour operators include Lancefield Bush Rides & Tucker (☎ 5429 1627), which offers a day trip to Hanging Rock with horse-riding and bush tucker for $85 (discounts for YHA members); and Echidna Walkabout (☎ 9646 8249), which runs day trips with bushwalking, wildlife-watching and an introduction to Aboriginal culture ($95 or less), as well as trips to the Grampians, the Great Ocean Road and the national parks of East Gippsland.

Wild-Life Tours (☎ 5439 5086) is another smaller company doing the Great Ocean Road and the Grampians, with the emphasis on wildlife. It also runs between Melbourne and Adelaide.

Bunyip Tours (☎ 9354 0861) has both camping and walking trips to Wilsons Promontory. The three-day trip costs $145 and has been recommended by a couple of readers.

Another outfit that gets good feedback is Eco Adventure Tours (☎ 5962 5115), which began offering wildlife tours of the Healesville area but now travels farther afield.

Bogong Jack Adventures (☎ (08) 8383 7198) has a wide range of cycling, bushwalking and skiing tours through the Victorian Alps and wine regions, involving either camping or other accommodation and various levels of skill and fitness.

Bike & Bush Escapes (☎ 5345 2552) offers supported rides in forests from half a

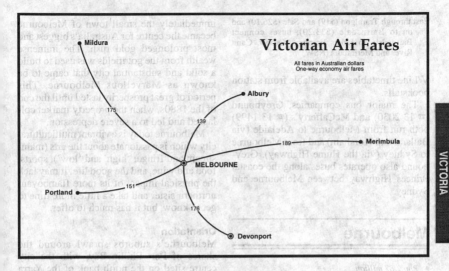

Victorian Air Fares

All fares in Australian dollars
One-way economy air fares

Mildura

Albury

175

139

189 — Merimbula

MELBOURNE

151

Portland

176

Devonport

VICTORIA

day ($25) to two days ($150) or longer, in the Creswick area and farther afield.

GETTING THERE & AWAY
Melbourne is the focal point for most transport into Victoria. Many international airlines fly into Melbourne, and Ansett (☎ 13 1300) and Qantas (☎ 13 1313) have flights between Melbourne and the other capital cities.

Greyhound (☎ 13 2030), McCafferty's (☎ 13 1499) and several other bus companies have regular services to Sydney and Adelaide, and V/Line (☎ 13 2232) operates the interstate rail links to Adelaide and Sydney (see Getting There & Away in the Melbourne section for more on transport into Victoria).

GETTING AROUND
Air
Kendell Airlines (bookings through Ansett on ☎ 13 1300) operates the main flights within Victoria, with services between Melbourne and Mildura, Albury, Portland and Merimbula (NSW). Southern Australia Airlines (bookings through Qantas on ☎ 13 1313) also flies between Melbourne and

Mildura, and Hazelton (bookings through Ansett) flies from Albury to Traralgon and Sale.

Train & Bus
V/Line (☎ 13 2232 between 7 am and 9 pm) has a fairly comprehensive rail network of country services radiating out of Melbourne – these are supplemented by (and increasingly supplanted by) V/Line buses. The main train routes, and economy fares from Melbourne, are:

West to Geelong ($8.40) then inland to Warrnambool ($33.20 from Melbourne); a bus runs along the Great Ocean Road from Geelong through Lorne ($10.90 from Geelong) and Apollo Bay ($17.50 from Geelong).
North-west to Ballarat ($13.40), Stawell ($30.70), Horsham ($40.10) and to Adelaide ($56 by overnight train, $49 by daylight train and bus) in South Australia; buses connect from Stawell to Halls Gap ($37.80) in the Grampians
North-west through Ballarat to Mildura ($52)
North through Bendigo ($20.20) to Swan Hill ($42.10)
North to Shepparton ($22.60) and Echuca ($26.10)
North along the Hume Highway to Albury-Wodonga ($37.80), continuing to Sydney; buses run from Wangaratta to Beechworth and Bright

East through Traralgon ($19) and Sale ($26.10) and on to Bairnsdale ($33.20); buses connect Bairnsdale to Lakes Entrance, Orbost, Cann River and Merimbula (NSW)

V/Line timetables are available from station bookstalls.

The major bus companies, Greyhound (☎ 13 2030) and McCafferty's (☎ 13 1499) both run from Melbourne to Adelaide (via Ballarat and Horsham) and from Melbourne to Sydney (via the Hume Highway). Greyhound also operates buses along the coastal Princes Highway between Melbourne and Sydney.

Melbourne

• *Pop 2.87 million*

Melbourne is Australia's second-largest city. Its birth and major period of development paralleled Queen Victoria's reign (1837-1901), and the city is in many ways a product of its formative era both architecturally and socially. It's a traditionally conservative city of elaborate Victorian-era buildings, gracious parks and gardens, and tree-lined boulevards.

Since WWII, the social fabric has been transformed by thousands of immigrants, and the city has been greatly enriched by the influence of people and cultures from around the world. Several building booms, most notably that of the 1980s, have altered the city physically so that it is now a striking blend of past and present, with ornate 19th-century buildings sitting alongside towering skyscrapers.

The first European settlement on Port Phillip Bay was established at Sorrento in 1803, although within a year it was abandoned and the settlers moved down to Tasmania. In 1835 a group of Tasmanian entrepreneurs returned and established a permanent settlement near the site of today's city centre.

In 1851 the colony of Victoria became independent of New South Wales and almost immediately the small town of Melbourne became the centre for Australia's biggest and most prolonged gold rush. The immense wealth from the goldfields was used to build a solid and substantial city that came to be known as Marvellous Melbourne. This period of great prosperity lasted until the end of the 1880s, when the property market collapsed and led to a severe depression.

Melbourne today is a vibrant multicultural city which is passionate about the arts (mainstream and fringe; 'high' and 'low'), sports, food and wine, and the good life. It may lack the physical impact of its more flamboyant northern sister and take a little more time to get to know, but it has much to offer.

Orientation

Melbourne's suburbs sprawl around the shores of Port Phillip Bay, with the city centre sited on the north bank of the Yarra River, about 5km inland from the bay. The city centre is laid out in a rectangular grid of wide boulevards (once known as the Golden Mile), interspersed with a network of narrow streets and alleys. The main shopping precinct is in the heart of the city, with the Bourke St Mall as its centre point. In the mall you'll find tourist information booths and the large department stores, and on the corner of Bourke and Elizabeth Sts is the main post office.

Bus travellers arrive at either the Spencer St Coach Terminal on the west side of the city (V/Line, Skybus, Firefly and McCafferty's buses), or the Melbourne Transit Centre at 58 Franklin St (Greyhound and Skybus airport buses) on the northern side of the city. Interstate and country trains operate from the Spencer St station, while the Flinders St station on the corner of Swanston and Flinders Sts is the main station for suburban trains. (Note that there's a station called Melbourne Central on the city centre's underground rail loop. This is *not* the main station – it's named after the shopping centre above it.)

Swanston St, which runs north-south through the city, is in part another pedestrian mall (although there are moves to have it revert to a road). After crossing the Yarra River, Swanston St becomes St Kilda Rd, a tree-lined boulevard that runs all the way south to St Kilda and beyond.

On Flinders St the big Federation Square project is underway, which might finally give Melbourne a decent city square. There will also be theatres, cinemas and the Museum of Australian Art, due to open in 2001.

Information

Tourist Offices In the city, the best places for information are the city council's information booths. The Bourke St Mall and City Square booths are open on weekdays from 9 am to 5 pm (on Friday until 7 pm), Saturday from 10 am to 4 pm and Sunday from 11 am to 4 pm. The Rialto observation deck booth is open on weekdays from 11 am to 5 pm and on weekends from 10 am to 4 pm.

The Victoria Visitor Information Centre (☎ 9658 9955) in the town hall on Swanston Walk has plenty of brochures, but it's mainly a booking office for tours and accommodation. Also in the town hall is the City Experience Centre, focussing on Melbourne and providing multilingual information. Both offices are open daily.

There are tourist information booths in the international terminal at Melbourne airport (Tullamarine).

The Age City Search web site is full of useful information. It's at citysearch.com.au.

Post & Communications The main post office (the GPO) is on the corner of Bourke and Elizabeth Sts; there's an efficient poste restante section and phones for interstate and international calls. Phone centres can also be found behind the main post office on Little Bourke St and down the road at 94 Elizabeth St.

The telephone area code for Melbourne and Victoria is (03).

Among the Internet cafes are: Melbourne Central Internet, Shop 133A, Level 2, Melbourne Central (noon to 6 pm daily); and The Internet Kennel, in a florist shop at 123 Acland St, St Kilda (11 am to 6 pm daily).

Gay & Lesbian Travellers Melbourne has a large and active gay scene. For information on events pick up a copy of *Brother & Sister*, a free mag which you'll find in many cafes in the city and inner suburbs. The Gay & Lesbian Switchboard (☎ 9510 5488) offers counselling (or just a chat) nightly between 6 and 10 pm (Wednesday from 2 to 10 pm) and there's a 24-hour recorded information service (☎ 0055 12504).

Useful Organisations The National Trust (☎ 9654 4711) has an office in the historic Tasma Terrace at 4 Parliament Place.

The YHA (☎ 9670 7991) has its helpful office at 205 King St, on the corner of Little Bourke St. The Travellers' Aid Society (☎ 9654 2600), on the 2nd floor at 169 Swanston St, offers assistance in emergencies.

Bookshops Melbourne's largest bookshops include Angus & Robertson Bookworld, 107 Elizabeth St; Collins Booksellers, 115 Elizabeth St; and Dymocks, on the corner of Bourke and Swanston Sts. The agreeably chaotic McGills at 187 Elizabeth St (opposite the main post office) is good for interstate and overseas newspapers.

Bowyangs Maps & Travel Guides at 372 Little Bourke St has the city's most extensive range of travel books and maps, and Information Victoria at 356 Collins St has a wide selection of books on Melbourne and Victoria, plus government maps.

There are dozens of good specialist bookshops, including Readings at 338 Lygon St, Carlton; Brunswick St Bookstore at 305 Brunswick St, Fitzroy; Cosmos Books & Music at 112 Acland St, St Kilda; and Black Mask Books at 78 Toorak Rd, South Yarra.

Medical Services The Traveller's Medical & Vaccination Centre (☎ 9602 5788), Level 2, 393 Little Bourke St, is open weekdays from 9 am to 5 pm (Monday, Tuesday and Thursday till 8.30 pm) and Saturday from 9 am to 1 pm (appointments necessary). There's another TMVC clinic (☎ 9437 7132) in the private wing of the Royal Melbourne

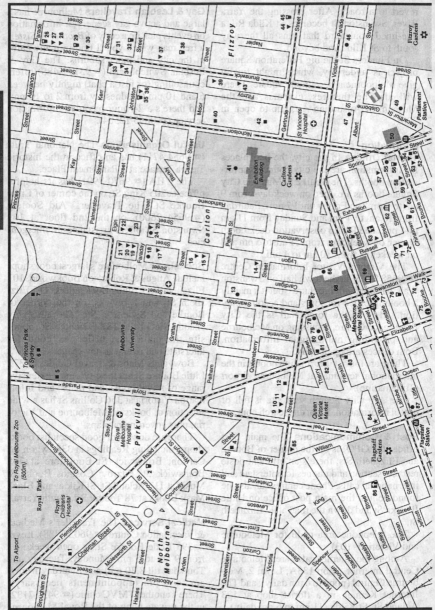

VICTORIA

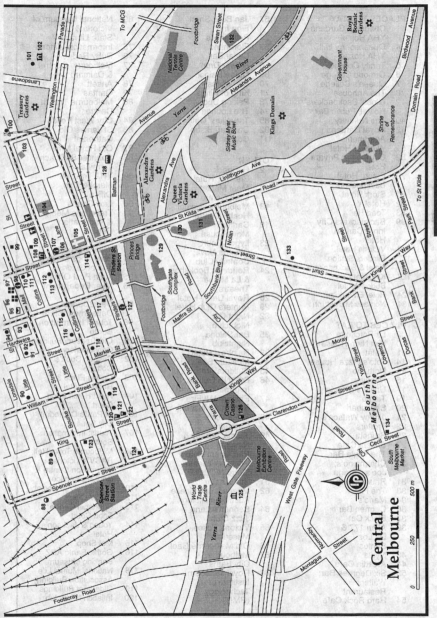

Central Melbourne

VICTORIA

PLACES TO STAY
1 Chapman Gardens
   YHA Hostel
4 Queensberry Hill
   YHA Hostel
5 Trinity College
6 Ormond College
7 Queen's College
8 The Arthouse
12 Global Backpackers'
   Hostel; Public Bar
40 The Nunnery
42 Royal Gardens
   Apartments
51 Windsor Hotel
52 City Centre Private
   Hotel
72 Exford Hotel
   Backpackers'
81 Stork Hotel
82 Hotel Y
83 Toad Hall
99 Backpackers City
   Inn & Carlton
   Hotel
109 Victoria Hotel
117 Flinders Station
   Hotel & Backpackers
123 Kingsgate
   Budget Hotel
124 Hotel Enterprize
134 Nomads Market Inn

PLACES TO EAT
9 La Porchetta
10 Viet Nam House
11 Dalat
14 Toto's Pizza House
15 Notturno
16 Nyonya
17 University Cafe
19 Tiamo
20 Shakahari
21 Jimmy Watson's
22 Trotters
25 Brunetti
27 Bakers Cafe
28 The Vegie Bar
30 Charmaine's;
   Joe's Garage
31 Rhumbarella's
33 The Fitz
34 Mario's
36 Carmen Bar
37 Black Cat
39 Akari 177 &
   De Los
   Santos
43 Nyala
44 Arcadia Cafe
53 Six Degrees Bar;
   Waiters
   Restaurant
54 Hard Rock Cafe

57 Jan Bo & Shark
   Finn Inn
58 Pellegrini's
59 Florentino
   Cellar Bar
60 Flower Drum
63 Cafee Balooè
70 Stalactites
71 King of Kings
73 Peking Duck
74 The Lounge
85 Travellers' Café
92 Campari Bistro
111 Gopals

OTHER
2 Redback
   Brewery Hotel
3 Meat Market
   Craft Centre
13 Melbourne Sexual
   Health Centre
18 Carlton
   Moviehouse
23 Lygon Court;
   Cinema Nova;
   Comedy Club
24 Readings Bookshop
   & La Mama
   Theatre
26 Royal Derby Hotel
29 Punters Club Hotel
32 Night Cat
   Nightclub
35 Bar Salona
   Nightclub
38 Rainbow Hotel
41 Museum Site
45 Builders Arms Hotel
46 DC&NR Outdoor
   Information Centre
47 Eastern Hill Fire
   Station & Museum
48 St Patrick's
   Cathedral
49 Tasma Terrace &
   National Trust
50 Parliament House
55 Princess Theatre
56 Metro Nightclub
61 Sadie's Bar
62 Museum of Chinese
   Australian History
64 Bennett's Lane
   Jazz Club
65 Victoria Police
   Museum
66 Old Melbourne Gaol
67 Melbourne
   City Baths
68 Royal Melbourne
   Institute of
   Technology
   (RMIT)

69 National Museum of
   Victoria &
   State Library
75 Information Victoria
76 Ruby Red
77 Melbourne Central
   & Daimaru
78 Ansett
79 Qantas
80 Melbourne Transit
   Centre
84 City West Police
86 St James Old
   Cathedral
87 Old Royal Mint
88 Spencer St Coach
   Terminal
89 YHA Travel &
   Membership
   Office
90 Law Courts
91 Traveller's Medical
   & Vaccination
   Centre
93 McGills
   Newsagency
94 Bowyangs Maps &
   Travel Guides
95 Main Post Office
96 Myer Department
   Store
97 David Jones
   Department Store
98 Tourist Information
   Booth
100 Old Treasury Building
101 Conservatory
102 Captain Cook's
   Cottage
103 Collins Place &
   Regent Hotel
104 Hyatt Hotel; Food
   Court
105 St Paul's Cathedral
106 City Square
107 Tourist Information
   Booth
108 Melbourne Town Hall;
   RACV's Victorian
   information Centre &
   Booking Service
110 Travellers' Aid Society
112 RACV Office
113 Sportsgirl Centre;
   Food Court
114 Young & Jackson's
   Hotel
115 Met Shop
116 Gothic Bank; ANZ
   Banking Museum
118 National Mutual Life
   Association Building
119 Olderfleet Buildings
120 Inflation Nightclub

121	Rialto Towers & Observation Deck	128	State Swimming Centre	132	Sports & Entertainment Centre
122	Grainstore Tavern	129	Melbourne Concert Hall	133	Malthouse Theatres
125	Polly Woodside Maritime Museum	130	Theatres Building		
126	Planet Hollywood	131	National Gallery of Victoria		
127	Parks Victoria				

Melbourne Walking Tour

Start at the intersection of Flinders and Swanston Sts, site of three landmarks. The grand old **Flinders St station** is the main train station for suburban trains – 'under the clocks' at the station entrance is a favourite meeting place. Across the road is one of Melbourne's best-known pubs, **Young & Jackson's**, which is famed mainly for the painting of *Chloe* hanging in the upstairs bar. Judged indecent at the Melbourne Exhibition of 1880, she has gone on to win affection among generations of drinkers. The third landmark on this corner, **St Paul's Cathedral**, is a masterpiece of Gothic revivalist architecture. A new landmark, **Federation Square**, is under construction on the south-east corner.

Stroll up Swanston St, which has been closed to cars to create **Swanston Walk**, a boulevard that pedestrians share with trams and commercial vehicles. In the block between Flinders Lane and Collins St is the temporary **City Square**, with its fountains and ponds, a statue of the ill-fated explorers Burke and Wills (on the Collins St side), and an information booth nearby. Across Collins St is the **town hall**.

Continue up to Swanston St and turn left into the **Bourke St Mall**. Like Swanston Walk, it's difficult for a pedestrian mall to work with 30-tonne trams barrelling through every few minutes, but despite this, the mall has become something of a focus for city shoppers.

Collect your mail from the main post office at the Elizabeth St end of the mall, then return to Swanston Walk and head north again. Across Little Lonsdale St you'll pass the **State Library** on your right, and in the next block is the **Royal Melbourne Institute of Technology**, with its rather bizarre architectural facades. Turn right into Franklin St and then another right into Russell St, and head down past the **Old Melbourne Gaol**. When you get to Little Bourke St, turn left and you've entered **Chinatown**. This narrow lane was a thronging Chinese quarter back in the gold-rush days and it's now a busy, crowded couple of blocks with excellent Chinese restaurants, Asian supermarkets and shops.

At the top end of Little Bourke St, turn right into Spring St, which has some of Melbourne's most impressive old buildings including the lovely **Princess Theatre**, the gracious **Windsor Hotel**, and the **State Houses of Parliament**. Built with gold-rush wealth, this building served as the national parliament while Canberra was under construction. There are free tours on weekdays when parliament is in recess (call ☎9651 8568 for dates and times).

Farther down Spring St, opposite Collins St, the 1853 **Old Treasury Building** is one of the finest 19th-century buildings in the city and houses an interesting exhibition on Melbourne's past and future (open daily; tours of the gold vault at 1 and 3 pm). The **Treasury Gardens**, beside this building, are full of healthy elm trees.

Cross Spring St and you'll enter what's known as the **Paris End** of Collins St – mainly because this stretch was once lined with plane trees, grand buildings and street cafés. The plane trees remain, but sadly many of the historic buildings have been demolished over the years.

On your left you'll see the soaring towers of Collins Place, which house **Hotel Sofitel**. The hotel's toilets on the 35th floor give spectacular views over the Melbourne Cricket Ground (MCG), parklands and shimmering suburbs, and are one of the city's prime (unofficial) attractions.

Continue down Collins St to Swanston Walk and turn left. Continue past Flinders St station, then turn right just before the river and stroll along the riverside boardwalk. An arched footbridge takes you across the river to the **Crown Casino** and the **Southgate** complex, with its restaurants, bars and cafés. South of Southgate is the **arts precinct**, and across St Kilda Rd are the parklands of the **Kings Domain** – a wonderful area to explore, if you still have the energy.

Other Walking Tours The City of Melbourne publishes a series of *Heritage Walk* brochures, available from the council's information booths, or the town hall, Swanston Walk (cnr Little Collins St).

The National Trust's *Walking Melbourne* booklet is particularly useful if you're interested in architectural heritage. ■

Hospital (enter from Royal Pde), open from 9 am to 5 pm on weekdays (to 8 pm on Wednesday). Both have accurate information on the vaccinations and precautions needed for most countries.

The Melbourne Sexual Health Centre (☎ 9347 0244) is at 580 Swanston St in Carlton – visits are free; appointments preferred.

Dangers & Annoyances Melbourne trams should be treated with some caution by car drivers. You can only overtake a tram on the left and you must always stop behind one when it halts to drop or collect passengers (except where there are central 'islands' for passengers). In the city centre at most junctions a peculiar left-hand path must be followed to make right-hand turns, in order to accommodate the trams. Note that in rainy weather tram tracks are extremely slippery; motorcyclists should take special care. Cyclists must beware of tram tracks at all times; if you get a wheel into the track you're flat on your face immediately, and painfully.

Tram passengers should be cautious when stepping on and off – a lot of people have been hit by passing cars, so don't step off without looking both ways. Pedestrians in Bourke St Mall and Swanston Walk should watch for passing trams too.

Tram Tours

When you tire of walking, consider buying a Zone 1 daily ticket and continuing your exploration by tram. For $4.30, you can spend the entire day travelling around the city and inner suburbs by tram – a bargain, and a great way to get a feel for Melbourne.

Try a ride on tram No 8. It starts off along Swanston St in the city, rolls down St Kilda Rd beside the Kings Domain and continues up Toorak Rd through South Yarra and Toorak. Another good tram ride is on No 16, which cruises right down St Kilda Rd to St Kilda.

There's also the free City Circle Tram, running along Flinders, Spring, Latrobe and Spencer Sts (the boundaries of the CBD). It's an old-style tram painted maroon.

City Buildings

Melbourne is an intriguing blend of the soaring new and the stately old. Epitomising this blend are buildings such as the **Melbourne Central** shopping complex on the corner of Latrobe and Elizabeth Sts. Opened in 1991, the centrepiece of the complex is the old **shot tower**, which still stands on its original site but is now enclosed within the new building. The **Block Arcade** is a gracious 19th-century shopping complex running between Elizabeth and Collins Sts.

The stretch of Collins St between William and King Sts is another embodiment of the old combined with the new. The **Rialto Towers** is an architectural landmark built during the boom of the 1980s. Beside it is the imaginative Le Meridien Hotel, which uses the facades of two old buildings and cleverly incorporates an old stone-paved alleyway that used to run between them. Next to the hotel are the **Olderfleet Buildings**, magnificent monuments to the Gothic revival architecture that dominated during the building boom of the late 19th century.

East along Collins St on the corner of Queen St are three bank buildings that are also fine examples of the extravagance of the land boom period. The 1887 **Gothic Bank** is regarded as the finest Gothic revival building in Melbourne, and the interior has been cleverly restored to highlight the intricate ceiling. Across the road is the impressive **National Mutual Life Association Building** (1891-1903).

Other old buildings in the centre include the 1872 **Old Royal Mint** beside Flagstaff Gardens, the 1842 **St James Old Cathedral** on King St (Melbourne's oldest surviving building), and **St Patrick's Cathedral**, one of the city's most imposing churches, behind the State Houses of Parliament. Victoriana enthusiasts may also find some very small buildings of interest – scattered around the city are a number of very fine cast-iron men's **urinals** (like French *pissoirs*). They date mainly from 1903 to 1914, and the one on the corner of Exhibition and Lonsdale Sts is classified by the National Trust.

Rialto Towers Observation Deck

This lookout is on the 55th floor of Melbourne's tallest building, the Rialto Towers on Collins St. The lookout platform offers spectacular 360° views. It's open daily from 11 am to 11.30 pm; entry costs $7.

State Library

Extending for a block between Swanston and Russell Sts, beside Latrobe St, are the State Library and Latrobe Library. The State Library has a gracious, octagonal, domed reading room and any book-lover will enjoy its hushed atmosphere. Its collection of more than a million books and other reference material is particularly notable for its coverage of the humanities and social sciences, as well as art, music, performing arts, Australiana and rare books.

The **National Museum**, which surrounds the State Library, has been closed to prepare for the move to a new (and controversial) building by the Exhibition Building in the Carlton (Exhibition) Gardens. It is due to open in 2000. The new museum was all set to be built on the banks of the Yarra but somehow a casino got built there instead ...

Old Melbourne Gaol

This gruesome old prison and penal museum is a block farther up Russell St. It was built of bluestone in 1841 and was used right up until 1929. In all, 135 prisoners were hanged here. It's a dark, dank, spooky place. The museum displays include death masks of noted bushrangers and convicts, Ned Kelly's armour, the very scaffold from which Ned took his fatal plunge, and some fascinating records of early 'transported' convicts. It is open daily from 9.30 am to 4.30 pm ($7, children $4, family tickets available).

Yarra River

Melbourne's prime natural feature, the Yarra, is a surprisingly pleasant river, enhanced by the parks, walks and bike tracks that have been built along its banks. Despite the cracks

about it 'running upside down', it's just muddy, not particularly dirty.

When the rowing eights are gliding down the river on a sunny day, or you're driving along Alexandra Ave towards the city on a clear night, the Yarra can look quite magical. Best of all you can cycle along the riverside without the risk of being wiped out by some nut in a Holden. The bike tracks follow the Yarra out of the city for some 20km (see the Getting Around section for bike-hire places).

A more leisurely way to see the river is on one of the tour boats that operate on the river from Princes Walk beside Princes Bridge (across from Flinders St station).

To the north-east of the city, the Yarra is bordered by parkland. At the **Studley Park Boathouse** in Kew, you can enjoy a meal and/or a drink and hire rowing boats, canoes and kayaks by the hour. In parts of **Studley Park** you could be out in the bush; it's hard to believe the city's all around you. Farther upstream at **Fairfield Park** there is another boathouse, restored to its Edwardian elegance, offering Devonshire teas and other snacks, and boats and canoes for hire. You might catch a performance in the outdoor amphitheatre next to the boathouse.

Southbank & the Casino

The area opposite the city centre on the southern side of the Yarra has been impressively redeveloped. The Southgate complex features three levels of riverside cafes, restaurants, a food hall and a shopping galleria. It's a great area for shopping, eating, drinking or just browsing, and there are good views of the city.

Next door to Southgate, the enormous Crown Casino masquerades under the name 'entertainment complex'. As well as acres of incredibly glitzy gambling there are plenty of bars, shops, places to eat and drink, cinemas and theatres. The casino is heartily disliked by those who see it as a temple of philistinism, and the contrast in philosophies behind the casino and the nearby arts precinct is staggering. However, if you're masochistic enough to enjoy a huge dose of kitsch, noise and flashing lights, it's worth a look.

Polly Woodside Maritime Museum

Close to Spencer St Bridge, immediately south of the city centre, is the *Polly Woodside*. Built in Ireland in 1885, it's an old iron-hulled sailing ship which carried freight in the dying years of the sailing era. The *Polly Woodside* is the centrepiece of the maritime museum, which is open daily from 10 am to 5 pm ($7, children $4).

Queen Victoria Market

Over on the northern side of the city, the Queen Victoria Market is on the corner of Peel and Victoria Sts. It's the city's main retail produce centre – a hectic and colourful multicultural scene on Tuesday, Thursday, Friday, and Saturday morning, when the stall operators shout, yell and generally go all-out to move the goods. On Sunday there are mostly general goods stalls – everything from cut-price jeans to second-hand records (see the Organised Tours section for walking tours of the market), though some fruit and vegie stalls and delicatessen shops are also open.

Royal Melbourne Zoo

Three kilometres north of the city centre in Parkville is Melbourne's excellent zoo. This is the oldest zoo in Australia and one of the oldest in the world but it is continually upgrading the standard of the prisoners' accommodation. It's open daily from 9 am to 5 pm ($13, children $7, family tickets available). The zoo is in **Royal Park** and you can get there on tram No 55 or 56 from William St in the city.

Scienceworks Museum

This is the science and technology section of the Museum of Victoria, and it has a huge array of tactile displays. It's at 2 Booker St, Spotswood, about 15 minutes walk from Spotswood train station, or just over the West Gate Bridge if you're driving. It's open daily from 10 am to 4.30 pm ($8, children $4).

Melbourne Cricket Ground

The MCG is Australia's biggest sporting stadium and was the central stadium for the 1956 Olympics. Set in Yarra Park, which stretches from the city and East Melbourne to Richmond, the stadium can accommodate about 100,000 spectators, and does so at least once a year. The big occasion is the annual Australian Rules football Grand Final in September. This is Australia's biggest sporting event and brings Melbourne to a fever pitch.

Cricket is, of course, the other major sport played at the MCG. International Test and one-day matches, as well as interstate Sheffield Shield and local district games, take place here over the summer months.

Hourly tours (☎ 9657 8879) are offered daily. These take in the **Australian Gallery of Sport & Olympic Museum**. Tours run between 10 am to 3 pm ($8, children $5).

Carlton Brewhouse

Carlton & United Breweries, maker of beers such as Fosters and Victoria Bitter, has a visitors centre with some interesting displays. It's on the corner of Nelson and Thompson Sts in Abbotsford, the next suburb east from Collingwood, and is open from Monday to Saturday ($5 including a tasting). On weekdays there are tours of the brewery at 10 and 11.30 am and 2 pm ($7.50). Book on ☎ 9420 6800.

Victorian Arts Centre & National Gallery

The arts centre is just south of the Yarra River and the city centre, alongside St Kilda Rd.

The building closest to the Yarra is the **Melbourne Concert Hall**, the city's main venue for the performing arts. Beside it, the **Theatres Building** houses the State Theatre, the Playhouse, the George Fairfax Studio and the Westpac Gallery. There are one-hour tours of the theatres complex ($11.25) each weekday at noon and 2.30 pm, as well as each Saturday at 10.30 am and noon. On Sunday, Backstage Tours (☎ 9281 8152) runs 1½-hour backstage tours ($12) at 12.15 and 2.15 pm.

The next building along, the **National**

Gallery of Victoria, houses a very fine collection. The stained-glass ceiling in the Great Hall is superb – best viewed from a supine position. The gallery is open daily from 10 am to 5 pm (admission is free). There are additional charges for some special exhibits.

Unfortunately, the gallery was due to close at the end of 1998 to undergo two years of renovation. Some of the collection may be loaned to regional galleries during this time, or a temporary gallery in Melbourne may be opened.

Parks & Gardens

Victoria has dubbed itself 'the garden state' and it's certainly true in Melbourne; the city has many swaths of green all around the central area. They're varied and delightful – formal gardens such as the Treasury and Flagstaff gardens; wide, empty parklands such as Royal Park; the outstanding Royal Botanic Gardens; and many others. Of poignant attraction to visitors from Europe are healthy old elm trees around the city. Dutch elm disease has arrived here but it has not destroyed many trees.

Royal Botanic Gardens Certainly the finest botanic gardens in Australia and among the finest in the world, this is one of the nicest spots in Melbourne. There's nothing more genteel than eating scones and cream by the lake on a Sunday afternoon. The beautifully laid out gardens are right beside the Yarra River; indeed the river once actually ran through the gardens and the lakes are the remains of curves of the river, cut off when the river was straightened out to lessen the annual flood damage. The site was chosen in 1845 but the real development took place when Baron Sir Ferdinand von Mueller took charge in 1852.

There's a surprising amount of fauna as well as flora in the gardens. Apart from the many water fowl and the frequent visits from cockatoos you may also see possums. In all, more than 50 varieties of birds can be seen in the gardens. A large colony of fruit bats has taken up residence in the trees of the fern gully.

Pick up guide-yourself leaflets at the park entrances; these are changed with the seasons and tell you what to look out for at the different times of year. The gardens are open daily from 7.30 am and they close at 5.30 pm from April to the end of October and 8.30 pm the rest of the year.

Over the summer movies are shown in the gardens; take a picnic and enjoy the twilight before the film begins. Call Ticketek (☎ 132 849) for bookings.

Kings Domain The Botanic Gardens form a corner of the Kings Domain, which is flanked by the Yarra River, St Kilda Rd, Domain Rd and Anderson St.

Beside St Kilda Rd stands the massive **Shrine of Remembrance**, a memorial to those who fought in WWI and other wars. It's worth climbing up to the top as there are fine views to the city along St Kilda Rd. The shrine's big day is Anzac Day, in April. The shrine is open to visitors daily from 10 am to 5 pm.

Across from the shrine is **Governor Latrobe's Cottage**, the original Victorian government house sent out from the UK in prefabricated form in 1840. The simple little cottage is open daily except Tuesday and Thursday from 11 am to 4.30 pm ($2).

The cottage is flanked by the **Old Observatory** and the **National Herbarium**. Among other things, the herbarium tests suspected marijuana samples to decide if they really are the dreaded weed. On some nights the observatory is open to the public for a free view of the heavens between 8 and 10 pm, but it is usually booked out months in advance.

The imposing building overlooking the Botanic Gardens is **Government House**, where Victoria's governor resides. It's a copy of Queen Victoria's palace on England's Isle of Wight. There are guided tours on Monday, Wednesday and Saturday (no tours from mid-December to the end of January) for $8 (children $4). Book through the National Trust (☎ 9654 4711).

Across the road from the herbarium on Dallas Brooks Drive is the **Australian**

Centre for Contemporary Art, which is open Tuesday to Friday from 11 am to 5 pm and weekends from 2 to 5 pm (admission is free). Up at the city end of the park is the **Sidney Myer Music Bowl**, an outdoor performance area in a natural bowl. On Christmas Eve it's the venue for the wonderful Carols by Candlelight; in winter it turns into an ice-skating rink.

Treasury & Fitzroy Gardens These two formal parks lie immediately to the east of the city centre – both have a large resident population of possums; you may see them in the early evening or at night.

The Fitzroy Gardens, with its stately avenues lined with English elms, is a popular spot for wedding photographs. The pathways in the park are laid out in the form of the Union Jack. The gardens contain several points of interest including **Captain Cook's Cottage**, which was uprooted from its native Yorkshire and reassembled in the park in 1934. Actually it's not certain that the good captain ever did live in this house, but never mind, it looks very picturesque. It's open daily from 9 am to 5 pm ($3, children $1.50).

Other City Parks The **Flagstaff Gardens** were the first public gardens in Melbourne. From a lookout point here, ships were sighted in the early colonial days.

On the northern side of the city, the **Carlton Gardens** are the site of the Exhibition Building, a wonder of the southern hemisphere when it was built for the Great Exhibition of 1880. Later it was used by the Victorian parliament for 27 years, while the Victorian parliament building was used by the national legislature until its parliament building in Canberra was finally completed. It's still a major exhibition centre. The new National Museum is being built next to the Exhibition Building.

Historic Homesteads
Como Overlooking the Yarra River from Como Park in South Yarra, Como was built between 1840 and 1859. An early occupant

writes of seeing Aborigines perform a cannibal rite from her bedroom window.

The home has been restored and furnished and, together with its extensive grounds, is operated by the National Trust. It is open from 10 am to 5 pm daily ($8, children $4.50); you can get there on tram No 8 from the city.

Ripponlea Ripponlea, 192 Hotham St, Elsternwick, close to St Kilda, is another fine old mansion, with elegant gardens inhabited by peacocks. It's open daily (except Monday) from 10 am to 5 pm ($8, children $4).

Other Galleries
At 7 Templestowe Rd in the suburb of Bulleen, the **Museum of Modern Art at Heide** is the former home of two prominent art patrons, John and Sunday Reed, and houses an impressive collection of 20th-century Australian art. The sprawling park is an informal combination of deciduous and native trees, with scattered sculpture gardens running right down to the banks of the Yarra. Heide is open from Tuesday to Friday between 10 am and 5 pm, and on Saturday and Sunday between noon and 5 pm. Bus No 203 goes to Bulleen, and the Yarra bike path runs close by.

In Eltham, the mud-brick and alternative lifestylers' suburb, **Montsalvat** on Hillcrest Ave (26km out from the city centre) is Justus Jorgensen's eclectic recreation of a European artists' colony, which today houses all manner of artists and artisans. It's open daily from dawn to dusk ($5, $2.50 children). It's a 2km walk from Eltham train station.

Other Museums
In Chinatown in the city centre the **Museum of Chinese Australian History** is housed in an 1890s warehouse on Cohen Place and traces the history of the Chinese people in Australia. It's open daily from 10 am to 4.30 pm, Saturday from noon ($5, children $3). The museum also conducts two-hour walking tours around Chinatown every morning, and these cost $15, or $28 with

lunch at a Chinatown restaurant. Phone ☎ 9662 2888 for bookings.

The **Jewish Museum of Australia**, 26 Alma Rd in St Kilda, preserves Jewish culture, art and customs; it's open Tuesday to Thursday from 10 am to 4 pm and Sunday from 11 am to 5 pm ($5).

Trams

If Melbourne has a symbol then it's a movable one – trams. The real Melbourne tram – green-and-yellow, ancient-looking and half the weight of an ocean liner – can still be seen, although most trams are now the less attractive (but more comfortable) modern beasts.

Trams are such a part of Melbourne life they've even been used for a play – Act One of *Storming Mont Albert by Tram* took place from Mont Albert to the city, Act Two on the way back. The passengers were the audience, the actors got on and off along the way. It wasn't a bad play! There's even a tram restaurant: the Colonial Tramcar Restaurant cruises Melbourne and you can have lunch ($65) or dinner ($55 to $90, depending on the time and night). Phone ☎ 9696 4000 for reservations.

Inner Suburbs

The inner suburbs surrounding Melbourne's centre are like a ring of villages, each with its own character. If you want to get a true feel for Melbourne you'll need to venture beyond the city centre – one of the best ways to explore these inner suburban areas is to jump on a tram or two and just go wherever the tracks take you.

Fitzroy Fitzroy is probably the most bohemian of the inner suburbs, with a large ethnic population living alongside lots of musicians, writers, artists and members of various subcultures. **Brunswick St** displays the liveliest array of cafes, restaurants, young designer clothes shops and bookshops in Melbourne. **Johnston St** is the Spanish quarter and the home of the annual Hispanic Festival, held every November, and **Smith St**, east of Brunswick St, is a diverse and multicultural streetscape with plenty of interesting and unusual offerings.

Carlton & North Melbourne Immediately north of the city, Carlton has one of the most attractive collections of Victorian-era architecture. It's also known as the Italian quarter, and busy **Lygon St** has enough Italian restaurants, coffee houses, pizzerias and gelaterias to satisfy the most rabid pasta and cappuccino freak. Carlton is flanked by gracious Parkville, home to the University of Melbourne; consequently, lots of students and members of the 'intelligentsia' live around here.

The Lygon St Festa is held annually in November and always gets a good turn-out. The greasy-pole-climbing competition is worth seeing.

West of Carlton is North Melbourne, a traditionally more working-class suburb that now combines Victorian-era architecture with some semi-industrial areas.

South Yarra & Toorak South (of the) Yarra is a bustling, trendy and style-conscious suburb. Nearby Toorak ('Trak') is the poshest suburb in Melbourne.

Running through and linking South Yarra and Toorak is the classy **Toorak Rd** shopping and restaurant strip. Running south from Toorak Rd in South Yarra is **Chapel St**; if the word for Toorak Rd is 'exclusive' then for Chapel St it's 'trendy'. The strip of Chapel St between Toorak and Commercial Rds is home to some of the most fashionable clothing and gift shops, bars and cafes.

Prahran Chapel St's trendiness fades as it crosses Commercial Rd and heads south into Prahran, although it's still a fascinating multicultural shopping strip all the way down to Dandenong Rd. The delightful Prahran Market is around the corner on Commercial Rd. Farther south you can turn right by the Prahran town hall and wander along Greville St to explore its retro and grunge clothing shops, galleries, junk shops and other offerings.

Prahran is something of a focal point for

VICTORIA

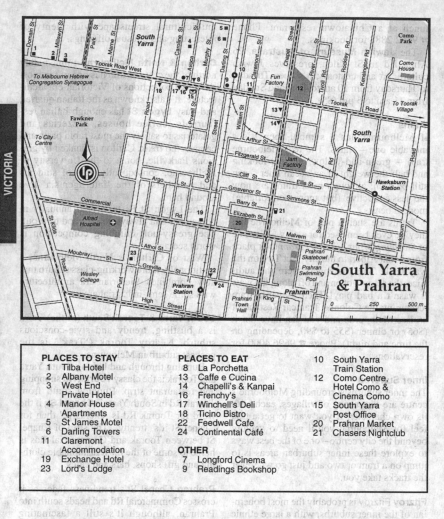

South Yarra & Prahran

PLACES TO STAY		PLACES TO EAT			10	South Yarra
1	Tilba Hotel	8	La Porchetta			Train Station
2	Albany Motel	13	Caffe e Cucina		12	Como Centre,
3	West End	14	Chapelli's & Kanpai			Hotel Como &
	Private Hotel	16	Frenchy's			Cinema Como
4	Manor House	17	Winchell's Deli		15	South Yarra
	Apartments	18	Ticino Bistro			Post Office
5	St James Motel	22	Feedwell Cafe		20	Prahran Market
6	Darling Towers	24	Continental Café		21	Chasers Nightclub
11	Claremont					
	Accommodation	**OTHER**				
19	Exchange Hotel	7	Longford Cinema			
23	Lord's Lodge	9	Readings Bookshop			

the gay community, with numerous bars, cafes and nightclubs along Commercial Rd.

Richmond As Carlton is to Italy so Richmond (just east of the city centre) is to both Greece and Vietnam. It is the Greek centre for the third-largest Greek city in the world, after Athens and Thessaloniki. Colourful **Victoria St** is known as Little Saigon.

crosses Commercial Rd and heads south into Prahran, although it's still a fascinating walk. **Bridge Rd** and **Swan St** are fashion centres, with shops where many Australian designers sell their seconds and rejects.

St Kilda Seaside St Kilda is Melbourne's most cosmopolitan suburb – it's an exuberant blend of stylish and seedy, alternative and arty, hip and hypnotic. **Fitzroy St** and **Acland St** are the main streets – both are a constant hive of activity, especially on weekends and late at night, and both are lined with interesting bars, cafes and restaurants.

St Kilda's foreshore areas have been impressively redeveloped, with several restaurants perfectly positioned along the beachfront. It's also very pleasant to stroll out along the **St Kilda Pier** – there's a cafe at the end, and you can hire boats and bikes or take a **ferry ride** across the bay to Williamstown. There's also a small **penguin colony**, tours of which operate from the pier.

Every Sunday the **Esplanade Sunday Market** features a huge range of art and craft stalls. With its famous 'laughing face' entry gates, the **Luna Park** amusement park is a local icon.

Held each February, the St Kilda Festival features local performing artists, bands and writers, with street stalls and parades, concerts and readings, and a fireworks display over the beach as a finale.

Once notorious as Melbourne's sin centre (a pale imitation of Sydney's Kings Cross), St Kilda's image has been given a major facelift in recent years, although it can still be somewhat perilous to wander the streets late at night, particularly for women.

Williamstown At the mouth of the Yarra, this is one of the oldest parts of Melbourne and it has many interesting old buildings and lots of waterside activity. Williamstown remained relatively isolated until the completion of the West Gate Bridge suddenly brought it to within a few minutes of the city centre.

Moored in Williamstown is the **HMAS Castlemaine**, a WWII minesweeper now preserved as a maritime museum and open on weekends from noon to 5 pm ($4, children $2).

The **Railway Museum** on Champion Rd, North Williamstown, has a fine collection of old steam locomotives. It's open weekends and public holidays from noon to 5 pm ($4, children $2).

There are various cruises from Williamstown – the information booth (☎ 9391 2970) on Nelson Pde has details.

Getting There & Away If you have a car, the quickest way from the city is across the West Gate Bridge, which provides great views of the city. Suburban trains run to Williamstown. Cyclists and pedestrians can't use the West Gate Bridge, but beneath the bridge and accessible via a cycle route from the city, a punt (☎ 015 304 470) will take you across the river Friday through Monday and during school holidays ($3, $5 return). Wave to attract the punter's attention.

Ferries run from Southgate to Williamstown four times a day ($10, $18 return, children half-price), and also from St Kilda Pier on weekends ($6, $10 return, children half-price). Phone the 24-hour information line (☎ 9506 4144) for times. The 60-year-old steam tug *Wattle* (☎ 9328 2739) runs across to Williamstown on Sunday from Station Pier in Port Melbourne, taking a meandering route. The return fare is $10 (children $7).

Other Suburbs South of the centre are other inner suburbs with many restored old homes, particularly the bayside suburbs of **South Melbourne**, **Middle Park** and **Albert Park**. Emerald Hill in South Melbourne is a whole section of 1880s Melbourne, still in relatively authentic shape. The parklands around **Albert Park Lake**, which stretch from Albert Park to St Kilda, were controversially redeveloped and are the venue for the Australian Formula One Grand Prix car race.

Port Melbourne is a traditional working-class suburb that has also been a target for gentrification. Station Pier is the departure point for ferries to Tasmania.

Sandwiched between the city and Richmond is the compact area of **East Melbourne**; like Parkville it's one of the most concentrated areas of old Victorian buildings around the city with numerous outstanding examples of early architecture. Wealthier inner suburbs to the east, which also contain some interesting shopping centres, include **Armadale**, **Malvern**, **Hawthorn** and **Camberwell**.

Beaches
The bayside beaches are reasonably good

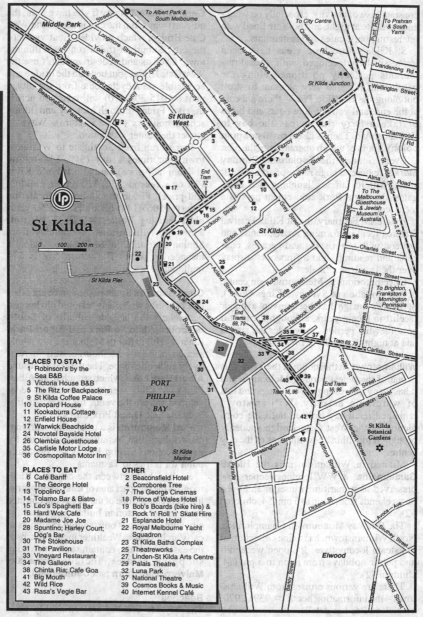

VICTORIA

St Kilda

0   100   200 m

PORT PHILLIP BAY

St Kilda Pier

St Kilda Marina

Middle Park

St Kilda West

St Kilda

To Albert Park & South Melbourne

To City Centre

To Prahran & South Yarra

St Kilda Junction

Dandenong Rd

Wellington Street

Chamwood Rd

To The Melbourne Guesthouse & Jewish Museum of Australia

To Brighton, Frankston & Mornington Peninsula

St Kilda Botanical Gardens

Elwood

Tram 16

Tram 12

Tram 12

End Tram 12

Tram 16,96

Tram 16,96

Tram 69, 79

Tram 69, 79

End Trams 16, 96

End Trams 69, 79

Tram 3, 67

Longmore Street

Fraser Street

Cowderoy Street

York Street

Park Street

Beaconsfield Parade

Pier Road

Centenary Road

Mary Street

Aughtie Drive

Light Rail 96

Queens Road

Punt Road

Fitzroy Street

Princes Street

Dalgety Street

Grey Street

Jackson Street

Eildon Road

Acland Street

The Esplanade

Robe Street

Clyde Street

Fawkner Street

Havelock Street

Carlisle Street

Foster St

Smith Street

Greeves Street

Barkly Street

Inkerman Street

Charles Street

Alma Road

St Kilda Road

Blessington Street

Blessington Street

Marine Parade

Jacka Boulevard

Herbert Street

Mitford Street

Barkly Street

Dickens St

Avoca Ave

Broadway

Southey Street

St Kilda Pier

PLACES TO STAY
1 Robinson's by the Sea B&B
3 Victoria House B&B
5 The Ritz for Backpackers
9 St Kilda Coffee Palace
10 Leopard House
11 Kookaburra Cottage
12 Enfield House
17 Warwick Beachside
24 Novotel Bayside Hotel
26 Olembia Guesthouse
35 Carlisle Motor Lodge
36 Cosmopolitan Motor Inn

PLACES TO EAT
6 Café Banff
8 The George Hotel
13 Topolino's
14 Tolarno Bar & Bistro
16 Leo's Spaghetti Bar
16 Hard Wok Cafe
18 Madame Joe Joe
28 Spuntino; Harley Court; Dog's Bar
30 The Stokehouse
31 The Pavilion
33 Vineyard Restaurant
34 The Galleon
38 Chinta Ria; Cafe Goa
41 Big Mouth
42 Wild Rice
43 Rasa's Vegie Bar

OTHER
2 Beaconsfield Hotel
4 Corroboree Tree
7 The George Cinemas
18 Prince of Wales Hotel
19 Bob's Boards (bike hire) & Rock 'n' Roll 'n' Skate Hire
21 Esplanade Hotel
22 Royal Melbourne Yacht Squadron
23 St Kilda Baths Complex
25 Theatreworks
27 Linden-St Kilda Arts Centre
29 Palais Theatre
32 Luna Park
37 National Theatre
39 Cosmos Books & Music
40 Internet Kennel Café

considering their proximity to the city. The bay itself tends to look murky, but it's clean enough for swimming, and the beaches have broad strips of sand. Closest to the city are the popular **Albert Park** and **Middle Park** beaches; farther around there's **St Kilda** and then **Elwood, Brighton** and **Sandringham**, which are all quite pleasant. Beyond Sandringham is the very good **Half Moon Bay** – well worth the half-hour drive from the city.

If you're looking for surf and spectacular ocean beaches, head for either the Mornington Peninsula or the Great Ocean Road (known as the 'east coast' and the 'west coast' respectively) – both are just over an hour's drive from the city centre.

Activities
There are two good indoor swimming pools in the city centre – the State Swimming Centre in Batman Ave and the Melbourne City Baths on the corner of Swanston and Victoria Sts (both open all year). Down in Albert Park, the new Sports & Aquatic Centre has a 75m pool (that's 50% longer than an Olympic pool) and many other facilities, including a wave pool. Outdoor pools include the Prahran Pool in Essex St and the Carlton Baths in Rathdowne St (both open October to April).

The 4km jogging track (known as 'the Tan') around the Kings Domain and Royal Botanic Gardens is one of the most popular running circuits. Albert Park Lake is also busy.

Inline skating is booming and the best tracks are those around Port Phillip Bay from Port Melbourne to Brighton. You can hire gear for about $8 an hour from places such as Rock 'n' Roll (☎ 9525 3434), 11 Fitzroy St, St Kilda.

There are sailing clubs all around Port Phillip Bay, and it's worth contacting them if you're interested in crewing on yachts. There are several places where you can learn to sail. Geoff Steadman's Melbourne Sailing School (☎ 9589 1433) is good and is based at the St Kilda Marina.

You can hire canoes or rowing boats for a gentle paddle on the Yarra at the Studley Park

Boathouse (off The Boulevard, accessible from Johnston St which runs through to kew from Fitzroy and Collingwood), and further upstream at the restored Fairfield Boathouse (see the Getting Around section for information on cycling).

Organised Tours
Companies such as Melbourne Sightseeing, Australian Pacific and Gray Line run conventional city bus tours, as well as trips to tourist destinations such as Sovereign Hill, Healesville Wildlife Sanctuary, Phillip Island and the Great Ocean Road. AAT/Kings (☎ 9663 3377) is another major company but they offer good discounts to YHA members (and probably to members of other hostel organisations as well). Their discounted city tour, including a river cruise, costs $37.

Two double-decker buses, the City Explorer and the City Wanderer (☎ 9563 9788), tour the city and inner suburbs. One-day passes cost $20 (two days costs $30), or you can get on or off wherever you choose. There's also the Southside Wanderer (south of the Yarra) and the Melbourne Explorer (night tours).

Queen Victoria Market Walking Tours (☎ 9320 5822) runs two-hour tours on Tuesday, Thursday, Friday and Saturday, departing from 513 Elizabeth St and costing $10 (10.30 am) to $15 (10 am).

City Cycle Tours (☎ 9585 5343) has a couple of guided bike tours, from $15 (bikes provided).

See the Getting Around section at the beginning of this chapter for tours that take you out of Melbourne.

Special Events
The Melbourne Music Festival is held during January. In March, Moomba is a family festival centred around the Yarra River.

Kicking off on April Fool's Day, the month-long International Comedy Festival features a great range of local and international acts at dozens of different venues. The marvellous Melbourne Film Festival is held during the depths of winter in June – the perfect time to be inside a cinema!

In September the Aussie Rules football finals dominate, and October features the outstanding Melbourne International Festival of the Arts, a world-class event that incorporates the Melbourne Writer's Festival and the Fringe Arts Festival (highlighted by the wild and crazy street party and parade along Brunswick St).

Places to Stay

You have a choice between backpackers' hostels, pubs and motels, B&Bs and guesthouses, serviced apartments and deluxe hotels. Once you've decided what you're looking for, the tricky part is deciding which area to stay in. The city centre is convenient and close to theatres, museums and the train and bus terminals, although it can be a little lifeless at night. The alternative is to stay in one of the inner suburbs that ring the city, each of which has its own character.

If you decide to stay longer, look in the *Age* classifieds on Wednesday and Saturday under 'share accommodation'. You could try the notice boards in the hostels, and various other places, including the universities, Readings bookshop in Carlton, Cosmos Books & Music and the Galleon cafe in St Kilda and the Black Cat cafe in Fitzroy.

Camping There are a few caravan parks and camping grounds in the metropolitan area, but none close to the centre. The most convenient is probably *Melbourne Holiday Park* (☎ 9354 3533) at 265 Elizabeth St in Coburg, 10km north of the city. It's well equipped and has tent sites from $17 for two people and cabins from $45 a double. The park is signposted from the corner of Sydney Rd and Murray Rd. From the city, take tram No 19 or 20 from Elizabeth St then bus No 526; the bus doesn't run on Sunday.

Farther from the city but much closer to beaches are the various caravan parks on the Mornington Peninsula (see the Around Melbourne section later in this chapter).

Hostels The hostel scene is fairly competi-

tive, and it can be hard to find a bed in one of the better places over summer, when prices rise by a dollar or two. Several of the larger hostels have courtesy buses that do pick-ups from the bus and train terminals.

City Centre The best of the city bunch is *Toad Hall* (☎ 9600 9010) at 441 Elizabeth St, within easy walking distance of the bus terminals. It's a quiet, well-equipped place with a pleasant courtyard and off-street parking ($5). A bed in a four or six-bed dorm costs from $16; single/twin/double rooms cost from $28/45/50.

At 199 Russell St, *Exford Hotel Backpackers'* (☎ 9663 2697) is a cheerful and well set-up hostel in the upper section of an old pub. You'll pay $11 in a 10-bed dorm to $15 in a four-bed dorm; twins/doubles cost from $42 a night. The same people are also due to open a big new hostel on the corner of Flinders Lane and Elizabeth St, called *Flinders Station Hotel & Backpackers*, with dorms from $13 and doubles from $39.

The *City Centre Private Hotel* (☎ 9654 5401), at 22 Little Collins St, is clean and quiet, if somewhat prim. All rooms have a shared bathroom and there's a TV lounge and kitchen on each floor. Backpackers pay from $17 in a three or four-bed room and doubles are $35; serviced singles/doubles are $35/50.

Backpackers City Inn (☎ 9650 2734), upstairs in the Carlton Hotel at 197 Bourke St, has dorms at $14 and singles/doubles for $28/35, although both the pub and accommodation are a bit rough around the edges.

Other places include *Downtown Backpackers* (☎ 9329 7525), 167 Franklin St; *Victoria Hall* (☎ 9662 3888), 380 Russell St; and the *Arthouse* (☎ 9347 3917), a pub on the corner of Elizabeth and Queensberry Sts, with live music most nights and a grunge/gothic atmosphere (dorms $12, doubles $26). On the edge of the city at 153 Hoddle St is *Packers Palace* (☎ 9428 5932).

Fitzroy Well located on the fringe of the city at 116 Nicholson St is the *Nunnery* (☎ 9419 8637; nunnery@bakpak.com; bakpak.com/nunnery), a converted Victorian building with good facilities. The dorms are spacious, although the rooms are small but clean and centrally heated. Costs are $17 in a 12-bed dorm to $20 in a three-bed dorm; singles are $35 to $40, twins and doubles are from $50 to $60. Take tram No 96 heading east along Bourke St, and get off at stop No 13.

North Melbourne The YHA hostels are both in North Melbourne, north-west of the city centre. Both offer discounts for a four-day or longer stay. From the airport you can ask the Skybus to drop you at the North Melbourne hostels. As with all YHA hostels, nonmembers are charged $3 more than members but there are several deals to make becoming a member relatively painless.

The YHA showpiece is the *Queensberry Hill Hostel* (☎ 9329 8599) at 78 Howard St. This huge 348-bed place has excellent facilities. Dorms cost $17 for members; singles/doubles are $45/55 and rooms with attached bathrooms cost $55/65. Breakfast and dinner are available, and office hours are 7 am to 10.30 pm, although there is 24-hour access once you have checked in. There's also a self-contained apartment sleeping four for $90 ($96 for nonmembers). Catch tram No 55 from William St and get off at stop No 11 (Queensberry St), or tram No 59 north up Elizabeth St to stop No 8 (Queensberry St).

Chapman Gardens YHA Hostel (☎ 9328 3595), 76 Chapman St, is smaller and older but can be a bit more intimate than Queensberry Hill. Dorms cost $15, twin rooms $35 and doubles $44.

Opposite the Queen Victoria Market at 238 Victoria St, *Global Backpackers' Hostel* (☎ 9328 3728) is in the top section of an old pub and has dorms ranging from $11 to $14, and singles/doubles for $25/35. The facilities include a good kitchen and an indoor rock-climbing wall. Note that the pub downstairs has bands most nights (free admission for residents) – great if you're into live music, not so great if you're an early sleeper.

South Melbourne *Nomads Market Inn* (☎ 9690 2220), 115 Cecil St, is opposite the South Melbourne Market in an old pub.

Unlike many other hostels in pubs, this is not just some bunks jammed into disused pub rooms but a well-equipped hostel with a good atmosphere. It isn't in the centre of everything but you can walk into the city and there's a nearby stop on the light-rail (tram) line running between the city and St Kilda. Dorms cost $15 and doubles (with TV) are $36.

St Kilda St Kilda has a good range of budget accommodation as well as plenty of restaurants and entertainment venues. From Swanston St in the city, tram No 16 will take you down St Kilda Rd to Fitzroy St, or there's the faster light-rail service (No 96 from Spencer St and Bourke St) to the old St Kilda railway station and along Fitzroy and Acland Sts.

Enfield House Backpackers (☎ 9534 8159), 2 Enfield St, is the original and probably the most popular of St Kilda's hostels. It's a huge Victorian-era building with over 100 beds and good facilities. Dorms cost from $15 and twins/doubles from $34. The courtesy bus picks up at the bus terminals and at Station Pier where the Tasmanian ferries arrive.

Olembia Guesthouse (☎ 9537 1412), 96 Barkly St, is more like a boutique hotel than a hostel. The facilities are very good and include a cosy guest lounge, dining room, a courtyard and off-street parking. The rooms are quite small but clean and comfortable, and all have hand basins and central heating. Dorm beds cost $16, singles are $35, and twins/doubles are $50 ($45 if you stay three nights). Book ahead.

At 169 Fitzroy St, the *Ritz for Backpackers* (☎ 9525 3501) is quite stylish, with comfortable lounges and a modern kitchen. Four to eight-bunk dorms cost $14, twins and doubles from $32. There's a good self-contained flat that sleeps eight people at $14 per person.

The *St Kilda Coffee Palace* (☎ 1800 654 098), 4 Grey St, is another long-running hostel that has been renovated and upgraded. It's a spacious place with its own cafe and a modern kitchen area. Dorms start at $13, twins/doubles are $32. Around the corner at 56 Jackson St is *Kookaburra Cottage* (☎ 9534 5457), a small and laid-back hostel. It's quite comfortable and has all the usual facilities; dorm beds are $14 and there are a couple of good twin/double rooms for $34.

On the corner of Grey and Jackson Sts is *Leopard House* (☎ 9534 1200), an old and roomy house with dorms at $14 and twins for $32. It has recently been renovated and many travellers consider it the best of the bunch in St Kilda.

South Yarra *Lord's Lodge* (☎ 9510 5658) is at 204 Punt Rd, which is a busy main road. This is a large, two-storey place with a range of accommodation, including six to eight-bed dorms with their own kitchen from $13 and doubles from $30 to $38.

Richmond The *Richmond Hill Guesthouse* (☎ 9428 6501), well located at 353 Church St, is another big old building with spacious living areas and clean rooms. Dorm beds cost $14 to $16 a night, singles/twins are $34/44. In the good B&B section rooms go for $54/69 a single/double or $89 a double with bathroom.

Also in Richmond is *Central House* (☎ 9427 9826) at 337 Highett St, with dorms for $12 a night and doubles from $28.

Preston *Terrace Travellers Hostel* (☎ 9470 1006) is at 418 Murray Rd, Preston, north of the city centre – it's not a bad hostel, but unless you've got relatives in Preston it's hard to think of a reason for staying all the way out here.

Hotels, Motels, B&Bs & Serviced Apartments As with cheaper accommodation, you have a choice between the convenience of the city centre and the often more pleasant surroundings of the inner suburbs.

City Centre The hotels along Spencer St are convenient for the bus and train terminals. It isn't the most salubrious end of town but it is starting to come up in the world. At 44 Spencer St, *Hotel Enterprize* (☎ 9629 6991)

is a refurbished hotel with budget singles/doubles from $40/50, or from $50/85 with en-suite.

At 131 King St, *Kingsgate Budget Hotel* (☎ 9629 4171) is a private hotel that has been renovated. It's a big old place with budget singles/doubles with shared bathroom from $29/45 or with en-suite from $60/80.

Hotel Y (☎ 9329 5188), run by the YWCA at 489 Elizabeth St, is close to the Franklin St bus terminal. It has basic bunk rooms for $25, singles/doubles for $65/75, and deluxe rooms for $75/90. Apartments sleeping four cost $140. Recently refurbished, the 'Y' has good facilities including a budget cafe, communal kitchen and laundry, gym and heated pool.

The *Stork Hotel* (☎ 9663 6237), nearby on the corner of Elizabeth and Therry Sts, is an old pub with simple rooms from $25/35, and a small guest kitchen. The *Duke of Wellington* (☎ 9650 4984) on the corner of Flinders and Russell Sts is a smallish old pub with rooms from $45/80, with breakfast.

The *Victoria Hotel* (☎ 9653 0441), 215 Little Collins St, is a notch up from the cheapest city hotels, and a bit of a Melbourne institution. Rates are from $42/55 to $85/130.

East Melbourne On the fringe of the city, East Melbourne has a pleasant residential feel with its tree-lined streets and grand old Victorian terrace houses.

Georgian Court Guesthouse (☎ 9419 6353), 21 George St, is an elegant and cosy B&B with singles/doubles at $59/69, to $89/99 with en-suite; prices include a buffet breakfast. At 2 Hotham St, the *East Melbourne Hotel* (☎ 9419 2040) has clean pub-style rooms upstairs from $35/45. There's a free car park and guest lounge, and a stylish restaurant and bar downstairs.

At 101 George St the *George Street Apartments* (☎ 9419 1333) is a secure and friendly place with serviced apartments from $65/90, all with bathroom, fridge and cooking facilities. The *East Melbourne Apartments* (☎ 9412 2555), at 25 Hotham St, are also good but more stylish, and cost from $119 to $145 a night for one or two people.

West Melbourne The *Miami Motor Inn* (☎ 9329 8499), 13 Hawke St, West Melbourne, is reasonably close to the city centre and is great value with singles/doubles starting at $36/52.

Fitzroy Well located in Royal Lane, one block back from the Exhibition Gardens, the stylish and spacious *Royal Gardens Apartments* (☎ 9419 9888) come in one, two or three-bedroom configurations, costing $165, $195 and $235 respectively.

South Yarra Tram No 8 from Swanston St in the city takes you along Toorak Rd into the heart of the chic suburb of South Yarra.

There are several places opposite leafy Fawkner Park. *Tilba* (☎ 9867 8844) on the corner of Toorak Rd West and Domain St is an elegant boutique hotel with gracious Victorian-era rooms ranging from $135 to $190 a double, depending on size – highly recommended for a splurge.

The *Albany Motel* (☎ 9866 4485) on the corner of Toorak Rd West and Millswyn St has units from $80/85. Nearby, the *West End Private Hotel* (☎ 9866 5375), 76 Toorak Rd West, has B&B with singles/doubles at $40/55 – it's pretty old-fashioned, but has a certain shabby charm.

Farther east at 189 Toorak Rd, the vast *Claremont Accommodation* (☎ 9826 8000) has recently been converted into a B&B. The rooms are bright and freshly painted, with polished-timber floors, heating and modern communal bathroom. Singles/doubles are from $44/58, including breakfast. *St James Motel* (☎ 9866 3701), 35 Darling St, is oldish but well located, and has rooms from around $75 a double and studio apartments from $85.

South Yarra is the serviced-apartment capital of Melbourne. Mostly converted blocks of flats, these can be rented overnight, weekly or long-term. Some of the more affordable ones include *Manor House Apartments* (☎ 9867 1266), 23 Avoca St, with a huge range, from studio apartments (from around $85) to two-bedroom apartments (from $135); and *Darling Towers* (☎ 9867 5200), 32 Darling St, with one-bedroom flats from $85.

St Kilda *Carlisle Motor Lodge* (☎ 9534 0591), 32 Carlisle St, has units from $55/60 and family rooms with kitchen facilities from $75. St Kilda also has some good serviced apartments. Opposite St Kilda Beach at 363 Beaconsfield Pde, *Warwick Beachside* (☎ 9525 4800) has 1950s-style holiday flats. They're not glamorous, but they're quite well equipped, and there's a laundry and off-street parking. A studio (sleeps up to three) costs from $70 and a two-bedroom apartment (sleeps up to five) starts at $90. Weekly rates for a two-person 'backpacker' apartment start at $220. *Cabana Court* (☎ 9534 0771), 46 Park St, has apartments from $90.

St Kilda has plenty of motels, but some of them are fairly dodgy. One of the more respectable places is the *Cosmopolitan Motor Inn* (☎ 9534 0781) at 6 Carlisle St, with rooms from $98 and family units with kitchenette from $108.

There are some good B&Bs in St Kilda. Opposite the beach at 335 Beaconsfield Pde, *Robinson's by the Sea* (☎ 9534 2683) is an elegant and impressive Victorian-era terrace house with three double en-suite rooms from $130 to $150. *Victoria House* (☎ 9525 4512), 57 Mary St, has two guest rooms with singles/doubles from $85/100.

Albert Park The *Hotel Victoria* (☎ 9690 3666), with a great position overlooking the bay from 123 Beaconsfield Pde, is a restored 1888 hotel with rooms with shared bathroom for $60 a double and rooms with en-suite from $90 to $150 a double. Ask for one of the corner rooms – the view is superb.

Colleges The venerable University of Melbourne is just to the north of the city centre in Parkville. Some colleges have accommodation in the summer vacation from late November to mid-February. Most of these

VICTORIA

colleges also have accommodation during semester breaks (July and the second half of September), although they are sometimes booked out by conferences. Ask about the possibility of cheaper student and weekly rates.

International House (☎ 9347 6655), $38 B&B, $45 full board
Medley Hall (☎ 9663 5847), $30, minimum three nights
Ormond College (☎ 9348 1688), $43 B&B
Ridley College (☎ 9387 7555)
Trinity College (☎ 9347 1044), $40 B&B, $50 full board
Whitley College (☎ 9347 8388), $30 B&B, $40 full board, with a $10 surcharge if you stay only one night (summer only)
Queen's College (☎ 9349 0500) sometimes has rooms but availability depends on conferences.

Ormond, Queen's and Trinity are impressive 19th-century piles – ask for a room in their old buildings.

Gay & Lesbian Accommodation There's quite a range of gay-only (usually aimed at men) and gay-friendly places: the *Laird* (☎ 9417 2832), 149 Gipps St, Collingwood (from $55 per room, including entry into the club downstairs); *163 Drummond St* (☎ 9663 3081), in Carlton (from $45/80, $105 with bathroom); and the *Exchange Hotel* (☎ 9867 5144), 119 Commercial Rd, Prahran ($45/60) – on Friday and Saturday it's pretty noisy until 3 am and on other nights the pub closes at 1 am.

Places to Eat
Melbourne is a wonderful place to have an appetite – and a terrible place to start a diet. Everywhere you go, there are restaurants, cafes, delis, markets, bistros and brasseries. Gastronomically you can travel the world here – go to Victoria St in Richmond for (very cheap) Vietnamese; Little Bourke St in the city for Chinese; Johnston St in Fitzroy for Spanish food; Swan St in Richmond for Greek; or for sheer variety, Brunswick St in Fitzroy, or Acland and Fitzroy Sts in St Kilda.

The restaurants listed are just a small selection of favourites that are in the main areas where travellers may be staying or visiting. If you want to make a more in-depth study of food in Melbourne, pick up a copy of the *Age Good Food Guide* or the *Age Cheap Eats in Melbourne*.

Most restaurants are either licensed to sell alcohol and/or BYO. Some BYO places charge a small fee for corkage.

For a reliable and inexpensive Italian restaurant, find the nearest member of the burgeoning *La Porchetta* chain, specialising in pizza and home-made pasta, with main courses around $6 or $7. There are La Porchettas in many areas, including: Brighton (3 Wells St), Brunswick (317 Victoria St), North Carlton (392 Rathdowne St), North Melbourne (302 Victoria St), South Yarra (93 Toorak Rd) and Williamstown (193 Nelson Place).

Chinatown The area in and around Chinatown, which follows Little Bourke St from Spring St to Swanston St, is one of the best and most diverse food precincts, with great Chinese restaurants as well as Italian, Malaysian, Thai and others. Some of these restaurants are expensive (such as the highly acclaimed *Flower Drum* (☎ 9662 3655), at 17 Market St) but many of the mid-range places have lost custom to the infamous casino and there are some good specials on offer. Just wander down and around Little Bourke St and see what the touts are offering.

Starting from the top end, *Jan Bo*, 40 Little Bourke St, has reasonably priced and authentic Chinese food, and serves great yum cha daily from 11 am to 3 pm. At No 50, *Shark Finn Inn* is also very popular, and stays open until 1.30 am. *Café K*, No 35, is an elegant European-style bistro with mains in the $8 to $15 range.

The low-key *Yamato*, 28 Corrs Lane, turns out excellent Japanese dishes at low prices, although it's tiny and often full.

King of Kings, 209 Russell St, is a cheap Chinese place which stays open until 2.30

am. *Peking Duck*, upstairs on the corner of Little Bourke and Swanston Sts, is a mid-range place specialising in, naturally, duck, carved at your table. Although a little old-fashioned it's spacious and relaxed and has good service.

Other City Centre Areas *Cafee Baloo*, 260 Russell St (just north of Lonsdale St), is perhaps the best budget eatery in the city centre. It's a funky little place with Indian/Italian food (strange combination but it works well) – great antipasto plates ($4.40), pastas ($5.40) and curries and stir-fries ($4.40 to $6.40). Rice and Indian breads cost between $1.30 and $2.20. There's a minimum charge of $4. There are plenty of choices for vegetarians and it's open daily from noon to 10 pm.

The *Lounge*, upstairs at 243 Swanston St, is a groovy cafe/club with pool tables and a balcony overlooking Swanston Walk; snags, stir-fries, satays and salads from $7.50.

The cheapest place in town is *Gopals*, 139 Swanston St, a vegetarian cafe run by the Hare Krishna sect. It's open for lunch and dinner and has a $9 all-you-can-eat deal plus much cheaper dishes.

Stalactites, on the corner of Lonsdale and Russell Sts, is a Greek restaurant best known for its bizarre stalactite decor and the fact that it's open 24 hours.

Off the top end of Bourke St at 20 Myers Place, the *Waiters Restaurant* serves good, cheap Italian food in unglamorous but cosy surrounds. Back on Bourke St at No 66 is another Melbourne institution – *Pellegrini's*. It's an old Italian bar with great apple strudel, pasta and risotto, and excellent coffee. The *Florentino Cellar Bar*, No 80, looks expensive but isn't, with daily specials for under $10 and main courses from $15, or you can just have coffee and snacks. Nearby at No 76, the busy *Nudel Bar* is dedicated to noodles from all sorts of European and Asian cuisines. The food is good and the prices reasonable – from $7.

As well as being a centre for outdoor adventure shops, Hardware St is lined with cafes with open-air tables. At No 25 *Campari*

Bistro is a busy Italian bistro with pastas for about $12 and other mains from $16 to $20.

There are some good food courts around the city. They include the *Hyatt Food Court* on the corner of Russell and Collins Sts, and the *Sportsgirl Centre* on Collins St just down from Swanston St. Melbourne's major department stores – Myer, David Jones and Daimaru – also have great food emporiums that should satisfy the most obscure craving.

Southgate Southgate, a stylish development on the south bank of the Yarra River beside the concert hall, is one of the best eating centres in Melbourne. The setting is great, there's a good range of styles and prices, and you can eat either indoors or outside overlooking the river and the city.

On the mid-level, the casual (but trendy and noisy) *Blue Train Café* serves breakfasts, pastas and risottos, pizzas and salads, all at reasonable prices. For example, calamari is $7, linguini is $10 and delicious pizzas cooked in a wood-fired oven cost between $4 and $10. There are outdoor tables with good views. It's open daily from breakfast until late. If you want to impress someone, take them to *Walter's*, upstairs.

St Kilda St Kilda has everything from all-night hamburger joints to stylish cafes, bars and restaurants. Most of the eateries are along Fitzroy and Acland Sts.

Up the beach end at 9 Fitzroy St, the very chic *Madame Joe Joe* is one of the best of the new breed of St Kilda restaurants – pricey, but great for a splurge. More affordable is the tiny and cheerful *Hard Wok Cafe*, No 49, with Asian stir-fries, laksas and curries for $7 to $11. At 55 Fitzroy St, *Leo's Spaghetti Bar* is a St Kilda institution, with a coffee bar, bistro and restaurant.

Across at No 42, the wonderful *Tolarno Bar & Bistro* has a good restaurant and a small bar/eatery with snacks and meals in the $5 to $15 range. *Topolino's*, 87 Fitzroy St, is the place to go for a pizza or a big bowl of pasta – it's usually crowded late at night and stays open until sunrise. On the corner of Fitzroy and Grey Sts, the trend-setting

George Hotel has a popular wine bar with good food and a restaurant.

Café Banff (☎ 9525 4114), 145 Fitzroy St near the corner of Grey St, is a small place (bookings advisable on Friday and Saturday nights) which has been in business a long time. The varied menu has an emphasis on healthy food and there are plenty of vegetarian dishes (eg huge salads for $9). Otherwise you can choose between dishes such as Thai green chicken curry ($12) and the Banff burger ($11). There are also snacks such as foccacias, frittatas etc. It's licensed (house wine $3.50 per glass, beer from $4) or you can BYO (bottled wine only) for a corkage of $2. It's open daily from 7 am to 11 pm, except Monday when it closes at 3 pm.

At 9 Carlisle St, the *Galleon* is a local favourite with its quirky decor and everything from toasted sandwiches and apple crumble to chicken and leek pie – all at very reasonable prices. Up Acland St on the Fawkner St corner, you'll find the trendy trilogy of the *Dogs Bar* (an in-vogue bar with good Italian food), *Harley Court* (delicious French pastries), and *Spuntino* (laid-back Italian-style street cafe).

If you're craving a steak, head for the unassuming *Vineyard Restaurant*, 71a Acland St – the grills are huge and cost from $15 to $28. At No 94, *Chinta Ria* combines wonderful Malaysian food with jazz and soul music – mains are $8 to $15. Next door the quirky *Cafe Goa* serves spicy Portuguese-Indian dishes for $7 to $13. *Scheherezade* at No 99 does good central European food in large quantities.

Acland St is renowned for it fine delis and cake shops – the window displays emanate so many calories you're in danger of putting on weight just walking past.

On the corner of Acland and Barkly Sts, *Big Mouth* is trendy but relaxed, with good service. There's a cafe downstairs and a restaurant upstairs – either is great for people-watching. The cafe has breakfast (from $3) and at lunch nothing is over $10. Upstairs main courses cost between $11 and $17 and there's an interesting menu with East-Asian influences. You can BYO, but

there's a massive corkage charge of $10. At the other end of Acland St, near the corner with Fitzroy St, *Il Fornaio* bakes and sells a wonderful range of delicious breads and cakes. Breakfast and light meals are also available.

Wild Rice, around the corner at 211 Barkly St, is a very good organic/vegan cafe with mains from $5 to $9 and a pleasant rear courtyard – it's open daily from noon to 10 pm. At 5 Blessington St, *Rasa's Vegie Bar* (mainly takeaways but a few seats) has tofu or lentil burgers for $5 and vegetarian stir-fries, curries and pastas from $8 to $11. It's open nightly from 5 to 10 pm.

Donovan's is a classy restaurant on the foreshore at 40 Jacka Blvd; mains are around $20 and up, and there's a cheaper takeaway section with great fish & chips and outdoor tables. Nearby, the *Stokehouse* also has a great outlook over the bay and is one of *the* places in St Kilda to see (and be seen). There's a pricey restaurant upstairs, and a big bustling bar/eatery downstairs with great food in the $10 to $16 range.

Last but by no means least is the wonderful *Espy Kitchen* way up the back of the Esplanade Hotel. It's always busy, the food is great (mains from $10 to $17), and after you've eaten you can play pool or check out one of the (usually free) live bands.

Fitzroy Brunswick St can't be beaten for sheer variety. It's one of the funkiest and most fascinating streets in Melbourne, and it has just about everything, including a huge range of cuisines.

At the city end at 113 Brunswick St, *Nyala* serves Ethiopian and other African food. The combination plate gives you an interesting variety of dishes to try, and you scoop them up with the spongy bread known as injera. At No 177, *Akari 177* is a Japanese restaurant with good-value set lunches and early dinners for $12 (order before 7 pm). Next door, the Spanish-influenced *De Los Santos* has good tapas, paella and other dishes.

Up at No 252, the famous *Black Cat Café* is an arty 1950s-style cafe, ideal for coffee and cake or snacks at late hours. *Thai Thani* at No 293 is an excellent place for lovers of hot and spicy Thai food.

Across Johnston St, the very hip *Mario's* is at No 303. Highly favoured by the locals, it has great Italian food day and night. *Café Cappadocia* at No 324 is an unpretentious and cheap Turkish restaurant. Other Brunswick St favourites include the *Fitz* at No 347, the barn-sized *Rhumbarella's*, No 342, with an art gallery upstairs; and *Joe's Garage* up at No 366. Next to Joe's, *Charmaine's* has simply sensational ice creams.

On the corner of Rose St, the *Vegie Bar* exudes delicious aromas and has a great range of vegetarian meals under $8 plus plenty of snacks and cakes. Servings are huge. It's open daily from breakfast until late and it's licensed (house wine $3 per glass, beer from $3.50), or you can BYO ($2.50 corkage).

Baker's, No 384, was one of the original trendy cafes on this strip. It's still a laid-back place serving mainly Italian-style food such as foccacia from $7 and pasta from $8. Breakfast starts at $5. Across the road at No 389, the *Hideout Café* has a wide range, from steaks ($17) to pasta to Chinese noodles, plus snacks. It's a very hip place – check out the crazy decor in the toilets.

Around the corner on Johnston St you'll find the small Spanish quarter. At No 74, the *Carmen Bar* (☎ 9417 4794) has authentic Spanish food, an outdoor barbecue, and flamenco and Spanish guitar from Wednesday to Saturday nights. There's also a cluster of small tapas bars.

A few blocks up Brunswick St you cross wide Alexandra Pde and are in North Fitzroy. At 248 St Georges Rd (the continuation of Brunswick St), on the corner of Scotchmer St, the *Tin Pot* is a friendly local eatery with excellent food at reasonable prices. Vegetarians are well catered for. It's open from breakfast to dinner daily (closed Monday evening). Diagonally opposite, *The Truffula Tree*, housed in a wonderfully angular old post office, serves good, inexpensive food. Live music is played here several nights a week.

Gertrude St in south Fitzroy has an inter-esting collection of galleries, art suppliers, costume designers and antique shops. At No 193, *Arcadia* is a groovy little cafe, and at 199 the very straightforward *Macedonia* does grills, goulash and other Balkan specialities.

Smith St also has some good eateries. It's an interesting multicultural streetscape, a lot less fashionable than Brunswick St (it's like Brunswick St was 10 years ago and Lygon St 20 years ago) and is worth exploring. *Café Birko* at No 123 is a rustic bar/restaurant with burgers, stir-fries, risottos and pastas for about $8. At 275 Smith St, the *Soul Food Vegetarian Café* is a popular and inexpensive vegan cafe with an organic grocery next door. *Friends of the Earth*, at No 312, operate a lunchtime-only organic/wholefood cafe in conjuction with a food cooperative (you don't have to be a member to buy here) and bookshop.

Farther north at No 354 Smith St, *Café Bohemio* is a quirky and laid-back Latin-American cafe with mains for $8 to $13. Upstairs there's a variety of activities (including Latin dance classes) and performances.

If you venture farther east on Johnston St you enter the untrendy working-class suburb of Collingwood (home of Australia's most famous Aussie Rules team). Here you'll find friendly *Jim's Greek Taverna*, 32 Johnston St, with some of the best Greek food in town. You don't get a menu – they bring you a succession of delicious courses (choose between lamb souvlaki and seafood for the main course) and you'll spend around $20 per person. It's open for dinner daily. Recommended, but not for vegetarians or those avoiding rich food.

Carlton Lygon St, the Italian centre, is all bright lights, big restaurants and flashy boutiques – a local writer calls it an antipodean Via Veneto. A one-time trend-setter in Melbourne's restaurant scene, nowadays Lygon St caters mainly to tourists and out-of-towners, although some of the long-running places are still worth searching out.

VICTORIA

Toto's Pizza House at No 101 claims to be the first pizzeria in Australia. Pizzas are cheap and good and it stays open till after midnight. After your pizza, head up to *Notturno* at No 177 for coffee and cake – it's open until 3 am.

At No 303 *Tiamo* is an old-fashioned Italian bistro with pastas for about $8 and great breakfasts just like mama used to cook ($8). *Trotters* at No 400 is a popular little bistro serving hearty Italian fare (from breakfast to dinner) in the $7 to $13 range.

Across at 333 Lygon St, *Jimmy Watson's* is a famous Melbourne institution. Wine and talk are the order of the day at this wine bar but the food is good too. It's always been a great spot for a long, leisurely lunch – and nowadays it is also open for evening meals.

Around the corner at 198 Faraday St, *Brunetti* serves wonderful Italian food. The service is excellent, the decor is chic, the coffee and cakes are arguably the best in town – and the prices won't break the bank. There are three sections, the pasticceria, the gelateria (both open daily) and the ristorante (closed Sunday). House wine costs $3 per glass, beer costs from $3.50 and you can BYO for $1 corkage. Pastas start at $9 and something like tornados rossini is $15. Across Faraday St is *Shakahari*, a long-running place in a new home, with outstanding vegetarian fare.

North Melbourne As well as several cafes at the Queen Vic Market, not to mention all the produce there, North Melbourne has some good eateries if you're prepared to search a little. Opposite the market, *Viet Nam House* at 284 Victoria St and *Dalat* at No 270 both have cheap Vietnamese food with lunches for about $5 and mains from $7. On the corner of Victoria and William Sts, the *Travellers' Café* has both information and good, cheap food. It's open from 7.30 am to 5 pm on weekdays and Sunday, closed Saturday.

Richmond Victoria St in Richmond, known as Little Saigon, is Melbourne's Vietnamese centre and it is lined with dozens of bargain-priced Vietnamese restaurants. Trams No 42 or 109 from Collins St in the city will take you there.

Don't expect vogue decor, but the food is fresh, cheap and lightning fast. You can have a huge steaming bowl of soup that is a meal in itself for about $5, and main courses are generally $4 to $8, so you can afford to be adventurous. Many places, even the more expensive, have lunch-time specials at around $5 for a meal. Or just grab a pork roll (about $2.50) from one of the bakeries. The supermarkets here are good if you're doing your own cooking and want exotic ingredients.

The very basic *Thy Thy 1* is the best known place, hidden away upstairs at No 142. It's something like a cafeteria but the food is exceptional, all sorts of people eat there and it's dirt cheap. *Thy Thy 2* at No 116 is a bit more upmarket – try the pork, chicken, prawn or vegetable spring rolls or the even better rice paper rolls.

The *Victoria* at No 311 is another good place to try, and also offers Thai and Chinese food. Down the city end at No 66 is the ultramodern *Tho Tho*. *Quán 88* at No 88 is also worth trying, with many dishes at $5 and not many over $8.

South Yarra & Prahran Take tram No 8 from Swanston St in the city to reach South Yarra. Along Toorak Rd you'll find some of Melbourne's most expensive restaurants – fortunately there are some more affordable places in between.

Tiny *Ticino Bistro*, No 16, has pizzas and pastas from just $6. *Winchell's Deli* at No 58 offers breakfast specials for $4.50, and if you're feeling indulgent, pop into *Frenchy's* at No 76 for a coffee and one of their sublime French pastries.

Don your designer shades and head down Chapel St – you'll find plenty of interesting cafes, bars and restaurants in among all the fashion boutiques. *Caffe e Cucina* (9827 4139), No 581, is one of the smallest, coolest and best cafe/restaurants in town, with great Italian meals in the $16 to $27 range – ring ahead, or expect to queue. It's closed on

LINDSAY BROWN

LINDSAY BROWN

Tasmania
Top: Victoria Dock, Hobart
Bottom: Stanley is a charming fishing village

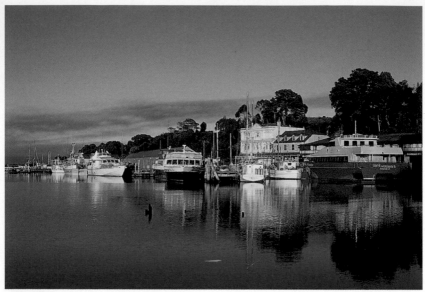

LINDSAY BROWN

RICHARD I'ANSON

RICHARD I'ANSON

Tasmania

Top:	Strahan, a picturesque town on the west coast
Left:	Sleepy Bay, Freycinet National Park
Right:	Cradle Mountain-Lake St Clair National Park

Sunday. Down at No 571 is the friendly *Chapelli's* – the food is pretty good and, most importantly, it's open round the clock. Right next door at No 569 is *Kanpai*, a neat little Japanese restaurant with modestly priced dishes.

The Prahran Market, on Commercial Rd, is a wonderful place to shop or just wander, with fresh fruit and vegies and plenty of little delis to explore.

Greville St, which runs off Chapel St beside the Prahran town hall, has an eclectic collection of grungy and groovy clothes boutiques, bookshops and music shops, and a few good eateries. Beside the railway tracks at No 95 is the ever-popular *Feedwell Cafe*, an earthy vegetarian cafe serving interesting and wholesome food in the $5 to $12 range. The *Continental Café* at No 132 has wonderful food at affordable prices and a hip, sophisticated atmosphere – it's open from 7 am until midnight.

Entertainment

The best source of 'what's on' info is the *EG* which comes out every Friday with the *Age* newspaper. *Beat*, *Inpress* and *Storm* are free music and entertainment magazines that have reviews, interviews, dates of gigs, movie guides and more.

Bass Victoria (☎ 11 500) is the main booking agency for theatre, concerts, sports and other events. If you're looking for cheap tickets, the Half-Tix booth in the Bourke St Mall sells half-price tickets on the day of the event. You have to visit in person and pay cash.

If you're here during the summer months watch out for the wonderful open-air theatre productions staged in the Royal Botanic Gardens.

Major venues include the Victorian Arts Centre, the National Tennis Centre, the outdoor Sidney Myer Music Bowl in the Kings Domain, and the Sports & Entertainment Centre.

Cinemas There are plenty of mainstream cinemas in the city, especially around the intersection of Bourke and Russell Sts.

You'll pay up to $11 for a ticket but on Tuesday most mainstream cinemas charge just $5. One of the cinemas in the Crown Casino complex has large, reclining seats for $20.

There are numerous independent cinemas that feature art-house, classic and alternative films. They include the wonderfully Art Deco *Astor Cinema* on the corner of Chapel St and Dandenong Rd, Prahran; the *George*, 133 Fitzroy St, St Kilda; the off-beat home of cult films, the *Westgarth*, 89 High St, Northcote; the *Carlton Moviehouse*, 235 Faraday St, and *Cinema Nova*, 380 Lygon St, both in Carlton; the *Kino*, 45 Collins St in the city; the *Longford*, 59 Toorak Rd, South Yarra; and the *Trak*, 445 Toorak Rd, Toorak. Check the *EG* or newspapers for screenings and times.

Theatre The *Victorian Arts Centre* (☎ 9281 8000) is the major venue for the performing arts. Flanked by the Yarra River on one side and the National Gallery on the other, the centre houses four theatres – the Melbourne Concert Hall, the State Theatre, the Playhouse and the George Fairfax Studio.

The Melbourne Theatre Company is the major mainstream theatrical company. *La Mama*, 205 Faraday St, Carlton, is a tiny, long-running experimental theatre and a great forum for new Australian works. The Playbox company, based at the *Malthouse Theatres* in Sturt St, South Melbourne, also stages predominantly Australian works.

Commercial theatres are numerous and include the *Athenaeum*, 188 Collins St, the *Comedy Theatre*, at 240 Exhibition St, *Her Majesty's Theatre*, 219 Exhibition St, the *Princess Theatre*, 163 Spring St, the *Universal Theatre*, 13 Victoria St in Fitzroy, and the *Gasworks Theatre* in Graham St in Albert Park.

Comedy Melbourne celebrates its place as Australia's comedy capital with the annual International Comedy Festival in April. At other times of the year, several places feature comedy acts on a fairly regular basis – check the *EG* for specific shows.

The *Comedy Club* (☎ 9348 1622), 380

Lygon St in Carlton, is another good cabaret-style comedy venue (between $20 and $30, more with dinner). Other regular (and considerably cheaper) comedy venues include the *Prince Patrick Hotel*, 135 Victoria Pde, Collingwood, the *Waiting Room* at the Esplanade Hotel in St Kilda, and the *Rex Hotel*, 145 Bay St, Port Melbourne.

Pubs & Live Music Melbourne has always enjoyed a thriving pub-rock scene and is widely acknowledged as the country's rock capital. The sweaty grind around Melbourne's pubs has been the proving ground for many of Australia's best outfits. To find out who's playing where, look in the *EG*, *Beat* or *Inpress*, or listen to the gig guides on FM radio stations such as 3RRR (102.7) and 3PBS (106.7), both of which are excellent noncommercial radio stations. Cover charges at the pubs vary widely: some gigs are free, but generally you'll pay $5 to $10.

In St Kilda is the famed *Esplanade Hotel*, on the Esplanade of course, which has live bands (often free) and other entertainment every night and Sunday afternoons. It's also a great place just to sit with a beer and watch the sun set over the pier, or have a meal in the Espy Kitchen out the back. You can't leave Melbourne without visiting the Espy.

Good music venues in Fitzroy are the *Punters Club*, 376 Brunswick St, the *Evelyn Hotel* at No 351 and the *Royal Derby* on the corner of Brunswick St and Alexandra Pde; the arty and cosy *Builders Arms*, 211 Gertrude St, is another good Fitzroy watering hole. The *Rainbow Hotel*, an old backstreet pub at 27 St James St, has (free) live bands nightly, ranging from jazz and blues to funk and soul.

The *Club*, 132 Smith St, Collingwood, attracts good bands and stays open until dawn, and the nearby *Gowings*, No 114, is also worth checking out. The *Africa Bar* at No 99 has music, often reggae, on Friday and Saturday.

The grungy *Great Britain Hotel*, 447 Church St, Richmond, is yet another icon of the local music scene. Speaking of grunge,

the *Public Bar* at 238 Victoria St opposite the Queen Vic Market has a nightly line-up of bands playing through until the early hours. Nearby on the corner of Queensberry and Elizabeth Sts, *Arthouse* at the Royal Artillery Hotel is the place to head if you're into death metal.

The *Continental* (☎ 9510 2788), above the cafe of the same name at 134 Greville St, Prahran, has great acts in a civilised environment. You have a choice of dinner-and-show deals (roughly $35 to $60) or standing-room ($10 to $25).

The *Limerick Arms* on the corner of Park and Clarendon Sts in South Melbourne is a funky and friendly little pub with jazz bands on Thursday and DJs on Friday and Saturday.

Bars Melbourne has a great collection of ultrafashionable bars – if you want to rub shoulders with dedicated funksters, the following places are all worth checking out (although a month can mean the difference between cool and passé): in the city, the *Six Degrees Bar* in Myers Place (off the top end of Bourke St), and *Sadie's Bar*, 1 Coverlid Place (off Little Bourke St near Russell St); in St Kilda, the *Dogs Bar*, 54 Acland St, and the *George Hotel* on the corner of Grey and Fitzroy Sts; and in Fitzroy, the *Gypsy Bar*, 334 Brunswick St, the *Provincial Hotel* on the corner of Johnston and Brunswick Sts, or any of the tapas bars along Johnston St.

Nightclubs The city centre is home to the mainstream clubs. The huge *Metro*, 20 Bourke St, is worth a visit on a Saturday night. King St is a busy but somewhat sleazy nightclub strip (with 'table dancing', 'gentlemen's clubs' and street fights), with clubs including *Inflation* at No 60, the *Grainstore Tavern* next door, and the *Sports Bar* at No 14.

The *Lounge*, upstairs at 243 Swanston Walk, is a hip, semialternative club with everything from Latin rhythms to techno and hip hop.

Fitzroy has some interesting clubs including *Bar Salona*, a Latin-style dance club at

48 Johnston St, and the very hip *Night Cat*, 141 Johnston St, with 1950s decor and jazz, groove, and soul bands.

Other good clubs include the long-running *Chasers*, 386 Chapel St, Prahran, still one of the hottest dance-music clubs; and *Dream*, 229 Queensberry St, Carlton, which goes gothic on Friday, indie/alternative on Saturday and has gay/S&M nights on Sunday.

Jazz & Blues Hidden down a narrow lane off Little Lonsdale St (between Exhibition and Russell Sts), *Bennett's Lane* is a quintessentially dim, smoke-filled, groovy jazz venue – well worth searching out. *Ruby Red*, a converted warehouse at 11 Drewery Lane, is also good.

Quite a few pubs have good jazz and blues sessions on certain nights – check the gig guide in the *EG*.

Gay & Lesbian Venues The *Exchange Hotel*, 119 Commercial Rd, Prahran, is one of the oldest venues. In Collingwood, the *Peel Dance Bar*, corner of Peel and Wellington Sts, stays open late for dancing, and the *Laird*, a gay men's pub, is at 149 Gipps St. Also in Collingwood, the *Glasshouse*, corner of Gipps and Rokeby Sts, is a women's pub with live bands. On the corner of Smith and Gertrude Sts, *Barracuda* is a queer venue housing a cocktail bar, disco and restaurant. Another good women's venue is *Rascal's Hotel*, 194 Bridge Rd, Richmond.

Casino The massive *Crown Casino*, which dominates the south bank of the Yarra across King St from the city centre, is open 24 hours a day. Plenty of pubs have poker machines – yawn.

Spectator Sports

When it comes to watching sports, Melburnians are about as fanatical as they come. You've probably heard the old expression that Aussie punters would bet on two flies crawling up a wall – well, at times it seems like half of Melbourne would queue up to watch two snails race, and most of them

In Australian Rules Football a free kick is awarded for a catch or 'mark'

wouldn't mind laying a bet on the outcome either.

Without a doubt, Australian Rules football – otherwise known as 'the footy' – is the major drawcard, with games at the MCG regularly pulling crowds of 50,000 to 80,000. If you're here between April and September you should try and see a match, as much for the crowds as the game. The sheer energy of the barracking at a big game is exhilarating. Despite the fervour, crowd violence is almost unknown.

During the summer months, the MCG hosts interstate and international one-day and Test cricket matches. Melbourne's Test traditionally begins on Boxing Day (26 December). The Australian Open tennis championship, one of the four international

The Melbourne Cup

If you happen to be in Melbourne on the first Tuesday in November, you can catch the greatest horse race in Australia – the prestigious Melbourne Cup, highlight of the city's Spring Racing Carnival. Although its status as the bearer of the largest prize for an Australian horse race is constantly under challenge, no other race can bring the country to a standstill.

For about an hour during the lead-up to the race each year, people all over the country get touched by Melbourne's spring racing fever. Serious punters and fashion-conscious racegoers pack the grandstand and lawns of the Victorian Racing Club's beautiful Flemington Racecourse; those who only bet once a year make their choice or organise Cup syndicates with friends; and the race is watched or listened to on TVs and radios in pubs, clubs and houses across the land. Australia virtually comes to a halt for the three or so minutes while the race is run.

The two-mile (3.2km) flat race attracts horses and owners from Europe, Asia and the Middle East, although often it's the New Zealand horses and trainers who leave with the coveted gold cup.

Some say that to be in Melbourne in November and not go to the Cup is like going to Paris and skipping the Louvre or to Pamplona and turning your back on the bulls. ■

Grand Slams, is held at the National Tennis Centre each January.

Melbourne's Spring Racing Carnival is always colourful, the highlight of course being the Melbourne Cup, held on the first Tuesday in November at Flemington Racecourse, a couple of kilometres west of the city centre.

Petrol heads and speed freaks are among the thousands who flock to the Australian Formula One Grand Prix held at the Albert Park circuit in March.

Things to Buy

There are a few places specialising in Aboriginal arts, crafts and souvenirs. The Aboriginal Gallery of Dreamings, 73-77 Bourke St, the Aboriginal Desert Art Gallery at 31 Flinders Lane, and Aboriginal Handcrafts on the 9th floor at 125 Swanston St, all sell a wide range of bark paintings, didjeridus and handicrafts from all over the country.

The best area for outdoor gear is around the intersection of Hardware and Little Bourke Sts. For nonspecialised outdoor gear (Akubra hats, Drizabone rain gear, boots etc) try Ofima at the Queen Victoria Market.

Chapel St in South Yarra (between Toorak and Commercial Rds) has the most fashionable boutiques. Other good areas include Brunswick St in Fitzroy (grunge gear and young designers), Toorak Rd in South Yarra (upmarket and quite pricey), and Swan St and Bridge Rd in Richmond (designer shops and factory outlets). Also good for clothes (and most other stuff) are the city's major department stores – Myer and David Jones in the Bourke St Mall, and the Melbourne Central complex three blocks north, which includes Daimaru.

If you're interested in the local craft scene, head for the Meat Market Craft Centre on the corner of Courtney and Blackwood Sts in North Melbourne (open Tuesday-Sunday from 10 am to 5 pm). The Esplanade Sunday Market in St Kilda is another good art and craft outlet, as is the Queen Victoria Market.

Getting There & Away

Air Melbourne airport at Tullamarine services both domestic and international flights. It's more spacious than Sydney's airport and also gets fewer flights, so if you make this your Australian arrival point you may get through immigration and customs a little more speedily.

Ansett (☎ 13 1300) and Qantas (☎ 13 1313) both have frequent connections between Melbourne and other state capitals – Melbourne to Sydney flights depart hourly during the airport's operating hours. Standard one-way full economy fares include Adelaide $260, Brisbane $441, Canberra

$222, Darwin $689, Perth $623 and Sydney $276. Connections to Alice Springs ($558) are via Adelaide or Sydney. Remember that hardly anyone pays the full fare (see the Getting Around chapter earlier in the book for details of discounted airfares).

Melbourne is the main departure point from the mainland to Tasmania. Flights to Hobart with Ansett or Qantas cost $247, and to Launceston they cost $214. Flights to Devonport cost $176 and are operated by Kendell Airlines (bookings through Ansett). Aus Air (☎ 9580 6166) also flies to Tassie from Moorabbin airport: destinations include Launceston (from $105), Devonport (from $95) and King Island (from $80).

The Qantas office is at 50 Franklin St. Ansett's is at 501 Swanston St. Both have smaller offices around the city.

Refer to the airfares chart in the introductory Getting Around section in this chapter for airfares within Victoria.

Bus Operating from the Melbourne Transit Centre at 58 Franklin St in the city, Greyhound (☎ 13 2030) has buses between Melbourne and Adelaide (10 hours, $56), Perth (48 hours, $285), Canberra (nine hours, $54), Brisbane (24 hours, $141) and Sydney (direct, 12 hours, $60; or via the Princes Highway, 15 hours, $70).

McCafferty's (☎ 13 1499) operates out of the Spencer St Coach Terminal, and has similar services but tends to be a few dollars cheaper. Firefly (☎ 9670 7500) also operates out of the Spencer St Coach Terminal, with services to Adelaide ($40) and Sydney ($45).

V/Line buses (☎ 13 2232) depart from the Spencer St Coach Terminal and go to all parts of Victoria (see the towns in this chapter for the appropriate fares).

There are some fun and scenic alternatives if you're travelling to Sydney or Adelaide. The Wayward Bus (☎ 1800 882 823) runs a three-day trip along the spectacular Great Ocean Road, running twice a week in each direction ($160). During summer they also have a six-day trip which does a loop up into the Grampians in Victoria. These trips include sightseeing, meals and camping accommodation (see the NSW chapter for information on the Wayward Bus Sydney-Melbourne route).

The Gypsy Bus (book at hostels) takes five days to get to Adelaide, running via an interesting inland route which includes the Grampians and Hattah Kulkyne National Park, then up to Broken Hill and the outback Mootwingee National Park and down to Adelaide via the wineries of the Clare Valley. The fare is around $245 plus accommodation and some meals.

Train Rail tickets for travel within Victoria or interstate can be booked by phoning V/Line on ☎ 13 2232 between 7 am and 9 pm (you may be on hold for 10 or 20 minutes at busy times!), or bought at most suburban stations and at Spencer St train station in Melbourne, from where the long-distance services depart.

Interstate Melbourne to Sydney takes 10¾ hours by *XPT* train, with the Melbourne-Sydney service operating during the day and the Sydney-Melbourne service overnight. Standard fares are $93 in economy, $130 in 1st class, and $225 for a 1st-class sleeper, although discounts of between 10% and 40% apply for advance bookings.

To get to Canberra by rail you take the daily *Canberra Link*, which involves a train to Wodonga and a bus from there. This takes about eight hours and costs as little as $47 in economy and $62 in 1st class.

The *Overland* operates between Melbourne and Adelaide nightly. The trip takes 12 hours and costs $58 in economy, $116 in 1st class and $182/362 for a single/twin 1st-class sleeper. You can transport your car on the *Overland* for $84. The *Daylink* to Adelaide involves a train to Bendigo and a bus from there. This trip takes 11 hours and costs $49 in economy, $57 in 1st class.

To get to Perth by rail from Melbourne you take the *Overland* to Adelaide and then the *Indian Pacific* (which comes through Adelaide from Sydney). The Melbourne to Perth trip takes two days and three nights, and fares are $286 for an economy seat, $548 for a seat

VICTORIA

to Adelaide and an economy sleeper to Perth and $936 for a 1st-class sleeper (all meals included).

Within Victoria See the Getting Around section at the start of this chapter for V/Line's network, and see sections on specific country towns for information on fares and travel from Melbourne. For travel within Victoria there are some discount fares, such as travelling at off-peak times.

Car Rental All the big car-rental firms operate in Melbourne. Avis, Budget, Hertz and Thrifty have desks at the airport and you can find plenty of others in the city. The offices tend to be at the northern end of the city or in Carlton or North Melbourne.

There are also rent-a-wreck-style operators, renting older vehicles at lower rates. Their costs and conditions vary widely so it's worth making a few enquiries before going for one firm over another. You can take the 'from $25 a day' line with a pinch of salt because the rates soon start to rise with insurance, kilometre charges and so on. Beware of distance restrictions; many companies only allow you to travel within a certain distance of the city, typically 100km.

Some places worth trying are Delta (☎ 13 1390) and Airport Rent-a-Car (☎ 9335 3355) which have branches around Melbourne. Other operators include Rent-a-Bomb (☎ 9428 0088) in Richmond. The *Yellow Pages* lists lots of other firms including some reputable local operators who rent newer cars but don't have the nationwide network (and overheads) of big operators.

Getting Around

To/From the Airport Tullamarine airport is 22km north-west of the city centre. There's one terminal: Qantas at one end, Ansett at the other, international in the middle. There are two information desks: one on the ground floor in the international departure area and another upstairs next to the duty-free shops.

The Tullamarine Freeway runs from the airport almost into the city centre, finishing in North Melbourne. A taxi between the airport and city centre costs about $25. There's also the regular Skybus (☎ 9662 9275) service, which costs $9 (children $4.50). The Skybus departs from Bay 30 at the Spencer St Coach Terminal and from the Melbourne Transit Centre at 58 Franklin St, with buses about every half-hour between 6 am and 10.30 pm (ring to confirm departure times).

Other buses run to the airport from various outer suburbs and a few larger regional towns.

Bus, Train & Tram Melbourne's public transport system, the Met, incorporates buses, trains and trams. The trams are the real cornerstone of the system; in all there are about 750 of them and they operate as far as 20km out from the centre. They're frequent and fun.

Buses are the secondary form of public transport, taking routes where the trams do not go, and replacing them at quiet weekend periods. Trains are the third link in the Met, radiating out from the city centre to the outer suburbs. The fast underground City Loop operates between Spencer St, Flinders St, Flagstaff, Museum and Parliament train stations.

There's quite an array of tickets, and they are all described in the Met's glossy *Travel Guide* brochure.

The same ticket allows you to travel on trams, trains and buses. The most common tickets are based on a specific period of travelling time – either two hours, one day, one week, one month or one year – and allow you unlimited travel during that period and within the relevant zone/s.

A new and automated ticketing system was introduced by the State Government in 1998. You can buy tickets on trams, or from train stations and retail outlets (including newsagents and milk bars). However, if buying a ticket on a tram, make sure you have enough coins (the machines don't accept notes). Only 2-hour tickets can be bought on trams.

Be warned: if you don't have a ticket there's a $100 fine.

The metropolitan area is divided into three zones, and the price of tickets depends on which zone/s you will be travelling in and across. Zone 1 covers the city and inner suburban area (including St Kilda), and most travellers won't venture beyond that unless they're going right out of town – on a trip to the Healesville Wildlife Sanctuary, for example, or down to the Mornington Peninsula. The fares are as follows:

Zones	2 Hours	All Day	Weekly
1	$2.20	$4.30	$18.60
2 or 3	$1.60	$2.90	$12.80
1 & 2	$3.80	$7.00	$31.40
1, 2 & 3	$5.20	$9.40	$38.40

Note that if you buy a weekly, monthly or yearly Zone 1 ticket, it also allows you unlimited travel in Zones 1, 2 and 3 on weekends. If you're heading into the city by train from Zone 2 or 3, you can get off-peak tickets for use after 9.30 am which take you into the city and then allow unlimited travel on trams and buses within the city area.

There are also Short Trip tickets ($1.60) which allow you to travel two sections on buses or trams in Zone 1, or you can buy a Short Trip Card ($12.50) which gives you 10 short trips. There are numerous other deals and you can check these out with the Met.

For information on public transport phone the Met Information Centre (☎ 13 1638), which operates daily from 7 am to 9 pm. The Met Shop at 103 Elizabeth St in the city also has transport information and sells souvenirs and tickets. It also has a 'Discover Melbourne' kit. If you're in the city it's probably a better bet for information than the telephone service, which is usually busy. Train stations also have some information.

The Met operates an information service for disabled travellers (☎ 9619 2355).

Bicycle Melbourne's a great city for cycling. It's reasonably flat so you're not pushing and panting up hills too often, and there are some interesting cycling routes throughout the metropolitan area. Two of the most scenic are the bike path that runs around the shores of Port Phillip Bay from Port Melbourne to Brighton, and the bike path that follows the Yarra River out of the city for more than 20km, passing through lovely parklands along the way. There are numerous other bicycle tracks, including those along the Maribyrnong River and Merri Creek.

Discovering Melbourne's Bike Paths ($14.95), has useful maps and descriptions of the city's bicycle paths. The *Melway Greater Melbourne* street directory is also useful for cyclists. Bicycles can be taken on suburban trains for free during off-peak times.

Quite a few bike shops and companies have bikes for hire – the following places are all worth trying:

St Kilda Cycles (☎ 9534 3074), 11 Carlisle St, St Kilda
Bob's Boards & Blades (☎ 9537 2118), 17 Fitzroy St, St Kilda
Cycle Science (☎ 9826 8877), 320 Toorak Rd, South Yarra
Bicycles for Hire (☎ 018 580 809), below Princes Bridge on the south side of the Yarra
Borsari Cycles (☎ 9347 4100), 193 Lygon St, Carlton

Around Melbourne

There are plenty of worthwhile destinations within about an hour's drive of Melbourne, including the fine beaches and seaside towns of the Bellarine and Mornington peninsulas, mysterious Hanging Rock, the scenic Yarra Valley with its wineries and excellent wildlife sanctuary, the verdant Dandenong Ranges, and Phillip Island with its famous penguin parade.

SOUTH-WEST TO GEELONG
It's a quick trip down the Princes Freeway to Geelong. As you leave Melbourne there are fine views of the city from the West Gate Bridge, although the rest of the trip is pretty dull. This road, crowded by Australian standards, has a high accident rate, so take care.

VICTORIA

VICTORIA

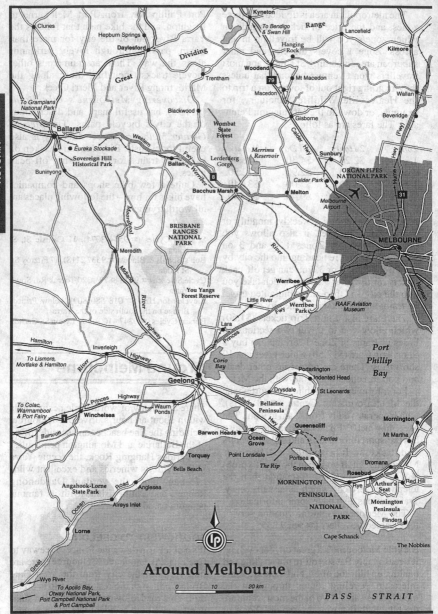

Around Melbourne

0   10   20 km

BASS   STRAIT

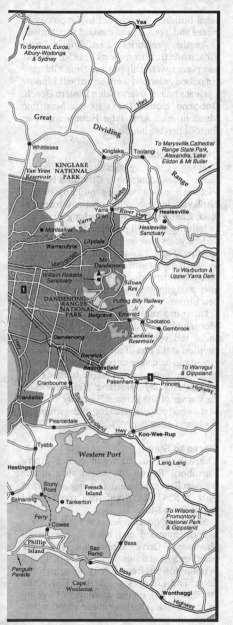

VICTORIA

Werribee Park & Zoo
Not far out of Melbourne you can turn off to Werribee Park with its free-range zoo and the huge Italianate **Werribee Park Mansion**, built in 1874. The flamboyant building is surrounded by formal gardens, with good picnic areas. Entrance to the gardens is free, but admission to the mansion is $8 (children $4). Safari bus tours of the zoo cost $14 (children $7). Werribee Park is open daily from 10 am to 3.45 pm (to 4.45 pm during summer).

You Yangs
You can also detour to the You Yangs, a picturesque range of volcanic hills just off the freeway. Walks in the You Yangs include the climb up **Flinders Peak**, the highest point in the park, with a plaque commemorating Matthew Flinders' scramble to the top in 1802. There are fine views from the top, down to Geelong and the coast.

Brisbane Ranges National Park
You can make an interesting loop from Melbourne out to the You Yangs and back through the Brisbane Ranges park and Bacchus Marsh. The scenic **Anakie Gorge** in the Brisbane Ranges is a short bushwalk and a good spot for barbecues. You'd be unlucky not to see koalas in the trees near the car park/picnic area or on the walk.

GEELONG (pop 125,382)
The city of Geelong began as a sheep-grazing area when the first white settlers arrived in 1836, and it initially served as a port for the dispatch of wool and wheat from the area. During the gold-rush era it became important as a landing place for immigrants and for the export of gold. Around 1900, Geelong started to become industrialised and that's very much what it is today – an industrial city, and Victoria's second-largest.

Melbourne people dismiss Geelong in much the same way that Sydney people dismiss Newcastle – as a small, dull, uncultivated, industrialised place. This is largely because all they see of it is the ugly highway strip that delays them on their way to the surf coast. In reality, Geelong isn't so bad. There's no sign of industry in the city centre or on the beaches at its doorstep. The atmosphere is relaxed, there's a real sense of history, and there are plenty of good eating places and some live music.

Information

The Geelong Otway Tourism Centre (☎ 5275 5797; 1800 620 888), on the corner of the Princes Highway and St George Rd 7km north of the city centre, is open daily from 9 am to 5 pm. There are also tourist offices in the National Wool Centre on Moorabool St and in the Market Square shopping complex. There's a web site at greatoceanrd.org.au.

If you want to buy camping gear, try the disposals and camping shops on Ryrie St between Moorabool and Gheringhap Sts.

Museums & Art Gallery

The impressive **National Wool Centre** on the corner of Brougham and Moorabool Sts is housed in a historic bluestone wool store and has a large and interesting museum, a number of wool-craft and clothing shops and a restaurant. It is open daily from 10 am to 5 pm and admission to the museum section is $7 (students $5.80, children $3.50).

The **Geelong Maritime Museum** on Swinburne St, North Geelong, is open daily, except Tuesday and Thursday, from 10 am to 4 pm ($2/50c). The **Geelong Art Gallery** on Little Malop St is open weekdays from 10 am to 5 pm and weekends from 1 to 5 pm and has an extensive collection of mainly Australian art; entry is $3 (free Monday).

Historic Houses

The city has more than 100 National Trust classified buildings. **Barwon Grange** on Fernleigh St, Newtown, was built in 1856. It's open on Wednesday, Saturday and Sunday from 2 to 5 pm; entry costs $4. The **Heights**, 140 Aphrasia St, is open from Wednesday to Sunday from 2 to 5 pm ($6, children $3, free under six). This 14-room timber mansion is an example of a prefabri-

cated building brought out to the colony in pieces and it features an unusual watchtower.

Another prefabricated building is **Corio Villa**, made from iron sheets in 1856. The bits and pieces were shipped out from Glasgow but nobody claimed them on arrival! It's now a private house, overlooking Eastern Beach. **Osborne House** (next to the Maritime Museum) and **Armytage House** are other fine old private buildings.

Other Attractions

Geelong's attractive botanic gardens (part of Eastern Park) contain the **Customs House**, Victoria's oldest wooden building, which displays telegraph equipment and memorabilia. **Eastern Beach** is Geelong's popular swimming spot and promenade where boats and bicycles can be hired on weekends in summer. There's a restaurant, cafe and kiosk, as well as swimming/diving platforms, sandy beaches and picnic lawns. There is also a signposted scenic drive along the beachfront.

Cunningham Pier at the end of Moorabool St is the centrepiece of a foreshore redevelopment, and the impressive pavilion at the end of the pier houses amusements and an eatery or two. It's worth a visit to see the carved and painted bollards. On hot summer days, **Norlane Waterworld** on the corner of the Princes Highway and Cox St is a good place to head for, with swimming pools and giant waterslides.

Places to Stay

There are four caravan parks along Barrabool Rd on the south side of the Barwon River, including *Billabong Caravan Park* (☎ 5243 6225), with sites from $12 and cabins from $40.

St Albans Backpackers (☎ 5248 1229), a historic mansion and horse-stud farm on Homestead Drive, Whittington, has bunk beds for $15 and one double at $40. Take a Whittington bus from the city – it stops at the door. The colleges at Deakin University (☎ 5227 1158), on the outskirts of Geelong towards Colac, also have cheap accommodation in the summer holidays.

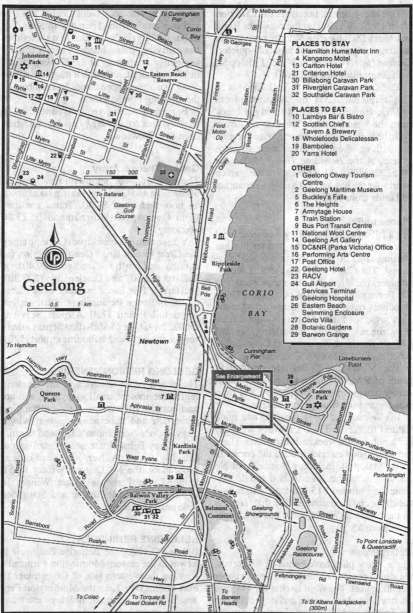

Geelong

0   0.5   1 km

PLACES TO STAY
3 Hamilton Hume Motor Inn
4 Kangaroo Motel
13 Carlton Hotel
21 Criterion Hotel
30 Billabong Caravan Park
31 Riverglen Caravan Park
32 Southside Caravan Park

PLACES TO EAT
10 Lambys Bar & Bistro
12 Scottish Chief's
   Tavern & Brewery
18 Wholefoods Delicatessan
19 Bamboleo
20 Yarra Hotel

OTHER
1 Geelong Otway Tourism
   Centre
2 Geelong Maritime Museum
5 Buckley's Falls
6 The Heights
7 Armytage House
8 Train Station
9 Bus Port Transit Centre
11 National Wool Centre
14 Geelong Art Gallery
15 DC&NR (Parks Victoria) Office
16 Performing Arts Centre
17 Post Office
22 Geelong Hotel
23 RACV
24 Gull Airport
   Services Terminal
25 Geelong Hospital
26 Eastern Beach
   Swimming Enclosure
27 Corio Villa
28 Botanic Gardens
29 Barwon Grange

Two cheap central hotels are the *Criterion Hotel* (☎ 5229 1104) on the corner of Ryrie and Yarra Sts, charging $25 per person, and the more impressive (and probably quieter) *Carlton Hotel* (☎ 5229 1954) at 21 Malop St, with singles/doubles at $30/40.

The *Kangaroo Motel* (☎ 5221 4365) at 16 The Esplanade has budget units from $43/53. However, while it's only a block from the waterfront it's less than that from both the highway and a busy flyover. Nearby, but with an altogether more relaxed atmosphere, is the *Hamilton Hume Motor Inn* (☎ 5222 3499), 13 The Esplanade, which overlooks the bay and has a pool, a restaurant and units from $75/79.

Places to Eat

For a filling budget meal try a counter meal at a pub. Many pubs have counter lunches starting at $3.50 (usually for crumbed sausages). The *Corio Hotel* on Yarra St is even cheaper, and also has bistro meals starting at $7. For a more upmarket pub meal ('Dress standards required at all times' is what the sign says, but I doubt that that's quite what they mean), try the interesting *Scottish Chief's Tavern & Brewery*, 99 Corio St. At lunch many dishes cost $7 or less.

The Moorabool St hill (Moorabool St south of Ryrie St) has a varied selection of eating places, mostly inexpensive. Go for a wander and see what takes your fancy.

Wholefoods, at 10 James St, has good natural tucker, and is open every weekday for lunch and on weekends for dinner. There are some good eateries around the corner in Little Malop St, including *Bamboleo* at No 86, with authentic Spanish food and decor – mains are around $15 but there's usually a lunch special for much less than that. *Lambys* in the National Wool Centre has lunch specials from $5.

Entertainment

Quite a few pubs have bands on weekends. Pick up a copy of *Forte*, a free weekly paper detailing gigs. The *Wool Exchange*, 44 Corio St, has a couple of venues and stays open late on Friday and Saturday. *Lambys*, not far away at the National Wool Centre, has DJs and live music from Thursday to Saturday. *Rebar*, 177 Ryrie St, is a club that sometimes has fairly big-name bands. There's usually something happening at the *Geelong Hotel* in Moorabool St, although it might be something like a guest appearance by members of the Geelong Football Club.

For Irish music from Wednesday to Sunday, visit *Irish Murphy's* pub at 30 Aberdeen St in Newtown.

Getting There & Away

There are frequent 'sprinter trains' between Melbourne and Geelong; the trip takes about an hour and costs $8.40. Trains continue from Geelong to Warrnambool ($23.80 economy).

V/Line also has buses from Geelong along the Great Ocean Road (see that section for details), and north to Bendigo ($29.40) via Ballarat ($9.50) and Castlemaine ($23.80). McHarry's Bus Lines services most places on the Bellarine Peninsula (see that section for details), and Gull Airport Services (☎ 5222 4966) at 45 McKillop St runs a daily service to and from Melbourne airport ($20).

GEELONG REGION WINERIES

The dozen or so wineries in the Geelong region are mostly small vineyards, and are particularly known for their outstanding pinot noir and cabernet-sauvignon wines. They include Scotchman's Hill and the historic Spray Farm Estate near Portarlington, the Idyll and Asher vineyards near Moorabool, the Mt Duneed Winery in Mt Duneed, the Tarcoola Estate Winery in Lethbridge, and Mt Anakie and Staughton Vale near Anakie.

BELLARINE PENINSULA

Beyond Geelong the Bellarine Peninsula is a twin to the eastern Mornington Peninsula, forming the western side of the entrance to Port Phillip Bay. Like the Mornington Peninsula, this is a popular holiday resort and boating venue.

Getting There & Away

McHarry's Bus Lines (☎ 5223 2111) operates the Bellarine Transit bus service with frequent services from Geelong to the Bellarine Peninsula; destinations include Barwon Heads and Ocean Grove (both $3.50), and Queenscliff and Point Lonsdale (both $5.40).

Portarlington, Indented Head & St Leonards

These three low-key family resorts on the northern peninsula front onto Port Phillip Bay (so there's no surf). Indented Head is where Matthew Flinders landed in 1802, one of the first visits to the area by a European. In 1835 John Batman landed at this same point, on his way to buy up Melbourne.

At Portarlington there's a fine example of an early steam-powered **flour mill**. Built in about 1856, the massive mill is owned by the National Trust and is open from September to May on Sunday from 2 to 5 pm.

Queenscliff (pop 3,832)

One of Melbourne's most popular seaside resort towns during the last century, Queenscliff has been 'rediscovered' in recent times and is again a fashionable getaway for the city's gentry. Many of the fine Victorian-era buildings have been restored into guesthouses and upmarket hotels; these are complemented by good cafes and restaurants, a great golf course and numerous other attractions.

Queenscliff was established in about 1838 as a pilot station to guide ships through the Rip at the entrance to Port Phillip Bay. The pilot station remains (on the bay beach near the cliff) and although the pilots' boats are infinitely safer than they were 150 years ago, piloting in these waters is still demanding and dangerous.

Fort Queenscliff was built in 1882 to protect Melbourne from the perceived Russian threat and, at the time, it was the most heavily defended fort in the colony. Today it houses the Australian Army Command and a military museum; there are guided tours on weekends at 11 am and 1 and 3 pm, and on weekdays at 1.30 pm ($5, children $2).

The **Marine Discovery Centre** (☎ 5258 3344) next to the ferry pier runs a range of trips, including 'snorkelling with the seals' ($35), two-hour canoe trips ($10), marine biology tours, rockpool rambles, nocturnal beach walks and lots more – ring to find out what's on. Queenscliff Dive School (☎ 5258 1188) also has trips to snorkel (or dive) with seals for the same price and offers an interesting learn-to-dive option. You can do a unit of the certificate course here (from $95) and do other units at other locations around Australia.

The **Queenscliff Maritime Museum**, next to the Marine Discovery Centre, is open weekends (1.30 to 4.30 pm) and during school holidays (10.30 am to 4.30 pm); admission is $4.

Railway enthusiasts will enjoy the **Bellarine Peninsula Railway**, which operates from the old Queenscliff station with a fine collection of old steam trains. On Sunday, public holidays and most school holidays steam trains make the 16km return trip to Drysdale four or five times a day (two hours, $12) and a shorter trip around Swan Bay (35 minutes, $8).

Places to Stay The *Queenscliff Point Lonsdale Caravan Park* (☎ 5258 1765) is on Mercer St; it has camp sites only.

The friendly *Queenscliff Inn* (☎ 5258 4600) at 59 Hesse St is a charming guesthouse with singles/doubles from $45/50, and lower rates for backpackers (these vary). The cosy *Athelstane House* (☎ 5258 1591) at 4 Hobson St has B&B from $35/60.

If you can afford to, stay at *Mietta's Queenscliff Hotel* (☎ 5258 1066), a jewel of old-world splendour with dinner B&B deals from $100 per person. Check out their web site at miettas.com.au.

Is Mietta's worth it? Yes, definitely, but be warned that the rooms are old-style pub rooms, and they don't have phone, radio or TV; in fact there's no TV or radio in the whole place. The rooms are beautifully decorated but they are very small and have shared bathrooms. In a way this is part of the attraction – rather than sit in your room watching TV you use the lovely public areas of the hotel and appreciate the service of the well-trained staff. And the food is superb.

Getting There & Away Ferries operate between Queenscliff and Sorrento and Portsea (see the Mornington Peninsula Getting There & Away section for details).

Around Queenscliff
Five kilometres south-west of Queenscliff, in the resort town of **Point Lonsdale**, a lighthouse and lookout overlook the turbulent waters of the Rip, which separates the Bellarine and Mornington peninsulas. Below the lighthouse is **Buckley's Cave** where the 'wild white man', William Buckley, lived with Aboriginal people for 32 years after escaping from the settlement at Sorrento on the Mornington Peninsula in 1803.

On the ocean side of the peninsula, **Ocean Grove** is another resort town full of holiday houses. There's good scuba diving on the rocky ledges of the Bluff, and farther out there are wrecks of ships that failed to get through the tricky entrance to Port Phillip Bay. Some of the wrecks are accessible to divers. The beach at the surf-lifesaving club is very popular with surfers. Just along from Ocean Grove is **Barwon Heads**, a smaller resort town, where there are both surf and quieter estuary beaches.

Accommodation options in all three towns include caravan parks, motels and holiday flats.

NORTH-WEST TO BENDIGO
It's about 160km north-west of Melbourne along the Calder Highway to the old mining town of Bendigo, and there are some interesting stops along the way.

You've hardly left the outskirts of Melbourne when you come to the turn-off to the surprisingly pretty and little-visited **Organ Pipes National Park** on the right, and the amazingly ugly Calder Thunderdome Raceway on the left.

The freeway skirts small towns such as **Sunbury**, where Test cricket's Ashes were created – there's a lovely little cricket ground. **Mt Macedon**, a 1013m-high extinct volcano, soon looms large on the right. The scenic route up Mt Macedon takes you past country mansions and lovely gardens to a lookout point at the summit; the road then continues down to Woodend and Hanging Rock.

Just north of Mt Macedon is **Hanging Rock**, a picnic spot made famous by the book and film, *Picnic at Hanging Rock*. At that mysterious picnic, three schoolgirls on a trip to the rock disappeared without trace; in an equally mysterious way one of the girls reappeared a few days later. The rocks are fun to clamber over and there are superb views from higher up. The Hanging Rock Picnic Races, held on New Year's Day and Australia Day, are a great day out.

To get there, take a train from Melbourne to Woodend ($8.40) – from there, a taxi to Hanging Rock will cost about $12, or it's an easy cycle – you might have to walk up one or two hills (see Organised Tours in the Victoria Getting Around section for day trips to the Hanging Rock area).

The highway skirts **Kyneton**, which has fine bluestone buildings. Piper St is a historic precinct, with antique shops, tearooms, and a historical museum. Another 11km brings you to **Malmsbury** with its bluestone railway viaduct and a magnificent ruined grain mill, which has been converted into a restaurant and gallery.

YARRA VALLEY & BEYOND
The Yarra Valley, beyond the north-eastern outskirts of Melbourne, is a place of great natural beauty and well worth exploring. It's a good area for bicycle tours or bushwalks, there are dozens of wineries to visit, and Healesville Wildlife Sanctuary is one of the best places in the country to see Australian wildlife.

Getting There & Away
McKenzie's Bus Lines (☎ 9853 6264) runs a daily bus service from the Spencer St bus

terminal through Healesville to Marysville, Alexandra and Lake Eildon.

Wineries

With more than 30 wineries sprinkled through the Yarra Valley, this area is a scenic and pleasant day trip from Melbourne. Wineries which open daily include Domaine Chandon, Lilydale Vineyards, De Bortoli, Fergussons, Kellybrook and Yarra Burn, and about 15 others are open on weekends as well as holidays.

Gulf Station

Gulf Station, a couple of kilometres north of Yarra Glen, is part of an old grazing run dating from the 1850s. Operated by the National Trust, it's open Wednesday to Sunday and public holidays from 10 am to 4 pm ($7). There is an interesting collection of rough old timber buildings plus the associated pastures and a homestead garden.

Healesville Wildlife Sanctuary

Near the pleasant town of Healesville, 65km from the centre of Melbourne, is the outstanding Healesville Wildlife Sanctuary (☎ 5962 4022). The nocturnal house, where you can see many of the smaller bush dwellers that come out only at night, is open from 10 am to 5 pm, as is the reptile house. The impressive 'birds of prey' presentation runs daily at noon and 3 pm. The whole park is open daily from 9 am to 5 pm ($13, children $7, family tickets available). There are barbecue and picnic facilities in a wooded park.

Getting There & Away From Melbourne, take a suburban train to Lilydale station, from where there's a connecting bus twice a day (once on Sunday). Phone the Met (☎ 13 1638) or the sanctuary for the times.

Warburton (pop 3446)

Beyond Healesville is Warburton, another pretty little hill town in the Great Dividing Range foothills. There are good views of the mountains from the Acheron Way nearby and you'll sometimes get snow on Mt Donna Buang, 7km from town.

Marysville (pop 626)

This delightful little town is a very popular weekend escape from Melbourne. It has lots of bush tracks good for walks: Nicholl's Lookout, Keppel's Lookout, Mt Gordon and Steavenson Falls. **Cumberland Scenic Reserve**, with numerous walks and the Cumberland Falls, is 16km east of Marysville. The cross-country skiing trails of **Lake Mountain Reserve** are only 10km beyond Marysville.

The **Cathedral Range State Park** is about 10km north-west of Marysville, and it offers good bushwalks and camping.

Places to Stay *Marysville Caravan Park* (☎ 5963 3433) is beside the river, and the rambling *Crossways Motel* (☎ 5963 3290) has motel-style units from $45/50. There are numerous upmarket guesthouses and B&Bs, including *Marylands Country House* (☎ 5963 3204), with dinner B&B from $150/240.

THE DANDENONGS

The Dandenong Ranges, just beyond the eastern fringe of Melbourne's suburban sprawl, are a favourite destination for day trips, scenic drives and picnics. Things can get a little hectic on weekends – midweek visits are much more relaxed.

The Dandenongs are cool owing to the altitude (Mt Dandenong is all of 633m tall) and lush because of the heavy rainfall. The area is dotted with lots of fine old houses, old-fashioned tearooms, restaurants, beautiful gardens and some fine short bushwalks. You can see the Dandenongs clearly from central Melbourne (on a smog-free day) and they're only about an hour's drive away.

The small **Ferntree Gully National Park** has pleasant strolls and lots of bird life. Unfortunately, the lyrebirds for which the Dandenongs were once famous are now very rare. The **Sherbrooke Forest Park** is similarly pleasant for walks and you'll see lots of rosellas. These parks, together with Doongalla Reserve, make up the Dandenong Ranges National Park, proclaimed in 1987.

The **William Ricketts Sanctuary** on

Olinda Rd is set in fern gardens and features the work of the sculptor William Ricketts, who died in 1993 aged 94. His work was inspired by the Aboriginal people and their affinity with the land – the sculptures rise like spirits out of the ground. The forest sanctuary is open daily from 10 am to 4.30 pm and is well worth the $5 admission.

Puffing Billy

One of the major attractions in the Dandenongs is Puffing Billy (☎ 9754 6800 for bookings; ☎ 9870 8411 for running times), a restored steam train which runs along a spectacular 13km track from Belgrave to Lakeside at the Emerald Lake Park. Puffing Billy was originally built in 1900 to bring farm produce to market.

Puffing Billy runs daily except Christmas Day. The round trip takes about 2½ hours ($17.50, children $9.50, family tickets available). You can get out to Puffing Billy on the regular suburban rail service to Belgrave.

Places to Stay

There are numerous motels, guesthouses and B&Bs in the Dandenongs, but the only budget accommodation in this area is *Emerald Backpackers* (☎ 5968 4086) on Emerald Lake Rd, a comfortable hostel with dorm beds for $13. The people here can often find work for travellers in the local nurseries and gardens.

MORNINGTON PENINSULA

The Mornington Peninsula is the spit of land down the eastern side of Port Phillip Bay, bordered on its eastern side by the waters of Western Port bay. Melbourne's suburban sprawl extends down the peninsula beyond Frankston to Mornington, but from there it's almost a continuous beach strip all the way to Portsea at the end of the peninsula, nearly 100km from Melbourne.

This is a very popular Melbourne resort area with many holiday homes; in summer the accommodation and camp sites along the peninsula are packed right out and traffic is heavy. On the northern side of the peninsula there is calm water on the bay beaches (the front beaches), and on the southern side there is good surf along the rugged and beautiful ocean beaches (the back beaches).

This is an acclaimed wine-growing region with some 30 wineries, many of which are open to the public. There are also bushwalking trails along the Cape Schanck Coastal Park. Other attractions include great golf courses, dolphin cruises, horse-riding ranches, craft markets, and the Mornington Peninsula National Park.

The tourist information centre in Dromana (☎ 5987 3078) on the Nepean Highway has a handy map of the peninsula for $2.

Getting There & Away

Train/Bus Take a suburban train from Melbourne down to Frankston to connect with the frequent buses of the Portsea Passenger Service (☎ 5986 5666) along the coastal highway from Frankston to Portsea ($6.80).

Ferry Peninsula Searoad Transport (☎ 5258 3244 in Queenscliff, 5984 4133 in Sorrento) operates the car and passenger ferry that links Sorrento with Queenscliff on the Bellarine Peninsula. It runs all year, departing Queenscliff every two hours from 7 am to 5 pm (with a 7 pm high-season service) and returning from Sorrento every two hours from 8 am to 6 pm (with an 8 pm high-season service). Cars cost $30 to $36 plus $3 per adult; a motorcycle costs $14 plus $3; and pedestrians cost $7 (children $5).

A passenger-only ferry (☎ 5984 1602) runs daily from Sorrento and Portsea to Queenscliff between Christmas and Easter, during school holidays and at weekends at some other times of the year ($7, $12 return, children $5/10).

Frankston to Blairgowrie

Beyond Frankston you reach **Mornington** and **Mt Martha**, both with some old buildings along the Mornington Esplanade and fine, secluded beaches in between. The **Briars** in Mt Martha is an 1840s homestead open to the public.

Dromana is the real start of the resort development and just inland a winding road leads up to **Arthur's Seat** lookout at 305m; in summer you can also reach it by a chair lift (weekends and holidays only). On the slopes of Arthur's Seat, near the township of McCrae, the **McCrae Homestead** is a National Trust property, dating from 1843. It is open daily from noon to 4.30 pm. **Coolart** on Sandy Point Rd, Balnarring, on the other side of the peninsula, is another historic homestead, also noted for the wide variety of its bird life.

Sorrento

Just as you enter Sorrento there's a small memorial and pioneer cemetery from the first Victorian settlement at pretty **Sullivan Bay**. The settlement party, consisting of 308 convicts, civil officers, marines and free settlers, arrived from England in October 1803, intending to forestall a feared French settlement on the bay. Less than a year later, in May 1804, the project was abandoned and transferred to Hobart, Tasmania.

Sorrento has a rather damp and cold little aquarium and an interesting small historical museum in the old **Mechanic's Institute** building on the Old Melbourne Rd. In the last century paddle-steamers ran between Melbourne and Sorrento. From 1890 through to 1921 a steam-powered tram operated from the Sorrento Pier to the back beach. The magnificent hotels built of local limestone in this period still stand – the Sorrento (1871), Continental (1875) and Koonya (1878).

Polperro Dolphin Swims (☎ 5988 8437) offers the opportunity to swim in the bay with dolphins ($50 or $35 as an observer) from September through to May.

Places to Stay *Bells Environmental YHA Hostel* (☎ 5984 4323) is a good place to stay. The owners, Ian and Margaret, are friendly hosts and organise activities including dolphin swims, coastal walks and bird-watching. Dorms cost $12 ($14 during summer) and there are also twins. *Carmel B&B* (☎ 5984 3512) has B&B from $100/120 and self-contained units from $90.

Portsea

At the tip of the peninsula, Portsea is where many of Melbourne's wealthier families have seaside summer mansions, and the small town has an unmistakable air of privilege. At the Portsea back beach (the surf side) there's the impressive natural rock formation known as **London Bridge**, plus a cliff where hang-gliders make their leap into the void. Portsea is a diving centre, and scuba-diving trips on the bay operate regularly from Portsea Pier.

The *Portsea Hotel* (☎ 5984 2213), overlooking the pier, is particularly popular in summer, and has B&B from $35/60/80 a single/twin/double, all with shared bathroom, rising to $50/80/105 from Christmas to the end of January. There are more expensive rooms with attached bathroom.

Mornington Peninsula National Park

After being off-limits to the public for over 100 years, most of the tip of the peninsula is now a national park. There's a visitors centre (☎ 5984 4276) where an entrance fee of $8.50 is payable. There are walking tracks or you can use the tractor-drawn transporter. Cheviot Beach, at the end of the peninsula, is where the Australian prime minister Harold Holt went for a swim in 1967 and was never seen again.

The Ocean Coast

The southern and eastern coasts of the peninsula face Bass Strait and Western Port bay. Walking tracks run all the way from London Bridge to Cape Schanck and Bushrangers Bay. Some stretches of the **Peninsula Coastal Walk** are along the beach (some are cut at high tide), and in its entirety the walk extends for more than 30km and takes at least 12 hours. The walk can be done in stages because the park is narrow and accessible at various points.

Cape Schanck is marked by the 1859 lighthouse and there are good walking possibilities around the cape. The rugged coast farther east towards **Flinders** and **West Head** has many natural features including a blowhole. Resort towns such as Flinders and

Hastings on this coast are not quite as crowded in the summer as those on Port Phillip Bay. There are dozens of good surf beaches – mostly beach breaks along Bass Strait, and mostly reef breaks in Western Port bay.

Off the coast in Western Port is **French Island**, once a prison farm, which is virtually undeveloped, although there are a few camp sites and a lodge. Koalas were introduced some years ago, and the thriving colony provides top-ups for depleted areas elsewhere in Victoria. The French Island Ferry (☎ 018 553 136) operates daily between Stony Point and Tankerton Jetty on French Island ($15.50 return).

PHILLIP ISLAND

At the entrance to Western Port, 137km south-east of Melbourne, Phillip Island is a very popular holiday island. Its main attractions are its excellent surf beaches and the famous (although somewhat commercialised) penguin parade. The island is joined to the mainland by a bridge from San Remo to Newhaven.

Orientation & Information

Cowes, the main town, is on the northern side of the island and has most facilities including banks, plus a good range of eateries and places to stay. The southern side of the island has surf beaches such as Woolamai, Cat Bay and Summerland, which is the home of the penguin parade.

There is an information centre (☎ 5956 7447) in Newhaven just after you cross the bridge to the island. It is open daily from 9 am to 5 pm (in summer to 6 pm).

Penguin Parade

Every evening at Summerland Beach in the south-west of the island, the tiny penguins which nest here perform their 'parade', emerging from the sea and waddling resolutely up the beach to their nests – totally oblivious of the thousands of sightseers. The penguins are there year-round but arrive in far larger numbers in the summer when they are rearing their young.

The parade takes place like clockwork a few minutes after sunset each day; it's a major tourist attraction. There are huge crowds so advance bookings should be made through either the tourist office, or the Penguin Reserve (☎ 5956 8300).

To protect the penguins everything is

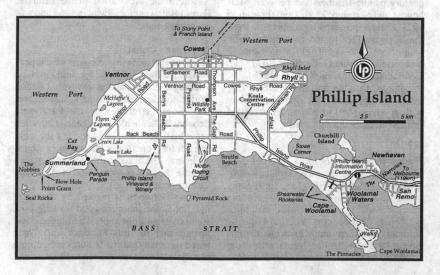

strictly regimented – keep to the viewing areas, don't get in the penguins' way and no camera flashes. There's a visitors centre with a walk-through simulated underwater display ($9, $4 children, family $24).

Wildlife Reserves

The **Phillip Island Wildlife Park**, on Thompson Ave about 1km south of Cowes, is a well-designed park with wallabies, wombats, emus and other native birds and animals. It's open daily from 9 am to dusk ($8, children $4). The **Koala Conservation Centre** at Fiveways on the Phillip Island Tourist Rd is open from 10 am to dusk ($5, children $2).

Seals & Shearwaters

A colony of fur seals inhabits **Seal Rocks**, off Point Grant at the island's south-western tip. There's a timber boardwalk along the foreshore and you can view the seals through coin-in-the-slot binoculars from the kiosk on the headland. The group of rocks closest to the island is called the **Nobbies**.

Phillip Island also has colonies of shearwaters, particularly in the sand dunes around Cape Woolamai. These birds, also known as mutton birds, are amazingly predictable; they arrive back on the island on exactly the same day each year – 24 September – from their migratory flight from Japan and Alaska.

Other Attractions

The island's old motor-racing circuit has been revamped and the **Australian 500cc Motorcycle Grand Prix** race is held here, usually around the beginning of October.

There are plenty of impressive walking tracks around the island at places such as rugged **Cape Woolamai**. Maps and brochures are available from the tourist office.

Churchill Island is a small island with a restored house and beautiful gardens. It was here in 1801 that the first building was constructed here by European settlers in Victoria. The island is connected to Phillip Island by a footbridge and the turn-off is signposted about 1km out of Newhaven. It's

open daily from 10 am to 4 pm ($5, children $2).

Organised Tours, Flights & Cruises

Island Scenic Tours (☎ 5952 1042) runs trips most evenings from Cowes to the penguin parade ($17, which includes entry). It also has three-hour scenic tours ($25) and five-hour tours of the island and various attractions ($35, including entrance fees). Amaroo Park Backpackers Inn (see Places to Stay) also runs trips to the penguin parade.

Phillip Island airport (☎ 5956 7316) operates scenic flights. Bay Connection (☎ 5952 3501) runs cruises to Seal Rocks ($35) and French Island ($40) from the Cowes jetty, as well as evening 'shearwater cruises' ($25) from San Remo, November through to March, when shearwaters (mutton birds) are in the area.

Places to Stay

Camping & Hostels The very friendly *Amaroo Park YHA Hostel* (☎ 5952 2548) on the corner of Church and Osborne Sts in Cowes is a good caravan park and YHA hostel. Dorms cost $13, twins $32 and tent sites $6. Cheap meals are available and there's a bar. It hires out bikes and will organise trips to the penguin parade and Wilsons Prom. The V/Line drivers all know this place and will usually drop you off at the door.

There are another half a dozen caravan parks, including *Kaloha Holiday Resort* (☎ 5952 2179) on the corner of Chapel and Steele Sts, which is about 200m from the beach and close to the centre.

Other Accommodation The *Isle of Wight Hotel* (☎ 5952 2301) on the Esplanade in the centre of Cowes has hotel rooms from $35/45 or motel units from $42/52. Not quite so central is the *Glen Isla Motel* (☎ 5952 2822) at 234 Church St (about 2km from the main street), where double rooms cost $40 to $80. A more upmarket option is the central *Continental* (☎ 5952 2316) at 5 The Esplanade, where double rooms cost $50 to $140. *Rhylston Park Historic Homestead*

(☎ 5952 2730), 190 Thompson Ave about 1km from the centre of Cowes, is a restored 1886 homestead with period-style guestrooms and B&B from $87 a double.

Places to Eat

Thompson Ave and the Esplanade in Cowes both have a good range of eateries. There are the usual takeaways, and at least three BYO pizza/pasta restaurants. The *Isle of Wight Hotel* has good-value counter meals and a buffet restaurant upstairs. Better again is the *Jetty*, on the corner of Thompson Ave and the Esplanade. This place is by no means cheap but the food is very good – especially the seafood.

Getting There & Away

Bus Amaroo Park Backpackers runs a free courtesy bus to the island, leaving from the YHA's Queensberry Hill Hostel in North Melbourne and outside the Coffee Palace on Grey St, Kilda, every Tuesday and Friday in the early afternoon; you should book (☎ 5952 2548).

V/Line has a daily train/bus service to Phillip Island (Cowes) via Dandenong. The trip takes 2¼ hours and costs $13.40.

Getting Around

There is no public transport around the island. Phillip Island Bike Hire (☎ 5952 2381), 11 Findlay St, Cowes, charges $6 for the first hour or $14 a day.

Great Ocean Road

For over 300km from Torquay (a short distance south of Geelong) to Warrnambool, the Great Ocean Road provides some of the most spectacular coastal scenery in Australia. The road, which took 14 years (1918-32) to complete, was built as a memorial to the soldiers who died in WWI. For most of the distance

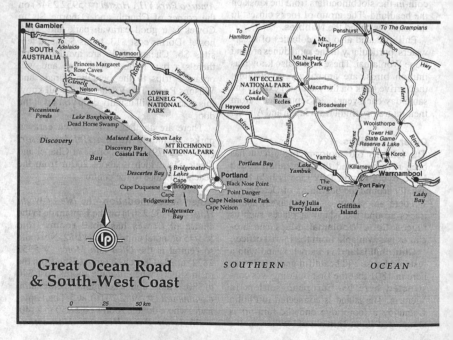

Great Ocean Road & South-West Coast

it hugs the coastline. Between Anglesea, Lorne and Apollo Bay the road features the beautiful contrast of the ocean beaches on one side and the forests and mountains of the Otway Ranges on the other. Farther west is Port Campbell National Park, with its amazing collection of rock formations.

If the seaside activities pall, you can always turn inland to the bushwalks, wildlife, scenery, waterfalls and lookouts of the Otway Ranges.

Surfing

Let's face it, surfing was the original cool activity and while other fads come and go surfing remains *numero uno*. But unless you were born near a surf beach it's impossible to learn, right? Wrong. Go Ride a Wave (☎ 5263 2111) teaches absolute beginners (including people with disabilities and even Poms) how to surf. The schools are at Lorne, Torquay and Anglesea on weekends and school and public holidays from November to April. Lessons cost $20 and most people learn to stand on a board after just one lesson. All instructors are qualified surf lifesavers.

Organised Tours

Various backpacker-oriented tours run through the area, including the Wayward Bus (see the earlier Victoria Getting There & Away section), Autopia and Mac's (see Organised Tours in the Victoria Getting Around section).

The Bells Beach Hostel (in Torquay) has a good three-day package from Melbourne, including transport, dorm accommodation, free entry to Surfworld, a trip to the Twelve Apostles plus either a surfing lesson (tour price $119), diving with seals ($142) or a short flight in a Tiger Moth biplane ($171). Wild-Life tours (☎ 5349 5086) has a variety of tours which include the Great Ocean Road, from one day ($75) to a four-day tour based in Warrnambool ($99 plus food and accommodation).

VICTORIA

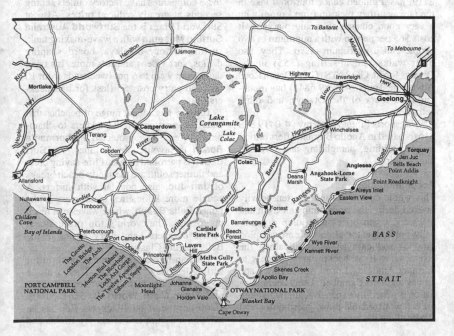

Otway Discovery Tours (☎ 9654 5432) runs day tours from Melbourne visiting many of the attractions for $50. Melbourne Sightseeing (☎ 9663 3388) has a wide range of day trips to Phillip Island, the Great Ocean Road and other destinations around Victoria, and offers discounts to YHA members.

If you get to the area under your own steam there are some good options. Eco-Logic (☎ 5263 1133) runs various educational trips, such as the Possum Prowl Nightwalk and the Creatures of the Night Rockpool Ramble costing as little as $5 (they also have daytime trips, but with less interesting names!).

Great Ocean Road Adventure Tours (☎ 5289 6841), based in Aireys Inlet, runs a range of activities, including cycling and canoeing. Blazing Saddles (☎ 5289 7322), based in Aireys Inlet, has various horse-riding tours, including a two-hour beach ride for $30.

Otwild Adventures (☎ 5289 1740 or 526 2119) has a guided canoe tour on a lake in the Otways (they pick up from Lorne) with a very good chance of seeing platypus. It costs $65 per person with a minimum of two people and a maximum of six. They also offer walks and abseiling ($55) in the Otways forest. GORATS (Great Ocean Road Adventure Tours; ☎ 5289 6841) has mountain-bike tours of the Otways, and other activities.

Wingsports Flight Academy (☎ 0419 378 616) is based in Apollo Bay and offers tuition in hang-gliding, paragliding and powered hang-gliding.

Accommodation

This whole coastal stretch is often heavily booked during the peak summer season and at Easter, when prices also jump dramatically. For budget travellers there are camping grounds and caravan parks all along the coast, as well as backpackers' hostels at Torquay, Anglesea, Lorne, Apollo Bay, Cape Otway and Port Campbell. Other accommodation is generally expensive, although there are a few affordable pubs, guesthouses and B&Bs along the route.

Getting There & Away

V/Line buses run from Melbourne to Geelong and then along the Great Ocean Road as far as Apollo Bay ($26.10) via Torquay ($10.90) and Lorne ($21.30) Monday to Friday three times daily, and on weekends twice-daily. On Friday (and Monday during December and January), a V/Line bus continues from Apollo Bay to Port Campbell ($37.80) and Warrnambool ($33.20).

McHarry's Bus Lines (☎ 5223 2111) has frequent bus services from Geelong to Torquay ($4.35).

TORQUAY (pop 5000)

On the coast 22km due south of Geelong, Torquay is a bustling holiday town and the capital of Australia's booming surfing industry. There are about a dozen surf shops in town, with the big names like Rip Curl and Quicksilver based at the **Surfworld Plaza** complex on the Surfcoast Highway. Both these companies have factory outlets selling seconds at greatly reduced prices. Also at Surfworld Plaza is the **Surfworld Australia Surfing Museum** with a wave-making tank, surfing history displays, board shaping demos, surf videos and lots more. It's open daily from 9 am to 5 pm (weekends from 10 am) and entry costs $6 (less for backpackers).

Torquay has a great range of beaches that cater for everyone from paddlers to champion surfers. The protected **Fisherman's Beach** is favoured by families, the **Surf Beach** is patrolled by a surf life-saving club, and farther south are the sandy beach breaks of **Jan Juc**, also popular with surfers. A couple more kilometres south-west is the famed **Bells Beach**, where waves can reach up to 6m. The world's top professional surfers compete here every Easter in the Bells Surfing Classic.

You can hire surfing gear or book in for surfing lessons at Surfworld. There's also a good golf course at the western end of town, and **Tiger Moth World** (☎ 5261 5100), 10km north-east on Blackgate Rd, has an aviation museum and offers joy flights and tours to the Twelve Apostles. For a short flight to Bells Beach the charge is $100 ($70 for backpackers) and you might get the odd loop and roll. You can also arrange tandem parachute jumps.

The **Surf Coast Walk** follows the coastline from Jan Juc to Aireys Inlet. The full distance takes about 11 hours, but can be done in stages. The Shire of Barrabool puts out a useful leaflet, available from tourist offices in the area.

Midway between Torquay and Anglesea there's a turn-off to **Point Addis** and the **Ironbark Basin**, a coastal nature reserve with some good walking tracks including the Koori Cultural Walk, an Aboriginal heritage trail.

Places to Stay

There are four caravan parks, including the big council-run *Torquay Public Reserve* (☎ 5261 2496) near the Surf Beach, with sites ($17 to $26) and cabins ($45 to $85); and *Zeally Bay Caravan Park* (☎ 5261 2400) near Fisherman's Beach, with tent sites ($13 to $18) and vans ($35 to $58).

There's a good new hostel, *Nomads Bells Beach Hostel* (☎ 5261 7070; email nomads @dove.mtx.net.au) near Surfworld at 51-53 Surfcoast Highway. Dorms are $17 and doubles $20. There's disabled access.

The *Torquay Hotel/Motel* (☎ 5261 6046) at 36 Bell St has motel units from $65/70 a single/double, and at 35 The Esplanade the *Surf City Motel* (☎ 5261 3492) charges from $80/90, up to $125 in season.

Places to Eat

There are numerous cafes and takeaways along Gilbert St (the main shopping centre). *Tapas Café* at No 14 is good for coffee or a snack, and farther down there's *Yummy Yoghurt*, a health-food cafe with good sandwiches, smoothies, felafels and cakes. Around the corner on Pearl St, *Pearly's* has been recommended as a good budget place.

Head to *Micha's*, 23 The Esplanade, for Mexican food, or try the *Torquay Thai Restaurant* at 45 Surfcoast Highway for Thai food. *Esperia Fish & Chips* on Bell St sells

the usual takeaways plus 'roovlakis', souvlakis made with kangaroo meat ($4.50).

ANGLESEA (pop 1995)

Anglesea, 16km south-west of Torquay, is another family-oriented seaside resort with good beaches and camping grounds. Backed by low hills, it's built around the Anglesea River.

The scenic Anglesea Golf Club is home to a large population of kangaroos that graze on the fairways, especially in the early morning and late afternoon. It's quite a sight. The entrance to the golf club is off Noble St.

The river has trout and bream, and to learn how to catch them contact Anglesea Outdoors & Angling (☎ 041 738 3656; 5263 3021 AH).

Places to Stay

Anglesea has three caravan parks. *Anglesea Family Caravan Park* (☎ 5263 1583), right on the foreshore and beside the river, has tent sites ($15 to $21) and cabins ($45 to $75).

There's a new hostel, *Anglesea Backpackers* (☎ 5263 2664), 40 Noble St, run by a house-proud local surfie. It's spotless, the facilities are good and there's disabled access. Dorms are $15 and a double with en-suite bathroom costs $20 per person. Noble St runs off the main through-road at the bridge over the river and the hostel is two-and-a-bit blocks along. In future there might be deals offering accommodation here and surfing lessons with Go Ride a Wave (see Surfing earlier in this section).

There's also a pub and several motels. On the main road, *Debonair Motel & Guesthouse* (☎ 5263 1440) offers a choice of old-fashioned guesthouse rooms or newer motel units, with tariffs ranging from $60 to $85 a double.

AIREYS INLET (pop 761)

Just south of Anglesea, the Great Ocean Road finally meets the coast and starts its spectacular coastal run. Aireys Inlet, midway between Anglesea and Lorne, is an interesting little town with the **Spit Point Lighthouse**, some fine beaches and walking tracks, a horse-riding ranch, a good pub and a motel.

Accommodation options include *Aireys Inlet Caravan Park* (☎ 5289 6230), with tent sites ($12 to $16) and cabins ($30 to $50). *Bush to Beach B&B* (☎ 5289 6538), a two-storey cedar cottage at 43 Anderson St (a little way east of town) has two en-suite guestrooms and singles/doubles from $60/80 with breakfast, and the owner offers guided nature walks. The *Lighthouse Keepers' Cottages* (☎ 5289 6306) by the lighthouse are available to rent.

The pub has good bistro meals, and the friendly *Ernie's Cantina* has a bar and tasty Tex-Mex tucker, with mains mostly $13 to $16.

AIREYS INLET TO LORNE

South of Aireys, the road is wedged between the ocean (with an excellent, long beach) and steep cliff faces and runs through a series of small townships – **Fairhaven**, **Moggs Creek** and **Eastern View**. Along this stretch there are some architecturally striking houses that seem to be performing amazing balancing acts on the hill side.

In Fairhaven, *Surf Coast Backpackers* (☎ 5289 6886) is close to the beach at 5 Cowan Ave, which meets the Great Ocean Road at the Fairhaven Surf Lifesaving Club. It's a good, new purpose-built place charging $15 ($20 in summer) in dorms.

This section of coast is ideal for hang-gliding, and there are usually one or two to be seen soaring above the road.

LORNE (pop 1082)

The small town of Lorne, 73km from Geelong, was a popular seaside resort even before the Great Ocean Road was built. The mountains behind the town not only provide a spectacular backdrop but also give the town a mild, sheltered climate all year round. Lorne has good beaches and surfing, and there are lovely bushwalks in the vicinity, especially in the Angahook-Lorne State Park. Lorne is the most fashionable resort on the coast, and it has a wide range of accommodation including camping grounds, a

good backpackers' hostel, guesthouses, cottages, and even a glossy resort complex, the Cumberland.

Climb up to **Teddy's Lookout** behind the town for fine views along the coast. The beautiful **Erskine Falls** are also close behind Lorne; you can either drive there (9km) and walk down from the top, or follow the walking trail beside the river, passing Splitter's Falls and Straw Falls on the way. It's about a three-hour walk each way. There are numerous other short and long walks around Lorne.

If you're in Lorne in early January and feeling fit, enter the 'Pub to Pier' swimming race. Some of the huge crowd of competitors take it very seriously, but others just appreciate a long swim in the ocean.

The helpful Lorne Visitor Information Centre (☎ 5289 1152) at 144 Mountjoy Pde is open daily from 9 am to 5 pm.

Places to Stay

Prices soar and the 'no vacancy' signs go out during the summer school-holiday season when half of Melbourne seems to move down to the coast. Even pitching a tent in one of the camp sites can prove difficult at peak periods.

The Lorne Foreshore Committee (☎ 5289 1382) manages four good camping grounds at Lorne. The *Erskine River Section* is pleasantly sited by the river and is right in the thick of things. The *Queens Park Section* is above it all, on the headland overlooking the pier. Tent sites cost from $12 in low season and cabins from $50/60 for two/four people. From late December to late January and at Easter there's a minimum stay of a week, with sites at $160 and cabins $600.

Great Ocean Road Backpackers YHA (☎ 5289 1809) is a collection of modern timber cottages in a bushy hillside setting, with lots of wildlife including possums and birds. The backpackers' section has dorm beds at $15 for YHA members ($23 during summer). There are also cosy, five-bed, self-contained cottages which range seasonally from $95 to $175 a night for two people. The hostel and cottages are up Erskine Ave behind the supermarket, which is where the V/Line bus stops. The same people also have more stylish studio apartments in a historic stone building with good views, from $75 to $165 for two.

The central *Sandridge Motel* (☎ 5289 2180) at 128 Mountjoy Pde has units from $75 to $150 a double, and the friendly *Ocean Lodge Motel* (☎ 5289 1330) at 6 Armytage St has cosy units from $70 to $100. The *Grand Pacific Hotel/Motel* (☎ 5289 1609) opposite the pier has spacious rooms from $55/65 ($90 in summer) – oldish and a bit shabby, but with great views.

Set in spacious grounds on the waterfront, *Erskine House* (☎ 5289 1209) is a 1930s-style guesthouse with bar, restaurant, tennis, croquet and bowling; B&B for singles/doubles ranges from $65/95 to $95/120 – try negotiating in the low season.

There are some great cottages and units for rent in town and in the hills behind Lorne. Contact an agency such as the Great Ocean Road Accommodation Centre (☎ 5289 1800), 136 Mountjoy Pde. Prices are highest from Christmas to late January and at Easter, but with a group they can be affordable. For example, a mid-range four-bedroom house

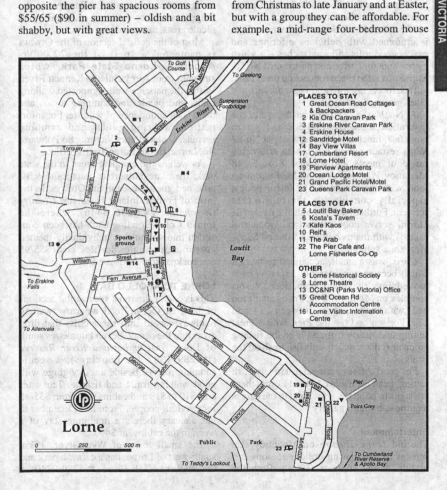

PLACES TO STAY
1 Great Ocean Road Cottages & Backpackers
2 Kia Ora Caravan Park
3 Erskine River Caravan Park
4 Erskine House
12 Sandridge Motel
14 Bay View Villas
17 Cumberland Resort
18 Lorne Hotel
19 Pierview Apartments
20 Ocean Lodge Motel
21 Grand Pacific Hotel/Motel
23 Queens Park Caravan Park

PLACES TO EAT
5 Loutit Bay Bakery
6 Kosta's Tavern
7 Kafe Kaos
10 Reif's
11 The Arab
22 The Pier Cafe and Lorne Fisheries Co-Op

OTHER
8 Lorne Historical Society
9 Lorne Theatre
13 DC&NR (Parks Victoria) Office
15 Great Ocean Rd Accommodation Centre
16 Lorne Visitor Information Centre

Lorne

costs $1025 per week in peak season, dropping by increments to $660 per week in winter. Between eight people that's less than $20 per night per person, even in peak season.

Places to Eat

Lorne is the gastronomic capital of the coast and has some fine (if somewhat pricey) cafes and restaurants along Mountjoy Pde. Most of these are open day and night during the holiday seasons, but you'll find the range more limited in the off season.

The *Loutit Bay Bakery*, 46 Mountjoy Pde, is crammed with delicious offerings and makes good rolls and sandwiches – it's also a great spot for coffee and pastries. At No 50, *Kafe Kaos* is the place for cooked breakfasts, jaffles, foccacias, tofu and vegie burgers and other gourmet goodies.

At No 94, the *Arab* cafe has been a Lorne institution since the mid-50s and serves breakfast, lunch and dinner, while at No 82 *Reif's* restaurant and bar has an affordable range of meals and snacks. *Kosta's*, 48 Mountjoy Pde, serves good Mediterranean food with mains about $18 (a bit pricey, especially considering the indifferent service). Further back towards the river, *The Marine* serves good meals (and wonderful cakes!) with mains between $18 and $25 – great for a splurge.

Chris' was a small, acclaimed restaurant which became considerably larger when it moved into the big Cumberland Resort complex on Mountjoy Pde. Prices aren't too bad, with main courses between $14 and $20. For seafood try the *Pier*, with a great setting and mains from $17, or the fishing co-op next door, which sells fish fresh off the boats.

For good coffee or a meal in a lovely bush setting, head for *Kudos*, behind Lorne; there are signs to point the way. Next to the cafe is a purpose-built art gallery.

Entertainment

The old *Lorne Theatre* on Mountjoy Pde screens movies during holiday seasons and nightly during summer ($7.50). Both the *Lorne Hotel* and the grungy *Grand Pacific Hotel* feature live bands, while *Reif's* restaurant often has live jazz and acoustic music.

OTWAY RANGES

These beautiful coastal ranges provide a spectacular backdrop to the Great Ocean Road, and if you have time it's worth heading inland to explore the area's rainforests, eucalypt forests, streams, waterfalls and walking trails. There are quite a few small and picturesque settlements scattered throughout the ranges, as well as galleries, tearooms, good picnic areas, and even a winery.

Most of the coastal section of the Otways is protected as part of the 22,000ha **Angahook-Lorne State Park**, which stretches from Aireys Inlet to Kennett River. Within the park are well-signposted walking trails, and picnic and camping areas, and there is an abundance of wildlife. For information, walking guides and camping permits, contact Parks Victoria, 86 Polwarth Rd, Lorne, or the Lorne Tourist office.

As well as the camping areas in the state park, there are numerous cottages, B&Bs, pubs and guesthouses in the Otways. In the town of Forrest, inland, is *Forrest Country Guesthouse* (☎ 5236 6446), where the former Colac Bowling Club has been converted into six quirky, individually themed guestrooms. Singles/doubles cost $55/95 and backpackers' beds are $15.

LORNE TO APOLLO BAY

This is one of the most spectacular sections of the Great Ocean Road, a narrow twisting roadway carved into sheer cliffs that drop away into the ocean. Seven kilometres south of Lorne is *Cumberland River Reserve* (☎ 5289 1382 for bookings), a scenic camping reserve beside a rocky gorge with good walking trails and fishing. Tent sites cost $10 to $19 and cabins start from $35/45 for two/four people. From late December to late January there's a minimum stay of a week in the cabins, at $400.

The small town of **Wye River**, 17km south-west of Lorne, has a caravan park and the *Rookery Nook Hotel* (☎ 5289 0240), a great little pub overlooking a pretty bay. On a sunny day the front balcony is a top spot for a meal and/or a drink, and there are simple motel units from $40/50 to $50/90 at peak times.

Twenty kilometres farther on is **Skenes Creek**, from where Skenes Creek Rd climbs steeply and takes you inland into the Otway Ranges. There's a simple camping reserve on the foreshore.

APOLLO BAY (pop 979)
The pretty little port of Apollo Bay, 118km from Geelong, is a fishing town and another popular resort. It's a little more relaxed than Lorne and a lot less trendy and, as well as all the fishing folk, quite a few artists and musicians live in and around the town.

The long sandy beaches and the surrounding Otway Ranges are the main attractions. There's a small **historical museum** (open afternoons on weekends and during holidays) and the Wingsports Flight Academy (☎ 5237 6486), a hang-gliding and paragliding school is based nearby. **Mariners Lookout**, a few kilometres from town, provides stunning views along the coast.

The tourist information centre (☎ 5237 6529), 155 Great Ocean Road, is open daily from 9 am to 5 pm. Enquire about nearby horse-riding ranches and boats offering cruises and/or fishing expeditions.

Places to Stay
There are five caravan parks. These include the *Recreation Reserve* (☎ 5237 6577), on the Great Ocean Road less than 1km from the centre of town. Tent sites cost from $12 to $15 (for up to four people) and vans from $25 to $40.

The new *Apollo Bay Backpackers*, also known as the *Bunkhouse* (no phone yet), is just a small house on the corner of Montrose Ave and Hobson St. It could be nice. *Surfside Backpackers YHA* (☎ 5237 7263) is close to the beach at 7 Gambier St. It charges around $12 ($15 at peak times) in dorms and from $35 for a double. Currently it's a house, but a purpose-built section should be built soon.

The *Apollo Bay Hotel* (☎ 5237 6250) in the centre of town has motel units from $45/55 to $60/65, and *Bayside Gardens* (☎ 5237 6248) at 219 Great Ocean Road has comfortable self-contained units from $55.

There are plenty of B&Bs in the area. On Tuxion Rd, 1km back from the coast, is the friendly *Lunabella B&B* (☎ 5237 7059), a bright farmhouse on a lovely hillside farmlet. Doubles cost from $85 to $100, which includes a home-cooked breakfast and great views.

The information centre takes accommodation bookings (needed well in advance for December and January) and if you don't want to camp or stay in a hostel, it's worth checking prices for houses or self-contained units. There are some bargains, with some two-bedroom places going for well under $100 a night in peak season and much less at other times. There'll probably be lengthy minimum stays at peak times, though.

Places to Eat
Bay Leaf Deli, in the centre of town at 131 Great Ocean Road, is an excellent gourmet deli with great coffee, breakfasts and homemade meals, while farther along at No 61, *Wholefoods Deli* is a health-food shop with soup, rolls, felafels and more. *Buff's Bistro*, nearby at No 51, is a bustling bistro that is open nightly (except Sunday) and has tasty and interesting mains from $15.

The *Apollo Bay Hotel* has bar meals from $6.50 and also a bistro. For a splurge, head for the stylish *Beaches Restaurant & Bar* at the Greenacres Country House – there is live jazz or acoustic music most nights in the piano lounge.

CAPE OTWAY
From Apollo Bay the road temporarily leaves the coast to climb up and over Cape Otway. The coast is particularly beautiful and rugged on this stretch, but it is dangerous and there have been many shipwrecks.

The forest-covered cape is still relatively untouched, and the scenic **Otway National Park** has walking trails and picnic areas at Elliot River, Shelly Beach and Blanket Bay; Blanket Bay also has a good camping ground. Although many of the roads through the park are unsurfaced and winding, they present no problems for the average car.

There are a number of scenic lookouts and nature reserves just off the main road. At the **Maits Rest Rainforest Boardwalk**, about 13km past Apollo Bay, you can stroll along an elevated boardwalk through a spectacular rainforest gully. A little farther on, an unsealed road heads north to the town of Beech Forest via **Hopetoun Falls** and **Beauchamps Falls**, while 7km farther on, another unsealed road heads 15km south to Cape Otway itself. The 1848 convict-built **Cape Otway Lighthouse** towers nearly 100m above a remote and windswept headland. The lighthouse and grounds are open daily and there are tours ($5). Contact Parks Victoria (☎ 5237 9240) for times, as they change.

After passing through the fertile Horden Vale flatlands, the Great Ocean Road meets the coast briefly at **Glenaire** before heading north to the tiny township of **Lavers Hill**, once a thriving timber centre. Six kilometres north of Glenaire is the turn-off to **Johanna**, which has camping and good surfing. Five kilometres south-west of Lavers Hill is the pretty little **Melba Gully State Park**, with its beautiful rainforest ferns, glow-worms and one of the area's last remaining giant gums – it's over 27m in circumference and more than 300 years old.

Farther south is **Moonlight Head**, starting point for the **Shipwreck Trail** – the treacherous coastline from here to Port Fairy is known as the Shipwreck Coast. At **Princetown**, the road rejoins the coast and runs along it through the spectacular Port Campbell National Park (see later in this section).

Places to Stay

Bimbi Park (☎ 5237 9246) is a camping ground and horse-riding ranch that offers trail rides through the national park and along the coast. Tent sites cost between $10 and $13 and there are cabins from $65 for four people. Bimbi Park is off the Cape Otway lighthouse road, about 7km after you turn off the Great Ocean Road. At Blanket Bay, also off the lighthouse road, there's a camping ground with picnic and barbecue facilities.

At *Cape Otway Lighthouse* (☎ 5237 9240), the former lighthouse keeper's sandstone cottage sleeps eight people and there are also studio apartments. All are fully equipped but BYO food. Two nights (the minimum) midweek cost $180 for two people, $330 for four; weekends (Friday, Saturday and Sunday nights) cost $245 for two and $445 for four. Prices drop in winter.

The *Shell Roadhouse* (☎ 5237 3251) in Lavers Hill has tent sites from $12 and basic bunk rooms at $20/40.

PORT CAMPBELL NATIONAL PARK

This narrow coastal park stretches through low heathlands from Moonlight Head to Peterborough. There's a Parks Victoria Information Centre (☎ 5598 6382) in Port Campbell.

This is the most famous section of the Great Ocean Road and features dramatic coastal scenery, including the bizarre rock formations known as the **Twelve Apostles**, huge stone pillars that soar out of the pounding surf (only seven of which can be seen from the lookouts). Nearby you can visit the 1869 **Glenample Homestead** (where the survivors of the famed *Loch Ard* shipwreck recovered) and check out their interesting maritime history displays. The homestead's original owner built **Gibson's Steps**, which lead down to an often treacherous beach.

Loch Ard Gorge has a sad tale to tell: in 1878 the iron-hulled clipper *Loch Ard* was driven onto the rocks offshore. Of the 50 or so on board only two were to survive – an apprentice officer and an Irish immigrant woman, both aged 18. They were swept into the narrow gorge now named after their ship. Although the papers of the time tried to inspire a romance between the two survivors, the woman, the sole survivor of a family of eight, soon made her way back to Ireland's safer climes. This was the last immigrant sailing ship to founder en route to Australia.

A little farther along the coast is **Port Campbell**, the main town in the area and,

The Shipwreck Coast
The Victorian coastline between Cape Otway and Port Fairy was a notoriously dangerous stretch of water in the days when sailing ships were the major form of transport. Navigation of Bass Strait was exceptionally difficult due to numerous barely hidden reefs and frequent heavy fog. More than 80 vessels came to grief on this 120km stretch in only 40 years.

The most famous wreck was that of the *Loch Ard* (see Port Campbell National Park in this chapter). Another was the *Falls of Halladale*, a Glasgow barque that ran aground in 1908 en route from New York to Melbourne. There were no casualties, but it lay on the reef, fully rigged and with sails set, for a couple of months.

Other vessels that came to grief included the *Newfield* in 1892 and *La Bella* in 1905.

All these wrecks have been investigated by divers, and relics are on display in the Flagstaff Hill Maritime Village in Warrnambool. ■

again, sited on a spectacular gorge. Port Campbell itself is nothing special, but it has a pleasant beach and calm waters, a good range of accommodation, and the **Loch Ard Shipwreck Museum**. Port Campbell Boat Charters (☎ 5598 6463) offers 1½-hour scenic tours to the Twelve Apostles and Bay of Islands ($30), fishing trips ($50 for four hours), and scuba-diving trips ($35 for one dive, $60 for two and $25 if you just want to snorkel). There's a dive shop in Lord St where you can hire gear.

Beyond Port Campbell, **London Bridge**, a bridge-like promontory arching across a furious sea, was once a famous landmark along this coast, but in 1990 it collapsed dramatically into the sea, stranding a handful of amazed – and extremely lucky – visitors at the far end. Other formations include the **Crown of Thorns** and, 8km past **Peterborough**, the beautiful **Bay of Islands**. After the bay the Great Ocean Road veers away from the coast and heads inland to Warrnambool, where it joins the Princes Highway.

Places to Stay
In Port Campbell, the *Port Campbell Caravan Park* (☎ 5598 6492) in Tregea St overlooks the gorge and has tent sites ($10 to $20) and cabins. Across the road the straightforward *Port Campbell YHA Hostel* (☎ 5598 6305) has dorm beds for $12. There are four motels to choose from, and the *Port Campbell Hotel* (☎ 5598 6320) will have

accommodation when the renovations are completed.

Macka's Farm (☎ 5598 8261), a working dairy farm about 5km inland from the Twelve Apostles, offers self-contained units from $85 a double (more in school holidays), while 3km inland from the Twelve Apostles is the friendly *Apostles View Motel* (☎ 5598 8277), with good motel units on a pleasant little farm costing $55 to $90.

Peterborough has a good riverside caravan park and the *Shomberg Inn Hotel* (☎ 5598 5285) has motel units out the back from $35/40 to $45/50.

Getting There & Away
V/Line runs from Melbourne to Port Campbell for $37.80.

South-West

The Great Ocean Road ends 12km east of Warrnambool where it meets the Princes Highway, which continues westwards towards South Australia. This stretch of Victoria's south-west coastline includes some of the earliest European settlements in the state.

You'll notice a tourist drive called the Mary MacKillop Trail in the area. Mary MacKillop founded an order of nuns, the Sisters of St Joseph, in the 1860s. The Vatican is expected to declare her Australia's first saint, after a very long process has been finished.

WARRNAMBOOL (pop 26,052)

Warrnambool is 264km from Melbourne and has sheltered beaches as well as surf beaches. It's the major town along the western coast, and a pleasant place in summer.

The tourist information centre (☎ 5564 7837) at 600 Raglan Pde is open daily from 9 am to 5 pm; you can pick up the useful *Warrnambool Visitors Handbook* and the *Heritage Trail* brochure.

Things to See

Gun emplacements intended to repel a Russian invasion that Australia feared in the 1880s can be seen near the lighthouse. This is now the site of the **Flagstaff Hill Maritime Village**, with a museum, restored sailing ships, maritime films, and port buildings of the era. It's open daily from 9 am to 5 pm ($9.50, students $8, children $4.50).

The **Warrnambool Art Gallery** on Timor St has a good collection of Australian art and is open Tuesday to Friday from noon to 5 pm ($3). Other attractions include the attractive **botanic gardens** on the corner of Queen and Cockman Sts; the **Lake Pertobe Adventure Playground** for kids (great flying foxes); and the National Trust classified **Proudfoot's Boathouse** on the Hopkins River, with a restaurant and tearooms (serving great scones!). **Hopkins Falls**, known locally as 'mini Niagara', are 13km north-east of Warrnambool.

The **Mahogany Walking Trail**, which starts at the Thunder Point coastal reserve, is a 22km coastal walk to Port Fairy, taking you past the possible site of the fabled Mahogany Ship. Historians have speculated that the shipwreck, of which there were numerous reported sightings between 1836 and 1870, could have been part of a secret Portuguese expedition in 1522. The search continues: if the Mahogany Ship is ever found Australian history would have to be rewritten.

The southern coast around Port Fairy and Warrnambool is where the **southern right**

whales *(Eubalagna glacialis)* come in large numbers every May or June, staying until around October. Whales have been sighted yearly off the Victorian coast since 1970, and at Logans Beach since 1982. By 1940 it was estimated that there were fewer than 1000 southern right whales left. Although the species has been protected since 1935, today it still numbers only about 1200 to 1500.

Places to Stay

Surfside Holiday Park (☎ 5561 2611) on Pertobe Rd is right on the beach, less than 1km south of the centre. Tent sites cost $13 to $23 and cabins from $40 to $75. Also on Pertobe Rd, the *Lady Bay Hotel* (☎ 5562 1544) has units from $30/40 to $40/50.

A good new hostel has opened at 17 Stanley St, close to the beach. *Great Ocean Road Backpackers* (☎ 5562 4874) is a member of the Nomad chain and has a huge lounge area, complete with a bar, dance floor and jukebox. Comfy bunks cost $15 and there are a couple of doubles for $30. There are disabled facilities. They offer horse-riding, with an overnight trip to Port Fairy (camping by the beach in a secluded bay) and there should by now be free bikes and fishing rods. And there's a friendly half-dingo called Cassie.

The *Stuffed Backpacker* (☎ 5562 2459), above Flaherty's chocolate shop at 52 Kepler St, is cheap at $12 a night, $30 a double including a light breakfast, and apple pie and ice cream at night.

One of the best of the many motels is the *Olde Maritime Motor Inn* (☎ 5561 1415) on Merri St opposite Flagstaff Hill; standard units are $75, suites cost $90 to $130. There are also numerous B&Bs in and around Warrnambool – check with the tourist office.

Places to Eat

Most of the eateries are along Liebig St, including the excellent *Fishtales Café* at No 63, with great value fish & chips, burgers (a huge range), Thai and vegetarian meals, foccacia and more. Next door, *Bojangles* is

VICTORIA

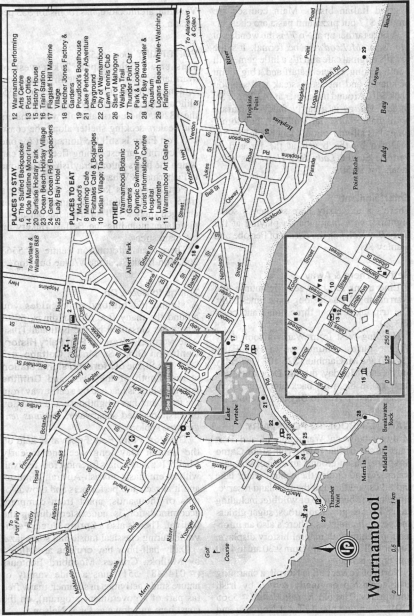

PLACES TO STAY
6 The Stuffed Backpacker
14 Olde Maritime Motor Inn
20 Surfside Holiday Park
23 Ocean Beach Holiday Village
24 Great Ocean Rd Backpackers
25 Lady Bay Hotel

PLACES TO EAT
7 McLeod's
8 Merribjo Cafe
9 Fishtales Cafe & Bojangles
10 Indian Village; Taco Bill

OTHER
1 Warrnambool Botanic
   Gardens
2 Olympic Swimming Pool
3 Tourist Information Centre
4 Hospital
5 Laundrette
11 Warrnambool Art Gallery

12 Warrnambool Performing
   Arts Centre
13 Post Office
15 History House
16 Train Station
17 Flagstaff Hill Maritime
   Village
18 Fletcher Jones Factory &
   Gardens
19 Proudfoot's Boathouse
21 Lake Pertobe Adventure
   Playground
22 City of Warrnambool
   Lawn Tennis Club
26 Start of Mahogany
   Walking Trail
27 Thunder Point Car
   Park & Lookout
28 Lady Bay Breakwater &
   Aquarium
29 Logans Beach Whale-Watching
   Platform

Warrnambool

a good Italian bistro. Main courses are around $17 but pizza and pasta are cheaper.

A little farther up at No 77 is the wonderful *Mac's*, or *McLeod's* to be formal. It's the town's original cafe and it's a little gem, with booth seating, efficient staff and a big menu of snacks and meals. A steak will set you back $10. Around the corner at 142 Timor St, *Indian Village* is a fairly fancy restaurant with main courses around $11, but sometimes has all-you-can-eat lunches for $7.50.

Down by the beach at the far end of Pertobe St, the *Lady Bay Hotel* has good meals for $6.50.

Entertainment
There's a university here so there's some nightlife, with major bands playing at the *Lady Bay Hotel* on the corner of Pertobe and Stanley Sts.

Getting There & Away
V/Line trains run between Melbourne and Warrnambool via Geelong three times daily. The trip takes about three hours and costs $33.20.

Heading west from Warrnambool, daily V/Line buses continue on to Port Fairy ($4.20) and Mt Gambier ($26.10). On Friday only (and Monday during December and January), a bus runs back along the Great Ocean Road to Apollo Bay and Geelong.

WARRNAMBOOL TO PORT FAIRY
Midway between Warrnambool and Port Fairy is the 614ha **Tower Hill State Game Reserve**, based around an extinct volcanic crater. A road circles the central crater lake and takes you through the bushland reserve, home to an abundance of wildlife, including emus, koalas, grey kangaroos, sugar gliders and peregrine falcons. There's also an information centre with natural history displays. Tower Hill is open daily from 9.30 am to 4.30 pm; entry is free.

North of Tower Hill is **Koroit**, a charming little township originally settled by Irish immigrants. The old *Koroit Hotel* (☎ 5565 8201), a unique blend of Art Nouveau and Victorian architecture, has rooms for $35 per person.

PORT FAIRY (pop 2625)
This small fishing port 27km west of Warrnambool was one of the first European settlements in the state, dating back to 1835, although there were temporary visitors from the 1820s. These first arrivals were whalers and sealers seeking shelter along the coast, and Port Fairy is still the home port for one of Victoria's largest fishing fleets. You can watch the boats unload crayfish and abalone at Fisherman's Wharf.

Port Fairy was known as Belfast for a time, and although the name was later changed there's still an Irish flavour about the place, including the Belfast Bakery on the main street.

There's an information centre (☎ 5568 2682) on Bank St, at the V/Line bus stop.

Things to See & Do
A signposted **history walk** guides you around the many fine old buildings, 50 of which are classified by the National Trust. Also worth a look are the **Port Fairy History Centre** on Gipps St, **Mott's Cottage** at 5 Sackville St, the **old fort and signal station** at the mouth of the river, and **Griffiths Island**, which is reached by a causeway from the town and has a lighthouse and a mutton bird (short-tailed shearwater, *Puffinus tenuirostris*) colony.

The **Port Fairy Folk Festival** is held on the Labour Day long weekend in early March. It's Australia's foremost folk festival, with an emphasis on Irish-Australian music, and it attracts top performers and crowds of tens of thousands; apart from camping, accommodation is nonexistent during the festival. There's also a **Spring Music Festival** featuring classical music and some jazz.

Daily half-hour bay **cruises** are offered by Mulloka Cruises. Moonbird Ecotours (☎ 014 481 551) runs a wide variety of nature study activities in summer, many free (as part of a government program), on the coast here and down as far as Nelson.

RICHARD I'ANSON

BETHUNE CARMICHAEL

Victoria
Top: The Melbourne skyline from Southgate
Bottom: Melbourne's delightful Royal Botanic Gardens

Victoria

Top Left: Rifle Brigade Hotel, Bendigo
Top Right: Sovereign Hill, Ballarat

Bottom Left: Wilson's Promontory
Bottom Right: Mt Speculation

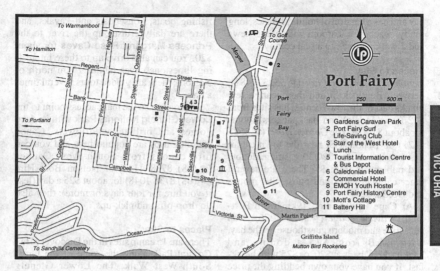

Port Fairy

0   250   500 m

1 Gardens Caravan Park
2 Port Fairy Surf
   Life-Saving Club
3 Star of the West Hotel
4 Lunch
5 Tourist Information Centre
   & Bus Depot
6 Caledonian Hotel
7 Commercial Hotel
8 EMOH Youth Hostel
9 Port Fairy History Centre
10 Mott's Cottage
11 Battery Hill

VICTORIA

Places to Stay & Eat

Gardens Caravan Park (☎ 5568 1060), Griffith St, is close to the beach; tent sites cost $12 to $14, and cabins $50 to $70.

The comfortable *EMOH YHA Hostel* (☎ 5568 2468), a stately little historic building at 8 Cox St, has a range of bunk rooms and newer units and charges from $13 a night.

There's also the old *Star of the West Hotel* (☎ 5568 1715) on the corner of Bank and Sackville Sts, with B&B for $20 per person and backpackers' beds for $12.

Port Fairy has a good collection of guesthouses, B&Bs and cottages for rent. The information centre has a full list and can make bookings. If you arrive after hours there's a list and a map in the window.

Lunch, beside the tourist office in Bank St, is an excellent gourmet deli serving breakfasts and lunches – highly recommended. Meals are available at five pubs.

Getting There & Away

Daily V/Line buses run between Warrnambool and Port Fairy ($4.20), continuing on to Mt Gambier in one direction and Melbourne ($35.40) in the other.

PORTLAND (pop 9664)

Portland is Victoria's oldest town. Whalers knew this stretch of coast long before the first permanent settlement was established here in 1834, and there were even earlier short-term visitors. Nowadays the town is a strange blend of the historic and the industrial, with its deep-water port, aluminium smelter, gardens and historic bluestone buildings.

The very helpful tourist information office (☎ 5523 2671; 1800 035 567) is in the old watch house on Cliff St. There's a Parks Victoria office (☎ 5523 1180) at 8 Julia St.

Things to See

Points of interest include **Burswood Homestead & Gardens**, 15 Cape Nelson Rd; the **botanic gardens** in Cliff St; a **historical museum** in Charles St; the **Powerhouse Car Museum** on the corner of Glenelg and Percy Sts; and the **old watch house** in Cliff St.

Eleven kilometres south of Portland is the small **Cape Nelson State Park** with some great walks and coastal views and a National Trust classified lighthouse.

Cape Bridgewater, 21km west of Portland, overlooks an idyllic and windswept bay and has a handful of holiday houses, long sandy beaches, a tearoom with great views and a walking track to a seal colony.

Places to Stay
Centenary Caravan Park (☎ 5523 1487), between Bentinck St and the ocean, a few blocks east of the town centre, has sites from $12 (four people) and backpackers' rooms for about $17/23. The *Gordon Hotel* (☎ 5523 1121) on Bentinck St near the town centre has pub rooms for $20/30 a single/double and pub meals from $5. There are several other caravan parks and pubs, plus motels and B&Bs.

At Cape Bridgewater, 19km from Portland, *Seaview Lodge* (☎ 5526 7276) is an attractive and modern guesthouse on the bay, with B&B from $75 a double and backpackers' beds at $20, or $25 with breakfast. If you have your own bedding the price might be a couple of dollars lower. The owners can often pick you up from Portland if you ring in advance.

PORTLAND TO THE SOUTH AUSTRALIAN BORDER
North of Portland, the Princes Highway heads inland. It's the quickest route to Mt Gambier in South Australia, but unless you're in a hurry there is a more interesting road that runs closer to the coast. This route passes a turn-off to the **Mt Richmond National Park** 20km west of Portland, and then runs parallel with the **Discovery Bay Coastal Park**, which incorporates the entire coastline from Cape Bridgewater to Nelson. The 250km **Great South-West Walk** starts in Portland and traverses the park. It's a very rewarding 10-day hike, or you can walk stages of it. Maps and information on the walk are available from the tourist office in Portland.

Fifty-five kilometres north-west of Portland and just before the border is the little township of **Nelson**, right on the Glenelg River and close to the coast. It's a sleepy, unspoilt and old-fashioned holiday and fishing town with a caravan park and a pub as well as a couple of motels. You can hire fishing boats, houseboats and kayaks, and there are daily cruises up the river to the **Princess Margaret Rose Caves** for about $20. You can also drive up to these interesting limestone caves (about 15km north of Nelson); there are guided tours several times a day.

Nelson is also the main access point to the **Lower Glenelg National Park** with its deep gorges and brilliant wildflowers. Canoe camping trips are popular here and you can hire canoes from South-West Canoes (☎ (08) 8738 4141) or Nelson Boat Hire (☎ (08) 8738 4048) for about $25 a day (less if you hire for four days or more); they also do drop-offs and pick-ups.

Places to Stay
There are 15 camp sites in the Discovery Bay Coastal Park along the route of the Great South-West Walk. The Lower Glenelg National Park has a number of very pretty camp sites with minimal facilities; bookings can be made through the information centre (☎ (08) 8738 4051). There are also camp sites and cabins at the Princess Margaret Rose Caves; contact the ranger for bookings (☎ (08) 8738 4171).

In Nelson, *River Vu Caravan Park* (☎ (08) 8738 4123) has tent sites ($14), cabins ($38) and a two-bedroom cottage (from $41 for two). The *Nelson Hotel* (☎ (08) 8738 4011) has straightforward rooms at around $20/30, and the *Pinehaven Chalet Motel* (☎ (08) 8738 4041) has double rooms from $45.

THE WESTERN DISTRICT
The south-west of the state, inland from the coast and stretching to the South Australian border, is particularly affluent sheep-raising and pastoral country. It's also said to be the third-largest volcanic plain in the world, and the area is littered with craters, lakes, lava tubes and other signs of its volcanic past.

Melbourne to Hamilton
On the eastern edge of the Western District is **Colac** (pop 9793) and there are many **volcanic lakes** in the vicinity of the town – a couple of lookouts give excellent views.

There's also a **botanical garden**, a tourist information office (☎ 5231 3730) and the **Colac Historical Centre**.

You can reach Hamilton, the 'capital' of the Western District, via Ballarat and the Glenelg Highway or you can go via Geelong along the Hamilton Highway. On the Glenelg Highway the **Mooramong Homestead** near Skipton is owned by the National Trust and open by appointment. Farther along the highway the small town of **Lake Bolac** is beside a large freshwater lake, a venue for water sports. **Inverleigh** is an attractive little town near Geelong along the Hamilton Highway.

The Princes Highway runs farther south, reaching the coast at Warrnambool. Winchelsea, on the Princes Highway, has **Barwon Park Homestead**, a rambling bluestone National Trust property. The stone Barwon Bridge dates from 1867. You can reach the Grampians from the south on a scenic route from **Dunkeld** on the Glenelg Highway.

Hamilton (pop 9248)

Hamilton is known locally as the 'Wool Capital of the World'. Sculptures at the Commonwealth Bank on Gray St display the relationship between wool and money.

The Hamilton Tourist Information Centre (☎ 5572 3746) is on Lonsdale St.

The impressive **Hamilton Art Gallery**, Brown St, is open daily (afternoons only on weekends). There's also the **History Centre** at 43 Gray St, open Sunday to Friday from 2 to 5 pm, and the **Sir Reginald Ansett Transport Museum** on Ballarat Rd, which is open daily.

The **Big Woolbales** on the Coleraine Rd has displays devoted to promoting the wool industry and things woolly; it's open daily (admission is free). There's a flora and fauna nature trail at Hamilton's **Institute of Rural Learning**, which is also the last refuge of the eastern barred bandicoot *(Perameles gunnii)*, a small, ground-dwelling marsupial.

Fifteen kilometres south of Hamilton is the **Mt Napier State Park**, with some fasci-nating volcanic remnants including the lava tubes of Byaduk Caves and Tunnel Cave.

Places to Stay There are a couple of caravan parks and pubs, including the *Commercial Hotel* (☎ 5572 1078), 145 Thompson Ave, with rooms for $20/33. Historic *Hewlett House* (☎ 5572 2494) at 36 Gray St has B&B from $65/100.

Getting There & Away V/Line has daily buses to Melbourne ($42.90) and also buses to Mt Gambier. There are weekday services south to Warrnambool and north to Horsham.

Mt Eccles National Park

About 45km south of Hamilton, Mt Eccles has numerous volcanic relics including lava caves, vents, craters and the very scenic Lake Surprise. There's a walking trail around the rim of the volcano and several other walks, plus a camping ground – contact the rangers on ☎ 5576 1338.

Lake Condah

Adjoining Mt Eccles, Lake Condah is an important site in the history of local Aboriginal tribes. Part of the legalistic argument behind the concept of *terra nullius*, which the English used to claim Australia as their own, was that as the Aboriginal people were nomads who didn't work the land or have permanent settlements they couldn't be said to have ever 'owned' Australia. The discovery of permanent stone dwellings and a complex system of stone canals and fish traps at Lake Condah proved that Aboriginal people lived here on a semipermanent basis.

During the last century when the Western District 'squattocracy' (land-grabbers who became wealthy pastoralists) quickly cleared the land of its people to begin intensive sheep farming, Lake Condah became the site of an Aboriginal mission. The site is now run by the Kerrup-jmara community, although the original mission buildings have long since disintegrated.

Lake Condah is closed to the public but

ask at the Hamilton information centre if Koori-run tours are in operation yet.

The Wimmera

The Wimmera region, in Victoria's far west, is mostly endless expanses of wheat fields and sheep farms. In the south are the spectacularly scenic mountains of the Grampians National Park. The region's other main points of interest are the Little Desert National Park and Mt Arapiles, Australia's most famous rock-climbing venue.

The main road through the Wimmera is the Western Highway, which is also the busiest route between Melbourne and Adelaide. It passes through Stawell, which is the turn-off point for the Grampians, and Horsham, the major town in the region.

ARARAT (pop 6890)

After a brief flirtation with gold in 1857, Ararat settled down as a farming centre. Its features include the **Langi Morgala Museum** (open weekends from 2 to 4 pm, $2), the **Alexandra Gardens**, an **art gallery** and some fine old bluestone buildings. Ararat's historic (and grisly) **J Ward**, a former prison for the criminally insane, is open for tours on weekdays at 11 am and on Sunday from 11 am to 3 pm ($5/2). The tourist information centre (☎ 5352 2096) is next to the town hall.

Fourteen kilometres east, the **Langi Ghiran State Park** has good walking tracks and climbs, plus a winery.

Places to Stay

Acacia Caravan Park (☎ 5352 2994), around 1km north of the town centre, has tent sites (from $11.50), vans (from $25) and cabins (from $40/45 a single/double). Five pubs on Barkly St have accommodation; cheapest is the *Shire Hall Hotel* (☎ 5352 1280) at $15/25.

On the Western Highway on the northern outskirts, the small *Chalambar Motel*

(☎ 5352 2430) is good value with singles/doubles from $32/38.

GREAT WESTERN

Midway between Ararat and Stawell, the small town of Great Western is at the centre of one of Australia's best known 'champagne' regions. You can tour the old underground cellars at Seppelt's Great Western, and also visit Best's and Garden Gully wineries.

At Allanvale, a sheep property 3km east of Great Western you can stay in restored shearers' quarters (☎ 5356 2201) for $15 per person.

STAWELL (pop 6272)

Stawell, another former gold town, is the turn-off for Halls Gap and the Grampians. The tourist information centre (☎ 1800 246 880), on the Western Highway just before the main turn-off (not the turn-off on the Ballarat/Melbourne edge of town), is the main information centre for the Grampians and has an accommodation booking service. It's open daily.

The town has a number of National Trust classified buildings, but it's best known as the home of the Stawell Gift, Australia's richest foot race, which attracts up to 20,000 visitors every Easter! The **Stawell Gift Hall of Fame** on Main St details the history of the event.

Bunjil's Cave, with Aboriginal rock paintings, is on the Pomonal road 11km south.

Places to Stay

There are two caravan parks and plenty of motels in town and along the highway. *Stawell Holiday Cottages* (☎ 5358 2868) sleeps up to six people and costs from $55 to $65 a double plus $7 for each extra person.

Getting There & Away

Stawell is on the Melbourne-Adelaide bus route and train line ($30.70 economy). The *Overland* train from Melbourne gets into Stawell at 1.43 am, but you'll be able to sleep in as the V/Line bus from Stawell to Halls Gap ($7.30) doesn't leave until 11.45 am

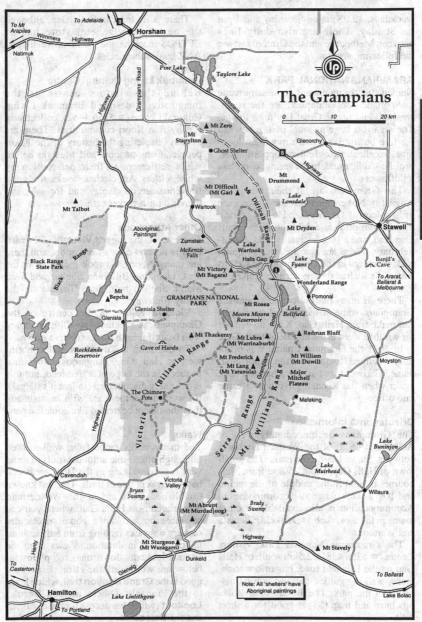

The Grampians

0   10   20 km

Note: All 'shelters' have Aboriginal paintings

weekdays, 12.05 pm on Saturday and 1 pm on Sunday. There are also daily links between Melbourne and the Grampians; see the following section.

GRAMPIANS NATIONAL PARK

Named after the mountains of the same name in Scotland, the Grampians are the south-west tail end of the Great Dividing Range. The area is a large national park renowned for fine bushwalks, superb mountain lookouts, excellent rock-climbing opportunities, prolific wildlife and, in the spring, countless wildflowers.

The Grampians are at their best from August to November when the flowers are most colourful. On a weekend in early spring there's a wildflower exhibition in the Halls Gap Hall, and a jazz festival is held in mid-February. There are also many Aboriginal rock paintings in the Grampians, as well as waterfalls such as the spectacular McKenzie Falls.

There are many fine bushwalks around the Grampians, some of them short strolls you can make from Halls Gap. Keep an eye out for wildlife, even in the middle of Halls Gap.

In 1991 the Grampians name was officially changed to include the Aboriginal name, Gariwerd, but it was changed back again when the Kennett government came into office.

Orientation & Information

The Grampians lie immediately west of Ararat and south of the Western Highway between Stawell and Horsham. The small town of Halls Gap, about 250km from Melbourne, is right in the middle of the region and has a wide range of accommodation. Accommodation is also available in other towns in the area, such as Dunkeld, Glenisla and Wartook.

The Grampians National Park Visitors Centre (☎ 5356 4381), 2.5km south of Halls Gap on the Dunkeld road, has information, maps, walking guides and audiovisual displays on the park. The *Wonderland Walks* brochure and map ($3) is good for a short visit.

There is no bank in Halls Gap, although the newsagency/general store has an EFTPOS machine and Commonwealth and ANZ bank subagencies.

Brambuk Living Cultural Centre

Behind the visitors centre is the imaginatively designed Brambuk Living Cultural Centre (☎ 5356 4452), collectively run by five Koori communities. There are displays depicting the history of the Koori people, from customs and lifestyle before white settlement to their persecution by white settlers. Art, clothes, books, tools and souvenirs are on display and for sale, and there's a bush-tucker cafe.

Other Attractions

To the west, the rugged **Victoria (Billawin) Range** is known for its red gums, and there are many Aboriginal rock paintings in the area, including Billimina Shelter and Wab Manja Shelter, both near Glenisla on the Henty Highway.

Victoria Valley, in the centre of the Grampians, is a secluded wildlife sanctuary with beautiful bush tracks to drive down.

To the north at **Zumstein**, 22km northwest of Halls Gap, kangaroos gather in a paddock in the hope of a free feed, but this is definitely discouraged (in fact it's illegal). Be warned that these are wild animals and they should not be treated like domestic pets.

Walks

The many walks range from well-marked (although often quite arduous) trails to some very rugged walking in the large areas that have been kept free of trails. The best known established trails are in the Wonderland Range area near Halls Gap, where you can scramble up and down some spectacular scenery on walks ranging from half an hour to four hours in duration. Views from the various lookouts down onto the plains far below are well worth the effort. Especially good is the **Grand Canyon trail**, which leads to the Pinnacle. Others include **Boroka Lookout** (which has access for the disabled) and the **Balconies**.

For more detailed information on the various walks available in the Grampians, check out Lonely Planet's *Bushwalking in Australia*, or buy Parks Victoria's booklets: *Wonderland Walks*, *Northern Grampians* and *Southern Grampians* ($3 each).

Other Activities & Tours

There's a wide range of organised activities and tours on offer, from walks (from $8), to abseiling (from $25), to bike rides (including a night ride, $20), to canoeing ($20). You can book them all at the Centre for Activities (☎ 5356 4556), in the Stony Creek Stores Centre, which is just before the main shopping strip in Halls Gap.

Grampians National Park Tours (☎ 5356 6221), based at the YHA hostel in Halls Gap, is one of several outfits running 4WD tours of the national park. They have a good package deal: for $70, you get the three-quarter-day tour, two nights dorm accommodation and return transport from Stawell to Halls Gap.

Lake Bellfield, just south of Halls Gap and covering the site of the original town, is a reservoir stocked with brown and rainbow trout.

Places to Stay

Camping There are more than 15 camp sites in the national park, all with toilets, picnic tables and fireplaces, and most with at least limited water. There's no booking system – it's first in, best site. Permits cost $7.50 and you can self-register or pay at the visitors centre.

Bush camping is permitted anywhere outside the designated camp sites except in water catchment areas. Check at the visitors centre.

When camping in the park pay close attention to the fire restrictions – apart from the considerable damage you could do to yourself and the bush, you stand a good chance of being arrested if you disobey them. Remember that you can be fined huge amounts or even jailed for lighting *any* fire, including fuel stoves, on days of Total Fire Ban, and the locals will be more than willing to dob you in.

For a more organised camping trip, try the site run by High Spirits outdoor Adventures (☎ 019 403 620). It's in Victoria Valley, by Moora Moora Reservoir and for $30 a day you get accommodation, meals, transport within the park and canoeing on the reservoir.

Halls Gap Halls Gap has a gaggle of guesthouses, caravan parks, motels, units and cottages, although during peak periods – especially Easter – it's a good idea to book. The Stawell & Grampians Information Centre (☎ 1800 246 880) operates an accommodation booking service.

Halls Gap Caravan Park (☎ 5356 4251) in the centre of town has tent sites from $13 and vans and cabins from $34 to $59. One kilometre from the centre of Halls Gap on the corner of Buckler St and Grampians Rd is the small *Halls Gap YHA Hostel* (☎ 5356 6221), with dorm beds ($13) and also family rooms. A new, larger YHA hostel will be built soon. Another hostel, operated by the Brambuk Centre, has opened on the main road across from the entrance to the visitors centre. *Brambuk Backpackers* (☎ 5356 4250 or 5356 4452) has dorms for $13.

Kingsway Holiday Flats (☎ 5356 4202) has good budget flats from about $45 a double, with additional people charged $6 each. The *Mountain Grand Guesthouse* (☎ 5356 4232) has B&B for $85 to $95 a double. The half-dozen motels include the central *Halls Gap Kookaburra Lodge* (☎ 5356 4395), with doubles from $72 to $85.

Places to Eat

The general store in Halls Gap has a cafe and takeaway section, and there's a well-stocked supermarket next door (open daily). *Flying Emu Café* is good for lunch or a snack, and *Golden Phoenix* has reasonable Chinese food.

The excellent *Kookaburra Restaurant* has a menu based on fresh local produce with mains ranging from $14.50 to $20. *Mountain Grand Guesthouse* has an upstairs buffet with meals at $20 a head and a 'jazz cafe' downstairs, and *Suzy's Halls Gap Tavern* is a modern bar/restaurant offering three-course set meals for $15.

Getting There & Away

The trip from Melbourne to Halls Gap with V/Line involves a train to Ballarat, a bus to Stawell then another bus to Halls Gap. This service operates daily, takes 4½ hours and costs $37.80.

The road from Stawell to Halls Gap is flat so it's an easy cycle of about 25km. You can take your bike on the *Overland* train (Melbourne to Adelaide) to Stawell, although it arrives in Stawell at 1.43 am. It's a longer and hillier ride from Ararat to Halls Gap (via Moyston) but still fairly easy.

HORSHAM (pop 12,591)

Horsham was first settled in 1842, and has grown to become the main commercial centre of the Wimmera. The **Horsham Art Gallery** collection includes works by significant Australian artists. The attractive **botanic gardens** are beside the Wimmera River, and **Olde Horsham Village** has antique displays, a gallery and a small fauna park. The **Wimmera Wool Factory**, out on the Golf Course Rd, produces ultrafine wool from merino sheep. There are daily tours.

The tourist information centre (☎ 5382 1832) is at 20 O'Callaghans Pde and is open daily. Pick up their *Horsham Historical River Walk* brochure. The Goolum Goolum Aboriginal Co-operative (☎ 5382 5033), 143 Baillie St, can provide information on ancient sites in the area.

Places to Stay & Eat

Horsham Caravan Park (☎ 5382 3476) is at the end of Firebrace St by the river, and has vans and cabins ($30 to $40) and tent sites ($10). The *Royal Hotel* (☎ 5382 1255), 132 Firebrace St, charges $20/35, and there are at least a dozen motels in the area as well.

Bagdad Café on Wilson St near the corner of Firebrace St is a great spot for a good coffee and a snack. It's a bit odd to find a place like this in such an archetypal country town. As one local told me, 'It's like a Mel-

bourne cafe – you know, weird'. *Bagdad House* (☎ 5382 0068), next door, is a hostel with dorms for $15, or $12 if you provide your own sleeping bag.

MT ARAPILES

Twelve kilometres west of Natimuk on the Wimmera Highway, Mt Arapiles (more commonly known as 'the Piles') lures rock climbers from around the world. There are more than 2000 climbs for all levels of skill, with colourful names such as Violent Crumble, Punks in the Gym and Cruel Britannia. It's usually alive with climbers and attracts an eclectic mix of people.

Mt Arapiles was called Djurite for several thousand years but the name was largely lost when most of the Drurid Balag people were killed or scattered when whites arrived. The people used the mountain as a quarry.

So great is its attraction that the sleepy town of **Natimuk** is now home to quite a few climbers who have moved into the area, bringing with them tastes and attitudes not often associated with small rural towns in Australia – the Natimuk pub must be one of the few to boast vegetarian pancakes on its counter-meal menu and the milkshakes at the local shops are famous.

Despite the mountain's fame as a spot for climbing, there is a sealed road right to the top for those unable to haul themselves up the hard way, and there are great views from the lookout. Not far away is the lone rocky outcrop of Mitre Rock, near to its namesake lake, and the Wimmera stretches into the distance.

There are several operators offering climbing and abseiling instruction, including the Climbing Company (☎ 5387 1329) and Arapiles Climbing Guides (☎ 1800 357 035; email climbacg@netconnect.com.au).

Places to Stay

There's a camp site (known as 'the Pines') in Centenary Park at the base of the mountain – facilities are limited to toilets and a washbasin. There's a caravan park 4km north of Natimuk, and in town the *National Hotel*

(☎ 5387 1300) has pub rooms at $15, or $25 with a cooked breakfast, and well-equipped self-contained units for $50 a double, with a discount if you stay three nights.

Seven kilometres east of Natimuk and midway between Horsham and Mt Arapiles, *Horsham-Arapiles Backpackers YHA* (☎ 5384 0236), usually known as *Tim's Place*, has dorm beds at $13 and two doubles at $30; it also hires out mountain bikes ($10 a day) and can arrange climbing and abseiling instruction. On Sundays there might be horse-riding.

DIMBOOLA (pop 1557)

The name of this quiet, typically Australian country town on the Wimmera River is a Sinhalese word meaning 'Land of the Figs'. Dimboola is an attractive town with some fine historic buildings, although its main interest to travellers is as the gateway to the Little Desert National Park, which starts 4km south of the town. Accommodation options include a caravan park, motels and pubs, including the excellent *Victoria Hotel* (☎ 5389 1630) on Wimmera St at $26/38 including a light breakfast.

The **Pink Lake** is a colourful salt lake beside the Western Highway about 9km north-west of Dimboola. The **Ebenezer Aboriginal Mission Station** was established in 1859 in Antwerp, 18km north of Dimboola. The ruins, complete with its small cemetery, are signposted off the road, close to the banks of the Wimmera River.

LITTLE DESERT NATIONAL PARK

Just south of the Western Highway and reached from Dimboola or Nhill, the Little Desert National Park is noted for its brilliant display of wildflowers in the spring. The name is a bit of a misnomer because it isn't really a desert nor is it that little. In fact with an area of 132,000 hectares it's Victoria's fifth-largest national park, and the 'desert' extends well beyond the national park's boundaries.

There are several introductory walks in the east block of the park: south of Dimboola is the **Pomponderoo Hill Nature Walk**;

south of Nhill is the **Stringybark Walk**; and south of Kiata there's the **Sanctuary Nature Walk**.

Places to Stay

You can camp in the park 10km south of Kiata, just east of Nhill, or on the Wimmera River south of Dimboola. Ring the rangers at Dimboola (☎ 5389 1204) for more information about camping.

Little Desert Lodge (☎ 5391 5232), in the park and 16km south of Nhill, has units for $55/70 for singles/doubles, including a light breakfast ($4 for a cooked breakfast) or you can camp for $9 per site ($11.50 with power). There are bunk rooms for $25 per person or $30 a single. There's an environmental study centre and the only aviary in the world housing the fascinating mallee fowl ($4 entry).

The Mallee

North of the Wimmera is the least populated part of Australia's most densely populated state. The Mallee forms a wedge between South Australia and New South Wales, and this area even includes the one genuinely empty part of Victoria. The contrast between the wide, flat Mallee, with its sand dunes and dry lakes, and the lush alpine forests of East Gippsland in eastern Victoria is striking.

The Mallee takes its name from the mallee scrub that once covered the area. Mallee roots are hard, gnarled and slow-burning. Some great Aussie kitsch can still be found – mallee-root egg cups and ashtrays – although they may have crossed that thin line from being kitsch to being collectable.

The Mallee region extends from around the Wyperfeld National Park in the south, all the way up to the irrigated oasis surrounding Mildura. Much of the northern area is encompassed in the Murray-Sunset National Park.

The main town in the Mallee is **Ouyen**, at the junction of the Sunraysia, Calder and Mallee highways, although Mildura is by far the largest town in the area. The north-west corner of the Mallee is known as 'Sunset Country' – a fine name for the edge of the arid wilderness that stretches right across the continent.

NATIONAL PARKS & RESERVES
Murray-Sunset National Park
Covering an area of 633,000 hectares in Victoria's north-west corner, this is the state's second-largest national park after the Alpine National Park.

Murray-Sunset is a largely untouched semi-arid wilderness area. Most of the tracks through the park are accessible only with 4WD, although conventional vehicles can take the 12km unsealed road leading from the Mallee Highway (60km west of Ouyen) up to the picnic and camping area at the Pink Lakes. There are no other facilities, but bush camping is allowed elsewhere in the park. Remember to carry water at all times. Temperatures are extreme during summer, and visits aren't recommended at that time. Contact the park rangers in Mildura (☎ 5022 3000) for more information.

Wyperfeld National Park
Best reached from Albacutya, north of Rainbow and west of Hopetoun, this large park (365,800ha) contains a chain of often-dry lakes, including Lake Albacutya. A combination of river gums on the flood plains, sandy mallee scrubland and treed plains supports a wide variety of wildlife, including emus and kangaroos. There are two 6km walking tracks, a 15km nature drive, and some good longer walks. The park information centre (☎ 5395 7221) can advise on these and it also has information on the area's flora and fauna, which of course includes the mallee fowl. There are four camping grounds with basic facilities.

Big Desert Wilderness
This large wilderness area (113,500ha) contains no roads, tracks or any other facilities, which makes it difficult and dangerous to travel in except for those with considerable wilderness experience. It consists of sand

dunes and mallee scrub, and wildlife abounds, particularly reptiles.

If you aren't equipped to venture into the wilderness, you can get a tantalising glimpse of the Big Desert along the dry-weather road which runs from Nhill north to Murrayville on the Ouyen Highway. There are camp sites and bore water at **Broken Bucket Reserve**, which is about 55km north of Nhill.

Hattah-Kulkyne National Park
With the near-desert of the mallee country, the woodlands, gum-lined lakes and the Murray River, Hattah-Kulkyne is a diverse and beautiful park of 49,690ha.

The Hattah Lakes system fills when the Murray floods and supports many species of water birds. There is a good information centre (☎ 5029 3253) at **Lake Hattah**, a few kilometres into the park from the small town of **Hattah**, on the Sunraysia Highway 35km north of Ouyen. The park is popular with bushwalkers, cyclists and canoeists. Canoes can be rented in Hattah. Walking tracks include the 10km Camel Pad Walk, which follows the old camel trails that were used to carry salt to riverboats on the Murray River. Check at the information centre on the condition of tracks in the park – many are impassable after rain.

There are camping areas at Lake Hattah and Lake Mournpall with toilets, picnic tables and fireplaces ($7 per site), but you need to bring drinking water. Camping is also possible anywhere along the Murray River frontage in the adjoining Murray-Kulkyne State Park.

Murray River

The mighty Murray River is Australia's most important inland waterway, flowing from the mountains of the Great Dividing Range in north-eastern Victoria to Encounter Bay, South Australia, a distance of some 2500km. For much of its route it forms the border between Victoria and New South Wales.

Some of Australia's earliest European

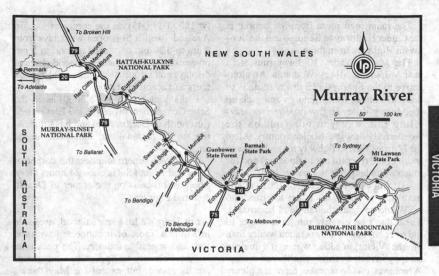

VICTORIA

explorers travelled along the Murray, including Mitchell, Sturt and Eyre. Later, before roads and railways crossed the land, the Murray became a great trade artery and an important means of opening up the interior. Echuca was Australia's leading inland port and the Murray an antipodean Mississippi, with paddle-steamers and riverboats carrying supplies between remote sheep stations, homesteads and the thriving river towns. The river and its surrounds provided an abundance of food for the explorers and settlers who arrived tens of thousands of years earlier, and there are important Aboriginal sites along it.

Today the Murray is of great economic importance, supplying the water for the irrigation schemes that have transformed huge tracts of bush and semidesert into prosperous dairy farms, vineyards, market gardens and citrus orchards.

The river is also famous for its magnificent forests of red gums, its plentiful wildlife and as a great place for canoe trips, riverboat cruises, houseboat holidays or river-bank camping.

Many of the river towns, particularly Echuca, have reminders of the Murray's colourful past, including preserved paddle-steamers, old buildings and museums.

The Murray is a slow-moving, meandering river, with many billabongs and patches of forest in the river bends. Many of these are state forest where camping is permitted.

Getting There & Away

Greyhound and McCafferty's both go through Mildura on the Sydney to Adelaide run.

V/Line has bus or combination bus/train services that connect Melbourne, Bendigo and Ballarat with the Murray River towns, and it also operates bus services running along the Murray between Albury and Mildura.

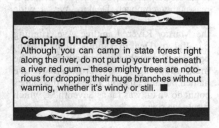

Camping Under Trees
Although you can camp in state forest right along the river, do not put up your tent beneath a river red gum – these mighty trees are notorious for dropping their huge branches without warning, whether it's windy or still. ∎

The main road route from Melbourne is the Calder Highway to Bendigo and the Sunraysia Highway from there.

The Murray Valley Highway runs from near Mildura to Albury-Wodonga. An alternative to the Sunraysia Highway route is to drive to Echuca from Bendigo and pick up the Murray Valley Highway. However, travelling this way you miss out on the wonderfully desolate Mallee country. Also, the Murray Valley Highway runs a little way south of the river (to avoid flooding) and for much of its length is not particularly attractive. If you want to travel along the river and have time to spare, it's better to cross into NSW and navigate the tangle of backroads. These don't necessarily run much closer to the river but the scenery is much wilder than on the Victorian side, where it's mainly scrappy irrigated farms. You'll need a map. Whichever route you take, there are plenty of opportunities to turn off into red gum forests.

MILDURA (pop 24,142)

Noted for its exceptional amount of sunshine, Mildura was chosen by the Chaffey brothers as the site of the first Murray River irrigation projects. Today it's something of an oasis in this arid region, and a tourist town with quite a few worthwhile attractions.

Mildura's festivals include Country Music Week in September, and the Jazz & Wine Festival in November over the Melbourne Cup weekend.

Orientation & Information

Once you penetrate the thick rind of tacky development which extends for kilometres from the city centre, downtown Mildura is reasonably compact. Deakin Ave, a wide boulevard, is the main street and runs east to the Murray River. Langtree Ave, running parallel to Deakin (and a block north) between Eleventh and Seventh Sts, is the main shopping street. Cross streets are named numerically, but note that the names count down only as far as Seventh St, which fronts the river.

The Mildura Tourist Information Centre

(☎ 1800 039 043) on the corner of Deakin Ave and Twelfth St is open weekdays from 9 am to 5.30 pm on weekdays and to 5 pm on weekends. This place has a good range of displays and information, and can also book tours and accommodation.

Parks Victoria (☎ 5022 3000) is in the State Government offices at 253 Eleventh St (just north of Deakin Ave) and has information on the national and state parks in the area.

The Coles supermarket on the corner of Lime and Eighth Sts is open 24 hours daily. The post office is on the corner of Deakin Ave and Eighth St.

Work There's a lot of casual work available in Mildura, most of it connected with the fruit and vegetable industry. The peak time is from February to April, when the grapes are harvested, but except for May there's usually something available. Some farmers provide accommodation, but take a tent if you're not sure. If you're working in a packing factory or earning a wage, the minimum rate is nearly $11 an hour, and the hours can be long. If you're being paid by the amount you pick, the money can be good but it depends on how you stand up to the backbreaking work.

The Commonwealth Employment Service is the place to arrange work but that department is in the process of being renamed, merged, corporatised and maybe privatised. And the Mildura office will also be shifting to a new address but no-one knows what it will be. Ask at the information centre. Backpackers staying at the Mildura International Backpackers will get a lot of help finding work.

Things to See & Do

The tourist office has a handy walking-tour brochure called *The Chaffey Trail*, which guides you around some of the more interesting sights including the **paddle-steamer wharf**, the **Mildura weir and lock**, **Old Mildura Homestead**, the **Mildara Blass Winery** and the **Old Psyche Bend Pump Station**.

Also on the trail, the **Mildura Arts Centre**

& Rio Vista complex is well worth a visit. There's a collection of Australian and European art and a historic homestead with interesting displays. It's on the corner of Chaffey and Curtin Aves, is open weekdays from 9 am to 5 pm and weekends from 2 to 4.30 pm, and costs $2.50.

There are a number of **wineries** in the area which offer cellar door sales and, at a couple, restaurants. The information centre has a brochure detailing opening times.

Orange World, 7km north of town (in New South Wales), has one-hour tours ($5) on tractor trains around the property and is a fascinating introduction to how citrus fruit is produced. The **Golden River Zoo**, 4km north-west, is open daily from 9 am to 5 pm ($12, children $6).

In summer you'll want to use the **swimming pool**, behind the information centre. In winter, when nights can be very chilly, you'll be pleased to hear that it's heated, and a new indoor heated pool and **wave pool** is being built at the same site.

Organised Tours & Cruises

Lest you forget that this is riverboat country, you can take **paddle-steamer trips** from the Mildura wharf. The historic steam-powered PS *Melbourne* has a daily two-hour cruise ($16, children $6), and the PV *Rothbury* does day trips to the Trentham winery ($34, children $14) and trips to the zoo ($30, children $14) during school holidays. Book on ☎ 5023 3300.

Several Aboriginal operators run tours of the area, concentrating on culture, history (which covers 45,000 years if you go to Lake Mungo) and wildlife. The best known is Harry Nanya (☎ 5027 2076), which has a wide range of tours, including a day trip to Mungo National Park for $45. Also good is Ponde Tours (book at the information centre).

On Wednesday and Friday, Sunraysia Bus Lines (☎ 5021 2882) has day trips from Mildura to Broken Hill, including a tour of Broken Hill ($59). Mallee Outback Experiences (☎ 5021 1621) runs various tours including day trips around Mildura on Thursday ($40), to Murray-Sunset National Park on Monday ($50), and to Mungo National Park on Wednesday and Saturday ($45).

Places to Stay

There are about 30 caravan parks in and near Mildura. You can expect prices to rise a little at peak times. *Buronga Riverside Caravan Park* (☎ 5023 3040), just across the river, has tent sites from $11, and cabins from $35. *Golden River Caravan Park* (☎ 5021 2289) is also on the river, 5km north-west of the town centre. Away from the river but reasonably close to the centre of town is *Crossroads Holiday Park* (☎ 5023 3239) on the corner of Fifteenth St and Deakin Ave, with sites from $12 and cabins from $36.

The good new *Mildura International Backpackers* hostel (☎ 5021 0133) is at 5 Cedar Ave. Cedar Ave runs between Twelfth and Eleventh Sts a block back from the information centre. All rooms have two beds (not bunks) in them, at $13 per person ($80 per week). Ros and Fi are good hosts who will help you find work, and their Saturday night barbecue (about $5) is worth waiting around for. The hostel has a van so you might be able to arrange a lift to work if you don't have a car.

The friendly *Rosemont Guest House* (☎ 5023 1535), 154 Madden Ave, is a cosy old timber guesthouse with simple units out the back. Doubles with attached bathroom cost from $40 and singles with shared bathroom cost $20. This place is also a YHA hostel and members are charged $15. All rooms have air-con, there's a good pool, and rates include a generous breakfast.

Mildura also has an abundance of motels. The *Riviera Motel* (☎ 5023 3696), opposite the train station (and the river) at 157 Seventh St, has singles/doubles from $38/40. The *Commodore Motor Inn* (☎ 5023 0241), well located on the corner of Deakin Ave and Seventh St (although this means traffic noise if you're facing the streets), charges from $55/65, and on the opposite corner the fine old *Grand Hotel* (☎ 5023 0511) has singles/doubles from $60/80 to

$100/130 and suites from $150 to $370. This place would probably be more comfortable than a motel in summer, as it was built to withstand the heat.

About 20 operators offer houseboats for rent and costs range upwards from around $400 for three nights for two people. Contact the information centre or the RACV for details.

See the information centre for a listing of B&Bs and farmstays.

Places to Eat

Langtree Ave is Mildura's main restaurant precinct. *Taco Bill* at No 36 has Mexican food (half-price on Tuesday), and across the road at No 35 *Siam Palace* has tasty Thai tucker with takeaway lunch boxes for $5 and mains courses from around $7.50.

The *Sandbar* on the corner of Langtree and Eighth Aves has a pleasant courtyard and meals from $8 to $13. *Restaurant Rendezvous*, 34 Langtree, is a modern, classy place with starters around $12 and main courses around $20, but there are also $10 special deals. Next door and run by the same people, *Liaisons* is a bar and bistro with a pleasant courtyard – and cheaper prices, including $6.50 specials.

On the corner of Seventh St and Deakin Ave, *Jackie's Corner* is a cheap Chinese takeaway. The *Mildura Workingman's Club* on Deakin Ave has lunch specials at $4.50 and other mains from $8 – this place once boasted the longest bar in the world, but some fool cut it down to fit in more poker machines.

Hungry fruit-pickers appreciate the all-you-can-eat deals at *Pizza Hut*, 237 Deakin Ave.

The Grand Hotel, at the river end of Deakin Ave, has several bars and dining rooms, including a casual wine bar and pizza cafe. Down in the old cellars of the hotel is the award-winning *Stefano's Cantina*, a candle-lit restaurant serving banquets of authentic northern Italian cuisine using fresh local produce. The cost is around $40 per person – great for a splurge.

Entertainment

Mildura has a small but lively nightlife scene, with several nightclubs in the town centre. *Sandbar* on the corner of Langtree and Eighth Aves has live music Wednesday to Saturday nights. *Dom's Nightclub*, a little farther along Langtree Ave, is also popular. The *Deakin Twin Cinema* (☎ 5023 4452) is at 93 Deakin Ave.

Getting There & Away

Air Kendell (book through Ansett, ☎ 13 1300) and Southern Australia (book through Qantas, ☎ 13 1313) connect Mildura with Melbourne, Adelaide and Broken Hill.

Bus Between Melbourne and Mildura, V/Line has a direct overnight bus every night except Saturday, as well as several daily train/bus services via Bendigo or Swan Hill. The trip takes about eight hours and costs $52. V/Line also has a bus service connecting all the towns along the Murray River.

Greyhound and McCafferty's both have daily services between Mildura and Adelaide ($35) and Mildura and Sydney ($74). Greyhound and Sunraysia Bus Lines have twice-weekly services to Broken Hill ($37).

AROUND MILDURA

Leaving Mildura you don't have to travel very far before you realise just how desolate the country around here can be. The Sturt Highway runs west arrow-straight and deadly dull to South Australia, about 130km away.

Going into New South Wales you follow the Murray west another 32km to **Wentworth**, one of the oldest river towns, where you can visit the Old Wentworth Gaol and the Pioneer Museum.

A very interesting excursion from Mildura is to **Mungo National Park** in New South Wales to see the strange natural formation known as the Walls of China (see the New South Wales chapter for details).

Red Cliffs, 17km south, is the home of Big Lizzie, a huge steam-engined tractor – a taped commentary tells her story. At Dareton, 19km north-west, the **Tulklana**

Kumbi Gallery has a good collection of locally made Aboriginal arts and crafts on sale.

SWAN HILL (pop 9385)

One of the more interesting towns along the Murray, Swan Hill was named by the early explorer Major Thomas Mitchell, who spent a sleepless night within earshot of a large contingent of noisy black swans.

The tourist information centre (☎ 5032 3033) is at 306 Campbell St (corner of Rutherford St) and is open daily.

Pioneer Settlement

The major attraction is the Swan Hill Pioneer Settlement, a recreation of a riverside port town of the paddle-steamer era. It's definitely worth a visit and is open daily from 8.30 am to 5 pm ($12, children $6). At night there's an hourly sound-and-light show, running from 7 pm (later in summer) for $8 ($4). The paddle-steamer *Pyap* makes short trips from the pioneer settlement for $8 ($4), at 10.30 am and 2.30 pm.

Other Attractions

Swan Hill's **art gallery** is opposite the entrance to the Pioneer Settlement.

The MV *Kookaburra* (☎ 5032 0003) offers two-hour luncheon cruises daily except Monday, costing $22 ($12).

The historic **Tyntynder Homestead**, 16km north of the town, has a small museum of pioneering and Aboriginal relics and many reminders of the hardships of colonial life, like the wine cellar! Admission is $5.50 (children $3), which includes a tour, and the homestead is open daily from 9 am to 4.30 pm.

There are a few **wineries** in the area, including Buller's at Beverford (15km north) and Best's at Lake Boga (17km south).

Places to Stay

Riverside Caravan Park (☎ 5032 1494) next to the river and the pioneer settlement has tent sites from $12 and vans and cabins from $30 to $75.

The *White Swan Hotel* (☎ 5032 2761) at 182 Campbell St has pub rooms at $22/35, or $30/40 with bathroom. The cheapest central motel is *Mallee Rest* (☎ 5032 4541) at 369 Campbell St, with doubles ranging from $44 to $54.

Places to Eat

Campbell St has plenty of eateries. One of the better ones is *Teller's Licensed Deli*, on the corner of McCrae St. It has good burgers and sandwiches, steaks, pastas and other meals ranging from $7 to $18. *Quo Vadis*, 259 Campbell St, is good for pizzas and pastas, and for a pub meal try the *White Swan Hotel*.

Getting There & Away

V/Line runs between Melbourne and Swan Hill ($42.10) via Bendigo. It also has buses four times weekly running between Swan Hill and Mildura ($38.50), Echuca ($17.50) and Albury-Wodonga ($33.60). These fares are on the V/Line Murray Link service.

KERANG (pop 3883)

Kerang is on the Murray Valley Highway about 25km south of the river, and is best known for the huge flocks of ibis that breed on the 50 or so lakes in the area. Middle Lake, 9km north of Kerang, is the best place to see the colonies, and there's a small hide. The town itself has a small historical museum, caravan parks and motels.

GUNBOWER STATE FOREST

The superb Gunbower State Forest, which is actually on a long 'island' enclosed by the Murray River and Gunbower Creek, features magnificent river red gums, abundant wildlife and plenty of walking tracks.

The town of **Cohuna**, 32km east of Kerang, is the main access point to the forest, although there are numerous marked tracks in from the highway. The tracks within the forest are all on old river mud which becomes impassable for conventional vehicles during wet weather.

Phone ☎ 5426 2266 to check on conditions.

Based 16km north-west of Cohuna,

Ganawarra Wetlander Cruises (☎ 5453 3000) runs cruises through these creeks and wetlands from mid-August to mid-May. Its two-hour afternoon cruise operates daily except Thursday at 2 pm ($15), and dinner cruises with live entertainment are offered most Saturday nights ($35).

ECHUCA (pop 10,014)

Strategically sited where the Goulburn and Campaspe rivers join the Murray, Echuca, which is an Aboriginal word meaning 'the meeting of the waters', was founded in 1853 by the enterprising ex-convict Henry Hopwood.

In the riverboat days this was the busiest inland port in Australia and the centre of the thriving river trade. In the 1880s the famous red-gum wharf was more than 1km long and there were stores and hotels all along the waterfront. At its peak there were more than 300 steamers operating out of the port here.

Today tourism is the main money-spinner. Echuca is the most interesting of the towns along the Murray, with numerous worthwhile attractions centred around the old port. There are also paddle-steamer cruises, museums and wineries to visit, and several impressive state forests nearby.

In mid-October Echuca hosts its annual Rich River Festival: seven days of entertainment and games. Over the Queen's Birthday weekend there's a big steam rally.

Information

The Echuca Tourist Information Centre (☎ 5480 7555; 1800 804 446) is open daily from 9 am to 5 pm. As well as local information and an accommodation booking service there is statewide information provided by Tourism Victoria and Tourism New South Wales.

For camping gear and other odds and ends, go to Echuca Camping or, next door, Echuca Disposals, on High St. The Coles supermarket on High St (corner of Darling St) never closes.

Historic Port of Echuca

The old port area has numerous attractions

along the riverfront. You start at the old Star Hotel (where you buy the tickets) with various old photographs on display, and the 1858 Bridge Hotel nearby, now a licensed restaurant.

Across the road at the wharf, there's a vintage train collection, a cargo shed with audiovisual displays, and the historic paddle-steamers PS *Pevensey* and PS *Adelaide*. The port is open daily from 9.15 am to 5 pm, and tickets cost $7.

Other Attractions

In the same street as the wharf are various other attractions, including the **Red Gum Works**, where wood is still worked using traditional machinery; **Sharp's Magic Movie House** ($8.50), which has old penny-arcade equipment, classic films projected on authentic equipment and displays relating to Australia's cinema industry; and a **Coach House & Carriage Collection** ($4). You can also take a short ride around the port in a horse-drawn carriage ($4).

A **paddle-steamer cruise** is almost obligatory, so head down to the river north of the old port and check out the sailing times. The steam-driven PS *Emmylou* (☎ 5482 3801) does 1½-hour cruises ($12; lunch extra) and overnight trips. Various boats, including the PS *Canberra* and PS *Pride of the Murray* have one-hour cruises ($9). There are also lunch and dinner cruises.

World in Wax, 630 High St, features 60 gruesome and famous characters, and is open daily from 9 am to 5 pm ($6). The **Historical Society Museum** in Dickson St is housed in the old National Trust classified police station and lock-up building (open daily from 1 to 3 pm). For car buffs, the **National Holden Museum** ($5/2.50) is in Warren St.

There are free wine-tastings at the port at **Murray Esplanade Cellars** in the old Customs House on the corner of Leslie St. There's also the **William Angliss Wine Tasting Centre**, on the corner of Radcliffe St and Murray Esplanade.

Activities

Based at the boat ramp, Echuca Boat &

Canoe Hire (☎ 5480 6208) has motorboats, kayaks and canoes for hire. It also offers canoe cruises – they drive you upstream, you paddle back. A day costs $50 for two people, and three-day, 80km trips cost $70 per person.

Several operators offer water-skiing trips and classes, and there's a go-kart track across the river in Moama.

There are pool tables, a bar and a cafe at Atomic Pool, Bar & Café, 207 Darling St.

Places to Stay

Echuca Caravan Park (☎ 5482 2157) on

Crofton St is the most central of the town's caravan parks and has vans from $35, cabins from $45 and tent sites at $12.

Echuca Gardens YHA (☎ 5480 6522), 103 Mitchell St, is a 10-minute walk from the centre. There are two sections – a small hostel with dorm beds for $16, and the pleasant *Echuca Gardens B&B*, with doubles with en-suite from $60/90 to $90/120. There are free bikes.

The *American Hotel* (☎ 5482 5044) on the corner of Heygarth and Hare Sts has budget rooms at $25/40. There's a stack of motels, the cheapest of which are the *Highstreet*

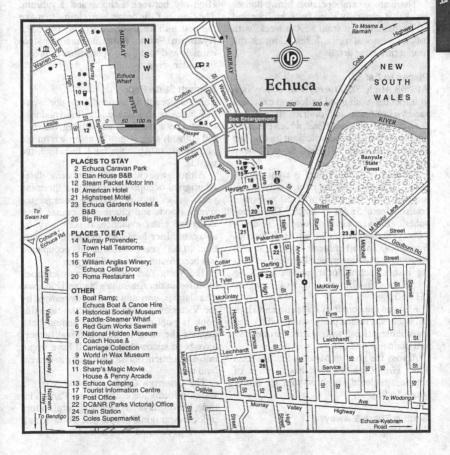

PLACES TO STAY
2 Echuca Caravan Park
3 Etan House B&B
12 Steam Packet Motor Inn
18 American Hotel
21 Highstreet Motel
23 Echuca Gardens Hostel & B&B
26 Big River Motel

PLACES TO EAT
14 Murray Provender; Town Hall Tearooms
15 Fiori
16 William Angliss Winery; Echuca Cellar Door
20 Roma Restaurant

OTHER
1 Boat Ramp; Echuca Boat & Canoe Hire
4 Historical Society Museum
5 Paddle-Steamer Wharf
6 Red Gum Works Sawmill
7 National Holden Museum
8 Coach House & Carriage Collection
9 World in Wax Museum
10 Star Hotel
11 Sharp's Magic Movie House & Penny Arcade
13 Echuca Camping
17 Tourist Information Centre
19 Post Office
22 DC&NR (Parks Victoria) Office
24 Train Station
25 Coles Supermarket

VICTORIA

Motel (☎ 5482 1013) at 439 High St and the *Big River Motel* (☎ 5482 2522) at 317 High St, both with singles/doubles from about $40/50. Not so cheap but in a historic building right in the port precinct, the *Steam Packet Motor Inn* (☎ 5482 3411) charges from $54/70. It's on the corner of Leslie St.

Etan House B&B (☎ 5480 7477) at 11 Connelly St is a beautifully restored homestead with a guest kitchen, grass tennis court and pool; doubles cost from $120. *Murray House B&B* (☎ 5482 4944) at 55 Francis St also has good rooms from $90/150 (no children).

There are several operators hiring houseboats that generally sleep between four and 10 people and cost from $800 a week, with lots of seasonal price hikes. Contact the tourist office for details.

Places to Eat
At 568 High St, *Murray Provender* is a gourmet deli with good coffee and excellent sandwiches, pies and pastries. For a pub feed, try the *American Hotel*, which has good bar meals from $7 and a pleasant bistro. The *Roma Restaurant*, 191 Hare St, is a cheap pizza/pasta joint.

Oscar W's at the Wharf is right on the wharf and overlooks the river. Prices aren't too bad, with snacks from $6.50 and main courses from $8.50 at lunch. The atmospheric *Echuca Cellar Door* at Tisdall's Winery, 2 Radcliffe St, has light lunches from $6.95 and other meals from $9 to $15. At dinner there's an impressive menu including dishes such as local yabbies and King Island brie in filo on a bed of mangoes ($13.50).

Fiori on the corner of Radcliffe and High Sts is a smart Italian place with good food at reasonable prices, with starters around $9 and mains around $20.

Across the river in Moama, the big *Rich River Golf Club* complex has a range of eateries, including a serve-yourself buffet (from $6.95).

Getting There & Away
Some long-distance buses operate from the post office or the train station. Others stop at the bus stop near the corner of Heygarth St and Cobb Hwy. V/Line has a daily service from Melbourne to Echuca ($26.10), changing from train to bus at Bendigo (just $6 from Echuca, thanks to a pricing anomaly). V/Line's Murray Link service connects Echuca with Albury-Wodonga ($20.40), Swan Hill ($17.50) and Mildura ($33.20).

AROUND ECHUCA
The indigenous people of this area called the Murray the **Tongala**, which is the name taken by a small town off the Murray Valley Highway between Echuca and Kyabram. The *Golden Cow* centre here claims to make the best milkshakes in Australia. The 55ha **Kyabram Fauna Park** has many native animals and birds, and specialises in breeding endangered species.

Barmah State Park
This very beautiful wetland area, north-east of Echuca, centres around the flood plains of the Murray and is forested with big, old river red gums. It's the largest remaining river gum forest in Australia (and, therefore, the world).

Although evidence in the area dates Aboriginal occupation at 'only' a thousand years or so, this is probably because the river's floods and changes of course have destroyed older evidence. It isn't very far away, on drier land, that evidence of more than 40,000 years of continuous occupation has been found. The mind boggles.

The Yorta Yorta people have (re)claimed the forest under Australia's Native Title laws. The claim is, unfortunately, being resisted by the Victorian government. By the time this book is published the courts should have decided the case. If the traditional owners have been successful, they will have imput into managment decisions relating to current land use.

The **Dharnya Centre** (☎ 5869 3302), a visitor information centre run by Parks Victoria, has displays on the heritage and culture of local Aboriginal people (the Yorta Yorta), as well as detailed track notes for the park's extensive walking trails. The centre is open daily from 11 am to 3 pm ($2), although if you just want information on the park you don't have to pay.

Canoeing is popular through here, and the *Kingfisher* (☎ 5869 3399) cruise boat offers two-hour discovery tours for $15 at 12.30 pm on Monday, Wednesday, Thursday and Saturday (perhaps more often in school holidays).

You can camp for free anywhere in the park or at the Barmah Lakes camping area. The *Dharnya Centre* (☎ 5869 3302) has good dorm accommodation at $15 per person but it's designed for groups and the minimum charge is $150. Still, with a group of, say, five that isn't too bad. BYO bedding and food.

Getting There & Away The park entrance is 9km from the small town of Barmah (pop 200).

YARRAWONGA (pop 3435)
About 40km east of Cobram on the banks of Lake Mulwala, Yarrawonga is known for its fine and sunny weather, for a host of aquatic activities, and as a retirement centre.

Lake Mulwala was formed by the completion in 1939 of Yarrawonga Weir, which was part of the massive Lake Hume project (near Albury) to harness the waters of the Murray for irrigation. Scenic cruises are available and you can hire canoes and other water-sports gear.

Yarrawonga was first settled by Elizabeth Hume, sister-in-law of the early explorer Hamilton Hume, in about 1842. Her **Byramine Homestead** is 15km west of the town.

There is a tourist information centre (☎ 5744 1989) on the corner of Belmore St and Irvine Pde.

Places to Stay
Yarrawonga Caravan Park (☎ 5744 3420) on the Murray River has sites (from $8) and vans (from $27), and the *Royal Mail Hotel* (☎ 5744 3033), 96 Belmore St, has units from $35/45. There are plenty of motels.

Gold Country

If you have transport, the well-signposted Goldfields Tourist Route takes in all the major centres involved in the rush of last century, and makes for an interesting excursion for a few days.

Ballarat and Bendigo are the two major towns on the route, but, in a clockwise direction from Ballarat, it goes through Linton, Beaufort, Ararat, Stawell, Avoca, Maryborough, Dunolly, Tarnagulla, Bendigo, Maldon, Castlemaine, Daylesford and Creswick.

BALLARAT (pop 64,831)
The area around present-day Ballarat (or Ballaarat, as it was originally spelled), Victoria's largest inland city, was first settled in 1838. When gold was discovered at nearby Buninyong in 1851 the rush was on and within a couple of years the town that grew out of the Ballarat diggings had a population of 40,000.

Ballarat's fabulously rich quartz reefs were worked by the larger mining companies until 1918. More than a quarter of the gold unearthed in Victoria came from Ballarat.

Today Ballarat has plenty of reminders of its gold-mining past, including some outstanding Victorian-era architecture. Other attractions include gorgeous gardens, a fine art gallery, good museums, and Sovereign Hill, probably the best attraction of its type in the country.

Information
The helpful Ballarat Tourism Centre (☎ 5332 2694) on the corner of Albert and Sturt Sts is open daily.

If you want to try finding some gold for yourself, visit the Gold Shop, 8A Lydiard St Nth, in the old Mining Exchange building. They sell miner's rights and hire out metal detectors.

Sovereign Hill
Ballarat's major tourist attraction is Sovereign Hill, a fascinating recreation of a

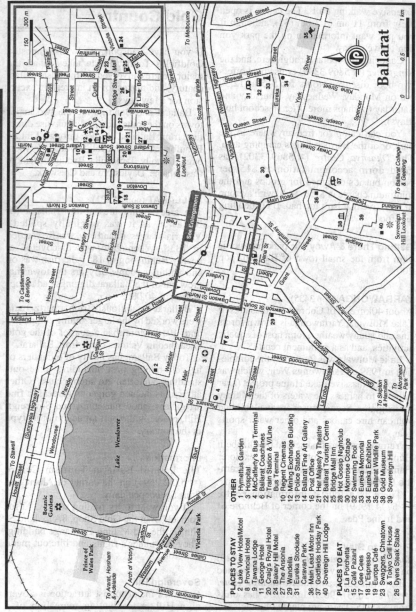

Ballarat

PLACES TO STAY
2 Lake View Hotel/Motel
8 Provincial Hotel
9 Tawana Lodge
11 George Hotel
20 Craig's Royal Hotel
24 Bakery Hill Motel
27 The Ansonia
29 Wandella
31 Eureka Stockade
36 Main Lead Motor Inn
37 Goldfields Holiday Park
40 Sovereign Hill Lodge

PLACES TO EAT
5 La Porchetta
15 Café Pazani
17 Gee Cees
19 L'Espresso
18 Europa Café
23 Swaggers, Chinatown
   & Tokyo Grill House
26 Dyers Steak Stable

OTHER
1 Hymettus Garden
3 Hospital
4 McCafferty's Bus Terminal
6 Ballarat Coachlines
7 Train Station & V/Line
   Bus Terminal
10 Regent Cinemas
12 Mining Exchange Building
13 Police Station
14 Ballarat Fine Art Gallery
16 Post Office
21 Her Majesty's Theatre
22 Ballarat Tourism Centre
25 Bridge Mall Inn
28 Hot Gossip Nightclub
30 Montrose Cottage
32 Swimming Pool
33 Eureka Memorial
34 Eureka Exhibition
35 Ballarat Wildlife Park
38 Gold Museum
39 Sovereign Hill

The Eureka Rebellion

Life on the goldfields was a great leveller, erasing all pre-existing social classes as doctors, merchants, ex-convicts and labourers toiled side by side in the mud. But as the easily won gold began to run out, the diggers began to recognise the inequalities between themselves and the privileged few who held land and government.

The limited size of claims, the inconvenience of licence hunts coupled with the police brutality that often accompanied searches, the very fact that while they were in effect paying taxes they were allowed no political representation, and the realisation that they could not get good farming land, fired unrest among the miners and led to the Eureka Rebellion at Ballarat.

In September 1854 Governor Hotham ordered that the hated licence hunts be carried out twice a week. A month later a miner was murdered near a Ballarat hotel after an argument with the owner, James Bentley.

When Bentley was found not guilty, by a magistrate who just happened to be his business associate, a group of miners rioted over the injustice and burned his hotel. Bentley was retried and found guilty, but the rioting miners were also jailed, which fuelled their mounting distrust of the authorities.

Peter Lalor

Creating the Ballarat Reform League, the diggers called for the abolition of licence fees, the introduction of the miner's right to vote and increased opportunities to purchase land.

On 29 November about 800 miners tossed their licences into a bonfire during a mass meeting, and then set about building a stockade at Eureka where, led by the Irishman, Peter Lalor, they prepared to fight for their rights.

On 3 December, having already organised brutal licence hunts, the government ordered troopers to attack the stockade. There were only 150 diggers within the makeshift barricades at the time, and the fight lasted only 20 minutes, leaving 30 miners and five troopers dead.

Although the rebellion was short-lived, the miners were ultimately successful in their protest. They had won the sympathy of most Victorians, and had the full support of the goldfields' population behind them. The government deemed it wise to acquit the leaders of the charge of high treason.

The licence fee was abolished and replaced by a miner's right, which cost one pound a year. This gave the right to search for gold; the right to fence in, cultivate and build a dwelling on a moderate-sized piece of land; and the right to vote for members of the Legislative Assembly. The rebel miner Peter Lalor actually became a member of parliament himself some years later. ∎

gold-mining township of the 1860s. It was the first and remains by far the best of the many similar recreations around the state, and you should allow at least half a day for a visit.

The main street features a hotel, post office, blacksmith's shop, bakery and a Chinese joss house. It's a living history museum with people performing their chores while dressed in costumes of the time. The site was actually mined back in the gold era so much of the equipment is authentic. There's a variety of above-ground and

underground mining works, and you can pan for gold in the stream.

Sovereign Hill is open daily from 9.30 am to 5 pm ($17.50, students $13, children $9, families $46).

The sound-and-light show 'Blood on the Southern Cross', a simulation of the Eureka Stockade events, takes in most of the large site. There are two shows nightly from Monday to Sunday; tickets cost $20.50 (children $10.50) or $38.50/24 with dinner. There's also a deal which includes daytime entry to Sovereign Hill, and an accommodation package. Bookings are essential (☎ 53 33 5777).

Gold Museum

Opposite Sovereign Hill, this museum has imaginative displays and samples from all the old mining areas in the Ballarat region. It's open from 9.30 am to 5.30 pm daily and is well worth the $4.80 admission (free if you have a Sovereign Hill ticket).

Eureka Stockade Memorial & Exhibition

The site of the Eureka Stockade is now a park on the corner of Eureka and Stawell Sts. There's a monument to the miners and a coin-in-the-slot diorama gives you an action replay of the events and causes of this revolt against British rule. A new interpretive centre is under construction.

Botanic Gardens & Lake Wendouree

Ballarat's lovely 40ha botanic gardens are beside Lake Wendouree, which was used as the rowing course in the 1956 Olympics. An original little paddle-steamer makes tours of the lake on weekends ($4). On weekends and holidays a tourist tramway operates around the gardens from a depot at the southern end.

Kryal Castle

Surprisingly, this modern bluestone 'medieval English castle' is very popular. It's no doubt helped along by the daily hangings (volunteers called for), regular 'whipping of wenches' and a weekly jousting tournament – kids love it. The castle is 8km from Ballarat, towards Melbourne, and is open daily from 9.30 am to 5.30 pm ($12.50, children $7 on weekends, a little less midweek).

Other Attractions

Lydiard St is one of the most impressive and intact streetscapes of Victorian architecture in the country, with many fine old buildings including Her Majesty's Theatre, the art gallery and Craig's Royal Hotel. The *Historic Lydiard Precinct* brochure is available from the tourist office.

The **Ballarat Fine Art Gallery**, 40 Lydiard

St North, is one of Australia's best provincial galleries and its Australian collection is particularly strong. You can also see the remnants of the original Eureka flag. The gallery is open daily from 10.30 am to 5 pm ($4).

The **Ballarat Wildlife Park** on the corner of York and Fussell Sts is home to wombats, koalas, Tasmanian devils, kangaroos, crocs and others; it is open daily from 9 am to 5.30 pm ($9/4.50). The **Great Southern Woolshed**, on the Western Highway on the eastern outskirts, has shearing demonstrations, trained dogs and woolly displays ($9/4).

Other attractions include **Montrose Cottage & the Eureka Museum** at 111 Eureka St, an **aviation museum** at the Ballarat airport, and the lovely **Hymettus Garden** at 8 Cardigan St.

Organised Tours

Timeless Tours (☎ 5342 0652) offers half-day guided tours around Ballarat's heritage sites ($20), as well as day trips to destinations farther afield including the Brisbane Ranges and Lerderderg Gorge – both well worth a visit.

Special Events

In early March Ballarat holds its annual Begonia Festival, which is 10 days of fun, flowers and the arts. Between August and November there's the Royal South Street Competitions, Australia's oldest eisteddfod.

Places to Stay

The Goldfields Accommodation Hotline (☎ 1800 240 077) books accommodation.

Camping *Goldfields Holiday Park* (☎ 5332 7888; 1800 632 237), 300m north of Sovereign Hill at 108 Clayton St, has tent sites ($14), vans ($35) and cabins ($43 to $58). Also convenient is the *Eureka Stockade Caravan Park* (☎ 5331 2281) next to the Eureka Stockade Memorial, with tent sites ($11), vans (from $25) and cabins ($39 to $44).

Hostels & Pubs Adjacent to Sovereign Hill, *Sovereign Hill Lodge YHA* (☎ 5333 3409) has eight to 10-bed bunk rooms at $16 and doubles for $37. There are some more expensive rooms with attached bathroom. The facilities are excellent and it's often fully booked.

The *Provincial Hotel* (☎ 5332 1845), opposite Ballarat train station at 121 Lydiard St, has basic pub rooms at $20/35 a single/double and backpackers' rooms at $10 per person. At 27 Lydiard St, the restored *George Hotel* (☎ 5333 4886) has good singles/doubles from $35/50, or $50/65 with en-suite (this pub has bands on weekends but it's pretty big so it might not be noisy). *Craig's Royal Hotel* (☎ 5331 1377), 10 Lydiard St South, has been restored to its original grandeur and has budget rooms at $40 and en-suite rooms from $65 to $160.

There's an excellent boutique hotel, the *Ansonia* (☎ 5332 4678), 28 Lydiard St Sth, with rooms from $90. It's a nonsmoking place.

Motels & B&Bs *Wandella* (☎ 5333 7046), 202 Dawson St Sth, is a big old guesthouse with B&B for $28/42/46 a single/double/twin. You pay 10% more on weekends and in school and other holiday periods, but 10% less if you stay more than one night. Bathrooms are shared.

The *Lake View Hotel/Motel* (☎ 5331 4592), by the lake at 22 Wendouree Pde, has singles/doubles from $46/56. The modern and central *Bakery Hill Motel* (☎ 5333 1363) on the corner of Humffray and Victoria Sts charges from $75/85, and close to Sovereign Hill, the *Main Lead Motor Inn* (☎ 5331 7533) at 312 Main Rd charges from $80/90.

Places to Eat
On the corner of Sturt and Drummond Sts there's a branch of the *La Porchetta* chain of good-value Italian restaurants. Farther towards the city centre on the corner of Sturt and Dawson Sts is *Gee Cees*, a reasonable cafe and restaurant carved out of the old Golden City pub. It's open from 11 am till late daily; pastas start around $8.50 and other

mains cost from $10 to $13. There are footpath tables.

L'Espresso, 417 Sturt St, is a funky little cafe with good food and coffee. It also sells (and plays) a great selection of jazz, blues and alternative music. A couple of doors south, *Europa Café* serves all-day breakfasts, lunches such as Turkish pita and Spanish omelettes, and Mediterranean-style dinner mains for about $17.

Café Pazani, on the corner of Sturt and Camp Sts, is a stylish European bar/restaurant. At 54 Lydiard St, near the Art Gallery, *Café Rendezvous* has healthy snacks and light meals.

There's a cluster of eateries in the Bridge St Mall: *Swaggers*, a steak-and-seafood joint, has pastas from around $6; *Chinatown* has all-you-can-eat deals; and *Tokyo Grill House* does sushi. For a great steak, head to *Dyer's Steak Stable* in Little Bridge St – it's expensive but very good.

Entertainment
Good live music venues include *Southern Star Saloon*, on the corner of Sturt and Drummond Sts, and the *Bridge Mall Inn* in Little Bridge St. If you're kicking on to a nightclub, try *21 Arms*, 21 Armstrong St, or *Hot Gossip*, 102 Dana St.

The wonderful *Her Majesty's Theatre* at 17 Lydiard St South is the main performing arts venue. The *Regent Cinemas* are at 49 Lydiard St North.

Getting There & Away
There are frequent daily trains between Melbourne and Ballarat, taking about 1¾ hours and costing $13.40 in economy. On weekdays V/Line buses go from Ballarat to Warrnambool ($17.50), Hamilton ($23.80), and Bendigo ($17.50) via Castlemaine ($13.40). There are also regular buses to Geelong ($9.50) and to Mildura ($45.40).

Passing through on the Melbourne to Adelaide run, Greyhound buses stop at the Ballarat Coachlines terminal near the train station, while McCafferty's buses stop at the Shell service station on the corner of Sturt and Pleasant Sts. Ballarat Coachlines

(☎ 5333 4181) has daily services to Melbourne airport for $20.

Getting Around

Timetables for the local Ballarat Transit bus service are available from the train station or the tourist office. The two main terminals are in Curtis St and Little Bridge St, on either side of the Bridge St Mall. Take bus No 9 to Sovereign Hill from the northern side of Sturt St, between Armstrong and Lydiard Sts. For the botanic gardens and Lake Wendouree, catch bus No 15 from Little Bridge St. Bus No 2 takes you to the train station.

The local taxi company (☎ 13 1008) runs 24 hours.

CLUNES (pop 846)

In June 1851 Clunes was the site of one of Victoria's very first gold discoveries. Although other finds soon diverted interest, many fine buildings are reminders of the former wealth of this charming little town.

The small hills around Clunes are extinct volcanoes. Nearby **Mt Beckworth** is noted for its orchids and bird life; you can visit the old gold diggings of **Jerusalem** and **Ullina**; and at **Smeaton**, between Clunes and Daylesford, an impressive bluestone water-driven mill has been restored (open Sunday afternoon only). This is a nice spot for a picnic.

MARYBOROUGH (pop 7381)

The district around Charlotte Plains was already an established sheep run, owned by the Simson brothers, when gold was discovered at White Hills and Four Mile Flat in 1854. A police camp established at the diggings was named Maryborough , and by the height of the gold rush the population had swelled to over 40,000. Gold mining ceased to be economical in 1918 but Maryborough had a strong manufacturing base by then and is still a busy town.

Built back in 1892, the magnificent Maryborough **railway station** was described by Mark Twain as 'a railway station with a town attached'. It now houses an impressive tourist complex, which includes the tourist office (☎ 5460 4511), a woodwork gallery, an antique emporium and a cafe.

Maryborough's Highland Gathering has been held every year on New Year's Day since 1857 and the annual 16-day Golden Wattle Festival is celebrated in September with literary events, music, the national gumleaf-blowing and bird-call championships, and street parades.

Places to Stay

The old *Bull & Mouth Hotel* (☎ 5461 1002), 119 High St, has pub rooms from $18/30, or $25/38 with en-suite; there are numerous other pubs, motels and caravan parks.

DAYLESFORD & HEPBURN SPRINGS (pop 6000)

Set among the scenic hills, lakes and forests of the Central Highlands, the delightful twin towns of Daylesford and Hepburn Springs are enjoying a booming revival as the 'spa centre of Victoria'.

The well-preserved and restored buildings show the prosperity that visited these towns during the gold rush, as well as the lasting influence of the many Swiss-Italian miners who expertly worked the tunnel mines in the surrounding hills.

The area's mineral springs were known before gold was discovered here, and by the 1870s Daylesford was a health resort attracting droves of fashionable Melburnians. It was claimed that the waters could cure any complaint.

The current trend towards healthy lifestyles (not to mention the proximity to Melbourne) has prompted a revival of interest in Daylesford and Hepburn Springs. There's the restored spa complex and the towns also boast masseurs, craft and antique shops, gardens, galleries, cafes and restaurants, and dozens of charming guesthouses, cottages and B&Bs. There's a healthy gay and (especially) lesbian scene.

Information

The Daylesford Information Centre (☎ 5348 1339) is next to the post office on Vincent St;

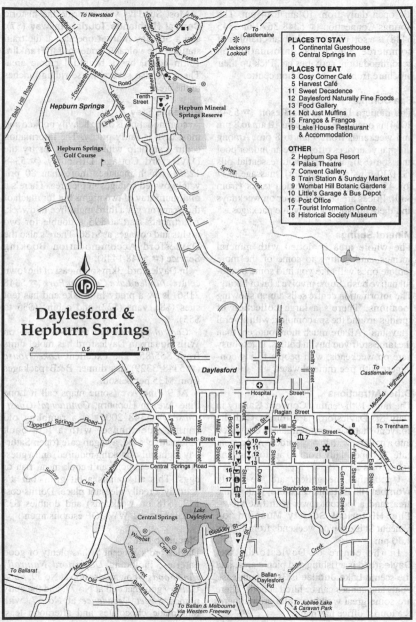

PLACES TO STAY
1 Continental Guesthouse
6 Central Springs Inn

PLACES TO EAT
3 Cosy Corner Café
5 Harvest Café
11 Sweet Decadence
12 Daylesford Naturally Fine Foods
13 Food Gallery
14 Not Just Muffins
15 Frangos & Frangos
19 Lake House Restaurant
& Accommodation

OTHER
2 Hepburn Spa Resort
4 Palais Theatre
7 Convent Gallery
8 Train Station & Sunday Market
9 Wombat Hill Botanic Gardens
10 Little's Garage & Bus Depot
16 Post Office
17 Tourist Information Centre
18 Historical Society Museum

VICTORIA

Daylesford &
Hepburn Springs

0   0.5   1 km

it's open daily from 10 am to 4 pm. The Springs Connection (☎ 5348 3670 or 5345 6448) is a sort of gay and lesbian chamber of commerce, which has information on accommodation, activities etc. Pick up their brochure from the information centre.

Spa Complex
The modern Hepburn Spa Resort (☎ 5348 2034) is open weekdays from 10 am to 8 pm and weekends from 9 am to 8 pm. Among the many services offered are an indoor pool and spa ($9), aero spas with essential oils ($21/30 for singles/doubles), massage ($47 for 45 minutes) and flotation tanks (from $30). Prices are slightly lower on weekdays and there are some good-value packages.

Mineral Springs
The whole area is dotted with mineral springs, and getting to some of the more remote ones will take you into some beautiful native bush. Some involve a bit of hiking. The information centre sells a map showing locations. There's a large collection of springs around the spa complex, with several 'flavours'. All are much more pungent than the tame stuff you buy in bottles. It gets busy here on weekends, with people filling containers with free mineral water.

Other Attractions
The huge 19th-century **Convent Gallery** in Daly St, Daylesford, is a former Catholic convent that has been brilliantly converted into a gallery, with lovely gardens and a great cafe. It's open daily from 10 am to 6 pm and entry costs $3.

Up behind the gallery are the lovely **Wombat Hill Botanic Gardens**, with picnic areas and a lookout tower with fine views. The **Historical Society Museum** on Vincent St is open on weekends from 1.30 to 4.30 pm.

In the centre of Daylesford, **Lake Daylesford** is a fishing and picnic area, and the scenic **Lake Jubilee** is 3km south-east; boats and canoes can be hired at both. There are some great **walking trails** around here; the tourist office has maps.

Most Sundays you can ride the historic **Central Highlands Tourist Railway** ($7), and a **Sunday market** operates at the train station. The volcanic crater of **Mt Franklin**, 10km north, has a beautiful picnic area. There are also several horse-riding ranches in the area.

Places to Stay
Accommodation is often heavily booked and most of it is fairly pricey. The information centre can help with bookings, or try the Daylesford Cottage Directory (☎ 5348 1255), which manages more than 80 privately owned cottages in the area. There's a minimum stay of two nights but for much of the year you get a third night free midweek. Apartments start at $95 a double for two nights and cottages at $180. There's also the Daylesford Accommodation Booking Service (☎ 5348 1448).

In Daylesford, 3km south-east of the town centre, *Jubilee Lake Caravan Park* (☎ 5348 2186) is by a pretty little lake and has tent sites ($8), vans ($22) and cabins ($35 to $55).

Central Springs Inn (☎ 5348 3134) on Wills Square in Daylesford has motel units from $55/85. The excellent *Lake House* (☎ 5348 3329) has dinner B&B packages from $135 per person.

At 9 Pine Ave (some maps call it Lone Pine Ave) in Hepburn, *Continental Guesthouse* (☎ 5348 2005) is a rambling old timber guesthouse, with a laid-back 'alternative' vibe, a vegan cafe (open Saturday night only, booking required) and a guest kitchen where you can't cook meat, fish or eggs. This all sounds a bit grim, but it's actually a really pleasant place. Dorms cost $17 ($18 on weekends) and doubles $35 ($40). This is a WWOOF establishment.

Places to Eat
Daylesford's Vincent St has plenty of good eateries, including *Daylesford Naturally Fine Foods* wholefoods shop at No 59, *Food Gallery* gourmet deli at No 77, and the aptly named *Sweet Decadence* at No 57, with handmade chocolates and afternoon teas.

Across the road is *Frangos & Frangos*, with an interesting but slightly pricey menu, or you can just have coffee and cake.

On Albert St, *Not Just Muffins* is famous for its home-made muffins and shortcakes, while across the road at No 29 is the laid-back *Harvest Café*, which specialises in organic foods. Overlooking Lake Daylesford is the *Lake House* (☎ 5348 3329), one of country Victoria's best restaurants – expensive but highly recommended.

In Hepburn Springs, the very popular *Cosy Corner Café* is at 3 Tenth St.

Getting There & Around

V/Line's trip between Melbourne and Daylesford ($11.90) takes two hours – you change from train to bus at Woodend. V/Line also has weekday buses to Ballarat ($8.40), Castlemaine ($4.20) and Bendigo ($8.40).

A shuttle bus runs back and forth between Daylesford and Hepburn Springs four times a day (weekdays only).

CASTLEMAINE (pop 6690)

Settlement of this district dates back to the 1830s when most of the land was taken up for farming. The discovery of gold at Specimen Gully in 1851 altered the pastoral landscape radically as 30,000 diggers worked a number of goldfields known, collectively, as the Mt Alexander diggings.

The township that grew up around the Government Camp, at the junction of Barkers and Forest creeks, was named Castlemaine in 1853 and soon became the thriving marketplace for all the goldfields of central Victoria.

Castlemaine's importance was not to last, however, as the district did not have the rich quartz reefs that were found in Bendigo and Ballarat. The centre of the town has been virtually unaltered since the 1860s when the population began to decline as the surface gold was exhausted.

These days Castlemaine is a charming town where the legacy of its rapid rise to prosperity lies in the splendid architecture of its public buildings and private residences

and in the design of its streets and many gardens.

Castlemaine XXXX, the beer that prompted jokes about Aussies not being able to spell 'beer', was first made here in 1859 but the brewer moved to Brisbane, taking the name with him.

The Castlemaine State Festival, one of Victoria's leading celebrations of the arts, is held every second October (even years), alternating with the Castlemaine Garden Festival (odd years).

Information

The tourist office (☎ 5470 6200), in a rotunda on Duke St (on the road in from the adjoining town of Chewton), is open daily.

Buda Historic Home & Gardens

Originally built by a retired Indian army officer in 1857, this is a superb example of Victorian-era colonial architecture. The house and magnificent gardens, extended in the 1890s by Hungarian gold and silversmith Ernest Leviny, are now open to the public and provide an insight into the town's refined and gracious past. Buda is on the corner of Urquhart and Hunter Sts, and is open daily from 9.30 am to 5 pm ($5).

Castlemaine Art Gallery & Museum

This gallery in Lyttleton St has an excellent collection of colonial and contemporary art and a museum featuring photographs, relics and documents. It's open daily from 10 am to 5 pm ($2).

Other Attractions

Dating back to 1861, the imposing **Old Castlemaine Gaol** looms over the town from a hilltop on Bowden St. The gaol now houses a gallery, a restaurant and a coffee shop and there's accommodation. It's open daily with hourly tours ($5, children $3) between 11 am and 5 pm. At least that's the theory. In practise you might find that tours run only on weekends.

The beautiful **botanic gardens** on Walker St were designed in the 1860s by the director of Melbourne's Royal Botanic Gardens,

Baron von Mueller, and it's well worth taking the time for a picnic by the lake or just a stroll among the 'significant trees' registered by the National Trust.

Castlemaine's original (and recently restored) **market building** on Mostyn St is now an art and craft market. Other places of interest include the **Camp Reserve**, the site of the original government camp during the gold rush; the **Burke & Wills Monument**, if you're into statues; a host of **gold-rush buildings**; and the **Kaweka Wildflower Reserve**.

Like several other towns in the goldfields area Castlemaine is attracting escapees from city life (including a couple of Lonely Planet staffers who commute to Melbourne) and there are services catering to citified tastes. Probably the best of them is the historic **Theatre Royal** (☎ 5472 1196), 30 Hargreaves St, now a cinema showing interesting movies (from $5). It also has a bar/restaurant, disco and band venue. It's worth ringing to find out what's on.

Places to Stay
Botanic Gardens Caravan Park (☎ 5472 1125), beside the gardens, has tent sites ($10.50) and vans ($26/31 a single/double).

You can stay in an old cell in *Old Castlemaine Gaol* (☎ 5470 5311); B&B tariffs are $45/65. The *Castle Motel* (☎ 5472 2433) at 1 Duke St (opposite the tourist office) has units from $60/70.

The *Midland Private Hotel* (☎ 5472 1085), opposite the train station at 2 Templeton St, is a fascinating blend of Victorian and Edwardian architecture with simple rooms from $45/90 (no smoking and no children).

Despite the name, *Bonkers on Barker* (☎ 5472 4454), 233 Barker St, is a refined place with singles from $75 and doubles from $85 to $100, including a great breakfast. Behind the Castlemaine Bookshop at 242 Barker St, the charming and self-contained *Bookshop Cottage* (☎ 5472 1557) charges $70 a double with breakfast.

Places to Eat
Tog's Place, 58 Lyttleton St, is a reasonably

priced cafe and the rustic *Capone's*, 50 Hargreaves St, is an affordable pizza/pasta joint.

The *Mad Cow*, next to the Theatre Royal in Hargreaves St, is a wine bar, gallery and cafe with a great seasonal menu. Main courses are around $8 to $12. The *Screaming Carrot* is a quirky-but-cool vegetarian restaurant with an emphasis on organic local produce. There's a great variety of food and it's fantastic value – mains start at $4.50 and don't go much over $8. Some nights there's live music.

For more upmarket dining, try the restaurant at *Bonkers on Barker* with a seasonal menu and mains between $12 and $16 – great value.

Getting There & Away
V/Line has daily trains between Melbourne and Castlemaine ($14.80), continuing on to Bendigo ($4.20), as well as weekday buses to Daylesford ($4.20), Ballarat ($13.40), Geelong ($23.80) and Maldon ($2.80).

AROUND CASTLEMAINE
The area around Castlemaine holds enough attractions – most of them related to the goldfields – to keep you going for a couple of days. You can visit the **Forest Creek Historic Gold Mine**, the remains of **Garfield's Water Wheel** and the **Dingo Farm**, all near Chewton; the **Heron's Reef Gold Diggings** at Fryerstown; the sombre **Pennyweight Children's Cemetery**, east of Castlemaine; the **Vaughan Springs** mineral springs and swimming hole; and the **Hilltop Cottage Garden** and **Tara Garden**, both at Guildford.

MALDON (pop 3100)
The small township of Maldon is one of the best preserved relics of Victoria's goldmining era. In 1966 the National Trust named Maldon the country's first 'notable town', an honour bestowed only on towns where the historic architecture is intact and valuable. Special planning regulations were introduced to preserve the town for posterity. It's flooded with visitors on weekends, and

it has its share of trendy (and overpriced) craft and antique shops. The Spring Folk Festival takes place every November.

The tourist information centre (☎ 5475 2569) on High St is open daily.

Things to See & Do

The tourist office has a handy *Historic Town Walk* brochure.

Carman's Tunnel Goldmine is 2km south of town; the 570m-long tunnel was excavated in the 1880s. There are candlelight tours through the mine on weekends and school holidays from 1.30 to 4 pm ($3.50, children $1.50).

Terry & Tangles offers horse-drawn wagon rides around town ($5/3) and picnic tours (bookings required ☎ 5475 2182; from about $30 a head). On Sunday and Wednesday you can ride a historic **steam train** along the old Maldon-Castlemaine line ($9/5).

The **historical museum** on High St is open daily from 1.30 to 4 pm. **Porcupine Township**, a recreation of an 1850s gold-rush town with timber-slab, mud-brick, tin and stone buildings, is open daily from 10 am to 5 pm and costs $7/4.

There are some good bushwalks around the town, and amateur gold hunters still scour the area with some success. There are good views from the tops of nearby **Anzac Hill** and **Mt Tarrengower**.

Places to Stay

Maldon Caravan Park (☎ 5475 2344) in Hospital St has tent sites ($10) and vans and cabins ($29 to $43). *Derby Hill Lodge* (☎ 5475 2033) in Phoenix St has motel-style rooms at $30/60 (weekends and school holidays only).

Most of the other accommodation is in B&Bs and guesthouses. *Palm House* (☎ 5475 2532) at 2 High St is one of the cheaper places, with B&B from $70 a double. The information centre has details of other places.

Getting There & Away

V/Line has a twice-daily bus service (week-days only) between Castlemaine and Maldon ($2.80).

BENDIGO (pop 59,936)

The solid, imposing and at times extravagant Victorian-era architecture of Bendigo is a testimony to the fact that this was one of Australia's richest gold-mining towns.

In the 1850s thousands upon thousands of diggers converged on the fantastically rich Bendigo diggings to claim the easily obtained surface gold, later turning their pans and cradles to Bendigo Creek and other local waterways in their quest for alluvial gold. The arrival of thousands of Chinese miners from 1854 (they called Bendigo 'Big Gold Mountain') caused a great deal of racial tension, but today Bendigo is one of the few places with significant reminders of its rich Chinese heritage.

By the 1860s the easily won ore was running out. Reef mining began in earnest and was dominated by the large and power-ful mining companies, who poured money back into the town as they extracted enor-mous wealth from their network of deep mine shafts. Reef mining continued up until the 1950s.

Today Bendigo is a busy and prosperous provincial city, with an interesting collection of mines, museums, historic buildings and other relics from the gold-mining era. It also has one of the best regional art galleries in Australia and some great wineries in the surrounding district.

Information

The Bendigo Tourist Information Centre (☎ 5447 7788) in the historic former post office on Pall Mall is open daily from 9 am to 5 pm. There are excellent historical dis-plays, and it's well worth a visit even if you don't want information.

There's an Internet cafe across the road from here, open daily.

Golden Dragon Museum

On Bridge St, the Golden Dragon Museum houses Loong and Sun Loong, the imperial Chinese dragons that are the centrepiece of

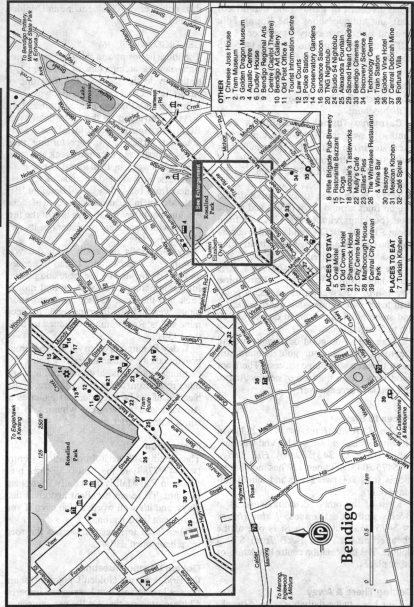

VICTORIA

Bendigo

To Bendigo Pottery,
Whipstick State Park
& Echuca

To Eaglehawk
& Kerang

To Marong,
Inglewood & Mildura

To Marong,
Inglewood & Mildura

To Castlemaine
& Melbourne

Rosalind Park

Queen
Elizabeth
Oval

See Enlargment

Lake
Weeroona

OTHER
1 Chinese Joss House
2 Tram Museum
3 Golden Dragon Museum
4 Aquatic Centre
6 Dudley House
9 Bendigo Regional Arts
  Centre (Capitol Theatre)
10 Bendigo Art Gallery
11 Old Post Office &
   Tourist Information Centre
12 Law Courts
13 Police Station
14 Conservatory Gardens
16 Sundance Saloon
20 TNG Nightclub
24 Studio 54 Nightclub
25 Alexandra Fountain
29 Sacred Heart Cathedral
33 Bendigo Cinemas
34 Discovery Science &
   Technology Centre
35 Train Station
36 Golden Vine Hotel
37 Central Deborah Mine
38 Fortuna Villa

PLACES TO STAY
5 Oval Motel
19 Old Crown Hotel
21 Shamrock Hotel
27 City Centre Motel
28 Marlborough House
39 Central City Caravan
   Park

PLACES TO EAT
7 Turkish Kitchen
8 Rifle Brigade Pub-Brewery
15 Ristorante Bazzani
17 Jogs
18 Jacquie's Tasteworks
22 Mully's Café
23 Gillies Pies
26 The Whirrakee Restaurant
   & Wine Bar
30 Rasoyee
31 Mexican Kitchen
32 Café Spiral

the annual Easter Fair parade, plus an impressive collection of Chinese heritage items and costumes. Loong is the oldest imperial dragon in the world and Sun Loong is the longest. The museum is open daily from 9.30 am to 5 pm; entry is $6.

The streets around the museum are being redeveloped with a Chinese theme, and there's a new (and still a bit raw) **Chinese Garden** across the road. Admission is free if you've paid the museum entry, otherwise it's $2.

Central Deborah Mine

This 500m-deep mine was worked on 17 levels and yielded about 1000kg of gold before it closed in 1954. There are lots of interesting exhibits and photographs, and you can do a self-guided surface tour ($5, children $3) or don a hard-hat for the 70-minute underground tour ($13/$6.50), which takes you 61m down to inspect newly commenced mining operations. The price includes the surface tour. The mine is on Violet St and is open daily from 9 am to 5 pm.

Bendigo Talking Tram & Tram Museum

A vintage tram makes a regular tourist run from the Central Deborah Mine through the centre of the city to the Tram Museum, with a commentary on the history of Bendigo. It departs daily at 9.30 and 11 am and 12.30, 2 and 3.30 pm from the Central Deborah Mine, or five minutes later from the Alexandra Fountain (more frequently during holidays). The fare is $7.50 adults, $4 children; you can also buy a combined ticket for the mine and the talking tram tour ($18.50/9.50).

Bendigo Art Gallery

Don't judge this gallery by its bland 1960s facade – behind is the lovely original gallery built in the 1880s. It has an outstanding collection of Australian colonial and contemporary paintings and 19th-century European art. The gallery is at 42 View St and is open daily from 10 am to 5 pm ($2, children $1).

A Bendigo Talking Tram trundles its way down to Bendigo's Central Deborah Mine

Chinese Joss House

Dating back to the 1860s and classified by the National Trust, this is one of the few remaining practising joss houses in the state, and features figures representing the 12 years of the Chinese solar cycle, commemorative tablets to the deceased, paintings and Chinese lanterns. It's in Finn St in North Bendigo and is open daily from 10 am to 5 pm ($3/1).

Other Attractions

Built in 1897, the magnificent **Shamrock Hotel** on Pall Mall is an outstanding example of the extravagance of late-Victorian architecture. Its size gives some indication of how prosperous the town was in the gold-mining era when, so the story goes, the floors were regularly washed down to collect the gold dust brought in on miners' boots. There are tours of the hotel on Saturday and Sunday at 2.30 pm; the $5 fee includes afternoon tea.

Opposite the Shamrock on Pall Mall are the equally elaborate former **post office** and **law courts** buildings. **Rosalind Park**, just north of Pall Mall, features open lawns and picnic tables, a lookout tower with great views, a fernery and the lovely **Conservatory Gardens**.

On High St, the **Sacred Heart Cathedral** is Victoria's largest Gothic-style building

Gold Fever

In May 1851 EH Hargraves discovered gold near Bathurst in New South Wales. Sensational accounts of the potential wealth of the find caused an unprecedented rush as thousands of people dropped everything to try their luck.

News of the discovery reached Melbourne at the same time as the accounts of its influence on the people of New South Wales. Sydney had been virtually denuded of workers and the same misfortune soon threatened Melbourne. Victoria was still being established as a separate colony so the loss of its workforce to the northern goldfields would have been disastrous.

A public meeting was called by the young city's businessmen and a reward was offered to anyone who could find gold within 300km of Melbourne. In less than a week gold was discovered in the Yarra River but the find was soon eclipsed by a more significant discovery at Clunes. Prospectors began heading to central Victoria and over the next few months the rush north across the Murray was reversed as fresh gold finds and new rushes became an almost weekly occurrence in Victoria.

Gold was found in the Pyrenees, the Loddon and Avoca rivers, at Warrandyte and at Bunninyong. At Ballarat in September 1851, the biggest gold discovery was made, followed by other significant discoveries at Bendigo, Mt Alexander, Beechworth, Walhalla, Omeo and in the hills and creeks of the Great Dividing Range.

By the end of 1851 about 250,000 ounces of gold had been claimed. Farms and businesses lost their workforces and in many cases were abandoned altogether as employers had no choice but to follow their workers to the goldfields. Hopeful miners left England, Ireland, Europe, China and the failing goldfields of California – during 1852 about 1800 people arrived in Melbourne each week.

The government introduced a licence fee of 30 shillings a month for all prospectors, whether or not they found gold. This entitled the miners to a claim, limited to eight feet square, in which to dig for gold, and it provided the means to enforce improvised laws for the goldfields.

The administration of each field was headed by a chief commissioner whose deputies, the state troopers, were empowered to organise licence hunts and to fine or imprison any miner who failed to produce the permit. Although this later caused serious unrest on the diggings, for the most part it successfully averted the lawlessness that had characterised the California rush.

There were, however, the classic features that seem to accompany gold fever: the backbreaking work, the unwholesome food and hard drinking, and the primitive dwellings. There was the amazing wealth that was to be the luck of some, but the elusive dream of others; and for every story of success there were hundreds more of hardship, despair and death.

In *Australia Illustrated*, published in 1873, Edwin Carton Booth wrote of the 1850s goldfields:

> ... it may be fairly questioned whether in any community in the world there ever existed more of intense suffering, unbridled wickedness and positive want, than in Victoria at [that] time ... To look at the thousands of people who in those years crowded Melbourne, and that most miserable adjunct of Melbourne, Canvas Town, induced the belief that sheer and absolute unfitness for a useful life in the colonies ... had been deemed the only qualification requisite to make a fortunate digger.

The gold rush had its share of rogues, including the notorious bushrangers who attacked gold shipments being escorted to Melbourne, but it also had its heroes who eventually forced a change in the political fabric of the colony (see The Eureka Rebellion in the Ballarat section).

Above all, the gold rush ushered in a fantastic era of growth and material prosperity for Victoria and opened up vast areas of country previously unexplored by whites.

In the first 12 years of the rush, Australia's population increased from 400,000 to well over a million, and in Victoria alone it rose from 77,000 to 540,000. To cope with the moving population and the tonnes of gold and supplies, the development of roads and railways was accelerated.

The mining companies that followed the independent diggers invested heavily in the region over the next couple of decades. The huge shantytowns of tents, bark huts, raucous bars and police camps were eventually replaced by the timber and stone buildings that were the foundation of many of Victoria's provincial cities, most notably Ballarat, Bendigo, Maldon and Castlemaine.

The gold towns reached the height of splendour in the 1880s. Gold production gradually lost its importance after that time, but by then the towns of the region had stable populations, and agriculture and other activities steadily supplanted gold as the economic mainstay.

Gold also made Melbourne Australia's largest city and financial centre, a position it held for nearly half a century. ■

outside Melbourne. Work was begun last century and completed in 1977.

Dudley House, 60 View St, is classified by the National Trust. It's a fine old residence with beautiful gardens and is open weekends and during school holidays from 2 to 5 pm. On Chum St the stately mansion, **Fortuna Villa**, with its lake and Italian fountain, was once owned by George Lansell, the Quartz King. It's open to the public on Sunday for a tour ($8) at 1 pm, including afternoon tea.

North of Bendigo, Eaglehawk also has some impressive historic buildings. The *Eaglehawk Heritage Trail* brochure, available from the information centre, guides you around many of them.

Special Events

Bendigo's annual Easter Fair, first held in 1871 to aid local charities, attracts big crowds and features a procession with Chinese dragons, a lantern parade, a jazz night and other entertainment. Bendigo's most curious event is the annual 'swap meet', held in November. It draws thousands of motoring enthusiasts from all over the country in search of that elusive vintage-car spare part.

Places to Stay

Central City Caravan Park (☎ 5443 6937), 362 High St, has tent sites from $10 and vans and cabins from $26 to $52, plus bunks at $12. It's about 2.5km south of the town centre – you can get there on a Kangaroo Flat bus from Hargreaves St.

Of the pubs offering accommodation, the central *Old Crown Hotel* (☎ 5441 6888), 238 Hargreaves St, is probably the best with singles/doubles with shared bathroom at $30/48, including breakfast. For a completely different sort of pub, consider a splurge at the very impressive *Shamrock Hotel* (☎ 5443 0333). Traditional rooms with shared bathroom are $50, en-suite rooms are $90, and the two-room suites cost $135 to $150.

There are plenty of motels. Two of the cheaper and more central ones are the *City*

Centre Motel (☎ 5443 2077), 26 Forest St (from $42/50), and the *Oval Motel* (☎ 5443 7211), opposite the Queen Elizabeth Oval at 194 Barnard St (from $42/52). The historic and elegant *Marlborough House* (☎ 5441 4142) on the corner of Rowan and Wattle Sts has B&B from $60/95.

Places to Eat

The small *Jacquie's Tasteworks*, 51 Bull St, is crammed with taste sensations: fresh pies and pastries, home-made salads and pastas, cooked breakfasts and more. *Green Olive Deli* in Bath Lane is the perfect spot for gourmet picnic supplies, with fine cheeses, patés, sandwiches and smallgoods.

Mully's Café, 32 Pall Mall, is nothing special, except that it's housed in an extraordinary old bank building, well worth a look.

In the Hargreaves St Mall, *Gillies'* pies are regarded by connoisseurs as among the best in Australia. A Bendigo institution, you queue at the little window, order one of their five or so varieties, then sit in the mall to eat it.

The popular *Rifle Brigade Pub-Brewery*, 137 View St, has bar meals for $7 and a good bistro with a courtyard. It also brews its own beers. The *Shamrock Hotel* has a pleasant corner bistro.

At 107 Pall Mall, *Clogs* is a stylish but affordable bar/restaurant with pizzas, pastas and a wide range of other meals – during the week it stays open until 1 am and on weekends until 4 am. *Café Spiral*, 95 Mitchell St, is a popular place serving Italian (and other) food at reasonable prices.

Mexican Kitchen, 28 High St, *Turkish Kitchen*, 159 View St, and *Rasoyee* Indian restaurant, 40 High St, all have filling main courses for about $10 and also do takeaways.

Ristorante Bazzani (☎ 5441 3777), Howard Place (by Pall Mall), is an excellent little restaurant and the prices aren't too bad, with main courses under $20 and vegetarian dishes under $15. The restaurant is open for dinner daily and there's also a cafe section open during the day, with pleasant outdoor tables.

Entertainment

For live music one of the best places is the *Golden Vine Hotel* on the corner of King and Myrtle Sts. *Sundance Saloon* on the corner of McCrae and Mundy Sts has pool tables and live bands on weekends, as does the *Rifle Brigade Pub-Brewery*. Bendigo's nightclubs include *Studio 54* on the corner of Williamson and Queen Sts, and *TNG* on the corner of Williamson and Hargreaves Sts.

The *Bendigo Regional Arts Centre*, in the beautifully restored Capitol Theatre at 50 View St, is the main venue for the performing arts. The *Bendigo Cinemas* are at 107 Queen St.

Getting There & Away

There are half a dozen trains between Melbourne and Bendigo on weekdays (fewer on weekends). The trip takes two hours and costs $20.20 in economy.

There's also a weekday V/Line bus service between Bendigo and Castlemaine ($4.20), Ballarat ($17.50) and Geelong ($29.40). Other destinations served by V/Line include Swan Hill ($22.60), Mildura ($45.50) and Echuca (just $6 – a bargain).

Getting Around

Bendigo and its surrounding area is well served by public buses. Check the route map at the bus stop on Mitchell St, at the end of the mall, or pick up timetables and route maps from the tourist centre or train station.

AROUND BENDIGO
Bendigo Pottery

Established in 1858, the oldest working pottery in Australia is on the Midland Highway, 7km north of Bendigo. The buildings are classified by the National Trust. There's a cafe, a sales gallery set among historic kilns, and you can watch potters at work in the studio. The pottery is open daily from 9 am to 5 pm; entry is free.

Whipstick State Park

Eight kilometres north of Bendigo, this small park conserves the distinctive Whipstick mallee vegetation. There are picnic areas, camp sites and walking tracks. Nearby, **Hartland's Eucalyptus Oil Factory** was established in 1890 and the production process can be inspected on Sunday.

Wineries

The brochure *Wineries of Bendigo & District* details 15 wineries that are open for sales and tastings, all within about half an hour's drive of Bendigo. These include Château Leamon (10km south of Bendigo), Balgownie (8km west) and Château Doré (8km south-west).

Heathcote

A quiet little town 47km south-east of Bendigo, Heathcote has a gold-mining past and a wine-making present and is surrounded by some excellent wineries including Jasper Hill, McIvor Creek, Zuber, Heathcote Winery and Huntleigh.

RUSHWORTH (pop 976)

This historic town, 100km north-east of Bendigo and 20km west of the Goulburn Valley Highway, was once a busy gold-mining centre and now has a National Trust classification. Apparently it was so named because the (gold) rush was worth coming to.

Seven kilometres south of town, in the Rushworth State Forest, is the gold-mining ghost town of **Whroo** (pronounced 'roo'). The small Balaclava open-cut mine yielded huge amounts of ore. At its peak the town had over 130 buildings, although today ironbark trees and native scrub have largely reclaimed the site.

The old cemetery (also National Trust classified) is an evocative place, and headstone inscriptions bear testimony to the hard life experienced by those who came in search of gold. There are a couple of signposted nature trails, one leading to a small rock water hole used by the Koories who inhabited this region. There's also a small mud-brick visitors centre and a camp site. Worth the detour.

North-East

LAKE EILDON

About 150km north-east of Melbourne, via the hill towns of Healesville and Marysville, is Lake Eildon, a massive lake created for hydroelectric power and irrigation purposes. It's a holiday area and one of Victoria's favourite water-sports playgrounds – water-skiing, fishing, sailing and houseboat trips are all available.

The township of **Eildon** is the main town on the southern end of the lake, and **Bonnie Doon** on one of the lake's northern arms also has some facilities. The main boat harbour is 2km north of Eildon township. On the western shores of the lake, the **Fraser National Park** has some good short walks including a guide-yourself nature walk. The 24,000ha **Eildon State Park** takes in the south-eastern shore area of Lake Eildon. On the eastern side of the lake is the old mining town of **Jamieson**.

Places to Stay

There's a stack of caravan parks in and around Eildon. There are also camp sites in the Fraser National Park and in the Eildon State Park – you'll need to book (☎ 5772 1293) during holiday periods.

In Eildon, the *Golden Trout Hotel/Motel* (☎ 5774 2508) has singles/doubles from $45/50. *Lakeside Leisure Resort* (☎ 5778 7252) in Bonnie Doon also has a *YHA Hostel* with bunks at $14.

Lake Eildon Holiday Boats (☎ 5774 2107) in Eildon is one of several outfits renting houseboats. As usual for houseboats, there's a huge array of rates and seasons. As an example, a six-berth boat (the smallest) costs from $550 to $670 for most weekends and for four days midweek.

Getting There & Away

McKenzie's (☎ 9853 6264) runs a daily service from Melbourne to Eildon ($17.50) via Marysville ($10.90) and Alexandra ($14.80).

MANSFIELD (pop 2526)

Mansfield is one of the best base-towns for Victoria's alpine country, with a good range of accommodation and eateries. In winter it offers easy access to the snowfields of Mt Buller and Mt Stirling, and at other times it's a good base for horse-riding, bushwalks and water sports on Lake Eildon.

The graves of three police officers killed by Ned Kelly at Tolmic in 1878 are in the Mansfield cemetery, and there's a monument to them in the town.

In late October, the Mansfield Mountain Country Festival features the Great Mountain Race, with the country's best brumbies and riders, and other activities. There's a tourist information centre (☎ 5775 1464) in the old railway station on High St.

Activities

Mountain Adventure Safaris (☎ 5777 3759) offers mountain-bike rides, white-water rafting, trekking, abseiling and more. High Country Camel Treks (☎ 5775 1591), 7km south, offers one-hour rides, as well as one, two and five-day alpine treks. The tourist centre has details of numerous other activities, including horse-riding ranches.

Places to Stay

James Holiday Park (☎ 5775 2705) on Ultimo St is the most convenient place to camp, with sites ($14 to $18) and cabins ($30 to $70).

Mansfield Backpackers Inn (☎ 5775 1800), in a restored heritage building at 112 High St, has good facilities. Bunks are $15 per person and singles/doubles with en-suite cost $30 per person. The *Mansfield Hotel* (☎ 5775 2101), 86 High St, and the *Delatite Hotel* (☎ 5775 2004), 95 High St, have B&B for $25 per person, and there are also a few motels in town.

Getting There & Away

V/Line buses operate daily from Melbourne for $26.10. During the ski season Mansfield-Mt Buller Bus Lines (☎ 5775 2606) has daily buses running up to Mt Buller ($18/29.70

one-way/return) and sometimes to Mt Stirling ($14.10/24.50).

GOULBURN VALLEY

The Goulburn River runs in a wide arc from Lake Eildon north-west across the Hume Highway, joining the Murray River just upstream of Echuca.

The army base of Puckapunyal, 9km west of Seymour, has the **RAAC Tank Museum** with a large collection of tanks and armoured vehicles. It is open daily.

South-west of **Nagambie** are two of the best known wineries in Victoria: Chateau Tahbilk, with its National Trust classified buildings and cellars, and the ultramodern Mitchelton, with its observation tower looming above the surrounding countryside.

Shepparton (pop 31,945)

Shepparton and its adjoining centre of Mooroopna are in a prosperous fruit and veg-etable-growing area irrigated by the Goulburn River.

The **Shepparton City Historical Museum** on the corner of High and Welsford Sts is open Sunday from 1 to 4 pm and is well worth a visit. There's also an **art gallery** in Welsford St, a fairly tacky **International Village**, and tours of the huge **Shepparton Preserving Company (SPC) cannery** (January to early April).

Most travellers come to Shepparton for casual fruit-picking work. The main season is January-April; contact the Harvest Office (☎ 5832 0151) for information.

There's a tourist information office (☎ 5832 9870) by the lake on Wyndham St, just south of the city centre.

Places to Stay & Eat *Victoria Lake Caravan Park* (☎ 5821 5431) is the most central of the six caravan parks. Tent sites cost from $8, vans from $30 and cabins $48. The *Victoria Hotel* (☎ 5821 9955), situated on the corner of Wyndham and Fryers Sts, charges $25/30 for singles/doubles ($40/50 with en-suite).

Getting There & Away V/Line has daily trains and buses between Melbourne and Shepparton ($22.60).

Kelly Country

In the north-east of Victoria is 'Kelly Country', where Australia's most famous outlaw, Ned Kelly, had some of his most exciting brushes with the law. Kelly and his gang of bushrangers shot dead three police officers at Stringybark Creek in 1878, and robbed banks at Euroa and Jerilderie before their lives of crime ended in a siege at Glenrowan. Ned and members of his family were held and tried in Beechworth, and Kelly was hung at the Old Melbourne Gaol.

Not far to the east of the Hume Highway are the Victorian Alps. In winter you'll catch glimpses of their snow-capped peaks from the highway near Glenrowan. ■

GLENROWAN (pop 343)

In 1880, the Kelly gang's exploits finally came to an end in a bloody shoot-out here, 230km north of Melbourne. Ned Kelly was captured alive and eventually hanged in Melbourne.

You can't drive through Glenrowan without being confronted by the commercialisation of the Kelly legend. The town has everything from a giant statue of Ned (complete with armoured helmet), colonial-style tearooms and souvenir shops, to **Kellyland**, an impressive animated computerised theatre ($15, children $8).

The ruins of the Kelly family homestead can be seen a few kilometres off the highway at Greta, though little remains of the slab bush hut.

WANGARATTA (pop 15,527)

'Wang', as it is commonly known, is at the junction of the King and Ovens rivers; it's also the turn-off point for the Ovens Highway to Mt Buffalo, Bright and the northern section of the Victorian Alps. The town has some pleasant parks, and bushranger Mad Dog Morgan is buried in the local cemetery.

Wang has a visitor information centre (☎ 5721 5711) on the corner of the Hume Highway and Handley St. A big Jazz & Blues Festival is held on the weekend before the Melbourne Cup horse race, which is on the first Tuesday in November.

Places to Stay

Painters Island Caravan Park (☎ 5721 3380) on the Ovens River has sites ($10) and cabins (from $35). The *Royal Victoria Hotel* (☎ 5721 5455), 25 Faithful St, has pub rooms for $20/30 and motel units from $32/45. A reader recommends the *Billabong Hotel* (☎ 5721 2353), $24/40. *Millers Cottage Motel* (☎ 5721 5755) on the highway north of the centre has units from $36/43.

Getting There & Away

V/Line has daily trains between Melbourne and Wang ($28.40), continuing on to Albury-Wodonga ($7.30). Wangaratta Coachlines (☎ 5722 1843) runs buses to Albury-Wodonga, Mt Beauty, Beechworth, Bright, Rutherglen etc.

CHILTERN (pop 1080)

Close to Beechworth and only 1km west off the Hume Highway between Wangaratta and Wodonga, Chiltern once swarmed with gold-miners in search of their fortunes. It's now a charming and historic town worthy of a visit.

Author Henry Handel Richardson's home, **Lake View**, and **Dow's Pharmacy**, a well-preserved old shop, are National Trust properties open on weekends and school and public holidays from 10 am to 4 pm.

RUTHERGLEN (pop 1904)

Close to the Murray River and north of the Hume, Rutherglen is the centre of one of Victoria's major wine-growing areas and has long been famous for its fortified wines. This is a great area for bike-touring – bikes can be hired from Walkabout Cellars, 84 Main St. Bogong Jack's Adventures (☎ (08) 8383 7198), also offers winery tours by bicycle.

Rutherglen itself is an attractive little town with a main street lined with old verandah-fronted buildings. There's a small **historical museum** (open Sunday), and the tourist office (☎ (02) 6032 9166), inside the historic Jolimont Wines complex on the corner of Main and Drummond Sts, is open daily from 9 am to 5 pm.

Festivals include the Winery Walkabout Weekend, held on the Queen's Birthday weekend in June, and the Tastes of Rutherglen Weekend, also in June.

Wahgunyah, 9km north-west, was once a busy port for the Ovens Valley gold towns. Its customs house is a relic of that era.

Wineries

A free map and brochure is available from Walkabout Cellars and the wineries. It guides you around the 15 or so wineries in the area, including **All Saints**, which is classified by the National Trust and has a wine museum; **Chamber's Rosewood**, an old family-run winery close to Rutherglen; **Gherig's Winery**, set around the historic Barnawartha Homestead; **Mt Prior**, with luxurious (and expensive) accommodation and a highly regarded restaurant; and **St Leonard's**, with an excellent bistro and a

Victorian Wineries

Some of Australia's best wines are made in Victoria. Grape growing and wine production began with the gold rush of the 1850s and, before the turn of the century, the fine reputation of Victorian fortified wines was established in Europe. Then phylloxera, a disease of grapevines, devastated the Victorian vineyards. Changing tastes in alcohol completed the destruction.

In the 1960s the Victorian wine industry started to recapture its former glory and produce fine table wines, as well as fortified wines.

Victoria's oldest established wine-producing region is in the north-east, particularly around Rutherglen, but extending to Milawa, Glenrowan and beyond. Other fine wine-growing areas include the Yarra Valley and the Mornington Peninsula near Melbourne; the Geelong region; central Victoria around Bendigo and Heathcote; the Goulburn Valley; the Great Western and Pyrenees ranges (between Stawell, Ararat and Avoca); the Macedon ranges north of Melbourne; and the Murray River valley. ■

very scenic picnic spot on a billabong by the Murray River.

Places to Stay & Eat

Rutherglen Caravan Park (☎ (02) 6032 8577) has vans from $24 and sites for $9. On Main St, the National Trust classified *Victoria Hotel* (☎ (02) 6032 8610) has B&B for $32/56 for basic rooms, $65/76 with en-suite.

The nearby *Star Hotel* (☎ (02) 6032 9625) is just as old but not quite as charming. It has rooms from $15/25 and motel-style units for $39 a double ($49 on weekends). Rutherglen's half-dozen motels include the modern *Wine Village Motor Inn* (☎ (02) 6032 9900), 217 Main St, with singles/doubles from $45/55.

There are tearooms and pubs along Main St and several of the wineries have good restaurants, including St Leonards, All Saints and Mt Prior.

At 152 Main St the *Shamrock* is open for dinner from Tuesday to Saturday, with mains in the $15 to $25 range.

Mrs Mouse's Pantry at Wahgunyah is another good place to eat.

Getting There & Away

V/Line has buses between Wangaratta and Rutherglen ($4.20) on Wednesday, Friday and Sunday.

WODONGA (pop 25,825)

The Victorian half of Albury-Wodonga is on the Murray River, the border between Victoria and New South Wales. The combined cities form the main economic and industrial centre of this region.

For tourist information there's the Gateway Tourist Information Centre (☎ (02) 6041 3875), on the Lincoln Causeway between Wodonga and the Murray (for more information, see the Albury section in the New South Wales chapter).

The excellent *Herb & Horse* (☎ (02) 6072 9553) is 45km away and it's a great place to stay. Again, see the Albury section for more information.

CORRYONG (pop 1215)

Corryong, the Victorian gateway to the Snowy Mountains and Kosciusko National Park, is close to the source of the Murray River, which at this point is merely an alpine stream.

Corryong's main claim to fame, however, is as the last resting place of Jack Riley, 'the Man from Snowy River'. Though some people dispute that Banjo Paterson based his stockman hero on Riley, a tailor turned mountain man who worked this district, the 'man' is nevertheless well remembered in Corryong.

Jack Riley's grave is in the town cemetery and the **Man from Snowy River Museum**, with local history exhibits, is open daily from 10 am to noon and 2 to 4 pm.

Places to Stay
The town has two caravan parks (both with vans and cabins), a pub and a couple of motels.

YACKANDANDAH (pop 592)
There's a saying around these parts that 'all roads lead to Yackandandah'. Indeed, if you were to get lost in the beautiful hills and valleys of this district you would find that most of the signposts do point to this charming little town.

This pretty little 'strawberry capital', 32km south of Wodonga, 23km from Beechworth and always on the way to somewhere, has been classified by the National Trust; not just the odd building but the entire town.

Yackandandah was a prosperous gold town and, back then, a welcome stopover on the old main road between Sydney and Melbourne. It has many fine old buildings, including the 1850 **Bank of Victoria**, which is now a museum.

There are tent sites ($10) and vans ($35) at the *Yackandandah Caravan Park* (☎ 6027 1380), on the Dederang Rd close to some good bushwalks.

BEECHWORTH (pop 2953)
This picturesque town set amid the rolling countryside of the Ovens Valley has been attracting tourists for a good many years. Way back in 1927 it won the Melbourne *Sun News Pictorial* 'ideal tourist town' competition.

It is still a pleasure to visit Beechworth and spend a few days enjoying its wide tree-lined streets with their fine and dignified gold-rush architecture, or exploring the surrounding forested valleys, waterfalls and rocky gorges. It's a perfect place for walking or cycling.

VICTORIA

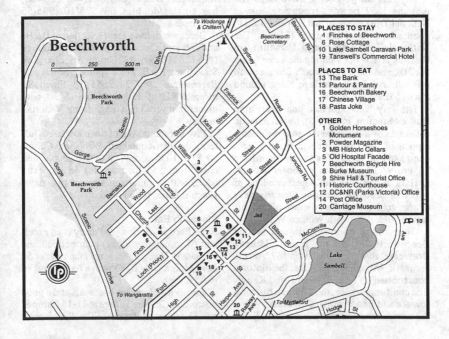

Beechworth

0   250   500 m

To Wodonga & Chiltem

Beechworth Cemetery

Beechworth Park

Beechworth Park

Gorge

Gorge

Scenic Drive

Sydney Road

Frederick Street

Kars Street

William Street

Street

Street

Street

Junction Rd

St

Bernard

Wood

Camp

Last

Church

Finch

Loch (Priory)

Ford

High

Scenic Drive

To Wangaratta

Jail

Billson Street

McConville

Harper Ave

Railway Ave

To Myrtleford

Hodge St

Lake Sambell

Ave

10

LP

PLACES TO STAY
4 Finches of Beechworth
6 Rose Cottage
10 Lake Sambell Caravan Park
19 Tanswell's Commercial Hotel

PLACES TO EAT
13 The Bank
15 Parlour & Pantry
16 Beechworth Bakery
17 Chinese Village
18 Pasta Joke

OTHER
1 Golden Horseshoes Monument
2 Powder Magazine
3 MB Historic Cellars
5 Old Hospital Facade
7 Beechworth Bicycle Hire
8 Burke Museum
9 Shire Hall & Tourist Office
11 Historic Courthouse
12 DC&NR (Parks Victoria) Office
14 Post Office
20 Carriage Museum

The town is 35km east of Wangaratta, and if you're travelling between Wang and Wodonga the detour through Beechworth makes a worthwhile alternative to the frenetic pace of the Hume Highway.

Information

The good Beechworth Visitor Information Centre (☎ 5728 3233) is inside the old shire hall on Ford St, and is open daily from 9 am to 5 pm.

Things to See

In the 1850s Beechworth was the very prosperous hub of the Ovens River gold-mining region. Signs of the gold wealth are still very much in evidence, reflected in the fact that 32 buildings are classified by the National Trust. They include **Tanswell's Hotel** with its magnificent old lacework, the **post office** with its clock tower, and the **training prison** where Ned Kelly and his mother were imprisoned for a while.

The 5km **Gorge Scenic Drive** takes you past the 1859 **powder magazine**, now a National Trust museum that is open 10 am to noon and 1 to 4 pm daily ($1.30). The National Trust's **Carriage Museum** on Railway Ave is open during the same hours ($1.50), and the **Beechworth Stagecoach** offers horse-drawn carriage rides around town ($5).

The very well-presented and interesting **Burke Museum**, in Loch St, has an eclectic collection of relics from the gold rush and a replica of the main street a century ago, complete with 16 shopfronts – well worth the $5 entry. The hapless explorer Robert O'Hara Burke was the superintendent of police in Beechworth during the early days of the gold rush before he set off on his historic trek north with William Wills.

Other things of interest in and around Beechworth include the historic **Murray Brewery Cellars**, established in 1872, on the corner of William and Last Sts; the **historic courthouse** on Ford St, site of Ned Kelly's first court appearance; the **Chinese burning towers** and **Beechworth Cemetery**, where the towers, altar and many graves are all that

remain of the town's huge Chinese population during the gold rush; and the **Golden Horseshoes Monument** to a local pioneer who made gold horseshoes for a friend who had won a seat in parliament to represent the local miners.

Woolshed Falls, just out of town on the Chiltern road, is a picnic area and the site of a major alluvial goldfield that yielded over 85,000kg of gold in 14 years. Farther west at **Eldorado** a gigantic gold dredge slowly rusts on the lake where it was installed in 1936.

Places to Stay

Lake Sambell Caravan Park (☎ 5728 1421), McConville Ave, has tent sites ($11), vans (from $28) and cabins ($47).

The *Old Priory* (☎ 5728 1024), 8 Priory Lane, charges $32/58 B&B and there is a dorm for groups only. There are also a couple of en-suite room in cottages for $80 a double B&B. German is spoken. At 30 Ford St, *Tanswell's Commercial Hotel* (☎ 5728 1480) has singles/doubles for $25/40 ($35/55 weekends).

Beechworth has a great selection of B&Bs and cottages. One of the best is *Rose Cottage* (☎ 5728 1069), 42 Camp St, charging $60/85 for B&B. For a splurge, *Finches of Beechworth* (☎ 5728 2655), 3 Finch St, offers B&B at 150 a double ($230 with dinner midweek) in a magnificent Victorian house.

Five kilometres out of town towards Chiltern, the self-contained *Woolshed Cabins* (☎ 5728 1035) sleeps up to five people, and costs from $55 for two plus $8 per extra adult, with a minimum stay of two days. Linen is extra, if you need it.

Places to Eat

At 69 Ford St, *Parlour & Pantry* is an excellent (if somewhat pricey) gourmet deli and restaurant. *Pasta Joke*, across the road at 52 Ford St, is a cosy BYO with a huge range of pasta dishes.

Tanswell's Hotel has bar meals and a good bistro, and *Chinese Village* at 11-15 Camp St has $5 takeaway lunches. The *Beechworth*

Beechworth Bakery on Camp St has an irresistible selection of hot bread, cakes and home-made pies. On a sunny morning, the tables on the footpath are the right place for a coffee and fresh croissant breakfast.

Beechworth's most upmarket restaurant is the *Bank*, housed in the historic Bank of Australasia building at 86 Ford St.

Getting There & Around
V/Line has daily services between Melbourne and Beechworth ($33.20) and Wangaratta Coachlines (☎ 5722 1843) runs buses to Albury-Wodonga, Bright and Rutherglen. Beechworth Bicycle Hire is on Camp St.

BRIGHT (pop 1898)
Deep in the Ovens Valley, Bright has become one of the focal points for adventure activities in the High Country. Renowned for its gorgeous setting, the town celebrates its contrasting seasonal beauty during the Bright Autumn Festival and the Alpine Spring Festival. In 1857 the notorious Buckland Valley riots took place near here; the diligent Chinese gold-miners were forced off their claims and given much less than a fair go. It is about an hour's scenic drive from town to the snowfields of Mt Hotham and Falls Creek, and half an hour to Mt Buffalo.

The tourist information centre (☎ 5755 2275) in Delany Ave is open daily from 9 am to 5 pm.

Activities
There are plenty of walking trails around here and the tourist office has a *Bright Walking Tracks* brochure, which details eight great walks from 1.5 to 5km long.

There are various places hiring bikes, and horse rides are available (see the information centre or the Bright Hikers Hostel).

This is a great place to try hang-gliding, with a launch ramp right up on top of Mt Buffalo, from where you can ride the thermals then land at Bright airport (just a mown field and a shed or two). Tandem hang-gliding is offered, and there are flights in powered hang-gliders (which fly up over the mountain then power-off and glide back down) and microlights. There are several operators and the Bright Hikers Hostel takes bookings. We had a great time with the Eagle School of Hang Gliding (☎ 5750 1174; 018 570 168).

Places to Stay
One of about a dozen caravan parks in town, *Bright Municipal Caravan Park* (☎ 5755 1141) on Cherry Lane also has a very good associate-YHA hostel with beds at $15. The park's tent sites cost $12 to $15 and cabins $36 to $60.

The modern and well-equipped *Bright Hikers Hostel* (☎ 5750 1244), in the centre of town at 4 Ireland St, has dorm beds at $15 and twins/doubles at $32. There's also a booking service for numerous activities.

The *Alpine Hotel* (☎ 5755 1366) at 7 Anderson St has motel units from $30/45 to $35/50, and the *Elm Lodge Motel* (☎ 5755 1144) at 2 Wood St is one of the best value motels with singles/doubles from $32/43. There are dozens of other accommodation options – the tourist centre runs a helpful booking service.

Places to Eat
Liquid Am-Bar on Anderson St is a fun cafe/bar with an interesting and affordable menu. *Alps Pasta & Pizza* on Gavan St has cheap pizzas, pastas and Mexican food.

Getting There & Away
Melbourne to Bright costs $37.80 with V/Line (train to Wangaratta and a connecting bus service daily except Saturday, continuing on to Beechworth).

The Alps

The Victorian Alps are the southern end of the Great Dividing Range, which runs all the way down Australia's east coast through Queensland and New South Wales into Victoria's north-east, finishing with a flourish at the Grampians in the state's west.

The Victorian ski fields are at lower altitudes than those in New South Wales, but they receive as much snow and have similar conditions above and below the snow line. The two largest ski resorts are Mt Buller and Falls Creek. Mt Hotham is smaller, but has equally good skiing, while Mt Buffalo and Mt Baw Baw are smaller resorts popular with families and novice to intermediate skiers. Lake Mountain, Mt Stirling and Mt St Gwinear are all mainly cross-country skiing areas with no overnight accommodation. Dinner Plain, near Mt Hotham, is an architect-designed village above the snow line (and it has a great pub!).

The roads are fully sealed to all ski resorts except Mt Baw Baw, Mt Stirling and Dinner Plain. In winter, snow chains must be carried to all ski resorts (you may be turned back if you haven't got them) and driving conditions can be hazardous. Other roads that crisscross the Great Dividing Range are unsealed for at least part of their way and only traversable in summer.

The skiing season officially commences on the first weekend of June, and skiable snow usually arrives later in the month. Spring skiing can be good as it is sunny and warm with no crowds, and there's usually enough snow until the end of September.

In the summer months, especially from December to February, the area is ideal for bushwalking, rock climbing, fishing, camping, and observing the native flora and fauna. Other activities include canoeing, rafting, hang-gliding, mountain biking, horse trekking and paragliding. This is the season most backpackers head for the hills.

Bushwalkers should be self-sufficient, with a tent, a fuel stove, warm clothes and sleeping bag, and plenty of water. In the height of summer, you can walk all day in the heat without finding water, and then face temperatures below freezing at night.

Accommodation

There are many places to stay, especially in the ski resorts, which have lots of accommodation. Overall, these are expensive in winter and many people prefer to stay in towns

below the snow line and drive up to the ski fields. In July and August it is advisable to book your accommodation, especially for weekends. In June or September it is usually possible to find something if you just turn up. Hotels, motels, chalets, self-contained flats and units, and caravan parks abound in the region. There is also a youth hostel at Mt Buller, plus backpackers' hostels in Bright and Mansfield.

Apart from these, the cheapest accommodation in the ski resorts is a bed in one of the club lodges, or it is possible to cut costs by cramming as many people as possible into a flat. The various accommodation-booking services at the resorts should be able to help you find a place. In summer, bushwalkers may find bargain accommodation in the skiing areas.

ALPINE NATIONAL PARK

The 646,000ha Alpine National Park was proclaimed in 1989. Victoria's largest national park, it covers most of the state's prime 'high country' stretching from Mansfield north-east to the New South Wales border, and is contiguous with the Kosciusko National Park in New South Wales. Most of the ski resorts in the state fall within the park's boundaries, and access is possible from many points.

Bushwalking and, in winter, cross-country skiing are the main activities within the park as it is largely undeveloped, and plans are to keep it that way. For many years large areas that are now part of the park were used for cattle grazing, but this is now being restricted.

The **Australian Alps Walking Track** is a walking trail that runs for 655km from Walhalla, near Mt Baw Baw, to the Brindabella Ranges on the outskirts of Canberra. For more information, visit a Parks Victoria office or contact the rangers in Bright on ☎ 5755 1577. The department also publishes an excellent 70-page colour guidebook called *Into the High Country* ($17.95). However, it's currently in short supply and no-one knows whether there will be a new edition. Several alpine walks are also

VICTORIA

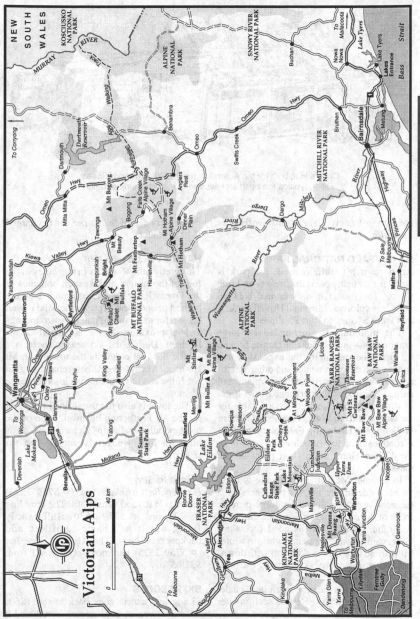

Victorian Alps

0   20   40 km

Craig's Hut, built for the Australian movie *The Man from Snowy River*, typifies the bush architecture of Victoria's alpine region

covered in Lonely Planet's *Bushwalking in Australia*.

MT BUFFALO NATIONAL PARK

Apart from Mt Buffalo itself, the park is noted for its many pleasant streams and fine walks. The mountain was named back in 1824 by explorers Hume and Hovell on their trek from Sydney to Port Phillip Bay.

The mountain is surrounded by huge granite tors – great blocks of granite broken off from the massif by the expansion and contraction of ice in winter and other weathering effects. There is abundant plant and animal life around the park, and over 140km of walking tracks. Leaflets are available for the **Gorge Nature Walk**, **View Point Nature Walk** and the **Dicksons Falls Nature Walk**. A road leads up to just below the summit of the 1720m Horn, the highest point on the massif.

In summer Mt Buffalo is a hang-gliders' paradise (definitely not for beginners) and the near-vertical walls of the gorge provide some of the most challenging rock climbs in Australia. **Lake Catani** is good for swimming, camping and canoeing, while in winter Mt Buffalo turns into a ski resort with downhill and cross-country skiing being the most popular activities.

Mt Buffalo has a camping ground, chalet and lodge (see the Ski Resorts section later in this chapter).

An entry fee of $6.50 per car is charged ($10 in winter).

HARRIETVILLE (pop 100)

This pretty little town sits in the valley at the fork of the eastern and western branches of the Ovens River, and is surrounded by the highest peaks in the Alps. Harrietville is well known for its beautiful natural surroundings and its proximity to the ski resort of Mt Hotham. During the ski season there is a shuttle bus that connects the town with Mt Hotham. Always check beforehand to find out if the road to Hotham is closed because of snow.

The town is also the usual finishing point for the Mt Feathertop bushwalk, one of the most popular walks in Victoria, and so is busy on long weekends outside the ski season.

Places to Stay

Harrietville Caravan Park (☎ 5759 2523) has sites ($10) and vans ($30). The rambling *Bon Accord* (☎ 5759 2530) isn't exactly flash, but it has basic facilities and backpackers' beds. The *Alpine Lodge Inn* (☎ 5759 2525) has motel-style B&B from $32/65.

SKI RESORTS

Skiing in Victoria goes back to the 1860s when Norwegian gold-miners introduced it in Harrietville. It has grown into a multi-million-dollar industry with three major ski resorts and six minor ski areas. None of these resorts is connected to another by a lift system, but it is possible for the experienced and well-equipped cross-country skier to go from Mt Hotham to Falls Creek across the Bogong High Plains. There is an annual race that covers this route.

The Alpine Resorts Commission (ARC; ☎ 9895 6900) is responsible for managing the ski resorts and on-mountain information centres. The entry fee at most resorts is $15 per car per day in winter. For cross-country skiers, there's a $5.25 trail-use fee at all resorts.

Falls Creek (1780m)

This resort sits at the edge of the Bogong High Plains overlooking the Kiewa Valley, a five-hour, 375km drive from Melbourne. Falls Creek is one of the best resorts in Victoria and the only ski village in Australia where everyone can ski directly from their lodge to the lifts and from the slopes back to their lodge.

The skiing is spread over two bowls with 30km of trails, 23 lifts and a vertical drop of 267m. Runs are divided into 17% beginners, 53% intermediate and 30% advanced. A day ticket costs $59, a seven-day ticket costs $340 and a daily lift and lesson package costs $80. Entry fees are $15 per car, and the ARC (☎ 5758 3224) has an information office in the lower car park.

You'll find some of the best cross-country skiing in Australia here. A trail leads around Rocky Valley pondage to some old huts from the cattle days. The more adventurous can tour to the white summits of Nelse, Cope and Spion Kopje. You can choose between ski-skating on groomed trails; light touring with day packs; and general touring with heavier packs, usually involving an overnight stay in a tent. Cross-country downhill, the alternative to skiing on crowded, noisy slopes, is also popular.

Summer in Falls Creek

In summer there are plenty of opportunities for alpine walking to places like Ruined Castle, Ropers Lookout, Wallaces Hut and Mt Nelse, which is part of the Australian Alps Walking Track. This can be affordable thanks to the great deal at Pfefferkorn Lodge (see Places to Stay).

Places to Stay & Eat There is very little cheap accommodation in Falls Creek in winter. Falls Creek Central Reservations (☎ 1800 033 079) can help you find accommodation on the mountain. They have a web site: skifallscreek.com.au.

Viking Lodge (☎ 5758 3247) charges just $80 a night for two people at peak times and has a communal kitchen. A number of ski lodges offer B&B plus dinner packages per week or weekend. One of the best and cheapest is the *Silver Ski Lodge* (☎ 5758 3375), costing from $480 to $680 per person weekly, depending on the season; however, it's normally fully booked during peak seasons. The small *Four Seasons Lodge* (☎ 5758 3254) costs from $35 to $60 per person daily, or $230 to $380 weekly.

In summer, *Pfefferkorn Lodge* (☎ 017 874 235 for bookings or book at a hostel) runs five-day trips to Falls Creek, including transport to/from Melbourne, accommodation (mostly in double rooms with TV and video) and all you can eat (cook-it-yourself) for $255. Numbers are restricted to 11 people. We get great feedback from travellers about this place. Maybe that's not surprising when you consider that the lodge is let for over $4000 a week in winter.

Café Max in the village bowl is a good bistro/bar, and *Winterhaven* is about the best restaurant. *Frying Pan* and the *Man* are both good nightspots, with live bands and other entertainment.

Four kilometres below Falls Creek, Sport & Recreation Victoria's *Howman's Gap Alpine Centre* (☎ 5758 3228) is an adventure activity camp also offering accommodation to individuals. Out of ski season the camp doesn't open for less than 10 people – if there are 10 people there, individuals are welcome. Daily costs are $31 per person in summer and $46 in winter, including all meals. There's also a self-contained unit sleeping eight which goes for $54 in summer and $90 in winter.

Getting There & Around During the ski season, Pyles Coaches (☎ 5754 4024) runs buses to and from Melbourne daily for $55/95 one-way/return, and it also has daily services to and from Albury ($25/48) and Mt Beauty ($13.50/25; same-day return $19). There is over-snow transport available from the car park to the lodges and back again.

Mt Baw Baw (1480m)
This is a small resort in the Baw Baw National Park, with eight lifts on the edge of the Baw Baw plateau. It is 173km and an easy three-hour drive from Melbourne, via Noojee. It's popular with novices and families and is more relaxed and less crowded than the main resorts. Runs are 25% beginners, 64% intermediate and 11% advanced, with a vertical drop of 140m. There are plenty of cross-country trails, including one that connects to the Mt St Gwinear trails on the southern edge of the plateau.

Car entry fees are $16 and a daily lift ticket costs $40; the ARC (☎ 5165 1136) office is in the village. The ARC can advise on accommodation options.

There is no public transport between Melbourne and Mt Baw Baw.

Mt Buffalo (1400m)
This magnificent national park (also covered earlier in this section) is 333km from Melbourne and takes about four hours. The winter entry fee is $10 per car.

It is another small place more suited to intermediate and beginner skiers, but it has challenging cross-country skiing. Tatra is a picturesque and not overly expensive village, but the downhill skiing is not very good and the snow does not last as long as at some of the other resorts. There are a number of cross-country loops, and one of the trails goes to the base of the Horn, which skiers climb on foot.

The walks are also interesting and take the walker beneath towering granite monoliths.

Places to Stay *Lake Catani Campground* (☎ 5755 1577) next to the lake has sites from $8 to $16. It's only open between 1 November and 1 May.

Mt Buffalo Chalet (☎ 5755 1500) was the first place built on the mountain and it still has the charm of the 1920s. Tariffs are $105 to $170 per person, including all meals.

The modern *Tatra Inn* (☎ 5755 1988) has backpackers' bunk rooms for $16 ($18 in winter), and dinner, B&B packages in lodge rooms ($65/70/75 per person in the low/middle/high seasons) and motel units ($75/95/105).

Getting There & Away The closest you can get by public transport is to Bright by bus – from there, a taxi to Mt Buffalo (018 589 370) costs $35.

Mt Buller (1600m)
Less than a three-hour drive from Melbourne and only 246km away, Mt Buller is the most popular (and crowded) resort in Victoria, especially on the weekends. It has a network of 26 lifts, including a chair lift that begins in the car park and ends in the middle of the ski runs. Runs are 25% beginners, 45% intermediate and 30% advanced, and there's even night skiing until 10 pm on Wednesday, Thursday and Saturday.

In years of light snow cover, Buller is skied out much sooner than Falls Creek or Mt Hotham, though snow-making equipment now extends the season on the main beginners' area. Cross-country skiing is possible around Buller and there is access to Mt Stirling, which has some good trails.

A day lift ticket costs $58, a seven-day ticket $325, and a daily lift and lesson package costs $79 ($58 for beginners). The entry fee is $17 per car, and the ARC (☎ 5777 6077) office is in the village.

Places to Stay There is plenty of accommodation. *YHA Hostel Lodge* (☎ 5777 6181) is, of course, the cheapest on the mountain. It's only open during the ski season, and the nightly rate is $45 for members. You'll need to book well in advance (from 1 March) although casual vacancies are often available. Outside the ski season make bookings on ☎ 9670 3802.

Club lodges are the best value, charging between $30 and $40 per person per night, with bunk accommodation and kitchen facilities; contact the Mt Buller Accommodation & Information office (☎ 1800 039 049). There's a web site at skibuller.com.au.

Getting There & Around V/Line has buses twice-daily from Melbourne to Mansfield ($26.10). In the ski season a V/Line service runs from Melbourne up to Mt Buller, with transport to the lodge included in the $49.60 fare. Mt Buller Snowcaper Day Tours (☎ 1800 033 023) has day trips on weekends ($99) and weekdays ($89), which include return transport from Melbourne, lift tickets and a lesson; gear hire is another $20.

In winter, there is an over-snow transport shuttle service that moves people around the village and to and from the car park; fares range from around $4 to $8. Day-trippers can take the quad chair lift from the car park into the skiing area and save time and money by bypassing the village. There are ski rental facilities in the car park. Cross-country skiers turn-off for Mt Stirling at the Mt Buller entrance gate at the base of the mountain. There are day facilities and fast food is available at Telephone Box Junction.

Mt Hotham (1750m)
Known as Australia's powder capital, Hotham does get the lightest snow in the country, but don't expect anything like Europe or North America. It's about a 5½-hour drive from Melbourne. You can take either the Hume Highway via Harrietville or the Princes Highway via Omeo – ring the ARC to check road conditions before setting off.

The lift system is not well integrated and some walking is necessary, even though the 'zoo cart' along the main road offers some relief. The skiing is good: there are 10 lifts, and runs are 23% beginners, 37% intermediate and 40% advanced. This is a skiers' mountain with a vertical drop of 428m and

the nightlife mainly happening in ski lodges. There is some good off-piste skiing in steep and narrow valleys. A day lift ticket costs $59, a seven-day pass $340, and a lift and lesson package $80 ($39 learn to ski package). Car entry costs $17. The ARC (☎ 5759 3550) has an information office in the village centre.

Cross-country skiing is good around Hotham and ski touring is very good on the Bogong High Plains, which you can cross to Falls Creek. This is also the starting point for trips across the Razorback to beautiful Mt Feathertop. Below the village, on the eastern side, there is a series of trails that runs as far as Dinner Plain. The biathlon (shooting and skiing) range is at Wire Plain, between Mt Hotham and Dinner Plain.

Places to Stay Most of the accommodation is in private and commercial lodges. It is possible to find beds in these or apartments through the Mt Hotham Accommodation Service (☎ 1800 032 061; hotham@netc.net.au; mt-hotham-accomodation.com.au) or Skicom (☎ 5759 3522).

Jack Frost Lodge (☎ 5759 3586) has one and two-bedroom apartments costing from $852 or $1218 per week, depending on the season and number of people. The huge *Arlberg Inn* (☎ 9889 0647) also has apartments sleeping from two to eight people; weekly rates start from $500 for two people and from $1300 for eight people. *Zirky's* (☎ 5759 3518) has six double rooms at $115 per person per night for B&B. Lawler's Apartments (☎ 5759 3606) are a cut above the usual bed-sits and cost $1320 a week, 40% less in the off season, for two people. A couple of places are open during summer – check with the booking services.

It is also possible to stay at Dinner Plain, 11km from Mt Hotham Village, where there are cabins, lodges and B&Bs; ring one of the booking services on ☎ 5159 6426 or ☎ 5159 6451.

Getting There & Around In winter, Trekset Snow Services (☎ 9370 9055) has daily buses from Melbourne to Mt Hotham (twice on Friday), costing $65/95 one-way/return. It also has daily services between Hotham and Myrtleford, Bright and Harrietville; fares range from $16 to $27, depending on when you're going.

The village was built on a ridge almost at the top of the mountain and is strung out along the road. Luckily, there are shuttle buses which run frequently all the way along the ridge from 7 am to 1 am (to 3 am on Saturday); the 'zoo cart' takes skiers from their lodges to the lifts between 8.15 am and 5.45 pm. Another shuttle service operates to Dinner Plain.

Other Resorts

There are five other snowfields, although they're mainly for cross-country skiing or sightseeing and have no accommodation. For more information, contact their respective information offices on the numbers given below.

Lake Mountain (☎ 5963 3288) is 120km from Melbourne via Marysville. The cross-country facility is world class, with over 40km of trails that are groomed daily.

Skiing for the experienced is found around the summit of Victoria's highest peak, **Mt Bogong**. Here, steep gullies tempt the cross-country downhill skier. Accommodation is in tents and in mountain huts. This area is not for beginners.

Mt St Gwinear (☎ 5165 3204) is 171km from Melbourne via Moe and has connecting cross-country ski trails with Mt Baw Baw. **Mt Stirling** (☎ 5777 5624) is a few kilometres from Mt Buller and is another cross-country ski area, with more than 60km of mostly groomed trails. **Mt Donna Buang** is the closest to Melbourne (95km via Warburton), but is mainly for sightseeing and tobogganing.

Gippsland

The Gippsland region is the south-eastern slice of Victoria. It stretches from Western Port, near Melbourne, to the New South Wales border on the east coast, with the Great Dividing Range to the north.

Named in 1839 by the Polish explorer Count Paul Strzelecki after Sir George Gipps, the former governor of New South Wales, Gippsland was first settled by prospectors in the 1850s, then by farmers after the completion of the railway from Melbourne in 1887.

The region can be divided into three distinct sections: West Gippsland, which is dominated by Victoria's industrial heartland, the Latrobe Valley; South Gippsland, which is largely dairy country but includes the wonderful Wilsons Promontory National Park; and East Gippsland, which includes the Gippsland Lakes (Australia's largest system of inland waterways) and with some of the wildest forests on the continent in the mountains behind the stunningly beautiful Wilderness Coast in the far east.

Getting There & Away

The Princes Highway runs from Melbourne to Bairnsdale through the Latrobe Valley, and then follows the coastline into New South Wales. For a slower but more scenic drive you could follow the South Gippsland Highway, which heads south-east from Melbourne towards Phillip Island and the Prom, rejoining the Princes Highway at Sale, 214km from Melbourne.

V/Line trains between Melbourne and Sale ($26.10) operate thrice-daily on weekdays and twice-daily on weekends; there are connecting bus services from Sale to Bairnsdale ($7.30). V/Line also operates the daily Sapphire Coast bus service along the Princes Highway as far as Narooma ($49) in New South Wales via Lakes Entrance ($16) and Genoa ($42.90). Greyhound also plies this coastal route.

WEST GIPPSLAND & THE LATROBE VALLEY

The Latrobe Valley contains one of the world's largest deposits of brown coal, and its mines and power stations supply most of Victoria's electricity, while the offshore wells in Bass Strait provide most of

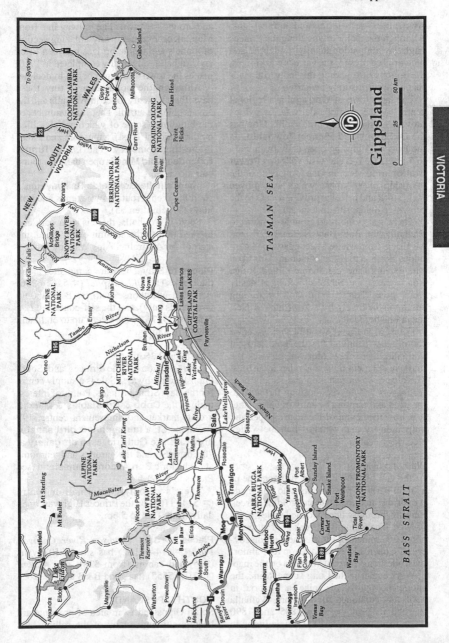

VICTORIA

Gippsland

Australia's petroleum and natural gas. Although the major towns along the Princes Highway are predominantly residential and industrial centres for the various workforces, the regions surrounding this industrial landscape are surprisingly beautiful.

The large town of **Warragul** is a regional centre for the district's dairy farms, which provide most of Melbourne's milk. **Moe** has the **Old Gippsland Pioneer Township**, on the Princes Highway, open daily from 9 am to 5 pm ($7). You can visit **Yallourn Power Station** from Moe, and the former site of the township of **Yallourn**, which was moved lock, stock and barrel to provide access to the brown-coal deposits underneath.

There's a scenic road from Moe north to Walhalla, the Baw Baw National Park and Mt Erica, from where a secondary road continues north across the Victorian Alps. You can get onto the panoramic Grand Ridge Road across the Strzelecki Ranges easily from either Trafalgar or Moe by turning south via the lovely little townships of Narracan or Thorpdale.

Founded in the 1880s as a supply centre for diggers heading for the goldfields at Walhalla, these days **Morwell** services the massive open-cut mine and other industries. **Traralgon** was a rest stop and supply base for miners and drovers heading farther into the gold and farming country of Gippsland. It is now the centre of the state's paper and pulp industry and a major Latrobe Valley electricity centre.

Walhalla (pop 30)

At the end of 1862 Edward Stringer, one of a small party of prospectors who had made it over the mountains, found gold in a creek running through a deep wooded valley north of Moe. The Stringer's Creek gold attracted about 200 miners but it was the later discovery of Cohen's Reef, an outcrop reef almost two miles long, that put Walhalla on the map.

Work began on the Long Tunnel Mine, the single most profitable mine in Victoria, in 1865 and continued for 49 years. Walhalla reached its peak between 1885 and 1890 when there were over 4000 people living in

and around the town. The railway line from Moe, incorporating a truly amazing section of tunnels and trestle bridges between Erica and Walhalla, was finally completed in 1910, just as the town's fortunes began to decline.

Although the population is tiny these days, there's plenty to see in Walhalla and the area is quite beautiful. There are a number of old buildings (some of which are classified by the National Trust), a museum and a very interesting cemetery. The **Long Tunnel Extended Gold Mine** is open daily for tours; entrance is $5.

The **Walhalla Goldfields Railway** runs a short but scenic route on weekends and holidays ($7, children $5).

South of Walhalla, there is a car park and marked trail to the summit of Mt Erica, the start of the Australian Alps Walking Track.

Places to Stay There are camp sites along the creek. The *Old Hospital* (☎ 5165 6246) is now a guesthouse with B&B at $60/90 (weekends only), and the self-contained *Log Cabin* (☎ 5176 2741) sleeps up to eight and costs $70 a night.

Sale (pop 13,366)

At the junction of the Princes and South Gippsland highways, Sale is a supply centre for the Bass Strait oilfields. Points of interest include the **Cobb & Co Stables & Market**, a craft market and amusement centre, 199 Raymond St; a **fauna park & bird sanctuary** near Lake Gutheridge; an **art gallery** at 70 Foster St; and the gardens and tearooms at the historic **Bon Accord Homestead** (see Places to Stay).

There's a tourist information centre (☎ 5144 1108) on the Princes Highway, open daily from 9 am to 5 pm.

Places to Stay *Thomson River Caravan Park* (☎ 5144 1102) has sites ($10), vans ($25) and cabins (from $28). *Bon Accord* (☎ 5144 5555) has good B&B at $90/120.

SOUTH GIPPSLAND

South Gippsland is an area of great natural beauty, although many of the rolling hills have been cleared for cows. There are still some forested mountains and a rugged and spectacular coastline. The area's major feature is Wilsons Promontory, one of Victoria's most loved national parks. The main road through here is the South Gippsland Highway, but the backroads through the hills, and the coastal route, are more scenic and worth exploring if you have time.

The Strzelecki Ranges

Between the Latrobe Valley and South Gippsland's coastal areas are the beautiful 'blue' rounded hills of the Strzelecki Ranges. The winding **Grand Ridge Road**, which runs along the ridge of these ranges and past the wonderful Tarra Bulga National Park, is a spectacular but rough scenic route through fertile farmland that was once covered with forests of mountain ash.

A good base for this area is the township of **Mirboo North**, which straddles the Grand Ridge Road south of Trafalgar. The town boasts the **Grand Ridge Brewery & Restaurant** in the old Butter Factory building. The complex not only produces a range of quality beers but also features a cosy bar and a good bistro. There's a caravan park opposite the shire hall, and the *Commercial Hotel* (☎ 5668 1552) has singles/doubles for $40/50.

Tarra Bulga National Park at the eastern end of the Grand Ridge Road is one of the last remnants of the magnificent forests that once covered this area. There are several good picnic areas and some lovely nature walks, and a visitors centre (☎ 5196 6166) open weekends and school holidays. The 1930s-style *Tarra Bulga Guesthouse* (☎ 5196 6141) charges $55 per person including meals or $35/65 a single/double B&B.

Korumburra (pop 2739)

The **Coal Creek Historical Village**, a recreation of a coal-mining town of the 19th century, is near Korumburra. Coal was first discovered in 1872 and the Coal Creek Mine operated from the 1890s right up to 1958. The **South Gippsland Railway** (☎ 5658

1888) runs steam (and diesel) trains between Nyora, Loch, Korumburra and Leongatha – 40km all up. The return fare along the whole route is a reasonable $16, or you can buy sections or an all-day pass. They even have a two-day course teaching you to drive a steam train.

WILSONS PROMONTORY

'The Prom' is one of the best loved national parks in Australia. It covers the peninsula that forms the southernmost part of the Australian mainland. The Prom offers more than 80km of walking tracks and a wide variety of beaches – whether you want surfing, safe swimming or a secluded beach all to yourself, you can find it here. Finally there's the wildlife, which abounds despite the park's popularity. There are wonderful birds (including emus), kangaroos and, at night, plenty of wombats. The wildlife around Tidal River is very tame and can even become a nuisance.

Information

The Parks Victoria office (☎ 5680 9555) at Tidal River is open daily from 8.30 am to 4.30 pm. The displays are excellent. The office is where you pay your park entry fee ($7 per car) if the main gate is not staffed.

Activities

It's probably walkers who get the best value from the Prom, though you don't have to go very far from the car parks to really get away from it all. The park office at Tidal River has free leaflets on walks ranging from 15-minute strolls from Tidal River to overnight and longer hikes. You can also get detailed maps of the park.

The walking tracks take you through ever-changing scenery: swamps, forests, marshes, valleys of tree ferns and long beaches lined with sand dunes. For serious exploration, it's really worth buying a copy of *Discovering the Prom on Foot* ($6.95) from the park office.

Don't miss the **Mt Oberon** walk. It starts from the Mt Oberon car park, takes one hour

VICTORIA

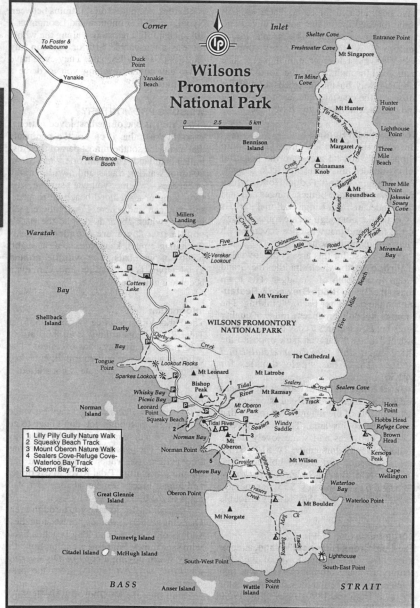

Wilsons Promontory National Park

Corner *Inlet*

To Foster &
Melbourne

Yanakie

Duck
Point

Yanakie
Beach

Shelter Cove

Entrance Point

Freshwater Cove

Mt Singapore

Tin Mine
Cove

Mt Hunter

Hunter
Point

Lighthouse
Point

Three
Mile
Beach

0   2.5   5 km

Bennison
Island

Park Entrance
Booth

Millers
Landing

Mt
Margaret

Chinamans
Knob

Three Mile
Point

Johnnie
Souey
Cove

Waratah

Five

Barry

Creek

Creek

Vereker
Lookout

Chinaman

Mile

Mt
Roundback

Road

Miranda
Bay

Cotters
Lake

Bay

Shellback
Island

Mt Vereker

WILSONS PROMONTORY
NATIONAL PARK

Five

Mile

Beach

Darby

Bay

Darby

Creek

The Cathedral

Tongue
Point

Lookout Rocks

Sparkes Lookout

Mt Leonard

Bishop
Peak

Mt Latrobe

Tidal
River

Mt Ramsay

Sealers

Sealers Cove

Creek

Horn
Point

Whisky Bay
Picnic Bay

Norman
Island

Leonard
Point

Squeaky Beach

Mt Oberon
Car Park

Track

Cove

Hobbs Head
Refuge Cove

1 Lilly Pilly Gully Nature Walk
2 Squeaky Beach Track
3 Mount Oberon Nature Walk
4 Sealers Cove-Refuge Cove-
   Waterloo Bay Track
5 Oberon Bay Track

2

Tidal River

Norman Bay

3

Sealers

Windy
Saddle

Brown
Head

Mt
Oberon

Kersops
Peak

Norman Point

5

Growler

Mt Wilson

Cape
Wellington

Oberon Bay

Great Glennie
Island

Oberon Point

Frasers

Lighthouse

Ck

Mt Boulder

Waterloo
Bay

Waterloo Point

Creek

Dannevig Island

Mt Norgate

Mes

Ck

Citadel Island

McHugh Island

Roaring

Meg

Track

Lighthouse

BASS

Anser Island

South-West Point

Wattle
Island

South
Point

South-East Point

STRAIT

and is about 3km each way. The views from the summit are superb.

It's a long day walk from the Mt Oberon car park to the south-east point of the Prom, and by prior arrangement (☎ 5680 9555) it's possible to visit the lighthouse. Another good walk is the Squeaky Beach Nature Walk, a lovely 1½-hour stroll around to the next bay from Tidal River and back.

The northern area of the park is much less visited, simply because all the facilities are at Tidal River. Most of the walks in this area are overnight or longer. All the camp sites away from Tidal River have pit toilets but nothing else in the way of facilities. Fires are totally banned (except in designated fire places in Tidal River between May and October) so you'll need to carry some sort of stove.

Places to Stay

To book accommodation phone ☎ 5690 9500. The high season is from 1 September to the end of April.

Camping The Tidal River camping ground has 500 sites, and at peak times (school holidays, Easter and long weekends) booking is essential. In fact for the real peak at Christmas a ballot is held in July allocating sites, so you can forget about a casual visit then (although a few sites are reserved for overseas visitors for one or two-night stays).

The charge is $14.50 per site (up to three people and one car), plus $3 per extra person, $4 per extra car.

Flats & Units Also at Tidal River are a number of self-contained flats, which are available on a weekly basis. Costs range from $57 a night to $60 in the high season for a six-bed hut with kitchenettes but shared bathrooms; BYO linen. There are also better cabins from $95 a double in the low season.

Getting There & Away

V/Line has daily buses from Melbourne to Foster ($21.30), 60km north of the Prom.

If you stay overnight in Foster at the *Little Mud Hut* (☎ 5682 2614), the owners run a postal/bus service to the Prom ($10 each way) at 9.30 am most mornings; they also have camping gear for hire. Beds in dorms cost $15 and there is one double at $35. Ring for details on their transport and accommodation package deals.

From Phillip Island, *Amaroo Park Backpackers* (☎ 5952 2548) runs day trips to the Prom for $30; you can also stay overnight in their cabin-tents at Tidal River.

THE GIPPSLAND LAKES

The Lakes District is the largest inland waterway system in Australia. The three main lakes, **Lake King**, **Lake Victoria** and **Lake Wellington**, are all joined and fed by a number of rivers that originate in the High Country. The lakes are actually shallow coastal lagoons separated from the ocean by a narrow strip of coastal sand dunes known as the Ninety Mile Beach.

The area is popular for fishing, boating, water-skiing and other water-oriented activities. Obviously, with more than 400 square kilometres of waterways, the best way to appreciate the area is from a boat. You can join a lakes cruise or hire a boat from various places including Lakes Entrance and Metung.

Most of the **Ninety Mile Beach** is part of the **Gippsland Lakes Coastal Park**. Within this area is the Lakes National Park and the bird-watchers' paradise of **Rotamah Island**.

A meteorological phenomenon known as the Fohn Effect means that this area enjoys warmer average temperatures than Melbourne but lower summer maximums. It's a nice place to be.

Sailing & Cruising

The lakes offer good boating and you can hire a yacht or a cruiser for overnight or longer trips. Most have showers, toilets, stoves and fridges.

You can't get into too much trouble sailing on the lakes, although running aground is a real possibility. After radioing Riviera Nautica to come and tow us off a sandbar (they gave us a bottle of champagne for consolation) we learned to read charts very quickly. There are some delightful places to tie up for the night, and sailing down Lake King in the early morning, accompanied by a pod of dolphins, was magic.

Riviera Nautica (☎ 5156 2243, 1800 815 127) in Metung has a range of yachts. There's a bewildering array of rates and seasons but as an example, hiring a Catalina 27 (sleeps four comfortably) for three days over a weekend outside public holidays and the December/January school holidays costs $780 or $690 in winter.

Though Riviera Nautica also rents cruisers, the longest-established name for cruisers on the lakes is Bull's (☎ 5156 2208), also based in Metung.

Cycling

The Howitt Bicycle Trail runs a mainly backroads route around the Gippsland Lakes region and extending as far east as Cape Conran and north into the mountains. It's a long cycle (around two weeks) and the mountain sections around Buchan and Omeo are tough, but there are plenty of flatter sections and shorter options, so you can pick and choose. A good booklet detailing the route is available at the larger information centres or write to the Howitt Trail Project Committee, 240 Main St, Bairnsdale, 3875.

Bairnsdale (pop 10,890)

Bairnsdale, a large commercial centre at the junction of the Princes and Omeo highways, is a handy base both for the mountains to the north and the lakes immediately to the south. The Aboriginal name for Bairnsdale was Wy-Yung, which is now the name of a small town on Bairnsdale's outskirts.

At 37 Dalmahoy St is the **Krowathunkoolong Keeping Place**, a cultural centre focusing on the heritage of local Aboriginal people. It is open on weekdays from 9 am to 5 pm ($3.50). Pick up a copy of the Bataluk Cultural Trail brochure (the larger fold-out one), which details some important sites in the area, some as much as 20,000 years old.

Howitt Park is a children's playground complete with flying foxes, and **St Mary's Catholic Church**, beside the information

centre, is covered in superbly mediocre murals and is worth a look.

Signposted 42km north-west of Bairnsdale is the **Mitchell River National Park** with the **Den of Nargun**, a small cave beneath a waterfall which, according to Aboriginal legend, was haunted by a strange, half-stone creature, known as a *nargun*. It's an atmospheric place and worth the steep walk from the car park.

There's a good tourist information centre (☎ 5152 3444) at 240 Main St, open daily from 9 am to 5 pm.

Places to Stay & Eat For a tent site (from $10) or cabin (from $29) try *Mitchell Gardens Caravan Park* (☎ 5152 4654) on the banks of the Mitchell River. The friendly *Bairnsdale Backpackers Hostel* (☎ 5152 5097), close to the train station at 119 McLeod St, has bunks at $15 including breakfast, while the *Commercial Hotel* (☎ 5152 3031) on the corner of Main and Bailey Sts has basic single rooms for $15 (although they're often all taken by permanents) and a good bistro downstairs.

The elegant *Riversleigh Country Hotel* (☎ 5152 6966), 1 Nicholson St, has heritage-style rooms from $70/80 and one of the best restaurants in country Victoria.

Getting There & Away There's a daily train/bus service between Bairnsdale and Melbourne ($33.20), and daily buses to Lakes Entrance ($7.30), Orbost ($17.50) and beyond.

Metung (pop 420)

This interesting little fishing village between Bairnsdale and Lakes Entrance is built on a land spit between Lake King and Bancroft Bay. The *Spray* and the *Gypsy* offer sailing cruises on the lakes.

If you want to splurge try the *Slipway* (☎ 5156 2469), which has excellent three bedroom, two-storey units right on the water's edge (guests get boat parking). From Christmas to the end of January (minimum stay one week) and at Easter (minimum four nights) they cost $210 per night and drop as low as $130 per night between May and the end of October (except in school holidays). Between six people that's a bargain.

Lakes Entrance (pop 5248)

A popular if somewhat old-fashioned tourist town, Lakes Entrance is the main centre of the Lakes District, and also Victoria's largest fishing port.

From the centre of town, a footbridge crosses Cunningham's Arm to the white-sand beaches of the Ninety Mile Beach; from the other side there's a scenic 2.3km walking track up to the actual 'entrance'. Apart from the beaches, fishing and surfing, the town's attractions include the **Kinkuna Country Fun Park**, the **Wyanga Park Winery & Bistro**, 10km north, and **Nyerimilang Park**, a historic homestead and property off the Metung road.

Lots of cruise boats operate from here to tour the rivers and lakes – the tourist office can advise you and make bookings. Boats can also be hired at various places.

The Lakes Entrance Fishermen's Co-operative, just off the Princes Highway, provides a viewing platform that puts you in the middle of the boats unloading their fish. Sunday morning is the best time to go. The co-op fish shop is guaranteed to sell the freshest fish in town.

There's a tourist information centre (☎ 5155 1966) on the Princes Highway, as you enter the town from the west.

Places to Stay & Eat Lakes Entrance has a huge array of accommodation, especially caravan parks and motels. *Riviera Backpackers YHA* (☎ 5155 2444), 5 Clarkes Rd, has dorms for $13 and doubles are available. *Silver Sands Backpackers* (☎ 5155 2343), 33 Myer St, charges just $13/26 a single/double. *Lakes Main Caravan Park* (☎ 5155 2365) in Willis St has tent sites ($10 to $17), vans ($18 to $40) and cabins ($20 to $80).

There are plenty of motels, with prices soaring over summer and some bargains available in winter. *Homlea Cottages* (☎ 5155 1998) at 32 Roadnight St has old, simple holiday cottages from $39 a double

in the off season to $600 a week (minimum) for up to six people in January.

Try *Tres Amigos*, 521 The Esplanade, for Mexican meals. The *Kalimna Hotel* has a good bistro overlooking the lakes, and for a seafood splurge try *Skippers Wine Bar & Restaurant*, 481 The Esplanade, or *Out of the Blue*, a floating restaurant off the Esplanade.

Getting There & Away There are daily V/Line buses between Lakes Entrance and Bairnsdale ($7.30), with bus/train connections to Melbourne ($40.20). V/Line and Greyhound also have buses continuing along the Princes Highway into New South Wales.

EAST GIPPSLAND

East Gippsland contains some of the most remote and spectacular national parks in the state, ranging from the coastal wilderness areas of Croajingolong to the lush rainforests of the Errinundra Plateau.

Although the area was always considered too remote for agriculture, it has been logged since late last century. Today, the logging of these forests (especially clear-felling for woodchipping) is a controversial issue and there are ongoing campaigns to stop the desecration of the old-growth forests. Huge bushfires in 1998 devastated hundreds of thousands of hectares in this region, but most of the remote forests survived.

Parks Victoria publishes a very good map/brochure, *East Gippsland: A Guide for Visitors*. The book *Car Touring & Bushwalking in East Gippsland* (paperback, $19.95) is also handy.

Eco Explorer Research Tours (☎ 5157 5751), based in Bruthen, runs interesting camping expeditions into the wilderness, where you get very close to some very shy wildlife, maybe helping with population surveys. Three-day trips cost $405 and five days costs $675.

Orbost (pop 2150)

Orbost is a logging service town with a very pretty location on the Snowy River. The Rainforest Information Centre (☎ 5161 1375) has information and displays on forests and national parks in East Gippsland. It is open on weekdays from 10 am to 4 pm, and during school holidays on weekends from 10 am to 4 pm.

The Slab Hut Tourist office (☎ 5154 2424) is on Nicholson St.

Places to Stay *Orbost Caravan Park* (☎ 5154 1097) on Nicholson St has both tent sites and vans. The *Commonwealth Hotel* (☎ 5154 1077), 159 Nicholson St, has B&B from $25/35. There are also a couple of motels.

Getting There & Away V/Line has daily buses to Bairnsdale ($17.50) and Genoa ($17.50).

Omeo (pop 298)

This small mountain town is on the Omeo Highway, the southern access route to the snowfields of Mt Hotham during winter. In summer it's a departure point for the Bogong High Plains. Rafting trips take place on the nearby Mitta Mitta River.

Omeo still has a handful of interesting old buildings despite the disastrous bushfire and two earthquakes that have occurred since 1885. Omeo's **log jail**, **courthouse** and **historical museum** are worth searching out. The town also had its own little gold rush.

Places to Stay *Holston Tourist Park* (☎ 51 59 1351) has tent sites from $10 and vans from $27. The basic *Hill Top Hotel* (☎ 5159 1303) charges $25 per person, with breakfast, *Colonial Bank House* (☎ 5159 1388) has four small self-contained units from $40/55, and the upgraded *Golden Age Hotel* (☎ 5159 1344) has B&B from $60/80.

Getting There & Away There is a weekday bus between Omeo and Bairnsdale ($22.80) operated by Omeo Buslines (☎ 5159 4231).

Marlo & Cape Conran

On the coast 15km south of Orbost is the sleepy little settlement of Marlo, at the mouth of the Snowy River. It's a popular fishing spot and the route along the coast to Cape Conran,

18km to the east, is especially pretty as it winds through stands of banksia trees. The beach at Cape Conran is one long beautiful deserted strip of white sand.

Places to Stay Marlo has a couple of caravan parks, and at Cape Conran Parks Victoria runs *Banksia Bluff Bush Camp* (☎ 5154 8438), with great sites ($6 to $12), and the superb *Cape Conran Cabins*, self-contained timber cabins that sleep up to eight and cost from $40 to $80 for four people plus $7 to $12 per extra adult; you'll need to book.

Baldwin Spencer Trail

This is a drive well worth doing: a 265km route through more superb forest, including Errinundra National Park, north of Orbost on the Bonang Highway.

The route follows the trail of Walter Baldwin Spencer, a noted scientist and explorer who led an expedition through here in 1889. A map/brochure is available from the Rainforest Information Centre in Orbost.

Buchan (pop 400)

There are a number of limestone caves around the tiny and beautiful town of Buchan, 55km north-west of Orbost. One-hour tours ($10) of Royal Cave or Fairy Cave are held daily, five times a day from October to March and three times a day the rest of the year. The rangers also offer guided tours to more remote and undeveloped caves in the area; phone ☎ 5155 9264.

Places to Stay There's a delightful camping ground at the Buchan Caves (☎ 5155 9264), with sites from $10 and self-contained units from $45.

There's also a pub and motels. Just out of town on Saleyard Rd is the good *Buchan Lodge Backpackers* (☎ 5155 9421), a modern homestead with dorms at $15.

Snowy River National Park

This is one of Victoria's most isolated and spectacular national parks, dominated by deep gorges carved through limestone and sandstone by the mighty Snowy River. The entire park is a smorgasbord of unspoilt and superb bush and mountain scenery.

The two main access routes are the Gelantipy Rd from Buchan and the Bonang Highway from Orbost. These roads are joined by McKillops Rd, which runs across the northern border of the park. Along McKillops Rd you'll come across **McKillops Bridge**, where you can have a dip in the river or camp on its sandy banks. The view from the lookout over **Little River Falls**, about 20km west of McKillops Bridge, is spectacular.

The classic canoe or raft trip down the Snowy River from Willis or McKillops Bridge to a pull-out point near Buchan offers superb scenery: rugged gorges, raging rapids, tranquil sections and great camping spots on broad sand bars.

Operators including Peregrine Adventures (☎ 9662 2700) and Snowy River Expeditions (☎ 5155 0220) run rafting trips on the Snowy.

At Gelantipy, right by the park and 39 km from Buchan on the Jindabyne road (heading towards McKillops Bridge), there's a *YHA Hostel* (☎ 5155 0220). It's on a cattle and sheep farm and activities such as rafting and rockclimbing are available. Facilites are good, and YHA members pay just $24 for a dorm bed and all meals, or $14 for a bed only. There's a double room with en suite for $40.

Errinundra National Park

This beautiful national park contains Victoria's largest areas of cool-temperate rainforest. The park is on a high granite plateau with a high rainfall, fertile soils and a network of creeks and rivers. There are walking trails throughout, and camp sites with minimal facilities. Access is via the Bonang Highway from Orbost or the Errinundra road from the hamlet of Club Terrace, both of which are unsealed, steep, slow and winding – note that roads through the park are closed from mid-June to the end of October. Contact the rangers at Bendoc (☎ (02) 6458 1456) or in Cann River (☎ 5158 6351) for more information and to check road conditions.

Croajingolong National Park

Croajingolong is a coastal wilderness park which stretches for about 100km along the easternmost tip of Victoria, and is one of Australia's finest national parks. Magnificent unspoiled beaches, inlets, estuaries and forests make this an ideal area for camping, walking, swimming, surfing or just lazing around. The diverse habitat supports a wide range of plants and animals, with over 250 species of birds recorded in the area.

There are several roads leading from the highway to different parts of the park. Some are quite rough and require 4WD; the Parks Victoria office at Cann River will give you more information about vehicular access.

There are camp sites within Croajingolong National Park at Wingan Inlet, Thurra River, Mueller River and Shipwreck Creek. Facilities are minimal and it's a good idea to make reservations with the Parks Victoria office in Cann River (☎ 5158 6351) or Mallacoota (☎ 5158 0219).

Mallacoota (pop 982)

Mallacoota is at the seaward end of a small lake system and is the main service town for this corner of the state. It's an old-fashioned holiday resort, with good fishing, walking trails, boating, and access to the Croajingolong National Park. Abalone and fishing are the town's mainstays, and there are fishing boats and houseboats for hire.

At Christmas and Easter the town becomes packed out with holiday-makers, but it's fairly peaceful at other times.

There is no public transport down to Mallacoota from the highway, although some accommodation places do pick-ups.

Organised Tours & Cruises Journey Beyond Eco-Adventures (☎ 5158 0166) offers a range of very good adventure tours, including sea kayaking trips (up to $95 for a full day) and mountain-bike rides (half-day, $35). They also hire mountain bikes and kayaks.

Wallagaraugh River Wilderness Cruises (☎ 5158 0555) has excellent five-hour cruises through the lakes and river system for

$40 including lunch; $30 children. Children under six aren't taken on this long cruise but there are shorter trips you can take them on.

Places to Stay *Mallacoota Caravan Park* (☎ 5158 0300) has hundreds of sites on the foreshore, ranging seasonally from $8.50 to $15. *Beachcomber Caravan Park* (☎ 5158 0233), 85 Betka Rd, has tent sites ($10 to $17), vans (from $22 for up to six people) and cabins ($30 to $55). The *Mallacoota*

Hotel/Motel (☎ 5158 0455) has motel units from $40/45 to $50/65. This place is also an associate YHA Hostel, with dorms at $13 and doubles at $30, more for nonmembers.

Other places include the good *Adobe Mud-brick Flats* (☎ 5158 0329), which cost from $40 to $60 for four people, plus $10 per extra adult; and *Karbeethong Lodge* (☎ 5158 0411), an old-fashioned guesthouse with doubles from $50 to $80 (plus $10 for en-suite) and family units from $60 to $110.

Western Australia

Western Australia (more commonly known as WA, or 'double-u-ay') is Australia's largest State. It's isolated from the country's eastern population and power centres, and many of its vast natural treasures are still being 'discovered'.

The region's position near the Indian Ocean trading routes led to very early European contact. The first known Europeans to land near the Western Australian coast were Dutch – including Dirk Hartog in 1616, and those previously shipwrecked on its wild shores (whose vessels are still being discovered). Abel Tasman was the first to chart parts of the WA coastline; he charted as far as the Gulf of Carpentaria in 1644.

William Dampier was the first Englishman to comprehensively chart the coast. He visited the area in 1688 on board the *Cygnet*, and his 1697 publication, *New Voyage around the World*, prompted funds for a subsequent trip in 1699 to what was then known as New Holland. On board the HMS *Roebuck*, he charted from the Houtman Abrolhos Islands as far north as Roebuck Bay, near Broome.

Dampier's reports of a dry, barren land discouraged attempts at settlement. It was not until 1829, three years after Britain had formally claimed the land, that the first British settlers arrived in the Swan Valley, later Perth. Their presence was intended to forestall settlement by other European nations, in particular France.

Because of its isolation, the region was seen as a natural prison, and in June 1850 the first group of convicts was transported to the new colony. For the next 18 years, convicts were used in the construction of public buildings and roads. When settlers spread out into the south-west, many convicts went as their labour force.

WA's development as a British colony was painfully slow – hardly surprising, given its distance from the main Australian settlements in the east. It was not until the gold

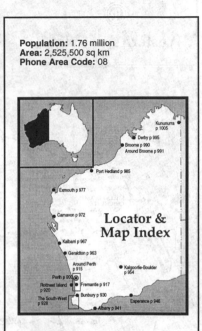

Population: 1.76 million
Area: 2,525,500 sq km
Phone Area Code: 08

Kununurra p 1005
Derby p 995
Broome p 990
Around Broome p 991
Port Hedland p 985
Exmouth p 977
Carnarvon p 972

Locator & Map Index

Kalbarri p 967
Geraldton p 963
Around Perth p 915
Kalgoorlie-Boulder p 954
Perth p 900
Rottnest Island p 920
Fremantle p 917
The South-West p 928
Bunbury p 930
Esperance p 946
Albany p 941

Highlights

- Exploring the harsh and beautiful Pilbara and interacting with marine life along Ningaloo Reef.
- Discovering the 'last frontier' of the Kimberley and relaxing in the tourist oasis of Broome, with its fascinating pearling past.
- Heading out to the mining and ghost towns of the goldfields region.
- Visiting the laid-back south-west, dotted with great surf and swimming beaches, historic towns, wineries and giant karri and tingle forests.
- Tackling the challenge of a lonely drive across the Nullarbor Plain.
- Experiencing vibrant Perth: sipping coffee in a Fremantle cafe, dining out in Northbridge, swimming at the beach or sailing on the Swan River.
- Seeing the spring wildflowers on the Midlands' Wildflower Way – perhaps the world's largest natural garden.

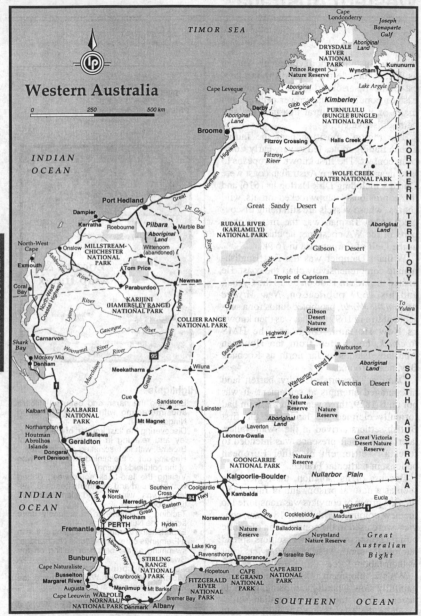

Sandgropers

You will often hear Western Australians colloquially referred to as sandgropers. The sandgroper is actually a subterranean insect known as a cylindrachetid, believed to be a descendant of the grasshopper group. Five species of sandgroper have been found in Australia.

Their bodies are perfectly adapted for 'groping' or burrowing in the sandy soils of the Swan Coastal Plain where they are found. They move through sand in a swimming motion, propelled by their powerful forelegs and with their mid and hind legs tucked away.

Similar to grasshoppers, sandgropers develop from egg to adult with no larval stage. They appear to be vegetarian, although some studies show that at least one species is omnivorous.

Humanoid sandgropers have a diet of Swan Lager, enjoy sunbathing and the footy, eat in Freo's cafe strip and holiday at the beach. They have yet to perfect the sand-swimming technique. ∎

rushes of the 1890s that the colony really began to progress. Today, a larger and far more technologically advanced mineral boom forms the basis of the State's prosperity. As a result, Western Australia is deeply embroiled in the native-title debate on Aboriginal land rights because of conflicting mining interests (see the Facts about the Country chapter for more information on land rights and native title).

ABORIGINAL PEOPLE

Western Australia has an Aboriginal and Torres Strait Islander population of over 47,250, which represents about 16% of the nation's total and is about the same number of Aborigines as when the Europeans arrived. About a quarter of these people live in the State's north-west and along its border with the Northern Territory.

Much evidence has been uncovered indicating that Aboriginal people lived as far south as present-day Perth at least 40,000 years ago. The State's archaeological record is rich, with a camp site (39,500 years old) unearthed at Swan Bridge, stone tools (30,000 years old) gathered from the Devil's Lair near Cape Leeuwin and ochre mined from Wilga Mia (30,000 years ago) in the Murchison as examples.

The arrival of the Europeans had disastrous consequences for the local Aboriginal people, who lived in harmony with nature, by hunting and gathering in small nomadic groups. Pushed off their traditional lands, many of the Aboriginal people who were not

killed by the colonisers died of European diseases, against which they had no immunity. Particularly hard hit were the Noongar people in the south-west.

From the end of WWII many Aboriginal people banded together in protest against their appalling treatment on the cattle stations. These protests were some of the first displays of a re-emerging consciousness.

In June 1992, the High Court of Australia recognised a form of native title which reflected the entitlement of the indigenous inhabitants of Australia to their traditional lands (known as the Mabo ruling). The Western Australian government was quick to pre-empt further legal restriction by rushing through its own Land Bill in December 1993. It also unsuccessfully challenged in the High Court the validity of the Commonwealth Native Title Act. Perhaps the mineral-rich State feels it has the most to lose in the short term.

Aboriginal people in WA have laid claims all across the State, mainly on Crown land. But injustices continue – Aboriginal people are 29 times more likely to be imprisoned than whites and many regional prisons, eg Roebourne and Broome, mainly have indigenous prisoners.

The full implications of the complex 1996 High Court Wik decision, which established that pastoral leases do not necessarily extinguish native title, have yet to be realised.

Permits

You need a permit to enter Aboriginal land

but getting one is only really a problem in the remote communities in the east of the State.

Permits are issued by the Aboriginal Affairs Department in Perth (☎ 9483 1222); individual Aboriginal people apparently can't give permission. However, access is often informally allowed.

Culture

Many tourists come wishing to see Aboriginal culture first-hand and many leave disappointed. Readers are encouraged to make contact with the Aboriginal communities they pass through.

As yet there are no major Aboriginal events or festivals in the West. National Aboriginal Islander Day Observance Committee (NAIDOC) Week, in early July, brings together many groups, with displays of indigenous art and cultural performances.

One of the finest collections of traditional and contemporary Aboriginal art and artefacts can be found in the Berndt Museum of Anthropology, in the Social Sciences Building, at the University of WA, Crawley. There is a fine indigenous publishing house in Broome – Magabala Books (☎ 9192 1991).

Tours on Aboriginal Land

Tours which incorporate aspects of Aboriginal life and culture are the best opportunity for travellers to make meaningful contact with Aboriginal people.

In the Kimberley, there are a number of options, mostly initiatives by local Aboriginal people. Operators include Over the Top Tours, Lombadina Tours, Darngku Heritage Cruise (Geikie Gorge), Kooljaman Resort and Wundargoodie Tours (see the Kimberley section for more details).

The Purnululu Aboriginal Corporation and CALM (Department of Conservation and Land Management) jointly manage the Purnululu (Bungle Bungle) National Park, one of the first attempts in Australia to balance the needs of local people and the demands of tourism. The traditional owners are planning to take tours into the Bungles.

In the Pilbara, Aboriginal people have worked closely with CALM in establishing a cultural centre in the Karijini National Park and an information centre about the Yinjibarndi people's culture in Millstream-Chichester National Park.

GEOGRAPHY

Western Australia takes up a third of the Australian land mass. It has a small fertile coastal strip in its south-west corner. As in the east of the country, hills rise behind the coast, but in WA they're much smaller than those of the Great Dividing Range. Farther north it's dry and relatively barren. Fringing the central-west coast is the Great Sandy Desert, an inhospitable region running right to the sea.

There are a couple of interesting variations, such as the Kimberley in the extreme north of the State – a wild and rugged area with a convoluted coastline and stunning inland gorges. It gets good annual rainfall, but all in the 'green' or wet season.

Farther south is the Pilbara, with magnificent ancient rock and gorge country – the treasure-house from which the State derives vast mineral wealth. Away from the coast most of WA is simply a vast empty stretch of outback: the Nullarbor Plain in the south, the Great Sandy Desert in the north, and the Gibson and Great Victoria deserts between.

CLIMATE

There are several different climate zones in WA, with the main three being tropical (in the north), semi-arid (in the interior) and mild 'Mediterranean' (in the south-west). In general the rainfall decreases the farther you get from the coast.

In the north the climate is characterised by the Dry and the Wet, rather than winter and summer. As the monsoon develops there is thunderstorm activity (the 'build-up'), followed by the occasional tropical cyclone which develops into rain-bearing depressions as it passes inland. Although it makes many roads impassable, the rain is generally welcomed. It is said that Port Hedland receives a cyclone at least every two years.

Farther south, there is little or no rainfall during summer and the winds are generally hot, dry easterlies, but in the afternoon coastal areas receive sea breezes such as the famed 'Fremantle Doctor'. Cold fronts and accompanying low-pressure systems produce most of the rainfall for southern districts and agricultural regions in winter.

INFORMATION

There are no interstate offices of the Western Australian Tourism Commission (WATC). Some States and Territories have WATC agencies:

ACT Goddard & Partners (☎ (02) 6248 9399), 40 Allara St, Canberra 2600
New South Wales NRMA Travel (☎ (02) 9260 9222), 151 Clarence St, Sydney 2000
Queensland Harvey World Travel (☎ (07) 3221 5022), 204 Adelaide St, Brisbane 4000
South Australia RAA Travel (☎ (08) 8202 4589), 41 Hindmarsh Square, Adelaide 5000
Victoria RACV (☎ (03) 9607 2233), 123 Queen St, Melbourne 3000

FLORA

WA is famed for its 8000 species of wild-flower, which bloom in greatest number from August to October. Even some of the driest regions put on a colourful display after a little rainfall, and at any time of the year.

You can find flowers almost everywhere in the State, but the jarrah forests in the south-west are particularly rich. The coastal national parks, such as Fitzgerald River and Kalbarri, also have brilliant displays. Near Perth, the Badgingarra, Alexander Morrison, Yanchep and John Forrest national parks are excellent choices. There's also a wildflower display in Kings Park, Perth.

ACTIVITIES
Bushwalking

There are a number of bushwalking clubs in Perth – the umbrella organisation is the Federation of WA Bushwalking Clubs (☎ 9362 1614; www.bushwalking.org.au/wapage. html). Popular areas for walking in WA include the Stirling Range and Porongurup national parks, both north of Albany. There are also good walking tracks in many coastal parks in the south and south-west, such as

Kangaroo paws can be seen along the Brand Highway north of Perth from late July to the end of November

Cape Le Grand, Fitzgerald River, Walpole-Nornalup and Cape Arid. To the north, the Kalbarri, Karijini (Hamersley Range) and Purnululu national parks also provide a great hiking environment.

There are interesting walks in the hills around Perth, and if you're a really enthusiastic walker there's the 640km Bibbulmun Track (see the Bibbulmun Track aside in this chapter), which runs along old forest tracks between Perth and Walpole (on WA's south coast). Information on this and many other tracks is available from CALM (☎ 1800 199 287), 50 Hayman Rd, Como, Perth. Two excellent CALM publications are *Wild Places, Quiet Places* (covering the south-west) and *North-West Bound* (covering Shark Bay to Wyndham). **Bird-watching** can be an integral part of bushwalking, and WA is a fascinating destination for avifauna

---

Bibbulmun Track

This walking track, often referred to as the 'Perth-Albany Track', winds it way from Kalamunda, near Perth, to Walpole. The first stages of the track were officially opened and first traversed by walkers in 1979 as part of the celebrations of 150 years of European settlement. When the final 180km section from Walpole to Albany is added in September 1988 the track will cover some 950km and pass through a variety of forest types. There will be camp sites spaced every 10km to 20km, most with a three-sided shelter sleeping eight to 12 people.

It's estimated that about 5000 walkers use the Bibbulmun each year, though most are only on the track for two or three days. For more information contact CALM on ☎ 9334 0265 or at bibtrack@calm.wa.gov.au. A new guide book and maps indicating camp sites and realigned sections of track will also be available from September 1998. ■

---

addicts. It is the only State with two RAOU (Royal Australian Ornithological Union) observatories – at Eyre and Broome, both splendid locations.

Cycling

This is a popular activity, with Rottnest Island, Perth and the south-west offering excellent conditions. For information contact the Cycle Touring Association through Bike West (☎ 9430 7550), 27-35 William St, Fremantle.

Rock Climbing & Caving

In the south, the sea cliffs of Wilyabrup, West Cape Howe and the Gap, and the huge cliffs of the Stirling and Porongurup ranges attract climbers. The noncommercial caves of the Margaret River region and the lesser known 'holes' of Cape Range National Park offer plenty of opportunities for speleologists.

Water Sports

Swimming & Surfing People in Perth often claim to have the best surf and swimming beaches of any Australian city. Popular surfing areas around WA include Denmark, near Albany; Bunbury and the coast from Cape Naturaliste to Margaret River in the south-west; and Geraldton to the north. There are fine swimming beaches all along the coast.

Diving Good diving areas include the large stretch of coast from Esperance to Geraldton, and between Carnarvon and Exmouth. You can get to the islands and reefs off the coast in small boats.

Fishing The coastal regions of WA offer excellent fishing. Some of the more popular areas include Rottnest Island, Albany, Geraldton and the Houtman Abrolhos Islands, Mackerel Islands, Shark Bay, Carnarvon, North-West Cape and Broome.

Fishing licences are only required if you intend catching marron and rock lobsters, or will be using a fishing net. Obtain licences ($55) from the Fisheries Department (☎ 9482 7333), the SGIO Building, 168 St George's Terrace, Perth, or its country offices.

Other Water Sports WA was once, briefly, the home of sailing's greatest prize, the America's Cup, and sailing is popular, especially on the sheltered Swan River.

The Amateur Canoe Association of WA (☎ 9387 5756) will provide information on the many good canoeing and kayaking rivers in the State. Sea kayaking is also coming of age and many paddlers are now exploring the more remote parts of the State's coastline. White-water rafting is not as widespread as on the eastern seaboard, but after heavy rains the State's rivers (such as the Murray, Avon and Ord) are challenging.

Windsurfing is very popular, especially along Perth's city beaches and up in windy Geraldton. Lancelin and Ledge Point are the true sailboarders' meccas.

Perhaps the most exciting water activity

that WA offers is interaction with marine creatures, such as whales and dolphins. You can do this at many places, including Monkey Mia and Perth.

GETTING THERE & AWAY

Western Australia is the largest, most lightly populated and most isolated State in the country. Yet despite vast distances, you can drive across the Nullarbor from the eastern States to Perth and then up the Indian Ocean coast and through the Kimberley to Darwin without leaving bitumen.

Even so, there's absolutely no way of covering all those kilometres cheaply, although the deregulation of the airline industry has certainly helped. Sydney to Perth is 3284km as the crow flies, and more like 4000km by road; a one-way economy rail ticket on the route is $380, a discounted air ticket costs about $600 return (less if you shop around), while a seat on a Greyhound Pioneer Australia bus costs around $335.

Hitching across the Nullarbor is not advisable; waits of several days are common. Driving yourself is probably the cheapest way of getting to WA from the eastern States – if you have a group. You'll probably spend around $500 on fuel, travelling coast to coast (see the Eyre Highway section later in this chapter).

Train The Indian Pacific is one of Australia's great rail journeys – a 65-hour trip between the Indian Ocean on one side of the continent and the Pacific Ocean on the other. Travelling this way you see Australia at ground level and by the end of the journey you either appreciate the immensity of the country or are bored stiff – perhaps both.

From Sydney, you cross New South Wales to Broken Hill and then continue on to Adelaide and across the Nullarbor. From Port Augusta to Kalgoorlie, the seemingly endless crossing of the virtually uninhabited centre takes well over 24 hours, including the 'long straight' on the Nullarbor – at 478km this is the longest straight stretch of railway line in the world. Unlike the Eyre Highway, which runs south of the Nullarbor along the

coast of the Great Australian Bight, the railway line actually crosses the Nullarbor Plain.

To Perth, one-way fares from Adelaide are $492 for an economy Holiday-class sleeper (no meals), $758 for a 1st-class sleeper or $230 in an economy seat ('coach') with no meals. From Sydney, fares are $763 economy, $1172 1st class or $378 in coach.

Heading west, the train departs from Sydney at 2.55 pm on Thursday and Monday, arriving in Perth at 7 am on Sunday and Thursday. Eastbound, it departs from Perth at 1.35 pm on Monday and Friday, arriving in Sydney at 9.15 am on Thursday and Monday.

Reservations for all services are made with Australian National Railways (☎ 13 2232).

GETTING AROUND
Air

Deregulation is making a difference to flying

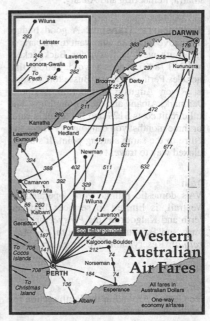

Western Australian Air Fares

All fares in Australian Dollars

One-way economy airfares

within WA. Ansett Australia and Skywest (☎ 13 1300) connect Perth to most regional centres. Qantas Airways (☎ 13 1313) has flights to Broome, Port Hedland, Kalgoorlie and Darwin.

See the airfares chart for the main domestic routes and flight costs.

Bus

Greyhound Pioneer (☎ 13 2030) buses run from Perth along the coast to Darwin ($415), and from Perth to Adelaide via Kalgoorlie and the Eyre Highway ($214). Perth Goldfields Express (☎ 9328 9199) goes from Perth via Kalgoorlie to Leonora ($90) and Leinster ($100).

South-West Coachlines (☎ 9322 5173) in the city bus port in Perth runs services from Perth to the south-west – Bunbury, Busselton, Nannup, Dunsborough, Augusta, Manjimup and Collie.

Westrail (☎ 13 2232) goes to Hyden, Geraldton, York, Esperance, Augusta, Meekatharra, Pemberton and Albany.

Backpackers' Transport A good budget alternative for those who want to see parts of the south-west is Easyrider Backpackers (☎ 9383 7848). It does a two-day circuit that includes Perth, Bunbury, Busselton, Margaret River, Augusta, Pemberton, Walpole, Denmark, Albany and the Porongurups. The full circuit costs $129 and the ticket is valid for three months; you can join anywhere and return to the same starting point. It's a fun, relaxed way to travel.

Train

WA's domestic rail network, operated by Westrail, is limited to services between Perth and Kalgoorlie (the *Prospector*), and Perth and Bunbury in the south (the *Australind*). Reservations are necessary (☎ 13 2232).

Car

See Getting Around in the Perth section for details on car rental.

Perth

- *Pop 1,097,000*

Perth is a vibrant and modern city, pleasantly sited on the Swan River, with the port of Fremantle a mere 20km downstream and the dormitory cities of Rockingham and Mandurah to the south. It's claimed to be the sunniest state capital in Australia and most isolated capital city in the world. Of WA's nearly 1.8 million people, around 80% live in and around Perth.

Perth was founded in 1829 as the Swan River Settlement. It grew very slowly until 1850, when convicts were brought in to alleviate the labour shortage.

Many of Perth's fine buildings, such as Government House and the Perth Town Hall, were built with convict labour. Even then, Perth's development lagged behind that of the eastern cities, until the discovery of gold in the 1890s increased the population fourfold in a decade and initiated a building boom.

More recently, WA's mineral wealth has contributed to Perth's growth, and the resultant construction boom has spread into the outer suburbs. A somewhat hick, squeaky-clean, nouveau-riche image has been tainted by political scandals in the 1980s and the crash of entrepreneurs, but this all seems to add to the city's frontier-town feel.

Orientation

The city centre is fairly compact, situated on a sweep of the Swan River, which borders the city centre to the south and east, and links Perth to its port, Fremantle. The main shopping precinct is along the Hay St and Murray St malls and the arcades that run between them. St George's Terrace is the centre of the city's business district.

The railway line bounds the city centre on the northern side. Immediately north of it is Northbridge, a popular restaurant and entertainment enclave with a number of hostels and other cheap accommodation. The western end of Perth slopes up to the pleasant

Perth Walking Tour

The civic mothers and fathers have been unkind to central Perth – charming old buildings have been bulldozed and replaced with giant concrete and glass towers. But if you look carefully you will find some remnants of the old Perth. This tour, which commences at the WATC tourist centre in Forrest Place, will help. You can use the free CAT buses to reach some of these places and get a map from the WATC.

If you cross Wellington St by the overpass, you will pass through the train station into a square containing the Western Australian Museum (and **Megamouth**), the Art Gallery of Western Australia and the Alexander Library.

Return to Forrest Place, pass the main post office, and proceed through one of the arcades to the Hay St Mall. Turn left and look out for **London Court** on your right. Between Hay St and St George's Terrace, the narrow, touristy London Court is a photographer's delight. Although it looks very Tudor English, it only dates from 1937. At one end of this shopping court St George and the dragon do battle above the clock each quarter of an hour, while at the other end knights joust on horseback.

Turn left at the end of the court and follow St George's Terrace to Barrack St. The **Central Government Buildings** on the corner of Barrack St and St George's Terrace, recognisable by their patterned brick, were built between 1874 and 1902 (at one stage they housed the GPO). Uphill on Barrack St, on the corner of Hay St, is the **Perth Town Hall** (1867-70).

Head back to St George's Terrace and turn left. On the corner of Pier St is the **Deanery**, built in 1859 and restored after a public appeal in 1980. It's one of the few cottage-style houses that have survived from colonial days; it is not open to the public. Across St George's Terrace are the Stirling Gardens. The old **courthouse**, next to the Supreme Court, is also here. One of the oldest buildings in Perth, it was built in Georgian style in 1836. A little further along St George's Terrace is **Government House**, a Gothic-looking fantasy built between 1859 and 1864.

Follow St George's Terrace to Hill St (at Victoria Ave, St George's Terrace becomes Adelaide Terrace). Turn left and head up to Hay St. The **Perth Mint** (☎ 9421 7425), on the corner of Hill and Hay Sts, and originally opened in 1899, has reopened for public tours. Visitors can mint their own coins and watch gold pours, held on the hour from 10 am to 3 pm on weekdays and 10 am to noon on weekends. Entry to the exhibition is $5 (children $3). The mint is open on weekdays from 9 am to 4 pm, and on weekends from 9 am to 1 pm.

Continue up Hill St to Goderich St. Turn left and head to Victoria Square where you'll find **St Mary's Cathedral** (1863), and a grassed area that's popular with office workers at lunch time. Follow Murray St, on the far side of the square, back to William St. Turn left into William St and head to St George's Terrace. On the corner of St George's Terrace is the grand and once extravagant **Palace Hotel** (1895), now a banking chamber. Turn right into St George's Terrace and head down to King St – on your left, at No 139, is the **Old Perth Boys' School** (1854), now a National Trust gift shop.

At King St turn right and follow it to Hay St. On the corner is the restored **His Majesty's Theatre** (1904); there are free daily tours of the 'Maj' between 10 am and 4 pm. Return to St George's Terrace and turn right. Walk a short distance and, on the right, are the **Cloisters** (1858), noted for their beautiful brickwork. Originally a school, they are now part of a modern office development.

The distinctive **Barracks Archway**, at the western end of St George's Terrace, is all that remains of a barracks built in 1863 to house the pensioner guards of the British army – discharged soldiers who guarded convicts.

On the far side of the Mitchell Freeway is **Parliament House**. Tours of the Parliament buildings can be arranged on weekdays through the parliamentary information officer (☎ 9222 7222) – you will of course get a more extensive tour when parliament is not in session. Take the Red CAT from Harvest Terrace to return to the city centre. Fit walkers may wish to proceed to **Kings Park**. ∎

Kings Park, which overlooks the city and Swan River.

Farther to the west, suburbs extend as far as the Indian Ocean beaches, such as Scarborough and Cottesloe.

Information

Tourist Offices The WATC's tourist centre (☎ 9483 1111, 1800 812 808) is in Albert Facey House on Forrest Place, next to the main post office and opposite the train station. The centre is open from Monday to Thursday from 8.30 am to 6 pm, Friday from 8.30 am to 7 pm, Saturday from 8.30 am to 5 pm and Sunday from 10 am to 5 pm. It has a wide range of maps and brochures on Perth and WA, and an

WESTERN AUSTRALIA

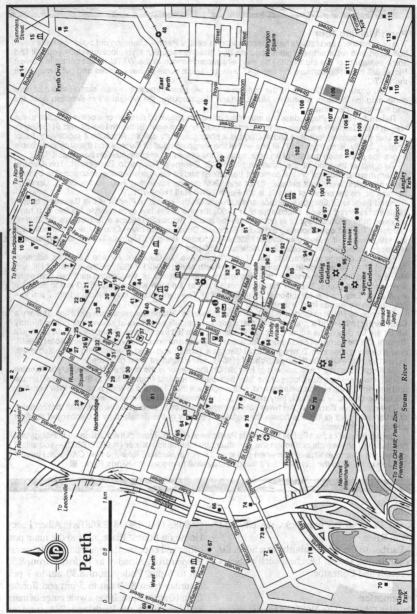

Perth

0   0.5   1 km

To Leederville

To Redbackpackers

To Rory's Backpackers

To North Lodge

Perth Oval

East Perth

Wellington Square

Russell Square

Northbridge

Stirling Gardens

Government House Grounds

Supreme Court Gardens

The Esplanade

Barrack Street Jetty

Swan River

Narrows Interchange

To The Old Mill; Perth Zoo; Fremantle

To Airport

Kings Park

West Perth

WESTERN AUSTRALIA

PLACES TO STAY
2 Budget Backpackers International
3 Lone Star - Perth Travellers Lodge
4 Paul & Scotty's Ozi Inn
5 Backpackers International
6 The Workhouse
12 Backpack City & Surf
13 The Shiralee
14 Cheviot Lodge
16 Rainbow Lodge
18 Britannia YHA Hostel
20 Northbridge YHA Hostel
21 Field Touring Hostel
23 Aberdeen Lodge
47 Court Hotel
57 Globe Backpackers
58 Royal Hotel
69 CWA House
70 Sullivan's Hotel
71 Adelphi Apartments Motel
72 Riverview on Mount Street
73 Mountway Holiday Flats
74 Mount St Serviced Apartments
91 Murray Street Hostel
92 Criterion Hotel
103 Townsend Lodge
104 City Waters Lodge Holiday Units
107 Downtowner Lodge
108 YMCA Jewell House
110 Airways City Hotel
111 Hay Street Backpackers
112 Exclusive Backpackers
113 East Backpackers

PLACES TO EAT
7 Sri Melaka & White Elephant Thai
8 City Fresh Food Co & Pho Van Reo
9 Asian Food Court
11 Dong Phuong
17 Villa Italia
19 Seoul Korean
24 The Street Cafe
25 Mamma Maria's
28 Lotus Vegetarian
34 Vinous
35 Northbridge Pavilion Food Hall
36 Trains, Planes & Automobiles
37 Old Shanghai Markets
38 Tequila Sunrise
39 Sylvana Pastry
41 Brass Monkey Bar & Brasserie
42 Tonic Cafe & Hare Krishna Food for Life
49 Depot Markets
51 Hayashi Japanese Barbecue
52 Gopals
53 Ann's Malaysian Food
62 Buzz Bar; Creations
64 Katong Singapore Restaurant; Taj Tandoor
65 Fast Eddy's
81 Fast Food Strip
83 Carillon Food Hall
85 Venice Cafe
90 Arcade Japanese Sushi Bar
93 Miss Maud's
96 Benardi's
100 Magic Apple Wholefoods
101 Stamina Indonesian

OTHER
1 The Bog
10 Mosque
15 Army Museum of Western Australia
22 Aberdeen Hotel
26 Kremlin
27 The Post Office
29 Rosie O'Grady's
30 Metropolis City Nightclub
31 Cinema Paradiso
32 Dual Control ('DC's)
33 Novak's Tavern, O2; Krush
40 Connections
43 Perth Institute of Contemporary Arts (PICA)
44 YHA Travel Centre
45 Art Gallery of WA
46 Western Australian Museum
48 Claisebrook Train Station
50 McIver Train Station
54 Central Perth Train Station
55 Western Australian Tourist Centre
56 Main Post Office
59 Wentworth Plaza (Bobby Dazzler's; Moon & Sixpence)
60 Wellington St Bus Station
61 Entertainment Centre
63 Club 418
66 Barracks Archway
67 Parliament House
68 It's a Small World Museum
75 Traveller's Vaccination & Medical Clinic
76 Cloisters
77 His Majesty's Theatre
78 City Bus Port
79 Old Perth Boy's School
80 Allan Green Plant Conservatory
82 Ansett Australia
84 Qantas Airways
86 London Court
87 Qantas Airways
88 Supreme Court
89 Perth Town Hall
94 Deanery
95 Government House
97 Ansett Australia
98 Perth Concert Hall
99 WA Fire Brigade Museum
102 Victoria Square; St Mary's Cathedral; Royal Perth Hospital
105 RACWA
106 Grosvenor Hotel
109 Perth Mint

accommodation and tours reservation service.

A number of guides to Perth, including *Hello Perth & Fremantle*, *What's on in Perth & Fremantle*, *West Coast Visitor's Guide*, *Your Guide to Perth & Fremantle* and *Tourist Maps: Perth & Fremantle*, are available free from the tourist centre, and hostels and hotels. The free *Tourist Guide to Western Australia* is also useful. Perth's tourist radio station broadcasts at 87.6 FM.

Fertile Internet sites include Your Guide to Perth & Fremantle (www.countrywide .com.au), CALM's NatureBase (www.calm. gov.au) and the WA Maritime Museum's site (www.mm.wa.gov.au).

Post & Communications Perth's main post office (☎ 9326 5211) is on Forrest Place, which is between Wellington St and the Murray St Mall. There are phones for international calls in the foyer.

Useful Organisations The Royal Automobile Club of Western Australia (RACWA; ☎ 9421 4444) is at 228 Adelaide Terrace. Membership is worth the reduced rate for its *WA Touring & Accommodation Guide*.

Disabled visitors can use the services of ACROD (☎ 9222 2961), 189 Royal St, East Perth. People with Disabilities (☎ 9386 6477, 1800 193 331) can also help.

The YHA (☎ 9227 5122) has its office at 236 William St in Northbridge.

Bookshops Some good city bookshops include Angus & Robertson, 199 Murray St and 625 Hay St; Dymocks, Hay St Mall; Boffins Bookshop, 806 Hay St; and the Down to Earth Bookshop, 790 Hay St.

Medical Services The Traveller's Vaccination & Medical Clinic (☎ 9321 1977) is at 5 Mill St, off St George's Terrace. The Royal Perth Hospital (☎ 9224 2244) on Victoria Square is close to the centre.

Kings Park

There are superb views across Perth and the river from this 4 sq km park. It includes a 17-hectare **Botanic Garden** that displays over 2500 different WA plant species, and a section of natural bushland. In spring, there's a display of WA's famed wildflowers.

Free guided tours of Kings Park and the Botanic Garden are available all year. The park also has a number of bike tracks; bikes can be rented from Koala Bicycle Hire

(☎ 9321 3061) at the western side of the main car park. An information centre, next to the car park, is open daily from 9.30 am to 3.30 pm. The park also has a restaurant with a pleasant coffee shop.

Get there on the Red CAT to Kings Park entrance or walk up Mount St from the city, then cross the freeway overpass.

Museums

On Francis St, north across the railway lines from the city centre, is the **Western Australian Museum**. The museum includes a gallery of Aboriginal culture, a marine gallery, vintage cars, a 25m blue whale skeleton and a large collection of meteorites, the biggest of which weighs 11 tonnes (many meteorites have been found in the outback). The complex also includes Perth's original prison, built in 1856 and used until 1888. Out in the courtyard, set in its own preservative bath, is **megamouth**, one of the largest species of shark – only five specimens of this benign creature have ever been recorded. The museum is open from Sunday to Friday from 10.30 am to 5 pm, and on Saturday from 1 to 5 pm (admission is free).

Three other museums close to the city are the **It's a Small World Museum**, 12 Parliament Place, which has the largest collection of miniatures in the country (open daily; entry is $5/4 for adults/children); the **Army Museum of WA** on the corner of Bulwer and Lord Sts, which has a display of army memorabilia (open on Sunday from 1 to 4.30 pm; free entry); and the **WA Fire Brigade Museum** on the corner of Irwin and Murray Sts, which has displays on fire safety and fire-fighting equipment (open on weekdays from 10 am to 3 pm; free entry).

Art Gallery of WA & PICA

Housed in a modern building which runs from James St through to Roe St, behind the train station, the gallery has a fine permanent exhibition of European, Australian and Asia-Pacific art and a wide variety of temporary exhibitions. It is open from 10 am to 5 pm daily (admission is free).

The Perth Institute of Contemporary Arts

(PICA; ☎ 9227 9339), 51 James St, promotes the creation, presentation and discussion of new and experimental art. It is open from Tuesday to Sunday from 10 am to 5 pm.

Perth Zoo

Perth's popular zoo is set in attractive gardens across the river from the city at 20 Labouchere Rd, South Perth. It has a number of interesting collections, including a nocturnal house which is open daily from noon to 3 pm, an Australian wildlife park, numbat display and conservation discovery centre.

The zoo (☎ 9367 7988) is open daily from 10 am to 5 pm ($8, children $3, family $25). You can reach the zoo on bus No 110 (or No 108 on weekends) from the city bus port, or by taking the ferry across the river from the Barrack St jetty.

Underwater World

Underwater World, north of the city at Hillarys Boat Harbour on West Coast Drive, Hillarys, is certainly not your run-of-the-mill aquarium. There is an underwater tunnel aquarium displaying 2500 examples of 200 marine species, including sharks and stingrays. Also in the complex are interactive displays such as a Touch Pool, Microworld and an audiovisual theatre. In season, staff conduct three-hour whale-watching trips ($25/$20 for adults/children on weekends, $20/$15 on weekdays). Underwater World is open daily from 9 am to 5 pm ($15.50, children $7.50, family $39).

Parks & Gardens

On the Esplanade, between the city and the river, is the **Allan Green Plant Conservatory**. It houses a tropical and semitropical controlled-environment display; entry is free.

Also close to the city, on the corner of St George's Terrace and Barrack St, are the **Stirling Gardens**, a popular place to eat lunch. The **Queen's Gardens**, at the eastern end of Hay St, is a pleasant little park with lakes and bridges; get there on a Red CAT bus.

Lake Monger in Wembley, north-west of the city centre, is another hang-out for local feathered friends, particularly the famous black swans.

Other Innercity Attractions

On Mill Point Rd, on the southern end of the Narrows Bridge, is one of Perth's landmarks: the finely restored **Old Mill** (☎ 9367 5788), built in 1835. The former flour mill is open every afternoon, except on Tuesday and Friday (admission is free). Catch bus No 108 or 109 from St George's Terrace.

The **Scitech Discovery Centre** on Railway Parade, West Perth, has over 160 hands-on and large-scale exhibits. It's open daily ($10, children $7, family $25).

Beaches

There are calm bay beaches on the Swan River at **Crawley**, **Peppermint Grove** and **Como**. Or you can try a string of patrolled surf beaches on the Indian Ocean coast, including the popular nude beach at **Swanbourne** – take bus No 205 or 207 from stand 44 on St George's Terrace.

Some of the other surf beaches include **Cottesloe**, a safe swimming beach; **Port**; **City**; **Scarborough**, a wide, golden and popular surf beach which is only for experienced swimmers; **Leighton**; **Floreat**; and **Trigg Island**, another surf beach that is dangerous when rough. See also the Rottnest Island section later in this chapter.

Markets

There are many lively markets in Perth – ideal if you're into browsing and buying. The **Subiaco Pavilion** on the corner of Roberts and Rokeby Rds and near the Subiaco train station is open from Thursday to Sunday. The **Wanneroo Markets**, north of Perth at 33 Prindiville Drive, Wangara, feature a large food hall and a variety of stalls; they're open on weekends from 9 am to 6 pm.

Other markets include the historic **Fremantle Market** (see the Fremantle section later in the chapter); the weekend **Stock Rd Markets** at Bibra Lake, south of Perth; the **Gosnells Railway Markets**, open

WESTERN AUSTRALIA

from Thursday to Sunday; and the **Depot Markets** in the East Perth food halls on the corner of Lord and Royal Sts, open from Friday to Sunday from 10 am to 5.30 pm (the food hall is open until 8 pm).

Perth Suburbs

Armadale The **Pioneer World** at Armadale, 27km south-east of the city, is a working model of a 19th-century colonial village; it's open daily ($4, children $2). You can get to Armadale on bus No 219 or by train from Perth station.

About 6km south of Armadale, **Tumbulgum Farm** has a number of Australian products for sale, and puts on farm shows and displays of Aboriginal culture. It is open from Wednesday to Sunday from 9.30 am to 5 pm ($8, children $4).

Up the Swan River There are many attractions up the Swan River. On Maylands Peninsula, enclosed by a loop of the river, is the beautifully restored **Tranby House**. Built in 1839, it is one of WA's oldest houses and a fine example of early colonial architecture. It's open daily from 2 to 5 pm ($2.50, children $1.50).

In West Swan the **Caversham Wildlife Park & Zoo** has a large collection of Australian animals and birds; it's open daily from 9 am to 5 pm ($5, $2 children). On Lord St, West Swan, is **Whiteman Park** (☎ 9249 2446), Perth's biggest reserve. It has over 30km of bikeways and paths, and there are tram and vintage steam train rides ($5 per car, and tram and train rides are extra).

Swan Valley **vineyards** are dotted along the river from Guildford to the Upper Swan. Many are open for tastings and cellar sales. Houghton Wines on Dale Rd, Middle Swan, was established in 1842 and produced its first vintage in 1859. Lamont's, Bisdee Rd, produces wines in the traditional manner (and prepares great lunches).

Other Suburbs In Subiaco, the **Museum of Childhood**, 160 Hamersley Rd, houses an interesting, nostalgic collection; it is open daily except Saturday. Across the Canning

River, towards Jandakot airport, on Bull Creek Drive there is the excellent **Aviation Museum**, with a collection of aviation memorabilia, including a Spitfire and a Lancaster bomber. It is open daily from 11 am to 4 pm ($5, children $2).

Adventure World, 15km south of Perth at 179 Progress Drive, Bibra Lake, is a large amusement park open daily ($20, $18 children). **Bungee West**, also on Progress Drive in Bibra Lake, is open daily. Throw yourself from a 40m tower; the less adventurous can abseil, the downright cowardly can just observe. Go on, jump! At **Cables Water Park**, Troode St, Spearwood (off Rockingham Rd), cables haul water-skiers along at 20 to 50 km/h. It is open daily; an hour's waterskiing costs $12.

There's a potpourri of other places to visit in the suburbs; enquire at the WATC tourist centre.

Organised Tours

Half-day city tours of Perth and Fremantle cost about $30, while for $55 you can get tours to the Swan Valley wineries, Cohunu Wildlife Park or Underwater World and the northern beaches.

A favourite is the free tour of the **Swan Brewery** (☎ 9350 0650), 25 Baile Rd, Canning Vale. The tour takes 1½ hours (followed by a beer) and starts at 10 am from Monday to Thursday, and there's 2.30 pm tours Monday through Wednesday. Reservations are essential.

Safari Treks (☎ 9271 1271) does a good half-day tour of the Swan Valley wineries and Yanchep Cave; it's not cheap at $80 but you cover a lot of territory. Coach Bush Eco Tours (☎ 9336 3050) includes national parks and lakes in its full-day tour ($96). On Saturday it has a great trip to the Dryandra Woodlands ($105), 160km south-east of Perth.

Cruises A number of cruise companies operate tours from the Barrack St jetty, including Captain Cook Cruises (☎ 9325 3341) and Boat Torque (☎ 9221 5844). Tours include scenic cruises on the Swan

River, winery visits, trips to Fremantle, lunch and dinner cruises.

From September to May, the Transperth MV *Countess II* departs daily, except Saturday, at 2 pm from the Barrack St jetty on a three-hour cruise of the Upper Swan ($15).

Boat Torque also has a full-day Swan Valley river cruise ($65, children $45), and Captain Cook Cruises has a three-hour scenic river cruise around Perth and Fremantle ($24/12).

Dolphin & Whale-Watching An informative whale-watching trip with Mills Charters (☎ 9401 0833) is run in conjunction with Underwater World. The tour searches for humpback whales on their return to Antarctic waters after wintering off north-western Australia. Run from September to November, it begins at Hillarys Boat Harbour and costs $25 and $20 on weekends and weekdays respectively (children $20 and $15).

Other whale-watching operators are Boat Torque (☎ 9246 1039), leaving from Hillarys, and Oceanic Cruises (☎ 9430 5127), from Fremantle. To get to Hillarys take the train to Warwick and then bus No 423 from there.

There are two-hour **dolphin-watching** cruises daily from the Val St jetty (☎ 0418 958 678) in Rockingham ($120).

Public Holidays & Special Events
Public holidays in WA that differ from the other States are: Labour Day (second Monday in March), Foundation Day (first Monday in June) and the Queen's Birthday (first Monday in October).

Every year around February/March the **Festival of Perth** offers music, drama, dance and films. The 'alternative' **Northbridge Festival** is also held around that time. The **Perth Royal Show** takes place every September/October, and the **Artrage Festival** is held in October. In early June, **West Week** is held to celebrate WA's foundation – there are historical re-creations, art and craft events, concerts and sporting fixtures.

Places to Stay
Camping Perth is not well-endowed with camp sites convenient to the city centre. There are many caravan parks in the suburbs, these includes:

Armadale Tourist Village (☎ 9399 6376; South-West Highway, Armadale; 27km south-east of Perth) has powered sites for $12 and holiday units for $38 for two

Forrestfield Caravan Park (☎ 9453 6378; 351 Hawtin Rd, Forrestfield; 18km east) has tent sites for $12 and cabins for $40 for two

Karrinyup Waters Resort (☎ 9447 6665; 467 North Beach Rd, Gwelup; 14km north) has tent/powered sites for $15/17, on-site vans from $29 and park cabins for $40 for two

Kenlorn Tourist Park (☎ 9356 2380; 229 Welshpool Rd, Queens Park; 9km south-east) has tent sites for $12 (weekly rates available), on-site vans for $20 and park cabins for $30 for two

Perth Central Caravan Park (☎ 9277 1704; 34 Central Ave, Redcliffe; 8km east) has tent/powered sites for $14/18 and on-site vans for $35 for two

Starhaven Caravan Park (☎ 9341 1770; 18-20 Pearl Parade, Scarborough; 14km north-west) has tent sites for $15, on-site vans for $28 and holiday units for $50 for two

Swan Valley Tourist Village (☎ 9274 2828; 6851 West Swan Rd, Guildford; 19km north-west) has tent/powered sites for $13/14, on-site vans from $28 and holiday units for $45 for two

Hostels – Northbridge There are many hostels and backpacker places in Perth – probably more than the city can support. As a result, competition is fierce. Some are good, others need lots of improvement. Most provide pick-ups from the airport or bus terminals.

A couple of places, run by travellers, are particularly good. *Rory's Backpackers* (☎ 9328 9958; also listed as Backpackers Perth Inn), 194 Brisbane St, is in two clean (and joined) renovated colonial houses with pleasant gardens and a barbecue area. Rory has done a lot to make his place comfortable, there is a range of good accommodation and the facilities have been entirely revamped. Dorm beds are $14, and twin, double and triple rooms are about $34.

Also good, probably as a result of its two capable owners, is *Paul & Scotty's Ozi Inn*

(☎ 9328 1222) at 282 Newcastle St. In the large renovated house, with all the necessary facilities and friendly staff, dorm beds are $14, and twins and doubles with TV and air-con are $34. Over the road is the *Workhouse* for longer-term (perhaps noisier) patrons. The Workhouse charges a weekly rate and is a little cheaper than Paul & Scotty's.

At 253 William St is the large, central and much-improved *Britannia YHA* (☎ 9328 6121). The better single-only rooms are at the back on the verandah, and rooms near the hallways can be noisy; dorm beds are from $14. Around the corner at 42-46 Francis St is the *Northbridge YHA* (☎ 9328 7794), popular with travellers who warm to the friendly staff. This ageing, but renovated, former guesthouse has all the facilities; again dorm beds are from $14.

The *Shiralee* (☎ 9227 7448), 107 Brisbane St, has been recommended by a number of readers. It is clean, has pleasant recreation areas, and the managers ensure that all facilities are shipshape; dorm beds are $14, air-conditioned twins and doubles are $34. A little farther east at 133 Summers St, East Perth is the pleasant *Rainbow Lodge* (☎ 9227 1818), a large rambling place with a number of recreation areas (and an offer of free breakfast); dorm beds are $12 ($75 per week), and twins and doubles are $28.

Redbackpackers (☎ 9227 9969), 496 Newcastle St, has been much improved (and it needed it). Like many backpacker places, the improvement has a lot to do with enthusiastic owners. Dorm beds are $14, twins are $32 and doubles $34. The small *Backpack City & Surf* (☎ 9227 1234), tucked away next to the Buddhist Centre at 41 Money St, is an unusual place with a large central corridor where travellers get together; it is well run and worth the $13 for dorm beds and $32 for twins and doubles. Staff arrange trips to Scarborough Beach, where their sister hostel is.

Another good alternative is the *North Lodge* (☎ 9227 7588) at 225 Beaufort St; it's clean, friendly, has all the usual facilities and comfortable dorm/twin rooms. Also in

Northbridge is *Cheviot Lodge* (☎ 9227 6817) at 30 Bulwer St; it's open 24 hours, is close to the interstate rail terminal and there are no bunk beds.

If these places don't satisfy your every whim, then try: the *Budget Backpackers International* (☎ 9328 9468), 342 Newcastle St, with a comfortable lounge and good kitchen facilities (dorm beds cost from $14 per night); the *Lone Star – Perth Travellers Lodge* (☎ 9328 6667), 156-158 Aberdeen St, made up of two recently renovated houses (dorm beds are $13, twins $30); *Aberdeen Lodge* (☎ 9227 6137), 79 Aberdeen St, which is central with four-bed dorms (you get what you pay your $10 for); *Field Touring Hostel* (☎ 9328 4692), 74 Aberdeen St (dorm beds for $13 and twins for $26); and *Backpackers International* (☎ 9227 9977) on the corner of Lake and Aberdeen Sts (dorm beds are from $12 and twins $28).

Brand-new is the *Witch's Hat* (☎ 9228 4228) on Palmerston St, Northbridge; please write and tell us about it (a dorm bed is $16, twins and doubles are $40).

Hostels – Inncercity The *Hay Street Backpackers*, 266-268 Hay St, East Perth, has all the facilities you would require but, as with all hostels in the city area, is separated from the action of Northbridge and Leederville – after 6 pm the centre closes down! But if good facilities, including a pool, attract you, then the dorm beds for $15 and doubles for $36 ($42 with en-suite) are probably good value.

Not far away, *12.01 East* (☎ 9221 1666) in a converted office building at 195 Hay St has dorm beds from $13, twins from $30 and doubles from $36; the rooms are clean as well as air-conditioned and some have fridges. Not far away at 158 Adelaide Terrace is *Exclusive Backpackers* (☎ 9325 2852) in a beautifully restored building. It lacked 'backpackers' when we visited – it costs about $15 for a dorm, $40 for a twin or double.

Closer to the city centre is the *Townsend Lodge* (☎ 9325 4143), 240 Adelaide Terrace; it is good value with dinner (Monday to

Friday) included in the $18 per person price for lockable single rooms. If you stay one week you get a free night. The *Murray Street Hostel* (☎ 9325 7627), 119 Murray St (dorm beds from $13), and *Globe Backpackers* (☎ 9321 4080), 479 Wellington St (dorm beds from $12), are both in an area that is busy during the day and, fortunately, within walking distance of Northbridge during the morgue-like city night.

The *YMCA Jewell House* (☎ 9325 8488), 180 Goderich St (as Murray St becomes after Victoria Square), has over 200 comfortable, clean and modern rooms; singles/doubles are $30/38 and weekly rates are six times the daily rate. It is open 24 hours and has off-street parking.

Hostels – Scarborough Close to the surf, Scarborough is a good alternative to Northbridge. *Mandarin Gardens* (☎ 9341 5431), 20-28 Wheatcroft St, has dorm rooms for $14. This hostel is within walking distance (500m) of popular Scarborough Beach and has a pool and sizeable recreational areas. It also has flats from $40 to $85 per night.

Backpack City & Surf (☎ 9245 1161), 119 Scarborough Beach Rd, needs a bit of work to make it comfortable; the plus is that the first night in a dorm is only $7 ($11 each night after); staff can transfer travellers from their city hostel on Money St, Northbridge.

The compact *Western Beach Lodge* (☎ 9245 1624), 6 Westborough St, is clean and airy; rates are $12 in dorms, $30 in doubles (with en-suite $34). Also in Scarborough, *Indigo Lodge* (☎ 9341 6655) on West Coast Highway has dorm beds for $13, singles for $22, and twin and double rooms for $36. To get there, take bus No 400 from the city bus port.

South of Scarborough, the *Swanbourne Lodge* (☎ 9341 6655) behind the hotel at 141 Claremont Crescent, Swanbourne, was still being renovated when we visited; tell us about it.

Guesthouses Centrally located, good value and recommended by readers is the *Downtowner Lodge* (☎ 9325 6973), 63 Hill St, opposite the Perth Mint. The rooms are clean and pleasant, and it's a tranquil, friendly, nonsmoking place; twin rooms cost $36 and there are weekly rates.

The *Country Women's Association (CWA) House* (☎ 9321 6081) is at 1174 Hay St, West Perth (the entrance is at the rear). The rooms are comfortable and some have good city views; all in all it's a most reasonable option at $35/60 for singles/doubles (some have en-suites). Families can get suites with connecting rooms for the children; a light breakfast is included in the price.

Out at Swanbourne, the gay-friendly *Swanbourne Guesthouse* (☎ 9383 1981), 5 Myera St, has excellent self-contained rooms from $55/65 (breakfast included).

Motels & Holiday Flats Perth and the surrounding suburbs have an abundance of motels and holiday flats (see the *Western Australia Accommodation & Tours Listing* available from the tourist centre for more information). A selection follows.

City Waters Lodge Holiday Units (☎ 9325 1566) at 118 Terrace Rd, by the river, is conveniently central and good value. Rooms have cooking facilities, bathroom, TV and laundry, and cost $72/77 for singles/doubles.

North of the city centre at 166 Palmerston St are the self-contained *Brownelea Holiday Units* (☎ 9227 1710) from $55 a double. The *Adelphi Apartments Motel* (☎ 9322 4666), 130a Mounts Bay Rd, has well-equipped units for $58/68.

The *Mount Street Inn Serviced Apartments* (☎ 9481 0866), 24 Mount St, West Perth, is between the city and Kings Park. It has magnificent views over the city and river and rooms are from $116 for two. Nearby, across the overpass, is the *Mountway Holiday Flats* (☎ 9321 8307) at No 36; singles/doubles cost from $39/45. In the vicinity is the *Riverview on Mount Street* (☎ 9321 8963) at No 42; rooms cost from $55/60.

Across the Narrows Bridge, on the South Perth side in Applecross, and about 7km south of the city centre, the *Canning Bridge Auto Lodge* (☎ 9364 2511), 891 Canning Rd, has rooms from $50 for two. The *Regency Motel* (☎ 9362 3000) at 61-69 Great Eastern Highway, Rivervale, has rooms from $38/45.

Hotels There are a number of old-fashioned hotels around the city centre. The *Criterion Hotel* (☎ 9325 5155), a refurbished Art Deco building centrally located at 560 Hay St, has friendly staff and clean renovated singles/doubles for $95/115, breakfast included. The *Royal Hotel* (☎ 9324 1510) on the corner of Wellington and William Sts has rooms from $30/45, and 'executive' rooms from $75. The *Court Hotel* (☎ 9328 5292), 50 Beaufort St, is a gay-friendly place with B&B from $30/60.

Sullivan's Hotel (☎ 9321 8022), 166 Mounts Bay Rd (about 2km from the centre and next to Kings Park), is a popular family-run place with comfortable rooms for $90. It has a pool, restaurant and off-street parking and is on the CAT route.

If you want something upmarket, you won't be disappointed in the city centre; ask at the tourist centre for more details. You could try the *Airways City Hotel*,195 Adelaide Terrace, which charges from $80 a double (☎ 9323 7799); it has been recommended by readers.

Places to Eat

Food Halls The *Down Under Food Hall*, downstairs from the Hay St Mall and near the corner of William St, has stalls offering Chinese, Mexican, Thai, Indian and many other types of food. It is open from Monday to Wednesday from 8 am to 7 pm and from Thursday to Saturday from 8 am to 9 pm.

The *Carillon Arcade Food Hall* in the Carillon Arcade off the Hay St Mall is slightly more upmarket than the Down Under Food Hall and has the same international flavour, with Italian, Middle Eastern and Chinese dishes costing from $6 to $8. It also has sandwich shops, a seafood stall and fast-food outlets. It is open until 9 pm every evening, although some of the food stalls do close around 7 pm.

The large *Northbridge Pavilion Food Hall*

on the corner of Lake and James Sts is also good value. It's open from Wednesday to Sunday and has some outdoor seating and a couple of bars; the juices at *Naturals* are truly refreshing.

On James St, at the back of the small Roe St Chinatown, are the *Old Shanghai Markets*. The *Victoria Gardens* food hall is on the corner of Aberdeen St, overlooking Russell Square, while there's the much smaller *Asian Food Court* on the corner of William and Little Parry Sts.

City Centre The city centre is a particularly good place for lunches and light meals. If, for you, this includes fast food then you will be well satisfied on the east side of William St between Murray and Hay Sts.

At the other end of the spectrum, *Magic Apple Wholefoods*, 445 Hay St, does delicious pitta sandwiches, cakes and fresh juices. The busy *Benardi's*, 528 Hay St, has good sandwiches, quiches, home-made soups and salads.

Ann's Malaysian Food at the northern end of Barrack St is a good place for a quick, economical lunch or takeaway. At 117 Murray St between Pier and Barrack Sts is a small, pleasant and reasonably priced sushi bar, the Arcade Japanese Sushi Bar, which is well worth a visit if you like raw fish. The *Hayashi Japanese Barbecue*, 107 Pier St, has excellent-value set lunches for around $11 and dinner for two is about $30. *Bobby Dazzler's* at the Wentworth Plaza has an Australian menu and is a good place for a bite and a drink.

The *Venice Cafe* at the St George's Terrace end of the Trinity Arcade (shop No 201) is a pleasant European-style cafe with tables out the front. Light meals, such as lasagne, quiche, home-made pies and salad, cost from $5 to $6.50. At 300 Murray St is the *Moon & Sixpence*, an English-style pub popular with the lunch-time office crowd (and backpackers), who feast on the $5-plus pastas.

Farther east of the malls, there are good lunch-time places, including the *Stamina Indonesian* in the Chateau Commodore

Hotel on Hay St, which has entrees from $3 and mains from $7.50.

Toward the western (Kings Park) end of the city centre, there's a string of places, including a cluster of restaurants near the corner of Murray and Milligan Sts. These include the deservedly popular *Fast Eddy's* on the corner of Murray and Milligan Sts (with great breakfasts and burgers); and the cheap, highly recommended *Katong Singapore*, 446 Murray St, for those tantalising nyonya delights (and let's not forget the reasonable Indian *Taj Tandoor* just beside it).

Shafto Lane, between Murray and Hay Sts, has the oh-so-chic *Buzz Bar*, for upmarket lunches, and *Creations*, a stylish outdoor cafe with a good lunch menu.

Marron, a local delicacy, is substantially larger than its relative the yabby, which is found in the eastern states

Northbridge The area bounded by William, Lake and Newcastle Sts is full of ethnic restaurants to suit all tastes and budgets. William St (and the streets which run west of it) is the hub.

Self-caterers will find *Cheapaway* on the corner of Roe and Fitzgerald Sts good value.

Starting west of the Perth train station is Roe St with its entrance to Chinatown. On the way you will pass *Tequila Sunrise*, a Mexican place that is open seven nights.

There is a real cornucopia of ethnic tastes on William St. Heading north from the Roe St corner you'll find a couple of Asian restaurants, the moderately priced and popular *Romany* – one of the city's long-running Italian eateries, and *Sylvana Pastry*, a comfortable Lebanese coffee bar with an amazing selection of sticky Middle Eastern pastries. You'll also pass the *Tonic Cafe* and the vegetarian *Hare Krishna Food for Life* at No 200. The latter has cheap ($4, or $3 with a concession) meals, including $2 meals on Tuesday and Friday between 5 and 6 pm.

On the left-hand side – in the next five blocks of William St heading north – you'll find the *Brass Monkey Bar & Brasserie*, with a great selection of beers and good-sized counter meals (lunches are about $7.50); the *Seoul Korean*, which is the sole Korean (with excellent lunches for about $7, dinners for about $15); the busy *Villa Italia*, which

serves fine coffee and light meals including good pasta; a string of Asian restaurants, including *Sri Melaka* (with nyonya choices and a full banquet for $17) at No 313, *White Elephant Thai* at No 323, and *Satay House* on the corner of Newcastle St.

Beyond Forbes St is the *City Fresh Food Co*, the place to buy healthy fruit and vegetables, and the Vietnamese *Pho Van Reo*, which serves tasty pho for $5.50 a bowl. The reliable *Dong Phuong*, 434A William St, is open every night (except Tuesday).

At the corner of James and Lake St is a large collection of places, most Italian, which give this sector of Northbridge a 'little Italy' feel. *Vinous*, open daily from 10 am until late, has a superb Aussie burger ($18), unlike any you've probably tasted – all the Australian food icons are represented here, from vegemite damper to kangaroo meat.

On Lake St between James and Francis Sts there are a number of sidewalk cafes including the *Street Cafe*, as well as landmarks like the *Northbridge Pavilion Food Hall*, *Trains, Planes & Automobiles* (with occasional all-you-can-eat specials) and *Kremlin*.

And notta' forget *Mamma Maria's*, 105 Aberdeen St. This place has a pleasant ambience and a deserved reputation as one of Perth's best Italian eateries. Its two-course weekday lunches are $12, and two people should be able to dine here for $40.

Appropriately plonked on the corner of

Milligan and James Sts is *Rosie O'Grady's*, a popular after-work venue; the meals are good value. A little farther down James St at No 220 is the new *Lotus Vegetarian* with an all-you-can-eat Australian, Malaysian, Indian and Chinese buffet for about $8.

Leederville The area of Oxford St between Vincent and Melrose Sts, and Newcastle St has earned popularity with the 'cappuccino set'. Many cafes and eateries, as well as the art-house *Luna Cinema*, are here.

Cafes include *Villa, Oxford 130, Mazzini's, Giardini* and *Fat Bellies* (which fulfils the promise in its name). The cuisines of the world are represented in an eclectic collection of eateries: *Cosmos Kebabs, Banzai Sushi & Noodle Bar, Woodstock Rock Pizzeria, Anna Vietnamese, Shalimar Indian* and *Hawkers Hut Asian*.

Nearby are the *Leederville Hotel* and *hip-e-club* entertainment venues.

Subiaco This enclave, known as 'Subi', boasts a number of eateries, most of which are on (or just off) Rokeby Rd. Heading north from Nicholson Rd you'll come to the *Little Lebanon* with its friendly staff and superb Middle Eastern fare.

Just before Bagot Rd are the reliable *Amarin Thai* and the busy *Rokeby's Bar & Café*. On the Barker St corner is the popular *Bridie O'Reilly's* pub and close by on Rokeby Rd is the *Witch's Cauldron* at No 89, with its renowned garlic prawns. Across from Forrest Way Mall on Churchill Ave is the small *Maggie's Kitchen*, a pleasant spot for a hearty cheap breakfast ($5.50). *Mezza Villa* on the corner of Railway and Rokeby Rds has good atmosphere, staff and food.

Entertainment

Perth has plenty of pubs, discos and night-clubs (see the Around Perth chapter for details of the Fremantle scene). *Xpress*, a weekly mag covering music, films, fashion, clubbing and other aspects of the entertainment scene, is available free at record shops and other outlets, and has a gig guide. Check the *West Australian* for listings of theatre, cinema and nightclub events.

Northbridge, Leederville and Subiaco are the places to go after dark. Weekend nights are witness to revelry, while the city centre is dead in spite of efforts to revitalise it.

Cinemas & Theatres For quality art-house films try *Cinema Paradiso* in the Galleria complex at 164 James St, Northbridge; *Luna* on Oxford St, Leederville; and the *Astor* on the corner of Beaufort and Walcott Sts in Mt Lawley. All of the Oscar-nominated favourites are on in the Hoyts, Greater Union and Village city and suburban cinemas; budget night is Tuesday.

Popular theatres include *His Majesty's Theatre* (☎ 93221 2721) on the corner of King and Hay Sts, the *Regal Theatre*, 474 Hay St, Subiaco, and the *Hole in the Wall* at the Subiaco Theatre Centre, 180 Hamersley Rd, Subiaco. Session times and programs appear daily in the *West Australian*.

Comedy The rear bar of the *Brass Monkey Bar & Brasserie* on the corner of William and James Sts in Northbridge seems to be the latest comedy venue (Wednesday and Thursday from 8.30 pm; entry $8).

Discos & Nightclubs Perth has plenty of places where you can dance into the wee small hours. In the city centre are the *Buzz Bar* in Shafto Lane; the *Racquet Club* on Piccadilly Square on the corner of Lord and Short Sts; *Club 418*, 418 Murray St (Friday and Saturday nights); and *Planet* at 329 Charles St, North Perth.

Northbridge has a few late-night venues for hard-core ravers. *Kremlin*, 69 Lake St, has its legion of fans, while *O2 (Oxygen)* in the James St nightclub at No 139 buzzes most buzzy nights. For rave, go to *Krush*, next door and upstairs from O2 (above Novak's Tavern). The *Post Office* on the corner of Parker and Aberdeen Sts handles a slightly older crowd with aplomb (especially on Thursday at the over-30s session).

Perth's glitzy *Burswood Casino*, over the Causeway from the city centre, is open all day on just about every day; it hosts a cavalcade of prominent local and foreign entertainers.

Concerts & Recitals The *Perth Concert Hall* (☎ 9325 9944) on St George's Terrace and the *Entertainment Centre* (☎ 9321 1575) on Wellington St are venues for concerts and recitals by local and international acts.

Find out more in the Perth Theatre Trust newsletter *Applause!* or the WASO *Concert Catalogue*, both free from the tourist centre.

Pubs & Live Music Some of the popular places for live music in Northbridge are the *Brass Monkey Bar & Brasserie* on the corner of William and James Sts; the *Metropolis City Nightclub* (☎ 9228 0500) at 146 Roe St, which really goes off most nights and is great for bands; *Novak's Tavern* on the corner of James and Lake Sts, which has cheap jugs for $4.50 during happy hour; *Rosie O'Grady's* on Lake St, which has Irish bands most nights of the week; The *Bog* (don't you just love the name) on Newcastle St, which is open until 6 am and where drinkers are serenaded through their hangovers with Irish tunes (ouch!); and the *Aberdeen Hotel*, 84 Aberdeen St, which has bands most nights.

On nearby Oxford St, the *Leederville Hotel* has a great Sunday afternoon session. On Monday and Tuesday many backpackers will be found at the *hip-e-club* behind the Leederville Village, enjoying free entry and a meal (eg macaroni, spaghetti bolognaise) and one complimentary drink – the club provides a free bus back to local hostels.

The Sunday blast at the *Ocean Beach Hotel* (the 'OBH'), on Marine Parade near North Cottesloe Beach never wavers in its ability to surprise even the most timid of drinkers.

Perth has the usual pub-rock circuit, with cover charges depending on the gig. Popular venues include the *Indi Bar & Bistro* on Hastings St, Scarborough, where 'slam' is king; the *Swanbourne Hotel*, 141 Claremont Crescent, Swanbourne; the *Shents*, 207 Nicholson Rd, Shenton Park; the *Junction* on Great Eastern Highway, Midland (Thursday to Sunday nights); and the *Grosvenor Hotel* on the corner of Hill and Hay Sts, East Perth, where music's belted out Wednesday to Sunday.

Gay & Lesbian Venues These include the revamped *Northbridge Hotel* on the corner of Lake and Brisbane Sts (live music on Wednesday and Sunday); the *Court Hotel* on the corner of Beaufort and James Sts (live music Friday and Sunday and gay-friendly accommodation); *Dual Control (DCs)*, 105 Francis St, for live shows on the weekend and a men-only night on Wednesday; and *Connections* ('Connies') on James St for dance music and floorshows. *Lola's Bar & Cafe*, 237 Queen Victoria St, North Fremantle, is a lesbian place open from Wednesday to Sunday from about 4 pm until late.

Look in the *Westside Observer (WSO)*, available from the above-mentioned places, for more venues and activities.

Spectator Sports

The people of Perth, like most other Australians, are parochial in their support of local sporting teams. The West Coast Eagles and the Fremantle Dockers, Perth's two representatives in the Australian Football League (AFL), and the Perth Wildcats, in the National Basketball League (NBL), regularly play interstate teams in Perth. Check the *West Australian* for game details.

International one-day cricket and test matches are played in Perth at the Western Australian Cricket Association (WACA) ground.

Things to Buy

Perth has a number of excellent outlets for Aboriginal arts and crafts, including the Creative Native Gallery, 32 King St; Ganada, 71 Barrack St; and Artists in Residence Gallery at the Lookout, Fraser Ave, Kings Park. Other crafts can be found at the various markets – see the Markets section earlier in this section.

Getting There & Away

Air Qantas Airways (☎ 13 1313) and Ansett

Australia (☎ 13 1300) have direct, one-way economy flights to and from Sydney ($694), Melbourne ($623), Adelaide ($557), Ayers Rock ($488) and Alice Springs ($539). In most cases, flights to Queensland (Brisbane and Cairns) involve stops in Melbourne or Sydney and flights to Darwin have one stop (either Port Hedland or Alice Springs). Both airlines have offices on Hay St and St George's Terrace.

However, major discounts on these fares are available: you should be able to get return tickets between Perth and Adelaide for around $440, Melbourne $510, Sydney $540 and Brisbane $660.

Ansett and Qantas also have flights to Perth from North Queensland via Alice Springs. An Apex return fare from Alice Springs is $503 and from Cairns $621. Darwin to Perth flights travel via Alice Springs or Port Hedland – Ansett Australia flies from Darwin to Perth along the coast daily (with possible stops at Broome, Karratha, Port Hedland or Kununurra); the Apex return fare from Perth to Darwin via Alice Springs is $699.

Skywest (☎ 9334 2288), out on the Great Eastern Highway, flies to smaller centres.

Bus Greyhound Pioneer (☎ 13 2030) operates daily bus services from Adelaide to Perth from the Westrail Centre at the East Perth terminal, West Parade, East Perth. The daily journey from Perth to Darwin along the coast takes about 56 hours by bus and costs $435. Greyhound also operates a thrice-weekly service to Port Hedland (with connections to Darwin) via the more direct, inland route through Newman. This trip is three hours shorter and is the same price.

Westrail (☎ 13 2232) has bus services from the East Perth terminal to a number of WA centres. South West Coachlines (☎ 9324 2333) travels from the city bus port to Bunbury, Margaret River and the capes.

Train Perth is the starting and ending point for the 65-hour trip between the Pacific and Indian oceans (see the Getting There & Away section earlier in this chapter).

The only rail services within WA are the limited *AvonLink* from Perth to York, the *Prospector* to Kalgoorlie and the *Australind* to Bunbury. Both the trains from the east coast and the domestic services run to or from the East Perth terminal in West Parade, East Perth, as do Westrail buses. Reservations can be made by phoning ☎ 13 2232.

The *Australind* has two services every day, except Sunday when there is one, in both directions. These leave Perth at 10 am and 7 pm, and Bunbury at 6.30 am and 3.40 pm.

The *Prospector* has at least one service in each direction every day and there are some other limited services during the week; the trip takes about 7½ hours. From Monday to Thursday it leaves around 9.30 am (it pays to check as this is only an indication) and on Friday and Sunday the train leaves at 4.10 pm from both ends; on Saturday the train departs from Perth at 6 pm and from Kalgoorlie at 7.15 am.

Hitching We *don't* advise hitching. But if you must, hostel notice boards are worth checking for lifts to points around the country. If you're hitching out of Perth to the north or east, take a train to Midland. For travel south, take a train to Armadale.

Getting Around

Perth's public transport organisation, Transperth, operates buses, trains and ferries. There are Transperth information offices (☎ 13 2213) in the Plaza Arcade (off the Hay St Mall), the city bus port on Mounts Bay Rd at the foot of William St, and at the Wellington St bus station. These offices are open from 7.30 am to 5.30 pm from Monday to Friday, but the Plaza Arcade office is open from 8 am to 5.30 pm on Saturday and noon to 6 pm on Sunday. The free *Public Transport to Tourist Spots Around Perth* is useful.

There's a free transit zone in the city, involving all Transperth buses and trains. You can travel free of charge within the area bounded by Northbridge in the north, the river in the south, Kings Park in the west and the Causeway in the east. For more information see the Bus section.

To/From the Airport The domestic and international terminals are 10km apart; taxi fares from them to the city are around $16 and $20 respectively.

The privately run airport bus (☎ 9479 4131) meets all incoming domestic and international flights and provides transport to the city centre, hotels and hostels. The airport bus costs $6 from the domestic terminal and $8 from the international terminal; a trip between the terminals costs $6/4 for adults/children. If you want to travel to the terminals, there are scheduled runs every two hours from 4.45 am to 10.30 pm. Call for more information on hotel and hostel pick-ups and timetables.

Alternatively, you can get into the city for $2.30 on Transperth bus No 200, 202, 208 or 209 to William St. The buses depart from the domestic terminal every hour or so (more frequently at peak times) from 5.30 am to 10 pm on weekdays, but less often on weekends. Buses leave from bus stand No 39, on St George's Terrace, for the domestic terminal. Staff from some backpacker places pick up travellers at the airport (generally you stay in their hostel that night).

Bus There are two free Central Area Transit (CAT) services in the city centre. The buses are state of the art and there are computer readouts (and audio services) at the stops telling you when the next bus is due. Using the two, you can get to most sights in the inner city.

The Red CAT operates east-west from Outram St, West Perth, to the WACA, in East Perth; the service runs every five minutes on weekdays from 7 am to 6 pm. The Blue CAT operates north-south from the river to Northbridge, roughly in the centre of the Red CAT route; services run every 7½ minutes on weekdays from 7 am to 6 pm. A modified version of the Blue CAT runs every 10 minutes on weekends – on Friday from 6 pm to 1 am, Saturday from 8.30 am to 1 am and Sunday from 10 am to 5 pm.

On regular buses, a short ride of one zone is $1.60, two zones $2.30 and three zones $3. Zone 1 includes the city centre and the inner suburbs (including Subiaco and Claremont) and Zone 2 extends all the way to Fremantle, 20km from the city centre. A Multirider ticket gives 10 journeys for the price of nine.

The Perth Tram (☎ 9367 9404) doesn't run on rails – it's a bus that takes you around some of Perth's main attractions in 1½ hours. It costs $12/6 for adults/children and leaves from 565 Hay St at least six times daily.

Train Transperth (☎ 13 2213) operates the Fastrak suburban train lines to Armadale, Fremantle, Midland and the northern suburb of Joondalup from around 5.20 am to midnight on weekdays, with reduced services on weekends. During the day, some of the Joondalup to Perth trains continue to Armadale and some Fremantle to Perth trains run through to Midland. Free train travel is allowed between the Claisebrook and City West stations.

All trains leave from the Perth train station on Wellington St. Your rail ticket can also be used on Transperth buses and ferries within its zone.

Car & Motorcycle In the city you will have no trouble getting fuel between 7 am and 9 pm from Monday to Saturday, but on Sunday it's a different story. You have to find out which fuel outlets are rostered to be open (usually from 7 am to 10 pm). For rostering details call ☎ 11573.

Hertz (☎ 9321 7777), Budget (☎ 13 2727), Avis (☎ 9325 7677) and Thrifty (☎ 94 81 1999) are all represented in Perth.

Bicycle Cycling is a great way to explore Perth. There are many bicycle routes along the river that carry on all the way to Fremantle and along the Indian Ocean coast. Get the free *Along the Coast Ride*, *Around the River Ride* and *Armadale to Perth* booklets from the tourist centre in Forrest Place.

At the WA Bicycle Disposal Centre (☎ 9325 1176) at 47 Bennett St, East Perth, you can buy a bike knowing that you will get a guaranteed buy-back price after a certain time. About Bike Hire (☎ 9221 2665), on

Riverside Drive near the Causeway Bridge, also rents cycles for about $15 per day.

Boat Transperth ferries (☎ 13 2213) cross daily from the Barrack St jetty to the Mends St jetty in South Perth every half an hour (more frequently at peak times) between 6.45 am and 7.15 pm for $1.60 (one zone). Take this ferry to get to the zoo.

Around Perth

FREMANTLE (pop 25,000)

Despite recent development, Fremantle ('Freo' to the locals) has a far more laid-back feeling than gleaming, skyscrapered Perth. It's a place with a real sense of history and a pleasant atmosphere.

Fremantle was founded in 1829, when the HMS *Challenger*, captained by Charles Fremantle, dropped anchor here. Like Perth, the settlement made little progress until it decided to take in convicts. This cheap and hard-worked labour constructed most of the town's earliest buildings, some of them among the oldest and most treasured in WA. As a port, Fremantle was abysmal until the brilliant engineer CY O'Connor built an artificial harbour in the 1890s.

In 1987, the city was the site of the unsuccessful defence of what was, for a brief period, one of Australia's most prized possessions – the America's Cup yachting trophy. Preparations for the influx of tourists associated with the competition certainly transformed Fremantle into a more modern, colourful and expensive city. However, many of the residents protested that their lifestyle and the character of their community were being damaged by development.

The town has numerous interesting old buildings, some excellent museums and galleries, lively produce and craft markets, and a diverse range of pubs, cafes and restaurants. A visit to Freo will be one of the highlights of your trip to WA. Make sure you allow enough time to explore, sip coffee in an outdoor cafe and soak in the atmosphere.

Orientation & Information

Fremantle, Perth's port, is at the mouth of the Swan River, about 20km south-west of the city centre. Over the years, Perth has sprawled to engulf Fremantle, which is now more a suburb of the city than a town in its own right.

The information centre in the Fremantle Town Hall shop was closed as a cost-cutting measure by the short-sighted local council. In the meantime the void is filled voluntarily by the Queen of Hearts Cafe (☎ 9335 9977) on Margaret St. You can get information on national parks at CALM's WA Naturally shop and information centre (☎ 9430 8600) at 47 Henry St.

Fremantle History Museum

The history museum, 1 Finnerty St, is housed in a building constructed as a lunatic asylum in the 1860s by convicts. It has a fine collection, including exhibits on Fremantle's Aboriginal history, the colonisation of WA and the early whaling industry. It also tells the intriguing story of the Dutch East India Company ships which first 'discovered' the western coast of Australia and in several instances were wrecked on its inhospitable shores. The museum is open from 1 am to 4 pm on weekdays, and from 1 to 5 pm on weekends (admission is by donation).

The arts centre, which occupies one wing of the building, is open every day from 10 am to 5 pm and on Wednesday evening from 7 to 9 pm (admission is by donation).

WA Maritime Museum

On Cliff St, near the waterfront, is the WA Maritime Museum, which occupies a building constructed in 1852 as a commissariat store. The museum has a display on WA's maritime history, with emphasis on the famous wreck of the *Batavia*. One gallery is used as a working centre where you can see the *Batavia* being preserved.

At one end of this gallery is the huge stone facade intended for an entrance to Batavia Castle in what is now Jakarta, Indonesia. It was being carried by the *Batavia* as ballast when the vessel sank. This intriguing

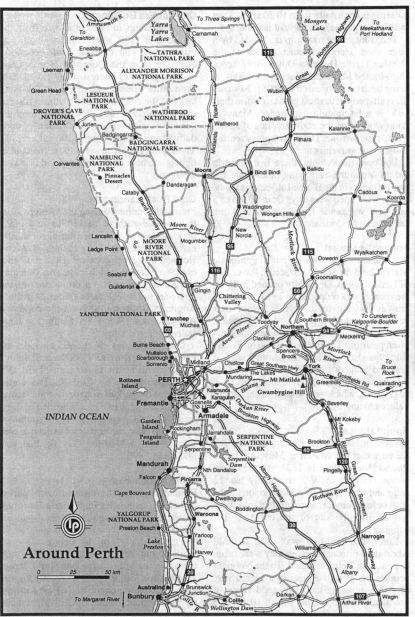

Around Perth

0   25   50 km

museum is open daily from 10.30 am to 5 pm (admission is free), and a visit is a must.

The front of the museum is shielded by a huge shed. Here, an exact replica of the *Duyfken* (Little Dove), a Dutch *jacht* (scout ship) for the Moluccan Fleet in the 1600s, is being built (as it appeared in 1606). To watch the craftspeople, the best in the world, at their task, is a fascinating experience. Many of them worked on the earlier replica of James Cook's *Endeavour*. There is no entry fee and some great souvenirs are sold.

For boat freaks only, there is a **Historic Boats Museum** displaying boats from the last 100 years in the B-Shed at Victoria Quay. The shed is open weekdays from 10 am to 3 pm, and weekends from 11 am to 4 pm (admission by donation).

Fremantle Market

A prime attraction is the colourful Fremantle Market held on South Terrace on the corner of Henderson St. Originally opened in 1892, the market was reopened in 1975 and draws crowds looking for everything from craft items to vegetables, jewellery and antiques; there is also a great tavern where buskers often perform. The market is open on Friday from 9 am to 9 pm, Saturday from 9 am to 5 pm, and Sunday from 10 am to 5 pm. Late Sunday afternoon is the time to buy fruit and vegetables, which are sold at cheap prices before closing time.

Round House

On Arthur Head at the western end of High St, near the WA Maritime Museum, is the Round House. Built in 1831, it's the oldest public building in WA. It actually has 12 sides and was originally a local prison (in the days before convicts were brought into WA). It was also the site of the colony's first hanging.

Later, the building was used to hold Aboriginal prisoners before they were taken to prison on Rottnest Island. To the Noongar people, the Round House is a sacred site. From the building there are good views of Fremantle. It is open daily from 10 am to 5 pm (admission is free).

Convict-Era Buildings

Many buildings in Fremantle date from the period after 1850, when convict labour was introduced. The *Convict Trail* brochure, available from the Queen of Hearts Cafe, outlines places of interest. They include **Old Fremantle Prison**, one of the first building tasks of the convicts and a maximum security prison until 1991. The entrance on the Terrace is picturesque. The prison is open daily from 10 am to 6 pm ($10, children $4). These prices apply also for the eerie candlelight tours, held on Wednesday and Friday at 7.30 pm.

Gold Rush Landmarks

Fremantle boomed during the Western Australian gold rush of the 1890s and many buildings were constructed during, or shortly before, this period. They include **Samson House**, a well-preserved 1888 colonial home on Ellen St, which is open on Thursday and Sunday from 1 to 5 pm – tours of the house are run by volunteer guides. **St John's Anglican Church** (1882) on the corner of Adelaide and Queen Sts features a large stained-glass window.

Other buildings of the era include the **Fremantle Town Hall** (1887) on St John's Square, and the Georgian-style **Old Customs House** on Cliff St. The **water trough** in the park in front of the train station has a memorial to two men who died of thirst on an outback expedition. The **Proclamation Tree** near the corner of Adelaide and Parry Sts is a Moreton Bay fig that was planted in 1890.

Other Attractions

Fremantle is well-endowed with parks, including the popular **Esplanade Reserve**, beside the picturesque boat harbour off Marine Terrace.

The city is a popular centre for craft workers and one of the best places to find them is at the imaginative **Bannister Street Workshops** on Bannister St. From the observation tower on top of the **Port Authority Building**, at the end of Cliff St, you can enjoy a panoramic view of the harbour. You

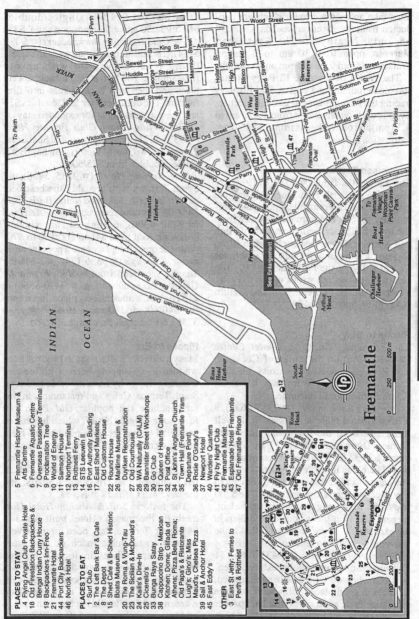

WESTERN AUSTRALIA

Fremantle

INDIAN OCEAN

PLACES TO STAY
4 Flying Angel Club Private Hotel
18 Old Firestation Backpackers &
Bengal Indian Curry House
19 Backpackers Inn-Freo
21 Fremantle Hotel
44 Port City Backpackers
46 Norfolk Hotel

PLACES TO EAT
1 Surf Club
2 The Left Bank Bar & Cafe
8 The Depot
15 Shed Cafe & B-Shed Historic
Boats Museum
20 The Roma & Vung-Tau
23 The Sicilian & McDonald's
24 Kailis's Dine-In
25 Cicerello's
33 Bunga Raya Satay
38 Cappuccino Strip - Mexican
Kitchen; Dome; Gilfada of
Athens; Pizza Bella Roma;
Old Papa's & Ristorante
Luigi's; Gino's; Miss
Maud's; Chelsea Pizza
39 Sail & Anchor Hotel
45 Fast Eddy's

OTHER
3 East St Jetty; Ferries to
Perth & Rottnest
5 Fremantle History Museum &
Arts Centre
6 Fremantle Aquatic Centre
7 Overseas Passenger Terminal
9 Proclamation Tree
10 World of Energy
11 Samson House
12 Northport Terminal
13 Rottnest Ferry
14 STS Leeuwin II
16 Port Authority Building
17 East Shed Markets;
Old Customs House
22 Round House
26 Maritime Museum &
Duyfken Reconstruction
27 Old Courthouse
28 WA Naturally (CALM)
29 Bannister Street Workshops
30 Go Club
31 Queen of Hearts Cafe
32 Post Office
34 St John's Anglican Church
35 Town Hall (Fremantle Tram
Departure Point)
36 Rosie O'Grady's
37 Newport Hotel
40 Warders' Quarters
41 Fly by Night Club
42 Fremantle Market
43 Esplanade Hotel Fremantle
47 Old Fremantle Prison

must take an escorted tour, which are conducted from the foyer on weekdays at 1.30 pm only. Nearby are the **East Shed Markets**, open from 10 am to 9 pm on Friday, and from 9 am to 5 pm on weekends.

The **World of Energy**, 12 Parry St, has some entertaining and educational displays tracing the development of gas and electricity. It is open on weekdays from 10.30 am to 4.30 pm, and on weekends from 1 to 4:30 pm (admission is free).

Organised Tours

The Fremantle Tram (☎ 9339 8719), very much like the Perth Tram, does a 45-minute historical tour of Fremantle with a full commentary for $7. The tram leaves daily from the town hall, near the intersection of High and Adelaide Sts, on the hour between 10 am to 5 pm; a harbour tour is also available for $7 and a Top of the Port tour for $10. You can combine the tour with a cruise to Perth, a tour of Perth on the Perth Tram and a return ticket to Fremantle for $34.

Places to Stay

The *Fremantle Village & Chalet Centre* (☎ 9430 4866) on the corner of Cockburn and Rockingham Rds has noisy en-suite sites/chalets for $20/70 for two. It's about 3.5km from central Fremantle.

Port City Backpackers (☎ 9335 6635), a YHA-affiliated place at 5 Essex St, is well located between the Esplanade and South Terrace. Dorm beds are $13/14 and double rooms $30/32 for YHA members/ nonmembers. There's an intimate courtyard, in which you can relax after that one-trip-too-many to Freo's cappuccino strips and pubs. The $200 trips out to Noongar country to select, prepare and then paint your own didjeridu are exceptional. They're a must if this is the souvenir you wish to take home.

Backpackers Inn-Freo (☎ 9431 7065), 11 Pakenham St, was undergoing extensive renovations when we visited. When completed, it will be a good place to stay with a secure recreation area, good cafe (with backpacker specials) and comfortable rooms. Dorm beds

or twins are $14.50, singles/doubles $19.50/32.50 and a 'honeymoon suite' $38.

The *Old Firestation Backpackers* (☎ 9430 5454), 18 Phillimore St, answers the question, 'What do you do with an old firestation?'. You turn it into a backpackers place and then turn backpackers into firefighters. The dorm beds are $12, doubles $30 and there are discounts for extended stays.

The *Flying Angel Club Private Hotel* (☎ 9335 5321) in the International Seafarers' Centre at 78 Queen Victoria St has B&B singles/doubles from $35/60.

The *Norfolk Hotel* (☎ 9335 5405), 47 South Terrace, with arguably the best beer garden in Perth, has good value B&B from $45/70. The fully restored *Fremantle Hotel* (☎ 9430 4300), 6 High St, has singles/ doubles priced from $45 to $60/$60 to $70.

Bed & breakfast places are a popular alternative. *Kilkelly's* (☎ 9336 1744), 82 Marine Terrace, has B&B from $65/85; *Fremantle Colonial Accommodation* (☎ 9430 6568) at 215 High St, a nonsmoking place, has rooms for $40/60; and *Danum House* (☎ 9336 3735), 6 Fothergill St, charges $75/85.

Places to Eat

Many a traveller's afternoon in Freo has been whittled away sipping beer or coffee and watching life go by from kerbside tables on South Terrace. Cafes and restaurants in this area include the popular *Old Papa's & Ristorante Luigi* at No 17, which has coffee and gelati (and is recommended by the great fast bowler Dennis Lillee – perhaps the pasta was his secret weapon); the trendy *Gino's* (the place to be seen) at No 1; *Dome*, which has a multicultural arts centre upstairs; and the large *Miss Maud's* at No 33.

The historic *Sail & Anchor Hotel* (formerly the Freemason's Hotel, built in 1854), 64 South Terrace, has been impressively restored to resemble much of its former glory. It specialises in locally brewed Matilda Bay beers, and on the 1st floor is a brasserie which serves snacks and full meals.

Also on South Terrace is the *Mexican Kitchen* next door to Old Papa's, with a range of Mexican dishes from $10 to $12 (half-price night on Tuesday). Across the road, *Chelsea Pizza* also has half-price specials on Tuesday night. Nearby is *Pizza Bella Roma* and the *Glifada of Athens* with tasty souvlaki.

The *Up-Market Food Centre* on Henderson St, opposite the market, has stalls where you can get delicious and cheap Thai, Vietnamese, Japanese, Chinese and Italian food from $7.50 for a large plate. It is open from Thursday to Sunday from about noon to 9 pm and can be busy, especially on market days. *Foodtown* at the top end of Essex St is another good choice.

Fast Eddy's at 13 Essex St, not far from South Terrace, has the best-value breakfast in town, with bottomless cappuccinos, and has a 24-hour licence. *Granita's* at the southern end of South Terrace in South Fremantle gets rave reviews from locals.

West End & Harbour The *Roma*, 13 High St, is a reliable Freo institution, which serves home-made Italian fare including its famous chicken and spaghetti. Even the rich and famous have to queue to eat here. For Vietnamese food, try the *Vung-Tau*, 19 High St, with meals, including a vegetarian menu, costing from $7 to $10. A little out of the restaurant belt is the *Bunga Raya Satay*, 8 Cantonment St, popular with locals and noted for its good food (although the servings are small). In the old firestation on Phillimore St is the *Bengal Indian Curry House* with great $6 lunch specials.

For fish & chips, *Cicerello's* and *Kailis's Dine-In* on the Esplanade by the fishing boat harbour are Fremantle traditions.

Again, if you want value for money, then the *Sicilian* beneath Sails Restaurant, near Cicerello's and Kailis's, is where you will probably end the evening – a huge plate of fish & chips and a mountain of salad costs $12. It is still as good as ever. If fast food takes your fancy, there is a *McDonald's* nearby – just look for the flocks of well-fed seagulls.

Other Areas The hipper-than-thou places are the *Left Bank Bar & Cafe* on Riverside Rd down from the East St jetty, and the beachy, trendy *Surf Club* (which has both cheap and expensive sections) out at North Fremantle Beach. The *Depot* on Beach St is a popular late-night place which also serves good meals.

Prickles on the corner of Douro Rd and South Terrace specialises in modern bush tucker – Aussie nouvelle cuisine (kangaroo, emu and crocodile) and a host of vegetarian dishes with a twist.

Entertainment

Freo fair buzzes at night. There are many venues in town with music and/or dancing.

Home of the 'big gig' is the much-lauded *Metropolis* on South Terrace (which has recently been replicated in Perth's Northbridge). The *Orient* on High St has bands pumping up the volume to drown out the opposition, and at the *Newport*, 2 South Terrace, there are bands most nights. On weekends, listen to indie and 'tribal roots' music with Freo's feral community down the road at the *Seaview Tavern* at No 282.

For Latin and folk music, try the *Fly by Night Club* on Parry St. This venue is frequented by talented musicians specialising in world music.

The *Go Club* on High St, entered with a free pass provided by the backpacker places, is a dance club with house and techno music. *Rosie O'Grady's*, an Irish pub on William St, has live music (washed down with Guinness) three or four nights per week.

Getting There & Around

The train between Perth and Fremantle runs every 15 minutes or so throughout the day for around $2.40. Bus Nos 106 (bus stand No 35) and 111 (bus stand No 48) go from St George's Terrace to Fremantle via the Canning Highway; or you can take bus No 105 (bus stand No 40 on St George's Terrace), which takes a longer route. Bus Nos 103 and 104 also depart from St George's Terrace (south side) but go to Fremantle via the north side of the river.

There are also daily ferries from Perth's Barrack St jetty to Freo for $14 one way.

The Fremantle Airport Shuttle (☎ 014 083 446) departs from Fremantle for the airport every two hours from 6 am to 10 pm; in the other direction it is every two hours from 7 am to 11 pm. The price of $10 includes drop off/pick up at your accommodation.

Bell Bike Hire (☎ 9430 5414) is a mobile set-up – ring and they deliver. The cost is $15 per day, or $30 per month.

ROTTNEST ISLAND (pop 400)

'Rotto', as it's known to the locals, is a sandy island about 19km off the coast from Fremantle. It's 11km long, 4.5km wide and popular with Perth residents and visitors. The island was discovered by the Dutch explorer Willem de Vlamingh in 1696. He named it Rats' Nest because of the numerous king-size 'rats' he saw there (in fact they were small wallabies called quokkas).

The Rottnest settlement was established in 1838 as a prison for Aboriginal people from the mainland – the early colonists had lots of trouble imposing their ideas of private ownership on the nomadic Aborigines. The prison was abandoned in 1903 and the island soon became an escape for Perth society. Only in the last 30 years, however, has it really developed as a popular day trip. The buildings of the original prison settlement are among the oldest in WA.

What do you do on Rotto? Well, you cycle around, laze in the sun on the many superb beaches, climb the low hills, go fishing or boating, ride a glass-bottomed boat (the waters off Rotto have some of the world's most southerly coral), swim in the crystal-clear water or go quokka spotting.

Information

There is a visitor centre (☎ 9372 9752) on Rotto, open on weekdays from 8.30 am to 5 pm, Saturday from 9 am to 4 pm and Sunday from 10 am to noon and 2.30 to 4 pm. It is just to the left of the jetty at Thomson Bay (the island's largest settlement) as you arrive. There, and at the museum, you can get useful publications detailing a walking tour of the old settlement buildings, heritage trails, various shipwrecks around the island and a cycling guide.

Get a copy of the informative *Rottnest: WA's Holiday Isle*. Rottnest is very popular in the summer, when ferries and accommodation are heavily booked – plan ahead.

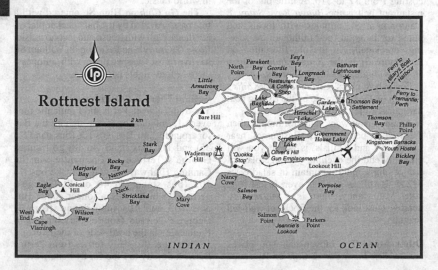

Things to See

The excellent little museum, open daily in summer from 10 am to 4 pm, has exhibits about the island, its history, wildlife and shipwrecks (entry is $2). You can pick up a walking-tour leaflet here and wander around the old convict-built buildings, including the octagonal 1864 'Quad'. Free guided walking tours depart from the visitor centre daily at 11.15 am and 2 pm.

Vlamingh's Lookout on View Hill, near Thomson Bay, offers panoramic views of the island. The main lighthouse, built on Wadjemup Hill in 1895, is visible 60km out to sea.

The island has a number of low-lying salt lakes and it's around these that you are most likely to spot **quokkas**. Bus tours have regular quokka-feeding points where the voracious marsupials appear on demand.

Also of interest is the restored **Oliver's Hill Gun Emplacement**, west of Thomson Bay. You can get to the battery on the Oliver Hill railway line; trains leave Thomson Bay four times daily. The cost of $9/4.50 for adults/children includes entry to the guns and tunnels.

Organised Tours

There are two-hour bus tours around the island for $9/4.50 for adults/children; they depart from the visitor centre daily at 11.15 am and 1.15 pm – again it is wise to book in the high season.

The *Underwater Explorer* is a boat with windows below the waterline for viewing shipwrecks and marine life. It departs hourly from the jetty at Thomson Bay; an interesting 45-minute trip costs about $15/8. Some of Rotto's shipwrecks are accessible to snorkellers but getting to most of them requires a boat. There are marker plaques around the island telling the grim tales of how and when the ships sank. Snorkelling equipment, fishing gear and boats can be hired from Dive, Ski & Surf (☎ 9292 5167) in Thomson Bay.

Places to Stay

Most visitors to Rotto come only for the day but it's interesting to stay on the island. You

Ospreys patrol the waters off Rottnest Island

can camp for $12 (two people) in hired tents with rubber mattresses or get tent sites for $10 at *Rottnest Camping* (☎ 9372 9737). Safari cabins are also available from $25 to $66 a night. Book in advance for a cabin or if you want a tent. The *Rottnest Island Authority* (☎ 9372 9715) has over 250 houses and cottages for rent in Thomson Bay and around Geordie, Fays and Longreach bays. Ocean-front villas (four beds) are $392 per week in winter, $492 in summer.

The *Kingstown Barracks Hostel* (☎ 9372 9780), 1.2km from the ferry terminal, is in an old barracks built in 1936; the cost per person is from $14 and doubles are $34, linen included. Units in the *Rottnest Lodge Resort* (☎ 9292 5161), based in the former Quad which is more inviting these days, cost from $130.

Places to Eat

Bring your own food if possible because there are slim pickings once you are on the island. *Rottnest Family Restaurant* has a pleasant balcony overlooking Thomson Bay and serves Chinese dishes, dim sum lunches and takeaways. In the same building, coffee and cakes are available from the *Bistro*. The island has a general store and a bakery that is famed for its fresh bread and pies but is only open during the day. There's also a fast-food centre in Thomson Bay.

Brolley's in the Rottnest Hotel also serve snacks and meals, and there's the licensed *Garden Lake* in the Lodge Resort.

Getting There & Away

Competition, bless it, has brought prices down for the ferry trip to Rotto. There are daily services and many more services on weekends. The Rottnest Express (☎ 9335 6406) departs from C Shed at Victoria Quay, Fremantle Port, daily at 7.30, 9.30 and 11.15 am and 3.30 pm; adult/child fares are $28/8 for same-day return, $33/12 for an extended stay.

Oceanic Cruises (☎ 9430 5127) has done some monopoly busting: its *Supercat*, which leaves the East St jetty in Fremantle, costs only $25/8 for adults/children for same-day return; the extended stay cost is $30/12. From Pier 2 at the Barrack St jetty in Perth it charges $35/12 for same-day return and $40/15 for extended stays.

Boat Torque (☎ 9430 7644, 9221 5844) leaves from Pier 4 at the Barrack St jetty, Northport in North Fremantle, the East St jetty and Hillarys Boat Harbour. Same-day return costs are slightly more expensive than those of Oceanic Cruises. To catch Boat Torque's speedy, luxurious *Star Flyte* ferry from Perth's Barrack St jetty costs $50/40 for a deluxe/economy return, and $33/28 from Northport, North Fremantle. To catch its *Sea Flyte* from Hillarys Boat Harbour (north of Perth) costs $37/27 for adults/backpackers.

Rottnest Airlines (☎ 9478 1322) has an $85 return special to Rotto, which includes lunch at the lodge and a two-hour guided tour of the island.

Getting Around

Bicycles are the time-honoured way of getting around the island. The number of motor vehicles is strictly limited, which makes cycling a real pleasure. Furthermore, the island is just big enough to make a day's ride fine exercise. You can bring your own bike over on the ferry (free of charge from the East St jetty) or rent one of the hundreds available on the island from Rottnest Bike Hire (☎ 9372 9722), in Thomson Bay, near the hotel. A deposit of $10 is required and locks and helmets, both necessary, are available for hire.

Two bus services, the Bayseeker ($2) and the Settlement bus (50c), run daily – the information centre has timetables.

SOUTH OF PERTH

The coast south of Perth has a softer appearance than the often harsh landscape to the north. This is a popular beach-resort area for Perth residents, many of whom have holiday houses along the coast.

Rockingham (pop 60,000)

Rockingham, just 47km south of Perth, was founded in 1872 as a port, but that function was taken over by Fremantle. Today, Rockingham is a dormitory city and popular seaside resort with both sheltered and ocean beaches. The beach at Point Peron is safe for young children.

Close by is **Penguin Island**, home to a colony of little blue (fairy) penguins from late October to May, and **Seal Island**. You can get to the islands with Rockingham Sea Tours (☎ 9528 2004), which departs from Mersey Point jetty, Shoalwater Bay, on Tuesday and Thursday (6 hours), Wednesday and Sunday (8 hours); the cost for adults/children is $46/36.

From Rockingham, you can also head inland to the Serpentine Dam and the scenic **Serpentine Falls**, where there are wildflowers and nice bushland. Get to Rockingham on bus No 120 from Fremantle, or No 116 (stand No 48) from St George's Terrace, Perth.

The tourist centre (☎ 9592 3464), 43 Kent St, is open on weekdays from 9 am to 5 pm, and weekends from 10 am to 4 pm.

The Australian sea-lion is highly territorial and aggressive during its breeding season, resulting in a high death rate among pups

Places to Stay & Eat The *Palm Beach Caravan Park* (☎ 9527 1515), 37 Fisher St, has powered sites for $14 and on-site vans for $35. Another budget place, the *CWA Rockingham* (☎ 9527 9560), 108 Parkin St, is operated by a friendly couple. There are two units available, each sleeping six, from about $50 per night.

The *Rockingham Motel Hotel* (☎ 9592 1828), 26 Kent St, has singles/doubles for $40/50. The *Leisure Inn* (☎ 9527 7777), on the corner of Read St and Simpson Avenue, has units for $560 for two.

For meals, try the local hotels. Otherwise, there is the *Promenade Cafe*, 43 Rockingham Rd, for al fresco dining or *Oliver's Cafe* at No 45. *Indian Delights*, 26 Flinders Lane, serves good-value curries.

Mandurah (pop 29,000)
Situated on the calm Mandurah Estuary and 74km south of Perth, Mandurah is yet another popular beach resort. Dolphins are often seen in the estuary, and the waterways in the area are noted for good fishing, prawning (March and April) and crabbing.

The tourist bureau at 5 Pinjarra Rd (☎ 9535 1155) has ferry schedules, maps and other information. To get to Mandurah, catch bus No 116 from stand 48 on St George's Terrace, Perth, or No 117 from Fremantle.

Things to see in town include the restored 1830s limestone **Hall's Cottage** on Leighton Rd (open Sunday afternoon) and the **Parrots of Bellawood Park** on Old Pinjarra Rd, open from Thursday to Monday from 10 am to 4 pm ($5/2.50 for adults/children). The latter is a fauna park where you can see and feed several species of parrot; there's also a breeding program for endangered species and a walk-in aviary.

Full-day and short cruises are available on the MV *Peel Princess* from the jetty in town. Prolific bird life can be seen on the Peel Inlet and the narrow coastal salt lakes, Clifton and Preston, to the south.

Places to Stay & Eat There is a string of caravan parks with tent sites and on-site vans, and several B&B places and resorts near town. *Albatross House* (☎ 9581 5597), 26 Hall St, has B&B for $45/90 for singles/doubles. The *Blue Bay Motel* (☎ 95 35 2743), on Oversby St about 200m from the beach, is good value at $50/75.

There are numerous good places to eat. The excellent BYO *Doddi's*, 115 Mandurah Terrace, is open for breakfast, lunch and dinner. A big and tasty serve of fish & chips ($3.50) is available at *Jetty Fish & Chips* by the estuary near the end of Pinjarra Rd. Next door is *Yo Yo's* for ice creams. *Pronto's*, on the corner of Pinjarra Rd and Mandurah Terrace, has an all-you-can-eat pasta night on Friday for $10 – live music is often provided.

Pinjarra (pop 1900)
Pinjarra, 86km south of Perth, has a number of old buildings picturesquely sited on the banks of the Murray River. The Murray tourist centre (☎ 9531 1438) in Pinjarra is in the historic **Edenvale**, on the corner of George and Henry Sts. About 4km south of town is **Old Blythewood**, an 1859 colonial farm and a National Trust property. Behind the historic post office is a pleasant picnic area and a suspension bridge – wobbly enough to test your coordination!

The **Hotham Valley Railway** (☎ 9221 4444) runs trains from Perth to Dwellingup via Pinjarra on Sunday in the 'steam season' (from May to October). These pass through blooming wildflowers and virgin jarrah forests. The Etmilyn Forest Tramway operates from Dwellingup on Tuesday, Thursday and weekends ($9, children $4.50).

The *Pinjarra Motel* (☎ 9531 1811) offers B&B singles/doubles for $40/50. The *Heritage Tearooms* has light meals, such as sandwiches and quiche, for around $6.50.

THE DARLING RANGE

The hills that surround Perth are popular for picnics, barbecues and bushwalks. There are also some excellent lookouts from which you can see across Perth and to the coast. The **Araluen Botanic Garden** with its waterfalls and terraced gardens (entry for cars/motorcycles is $5/2), the **Mt Dale** fire lookout and **Churchman's Brook** are all off the Brookton Highway. Other places of interest include the hairpin bends of the former **Zig Zag** railway at Gooseberry Hill and the walking trails of **Lake Leschenaultia**. CALM provides a good free pamphlet *The Hills Forest*, detailing regional attractions.

From **Kalamunda** there are more fine views over Perth. You can get there from Perth on bus No 300 or 302, via Maida Vale, from stand No 43 on St George's Terrace, or on bus No 292 or 305, via Wattle Grove and Lesmurdie, also from stand No 43. Taking one route out and the other back makes an interesting circular tour of the hill suburbs.

Mundaring Weir (pop 1900)

Mundaring, in the Darling Range only 35km east of Perth, is the site of the Mundaring Weir, built at the turn of the century to supply water to the goldfields over 500km to the east. The reservoir has an attractive setting and is a popular excursion for Perth residents. There are a number of walking tracks. The **CY O'Connor Museum** has models and exhibits about the water pipeline to the goldfields – which in its time was one of the country's most audacious engineering feats. It is open on weekdays from 10.30 am to 3 pm (closed on Tuesday), Saturday from 1 to 4 pm and Sunday from 12.30 to 5 pm.

The **John Forrest National Park** near Mundaring has protected areas of jarrah and marri trees, native fauna, waterfalls, a swimming pool and an old railway tunnel (admission is $5/3 for cars/motorcycles).

Places to Stay The *Mundaring Caravan Park* (☎ 9295 1125), 2km west of town on the Great Eastern Highway, has powered sites for $7 for two. A room at the *Djaril Mari YHA Hostel* (☎ 9295 1809), on Mundaring Weir Rd, 8km south of town, costs from $11 (meals are available).

The *Mundaring Weir Hotel* (☎ 9295 1106) is exceedingly popular with Perth residents for weekend breaks. Its quality rammed-earth units cost from $60 for two. The historic *Mahogany Inn* (☎ 9295 1118) on the Great Eastern Highway is worth the $80/120 for single/double B&B.

AVON VALLEY

The green and lush Avon Valley, about 100km north-east of Perth, looks very English and was a delight to homesick early settlers. In the spring, this area is particularly rich in wildflowers. The valley was first settled in 1830, only a year after Perth was founded, so there are many historic buildings. The picturesque Avon River is very popular with canoe enthusiasts.

Getting There & Away

The Avon Valley towns all have bus connections to Perth with AvonLink; contact Westrail (☎ 9326 2222) for timetable details. The fare to York is $9.70. You can take the *Prospector* to Northam ($11.40). The best way to see the valley, however, is in your own car.

Toodyay (pop 800)

There are numerous old buildings in this charming and historic town, many built by convicts. The tourist centre (☎ 9574 2435) is on Stirling Terrace, in the 1870s **Connor's Mill**, which still houses a working flour mill. It is open daily from 9 am to 5 pm (Sunday from 10 am).

The **Old Newcastle Gaol Museum** on Clinton St is open in the afternoon and the

Moondyne Gallery tells the story of bush-ranger Joseph Bolitho Johns (Moondyne Joe). Close to town is an old winery, **Coorinja**, which dates from the 1870s; it is open daily, except Sunday.

Places to Stay & Eat *Toodyay Caravan Park Avon Banks* (☎ 9574 2612), Railway Rd, on the banks of the Avon River, has tent/powered sites for $8/12, air-conditioned on-site vans and chalets. It is noisy and the tent sites are as hard as rock. The *Broadgrounds Park* (☎ 9574 2534) has tent/powered sites for $5/15 and a campers' kitchen.

The *Freemasons Hotel* (☎ 9574 2201), on Stirling Terrace, has basic B&B for $25 per person. On the same street is the *Victoria Hotel/Motel* (☎ 9574 2206) with singles/doubles from $20/40 (add $10 if you want a motel room); meals are available from $10.

There are eating places on Stirling Terrace, including the *Wendouree Tearooms*, the *Stirling House Cafe* and the *Lavender Cafe*. *Connor's Restaurant* is the best place in town and popular with day-trippers.

Avon Valley National Park

This national park, downriver from Toodyay, is an area of granite outcrops, diverse fauna and transitional forests. It is the northern limit of the jarrah forests, and jarrah and marri are mixed with wandoo woodlands. There are camp sites with basic facilities such as pit toilets and barbecue; contact the ranger (☎ 9574 2540). A camp site is $5 for two and entry to the park is free.

Northam (pop 6300)

Northam, the major town of the Avon Valley, is a farming centre on the railway line to Kalgoorlie. At one time, the line from Perth ended abruptly here and miners had to trek hundreds of kilometres to the goldfields by road. Every year Northam is packed on the first weekend in August for the start of the gruelling 133km Avon Descent race for power boats and canoeists.

The friendly tourist bureau (☎ 9622 2100), on Minson Ave near the suspension bridge, is open daily from 9 am to 5 pm.

The 1836 **Morby Cottage** served as Northam's first church and school, and it now houses a museum, open on Sunday from 10.30 am to 4 pm ($1). The **old train station**, listed by the National Trust, has been restored and turned into a museum; it is open on Sunday from 10 am to 4 pm ($2). Also of interest in town is the colony of **white swans** on the Avon River, the descendants of birds introduced from England early this century.

If you have the funds, then try **ballooning** over the Avon Valley (March to November); it costs $160 per person.

Places to Stay The *Northam Guesthouse* (☎ 9622 2301), 51 Wellington St, has cheap accommodation from $15 per person for the first night and $10 thereafter.

The *Avon Bridge Hotel* (☎ 9622 1023) is the oldest hotel in Northam and has singles/twins for $20/40 and counter meals from $5. The only motel in town, aptly named the *Northam* (☎ 9622 1755), is at 13 John St; singles/doubles are $48/57. The *Shamrock Hotel*, 112 Fitzgerald St, is the best place in town, with elegant en-suite bedrooms; a double costs from $99.

An excellent out-of-town choice is the farmstay *Egoline Reflections* (☎ 9622 5811), 7km out on the Toodyay road, which has singles/doubles from $85/110.

Places to Eat *Bruno's Pizza Bar* on Fitzgerald St does tasty pizza to eat in or take away. The *Whistling Kettle*, 48 Broome Terrace overlooking the river, is a great place to enjoy some home-cooked food; it is open daily from 10 am to 5 pm. The Shamrock Hotel is the best breakfast choice in town ($7.50) and its upmarket *Gallery Restaurant* has Avon Valley yabbies for $14. If you want a steak try the *Stonecourt*, on the corner of Gordon and Chidlow Sts.

York (pop 1900)

The oldest inland town in WA, York was settled in 1831. It is one of the highlights of the Avon Valley even though its efforts to preserve its Englishness are a bit sickly. A stroll down the main street, with its many restored old buildings, is a step back in time. The town is classified by the National Trust. The tourist centre (☎ 9641 1301), 105 Avon Terrace, is open daily from 9 am to 5 pm.

York is the State's festival town, with no fewer than a dozen major annual events. The better-patronised ones are the Jazz Festival in October and the Flying 50s Vintage & Veteran car race in August.

There are many places of historic interest in this town. The excellent 1850s **Residency Museum** is open from Tuesday to Thursday from 1 to 3 pm, and on weekends from 1 to 5 pm ($2, children $1). The old **town hall** and Castle Hotel (which dates from coaching days) are photogenic, as are the police station, gaol, courthouse and Settlers House.

The classy **Motor Museum**, a must for vintage-car enthusiasts, houses Australia's best collection of vintage, classic and racing cars, including the Saudi Williams driven by former world champion Alan Jones ($7, children $2).

Places to Stay The only caravan park around town is the *Mt Bakewell Caravan Park* (☎ 9641 1421), with tent/powered sites at $12/14 and on-site vans for $30 for two.

The old section of the historic, renovated *Castle Hotel* (☎ 9641 1007), on Avon Terrace, is good value with B&B singles/doubles from $30/60. The *Settlers House* (☎ 9641 1096), 125 Avon Terrace, has stylish B&B for $69/98.

There are a number of quality B&Bs and farmstays in the region charging from about $50 to $90 for two; enquire at the tourist centre.

Places to Eat From the wide selection of places along Avon Terrace, try the *Settlers House* for breakfast, *Cafe Bugatti* for cappuccino and Italian food, *York Village Bakehouse* for freshly baked bread and cakes (including delicious vanilla slices) and *Jule's Shoppe* for delicious 'LP road-tested' homemade pasties. The *Castle Hotel* serves good

counter meals (from $10) and has an à la carte restaurant.

Beverley (pop 1500)

South of York, also on the Avon River, is Beverley, founded in 1838 and noted for its fine **aeronautical museum**, open daily from 9 am to 4 pm. Exhibits include a locally built biplane, *Silver Centenary*, constructed between 1928 and 1930. The tourist bureau (☎ 9646 1555) is housed in this building, which is impossible to miss as it has a Vampire jet mounted outside the door.

The 7 sq km **Avondale Discovery Farm**, 6km west of Beverley, has a large collection of agricultural machinery, a homestead, a workshop and stables.

The **lonely grave**, 3km south of town, is the solitary last resting place of a baby who died in January 1883. Why here? There was no town cemetery at the time.

Places to Stay The *Beverley Caravan Park* (☎ 9646 1200), on Vincent St, has powered sites for $12 for two. The ordinary *Beverley Hotel* (☎ 9646 1190), 137 Vincent St, has singles/doubles for $24/47.

NORTH OF PERTH

The coast north of Perth is scenic, with long sand dunes, but quickly becomes the inhospitable terrain that deterred early explorers. The **Yanchep National Park**, 51km north of Perth, has natural bushland, a colony of 'imported' koalas, some fine caves (including the limestone Crystal and Yondemp caves), Loch McNess and the Yaberoo Budjara Aboriginal Heritage Trail. The town of Yanchep has an atmospheric pub and nearby is the Two Rocks fishing marina with attached shopping complex.

There are a handful of places to stay, including the *Yanchep Lagoon Lodge* (☎ 9561 1033), 11 Nautical Court, which has dinner and B&B from $60 for two. On weekdays, one bus goes to Yanchep from Perth's Wellington St bus station.

Some 43km north of Yanchep is **Guilderton**, a popular holiday resort beside the mouth of the Moore River. The *Vergulde*

Draeck (Gilt Dragon), a Dutch East India Company ship, ran aground near here in 1656.

The coast road ends at **Lancelin**, a small fishing port 130km north of Perth, but coastal tracks continue north and may be passable with a 4WD. Windswept Lancelin is the end of the annual Ledge Point Windsurfing Race. There are many opportunities in Lancelin to learn **windsurfing**.

A tidy, purpose-built backpackers place, the *Lancelin Lodge* (☎ 9655 2020), is on Hopkins St. It is run by two travellers, Trish and Trev – many of the features in the place are those they would have wished to have seen in places they stayed in on the road (such as the fully equipped kitchen). A comfortable dorm bed is $15 and neat doubles are $40 ($50 in peak season).

Pinnacles Desert

The small seaport of **Cervantes**, 257km north of Perth, is the entry point for the unusual and haunting Pinnacles Desert. Here, in coastal **Nambung National Park**, the flat sandy desert is punctured with peculiar limestone pillars, some only a few centimetres high, others towering up to 5m. The park is the scene of an impressive wildflower display from August to October.

Try to visit the Pinnacles Desert early in the morning. Not only is the light better for photography but you will avoid the crowds that can detract from your experience of the place later in the day, especially in peak holiday times.

Check in Cervantes before attempting to drive the unsealed road into the park – if conditions are bad, a 4WD may be necessary, but usually the road is OK, if somewhat bumpy, for normal vehicles. A coastal 4WD track runs north to **Jurien**, a crayfishing and holiday centre, and south to Lancelin.

Organised Tours Cervantes Pinnacles Adventure Tours (☎ 9652 7236) includes a 4WD jaunt along the beach from Hangover Bay, refreshments, entrance fee to the Pinnacles and commentary in its tour ($27.50).

There is another thrilling 4WD trip (also $27.50) up and over sand dunes, down narrow overgrown tracks to a 'rollercoaster hill' where the 4WD tackles the dunes. Once at the top you sandboard down a few times, before having a relaxing snack at a secluded beach. A combined trip – Pinnacles and sandboarding – is $44. If you drive into the Pinnacles Desert yourself, there is a $5 car entrance fee.

Places to Stay There is accommodation in Cervantes but not in the national park. The *Pinnacles Caravan Park* (☎ 9652 7060) on the beachfront has tent/powered sites at $10/13 and on-site vans from $25. The purpose-built *Pinnacles Beach Backpackers* (☎ 9627 7377), 91 Seville St, was much needed. It has a well-equipped, airy kitchen, plenty of recreation space and tidy rooms; dorm beds are $15, en-suite doubles $50 and family rooms $40 for two (a child is $8 extra – this can add up!) The *Cervantes Pinnacles Motel* (☎ 9652 7145), 227 Aragon St, has doubles from $75.

The South-West

The south-west of WA has a magnificent coastline with two prominent capes and many forest national parks, including the region of 'tall trees'. These are green, fertile areas which contrast with the dry and barren country found in much of the State. There are also whale-watching opportunities, famous surfing beaches, prosperous farms, the Margaret River wineries and, in season, beautiful wildflowers.

Getting There & Away

Westrail (☎ 13 2232) buses go daily from Perth to Bunbury ($16.30), Busselton ($21.30), Yallingup ($24.50), Margaret River ($24.50) and Augusta ($29.10).

South-West Coachlines (☎ 9324 2333) also services the region and travels daily from Perth to Bunbury ($16), Busselton ($20), Dunsborough ($22), Margaret River

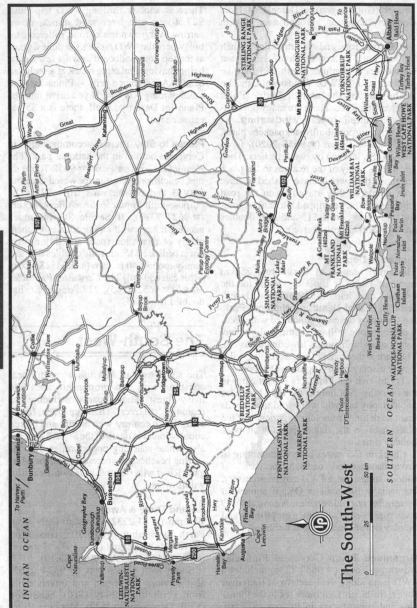

The South-West

RICHARD I'ANSON

MARGARET JUNG

Victoria
Top: Twelve Apostles, Port Campbell National Park
Bottom: Fishing vessels at Apollo Bay

ROB VAN DRIESUM

ROB VAN DRIESUM

JEFF WILLIAMS

Western Australia
Top: Perth's modern skyline
Left: The 15-metre-high Wave Rock is shaped like a perfect wave
Right: After rain, wildflowers bloom in the outback

($23) and Augusta ($28); from Monday to Friday, it has services to Collie ($20), Donnybrook ($20), Balingup ($23), Bridgetown ($23), Nannup ($24) and Manjimup ($27).

The Easyrider Backpackers' bus (☎ 9383 7848) also stops off at hostels at a dozen south-west towns ($129 for a loop pass).

SOUTH-WEST HINTERLAND

Inland from the south-west coast, the town of **Harvey** (pop 2500) is in a popular bushwalking area of rolling green hills north of Bunbury. This is the home of WA's **Big Orange**, standing 20m high at the Fruit Bowl on the South-Western Highway. There are dam systems and some beautiful waterfalls nearby, and the **Yalgorup National Park**, with its peculiar stromatolites, is north-west of the town. The tourist bureau (☎ 9729 1122) is on the South-Western Highway.

South of Bunbury is **Donnybrook**, in the centre of an apple-growing area. Its tourist centre (☎ 9731 1720) is in the old train station. Apple-picking work is available most of the year. There are two backpacker places in Donnybrook – *Brook Lodge* (☎ 9731 1520) and *Donnybrook Backpackers* (☎ 9731 1844); both charge $12 per dorm bed. Their staff can arrange picking work for you.

Collie (pop 7660), WA's only coal town, has an interesting replica of a coal mine, and mining and steam-locomotion museums. There is pleasant bushwalking country around the town and plenty of wildflowers in season. The tourist bureau (☎ 9734 2051), Throssell St, is open on weekdays from 9 am to 5 pm and on weekends from 10 am to 4 pm.

Places to Stay

The *Rainbow Caravan Park* (☎ 9729 2239), 199 King St in Harvey, has tent sites and on-site vans, as does the *Mr Marron Holiday Village* (☎ 9734 5088), on Porter St, Collie.

In Donnybrook, the *Brook Lodge* (☎ 9731 1520), on Bridge St, is a private lodge with kitchen and laundry facilities. If you are picking fruit you may like to stay here ($70 per week).

BUNBURY (pop 25,000)

As well as being a port, an industrial town and a holiday resort, Bunbury is noted for its blue manna crabs and dolphins. The tourist bureau (☎ 9721 7922) is in the old 1904 train station on Carmody Place. It has detailed brochures of walking and driving tours around town and the region.

Things to See

The town's **old buildings** include King Cottage at 77 Forrest Ave, which houses a museum, the Rose Hotel and St Mark's Church (1842). The interesting Bunbury

---

Swimming with Dolphins

You don't have to go to Monkey Mia to commune with dolphins – you can also do this at the Dolphin Discovery Centre (☎ 9791 3088) on Koombana Beach. This can be a rewarding experience. Visits from three pods of about 100 bottlenose dolphins *(Tursiops truncatus)* that regularly feed in the Inner Harbour usually occur several times a day but less frequently in winter; a flag is hoisted when the dolphins are in. I rate the 'encounter' better than that at Monkey Mia, and it happens much closer to Perth!

The area, staffed during the day by helpful volunteers, was set up in 1989 and dolphins started to interact with the public in early 1990. The centre is housed in a new building near the beach. A brochure explains the simple rules of contact with dolphins; otherwise ask a volunteer. The centre's museum and audiovisual is a must (casual entry is $5/4 for adults/children).

You can literally dance with the dolphins on a trip in the jet-propelled *Dolphin Dancer* (☎ 9791 1827); the cost is $12.50/7.50. Or you can watch the high jinks of the dolphins in a more leisurely fashion on the *Naturaliste Lady*. Trips go out daily, weather permitting, at 11 am and 2 pm; the cost is $15/10. In summer catch the boat outside the discovery centre and in winter catch it from the wharf.

Jeff Williams

Regional Art Galleries, Wittenoom St, are in a restored convent.

The **Big Swamp Wildlife Park** (☎ 9721 8380) on Prince Philip Drive is open daily from 10 am to 5 pm and includes many examples of native fauna. There is a nearby boardwalk through the white mangroves of Big Swamp.

At Australind, 7km north of Bunbury, is the **St Nicholas Church**, which, at just 4m by 7m, is said to be the smallest church in Australia. There is a scenic drive between Australind and Binningup along the shores of the **Leschenault Inlet**.

Places to Stay

There are four caravan parks in town and two out of town. Two in town are the *Bunbury Village* (☎ 9795 7100) on Washington Ave, with tent/powered sites for $12/13 for two and chalets from $55; and the *Koombana Bay Holiday Resort* (☎ 9791 3900) on Koombana Drive, with sites for $13/15 and chalets from $100. The *Punchbowl Caravan Park* (☎ 9721 4761) is on Ocean Drive and has tent/powered sites for two people for $11/13 (extra person $3).

The efficiently run and friendly *Wander Inn – Bunbury Backpackers* (☎ 9721 3242)

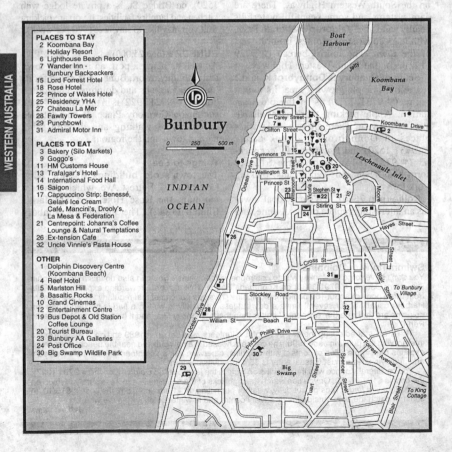

PLACES TO STAY
2 Koombana Bay
   Holiday Resort
6 Lighthouse Beach Resort
7 Wander Inn -
   Bunbury Backpackers
15 Lord Forrest Hotel
18 Rose Hotel
22 Prince of Wales Hotel
25 Residency YHA
27 Chateau La Mer
28 Fawlty Towers
29 Punchbowl
31 Admiral Motor Inn

PLACES TO EAT
3 Bakery (Silo Markets)
9 Goggo's
11 HM Customs House
13 Trafalgar's Hotel
14 International Food Hall
16 Saigon
17 Cappuccino Strip: Benessé,
   Gelaré Ice Cream
   Café, Mancini's, Drooly's,
   La Mesa & Federation
21 Centrepoint: Johanna's Coffee
   Lounge & Natural Temptations
26 Ex-tension Cafe
32 Uncle Vinnie's Pasta House

OTHER
1 Dolphin Discovery Centre
   (Koombana Beach)
4 Reef Hotel
5 Marlston Hill
8 Basaltic Rocks
10 Grand Cinemas
12 Entertainment Centre
19 Bus Depot & Old Station
   Coffee Lounge
20 Tourist Bureau
23 Bunbury AA Galleries
24 Post Office
30 Big Swamp Wildlife Park

Bunbury

INDIAN

OCEAN

WESTERN AUSTRALIA

is close to the city centre at 16 Clifton St (two blocks from both the tourist office and the Indian Ocean). It charges $14 for a dorm bed, $32 for a double or twin. A trip to the forests, waterfalls and wildflowers around Wellington Dam, especially suited to backpackers, costs $15/25 for a half-day/day. Phone ☎ 1800 064 704 for a free pick-up from the train station.

The *Residency YHA* (☎ 9791 2621) is on the corner of Stirling and Moore Sts in an historic residence. Good dorm beds in this clean hostel are $15 ($13 for members), doubles are $28 and a family room is $35.

The *Prince of Wales* (☎ 9721 2016) on Stephen St has B&B doubles for $60. The *Rose Hotel* (☎ 9721 4533) on Victoria St is a clean, lavishly restored place, yet the rooms, $53/66 for singles/doubles with breakfast, are rough and ready.

Close to the centre are the *Admiral Motor Inn* (☎ 9721 7322) at 56 Spencer St, with singles/doubles for $70/80; and the *Lighthouse Beach Resort* (☎ 9721 1311) on Carey St, with rooms from $50/70 and suites from $90 for two. On Ocean Drive are the *Chateau La Mer* (☎ 9721 3166), the *Ocean Drive* (☎ 9721 2033) and the courageously named *Fawlty Towers* (☎ 9721 2427); singles/doubles are about $45/60 at these places.

Places to Eat

On Victoria St is the popular *HM Customs House*, which has four outlets including a brasserie. There are a number of cafes and food outlets in the Centrepoint shopping centre, including *Johanna's Coffee Lounge* and *Natural Temptations*.

There are lots of cafes on Victoria St, aptly named the 'cappuccino strip'. *Mancini's*, *Benessé* ($8 breakfasts), *Gelaré Ice Cream Café*, *Drooly's*, *La Mesa* and The *Federation* are here. The *Old Station Coffee Lounge* is in Carmody Place, trendy *Goggo's* is at 18 Wittenoom St and the *Ex-Tension Cafe* on Ocean Drive, overlooking the sea, is open daily from 7 am.

Drooly's, 70 Victoria St, does great pizzas for moderate prices and is open from 5 pm until late. The *Rose Hotel* on Wellington St does good counter meals and has nine beers on tap. Those wanting to try tasty Vietnamese pho for $6.50 a huge bowl should go to the *Saigon* on Victoria St.

A popular Italian place is *Uncle Vinnie's Pasta House*, 113 Spencer St; spaghetti slurpers can escape satisfied from here for $15. Bistro meals in the lounge of the *Trafalgar's Hotel*, 36 Victoria St, come recommended – there is always a fish of the day ($12) and unrestricted access to the salad bar.

Popular night spots are the *Lord Forrest*, *Rose* and *Trafalgar's* hotels. The *Reef Hotel*, 8 Victoria St, is currently the social focus for the nocturnal set – the verdant Reef Bar is the place for a drink.

Getting Around

Bunbury City Transit (☎ 9791 1955) covers the region around the city as far north as Australind and south to Gelorup.

BUSSELTON (pop 10,600)

Busselton, on the shores of Geographe Bay, is another popular holiday resort. The town has a 2km jetty once reputed to be the longest timber jetty in Australia. The Busselton tourist bureau (☎ 9752 1288) is on the corner of Causeway Rd and Peel Terrace.

The old **courthouse** has been restored and now houses an impressive arts centre; it is open from 9 am to 5 pm daily (admission is free). **Wonnerup House**, 10km east of town, is an 1859 colonial-style house, lovingly restored by the National Trust. It is open from 10 am to 4 pm daily ($4, children $2).

To get to Busselton you can take a Westrail (☎ 13 2232; $21.30) or South-West Coachlines bus ($20). Geographe Bay Coachlines (☎ 9754 2026) has day tours to Cape Naturaliste ($50) and to Augusta/Margaret River ($50).

Places to Stay

The most central of the many caravan parks, *Kookaburra* (☎ 9752 1516), 66 Marine Terrace, has powered sites for $12, on-site vans for $20 and cabins for $30 for two.

The quite small *Busselton Backpackers*

(☎ 9754 2763), 14 Peel St, is a private house with limited kitchen facilities ($12 for dorm beds); ask at the tourist office for details.

The often booked-out *Motel Busselton* (☎ 9752 1908), 90 Bussell Highway, has comfortable units from $35 per B&B double. *Villa Carlotta Private Hotel* (☎ 9754 2026), 110 Adelaide St, is good, friendly, organises tours and has singles/doubles for $40/60 with breakfast.

There are a number of holiday resorts with a bewildering variety of accommodation in the region. One example is the *Busselton Beach Resort* (☎ 9752 3444), on the corner of Geographe Bay Rd and Guerin St, which has single/doubles from $80/100.

Places to Eat

There are lots of takeaway places along this coastal strip, which cater for travellers and the hordes that descend upon the place during holiday periods. *Geographe Pizza* is on Queen St, *Red Rooster* is on the Bussell Highway, and *Presto Pizza* is in the Boulevarde shopping centre.

Hotels such as the *Ship Resort* on Albert St and the *Esplanade* on Marine Terrace are good for counter meals. A local favourite is the *Equinox Café* on the beachfront; staff serve light meals and dinners.

DUNSBOROUGH (pop 1150)

Dunsborough, just to the west of Busselton, is a pleasant little coastal town dependent on tourism. The tourist bureau (☎ 9755 3299) is in the shopping centre.

North-west of Dunsborough, the Cape Naturaliste Rd leads to excellent beaches such as **Meelup**, **Eagle Bay** and **Bunker Bay**, some fine coastal lookouts and the tip of **Cape Naturaliste**, which has a lighthouse and some walking trails. The lighthouse is open daily, except Monday, from 9.30 am to 4 pm; entry is $5/2 for adults/children. In season you can see humpback and southern right whales and dolphins from the lookouts over Geographe Bay. At scenic **Sugarloaf Rock** is the southernmost nesting colony of the rare red-tailed tropicbird.

Places to Stay & Eat

Green Acres Beachfront Caravan Park (☎ 9755 3087) in Dunsborough has tent/powered sites for $11/12, as well as on-site vans from $30 to $60, cabins from $40 to $75 for two and park cabins from $30 to $60; prices go up 25% in the high season.

In Quindalup, near Dunsborough, is the *Three Pines Resort YHA* (☎ 9755 3107), which is well-positioned on the beachfront at 285 Geographe Bay Rd. It charges $16 for dorm beds, while twin and family rooms are $18 per person. Staff hire out bikes ($6 per day) and canoes ($5 per hour).

The *Forum Food Centre* has a variety of eating places, including a fine bakery. *Dunsborough Health Foods* in the shopping centre sells wholemeal salad rolls and delicious smoothies and juices. The *Little Havana* has introduced Tex-Mex and Cajun food to a former culinary wasteland. On Commonage Rd is *Simmo's Ice Creamery* with 21 home-made flavours.

YALLINGUP (pop 500)

Yallingup, a mecca for surfers, is surrounded by spectacular coastline and some fine beaches. Surfers can get a copy of the free *Down South Surfing Guide* from the Dunsborough tourist centre. Nearby is the stunning **Ngilgi Cave** which was discovered, or rather stumbled upon, in 1899. The cave is open daily from 9.30 am to 3.30 pm and you can look around by yourself or take a guided tour ($9, children $4) that explores parts of the cave not usually open to visitors.

The *Yallingup Beach Caravan Park* (☎ 9755 2164) on the beachfront at Valley Rd has tent sites for $10 and on-site vans for $30. On Caves Rd, *Caves House Hotel* (☎ 9755 2131), established in 1903, is an old-world lodge with ocean views and English garden. As Yallingup means 'place of lovers', the units at Caves House are perfect for honeymooners but are not cheap at $120. The popular *Yallingup Siding Carriages* (☎ 9755 1106) are on Glover Rd. These quaint, recycled dwellings are good value at $75 to $105 for two, depending on the season.

The *Yallingup Store* is known for its burgers. The expensive brasserie at *Wildwood Winery* is 8km south of Yallingup on Caves Rd.

MARGARET RIVER (pop 2800)

Margaret River is a popular holiday spot due to its proximity to fine surf (Margaret River Mouth, Gnarabup, Suicides and Redgate) and swimming beaches (Prevelly and Gracetown), some of Australia's best wineries and spectacular scenery.

The Margaret River-Augusta tourist office (☎ 9757 2911) is on the corner of the Bussell Highway and Tunbridge Rd. It has a wad of information on the area, including an extensive vineyard guide ($2.50) and info on the many art and craft places in town. CALM produces an informative, free booklet, *Leeuwin-Naturaliste National Park*.

Eagles Heritage, 5km south of Margaret River on Boodjidup Rd, has an interesting collection of raptors (birds of prey) in a natural setting; it is open daily from 10 am to 5 pm ($4.50, children $2.50).

The **old coast road** between Augusta, Margaret River and Busselton is a good alternative to the direct road which runs slightly inland. The coast here has real variety – cliff faces, long beaches pounded by rolling surf, and calm, sheltered bays.

An interesting three-hour tour, conducted by Helen of **Cave Canoe Bushtucker**

Tours (☎ 9757 9084) at Prevelly Park, takes you on a search for forest secrets. The tour combines walking and canoeing up the Margaret River, entering deep inside a wilderness cave and learning Aboriginal culture, bushcraft, flora and fauna; it costs $20 (children $10) and is well worth it.

Places to Stay

Less expensive possibilities include the *Margaret River Caravan Park* (☎ 9757 2180) on Station Rd, which has tent/powered sites for $12/14 and on-site vans for $33 for two; and the *Riverview Caravan Park* (☎ 9757 2270) on Willmott Ave.

The *Margaret River Lodge* (☎ 9757 2532), a backpacker hostel, is about 1.5km south-west from the town centre at 220 Railway Terrace. It's clean and modern with all the facilities (and doesn't mind family groups); dorm beds are $12, four-bed bunkrooms are from $15 per person and doubles from $35 for two.

The name says it all: the *Margaret River Inne Town Backpackers* (☎ 9757 3698), 93 Bussell Highway, is in town. It is in a converted house, slowly being extended, but has a great patio; dorm beds are $14, twins and doubles $32 and a trio room $39.

One of the nicest backpacker places you could hope to stay in is the *Surf Point Lodge* (☎ 9757 1777) on Riedle Drive at Gnarabup Beach. In addition to the plus of its beachside

Surfing

The beaches between the Capes Leeuwin and Naturaliste offer powerful beach and reef breaks, both right and left-handers. The wave at Margaret River ('Margaret's') has been described by surfing supremo Nat Young as 'epic', and by world-surfing champ Mark Richards as 'one of the world's finest'.

The better locations include Rocky Point (short left-hander), The Farm and Bone Yards (right-hander), Three Bears (Papa, Mama and Baby, of course), Yallingup ('Yal's'; breaks left and right), Injidup Car Park and Injidup Point (right-hand tube on a heavy swell; left-hander), Guillotine/Gallows (right-hander), South Point (popular break), Left-Handers (the name says it all) and Margaret River (with Southside or 'Suicides').

You can get a free copy of the *Down South Surfing Guide*, which indicates wave size, wind direction and swell siz, from the Dunsborough and Busselton tourist bureaux. The Margaret River Surf Classic is held in November. Josh Palmateer (current WA champ) runs Josh Palmateer's Surf Academy (☎ 9757 1850), PO Box 856, Margaret River; a two-hour lesson at either Margaret's or Yal's with one of WA's best is $25. ■

location, the place has an air of class – it has a large, fully equipped kitchen and many recreation areas; surfers will love the theme. There is also a courtesy bus to and from Margaret River. Dorm beds in four/eight-bed rooms are $15/16, twins and doubles are $40 and en-suite rooms $59.

There are many other cottages, B&Bs and farmstays; enquire at the tourist offices or check the free *Margaret River Regional Accommodation Guide*.

Places to Eat

Among the many places to eat in Margaret River is the *Settler's Tavern*, on Bussell Highway, which has good counter meals from $10 to $12 – there's also live music on weekends. The Margaret River Motel Hotel has counter meals in its *Rivers Bistro*.

There is a great number of eateries along the section of the Bussell Highway between the tourist office and Wallcliffe Rd. At the southern end is the *Margaret River Tuckshop*, a bit of an institution with friendly owners, and the *Arc of Iris*, a quick bypass to the Aquarian generation – a Thai meal will cost from $8 to $12. *Cafe Forte* on the Bussell Highway serves great Aussie cuisine and a hearty meal costs $15 or so.

Getting Around

The Wanderer Bus can get you around town, out to Surf Point Lodge, the beaches (Gnarabup and Surfers' Point) and perhaps the wineries (eg Cape Mentelle); the cost for a single trip is $3 (or $6 round trip). Catch it outside the tourist office.

Bikes can be rented by the hour or day from the Margaret River Lodge.

AUGUSTA (pop 1080)

A popular holiday resort, Augusta is 5km north of Cape Leeuwin. The cape, the most south-westerly point in Australia, has a rugged coastline and a **lighthouse** (open daily, except Monday, from 9 am to 4 pm; entry $3) with views extending over two oceans (the Indian and the Southern). Not far away is a salt-encrusted **water wheel**, built in 1895.

Cape Leeuwin took its name from a Dutch ship which passed here in 1622. The **Matthew Flinders memorial** on Leeuwin Rd commemorates Flinders' mapping of the Australian coastline, which commenced at the cape on 6 December 1801.

The tourist office (☎ 9758 1695), 70 Blackwood Ave, is open daily from 9 am to 5 pm.

Whale-watching is good from Cape Leeuwin between May and September. Naturaliste Charters (☎ 9755 2276) has three-hour trips to see southern right as well as humpback whales, bottlenose dolphins and a colony of NZ fur seals on Flinders Island (June to September); the cost is $40/20 for adults/children. The *Leeuwin Lady* (☎ 9758 1770) also has three-hour tours for $40; you can book at the dive shop on Blackwood Ave.

There are more sedate cruises up the Blackwood River on the *Miss Flinders* (☎ 9758 1944) leaving from the Ellis St jetty. From September to June it leaves at 2 pm on Tuesday, Thursday and Saturday, while between Christmas and Easter it has an extra Wednesday service; the cost is $14/7 for adults/children.

Leeuwin-Naturaliste Caves

There are a number of limestone caves dotted throughout the Leeuwin-Naturaliste Ridge between the capes. In **Mammoth Cave**, 21km south of Margaret River, a fossilised jawbone of *Zygomaturus trilobus*, a giant wombat-like creature, can be touched. Limestone formations are reflected in the still waters of an underground stream in the **Lake Cave**, 25km from Margaret River. The vegetated entrance to this cave is spectacular and includes a karri tree with a girth of 7m. The interpretive centre, CaveWorks (☎ 9757 7411), has state-of-the-art computerised displays, a cave model, audio-visuals and a boardwalk. Fossilised remains of a Tasmanian tiger *(thylacine)* have been discovered in the **Jewel Cave**, 8km north of Augusta. **Moondyne Cave**, also 8km north of Augusta, is unlit and a guide takes visitors on a two-hour caving adventure ($25).

Guided cave tours, the only way to see these caves, run daily for $9 (Jewel $10). Both Jewel and Lake are open on the half-hour from 9.30 until 4 pm, Mammoth is open on the hour from 9 am until 4 pm and Moondyne at 10 am and 2.30 pm (these times vary, so contact CaveWorks).

Places to Stay & Eat

The *Doonbanks Caravan Park* (☎ 9758 1517) is the most central caravan park, with tent/powered sites for $12/13, on-site vans for $25 and park cabins from $40 for two. There are a number of basic camp sites in the Leeuwin-Naturaliste National Park including one on Boranup Drive, Point Rd and Conto's Field, near Lake Cave; camping costs $5 per person.

The purpose-built, Federation-style *Baywatch Manor Resort* (☎ 9758 1290), 88 Blackwood Avenue, has all the facilities and comfortable rooms, but it is definitely not a party place. It's equipped for disabled travellers, and dorm beds cost $15 and double and twin rooms cost $36 for two (linen included).

Squirrels serves delicious burgers (piled high with salad), Lebanese sandwiches and various health foods. The bakery is known for its pizzas (from $8 to $16), buns and home-baked pies. *Cosy's Corner* has $6 breakfasts and tasty focaccia.

SOUTHERN FORESTS

A visit to the forests of the south-west is a must for any traveller to WA. The forests are magnificent – towering jarrah, marri and karri trees protect the natural, vibrant garden beneath. Unfortunately, parts of these forests are threatened by logging.

The area of 'tall trees' (not 'tall timber', as that predetermines their fate) lies between the Vasse Highway and the South-Western Highway, and includes the timber towns of Bridgetown, Manjimup, Nannup, Pemberton and Northcliffe. A trip will be more rewarding if you have CALM's free brochure *Karri Country*.

Getting There & Away

Westrail's (☎ 13 2232) Perth-Pemberton buses run daily, via Bunbury, Donnybrook and Manjimup; the trip takes about five hours. From Albany it takes three hours and the service is twice weekly. Westrail has a daily train service from Perth via Bunbury and South-West Coachlines has a weekday service from Perth.

Nannup (pop 1100)

Some 50km west of Bridgetown, Nannup is a quiet, historical and picturesque town in the heart of forest and farmland. The tourist centre (☎ 9756 1211) in the old 1922 police station on Brockman St is open daily from 9 am to 3 pm. Its excellent booklet (50c) points out places of interest around town and details a range of scenic drives in the area, including numerous forest drives.

There is a jarrah sawmill, an arboretum, some fine old buildings and several craft shops. The descent of the **Blackwood River**, from the forest to the sea, is one of Australia's great canoe trips.

The town's backpackers lodge is the permaculture-conscious and rustic *Black Cockatoo Eco-Stay* (☎ 9756 1035), 27 Grange Rd, with beds for $12. The people who run this place are cool and contribute to its laid-back atmosphere. There is a large back yard with a stream as one border.

The *Blackwood Cafe* serves light meals, such as quiche, soup and sandwiches. *Old Templemore* serves great cafe-style food and the *Good Food Shop* has scrumptious trout rolls ($4).

Bridgetown (pop 2000)

This quiet country town on the Blackwood River is in an area of karri forests and farmland. Bridgetown has some old buildings, including the mud-and-clay **Bridgedale House**, built by the area's first settler in 1862. There is a local history display in the tourist bureau (☎ 9761 1740) on Hampton St.

Interesting features of the Blackwood River valley are the burrawangs (grass trees) and large granite boulders. In **Boyup Brook**,

31km north-east of Bridgetown, there is a flora reserve, a country and western music collection (some 2000 titles) and a large butterfly and beetle display. Nearby is **Norlup Pool** with glacial rock formations.

Places to Stay *Bridgetown Caravan Park* (☎ 9761 1053) on the South-Western Highway has tent/powered sites for $12/14 and on-site vans for $28. The *Old Well* (☎ 9761 2032) on Gifford St has B&B singles/doubles for $35/65 and the *Bridgetown Motel* (☎ 9761 1641), 38 Hampton St, has rooms from $58 to $130 a double.

About 20km north in Greenbushes, the *Exchange Hotel* (☎ 9764 3509) has budget rooms, and units for $35/45.

Manjimup (pop 4400)

Manjimup, the agricultural centre of the south-west, is noted (and sometimes vilified) for its woodchipping industry. The **Timber Park Complex**, on the corner of Rose and Edwards Sts, includes museums, old buildings and the tourist bureau (☎ 9771 1831). The latter, open daily from 9am to 5 pm, is just an apologia for the local timber industry.

One Tree Bridge, or what's left of it after the 1966 floods, is 22km down Graphite Rd. It was constructed from a single karri log. The **Four Aces**, 1.5km from One Tree Bridge, are four superb karri trees believed to be over 300 years old. **Fonty's Pool**, a cool swimming spot, is 10km south-west of town along Seven Day Rd.

About 9km south of town along the South-Western Highway is the 51m-high karri **Diamond Tree**. You can climb most of the way up to a platform from where there are great views over forest and farmland.

Perup, 50km east of Manjimup, is in the centre of a forest that boasts six rare mammals – the numbat, chuditch, woylie, tammar wallaby, ringtail possum and southern brown bandicoot. Contact Perup Tours (☎ 9776 7273) for details of its weekend excursions ($95).

Places to Stay & Eat The caravan park (☎ 9771 1575) has a hostel with dorm beds

and cooking facilities for $12 per night – it can get busy in apple-picking season (March to June). It also has powered sites for $13 and on-site vans for $26. The austere *Barracks Backpackers* (☎ 9771 1154) has opened at 8 Muir St; twin rooms cost $30 (write and tell us about it).

The *Manjimup Hotel* (☎ 9771 1322) on Giblett St, designed to slake the thirst of raucous timber millers, can be noisy. The staff are friendly and the singles/doubles, most with bathrooms, are worth the $35/48.

If you have transport go to Pemberton for dinner. Otherwise, on Mottram St, across the railway line from the hotel, is the garish, pulsating *Manji-Mart Takeaway*.

Pemberton (pop 1000)

Deep in the karri forests is the delightful township of Pemberton. The child-friendly, well-organised Karri visitors centre (☎ 9776 1133) on Brockman St incorporates the tourist centre, pioneer museum and karri forest discovery centre.

You need a day pass to go into the national parks. They are available from the CALM office on Kennedy St and cost $5 per car or $2 for people in tour groups.

Pemberton has some interesting **craft shops**, the pretty **Pemberton Pool** surrounded by karri trees (ideal on a hot day) and a **trout hatchery** that supplies fish for the State's dams and rivers.

If you are feeling fit, you can make the scary 60m climb to the top of the **Gloucester Tree**, one of the highest fire lookout trees in the world. This is not for the faint-hearted and only one visitor in four ascends. The view makes the climb well worthwhile. To get there, just follow the signs from town.

Also of interest in the area are the cascading **Cascades** (only so when the water level is high); **Beedelup National Park**; the 100-year-old forest (it was logged over 100 years ago and has since regrown), which stands as a defence against the supposed low impact of careful logging; and the **Warren National Park**, where camping is allowed in designated areas. The **Dave Evans Bicentennial**

Tree, at 68m the tallest of local 'climbing trees', is in this park.

Organised Tours The scenic **Pemberton Tramway** is one of the area's main attractions. Trams leave Pemberton train station for Warren River ($12.50, children $6.50) daily at 10.45 am and 2 pm, and for Northcliffe ($19.50, children $9.50) at 10.15 am on Tuesday, Thursday and Saturday. The route travels through lush marri and karri forests and there are occasional picture stops.

Southern Forest Adventures (☎ 9776 1222) has 4WD tours of the forest and coastal areas around Pemberton from $40.

For diametrically opposed views on the forests, Andy Russell (☎ 9776 1559) takes short walks through beautiful stands of karri, while Forest Discovery Tours (☎ 9771 2915) does forest industry tours ($10, children $2).

Places to Stay Camping is permitted in Warren National Park (☎ 9776 1207) and some areas of the Pemberton Forest (☎ 9776 1200). The picturesque caravan park (☎ 9776 1300) has tent/powered sites costing $11/13, on-site vans for $26 and cabins for $34 for two.

Pimelea Chalets YHA (☎ 9776 1153) in a beautiful forest location at Pimelea charges $14 a night (nonmembers $15). It's 10km north-west of Pemberton – readers have reported problems getting transport to this hostel. The place was not attended when we visited (for the second time).

In town, the centrally located *Warren Lodge* (☎ 9776 1105) on Brockman St has backpacker beds from $13 and twins/doubles for $30/38. It requires some tender loving care and an augmentation of facilities. And remember, you are the paying guest and should be treated as such.

Flush Perth-ites head for the *Karri Valley Resort* (☎ 9776 2020) on the Vasse Highway. This is a beautiful place sited at the edge of a lake and surrounded by magnificent karri forest. It has motel rooms from $131 and chalets from $181.

For more information on the plethora of farmstays, cottages and B&Bs, enquire at the Karri visitors centre. Readers recommend the fine *Marima Cottage Retreat* (☎ 9776 1211) on Old Vasse Rd in Warren National Park; single and double B&B costs from $90.

Places to Eat The town, for its size, has many places to eat; most have local trout and marron on their menus. The *Pemberton Patisserie* has tasty pies and cakes, the *Country Kitchen* near the hotel has good old-fashioned home cooking, while the *Mainstreet Cafe* on Brockman St has basic, cheap food such as hamburgers and Lebanese rolls.

Shannon National Park

This 535 sq km national park on the South-Western Highway, 50km south of Manjimup, is well worth a visit. There is a covered information shelter on the north of the highway (near the entrance to the drive); the free CALM publication *Shannon National Park and the Great Forest Trees Drive* is informative.

CALM has markedly improved facilities and the 48km **Great Forest Trees Drive** is well worth doing. On the drive you can learn about the old-growth karri forest by tuning into 100FM when you see the signs (there are eight). Those wishing to know more could consult *The Great Forest Trees Drive* ($12.95), a detailed guidebook.

There is a fine camping area (☎ 9776 1207) in the spot where the original timber milling village used to be (it was closed in 1968). Camping fees are $8 for two adults ($3 for an additional adult) and $1 for school-age children. If you use a hut, equipped with pot belly stoves, it costs $5 – all fees are on a self-registration basis.

Northcliffe (pop 800)

Northcliffe, 32km south of Pemberton, has a **pioneer museum** and a nearby **forest park**, with good walks through stands of grand karri, marri and jarrah trees. The tourist centre (☎ 9776 7203) is by the pioneer museum on Wheatley Coast Rd.

Windy Harbour on the coast 29km south of Northcliffe has prefabricated shacks and a sheltered beach; true to its name, it is windy. The cliffs of the fine **D'Entrecas-teaux National Park** are accessible from here.

Opposite the school, the caravan park (☎ 9776 7193) has tent sites for $5.50. At Windy Harbour, the camping area (☎ 9776 7056) has basic tent sites for $4.

The South Coast

To the east of the capes and the karri forests is the vast area of the South Coast, sometimes called the Great Southern. It includes the coastline from Walpole-Nornalup in the west to Cape Arid, east of Esperance. The scenery is magnificent and the main scenic road often hugs the coastline.

This large area has some of the State's best coastal parks and inland, north of Albany, are two of the best mountain parks in Australia – the 'ecological islands' of the Stirling Range, which rise abruptly 1000m above the surrounding plains and the ancient granite spires of the Porongurups.

Getting There & Away
Skywest (☎ 9334 2288) flies daily from Perth to Albany (☎ 9841 6655) and Perth to Esperance (☎ 9071 2002).

Westrail's (☎ 13 2232) daily service from Perth to Albany via the south coast ($44.70), which passes through Denmark ($39.30), takes about seven hours. Perth to Denmark, via Albany, also costs $39.30. It costs $36.70 to get to Walpole, by a combination of the *Australind* and coach.

The daily six-hour Westrail service from Perth to Albany via Williams stops daily in Mt Barker ($30.60); by this route the fare from Perth to Albany is $35.10 one way.

Westrail has a bus three times a week from Kalgoorlie to Esperance ($33.50) and an Esperance to Albany service ($45.90). Its 10-hour Perth to Esperance service ($52.60) runs via Jerramungup on Monday, via Lake Grace on Wednesday and Friday, and via Hyden on Tuesday and Thursday. On the latter services, it costs $18 to travel from Esperance to Norseman, where connections with Greyhound Pioneer can be made.

WALPOLE-NORNALUP AREA
The heavily forested **Walpole-Nornalup National Park** covers 180 sq km around the Nornalup Inlet and Walpole; it contains beaches, rugged coastline, inlets and the famous Valley of the Giants.

Scenic drives include Knoll Drive and the Valley of the Giants Rd. About 13km from Walpole via Crystal Springs is **Mandalay Beach**, where the wreck of the *Mandalay*, a barque wrecked here in 1911, can sometimes be seen protruding through the sand.

You can get more information from the Walpole tourist bureau (☎ 9840 1111) or CALM (☎ 9840 1027); both are on the South Coast Highway.

Cape to Cape Ecotours (☎ 9752 2334) runs day trips around the area for $60, which includes lunch on the Nornalup Inlet. Wilderness Cruises (☎ 9840 1036) runs daily trips through the inlets and river systems at 10 am; it charges $15/8 for adults/children.

Valley of the Giants
Four species of rare eucalypts grow within 4km of each other in this region and nowhere else in the world: red, yellow and Rates tingle (*Eucalyptus jacksonii, E. guilfoylei, E. cornuta*), in inland areas, and the red flowering gum (*E. ficifolia*), closer to the coast.

The Valley of the Giants is the best place to see the giant tingle trees. Recently an impressive **Tree Top Walk**, a 600m-long ramp structure, was built, allowing visitors to get high up into the canopy of the giant trees. At its highest point it is 40m above the ground; the views below and above are simply stunning. (It's wheelchair accessible.)

At the right end of the ramp is the entrance to the **Ancient Empire**, a boardwalk at the base of the giant trees, some of which are 16m in circumference. Children particularly love to look for the faces of 'forest giants' in the gnarled tree roots.

The site (☎ 9840 8263) is open 9 am to 5 pm, March to November, and from 8 am to

6 pm, December to February; entry to the Tree Top Walk costs $5/2/12 for adults/children/families. The Ancient Empire walk is free.

Places to Stay & Eat

There are a number of camping grounds in the Walpole-Nornalup National Park, including tent sites ($5) at Peaceful Bay, Crystal Springs and Coalmine Beach, and CALM huts at Fernhook Falls and Mt Frankland. The *Rest Point Tourist Centre* (☎ 9840 1032), perfectly sited on the Walpole Inlet, has cottages which sleep six for $95.

The *Tingle All Over Backpackers* (☎ 9840 1041) in Walpole has dorm beds for $12 – if you are lucky and find it open! There is also the *Dingo Flat YHA* (☎ 9840 8073) on Dingo Flat Rd off the Valley of the Giants Rd, 18km east of Walpole. They *say* they pick you up at Bow Bridge (there is a public phone in the local shop); rustic beds are $11.

You can get counter meals at the *Walpole Motel/Hotel* but be careful when enquiring about the 'thing' above the bar.

DENMARK (pop 1900)

Denmark, or Koorabup ('place of the black swan'), has some rare evidence of Aboriginal settlement in its Wilson Inlet – 3000-year-old fish traps. Named Denmark by an early explorer to commemorate a friend, the town was first established to supply timber for goldfields developments. About 54km west of Albany, it has some fine beaches (especially Ocean Beach for surfing) and is a good base for trips into the tingle forests.

The tourist office (☎ 9848 2055) on Strickland St provides heritage trail brochures. **Trails** include the Mokare Trail (a 3km trail along the Denmark River) and the Wilson Inlet Trail (a 6km trail that starts from the river mouth).

The **William Bay National Park**, 15km west of Denmark, has fine coastal scenery of rocks and reefs. Green's Pool and Elephants Rocks are both calm and safe for swimming.

Places to Stay

There are several caravan parks in town, the closest being the idyllic *Rivermouth Caravan Park* (☎ 9848 1262), 1km south of the town centre on Inlet Drive; tent/powered sites are $10/13 and on-site vans are from $28 for two.

The associate-YHA hostel at the Wilson Inlet Caravan Park (☎ 9848 1267), over 4km south of Denmark, isn't much chop. Beds in the dingy dorm in the park's most dilapidated building are $10 per night – four or so people could get together and get something better in town.

Edinburgh House (☎ 9848 1477, 1800 671 477) on the South Coast Highway in the centre of town is a friendly place with a large TV lounge and clean single/double en-suite rooms for $45/70.

There are many types of farmstays, B&Bs, chalets and cottages in the Denmark area; the tourist office keeps a current list.

Places to Eat

There are three bakeries: *Bill's* and *Day's Lunch Bar* on the highway, and the *Denmark* on the corner of Fig Tree Square. *Russell's Hunger Buster*, a fast food place, is near the corner of Walker and Strickland Sts and *Kettles Deli* is on the corner of the highway and Holling Rd.

Bellini's, also on Holling Rd, has a great balcony with views of the river. The food is Greek even though the name is Italian and you are in Denmark, Australia. It is open daily for lunch and dinner, except Tuesday; a meal will set you back about $20. The *Hillside Restaurant* (☎ 9848 1147) out on Inlet Drive has large fish baskets for about $20; bookings are essential.

The *Mary Rose* on North St is a quaint place with a pleasant balcony and serves tasty light meals – it also has vegetarian dishes.

MT BARKER (pop 4500)

This pleasant town is 50km north of Albany and about 64km south of the Stirling Range. The tourist bureau at 57 Lowood Rd (☎ 9851 1163) opens on weekdays from 9 am to 5 pm, Saturday from 9 am to 2 pm and Sunday from 10 am to 3 pm.

You can get a panoramic view of the area from the **Mt Barker Lookout**, 5km south of town. South-west of town is the picturesque **St Werburgh's Chapel**, constructed from local materials in 1873.

The region has a reputation for wine and there are many **wineries** with cellar sales within a few kilometres of the town – the tourist bureau has locations and opening times.

Places to Stay

The caravan park (☎ 9851 1691) on Albany Highway has tent/powered sites at $10/12 and park homes from $32 for two. The *Plantagenet Motel Hotel* (☎ 9851 1008), 9 Lowood Rd, has singles/doubles from $20/36 (in the older section) and good counter meals for around $10.

PORONGURUP & STIRLING RANGES

The beautiful **Porongurup National Park** (24 sq km) has panoramic views and scenery, large karri trees, 1100-million-year-old granite outcrops and some excellent bushwalks. Walking trails range from the short Tree in the Rock stroll and the intermediate Castle Rock walk (2 hours) to the harder Haywards and Nancy Peaks (4 hours) and the excellent Devil's Slide and Marmabup Rock (3 hours) walks. A scenic 6km drive along the park's northern edge starts at the ranger's residence.

In the **Stirling Range National Park** (1156 sq km), Toolbrunup Peak (for views and a good climb), Bluff Knoll (at 1073m, the highest peak in the range) and Toll Peak (good wildflowers) are popular half-day walks. The 96km range is noted for its spectacular colour changes through blues, reds and purples. The mountains rise abruptly from the surrounding flat and sandy plains, and the area is known for its fine flora and fauna – the Stirling Bells are especially magnificent in bloom.

For further information contact the CALM offices on Bolganup Rd, Mt Barker; Chester Pass Rd, Stirling Range; or Albany Highway, Albany.

Places to Stay & Eat

There is no camping in the Porongurups but there's a tourist park (☎ 9853 1057) in the township. There are backpacker beds at the friendly *Porongurup Shop & Tearooms* (☎ 9853 1110) for $13; this place is run by informative, seasoned travellers. The *Karribank Lodge* (☎ 9853 1022) has singles and doubles from $55 to $90.

You can camp in the Stirling Range National Park on Chester Pass Rd near the Toolbrunup Peak turn-off; call the ranger (☎ 9827 9278) for details. Facilities are limited and tent sites cost $5 for two.

The *Stirling Range Caravan Park* (☎ 9827 9229) on the northern boundary of the park is also on Chester Pass Rd. Tent/powered sites are $10/14, on-site vans $30, self-contained rammed-earth cabins $49 and chalets $67; all prices are for two people.

ALBANY (pop 20,500)

The commercial centre of the southern region, Albany is the oldest European settlement in the State, having been established shortly before Perth in 1826. The area was occupied by Aboriginal people long before and there is much evidence, especially around Oyster Harbour, of their earlier presence.

With its excellent harbour on King George Sound, Albany was until the late 1970s a thriving whaling port. When steamships started travelling between the UK and Australia, Albany was also a coaling station for ships bound for the east coast. During WWI, it was the gathering point for troopships of the 1st Australian Imperial Force (AIF) before they sailed for Egypt; the soldiers eventually fought in the Gallipoli campaign.

The coast near Albany has some of the country's most rugged and spectacular scenery.

Information

The impressive tourist bureau (☎ 9841 1088, 1800 644 088) in the old train station on Proudlove Parade is open on weekdays from 8.15 am to 5.30 pm and on weekends from 9 am to 5 pm. The CALM and RACWA offices are on the Albany Highway.

Old Buildings

Albany has some fine colonial buildings – **Stirling Terrace** is noted for its Victorian shopfronts. The 1851 **Old Gaol** on Lower Stirling Terrace is now a folk museum and is open daily from 10 am to 4.15 pm. The charge of $3.50 includes entry into the 1832 wattle-and-daub **Patrick Taylor Cottage** on Duke St, the oldest dwelling in WA, also open daily.

The **Albany Residency Museum**, opposite the Old Gaol, was originally built in the 1850s as the home of the resident magistrate; it is open daily from 10 am to 5 pm. Displays include seafaring subjects, flora and fauna and Aboriginal artefacts. Housed in another building is 'Sea & Touch', a great hands-on experience for children and adults.

Next to this museum is a full-scale replica of the brig *Amity*, the ship that brought Albany's founders to the area in 1826 ($2, children 50c).

The restored **post office** (1870) on Lower Stirling Terrace houses the Inter-Colonial Museum, with its collection of communications

WESTERN AUSTRALIA

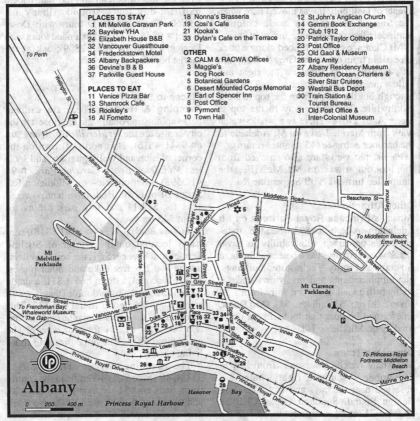

PLACES TO STAY
1 Mt Melville Caravan Park
22 Bayview YHA
24 Elizabeth House B&B
32 Vancouver Guesthouse
34 Frederickstown Motel
35 Albany Backpackers
36 Devine's B & B
37 Parkville Guest House

PLACES TO EAT
11 Venice Pizza Bar
13 Shamrock Cafe
15 Rookley's
16 Al Fornetto

18 Nonna's Brasseria
19 Cosi's Cafe
21 Kooka's
33 Dylan's Cafe on the Terrace

OTHER
2 CALM & RACWA Offices
3 Maggie's
4 Dog Rock
5 Botanical Gardens
6 Desert Mounted Corps Memorial
7 Earl of Spencer Inn
8 Post Office
9 Pyrmont
10 Town Hall

12 St John's Anglican Church
14 Gemini Book Exchange
17 Club 1912
20 Patrick Taylor Cottage
23 Post Office
25 Old Gaol & Museum
26 Brig Amity
27 Albany Residency Museum
28 Southern Ocean Charters & Silver Star Cruises
29 Westrail Bus Depot
30 Train Station & Tourist Bureau
31 Old Post Office & Inter-Colonial Museum

Albany

0   200   400 m

Princess Royal Harbour

equipment from WA's past; it is open daily from 10 am to 4 pm (admission is free).

Other historic buildings include **St John's Anglican Church**, the elegant home **Pyrmont** and the **courthouse**. A brochure ($2) detailing a walking tour of Albany's colonial buildings is available from the tourist bureau.

Views

There are some very fine views over the coast and inland from the twin peaks, **Mt Clarence** and **Mt Melville**, which overlook the town. On top of Mt Clarence is the Desert Mounted Corps Memorial, originally erected in Port Said as a memorial to the events of Gallipoli. It was moved here when the Suez Crisis (1956) made colonial reminders less than popular in Egypt.

Mt Clarence can be climbed along a track accessible from the end of Grey St East; turn left, take the first street on the right and follow the path by the water tanks. The walk is tough but the views from the top make it worthwhile. The easier way to the top is along Apex Drive. There is a whale-watch walk from Marine Drive on Mt Adelaide to the harbour entrance (45 minutes return).

Panoramic views are also enjoyed from the lookout tower on Mt Melville; the signposted turn-off is off Serpentine Rd.

Other Attractions

Albany's **Princess Royal Fortress** on Mt Adelaide was built in 1893 when the strategic port's perceived vulnerability to naval attack was recognised as a potential threat to Australia's security. The restored buildings, gun emplacements and fine views make it well worth a visit. It is open daily from 7.30 am to 5.30 pm ($3, children $1). **Dog Rock**, a deformed boulder that looks like a dog's head, is on Middleton Rd.

Organised Tours

The whale-watching season is from July to September – southern right whales are observed near the bays and coves of King George Sound. Southern Ocean Charters (☎ 9841 7176) takes trips out in the *Pamela*

to the whales (adults $20, children $12) and also operates diving, fishing, underwater photography and snorkelling tours on demand. You might also see dolphins, sea lions and seals.

Two other operators are Silver Star Cruises (☎ 9841 3333) and Spinners Charters (☎ 9841 7151). The *Silver Star* leaves the town jetty four times weekly for a 2½-hour cruise around King George Sound; the cost is $22/12 for adults/children. Spinners Charters departs from the Emu Point marina, and Southern Ocean Charters leaves from the town jetty.

Escape Tours (☎ 9841 2865) operates from the tourist bureau and has many local half/full-day tours around Albany for $30/60. There are 4WD tours with Do-a-Tour (☎ 9844 3509) and extended tours with Design a Tour (☎ 9842 2809); ask at the tourist bureau.

Places to Stay

Camping & Hostels There are caravan parks aplenty in Albany and the closest to the city centre are the *Mt Melville Caravan Park* (☎ 9841 4616), 1km north of town on the corner of Lion and Wellington Sts; and spotless *Middleton Beach Caravan Park* (☎ 98 41 3593) – our choice – on Middleton Rd, 3km east of town. Both have tent/powered sites for $12/14 and tidy park cabins for about $45 for two.

Albany Backpackers (☎ 9841 8848), centrally located on the corner of Stirling Terrace and Spencer St, is the best travellers' option – it has free cake and other pluses. With a discount, a dorm bed is $11, a single room is $20 and a twin/double (that is, 'with a friend'/'with a good friend') is $32. This place has all the necessities; staff hire mountain bikes for $12/24 for a day/week. The cafe below offers half-price pizzas to those living above.

The rambling *Bayview YHA* (☎ 9842 3388), 49 Duke St, is 400m from the centre; dorm beds cost $13, single rooms are $20, and twins and doubles are $32 for two (children are $8 extra). Staff rent out items such as surfboards ($10 per day), bicycles ($10) and kites ($2).

Guesthouses, Motels & Hotels Albany also has a number of reasonably priced guesthouses and B&B places; enquire at the tourist office. Some places on the tourist office's list are: *Parkville Guest House* (☎ 9841 3704), 136 Brunswick Rd, which charges from $25/38 for singles/doubles, including breakfast; and divine *Devines Guesthouse* (☎ 9841 8050), 20 Stirling Terrace, which charges $35/55. *Elizabeth House B&B* (☎ 9842 2734) on Festing St is good value at $28/50; and the *Vancouver Guesthouse* (☎ 9842 1071) on Stirling Terrace has similar prices.

In town there is the *Frederickstown Motel* (☎ 9841 8630), near the corner of Frederick and Spencer Sts, with singles/doubles from $62/72.

The town's finest (and most expensive) accommodation is the *Mercure Grand Hotel* (☎ 9842 1711) at Middleton Beach; rooms, with everything that opens and shuts, are from $129 to $199 (but there are all sorts of weekend and other specials).

Places to Eat
You will not starve if you wander along Stirling Terrace. *Dylan's Café on the Terrace* at No 82 has an excellent range of light meals, including hamburgers and pancakes, at reasonable prices; it is open late most nights, early for breakfast and has a takeaway section. Also on the terrace is *Kooka's* at No 204 in a restored old house, where you pay about $35 for an excellent three-course meal.

Breakfasts at *Eatcha Heart Out* at 154 York St and *Cosi's Cafe* on Peel Place are recommended by us (the tasters). The *Shamrock Cafe* on York St is a favourite of the impecunious; breakfasts are $4 and a bottomless coffee or tea is $1.60.

There are also a couple of pizza places on York St, including *Al Fornetto* and the *Venice Pizza Bar* (open daily); the latter wins our Silver Fork Award for value.

Rookley's, 36 Peel Place, has an alfresco courtyard and specialises in lunches, deli meals and fine takeaways. It is not open in the evenings. Expect to pay $5 to $7 for a tasty roll with unusual ingredients.

At Middleton Beach there is the trendy *Beachside Cafe* – with great fish & chips – and the *Middleton Beach Fish & Chips*, close to the Mercure Grand. The latter has crisp chips and a diverse catch of groper, snapper, shark and flounder.

Maggie's, 338 Middleton Rd, and *Club 1912*, 120 York St, are the latest of the late-night venues – Maggie's has bands from Thursday to Sunday. There are bands at the *Earl of Spencer Inn* on the corner of Earl and Spencer Sts on weekends.

Getting Around
Love's runs bus services around town from Monday to Friday and on Saturday morning. Buses will take you along Albany Highway from Peel Place to the main roundabout; other services go to Spencer Park, Middleton Beach, Emu Point and Bayonet Head (once a week).

You can rent bicycles from Albany Backpackers on Stirling Terrace; the cost is $12 per day. Emu Beach Caravan Park also rents out bikes (see the Places to Stay section).

AROUND ALBANY
South of Albany, off Frenchman Bay Rd, is a stunning stretch of coastline. It includes the **Gap** and **Natural Bridge** rock formations; the **Blowholes**, which are especially interesting in heavy seas when air is blown with great force through the surrounding rock; the **rock-climbing** areas of Peak Head and West Cape Howe; steep, rocky coves such as **Jimmy Newhill's Harbour** and **Salmon Holes** (popular with surfers, although these coves are considered quite dangerous); and **Frenchman Bay**, which has a caravan park, a fine swimming beach and a grassed barbecue area with plenty of shade. This coastline is dangerous; beware of king-sized waves.

Whaleworld Museum
The Whaleworld Museum at Frenchman Bay, 21km from Albany, is based at the

WESTERN AUSTRALIA

Cheynes Beach Whaling Station (which only ceased operations in November 1978). There's the rusting *Cheynes IV* whalechaser and station equipment (such as whale oil tanks) to inspect outside. The museum screens a gore-spattered film on whaling and it has harpoons, whaleboat models as well as scrimshaw (etching on whale bone and teeth).

It is open daily from 9 am to 5 pm ($5, children $2). The museum also has a superb collection of marine mammal paintings by noted US artist Richard Ellis. Listen carefully and you will hear the haunting, mournful songs of the humpbacks out at sea.

National Parks & Reserves

There are a number of excellent natural areas along the coast both west and east of Albany where you can explore many different habitats and see a variety of coastal scenery.

West Cape Howe National Park is a playground for naturalists, bushwalkers, rock climbers and anglers. **Torndirrup National Park** includes the region's two popular attractions, the Natural Bridge and the Gap, as well as the Blowholes, Jimmy Newhill's Harbour and beach, and Bald Head. Southern right whales can be seen from the cliffs during the season.

East of Albany is **Two People's Bay**, a nature reserve with a good swimming beach, scenic coastline and a small colony of noisy scrub-birds, a species once thought extinct.

Probably the best of the national parks, but the least visited, is **Waychinicup** which includes Mt Manypeaks and other granite formations. Walking in the area is currently restricted because of dieback, a fungal disease that attacks the roots of plants and causes them to rot. Its spread can be prevented by observing 'no go' road signs and by cleaning soil from your boots where you're instructed to do so.

ALBANY TO ESPERANCE (476km)

From Albany, the South Coast Highway runs north-east along the coast before turning inland to skirt the Fitzgerald River National Park and ending in Esperance.

Ongerup, a small Wheatbelt town 153km north-east of Albany, has an annual wildflower show in September/October with hundreds of local species on display. In **Jerramungup**, north-east of Albany on the South Coast Highway, you can visit an eclectic Military Museum.

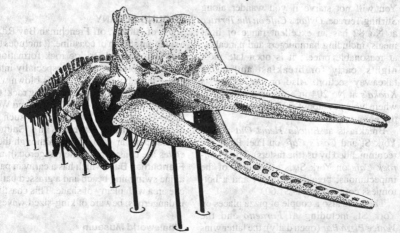

This 11m sperm whale was one of the last killed by the Cheynes Beach Whaling Company in 1978

Bremer Bay (pop 200)
This fishing and holiday town, at the western end of the Great Australian Bight, is 61km west of the South Coast Highway. It is a good spot to observe southern right whales. Information is available from the BP Roadhouse (☎ 9837 4093).

The caravan park (☎ 9837 4018) has powered sites for $14 and on-site vans for $30 for two. A nice place to stay in the Fitzgerald River National Park is *Quaalup Homestead* (☎ 9837 4124), 18km east of Bremer Bay; camping costs $10, single/double units are $47.50/60, chalets are $55 and a cottage is from $85 to $100.

Ravensthorpe & Hopetoun (pop 450)
Ravensthorpe was once the centre of the Phillips River goldfield. Copper mining followed. Nowadays, the area is dependent on farming. The ruins of a disused smelter and the Cattlin Creek copper mine are near town, and there are drives in the region from which many **wildflowers** can be seen; there is a wildflower show in the first two weeks of September. The Going Bush information centre (☎ 9838 1277) on Morgans St is open daily from 8.30 am to 5 pm.

Hopetoun, 50km south of Ravensthorpe, centres on fine beaches and bays and is the eastern gateway to the Fitzgerald River National Park. The information centre (☎ 9838 3228) is in Chatterbox Crafts on Veal St.

About 150km north of Ravensthorpe, the **Frank Hann National Park** has a range of typical sandplain flora.

Places to Stay & Eat The *Ravensthorpe Caravan Park* (☎ 9838 1050) has tent/powered sites for $10/11 and on-site vans at $25 for two. The *Palace Motor Hotel* (☎ 9838 1005), classified by the National Trust, has backpacker beds for $20; single/double motel units are $38/48.

The *Hopetoun Caravan Park* (☎ 9838 3096) has tent/powered sites for $11/13 and on-site vans for $27 for two. The *Port Hotel* (☎ 9838 3053) on Veal St has singles/doubles for $15/30 ($10 for backpackers).

At Munglinup, 90km east of Ravensthorpe, is the *Singing Winds* (☎ 9075 1018), which provides B&B at reasonable rates for long-distance cyclists.

There is a sumptuous cake selection at the *Country Kitchen* in Ravensthorpe and at *Marg's Cafe* in Hopetoun.

Fitzgerald River National Park
This 3300 sq km park contains beautiful coastline, sand plains, the rugged Barren mountain range and deep, wide river valleys. The bushwalking is excellent and the wilderness route from Fitzgerald Beach to Whalebone Beach is recommended – there is no trail and no water but camping is permitted. Clean your shoes at each end of the walk to discourage the spread of dieback.

The park contains half of the orchid species in WA (over 80 species, 70 of which occur nowhere else), 22 mammal species, 200 species of birds and 1700 species of plants. It is also the home of those floral marvels the royal hakea and Quaalup bell, and southern right whales can be seen offshore (August to September).

You can gain access to the park from Bremer Bay and Hopetoun or from the South Coast Highway along Devils Creek, Quiss and Hamersley Rds. There is accommodation in Bremer Bay, Quaalup and Hopetoun.

ESPERANCE (pop 8600)
Esperance, or the Bay of Isles, has become a popular resort due to its temperate climate, magnificent coastal scenery, blue waters, good fishing and dazzling white beaches. Distinctive Norfolk Island pines line the town's foreshore. It is 721km south-east of Perth and 200km south of Norseman.

Although the first settlers came to the area in 1863, it was during the gold rush in the 1890s that the town really became established as a port. When the gold fever subsided, Esperance went into a state of suspended animation until after WWII. In the 1950s, it was discovered that adding missing trace elements to the soil around Esperance restored it to fertility; since then the town has rapidly become an agricultural centre.

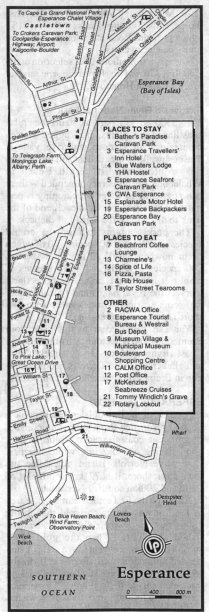

PLACES TO STAY
1 Bather's Paradise Caravan Park
3 Esperance Travellers' Inn Hotel
4 Blue Waters Lodge YHA Hostel
5 Esperance Seafront Caravan Park
6 CWA Esperance
15 Esplanade Motor Hotel
19 Esperance Backpackers
20 Esperance Bay Caravan Park

PLACES TO EAT
7 Beachfront Coffee Lounge
13 Charmeine's
14 Spice of Life
16 Pizza, Pasta & Rib House
18 Taylor Street Tearooms

OTHER
2 RACWA Office
8 Esperance Tourist Bureau & Westrail Bus Depot
9 Museum Village & Municipal Museum
10 Boulevard Shopping Centre
11 CALM Office
12 Post Office
17 McKenzies Seabreeze Cruises
21 Tommy Windich's Grave
22 Rotary Lookout

Information

The helpful tourist bureau (☎ 9071 2330) on Dempster St is open daily from 9 am to 5 pm and can book tours to the islands and the surrounding national parks. The post office is on the corner of Andrew and Dempster Sts.

Things to See & Do

The **municipal museum** contains the tourist bureau and various old buildings, including a gallery, smithy's forge, cafe and craft shop. The museum itself, between the Esplanade and Dempster St, is open daily from 1.30 to 4.30 pm. There's also a Skylab display – Skylab, a US space station which was launched in May 1973, crashed to earth in 1979 right over Esperance.

The 36km scenic **Great Ocean Drive** includes vistas from Observatory Point and the Rotary Lookout on Wireless Hill; the popular swimming spots of Twilight Bay and Picnic Cove; and the **Pink Lake**, stained by a salt-tolerant algae called *Dunalella salina*.

There are about 100 small islands in the **Recherche Archipelago**, home to colonies of fur seals, penguins and a wide variety of water birds. There are regular trips to Woody Island, a wildlife sanctuary; for more information see the Organised Tours section.

Organised Tours

Vacation Country Tours (☎ 9071 2227) runs tours around Esperance, including a town-and-coast tour for $22 and a Cape Le Grand tour for $38. More adventurous alternatives are Aussie Bight Expeditions (☎ 9071 7778) which, as the name suggests, have 4WD safaris to secluded beaches and bays, and to national parks.

Tours on the waters of the Bay of Isles are a must. McKenzies Marine's *Seabreeze* (☎ 9071 5757) regularly tours the bay ($39, children $16). Expect to see NZ fur seals, Australian sea lions, sea eagles, Cape Barren geese, common dolphins and a host of other wildlife on these cruises. McKenzies operates the daily ferry to Woody Island in January and February ($25, children $13). Book tours at its Esplanade office.

The Esperance Diving Academy (☎ 9071

5111) conducts dive charters and diving courses. It has island cruises in its *Southern Image* over the Christmas school holidays ($28, children $14).

Places to Stay
There are half a dozen caravan parks around Esperance that provide camp sites and on-site vans and cabins; the usual rates for tent/powered sites are $12/14, on-site vans are $25 and park cabins are $40 for two.

The most central of the parks are the *Esperance Bay Caravan Park* (☎ 9071 2237) on the corner of the Esplanade and Harbour Rd, near the wharf, and the *Esperance Seafront Caravan Park* (☎ 9071 1251) on the corner of Goldfields and Norseman Rds. The well-kept and efficiently run *Crokers* (☎ 9071 4100), 629 Harbour Rd, deservedly wins accommodation awards.

The large, popular *Blue Waters Lodge YHA* (☎ 9071 1040) on Goldfields Rd is 2km north of the centre. It charges $14 for dorm beds and $32 for single and twin rooms. It has a nice breakfast area with views over the water.

Also good value is the tidy, comfortable *Esperance Backpackers* (☎ 9071 4724, 018 93 4541), 14 Emily St. It has all the facilities: dorm beds for $14, and twins and doubles for $30. Staff run tours for the guests: trips to the national parks (with 'scurfing' included) are $40, while fishing tours are $25.

The well-run *Esperance Travellers' Inn Hotel* (☎ 9071 1677) on the corner of Goldfields Rd and Phyllis St has clean singles/doubles for $40/50. The *CWA Esperance* (☎ 9071 1364), 23 the Esplanade, has units from $25 to $40; and the *Esperance Chalet Village* (☎ 9071 1861), 6km east of town on Frank Freeman Drive, off Goldfields Rd, has self-contained A-frame chalets from $50 to $95 (depending on the season).

There are many motels with rates from about $55/70 for singles/doubles; the tourist bureau has a list of these and local B&Bs.

Places to Eat
The town has a good number of cafes. Sip at the *Beachfront Coffee Lounge, Taylor Street* *Tearooms* or the *Village Cafe*; the latter is in the museum enclave. The best known of the takeaways is *Pizza, Pasta & Rib House* on the corner of William and Dempster Sts, but there are also a number of fish and chip places. If you like cooking fish then buy fillets of gnanagi – coat them in flour and lightly cook in butter with a sprinkling of lemon and pepper.

Coffee lounges serving meals include *Island Fare* in the Boulevard shopping centre and *Charmeine's* in the Dutton Arcade, Dempster St. The *Spice of Life* on Andrew St has a varied health-food menu including zucchini slice, vegetarian pasties and Lebanese rolls chock full of salad.

Getting Around
There is a taxi rank by the post office. Hire bicycles from Esperance Mini Golf (☎ 9071 5875) on the Esplanade for $6 per hour ($22 daily).

AROUND ESPERANCE
There are four national parks in the Esperance region. The closest and most popular is **Cape Le Grand**, extending from about 20km to 60km east of Esperance. The park has spectacular coastal scenery, some good beaches and excellent walking tracks. There are fine views from **Frenchman's Peak**, at the western end of the park, and good fishing, camping and swimming at Lucky Bay and Le Grand Beach.

Farther east is the coastal **Cape Arid National Park**, at the start of the Great Australian Bight and on the fringes of the Nullarbor Plain. It is a rugged and isolated park with abundant flora and fauna, good bushwalking, beaches and camp sites. Most of the park is only accessible by 4WD, although the Poison Creek and Thomas River sites are accessible in normal vehicles.

Other national parks include **Stokes**, 92km west of Esperance, with an inlet, long beaches and rocky headlands; and **Peak Charles**, 130km north. For more information on all parks, contact CALM (☎ 9071 3733), Dempster St, Esperance.

If you are going into the national parks,

WESTERN AUSTRALIA

take plenty of water, as there is little or no fresh water in most of these areas. Also, be wary of spreading dieback; get information about its prevention from park rangers.

Places to Stay & Eat
Limited-facility tent sites are $8 at Cape Le Grand (☎ 9075 9022) and free at Cape Arid (☎ 9075 0055); apply for permits at the park entrances. There are basic camp sites at Stokes ($8) and Peak Charles (free; ☎ 9076 8541).

Between Cape Le Grand and Cape Arid is the *Orleans Bay Caravan Park* (☎ 9075 0033), a friendly place to stay; sandy tent/powered sites are $11/13, cabins are from $30 for two and chalets are $50 for four.

Just off Merivale Rd, on the way to Cape Le Grand, tasty cakes and tortes are available from *Merivale Farm*.

The Midlands

This huge area stretches from the base of the Pilbara down to the Wheatbelt towns some 300km or so south of the Great Eastern Highway. Much of it is commonly referred to as the Wheatbelt. The area is noted for its unusual rock formations (the best known of which is the somewhat overrated Wave Rock near Hyden), many Aboriginal sites and *gnamma* (water holes), and magnificent displays of wildflowers in spring.

WILDFLOWER WAY
The best place to see the famous carpet of wildflowers, mainly everlastings, is in the Midlands, north of Perth. Follow the Great Northern Highway (SH95) via New Norcia to Dalwallinu. From here, turn due north on the Wildflower Way to Mullewa. You can return to Perth on the Midland Road (SH116) via Mingenew or on the Brand Highway (Highway 1) via flora-rich sand-plain parks.

New Norcia (pop 80)
The small, meditative community of New Norcia is an incongruity, Australia's very own setting for Umberto Eco's *The Name of the Rose*. Established as a Spanish Benedictine mission in 1846, it has changed little since and boasts a fine collection of buildings with classic Spanish architecture.

The building housing the museum and art gallery (both worth seeing for their old paintings, manuscripts and religious artefacts) also contains the tourist office (☎ 9654 8056). Daily tours of the monastery ($10, children $5) take in the interior of chapels and other cloistered and secret places. You can buy a snack of sourdough or olive bread at the museum.

Also at the museum, you can get the *New Norcia Heritage Trail* brochure ($2) which traces the development of the settlement. Just past the museum is the historic *New Norcia Hotel* (☎ 9654 8034), which has interesting décor, including a grand staircase; singles/doubles here cost $33/50. Benedictine monks still live and work in New Norcia. You can experience monastery life by staying in their guesthouse; the cost is $40 per person for bed and all meals.

Midlands Scenic Roads
To the north of New Norcia is **Moora**, a farming community in an area known for its colourful spring wildflowers. In the nearby Berkshire Valley, an old cottage and flour mill built in the mid-19th century have been restored and now operate as a museum (☎ 9654 9040), open on Sunday from noon to 4 pm.

Towns such as **Dalwallinu**, **Perenjori**, **Morawa** and **Mullewa** are part of the Wildflower Way – famous for its brilliant spring display of wildflowers, including wreath leschenaultia, foxgloves, everlastings and wattles. This area is the gateway to the Murchison goldfields; there are gold-mining centres and ghost towns near Perenjori.

The return option is SH116 farther west, known locally as the Midlands Scenic Way. It's a good alternative route for travel between Perth and Geraldton – the scenery is more interesting than along the Brand Highway and there are a number of small towns along the way. At **Watheroo**, the old

Watheroo Station Tavern (☎ 9651 7007) offers accommodation, meals and activities such as bushwalking, wildflower walks, tennis and horse-riding. It's worth the detour.

Coorow is 262km north of Perth and nearby is the **Alexander Morrison National Park**. **Carnamah** is noted for its bird life. It is near the Yarra Yarra Lakes.

Mingenew has an historical museum in an old primary school. The tourist centre (☎ 9928 1081) is on Midlands Rd.

GREAT NORTHERN HIGHWAY

Although most people heading for the Pilbara and the Kimberley travel up the coast, the Great Northern Highway is much more direct. The highway extends from Perth to Newman and then skirts the eastern edge of the Pilbara on its way to Port Hedland; the road is sealed all the way. The total distance is 1636km – longer if you take the gravel detour through Marble Bar.

The highway is not the most interesting in Australia, mainly passing through flat and featureless country. The Murchison goldfields and towns of Mt Magnet, Cue, Meekatharra and Mt Newman punctuate the monotony.

Getting There & Away

Skywest (☎ 13 1300) has flights from Perth to Mt Magnet, Cue and Meekatharra. Greyhound Pioneer (☎ 13 2030) goes from Perth to Port Hedland on Friday, Wednesday and Sunday. Westrail (☎ 13 2232) has a weekly service from Perth to Meekatharra ($67.30), stopping at Mt Magnet ($56) and Cue ($60.50).

Mt Magnet Area

Gold was found at Mt Magnet in the late 19th century and mining is still the town's lifeblood. Some 11km north of town are the ruins of **Lennonville**, once a busy town. There are some interesting old buildings of solid stone in **Cue**, 80km north of Mt Magnet, and **Walga Rock**, 48km to the west, is a large monolith with a gallery of Aboriginal art (walga means 'ochre painting' in the local Warragi language).

Wilgie Mia, 64km north-west of Cue via Glen Station, is the site of a 30,000-year-old Aboriginal red ochre quarry.

The oft-unattended *Mt Magnet Caravan Park* (☎ 9963 4198) has tent/powered sites for $7/13 and shocking, leaky on-site vans. There are a couple of hotels in Mt Magnet's main street. *Cue Caravan Park* (☎ 9963 1107) has sites at $7/12 and the *Murchison Club* (☎ 9963 1020), Austin St, also in Cue, has singles/doubles for an inflated $80/95.

Meekatharra (pop 1270)

Meekatharra is still a mining centre. At one time it was a railhead for cattle brought down from the Northern Territory and the east Kimberley along the Canning Stock Route. There are ruins of various old gold towns and operations in the area. From Meekatharra, you can travel south via Wiluna and Leonora to the Kalgoorlie goldfields. It's over 700km to Kal, more than half of it on unsealed road.

The *Meekatharra Caravan Park* (☎ 9981 1253) has tent/powered sites at $11/12.50 for two. The *Royal Mail Hotel* (☎ 9981 1148) on Main St charges $55/75 a single/double.

GREAT EASTERN HIGHWAY

An earthquake in 1968 badly damaged **Meckering**, a small town 24km west of Cunderdin. The museum on Forrest St in **Cunderdin** has exhibits relating to that event, as well as an interesting collection of farm machinery and equipment. The museum is in an old pumping station formerly used on the goldfields water pipeline.

Merredin (pop 3500), the largest centre in the Wheatbelt, is 260km east of Perth. It has a tourist centre (☎ 9041 1666) on Barrack St. The 1920s train station is now a charming museum with a vintage 1897 locomotive and an old signal box.

There are interesting **rock formations** around Merredin: Kangaroo Rock is 17km south and Burracoppin Rock is to the north. Sandford Rocks is 11km east of Westonia.

Although the gold quickly gave out, **Southern Cross**, farther east, was the first gold-rush town on the WA goldfields. The big rush soon moved east to Coolgardie and

Kalgoorlie. Like the town itself, the streets of Southern Cross are named after the stars and constellations. The **Yilgarn History Museum** in the courthouse has local displays which are worth a visit. If you follow the continuation of Antares St south for 3km, you'll see a couple of active open-cut mines.

Southern Cross, some 368km east of Perth, is really the end of the Wheatbelt and the start of the desert; when travelling by train the change is noticeable. In the spring, the sandy plains around Southern Cross are carpeted with wildflowers.

Places to Stay & Eat
The *Cunderdin Motor Hotel* (☎ 9635 1104) on Olympic Ave has singles/doubles for $40/60.

The *Merredin Caravan Park* (☎ 9041 1535) on the Great Eastern Highway has tent/powered sites at $10/13 and on-site vans for $28. The *Merredin Motel* (☎ 9041 1886) on Gamenya Ave costs $40/50. The *Commercial Hotel* on Barrack St has counter meals, and the *Gum Tree* in the Merredin Motel is a good choice for dinner.

In Southern Cross, there is a caravan park (☎ 9049 1212) on Coolgardie Rd, two hotels on Antares St and a motel on Canopus St. The *Palace Hotel* (☎ 9049 1555) on Antares St has been restored and is a great place to stay, with real country charm, a large bar and restaurant; rooms are $30 per person.

WAVE ROCK & HYDEN (pop 190)
Wave Rock is 350km south-east of Perth and 3km from the tiny town of Hyden. It's a real surfer's delight – the perfect wave, 15m high and frozen in solid rock marked with different coloured bands. But it hardly justifies the 700km return trip from Perth, although many people make it in a day.

Other interesting rock formations in the area bear names like the **Breakers**, **Hippo's Yawn** and the **Humps**. **Mulka's Cave** has Aboriginal rock paintings. The information centre (☎ 9880 5182) is in the Wave Rock Wildflower Shop.

At Wave Rock, the *Wave Rock Caravan Park* (☎ 9880 5022) has tent/powered sites

for $9/12 and on-site cabins for $52. The revamped *Hyden Hotel* (☎ 9880 5052) on Lynch St has singles/doubles for $50/70. The nearest backpackers is *Wave-a-Way* (☎ 9880 5103), on the corner of Kalgarin Lake and Worlands Rds in Kalgarin, a 30-minute drive south-west of the rock; dorm beds are $15.

A Westrail (☎ 13 2232) bus to Hyden via the town of Bruce Rock leaves Perth on Tuesday and returns on Thursday; the trip costs $30.60 one way and takes five hours.

OTHER WHEATBELT TOWNS
Most sizeable Wheatbelt towns have a caravan park, a pub that serves counter meals, a motel, a takeaway, a trio of wheat silos, a pervading ennui and little else.

There is a fine rock formation, known as **Kokerbin** (Aboriginal for 'high place'), 45km west of Bruce Rock. **Corrigin**, 68km south of Bruce Rock, has a folk museum, a 'Buried Bone' canine cemetery (can you believe it?), a craft cottage and a miniature railway. **Jilakin Rock** is 18km from Kulin, while farther south-east there's **Lake Grace**, near the eponymous lake.

Narrogin, 189km south-east of Perth, is an agricultural centre with a courthouse museum, a railway heritage park and the **Albert Facey Homestead**, 39km to the east and close to Wickepin, which is well worth a visit, especially if you have read Facey's popular book *A Fortunate Life*. The helpful Narrogin tourist centre, staffed by volunteers, (☎ 9881 2064) is on Egerton St.

Some 26km north of Narrogin is the magnificent **Dryandra Woodland**, a remnant of the open eucalypt woodlands which once covered most of the Wheatbelt. It now supports many animal species, including numbats, and is good for bird-watching, walking and, in season, wildflowers.

Dumbleyung, south-east of Narrogin, also has a museum. Near the town is the lake upon which Donald Campbell broke the world water-speed record (444.66 km/h) in 1964; today it hosts a variety of bird life.

Wagin, 229km south-east of Perth, has a kitsch 15m-high fibreglass ram (a tribute both to the surrounding merino industry and civic bad taste). It is the biggest in the southern hemisphere – are there actually more? The Wagin tourist centre (☎ 9861 1177) on Arthur Rd will reveal more regional delights.

There is bushwalking around **Puntapin Rock** and **Mt Latham** (called 'Badjarning' in an Aboriginal dialect), both 6km from Wagin.

Katanning, south of Wagin, has a large Muslim community (Christmas Islanders), and a mosque built in 1980. The old flour mill on Clive St houses the tourist centre (☎ 9821 2634); it is open on weekdays from 10 am to 4 pm, and Saturday from 10 am to noon.

Southern Outback

The Southern Outback is a vast area stretching from the goldfields city of Kalgoorlie-Boulder (and the gold and nickel towns to the north and south) all the way across to South Australia and the Northern Territory. It includes the long and lonely Eyre Highway and the Trans-Australia Railway which link WA to the eastern States.

Fifty years after its establishment in 1829, the Western Australian colony was still going nowhere, so the government in Perth was delighted when gold was discovered at Southern Cross in 1887. That first strike petered out quickly, but more discoveries followed and WA profited from the gold boom for the rest of the century. Gold finally gave WA the population to make it viable in its own right, rather than being just a distant offshoot of the east-coast colonies.

The major strikes were made in 1892 at Coolgardie and nearby Kalgoorlie, but in the goldfields area today Kalgoorlie is the only large town remaining.

Coolgardie's period of prosperity lasted only until 1905 and many other gold towns went from nothing to populations of 10,000 then back to nothing in just 10 years. Nevertheless, the towns capitalised on their prosperity while it lasted, as the many magnificent public buildings grandly attest.

Life on the early goldfields was terribly hard. This area of WA is extremely dry – rainfall is erratic and never high. Even the little rain that does fall quickly disappears into the porous soil. Many early gold-seekers, driven more by enthusiasm than common sense, died of thirst while seeking the elusive mineral. Others succumbed to diseases in the unhygienic shanty towns. The supply of water to the goldfields by pipeline in 1903 was a major breakthrough and ensured the continuation of mining.

Today, Kalgoorlie is the main goldfields centre and mines still operate there. Elsewhere, a string of fascinating ghost and near-ghost towns and modern nickel mines make a visit to WA's gold country a must.

COOLGARDIE (pop 1260)
A popular pause in the long journey across the Nullarbor, and also the turn-off for Kalgoorlie, Coolgardie really is a ghost of its former self. You only have to glance at the huge town hall and post office building to appreciate the size that Coolgardie once was.

Gold was discovered here in 1892, and by the turn of the century the population had boomed to 15,000. The gold then petered out and the town withered away just as quickly. However, there's still plenty to interest the visitor and improved mining techniques have seen a resurgence in the population.

The tourist office (☎ 9026 6090) in the Warden's Court on Bayley St is open daily from 9 am to 5 pm.

Historical Buildings
The many historical markers scattered in and around Coolgardie describe the past history of its buildings and sites. The **Goldfields Exhibition**, in the same building as the tourist bureau, is open daily from 9 am to 5 pm and has a fascinating display of goldfields memorabilia. You can even find out about former US president Herbert Hoover's days on the WA goldfields. It's worth the $3/1 entry for adults/children, which includes a film shown at the tourist bureau.

The **train station** also operates as a

museum, and there you can learn the incredible story of the miner who was trapped 300m underground by floodwater in 1907 and rescued by divers 10 days later.

Warden Finnerty's Residence, restored by the National Trust, is open daily from 1 to 4 pm and from 10 am to noon on Sunday, but is closed on Monday ($2).

One kilometre west of Coolgardie is the **town cemetery**, which includes many old graves such as that of explorer Ernest Giles (1835-97). It's said that 'one half of the population buried the other half' due to unsanitary conditions and violence.

Places to Stay & Eat

The *Coolgardie Caravan Park* (☎ 9026 6009), 99 Bayley St, has excellent tent/powered sites for $9/12 and on-site vans for $32. There is budget accommodation at the *Goldrush Lodge* (☎ 9026 6446), 75 Bayley St, with singles/doubles for $25/35. The *Denver City Hotel* (☎ 9026 6031) on Bayley St has rooms for $30/45 and the *Coolgardie Motor Inne* (☎ 9026 6031) on Bayley St has good rooms for $55/70.

The *Denver City* does counter lunches and teas and the pizza shop next door has the doughy things from $12 to $18.

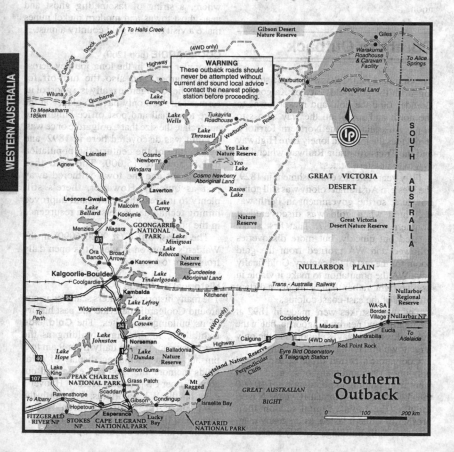

Getting There & Away

Greyhound Pioneer (☎ 13 2030) passes through Coolgardie on the Perth to Adelaide run; the one-way fare from Perth to Coolgardie is $85, and from there to Adelaide it's $207. Perth Goldfields Express (☎ 9021 2655) runs on weekdays from Kalgoorlie to Coolgardie; the fare is $2.75.

The *Prospector* train from Perth to Kalgoorlie stops at Bonnie Vale train station, 14km away, daily except Saturday; the one-way fare from Perth is $56.50, including a meal. For bookings call the tourist bureau or Westrail (☎ 9326 2222).

KALGOORLIE-BOULDER (pop 28,000)

Kalgoorlie ('Kal' to the locals) is a real surprise – a prosperous, humming metropolis. It is a raw city exuding all the atmosphere of a frontier mining town. Tattoos, 'skimpies' (scantily clad bar staff), gambling, brothels, Harley Davidsons and mass consumption of alcohol are *de rigueur*.

The longest-lasting and most successful of WA's gold towns, Kalgoorlie rose to prominence later than Coolgardie. In 1893, Paddy Hannan, a prospector from way back, set out from Coolgardie for another gold strike but stopped at the site of Kal and found enough surface gold to spark another rush.

As in so many places, it became increasingly harder to retrieve surface gold, but at Kal the miners went deeper and more and more gold was found. There weren't the story-book chunky nuggets of solid gold – Kal's gold had to be extracted from the rocks by costly and complex processes of grinding, roasting and chemical action – but there was plenty of the mineral.

Kalgoorlie quickly reached fabled heights of prosperity, and the enormous and magnificent public buildings constructed around the turn of the century are evidence of its fabulous wealth. After WWI, however, increasing production costs and static gold prices led to Kal's slow but steady decline.

Kal is the largest producer of gold in Australia, thanks in part to new technology which has allowed the mining of lower-grade deposits. The price of gold has recently slumped, however, and it is not known what the future effect will be on the city. Large mining conglomerates have been at the forefront of new open-cut mining operations in the Golden Mile – gone are the old headframes and corrugated iron homes. Mining, pastoral development and a busy tourist trade ensure Kal's continuing importance as an outback centre.

Orientation

Although Kalgoorlie sprang up close to Paddy Hannan's original find, the mining emphasis soon shifted a few kilometres away to the Golden Mile, a square mile that was one of the wealthiest gold-mining areas for its size in the world. The satellite town of Boulder, 5km south of Kal, developed to service this area. The two towns amalgamated in 1989 into Kalgoorlie-Boulder city.

Kalgoorlie itself is a grid of broad, tree-lined streets. The main street, Hannan St, is flanked by imposing buildings and is wide enough to turn a camel train – a necessity in turn-of-the-century goldfields towns. You'll find most of the hotels, restaurants and offices on or close to Hannan St.

Information

There's a helpful tourist centre (☎ 9021 1966), on the corner of Hannan and Cassidy Sts, where you can get a free map of Kal; a number of maps of other areas are for sale. It is open on weekdays from 8.30 am to 5 pm and on weekends from 9 am to 5 pm. Kal's daily newspaper is the *Kalgoorlie Miner* ($0.60).

Kal can get very hot in December and January; overall the cool winter months are the best time to visit. From late August to the end of September, however, the town is packed because of wildflower tours and the local horse races, and accommodation of any type can be difficult to find.

The RACWA office (☎ 9021 1511) is on the corner of Porter and Hannan Sts.

Hannans North Tourist Mine

This mine is one of Kal's biggest tourist attractions. You can take the lift-cage down

WESTERN AUSTRALIA

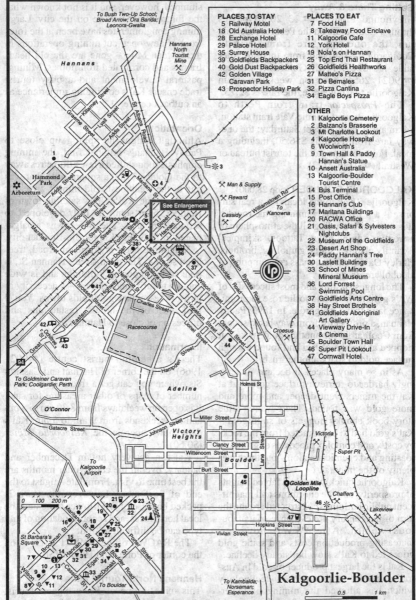

To Bush Two-Up School;
Broad Arrow; Ora Banda;
Leonora-Gwalia

Hannans North Tourist Mine

Hannans

Hammond Park

Arboretum

See Enlargement

Kalgoorlie

Man & Supply

Reward

Cassidy

To Kanowna

Williamstown Rd

Eastern Bypass Road

Croesus

Racecourse

To Goldminer Caravan Park; Coolgardie; Perth

O'Connor

Adeline

Hampden Street

Holmes St

To Kalgoorlie Airport

Victory Heights

Johnson Street

Miller Street

Clancy Street

Wittenoom Street

Burt Street

Boulder

Lane Street

Victoria

Super Pit

Golden Mile Loopline

Chaffers

Lakeview

To Kambalda;
Norseman;
Esperance

Vivian Street

Hopkins Street

St Barbara's Square

To Boulder

0   100   200 m

0   0.5   1 km

Kalgoorlie-Boulder

PLACES TO STAY
5 Railway Motel
18 Old Australia Hotel
28 Exchange Hotel
29 Palace Hotel
35 Surrey House
39 Goldfields Backpackers
40 Gold Dust Backpackers
42 Golden Village Caravan Park
43 Prospector Holiday Park

PLACES TO EAT
7 Food Hall
8 Takeaway Food Enclave
11 Kalgoorlie Cafe
12 York Hotel
19 Nola's on Hannan
25 Top End Thai Restaurant
26 Goldfields Healthworks
27 Matteo's Pizza
31 De Bernales
32 Pizza Cantina
34 Eagle Boys Pizza

OTHER
1 Kalgoorlie Cemetery
2 Balzano's Brasserie
3 Mt Charlotte Lookout
4 Kalgoorlie Hospital
6 Woolworth's
9 Town Hall & Paddy Hannan's Statue
10 Ansett Australia
13 Kalgoorlie-Boulder Tourist Centre
14 Bus Terminal
15 Post Office
16 Hannan's Club
17 Maritana Buildings
20 RACWA Office
21 Oasis, Safari & Sylvesters Nightclubs
22 Museum of the Goldfields
23 Desert Art Shop
24 Paddy Hannan's Tree
30 Laslett Buildings
33 School of Mines Mineral Museum
36 Lord Forrest Swimming Pool
37 Goldfields Arts Centre
38 Hay Street Brothels
41 Goldfields Aboriginal Art Gallery
44 Viewway Drive-In & Cinema
45 Boulder Town Hall
46 Super Pit Lookout
47 Cornwall Hotel

into the bowels of the earth and make a tour around the drives and crosscuts of the mine, guided by an ex-miner.

The $15 (children $7.50, family $38) entry covers the underground tour, an audio-visual, a tour of the surface workings, and a gold pour. Underground tours are run daily (according to demand and more regularly during high seasons) and the complex is open daily from 9.30 am to 4.30 pm. Fully enclosed shoes must be worn underground.

Golden Mile Loopline Railway

You can make an interesting loop around the Golden Mile by catching the 'Rattler', a ramshackle tourist train complete with commentary, which makes an hour-long trip daily at 10 am. On Sunday it also leaves at 11.45 am. It departs from the Boulder train station (☎ 9021 7077), passing the old mining works ($9, children $5).

Museum of the Goldfields

The impressive Ivanhoe mine headframe at the north-eastern end of Hannan St marks the entrance to this excellent museum. It is open daily from 10 am to 4.30 pm (entry by donation) and has a wide range of exhibits, including an underground gold vault and historic photographs. The tiny **British Arms Hotel** (the narrowest hotel in Australia) is part of the museum.

Other Attractions

Kalgoorlie has a legal **two-up school** in a corrugated-iron amphitheatre; it is 6km out along the Menzies road – follow the signs from Hannan St. A lot of money changes hands in this frenetic Australian gambling game, where two coins are tossed and bets are placed on the heads or tails result. It is open from 4 pm until after dark.

A few blocks north-west of Hannan St is **Hay St**, one of Kal's more famous 'attractions'. Although it's quietly ignored in tourist brochures, this is a block-long strip of brothels where working ladies beckon passing men to their true-blue (sometimes pink) galvanised-iron doorways. A blind eye has been turned to this activity for so long

that it has become an accepted, historical part of the town.

The **Mt Charlotte Lookout** and the town's reservoir are only 200m from the north-eastern end of Hannan St. The view over town is good but there's little to see of the reservoir, which is covered to limit evaporation.

The **Super Pit** lookout, just off the Eastern Bypass Road near Boulder, gives a good insight into modern mining practices; it is open daily from 6 am to 6 pm (but is closed when blasting is in progress).

Along Hannan St, you'll find the imposing **town hall** and the equally impressive **post office**. There's an art gallery upstairs in the decorative town hall, while outside is a replica of a statue of Paddy Hannan holding a water bag. The original is inside the town hall, safe from nocturnal spray-painters.

On Outridge Terrace is **Paddy Hannan's tree**, marking the spot where the first gold strike was made. **Hammond Park**, a small fauna reserve with a miniature Bavarian castle, is open daily from 9 am to 5 pm. Not far away is a pleasant, shady **arboretum**.

Organised Tours

Goldrush Tours (☎ 9021 2954) is the main tour operator in Kal. It has tours of Kal ($35), Coolgardie and nearby ghost towns. There's also a gold-detector tour for avid fossickers, and August and September wildflower tours. Book through the tourist centre or through the Goldrush Tours offices on St Barbara's Square and on Boulder Rd.

Geoff Smith's Bush Tours (☎ 9021 2669) include the yarns and lore of the bushies. Also recommended are Geoff Stokes' (☎ 9093 3745) Aboriginal bush tours.

You can see the Golden Mile mining operations from above with Goldfields Air Services (☎ 9093 2116) and AAA Charters (☎ 9021 6980); flights cost from $25 per person (minimum of two).

Places to Stay

Camping & Hostels There are a number of caravan parks in Kal; all prices below are for two people. The closest to the city centre are the *Golden Village Caravan Park* (☎ 9021 4162), 406 Hay St, 2km south-west of the train station, which has tent/powered sites for $14/17.50, and chalets and villas for $65 ($70 in peak season); and the *Prospector Holiday Park* (☎ 9021 2524) on the Great Eastern Highway, with tent and powered sites for $15, and standard and en-suite cabins for $42/48. The Prospector has a pool, a grassed area for campers and a campers' kitchen – it's one of the best in WA and gets a thumbs-up from us.

There are two good purpose-built hostels on Hay St; both pick up travellers from the bus or train on request. *Goldfields Backpackers* (☎ 9091 1482, 017 110 001) at No 166 has a pool, fully equipped kitchen and comfy TV lounge; dorm beds (with comforts such as linen, mirrors and towel racks) are $15, doubles are from $36 to $38 and trios are $18 per person. The character-filled *homestay* (☎ 9091 1482), next door at No 164, is based in a former brothel; B&B rooms cost $30/50.

The *Gold Dust Backpackers* (☎ 9091 3737) at No 192 is similar to Goldfields Backpackers in facilities; dorm beds are $15, twins $30, doubles $35 and triples $45. *Surrey House* (☎ 9021 1340), 9 Boulder Rd, has shared rooms for $20 per person; it's an option if the purpose-built places are full.

Hotels & Motels There are several pleasantly old-fashioned hotels right in the centre of Kal, including the *Palace Hotel* (☎ 9021 2788), on the corner of Maritana and Hannan Sts, with en-suite singles/doubles for $40/60. The *Exchange Hotel* (☎ 9021 2833), also on the corner of Maritana and Hannan Sts, has rooms from $35/50; it is well placed in the heart of town. Also good is the *Old Australia Hotel* (☎ 9021 1320) diagonally opposite the Palace; it charges from $70/85.

Perhaps the town's nicest accommodation is the *Railway Motel* (☎ 9088 0000), 51 Forrest St; standard rooms are $124, rooms with kitchenettes $130, and deluxe spa units $145 (all rooms are $30 less on weekends).

Places to Eat
The tourist office produces a small restaurant guide – a good place to start. There is a food hall on Brookman St with a selection of about six types of food; it is open from 11.30 am to 2.30 pm and from 5 to 9 pm.

On Wilson St, between Brookman and Hannan Sts, is a small enclave of takeaway places, including the *Fu Wah* Chinese restaurant, a bakery and a takeaway *Pizza Hut*. At 277 Hannan St is the *Kalgoorlie Cafe*, which has burger-type fast food. For pizza, try *Pizza Cantina*, 211 Hannan St; *Matteo's* at No 123; or *Eagle Boys* on Boulder Rd.

There are plenty of counter-meal pubs (where they skimp on clothing and not the servings), restaurants and cafes in Kal, particularly along Hannan St. The *York Hotel* on Hannan St has counter meals in its Steak House for $14, and meals in the saloon bar for around $7.50.

Goldfields Healthworks, 75 Hannan St, has a lunch bar with an interesting menu – most of it vegetarian. Nearby, the *Top End Thai*, 71 Hannan St, is good for a splurge – it has a wide range of prawn, curry and noodle dishes which cost from $14 to $18. Across the road at No 84 is *Nola's on Hannan*, a BYO Italian place with hearty soups for $4.50 and daily pasta specials from $10.

The more upmarket *De Bernales*, 193 Hannan St, does tasty food (and game specials) from $12 to $16 and has a pleasant verandah opening onto Hannan St – a good place to sip a beer and watch life go by.

Entertainment
Pubs feature heavily in the night scene. *Balzano's Brasserie*, in the Tower Hotel at 11 Maritana St, and *De Bernales* on Hannan St are great places for an ale. Nightclubs include the *Oasis*, *Safari* and *Sylvesters* – all in the same building at the top end of Hannan St. Careful, it gets rough at times.

Things to Buy
The Goldfields Aboriginal Art Gallery on Dugan St and the Desert Art shop, next to the Museum of the Goldfields, have craft for sale. Kal is a good place to buy gold nuggets

fashioned into relatively inexpensive jewellery – shop along Hannan St.

Getting There & Away

Air Ansett (☎ 13 1300) flies from Perth to Kal and return several times daily. The Ansett Australia office is at 314 Hannan St.

Skywest (☎ 13 1300) has a direct flight daily – it has discounts such as special weekend fares ($196 return for a 21-day advance purchase). To contact Skywest and Ansett, call ☎ 13 1300. Stoddart's (☎ 9021 2796), 248 Hannan St, is the Qantas agent; you can also call Qantas on ☎ 13 1313

Bus Greyhound Pioneer (☎ 13 2030) buses operate through Kalgoorlie on their services from Perth to Sydney, Melbourne and Adelaide. Goldfields Express (☎ 9021 2954) has a twice-weekly Perth to Kal service which also heads north to Laverton ($50 from Kal), Leinster ($55) and Leonora ($35). Check timetables carefully as some of these buses pull into Kal at an ungodly hour when everything is closed and finding a place to stay can be difficult.

Westrail (☎ 9021 2023) runs a bus three times a week from Kal to Esperance – once via Kambalda and Norseman and twice via Coolgardie and Norseman; the trip takes 5½ hours and costs $18 to Norseman, $33.50 to Esperance. There are daily Westrail services between Perth and Kal (see the Getting Around section earlier in the chapter).

Train The daily *Prospector* service from Perth takes around 7½ hours and costs $58.80, including a meal. From Perth, you can book seats at the WATC tourist centre on Forrest Place or at the Westrail East Perth terminal (☎ 9326 2222). The Indian-Pacific train also goes through Kal twice a week.

Getting Around

Between Kal and Boulder, there's a regular bus service (get a timetable from the tourist office). Goldenlines (☎ 9021 2655) travels to Boulder, either directly or via Lionel St, between 8 am and 6 pm. There are also daily

buses to Kambalda and Coolgardie (during school term only).

You can hire bicycles from Johnston Cycles (☎ 9021 1157), 76 Boulder Rd, and Hannan Cycles (☎ 9021 2467) on Maritana St; a deposit is required.

NORTH OF KALGOORLIE-BOULDER

The road north is surfaced from Kal all the way to the three 'Ls' – Leonora-Gwalia (237km away), Laverton (368km) and Leinster (361km). Off the main road, however, traffic is virtually nonexistent and rain can quickly close dirt roads. Skywest (☎ 13 1300) has regular flights from Perth to Leinster ($248), Laverton ($282), Leonora ($246) and Wiluna ($293).

Towns of interest include **Kanowna**, just 18km north-east of Kalgoorlie-Boulder along a dirt road. In 1905, this town had a population of 12,000, 16 hotels, many churches and an hourly train service to Kal. Today, apart from the train station and the odd piles of rubble, not much remains.

Broad Arrow, farther north, has a population of 20, compared with 2400 at the turn of the century. One of the town's original eight hotels operates in a virtually unchanged condition. **Ora Banda**, just west of Broad Arrow, has gone from a population of 2000 to less than 50 today. There is a tavern for drinks and meals.

Menzies, 132km north of Kal, has about 110 people today, compared with 5000 in 1900. Many early buildings remain, including the train station with its 120m-long platform and the town hall with its clockless clock tower – the ship (SS *Orizaba*) bringing the clock from England sank en route.

With a population of 1200, **Leonora** serves as the railhead for the nickel from Windarra and Leinster. In adjoining **Gwalia** (once a ghost town), the Sons of Gwalia gold mine, the largest in WA outside Kalgoorlie, closed in 1963 and much of the town closed with it; however, due to the increase in gold prices and new technology the mine has reopened. At one time, the mine was managed by Herbert Hoover, who was later to become president of the USA. The Gwalia

Historical Society is housed in the 1898 mine office – this fascinating local museum is open daily. Also of interest is the restored State Hotel, built in 1903.

South of Leonora-Gwalia, 25km off the main road, is **Kookynie**, another interesting once-flourishing mining town with just a handful of inhabitants. The 1894 *Grand Hotel* (☎ 9031 3010) has full board for $60 per person. Nearby **Niagara** is also a ghost town; the Niagara Dam was built with cement carried in by a 400-strong camel train.

From Leonora-Gwalia, you can turn north-east to **Laverton**, where the surfaced road ends. The population here declined from 1000 in 1910 to 200 in 1970, when the Poseidon nickel discovery (beloved of stock-market speculators in the late 60s and early 70s) revived mining operations in nearby Windarra. The town now has a population of 1500, and there are many abandoned mines in the area. From here, it is just 1710km to Alice Springs via the Warburton road.

North of Leonora-Gwalia, the road is surfaced to **Leinster** (pop 1000), another modern nickel town. Nearby, **Agnew** is another old gold town that has all but disappeared. From here, it's 170km north to **Wiluna** (pop 250) and then another 185km west to Meekatharra and the surfaced Great Northern Highway, which runs 765km south-west to Perth or 860km north to Port Hedland. Throughout the 30s, due to the mining of arsenic, Wiluna had a population of 9000 and was a modern, prosperous town. The ore ran out in 1948 and the town quickly declined. There is a caravan park (☎ 9981 70 21), and the *Club Hotel/Motel* (☎ 9981 7012) has single/double units for $80/95.

Warburton Road

For those interested in an outback experience, the unsealed road from Laverton to Yulara (the tourist development near Uluru), via Warburton, provides a rich scenery of red sand, spinifex, mulga and desert oaks. The road, while sandy in places, is suitable for conventional vehicles, although a 4WD would give a much smoother ride. Although

this road is often called the Gunbarrel Highway, that rough, unmaintained road actually runs some distance to the north.

You should take precautions relevant to travel in such an isolated area – tell someone reliable of your travel plans and take adequate supplies of water, food, petrol and spare parts. The longest stretch without fuel is between Laverton and Warburton (568km). Don't even consider doing it from November to March when the heat is extreme. Conditions should not be taken lightly – in 1994 a Japanese motorcyclist, equipped with just four leaky 1L milk bottles, nearly met his end here. See the Getting Around chapter for more details on outback travel.

Petrol is available at Laverton, Warburton (where basic supplies are also available), Docker River and Yulara. At **Giles**, about 105km west of the Northern Territory border, is a weather station with a friendly 'Visitors Welcome' sign and a bar.

As this road passes through Aboriginal land, permits from the Central Land Council in Alice Springs (☎ (08) 8951 6211) are required before you can travel along it. These permits take up to two weeks to issue.

SOUTH OF KALGOORLIE-BOULDER
Kambalda (pop 1200)

Kambalda, south of Kalgoorlie-Boulder, died as a gold-mining town in 1906, but nickel was discovered in 1966 and today it is a major mining centre. There are two town centres, Kambalda East and Kambalda West, about 4km apart. The town is on the shores of **Lake Lefroy**, a large saltpan and a popular spot for land yachting.

The tourist bureau (☎ 9027 1446) on Emu Rocks Rd in Kambalda West can provide information and a map of the region. There is a caravan park and motel in Kambalda West.

South of Kambalda is the idiosyncratic outback town of **Widgiemooltha**, which has limited accommodation and a roadhouse/tavern; the 'truckies brekkie' at the roadhouse is a must for the famished and the tavern an oasis for the thirsty.

Norseman (pop 1500)

Norseman is a major crossroads town from where you can head east on the Eyre Highway (Nullarbor) journey. The tourist bureau (☎ 9039 0171), 68 Roberts St, is open daily from 9 am to 5 pm. Nearby is a rest park, also open from 9 am to 5 pm.

The **Historical & Geological Collection** in the old School of Mines has items from the gold-rush days; it's open on weekdays from 10 am to 4 pm ($2, $1 children).

You can get an excellent view of the town and the surrounding salt lakes from the **Beacon Hill Mararoa Lookout**, down past the mountainous tailings dumps, one of which contains 4.2 million tonnes of rock, the result of 40 years of mining.

Also worth a look are the views at sunrise and sunset of the dry, expansive **Lake Cowan**, north of the town. South of Norseman, just under halfway along the road to Esperance, is the small township of **Salmon Gums**, named after the gum trees, prevalent in the area, which acquire a rich, pink bark in late summer and autumn.

Places to Stay & Eat The tidy *Gateway Caravan Park* (☎ 9039 1500) on Princep St has tent/powered sites for $13/15 and on-site vans/cabins for $28/36 for two. The $15 dorm beds at *Lodge 101* (☎ 9039 1541), 101 Princep St, will suit unfussy cross-Nullarbor cyclists.

The *Norseman Hotel* (☎ 9039 1023) on the corner of Robert St and Talbot Rd has B&B singles/doubles for $30/50, and the *Norseman Eyre Motel* (☎ 9039 1130) on Robert St charges $62/69.

Bits & Pizzas on Robert St serves eat-in or takeaway meals; the BP and Ampol roadhouses at the start of the Eyre Highway have a wide range of food, including tasty fish & chips. *Pure Health*, 91B Roberts St, is the best choice for wholefood.

EYRE HIGHWAY

It's a little over 2700km between Perth and Adelaide – not much less than the distance from London to Moscow. The long and sometimes lonely Eyre Highway crosses the southern edge of the vast **Nullarbor Plain** – Nullarbor is bad Latin for 'no trees' and indeed there is a small stretch where you see none at all. Surprisingly, the road is flanked by trees most of the way as this coastal fringe receives regular rain, especially in winter.

The road across the Nullarbor takes its name from John Eyre, the explorer who, in 1841, was the first European to make the east-west crossing. It was a superhuman effort that involved five months of hardship and resulted in the death of Eyre's companion, John Baxter. In 1877, a telegraph line was laid across the Nullarbor, roughly delineating the route the first road would take.

Later in the 19th century, miners en route to the goldfields followed this telegraph-line route across the empty plain. In 1896, the first bicycle crossing was made and in 1912 the first car was driven across.

In 1941, WWII inspired the building of a transcontinental highway, just as it had the Alice Springs to Darwin route. It was a

rough-and-ready track when completed, and in the 50s only a few vehicles a day made the crossing. In the 60s, the traffic flow increased to more than 30 vehicles a day and in 1969 the WA government surfaced the road as far as the South Australian border. Finally, in 1976, the last stretch was surfaced and now the Nullarbor crossing is an easier, but still long, drive.

The surfaced road runs close to the coast on the South Australian side. Here, the Nullarbor region ends dramatically at the cliffs of the Great Australian Bight.

The Trans-Australia Railway runs north of the coast and actually on the Nullarbor Plain – unlike the main road, which only fringes the great plain.

From Norseman, where the Eyre Highway begins, it's 725km to the WA-SA border, near Eucla, and a farther 480km to Ceduna (meaning 'a place to sit down and rest' in an Aboriginal dialect) in South Australia. From Ceduna, it's still another 793km to Adelaide via Port Augusta. It's a bloody long way!

Crossing the Nullarbor

Although the Nullarbor is no longer the torture trail of old, it's wise to prepare adequately to avoid difficulties.

The longest distance between fuel stops is about 200km, so if you're foolish enough to run low on petrol midway, it can be a long trip to get more. Getting help for a mechanical breakdown can be very expensive and equally time-consuming, so make sure your vehicle is in good shape and that you have plenty of petrol, good tyres and at least a basic kit of simple spare parts. Carry some drinking water (4L per person) just in case you do have to sit it out by the roadside on a hot summer day.

Take it easy on the highway – many, trying to set speed records, have dented their cars by hitting kangaroos, particularly at night.

Norseman to Eucla

From Norseman, the first settlement you reach is **Balladonia**, 193km to the east. After Balladonia, near the old station, you can see the remains of stone fences built to enclose stock. Clay saltpans are also visible in the area. The *Balladonia Hotel Motel* (☎ 9039 3453) has singles/doubles from $58/68 and its dusty caravan facility has tent/powered sites for $10/14. The road from Balladonia to Cocklebiddy is one of the loneliest stretches of road across the Nullarbor.

Between Balladonia and Caiguna is one of the longest stretches of straight road in the world – 145km. At **Caiguna**, the *John Eyre Motel* (☎ 9039 3459) has rooms for $50/65, and a caravan facility with tent/powered sites from $5/12 for two.

At **Cocklebiddy** are the stone ruins of an Aboriginal mission. Cocklebiddy Cave is the largest of the Nullarbor caves – in 1983 a team of French explorers set a record there for the deepest cave dive in the world. With a 4WD, you can travel south of Cocklebiddy to Twilight Cove, with its 75m-high limestone cliffs. The *Wedgetail Inn Motel Hotel* (☎ 9039 3462) at Cocklebiddy has expensive fuel, tent/powered sites for $6/12 and pricey rooms from $66/76 for two/three.

The RAOU's *Eyre Bird Observatory* (☎ 9039 3450), housed in the former **Eyre Telegraph Station**, 50km south of Cocklebiddy on the bight, is a haven for twitchers. Full board is $60 per person per day. Return transport from the microwave tower on the escarpment costs $30, otherwise you will need to be a competent 4WD driver.

Madura, 90km east of Cocklebiddy, is close to the Hampton Tablelands. At one time, horses were bred here for the Indian Army. There are good views over the plains from the road. The *Madura Pass Oasis Inn* (☎ 9039 3464) has tent/powered sites from $8/15 and rooms (not their 'units of a lesser classification') cost from $49 to $76 for two.

Mundrabilla, 116km to the east, has a caravan facility, with tent/powered sites from $8/12 and cabins for $30, while the *Mundrabilla Motel Hotel* (☎ 9039 3465) has singles/doubles from $45/55.

Just before the South Australian border is **Eucla**. Just south of the town, on the Great Australian Bight, are picturesque ruins of an old **telegraph repeater/weather station**, first opened in 1877. The telegraph line now

RICHARD I'ANSON

RICHARD I'ANSON

Western Australia
Top: Twilight Cove, Esperance
Bottom: Morning mist in Karri Forrest, Warren National Park

ROB VAN DRIESUM

RICHARD I'ANSON

RICHARD I'ANSON

Western Australia
Left: Windjana Gorge and the Lennard River
Right: Bungle Bungle (Purnululu) National Park
Bottom: Mitchell Falls, Mitchell Plateau, Kimberley

runs along the railway line, far to the north. The station, 5km from the roadhouse, is gradually being engulfed by sand dunes (just the chimneys protrude).

The Eucla area has many caves, such as the famous **Koonalda Cave** with its 45m-high chamber. Like most Nullarbor caves, it's only for experienced speleologists.

Many people have their photo taken at Eucla's famous sign which pinpoints distances to international destinations. For connoisseurs of kitsch there's a ferro-cement sperm whale (a species seldom seen in these parts) and a 5m-high fibreglass kangaroo.

The *Amber Motor Hotel* (☎ 9039 3468) has double rooms from $68; its Eucla Pass economy section has tent/powered sites costing $4/10 (showers are $1) and basic rooms for $15/30. The *WA-SA Border Village* (☎ 9039 3474) has tent/powered sites from $6/10, cabins from $35 a double and single/double motel units from $60/68.

Eucla to Ceduna (SA)

Between the WA-SA border and the pit-stop of Nullarbor (184km to the east in South Australia), the Eyre Highway runs close to the coast and there are fine lookouts over the **Great Australian Bight** – stop at one or two.

At **Nullarbor**, the *Nullarbor Hotel Motel* (☎ 8625 6271) has a restaurant, budget rooms, tent sites, and single/double units from $55/68. Just look for the diminutive fibreglass southern right whale. There are opportunities to see whales from here, either from cliff lookouts or from the air (see the South Australia chapter).

The road passes through the **Yalata Aboriginal Reserve**, and Aboriginal people often sell souvenirs by the roadside. **Nundroo** is on the edge of the Nullarbor. Its *Nundroo Inn* (☎ 8625 6120) has a caravan park, restaurant and pool.

Between Nundroo and Penong is the ghost town of **Fowlers Bay**, with its good fishing, and nearby Mexican Hat Beach. The *Penong Hotel* (☎ 8625 1050) has beds and serves meals. The service station across from it has a restaurant/takeaways.

Make a short detour south of Penong to the **Pink Lake**, **Point Sinclair** and **Cactus Beach** – a surf beach with left and right breaks that is a must for the serious surfer. Although the point is private property, you can camp there for $5 (bring water).

Eastbound from Penong to Ceduna, there are places with petrol and other facilities. **Ceduna** is effectively the end of the solitary stretch from Norseman, and is equipped with supermarkets, banks, and all the comforts (see the Ceduna section in the South Australia chapter).

Central West Coast

After leaving Perth's north coastal region, the North-West Coastal Highway (Highway 1) passes through three interesting regions – the Batavia Coast (evoking memories of the area's many shipwrecks, and including the towns of Geraldton and Kalbarri); the Shark Bay World Heritage region; and the Gascoyne, with Carnarvon and Mt Augustus. Inland are the Murchison goldfields, linked by the Great Northern Highway.

DONGARA & PORT DENISON (pop 2000)

The Brand Highway hits the coast at Dongara. This is a pleasant little port with fine beaches, lots of crayfish, a main street lined with Moreton Bay fig trees, and a tourist centre (☎ 9927 1404) housed in the old police station at 5 Waldeck St. **Russ Cottage**, built in 1870, is open on Sunday from 10 am to noon.

Just over the Irwin River is Port Denison. The mouth of the Irwin is a great place to watch birds such as pelicans and cormorants.

Places to Stay & Eat

There are four caravan parks in these twin coastal towns. Two recommended ones are the *Dongara Denison Beach* (☎ 9927 1131) on Denison Beach, with powered sites/on-site vans for $14/28, and the friendly *Seaspray* (☎ 9927 1165), 81 Church St, with powered sites/on-site vans for $12/26. The latter is sheltered from the sea breezes by a large, grassed wall.

The *Dongara Backpackers* (☎ 9927 1581) is at 32 Waldeck St. It is a comfortable, friendly place with rooms in an old house or in a nearby train carriage. There is a pleasant verandah overlooking the volleyball court; the cost is $12/26 for dorm/twin rooms.

The *Priory Lodge Historic Inn* (☎ 9927 1090), 9 St Dominics Rd, is a good accommodation alternative (it was built in 1881) with singles/doubles for $20/30; and *Obawara B&B* (☎ 9927 1043), 5km east of Dongara, is a farm property with doubles for $60 (B&B, including dinner, is $90 for two).

New Age devotees will find inspiration in the ley lines and chakra points of the *Iona Lodge: Celestial Dolphin Centre* (☎ 9927 1206), to the north-west of Dongara. Single/double B&B accommodation here costs $30/50.

In Dongara, try *Toko's Restaurant* at 38 Moreton Terrace. Also on Moreton Terrace, opposite the hotel, is the *Sea Jewels Seafood & Takeaway*, which has delicious fish & chips, chilli mussels and garlic prawn rolls. On a fine day the verandah at *Dooley's* on Ocean Drive in Denison is popular.

GREENOUGH (pop 100)

Farther north, only about 20km south of Geraldton, is Greenough, once a busy little mining town but now a quiet farming centre. The **Greenough Historical Hamlet** contains 11 buildings constructed in the 19th century and now restored by the National Trust; guided tours are run daily ($4/2 for adults/children) and it is well worth a visit. The Pioneer Museum, open daily from 10 am to 4 pm, has some fine historical displays. In the local paddocks, look out for flood gums, the 'leaning trees' *(Eucalyptus camaldulensis)* caused by salt winds off the ocean.

The *Greenough Rivermouth Caravan Park* (☎ 9921 5845) has tent/powered sites for $12/15 and on-site vans for $25. The *Greenough River Resort* (☎ 9921 5888) has singles/doubles for $60/75.

GERALDTON (pop 25,000)

Geraldton, the major town in the mid-west, is on a rugged stretch of coast, with the mystical Houtman Abrolhos Islands offshore. It's 421km north of Perth and the area has a fine climate, particularly in winter. If you are tempted by fresh lobster or are a windsurfing enthusiast then this is the place to visit. But beware: it is extremely windy.

Information

The Geraldton-Greenough tourist bureau (☎ 9921 3999) in the Bill Sewell complex on Chapman Rd is almost diagonally across from the train station. It is open on weekdays from 8.30 am to 5 pm, Saturday from 9 am to 4.30 pm, and Sunday from 9.30 am to 4.30 pm. The main post office is on Durlacher St and most of the banks are in the Mall, on Marine Terrace between Cathedral and Durlacher Sts.

Geraldton Museum

The town's captivating museum is in two adjacent buildings on Marine Terrace. The Geraldton Maritime Museum tells the story of the early wrecks and has assorted relics from the doomed Dutch ships, including the *Batavia* and the *Zeewijk*. A feature item is the carved wooden sternpiece from the *Zuytdorp*, found in 1927 on top of cliffs near where the ship had grounded.

The Geraldton Regional Museum is in the old railway building and has displays on flora, fauna and the settlement of the region by both Aborigines and Europeans. The museum complex is open daily from 10 am to 4 pm (admission is free).

St Francis Xavier Cathedral

Geraldton's cathedral is just one of a number of buildings in Geraldton and the mid-west designed by Monsignor John Hawes, a strange priest-cum-architect who left WA in 1939 and spent the rest of his life as a hermit on an island in the Caribbean (he died in Florida in 1956). Construction of the Byzantine-style cathedral commenced in 1916, a year after Hawes arrived here, but his plans

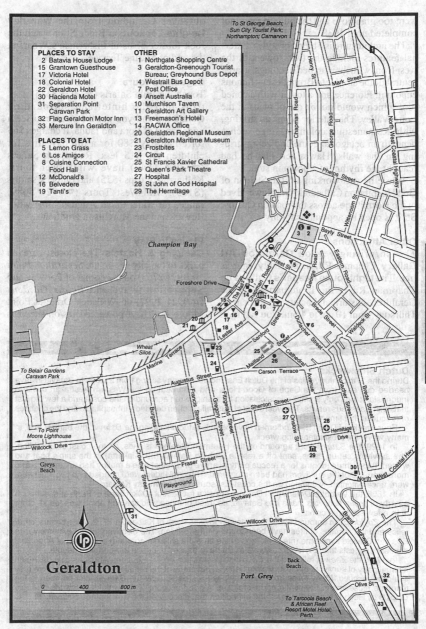

PLACES TO STAY
2 Batavia House Lodge
15 Grantown Guesthouse
17 Victoria Hotel
18 Colonial Hotel
22 Geraldton Hotel
30 Hacienda Motel
31 Separation Point
   Caravan Park
32 Flag Geraldton Motor Inn
33 Mercure Inn Geraldton

PLACES TO EAT
5 Lemon Grass
6 Los Amigos
8 Cuisine Connection
   Food Hall
12 McDonald's
16 Belvedere
19 Tanti's

OTHER
1 Northgate Shopping Centre
3 Geraldton-Greenough Tourist
   Bureau; Greyhound Bus Depot
4 Westrail Bus Depot
7 Post Office
9 Ansett Australia
10 Murchison Tavern
11 Geraldton Art Gallery
13 Freemason's Hotel
14 RACWA Office
20 Geraldton Regional Museum
21 Geraldton Maritime Museum
23 Frostbites
24 Circuit
25 St Francis Xavier Cathedral
26 Queen's Park Theatre
27 Hospital
28 St John of God Hospital
29 The Hermitage

To St George Beach;
Sun City Tourist Park;
Northampton; Carnarvon

Champion Bay

Foreshore Drive

Wheat
Silos

To Belair Gardens
Caravan Park

To Point
Moore Lighthouse

Willcock Drive

Greys
Beach

Playground

Willcock Drive

Geraldton

0   400   800 m

Port Grey

Back
Beach

To Tarcoola Beach
& African Reef
Resort Motel Hotel;
Perth

WESTERN AUSTRALIA

were too grandiose and the building was not completed until 1938.

The architecture is a blend of styles. External features include the twin towers of the west front with their arched openings, a large central dome similar to Brunellesci's famous cupola in Florence and a tower with a coned roof which would not be out of place in the Loire Valley. The interior is just as striking, with Romanesque columns, huge arches beneath an octagonal dome and zebra striping on the walls. Hawes felt that he had 'caught the rhythm of a poem in stone'.

While he was working on the St John of God Hospital on Cathedral Ave, Hawes lived in the **Hermitage** across the road on Onslow St; it is open by appointment only.

Other Attractions

The surprisingly good **Geraldton Art Gallery**, Chapman Rd, is open daily; entry is free. The **Lighthouse Keeper's Cottage** on Chapman Rd is the headquarters of the Geraldton Historical Society and open on Thursday from 10 am to 4 pm. You can look out over Geraldton from the **Waverley Heights Lookout** on Brede St or watch the rock lobster boats at Fisherman's Wharf at the end of Marine Terrace.

Organised Tours

Touch the Wild Safaris (☎ 9921 8435) does trips into the hinterland surrounding Geraldton, and you get the chance to see a wide range of flora and fauna. It charges $65 for a half-day, $80 for a full day; trips for children are $15 less. Red Earth Safaris (☎ 9964 1543) have wildflower tours, Kalbarri day trips ($55) and outback safaris ($165). Mid-West Tours (☎ 9921 5089) ranges far wider to Mt Augustus, the wildflowers and the Murchison goldfields.

Places to Stay

Camping & Hostels The closest caravan parks to the city centre are *Separation Point* (☎ 9921 2763) on the corner of Portway and Separation Way, and *Belair Gardens* (☎ 9921 1997) on Willcock Drive at Point Moore; both have powered sites/on-site vans

---

Dutch Shipwrecks

During the 17th century, ships of the Dutch East India Company sailing from Europe to Batavia in Java headed due east from the Cape of Good Hope and then beat up the Western Australian coast to Indonesia. It took only a small miscalculation for a ship to run aground on the coast and a few did just that, with disastrous results. The west coast of Australia is often decidedly inhospitable and the chances of rescue at that time were remote.

Four wrecks of Dutch East Indiamen have been located, including the *Batavia*, the earliest and, in many ways, the most interesting wreck.

In 1629, the *Batavia* went aground on the Houtman Abrolhos Islands, off the coast of Geraldton. The survivors set up camp, sent off a rescue party to Batavia (now Jakarta) in the ship's boat and waited. It took three months for a rescue party to arrive and in that time a mutiny had taken place and more than 120 of the survivors had been murdered. The ringleaders were hanged and two mutineers were unceremoniously dumped on the coast just south of modern-day Kalbarri.

In 1656, the *Vergulde Draeck* (Gilt Dragon) struck a reef about 100km north of Perth and, although a party of seven survivors made it to Batavia, no trace of those who stayed behind was found, other than a few scattered coins.

The *Zuytdorp* ran aground beneath the towering cliffs north of Kalbarri in 1712. Wine bottles, other relics and the remains of fires have been found on the cliff top. The discovery of the extremely rare Ellis van Creveld syndrome (rife in Holland at the time the ship ran aground) in children of Aboriginal descent suggests that *Zuytdorp* survivors might have passed the gene to Aboriginal people.

In 1727, the *Zeewijk* followed the *Batavia* to destruction on the Houtman Abrolhos Islands. Again a small party of survivors made its way to Batavia, but many of the remaining sailors died before they could be rescued. Many relics from these shipwrecks, particularly the *Batavia*, can be seen in the maritime museums in Fremantle and Geraldton. A good account of the wrecks is *Islands of Angry Ghosts* by Hugh Edwards, leader of the expedition that discovered the wreck of the *Batavia*. ■

for about $13/30 for two. The excellent *Sun City Tourist Park* (☎ 9938 1655) on Bosley St, Sunset Beach, is a little way north of town but well worth it for its beach location; tent/powered sites are $12/15, on-site vans $24 for two and tidy park cabins are from $45 for two. This writer highly recommends this park.

The *Batavia House Lodge* (☎ 9964 3001), on the corner of Chapman Rd and Bayly St in the Bill Sewell complex, has good facilities and beds for $12 per night; a double is $25. The *Chapman Valley Farm Backpackers* (☎ 9920 5160), 25km out of town, is in an historic homestead. Staff pick up travellers from Geraldton at 11 am; beds are $12.

Guesthouses, Hotels & Motels The *Grantown Guesthouse* (☎ 9921 3275) at No 172 has singles/doubles for $22/44, including breakfast. Cheap rooms are also available at some of the older-style hotels such as the *Colonial* on Fitzgerald St, the *Victoria* on Marine Terrace, and the *Geraldton* ('the Gero') on Gregory St; count on about $20 per person.

The *Hacienda Motel* (☎ 9921 2155) on Durlacher St has singles/doubles for $50/60; family units are available. The *Flag Geraldton Motor Inn* (☎ 9964 4777), 107 Brand Highway, is an old favourite of travelling salespersons. The rooms, with all comforts, are from $70 to $80; breakfast is included. The *Mercure Inn Geraldton* (☎ 9921 2455) on the Brand Highway charges $96 a double.

The *African Reef Resort Motel Hotel* (☎ 9964 5566), 5 Broadhead Ave, Tarcoola Beach, is the best of the city's places to stay, with every facility imaginable; holiday units are from $55 to $80 and comfortable rooms are from $90 to $95 for two.

For information on B&Bs, contact the tourist bureau.

Places to Eat
The *Cuisine Connection* on Durlacher St is a food hall with Indian, Chinese and Italian food, roasts and fish & chips. The food is excellent and you should be able to get a good feed for $7. Fast-food junkies who have made the long haul from Darwin will think they have entered nirvana: *Chicken Treat, Hungry Jacks, Pizza Hut, McDonald's, KFC* and *Red Rooster* all occupy real estate in this town.

There are a number of small snack bars and cafes along Marine Terrace, including *Thuy's Cake Shop* at No 202, which is open from 6 am for breakfast; and *Belvedere* at No 149, with standard cafe food at down-to-earth prices.

Lemon Grass Thai, 18 Snowdon St, and *Tanti's*, 174 Marine Terrace, are both popular Thai restaurants; expect to pay from $14 for a main meal. At 105 Durlacher St, *Los Amigos* is a good, licensed Mexican place; it's popular, and deservedly so.

Entertainment
Occasionally a live band plays at the *Gero* on Gregory St and, if you recently turned 20, chances are you would be meeting friends at the *Freemason's* ('the Freo') in the Mall, or at the *Frostbites* and *Circuit* nightclubs on Fitzgerald St.

Getting There & Around
Skywest (☎ 13 1300) has flights from Perth to Geraldton daily. There are also flights from Geraldton to Broome, Carnarvon, Karratha and Exmouth on Tuesday and Thursday.

Westrail (☎ 13 2232) and Greyhound Pioneer (☎ 13 2030) have regular bus services from Perth to Geraldton for around $40 one way. Westrail services continue northeast to Meekatharra (twice weekly) or north to Kalbarri (three weekly). Greyhound Pioneer continues on Highway 1 through Port Hedland and Broome to Darwin. Westrail (☎ 13 2232) stops at the train station, while Greyhound Pioneer (☎ 13 2030) stops at the Bill Sewell complex.

There is a local bus service (☎ 9921 1034) which provides access to all nearby suburbs. Try at Sun City Bike Hire (☎ 9921 3999) if you need two unpowered wheels.

HOUTMAN ABROLHOS ISLANDS (pop 0)

There are more than 100 islands in this group, located about 60km off the Geraldton coast, and they are a bird-watcher's paradise. The beautiful but treacherous reefs surrounding the islands have claimed many ships over the years. The islands are also the centre of the area's lobster industry. Much of the beauty of the Abrolhos lies beneath the water, where the *Acropora* family of corals abounds. Air and diving tours to these protected, spectacular islands can be taken from Geraldton – ask at the tourist bureau.

NORTHAMPTON (pop 842)

Northampton, 50km north of Geraldton, has a number of historic buildings and provides access to good beaches at **Horrocks** (22km west) and **Port Gregory** (47km north-west). The town was founded to exploit the lead and copper deposits discovered in 1848. Today it is an agricultural centre, now with an embryonic tourism industry.

An early mining home, **Chiverton House**, is a fine municipal museum ($2 entry). The tourist bureau (☎ 9934 1488) is in the old library on the main road.

The **Lynton Convict Settlement**, about 40km west of Northampton, was established as a convict-hiring facility in 1853 and abandoned some four years later. Only ruins exist.

Places to Stay

There are caravan parks near Northampton (☎ 9934 1202), Port Gregory (☎ 9935 1052) and Horrocks (☎ 9934 3039); all have tent sites, and the Horrocks and Port Gregory caravan parks have on-site vans. The *Killara Cottages* (☎ 9934 3031) at Horrocks charges from $200 per week.

There are budget beds in the *Nagle Centre* (☎ 9934 1488), formerly the Sacred Heart Convent, for $12 per person in two and four-bed rooms; it has all the usual facilities.

The hotels in town all offer rooms. The *Lynton Homestead B&B* (☎ 9935 1040), next to the convict settlement, charges a reasonable $25 a night and has backpacker beds in a bunkhouse for $15 per person.

KALBARRI (pop 1800)

A popular spot with backpackers, Kalbarri is on the coast at the mouth of the Murchison River, 66km west of the main highway. The area has an alluring coastline, scenic gorges and haunting Dutch shipwrecks. The *Zuytdorp* was wrecked about 65km northwest of Kalbarri in 1712; earlier, in 1629, two *Batavia* mutineers were marooned at Wittecarra Gully, an inlet just south of the town. Although diving around the *Zuytdorp* is very difficult, as a heavy swell and unpredictable currents batter the shoreline, divers from the Geraldton Museum managed to raise artefacts in 1986.

The tourist bureau (☎ 9937 1104), Grey St, is open daily from 9 am to 5 pm; it has plenty of information and handles bookings for local activities.

Kalbarri National Park

This park has over 1000 sq km of bushland including some scenic gorges on the **Murchison River**. From Kalbarri, it's about 40km to the **Loop** and **Z-Bend**, two impressive gorges. Short walking trails lead down into the gorges from road access points but there are also longer walks. It is a two-day walk between the Z-Bend and the Loop.

Farther east along the Ajana-Kalbarri road are two lookouts: **Hawk's Head** (a must) and **Ross Graham**. The park has a particularly fine display of wildflowers in spring, including everlastings, banksias, grevilleas and kangaroo paws.

Other Attractions

The **Rainbow Jungle** is an interesting rainforest and bird park 4km south of town towards Red Bluff ($5; children $2). Boats can be hired (☎ 9937 1245) and tours taken on the river aboard the *Kalbarri River Queen* ($14/7 for adults/children).

South of the town is a string of rugged **cliff faces**, including Red Bluff, Rainbow Valley, Pot Alley, Eagle Gorge and Natural Bridge. They can all be reached by car and the road to them has recently been sealed.

There are some excellent surfing breaks

along the coast – **Jakes Corner**, 3.5km south of town, is among the State's best.

Organised Tours

For views of the Murchison River gorges, take a flight with Kalbarri Air Charter (☎ 9937 1130); these cost from $29.

Kalbarri Coach Tours visits the Loop, Z-Bend and ocean gorges ($30). It also runs a canoeing adventure tour into the gorges ($40) which takes in the Fourways gullies. Kalbarri Safari Tours (☎ 9937 1011) is a new and untested outfit – it visits the Murchison River gorges for $35 (write and let us know

how the trip was). The more adventurous can abseil into the gorges with Gordon ($40). The tourist office staff will provide details.

Places to Stay

Kalbarri is a popular resort and accommodation can be tight at holiday times.

There are several caravan parks. A favourite is *Red Bluff* (☎ 9937 1080) on Red Bluff Rd, 4km south of town, with on-site vans/chalets from $28/35 for two. It puts on barbecues on Wednesday and Saturday nights with hearty serves of meat and salads.

The clean, modern and 'kid-friendly'

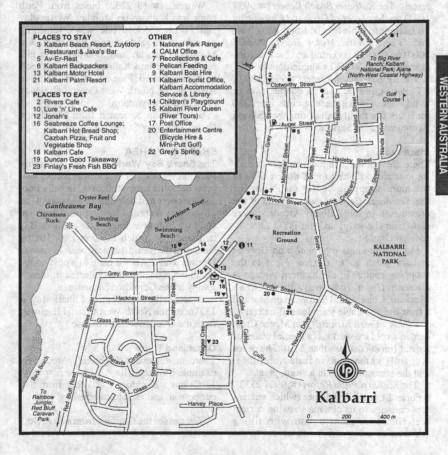

PLACES TO STAY
3 Kalbarri Beach Resort, Zuytdorp Restaurant & Jake's Bar
5 Av-Er-Rest
6 Kalbarri Backpackers
13 Kalbarri Motor Hotel
21 Kalbarri Palm Resort

PLACES TO EAT
2 Rivers Cafe
10 Lure 'n' Line Cafe
12 Jonah's
16 Seabreeze Coffee Lounge; Kalbarri Hot Bread Shop; Cazbah Pizza; Fruit and Vegetable Shop
18 Kalbarri Cafe
19 Duncan Good Takeaway
23 Finlay's Fresh Fish BBQ

OTHER
1 National Park Ranger
4 CALM Office
7 Recollections & Cafe
8 Pelican Feeding
9 Kalbarri Boat Hire
11 Kalbarri Tourist Office, Kalbarri Accommodation Service & Library
14 Children's Playground
15 Kalbarri River Queen (River Tours)
17 Post Office
20 Entertainment Centre (Bicycle Hire & Mini-Putt Golf)
22 Grey's Spring

WESTERN AUSTRALIA

Kalbarri

0   200   400 m

Kalbarri Backpackers (☎ 9937 1430), 2 Mortimer St, has dorm beds from $11, and family and disabled units from $40; it has been recommended by many travellers and would have to be one of the best of its type in WA. The owners organise snorkelling gear free of charge and point you in the right direction for other activities. *Av-Er-Rest* (☎ 9937 1101), also on Mortimer St, has dorm beds for $13 and singles for $18 – but it lacks the communal spirit of many good backpacker places.

As would be expected in a holiday destination, there are plenty of holiday units and resorts. The *Kalbarri Beach Resort* (☎ 9937 1061) on the corner of Grey and Clotworthy Sts has comfortable two-bedroom units from $65. The *Kalbarri Motor Hotel* (☎ 9937 1000) on Grey St is central and has comfortable rooms for $40/50 a single/double.

The *Kalbarri Palm Resort* (☎ 9937 2333), 8 Porter St, has 50 units; a double, twin or family unit with kitchenette costs from $50 for B&B. For family villas, ring the Kalbarri Accommodation Service (☎ 9937 1072).

Places to Eat

There are four cafes in town and all specialise in seafood dishes: the *Kalbarri Cafe* in the main shopping centre on Porter St; the *Seabreeze Coffee Lounge*, home of the prawn roll, in the Kalbarri Arcade; *Rivers Cafe* near the jetty; and the BYO *Lure 'n' Line* on Grey St.

For fish & chips try *Jonah's* on Grey St and for pizza go to *Cazbah Pizza* in the shopping centre. In the Kalbarri Arcade is *Duncan Good Takeaway*, with cheap Mexican, Chinese and European dishes, and a fruit and vegetable shop for self-caterers.

Finlay's Fresh Fish BBQ on Magee Crescent in an old ice works, is a special place for a meal (most cost less than $10). The decor is no frills but the meals and salads are filling, and the atmosphere is, in a word, great.

The *Kalbarri Palm Resort* (☎ 9937 2333), 8 Porter St, has a $10 dinner (which guarantees entrance to its cinema showing current reel films). A giant potato with filling (chicken or meat curry) and access to the salad bar is included. It is the only licensed cinema in Australia – book early for the front couches.

Behind the Zuytdorp Restaurant in the Kalbarri Beach Resort is *Jake's*, a 1970s-style bar, with great counter meals ($9).

Getting There & Around

Western Airlines (☎ 1800 998 097) has return flights from Perth on Monday, Wednesday and Friday; the one-way/return fare is $167/334. The fare is $86 from Kalbarri to Monkey Mia (or $498 Perth-Kalbarri-Monkey Mia-Perth).

Westrail (☎ 13 2232) buses from Perth come into Kalbarri on Monday, Wednesday and Friday ($59.40 one way), returning Tuesday, Thursday and Saturday. On Monday, Thursday and Saturday there is a return shuttle into Kalbarri which connects with Greyhound Pioneer (☎ 13 2030) at Ajana on the North-West Coastal Highway ($13/24 one way/return).

Bicycles can be rented from Murchison Cycles on Porter St.

SHARK BAY AREA

The **Shark Bay World Heritage & Marine Park** has spectacular beaches, important sea-grass beds, the stromatolites at Hamelin Pool and the overrated dolphins of Monkey Mia.

The first recorded landing on Australian soil by a European took place at Shark Bay in 1616 when Dutch explorer Dirk Hartog landed on the island that now bears his name. He nailed an inscribed plate to a post on the beach but a later visitor collected it; there's a copy in the Geraldton Museum.

Denham, the main centre of Shark Bay, is 132km off the North-West Coastal Highway from the Overlander Roadhouse.

Organised Tours

There are numerous 'flightseeing' tours, for example Monkey Mia Air Charter (☎ 9948 1307) has a Zuytdorp Cliffs tour from $47 per person, and an 'around the bay' tour for $67.

You can see the dolphins from a boat. Both the *Aristocat* and *Shotover* cruise to the dolphins ($29) or do a four-hour trip around the bay ($34). The *Shotover* sails out to the dugongs and in the 2½-hour trip you'll probably see these shy mammals ($34/17 for adults/children). Contact the Shark Bay Tourist Centre in Denham (☎ 9948 1253) for more information on these trips.

There are also Monday trips to Dirk Hartog Island on the *Sea Eagle* (☎ 9948 1113, $100), and cruises to Steep Point for fishing with Explorer Charters & Cruises (☎ 9948 1246; $110).

There are a number of Shark Bay Discovery 4WD tours from the resort (☎ 9948 1320). The full-day Péron/Project Eden tour is the best, as it covers the cape's native mammal reintroduction program and ends with a dip in the hot tubs ($70/30). The Steep Point and Zuytdorp Cliffs trip involves a scenic flight and 4WD trip to the 60m-high cliffs ($149/89).

Getting There & Away

Western Airlines (☎ 1800 998 097) has return flights from Perth on Monday, Wednesday and Friday; the one-way fare is $167 to Kalbarri and an extra $86 to Monkey Mia.

North from Kalbarri, it's a fairly dull, boring and often very hot run to Carnarvon. The Overlander Roadhouse, 290km north of Geraldton, is the turn-off to Shark Bay. Greyhound Pioneer (☎ 13 2030) has a bus service from Denham to the Overlander to connect with interstate buses on Saturday, Monday and Thursday (both north and southbound). The fare from Perth to Denham is $120. It's $23/42 one way/return from Denham and Monkey Mia to the Overlander.

A daily local bus departs Denham (near the tourist office on Knight Terrace) at 8.45 and 5 pm for Monkey Mia and returns at 9.15 am and 5.30 pm; the fare is $14 return. There is also another daily service at 8 am (7.15 am Friday) for $14; for more details ask at the tourist office.

Overlander Roadhouse to Denham

Once you are off the highway, headed west for Monkey Mia and Denham, the first turn-off (27km from the highway) is the 6km road to **Hamelin Pool,** a marine reserve which has the world's best-known colony of **stromatolites** (see the Stromatolites aside in this chapter). Information on these unique living-rock formations can be obtained from the 1884 **Telegraph Station** (☎ 9942 5905). The station served as a telephone exchange until 1977. Camping, caravan sites and food are also available there.

The 110km-long stretch of **Shell Beach** consists of solid shells nearly 10m deep! In places in Shark Bay, the shells *(Fragum erugatum)* are so tightly packed that they can be cut into blocks and used for building construction. **Nanga Station** has a pioneer museum and at **Eagle Bluff,** halfway between Nanga and Denham, there are superb cliff-top views.

At the *Nanga Bay Holiday Resort* (☎ 9948 3992), there are tent and powered sites, backpacker beds for $12, cabins for $45 and chalets from $80.

Denham (pop 1140)

Denham, the most westerly town in Australia, was once a pearling port. Today, prawns and tourism (both best raw!) are the local moneymakers. The Shark Bay tourist centre (☎ 9948 1253) on Knight Terrace is open daily from 8.30 am to 6 pm. The CALM office (☎ 9948 1208), also on Knight Terrace, has a great deal of information on the World Heritage area. There are some buildings in town made of shell blocks.

About 4km from Denham on the Monkey Mia Rd is the turn-off to the fascinating, wild **François Péron National Park.** The park is known for its arid scenery, wilderness feel and landlocked salt lakes. Entry to the park is $3 for a day visit and $20 for a vehicle with four passengers for seven nights. There are two **artesian bore tanks,** one which has water at 35°C and the other at a hot 43°C in the grounds of the Péron Homestead – you may soak in one of these (sunset is a great time). The station is a reminder of the peninsula's former use for grazing. Camp sites with limited facilities are located at Big

Lagoon, Gregories, Bottle Bay, South Gregories and Herald Bight.

The road to the homestead is suitable for 2WD vehicles but a 4WD will be necessary to go any farther into the park. Stick to the roads and *don't* try to cross a *birrida* (salt pan) – you will get bogged. For those without 4WD, try Shark Bay Safari Tours (☎ 9948 1593).

Places to Stay & Eat Accommodation can be very tight and expensive during school holidays. You can camp at Denham or 55km south at Nanga Station. The *Seaside Caravan Park* (☎ 9948 1242) on Knight Terrace is a friendly place on the foreshore with tent/powered sites for $11/13 and cabins from $33.

The recently renovated *Bay Lodge* (☎ 9948 1278), a budget place at 95 Knight Terrace on the foreshore, has beds in shared units which cost $12, and two-bedroom self-contained units for $46.

The friendly, well-run *Shark Bay Holiday Cottages* (☎ 9948 1206) on Knight Terrace has backpacker beds in four-bed, self-contained rooms for $12, as well as cottages for $40 for two. The *Old Pearler Restaurant* on Knight Terrace has a full à la carte menu with local seafood (lunch specials are $10).

Monkey Mia
This pleasant spot is 26km north-east of Denham on the other side of the Péron Peninsula. The Dolphin Information Centre (☎ 9948 1366), near the beach viewing area, has lots of information on dolphins and also screens a 45-minute video on Shark Bay. The high farce begins when the eager 'cross-channel communicators' reach out to get answers, a sign, whatever, from dolphins which venture inshore for a fish handout.

It's believed that bottlenose dolphins have been visiting Monkey Mia since the early 1960s, although it's only in the last 15 years that their visits have become famous.

Monkey Mia's dolphins swim right into knee-deep water, nudge up against you, chuckle and even take a fish if it's offered. The dolphins generally come in every day during the winter months, less frequently during the summer and more often in the morning. They may arrive alone or in groups of five or more; as many as 13 were recorded on one occasion. The entry fee to the reserve is $5 per vehicle. Observe human rules of behaviour – outlined in your entry brochure.

Places to Stay & Eat *Monkey Mia Dolphin Resort* (☎ 9948 1320) has a wide range of accommodation including tent/powered sites from $15/17.50 for two (a beachfront site is a whopping $21.50), backpacker beds in two-tented condos for $12, on-site vans from $25 and chalets from $130 for three; discounts apply in the off season.

Stromatolites

The dolphins at Monkey Mia didn't solely contribute to the listing of Shark Bay as a World Heritage region. The most significant feature was the stromatolites at Hamelin Pool. These rocky masses, consisting of layers of calcareous material formed by the prolific growth of microbes, are thousands of years old. What's more, their evolutionary history spans an amazing 3.5 billion years, right back to the dawn of life on Earth.

Hamelin Pool is suited to the growth of stromatolites because of the clarity and hypersalinity of the water. Each stromatolite is covered in a form of cyanobacterial microbe shaped like algae which, during daily photosynthesis, wave around. At night the microbes fold over, trapping calcium and carbonate ions dissolved in the water. The sticky chemicals they exude constantly add new layers to the surface of the stromatolite.

These are the most accessible stromatolites in the world, spectacularly set amid the turquoise waters of Hamelin Pool. There is now a boardwalk across the site – observe the regulations and be careful not to disturb them. ∎

WESTERN AUSTRALIA

At the *Bough Shed* in Monkey Mia, join the elite and watch the dolphins feed as you do. There is a more economical takeaway and a small grocery shop nearby.

CARNARVON (pop 6300)

Situated at the mouth of the Gascoyne River, Carnarvon is a nondescript place noted for its tropical fruit (particularly bananas) and fine climate – although it can become very hot in the middle of summer and is periodically subjected to floods and cyclones. Subsurface water, which flows even when the river is dry, is the lifeblood of riverside plantations but anathema to the salt piles produced at nearby Lake Macleod.

The main street, Robinson St, is 40m wide and a reminder of the days when camel trains used to pass through; it now suits 'hoons' doing 'doughnuts' in hotted-up cars. The **Fascine esplanade**, lined with palm trees, is a pleasant place to take a stroll and the 'one mile' jetty is a popular fishing spot, as is the little jetty at the prawning station south-west of town.

Carnarvon's tourist bureau (☎ 9941 1146), in the council chambers on the corner of Robinson and Stuart Sts, is open daily from 8.30 am to 5.30 pm; during the off season its hours are 9 am to 5 pm.

Organised Tours

Tropical Tripper Tours (contact the tourist bureau) departs from the tourist office and has half-day tours around town for $15 and an all-day tour that includes Lake Macleod, Cape Cuvier, the *Korean Star* wreck and blowholes for $40.

There are helicopter scenic flights from Carnarvon airport with Gascoyne Helicopter Services (☎ 9941 2494); these cost from $50 per person (minimum of two).

Places to Stay

You shouldn't have any trouble finding a caravan park in Carnarvon as there are seven of them; the closest to the centre of town is the *Carnarvon Tourist Centre Caravan Park* (☎ 9941 1438), 90 Robinson St, which has

powered sites/on-site vans at $13.50/29 for two.

Carnarvon Backpackers (☎ 9941 1095), 46 Olivia Terrace, has dorm beds from $10 (it is a good place to find picking work). *Backpackers' Paradise* (☎ 9941 2966), an associate-YHA hostel on Robinson St, has shared accommodation from $12; it also has doubles (which can be family rooms) from $30. The adjoining Old Post Office Café has good value meals.

There are self-contained holiday units at the *Carnarvon Close Holiday Resort* (☎ 99 41 1317), 96 Robinson St, for $55 for two. The *Fascine Lodge Motel* (☎ 9941 2411), 1002 David Brand Drive, has rooms for $80/85 a single/double, while the *Hospitality Inn Motel* (☎ 9941 1600) on West St charges from $74 for a double.

The Outcamp (☎ 9941 2421), 16 Olivia Terrace, on the Fascine is a luxurious B&B in the town's best location. It charges a mere $45/75 for singles/doubles for its great facilities, so treat yourself.

Places to Eat

On Robinson St are *Fascine* and *Kaycee's*, both standard coffee lounges. Readers recommend the *Old Post Office Café* at Backpackers' Paradise, which is open from 6 pm until late and also for Sunday breakfast.

The *Carnarvon Bakery*, 21 Robinson St, has home-made pies and sandwiches, as does *Jenny's Hot Bread Kitchen* on the corner of Robinson and Angelo Sts in the Supa Valu supermarket. The *Northern Heritage Tearooms*, 44 Olivia Terrace, comes and goes; when it is resurrected it has great home-made meals. For seafood, try the *Harbour View Cafe* at the fishing port on Douglas St.

Getting There & Around

Skywest (☎ 13 1300) flies to Carnarvon from Perth daily. Greyhound Pioneer (☎ 13 2030) passes through Carnarvon on its way north or south. The one-way fare from Perth to Carnarvon is $114 ($202 return).

Bicycles and helmets are available for hire from Backpackers' Paradise.

GASCOYNE AREA

There are daily tours to **banana plantations** (on South River Rd or Robinson St, just out of Carnarvon) which culminate with the almost obligatory eating of a chocolate-coated banana. You can buy a banana cookbook which includes cures for such ills as diarrhoea, ulcers and depression.

Pelican Point, 5km to the south-west, is a popular swimming and picnic spot. Other good beaches, also south and off the North-West Coastal Highway, are **Bush Bay** (turn-off 20km) and **New Beach** (37km).

Bibbawarra Bore, 14km north of Car-narvon, is an artesian well sunk to a depth of 914m which is being turned into a spa bath.

The frenzied **blowholes**, 70km to the north of Carnarvon, are well worth the trip. There's a fine beach about 1km south of the blowholes with a primitive camping ground (no fresh water available). You can camp at *Quobba Station* for about $5 – power is limited but water is available. About 1km south of the homestead is the **HMAS Sydney Memorial** to the ship sunk here by the German raider *Kormoran* in 1941.

Cape Cuvier, where salt is loaded for Japan, is 30km north of the blowholes, and

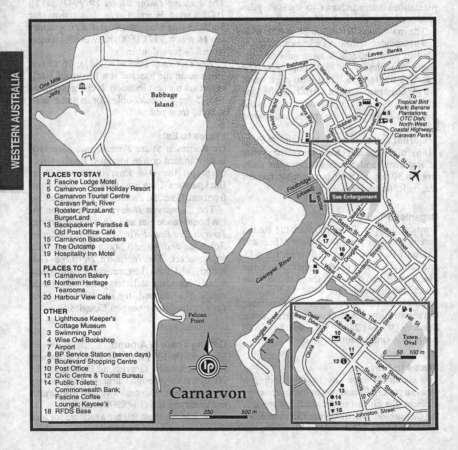

PLACES TO STAY
2 Fascine Lodge Motel
5 Carnarvon Close Holiday Resort
6 Carnarvon Tourist Centre Caravan Park; River Rooster; PizzaLand; BurgerLand
13 Backpackers' Paradise & Old Post Office Café
15 Carnarvon Backpackers
17 The Outcamp
19 Hospitality Inn Motel

PLACES TO EAT
11 Carnarvon Bakery
16 Northern Heritage Tearooms
20 Harbour View Cafe

OTHER
1 Lighthouse Keeper's Cottage Museum
3 Swimming Pool
4 Wise Owl Bookshop
7 Airport
8 BP Service Station (seven days)
9 Boulevard Shopping Centre
10 Post Office
12 Civic Centre & Tourist Bureau
14 Public Toilets; Commonwealth Bank; Fascine Coffee Lounge; Kaycee's
18 RFDS Base

Carnarvon

Station Stays

If you really want to sample a slice of genuine outback life, then try a station stay.

The 2650 sq km Giralia Station (☎ 9942 5937) on the Bullara-Giralia road, 43km from the North-West Coastal Highway is one possibility. There is a variety of accommodation here, including dinner and B&B from $60 (bookings essential and BYO), beds in the shearers' quarters from $10 to $15 and camping and caravan sites for $6; all prices are per person. The homestead is near many of the Pilbara and Gascoyne regions' best attractions. If you want to sample work on the station, which runs 25,000 merino sheep, just ask.

There are plenty of other places in the region (many are covered in this chapter): Mt Sandiman Station (☎ 9943 0550) is in the Kennedy Ranges; Manbery Station Stays (☎ 9942 5926) and Gnaraloo (☎ 9942 5927) are north of Carnarvon; Nallan Station (☎ 9963 1054) is near Cue; Erong Springs (☎ 9981 2910) is east of Gascoyne Junction; Eurady Station (☎ 9936 1038) is just off the North-West Coastal Highway; Yalardy (☎ 9942 5904) is north-east of the Overlander Roadhouse; Wooleen Station (☎ 9963 7973) is on the Murchison River; and Cobra Station (☎ 9943 0534) and Mt Augustus Station (☎ 9943 0527) are at the head of the Gascoyne River.

Get a copy of the free *Gascoyne Station Stays* from tourist offices, and go outback! ∎

nearby is the wreck of the *Korean Star*, grounded in 1988 (do not climb over the wreck as it is dangerous).

Remote Gascoyne Junction, 164km inland (east) of Carnarvon in the gemstone-rich **Kennedy Range**, has the welcome *Junction Hotel* (singles/doubles for $40/50). From here, the adventurous can continue through the outback to **Buringurrah National Park**, 450km from Carnarvon, to see **Mount Augustus**, the biggest – but certainly not the most memorable – rock (or monadnock) in the world. The rock can be climbed in a day and you can see Aboriginal rock paintings.

At *Cobra Station* (☎ 9943 0565), 50km from the rock, singles/doubles in the guesthouse (with tea and coffee-making facilities, and communal fridge) are from $35/45 and motel unit singles/doubles (with toilets, showers, tea and coffee-making facilities, and fridges) are $50/60. At the *Mt Augustus Outback Tourist Resort* (☎ 9943 0527) tent/powered sites are $12/16 for two and single/double units are $40/60.

Coral Coast & Pilbara

The Coral Coast extends from Coral Bay to Onslow and is, without doubt, one of the richest eco-tourism destinations in the world, with scintillating Ningaloo Reef and the rugged Cape Range National Park. Here you can snorkel over the world's largest west-coast reef, only metres from the shore, and swim with benign whale shark, dugongs, manta rays and a host of tropical fish.

The Pilbara, composed of the oldest rocks in the world, is an ancient, arid region with a glut of natural wonders. It stretches along the coast from Onslow to Port Hedland and inland beyond the Millstream-Chichester and Karijini national parks, and includes several hoary mining towns. Be careful: the Pilbara is alluring.

NINGALOO MARINE PARK

Running alongside of the North-West Cape for 260km, from Bundegi Reef in the north-east to Amherst Point in the south-west, is the stunning Ningaloo ('Point of Land') Reef. This miniaturised version of the Great Barrier Reef is actually more accessible – in places it is less than 100m offshore. The lagoons enclosed by the reef vary in width from 200m to 6km.

Within the marine park are eight sanctuary zones, where fishing is banned – you can only observe. You can see greenback turtles laying their eggs along the beaches, placid whale sharks swimming beyond the reef's waters, and dugongs.

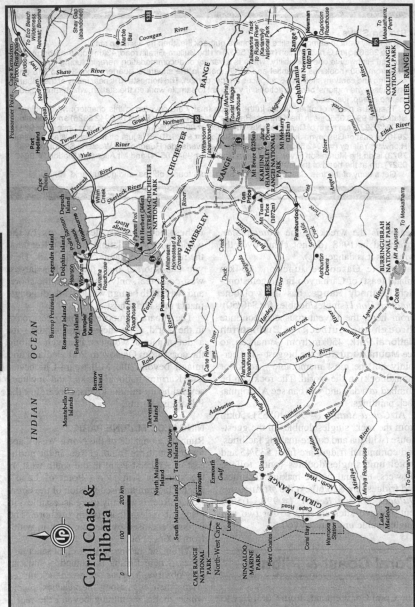

WESTERN AUSTRALIA

Coral Coast &
Pilbara

0   100   200 km

INDIAN OCEAN

Dugongs graze in seagrass meadows and for this reason are often called sea cows.
Their eating habits restrict them to shallow coastal waters and estuaries;
they are threatened by accidental capture in fishing nets.

Over 220 species of coral have been recorded in the waters of the park, ranging from the slow-growing bommies to delicate branching varieties. For eight to nine nights after the full moon in March, there is a synchronised mass spawning of coral, with eggs and sperm being released into the water simultaneously. For more information, see CALM's *Coral Reefs of WA* ($3).

Every year, humpback whales pass close by the coast on their way north in June and July to their calving grounds, probably near the Montebello Islands. In October and November they return to Antarctica.

Between November and January, near the top of North-West Cape, turtles come up the beaches at night, when the tide is right, to lay their eggs.

Contact the CALM office (☎ 9949 1676) for more specific information. Get a copy of the excellent *Parks of the Coral Coast* pamphlet from there; special fishing regulations apply in this park.

Coral Bay (pop 150)

This town, 150km south of Exmouth, is at the southern end of the Ningaloo Marine Park and a great place for snorkelling, swimming and sunbathing. The tourist bureau (☎ 9942 5988) is in Coral Bay Arcade; get a copy of *Coral Bay: Ningaloo Reef*.

Coral Dive (☎ 9942 5940), Ningaloo Reef Dive (☎ 9954 5836) and Dominator (☎ 9942 5995) arrange scuba adventures, operate PADI dive courses, fill tanks and rent out equipment. A good time to dive is during the coral spawning in March and April. You can rent snorkelling equipment for $10 per day at the beach or go 'snuba' diving (using an air hose) for $40/20 for adults/children.

Glass Bottom Boats (☎ 9942 5885) and Sub-Sea Explorer (☎ 9942 5955) trips allow you to see beneath the waves without getting wet; they cost $25 for three hours.

Places to Stay & Eat The *Bayview Holiday Village* (☎ 9942 5932) has tent/powered

WESTERN AUSTRALIA

Interacting with Marine Life

Visitors to Australia are often morbidly fascinated by sharks, especially the deadly great white shark which frequents the Southern Ocean. The **whale shark** *(Rhiniodon typus)* is the largest of the sharks, but it is a gentle giant. One of the few places in the world where you can come face to face underwater with this leviathan is off Ningaloo Reef, near Exmouth. To swim with these sharks is to experience one of the natural wonders of the world.

The whale shark weighs up to 40,000kg, is up to 18m long and drifts slowly on ocean currents filtering water through its 300 or more bands of minute teeth for the plankton and small fish on which it feeds. These sharks also eat an awful lot of rubbish: a wallet, boot, bucket and part of an oar were found in the stomach of one.

Whale-shark observing goes on from late March to the middle of June. The largest number of whale sharks are seen off the Tantabiddi and Mangrove Bay areas. The season begins at the time of coral spawning, when there is also a plankton bloom. The best way to see them is by licensed charter vessel (after they have been initially spotted by aircraft).

About 12 boats were allowed to take trips out to them in 1997. Exmouth Diving Centre (☎ 9949 1201) provides full equipment and daily refreshment for $250. This company has a good encounter rate.

Other reputable operators and their charges for a trip out to the whale sharks are:

Diving Ventures (☎ 9421 1052, $214)
King Dive (☎ 9949 1094), $199
Ningaloo Blue (☎ 9949 1119), $199
Ningaloo Deep (☎ 9949 1663), $250
Sea-Trek Diving Ventures (☎ 9949 2635), $214
Willie and the Whale Shark (☎ 9949 1004), $199

A normal dive charter costs $30 per dive, $60 with a daily rental of equipment. **Manta rays** are seen from July to November, and to 'fly' with one is an awesome experience. However, it is not guaranteed that you will see them every day.

Exmouth Diving Centre organises trips to the Muiron Islands, 10km north-east of the cape, on demand. These islands are a breeding sanctuary for three species of turtle: green, loggerhead and hawksbill. During dives you can hand feed the 1.5m-long potato cod *(Epinephalus tukula)* at the 'cod house'.

Other marine life you might see include humpback whales, dugongs and a few species of turtles, as well as a host of fish species. If you're interested in identifying fish consider getting *The Marine Fishes of North-West Australia* by G Allen & R Swainston. ■

sites from $13/15. There is a backpacker place, with kitchen facilities, which charges $14 a night. *Coral Bay Backpackers'* (☎ 99 42 5934) is behind the Ningaloo Reef Resort; as well as a basic bed, you get access to the resort's pool and bar for $15.

The *Coral Bay Lodge* (☎ 9942 5932) on the corner of Robinson and French Sts is associated with the Bayview. It has double units from $86 to $110. The *Ningaloo Reef Resort* (☎ 9942 5934) has tidy, well-appointed rooms from $95 for two ($10/5 for an extra adult/child).

The *Coral Bay Supermarket* has fresh bread, milk, fish and meat for self-caterers. *Fin's Cafe* opens early for those needing a caffeine fix before heading off to fish or dive; it has a nice alfresco dining area.

EXMOUTH (pop 3050)

Exmouth was established in 1967 largely as a service centre for the huge US navy communications base. The Yanks have gone and it now provides a good focus for the many great eco-activities in the area. On no account should it be allowed to become a supply and administrative centre for multinational companies drilling in and around Ningaloo Marine Park!

The helpful Exmouth tourist office (☎ 9949 1176), recently relocated to the Exmouth Cape Tourist Village caravan park on Murat Rd has a video on all aspects of the reef. It's open daily from 8.30 am to 5 pm. CALM (☎ 9949 1676) has an office on Maidstone Crescent.

The town beach at the end of Warne St is a popular swimming spot. About 13km south of town is **Pebbly Beach**, a safe swimming beach covered in colourful pebbles. The wreck of the **SS Mildura**, beached in 1907, and the **Vlaming Head Lighthouse** are north of town and have sensational views.

Part of North-West Cape is dominated by the 13 low-frequency transmitter stations of the Harold Holt Communications Station. Twelve are higher than the Eiffel Tower (321m) and serve to support the 13th, which is 396m high.

Organised Tours

There is a host of tours in the area, ranging from gulf and gorge safaris to reef and fishing tours. Perhaps the most informative is run by Neil McLeod's Ningaloo Safari

Tours (☎ 9949 1550). The full-day safari, called 'Over the Top' (10 hours; $95), has been recommended by many travellers (including this writer); it takes in Cape Range, Ningaloo Reef, Yardie Creek and Vlaming Head lighthouse. Neil's mum makes a great boiled fruit cake.

Tour operators with similar itineraries are Exmouth Eco Tours (☎ 9949 2809; $95), West Coast Safaris (☎ 9949 1625; $95) and WestTrek Safaris (☎ 9949 2659; $85).

The Ningaloo Coral Explorer (☎ 9949 2424), a glass-bottomed boat, operates coral viewing trips over Bundegi Reef on the east coast. Ningaloo Ecology Cruises (☎ 9949 2255) operates tours from Tantabiddi on the west coast. It charges $20/45 for adults/a family.

Sea Kayak Wilderness Adventures (☎ 9949 2952, 0417 942 017) runs a great full-day sea kayak paddle from Tantabiddi to Turquoise Bay; it charges $130, all equipment included.

WESTERN AUSTRALIA

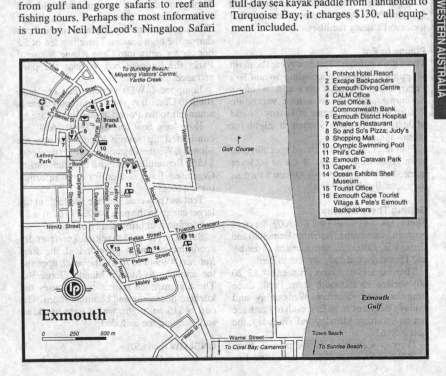

1 Potshot Hotel Resort
2 Excape Backpackers
3 Exmouth Diving Centre
4 CALM Office
5 Post Office & Commonwealth Bank
6 Exmouth District Hospital
7 Whaler's Restaurant
8 So and So's Pizza; Judy's
9 Shopping Mall
10 Olympic Swimming Pool
11 Phil's Café
12 Exmouth Caravan Park
13 Caper's
14 Ocean Exhibits Shell Museum
15 Tourist Office
16 Exmouth Cape Tourist Village & Pete's Exmouth Backpackers

Exmouth

0   250   500 m

Golf Course

Exmouth Gulf

Town Beach

Warne Street
To Coral Bay; Carnarvon
To Sunrise Beach

Places to Stay

The well-kept, tidy *Exmouth Cape Tourist Village* (☎ 9949 1101) on the corner of Truscott Crescent and Murat Rd has powered/en-suite sites for $17/21, cabins with cooking facilities from $32 to $46 and comfortable self-contained chalets for $60. Some chalets have been converted into a backpacker place and beds are $14 per night (this includes access to a very cold pool).

The *Exmouth Caravan Park* (☎ 9949 1331) on Lefroy St was once a poor choice but the local council has promised that the park will improve. It has tent/powered sites for $12/15, on-site vans for $35 and park cabins for $45; all prices are for two.

The huge *Potshot Hotel Resort* (☎ 9949 1200) on Murat Rd has all types of accommodation. The *Excape Backpackers* (☎ 9949 1201) looks as though it is the old staff quarters for the Potshot; the plus is that $15 gets the budget traveller access to all of the resort's fancy facilities.

Places to Eat

There are a number of takeaways in the main shopping area of town including *So and So's Pizza*, *Three Palms*, *Judy's* and *Whaler's Restaurant*, which has a nice verandah. *Phil's Café* on the corner of Lefroy St and Maidstone Crescent is open at night for takeaways.

Fish & chips are a regional speciality. In town go to *Caper's Fish & Chips* – clever name, but bring your own tomato sauce as they actually charge for it!

Getting There & Away

There are Skywest (☎ 13 1300) services between Learmonth (37km from Exmouth) and Carnarvon, Geraldton and Karratha (Tuesday and Thursday), and daily services to Perth.

There is a Greyhound Pioneer (☎ 13 20 30) service to Exmouth from Perth three times a week (Sunday, Wednesday and Friday). Services from Exmouth to Perth are run on Saturday, Monday and Thursday; the cost is $167.

There is a shuttle bus (the postie), from Monday to Saturday, which goes from Ex-mouth to Minilya roadhouse on the North-West Coastal Highway, to meet Greyhound Pioneer buses. The one-way cost is $15 and the bus is a good option if you don't have your own vehicle.

Hitching is not really an option around here. It is better to have your own transport.

CAPE RANGE NATIONAL PARK

This 510 sq km park, which runs down the west coast of the cape, includes the modern Milyering visitor centre, a variety of flora and fauna, good swimming beaches, several gorges (the Shothole, Charles Knife and scenic Yardie Creek), Owl's Roost Cave and rugged scenery.

Milyering visitor centre (☎ 9949 2808) is built in the rammed-earth style, is solar powered and has environmentally thoughtful waste disposal. You can see a comprehensive display of the area's natural and cultural history here. It is usually open daily (except Tuesday and Saturday) from 10 am to 4 pm during the high season. There is a fee of $5 per car for entry into Cape Range National Park; the honesty box is near the park entrance.

Equipped (4WD) vehicles can continue south to Coral Bay via the coast and there is a turn-off to the Point Cloates lighthouse.

Hour-long boat tours (☎ 9949 2659) are conducted up scenic **Yardie Gorge** on Monday, Wednesday and Saturday; they cost $15/8 for adults/children. See the earlier Organised Tours section for more information on tours.

Tent and powered sites are available at the larger camps in the park (☎ 9949 1676) at $5 per double (but bring plenty of water).

Safari-style and backpacker-friendly accommodation is provided at the *Reef Retreat* (☎ 9949 1776) on the beach opposite the entrance to Mandu Mandu Gorge Rd. The big marquee (circus tent) houses the kitchen, bedrooms and common room. The cost is $15 per night, with a light breakfast and camping fee included.

ONSLOW (pop 650)

Onslow has the dubious distinctions of being

Montebello Islands

The Montebellos are a group of more than 100 flat limestone islands off the north-west coast of Western Australia between Onslow and Karratha. In 1992 they were gazetted as a conservation park.

In 1622, the survivors of the shipwrecked *Tryal* camped here before setting off to the East Indies. The islands were named in 1801 after the battle of Monte Bello, by the French explorer Baudin. The pearlers who came next introduced the black rat and the cat, which ensured the extinction of the golden bandicoot and the spectacled hare-wallaby on the island.

In 1952, the British detonated an atomic weapon mounted on HMS *Plym*, anchored in Main Bay off Trimouille Island. Two further atomic tests were carried out in 1956, on Alpha and Trimouille islands. Some 40 years later you can now step ashore and get close to the point of detonation. It will be interesting to see how long the radiation warning signs last before being souvenired by collectors of the macabre.

Nature is resilient and the islands have thriving populations of both land and marine fauna and more than 100 plant species, including a stand of mangroves. The legless lizard *Aprasia rostrata* is found on Hermite Island (was it legless before 1952?). Two species of marine turtle are known to nest on the islands, as are a number of seabirds. Vignerons will love the names of many of the bays – Hock, Champagne, Burgundy, Claret and Moselle, for example.

'Beautiful Mountains' the islands are not. They are, rather, silent witness to the awesome destructive power of nuclear fission, and to the miraculous, recuperative powers of nature. ■

the southernmost Western Australian town to be bombed in WWII and later of being used as a base by the British for nuclear testing in the Montebello Islands.

There is good swimming and fishing in the area. The **Old Onslow ruins**, 48km south-west of the town, were abandoned in 1925. They include a gaol and post office, and are worth a look.

The *Ocean View Caravan Park* (☎ 9184 6053) on Second Ave has tent/powered sites for $12/14 and on-site vans from $30. The *Beadon Bay Village* (☎ 9184 6007) on Beadon Creek Rd also has tent and powered sites. There are expensive resorts on the Direction and Mackerel islands, 11km and 22km offshore, respectively; for more information contact Onslow Sun Chalets (☎ 9184 6058).

KARRATHA (pop 10,000)

Karratha (Aboriginal for 'good country') is the commercial centre of the area. The town was developed due to the rapid expansion of the Hamersley Iron and Woodside LNG projects.

The area around Karratha is replete with evidence of Aboriginal occupation – carvings, grindstones, etchings and middens can

be found on the 3.5km **Jaburara Heritage Trail**, which starts by the information centre. *Terminalia canescens*, the trees which grow in the creek beds here, are a reminder of the area's former tropical climate.

The Karratha & District Information Centre (☎ 9144 4600) on Karratha Rd, just before you reach the T-junction of Karratha and Millstream Rds, has heaps of info on what to see and do in the Pilbara.

The **Fe-NaCl-NG Festival** is held in August each year. The title combines the chemical abbreviations of the region's main natural resources – iron, salt and natural gas.

Places to Stay & Eat

There are three caravan parks in Karratha, including *Fleetwood's Balmoral Rd* (☎ 9185 3628), a permanent residents' haunt, and *Fleetwood's Rosemary Rd* (☎ 9185 1855) a temporary residents' haunt – this writer's experience in one of the shoddiest caravans ever rented was very temporary. At the latter, powered/en-suite sites are $16.50/24 and on-site vans are $47.50.

Sadly, we have had lots of letters saying that *Karratha Backpackers* (☎ 9144 4904) on Wellard Way is tainted by beer-swilling semi-permanents who are rude to foreign female travellers. It seemed OK on our visit, with a friendly host, and the rooms and facilities (laundry, TV room, etc) were good value ($15 for a dorm bed, $30 for a single room, $50 for a family room). Let us know more. The upmarket choices in town are expensive.

On Balmoral Rd, *Los Amigos*, opposite the BP station, has Mexican food (Wednesday is 'el cheapo' night with four courses for $12.50). For snacks, there are cafes and takeaways in the Karratha shopping centre.

Getting There & Away

By far the most convenient way to Karratha is by air and Qantas/Airlink (☎ 13 1313) and Ansett (☎ 13 1300) have direct daily services from Perth. Skywest (☎ 13 1300) operates periodic services to Broome, Exmouth and Port Hedland. The Karratha Backpackers (☎ 9144 4904) has a courtesy bus from the terminal.

Greyhound Pioneer (☎ 13 2030) has daily services (about $126) from Perth; it uses the Shell Roadhouse on Searipple Rd as its depot. Most people coming to Karratha, however, arrive by car.

A local taxi is $33 from Karratha to Dampier.

DAMPIER (pop 1400)

Dampier is on King Bay, across from the 41 islands of the Dampier Archipelago (named after William Dampier, who visited the area in 1699). It is a Hamersley Iron town, the port for Tom Price and the Paraburdoo iron-ore operations. (It will also be the port for the huge Marandoo mineral project.) Gas from the natural-gas fields of the North-West Shelf is piped ashore nearby on the Burrup Peninsula. From there, it is piped to Perth and other parts of the Pilbara, or liquefied as part of the Woodside Petroleum project and exported to Japan and South Korea.

An inspection of the port facilities can be arranged (☎ 9144 4600); the cost is $5/2 for adults/children. The William Dampier Lookout provides a fine view over the harbour. The Woodside LNG visitor centre

(☎ 9183 8100) is open on weekdays from 10 am to 4 pm during the tourist season.

The **Burrup Peninsula** has some 10,000 Aboriginal rock engravings depicting fish, turtles, kangaroos and a Tasmanian tiger.

The **Dampier Archipelago** is renowned as a game-fishing mecca and each year in August it hosts the Dampier Classic.

Places to Stay & Eat

Apart from the *transit caravan park* (☎ 9183 1109) on the Esplanade, which has tent/powered sites for $7/14 for two, there is a backpacker place in the *Peninsula Palms* (☎ 9183 1888) on the Esplanade. It charges $15 a night to stay in a building we only saw before it was fully renovated (write and tell us about it); enquire at the main hotel desk.

Barnacle Bob's, also on the Esplanade and overlooking Hampton Harbour, is good for fish & chips ($8.50).

ROEBOURNE AREA

The Roebourne area is a busy little enclave of historic towns and modern port facilities. Information is available from the tourist bureau (☎ 9182 1060) in the Old Gaol on Queen St in Roebourne. In Cossack, Heritage Council of WA officials will help.

Roebourne (pop 1700)

Roebourne is the oldest existing town in the Pilbara. It has a history of grazing, and gold and copper mining, and was once the capital of the north-west region. There are still some fine old buildings, including the **Old Gaol**, an 1894 church and the Victoria Hotel, which is the last of five original pubs. The town was once connected to Cossack, 13km away, by a horse-drawn tram.

The *Harding River Caravan Park* (☎ 9182 1063) has tent/powered sites at $10/12 for two. The *Mt Welcome Motel Hotel* (☎ 9182 1001) on Roe St is the main accommodation, with singles/doubles for $45/65.

Cossack (pop 30)

Originally known as Tien Tsin Harbour, Cossack, at the mouth of the Harding River, was a bustling town and the main port for the district in the mid to late 19th century. Its boom was short-lived and Point Samson soon supplanted it as the chief port for the region. The sturdy old buildings date from 1870 to 1898, and much of the ghost town has been restored.

The town has an **art gallery**, **museum** and budget accommodation. Beyond town, there's a **pioneer cemetery** with a small Japanese section dating from the old pearl-diving days. In fact, this is where WA pearling actually began; it later moved on to Broome in the 1890s. There are good look-outs and excellent beaches in the area; the cooler, drier months are best for a visit.

The *Cossack Backpackers* (☎ 9182 1190) is still one of those gems of the road. It's housed in the old police barracks administered by the Heritage Council of WA. Dorm rooms are $12, family rooms are $35, and there is a kitchen, refrigerators and hot showers. There is also a small shop nearby. As there are no places to eat, bring your own food. If you ring in advance the proprietors will pick you up from Wickham.

Wickham & Point Samson

Wickham (pop 1650) is the Robe River Iron company town. The company handles its ore-exporting facilities 10km away at Cape Lambert, where the jetty is 3km long. Ore is railed to the coast from the mining operations inland at Pannawonica.

Point Samson (pop 200), beyond Wickham, took the place of Cossack when the old port silted up. In turn, it has been replaced by the modern port facilities of Dampier and Cape Lambert. There are good **beaches** at Point Samson and at nearby Honeymoon Cove.

The *Solveig Caravan Park* (☎ 9187 1414) on Samson Rd next to the tavern in Point Samson has tent/powered sites for $13/15. *Delilah's B&B* (☎ 9187 1471) in Point Samson charges $45/85 for singles/doubles.

It's worth detouring to Point Samson for its seafood. At *Moby's Kitchen* you can get excellent fish & chips and salad ($8).

Whim Creek

The first significant Pilbara mineral find was at Whim Creek, 80km east of Roebourne. It once had a copper mine but today all that is left is the *Whim Creek Hotel* (☎ 9176 4953) which has accommodation and a restaurant; tent sites are $10 for two, backpacker beds are $12 and singles/doubles are from $30/35.

MILLSTREAM-CHICHESTER NATIONAL PARK

This impressive 2000 sq km national park, in the middle of a semi-arid environment, includes a number of freshwater pools, such as **Python Pool**. This was once an oasis for Afghani camel drivers and is still a good place to pause for a swim. The **Millstream Homestead** is 150km south of Roebourne and 21km from the turn-off from the Wittenoom road. It has been converted into an information centre, with much detail on the Millstream ecosystems and the lifestyle of the Yinjibarndi people.

The **Chinderwarriner Pool**, near the information centre, is a pleasant oasis with pools, palms (including the unique Millstream palm) and lilies; it is well worth a visit. The lush environment is a haven for birds and other fauna, such as flying foxes and kangaroos. Over 20 species of dragonfly and damselfly have been recorded here.

The park also has a number of walking/driving trails including Cliff Lookout Drive, the Murlunmunyjurna Trail (6.8km) and the 8km Chichester Range Camel Track.

The basic camp sites (☎ 9184 5144) at Snake Creek, Crossing Pool and Deep Reach have gas barbecues, fire rings and pit toilets; tent sites are $5 ($3 for each extra adult).

KARIJINI NATIONAL PARK

Like other gorges in central Australia, those of Karijini (Hamersley Range) National Park are spectacular both in their sheer rocky faces and varied colours. In early spring, the park is often carpeted with colourful wildflowers.

There is an interpretive centre (☎ 014 511 1285) at the junction of Juna Downs, Joffre

Falls and Yampire Gorge roads, in the south-east corner of the park. It is run by Aboriginal people, the traditional dwellers of Karijini, and they are enthusiastic and informative. Get a copy of the free *Karijini: Visitor Information/Walk Trail Guide* to assist in planning your visit.

The 10km road into **Dales Gorge** starts just south of the interpretive centre. About 200m along the Dales Gorge track is a turn-off to a giant termite mound. By this same route, you can get to **Circular Pool** and a nearby lookout, and, by a footpath, to the bottom of the **Fortescue Falls**. The walk from Circular Pool along Dales Gorge to the falls is recommended; you will be surprised by the permanent water in the gorge.

The Joffre Falls road leads to **Knox Gorge**; nearby is a 1.5km return walk to Red Gorge lookout. From the Joffre Falls turn-off it is 16km to the truly spectacular **Oxers Lookout**, at the junction of the Red, Weano, Joffre and Hancock gorges, one of Australia's great sights. If you wish to get down into the gorge proper, take the steps down to Handrail Pool (turn to the right at the bottom) in Weano Gorge.

In the north-west of the park on the Nanutarra-Munjina road, you pass through the small **Rio Tinto Gorge**, and just beyond this is the **Hamersley Gorge**, only 4km from the main road. Mt Meharry (1250m), the highest mountain in WA, is near the south-eastern border of the national park.

The ghost town of Wittenoom is at the northern end of the park and **Wittenoom Gorge**, infamous because of many asbestos-related deaths in the region, is immediately south of the town. A road runs the 13km into the gorge, passing old asbestos mines, small gorges and pretty pools.

Some 18km from the Great Northern Highway is the turn-off to the **Yampire Gorge**, where blue veins of asbestos can be seen in the rock. Fig Tree Soak, in the gorge, was once used by Afghani camel drivers as a watering point. This road is no longer looked after and can only be negotiated by 4WD – it should not be used as a means of entry to the park. The best entry is via the sealed road from the Great Northern Highway, some 35km south of the Auski (Munjina) Roadhouse and 160km north-west of Newman.

Warning

Even after 25 years, there is a health risk from airborne asbestos fibres in Wittenoom township, and in the Wittenoom and Yampire gorges. Avoid disturbing asbestos tailings in the area and keep your car windows closed on windy days. If you are concerned, seek medical advice before going to Wittenoom.

Places to Stay

There are several basic camp sites within Karijini, including Dales Gorge at the Weano Gorge and Joffre intersection ($5 for a site) – call ☎ 9189 8157 for information.

On the Great Northern Highway is the asbestos-free *Auski Tourist Village* (☎ 9176 6988); tent sites are $10 for two, austere cabins $45 and overpriced motel rooms $110. *Mt Florance Station* (☎ 9189 8151), halfway between the Millstream-Chichester and Karijini national parks, has camp sites for $5 per person and beds in the shearers' quarters for $12.

There are several places to stay in Tom Price and Mt Newman (see the Company Towns entry later in the section).

Organised Tours

Dave's Gorge Tours (☎ 9189 7026) receives rave reviews from our readers. Design-a-Tour (☎ 9144 1460) has one-day tours of Karijini and the gorges for $70, including lunch. Snappy Gum Safaris (☎ 9185 1278) runs two-day camping safaris to Karijini ($190) and Lestok Tours (☎ 9189 2032), based in Tom Price, has a day trip to Karijini for $35/15 for adults/children.

Scenic helicopter flights (☎ 9176 6979) over the gorges depart from the Auski (Munjina) Roadhouse; a 30-minute flight is $135 (minimum of two people).

COMPANY TOWNS

There are two large, company-run, iron-ore towns near Karijini – Tom Price (pop 3550), to the west, and Paraburdoo (pop 2350), to the south-west. Another, Newman (pop 5500), is 450km south of Port Hedland, to the south-east of Karijini. Pannawonica, very much a 'closed' town, is 46km east of the North-West Coastal Highway.

Company towns usually have sports facilities, which are second in popularity to the tavern or workers' club. SkyTV, dirt-bike racing, stock cars, takeaways and 'porno' videos have all found a comfortable niche.

In **Tom Price**, check with Hamersley Iron (☎ 9189 2375) about inspecting the mine works – if nothing else, the scale of it will impress you; tours cost a hefty $12/6 for adults/children. Mt Nameless, 4km west of Tom Price, offers good views of the area, especially at sunset. **Paraburdoo** has mine tours, a hotel and caravan park; its airport is the closest to Karijini.

At **Newman**, a town which only came into existence in the 1970s, the iron-ore mountain, Whaleback, is being systematically taken apart and railed north to the coast. Guided 1½-hour tours (☎ 9175 2888) of these engrossing operations leave across from the tourist centre daily at 8.30 am and 1 pm; safety helmets are provided.

Newman is a modern company town built to service the mine but it has a helpful tourist centre on the corner of Fortescue Ave and Newman Drive.

The scenic drive through the **Ophthalmia Range** is spectacular in wildflower season.

Places to Stay & Eat

In Tom Price, the caravan park (☎ 9189 1515) has tent/powered sites for $12/14 for two and on-site vans for $40. The *Hillview Lodge* (☎ 9189 1110) has budget/deluxe rooms for two for $50/119.

In Newman, *Dearlove's Caravan Park* (☎ 9175 2802) on Cowra Drive has tent/powered sites for $10/15 and on-site vans from $30. The *Mercure Inn Newman* (☎ 9175 1101) has backpacker beds for $30.

The *Red Emperor* in the Tom Price shopping mall provides reasonable food and the *Mercure Inn Tom Price* has counter meals. In Newman, there are roadhouses, Asian places

and takeaways. You get good counter meals (with an excellent salad bar) in the *All Seasons Newman Hotel*.

MARBLE BAR (pop 350)

Reputed to be the hottest place in Australia, Marble Bar had a period in the 1920s when for 160 consecutive days the temperature topped 37°C. On one day, in 1905, the mercury soared to 49.1°C. From October to March, days over 40°C are common.

The town, 203km south-east of Port Hedland, is the centre of a 377,000 sq km shire (larger than New Zealand). It takes its name from the red jasper bar across the Coongan River, 5km to the west. The tourist centre (☎ 9176 1041) is across from the Ironclad Hotel.

In town, the 1895 government buildings, made of local stone, are still in use. In late winter, as the spring wildflowers begin to bloom, Marble Bar is actually quite a pretty place and one of the most popular towns in the Pilbara to visit. The **Comet Gold Mine**, 10km south of Marble Bar, still in operation and with a mining museum, is open daily.

The caravan park (☎ 9176 1067), Contest St, has tent sites/on-site vans for $15/35 for two. There's a range of rooms at the *Ironclad Hotel* (☎ 9176 1066), one of the area's colourful drinking spots; backpacker beds cost from $20.

PORT HEDLAND (pop 13,000)

This port handles a massive tonnage, as it is the place from where the Pilbara's iron ore is shipped overseas. The town is built on an island connected to the mainland by causeways. The main highway into Port Hedland enters along a 3km causeway.

Even before the Marble Bar gold rush of the 1880s, the town had been important. It became a grazing centre in 1864 and during the 1870s a fleet of 150 pearling luggers was based here. By 1946, however, the population had dwindled to a mere 150.

Information

The helpful tourist bureau (☎ 9173 1711), which has showers ($1.50), is at 13 Wedge

St, across from the post office. It's open from 8.30 am to 5 pm during the week, and from 8.30 am to 4.30 pm on weekends. It provides an excellent map of the town.

Things to See & Do
You can visit the wharf area or view it from the 26m **observation tower** behind the tourist office (you have to sign a waiver to climb it and you'll need closed-in shoes; $2, children $1). Below are huge ore carriers, stockpiles of ore and a town encrusted in red Pilbara dust. The iron-ore trains are up to 2.6km in length. From Monday to Friday, at 10 am, there's the 1½-hour BHP Iron Ore & Port Tour which leaves from the tourist office ($10, children $2).

Pretty Pool, 7km east of the town centre on the waterfront, is a tidal pool where shell-collectors have fun, but beware of stonefish.

There are **Aboriginal petroglyphs** (rock engravings), including turtles and a whale, near the BHP gate at Two-Mile Ridge; contact the Department of Aboriginal Affairs office in the Boulevard shopping centre on Wilson St for permission to enter.

Whale & Turtle-Watching Between October and March **flatback turtles** nest on some of the nearby beaches, including Munda, Cooke Point, Cemetery and Pretty Pool. Their nesting density is low on city beaches, with only a few turtles nesting each night. At Munda, up to 20 turtles may nest in a night. Enquire at the tourist office about the turtles' location during the nesting season.

Whale-watching trips are operated by Big Blue Dive (☎ 9173 3202). These take four hours, leave on weekdays and cost about $60 per person; trips are dependent on tides and numbers. Majestic humpbacks are often seen in pods of five to six.

Places to Stay
You can camp by the airport at *Dixon's Caravan Park* (☎ 9172 2525) when space permits; powered sites are $16 for two. More convenient is the revamped *Cooke Point Caravan Park* (☎ 9173 1271) on Athol St, which is also close to Pretty Pool; powered

sites in this presentable park are $17 for two and excellent park cabins are $65.

The dusty *Port Hedland Backpackers* (☎ 9173 3282) is at 20 Richardson St, between Edgar and McKay Sts. The homely atmosphere and friendly hosts make up for the lack of luxuries. Dorm beds/twin rooms cost $14/32 and the place has a kitchen and (in these parts) much-needed laundry facilities. Staff run economical three-day camping trips to Karijini for $220.

The *Harbour Lodge* (☎ 9173 2996), 11 Edgar St, has a fully equipped kitchen; double/family rooms are $40/45.

Natalie's Waterside Lodge (☎ 9173 2635), 7 Richardson St, is a good choice because you at least get what you pay for; comfortable doubles are $80 or $420 per week (the views of the ore piles are free).

The most expensive motels are the *Hospitality Inn* (☎ 9173 1044) on Webster St, with singles and doubles from $138, and the *Mercure Inn Port Hedland* (☎ 9173 1511) on Lukis St, with rooms for $139.

Places to Eat
There are plenty of supermarkets if you want to fix your own food and also a number of coffee bars and other places where you can get a pie or pastie.

Natalie's Bakehouse on Richardson St has been heartily recommended for its home-made salad rolls. Nearby is the *Coral Trout*, with a BYO restaurant and takeaway section where you can get fish & chips; the mackerel is superb. *Kath's Kitchen* on Wedge St is open from 5 am to 8.30 pm and has basic, good meals such as gigantic breakfasts for about $8. The *Oriental Gallery* on the corner of Edgar and Anderson Sts does a good-value weekday lunch.

Getting There & Away
Qantas (☎ 13 1313) has at least one service daily to Perth. Ansett (☎ 13 1300) has daily flights to Perth and also frequent flights, many operated by Skywest, to and from Broome, Derby, Geraldton, Karratha and Kununurra.

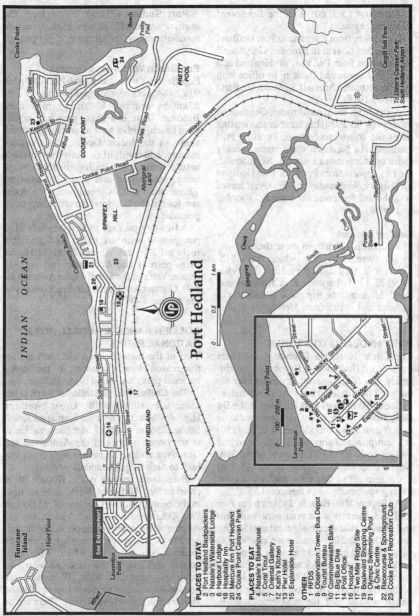

Port Hedland

0   0.5   1 km

PLACES TO STAY
2   Port Hedland Backpackers
3   Natalie's Waterside Lodge
18 Harbour Lodge
20 Hospitality Inn
22 Mercure Inn Port Hedland
24 Cooke Point Caravan Park

PLACES TO EAT
4   Natalie's Bakehouse
5   Coral Trout
7   Oriental Gallery
12 Kath's Kitchen
13 Pier Hotel
15 Esplanade Hotel

OTHER
1   RFDS
8   Observation Tower; Bus Depot
9   Tourist Bureau
10 Commonwealth Bank
11 Big Blue Dive
14 Post Office
16 Hospital
17 Two Mile Ridge Site
19 Boulevard Shopping Centre
21 Olympic Swimming Pool
    & Civic Centre
22 Racecourse & Sportsground
23 Cooke Point Recreation Club

WESTERN AUSTRALIA

Ansett (☎ 13 1300) is in the Boulevard shopping centre.

It's 230km from Karratha to Port Hedland and a farther 604km to Broome. Greyhound Pioneer runs from Perth to Port Hedland and north to Broome and Darwin. Its office is in the Homestead, Throssell St, South Hedland (☎ 9140 1919).

Apart from the coastal route, Greyhound Pioneer (☎ 13 2030) has another service that takes the inland route from Perth to Port Hedland via Newman three times weekly (with connections to Darwin). Northbound, the bus departs from Perth for Port Hedland on Sunday, Wednesday and Friday; it leaves southbound for Perth on Sunday, Tuesday and Friday.

Getting Around
The airport is 13km from town; the only way to get there is by taxi, which costs $15. There's a Hedland Bus Lines service (☎ 9172 1394) between Port Hedland and South Hedland; the trip takes 40 minutes to an hour and is run from Monday to Friday ($2.20).

PORT HEDLAND TO BROOME
The Great Northern Highway continues from Port Hedland to Broome. Unfortunately, this 604km stretch is a contender for the most boring length of road in Australia.

Some 84km from Port Hedland is the **De Grey River**, where many bird species can be seen. *Pardoo Station* (133km; ☎ 9176 4930) has tent/powered sites for $7/9 for two and budget beds for $15/7 for adults/children. Not far from the Pardoo Roadhouse (154km) is the turn-off to **Cape Keraudren**, a great fishing spot; camp sites there cost $5.

At **Eighty Mile Beach**, 245km from Port Hedland, there is a caravan park with tent and powered sites and budget cabins ($35 for two). The Sandfire Roadhouse (295km) is very much an enforced fuel stop for most – pack your own sandwiches rather than eat the expensive food sold here (there is also accommodation). The Droughtmaster Bar is worth a look and the neoprene stubby-holders sold here are prized souvenirs.

Port Smith (477km), 23km from the highway turn-off, comes highly recommended; unpowered sites are $6 per person.

Eco Beach Wilderness Retreat
Eco Beach Yardoogarra (☎ 9192 4844; fax 9192 4845; ecobeach@tpgi.com.au) is only 27km by sea and 130km by road from Broome. There is a 15km stretch of white-sand beach, timber huts on stilts with superb views of the Indian Ocean, and abundant marine and bird life. Activities include nature walks, horse-riding, fishing, swimming, snorkelling and generally relaxing. There are no TVs, telephones or room service but the fare-for-yourself theme compensates.

A two-day package to Eco Beach is $199 per person with all meals and transfers included. Singles/twins are $100 ($10 for an extra person) and 4WD transfers are $40 return. You can fly with Broome Aviation for $60. Contact Eco Beach for directions if you are driving a 4WD.

COLLIER RANGE & RUDALL RIVER NATIONAL PARKS
Two of the most isolated and, perhaps for that reason alone, interesting, of the State's national parks are found in the Pilbara.

The **Collier Range National Park** is the more accessible, as the Great Northern Highway bisects it near the Kumarina Roadhouse, 256km north of Meekatharra. Here, at the upper reaches of the Ashburton and Gascoyne rivers, the ranges vary from low hills to high ridges bounded by cliffs.

Even more remote is the **Rudall River (Karlamilyi) National Park**, a breathtakingly beautiful desert region of 15,000 sq km, 300km east of Newman. Visit in July and August when daytime temperatures are tolerable – although the nights can be exceptionally cold. The Martu Aboriginal people still live in the park. At least two vehicles, equipped with HF radios, are needed for off-road trips into these parks and visitors must be self-sufficient. There are no facilities.

The Kimberley

The rugged Kimberley, at the northern end of WA, is one of Australia's last frontiers. Despite enormous advances in the past decade this is still a little-travelled and remote area of great rivers and magnificent scenery. The Kimberley suffers from climatic extremes – heavy rains in the Wet followed by searing heat in the Dry – but the irrigation projects in its north-east have made great changes to the region.

Rivers and creeks can rise rapidly following heavy rain and become impassable torrents within 15 minutes. Unless it's a brief storm, it's quite likely that watercourses will remain impassable for some days. After two or three days of rain the Fitzroy River can swell from its normal 100m width to over 10km. River and creek crossings on the Great Northern Highway on both sides of Halls Creek become impassable every Wet.

The best time to visit is between April and September. By October it's already getting hot (with daily temperatures of 35°C), and later in the year temperatures of more than 40°C are common until it starts to rain. On the other hand, the Wet is a spectacular time to visit – ethereal thunderstorms, lightning, flowing waterfalls close to the towns and the magic carpet of the green rejuvenated landscape.

Kimberley attractions include idyllic Broome, the spectacular Fitzroy River gorges, the Wolfe Creek meteorite crater, the Gibb River Road and the Bungle Bungles.

BROOME (pop 11,500)

For many travellers, Broome is Australia's true getaway, with palm-fringed beaches and a cosmopolitan atmosphere. This small, dusty old port is noted for its Chinatown and the influences of early Japanese pearlers. Although still isolated, Broome has certainly been discovered. Today it is something of a travellers' centre, with the attendant good and bad characteristics.

Pearling in the sea off Broome started in the 1880s and peaked in the early 1900s, when the town's 400 pearling luggers, worked by 3000 men, supplied 80% of the world's mother-of-pearl (used mainly for buttons). Today only a handful of boats operates. The divers were from various Asian countries and rivalry between the nationalities was always intense and sometimes ugly. The *Broome Heritage Trail* pamphlet merges the past with the present.

Information

The efficient tourist bureau (☎ 9192 2222) is on the corner of Broome Rd and Bagot St. It's open daily from 8 am to 5 pm from April to November, and from 9 am to 5 pm on weekdays and from 9 am to 1 pm on weekends during the rest of the year. The bureau publishes a useful monthly guide to what's happening in and around Broome, *Discover Broome* and the annual *Kimberley Holiday Planner*. Also free is *Broome Time*.

The post office is in the Paspaley shopping centre and there are banks on Carnarvon St.

Chinatown

The term 'Chinatown' refers to the old part of town, although there is really only one block or so that is truly multicultural and historic. Some of the plain and simple wooden buildings that line Carnarvon St still house Chinese merchants, but most are now restaurants and tourist shops. The bars on the windows of the shops aren't there to deter outlaws but to minimise cyclone damage.

The men in the **statue** on Carnarvon St were involved in the cultured pearl industry.

Pearl Fishing

An authentic pearling lugger can often be seen at Streeters jetty off Dampier Terrace.

The **Broome Historical Society Museum** on Saville St has exhibits both on Broome and its history and on the pearling industry and its dangers. It's in the old customs house and is open on weekdays from 10 am to 4 pm, and on weekends from 10 am to 1 pm (April to November), with reduced hours from November to May.

Mother-of-pearl has long been a Broome

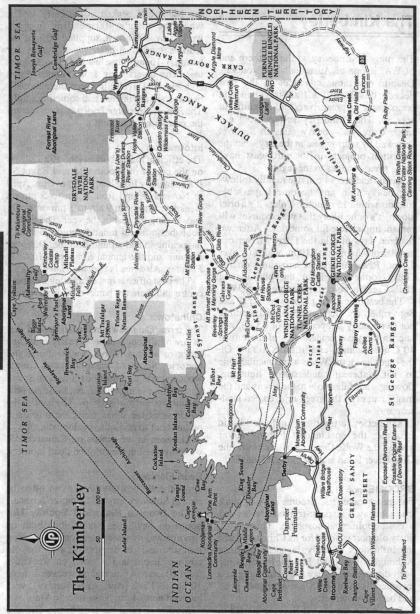

The Kimberley

speciality. There are pearl shops along Dampier Terrace, and Short and Carnarvon Sts in Chinatown.

The **cemetery**, near Cable Beach Rd, testifies to the dangers that accompanied pearl diving when equipment was primitive and the knowledge of diving techniques limited. In 1914 alone, 33 divers died of the bends, while in 1908 a cyclone killed 150 seamen caught at sea. The Japanese section is one of the largest and most interesting; it was renovated in 1983.

Cable Beach

The most popular swimming beach in Broome, Cable Beach is about 4km from town. It's a classic – white sand and turquoise water as far as the eye can see. You can hire surfboards and other beach equipment there – parasailing ($50) is a favourite activity. The northern side beyond the rock is a popular nude-bathing area. You can also take vehicles (other than motorbikes) onto this part of the beach, although at high tide access is limited because of the rocks – don't get stranded.

Tandem skydiving is really popular at Cable Beach and the WA Skydiving Academy has tandem freefall jumps for $285 with a video and T-shirt ($190 without freefall); contact the tourist bureau for more information.

Two companies, Red Sun and Ships of the Desert, operate camel rides on the beach; the best time is sunset. The cost is $25 per hour; again, book at the tourist bureau.

Also on Cable Beach Rd is the **Broome Crocodile Park** (☎ 9192 1489). It's open from May to November daily from 10 am to 5 pm, with reduced hours the rest of the year. There are guided tours; entry is $10 (children $5).

The long sweep of Cable Beach eventually ends at **Gantheaume Point**, 7km south of Broome. The cliffs here have been eroded into curious shapes. At extremely low tides **dinosaur tracks**, 120 million years old, are exposed. At other times you can inspect casts of the footprints on the cliff top. Anastasia's Pool is an artificial rock pool, on the northern side of the point, built by the lighthouse keeper for his crippled wife.

Other Attractions

Across Napier Terrace from Chinatown is Wing's Restaurant with a magnificent **boab tree** beside it. There's another boab tree behind, outside what used to be the old police lock-up, with a rather sad little tale on a plaque at its base. The tree was planted by a police officer when his son (later killed in France in WWI) was born in 1898. The boab tree is still doing fine.

The 1888 **courthouse** (entrance on Hamersley St) was once used to house the transmitting equipment for the old cable station. The cable ran to Banyuwangi on Java, the ferry port across from Bali.

Farther along Weld St, by the library and civic centre, is a **Wackett aircraft** that used to belong to Horrie Miller, founder of MacRobertson Miller Airlines (now part of Ansett). The plane is hidden away in a modern, absurdly designed building.

There's a **pioneer cemetery** near Town Beach at the end of Robinson St. The 1900 **Matso's Store** on the corner of Hamersley and Anne Sts has been beautifully restored and now houses an art gallery and restaurant.

If you're lucky enough to be in Broome on a cloudless night when a full moon rises you can witness the **Staircase to the Moon**. The reflections of the moon from the rippling mud flats create a wonderful golden stairway effect, best seen from Town Beach. The effect is most dramatic about two days after the full moon, as the moon doesn't rise until after the sky has had a chance to darken. A lively evening market is held and the town takes on a carnival air. Check with the tourist bureau for dates and times.

Organised Tours

There are a number of tours to make in and around Broome. The *Spirit of Broome* (☎ 9193 5025) is a small hovercraft which makes daily one-hour trips around Roebuck Bay ($45). You can take twilight cruises in the original pearl lugger *Cornelius* ($65) or in the replica lugger *Willie* ($45).

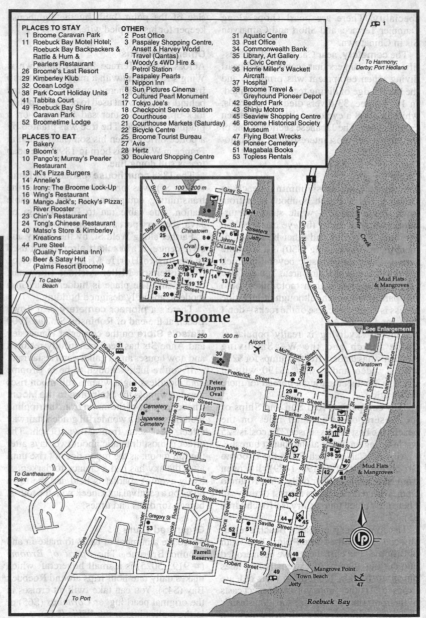

PLACES TO STAY
1 Broome Caravan Park
11 Roebuck Bay Motel Hotel;
  Roebuck Bay Backpackers &
  Rattle & Hum &
  Pearlers Restaurant
26 Broome's Last Resort
29 Kimberley Klub
32 Ocean Lodge
38 Park Court Holiday Units
41 Tabbita Court
49 Roebuck Bay Shire
  Caravan Park
52 Broometime Lodge

PLACES TO EAT
7 Bakery
9 Bloom's
10 Pango's; Murray's Pearler
  Restaurant
13 JK's Pizza Burgers
14 Annelie's
15 Irony: The Broome Lock-Up
16 Wing's Restaurant
19 Mango Jack's; Rocky's Pizza;
  River Rooster
23 Chin's Restaurant
24 Tong's Chinese Restaurant
40 Matso's Store & Kimberley
  Kreations
44 Pure Steel
  (Quality Tropicana Inn)
50 Beer & Satay Hut
  (Palms Resort Broome)

OTHER
2 Post Office
3 Paspaley Shopping Centre,
  Ansett & Harvey World
  Travel (Qantas)
4 Woody's 4WD Hire &
  Petrol Station
5 Paspaley Pearls
6 Nippon Inn
8 Sun Pictures Cinema
12 Cultured Pearl Monument
17 Tokyo Joe's
18 Checkpoint Service Station
20 Courthouse
21 Courthouse Markets (Saturday)
22 Bicycle Centre
25 Broome Tourist Bureau
27 Avis
28 Hertz
30 Boulevard Shopping Centre

31 Aquatic Centre
33 Post Office
34 Commonwealth Bank
35 Library, Art Gallery
  & Civic Centre
36 Horrie Miller's Wackett
  Aircraft
37 Hospital
39 Broome Travel &
  Greyhound Pioneer Depot
42 Bedford Park
43 Shinju Motors
45 Seaview Shopping Centre
46 Broome Historical Society
  Museum
47 Flying Boat Wrecks
48 Pioneer Cemetery
51 Magabala Books
53 Topless Rentals

Broome

There are also some good guided **bushwalks**. Paul Foulkes (☎ 9192 1371) concentrates on environmental features close to Broome, such as the palaeontologic-ally important dinosaur footprints (\$15/7.50 for adults/children), the mangroves (\$25/12.50), remnant rainforest (\$25/12.50) and a hidden valley (\$25/12.50).

Other unusual options include Harley Davidson motorcycle tours with the incom-parable Roger (\$25), jet boat tours up Dampier Creek (\$30/20), and Astro Tours, examinations of the star-studded Kimberley night sky (\$30). Enquire at the tourist office.

Places to Stay

Camping The *Roebuck Bay Shire Caravan Park* (☎ 9192 1366) is conveniently central; tent/powered sites are \$14/16.50 for two and on-site vans are \$40. *Broome Vacation Village* (☎ 9192 1057) on Port Drive has powered/en-suite sites from \$15/18 for two; fortunately it has new owners trying their best to overcome the place's former bad rep-utation. *Broome Caravan Park* (☎ 9192 1776) on the Great Northern Highway, 4km from town, has tent/powered sites from \$10/13 for two, on-site vans from \$25 and cabins from \$54.

Cable Beach Caravan Park (☎ 9192 2066) on Millington Rd has tent/powered sites for \$15/18 for two. *Tarangau Art Village* (☎ 9193 5084), also on Millington Rd, has sites for \$12/18 and on-site vans.

Hostels The new *Kimberley Klub* (☎ 9192 3233; fax 9192 3530) on Frederick St has purpose-built backpacker accommodation (family friendly). It's impressive, with a fully equipped kitchen, a bar and barbecue area overlooking the swimming pool, sand volleyball court, a big TV/games room, travel advisory service, shuttle bus and so on. In eight/four/two-bed rooms, a bed costs \$14/16/19 per person. There are singles and doubles for \$45 per room (all high-season prices).

On Bagot St, close to the centre and just a short stagger from the airport, is *Broome's*

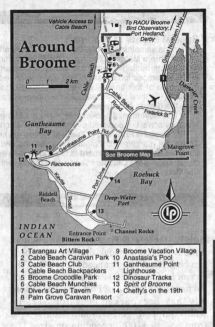

Around Broome

0   1   2 km

Vehicle Access to Cable Beach

To RAOU Broome Bird Observatory; Port Hedland; Derby

Great Northern Hwy

Cable Beach

Cable Beach Road

Frederick St

Gantheaume Bay

Gantheaume Point Rd

Dampier Creek

Mangrove Point

See Broome Map

Racecourse

Roebuck Bay

Kavite Road

Port Drive

Riddell Beach

Deep-Water Port

INDIAN OCEAN

Entrance Point
Bittern Rock

Channel Rocks

1 Tarangau Art Village
2 Cable Beach Caravan Park
3 Cable Beach Club
4 Cable Beach Backpackers
5 Broome Crocodile Park
6 Cable Beach Munchies
7 Diver's Camp Tavern
8 Palm Grove Caravan Resort
9 Broome Vacation Village
10 Anastasia's Pool
11 Gantheaume Point Lighthouse
12 Dinosaur Tracks
13 Spirit of Broome
14 Cheffy's on the 19th

Last Resort (☎ 9193 5000), which seem-ingly caters for the overflow of the Kimberley Klub's noisier patrons. It has a pool, pokey kitchen and oodles of character. Dorm beds are from \$12 and doubles (some with air-con) are \$38; all rooms have shared facilities.

The *Roebuck Bay Backpackers* (☎ 9192 1183), part of the Roebuck Bay Motel Hotel on Napier Terrace, is, if nothing else, central. A dorm bed is \$10 and budget doubles, still suffering from leaky showers and musty carpets, are \$38 for two.

Cable Beach Backpackers (☎ 9193 5511), 33-37 Lullfitz Rd, is an ideal place with an open-plan, fully equipped large kitchen, plenty of amusements, and a pool and vol-leyball court. It is connected to town by local bus, and staff can pick you up from the Greyhound Pioneer depot. Only 200m from the beach, it's the best budget alternative at Cable Beach. You'll pay \$15 to stay in four-bed dorm rooms (or \$40 in a twin).

WESTERN AUSTRALIA

Special Events in Broome

Broome is something of a festival centre. There are many excuses to party.

The **Shinju Matsuri** (Festival of the Pearl) commemorates the early pearling years and the town's multicultural heritage. During the festival (usually around August and September), the population swells and accommodation is hard to find, so book ahead. It's well worth trying to juggle your itinerary to be in Broome at this time. Many traditional Japanese ceremonies are featured, including the **O Bon Festival** (Festival of the Dead). It concludes with a beach concert and a huge fireworks display. Don't miss the dragon-boat races.

In late November the town celebrates the **Mango Festival**, commemorating that sticky sweet fruit loved by some but deplored by parents of small children.

The **Broome Fringe Arts Festival**, where the alternative lifestylers have their day, is in early June. There are markets, Aboriginal art exhibitions and impromptu jamming sessions. There is also the **Broome Sailfish Tournament** (a tag and release event) in July, the **Chinatown Street Party** in March, the **Dragon Boat Classic** in early April, and evening markets on the many nights of the Staircase to the Moon. ■

Hotels, Motels & Resorts During school holidays and other peak times, getting beds can be difficult; book ahead if possible. The *Ocean Lodge* (☎ 9193 7700) on Cable Beach Rd near the junction of Port Drive occasionally has backpacker beds for $12; its well-equipped, self-contained units cost from $55 to $100, depending on size. The swimming pool is this place's biggest plus.

The once legendary *Roebuck Bay Motel Hotel* (☎ 9192 1221) on the corner of Carnarvon St and Napier Terrace has single/double motel units for $65/85. The *Broometime Lodge* (☎ 9193 5067), 59 Forrest St, has tiny singles/twins/doubles with fan and air-con for $50/70/80. It's a neat, quiet place but overpriced for its obscurity and poor location, although the travellers we spoke to there seemed happy enough.

The *Park Court Holiday Units* (☎ 9193 5887) on Haas St has units with all facilities from $50 to $130 (and cheaper weekly rates).

B&B options are *Harmony* (☎ 9193 7439) on Broome Rd (5km north of town), which charges $70/100 for doubles/triples; and *Tabbita Court* (☎ 9193 6026) on Anne St, with doubles from $100 ($120 in the high season).

The upmarket *Cable Beach Club* (☎ 9192 0400) is a beautifully designed place covering a large area; a studio room costs from $255 (low season).

Places to Eat

Light Meals & Fast Food *Bloom's* on Carnarvon St serves a generous cappuccino and has excellent croissants. *Mango Jack's* on Hamersley St has hamburgers and kebabs and also dispenses fish & chips. Near Mango Jack's, there's a *River Rooster* and *Rocky's Pizza*, which turns out distinctly average pizzas. Another pizza place is *JK's Pizza & Burgers* on Napier Terrace, which is open from 8 pm until late.

There's an average, pricey bakery in Chinatown on the corner of Carnarvon and Short Sts. The Seaview shopping centre also has a bakery, as well as a Charlie Carter's supermarket (there is also a Charlie Carter's in the Paspaley centre). *Tanami Moon* on Johnny Chi Lane has economical lunches.

Cable Beach Munchies at the beach is open daily for breakfast, lunch and dinner.

Pubs & Restaurants The Roebuck Bay Motel Hotel (the 'Roey') has *Pearlers Restaurant*, with an alfresco dining area, while the Palms Resort Broome has the buzzing *Beer & Satay Hut* and the Quality Tropicana Inn has the popular *Pure Steel*.

Chin's Restaurant on Hamersley St has a variety of dishes from all over Asia. Prices range from $7 for a nasi goreng to $12 for other dishes. The takeaway is popular. Other Chinese specialists are *Wing's Restaurant* on

Napier Terrace; *Tong's* around the corner on Broome Rd; *Son Ming* on Carnarvon St; and *Murray's Pearler* on Dampier Terrace.

Annelie's is a continental restaurant on Napier Terrace opposite the Roey; reports from locals are all good and the lunches are cheap – eg turkey, camembert and avocado in a huge roll for $4.50. The *Tea House* in a mud-brick building with an outdoor dining area is at the end of Saville St. It has a great range of Thai and seafood dishes and BYO is permitted. *Irony: The Broome Lock-Up* on Carnarvon St serves vegetarian meals such as quiche and lasagne, and also has cakes and a wide variety of coffees. *Pango's* on Dampier Terrace is a new place and a little slice of Bali with an Asian menu and Pindan décor; an entree is about $9, and a main meal from $14 to $15.

Cheffy's at the 19th (☎ 9192 2092) at the golf course overlooking Roebuck Bay has meals from $5, a buffet roast for $10 and the greatest of garlic prawns.

Entertainment

Sun Pictures on Carnarvon St is an open-air cinema dating from 1916. It screens recent releases and watching the 'flicks' here is a must. The *Roey* still rocks along and back-packers are well protected in its *Rattle & Hum*; they get free entry and a meal voucher for a $4 dinner.

Broome's nightclubs (of the disco type) are the *Nippon Inn*, Dampier Terrace, and

Tokyo Joe's on Napier Terrace (entry to either is $5).

Getting There & Away

Ansett (☎ 9193 6855) flies to Broome regularly on its Perth to Darwin route, and its office is in the Paspaley shopping centre on Short St. Qantas' Broome agent is Harvey World Travel (☎ 9193 5599), also in the Paspaley centre.

Greyhound Pioneer operates through Broome on its daily Perth-Darwin service; its terminal (☎ 9192 1561) is near the corner of Haas and Hamersley Sts.

Getting Around

There are plenty of taxis at the airport. A taxi into Chinatown costs $5 and to the beach $11. The Kimberley Klub and Last Resort are within walking distance of the airport.

The Pearl Town Bus (☎ 9193 6000) plies hourly between the town, Cable Beach, the port and Gantheaume Point (Red Line service only). A sector fare is $2 ($1.50 for each additional sector, $1 per sector for children and $25 for a week of unlimited travel). The bus stops close to most places to stay.

Cycling is the best way to see the area. There are a number of places that hire bicycles for $6 to $12 a day, including the backpacker places. Staff at the Broome Cycle Centre on the corner of Hamersley and Frederick Sts hire out bikes, do repairs and give advice.

Bird-Watching at Roebuck Bay

Roebuck Bay is the most significant site in Australia for observing migratory waders – some 800,000 birds migrate here annually. The wide variety of habitats encourages a vast range of species: over 270 species have been recorded, which is about one-third of Australia's species. Of these, the 48 species of waders represent nearly a quarter of all wader species in the world, and 22 of the 24 raptor (birds of prey) species found in Australia can be observed here.

The Royal Australian Ornithological Union (RAOU) has established an observatory (☎ 9193 5600) on Crab Creek Rd, not far from the shores of Roebuck Bay. You can stay here and organise economical tours with the observatory staff. The Shorebird, Mangrove Bird and Bush Bird tours are $42 if taken from Broome, or $25 if you leave from the observatory. Tent/powered sites are $12/16, double bunk rooms are $28 and a five-bed, self-contained chalet is $60 a double.

George Swann of Kimberley Birdwatching (☎ 9192 1246) has a number of excellent bird-watching tours. Happy twitching! ■

Hertz, Budget, ATC and Avis have rent-a-car desks at the airport. Topless Rentals (☎ 9193 5017) on Hunter St, Woody's (☎ 91 92 1791) on Napier Terrace and Broome Broome (☎ 9192 2210) on Carnarvon St are all local operations.

DAMPIER PENINSULA

The **Willie Creek Pearl Farm** is 38km north of Broome, off the Cape Leveque Rd. It offers a rare chance to see a working pearl farm and is worth the trip (entry costs $17.50). During the Wet the road is open only to 4WD vehicles. Broome Coachlines (☎ 9192 1068) has daily tours ($40).

It's about 200km from the turn-off 9km out of Broome to the Cape Leveque Lighthouse at the tip of the Dampier Peninsula. This flora and fauna paradise is a great spot for humpback whale-watching. On the west coast of the peninsula is **Coulomb Point Nature Reserve**, established to protect the unique pindan vegetation and the rare bilby. You can see bilbies in the CALM nocturnal house on Herbert St, Broome.

About halfway to the lighthouse (120km) is a diversion to the **Beagle Bay Aboriginal community** (☎ 9192 4913), which has a beautiful church in the middle of a green. Inside is an altar stunningly decorated with mother-of-pearl. A fee of $5 is charged for entry to the community; fuel is available from 8 am daily (except Sunday).

Just before Cape Leveque is the **Lombadina Aboriginal community** (☎ 9192 4942), which has a church built from mangrove wood. One-day and overnight mud-crabbing and traditional fishing tours are available with the Bardi people; the Broome tourist bureau has details on the tours and accommodation. Petrol and diesel are available on weekdays. A $5 car permit is required from the office. You can stay here in backpacker units for $35 per person (linen and towels provided).

Cape Leveque itself, about 200km from Broome, has a lighthouse and wonderful beaches. Sunset here is truly memorable and a great photo opportunity. There is accommodation at *Kooljaman* (☎ 9192 4970). In the high season, tent/powered sites are $10/15, exotic beach shelters are $30 for two and family units are $50; all prices, except for camping, drop in the off season. Bushtucker and mud-crabbing tours are available, as are vehicle fuels (except LPG).

Take note that the communities won't want you to stay on their land, but if you want to see their churches or buy something from their shops they will be helpful. Permission to visit other areas must be obtained in advance; check with the Broome tourist bureau about road conditions and permits.

Organised Tours

Halls Creek and Bungle Bungle Tours (☎ 9193 6802), Over the Top Adventure Tours (☎ 9193 7257) and Flak Track in Broome (☎ 9192 1487) all operate tours to the peninsula. Expect to pay about $170/290 for a one/two-day 4WD trip.

DERBY (pop 3200)

Only 220km from Broome, Derby is a major administrative centre for the west Kimberley and a good point from which to travel to the spectacular gorges in the region. The Great Northern Highway beyond Derby continues inland to Fitzroy Crossing (256km) and Halls Creek (288km farther on). Alternatively, there's the much wilder Gibb River Road. Derby is on King Sound, north of the mouth of the mighty Fitzroy, which drains the west Kimberley.

The tourist bureau (☎ 9191 1426), 1 Clarendon St, is open on weekdays between April and October from 8.30 am to 4.30 pm, and on weekends from 9 am to 1 pm (in the other months it's open for the same hours on weekdays but only on Saturday from 9 am to noon on weekends).

Things to See

Derby's cultural centre and botanic garden are just off Clarendon St. There's a small museum and art gallery in **Wharfinger's House** at the end of Loch St. This has been restored as an example of early housing in the area. Derby's lofty **wharf** has not been used since 1983 for shipping, but it provides a handy fishing spot for the locals. The whole town is surrounded by huge expanses of mud flats, baked hard in the Dry and occasionally flooded by king tides.

The **Prison Tree**, near the airport, 7km south of town, is a huge boab tree with a hollow trunk 14m around. It is said to have been used as a lock-up years ago. Nearby is **Myall's Bore**, a 120m-long cattle trough.

Organised Tours

From Derby there are flights over King Sound to **Koolan** and **Cockatoo** islands, both owned by BHP. You can't go there unless invited by a resident, but scenic flights are available to the adjoining islands of the **Buccaneer Archipelago**. Aerial Enterprises (☎ 9191 1132) and Derby Air Services (☎ 9193 1375) provide these two-hour flights for about $120 (minimum of four).

Buccaneer Sea Safaris (☎ 9191 1991) does extended tours up the Kimberley coast (including the horizontal falls of Talbot Bay) in a large aluminium mono-hull.

Bush Track Safaris (☎ 9191 4644) operates four to 10-day tours into the remote Walcott Inlet area; these cost from $175 per day. West Kimberley Tours (☎ 9193 1442) goes to the Devonian Reef gorges ($80) and Gibb River Road gorges ($290 for two days).

Places to Stay

The *Kimberley Entrance Caravan Park* (☎ 9193 1055) on Rowan St has tent/powered sites for $12/15 for two, and on-site vans for $40 a double. It is a nice, friendly place with free barbecues. *Aboriginal Hostels Ltd* (☎ 9191 1867) at 233-235 Villiers St charges $12 per person; dinner costs $8.50.

West Kimberley Lodge (☎ 9191 1031) at the edge of town on the corner of Sutherland and Stanwell Sts has singles/doubles for $30/45. A little out of town at Lot 4 Guildford St is *Goldsworthy Connection* (☎ 9193

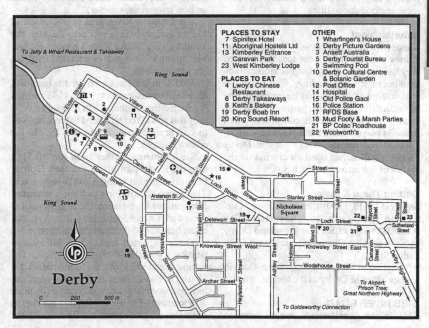

PLACES TO STAY
7 Spinifex Hotel
11 Aboriginal Hostels Ltd
13 Kimberley Entrance Caravan Park
23 West Kimberley Lodge

PLACES TO EAT
4 Lwoy's Chinese Restaurant
6 Derby Takeaways
8 Keith's Bakery
19 Derby Boab Inn
20 King Sound Resort

OTHER
1 Wharfinger's House
2 Derby Picture Gardens
3 Ansett Australia
5 Derby Tourist Bureau
9 Swimming Pool
10 Derby Cultural Centre & Botanic Garden
12 Post Office
14 Hospital
15 Old Police Gaol
16 Police Station
17 RFDS Base
18 Mud Footy & Marsh Parties
21 BP Colac Roadhouse
22 Woolworth's

1246); there are also self-contained homes/cottages for $25/20 per person (there are minimum numbers).

The *Spinifex Hotel* (☎ 9191 1233), known as 'the Spinny' to all, on Clarendon St has budget rooms at $40/50, motel units at $50/65 and backpacker beds in the bunkhouse from $11 per person (fourth night free).

Places to Eat

Keith's Bakery, near the tourist bureau, is good for lunch and has a fine selection of sandwiches. The air-conditioned *Jabiru Cafe* has a nice garden setting; *Derby Takeaways* is open daily until 11 pm, and *Albert's Kitchen* has cheap, tasty curries. All these places are on Clarendon St.

The *Spinny, Derby Boab Inn Hotel* and the *King Sound Resort Hotel* all do counter meals.

At the end of Loch St there's *Lwoy's Chinese Restaurant*, and at the jetty is the BYO *Wharf Restaurant & Takeaway* with local seafood specialities.

Entertainment

Bands (or a disco) can usually be heard at the *Spinny* on weekends. If the locals get bored they will probably start a cockroach race (and bet on it) – no kidding.

If you are lucky you may be invited to one of the impromptu 'marsh parties', when barbecues are set up, beer is consumed, 'mud footy' is played and a band plays furiously.

Less wild are the 'flicks' at the *Derby Picture Gardens*, an open-air cinema on the corner of Johnston and Loch Sts.

Getting There & Away

Skywest (☎ 13 1300) flies to Broome, Carnarvon, Exmouth and Karratha. The Ansett/Skywest office is at Traveland Derby in Shop 6 in the Clarendon Arcade on Clarendon St.

Greyhound Pioneer's daily Perth-Darwin service stops in Derby at the tourist office.

GIBB RIVER ROAD

This is the 'back road' from Derby to Wyndham or Kununurra. At 667km it's more direct by several hundred kilometres than the Fitzroy Crossing to Halls Creek route. It's almost all dirt, although it doesn't require a 4WD if it happens to have been recently graded. However, in the Wet the road is impassable. You can also reach many of the Kimberley gorges from this road without a 4WD. The Kimberley gorges are the major reason for taking this route.

Get a copy of *The Gibb River and Kalumburu Roads Travellers Guide* from information centres. There's no public transport along the Gibb River Road – in fact, there's little traffic of any sort, so don't bother trying to hitch.

Derby to Mt Barnett Station

From Derby the bitumen extends 62km. It's 119km to the Windjana Gorge (21km) and Tunnel Creek (51km) turn-off and you can continue down that turn-off to the Great Northern Highway near Fitzroy Crossing (see the Devonian Reef National Parks section later in the chapter).

The Lennard River bridge is crossed at 120km and at 145km you pass through the Yamarra Gap in the King Leopold Range. The country is rugged, punctuated by huge granite outcrops.

At 184km you can turn off to the beautiful **Mt Hart Homestead** (☎ 9191 4645) which is reached by a farther 50km of rough 4WD-only dirt road. You will need to have booked to stay here; dinner and B&B is $95/50 for adults/children.

Six kilometres farther from the Mt Hart turn-off is the turn-off to the **Bell Gorge**, 8km off the road along a 4WD-only track. This gorge is 5km long and has a waterfall just north of its entrance; the nearby pool is great for a quick, refreshing dip. You can camp here for $5/1 for adults/children.

The signposted turn-off to **Mt House Station** (☎ 9191 4649) is at 246km. The station, nestled below the odd-shaped Mt House, is about 10km down a side road and has fuel, stores and accommodation (by prior arrangement). Dinner and B&B in the station homestead, with shared facilities (and the

The blue heeler – great Australian cattle dog

shadiest of verandahs), costs from $67 to $77 per person. The adventurous can push on from Mt House to the **Old Mornington Cattle Station** (☎ 9191 7035) on the Fitzroy River; comfortable tent accommodation (with hot showers) is $85, fully inclusive.

At the 251km mark is the road into **Beverley Springs Homestead** (☎ 9191 4646). This is a working farm and station, 43km off the Gibb River Road, with a variety of accommodation; camping costs $8 per person, chalets with dinner and B&B are $80, homestay with dinner and B&B is also $80 and self-contained two-bedroom homes are $85 a night.

The turn-off to **Adcock Gorge** is at 267km. This gorge is 5km off the road and is good for swimming. You can camp here, although the site is rocky and there's little shade.

Horseshoe-shaped **Galvans Gorge** is less than 1km off the road, at the 286km mark. The small camp site here has some good shade trees and the gorge itself has a swimming hole. The distance from Derby to Mt Barnett Roadhouse is 306km.

Mt Barnett & Manning Gorge

The Mt Barnett Roadhouse (☎ 9191 7007) is at the 306km point and is owned and run by the Kupingarri Aboriginal community. The roadhouse (ice is available) and small general store are open seven days a week from 7 am to 6 pm, from May to October. It's also the access point for **Manning Gorge**, which lies 7km off the road along an easy dirt track. There's an entry fee of $5/10 per person/family which also covers camping.

The camp site is by the waterhole, but the best part of the gorge is about a 1¼-hour walk along the far bank – walk around the right of the waterhole to pick up the track, which is marked with empty drink cans strung up in trees. It's a strenuous walk; carry some drinking water.

Mt Barnett to Wyndham-Kununurra Rd

There is a turn-off to the **Barnett River Gorge**, after Mt Barnett, at 328km. This is another good swimming spot, 3km down a side road. The **Mt Elizabeth Station** (☎ 9191 4644) lies 30km off the road at the 338km mark. Homestead accommodation is available but this must be arranged in advance ($90/45 per adult/child for dinner and B&B). Camping is $7 per person.

At 406km you come to the turn-off to the spectacular **Mitchell Plateau** (172km) and the **Kalumburu Aboriginal community** (267km). This is remote, 4WD-only territory and should not be undertaken without adequate preparation; an entry permit is required (see the Kalumburu Road section later in the chapter).

There's magnificent scenery between the Kalumburu turn-off and Jack's (Joe's) Waterhole on **Durack River Station** (☎ 9161 4324) at 524km. There is no camping at Campbell Creek (451km) and at the Durack River (496km). At 476km there is a turn-off to **Ellenbrae Station** (☎ 9161 4325), 6km farther down a side road; camping costs $7 and dinner and B&B is $80 per person.

Jack's Waterhole is 8km down a side road at 524km and, apart from fuel, there's also homestead accommodation and camping here. Camping costs $6/1 per adult/child and dinner and B&B is $75 per person.

At 579km you get some excellent views

of the Cockburn Ranges to the north, as well as the Cambridge Gulf and the twin rivers (the Pentecost and the Durack). Shortly after (2km or so) is the turn-off to **Home Valley Station** (☎ 9161 4322) which has camping ($6/1 for adults/children) and dinner and B&B in the homestead for $50 per person.

The large **Pentecost River** is forded at 590km and this crossing can be dodgy if there's water in the river.

El Questro Station & Wilderness Park (☎ 9169 1777) is another place offering a variety of accommodation – from single/double bungalows for $97/130 to expensive homestead beds for a whopping $840/1280, all trips inclusive. For the poorer, riverside camping is $10 per person. El Questro lies 16km off the road at the 614km mark.

The last attraction on the road is **Emma Gorge** at 623km. The pleasant camp site lies 2km off the road and from here it's about a 40-minute walk to the spectacular gorge. Near the gorge is great wilderness cabin accommodation, run by El Questro; singles/doubles/family rooms are $62/98/146. There's a licensed restaurant, bar and pool.

At 630km you cross King River (camping for crocodiles only) and at 647km you finally hit the bitumen road; Wyndham lies 48km to the north-west, while it's 52km east to Kununurra. The distance from the Mt Barnett Roadhouse to the Wyndham-Kununurra Rd is 341km.

KALUMBURU ROAD

This is a natural earth road which traverses extremely rocky terrain in an isolated area. Distances in the following description are given from the junction of the Gibb River and Kalumburu roads, where the road commences. The junction is 419km from the Derby Highway or 248km from the Great Northern Highway (Wyndham to Kununurra).

It's recommended that you get a permit before entering Kalumburu Reserve. Phone the community on ☎ 9161 4300 (or fax 9161 4331) from 7 am to noon on weekdays.

Gibb River Road to Mitchell Plateau
The Gibb River is crossed at 3km and Plain Creek at 16km. The first fuel is at the **Drysdale River Station** (☎ 9161 4326) at 59km; the homestead is 1km down a side road. You can also buy supplies and leave trailers and caravans at the homestead ($2 per day or $10 per week).

At 62km you can turn off to the **Miners Pool** picnic area. It is 3.5km to the river and the last 200m is slow going; there is an entrance fee of $2/1 for adults/children.

The road passes a couple of entrances to stations in the next 100km until it reaches the Mitchell Plateau turn-off at 172km. From this junction it is 70km along the Mitchell Plateau Road to the turn-off to the spectacular, multi-tiered **Mitchell Falls**. The falls are a farther 16km downhill from this turn-off; from the last car park (13km) you need to walk for a farther 3km (allow a full day for the excursion). You usually cannot get into the falls until late May (when the Wet ends).

As this is a remote area, be sure to bring a large swag of basic necessities. In the Dry the falls are like any other, with water falling from the centre of the terraces. In the Wet they are vastly different – the muddied water stretches from escarpment to escarpment and thunders down submerged terraces.

You can camp at the King Edward River (don't use soap in the watercourse), at Camp Creek (away from the Kandiwal Aboriginal community) and at Mitchell Falls car park.

Mitchell Plateau to Kalumburu
From the Mitchell Plateau turn-off, the road heads north-east towards Kalumburu, crossing the Carson River at 247km. About 1km farther is a road to the east to the Carson River Homestead on the fringe of the Drysdale River National Park. There is no access without prior approval from the Kalumburu Aboriginal Corporation.

The **Kalumburu Aboriginal community** (☎ 9161 4300) is at 267km, about 5km from the mouth of the King Edward River and King Edward Gorge. The picturesque mission is set among giant mango trees and coconut palms. There is accommodation (entry is $25 per vehicle and there's an additional fee to camp at McGowan's Island and Honeymoon Beach) and a store; food and all types of fuel are available from Monday to Friday from 7 to 11 am and 1.30 to 4 pm, and on Saturday from 7 to 11 am.

The distance between the Mitchell Plateau turn-off and Kalumburu is 95km.

Drysdale River National Park
Very few people get into Drysdale River, WA's most northern national park, which is 150km west of Wyndham. Apart from being one of the most remote parks in Australia – it has no road access – it is also the largest park in the Kimberley, with an area of 4000 sq km. Furthermore, it is also the home of the mysterious, ancient Bradshaw art figures and the more recent Wandjina art figures.

The park has open woodlands, rugged gorges, waterfalls (Morgan and Solea) and the wide, meandering Drysdale River. Rainforest, which until 1965 was thought not to exist in WA, is found in pockets along the Carson Escarpment and in some gorges.

The King George River drains the northern part of the reserve. At the mouth of this river are the spectacular, split **King George Falls**, best seen from the air.

A permit is necessary to enter this national park; get one from the CALM offices in Derby or Kununurra.

Prince Regent Nature Reserve
This 6000 sq km wilderness is one of Australia's most isolated reserves, and there are no roads into it; it is best seen from the air or its edges explored by boat. Notable features include the mesa-like Mts Trafalgar and Waterloo, the near-vertical cliffs of the straight Prince Regent River and extremely photogenic King Cascade.

Several companies operate flights over the region, including Kingfisher Aviation (☎ 9168 6160) and King Leopold Air (☎ 9193 7997); a half-day flight is about $350.

Organised Tours
Kununurra's Desert Inn (☎ 1800 805 010) runs budget five-day camping trips along the Gibb River Road for $425. Kimberley Wilderness Adventures (☎ 9168 1711) has a five-day Gibb River Road Wanderer 4WD safari ($745) which leaves from Kununurra and finishes in Broome. Its six-day Mitchell Plateau Explorer, which includes a fair slice of the Gibb River Road, is $895.

There are guided full-day trips to the Mitchell Plateau from Kununurra. Kimberley Air Safaris (☎ 9169 1326) departs from Kununurra at 6 am and returns at 5 pm; transport from the plateau airstrip to the falls is by 4WD. The total cost is $350 per person.

DEVONIAN REEF NATIONAL PARKS
The west Kimberley boasts three national parks, based on gorges which were once part of a western coral 'great barrier reef' in the Devonian era, 350 million years ago. The magnificent **Geikie Gorge** is just 18km north-east of Fitzroy Crossing. Part of the gorge, on the Fitzroy River, is in a small national park. During the Wet the river rises nearly 17m and in the Dry it stops flowing, leaving only a series of water holes.

The vegetation around this beautiful gorge is dense and there is also much wildlife, including freshwater crocodiles, wallaroos and the rare black-footed wallaby. Sawfish and stingrays, usually only found in or close to the sea, can also be seen in the river. Visitors must at all times stick to the prescribed 1.5km west-bank walking track.

During the Dry (April to November) there's a 1½-hour boat trip up the river daily at 8 and 11 am and 3 pm. It costs $18 (children $2) and covers 16km of the gorge.

You can go to the gorge with the people from Darngku Heritage Cruise (☎ 9191 5355), who show you a lot more than just rocks and water. These Bunuba people reveal secrets of bush tucker and tell stories of the region and Aboriginal culture. The cost of $75 includes the ride from Fitzroy Crossing, the river trip and lunch.

You can visit the spectacular formations of Windjana Gorge and Tunnel Creek from the Gibb River Road, or make a detour off the main highway between Fitzroy Crossing

Tidal Waterfalls

The Kimberley coastline is made up of sheer sandstone cliffs and basalt promontories with deep indentations made by inlets and bays. It is one of the remotest coasts in the world, mainly inaccessible from the land, and certainly one of the most treacherous. The tidal variation is enormous, fluctuating up to 10m, and the region is often hit by fierce cyclonic storms. It is as if nature constructed its own fortified Maginot Line to keep its beauty and wonders secret.

One of the most remarkable features of this coastline are the spectacular tidal 'waterfalls', which are not actual waterfalls but immense tidal currents that hurtle through the narrow coastal gorges. The speed they attain, from 20 to 30 knots in places, gives the impression of a waterfall flowing horizontally.

The waterfalls are spectacular at **Talbot Bay**, north of King Sound. At the south end of the bay, two constricted gorges, both about 30m high and constructed of hard sandstone, protect the Inner and Outer bays (flooded valleys). The high tide fills both bays with water and, when the tide is outgoing, the water in the bays is released. The narrow gorges restrict the outflow, resulting in a vertical difference of 1m between the first bay and the open sea of Talbot Bay, and of 2m between the first and second bays. Water then thunders through both the outer 70m-long gorge and the impressive 100m-long inner gorge.

The Aborigines of the now-extinct Meda tribe and the Worora people knew the waterfalls as 'Wolbunum' and once had a system of *bidi* (tracks) running to these valleys as food was abundant there. Nowadays, many people see the waterfalls from the air and, occasionally, some brave the waterfalls in a powerful motor boat or in a rubber raft. The landward journey to the falls is considered extremely difficult, as harsh terrain, a lack of water and the tangle of vegetation all combine to impede progress.

Kimberley Wilderness Promotions, based in Talbot Bay from April to November, plans to offer rafting trips through the horizontal falls in specially designed rafts. Contact the Derby tourist office on ☎ 9191 1426 for the latest developments. ■

---

and Derby onto Leopold Station Road, which only adds about 40km to the distance.

The walls at the **Windjana Gorge** soar 90m above the Lennard River, which rushes through in the Wet but becomes just a series of pools in the Dry. More than likely the deafening screech of corellas and the persistent horseflies will keep you out of the gorge during the middle of the day. Three kilometres from the river are the ruins of **Lillimilura**, an early homestead and, from 1893, a police station. Nightly camping fees for this gorge are $5 (children $1).

Tunnel Creek is a 750m-long tunnel which the creek has cut through a spur of the Napier Range. The tunnel is generally from 3m to 15m wide and you can walk all the way along it. You'll need a good light and sturdy shoes; be prepared to wade through cold, chest-deep water in places. Don't attempt it during the Wet, as the creek may flood suddenly. Halfway through, a collapse has created a shaft to the range's top.

Over the Top Adventure Tours (☎ 9193 7700) operates popular two-day trips com-

bining Windjana and Tunnel Creek with Geikie Gorge, a good way of seeing three sites in one trip; the cost is $190. It also includes the Mimbi Caves of the Gooniyandi people, the Dreamtime place of the blue-tongued lizard. In Broome, staff at the Kimberley Klub and Broome's Last Resort can advise on popular tours to the gorges.

FITZROY CROSSING (pop 1200)

A tiny settlement where the Great Northern Highway crosses the Fitzroy River, this is another place from which you can get to the gorges and water holes of the area. The old town site is on Russ St, north-east of the present town. The Crossing Inn, near Brooking Creek, is the oldest pub in the Kimberley.

The new, large Fitzroy Crossing tourist bureau (☎ 9191 5355) is on the highway next to the service station. It is open daily from April to November (but for fewer hours during the Wet).

Places to Stay & Eat

The *Fitzroy River Lodge Motel Hotel &*

Jandamarra ('Pigeon')

Windjana Gorge, Tunnel Creek and Lillimilura were the scene of the adventures of an Aboriginal tracker, Jandamarra, nicknamed 'Pigeon'. In November 1894, Pigeon shot two police colleagues and then led a band of dissident Aboriginal people who skilfully evaded search parties for more than two years.

During this time Pigeon killed another four men, but in early 1897 he was trapped and killed at Tunnel Creek. He and his small band had hidden in the seemingly inaccessible gullies of the adjoining Napier Range.

For the full story, get a copy of the *Pigeon Heritage Trail* from the Derby or Broome tourist bureaux ($1.50), or *Jandamarra and the Bunuba Resistance* by Howard Pedersen & Banjo Woorunmurra. ■

Caravan Park (☎ 9191 5141), 2km east of town on the banks of the Fitzroy River, has tent/powered sites for $8.50/17 for two and you are allowed to use the motel pool for free. Single/double air-con safari tents cost $75/90, while motel units cost $100/115.

In the Old Post Office on Geikie Gorge Rd, about 4km from town, you'll find *Darlngunaya Backpackers* (☎ 9191 5140) well in need of a spring clean; dorm beds are $12. All backpackers get picked up and returned to the bus stop at the roadhouse (usually at some ungodly hour of the night).

The *Crossing Inn* (☎ 9191 5080) has B&B singles/twins for $70/85. It can get pretty noisy as there is a rather colourful, if a little unsavoury, bar next door. If you stay here, there's a good chance you will meet the friendly Bunuba people. They may even invite you to a barbecue or on a fishing trip.

It is cheaper to prepare food for yourself in this town. If your margarine is runny and the cheese you bought yesterday stinks then *Maxine's* in the Fitzroy River Lodge serves reasonable meals.

HALLS CREEK (pop 1260)

Halls Creek, in the centre of the Kimberley and on the edge of the Great Sandy Desert, was traditionally the land of the Jaru and Kija people. Graziers took over in the 1870s and virtually turned these people into slave labourers on the stations. When the stations were sold, about 100 years later, the Aboriginal people drifted to the nearby town and its associated boredom and alcohol. The region

was the site of the 1885 gold rush, the first in WA. The gold soon petered out and today the town is a cattle centre, 14km from the original crumbling site.

Five kilometres east of Halls Creek and then about 1.5km off the road there's the natural **China Wall** – so called because it resembles the Great Wall of China. This subvertical quartz vein is short, but picturesquely situated.

Halls Creek **Old Town** is a great place for fossicking. All that remains of the once bustling mining town are the ant-bed and spinifex walls of the old post office, the cemetery and a huge bottle pile where a pub once stood. 'Old Town' is in fact the general term for the hilly area behind Halls Creek, and gold might be found anywhere there. You can swim in Caroline Pool, Sawpit Gorge and Palm Springs.

Although Halls Creek is a comfortable enough little place it's as well to remember that it sits on the edge of a distinctly inhospitable stretch of country. The Halls Creek tourist centre (☎ 9168 6262) on the Great Northern Highway is open daily from 8 am to 4 pm, from April to September; it has lots of information and handles bookings for tours.

Places to Stay & Eat

The caravan park (☎ 9168 6169) on Roberta Ave has tent/powered sites for $12/14 and on-site vans for $38 for two.

Opposite is the *Kimberley Hotel* (☎ 9168 6101). It has a variety of overpriced rooms

WESTERN AUSTRALIA

from $80/95. On the Great Northern Highway, the *Shell Roadhouse Cabins* (☎ 9168 6060) charges $50 and the *Halls Creek Motel* (☎ 9168 6001) has units for $65/80.

The Kimberley Hotel has a pleasant bar with standard counter meals at $10; you can eat outside. Inside there's a swish restaurant with smorgasbord meals at $15.

Getting There & Away
Greyhound Pioneer buses pass through Halls Creek early in the morning (northbound) and late at night (southbound).

WOLFE CREEK METEORITE CRATER
The 835m-wide and 50m-deep Wolfe Creek meteorite crater is the second-largest crater in the world where meteorite fragments have been found. To the local Jaru Aboriginal people, the crater, which they call 'Kandimalal', marks the spot where a huge snake emerged from the ground.

The turn-off to the Wolfe Creek Crater is 16km out of Halls Creek towards Fitzroy Crossing and from there it's 130km by unsealed road to the south. It's accessible without 4WD (with care), but you'll need to carry enough fuel, food and water for a return trip, as there are no supplies available at the park. If you can't handle one more outback road, you can fly over the crater from Halls Creek for $100 (per person) with these local operators: Oasis Airlines (☎ 9168 6462), Kingfisher Aviation (☎ 9168 6162) and Crocodile Air (☎ 9168 6250).

From Carranya Station Homestead the road, known as the **Tanami Track**, goes all the way to Alice Springs nearly 900km away.

BUNGLE BUNGLE (PURNULULU) NATIONAL PARK
The 3000 sq km Bungle Bungle (Purnululu) National Park, which shouldn't be missed, is an amazing spectacle with its spectacular rounded rock towers, striped like tigers in alternate bands of orange (silica) and black (lichen). The only hitches are that the range is hard to get to, and because the rock formations are fragile you are not allowed to climb them. The name purnululu means sandstone in the local Kija dialect and bungle bungle is a misspelling of bundle bundle, a common grass.

Echidna Chasm in the north or **Cathedral Gorge** in the south are only about a one-hour walk from the car park at the road's end. However, the soaring **Piccaninny Gorge** is an 18km round trip that takes eight to 10 hours to walk. Access to the park costs $11/1 per adult/child; this entitles you to seven nights in the park and fuel for campfires. The restricted gorges in the northern part of the park can only be seen from the air, but they are a memorable sight.

From the main highway it's 55km to a track junction known as Three Ways. From here it's 20 minutes' north to *Kurrajong Camping Area* and 45 minutes' south to *Bellburn Camping Area*. Fire sites and firewood are supplied. Kurrajong, for casual visitors, has long-drop toilets, supplied drinking water and fireplaces with firewood supplied. Bellburn is mainly for tour groups and is similarly equipped.

Scenic Flights
As the range is so vast, flights and helicopter rides over the Bungles are popular – it's money well spent. The chopper rides cost $120 for a 45-minute flight from Wilardi camp site or $130 in a faster helicopter from Turkey Creek on the main highway. This latter flight is a popular option for people without a 4WD. The chopper rides, operated by Heliwork WA (part of Slingair; ☎ 9168 1811), are most impressive because they fly right in, among and over the deep, narrow gorges, while light planes have to remain above 700m.

Flights from Kununurra are $150/160 in a land/float plane; they fly over Lake Argyle and the Argyle Diamond Mine. Out of Halls Creek, flights to the Bungles only are $110.

Getting There & Away
The 55km-track from Highway 1 to Three Ways requires a 4WD and takes two hours. From Three Ways it's 20km north to Echidna Chasm, 30km south to Piccaninny Creek.

The best option if you don't have a 4WD is to take a tour from Kununurra or Halls Creek. Desert Inn 4WD Adventures (☎ 1800 805 010) has two-day and three-day tours from $220/365. With East Kimberley Tours (☎ 9168 2213) it is $295/425 for a day/overnight combined flight-4WD trip.

WYNDHAM (pop 850)

Wyndham, a sprawling town, is suffering from Kununurra's boom in popularity but its **Five Rivers Lookout** on top of Mt Bastion is still a must. From there you can see the King, Pentecost, Durack, Forrest and Ord rivers enter the Cambridge Gulf. The view is particularly good at sunrise and sunset.

When the tide is right you can observe (from a distance) large saltwater **crocodiles** near the water. A hideous 20m concrete croc greets you as you arrive in town.

The **Moochalabra Dam** is a popular fishing and picnic spot about 25km away. Near the dam are some Aboriginal paintings and another prison boab tree.

Not far from Wyndham is the **Marlgu Billabong** of Parry Lagoons Reserve, a wetlands which hosts many bird species.

Highly recommended by a number of readers is Wundargoodie Aboriginal Safaris (☎ 9161 1336) on O'Donnell St, Wyndham Port. Half-day/one-day tours cost $60/100 and include bush medicine, bush tucker and Aboriginal rock art.

Places to Stay

The *Three Mile Caravan Park* (☎ 9161 1064) has tent/powered sites for $10/12 and shade trees for campers. At the *Wyndham Town Hotel* (☎ 9161 1003) on O'Donnell St doubles are $80, or you can try the *Wyndham Community Club Hotel* (☎ 9161 1130) for cheaper but more basic rooms; singles/ doubles are from $45/55.

KUNUNURRA (pop 4800)

In the Miriwoong language, this region is known as 'gananoorrang' – Kununurra is the European version of this word. Founded in the 1960s, Kununurra is in the centre of the Ord River irrigation scheme and is quite a modern and bustling little town. In the past it was just a stopover on the main highway and there was little incentive to linger. That's all changed with the increase in tourism.

WESTERN AUSTRALIA

The boab tree *(Adansonia gegorii)* is closely related to the baobab of Africa

There are now enough recreational activities, mostly water-based, to keep you busy for a week.

This is a popular place to seek work. The main picking season starts in May and ends in September. Ask at the Kununurra Backpackers, Desert Inn International or at the tourist bureau.

Information
The tourist bureau (☎ 9168 1177) on Coolibah Drive has information on the town and the Kimberley. It's open on weekdays from 8 am to 5 pm, and on weekends from 8.30 am to 4 pm. There's a 1½-hour time difference between Kununurra and Katherine in the Northern Territory. Strict quarantine restrictions apply when entering WA.

Lake Kununurra (Diversion Dam)
Lily Creek Lagoon is a mini-wetlands beside the town and has plenty of bird life. Lake Kununurra, also called the Diversion Dam, has picnic spots and is popular with water-skiers and boating enthusiasts. There's good fishing below the Lower Dam (watch for crocodiles) and also on the Ord River at **Ivanhoe Crossing**. If you dare to swim there, be careful of the crocs.

Other Attractions
There are good views of the irrigated fields from **Kelly's Knob**, close to the centre of town. During the Wet, distant thunderstorms are spectacular when viewed from the lookout, although caution is needed as the knob is frequently struck by lightning.

Hidden Valley, in **Mirima National Park** and only 2km from the town centre, is a wonderful park with a steep gorge, great views and short walking tracks. The banded formations in the park are reminiscent of the Bungle Bungles and are of great spiritual importance to the Miriwoong people.

The **Packsaddle Plains**, 6km south-east of town, has the touristy Zebra Rock Gallery. Farther along this road you'll find farms (producing bananas and mangos) that are open to the public.

Organised Tours & Flights
Canoe trips on the Ord River, between Lake Argyle and the Diversion Dam, are popular with travellers. A recommended operation, Kimberley Canoeing Experience (☎ 1800 641 998), has three-day tours for $120, with gear supplied, including transport to the dam.

Barramundi is the major **fishing** attraction, but other fish are also caught. Full-day boat trips operated by Ultimate Adventures (☎ 9168 2310) cost about $200. Triple J Tours (☎ 9168 2682) operates high-speed boats along the Ord between Lake Argyle and Kununurra (55km). These are a real thrill and pass through beautiful scenery. The cost is $90/55 for an adult/child (with lunch), including a return by bus.

Duncan's Ord River Tours (☎ 9168 1823) cruises on Lake Kununurra, visiting banana plantations on Packsaddle Plains, the zebra rock gallery and areas where bird life is prolific; the cost of the four-hour tour is $50/30 for adults/children.

R&B Kimberley Ecotours (☎ 9168 2116) has two really interesting and informative wildlife tours, both thoroughly recommended. The morning tour (6 to 8 am) focuses on wetland bird species ($30) and the evening tour (5 to 7 pm) on crocodile biology and nocturnal wildlife ($35).

Flights over Purnululu are popular and cost about $150 a person (discounts apply). They take about two hours and also fly over Lake Argyle, the Argyle and Bow River diamond projects and the irrigation area north of the town. Contact Alligator Airways (☎ 9168 1333) or Slingair (☎ 9169 1300) in Kununurra; Heliwork WA (☎ 9168 1811) in Turkey Creek; or Ord Air Charter (☎ 9161 1335) in Wyndham.

Places to Stay
The *Town Caravan Park* (☎ 9168 1763) on Bloodwood Drive has tent/powered sites from $7/16 and on-site vans for $45. *Hidden Valley Caravan Park* (☎ 9168 1790) on Weaber Plains Rd and *Kimberleyland Caravan Park* (☎ 9168 1280) on the lake's edge near town both charge $14/16. The

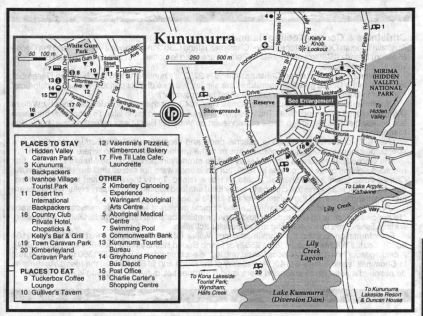

Ivanhoe Village (☎ 9169 1995) on Ivanhoe Rd was previously the 'Coolibah' and has tent sites for \$15 for two.

Kona Lakeside Tourist Park (☎ 9168 1031), the pick of the parks, is about 1km from town and also on the lake. Kona is a great place for bird-watchers and it is likely that you will see the comb-crested jacana darting around beside the lake. Tent/powered sites are \$7/15, on-site vans are \$45, and park cabins and bungalows are from \$65 to \$85.

The *Desert Inn International* (☎ 9168 2702) is on Tristania St, opposite Gulliver's Tavern in the centre of town; dorm beds are \$14 and twins are \$30. This purpose-built complex, with full facilities including a spa pool, is a friendly and popular place.

Kununurra Backpackers (☎ 9169 1998) is at 112 Nutwood Crescent. It's in a couple of adjacent houses about five-minutes walk from the town centre; dorm beds are \$13 and rooms \$30 for two. The shaded pool is a big drawcard.

Hotel accommodation is expensive, with a big variation between low and high season tariffs. The *Country Club Private Hotel* (☎ 9168 1024), 76 Coolibah Drive, is the cheapest but, at \$50/60 a single/double for small air-con rooms with no facilities, even it is overpriced.

Duncan House (☎ 9168 2436), 1921 Melaleuca Drive, is close to the lake; B&B in comfortable singles/doubles is \$60/75.

For more accommodation information, see the tourist bureau.

Places to Eat

The *Five Til Late Cafe* on Banksia St offers takeaway tucker and light meals, and *Valentine's Pizzeria* and the *Kimbercrust Bakery*, both on Cottontree Ave, are open daily. Just off Coolibah Drive, the *Tuckerbox Coffee Lounge* serves good salads and excellent salad rolls (\$2.50), and its small lunches at \$3.50 are unbeatable value.

Gulliver's Tavern on Konkerberry Drive

Christmas & Cocos (Keeling) Islands

Australia's Indian Ocean protectorates – Christmas Island (2300km north-west of Perth) and the Cocos (Keeling) Islands (2750km north-west of Perth) – are often forgotten. Both places are island paradises with abundant wildlife.

The average temperature on Christmas Island is 27°C, it's humid and rain falls between December and April. In the Cocos group temperatures are similar, with two distinct periods: the sultry 'doldrums' (October to March) and the cooler 'trades' (April to September).

Christmas Island was named on Christmas Day 1643, but the first recorded landing, by William Dampier, did not occur until 1688. Today tourism plays a large part in the island's prosperity and there is a backpackers' hostel, lodge and a casino/resort on Waterfall Bay (it was recently closed but is due to reopen).

Over 60% of Christmas Island is national park, and each year in December/January there is a spectacular migration of millions of red crabs from the rainforest to the ocean where they spawn.

The Cocos Islands have a Cocos-Malay culture strongly influenced by the Muslim faith. The first recorded sighting of the Cocos was in 1609, but the islands were not settled until the 1820s, when the Clunies-Ross family established an estate on Home Island. Today there is limited tourist accommodation on West Island and the chance to enjoy local seafood cooked in the Malay style. Travellers are just beginning to learn of the existence of this idyllic island group.

On the islands of both groups you can see tropical rainforest and orchids, masses of land crabs (18 species are found on Christmas Island alone), reptiles, bats and rare seabirds. Diving, snorkelling, surfing, fishing and beachcombing are all popular activities.

For information, contact the Christmas Island Visitor Information Centre (☎ 9164 8382; fax 9164 8080), Coates Wildlife Tours (☎ 9324 2552) or Island Bound Holidays (☎ 91800 804 420, 9381 3644). A package tour from Perth to Cocos Island with lodge accommodation is $1090/1330 for six/14 nights; to Christmas Island it costs $1140/1410 to stay at the lodge and $1300/1780 at the resort. Australians do not need a passport to enter and there is no departure tax; duty-free shopping is possible. ■

is a popular drinking place and has good meals (fish & chips for $6.50). The Country Club has the Chinese *Chopsticks* (main courses for $17.50) and at its *Kelly's Bar & Grill*, in its tropical setting, you get excellent steaks with potato and salad for $16.50.

Getting There & Away

The Ansett office (☎ 9168 1622) is in the Charlie Carter's shopping complex; the airline has flights to Darwin and Perth daily. There are daily flights to Broome (except Tuesday) by either Ansett or Skywest. Skywest flies to Derby daily except Tuesday and Thursday. There is a cheap one-way fare from Kununurra to Darwin on Wednesday ($92).

Greyhound Pioneer (☎ 13 2030) passes through Kununurra on the Darwin-Perth route; its depot is in the shire office car park.

LAKE ARGYLE

Created by the Ord River Dam, Lake Argyle is the second-biggest storage reservoir in Australia, holding nine times as much water as Sydney Harbour. Prior to its construction, there was too much water in the Wet and not enough in the Dry. By providing a regular water supply the dam has encouraged agriculture on a massive scale.

At the lake there's a **pioneer museum** in the old Argyle Homestead, moved here when its original site was flooded. The *Lake Argyle Village* (☎ 9168 7360) has tent/powered sites for $9/12 for two and relatively expensive rooms for $65 a double ($15 for an extra person).

Downstream from the lake there is now green farmland. Encircling these flat lands are the reddish mountains typical of the region. There are two lake cruises: the *Bowerbird* does a two-hour cruise ($25/12.50 for adults/children) and the *Silver Cobbler* a half-day cruise ($80/50). These cruises are thoroughly recommended – the immensity of this inland sea is not fully appreciated until you are out in the middle of it all.

About 150km south of Kununurra is the

huge **Argyle Diamond Mine**, which produces around 35% of the world's diamonds, although most are only of industrial quality.

There is no public access and the six-hour tour, which must be booked through Belray's (☎ 9168 1014), costs about $285 per person.

Index

Maps

TEXT

Map references are in **bold** type

Aboriginal people 16, (NT) 347-51, (Qld) 435, (SA) 609, (Tas) 689, (Vic) 770, (WA) 893
  ancient sites 17
  art 129-48, (NT) 380
  assimilation 27
  beliefs & ceremonies 61
  books 93
  culture 60-4
  devastation of 21
  land rights 46-9
  language 63-4
  Mabo 27, 48
  religion 62-3
  stolen generation 25
  Wik 48
Aboriginal rock art
  Arnhem Land (NT) 388
  Brisbane Water NP (NSW) 265
  Bunjil's Cave (Vic) 836
  Burrup Peninsula (WA) 980
  Carnarvon NP (Qld) 518
  Chillagoe (Qld) 568
  Ewaninga (NT) 423
  Grampians (Vic) 838
  Kakadu NP (NT) 380
  Karratha (WA) 979
  Lakefield NP (Qld) 587
  Lawn Hill NP (Qld) 593
  Manyallaluk (NT) 391, 394
  Marrawah (Tas) 752
  Mootwingee NP (NSW) 338
  Mount Augustus (WA) 973
  Mt Chambers Gorge (SA) 676
  Mt Grenfell (NSW) 337
  Mulka's Cave (WA) 950
  N'dhala Gorge Nature Park (NT) 417
  Nitmiluk NP (NT) 393
  Nourlangie (NT) 383
  Port Hedland (WA) 983
  Quinkan Aboriginal Rock-Art Galleries (Qld) 587
  Red Hand Cave (NSW) 259

Sacred Canyon (SA) 674
Tasmanian Aboriginal Culture & Art Centre 744
Ubirr (NT) 382
Walga Rock (WA) 949
Wallace Rockhole (NT) 419
activities, *see individual activities*
Aboriginal Tent Embassy (ACT) 181
accommodation 117-22
  station stays 973
Adelaide (SA) 612, **613**
  entertainment 624
  getting there & away 625
  information 612
  places to eat 622
  places to stay 619
Adelaide Festival of the Arts (SA) 619
Adelaide Hills (SA) 628-3, **629**
Adelaide River (NT) 389
Adelaide River Crossing (NT) 373
Agnes Water (Qld) 507
Agnew (WA) 958
air travel
  to/from Australia 149-53
  within Australia 155-8
Aireys Inlet (Vic) 823
Airlie Beach (Qld) 524-8, **525**
Albany (WA) 940, **941**
Albury (NSW) 323-4
Albury-Wodonga (Vic) 870
Alexandra Headland (Qld) 481
Alice Springs (NT) 399-415, **400**, **416-17**
Alice Springs Desert Park (NT) 406
Alligator (NT) 381
Alligator Gorge (SA) 650
Alpine NP (Vic) 874
Alpine Way (NSW) 320
Alyangula (NT) 388
American River (SA) 640
Anakie (Qld) 517
Anakie Gorge (Vic) 809

Andamooka (SA) 679
Angahook-Lorne State Park (Vic) 826
Angaston (SA) 645
Anglesea (Vic) 823
Anna Bay (NSW) 272
Annaburroo (NT) 374
Anxious Bay (SA) 668
Apollo Bay (Vic) 827
Arakoon State Recreation Area (NSW) 279
Ararat (Vic) 836
Arcadia (Qld) 541
archaeological sites 17
architecture 53-4
Ardrossan (SA) 663
Arkaroo Rock (SA) 675
Arkaroola (SA) 677
Arltunga Historical Reserve (NT) 417
Armidale (NSW) 304
Arnhem Land (NT) 384-6
Arno Bay (SA) 667
Aroona Valley (SA) 676
Arrawarra (NSW) 286
Arthur River (Tas) 752
Arthur's Seat (Vic) 817
art galleries, *see* galleries
arts 50-5, 129-48
Asbestos Range NP (Tas) 747
Atherton (Qld) 569
Atherton Tableland (Qld) 557-71
Attack Creek (NT) 396
Auburn (SA) 647
Augusta (WA) 934
Aussie rules football 126, 792
Australian Capital Territory (ACT) 175, **176**
Australian Institute of Sport (ACT) 185
Australian War Memorial (ACT) 184
automatic teller machines 88
automobile associations 169
Avon Valley (WA) 924
Ayers Rock (NT) 423-6
Ayr (Qld) 533

National Parks & Reserves

THANKS

Many thanks to the travellers who used the last edition and wrote to us with helpful hints, useful advice and interesting anecdotes. Your names follow:

Noriko Abe, Sara Adamson, Mattias Agren, Sharon Allerton, Eve Alpern, A Anderson, Mikael Andersson, P Andrews, April Andrews, Robert Arnold, R Arthur, Ian Asbury, Joanne Ashburn, Emma Astrom, Nicole Avard, Courtney Babcock, Monique Baeten, Jan Bailey, Jon & Tracy Baker, Catherine Baker, Lisa Bannocks, N Barbour, Jacopo Bargellini, Todd & Kerri Barnsley, Rob Barouque, Julie Barter, Gary & Cheryl Beemer, David Beeusaert, Malia Bell, Holly Bendal, Philip Bergluf, Julian Best, Karena Bett, Dr Thomas Betz, Martin Beversluis, G Biggs, Kerstin Bilgmann, Belinda Bird, Helen Black, Amy Boardman, Jens Bodensohn, S Bolton, Paul Bouloudas, Rob Bourque, Rose Boutin, Jane Boyle, Darran Bragg, Eric Brahm, Mark Brailsford, Manuela Braun, Val Braun, Margaret Bremner, Bernhard Brendel, Henning Breuise, Rachel Brew & Co, Christopher Broad, Lisa Brooke, Matti Brotherus, Karl Brown, Angela Brown, Georgina Brown, D Buchweld, Neil Buhrich, Wilma Burgess, Lenny & Wendy Burnett, Ingeborg Buschmann, Michael Butterworth, N Byrne, Elkie Calcetas, A & F Calde, S Cameron, Guy Canessa, N Carnegie, D Carrasco, Elaine Carty, C J P Cass, Tom Cassidy, Michael & Pat Cavey, H B Charman, Rachel Chesme, Britta Cierniak, Al & Lorraine Cleveland, Hannah Coffey, John Cogill, Tim Colborn, Janine & Mark Collidge, Ken Collier, Jason Com, Jean Compton, Carmela Conroy, Karen Cooper, Antonio Cornet, Gerald Coulter, B T Cousins, C A Coyle, Kathleen Crisley, Pauline Crowley, Janice Cullen, Michael Cummins, Diane Cunningham, Pat Dagger, Dave Darrah, Alison Davie, Kirsty Davies, Keith Davies, Andrew Davis, Wilco de Brouwer, Francis Delissen, Michael Delman, Tina Dembek, Audrey Dewhurst, Patrick D'Haese, Sue Dickery, J D Dickinson, A Dillon, Jan Doms, Michael Donovan, Ian Doran, J Dougall, Roslyn Doyle, Amy Drapeau, M Dreher, Kirsten Dreyer, Mindy Dubin, Margaret Dudley, Jim Dunn, Peter Durand, Steve Dyer, Marc Dyer, William Dyson, Kathryn Earle, Ulf Ellervik, Rob & Margaret Elvidge, Jacob & Jesper Ernst, S Evans, Amir Even-Zur, Ken Everett, B Evers, Charlie Ewer-Smith, Mick Feldon, Jan-Howard Finder, Dawn Finnie, Paul Fitz-Patrick, Nick Fletcher, Marcelo Follari, Joanne Ford & Friends, Stuart Forder, Sonia Forster, Nigel Fosker, Bruce Freer, Peter Fremmer, Lisa Gagyi, F & A Gallagley, Joanne Gallimore, Lisa Gani, Y George, John Giba, Ruth Gibson, Iris Glatthaar, Diane Godfrey, Nathalie Goerke, Leigh Goldstein, Tania Goodmund, Sally Gordon, Frances Graham, Peter Grant, Eddie & Margaret Grantham, David Green, Richard Green, Leigh Green, David Greenyer, Justine Greeson, Jason Greif, Jackie Gridley, Martin Griffiths, Neil Griffiths, Leslie Grossman, E J Grove, Maxi Gruchot, Beverley Gryting, Monica Gupta, C Haddon, Iain Haddow, Kerry Hagen, Bill Haigh, Elizabeth Haigh, Ossy Halachmy, Neville Hallam, Sharyn Hammond, Glanda Hanbury, Teresa Hannon, Jillian Hardy, Philip Harle, Diane Hart, Claire Hawkins, Lucinda Hawksley, A Hayes-Griffin, Inga Hellings, Celia Hemmings, L Heng, Hilary Herdman, Markus Herren, Elisabeth Herreria, Rev Ian Higgins, T High, Jane Hill, P Hiscock, Fraser & Jean Hocking, Sara Hogg, R Holchan, Kirsi Holmes, Michael Huber, Anneti Hyronen, Ellen Ijspeert, Brian & Laura Inder, Mark Irish, Carol Jadraque, Annette James, Alex Jansen, M Jensen, Don & Reggie Johnston, Louisa & Stewart Johnstone, Gregory Jones, Lisa Jones, M Jonkman, L Jonsson, Marc Kammerer, Carrie Kangro, Wolf-Peter Katz, Mel Kay, Norma Kay, Liam Keating, Laura Keller, Harry & Ruth Kellerman, Jane Kelley, Jane Kernot, John Kerr, Dr H Ketelaars, Alexander Kick, Herb Kieklak, Hyung-Uk Kim, Ken & Carolyn Kimpton, Hugh Kingham, Jan Kirchhof, Isabella Klegger, Ute Koppmann, Magnus Kraemer, Amman Krishnamurthy, S L Munro, Lance & Mitch, Leon & Linda, Lassen & Martin, Isabelle Laliberte, Gordon Lang, Andreas Larsson, J Laycock, Marianne Leimert, Gordon Lennox, Dara Levine, George & Ann Levinger, David Lilagstaff, Birgit Lindberg, Ruth Lippiatt, Philip Lisamer, Andrea Ilari, Denise Lochner, Christian Loffler, S Logan, Ina Lonnies, Nicky Lowry, Georgina Lucocq, Jason Lunden, Megan Lynch, Paul MacEachern, Rainer Mack, Rodney Maier, Nadine Malfait, Dan & Amy Marcus, Nigel Marsden, Judith Marshak, Audrey Martin, Roy & Susan Masters, Barbara Mather, Steven Mathieson, Isibeal McCoy, Dudley McFadden, Tracey McGowan, Glenn McGregor, Melanie McLaren, H McLenaghan, Russell McNally, Finlay & Clare McNicol, F & C McNicol, Simone Mendes, Michael Meyden, Josephine Middleton & Co, Sara Mikkonen, Franz Miltenburg, Jorg & Grit Moller, Jennifer Monkhouse, B Monsma, Frederica Monsone, Philip Mooney, Michael Moore, Priska Moosbauer, Alison-Jayne Morgan, Angela Morris, Katalin Morvai, Michael Mowry, Nadja Muggli, Krista Mulder, Miklos Muller, Linda Mylins, R E Ness, Pat & Julie Nethercoat, Gordon Newlands, Jacqueline Newman, V Nicholas, Sara Nowell, Ben Odbert, Jo O'Flaherty, Karen Oliver, Eileen O'Meara, Barb & Frank O'Neal, T Oosterhout, Alisa & Aluf Orell, K Osborn, Birgit Paehlke, Ros Passmore, G Paton, V A Peck, K Pedersen, Roger Perras, Roland Phillips, Alan Phillips, J Pieters, Jo Pilkington-Down, David Pindar, Trent Pingenot, Alex S Pinto, Jeremy Polmear, A F Pooley, Sue Popesku, Bo Powell, Michael Powrie, Ashley Pridgeon, Emma Quinn, Peter Quirke, Denise Radomile, R V Rakcowski, Kate Ramsden, Peter Ratcliffe, A Reddaway, Yvonne Reeves, M & R Renner, Hanjoerg Resa, Eleanor Reza, Andy Rhodes,

Peter Rich, Jane Richardson, Elizabeth Richardson, Joe & Bea Rizzo, Ilona Roberts, Seth Robey, Elizabeth Robinson, Jason Rodgers, Carlos Rodriguez, P A Roe, Lisa Roell, Amanda Roll-Pickering, Aletta Roorda, Johan Ros, Stephen Roso, A Ross, San & Darren, Sarah Ross, Elisabeth Rothleaner, Janet Roxx, Susan Ruben, Lee Rubinstein, Virginia Sanz, Bernard Sarosi, Maria Sartori, Volker Sauer, Bernd & Elke Scheffler, John Schlamm, Peter Schmidt, Dr Ulrike Schnepf, Richard Schoonraad, Fiona Scott, Alan Scott, Anne Scott, Tim Searle, Lucie Seaton, Steve Seifert, Jo Selwyn, Dr N Shah, Robby Sharp, Florence & Peter Shaw, Kate Sheather, Shirley Sheehan, J G & I E Sims, Sarah Skerp, Tara Skey, Elaine Slade, Matthew Slater, Mar'jke Sleeckx, Ed Smeaton, Heidi Smith, Angela Smith, Simon Smith, Heather Smith, Stuart Smith, Rachel Smith, Preston Smith, Sam Soppitt, A Sorensen, Dana Spanierman, M Speck-Weisshaupt, Harley Spiller, Jaroslaw Stachiw, Christina Stansfield, Julie Staplehurst, Ed Starkie, R. Stauffer, D J Staveley, Neil Stead, Keith Stead, Nick Steadman, Judith Steele, Charlotte Steiner, David Stevens, Bill Stoughtan, A Streicher,

Abbie Stringer, Joseph Stubbins, Karen Sue, Mark Susan, Donna Swarbrick, Mark Swatek, Kate Swinburn, C Swindells, Robert Takiguchi, Helen Tapping, Cilla Taylor, G Taylor, Daniel Taylor, Simon Thomas, Patricia Thompson, Kate Thompson, Natasha Thorp, Narell Thrower, Andrew Tink, Sherry Lynn Tischler, Greg Tom, Rory Towler, Jim Trepka, Rachel Tucker, Kylie Turner, Colin Twomey, C Urban, Marc Urban, Kees van der Braak, Johan van den Hoorn, Yves & Els Vandijk, Harold van Voornveld, Laura Vates, Jonas Vejlo, Michael Venter, Rachel Vergette, Shelly Walcock, Jim Walker, Irmi Wanke, Doris Waring, Carolyn Webb, Edward Webber, Kerstin Weidner, P Weisshaupt, Henrik & Kanna Wellejus, Debbie Wells, Cy West, C Westgeest, A Whiteside, Hakan Widerstrom, Thomas Wiegold, Dimity Williams, Sarah Williams, Ann-Marie Williams, Sally Willis, Anne Wilshin, Norm Wilson, Alexander Winter, Dieter Wiobel, Ray Wittert, Sarah Wood, Paul & Fiona Woodhouse, Emma Woods, Vicky Woods, S Wright, Sara Wyatt, Karen Young, Thomas & Rocio Zeiler, Andrea Zimmermann.

LONELY PLANET PHRASEBOOKS

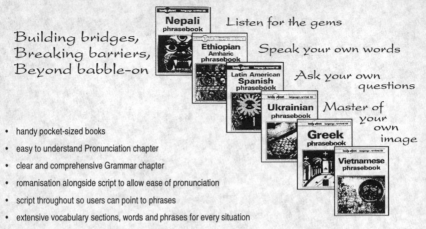

Building bridges,
Breaking barriers,
Beyond babble-on

Listen for the gems

Speak your own words

Ask your own
                questions

Master of
        your
        own
        image

- handy pocket-sized books
- easy to understand Pronunciation chapter
- clear and comprehensive Grammar chapter
- romanisation alongside script to allow ease of pronunciation
- script throughout so users can point to phrases
- extensive vocabulary sections, words and phrases for every situation
- full of cultural information and tips for the traveller

'...vital for a real DIY spirit and attitude in language learning' – **Backpacker**

'the phrasebooks have good cultural backgrounders and offer solid advice for challenging situations in remote locations' – **San Francisco Examiner**

'...they are unbeatable for their coverage of the world's more obscure languages' – *The Geographical Magazine*

Arabic (Egyptian)
Arabic (Moroccan)
Australia
  Australian English, Aboriginal and
  Torres Strait languages
Baltic States
  Estonian, Latvian, Lithuanian
Bengali
Brazilian
Burmese
Cantonese
Central Asia
Central Europe
  Czech, French, German, Hungarian,
  Italian and Slovak
Eastern Europe
  Bulgarian, Czech, Hungarian, Polish,
  Romanian and Slovak
Ethiopian (Amharic)
Fijian
French
German
Greek

Hindi/Urdu
Indonesian
Italian
Japanese
Korean
Lao
Latin American Spanish
Malay
Mandarin
Mediterranean Europe
  Albanian, Croatian, Greek,
  Italian, Macedonian, Maltese.
  Serbian and Slovene
Mongolian
Nepali
Papua New Guinea
Pilipino (Tagalog)
Quechua
Russian
Scandinavian Europe
  Danish, Finnish, Icelandic, Norwegian
  and Swedish

South-East Asia
  Burmese, Indonesian, Khmer, Lao,
  Malay, Tagalog (Pilipino), Thai and
  Vietnamese
Spanish (Castilian)
  Basque, Catalan and Galician
Sri Lanka
Swahili
Thai
Thai Hill Tribes
Tibetan
Turkish
Ukrainian
USA
  US English, Vernacular,
  Native American languages and
  Hawaiian
Vietnamese
Western Europe
  Basque, Catalan, Dutch, French,
  German, Irish, Italian, Portuguese,
  Scottish Gaelic, Spanish (Castilian)
  and Welsh

LONELY PLANET JOURNEYS

JOURNEYS is a unique collection of travel writing – published by the company that understands travel better than anyone else. It is a series for anyone who has ever experienced – or dreamed of – the magical moment when they encountered a strange culture or saw a place for the first time. They are tales to read while you're planning a trip, while you're on the road or while you're in an armchair, in front of a fire.

JOURNEYS books catch the spirit of a place, illuminate a culture, recount a crazy adventure, or introduce a fascinating way of life. They always entertain, and always enrich the experience of travel.

ISLANDS IN THE CLOUDS
Travels in the Highlands of New Guinea
Isabella Tree

Isabella Tree's remarkable journey takes us to the heart of the remote and beautiful Highlands of Papua New Guinea and Irian Jaya – one of the most extraordinary and dangerous regions on earth. Funny and tragic by turns, *Islands in the Clouds* is her moving story of the Highland people and the changes transforming their world.

Isabella Tree, who lives in England, has worked as a freelance journalist on a variety of newspapers and magazines, including a stint as senior travel correspondent for the *Evening Standard*. A fellow of the Royal Geographical Society, she has also written a biography of the Victorian ornithologist John Gould.

'*One of the most accomplished travel writers to appear on the horizon for many years . . . the dialogue is brilliant*' – Eric Newby

SEAN & DAVID'S LONG DRIVE
Sean Condon

Sean Condon is young, urban and a connoisseur of hair wax. He can't drive, and he doesn't really travel well. So when Sean and his friend David set out to explore Australia in a 1966 Ford Falcon, the result is a decidedly offbeat look at life on the road. Over 14,000 death-defying kilometres, our heroes check out the re-runs on tv, get fabulously drunk, listen to Neil Young cassettes and wonder why they ever left home.

Sean Condon lives in Melbourne. He played drums in several mediocre bands until he found his way into advertising and an above-average band called Boilersuit. *Sean & David's Long Drive* is his first book.

'*Funny, pithy, kitsch and surreal . . . This book will do for Australia what Chernobyl did for Kiev, but hey you'll laugh as the stereotypes go boom*'
– *Time Out*

LONELY PLANET TRAVEL ATLASES

Lonely Planet has long been famous for the number and quality of its guidebook maps. Now we've gone one step further and in conjunction with Steinhart Katzir Publishers produced a handy companion series: Lonely Planet travel atlases – maps of a country produced in book form.

Unlike other maps, which look good but lead travellers astray, our travel atlases have been researched on the road by Lonely Planet's experienced team of writers. All details are carefully checked to ensure the atlas corresponds with the equivalent Lonely Planet guidebook.

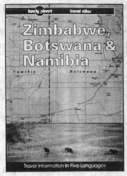

The handy atlas format means no holes, wrinkles, torn sections or constant folding and unfolding. These atlases can survive long periods on the road, unlike cumbersome fold-out maps. The comprehensive index ensures easy reference.

- full-colour throughout
- maps researched and checked by Lonely Planet authors
- place names correspond with Lonely Planet guidebooks
  – no confusing spelling differences
- legend and travelling information in English, French, German, Japanese and Spanish
- size: 230 x 160 mm

Available now:
Chile & Easter Island • Egypt • India & Bangladesh • Israel & the Palestinian Territories •Jordan, Syria & Lebanon • Kenya • Laos • Portugal • South Africa, Lesotho & Swaziland • Thailand • Turkey • Vietnam • Zimbabwe, Botswana & Namibia

---

LONELY PLANET TV SERIES & VIDEOS

Lonely Planet travel guides have been brought to life on television screens around the world. Like our guides, the programmes are based on the joy of independent travel, and look honestly at some of the most exciting, picturesque and frustrating places in the world. Each show is presented by one of three travellers from Australia, England or the USA and combines an innovative mixture of video, Super-8 film, atmospheric soundscapes and original music.

Videos of each episode – containing additional footage not shown on television – are available from good book and video shops, but the availability of individual videos varies with regional screening schedules.

Video destinations include: Alaska • American Rockies • Australia – The South-East • Baja California & the Copper Canyon • Brazil • Central Asia • Chile & Easter Island • Corsica, Sicily & Sardinia – The Mediterranean Islands • East Africa (Tanzania & Zanzibar) • Ecuador & the Galapagos Islands • Greenland & Iceland • Indonesia • Israel & the Sinai Desert • Jamaica • Japan • La Ruta Maya • Morocco • New York • North India • Pacific Islands (Fiji, Solomon Islands & Vanuatu) • South India • South West China • Turkey • Vietnam • West Africa • Zimbabwe, Botswana & Namibia

The Lonely Planet TV series is produced by:
Pilot Productions
The Old Studio
18 Middle Row
London W10 5AT UK

For video availability and ordering information contact your nearest Lonely Planet office.

Music from the TV series is available on CD & cassette.

PLANET TALK

Lonely Planet's FREE quarterly newsletter

We love hearing from you and think you'd like to hear from us.

When...is the right time to see reindeer in Finland?
Where...can you hear the best palm-wine music in Ghana?
How...do you get from Asunción to Areguá by steam train?
What...is the best way to see India?

For the answer to these and many other questions read PLANET TALK.

Every issue is packed with up-to-date travel news and advice including:

* a letter from Lonely Planet co-founders Tony and Maureen Wheeler
* go behind the scenes on the road with a Lonely Planet author
* feature article on an important and topical travel issue
* a selection of recent letters from travellers
* details on forthcoming Lonely Planet promotions
* complete list of Lonely Planet products

To join our mailing list contact any Lonely Planet office.

Also available: Lonely Planet T-shirts. 100% heavyweight cotton.

LONELY PLANET ONLINE

Get the latest travel information before you leave or while you're on the road

Whether you've just begun planning your next trip, or you're chasing down specific info on currency regulations or visa requirements, check out Lonely Planet Online for up-to-the minute travel information.

As well as travel profiles of your favourite destinations (including maps and photos), you'll find current reports from our researchers and other travellers, updates on health and visas, travel advisories, and discussion of the ecological and political issues you need to be aware of as you travel.

There's also an online travellers' forum where you can share your experience of life on the road, meet travel companions and ask other travellers for their recommendations and advice. We also have plenty of links to other online sites useful to independent travellers.

And of course we have a complete and up-to-date list of all Lonely Planet travel products including guides, phrasebooks, atlases, Journeys and videos and a simple online ordering facility if you can't find the book you want elsewhere.

www.lonelyplanet.com
or
AOL keyword: lp

LONELY PLANET PRODUCTS

Lonely Planet is known worldwide for publishing practical, reliable and no-nonsense travel information in our guides and on our web site. The Lonely Planet list covers just about every accessible part of the world. Currently there are nine series: *travel guides, shoestring guides, walking guides, city guides, phrasebooks, audio packs, travel atlases, Journeys – a unique collection of travel writing and Pisces Books - diving and snorkeling guides.*

EUROPE

Amsterdam • Austria • Baltic States phrasebook • Britain • Central Europe on a shoestring • Central Europe phrasebook • Czech & Slovak Republics • Denmark • Dublin • Eastern Europe on a shoestring • Eastern Europe phrasebook • Estonia, Latvia & Lithuania • Finland • France • French phrasebook • Germany • German phrasebook • Greece • Greek phrasebook • Hungary • Iceland, Greenland & the Faroe Islands • Ireland • Italian phrasebook • Italy • Lisbon • London • Mediterranean Europe on a shoestring • Mediterranean Europe phrasebook • Paris • Poland • Portugal • Portugal travel atlas • Prague • Romania & Moldova • Russia, Ukraine & Belarus • Russian phrasebook • Scandinavian & Baltic Europe on a shoestring • Scandinavian Europe phrasebook • Slovenia • Spain • Spanish phrasebook • St Petersburg • Switzerland • Trekking in Spain • Ukrainian phrasebook • Vienna • Walking in Britain • Walking in Italy • Walking in Switzerland • Western Europe on a shoestring • Western Europe phrasebook

Travel Literature: The Olive Grove: Travels in Greece

NORTH AMERICA

Alaska • Backpacking in Alaska • Baja California • California & Nevada • Canada • Chicago • Deep South • Florida • Hawaii • Honolulu • Los Angeles • Mexico • Mexico City • Miami • New England • New Orleans • New York City • New York, New Jersey & Pennsylvania • Pacific Northwest USA • Rocky Mountain States • San Francisco • Southwest USA • USA phrasebook • Washington, DC & the Capital Region

Travel Literature: Drive thru America

CENTRAL AMERICA & THE CARIBBEAN

•Bahamas and Turks & Caicos •Bermuda •Central America on a shoestring • Costa Rica • Cuba •Eastern Caribbean •Guatemala, Belize & Yucatán: La Ruta Maya • Jamaica

SOUTH AMERICA

Argentina, Uruguay & Paraguay • Bolivia • Brazil • Brazilian phrasebook • Buenos Aires • Chile & Easter Island • Chile & Easter Island travel atlas • Colombia Ecuador & the Galápagos Islands • Latin American Spanish phrasebook • Peru • Quechua phrasebook • Río de Janeiro • South America on a shoestring • Trekking in the Patagonian Andes • Venezuela

Travel Literature: Full Circle: A South American Journey

ISLANDS OF THE INDIAN OCEAN

Madagascar & Comoros • Maldives• Mauritius, Réunion & Seychelles

AFRICA

Africa - the South • Africa on a shoestring • Arabic (Moroccan) phrasebook • Cairo • Cape Town • Central Africa • East Africa • Egypt • Egypt travel atlas• Ethiopian (Amharic) phrasebook • Kenya • Kenya travel atlas • Malawi, Mozambique & Zambia • Morocco • North Africa • South Africa, Lesotho & Swaziland • South Africa, Lesotho & Swaziland travel atlas • Swahili phrasebook • Tunisia Trekking in East Africa • West Africa • Zimbabwe, Botswana & Namibia • Zimbabwe, Botswana & Namibia travel atlas

Travel Literature: The Rainbird: A Central African Journey • Songs to an African Sunset: A Zimbabwean Story

MAIL ORDER

Lonely Planet products are distributed worldwide. They are also available by mail order from Lonely Planet, so if you have difficulty finding a title please write to us. North American and South American residents should write to 150 Linden St, Oakland CA 94607, USA; European and African residents should write to 10a Spring Place, London NW5 3BH; and residents of other countries to PO Box 617, Hawthorn, Victoria 3122, Australia.

NORTH-EAST ASIA

Beijing • Cantonese phrasebook • China • Hong Kong • Hong Kong, Macau & Guangzhou • Japan • Japanese phrasebook • Japanese audio pack • Korea • Korean phrasebook • Mandarin phrasebook • Mongolia • Mongolian phrasebook • North-East Asia on a shoestring • Seoul • Taiwan • Tibet • Tibet phrasebook • Tokyo

Travel Literature: Lost Japan

MIDDLE EAST & CENTRAL ASIA

Arab Gulf States • Arabic (Egyptian) phrasebook • Central Asia • Central Asia phrasebook • Iran • Israel & the Palestinian Territories • Israel & the Palestinian Territories travel atlas • Istanbul • Jerusalem • Jordan & Syria • Jordan, Syria & Lebanon travel atlas • Lebanon • Middle East • Turkey • Turkish phrasebook • Turkey travel atlas • Yemen

Travel Literature: The Gates of Damascus • Kingdom of the Film Stars: Journey into Jordan

ALSO AVAILABLE:

Brief Encounters • Travel with Children • Traveller's Tales

INDIAN SUBCONTINENT

Bangladesh • Bengali phrasebook • Delhi • Goa • Hindi/Urdu phrasebook • India • India & Bangladesh travel atlas • Indian Himalaya • Karakoram Highway • Nepal • Nepali phrasebook • Pakistan • Rajasthan • Sri Lanka • Sri Lanka phrasebook • Trekking in the Indian Himalaya • Trekking in the Karakoram & Hindukush • Trekking in the Nepal Himalaya

Travel Literature: In Rajasthan • Shopping for Buddhas

SOUTH-EAST ASIA

Bali & Lombok • Bangkok • Burmese phrasebook • Cambodia • Ho Chi Minh City • Indonesia • Indonesian phrasebook • Indonesian audio pack • Jakarta • Java • Laos • Lao phrasebook • Laos travel atlas • Malay phrasebook • Malaysia, Singapore & Brunei • Myanmar (Burma) • Philippines • Pilipino phrasebook • Singapore • South-East Asia on a shoestring • South-East Asia phrasebook • Thailand • Thailand's Islands & Beaches • Thailand travel atlas • Thai phrasebook • Thai audio pack • Thai Hill Tribes phrasebook • Vietnam • Vietnamese phrasebook • Vietnam travel atlas

AUSTRALIA & THE PACIFIC

Australia • Australian phrasebook • Bushwalking in Australia • Bushwalking in Papua New Guinea • Fiji • Fijian phrasebook • Islands of Australia's Great Barrier Reef • Melbourne • Micronesia • New Caledonia • New South Wales • New Zealand • Northern Territory • Outback Australia • Papua New Guinea • Papua New Guinea phrasebook • Queensland • Rarotonga & the Cook Islands • Samoa • Solomon Islands • South Australia • Sydney • Tahiti & French Polynesia • Tasmania • Tonga • Tramping in New Zealand • Vanuatu • Victoria • Western Australia

Travel Literature: Islands in the Clouds • Sean & David's Long Drive

ANTARCTICA

Antarctica

THE LONELY PLANET STORY

Lonely Planet published its first book in 1973 in response to the numerous 'How did you do it?' questions Maureen and Tony Wheeler were asked after driving, bussing, hitching, sailing and railing their way from England to Australia.

Written at a kitchen table and hand collated, trimmed and stapled, *Across Asia on the Cheap* became an instant local bestseller, inspiring thoughts of another book.

Eighteen months in South-East Asia resulted in their second guide, *South-East Asia on a shoestring*, which they put together in a backstreet Chinese hotel in Singapore in 1975. The 'yellow bible', as it quickly became known to backpackers around the world, soon became *the* guide to the region. It has sold well over half a million copies and is now in its 9th edition, still retaining its familiar yellow cover.

Today there are over 350 titles, including travel guides, walking guides, language kits & phrasebooks, travel atlases and travel literature. The company is the largest independent travel publisher in the world. Although Lonely Planet initially specialised in guides to Asia, today there are few corners of the globe that have not been covered.

The emphasis continues to be on travel for independent travellers. Tony and Maureen still travel for several months of each year and play an active part in the writing, updating and quality control of Lonely Planet's guides.

They have been joined by over 80 authors and 200 staff at our offices in Melbourne (Australia), Oakland (USA), London (UK) and Paris (France). Travellers themselves also make a valuable contribution to the guides through the feedback we receive in thousands of letters each year and on our web site.

The people at Lonely Planet strongly believe that travellers can make a positive contribution to the countries they visit, both through their appreciation of the countries' culture, wildlife and natural features, and through the money they spend. In addition, the company makes a direct contribution to the countries and regions it covers. Since 1986 a percentage of the income from each book has been donated to ventures such as famine relief in Africa; aid projects in India; agricultural projects in Central America; Greenpeace's efforts to halt French nuclear testing in the Pacific; and Amnesty International.

'I hope we send people out with the right attitude about travel. You realise when you travel that there are so many different perspectives about the world, so we hope these books will make people more interested in what they see. Guidebooks can't really guide people. All you can do is point them in the right direction.'

– Tony Wheeler

LONELY PLANET PUBLICATIONS

Australia
PO Box 617, Hawthorn 3122, Victoria
tel: (03) 9819 1877 fax: (03) 9819 6459
e-mail: talk2us@lonelyplanet.com.au

USA
150 Linden St
Oakland, CA 94607
tel: (510) 893 8555 TOLL FREE: 800 275-8555
fax: (510) 893 8572
e-mail: info@lonelyplanet.com

UK
10a Spring Place,
London NW5 3BH
tel: (0171) 428 4800 fax: (0171) 428 4828
e-mail: go@lonelyplanet.co.uk

France:
71 bis rue du Cardinal Lemoine, 75005 Paris
tel: 01 44 32 06 20 fax: 01 46 34 72 55
e-mail: bip@lonelyplanet.fr

World Wide Web: http://www.lonelyplanet.com
or *AOL keyword: lp*